COURTLY GARDENS IN HOLLAND 1600-1650

COURTLY GARDENS IN HOLLAND 1600-1650

THE HOUSE OF ORANGE AND THE HORTUS BATAVUS

Vanessa Bezemer Sellers

Architectura & Natura Press, Amsterdam
Garden Art Press, Woodbridge

... Nu door het velt te gaen, dan weder in de boecken
Den aert van alle dingh te mogen ondersoecken
En Godt daer in te sien ...

... Now going through the fields, than through the books again,
being able to probe the core of everything
and seeing God therein ...
   (Jacob Cats, *Ouderdom, buyten-leven en hof-gedachten,* 1656)

CONTENTS

Acknowledgements 7

Introduction 9

CHAPTER I
The History of the Gardens of Frederik Hendrik and Amalia: Honselaarsdijk 15

CHAPTER II
The Palace and Gardens of Ter Nieuburch at Rijswijk 61

CHAPTER III
The Other Gardens of Frederik Hendrik and Amalia 101

CHAPTER IV
Architecture, Theory and Practice at the Stadholder's Court 151

CHAPTER V
Style and Form of the Stadholder's Gardens 185

CHAPTER VI
An Iconological Interpretation of the Dutch Courtly Garden: Sculptural Ornamentation and the Motif of the Twin Circles 223

Conclusion 262

Notes 270

Appendix 327

Bibliography 395

List of Illustrations 407

List of Abbreviations 413

Index 414

COURTLY GARDENS IN HOLLAND 1600-1650

ACKNOWLEDGEMENTS

It is with great pleasure that I extend these words of gratitude to all who have assisted me in writing this book. Especially my husband, Gianni, needs to be applauded for his many hours of editorial work, and for his wonderful patience and support during the years of research and writing. Our children, Erica and Alexander, helped me to keep a clear view of the actual use and enjoyment of parks and gardens throughout the ages.

I should also like to thank Elsa Fabbrizzi-Messing, who alleviated my work in many ways. In Holland my parents Tammo and Hilde Bezemer, as well as Jan and Mary-An de Jong-Bezemer and Katrijne Bezemer, provided encouragement and were most helpful in collecting material from the various libraries and archival institutions overseas. Enthusiastic support and important suggestions were given by several colleagues and friends in Holland, especially Professor Koenrad A. Ottenheym and, during my years at Leiden University, Professor Jan J. Terwen and Professor Th.H. Lunsingh Scheurleer.

At Princeton University I was greatly inspired, in the first place, by my adviser Professor David R. Coffin, and also by Professor John A. Pinto of the Department of Art and Archaeology. I am most grateful for their invaluable suggestions and continued encouragement during the completion of my original dissertation, out of which this book has grown. Professor Egbert Haverkamp-Begeman and Betsy Rosasco read the original manuscript, and Shay Alster prepared the reconstruction diagrams for this final published version. Danielle Kisluk-Grosheide, associate curator at the Metropolitan Museum of Art, was always available for discussions and her enthusiasm was most uplifting.

Over the years I was kindly helped by the staffs of many libraries and archives, among them Mr. B. Woelderink of the Koninklijk Huisarchief, the staffs of the Koninklijke Bibliotheek, the Algemeen Rijksarchief, the Gemeentearchief and the Topographical Department of the Rijksbureau voor Kunsthistorische Documentatie in The Hague. In Leiden Mr. D. de Vries of the Collectie Bodel Nijenhuis of the Leiden University Library, and in Wageningen Mrs. C. Oldenburger-Ebbers of the Wageningen University Library were most helpful.

In the United States I am equally indebted to the staffs of the various libraries and departments of Rare Books and Prints. Especially important were the Marquand Library and Firestone Library of Princeton University, as well as the Butler Library and Avery Library of Columbia University and the Department of Drawings and Prints of the Metropolitan Museum of Art in New York.

Much credit for the readability of the text goes to my editor H.J. Scheepmaker, whose uncanny eye for discovering even the smallest error greatly improved the final product. I am also grateful for Caroline van Eck's directions regarding the larger theoretical-philosophical content of my work.

Finally, I wish to thank Andrea and Alexei Bayer, Eugene Kisluk, Nora Laos, Mariette Westermann-Pardoe, Frédérique Westerhoff-König, Francisca Bongaerts-Verdonk, Ruth Milvaney and Peninah Petruck-Jacobson, who in many ways were instrumental in bringing this book to its completion.

Respublica HOLLANDIÆ, et Urbes.

LVGDVNI BATAVORVM, Ex officina
IOANNIS MAIRE. Anno cIɔ Iɔc xxx.

INTRODUCTION

All that is known as Holland are but cities few
And Holland's friends themselves but a little crew
And, 'though everything on a small scale,
There are many wonders to unveil.
So whoever enters the ring of Holland's coasts,
Of a beautiful Arbour of pleasures he will boast;
All that heaven sends, or the earth brings forth,
Is brought here by the sea and floats into the ports.
God is like a sun who sends his thousand rays
To shine on this small garden throughout the days!
What ever grew on trees, or the fields did clothe
Comes here to the people fallen into their mouths.[1]

1. Title-page of Hugo de Groot's *Respublica Hollandiae et Urbes*, 1630, depicting Holland as an enclosed garden guarded by the rampant Dutch Lion which represents the Stadholder.
The Folger Shakespeare Library, Washington, D.C.

In these verses the popular seventeenth-century Dutch poet Jacob Cats expressed the idea, commonly found in contemporary art and literature, of Holland as a garden *(fig. 1)*[2] recovered from the sea and brought to flower, yet still in constant danger of inundation.[3] The fight for land, the constant effort to keep it safe from the sea and foreign intruders, whether perceived as a real or an abstract threat, is one of the central themes and thoughts which have permeated not only Dutch culture in general but the art of Dutch gardening in particular. Land reclamation and cultivation and the creation of a peculiarly Dutch geometrical landscape interspersed with canals lay at the foundation of the art of gardening in Holland, so much so that the country itself became identified with a garden and its people with gardeners. As Mountague stated: 'The Dutch are great improvers of Land, and Planters of Trees of Ornament as well as Profit'.[4] Indeed, it almost might be said that the Dutch made Holland, since most of the land was reclaimed from the North Sea through hard work by its inhabitants.[5]

Paradoxically, while the sea constantly threatened the very existence of the Dutch landscape, it also was its source, since much of the wealth used to pay for the layout of the gardens came from moneys collected through official state piracy.[6] The development of the Dutch garden and country-house culture also should be seen as a response to Holland's rapid urbanization.[7] This development was accompanied by the rethinking of the existing ideals of building and gardening and the birth of a true 'science of architecture'. At the Dutch court this resulted in the adaptation of a new, classically-inspired vocabulary or, as the Stadholder's architect Pieter Post described it, 'the building after the antique or Roman manner'.[8]

The gardens of Stadholder Frederik Hendrik, Prince of Orange-Nassau (1584-1647), the creation of which coincided with the foundation of the Dutch Republic itself, offer a unique opportunity to study larger aspects of Dutch seventeenth-century culture. The

Stadholder's grand geometrical gardens were the first truly monumental expression of this art form in the Northern Netherlands, contributing to a new, representative ambience of courtly residences. It is also significant that the Dutch courtly garden was an ideal setting for other artistic media, such as sculpture and painting, and thus was not simply a place of 'nature adorned' but truly the ancient *museion* re-created.[9] In this context, the Stadholder's gardens illustrate the phenomenon described by Huizinga[10] of a nation which reaches its cultural peak soon after its very creation. A Landscape of War and Peace,[11] both in a literal and in a metaphorical sense, the Stadholder's gardens are a reflection *par excellence* of contemporary history and culture.

The current surge of interest in the seventeenth-century Dutch garden, as shown by a large number of recent publications, including a special yearbook on garden art,[12] provides an opportunity to come to a new assessment of Dutch garden architecture. With the exception of a few important articles,[13] however, most of these new publications concentrate on late-seventeenth-century garden architecture in Holland and mention the early-seventeenth-century garden architecture only in passing.[14] For this earlier period of Dutch garden architecture we must for a large part still rely on books which were written more than fifty years ago, such as *Oude Hollandsche tuinen* by A.G. Bienfait, *Het Huis Honselaarsdijk* by Th. Morren and *De paleizen van Frederik Hendrik* by D.F. Slothouwer. These works give a general description of Dutch garden art during this period, but are still coloured by the nineteenth-century bias towards geometric garden art as being too artificial. Also, perhaps due to a general distrust of classicism as being inherently 'un-Dutch', these studies fail to stress the importance of classical inspiration in early-seventeenth-century Dutch art and architecture.[15] Furthermore, they do not give a detailed survey of the gardens surrounding Frederik Hendrik's palaces in particular, nor do they discuss origin, future development and underlying symbolism of these important garden layouts. An attempt will be made here to correct this neglect and to fill the gap in art-historical research of a period generally known as the Dutch Golden Age, which includes not only the art of painting and sculpture but also the art of gardening.

While focusing our analysis on garden art during the first part of the century, the layout and decoration of the stadholderly gardens of Honselaarsdijk and Ter Nieuburch will be discussed in detail, together with other gardens in and around The Hague, such as the Oude Hof or Paleis Noordeinde and the Huis ten Bosch, which show the most important garden layouts of the seventeenth century. The history of the gardens of Honselaarsdijk and Ter Nieuburch is the core of our research, as their layouts represented the model for garden designs throughout the seventeenth century. Other gardens which will be studied include the courtly gardens at Breda, Buren, Zuylesteyn and Ysselsteyn, all of which played a crucial role in the creation and flowering of garden architecture in The Netherlands. Finally, it will be shown that the influence of the Dutch courtly gardens created under Frederik Hendrik has exceeded Holland's borders into France, Denmark, Germany and Sweden.[16]

In spite of Frederik Hendrik's wish to leave his palaces and gardens intact for posterity, none of the above-mentioned palace complexes have survived, except for the Huis ten Bosch and the Paleis Noordeinde. Thus, in order to reconstruct the gardens around Frederik Hendrik's former palaces, this study relies on written sources, such as account books, travel journals and country-house poetry. In addition, visual material is provided by maps, prints, drawings and paintings. The Archives of the Nassau Domains and various topographical departments afford a wealth of material about the Stadholder's gardens which has not been systematically studied before.[17] To further our understanding of Dutch garden architecture this new documentary and visual evidence will be set against a wider

2. Frederik Hendrik portrayed in a garland of orange blossom, with verses glorifying his deeds and with his personal motto 'Patriaeque Patrique'.
Universiteitsbibliotheek, Amsterdam

Patriæque   Patrique

Fredrick Hendrick Prins Van Oranje Graef Van Nassow Gouverneur Van Hollandt en Zeelandt &c.

ICk in het Veldheers-ampt mijn' Broeder nagetreden
  Heb op sijn spoor mijn stuck oock mannelijck verricht;
Dat tuygen Bosch, Maestricht en soo veel and're steden,
  Dat ickse niet en weet te vatten in gedicht.
Dees' Helden-dapperheyd brengt Spaenjen tot bedaren,
  En dwingt den Iber 't stael te steken in de schee:
En ick van arbeyd mat, en sat van hooge jaren
  Sinck wel vernoegt in 't graf op 't rijsen van den Vré.

cultural-artistic background, involving contemporary architectural theory, advances in science and technology and religious and socio-political developments in The Netherlands and in Europe at large.

The role and personality of the Stadholder himself *(fig. 2)*,[18] as well as of his wife and consort Amalia van Solms-Braunfels (1602-1675), are of central importance to the history of the princely Dutch gardens. Educated according to the humanist tradition in the arts and (military) sciences, already at an early age Frederik Hendrik expressed a great interest in the art of building, city planning and gardening. Having completed his studies at the University of Leiden at the turn of the seventeenth century, Frederik Hendrik – 'Henry de

Nassau' or simply 'Henry' as he would sign his name – soon followed in the footsteps of his brother Prince Maurits and became preoccupied with the science of warfare, without, however, neglecting his varying interests in the peaceful arts.[19] Throughout his life the Stadholder was a passionate art collector. His extensive collections of *artificia* and *naturalia* indeed reflect the ideal of the perfect gentleman-virtuoso, who, according to Francis Bacon, in addition to having 'a most perfect and general library [and] a spacious and wonderful garden replete with rare birds, beasts and fish of all kind', also was said to own a universal art cabinet.[20]

In his book *Ouderdom, buyten-leven en hof-gedachten* (Age, Country Life and Garden Thoughts), Jacob Cats defined the Stadholder as 'een vorst tot planten seer genegen' (a sovereign much inclined to gardening). Each time Frederik Hendrik would visit Cats's estate outside The Hague, the latter would urge the Stadholder to reclaim and improve lands. As befits 'a man of means and status', the Stadholder should design great pleasure gardens, not only for his own delight but for the benefit of Holland at large, according to Cats:

> Prince Henry being a sovereign to gardening much inclined
> Often came to see God's great blessings here to find.
> His Highness was amazed when he would then discover
> That rich and sumptuous woods once empty grounds did cover.
> I told him, mighty Sovereign, you're buying various lands
> And that at high a cost, but getting barren sands.
> Do turn them into woods, and from this dust despised
> Create a handsome arbour, let pleasure gardens rise.
> This is true Princely work, with Holland's good in mind,
> And leads you to be praised for what you left behind.
> This would not benefit just one individual
> But also serve the Fatherland in general.[21]

By encouraging the Stadholder to lay out gardens on barren rather than fertile grounds, and by insisting upon their function as a common rather than private good, Cats perpetuated the contemporary Dutch notion of creating wondrous lands out of nothing,[22] and to cultivate gardens to declare Holland's national identity. Indeed, it was the re-creation of the ancient 'Land of the Batavians', metaphorically the *Hortus Batavus* or 'Garden of Holland', which Cats had in mind when speaking of the Stadholder's princely obligations. Frederik Hendrik would acquit himself well of his princely task to build, aware of the need to establish a truly representative *Architectura Recreationis*.[23] In laying out his palace and garden complexes he chose architectural formulae from the Italian Renaissance and Graeco-Roman past. His choice of the classical *canon* is of interest, for it implies a new intellectual attitude, reflecting the Stadholder's notion that the use of age-old and more 'absolute' aesthetical principles would command respect and lend stability to his country and his reign. The Stadholder's concern to have his heritage and that of his father, the legendary William the Silent, secured and not let it fall into oblivion would thus find its visual expression in palace and garden architecture.

In 1625, after Maurits's death, Frederik Hendrik succeeded his brother as Prince of Orange, Captain-General and Admiral of the United Provinces and Stadholder of the Dutch Republic. Though various military campaigns compelled him to spend much of his time on the battlefield as commander of the Dutch army, the Stadholder nevertheless managed to engage in an impressive building campaign which involved the restoration and construction of palaces and gardens throughout the Dutch Republic. It is in the Stadholder's correspondence from the battlefield to his secretary and close adviser Constantijn Huygens that Frederik Hendrik's fascination for art and architecture is expressed. Many a letter written by Huygens to Frederik Hendrik and his wife Amalia van Solms shows the Stadholder's passion for building and laying out gardens, which was his most cherished pastime:

> Après l'heure de soupper il passa le temps à veoir des figures de ma maison à la Haye,[24] et autres choses touchant L'Architecture, qui est un de ses plus aggreables divertissements.[25]

In building his palaces and gardens, Frederik Hendrik was to herald a more unified architectural style, generally defined as Dutch Classicism or Classical Baroque,[26] which gradually developed during the first decades of the seventeenth century. The search for a new architectural vocabulary and the creation of an all-encompassing architectural standard coincided with greater political and cultural unity under the new Stadholder, whose title became hereditary in 1630.[27] Thus, the history of seventeenth-century Dutch architecture and garden architecture cannot be explained without understanding the significance of Frederik Hendrik's building commissions.[28] While the leading architects of the time, Hendrick de Keyser and Lieven de Key,[29] did not leave a permanent mark on Dutch architecture, Frederik Hendrik's court at The Hague left an indelible mark on seventeenth-century architectural design.[30] The new architectural development is all the more intriguing if studied in the context of the increasingly international atmosphere of the court at The Hague. This internationalism was due to Frederik Hendrik's own family background, especially his French mother, Louise de Coligny, and French godfather, King Henri IV of France, as well as to several external circumstances. These include the arrival in 1620 in The Hague of Friedrich V, Elector Palatine, and Elizabeth Stuart (later Queen of Bohemia), daughter of King James I of England.[31] Their presence in The Hague, after their flight from Bohemia and Heidelberg, helped to lend an air of royalty to the Stadholder's court.[32] It was one of Elizabeth's maids of honour, Amalia van Solms, who, as Frederik Hendrik's wife, would have a great impact on the creation of palaces and gardens in and around the Residence.

The layout of Frederik Hendrik's gardens was the impetus for the proliferation of country estates and gardens of the wealthy merchants and bourgeoisie throughout The Netherlands.[33] These gardens expressed the wish to imitate the Stadholder's gardens in their general layout and decoration, as well as in their plantation, which contained an abundance of rare flowers and trees. The prominence of rare flowers, collected from all corners of the world, shows the all-important role of Holland in the development of horticulture at the time, and the direct stimulus the Stadholder and his advisers gave to the advancement of botanical as well as zoological collections.[34] An overview of the plant material of Frederik Hendrik's gardens, collected from the archives of the Nassau Domains, compared with later botanical illustrations in the *Hortus Regius Honselaerdicensis*,[35] will be discussed here to complement the purely aesthetic features of the stadholderly gardens.

In reconstructing the form, layout and plantation of Frederik Hendrik's gardens, we immediately encounter a number of methodological problems which need to be resolved. Firstly, the traditional method of defining artistic change by arranging works of art into periods of time and according to stylistic development and national origin does not precisely fit into an analysis of garden architecture. In this book an attempt is made to further the appreciation of Dutch garden architecture as an individual form of garden art, connected in part with, yet separate from, Italian and French architecture and their stylistic developments. The individual traits of the Dutch garden style must be carefully weighed against the topographical peculiarities of Holland's wet and flat countryside. Natural conditions and the geographical situation have a greater impact on the style, form and decoration of gardens, which consist for a large part of organic material, than is generally admitted. Secondly, the design of gardens is influenced by local gardening traditions and practices, which in the case of the Stadholder's gardens centred on a complicated system of teamwork, involving land-surveyors and map-makers as well as local workmen and artisans. As a consequence, the method of looking for 'one genius' as designer is not entirely applicable and in general is misleading for the history of Frederik Hendrik's gardens. In fact, in Holland the lack of trained garden architects or specialized designers made the role of the dilettante architect particularly important. Thirdly, the role of books and prints is significant and needs to be considered closely to determine the dissemination of art forms throughout Europe and the implications for the penetration of style forms in Dutch gardens.

In reaching a new assessment of Frederik Hendrik's gardens we will not only concentrate on the most important features of the gardens themselves but approach their layout as an extension to the palace proper. Indeed, in the palace and garden complexes of the Stadholder, and for the first time in Dutch architectural history, the wish to relate building and garden within one unified design is so clearly made manifest. As we shall see, the relationship between building and garden is not only expressed in the form and layout of the interior and exterior spaces but also in their decoration, which, centring on the celebration of the owner, places palace and garden in a larger cosmological setting.

This book consists of two main parts: the first is descriptive, the second analytical in content. The first part (chapters I-III) discusses the general history of the Stadholder's gardens, concentrating on Honselaarsdijk and Ter Nieuburch, followed by the history of the other stadholderly gardens. This section relies heavily on the payment accounts and the decrees of the comptroller and estate stewards of the Nassau Domains, gathered in a comprehensive Appendix to provide a valuable separate source of information. The second part of the book (chapters IV-VI) offers a deeper analysis of the gardens, their layout and sculptural decoration, while containing an overview of the contemporary theoretical and practical backgrounds of garden designing. Seventeenth-century architectural theory and building practices are discussed, followed by an analysis of the style and form of the Stadholder's gardens. Finally, tying all material together, the last chapter provides an iconological analysis of Frederik Hendrik's gardens, appropriately concentrating on the form of the circle as an all-encompassing image.

CHAPTER I

THE HISTORY OF THE GARDENS OF FREDERIK HENDRIK AND AMALIA: HONSELAARSDIJK

Frederik Hendrik began his building activities with the construction and layout of the palace and gardens of Honselaarsdijk.[1] In doing so, he had to take into account the existing older structures on the site and consider certain topographical factors which conditioned the development of Honselaarsdijk. Among the particular characteristics of the surrounding countryside which influenced the layout of palace and gardens were the proximity to the sea, the total flatness of the country, the abundance of water and the lack of natural rock in the low-lying, humid grounds. To get a clear impression of the situation of the estate in the landscape and its relation to the neighbouring cities and towns it is best to use both a contemporary mid-seventeenth-century and an early-eighteenth-century map of this polder area called Delfland *(figs. 3, 4, 4a and 5)*, drawn by Floris Jacobsz or Pieter Florisz van der Sallem,[2] Nicolaas Cruquius and Cornelis Koster, respectively.[3] Honselaarsdijk is situated immediately to the north of the town of Naaldwijk, circa seven miles south-west of The Hague, about the same distance west of Delft and a few miles south of the town of Monster.[4] The estate is laid out in the region called the Westland,

3. Map of the Westland by Floris Jacobsz or Pieter Florisz van der Sallem, c. 1638, with Honselaarsdijk in the centre, the North Sea on top.
Hoogheemraadschap Delfland, Delft

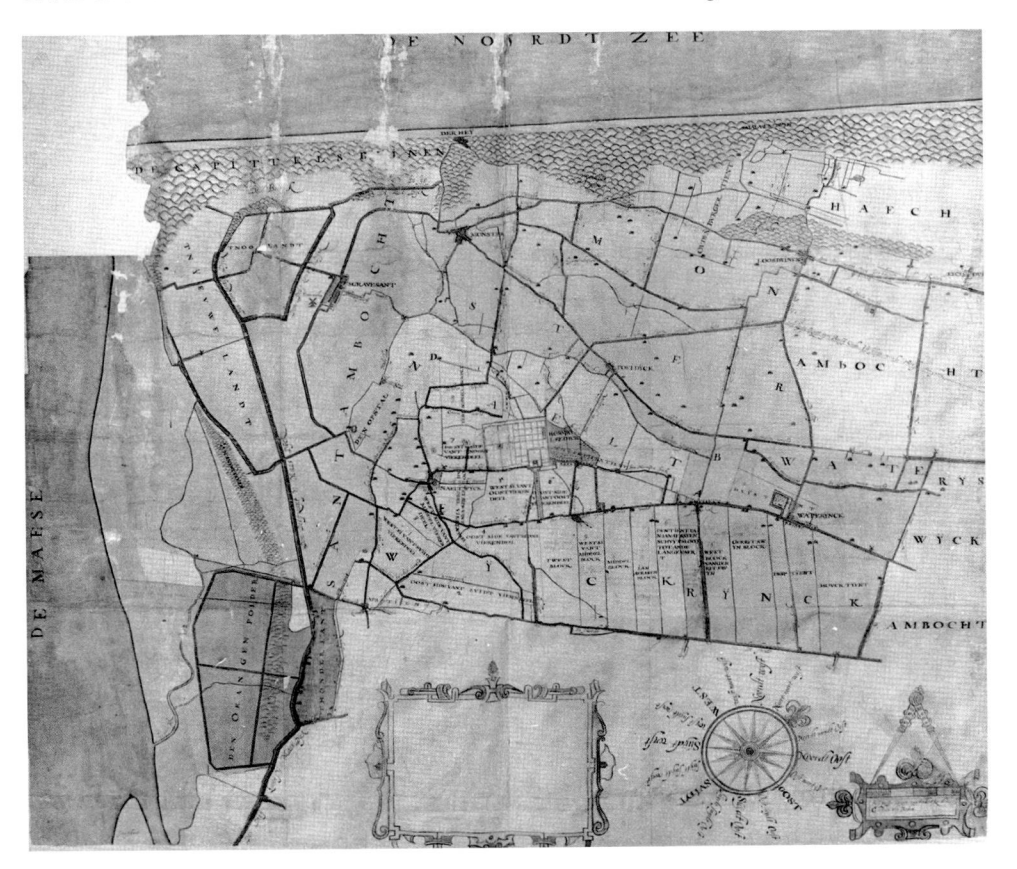

4. Map of the Hoogheemraadschap of Delfland by Nicolaas Cruquius, 1712, showing the situation and extended layout of Honselaarsdijk and its surroundings. Gemeentearchief, The Hague

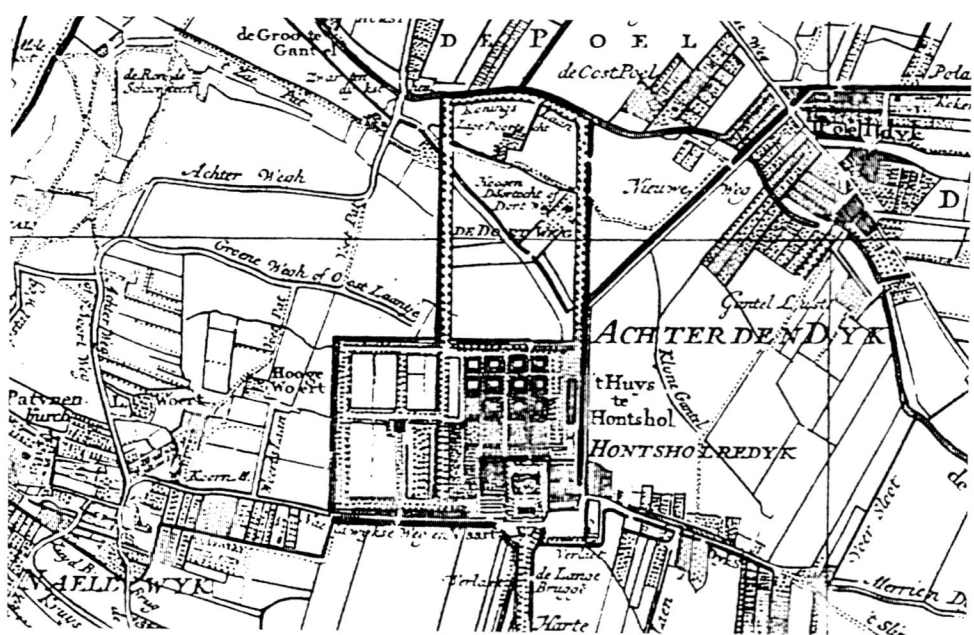

4a. Detail of the map of the Hoogheemraadschap of Delfland by Nicolaas Cruquius, showing the early-eighteenth-century layout of the Honselaarsdijk garden. Gemeentearchief, The Hague

COURTLY GARDENS IN HOLLAND 1600–1650

5. Map of the Hoogheemraadschap of Delfland made by Cornelis Koster after Nicolaas Cruquius's map of 1712 and published by Isaac Tirion, c. 1750, showing Honselaarsdijk and Ter Nieuburch among rows of country estates in the polderlands surrounding Delft and The Hague. Rijksprentenkabinet, Atlas Ottens, Rijksmuseum, Amsterdam
see colour plate 1

which consisted of humid but fertile grass- or polderland extending behind the dunes. The dunes protected the lowlands against the North Sea in the north-west, visible on the upper edge of the map, while the large river Maas formed the south-west border, visible on the left.

Though Frederik Hendrik purchased Honselaarsdijk officially in 1612,[5] as early as 1610 he sent out his councillor and his steward into the Westland to collect information concerning the estate of Honselaarsdijk. In the favourable report which was drawn up on that occasion, and led to negotiations resulting in the acquisition of the Seigniory, Honselaarsdijk was described as follows:

> The Manor proper or Castle of Honsholredijk with its canals, moats, plantations, lower court, orchards, flowers, herbal court, pigeon house and fishing grounds ... yearly yielding 500 ar. [pounds artois].[6]

This document shows that when Frederik Hendrik acquired the estate and began his improvements the property of Honselaarsdijk already comprised kitchen and herbal gardens and orchards. These were most likely simple gardens and orchards which already may have belonged to the original, medieval *burcht*, or castle, of the Lords of Naaldwijk.[7] They owned Honselaarsdijk until the beginning of the sixteenth century and had used the property primarily as a hunting reserve.[8] Subsequently, Honselaarsdijk became the property of the Counts of Aremberg, which it remained until 1583 when it was confiscated by the States of Holland.[9] From 1589 to 1609[10] the States placed Honselaarsdijk at the disposal of Stadholder Prince Maurits (1567-1625), Frederik Hendrik's older half-brother, 'to be used [by him] as his country estate *(uythof)*, for his service and pleasure'.[11] It was in the context of an estate still essentially used for hunting that the young Frederik Hendrik came to know and enjoy Honselaarsdijk. During his ownership it grew to become a monumental palace with pleasure gardens, acquiring added function and status as a grand country retreat.

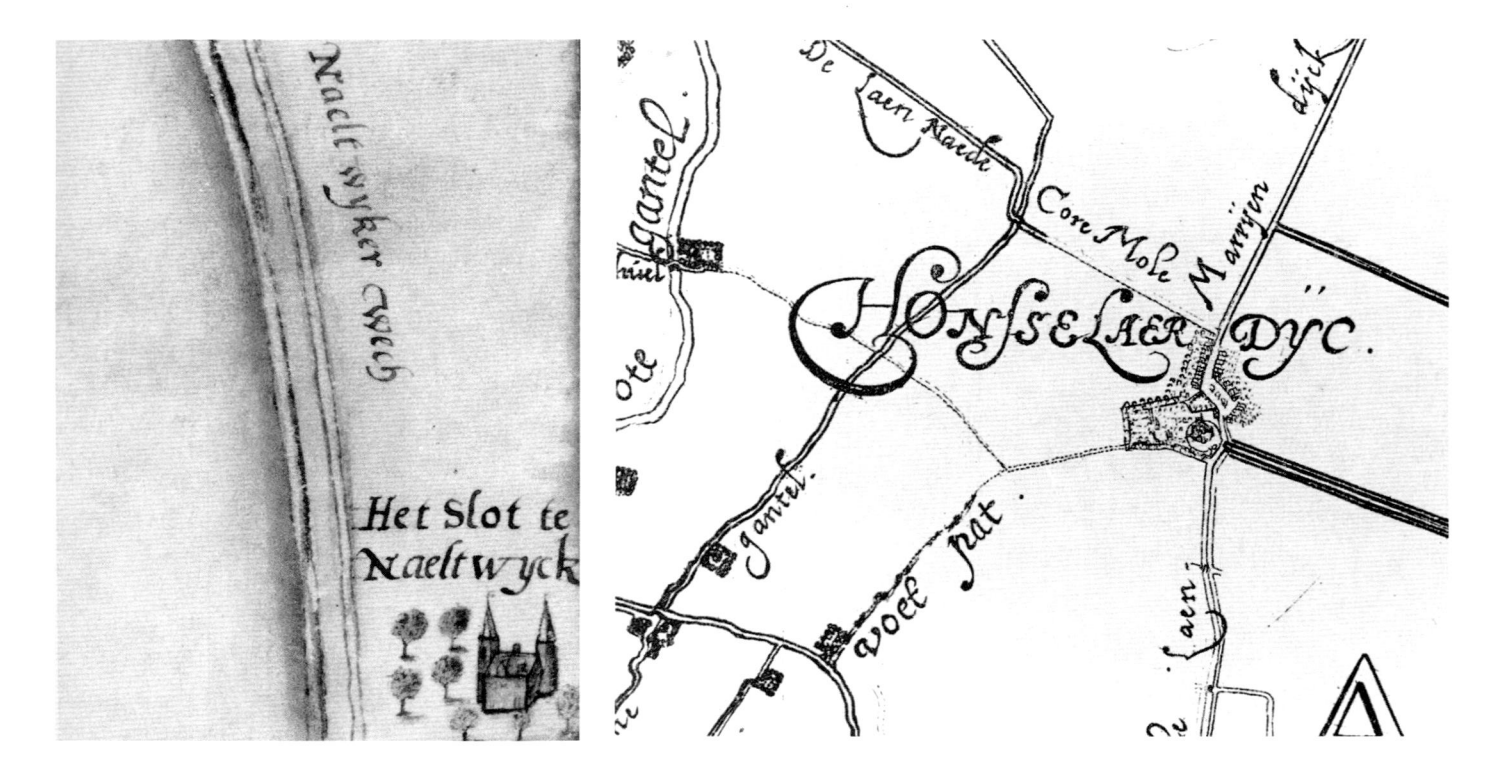

Our knowledge of the building structures and ground division before Frederik Hendrik made his changes is fragmentary. The oldest surviving document, a map of 1609 by Jan Pietersz Dou from the map book of the St. Catharijne Gasthuis in Leiden *(fig. 6)*,[12] gives a rough sketch of the layout of the grounds prior to their improvement and extension. The map vaguely shows a rectangular central building flanked on either side by two (possibly octagonal) towers with pointed roof structures.[13] One may recognize a wooded area or orchard in the line of trees surrounding the house, but we cannot draw any further conclusions as to the precise divisions of the grounds at the time. A somewhat clearer, though still rather sketchy overview of the estate is offered by a map of Delfland by Floris Balthasars, dated 1611 *(fig. 7)*.[14] On this map the old castle of 'Honsholredijk' is depicted as a round stronghold in the water, surrounded by grounds held within an irregular, rectangular framework. The estate was bordered to the left, roughly on the west side, by a dike or waterway and to the south by the main road leading to the village of Naaldwijk. Access to the stronghold was provided by two bridges, one to the north from the orchards and gardens and one to the east from a kind of forecourt, right in the bend of the road leading to the main square of the village of Honselaarsdijk.[15]

A more precise overview of early-seventeenth-century Honselaarsdijk is given in a series of maps in the *Kaartboek van Naaldwijk*, which includes maps of the larger Naaldwijk area in circa 1620 *(figs. 8 and 9)*.[16] These maps were presumably commissioned by Frederik Hendrik himself and must have been prepared in connection with his extension plans, for administrative purposes and to have a clear, general overview of his property.[17] The plans in this map book distinctly show the original system of dikes and canals surrounding the castle and a simple layout of gardens and orchards. The castle, still situated on a circular

6. Earliest map of the Castle, or Slot, at Naaldwijk by Jan Pietersz Dou, 1609. Map book of the St. Catharijne Gasthuis. Gemeentearchief, Leiden

7. Map of Delfland by Floris Balthasars, 1611, showing the old situation of Honselaarsdijk as a round 'donjon', with old dike system and avenues. Gemeentearchief, The Hague

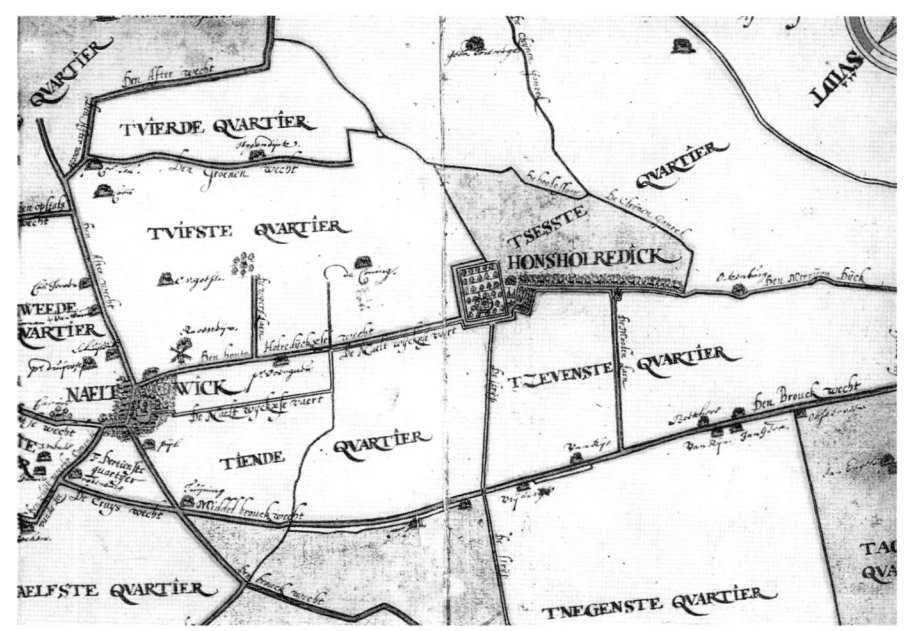

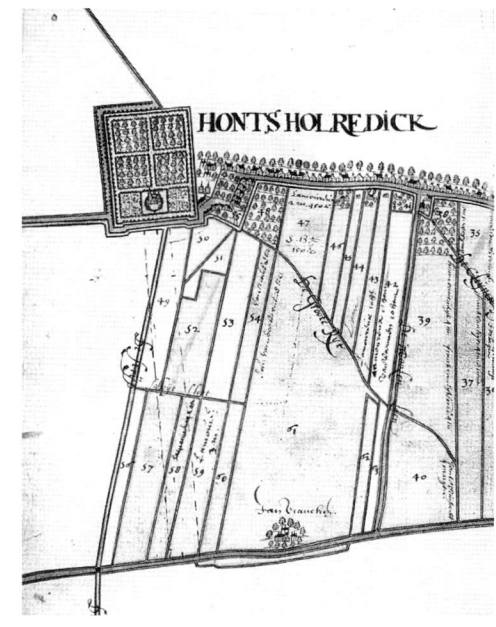

8. Map from the map book of Naaldwijk, showing Honselaarsdijk c. 1620, with orchards and castle in round pond prior to the large-scale improvements.
Gemeentearchief, Naaldwijk

9. Map from the map book of Naaldwijk, showing Honselaarsdijk in 1620-25 with the first changes made to the garden layout and the approach avenue.
Gemeentearchief, Naaldwijk
see colour plate 2

10. Map by Floris Jacobsz van der Sallem, c. 1615, showing the situation of the castle on a round island and first indications of a grand avenue.
Algemeen Rijksarchief

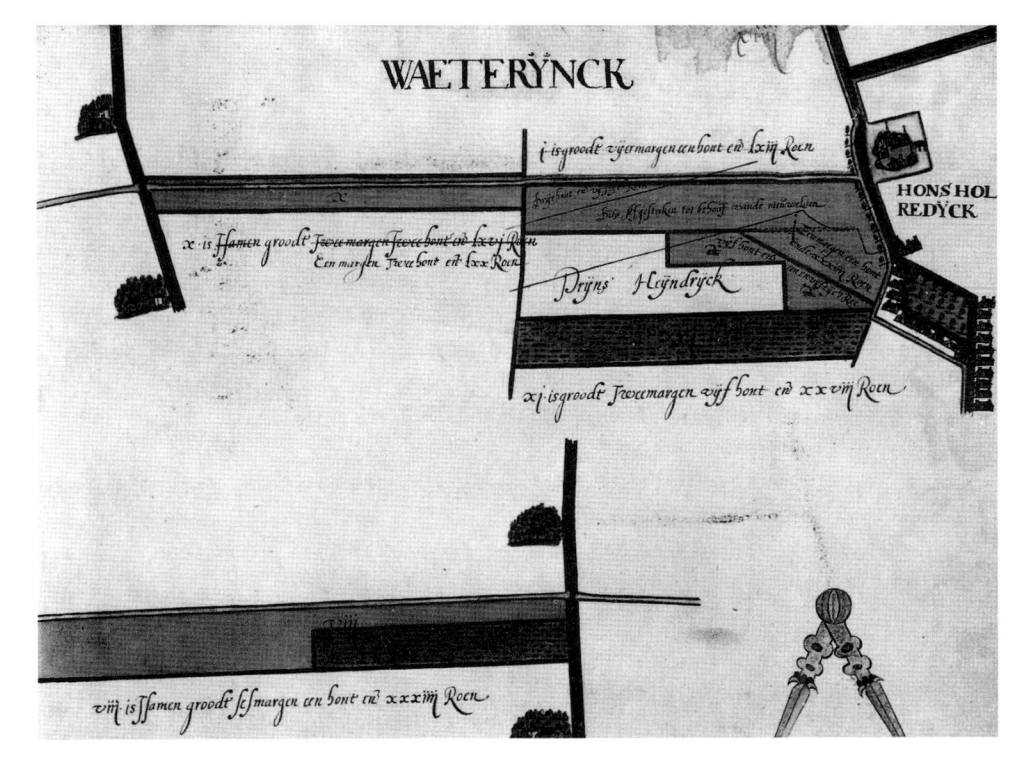

island, consisted of an irregular agglomeration of buildings. The old dike, visible on the left and enclosing the west and part of the north sides of the property, is worth noting as an important former barrier. This barrier would not only dictate the basic size and form of the main pleasure garden under Frederik Hendrik, but would continue to influence the layout throughout its further development history.

Though records of payments indicate that major building activities at Honselaarsdijk did not take place until 1621, some important changes were begun soon after 1612. Visual evidence shows that Frederik Hendrik started his activities by planning a monumental access way to his property. A map by Floris Jacobsz van der Sallem dated circa 1615 *(fig. 10)*[18]

I. HONSELAARSDIJK

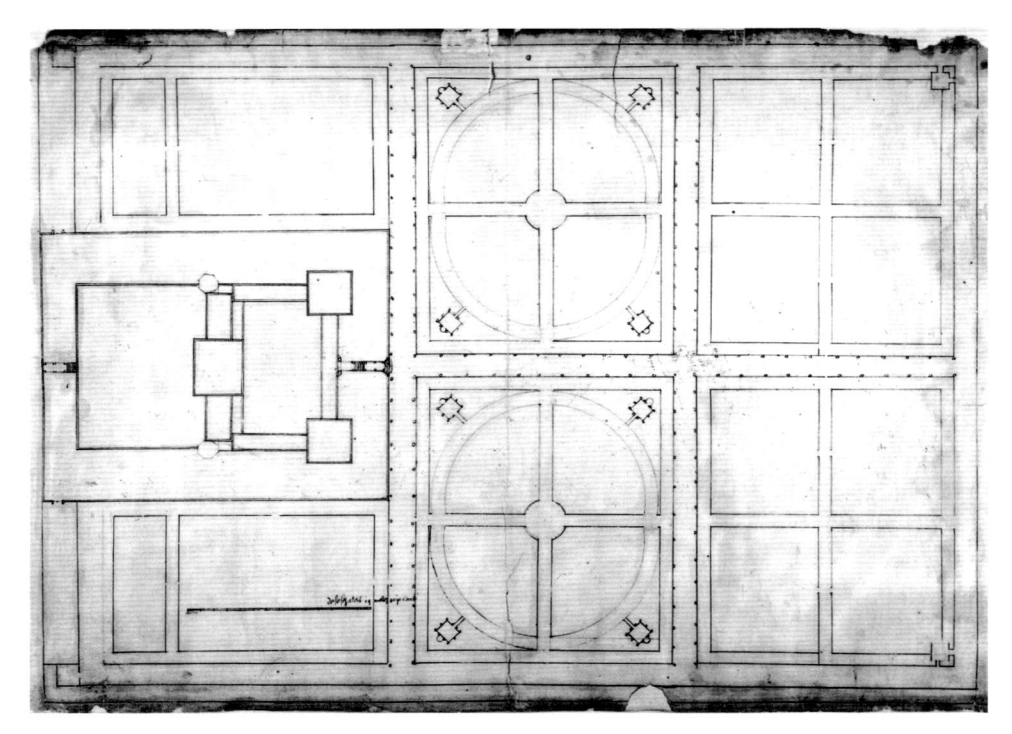

11. Original plan of the new layout of Honselaarsdijk, c. 1633, showing the geometrical garden compartments and circular *berceaux*.
Algemeen Rijksarchief

shows the newly-acquired, elongated strip of land outlining the area for the layout of the grand entrance avenue. This strip is described on the map as belonging to 'Prijns Heijnrijck' and as 'Dito Afgesteeken tot behoef van de nieue Laen' (also marked off for the sake of the new avenue). At that time, in order to create new gardens, first steps must also have been undertaken to change and expand the grounds. This was done by filling in ditches and canals, rearranging and heightening low-lying fields and polder areas. Only when the land was thus reclaimed and prepared could the arrangement of the ground in plots begin, resulting in a garden layout proper.

In order to modernize his property still further, Frederik Hendrik developed plans for the construction of a new palace, a final, toned-down version of which was to be completed only after his death. The creation of the whole palace complex was realized over a long period, during three major building campaigns stretching from the early 1620s to the late 1640s.[19] In the first phase, the old castle was demolished in stages during what may be called the first great building campaign of 1621-31, its original form still visible on the maps shown above dated shortly before 1620 *(see figs. 9 and 10)*. As seen on these early maps, the old moated castle did not have a unified form but consisted of a complex of separate building structures grouped together on a round island. The form and character of the whole complex remind one of the age-old type of medieval *donjon*. As will be seen in some detail, it was this complex which, after it had been partly demolished and its building material partly reused, was the basis of the later palace of Honselaarsdijk.

How comprehensive the changes at Honselaarsdijk were can be seen by comparing the plans from the *Kaartboek van Naaldwijk* with two later plans of the Honselaarsdijk garden shown in an undated, anonymous drawing *(fig. 11)*[20] and in a print by Balthazar Florisz van Berckerode, dated circa 1638 *(fig. 12)*.[21] The anonymous drawing and Van Berckerode's print are the earliest representations of the Honselaarsdijk palace and garden after Frederik Hendrik's second building campaign, which took place circa 1633-39 and comprised the further embellishment of building and garden. The drawing is set up as a rough, preliminary sketch-plan of the new layout and gives a clear, schematic overview of the moated palace and the main pleasure garden. The new garden is designed in carefully

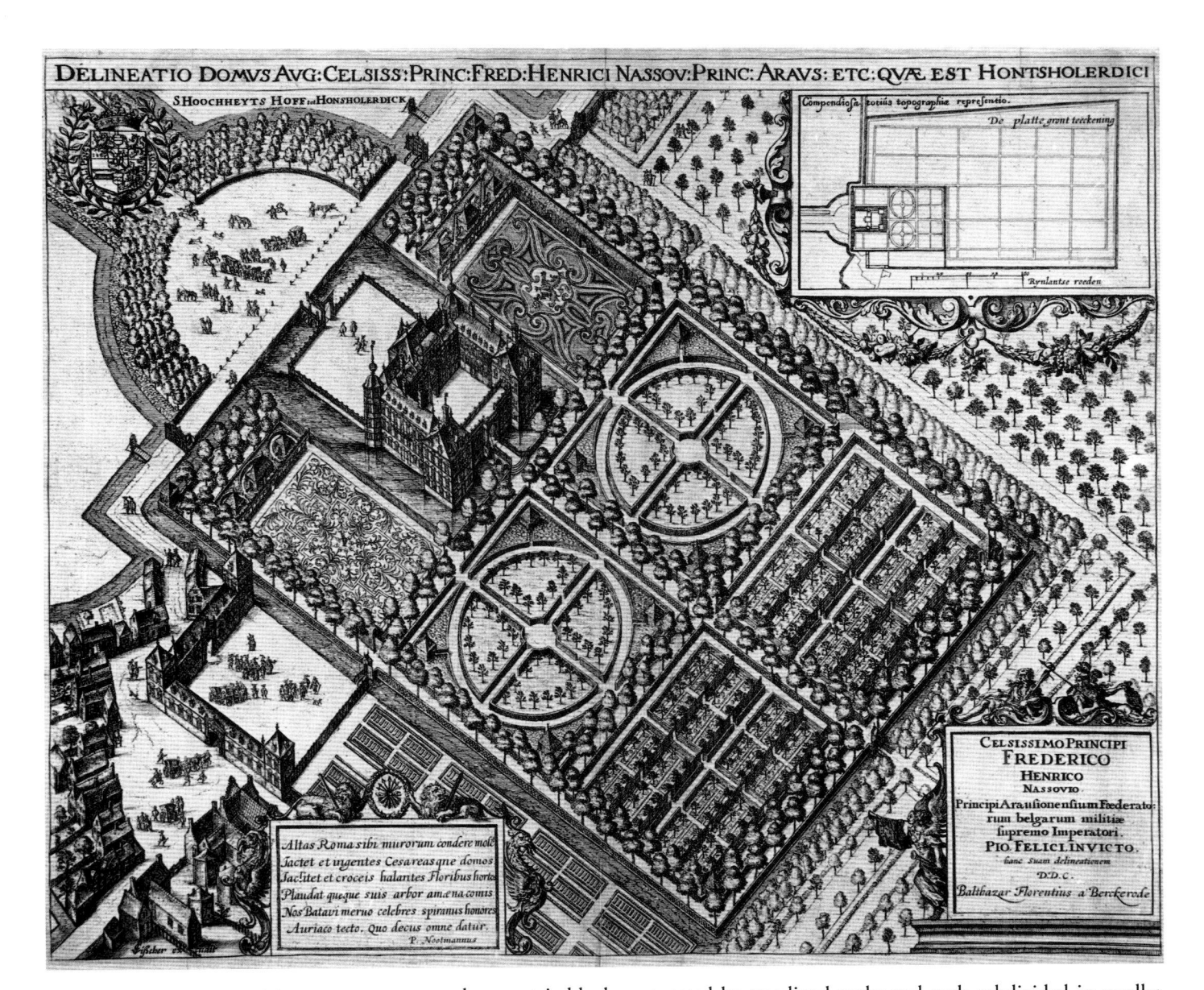

12. The gardens of Honselaarsdijk in Balthazar Florisz van Berckerode's bird's-eye view, c. 1638, showing the completion of the first geometrical garden layout under Frederik Hendrik.
Gemeentearchief, The Hague
see colour plate 3

arranged geometric blocks, separated by tree-lined paths and each subdivided in smaller sections. The garden compartments immediately behind the building contain two large circles which, as comparison with the Van Berckerode print shows, represent two circular *berceaux*. The print, providing a first, clear bird's-eye view of the whole layout, shows the newly-completed palace and gardens in all their detail and with remarkable precision. Van Berckerode dedicated the print to Frederik Hendrik; it was executed by Claes Jansz Visscher (1587-1652) and is accompanied by a poem by Pieter Nootman (1601-before 1652),[22] which refers to Honselaarsdijk as to a 'new Rome'. In the top left-hand corner one recognizes the Orange family's coat of arms, encompassed by the emblem of the Order of the Garter bearing the well-known motto 'Honi soit qui mal y pense'. Van Berckerode's print is a unique document, as it is one of the earliest examples of a monumental panoramic view, a specific Dutch seventeenth-century tradition of depicting an estate, which was to become widely popular in the second half of the century.[23] Of great artistic value, this representation of Honselaarsdijk at the same time had an important political purpose: it propagated the ancientness and power of the Dutch Republic as a new Batavian stronghold, the *Hortus Batavus* with the House of Orange as its protector.

I. HONSELAARSDIJK

Though one cannot call the garden depicted in Van Berckerode's print a 'finished product', since several later changes and extensions would take place during the building campaigns of the 1640s, one can get a good impression of the general ideals of architecture and garden art around the Dutch court at the time. In short, these ideals embraced classical architectural theory of form and proportion, while retaining traditional Dutch methods of land division. The successful combination of classical ideals and Dutch gardening tradition at Honselaarsdijk did not remain unnoticed even to the critical French eye. In fact, in addition to the building and its interior, the extensiveness of the Honselaarsdijk garden, the beauty of its flowers and *berceaux*, the function of its many paths and avenues as ideal walking places are recorded with enthusiasm in de la Serre's account of Maria de' Medici's visit to The Netherlands in 1638:

> Cette Maison superbe et splendide, est bastie a quatre pavillons qui ne font toutesfois qu'un seul corps de bastiment, par la liaison de deux belles galleries qui les joygnent ensemble de deux costez. La basse court de l'entree de fort large estandue faisant montre d'abord d'un nombre infiny de statues, marque la magnificence de ce Palais. L'escallier a jour de marbre est fait si artistement, que dans le pays on ne treuve point son semblable. On y voit depeint au plus haut tout a l'entour, un baslustre, ou un grand nombre de personnes de differentes nations, y paressent si vivement, que d'abord on en prend la peinture pour relief; … Il y a un fort beau Jardin partagé en deux, sa moitié fait voir diverses sortes de parterres remplis avec ordre en toute saison de mille belles fleurs qui se font également aymer, et par leur beauté, et par leur odeur. L'autre moitié a ses allees a perte de veuë, bornees de deux costez de pallisades tousjours vertes, dont la hauteur et l'espaisseur servent d'abry aux ombres, la plus grande partie de la journee, contre les attaintes du Soleil. On y voit aussi un Parc de longue estanduë, peuplé d'un nombre infiny de bestes sauvages, et tout cela ensemble est environné d'un large fossé plain d'eau, ayant une chausee de chasque costé qui fait encore un beau lieu de promenade.[24]

In his account of the Honselaarsdijk estate, de la Serre mentions all the essential features of the garden, including the perpetually green and shady palisades or *berceaux*, the fragrant flower parterres, the long alleys, as well as the enclosing canals with fresh water. Also admired was the deer park, which apparently functioned as a zoo or menagerie, with a collection of wild animals. Maria de' Medici never knew a dull moment here, de la Serre assures us, and, accompanied by her ladies-in-waiting or by *Son Altesse* Frederik Hendrik himself, often enjoyed walking through these beautiful gardens and the great park, where 'tous les objects champestres qui pouvoient contenter l'esprit par les yeux, s'y trouvoient en abondance'.[25]

As shown by de la Serre's description and Van Berckerode's print, by 1638 the entire layout of Honselaarsdijk covered a large rectangular area containing a smaller rectangular pleasure garden which was enclosed by a canal with a moated palace in the centre. The section with the main pleasure garden, represented on the original sketch-plan *(see fig. 11)* and shown in the top right-hand corner of Van Berckerode's print, was but a small part (approximately one sixth) of the total plantation area of Honselaarsdijk. Indeed, the larger plantation or park area measured circa 125 acres or 50 hectares, while the main pleasure garden, immediately surrounding the palace, was about 20 acres or eight hectares large.[26] The whole pleasure garden was symmetrically laid out round a central axis running north-south, beginning with the avenue, crossing the bridge, cutting through the middle of the palace building and continuing over the rear drawbridge into the garden proper and from

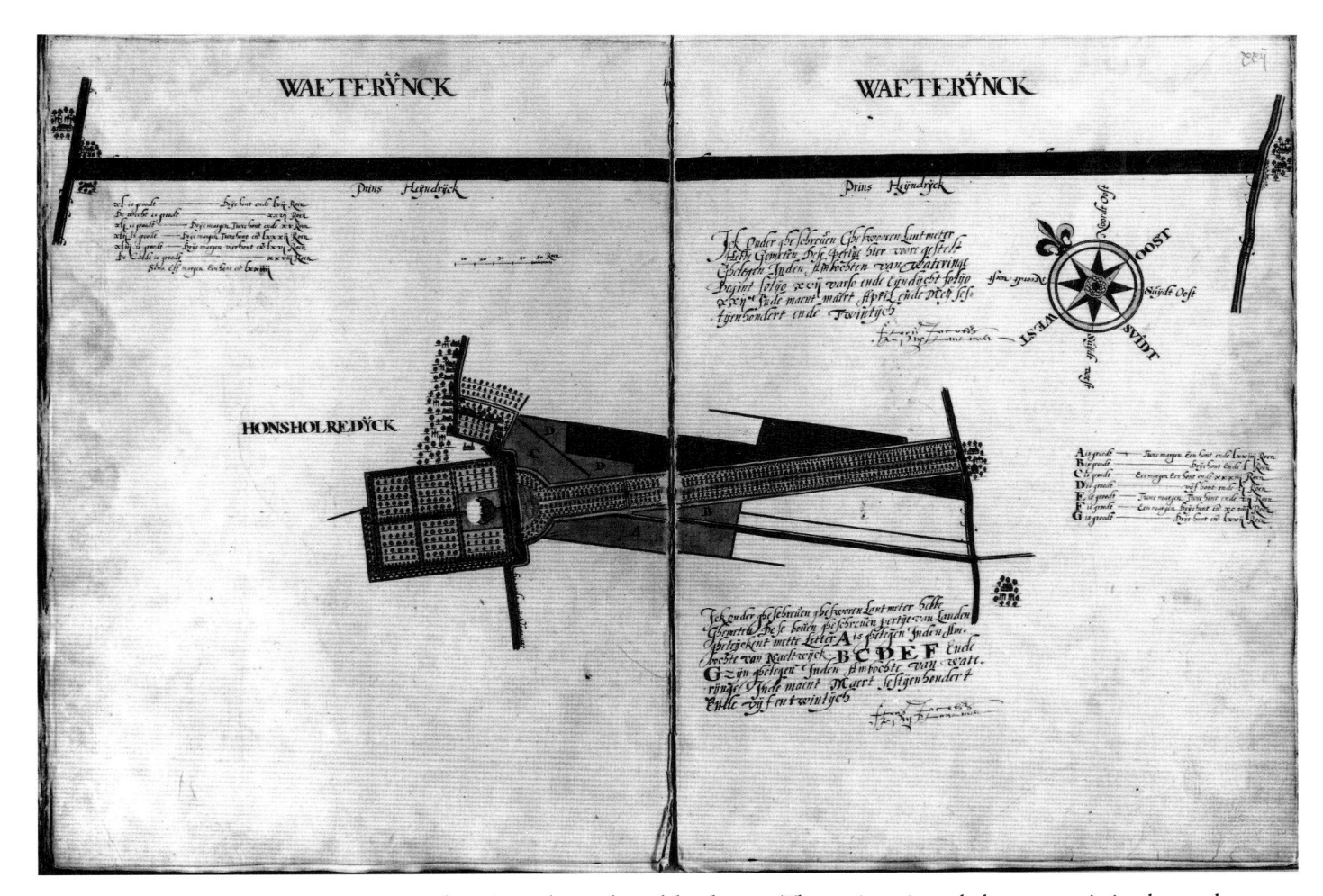

13. Map of the front approach avenue of Honselaarsdijk by Floris Jacobsz van der Sallem, signed and dated 1625. Algemeen Rijksarchief
see colour plate 4

there into the park and landscape. The main axis and the cross axis in the garden were accentuated by a double row of trees. The garden as a whole was divided into three parts. The first part comprised the sections or garden plots with arbours and decorative parterres, situated on either side of the central, moated castle. On the outer west and east corners two little 'watch-towers' – in fact little houses or arbours built of wood – extended into the moat. The second garden part, situated directly behind the palace, consisted of two large square plots, each inscribed by high circular hedges, with arbours in the corners. The last of the three garden parts was planted with trees and espaliers, arranged in two square sections, each again divided into four smaller plots. All garden sections were neatly enclosed by wooden fences, thus forming a system of separate garden 'enclaves'. The garden in its entirety was not only enclosed by a fence and the moat, but also by a double row of trees, on the north and west sides even with added rows. This 'green screen' may have protected the garden from harsh north-westerly winds, yet must also have obstructed the view into the surrounding park.

The aesthetic pleasure which Honselaarsdijk gave to the inhabitants and visitors as they approached along the long, shaded avenue towards the palace must have been one of colourful festivity: the red brick of the building, its dark-green shutters, the coloured tiles in the courtyards and terraces, the gilded pinnacles on the lead-blue roof, all stood out against a screen of greenery and a varying blue-grey sky. The many colourful flowers in vases on the balustraded terraces and in the parterre borders reflected the colours of the building, while the gilded statues harmonized with the shiny pinnacles and the sparkling water in ponds and canals. In addition to the sweet *odeur* of the flowers themselves,[27] a fresh breeze with a whiff of salt from the sea glided over the fields, while the sound of exotic birds in the menagerie and the splattering fountains filled the air, delighting the visitor's senses as well as refreshing his mind.

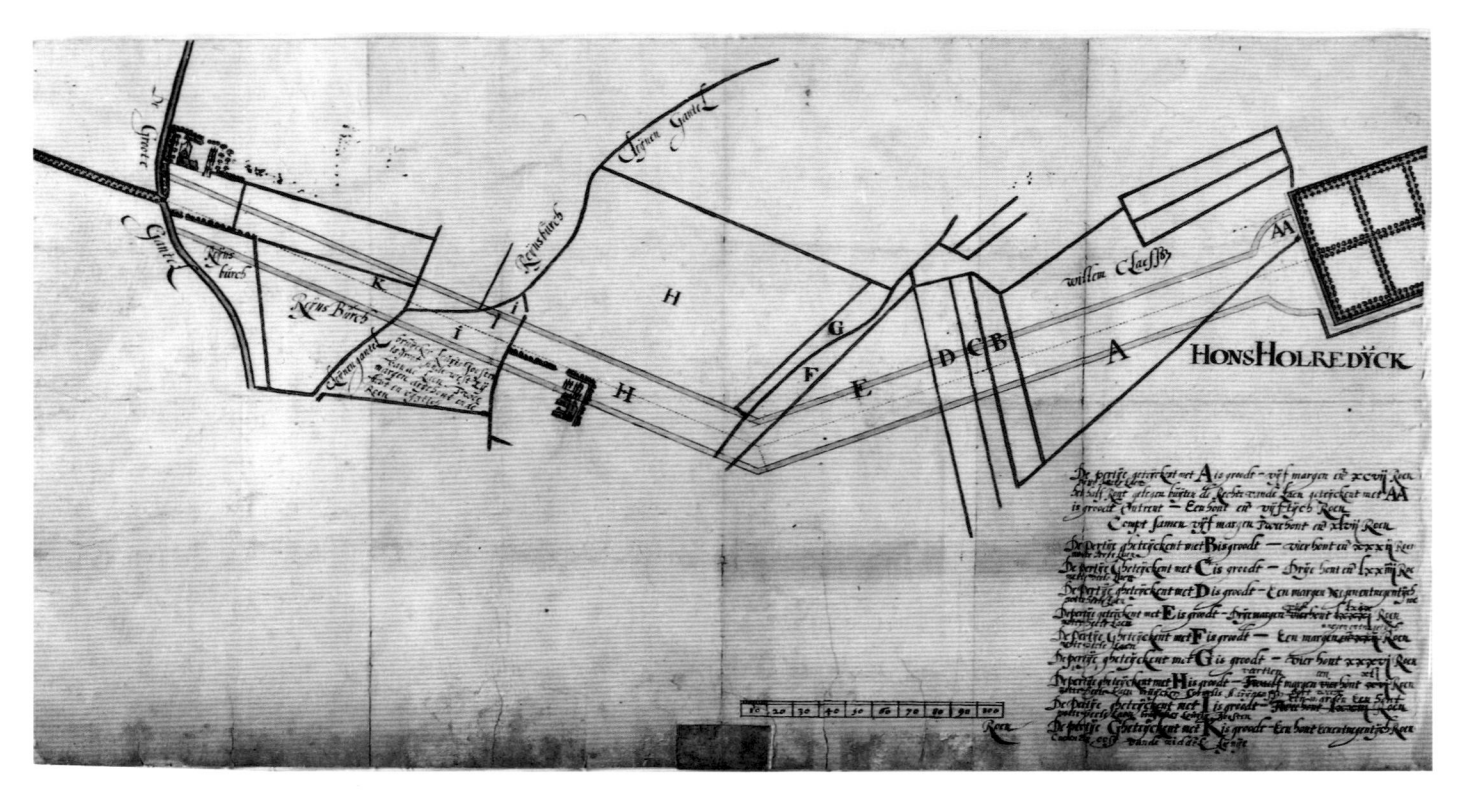

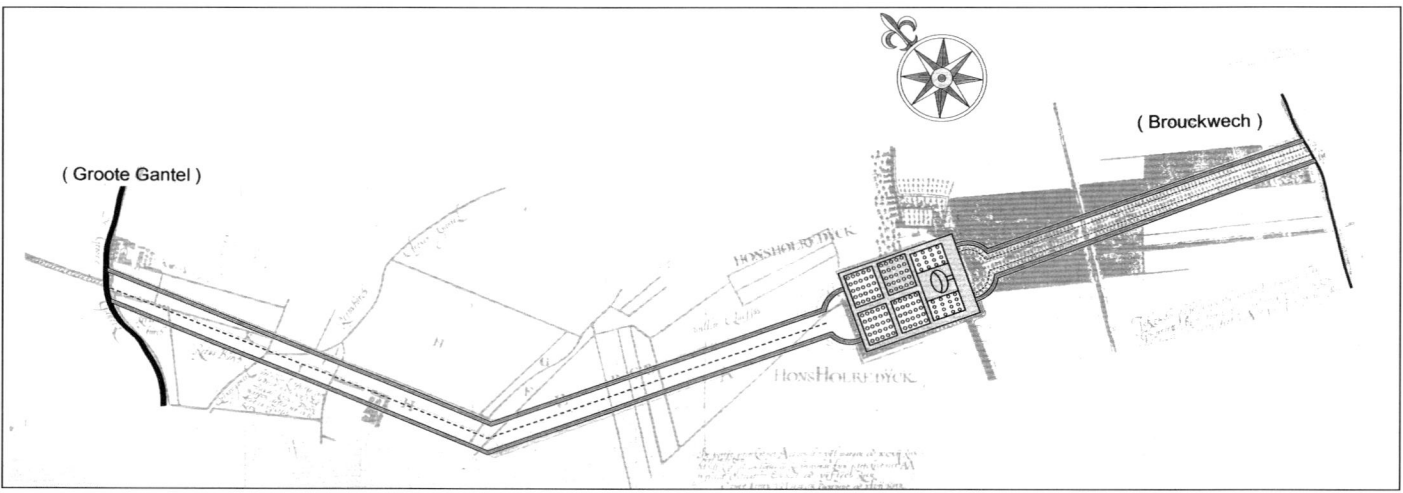

When it comes to the actual garden design, if one compares Van Berckerode's print with the *Kaartboek van Naaldwijk* drawn twenty years earlier, one realizes that – except for the layout of the *parterres de broderie*, the circular hedges and certain details of planting – the inner organization of the garden proper had not changed much. The layout of the various garden plots basically follows the age-old principle of quadrature, the system of dividing the grounds into simple square plots or sections. New elements in Van Berckerode's print, such as the parterres and circular *berceaux*, will be discussed at greater length in the following chapters, but some preliminary comments should be made here on the now completed, huge and costly avenue[28] ending in a semicircle.

24   COURTLY GARDENS IN HOLLAND 1600-1650

14. Unexecuted plan of the rear approach avenue of Honselaarsdijk, creating a monumental system of axes crossing the surrounding landscape.
Algemeen Rijksarchief

15. Reconstruction drawing of the combined front and rear avenues of Honselaarsdijk extending over several kilometres into the surrounding polder landscape.

The finished approach avenue, defined by a canal and double rows of trees on either side, is drawn in great detail by Floris Jacobsz van der Sallem, in a map signed and dated 1625 *(fig. 13)*.[29] This avenue not only bestowed monumentality on the layout of Honselaarsdijk, it also influenced the spatial pattern of the whole surrounding area, as can be clearly seen on maps of the larger Westland area *(see figs. 3 and 4)*. Contrary to what has generally been believed – that the French garden architect André Mollet, who worked at Honselaarsdijk from 1633 to 1635, was responsible for designing such a grand entry – the avenue was completed long before his arrival in Holland, as Hopper first pointed out.[30] Indeed, as is shown by the map dated c. 1615 *(see fig. 10)*, a monumental driveway was one of the first steps in planning the improvement of Honselaarsdijk. More remarkable, however, and hitherto unknown, is the fact that, in conjunction with the front entry, another prominent avenue was originally planned to approach the palace from the rear *(fig. 14)*.[31] For unknown reasons this rear entrance road was never executed, perhaps because one major entry avenue in front was deemed enough. In any case, if the rear driveway had been executed, the whole complex of entry avenues would have formed an unprecedented and powerful system of axes, which, with a combined length of about three kilometres, would have completely dominated the surrounding landscape, as is shown in a reconstruction drawing *(fig. 15)*.[32] Apart from aesthetic and spatial considerations, practical reasons may have led to the idea of designing two large approach avenues. Such a system of double avenues would have provided an easy access to the network of roads in the Westland, facilitating the flow of visitors to Honselaarsdijk. Another aspect which must have prompted the original design for a monumental entrance at the rear of the building is the form of the palace itself – a consideration which brings us to look in greater detail at the development of Frederik Hendrik's new palace structure and its composition.

Turning to the building visible on Van Berckerode's print *(see fig. 12)*, we can see that its design was based on a palace form which had evolved in France; it consisted of four corner pavilions connected by three wings and a low entrance wing, surrounding a court, or *cour d'honneur*. As a type, and in its block-like, severe appearance, the Honselaarsdijk palace and garden complex reminds one of layouts such as Ancy-le-Franc and Charleval, depicted in Jacques Androuet Du Cerceau's *Les Plus Excellents Bastiments de France* (1576-79).[33] However, probably due to the natural form of the island itself, its traditional accessibility by means of a bridge on the rear or garden side[34] and to the situation of the old castle on whose foundations the new palace was rebuilt,[35] the composition of this traditional French palace form is reversed at Honselaarsdijk. Crossing a small bridge from a semicircular forecourt, instead of entering through an entrance pavilion into the *cour d'honneur*, one finds oneself in an unadorned square forecourt on the island, immediately facing the main *corps de logis*, which is normally located on the opposite side of the interior court, facing the garden. At Honselaarsdijk the low 'entrance wing', usually situated in front, lay at the back of the building block facing the gardens, and consisted of an open arcade topped by a terrace. Given these specific 'reversed' architectural features, it is not surprising that Frederik Hendrik wished to have an alternative main entrance in the garden or rear façade which, if the traditional French palace composition had been followed exactly, would function as the front entrance to his palace. Hence the attempt to create a monumental avenue ending at the rear of the building, as demonstrated by the plan shown above *(see fig. 14)*.

The palace visible on Van Berckerode's print constitutes the situation after the second, major building campaign of 1633-39; it shows an improved façade, consisting of a large central pavilion with adjoining wings flanked by octagonal towers. These may be remains of the old castle *(see figs. 6 and 9)*, though this cannot be determined with certainty.[36] The preservation of certain architectural details, such as these towers and the drawbridges, expresses a desire to maintain feudal pretensions. Actually, the aspect of holding on to traditional forms with particular 'power connotations' can also be recognized in Frederik Hendrik's gardens, as will be seen below.

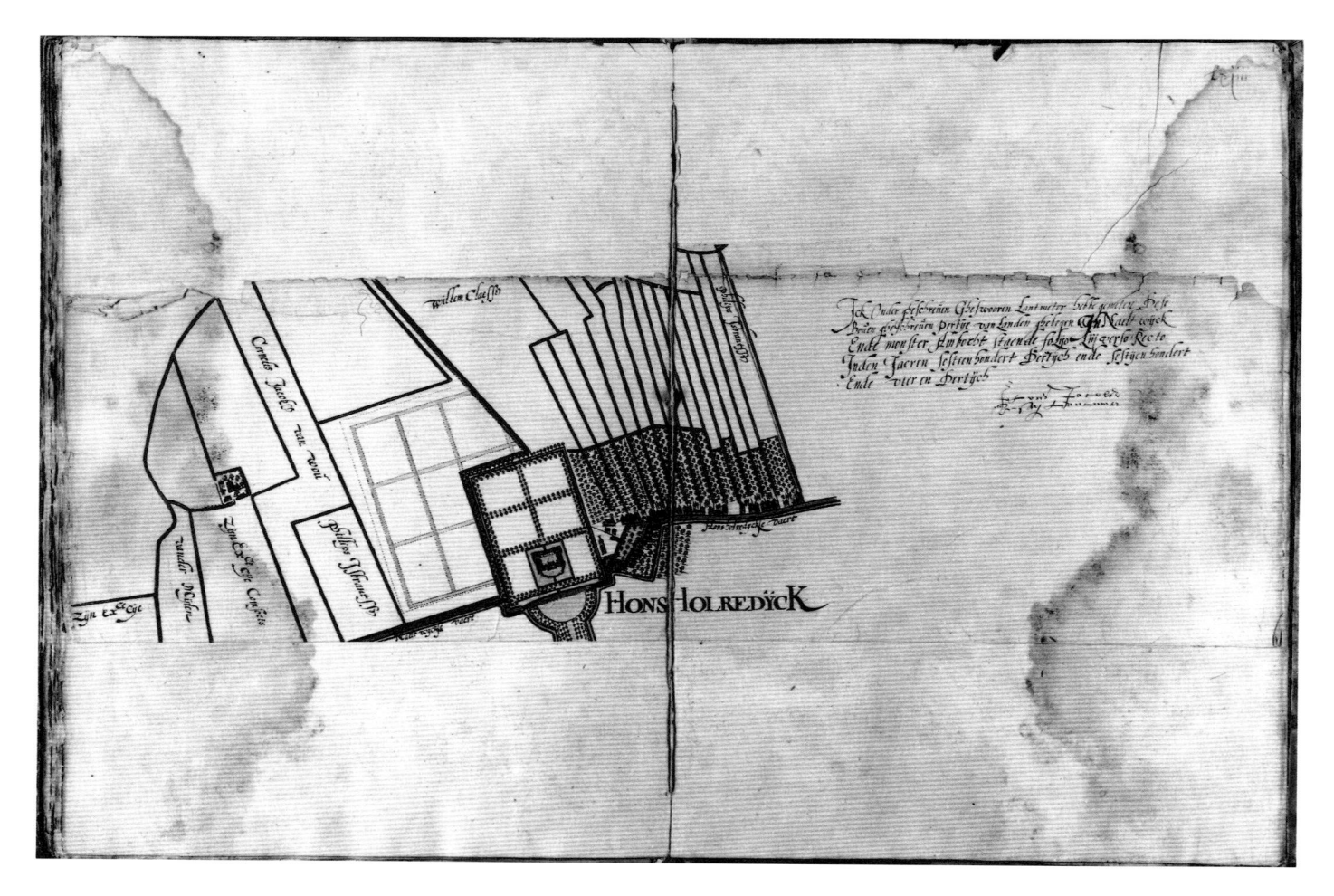

The construction of the Honselaarsdijk façade is clearly documented in the account books (1036 fol. 155), which record that during the years 1621-24 three pavilions were completed. The completion of this main façade can be seen on Floris Jacobsz's map of 1625 *(see fig. 13)*. This map is also important for showing a particular stage in the construction of the palace: the rear half of the round 'island' is still visible as a white section, or empty, unbuilt area. The record books (1039 fol. 214vo) also indicate that the extension of the building with a north-east pavilion and gallery was begun in the mid-1620s, gradually filling in the empty section on the island. The opposite north-west pavilion and its gallery were built only five years later, in 1629, and completed in 1633-34 (1038 fol. 202).[37] At the same time the open arcade running along the garden and connecting the two rear pavilions was finished. Another map made by Floris Jacobsz, signed and dated 1634 *(fig. 16)*,[38] for the first time shows the completed building block surrounding an interior court. However, the shape of the original *donjon* or island is still recognizable in the half-round form of the ground in front of the new palace façade. This area, the place of the later square forecourt visible on Van Berckerode's print, would only acquire its rectilinear form around 1634-35, probably on the advice of the French architect Simon de la Vallée who worked at Honselaarsdijk from 1633 to 1637.

In 1635, only halfway through the second major building campaign, Constantijn

16. Map by Floris Jacobsz van der Sallem, 1634, showing the finished building block of the castle and the further extension of the gardens.
Algemeen Rijksarchief

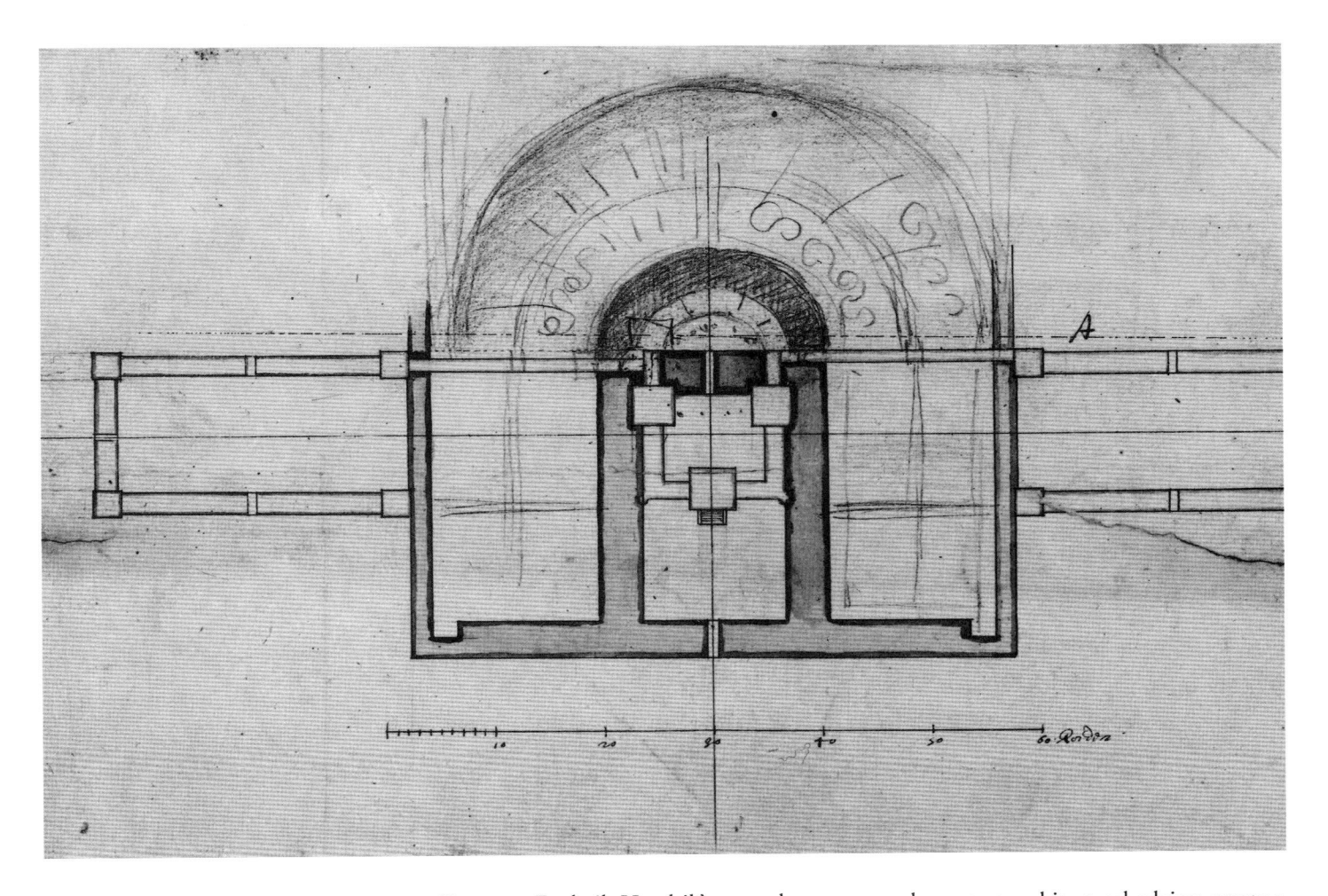

17. Plan by Pieter Post, 1646, for the connection of the Honselaarsdijk palace and annexes with extensive semicircular gardens.
Algemeen Rijksarchief

Huygens, Frederik Hendrik's trusted secretary and constant architectural adviser, wrote a letter to his brother-in-law and special supervisor of the works, David de Wilhem, expressing the Prince's dissatisfaction with the fact that the building would not be finished that same year: '... aliquid hoc anno ad perfectionem Honselardici reliquum fore.'[39] Frederik Hendrik's eagerness to enjoy his palaces and gardens as quickly as possible resulted in repeated admonitions to complete the work at an accelerated pace, as can be gleaned from another letter by Huygens to de Wilhem, written in the autumn of 1636: 'Take good care of the cultivation of the grounds at Honselaarsdijk; the Prince is annoyed that no care was taken of it the previous year.'[40] De Wilhem replied, somewhat piqued, that 'everyone was doing his best at Honselaarsdijk', but that the work had slowed down for various reasons, one of them being that the recalcitrant estate manager Simon van Catshuysen had refused to plant the trees without exact further orders from the Stadholder himself. Moreover, de Wilhem added, Huygens must realize that he could not stay at Honselaarsdijk all day long to supervise the work without risking being infected by the plague, which raged through The Hague at the time.[41] Neither Huygens nor de Wilhem could have foreseen that only a few years after their latest efforts new extension plans would be undertaken, comprising Frederik Hendrik's last building activities, when not only part of the just completed palace façade would again be destroyed but the grounds and gardens would also be laid out and decorated anew.

During this last building campaign of 1640-46 Pieter Post (1608-1669), the court architect at that time, designed several plans for the renewal of the façade and the extension of the whole complex by adding two annexe service quarters. This design, if completed, would have totally changed Honselaarsdijk's block-like *donjon* character to embrace the latest French type of elongated palace form, already successfully employed by the Stadholder in the design of the Huis ter Nieuburch at Rijswijk.[42] Post's detailed design for the extension of Honselaarsdijk's façade shows similar solutions based on French architectural form principles: by replacing the octagonal towers with two square corner pavilions which corresponded with the northern pavilions at the rear of the building,[43] and by subsequently rebuilding the octagonal towers at the end of galleries constructed at a right angle to the main building, a real *cour d'honneur* would finally be created, vying with the grand palaces of France.[44] However, due to the death of Frederik Hendrik in 1647, only part of the plans were executed. When it comes to the façade, merely the two square corner pavilions were realized, while the end-towers and connecting galleries were never built.[45] The annexe buildings, instead of being connected by means of long hallways to the main building block, would remain separate structures on the adjoining terrain flanking the palace. The construction of these annexes or lower courts (to the west known as the Domeinhof; to the east, the Nederhof) flanking the palace and containing stables, kitchens, a chapel, a picture gallery and, notably, 'antique' bath apartments[46] would not be completed until the mid-1640s. Except for a detail of the eastern lower courts, these buildings are therefore not yet shown in Van Berckerode's print. Since the lower courts were separated from the main building by the moat there was no easy, direct access from the palace to the stables and the other living quarters. Frederik Hendrik tried to remedy this on various occasions by commissioning his architects to design connecting structures.

In this context, and considering Frederik Hendrik's last building activities undertaken between 1640 and 1646, one should mention the problem of accessibility of these lower courts, since they relate to new ideas about Honselaarsdijk's garden layout. Two most interesting but relatively little-known plans designed by Pieter Post for the connection of the palace with the lower courts survive today, one of which is reproduced here *(fig. 17)*, the other in the next chapter.[47] Post's designs, containing massive, all-embracing semicircular building and garden structures, are unusual in that they show a monumental scheme which ingeniously blends architecture and nature at Honselaarsdijk. These designs *(see fig. 17)* have been criticized, perhaps not without reason, as lacking a sense of reality.[48] Yet they leave one wondering what the next step would have been in the extension of Honselaarsdijk's house and garden, had the Stadholder not died in the midst of his building activities. Comparison of Post's bold designs with new findings in contemporary archival documents will make it possible to answer this question in the analytical sections of chapters IV and V.

By reading the estates' account books and looking at the maps, one can obtain a rare insight not only into seventeenth-century work processes in general but also into the methods applied, the work divisions and techniques of building and the creation of garden architecture. As was mentioned briefly in the introduction, the development of Honselaarsdijk can also be seen in connection with Holland's legendary prowess on the high seas. Of particular importance was the capture of a Portuguese ship of the *Zilvervloot*, or Silver Fleet, one of several 'sea prices' with which the Stadholder's high building costs were covered, according to many entries in the account books (992 fols. 185, 277 and 278).[49]

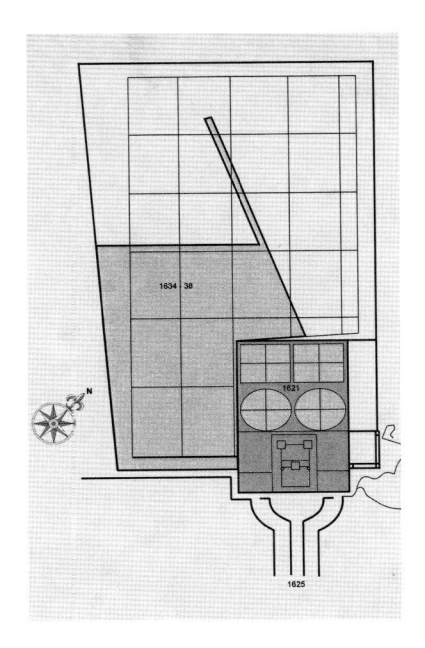

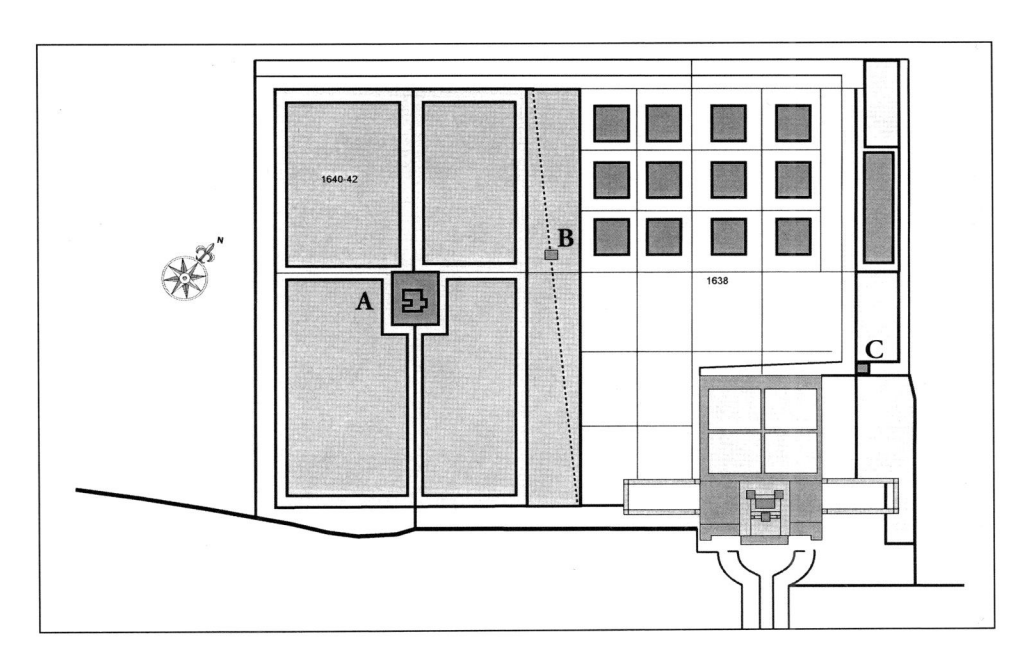

18. Reconstruction drawing showing the charges and further extension of the Honselaarsdijk garden between c. 1620 and 1638.

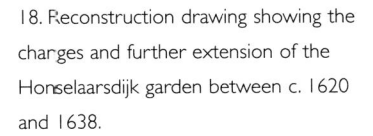

19. Reconstruction drawing showing the further extension of the Honselaarsdijk garden to the east and to the west, c. 1638-42.

THE DEVELOPMENT OF THE HONSELAARSDIJK GARDEN: INITIAL CONSTRUCTION PROGRAMME

The early development of the Honselaarsdijk garden can be characterized as a constant struggle with water. This was particularly evident in the mounting concern for an appropriate drainage system, the lack of which in the first years of the new garden layout had resulted in the death of most newly-planted trees from salt water which had seeped into the ground. Another aspect of the garden's first creation was the large-scale acquisition of surrounding fields, both uncultivated tracts and arable land, in order to expand the actual pleasure garden and the plantations around it. Comments in letters and accounts lament the loss of valuable trees and the spoiling of the ground on these newly-acquired lands in the summer of 1631, which prompted the need for a more advanced drainage system:

> ...Paid the sum of forty-seven pounds five shilling artois ... for the surveying and contracting of the work of large sewers in the Garden of Honselaarsdijk serving for the drainage of redundant water which spoils the trees there ... (1040 fol. 209).

And:

> ...Paid the sum of eighteen hundred eleven pounds sixteen shilling ... for the construction and completion of the large and small drains in the Garden of Honselaarsdijk done by Jan Gijbersch, Laurens Arentsz and Cornelis Jansz, masons ... to complete the drains in the two palm gardens laying next to the house Honselaarsdijk ...(1040 fol. 209vo).

As the garden was further expanded and embellished, the drains and water channels had to be improved accordingly. In 1631 Frederik Hendrik's special commissioners were once again sent into the field to check the latest water damage to the trees and prepare plans for a network of new sewers in the garden of Honselaarsdijk (1040 fols. 209, 209vo). Similar measures had to be taken a few years later, when André Mollet, fearing the drowning of his intricate boxwood parterre gardens on either side of the palace, insisted on appropriate new

I. HONSELAARSDIJK

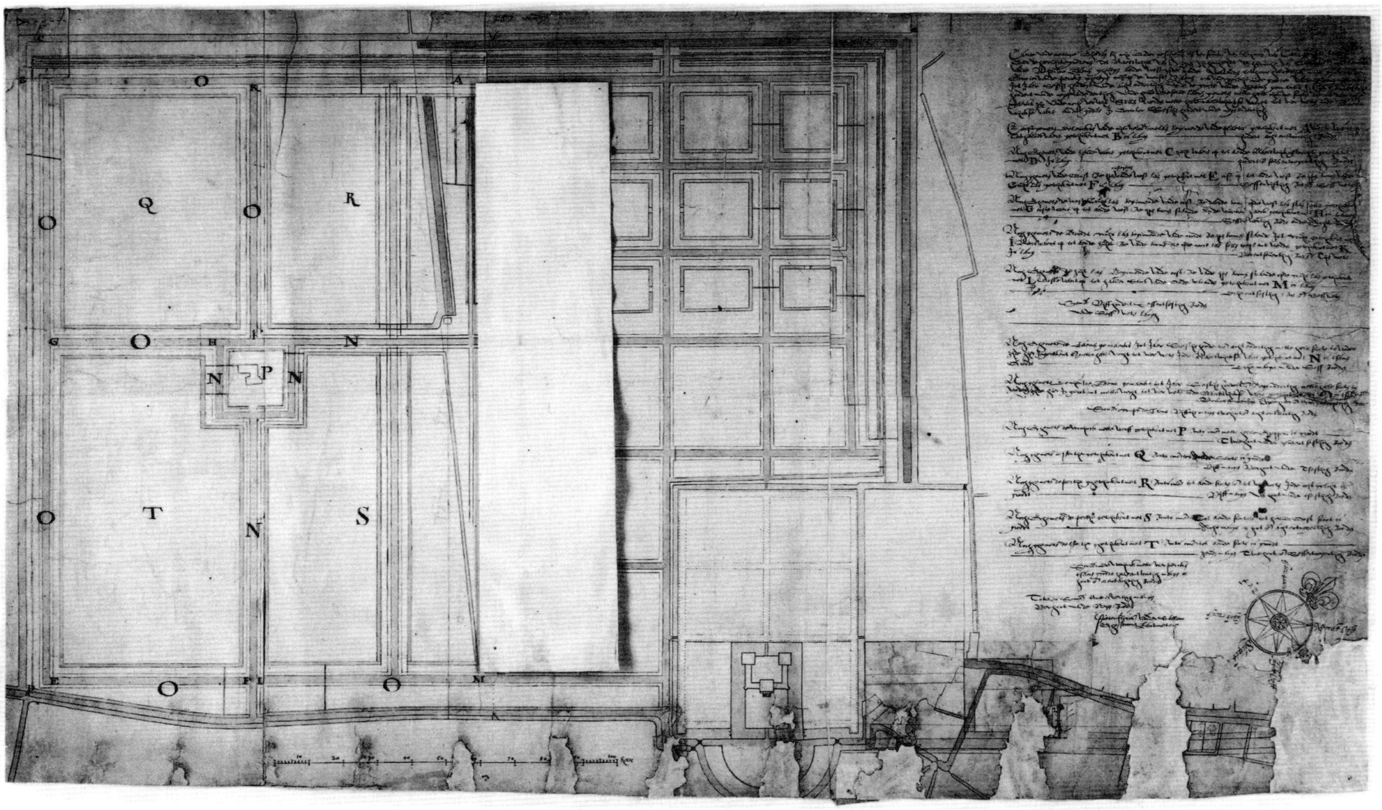

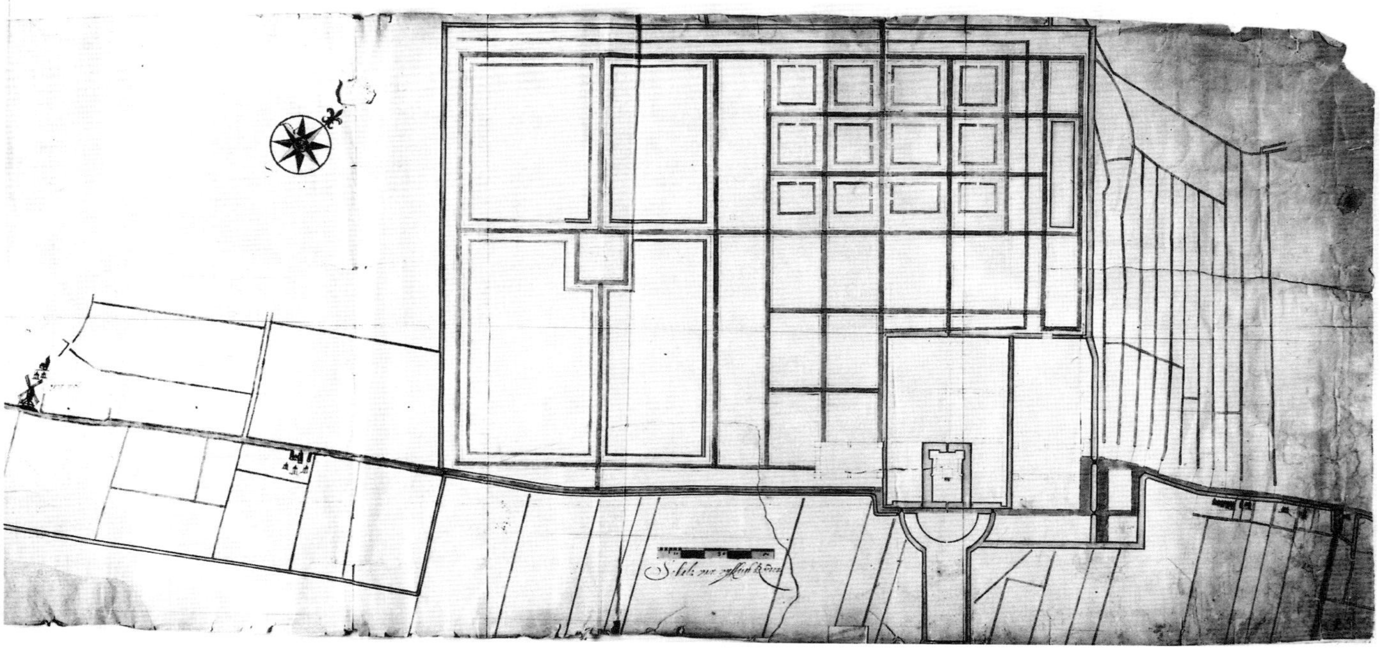

20. Plan of the Honselaarsdijk garden by Pieter Florisz van der Sallem, 1639, showing the old and the new situation of the west gardens.
Algemeen Rijksarchief

21. Completed extension plans and exact regulation of compartments in straight blocks in a map by Pieter Florisz van der Sallem, 1640-42.
Algemeen Rijksarchief

drainage systems in the main ornamental garden.[50] A remark in the late-seventeenth-century travel journal of the Swedish architect Nicodemus Tessin, which described the forlorn state of all the plantations in the Orangerie at Honselaarsdijk due to salt-water seepage, reflects this recurring problem in spite of enhanced water drainage systems: 'In der Orangerie wahr dass beste von gewächsten verdorben wegen dem saltzen wasser.'[51] Significantly, at the very time the Stadholder was building his palaces, the architect Salomon de Bray in *Architectura moderna*[52] drew attention to the problem of the soft, swamp-like ground and the lack of natural stone as the main obstacles in creating grand buildings in Holland.[53]

To give a clear, immediate survey of the extension and improvement of Honselaarsdijk's garden, a series of reconstruction drawings, combining evidence from contemporary maps and account books, must be described *(figs. 18 and 19)*. Figure 18 shows the garden in its original form about 1620, before Frederik Hendrik's extension plans, consisting of a garden plot set within a moated rectangular framework. The area to the west of the garden depicts the first stage of a major extension, shown also on the 1634 map by Floris Jacobsz van der Sallem *(see fig. 16)* and referred to in the accounts as the 'nieuwe perck' (new bounds) (1043 fols. 218, 218vo, 219ff.). The area which is left blank in this reconstruction drawing corresponds to the layout visible in the top right-hand corner of Van Berckerode's print, showing the boundary of the park about 1638. The continued extension of this north-west area of Honselaarsdijk is clearly shown in the reconstruction drawing of figure 19, which can be directly compared with maps drawn by Pieter Florisz van der Sallem *(figs. 20 and 21)*.[54] These two maps, dated 1639-40, show the various stages of land improvement in the west corner of the Honselaarsdijk garden during the late 1630s and early 1640s. The development of this area can also be followed closely by studying the account books over those years. It becomes clear that, after the task of basic land-surveying was completed, plans were made to rearrange and straighten out the existing erratic division of plots of land in order to create an area consisting of a neatly arranged conglomerate of squares and rectangles, bordered by canals. The improvement of the land often first entailed reclaiming the humid grounds by means of drainage systems, digging out ditches and throwing up earthen walls and small dikes to protect the land (992 fols. 36, 148). As can be seen on the maps, waterways and small canals which first crossed the land in irregular patterns were either drained and filled with earth or brought together to create a framework for orderly arranged, rectilinear plots of land. When the grounds were thus divided, trees and bushes were planted in each section and, lastly, garden structures were built and sculpture added to change the new plantation into a pleasure garden proper.

While one often expects aesthetic elements primarily to dominate the form and layout of gardens, as the above explanation shows, at Honselaarsdijk this was not the case. Obviously other factors than solely artistic ones were the basis for the creation of new garden sections, here as well as in the other stadholderly gardens. Careful adjustments to specific topographical conditions, the cold and wet climate and certain methods of land division and reclamation were essential. These factors had an impact on the size and shape of the garden as well as on the choice of plant material. This is not to say that artistic considerations had no influence on the development of the Honselaarsdijk garden, but that aesthetic awareness had to be balanced against, or fitted to, the particular natural conditions of the Westland and of Holland at large.

The newly-reclaimed and replanted polder and farm lands were quickly absorbed in the Honselaarsdijk total garden layout. As early as 1637 the accounts refer to the newly-planted west area as the 'nieuwe warande' (new pleasure garden) (992 fol. 145) and also to the new 'Noordwesthouck vant bosch' (north-west corner of the park or wood) (992 fol. 36).[55] The

t'Koningins Speelhuys met de Prielen.

new plots of land were bought by Frederik Hendrik from the proprietors Van Heemskerck, Van Wou and Boon Dircksz, all of whose names appear on the map showing their respective lands.[56] The transactions between these landowners and Frederik Hendrik are described in great detail in the account books dating from the autumn of 1637 onward. One plot of land, extending along the new avenue in front of Honselaarsdijk, was made into a track or mall called *maliebaen*, also spelled *maillebaan*; it was used for walking and the game of pall-mall. Soon it developed into one of the court's favourite pastimes and the *maillebaan* would grow out to become a standard feature in seventeenth-century Dutch gardens, exemplified by the later gardens laid out by William II and William III at Dieren and Het Loo. In the spring of 1638 workers at Honselaarsdijk were paid for levelling the ground and supplying wood and iron to complete this *maillebaan* of circa 200 Rijnlandse roeden, or 750 metres (992 fols. 142a, 144). In the records of the account books the treasurer frequently refers to particular maps and precise measurements made by the land-surveyor Pieter Florisz van der Sallem, which must have included some of the very maps shown above *(see figs. 20 and 21)*.[57]

As shown in the reconstruction drawings *(see fig. 19)*, apart from the palace and the lower courts three smaller buildings can be distinguished, designated as A, B and C. The small square house marked B is the house for the estate manager and forester Dirck de Milde, whose name one encounters frequently in the accounts. The other two structures

22. The pleasure house, or *speelhuys*, in the east garden of Honselaarsdijk, shown in a print published by J. Covens and C. Mortier, c. 1690.
Historisch Museum, Stichting Atlas van Stolk, Rotterdam

COURTLY GARDENS IN HOLLAND 1600-1650

Map of Delfland by C. Koster after Cruquius's map of 1712, published by I. Tirion c. 1750. RPK (see fig. 5)

Map of Honselaarsdijk, 1620-25, from the Kaartboek of Naaldwijk. GAN (see fig. 9) *(next page)*

COURTLY GARDENS IN HOLLAND 1600-1650

COURTLY GARDENS IN HOLLAND 1600-1650

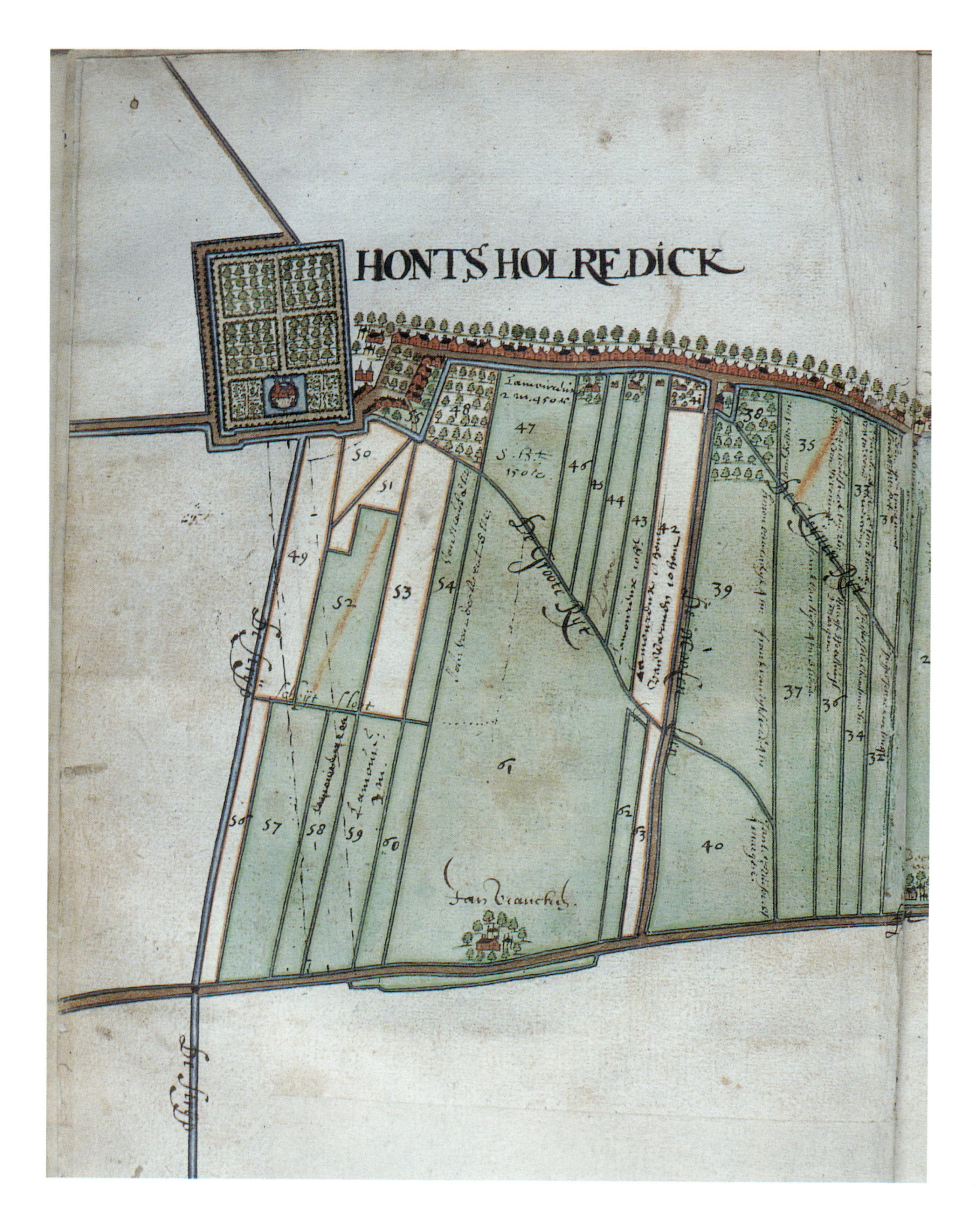

are both pleasure houses, the larger one of which, marked A, must have been a rebuilt and decorated pleasure house made from an already existing home of one of the abovementioned landowners, Boon Dircksz (992 fols. 51-52). This house, referred to in the accounts as 'the new pleasure house in the north-west corner of the wood at Honselaarsdijk' (992 fol. 36), in future years is found to be part of the Faisanterie, visible in later seventeenth-century prints of Honselaarsdijk. The smaller pleasure house, marked *c* on the map, was constructed in conjunction with the extension of the grounds on the east side of the palace of Honselaarsdijk, and is featured as the main *speelhuys*, or pleasure house, in all later seventeenth-century engravings *(fig. 22)*. This is the house referred to in the accounts of 1642 as 'the pleasure house in the new garden'. The interior must have been like a garden room itself, decorated with 'various landscapes, fruits, flowers and birds' (993 fol. 151). This pleasure house was also the object of Frederik Hendrik's frustration when new building delays occurred, as described in a letter by Huygens to Amalia of August 1640:

> Ceste après disnée il est venu une lettre de V.A. à Monseigneur qui s'etonne et se fasche à bon escient de ceque Catshuijsen [estate manager][58] et surtout 'sHerwouters [comptroller][59] demeurent tant en faulte de l'advertir de cequi se faict en ses bastiments et autres ouvrages, qui de vraij est chose estrange. S.A. leur ayant tant de fois commandé et faict escrire par moy, qu'ils eussent a la tenir advertie de jour à autre de ce qu'ils avancent ou n'avancent point. S'il plaisoit à V.A. y interposer l'authorité de ses commandemens de bouche, aveq ce qu'il convient de severité à de si longues impertinences, ce seroit oster autant de subjects de mauvaise humeur à S.A. qui n'ij peut penser sans s'en courroucer, disant que puis qu'elle paije tout, on debvroit bien luij rendre compte de ce qui se faict de son argent, mais qu'on n'ij songe non plus que si elle n'estoit pas au monde.[60]

Apparently, the building undertakings at Honselaarsdijk did not always proceed as smoothly as one had hoped, even though the builder was the Prince of Orange himself and Princess Amalia personally came to survey the work. Enthusiasm for the construction programme was often lacking and workmen did not appear to have been particularly motivated in completing their work on schedule, perhaps not without reason because they were generally paid years later, and only after repeated, urgent requests. Furthermore, the work at Honselaarsdijk definitely met with opposition, since it involved forced acquisition of surrounding farm lands and living quarters in town. Indeed, from 1637 onward frequent mention is made in the account books of the acquisition not only of farm lands (992 fol. 149) but also of a whole series of houses still inhabited by local residents. After buying out the owners, these houses were demolished in order to create space for the extension of the stables and newly-planned orchard and herb and kitchen gardens.

THE NEW EAST GARDENS AND PRINCESS AMALIA'S INVOLVEMENT

To construct a viable new garden on the east side of Honselaarsdijk, standard methods were again applied, involving ground measuring, surveying, mapping and drainage. New canals were dug (992 fol. 58), earth banks and dikes were built and after the grounds were divided into neatly defined, regular plots, trees were planted. These activities can be followed step by step by reading a newly-discovered *besteck*, or builder's estimate, for the forester-in-chief

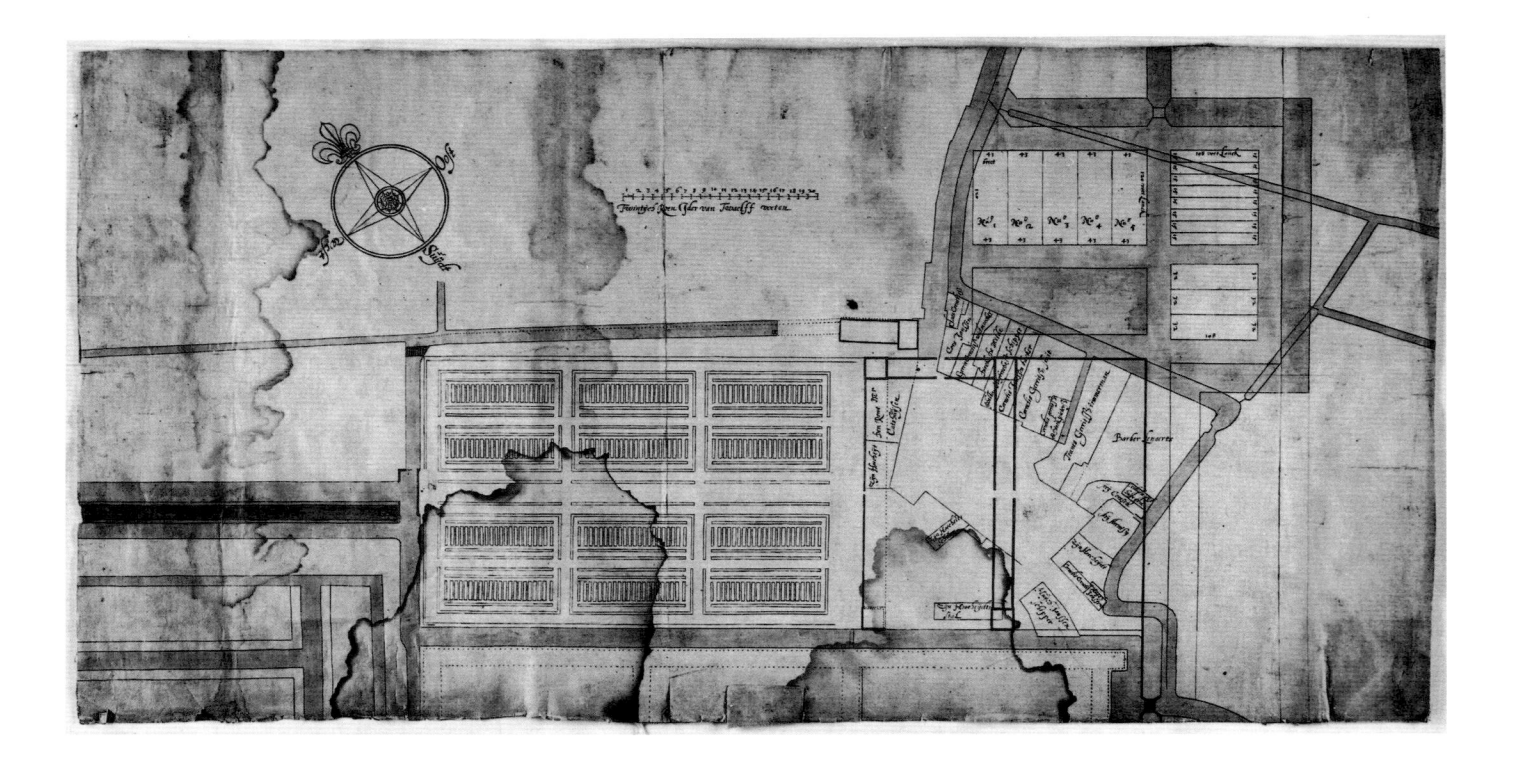

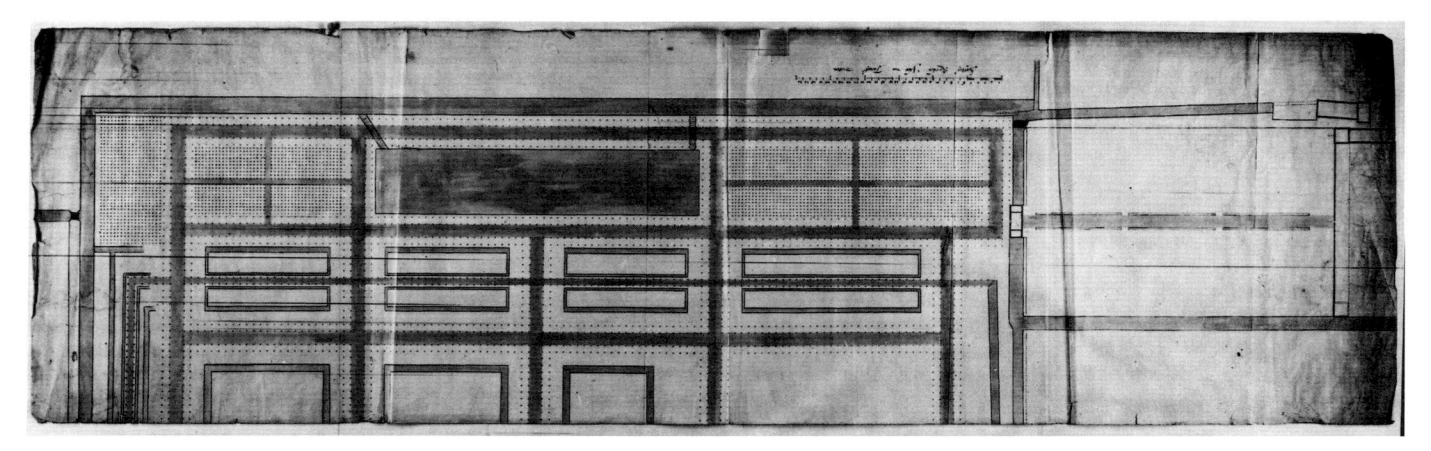

Dirck de Milde, entitled *Estimate for Making and Digging a New Garden (see Appendix, Document I).*[61] This *besteck* can be compared with a series of designs kept in the Map Department of the General State Archives, or Algemeen Rijksarchief, in The Hague, the description of two of which must suffice here. One of these designs *(fig. 23)*[62] shows a detailed extension plan for the stables or east lower courts, as well as the layout of new orchards and kitchen gardens, divided into small elongated beds known as *pulvilus* and situated north and east of the lower courts. The original row of houses standing on the spot are still visible shortly before their demolition. The other plan *(fig. 24)*[63] is a design for the whole eastern extension of the garden, including the exact division of the various garden sections. It shows the planting of trees in rigid lines and precisely organized plots, a large rectangular pond and the above-mentioned small pleasure house.

Based on the comparison of the various maps and the information from the account books, these three plans can be dated about 1640[64] and, judging by their style, may be attributed to Pieter Florisz van der Sallem, who took over the work from his then very old father Floris Jacobsz.[65] It is important to realize that a land-surveyor or map-maker, not an

23. Extension plans of the new east garden and annexe buildings at Honselaarsdijk, replacing existing houses.
Algemeen Rijksarchief

24. Plan of the kitchen gardens, orchard and fish-pond in the new east garden of Honselaarsdijk, in accordance with strict geometrical arrangement.
Algemeen Rijksarchief

architect, was responsible for the design and layout of new garden plots. Furthermore, the documents indicate that the head gardener Anthony van Thooren was paid for 'drawing and planting' the parterres on the west side of the house, as well as 'drawing and making' a new parterre in the 'oude thuyn' (old garden) at Honselaarsdijk (995 fols. 46a[vo], 46b[vo]). The personality of the supervisor of all these new works is also of interest. There is a letter written in connection with the new layout of the easterly gardens indicating that Amalia was directly involved in these changes at Honselaarsdijk. In this letter Constantijn Huygens writes to her that Frederik Hendrik had ordered the estate manager Catshuysen to prepare that section of the park which Her Highness, Amalia, believed to be the most convenient for the layout of the new garden at Honselaarsdijk. Thus it would appear that Amalia was free to choose the form and layout of new garden sections:

> J'escris presentement par ordre de S.A. [Son Altesse, Frederik Hendrik] à Catshuysen, qu'il ayt à faire preparer tel parcq, que V.A. [Votre Altesse, Amalia] jugera le plus convenable pour le nouveau jardin à Honselardijck.[66]

Not only at Honselaarsdijk but also at Ter Nieuburch did Amalia coordinate the work proceedings and the hire of necessary personnel, from the estate steward to the *concierge*.[67] The crucial role Amalia played in the coordination of both state affairs and building projects, and the influence she had on the Prince's decision-making, are described by her nephew Frederik van Dohna, who knew her well, as follows:

> Cependant le grand ascendant que la princesse avait sur l'esprit de ce grand prince lui attirait les voeux et les respects de toute la terre. Non seulement les officieux et les directeurs de l'Etat mais encore les ministres étrangers n'entamaient aucune affaire importante sans avoit auparavant consulté l'oracle chez cette princesse; comme elle était extrêmement habile, elle ménageait les esprits avec une adresse et elle réglait toutes leurs démarches au grand soulagement de son mari.[68]

The east gardens of Honselaarsdijk completed Amalia and Frederik Hendrik's extension plans, the size and form of which *(see fig. 21)* would remain unchanged, defining the outline of the whole estate over the following centuries.[69] The inner layout of the garden would change, however, and the main garden behind the palace would once again be modernized – this time according to the then prevalent French fashion – into a monumental and transversely placed hippodrome-shaped area. This undertaking, begun at the end of the Stadholder's life, would be completed during the short reign of William II (1647-1650), under the guiding eye of Amalia.

THE GARDEN ORNAMENTATION AND THE ROLE OF ANDRÉ MOLLET

One of the most interesting aspects of the decoration of the Honselaarsdijk garden was the arrival in the early 1630s of the French garden architect André Mollet and his fellow-countrymen, the architect Simon de la Vallée[70] and the *grottier-fontainier* Joseph Dinant. While de la Vallée was primarily responsible for work on the interior of the palace of Honselaarsdijk, in particular the construction of a monumental stone staircase,[71] and Dinant for waterworks, Mollet's fame rested on his design of the Honselaarsdijk parterre gardens. Because Mollet's exact role as garden architect at the Stadholder's court, though not entirely clear, is crucial for a proper analysis of Dutch gardens, it will receive some preliminary attention here, prior to a detailed consideration of architects-designers in chapter IV. It should be stressed, first, that André Mollet was not the architect of the whole Honselaarsdijk garden, inviting as this thought may be. As can be seen from the maps shown above, which date from about 1630, the garden's main composition was already completed before his arrival.[72] What can be said is that Mollet was primarily responsible for designing the parterres at Honselaarsdijk, not for the design of the whole garden, as is erroneously stated in most older – and also some fairly recent – literature.[73] Even Slothouwer himself, in his otherwise careful text, and in spite of the wealth of archival information available to him, omitted a detailed description of the artistic development of the gardens at Honselaarsdijk and simply stated that they were laid out by François [sic] Mollet.[74]

André Mollet was already known in parts of Northern Europe for his work together with his father Claude – at Fontainebleau, the Tuileries and Saint-Germain-en-Laye. It was not surprising, therefore, that this son of the gardener to the French king was invited to Holland to work at the court. At a later date André Mollet would become even more widely known as the author of *Le Jardin de plaisir*.[75] In this treatise, published in 1651, Mollet even refers to his work in Holland and shows two ideal garden plans, one of which can actually be compared with the layout of Honselaarsdijk,[76] while the other also appears to be related to a Dutch design, namely Ter Nieuburch, as we shall see. Mollet himself is described in Frederik Hendrik's records, not without a certain pride, as the 'Franschen architect hovenier' (French horticulturist) (1042 fol. 231vo), and in one of the letters written by David de Wilhem to Huygens as 'l'intendant et desseigneur des jardins'.[77] Mollet was not only responsible for laying out the parterres at Honselaarsdijk; he also designed parterres for Buren and, what is less known, for Zuylesteyn,[78] where since 1632 large building and garden improvements were undertaken.[79] It is interesting and intriguing to note that Mollet was paid for a series of designs he made for Frederik Hendrik, probably further parterre designs or new garden sections, though this cannot be verified with certainty.[80]

Mollet received a yearly income of 800 pounds artois,[81] a considerable sum, taking into account that the yearly income of Frederik Hendrik's Dutch gardeners was about 300 pounds,[82] while de la Vallée was promised 400 for his initial travel to and stay in Holland[83] and the *fontainier-grottier* Joseph Dinant received 500 pounds yearly.[84] Mollet is not only referred to in the accounts as the French architect-gardener but also as the supervisor[85] and director[86] of Frederik Hendrik's gardens. The payment records clearly express Frederik Hendrik's and Amalia's interest in, and admiration for, Mollet's work, which is described as being 'seer aardigh' (very delightful) (1042 fol. 232). A letter written in the autumn of 1635 to Huygens by David de Wilhem, who supervised the activities at Honselaarsdijk, shows Frederik Hendrik's direct involvement with and specific ideas for the Mollet's parterre designs:

> I received your letter with the order of His Highness concerning the parterres. The manager [*intendant*] André Mollet will organize it. But one should also take care of the water drainage. Catshusen [*sic*] promises to do his utmost at Honselaersdijk.[87]

In another passage of this letter, which was omitted by Worp in his *Briefwisseling*, André Mollet's role as garden architect is further detailed:

> J'ai receu celles qu'il vous a pleu m'escrire concernant l'ordre de S.E. [Son Excellence,

the Stadholder] des parterres en qu'elles je reconnoi vostre bonne affection et mon endroit et vous en ai de l'obligation. Les parterres des Gasettes [*sic*, Gazon] est en son entier, et nullement ruins. Pour l'autres And. Mollet l'Intendant et desseigneur des jardins dit qu'il tachera de trouver tant de gros buis pour le faire tout des gros buis, afin qu'il puisse mieux resister a l'injure du temps; et en cas qu'il ne trevus [*sic*, trouve] tant de prevision il le sera de petit buis comme il a ete fait par ci devant avec le bord de gros buis. Mais il juge necessaire qu'on fais une riole pour degorger l'eau tout dulong par deux conduits dans la fosse dela maison. La riole seroit de 3 pieds de largeur & 4 1/2 de profond et de 22 verges de longeur de sort que vingt F la verger il monteroit avec le C [tous] des plus a la sommer de cincq cent francs. A faults de la Riole le buis mourira derechef comme il a fait parci devant daultant que l'eau ne peut passer ou se vuider [*sic*, fuir] par la muraille a cement et par ainsi fait mourir le buis. La dessus il vous plaira nous faire avoir l'ordre de S.E.[88]

From this text it can be concluded that Mollet, referred to here as 'intendant et desseigneur des jardins', did not merely contribute to the pure decorative aspects of the garden.[89] Though Mollet was not the overall designer of Honselaarsdijk's basic garden and framework, as indicated above, he did function as the most important *opsichter*, or general supervisor (1042 fol. 250), of the garden's interior layout and decoration from 1633 to 1635. In addition to being the actual designer of the boxwood parterres, he gave general practical directions for the larger preparatory work, which involved the levelling of the grounds and the construction of drainage systems, as well as the actual acquisition of the plant material for the pleasure gardens at Honselaarsdijk.[90] Another recently discovered document detailing Mollet's efforts[91] includes a copy of Mollet's own original work account and corroborates Frederik Hendrik's and especially Amalia's direct involvement with Mollet's parterre layouts, the total cost of which was found very reasonable, or 'not exorbitant by any means'[92]:

The above-mentioned M[r]. Brouaert Councillor and Treasurer General responding to the order of Madam the Princess that when Andre Mollez [*sic*], son of the gardener to the King of France, would complete the ordering of and making of the parterres at Buren and Honsholredijck, that one should pay him for his travel expenses, efforts, and other expenses incurred by him. This including the manual workers or labourers who have worked on them [parterres]. And in view of the following declaration handed over by Andre Mollez[93]:

For the parterres of the Castle of Buren which are on two sides, the same three hundred livres of which I make account and fifty which Mr. Dinance [Dinant] has received for himself   300 L.

And further for the parterres en broderie and compartiments de gazon [grass compartments] of Honsholredick [*sic*] four hundred livres   400 L.

Further for his travels three hundred livres   300 L.

And for his expenditures made at The Hague during the making of the aforesaid designs fifty Livres   50 L.

[to the total of]   1050 L.[94]

And since the aforesaid declaration is not judged to be exorbitant, amounting to ten hundred fifty guilders, it is agreed that the aforesaid Counsellor and Treasurer General

25. Detail of the Berckerode print, c. 1638, showing André Mollet's *parterres de broderie* at Honselaarsdijk, including the Rampant Lion made of boxwood, with the classical statue of Hercules and Cacus at the centre.

may satisfy the aforesaid Mollez, in reduction of which he may already have received and which is partly mentioned above.[95]

In the engraving by Van Berckerode, details of Mollet's *parterres de broderie* laid out at Honselaarsdijk can be clearly recognized on either side of the palace. Both parterre layouts consisted of highly intricate, swirling, arabesque-like designs, with the one in the west garden centring upon the representation of the Dutch Lion *(fig. 25)*.[96] They consisted primarily of low boxwood hedges, while the one in the west garden was also filled in with turf and coloured stones, gravel and shells, in red, black and white.[97]

In his treatise *Le Jardin de plaisir*, published nearly twenty years after the completion of his work in Holland, Mollet still considered his parterre design for Honselaarsdijk so important that he published it as an ideal model.[98] Indeed, not just one, but two parterre models depicted in his book – folio 23 *(fig. 26)* and, unnoticed before, folio 14 *(fig. 27)*[99] – represent the very two parterres laid out at Honselaarsdijk. The parterre made of 'palm ende soden' described in the Nassau account book (1042 fol. 232vo), situated on the left or west side of the palace, is exactly identical with Mollet's design shown in folio 23, except

26. Design for a parterre from André Mollet, *Le Jardin de plaisir*, plate 23, used for the layout of the west parterre at Honselaarsdijk in 1632-33.
The Metropolitan Museum of Art, New York

27. Design for a parterre from André Mollet, *Le Jardin de plaisir*, plate 14, used for the layout of the east parterre at Honselaarsdijk in 1632-33. The Metropolitan Museum of Art, New York

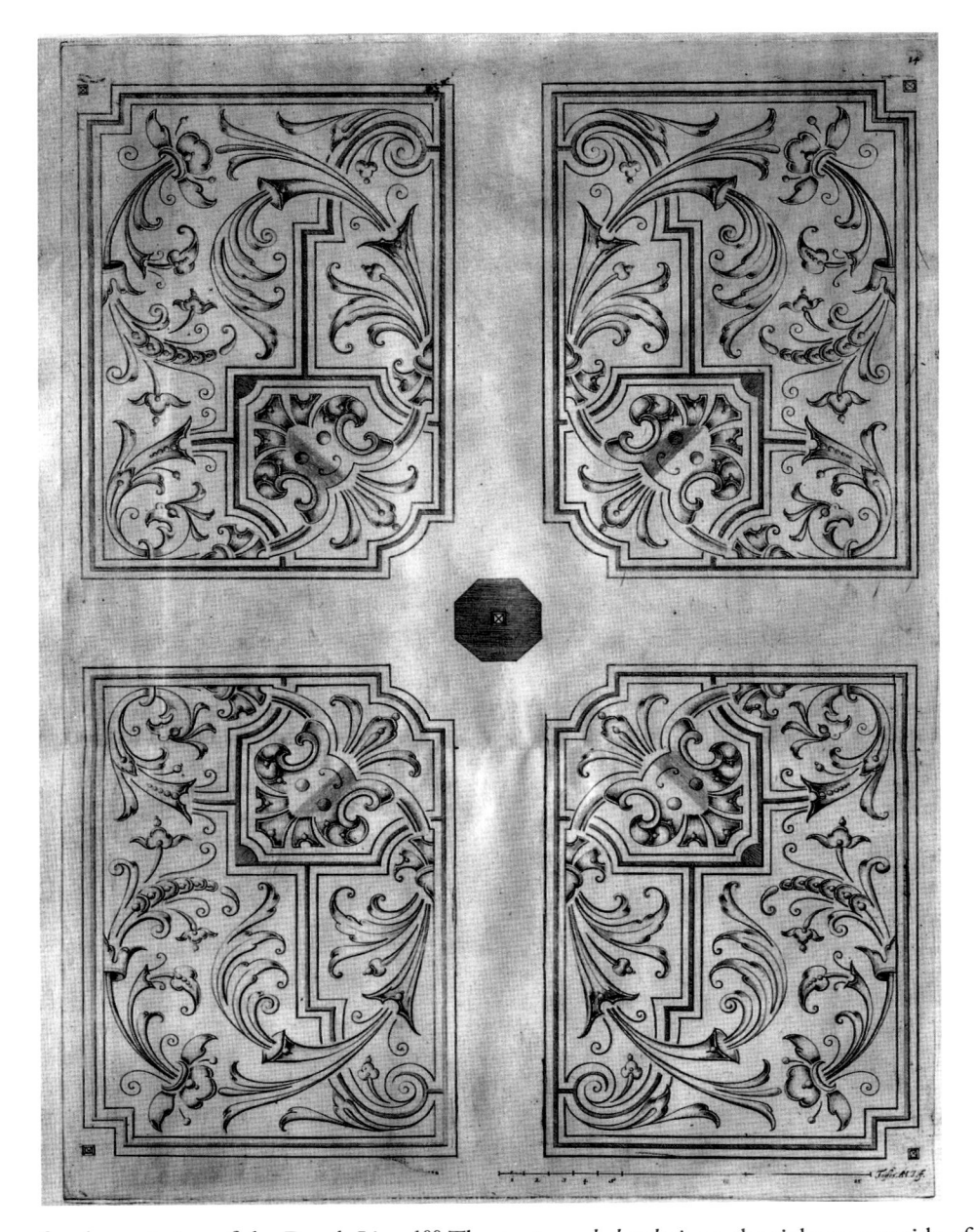

for the omission of the Dutch Lion.[100] The *parterre de broderie* on the right or east side of the Honselaarsdijk palace, described in the account book of 1633 as 'geheel van palm' (entirely made of boxwood), follows exactly Mollet's design depicted in folio 14, though on a somewhat smaller scale.[101] Moreover, as mentioned before, Mollet did not only represent the parterres but the whole shape of the Honselaarsdijk garden which, completed before his arrival, apparently impressed him to such an extent that he based one of his ideal garden plans on its general form and layout.[102]

After the parterres were finished, wooden fences or balustrades and eight arbours or cabinets (992 fol. 148)[103] as well as wooden arcades or trellis-work *berceaux* were constructed in and round these two garden plots.[104] These trellis-work structures are visible in Van Berckerode's print and stress again the enclosed nature of the separate garden sections. Apart from Mollet's *parterres de broderie*, other ornaments contributed to the general decoration of the Honselaarsdijk garden. For some of them – those involving the fountain works and grotto – another Frenchman, Joseph Dinant, was responsible.

28. Drawing by Jan de Bisschop, c. 1660, showing the statue of Hercules and Cacus in the west parterre of Honselaarsdijk. Rijksprentenkabinet, Rijksmuseum, Amsterdam
see colour plate 5

The grotto is not represented in the Van Berckerode print; this can be explained by the fact that it was built after the print was made. It is also possible that the grotto was incorporated in another building structure, as was the case at Ter Nieuburch, where the grotto was part of the Orangerie, as the account books imply.[105] Though the accounts do not provide much information about the grotto's appearance and decoration, they do contain the important detail that exotic shells from overseas and special fountain stone (*fonteijnsteen*)[106] from Tivoli were used to create this grotto and other waterworks, that is, the three fountains in the garden (994, fols. 85vo, 90). Another entry shows that Dinant received the large amount of 3,277 guilders for his expenses on the 'grottoes [plural!] and fountains at Honselaarsdijk' (994 fol. 168vo). A more detailed analysis of the grottoes in the Stadholder's gardens will follow in the next chapter.

Whereas André Mollet and Simon de la Vallée left Holland in 1635 and 1637 respectively, Joseph Dinant stayed on and had a career at the Dutch court. Apart from the *fontainier-grottier*, he also became the general caretaker (*concierge*, 994 fol. 112) of the palace at Rijswijk, where he was still mentioned in 1653 (995 fol. 114vo) and 1657 (995 fol. 221), at which time one of his relatives had taken over his responsibilities.[107]

SCULPTURE IN THE HONSELAARSDIJK GARDEN

Since no separate, systematic study of the Orange family's extensive sculpture collection has been undertaken, little information is available on the sculptural decoration of the Stadholder's gardens.[108] However, newly-found archival documentation combined with information from the now published Orange family inventories[109] sheds further light not only on the statues in the Honselaarsdijk garden but also on Frederik Hendrik as a collector of sculpture, about which the well-known seventeenth-century historiographer Sandrart remarked:

> Ingleichen befinden sich viel rare Statuen in Niederland, … überall in Holland bei den Liebhabern, jedoch am meisten in des Durchleuchtigen Prinzen von Oranien Lustgarten in Grafenhag zu Reswick und Hontslardick von antichen und modernen.[110]

While this topic will be discussed in detail in chapter VI, it is important to realize here that the gardens of the Stadholder were famous not only for their layout but also for their collection of antique and modern sculpture. Actually, a direct reference to antique sculpture can be found in the account book's entry of April 1638, describing, in addition to three Italian 'children' or putti (usually called *Kinderkens* or *Cupidoken*), the arrival at Honselaarsdijk of no fewer than six antique heads (992 fol. 133). Documentary evidence confirms that the statues in the Stadholder's collection were indeed classical in style and form, or direct copies after antique originals. It is also significant that most of the sculpture for Frederik Hendrik's gardens, including Honselaarsdijk, came from abroad, in particular from France. Entries in the commission book of May 1639 state that the architect Jacob van Campen and the stonemason Bartholomeus Drijffhout with their workmen were paid 'for the unpacking and carrying into the garden of all the cast statues and busts, which were sent to His Highness from France, and of which nine statues were brought to Honselaarsdijk' (992 fol. 277).

Another entry in the commission book, dated May 1639, states that Bartholomeus Drijffhout was to receive payments for the 'transportation and placing of some vases and statues on pedestals' in the Honselaarsdijk garden (992 fol. 278). As early as 1634, a group of three stone statues were 'bronzed', that is gilded, by Otto Reijersen, which added an element of sparkle to the terrace and west parterre garden, where they were put (1043 fol. 225). One of the statues referred to here as standing in the west garden was depicted in a drawing by Jan de Bisschop of circa 1660 *(fig. 28)*.[111] This drawing clearly shows a statue *à l'antique* of a man slaying another person, identified as Hercules and Cacus.[112] Remarkably, this statue can be recognized in Van Berckerode's print of circa 1639. It is hidden under the front leg of the Rampant Lion in the westerly parterre garden, and its presence in the print corroborates archival descriptions of the placement of a gilded stone statue in this section of the Honselaarsdijk garden in 1634 (1043 fols. 225, 228vo). Apart from this, and several other sketchy illustrations, de Bisschop's drawing is a rare picture of a specific statue in the Stadholder's garden.

Other important sculptural works were commissioned by the Stadholder from the Flemish sculptor François Dieussart, who, coming to The Hague from the English court in 1641, exemplified a group of 'itinerant' court artists, among them several Flemish-born sculptors, working for the Stadholder. While the Stadholder immediately acquired Dieussart's busts of King Charles I and Princess Henrietta Maria of England for 1,500 pounds (993 fol. 90), he also commissioned his own effigies, some of which may have been placed in the garden. This was perhaps the case with the life-size figures of the four Princes of Orange placed at the Huis ten Bosch,[113] for the marble slabs of which Dieussart received 900 Carolus guilders in 1646 (993 fol. 428[vo]), followed by 4,000 guilders in 1651 (995 fol. 31) after completion of the statues; a later copy was indeed placed in the garden of the Stadholder's daughter.[114] In May 1640 Constantijn Huygens was reimbursed for ordering as many as five statues in Antwerp (992 fol. 400), probably also meant to decorate the Stadholder's gardens. This would not only confirm Huygens's involvement in the

29. Exotic plants at Honselaarsdijk, in a water-colour album entitled *Hortus Regius Honselaerdicensis*, attributed to Stephanus Cousyns, c. 1685.
Biblioteca Nazionale, Florence

acquisition of sculpture for the court, but also Antwerp's importance as a supplier of statues.

In addition to these statues, a large quantity of lead vases and pots were acquired for the ornamentation of the garden. A series of vases, or *potten* (992 fol. 442), and flowerpots and bowls (*blompotten en commen*, 992 fol. 14) were filled with 'various kinds of flowers' (992 fol. 442). These vases are clearly visible in the various prints; they may be the same as those mentioned in a later inventory of the Honselaarsdijk property as 'thirty-three [iron pots] on the wall of the front courtyard'.[115] Together with the plants and flowers planted in the borders or *rabatten* of the parterres, the flowerpots set on the balustraded terraces surrounding the palace added to the general colourfulness of the whole garden.[116]

THE HONSELAARSDIJK GARDEN AND HORTICULTURE

The account books provide an excellent picture of most of the plants in the Honselaarsdijk garden during Frederik Hendrik's lifetime. In addition, information from two other, slightly later sources is most important. Of particular interest are the gardener's contract or *Reglement van Meester Hendrick Quellenburch in het onderhouden van alle de Thuijnen van het huys Honsholredijck* ('Regulations for Mr. Hendrick Quellenburch to keep the Gardens of the House Honselaarsdijk'; *see Appendix, Document II*),[117] and the collection of late-seventeenth-century water-colour drawings in the album *Hortus Regius Honselaerdicensis (fig. 29)*,[118] depicting many rare plants grown at Honselaarsdijk under William III, who continued the tradition established by his grandfather. Information from Jan van der Groen's treatise *Den Nederlandtsen Hovenier*, which includes a list of plants known in Holland in the second half of the seventeenth century, can be added to these sources; because Van der Groen was gardener of the Orange family, his list includes plants grown in the Stadholder's gardens. Finally there also exists a late-seventeenth-century document written by the famous English garden architect George London, describing plants in some important Dutch gardens, including Honselaarsdijk.[119] Though these sources are dated later in the century, they nevertheless are helpful in shedding light on the otherwise little-known procedures involving planting and upkeep of the gardens. Moreover, the detailed description of many exotic plants and flowers is a good indication of the active role Holland played in introducing unknown plant species in Europe, and of the Orange family's own interest and expertise in these horticultural matters.

The *Reglement* for gardener-in-chief Hendrick Quellenburch describes in detail how the gardener had to keep and improve the gardens, showing what floral elements as well as architectural structures (trellis-work) enhanced the garden's decoration. At all times the gardener had to clean out the weeds and neatly keep all the parterres, borders, flowerbeds and paths. Extra diligence had to be applied towards the proper growth of late and early fruits and vegetables, including grapes and cherries, planted in the hotbeds and hothouses supplied for this purpose.[120] At set times he had to bring specially indicated vegetables and fruits to the court at The Hague. Furthermore, he was required to cut and trim the *berceaux* and hedges and mow the grass parterres, while replacing old flowers with new ones. The plants, bulbs and seeds that had been supplied to him had to be kept carefully, and he had to put his best efforts into their increase as well as their continuous flowering, in all seasons, so that each week two to three bouquets could be delivered to Her Highness.[121]

Apart from these flowers, the orange, lemon and pomegranate, jasmin and other exotic plants and trees required extra care and watering. The flowers and fruits coming from these rare plants, including melons, had to be cut with great care and brought to The Hague by the gardener, who was specifically warned not to steal or sell them. For the transportation of the plants and vegetables a wagon and horse were at his disposal, and he had to use the horse also for pumping water into the garden's fountain basins. Finally, the sand, dung and the peat for heating the eight stoves in the hothouses would be supplied to him, but the necessary tools to perform his tasks were the gardener's own responsibility. Quellenburch's yearly salary was set at 800 Carolus guilders, with an added 780 for five assisting gardeners, plus 468 guilders for three extra helpers during the nine spring and summer months.

Not specifically mentioned in this gardener's contract, but not to be overlooked in the

Honselaarsdijk and other garden layouts, is the importance of trees. Their function was twofold: they were planted both for aesthetic and for economic reasons. In part grown for timber production, trees had an additional 'economic' function at the Honselaarsdijk estate. The menagerie and deer park, which was a kind of venison park, also played an economic role, serving as a last reminder of Honselaarsdijk's original function as a hunting reserve.[122]

Archival documents prove that already from 1633 onward, especially about 1640, considerable sums were spent on shrubs and trees to be planted at Honselaarsdijk. Many of the trees mentioned in the accounts coincide with those referred to in these later seventeenth-century documents. In 1634 as many as 6,000 beech trees and young shrubs arrived at Honselaarsdijk. They were followed by more than 55,000 elm and white poplar trees in 1638 and, in 1640, by three full shiploads of thousands of oak and beech trees which were to be added to the plantation. In 1647 the records mention payment of no fewer than 36,000 beech trees and other plants (994 fol. 41) to be brought over to the Westland.

Most interesting is the reference to the planting of the parterres in the above-cited letter quoting remarks by André Mollet,[123] from which can be inferred that, in spite of the architects' exertions, it was not always possible to acquire the needed plant material, even though the decoration of the gardens depended on certain vegetational components. Appropriate plants for the vertical accentuation of the borders, or, as Mollet had remarked, 'des gros buis pour mieux resister a l'injure du temps' – referring to dwarf trees which could better stand the climate – were crucial for the successful completion of the grand parterres at Honselaarsdijk.

It was Dirck de Milde, frequently referred to in the records from 1637 onward as the forester-in-chief and supervisor of the larger park and wood area, who was responsible for the new plantations at Honselaarsdijk. During the late 1630s, and all through the 1640s, de Milde received large monthly payments for 'expenses in the garden and woods of Honsholredijck' (992 fols. 155 ff). The older Gijsbrecht Theunissen, mentioned as gardener of the 'old garden' and residing at Honselaarsdijk since 1622, worked together with de Milde[124] and received yearly payments for the upkeep of Mollet's parterres (1042 fol. 24 and 1043 fols. 232-33). Extra workers were also hired, for example two Englishmen, Jan Aderen and Rosier Hirver, who were paid for planting trees in the gardens (993 fols. 25-26).[125]

The trees themselves are all specified in the account book, among them not only the more indigenous Dutch trees, such as the elm, lime-tree, oak, poplar and willow, but also a large number of delicate fruit-trees, such as apricot, cherry, fig and peach. Some of these fruit-trees were planted along the *espaliers* in the main pleasure garden, visible in the Van Berckerode print, others in separate orchards in the surrounding, larger plantation area created in the late 1630s. The beeches, elms and lime-trees and, of course, the oaks, pines and poplars seem to have been favoured at Honselaarsdijk. However, in addition to these sturdy indigenous trees, the account books also describe the cultivation of exotic trees, such as orange- and lemon-trees, which later in the century, fully grown, would attract much attention.

The plants and trees collected for Honselaarsdijk were sent by water from several Dutch cities and counties, particularly those in the south-east, such as Diest and Meurs. Other plants and trees were imported from Flanders, while some were sent from considerable distances, even as far as France.[126] The orange-trees were shipped from Antwerp; they were sent by the 'gardener at Antwerp', Balthasar van Engelen,[127] and by a certain Hilario Oliva, who also provided rare, unspecified Chinese trees (*chineesche boomkens*, 992 fol. 53). Other plants grown at Honselaarsdijk, both for beauty and for use, included asparagus, various kinds of berries, and fig-trees. Eglantine, honeysuckle and rose-bushes, among other plants, filled the garden with their fragrance, and an impressive amount of tulips added colour to the greenery. At Honselaarsdijk the gardener with the appropriate name of Arent Pietersz Blom was primarily responsible for the supply of seed and for the upkeep of flowers and parterres. In 1644 he planted more than a thousand tulip bulbs, an expensive commodity at the time.[128]

In May 1641 Frederik Hendrik appointed a special plantation master, Hendrick van Hattem, responsible not only for the estates' plantations, but also for the cultivation of flowers and exotic plants at Rijswijk, Buren, Zuylesteyn and Ysselsteyn.[129] This plantation master, or *plantagueur*, played an important role in the total supply of plants in the Stadholder's gardens; besides de Milde, he is the one whose work is most regularly mentioned in the accounts during the early 1640s.

The importance of Honselaarsdijk as tree-growing centre is reflected in the recurring references to the transportation of fruit- and other trees from Honselaarsdijk to the gardens at Buren, Ysselsteyn and Zuylesteyn. In the latter part of the century Honselaarsdijk would continue to fulfil this role, for instance when William III sent shiploads of trees and plants to his gardens in England (999 fols. 75vo, 155). The amount of trees planted at Honselaarsdijk is a good indication of the size of the place and provides us with an idea of the spatial, alternately vertical (trees, hedges) and horizontal (parterres) effect of the layout and its overall 'wooded' impression.

IDEAL COUNTRY LIFE AND *UTILE DULCI* AS EXPRESSED IN THE COURTLY GARDENS

The importance attached to woods and orchards at Honselaarsdijk and other courtly gardens reminds one of the aspect of combining utility with pleasure manifest in many early-seventeenth-century gardens. The dual function or purpose of the garden, for pleasure and for the provision of the table, was favoured at the time and described in detail by the French garden architect Jacques Boyceau de la Barauderie in his *Traité du jardinage selon les raisons de la Nature et de l'Art*.[130] The title of this book is indicative of its content, as a distinction is made between Art and Nature. Boyceau clearly distinguishes between the *jardin de plaisir* and the *jardin utile*, one for *le plaisir & la beauté*, the other for the cultivation of the grounds. The pleasure garden is filled with fountains, canals, grottoes, *volières, berceaux, bosquets*, parterres and grass areas for exercise, such as the *jeux de ballon* and the *jeux de palmail*.[131] The latter garden, laid out for utilitarian purposes, is filled with 'arbres fruitiers ... les herbes potageres', yet is not without its own proper 'embellissemens d'artifices', containing *allées* and *berceaux*, while the plants and trees also provide beauty by the diversity of their shapes and colours: 'donnera aussi de beaux ornemens par leurs formes et couleurs diverses'.[132]

The layout of Honselaarsdijk in many ways reflected Boyceau's description. At Honselaarsdijk the woods were not only planted for their beauty in the otherwise barren polderland but also for the fruit they provided for the table and for the timber production, as well as for the protection of the garden from harsh winds. As mentioned above, apart from fruits and vegetables the garden provided many kinds of game and fowl, kept in the menagerie (992 fols. 149b, 272) and the deer park. It also provided fresh fish, reared in the large rectangular pond and in the canals surrounding the property (992 fols. 241, 269 ff).

The aspect of the *utile dulci*, the combination of the practical and the pleasurable, as expressed in the Honselaarsdijk garden is not only the topic of Boyceau's treatise but the central theme in contemporary country-house poetry, including Constantijn Huygens and Jacob Cats's own poems. The regard for nature and country life, largely derived from ideals formulated by the classical writers Columella, Varro and Virgil, found its expression in a new Dutch literary genre, the country-house poem.[133] Good examples are Huygens's *Hofwijck*, Jacob Cats's *Ouderdom, buyten-leven en hof-gedachten, op Sorghvliet* ('Age, Country Life and Garden Thoughts on Sorgvliet') and Petrus Hondius's *Dapes inemptae, of de Moufe-schans, dat is, de soeticheydt des buyten-levens vergheselschapt met de boucken* ('Dapes inemptae, or the Moufe-schans, that is, sweetness of country life accompanied by books'), the titles of which alone are evidence of the all-embracing quality of the country-life topos. The cultivation of the orchard and the reclamation of land to be turned into fertile garden grounds, described in the above-cited verses by Cats as the leading responsibility of the Stadholder, were the central theme in the Calvinist-humanist realm of thought, in which the circle round Huygens was steeped and with which the Stadholder certainly was conversant. Nature as God's revelation and country life as peaceful existence away from the corrupt world are central topoi of humanist philosophy and literature, describing man's relation to and involvement in the great natural cycles through his labour and the cultivation of land. Ultimately, tending the garden and orchard was seen as a divine responsibility given to mankind. In this context, the effort extended to land reclamation, water drainage and cultivation of the orchards at Honselaarsdijk, Ter Nieuburch and other gardens takes on a completely different meaning, having specific religious and philosophical connotations.

These age-old notions of ideal country life and cultivation of the land prevailed throughout the seventeenth century and were summarized by Jan van der Groen: 'According to many learned people, gardening and country life are the most delightful, the most advantageous and the healthiest, oft-times also the most blessed life one could wish for the person who is not bound by his profession to the city.'[134] While the Stadholder and his courtiers drew pleasure from the pure splendour of their plants and trees, it also was with such loftier thoughts in mind that they observed the whole layout and plantation of their gardens and orchards.

FREDERIK HENDRIK AND HIS GARDEN AT HONSELAARSDIJK

Having combined the evidence from archival documents with details from the Van Berckerode print, within the context of current literary and philosophical thought on gardening, one is now able to get a clear picture of the courtly garden layouts and their significance in mid-seventeenth-century Holland. The pleasure Frederik Hendrik drew from his newly-planted and decorated estate of Honselaarsdijk can be gleaned from the many letters Huygens wrote over the years to Amalia, describing the Stadholder's thoughts, moods and ideas. One letter, written in the summer of 1637, shows how Honselaarsdijk was used as a standard in comparing other layouts, for example the new buildings at Breda:

> Monsieur le Prince Electeur et tout le reste de sa cour angloise ont vuidé la maison et tentes de S.A. [at Breda] depuis hier au soir, de sorte qu'on s'y trouve plus au large, nommement par le nouveau bastiment que S. Alt^e. y a faict adjouster d'une belle chambre de bois, aveq un joli cabinet, le tout gazonné au dehors, ou il se plaist à merveilles, et proteste de l'admirer plus que Honselerdijck. Aussi est-ce une superbe structure, et digne que les grands Architectes la viennent contempler.[135]

Other letters written in the same vein confirm Frederik Hendrik's deep involvement and extensive personal interest in the building activities and garden layout of Honselaarsdijk:

> Charles Lannoy[136] revint hier et donna contentement à S.A. de beaucoup de choses, concernant les ouvrages à la Haye et Honselardijck, hormis la garderobbe de S.A. et la maisonnette de bois au jardin, voyant qu'on tarde tant à y mettre seulement la main. Parmi les occupations de S.A. c'est le premier et plus aggreable de ses divertissements, que d'estre entretenue de ces matieres.[137]

Clearly, Frederik Hendrik was pleased to hear about the progress of the work at Honselaarsdijk. As Huygens states here, among all Frederik Hendrik's occupations the first and most agreeable one was to converse about matters concerning architecture and garden art. In 1633 the Councillor and Treasurer of the Domains, a certain Brouart, was ordered to come to the army camp and take along all the architects of the buildings and gardens to discuss matters with the Stadholder (1042 fol. 205). Several letters in the Huygens correspondence stress the point that the Stadholder would find relaxation in discussing palace and garden improvements:

30. Bird's-eye view of Honselaarsdijk by A. Bega and A. Blooteling, c. 1680, showing the garden as originally planned by Frederik Hendrik.
Koninklijk Huisarchief
see *colour plate 6*

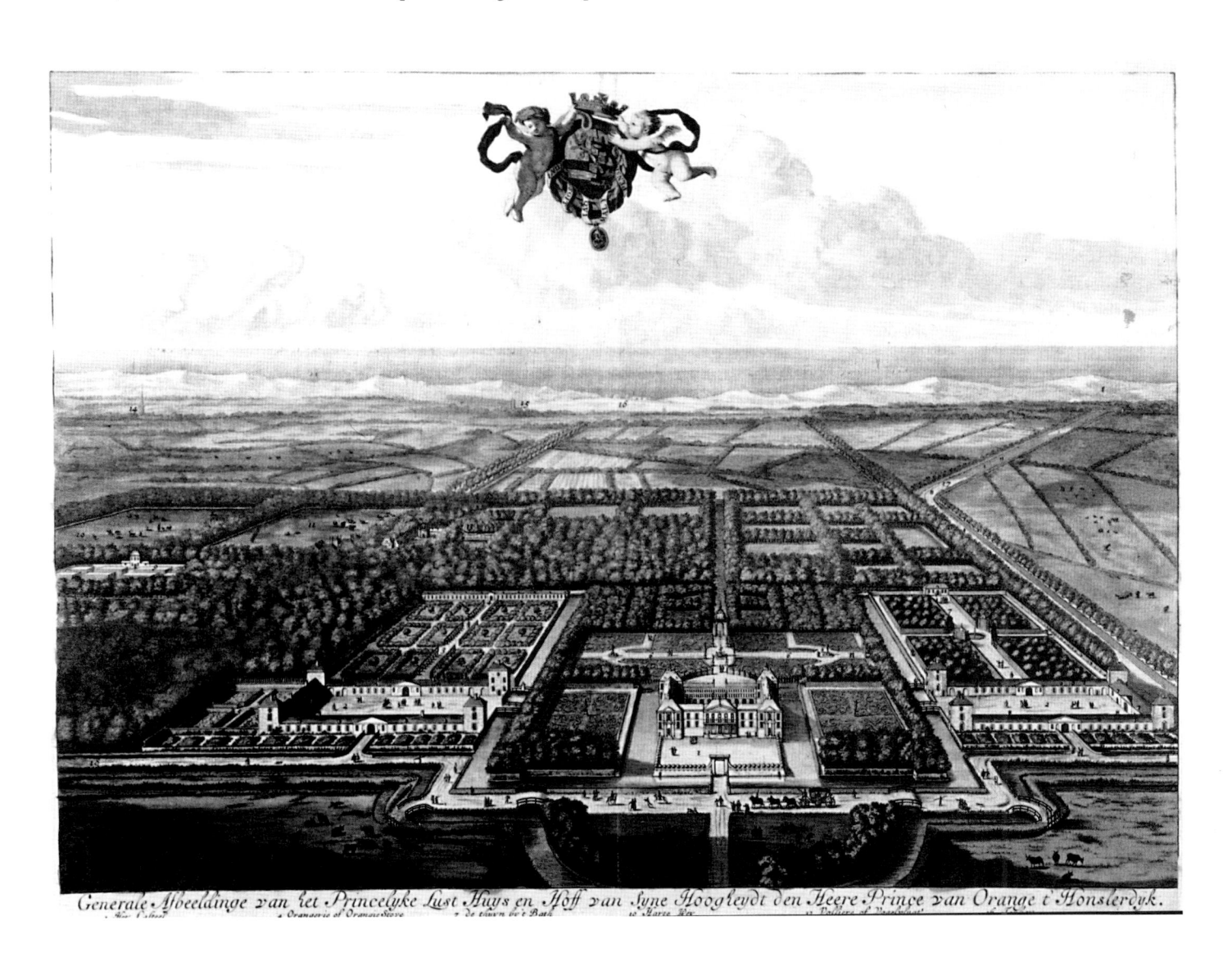

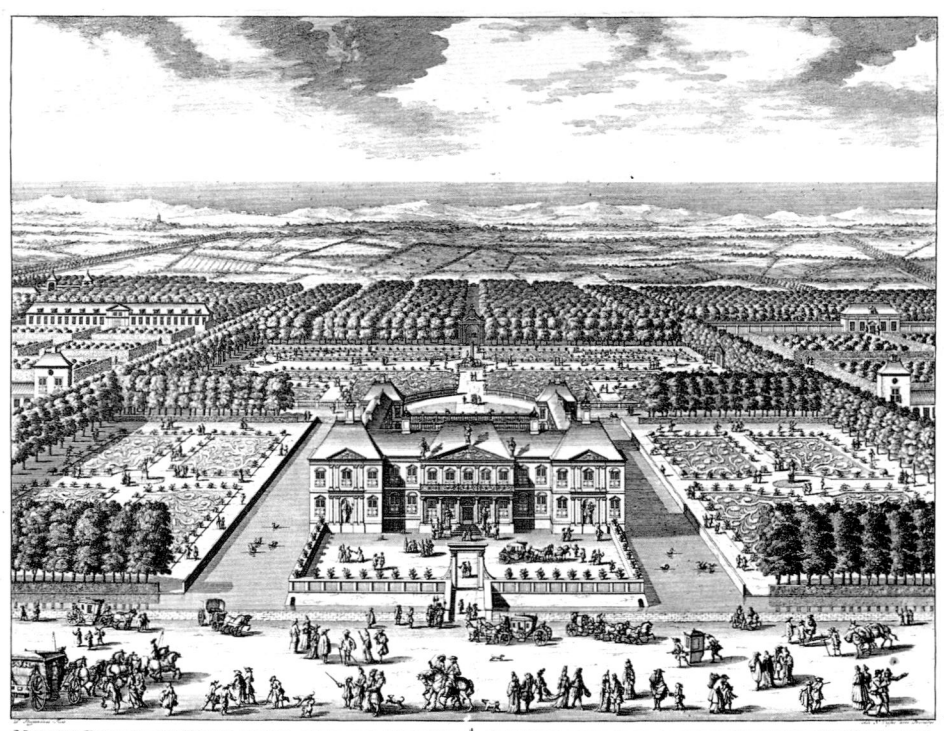

31. Bird's-eye view of Honselaarsdijk by Daniel Stoopendael, c. 1685-90, showing the situation of the garden and details of Honselaarsdijk's façade.
Gemeentearchief, The Hague

32. Drawing attributed to Cornelis Pronk, c. 1730, of Honselaarsdijk's garden façade, with a view over the fountain with the eight gilded statues.
Private collection

> Avant hier au soir, comme S.A. eut escrit sa lettre que V.A. en aura maintenant receue soubs ma couverte, il souppa, – tres bien, peut estre trop bien – et demeura bien deux heures à ordonner les jardins et Bastimens de Honselardick.[138]

Until the very end of his life Frederik Hendrik was actively following building activities and garden layouts of Honselaarsdijk, sometimes fully approving of certain changes, at other times favouring his own ideas. He did not have the opportunity to enjoy the completion of all his garden ideas at Honselaarsdijk and see the plantations in their full-grown glory. The last prolonged visit he paid to Honselaarsdijk with his whole retinue was in the spring

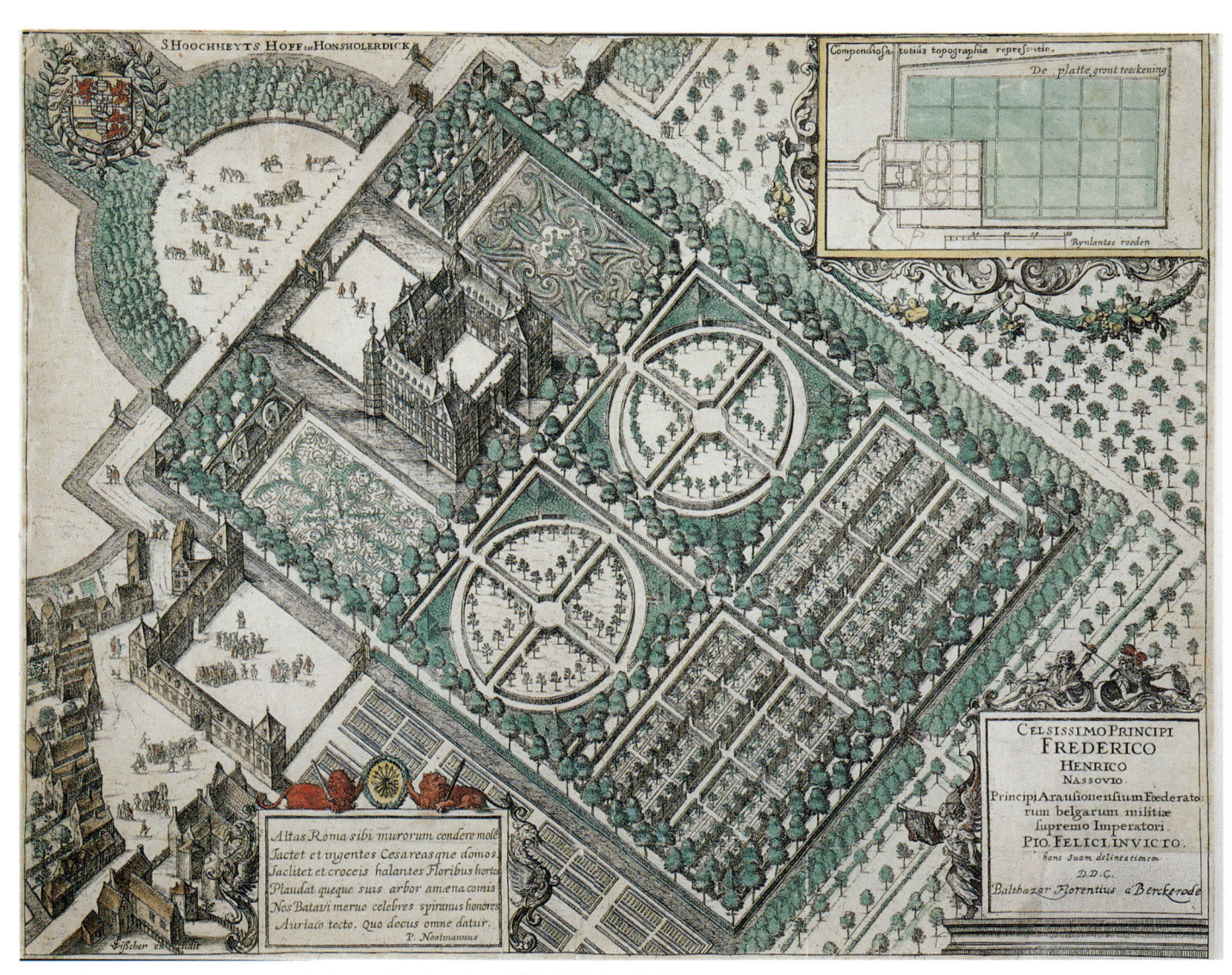

View of Honselaarsdijk by Balthazar Florisz van Berckerode, c. 1638. GAH (see fig. 12)

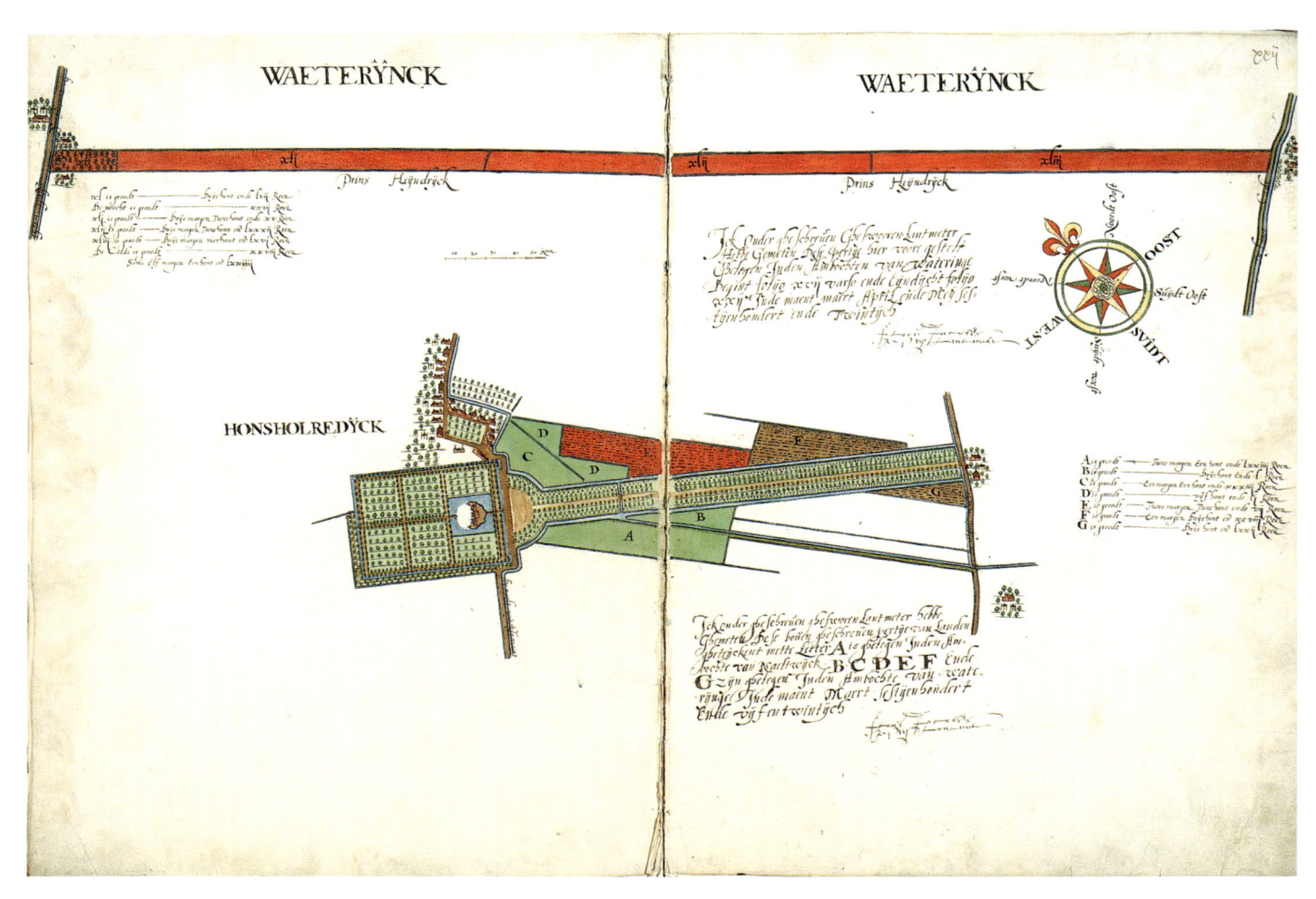

Map of Honselaarsdijk and its approach avenue by Floris Jacobsz van der Sallem, 1620-25. ARA (see fig. 13)

33. Honselaarsdijk's parterre garden with central fountain as originally envisaged by Frederik Hendrik. Print by Petrus Schenck, c. 1690.
Bibliotheek Landbouwuniversiteit, Wageningen

of 1646.[139] At that time, work was continuing on the last great alteration of the main garden behind the palace, and the old garden compartments were completely modernized following contemporary French fashion in the field of garden architecture.

This significant event of the renovation of the Honselaarsdijk garden in the late 1640s has escaped the attention of previous authors. It is all the more unfortunate since the changes in the garden involved a remarkable stylistic development from lingering late Renaissance tendencies to early classical French baroque principles. This neglect also reflects certain methodological deficiencies in art history, owing to which a garden is too often approached as a finished product: the garden's inherent continual growth and development are ignored, in favour of one particular moment or status quo chosen for a stylistic analysis. The new early French baroque principles referred to here involved the introduction of large open garden spaces containing monumental parterres.[140] This new approach to designing the Stadholder's gardens can be recognized by comparing the C. 1638 Van Berckerode print with later ones, such as those by A. Blooteling and A. Bega, D. Stoopendael, and P. Schenck *(figs. 30, 31 and 33)*,[141] showing the more monumental use of space, when the small enclosed garden compartments (including the two circular *berceaux*) were demolished to create one large open parterre area. The parterres were no longer cut up in separate pieces, but followed one large design encompassing the whole pleasure garden, which was seen as an ensemble with the building and provided unobstructed views over the whole width of the garden and the surrounding countryside.

Most important, the new layout was the result of a direct collaboration with French architects, as can be gathered from a contemporary letter asking for suggestions and designs from 'the best architects in France'. This letter holds interesting documentary evidence regarding the last alterations undertaken by Frederik Hendrik in his gardens, which involved the extension of the annexe buildings, their connection with the palace and the construction of a chapel. The letter says that the old garden, situated 'to the right of the palace', needs redressing according to the latest fashion, or, as Huygens put it, 'un habit neuf, qui maintenant se pourra tailler à la mode':

> Dans ce gros pacquet que S.A. me commande de vous envoyer, vous trouverez les plans des deux estages de la maison de Honselardijck, aveq un troisiesme plus estendu et comprenant l'escurie aveq les jardins. L'intention de S.A. est que vous le communiquiez à de vos meilleurs architectes et jardiniers separément, pour les faire ordonner dessus ce qu'ils estimeroyent s'y pouvoir appliquer pour plus grand embellissement du lieu. Les Escuries que vous verrez d'un costé y ont esté adjoustées depuis peu, et enferment une cour bien ample. La question est, comment ceste piece se pourroit attacher aveq grace au grand logis. Le jardin que vous y aurez veu à droict de la maison est desja vieulx, et requiert un habit neuf, qui maintenant se pourra tailler à la mode qu'on voudra. Et pour la maison comme il y manque une chapelle, que d'aucuns ont jugé se pouvoir faire par dessûs le pont du jardin, de sorte que leurs Altesses y pourroyent avoir leurs oratoires en hault, et y entrer par le plombé de la galerie, qui est une belle communication des quartiers, S.A. desire que là dessus specialement les Architectes disent leurs sentiments et en quel endroict ils jugent qu'une chapelle se pourroit le mieulx placer tant pour la bienseance du bastiment que pour la commodité des Princes.[142] Quand vos gens auront mis la main à la plume, nous attendons leurs desseins par V.[tre] moyen, et ne manquerons pas de les bien salarier. Si vous vous souvenez de l'humeur du M.[tre] vous scaurez qu'il convient le servir promptement. C'est ce que je vous recommande surtout aveq asseurance que je suis tousjours veritablement ...[143]

The renovation of the garden mentioned by Huygens involved the layout of a monumental parterre over the whole width of the main pleasure garden, replacing the older square compartments with circular *berceaux* and incorporating the orchard behind it. This conclusion can be made when we combine the content of the above letter with information from the records of payments describing the construction of three octagonal fountains by Joseph Dinant, which, as later prints show, formed the central decoration of this grand parterre garden.

These changes to the garden and the description provided by Huygens's letter must also be related to the previously mentioned designs by Pieter Post for the connection of the new annexe buildings with the palace proper, unifying them in a dramatic, amphitheatre-shaped setting *(see fig. 17)*. Belonging to these renovation plans are Pieter Post's *bestecken* or detailed estimates describing the new layout of the 'grooten ende cleynen thuyn', the large and small garden of Honselaarsdijk, referred to in contemporary correspondence.[144] Unfortunately these *bestecken* for the gardens have not come down to us, but it is significant that they were made by the architect Post, who apparently also ventured out into the area of garden architecture.

Though we do not know the direct reply to the French letter or the degree of Post's influence in Honselaarsdijk's last major garden improvements, we do know the ultimate result: the reorganization and decoration of the main pleasure garden behind the palace leading to one expansive parterre area interrupted only by three fountains set on the transverse axis. The bird's-eye view by Bega and Blooteling of circa 1680 *(see fig. 30)*[145] clearly shows the new situation originally planned by Frederik Hendrik. By comparing this print with the print made forty years earlier by Van Berckerode *(see fig. 12)*, one can clearly see that the main pleasure garden behind the palace had lost its remarkable shape of two circular *berceaux* which typified the early-seventeenth-century garden layout. Instead of enclosed square plots, the garden consisted of a large open area cut through by a system of two perpendicular axes.

The new garden was decorated with parterres which centred on the three fountains set on the transverse axis. The total form of the extensive new parterre garden resembled the layout of the age-old hippodrome. Furthermore, the remarkable shape of the new, semicircular open terrace that was reached on entering the garden, and that was borrowed from Post's design, mirrored the exedra of the main driveway in front of the palace. The two parterre gardens flanking the palace were modernized and divided into four smaller plots. The larger plantation areas outside the garden island proper are now visible in their full-grown form. Also new in Bega's print are the Orangerie and its garden behind the westerly lower courts or annexe buildings; they, too, are now shown in their completed form. On the opposite or east side, a garden section filled with fountains and trellis-work structures stretched in front of the pleasure house. Clearly visible are vegetable and herb gardens, planted in neatly arranged plots in front of, or south of, both lower courts. More to the west, where the woods and the deer park extended, two groups of buildings can be seen: one is the old menagerie, now called Faisanterie, the other, more to the north, the old forester's house.

From the mid-1640s onward considerable expenditure is recorded for the planting and decoration of the new east and west gardens ('nieuwe West Thuijn').[146] Large payments for the embellishment of the garden with sculpture, waterworks and other ornaments continued unabated into the late 1640s. Indeed in 1647, shortly before his death, Frederik Hendrik commissioned Joseph Dinant, the French *fontainier-grottier*, to make the three fountains, the stone for which was imported from Italy – it actually came from Tivoli[147] – to decorate the newly-planned parterre garden. Only his grandson William III, however, would later in the century draw pleasure from these grand parterres and fountains. In fact, he would enhance their ornamentation and, with the help of Huygens's son Christiaan, the famous scientist, would improve the effect of the fountains and other waterworks by developing more sophisticated pump systems in the garden.[148]

HONSELAARSDIJK AFTER FREDERIK HENDRIK, UNDER WILLIAM II AND WILLIAM III

After the death of Frederik Hendrik in 1647, Honselaarsdijk came into the possession of William II, who, guided by Amalia, completed most of the work in progress. There did not change much in the gardens during his reign; his early death in 1650 did not leave time for many changes and his preference lay in the newly-acquired estate of Dieren in the province of Gelderland, an ideal place for the hunt. In the interim period between William II's death and the appointment of his son William III as new Stadholder in 1672, the activities at Honselaardijk can be defined as maintaining the status quo. However, during these interim years mention is made of an 'eerste en tweede nieuwe thuyn' (first and second new garden) at Honselaarsdijk (996 fols. 10vo, 11-13). While it is not clear to which section of the garden the records refer, this reference most likely concerns the upkeep of the earlier-mentioned 'new gardens', or the new plantations on the west and east sides of the estate, begun in the 1640s. Other entries confirm that no major new building activities were undertaken and that expenditures were limited to the most necessary repairs of house and gardens, which could no longer be delayed (996 fol. 19).

Besides a few new labourers and gardeners,[149] a large number of familiar names recur in the accounts and many individuals originally employed by Frederik Hendrik continued to work at Honselaarsdijk, among them the architect Pieter Post and the land-surveyor Pieter Floris van der Sallem. One name that should be singled out is that of Jan van der

de Fonteyn ende Goude Beelden in de Groote Thuyn.

34. Honselaarsdijk's grand parterre garden with mid-seventeenth-century fountain and statues as they were under William III, with Jacob Roman's triumphal arch.
Gemeentearchief, The Hague

de Orangerie.

35. The Orangerie at Honselaarsdijk, built under William III by Johan van Swieten and Jacob Roman in sober brick style. Print by C. Danckerts.
Bibliotheek Landbouwuniversiteit, Wageningen

36. The new Orangerie at Honselaarsdijk as rebuilt under Prussian reign, in an engraving by Pierre Loofs, c. 1715. Rijksprentenkabinet, Rijksmuseum, Amsterdam

Groen (996 fols. 220vo, 232ff.), who would come to be known for his treatise on garden art entitled *Den Nederlandtsen Hovenier*, first published in 1669. This treatise is of value as a general survey of what was considered important in garden art at the time, and, as we have seen, it was of interest for its description of the choice of flora at the Dutch court, particularly at Honselaarsdijk.

A whole series of prints of Honselaarsdijk, all dating from the 1680s and 1690s, provides us with a visual overview of important changes in the gardens after Frederik Hendrik. Some further renovations apparently occurred about 1669, when Cosimo III de' Medici during his visit at Honselaarsdijk saw work in progress in the gardens:

> La mattina de' 21 andò l'A.S. sei miglia lontano a vedere una villa del Principe d'Oranges, chiamata Onselerdic, che è assai galante per la moltiplicita de' boschi, statue e fontane deliziose, aggiuntovi un parco non grande ma bene inteso, il che tutto andavano mettendo in stato migliore.[150]

The modernization of the garden must have included further improvement of the large, open parterre area with three fountains and the cutting of a new avenue through the orchard behind it, providing a vast view into the surrounding fields and dunes. A bird's-eye view by Daniel Stoopendael of the whole estate *(see fig. 31)*[151] clearly shows the exact layout of the garden parts and their decoration, including statues such as the *Hercules and*

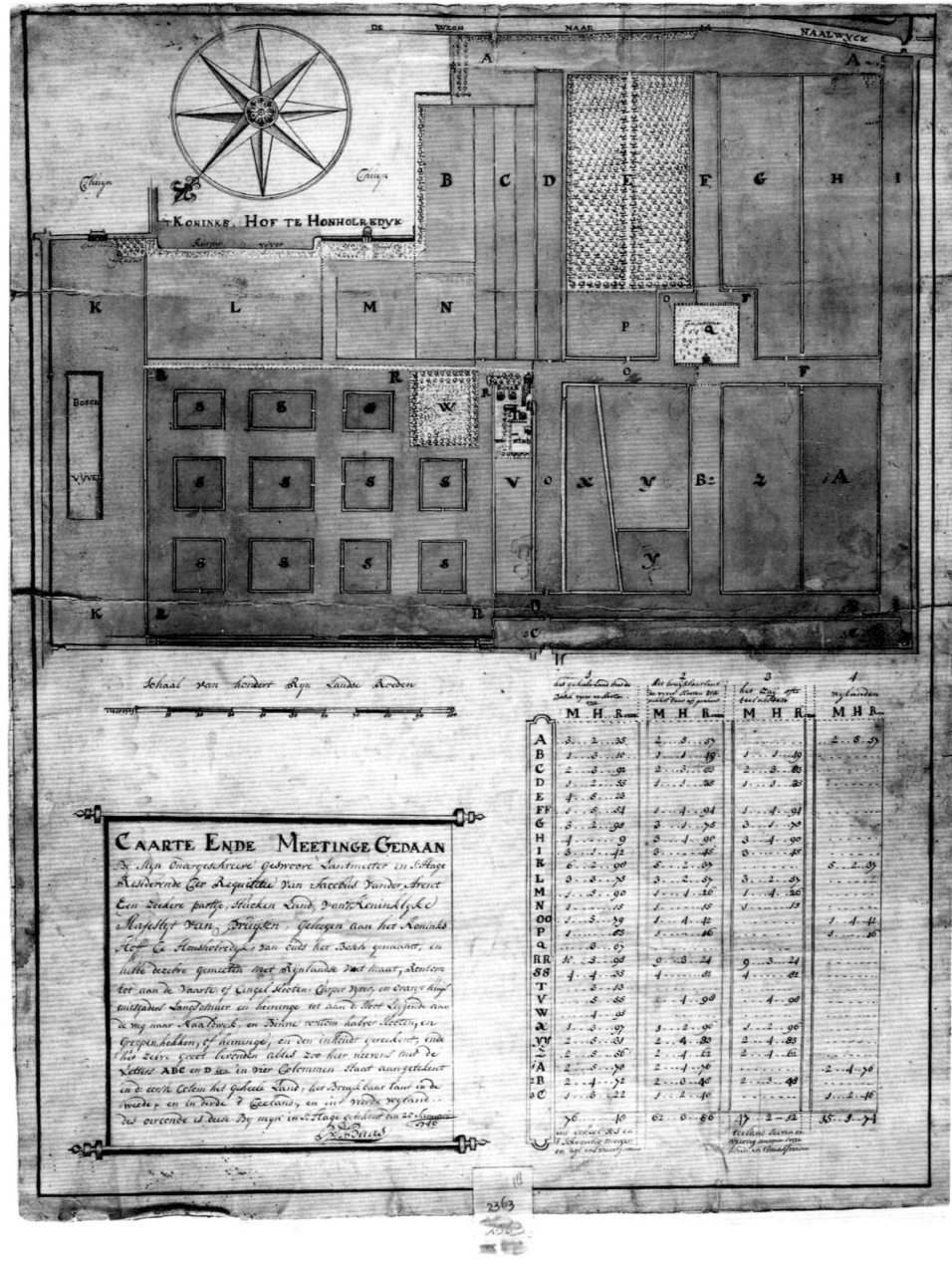

37. Plan of Honselaarsdijk by B. de Baes, 1746, showing the larger utilitarian garden sections with orchards, woods and fishpond.
Algemeen Rijksarchief

Cacus, about the year 1685 and under William III. The print affords a good impression of the fortress-like appearance of the moated palace, showing the elevation of the façade of the building in all its detail. The entrance bridge, decorated by the early-seventeenth-century sculptures on pedestals and a portico crested by lions holding an escutcheon, led to the square forecourt whose decoration still consisted of the old sculptured, lead vases planted with flowers set on the surrounding balustrade. The decoration of the main façade, begun under Frederik Hendrik and completed under William II, is also visible. The central pavilion holds the main entry, accentuated by a portico topped by a balcony. The roof pediment is crowned by three statues of classical female figures. Two other statues, a *Mars* and a *Venus* by the Antwerp sculptor Artus Quellinus, originally placed there in 1634, flank the stairs leading up to the main entry. Continuing one's path through the whole palace complex into the garden, one entered the semicircular terrace framed by a balustrade, from

54   COURTLY GARDENS IN HOLLAND 1600-1650

38. Large plan of Honselaarsdijk attributed to B. de Baes, showing the new plantations and avenues in the garden during Prussian ownership.
Collectie Bodel Nijenhuis, Universiteitsbibliotheek, Leiden
see colour plate 7

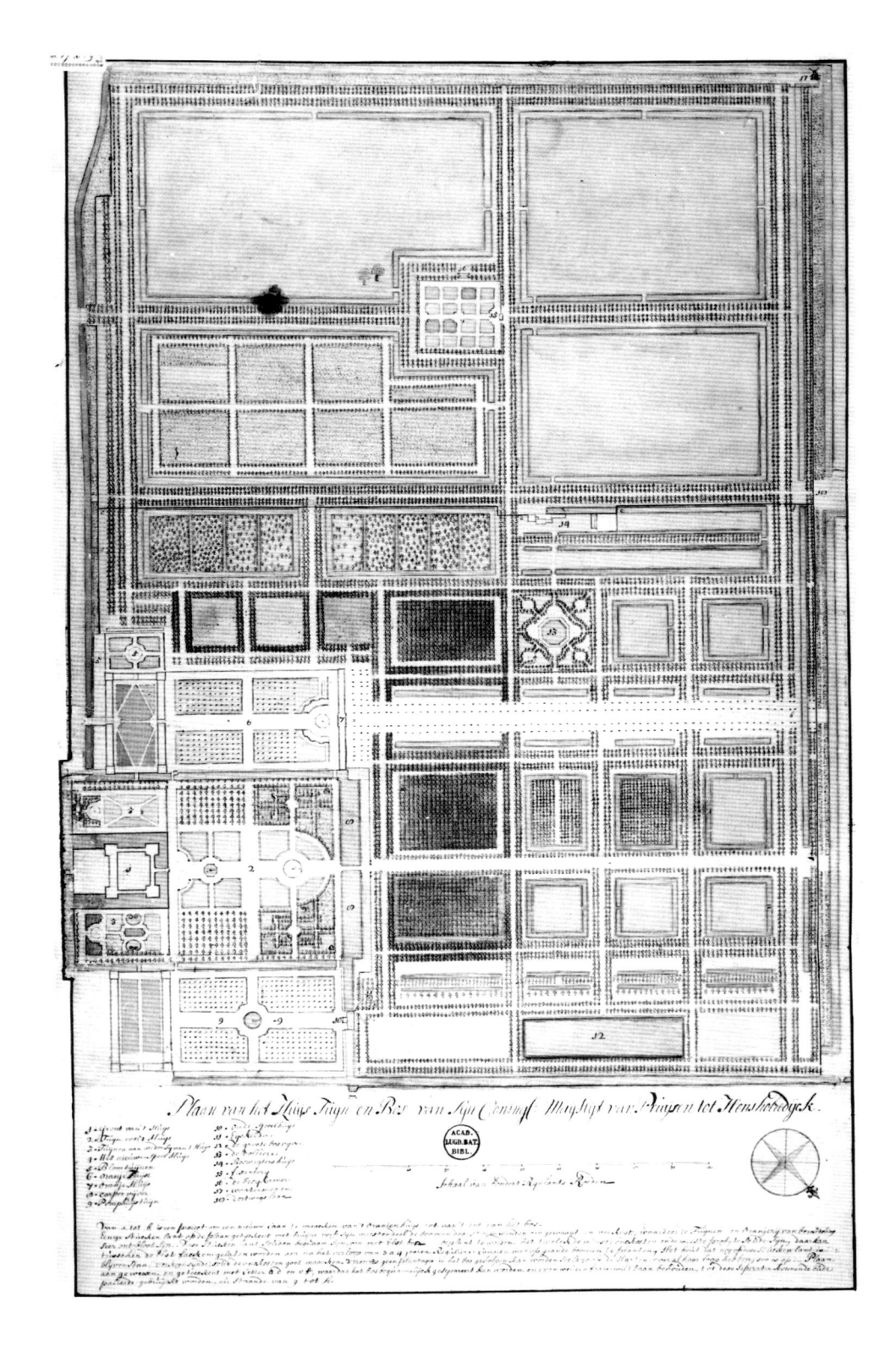

1. HONSELAARSDIJK

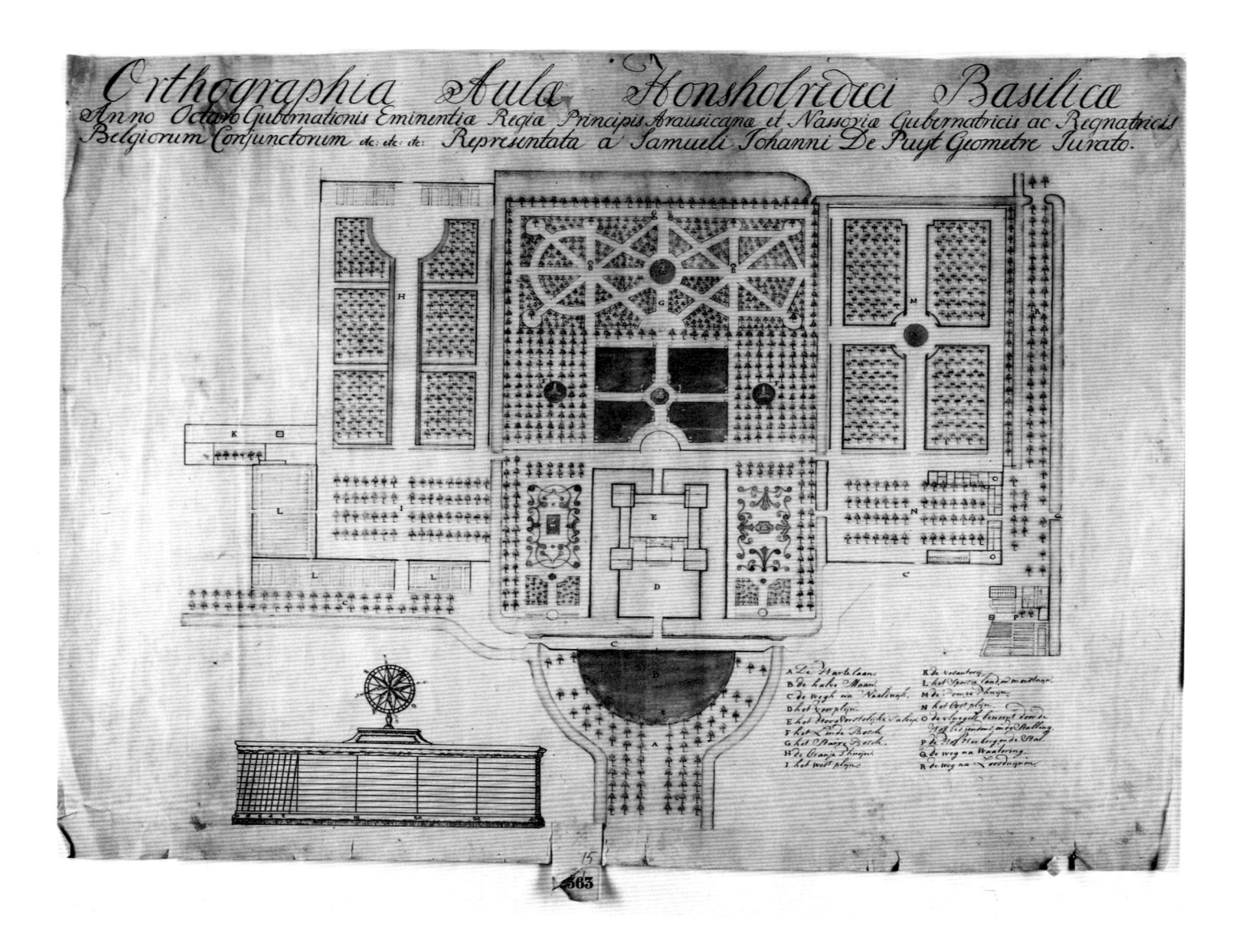

where one could oversee the whole parterre layout.

A little-known drawing, probably by Cornelis Pronk,[152] depicts the rear elevation or garden façade of early-eighteenth-century Honselaarsdijk. It shows the main parterre garden as constructed at the end of Frederik Hendrik's life and worked out by William II and III *(see fig. 32)*. Its decoration with statues, vases and fountains is shown in a print by Petrus Schenck *(see fig. 33)*,[153] offering an added spatial impression of this open parterre area.

Within the pleasure garden the main transverse axes now were accentuated by what appear to be trellis-work structures, designed in the form of huge porticoes representing triumphal arches *(see fig. 34)*.[154] The records show that these porticoes were designed by Jacob Roman (1640-1716) in 1684, even before his official appointment as royal architect five years later (998 fol. 7).[155] Before Roman's appointment, Johan van Swieten worked as designing architect at Honselaarsdijk; he was primarily responsible for the building of the new Orangerie (997 fol. 255 and 998 fol. 6). The Orangerie, first shown in Bega's print north of the left-hand annexe *(see fig. 30)*, later was engraved in detail by C. Danckerts *(fig. 35)*.[156] This elongated building, the plain façade of which adhered to the typical late-seventeenth-century Dutch sober brick style, in itself is nothing exceptional, but it is

39. Map of Honselaarsdijk by Johannes de Puyt, 1762, showing the 'picturesque' layout of the pleasure garden with sculpture in chinoiserie style.
Algemeen Rijksarchief

56 COURTLY GARDENS IN HOLLAND 1600-1650

40. Eastern lower courts or stables at Honselaarsdijk, still known as 'Nederhof', the only remaining structure of the palace complex.
Photo courtesy Rijksdienst voor de Monumentenzorg, Zeist, 1978

41. Map of the Honselaarsdijk area as it is today, intersected by a motorway and built over by greenhouses, its original framework of canals still visible.
Provinciale VVV Zuid-Holland

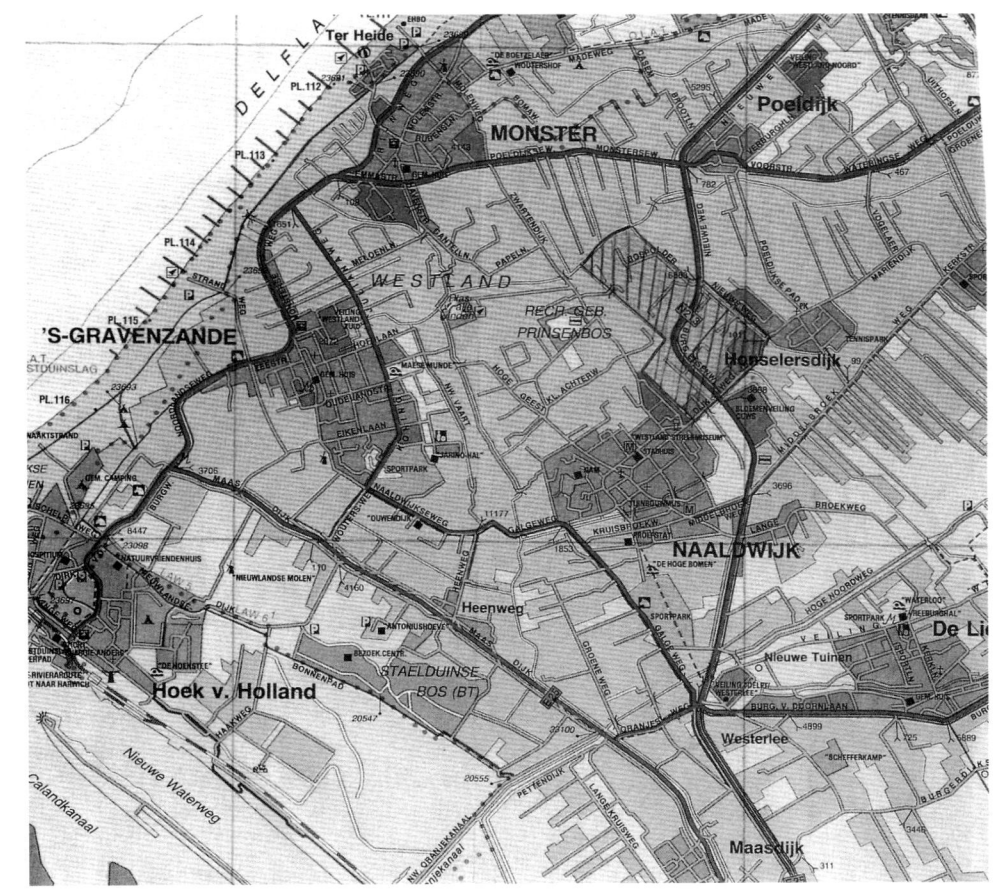

I. HONSELAARSDIJK

remarkable for its contents: the orange-, lemon- and other exotic trees and plants which were cultivated within its walls. According to William III's trusted friend and adviser Hans Willem Bentinck, the Earl of Portland, Honselaarsdijk's orange-trees compared favourably even with Louis XVI's orange-trees at Versailles.[157]

The correspondence between William III and Hans Willem Bentinck also indicates how important horticulture and garden architecture again were to William III; with hunting, he called them his 'greatest passion'.[158] Like his grandfather Frederik Hendrik, William III was directly involved in garden art round his estates. Moreover, as had been the case in the early part of the century under Frederik Hendrik, through William and a close circle of courtiers new French style forms would be absorbed in late-seventeenth-century Dutch garden art and from there spread to other European countries.[159]

HONSELAARSDIJK AFTER 1700

A series of three little-known maps and prints of Honselaarsdijk must suffice to give a picture of the estate's garden layout in the eighteenth century *(figs. 37, 38 and 39)*.[160] After William III's childless death in 1702, Friedrich I of Prussia, son of Frederik Hendrik's eldest daughter, claimed Honselaarsdijk.[161] Under Friedrich I (1702-1713) certain changes were made in the house and garden, the most noteworthy of which involved the construction of a new Orangerie *(fig. 36)*.[162] However, the basic division of the grounds remained unchanged from the mid-eighteenth century onward, as can be seen by comparing a series of old maps *(see figs. 20 and 21)* with a map by B. de Baes *(fig. 37)*, dated 1746 and showing the wooded area behind the castle.[163] Visible on this map are also (from left to right) the old pleasure house (*speelhuys*) in the east garden, now flanked by an ice cellar, and the new Orangerie with its central cupola.

A larger map of the whole garden, also dating from the first half of the eighteenth century and probably again drawn by B. de Baes *(fig. 38)*,[164] clearly shows the alterations in the main pleasure garden during Prussian ownership. The central parterre area, the hippodrome-shaped outline of which originally extended parallel to the façade of the building *(see fig. 31)*, was now turned and aligned with the main north-south axis. Though the parterre opened up in a semicircle towards the north, tree plantations encroached on its sides, limiting the unobstructed side view which had characterized its late-eighteenth-century layout. Trees increasingly came to dominate the whole garden layout in the later part of the eighteenth century; actually they seemed to become the garden's main *raison d'être*.

The importance of tree cultivation for timber production at eighteenth-century Honselaarsdijk is also evidenced by the accompanying text on the map shown above *(see fig. 38)*. It mentions where further plantation should be added and which woods could best be cut down and sold for profit, at a time when the cost to keep up such extensive gardens became exorbitant. Matters worsened as the century wore on: having installed his envoy at Honselaarsdijk and rarely visiting the place himself, Friedrich Wilhelm, the King of Prussia's successor, had not the opportunity to draw any aesthetic pleasure from the gardens. In fact, by the mid-eighteenth century he seemed to be mainly concerned with the cultivation of trees and plants at Honselaarsdijk for sustenance and for making profit through the sale of wood. The pleasure gardens proper were neglected and the alabaster statues of the Princes of Orange became overgrown with moss – 'everything was smelling of the Prussian reign', according to Albrecht Haller's travel account.[165] Thus, during Friedrich Wilhelm's ownership from 1713 to 1754, a combination of distance (between

The Hague and the Prussian residence in Berlin), disinterest and need to economize resulted in the increasing deterioration of the Honselaarsdijk estate.[166] An inventory drawn up in 1754, when the estate was bought back by the Orange family, describes the dilapidated state of Honselaarsdijk, the house and garden of which were in need of extensive restoration.[167] Yet, in the hands of the Orange family again, the Honselaarsdijk garden experienced a brief period of flowering, prior to its total ruin and the demolition of the castle in the early nineteenth century. Johannes de Puyt's map *(fig. 39)*, dated 1762,[168] shows the newly-decorated garden. Following the fashion of the time, an extensive wooded area (Starrebosch) dominated the main pleasure garden which, in addition to the traditional seventeenth-century sculpture, was now partly decorated with Chinese pagodas. They were set on small mounds in the lime-tree wood, on either side of the central axis. The style of the garden can be called eclectic, as landscape features alternated with parterres in late rococo style in what was basically still the formal garden layout created under Frederik Hendrik. In 1778 the gardens would undergo their final metamorphosis when, in order to improve the pleasure garden, the badly-kept grass parterres were replaced with a 'so-called English flower and shrubbery garden'.[169] By that time, however, most of the buildings in the garden had disappeared – among them the Orangerie and pleasure house, which were demolished about 1750 and consequently missing on de Puyt's map of 1762 *(see fig. 39)*. Sadly, the entire lower courts on the west side of the castle, and part of those on the east side which are no longer found on this map, were demolished about the same time. Recently restored, the remains of these eastern lower courts, still known as 'Nederhof', survive today as the sole reminder of the once famous palace of Honselaarsdijk *(fig. 40)*.[170] The outline of the gardens themselves, now taken over by modern greenhouses and factories and cut through by a motorway,[171] can still be recognized on today's maps of the area *(fig. 41)*,[172] which show the elongated rectangular form of the original layout, bordered by the old seventeenth-century canals.

COURTLY GARDENS IN HOLLAND 1600-1650

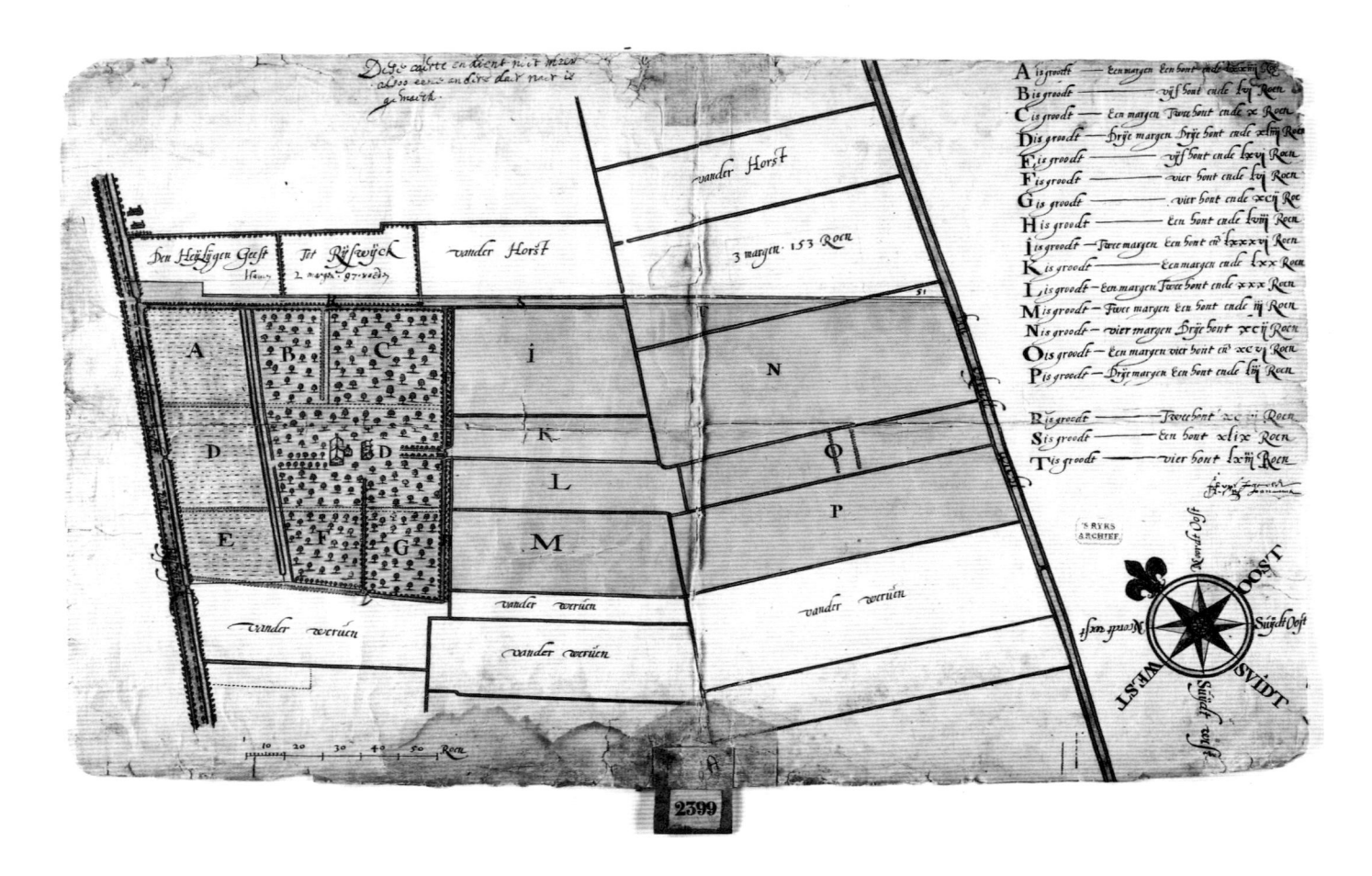

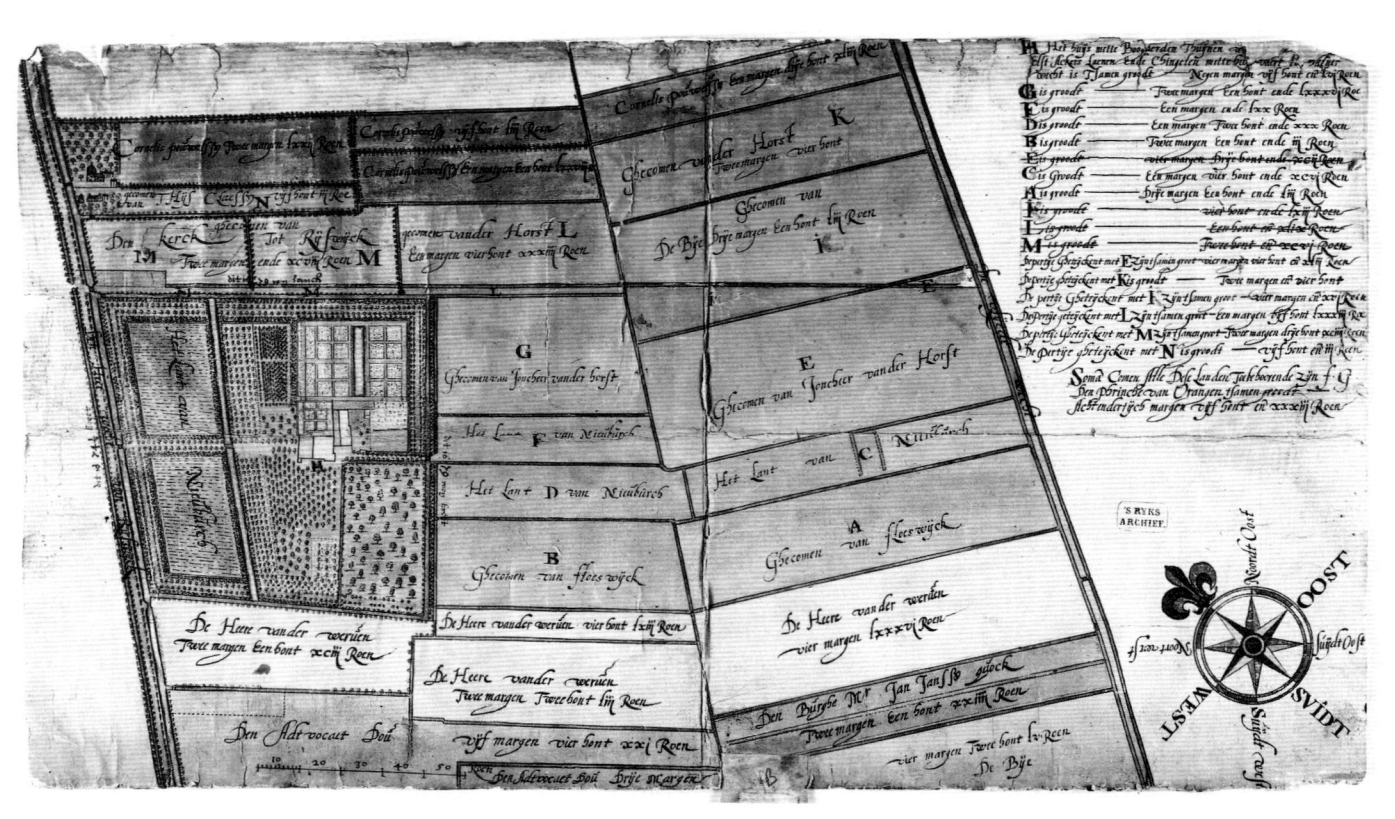

CHAPTER II

THE PALACE AND GARDENS OF TER NIEUBURCH AT RIJSWIJK

42. Map of Ter Nieuburch by Floris Jacobsz van der Sallem, c. 1630, with old orchards and farm shortly before the improvements by Frederik Hendrik.
Algemeen Rijksarchief
see *colour plate 8*

43. Map of Ter Nieuburch by Floris Jacobsz van der Sallem, c. 1630, showing the first improvement of grounds and newly-acquired parcels of land.
Algemeen Rijksarchief

The history of Ter Nieuburch, Frederik Hendrik's estate on the outskirts of The Hague, in many respects mirrors the history of Honselaarsdijk. The extensive gardens were laid out in the 1630s and many of the workmen, gardeners and map-makers who had been involved at Honselaarsdijk were again present here. Indeed, the procedure followed in creating the Huis ter Nieuburch can be compared with the way Honselaarsdijk was created; it can also be told from the account books and a series of *bestecken*, or builder's estimates and specifications, recovered in the Algemeen Rijksarchief.[1] However, there are not only similarities but also distinct differences between the two layouts and their decorations, of both building and garden. Whereas Honselaarsdijk's total layout could be defined as a 'classical canal garden' which, with its fortress-like appearance, was the domain of late-sixteenth-century Franco-Italian architecture, Ter Nieuburch exhibited more 'modern' tendencies anticipating later architectural style developments, generally defined as the Franco-Dutch classical baroque.

Part of these stylistic differences may be due to the fact that Honselaarsdijk was built on the grounds of an existing palace and garden, whereas Ter Nieuburch was designed from scratch on largely unbuilt terrain, the form of which was not determined by the necessity to incorporate existing parcels and plantations. Furthermore, palace and garden were more closely related and not separated by a moat, as at Honselaarsdijk. The Ter Nieuburch garden layout for the first time expresses the wish to integrate the garden with the surrounding landscape, as well as to merge all the garden's features by means of embracing architectural forms. At Ter Nieuburch we recognize a first, hesitant departure from the traditional grid system with its successive cumulative impression characteristic of Honselaarsdijk's early garden layout and an attempt at larger baroque solutions.

While both estates ultimately served as representative country seats and places for official state receptions, Ter Nieuburch, originally built as a summer residence, would acquire international renown as the place where the Rijswijk Peace Treaty was signed in 1697, formalizing a new alliance between England, France and Holland. In spite of this important historical event, Ter Nieuburch suffered the same unfortunate fate that struck Honselaarsdijk and was demolished in the late eighteenth century. The only object reminding us of this once magnificent estate is a lonely obelisk in what nowadays is the Rijswijk public park.

EARLY HISTORY AND DEVELOPMENT OF TER NIEUBURCH

Two enthusiastic descriptions of the general situation, plantation and interior decoration of Ter Nieuburch – one by an Englishman, the other by a Frenchman – make good introductions to the estate. Sir William Brereton, who travelled through The Netherlands in 1634, was the first to describe the newly-constructed, if not quite finished, palace and garden complex:

> Hence [from The Hague] I went to a dainty new house of the Prince of Orange, erecting and almost finished: it is about an English mile from the place where we left the scute [*schuit*, or towed barge], and as far from The Hague. This house was intended a story higher, but that the foundation would not admit.[2] It is most proportioned in length; … Here are mighty spacious garden plots here, sowed with herbs and roots; one or two English acres. Here is also leading from the highway to the court … a spacious piece of ground containing about four English acres, wherein are planted sycamore-trees curiously and in such order, as which way soever you look, they stand in order and rank.[3]

While Brereton admired the palace's exterior and commented on the spaciousness of the garden compartments and the orderliness of the tree plantations, the Frenchman Jean de Parival, in his *Les Délices de la Hollande* of 1651, seemed most struck by the interior of the palace, decorated by 'the greatest masters of the world':

> Ryswic est aussi un beau Village tout proche de la Haye, où ledit Prince a fait encore bastir un beau chasteau qui découvre la prairie & qui resjouit beaucoup la veuë de tous ceux qui viennent de Delft. On y voit quantité de très rares peintures & des pieces des plus grands maistres du monde.[4]

The silhouette of Ter Nieuburch seen from Delft and its situation on the flat holm grounds as evoked by these texts fit the descriptions of the early layout of palace and garden in the account books of the Nassau Domains. The first important entry concerning Ter Nieuburch was in the summer of 1630. That year the estate Ter Nieuburch, also called Huis te Rijswijk, was acquired by Frederik Hendrik. Apparently the site already included an old house, or *hofstede*, with orchards and gardens,[5] all of which were demolished to make room for the new palace and gardens:

> In July 1630 His Highness has bought from Filibert Vernatti[6] a house called Ter Nieuburch near Rijswijk including its orchards, canals, gardens and belonging to it fourteen morgen one hond ninety-six roeden land, and this for the price of thirty thousand pounds artois … the house of which His Highness had completely demolished and in its place constructed a remarkable building …[7]

This text tallies with two contemporary maps by the already familiar surveyor Floris Jacobsz van der Sallem *(figs. 42 and 43)*.[8] From 1630 onward he is frequently mentioned in the records of Ter Nieuburch as having received payments in February of 1631 and 1632 for measuring plots of land in the manor (*ambacht*) of Rijswijk and for making several maps of the area (1040, fol. 214 and 255[vo]). The maps mentioned in the records must have included the two shown here, which were made in conjunction with the Stadholder's plans to acquire the Ter Nieuburch estate. The two maps clearly show the early situation, size and layout of Ter Nieuburch before the extension and embellishment of the property under Frederik Hendrik. The first map depicts the original farmstead, displaying a simple layout consisting of orchards without a specific delineation of a pleasure garden. The second map shows Ter Nieuburch in the next stage of its development from a modest farmstead to a country estate. However, this second map may also be just a more detailed version of the first one.[9] In the second, more refined plan the grounds are divided into neatly arranged compartments, while the old farmhouses are enlarged and surrounded by a garden consisting of square plots and a long, rectangular pond. This map gives a clear overview of

44. Map of Delfland (detail) by Nicolaas Cruquius, 1712, showing the extension of Ter Nieuburch (left of centre) between Zandvaert and Rijswijkse Vaart (Vliet). Gemeentearchief, The Hague

45. Reconstruction drawing of the extension of Ter Nieuburch by the acquisition of land parcels between Zandvaert and Vliet. (orientation reversed)

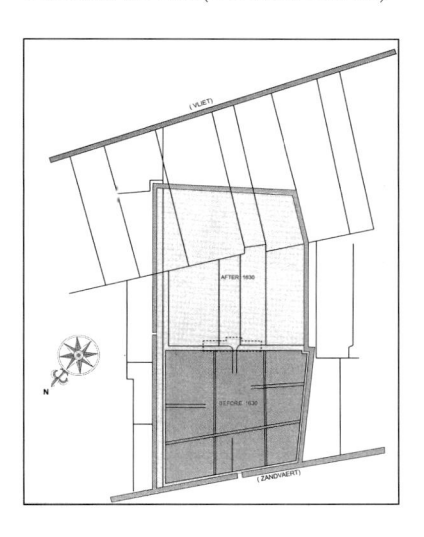

the planned division and boundary of the new grounds, laid out on land parcels numbered A to N on the old maps and totalling roughly 'thirty-eight morgen', which equals thirty-three hectares, or about eighty acres. The actual size of the later pleasure garden, measuring circa 620 by 310 metres, would total roughly twenty hectares, or about fifty acres – approximately twice the size of the main pleasure garden at Honselaarsdijk.[10]

When comparing these two early maps by Floris Jacobsz van der Sallem with the Delfland map by Nicolaas Cruquius of 1712 *(fig. 44)*, one can see the precise extension plan of the new layout. The outline and division of the parcels of land featured on the early-seventeenth-century maps by Floris Jacobsz[11] are replicated in the Cruquius map. The extension and the development of the grounds are clarified by an added reconstruction drawing *(fig. 45)*, showing both the originally planned and the completed layouts of Ter Nieuburch. As is shown by these maps, the whole property of Ter Nieuburch extended between two major waterways, the Zandvaert and the Vliet; along them ran two important roads, the Zandwegh (originally called Heerewegh) and the Vlietwegh or Kleiwegh, known today as the Van Vredenburchweg and the Winston Churchill-laan, respectively. The situation of Paleis ter Nieuburch and the atmosphere of the windswept holm grounds interspersed with oak groves are admirably rendered in a painting by Anthony Jansz van der Croos *(fig. 46)*.[12] Made after a drawing of circa 1634 by the same artist, the painting shows the gardens as unfinished, while the building's silhouette appears to be finished entirely.

What the garden of Ter Nieuburch looked like in detail after its completion under Frederik Hendrik can be seen in an engraving by J. Julius Milheusser, signed and dated 1644 *(fig. 47)*.[13] This print gives a bird's-eye view of the whole layout, showing palace and

46. Painting by Anthony Jansz van der Croos based on a sketch of c. 1634, depicting the recently completed Ter Nieuburch palace with still unfinished gardens, in a wooded holm-ground setting. Photo Collection Museum 'Het Tollenshuis', Rijswijk
see *colour plate 9*

garden in all their new splendour. The layout of Ter Nieuburch in its entirety, still rather 'regimented' and in this sense comparable to other early-seventeenth-century Dutch gardens, is characterized by a grid system of squares and rectangles which is enclosed by the framework formed by a canal, rows of trees and a raised path, from where one could overlook the whole garden layout. Across the width of the building, extending southward, lay a central parterre area, which – each decorative detail intricately depicted on the Milheusser print *(fig. 48)*[14] – was divided into three square plots and ended in a semicircular, exedra-like *berceau*. This hippodrome-shaped parterre area was flanked by an equally large compartment consisting of two pairs of symmetrically arranged rectangular ponds bordered by two lateral *bosquets* with arbours in the four outer corners. In front of the palace, looking northwards, the grounds were carefully divided into geometrical, primarily square compartments planted with lime-trees. Approaching the house along an avenue through the lime-tree plantation, one entered a large, rectangular forecourt enclosed by a crenellated wall with pavilions in its corners (the lodge of the manager and the gardener); it was flanked by two *giardini segreti* filled with interlaced knot parterres.

To the south, immediately next to the palace, on either side of a raised balustraded terrace, lay two rectangular gardens. They were called the Rock and the Mellon Garden in a later reprint of the Milheusser engraving.[15] Behind the crenellated wall of the Rock Garden stood a gatehouse; it functioned not only as the dovecote but also as the pump house, providing water for the fountain works. Next to this building, on either side of the path behind the palace, a wall of decorative trellis-work, forming a kind of arcade, gave a screened view of the surrounding countryside. Such intricate, architectural trellis-work structures, topped by decorative pinnacles, were spread throughout the garden, accentuating all major intersections.

The composition of the building, well suited to the site, consisted of a large central pavilion with smaller, square side pavilions, connected by lateral galleries. The front façade was practically flat, apart from elements of rustication in the lower storey, while the south or garden façade decidedly protruded. This three-dimensional effect was especially encouraged by the central loggia projected onto the open arcade of the main pavilion. At

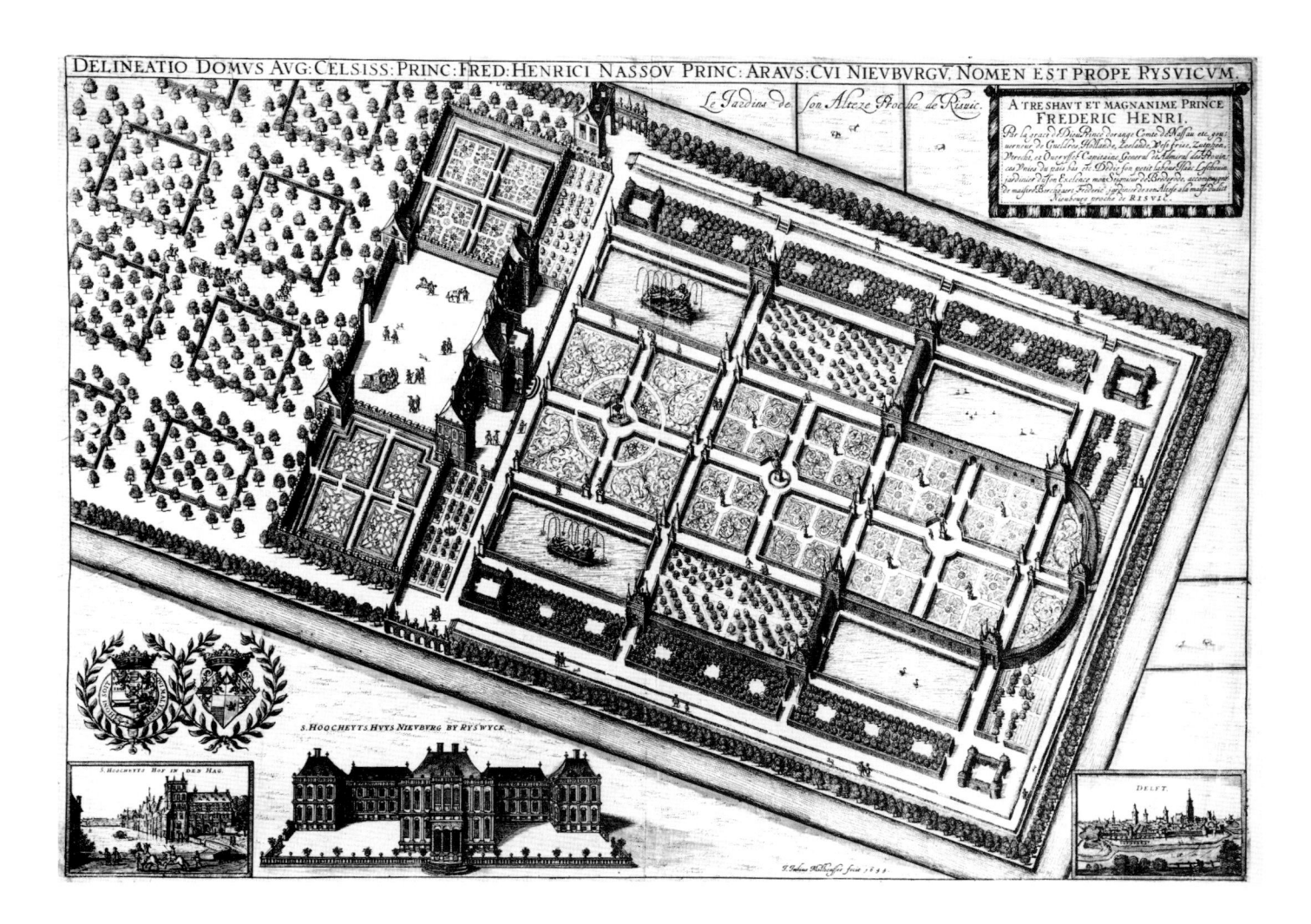

47. Bird's-eye view by J. Julius Milheusser, 1644, showing the palace and gardens of Ter Nieuburch as completed under Frederik Hendrik.
Gemeentearchief, The Hague
see colour plate 10

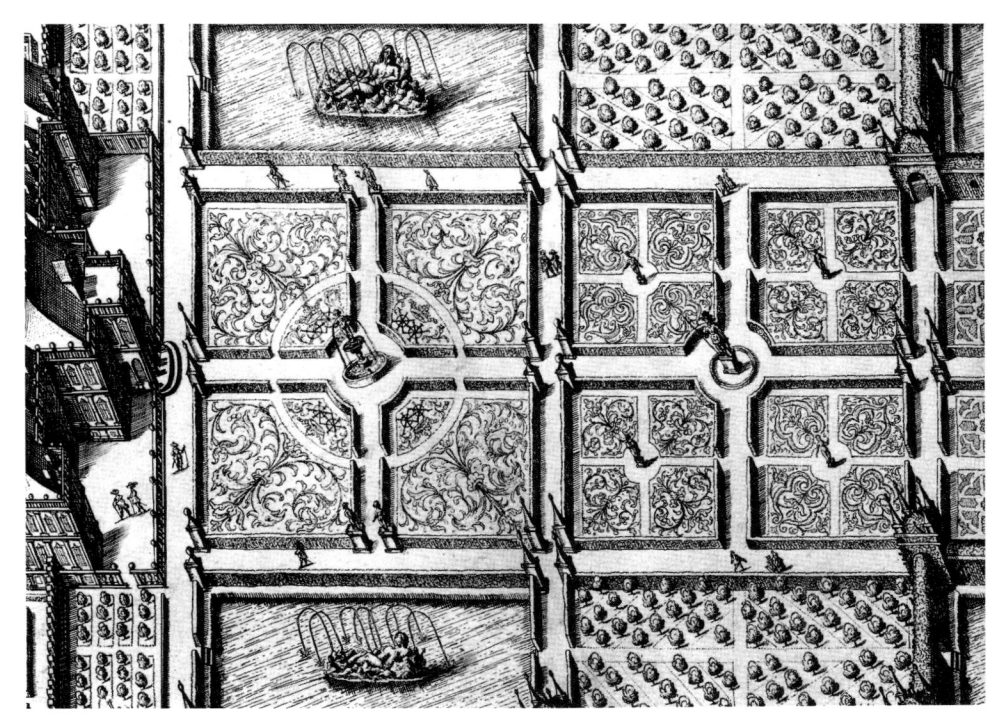

48. Ter Nieuburch's *parterres de broderie* and sculpture, the River Gods, Venus-Ceres fountain and Minerva statue. Detail of Milheusser print, 1644.
Collectie Bodel Nijenhuis, Universiteitsbibliotheek, Leiden

II. TER NIEUBURCH

first glance the whole concept of the layout, especially the elongated palace façade, strikes one as being quite unusual for Holland at that time and reminds one of French or possibly Italian prototypes. This first impression is reinforced when one looks at a drawing by Jan de Bisschop, dated about 1660 *(fig. 49)*[16] and showing the elongated form of the palace, reflected as it were as a *scenae frons* in still water surfaces, within an extensive garden space. The drawing gives a good idea of the strong plasticity of the building's garden façade, culminating in the open, Italianate stone loggia of the central pavilion. Jan de Bisschop tried to express the dramatic effect created by the play of light and shadow over the building blocks or masses – an effect which in all respects seems more Franco-Italian than Dutch.

When we look at Ter Nieuburch's total layout as shown on the Milheusser print from an architectural point of view, the correlation of house and garden, brought on by careful mathematical arrangement of the parts and unifying architectural features, strikes us as most remarkable. This unifying effect is created not only by the geometrical form of the compartments but also by architectural structures in the garden itself. For example, the form of the stepped exedra *berceau*, constituting the central framework of the pleasure garden, reflects the protruding silhouette of the palace's garden elevation. At the same time the vertical construction of this *berceau* forms the barrier between the 'aesthetic' and the 'useful' sections of the garden, as it divides the parterre compartments from the rear fishponds and kitchen gardens. Thus, at Ter Nieuburch one can recognize again the aspect of *utile dulci*, which could also be found in the layout of Honselaarsdijk. Another aspect of the Ter Nieuburch garden which also typified the Honselaarsdijk garden layout is the surprising enclosed character of the various garden plots. Each compartment, usually a

49. Drawing by Jan de Bisschop, overlooking the ponds from the garden southward, to the garden façade of Ter Nieuburch's palace.
Private collection

50. Print by J. Gole showing the symbolic axis running from the garden of Ter Nieuburch to the Grote Kerk at Delft with monument of William I.
Koninklijk Huisarchief, The Hague

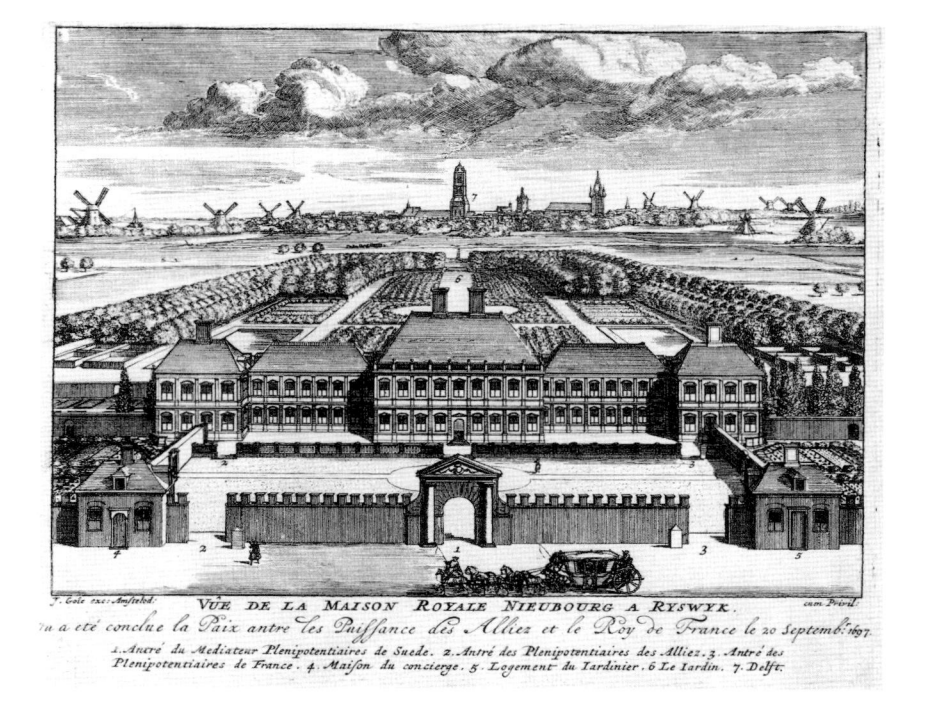

square area bordered by hedges with statues or trellis-work in the corners, was a separate entity. However, the prominent central axis as well as the form of the semicircular *berceau* at the end of the parterres of Ter Nieuburch relieves this sense of isolated garden spaces by holding all separate sections together.

This central axis constituted one of the leading thoughts behind the choice of terrain, the composition of the building and the orientation of the layout. The axis of the Ter Nieuburch palace and garden complex focused on the church tower of the Nieuwe Kerk at Delft, mausoleum of Frederik Hendrik's legendary father William the Silent, the founder of the Dutch Republic.[17] The orientation of the main axis on the tower of the Nieuwe Kerk is indeed clearly visible in a rare print made by J. Gole sometime in the early years of the eighteenth century *(fig. 50)*.[18] Stressing the correlation between form and meaning of Ter Nieuburch's layout, the printmaker must have well understood the important historical and iconographical implications of such an orientation.

DESIGNS FOR THE PALACE AND GARDEN OF TER NIEUBURCH

The single most important discovery for a historical and stylistic reconstruction of Ter Nieuburch is a series of coloured drawings found in the Gemeentearchief and the Algemeen Rijksarchief at The Hague,[19] among them a rare set of eight different plans showing alternative designs for a new palace and garden at Ter Nieuburch *(figs. 51-59)*. Except for one of them,[20] these drawings have not been published before. They are the only surviving examples of a group of twenty-one designs for Ter Nieuburch's layout under Frederik Hendrik.[21] Unfortunately the drawings are not signed and, though two carry a date *in dorso* of 1636 and 1643 respectively,[22] cannot be dated precisely. Yet comparisons with information from the account books and other documents result in a date between 1630 and 1640, when the Stadholder was studying the various design ideas for his new house and garden at Rijswijk.

51. Plan referred to as 'French plan' for the new layout of Ter Nieuburch based on the Palais and Jardin du Luxembourg in Paris. Algemeen Rijksarchief

52. Copy of the 'French plan' for the layout of Ter Nieuburch, showing in stylized form the adaptation of the Palais and Jardin du Luxembourg in the Dutch polderland. Gemeentearchief, The Hague

These drawings give a unique opportunity to examine sources for architectural inspiration and to study the contemporary artistic process of choosing and changing design ideas until the final version is reached. In order to fully comprehend this artistic process, as well as the Stadholder's own contribution and thoughts on garden architecture, a short critical analysis of the style of these drawings will precede a further detailed study of the garden's decoration and plantation.

This style analysis revolves round a few important findings, the first of which is that one of the drawings must be of French origin since the measurements indicated on the plan are in the French toise instead of the local Dutch Rijnlandse voet *(fig. 51* and its copy, *fig. 52)*.[23] Equally important are remarks in a letter by Huygens written in 1638, showing that not only the architect Jacob van Campen but also Frederik Hendrik himself made a design for the gardens at Ter Nieuburch:

53. Plan of the new layout of Ter Nieuburch's palace. Rudimentary design, showing the concept of a central pavilion connected with side pavilions.
Algemeen Rijksarchief

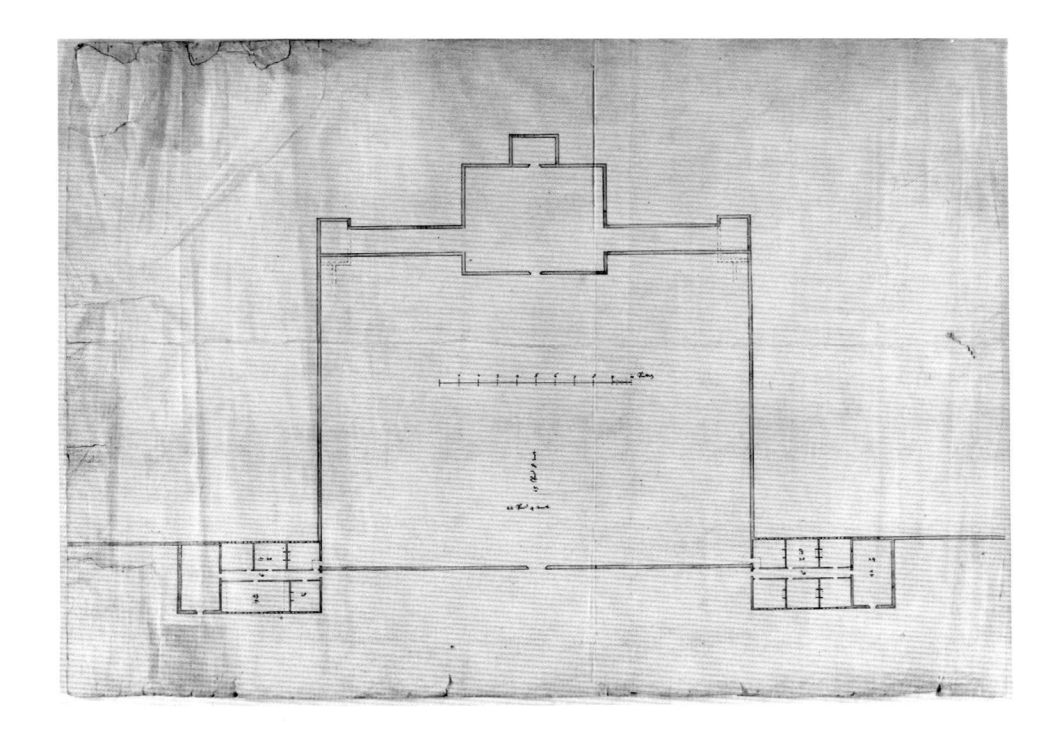

Son Altesse vient de recevoir une lettre de V.A. par un messager parti de Buren hier, et me commande d'en envoyer un expres pour porter ceste boitte, et deux plans du jardin à Rijswijck, pour lequel M. van Campen avoit encore formé un autre dessein, qui plaisoit assez, mais S.A. a preferé ceux-ci qui sont de sa propre ordonnance …[24]

From this letter it can be concluded that at least two, possibly as many as four different design ideas were made for the Ter Nieuburch garden. One alternative idea was offered by Van Campen, while other designs apparently were from the Stadholder himself. It is important to note that, though Van Campen's plan generally pleased the Stadholder, he preferred his own designs in the end. Consequently it seems logical that the layouts of the Ter Nieuburch gardens as shown in the Milheusser print were based at least in part on Frederik Hendrik's own ideas. Bearing this in mind, and considering the connection between Huygens's letter and the newly-discovered drawings, it is curious to see that one of the drawings, the one in French toises (henceforth called the 'French drawing'), shows a truly monumental approach for the layout of palace and garden *(see figs. 51 and 52)*, while another, more toned-down version *(see fig. 58)* shows distinct similarities to the final layout depicted in the Milheusser print.

It is not known who designed the 'French plan', but it must have been someone familiar with the latest architectural developments in France, since the drawing is based on a French prototype. It is indeed significant to note that the plan of the building and garden is a direct copy of the Palais du Luxembourg, built for Maria de' Medici by Salomon de Brosse from 1615 onward and one of the most admired architectural designs at the time.[25] Our 'French plan' has the date 1636 vaguely indicated *in dorso*. However, in view of the accession of the estate and the character of the drawing, the actual concept of the 'French plan' must date from the early 1630s, when the first design ideas for a new layout were developed. At this time several French artists and architects worked at Ter Nieuburch; one of them may have been the plan's designer. André Mollet and Simon de la Vallée immediately come to mind – they both arrived in Holland in 1633 to enter the service of

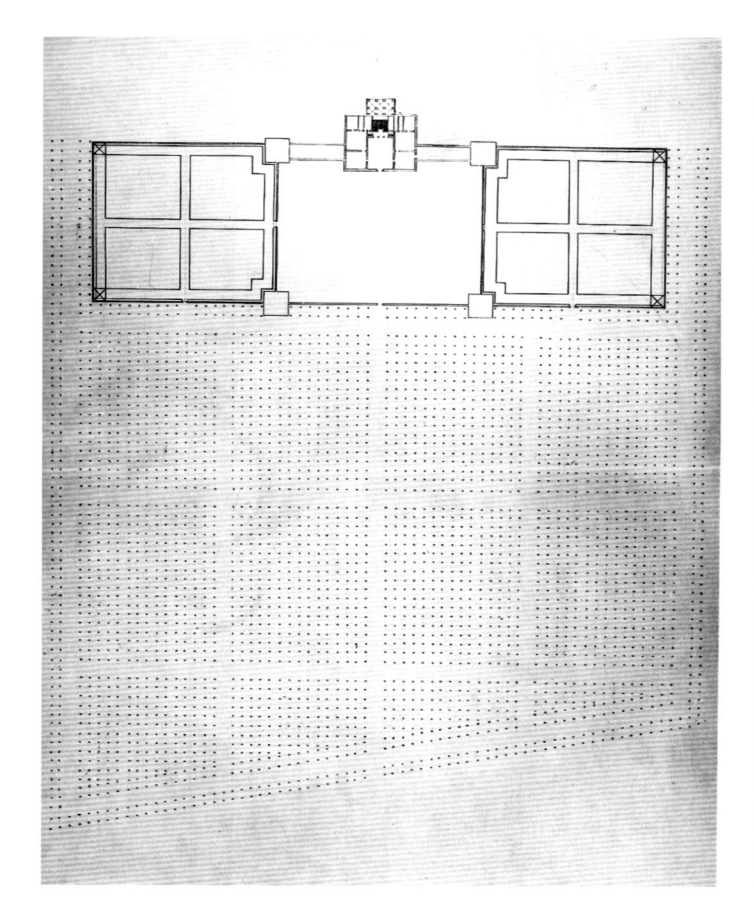

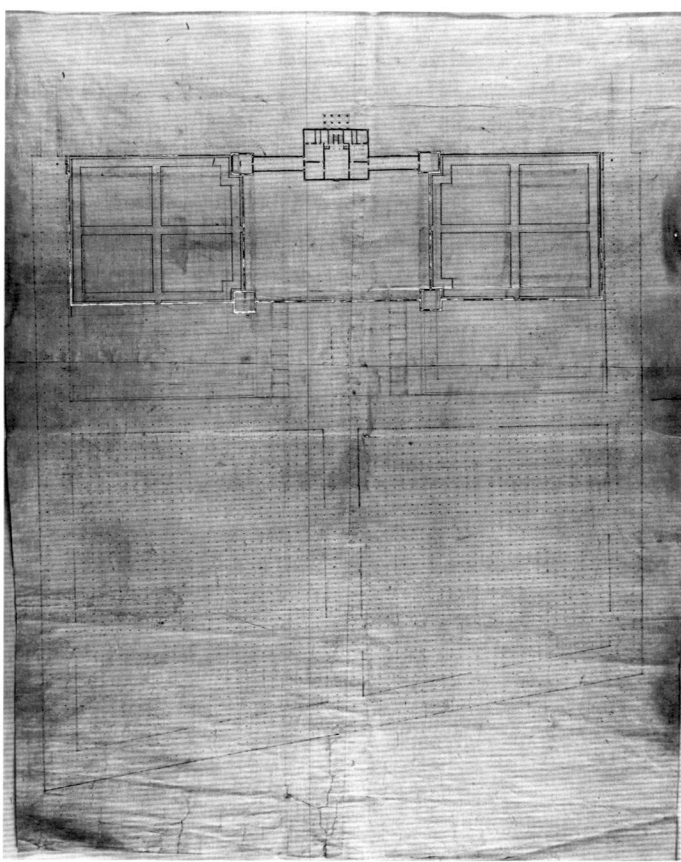

Frederik Hendrik. In this context one should in the first place consider André Mollet's involvement at Ter Nieuburch as the Stadholder's supervisor of the garden, and payments made to Mollet in 1633 for 'a series of drawings made for His Highness's (1042 fol. 232vo).

On the other hand, Simon de la Vallée, who since 1634 was officially called 'the Stadholder's architect', and who held that function until his departure to Sweden in 1637, is another good possibility.[26] In 1633 de la Vallée, who was primarily involved in the building activities at Honselaarsdijk, is also mentioned as the general supervisor of the works at Ter Nieuburch (1042 fol. 298). Not surprisingly, he was once believed to be the designer of Ter Nieuburch, though this notion subsequently was refuted.[27] However, there still remains a case for Simon de la Vallée's involvement in Ter Nieuburch's design, as is shown by his later work in Sweden, which was inspired by French architecture.[28] Actually the design of de la Vallée's Swedish buildings, such as the Riddarhuspalatset and the palace and garden of Ekolsund, like Ter Nieuburch, relied heavily on the plan of the Luxembourg.[29]

Another Frenchman who might be considered as the possible designer of the 'French plan' is Joseph Dinant, the Stadholder's *fontainier-grottier*, who arrived in Holland in 1634 and was responsible for designing and laying out the grottoes of Honselaarsdijk and Ter Nieuburch during the following years. It is not known whether Dinant would have been capable of drawing such monumental architectural designs as the one for Ter Nieuburch. Still, he should be considered, for his role exceeded that of a mere *grottier:* as *concierge* of Ter Nieuburch he served the Stadholder's court for more than twenty years and in that capacity also supervised the works at Ter Nieuburch and Honselaarsdijk.[30]

It is difficult to point out one of these three Frenchmen as the definite author of the design under discussion. Besides, the scenario may have been completely different. The

54. Plan of Ter Nieuburch's palace structure with central loggia, front and lateral courts, and the layout of the orchard in strict compartments.
Gemeentearchief, The Hague

55. Alternative plan of Ter Nieuburch's palace, pavilions and lateral courts, including the stables in front of the courtyard.
Algemeen Rijksarchief

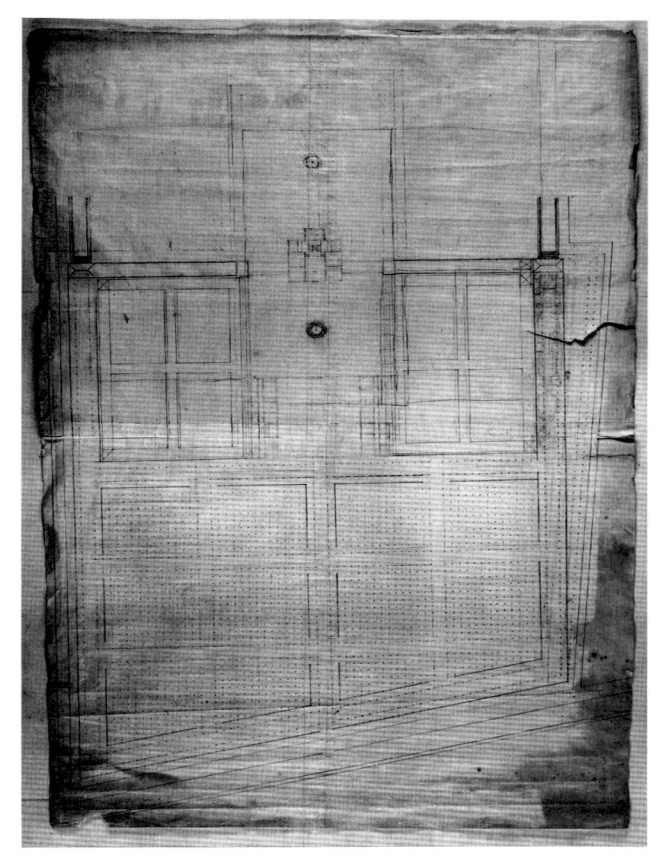

56. Plan or 'great fountain design' of Ter Nieuburch's palace and garden, including lateral courts, stables and two central fountains.
Algemeen Rijksarchief

58. Final plan of the garden of Ter Nieuburch with central parterre area, four ponds, lateral arbours, surrounding terrace and canal system.
Algemeen Rijksarchief

57. Alternative design for the garden of Ter Nieuburch, showing its geometrical, square compartments, lateral ponds and enclosing canals.
Algemeen Rijksarchief

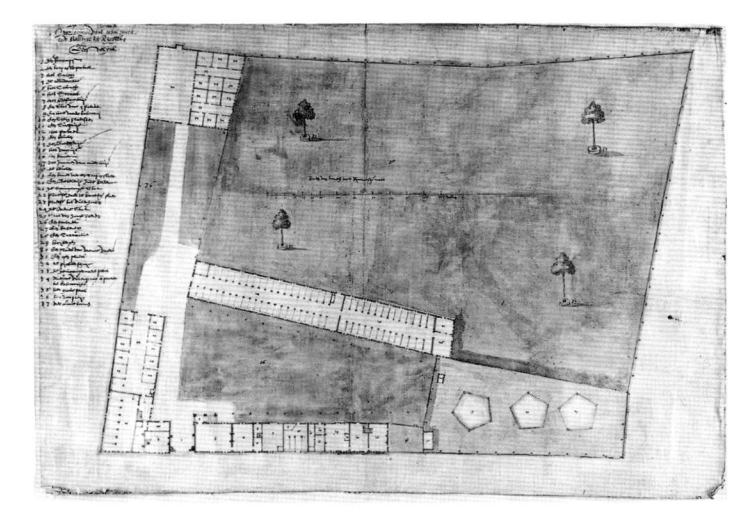

59. Design for the stables at Ter Nieuburch, the precise location of which on the Ter Nieuburch estate is not clear.
Algemeen Rijksarchief

II. TER NIEUBURCH

'French plan' may very well have been sent directly from France. It should be remembered that Frederik Hendrik was in the habit of sending designs for his palaces and gardens to France to be judged by the best architects and gardeners there. As we have seen in the case of Honselaarsdijk, Frederik Hendrik sent plans for the extension of the adjacent stables to France in order that Tassin, intendant of the Duc d'Orléans and agent of the Orange family in France, should show them to the best architects and gardeners for their opinion:

> … le communiquiez à de vos meilleurs architectes et jardiniers separément, pour les faire ordonner dessus ce qu'ils estimeroyent s'y pouvoir appliquer pour plus grand embellissement du lieu.[31]

The 'meilleurs architectes et jardiniers' in France at the time were those involved in the building projects at the French court, including the Louvre, the Tuileries and the Palais du Luxembourg, which constituted the examples *par excellence* for palace designs in Northern Europe.

Similar comments, entirely matching the tone of Frederik Hendrik's letter to Tassin, are found in the correspondence of the scientist-philosopher René Descartes (1596-1650). Descartes, who lived in Holland from 1639 to 1649 and was a close friend of Constantijn Huygens, was much appreciated at the Dutch court for his architectural and mathematical expertise. He not only enjoyed studying Dutch architecture, but actually visited gardens in the company of Huygens[32] and on several occasions assisted the Stadholder in the extension of his gardens by resolving disputes over land divisions.[33]

Most interesting in the context of Frederik Hendrik's building plans for Ter Nieuburch were Descartes's more or less concurrent reaction to the question of how best to design a Dutch estate and his apparent inclination towards a French design. When consulted by his friend Anthonis van Zurck on how to lay out the gardens of his estate at Bergen, north-west of Alkmaar in the province of Noord-Holland, Descartes suggested the layout of the Luxembourg palace complex as the most ideal design to be followed.[34] In a letter written in 1641 to his agent in France, Marin Mersenne, Descartes ordered prints and drawings of the Luxembourg. A good and detailed representation of the building and grounds, especially of the gardens, was of foremost importance, Descartes explained, since the proper arrangement of the trees and the parterres was what one was principally concerned with:

> J'ai une prière à vous faire de la part d'un de mes intimes amis [Van Zurck], qui est de nous envoyer le plan du Jardin de Luxembourg, et même aussi des bâtiments, mais principalement du Jardin. On nous a dit qu'il y en avait des plans imprimés; si cela est, vous m'obligerez, s'il vous plaît, de m'en envoyer un; ou, s'il n'y en a point, de le faire demander au jardinier [Jacques Boyceau] même qui l'a fait; ou enfin si vous ne pouvez mieux, de le faire tracer par le jeune homme [Frans van Schooten] qui a fait les figures de ma *Dioptrique*, et lui recommander qu'il observe bien toute l'ordonnance des arbres et des parterres, car c'est principalement de cela qu'on a affaire.[35]

Descartes's interest in obtaining visual information on the Luxembourg palace coincides with the same effort undertaken by the Dutch court to receive prints of this palace complex. Moreover, Descartes's letters and Anthonis van Zurck's activities at Bergen date from approximately the same period, less than a decade after the 'French plan' of Ter Nieuburch (basically a copy of the Luxembourg) was first drawn up.

Though Ter Nieuburch was already completed, its building history can be linked further to Huygens and Descartes's contacts with France in the early 1640s. In response to their urgent entreaties to obtain the latest French garden-architectural designs, Huygens received a French book, the title of which is unfortunately not mentioned in the correspondence. The book is referred to simply as 'un grand livre des Parterres ou Jardins de France'[36] and was forwarded to Descartes after having been mislaid in a trunk of books sent to the Stadholder in the army camp.[37] One must suppose that the book in question was *Traité du Jardinage* by the French royal gardener Jacques Boyceau, published in Paris in 1638 and the only 'large volume' on the topic of gardens published in that period.[38] Boyceau's richly illustrated treatise does contain prints of the gardens and *grand parterre* of the Luxembourg, for the design and layout of which Boyceau himself was largely responsible. Through the dissemination of such printbooks the latest French garden-artistic style principles would become more generally known in Holland and were diffused slowly throughout Europe.

Another source for Dutch knowledge of the latest French architectural style principles was the 'Grand Tour', or travels undertaken by gentlemen to complete their education abroad. For a better understanding of Ter Nieuburch's design and of contemporary taste at the Dutch court, it is helpful to see how a few Dutch gentlemen studying architecture in France responded to the Luxembourg palace layout:

> Le 28e, nous fusmes la pourmenade aux Thuileries; c'est le jardin du Louvre dont nous avons desia parlé. Il y a sans doute quelque chose de tout à fait magnifique, grand et extraordinaire; mais il est d'une beauté entierement differente de celle du Luxembourg, qui est plus à la moderne, mieux compassée et disposée avec plus d'art, au lieu qu'en celui-cy on voit quelque chose de plus sauvage et de plus champestre.[39]

Comparing the beauty of the Tuileries garden with that of the Luxembourg, the Dutch travellers remarked on the latter's 'modernity', finding its layout better set-out, divided and arranged and filled with more art than the garden of the Tuileries, which is less regulated and somewhat 'wild and more rustic'. From the above it can be concluded that the so-called French plan of Ter Nieuburch is more than just a French-inspired design: it sheds light on the whole issue of contemporary Northern European taste for 'modern architecture' and inaugurates, as it were, the fashion to imitate the Luxembourg as the most popular of early-seventeenth-century building projects.

The lack of certainty about the identity of the designer of the Ter Nieuburch 'French' drawing should not distract us from the fact that in itself this drawing is the first example of the direct use of the Luxembourg palace complex for a Dutch palace design. Indeed, the design must stem from the circle of Salomon de Brosse[40] or originate from the school of Jacques Boyceau and the Mollets. Given Mollet's and de la Vallée's presence at the Dutch court, it is important to remember their training in this artistic group. Mollet received his basic training as garden architect from his father Claude Mollet, who as Premier Jardinier de France[41] was responsible for Henri IV's royal gardens. Concurrently, Simon de la Vallée was trained by his father Marin de la Vallée, who had replaced de Brosse in 1626 as main contractor of the Luxembourg palace.[42] Several of Simon's later designs, as well as those of his son Jean for the court of Sweden,[43] not only resemble the Ter Nieuburch design but also reflect inspiration from the same, increasingly international French artistic milieu.

An early plan of the Luxembourg, dating from before 1627 *(fig. 60)*,[44] can be related stylistically to the Ter Nieuburch 'French plan', as it shows a similar rudimentary design for the heightened, semicircular terraces with oval stairs.[45] The final layout of the Jardin du Luxembourg *(fig. 61)*[46] incorporated a grand ornamental parterre with monumental vista,

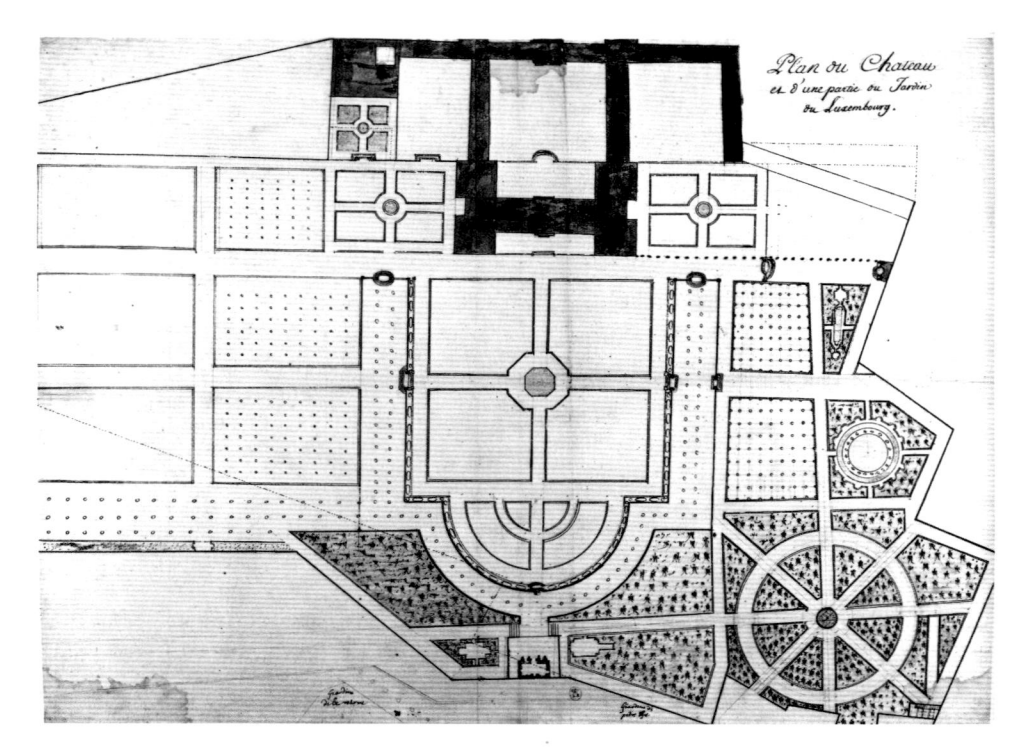

60. Plan of the Luxembourg palace and garden complex, shortly before 1627, showing the rudimentary design for gardens with surrounding terraces.
Bibliothèque Nationale, Paris

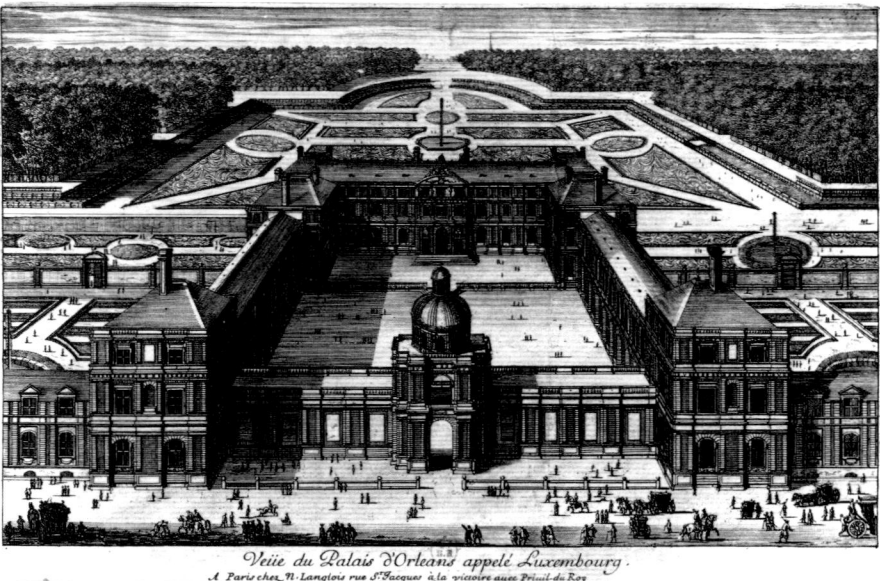

61. Print of the Palais du Luxembourg, with semicircular enclosed gardens and parterres, used in Ter Nieuburch's original 'French design'.
Bibliothèque Nationale, Paris

enhanced by the enclosing semicircular promenade. The garden layout shown here is generally attributed to Jacques Boyceau, who published engravings of the Luxembourg parterres in his *Traité du jardinage (fig. 62)*.[47] While Boyceau, because of these engravings and in his role of Intendant des Jardins, must be considered as the designer of the Luxembourg gardens, their basic outline also may have been determined by Salomon de Brosse,[48] assisted by the Italian engineers-*fontainiers* Tommaso and Alessandro Francini for the waterworks.

Leading Dutch architectural historians such as Slothouwer and Vermeulen have argued the relationship between the overall architectural design of the Ter Nieuburch and Luxembourg palaces. Much of the stylistic analysis of early-seventeenth-century palaces and gardens as 'French' hinges on the layout of Ter Nieuburch, though nobody was aware

COURTLY GARDENS IN HOLLAND 1600-1650

62. The central parterre of the Jardin du Luxembourg, designed by Jacques Boyceau, as published in his *Traité du jardinage*, 1638. The Metropolitan Museum of Art, New York

of the 'French plan' considered here. Slothouwer and Vermeulen pointed out Ter Nieuburch's elongated façade, the arrangement of galleries and pavilions and such specific features as the heightened terrace in the entrance courtyard, the rustication of the lower storey, the use of orders, as well as the balustraded roof – all of which copied the Luxembourg palace structure. By adding these architectural similarities to the interesting find of the 'French plan' itself, direct French inspiration can now be reconfirmed and, more important, extended to the layout of the gardens.

The resemblance between the two palaces begins with their topographical situation, as both are built on flat and humid grounds. Then the peculiar sloping outline of the Ter Nieuburch property, caused by an existing road along its northern border (Heerewegh), happens to resemble the outline of the Luxembourg estate (bordered by the Rue de Vaugirard). Because of these topographical similarities, F. Hamilton Hazlehurst at first wondered if our 'French plan' of 1636 had to refer specifically to a Dutch site or whether this drawing might picture an alternative plan for the Luxembourg itself.[49] As we have seen, the 'French plan' depicts the exact site of the Ter Nieuburch estate, a fact which is confirmed if we compare this drawing with the earlier maps by Floris Jacobsz van der Sallem and the reconstruction drawing *(see figs. 43, 45 and 51)* showing exactly the same parcel division of the surrounding meadows.

In addition to the architectural and topographical resemblances, the garden ornamentation is also similar. The style and form of the parterre in the 'French drawing', though not realized in Ter Nieuburch's final design, are directly comparable to those of the Luxembourg main parterre as depicted in Jacques Boyceau's *Traité du jardinage*.[50] Both parterre layouts repeat the mathematical formula of superimposed squares (octagonals in the case of Ter Nieuburch) composed of parallelograms, cut in their centres by circles.[51]

Finally there are two important differences between the Ter Nieuburch preliminary garden design as shown in the 'French plan' and its counterpart: the Ter Nieuburch garden was to form a perfect rectangle, containing an agglomerate of small, square parterres instead of one monumental compartment as at the Luxembourg. Ter Nieuburch's layout is defined by the typically Dutch rectilinear framework of terraces and canals, separating the garden from the surrounding landscape. Its French counterpart exhibited more dramatic form features, designed as it was round only one monumental parterre in the centre of a layout which, despite the framing terraces, opened up towards the countryside.

The seven remaining drawings of Ter Nieuburch *(see figs. 53-59)* all are alternative designs for the palace and garden layout and demonstrate continued concern for the proper interrelationship of garden and architectural structure within a given geographical location. Indeed, the drawings are an excellent example of the contemporary interest in and search for a common mathematical denominator, when palace and garden are carefully arranged in corresponding geometrical blocks.

Though it is not known who made these drawings, they are stylistically related and must be of Dutch origin.[52] Each drawing is a clear representation of the palace's ground-plan. A closer study of the inner layout of Ter Nieuburch, particularly the central pavilion and the double staircase, described by Brereton as 'a dainty stair-case, there being two pair of stairs which come out of the hall, and land both at one stair-head',[53] reveals undeniable similarities to the plans of the Mauritshuis and Huygens's house in The Hague. Both were built at the same time as Ter Nieuburch and involved the same group of individuals – Huygens, Van Campen, de la Vallée, as well as the patrons Frederik Hendrik and his nephew Johan Maurits. The Mauritshuis, built between 1634 and 1644 by Jacob van Campen in collaboration with the owner Johan Maurits van Nassau-Siegen (1604-1679) and Constantijn Huygens, was to become the prototype of a new architectural language developed at court, generally defined as the Dutch classical baroque. It is revealing to see that not the Mauritshuis but Ter Nieuburch first introduced new classical style forms, the history of which will be discussed in greater detail in chapter IV, as it relates to the development of garden architecture.

Considering the parallels between the Hague city palaces and the Ter Nieuburch palace, it is not surprising to see that Jacob van Campen, in addition to Simon de la Vallée, was involved in the construction of Ter Nieuburch, functioning as general supervisor of its inner decoration (1042 fol. 298 and 992 fol. 129).[54] Moreover, Huygens's letter quoted above *(see page 69)* indicates that Van Campen also made actual designs for Ter Nieuburch's garden and grounds: '… du jardin à Rijswijk, pour lequel M. van Campen avoit encore formé un autre dessein …' This being so, it is justified to regard Jacob van Campen as the designer of part of Ter Nieuburch's garden layout. Nevertheless, despite the fact that he surely knew of all the preliminary designs, we cannot recognize his hand in any of the surviving drawings, because we lack more information on his drawing style.[55]

Among the remaining preliminary designs for Ter Nieuburch there is a rather rudimentary plan *(see fig. 53)*[56] which shows that certain basic problems concerning the layout of the main building block and the connection of lateral pavilions with galleries had not been solved yet. However, the garden loggia is already a fixed feature; it is also recognizable in all the subsequent designs. Three of the drawings *(see figs. 54, 55 and 56)* show further experimenting with the layout of this main building block and the side pavilions, forecourt and lateral enclosed gardens. In these drawings the architect obviously tried to find solutions for the division of the terrain in front of the building, which had to contain tree plantations as well as stables.

A first drawing *(see fig. 54)*[57] shows the central pavilion flanked by two short galleries ending in small square pavilions which correspond to those in the outer corners of a rectangular forecourt. The two lateral walled-in *giardini segreti* are divided into four compartments with two arbours in the outer corners. The second drawing *(see fig. 55)*[58] basically follows this plan, but omits the arbours and adds stables between the forecourt and a shortened plantation area. Of special interest, since it displays ideas for the layout of the pleasure garden behind the palace, is another alternative design *(see fig. 56)*.[59] Herein the main garden consisted of a relatively small rectangular area divided into four square compartments which surround a central fountain. The fountain was placed on the main axis and corresponded to the fountain at the centre of the forecourt. In this design, which we shall call the 'great fountain design', the lateral *giardini segreti* have been extended to incorporate the stables. In the end, other solutions were found for the construction of these stables, which obviously would have ruined the aesthetic appeal of the whole entrance area. Where the stables were finally constructed is unknown, but the Stadholder may have had to contend himself with existing stables elsewhere on the estate *(see fig. 59)*.[60]

The most important aspects of the 'great fountain design' *(see fig. 56)* are the clear relationship between garden and building and the heightened terrace enclosing the garden, aspects which can be found in the finally executed garden shown in the Milheusser print. Two large rectangular garden pavilions, in front of them a complex of stairs leading up to a terrace, were planned at the end of the transverse axis running parallel to the palace's garden façade. A subsequent design *(see fig. 57)*,[61] clearly a variation on the previous one, shows the division of the garden behind the palace, the silhouette of which was cut out. For the first time the two rectangular ponds, predecessors of the later four and mentioned in the bundle of builder's estimates dated 1636,[62] are incorporated in the plan as flanking four square garden sections, each subdivided into four smaller parts.

Most of the elements found in these preliminary designs were ultimately translated into the final design of Ter Nieuburch, a rough version of which is shown in the last, and most important, drawing *(see fig. 58)*.[63] The building is shown in its completed form, with the monumental garden façade stretching over a length of more than 100 metres.[64] The purpose of this drawing was to show the construction of a 'new grotto'[65] distinguishable in the enclosed garden east of the palace. At the same time, the drawing offers the earliest depiction of Ter Nieuburch's final garden design, including the semicircular parterre area flanked by four ponds and decorative arbours which were to remain the distinguishing features of the garden until the end of the century.

LATER DEVELOPMENT OF THE TER NIEUBURCH GARDEN

The step-by-step creation of the Ter Nieuburch palace and garden shown by this series of drawings may also be illustrated by further documentary evidence, collected from the records of payments and order books of the Nassau Domains and from descriptions of contemporary visitors. Important new information on the construction and decoration of building and garden may be extracted from a remarkable series of *bestecken*, recently recovered in the Algemeen Rijksarchief and dating from the early 1630s. For our purpose one of these documents, the 'Conditions and Stipulations of the Gardener Louis D'Anthoin [Anthoni]' *(see Appendix, Document III)*,[66] is particularly significant, as it describes in detail the basic care for the garden in its earliest state and the exact responsibilities of the first gardener. In this document, dated February 1632, mention is made of new canals and ditches which the gardener would have to dredge and clean, as well as of the seeds, fruits, vegetables, lime- and elm-trees he was to plant and tend. In the first year (1632) and until further notice, the still barren grounds were to be laid out in beds and square plots. Already in place were plans to decorate the garden with all kinds of 'works of *plaisanterie*', including arbours, pyramids, portals and other *fraijicheden*, or handsome structures and topiary work which the gardener would have to cut and bind carefully. If the Prince desired to change any arrangements or plantings, the gardener had to be ready to improve their layout accordingly. None of the fruits of the garden were to be enjoyed by the gardener himself, because all were to be 'for the profit and at the disposition' of the Stadholder and his household. However, in addition to a yearly income of 600 Carolus guilders the gardener would enjoy free lodging. Unbuilt as yet, this abode was ultimately to be one of the entrance pavilions indicated as 'The House of the Gardener' in subsequent prints of Ter Nieuburch.

From 1630 onward, as we have seen, Frederik Hendrik acquired extensive parcels of land from a variety of owners in order to expand his property; some of these plots are indicated on Floris Jacobsz van der Sallem's map *(see fig. 43)*. In addition to land bought from the Rijswijk church,[67] the parcels came from Jonkheer Lambert van der Horst, Barthout van Vlooswijck, Vander Werven, Jacob de Bye and Cornelis Pauwelsen, whose deeds of purchase are also mentioned in the accounts (1040 fols. 222[vo] and 224[vo]). Written on parchment and marked with a seal, several of these original deeds are still kept in the Algemeen Rijksarchief,[68] presenting a complete picture of all square feet purchased by the Stadholder to add to his property, and the exact costs incurred.

The first changes at Ter Nieuburch before the actual 'gardening' could begin comprised again, as at Honselaarsdijk, the general improvement of the newly-acquired terrain by filling up old ditches and digging new canals and, where necessary, throwing up earthen embankments while raising or levelling the grounds (1039 fols. 214, 215, 219). In February 1631 the Oost Thuijn (East Garden) and West Thuijn (West Garden) on either side of the newly-planned palace were raised and secured and provided with drainage systems (1040 fol. 215).

One of the first projects undertaken after the basic improvements to the grounds had been made was the demolition of the old orchard and the plantation of a new wooded area, primarily consisting of lime-trees (1039 fol. 220 and 1040 fol. 213). The layout of this new lime-tree plantation was begun in 1630 in the large open area situated between the newly-constructed palace and the *gemene wech* (public road), where the old farmhouse had been. As indicated in the newly-discovered drawings discussed above *(see figs. 53-56)*, the design was altered many times; it consisted of eight compartments with trees planted in a quincunx arrangement bordered by hedges *(see fig. 47)*. The lime-tree plantation – whose beauty was already admired in 1641 by John Evelyn, describing it as 'delicious walkes planted with lime trees'[69] – later would grow out to become a densely wooded area cut through by three wide avenues leading up to the palace. Its layout would play an important symbolic part in the protocol of the Rijswijk Peace Treaty, as the two adversaries would approach the palace (also divided in this manner) along the two outer roads, which were divided by the central one taken by the mediator.

In the spring of 1631 most of the newly-created gardens were extensively fertilized and subsequently filled with many types of plants and rare fruit-trees, among them wild fig-trees,[70] pear-, peach- and cherry-trees (1040 fol. 216vo). Furthermore, a large quantity, a thousand feet, of *groene palm* or boxwood was paid for in May 1631 (1040 fol. 216vo), which seems to indicate the starting-point of large-scale parterre layouts. About the same time, and probably in order to plant the bosquet area surrounding the parterre garden, no fewer than a hundred thousand *plansoenen*, beds of hornbeam and dwarf trees, were brought from the town of Meurs to Ter Nieuburch, while the remaining trees were transported to Zuylesteyn (1040 fol. 221).

Evidently an important aspect of the Ter Nieuburch garden were the *moesthuijnen*, or kitchen gardens, specifically recorded in the archival documents and already hinted at in the 'Conditions and Stipulations' of the first head-gardener Louis D'Anthoni. Laid out and fertilized in 1631 (1040 fol. 217vo), these kitchen gardens provided sustenance for the Stadholder's table. This element of *utile dulci* would continue to define the function of the Ter Nieuburch garden throughout the century, as can also be gathered from another little-known and previously unpublished document in the archives of the Nassau Domains, dated 4 February 1686 and entitled *Reglement waernaer Mr Willem Brederoo als hovenier ende Casteleyn in het onderhouden van S. hooch^{ts} huys ende thuynen van het selve huys Ter Nieuburch gelegen by Ryswyck sich sal hebben te reguleren* (Regulations for the Gardener and Castellan Willem Brederoo ... for the Upkeep of the Gardens of Ter Nieuburch) *(see Appendix, Document IV)*.[71] Describing the situation of the garden at the time of Frederik Hendrik's grandson William III, this document constitutes an important addition to Louis D'Anthoni's contract written half a century earlier. While of specific horticultural interest, references to the various garden sections (the Small Gardens, or walled-in gardens, on either side of the house and the main or Great Garden) and particularly the mention of certain structures in the garden (the four ponds, dikes, terraces, arbours, trellis-work, hotbeds, various kinds of parterres) are of historical importance. Moreover, they help to complete our picture of the architectural elements in the garden and reconfirm the reliability of the prints of Ter Nieuburch. The precise horticultural descriptions in this gardener's contract can in many ways be related to the contemporary contract for the gardener Hendrick Quellenburch at Honselaarsdijk *(see Appendix, Document II)*; all together they provide an excellent insight into the whole culture of contemporary gardening. As can be deduced from this text – and from remarks by visitors to be quoted presently – flowers, fruits and vegetables were not only used in the kitchen but also had an aesthetic purpose, decorating the halls and tables.[72]

The kitchen gardens referred to in both gardener's contracts are not yet clearly depicted in the Milheusser print, where only the area behind the curve of the large central *berceau* seems to contain kitchen-garden beds. Only the later engravings of Ter Nieuburch show that the enclosed knot-gardens on either side of the forecourt, featuring as vegetable gardens in the above-mentioned contract, were also used as kitchen gardens. As at Honselaarsdijk, the four ponds in the Ter Nieuburch garden, apart from their aesthetic purpose, also provided nourishment, as appears from the payments received by the fishmonger Dirck

Pietersz for bringing freshwater fish in 'the pond at Ter Nieuburch' (993 fol. 189).

The *nieuwe Graften ende Slooten* (new canals and ditches), first mentioned in D'Anthoni's contract as requiring regular dredging, were followed by the construction of new embankments. The heightened dikes or terraces surrounding the garden, clearly described for the first time in the account books of the late 1630s, still featured as the main architectural boundary of the garden in Brederoo's late-seventeenth-century contract, which describes them as 'dikes to be kept clean and in good condition'. These embankments were constructed as part of a second wave of earthwork activities involving the further cultivation of newly-acquired meadows to procure fertile garden grounds (1042 fols. 284, 288 and 1043 fol. 292vo). Descriptions of these earthworks are often very detailed and explain the proceedings and methods of preparing grounds for garden layouts at the time. According to the accounts, the broad moat or canal (*sloot*) was 30 'roeden voeten' (circa nine metres) wide[73] and 'proportionally deep'. All along this canal an embankment was thrown up constructed of sturdy clay and clay-earth, reaching a height of three Rijnlandse voeten (circa one metre) and a width of 24 Rijnlandse voeten (circa four metres).[74] Interestingly, this description of the surrounding canals and embankments (992 fols. 24, 41) exactly matches the representation of these heightened promenades in the preliminary garden designs *(see figs. 56 and 57)* and the later Milheusser print *(see fig. 47)*.

The records of payments for Ter Nieuburch show that – as the embankments were thrown up, other ground parcels levelled and a proper water drainage system was constructed – planting of the garden continued at a great pace into the early 1640s. Apart from the indigenous and exotic trees mentioned above, a large quantity of fruit-trees arrived at Ter Nieuburch in 1638 (992 fol. 132), and the spring of 1640 saw the arrival of as many as 640 elm-trees and 4,000 hornbeams (992 fol. 400), to which another 1,700 elm-trees were added a year later (993 fol. 21). Lastly, in 1646, as part of the larger planting project involving all of Frederik Hendrik's gardens (993 fol. 414), Hendrick van Hattem, the 'plantage master', was paid a total sum of 3,700 Carolus guilders, which included the planting of flowers at Ter Nieuburch.

While the decoration of the garden with tree and plant material continued unabated during the 1630s, as evidenced by payments to the head-gardeners Louis D'Anthoni (1041 fol. 278vo and 1043 fol. 278) and Borchgaert Frederic (993 fols. 190, 244, 245), as well as to other gardeners and workmen, the construction of the palace building itself was often interrupted. The central pavilion and its balustraded terrace and courtyard, situated in front and at the rear of the building, were completed in 1633 (1041 fol. 271).[75] Yet much of the rest of the palace was still in its projected state (*in proiect staet*) in January 1633, in spite of Frederik Hendrik's incessant demands to expedite the works and send all designs immediately to the army to be reviewed and approved by him (1042 fol. 258vo).[76] From this period also date the previously mentioned series of *bestecken*,[77] which is evidence of a concerted effort in the spring of 1633 to complete the palace without further delay. Stagnation in the building may have been due to the fact that, apart from brick, the less readily available natural sandstone or *Bentheimer steen* was used in constructing the rustication of the lower part of the palace, as shown by the prints and described in contemporary travel journals. Another reason may have been that certain details of the design had not been decided upon by the Stadholder, who, as appears from the preliminary designs of the building and its connecting pavilions, liked to study various alternatives before making up his mind. Thus, by the time the central pavilion was completed, workmen had just begun to lay the foundations for the two outer pavilions and connecting galleries (1041 fol. 284vo), which were not finished until the end of 1634 (1043 fols. 281vo, 282). The preliminary drawings discussed above, showing alternative designs for the palace and its connecting pavilions, must therefore predate 1635.

At the beginning of 1635, or shortly after, the precise form, inner layout and basic plantation of the garden must have been determined, since it was largely completed four years later, in 1638, according to a description by a French visitor. In his travel journal, the Frenchman Dubuisson-Aubenay describes the exterior decoration of the palace and the state of the gardens in detail,[78] adding vitality to the somewhat dry information from the account books. Like the gardener's contract, Dubuisson's description also substantiates the accuracy of the depiction of Ter Nieuburch in the various prints. Of particular interest are Dubuisson's critical remarks on style, comparing Ter Nieuburch's structure with contemporary buildings in France, especially the Luxembourg palace. From his text one can conclude that the architecture of the palace of Ter Nieuburch was praised for its classical style, in particular its 'regularity', referring to its balanced, symmetrical layout and the correct handling of the classical orders. Dubuisson also commented on the rustication or treatment of the façades with natural Bentheimer stone, the use of which was indeed quite exceptional in Holland, where natural stone had to be imported and brick was the common building material.

Hence, both the form and the treatment of the palace of Ter Nieuburch compared favourably with what this French visitor knew about the latest architecture in his own country. French origins also were recognized in the relationship between house and garden; according to Dubuisson, the latter could be reached from the palace through the central tripartite entrance under the staircase, 'just like in the Luxembourg of Paris':

> Comme vous entrez par une grande porte de ce corps de logis, vous trouvez un vestibule qui par 3 arcades de colonnes et arceaux de marbre jaspé vous maine en celuy du milieu par un portique qui est derrière (comme à Luxembourg de Paris) dans le jardin des broderies et parterres, qui est fort grand et abouté de deux viviers, et quand il sera achevé, il sera par les 3 cotés environné d'une aultre levée avec un large fossé tout autour.[79]

The layout of the garden itself was admired for its extensive parterres bordered by two pairs of lateral ponds and enclosed on three sides by a heightened terrace with a wide canal behind it. According to Dubuisson's description, the garden was not yet finished in all its detail by 1638, since gardeners and other workmen were still busy completing the embankments and the surrounding canals. This remark coincides with contemporary entries in the account books referring to the completion of '40 or 50 roeden embankments or dikes, situated along the east and west sides of the acquired lands to the south side of the House Ter Nieuburch' (992 fols. 24, 41).

Dubuisson-Aubenay's account reveals that the treatment of the interior of Ter Nieuburch was also very impressive, with its coloured marble floors, sculptural ornamentation, wood-carved walls and ceilings, rich furniture and impressive collection of tapestries and paintings. This description supports the detailed builder's estimates dated 1633 and 1636 respectively, providing precise directions on the layout of marble and stone floors and decoration of the walls and ceilings with wood-carvings 'in the antique manner'.[80] In addition to Constantijn Huygens, Jacob van Campen was involved in the interior's painted decorations (992 fol. 129), set admirably into the classical architectural framework of the wall to create a rich, unified whole.[81] That the richness of Ter Nieuburch's interior decoration must have rivalled that of Honselaarsdijk is confirmed by another French account of Ter Nieuburch by the Sieur de la Serre, who extolled the beauty of the palace while describing the visit of Maria de' Medici to Rijswijk in 1638:

La Reyne ayant fait dessain d'aller a Ryswick [*sic*], pour voir la belle maison de son Altesse, Elle y accompagna sa Majesté, suivie de toute sa Court. Cette maison est assise a demy lieuë de la Haye. Les salles, les chambres et le cabinets parez superbement de diverses sortes de tapisseries, toutes de haut prix, ont encore un nouvel ornement de peintures, que l'artiste main de Honthorst, un des plus fameux peintres de ce siecle, met au rang de ses raretez. On y voit encore deux Galleries, l'une remplie de portraitz des plus grands Monarques de la terre, et de leurs Espouses; et l'autre de Statues de pierre, et de bronse, qui se font égallement admirer des moins curieux. Et ce qui et digne de remarque encore, c'est qu'au dessoubs des vitres les principalles victoires de tous ces grands Princes y sont representez d'un art inimitable. ... Elle entra dans une salle ou les quatre saisons a l'envy l'une de l'autre, avoient estallé sur une grande table tout ce qu'elles produissent de plus excellent; de maniere que les fruits les plus rares y paressoient en nombre, nouvellement cueillis, dans divers bassins.[82]

De la Serre's description of the interior decoration of Ter Nieuburch mentions Gerard Honthorst's innovative paintings and decorations, among them the famous illusionistic ceiling painting filled with musicians and people, exotic flora and fauna representing the Four Corners of the World.[83] Of special iconographical importance is de la Serre's description of the decoration of the galleries holding antique bronzes and marble statues as well as a representation of the Four Seasons in the form of actual rare flowers and fruits. Much of the decoration centred on the portrayal of the reigning houses of Europe and their principal victories within the larger cycles of nature. Of further significance is the fact that the decoration of these galleries was invented and arranged following Frederik Hendrik and Amalia's own ideas[84] and that the same themes – the representation of nature and the rule of the House of Orange – would form the core of the garden ornamentation.

Another curious detail of Ter Nieuburch's inner decoration, according to de la Serre, relates to the adornment of the palace with flowers and fruits from the gardens. The table in one of the main rooms was filled with a great variety of flowers and fruits – produce picked from the Stadholder's own gardens, we may assume, which, exhibited in large basins, represented the Four Seasons. There was such a great quantity and variety of *confitures* that even 'the servants could not eat or carry them along any more', de la Serre boasted.

For the purpose of this study it is of special interest that, in addition to a Frenchman describing the beauty of the gardens, several other French individuals were involved in the interior decoration of Ter Nieuburch. Among them were the sculptor Jacques Martin,[85] responsible for ornamental wood-carvings (1043 fol. 287), and the familiar *grottier-fontainier* Joseph Dinant, responsible for a special kind of sculptural decoration made of pressed paper (1042 fol. 298). Dinant's main responsibility, however, concerned the design and interior embellishment of the grotto.

THE ORANGERIE AND GROTTO IN THE GARDEN OF TER NIEUBURCH

In 1633 the construction and interior decoration of Ter Nieuburch had obviously advanced far enough to allow for an official visit by foreign dignitaries, the Gentlemen Deputies from Ireland, who were invited to inspect the new palace while enjoying a meal there (1042 fol. 269[vo]). At the time, workmen were completing the large terrace and

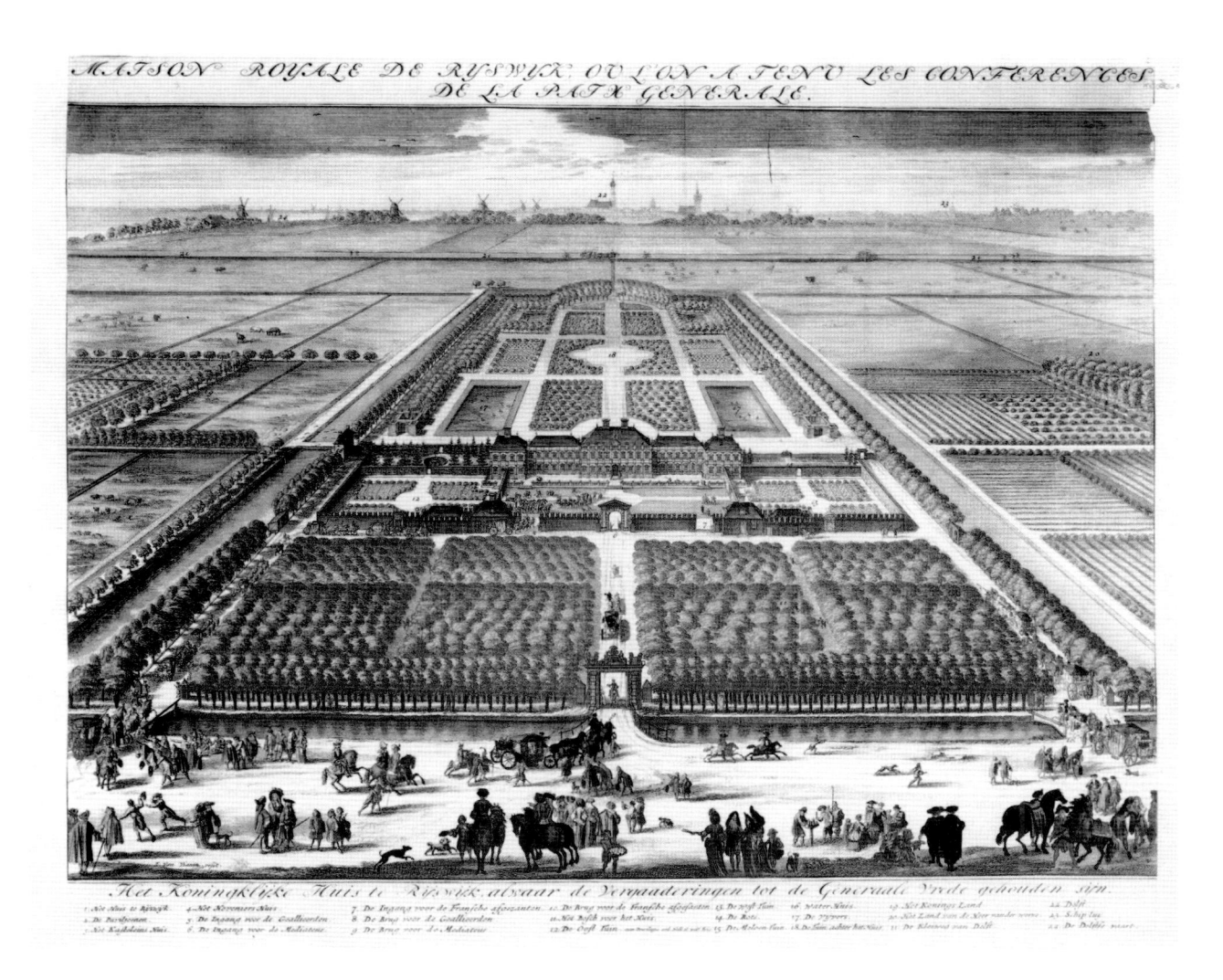

63. Print by I. van Vianen and A. Beek of Ter Nieuburch, showing the entry of the plenipotentiaries negotiating the Peace of Rijswijk in 1697.
Koninklijk Huisarchief, The Hague
see colour plate 11

balustrade along the palace's north façade, creating a unity between the lower forecourt and the higher entrance level of the building (1042 fols. 291, 292). Similar terraces, or *buiten bordessen*, were built along the south or garden façade and on either side of the outer west and east pavilions (1043 fol. 271vo). Functioning as a walking area (*wandelplaets*), these terraces were an ideal transitional spatial structure between the stone of the building and the landscape of the garden, as can be seen in later engravings of Ter Nieuburch (*figs. 63 and 64*)[86] showing, respectively, a bird's-eye view of the estate and a side view of the garden façade. In a print dated 1697 by J.A. Rietkessler (*fig. 65*),[87] the front and rear façades of the palace are depicted in all their detail, along with the courtyard and lateral gardens, then laid out as kitchen gardens.

In 1639 first mention is made of the construction and decoration of an Orangerie at Ter Nieuburch (992 fols. 335, 376, 388, 409ff.). Of particular interest is the setting of an exotic, shell- and coral-filled grotto in this Orangerie, as can be concluded from the description of the work in the accounts. Joseph Dinant, the *grottier*, received considerable sums for his acquisition of 'Indian conches and shells' as well as 'coral and black granite' to be used in the grotto-work at Ter Nieuburch in 1639-40 (992 fols. 376, 409). Important for our understanding of the efforts needed to complete such a task, especially when there was no stone available in the country itself, is a following entry, stating payment of as much as 1,217 guilders to Joseph Dinant for providing 'fountain stone' bought by him at Tivoli, outside Rome, and delivered at Ter Nieuburch for the completion of the grotto (992 fol.

II. TER NIEUBURCH

64. Side view of Ter Nieuburch's rear elevation and garden, as designed under Frederik Hendrik and planted under William III, looking south-westward over the clipped *berceaux* and low shrubbery.
Koninklijk Huisarchief, The Hague

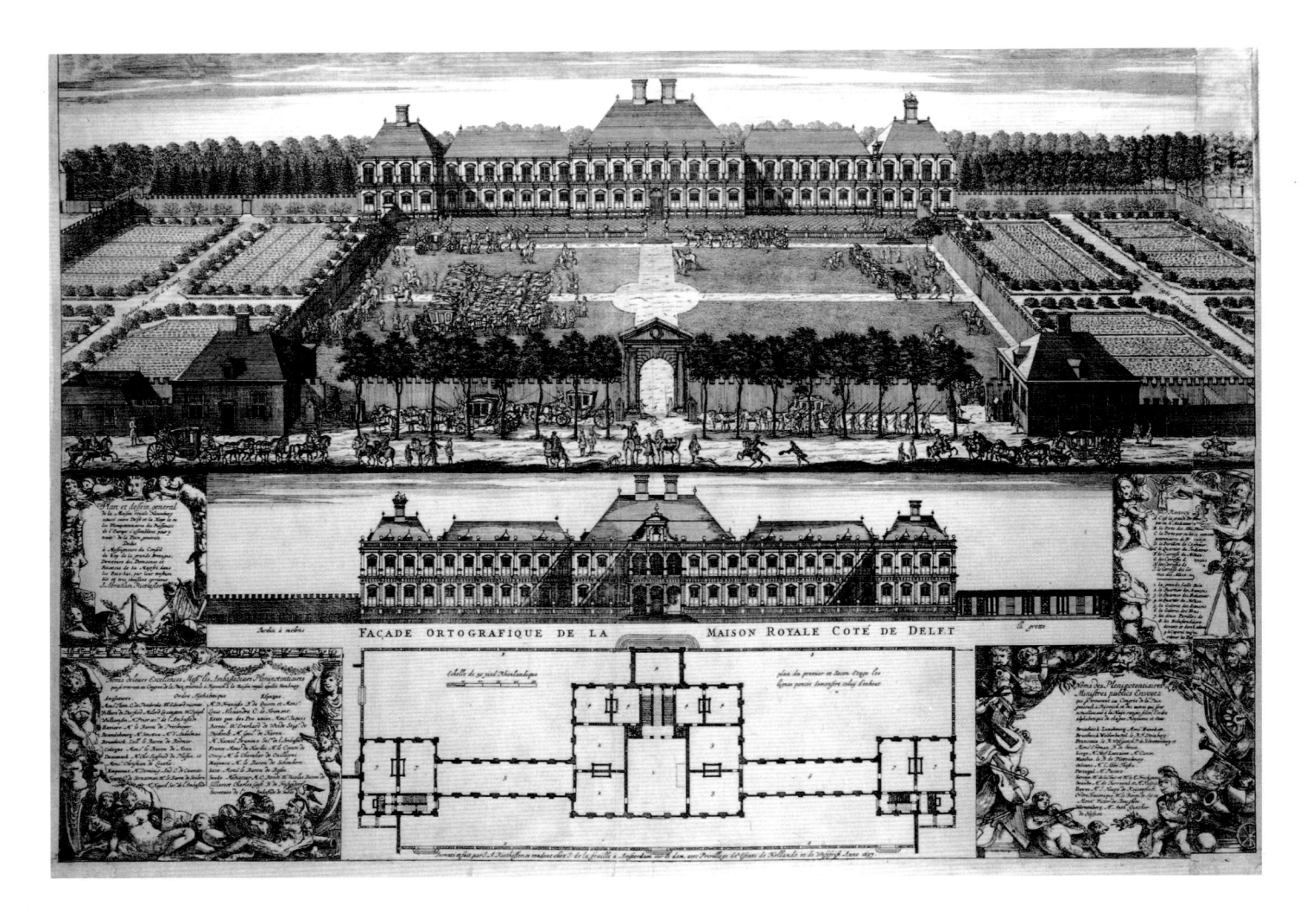

65. Print by J.A. Rietkessler, 1697, of Ter Nieuburch, showing the plan and elevation of the palace and courtyard with lateral, enclosed gardens.
Koninklijk Huisarchief, The Hague

COURTLY GARDENS IN HOLLAND 1600-1650

66. Detail of J.A. Rietkessler's print of Ter Nieuburch, showing the grotto wall in the east or Orangerie garden beside the palace.
Koninklijk Huisarchief, The Hague

439). Also imported from abroad were the orange-trees to be set in the Orangerie. Balthasar van Engelen, the 'gardener at Antwerp', whom we met already as the chief provider of exotic trees at Honselaarsdijk, also regularly sent or brought orange-trees to Ter Nieuburch. In the early 1640s he sent more than twenty-five, for which he received the large sum of close to one thousand guilders, each tree costing between thirty and forty guilders (992 fol. 448 and 993 fols. 23, 213).

Some uncertainty has always surrounded the existence of this 'Orangerie cum Grotto'. No historian seemed to be able to recognize the Orangerie and grotto in the engravings and plans of Ter Nieuburch. Indeed, in the Milheusser print of 1644 the Orangerie and grotto are not found. However, a close study of the drawing with a 'new grotto' *(see fig. 58)* and some later and little-known prints, such as the one Rietkessler published in 1697 *(see fig. 65)*, combined with information from the account books, has now made it possible to locate this grotto. Though it was designed in the early 1630s *(see fig. 58)*, it was not clearly depicted until Rietkessler's print, a detail of which is reproduced here *(fig. 66)*.[88] This print shows it as a kind of 'wall-grotto', consisting of a wall surface interrupted by semicircular window openings. The closed sections or wall surfaces were decorated with *rocaille* and pumice-stone, shells and coral, while the window openings were filled with decorative grills of wrought iron, exposing the gardens on either side through an embroidered screen.

This grotto-wall, clearly represented and, in fact, indicated as *la grotte* in the Rietkessler print *(see fig. 66)*, was situated to the right or next to the east pavilion of the palace. That this grotto and Orangerie must indeed have been in that place is further substantiated by a payment to Arent Laurensz (or Lourisz), carpenter at Rijswijk, for making two doors in the east pavilion 'so that His Highness can reach the Orangerie directly from his own quarters' (993 fol. 446). Furthermore, under Joseph Dinant's direction the pumpmaker Simon de Wilde and the carpenters Arent Laurensz and Pieter Cornelisz van Couwenhoven, in order to supply this grotto and the fountains in the garden with water, constructed a pump house (993 fols. 48, 145) between the east or Orangerie garden and the outer canal.[89]

From the accounts it can be inferred that this Orangerie was not then an actual building but an Orangerie garden, comprising the whole enclosed garden area to the east of the palace. This is confirmed by a reference to the completion of the 'pavement round the beds in the Orangerie' (993 fol. 47c). However, some uncertainty as to the precise layout of this Orangerie garden remains. It is not clear what exactly is meant by the construction of a wooden *logie* for the Orangerie, for which the carpenters Laurensz and Van Couwenhoven received payment in the spring of 1640 (992 fol. 376). At the same time they were also paid for the repair of the 'south wall of the Orangerie'. This south wall must have been the wall separating the Orangerie garden from the main parterre garden, and it was this wall which must have contained the grotto and fountain works. Presuming that the placement of the grotto was not changed since Frederik Hendrik's death,[90] it was the grotto in this southern wall, originally designed by Joseph Dinant, which was later depicted in the Rietkessler print *(see fig. 65)*.

For the artistic background of Frederik Hendrik's garden ornamentation it is important to look in greater detail at the decoration of Ter Nieuburch's grotto and fountain works. Not much is known about their layout apart from the short description in the account books and an illustration of the exterior wall shown in the Rietkessler print. However, an idea of the appearance of grottoes at the Dutch court can be had by studying contemporary grottoes laid out by the Stadholder's family members at The Hague, such as those in the Buitenhof and Mauritshuis gardens and the ones laid out by the Stadholder's daughters in their German estates. Another famous contemporary example outside Holland was the

67. Design by Jacques de Gheyn II for the grotto in the Buitenhof garden, c. 1620, showing a phantasmagoria of sea monsters, shells and organic shapes.
The Pierpont Morgan Library, New York

68. Grotto design for one of the Stadholder's gardens. Classic architectural design, with bust of the Stadholder and famous monogram.
Rijksprentenkabinet, Rijksmuseum, Amsterdam
see colour plate 12

69. Grotto design by G.H. van Scheyndel (attributed), with portraits of William I and Prince Maurits and details of coral and pumice-stone.
Rijksprentenkabinet, Rijksmuseum, Amsterdam

grotto in the garden of the Nassau palace at Idstein in Germany.[91] The grotto to be considered here is the one begun by Frederik Hendrik's brother Maurits and finished by Frederik Hendrik himself, in the Buitenhof garden at The Hague.

Prince Maurits's grotto, which was set in the gallery of the Buitenhof garden and completed between 1625 and 1630, had a wall structure with narrow basin covered with pumice-stone, coral and shells similar to that of the grotto at Ter Nieuburch. According to a description by Huygens[92] – which will be discussed in greater detail in the next chapter – the Buitenhof garden and grotto were designed by Jacques de Gheyn II (1565-1629) who later also worked for Frederik Hendrik, for whom, we may presume, he was involved in the ornamentation of gardens as well. The grotto structure in the Buitenhof garden consisted of a 'clever imitation of steep rock standing in water after the example of the Italians', as Huygens wrote. To Huygens's description may be added that of John Evelyn, who admired the garden's ornamentation, especially the 'grotts, fountains and artificiall musiq',[93] and the description by the Italian brothers De Bovio, who again admired the rock formations of the grotto.[94]

Such descriptions not only enable us to envisage the general appearance of grottoes at the Dutch court, but they also give us a good sense of their peculiar, mysterious atmosphere, including amorphous figures, grotesques and strange sounds or music. In displaying natural wonders and artificial objects, the grotto seems to have served both as a cool-water area and as a kind of open-air museum.[95] It is this very element of 'the marvellous', a certain obscurity, wildness and general 'bizarreness' which is extolled in contemporary treatises, for example Jacques Boyceau's *Traité du jardinage*, as befitting the realm of the grotto:

> Les Grotes sont faites pour representer les Antres sauvages, soit qu'elles soient taillées dans les rochers naturels, ou basties expressément autre part: aussi sont elles ordinairement tenuës sombres, & aucunement obscures. Elles sont ornées d'ouvrages rustiques, & d'étoffes convenantes à cette maniere, comme pierres spongieuses & concaves, especes de rochers, & cailloux bigearres, congelations, & petrifications estranges ...[96]

The aspect of artifice and a certain capriciousness, characteristic of sixteenth- and early-seventeenth-century grottoes filled with 'marvels' and 'curiosities', is also exhibited in three contemporary drawings representing designs for grotto layouts. One of the drawings is by Jacques de Gheyn and shows a design for the grotto in the garden of the Buitenhof at The Hague *(fig. 67)*,[97] while the other designs are by unknown artists for unidentified gardens *(figs. 68 and 69)*.[98] De Gheyn's drawing is a blend of the fantastic and the weird, centring on a rock with a bearded man and two lateral caverns, also populated by strange creatures and animals. In typical mannerist fashion, the composition dissolves into a monstrous head, the caverns forming the eye sockets.[99] The source for such grotesque double images lay in sixteenth-century Flemish art, exemplified by the work of Cornelis Floris.[100] Similar grotesque heads feature in the contemporary designs of the Franco-Flemish architect Salomon de Caus (1576-1626),[101] whose work may have been inspired by the same Flemish source or its Italian prototypes.[102] The grottoes of the Heidelberg gardens were widely known and, like the rest of the garden, described with great admiration in Huygens's 1620 travel journal:

> ...nous mena veoir les beaux jardins du palais,... tel qu'à present il est, portant fleurs, figuiers, orangiers etc. en abondance. Au bout du jardin se monstrent les grottes et

fontaines, de l'invention de Salomon de Caus, qui se parangonnent, voire et se preferent à toutes celles de France; tant la capacité en est grande, l'ouvrage mosaïque relevé et bizearre, et les eaux fortes et abondantes.[103]

From this letter it can be concluded that the gardens of Heidelberg, especially their waterworks, were considered the high point of garden art at the time. It also shows that, in addition to water-power, the element of 'bizarreness' was highly esteemed in grotto designs by 1620. It is important to remember that, if we consider Huygens an arbiter, this Northern European example of gardening was preferred to contemporary French layouts, usually believed to be the absolute model. However, while such elements as the 'bizarreness' expressed in the first grotto design may have lingered in the Stadholder's gardens, their decoration was also typified by calmer, classical style forms, such as those displayed in the two further grotto designs.

These two designs *(see figs. 68 and 69)*, which are stylistically related and show the same basic layout, show a wall divided into three sections by classical architectural features, accentuated by lion's heads holding draperies. Both grotto decorations, centring on the portraits of William the Silent and Prince Maurits, respectively, and a bust of Frederik Hendrik, were designed to celebrate the Princes of Orange. As such, they would fit well in the gardens of Honselaarsdijk and Ter Nieuburch, where the glorification of the House of Orange is the central theme of the palace's interior and exterior decoration. Stylistically the designs fit the kind of grotto which was constructed at Ter Nieuburch – a grotto which, like the drawings, is more appropriately defined as a 'shell-pavilion'[104] or 'wall-grotto', since there are no deep caverns generally associated with grottoes. Like the wall-grotto at Ter Nieuburch, both designs consisted basically of a two-dimensional wall surface, in one case with blind porticoes just deep enough to hold a statue. Only the lower part of the wall surface in both designs was decorated with pumice-stone, shells and coral.

In many other respects these designs can be associated with the grotto works undertaken at Ter Nieuburch and Honselaarsdijk, especially when it comes to the choice of building material.[105] Indeed, payments to Joseph Dinant (992 fols. 335, 409 and 993 fol. 442[vo]) specifically mention pumice-stone, shells, white coral and black granite, as well as special limestone from Tivoli, materials which are all represented in the above-mentioned drawings. A direct association between these designs and the Stadholder's grottoes is supported by the recurrence of the combined monogram of Frederik Hendrik and Amalia in one of the drawings *(see fig. 68)*. In this drawing the two armorial cartouches in the lower half of the two lateral niches carry the entwined H (Hendrik), A (Amalia) and O (Orange), which formed the central ornamental motif in the Stadholder's palaces and gardens. In point of fact, at Ter Nieuburch this monogram was the decorative and symbolic focus of the main parterre layout. At Honselaarsdijk the same monogram was to be found in the chapel, carved in the wood of the pulpit.[106] Later, at the Huis ten Bosch, we will find the monogram once again at the centre of the cupola paintings and, just as at Ter Nieuburch, as focal point of the boxwood ornamentation of the garden's main parterre.[107]

The link between the drawings and the grottoes built in the Stadholder's gardens is further borne out by the use of the same standard measure, the Rijnlandse voet. One of the designs *(see fig. 68)* has a scale in Rijnlandse voeten; converted, it would give a total length of circa eight metres for the whole grotto wall. Thus the design would be too small for the wall space of the grotto at Ter Nieuburch, unless it related solely to part of the wall decoration, for example the shorter side-wall of the Orangerie. This eastern side-wall, measuring indeed about eight metres, is shown in the Milheusser print *(see fig. 47)* as being divided into three shallow arch-shaped niches comparable to the division of the wall in one of the preliminary grotto designs *(see fig. 68)*. However, the drawing could also be a design for the grottoes laid out somewhat later at Honselaarsdijk, between 1646 and 1650 (993 fol. 452vo and 994 fols. 85vo, 168vo). Another possibility is that the design belongs to the grotto in the garden of the Paleis Noordeinde built in the early 1650s by Joseph Dinant and Pieter Post, general supervisor of the works (995 fol. 90vo). A point in favour of putting the design in the context of the grotto works in these last two palaces rather than in that of the Ter Nieuburch grottoes begun much earlier (1639-41), is that they were executed after Frederik Hendrik's death in 1647 and so could account for one peculiar detail in the design: the sign of mourning expressed by tears running down the columns flanking the bust of Frederik Hendrik *(see fig. 68)*. These tears would fit a design made for Amalia, who, as we shall see, soon after her husband's death turned the Huis ten Bosch into a veritable mausoleum, and who in various other works of art (such as Gerard van Honthorst's portrayal of the mourning Artemisia in the Princeton University Art Museum) referred to herself as an inconsolable widow.[108] Likewise Amalia may have decorated certain grottoes, for instance the one in her flower garden at the Noordeinde, thus extending the iconography of mourning from the inner palace rooms to the exterior garden spaces.

A possible connection between the above-shown grotto designs and the grotto of Ter Nieuburch is also confirmed by new findings, involving a *Decree for the Utilization of Ter Nieuburch (see Appendix, Document V)*[109] and a set of statues in the German estates of Frederik Hendrik and Amalia's daughters. In the document, which grants long-term use of Ter Nieuburch to Willem van Nassau-Odijk, care is urgently requested for the objects in the grottoes decorated with 'Statues [!], Shellwork and other rarities'. The statues could refer to a set of busts which, standing in the Gothic House at Wörlitz today,[110] originally decorated one of the Stadholder's grottoes, possibly at Ter Nieuburch. One of the three statues is a bust of Frederik Henrik himself which, remarkably, appears to be identical with the bust represented in the grotto design *(see fig. 68)*.[111] The rediscovery in Germany of garden statues from the Orange family's gardens will be considered further in chapter VI and is of special significance for shedding new light on the history, purpose and meaning of the Stadholder's garden sculptures and the grottoes they decorated.

PARTERRES AND FURTHER GARDEN ORNAMENTATION

When it comes to the further embellishment of the Ter Nieuburch garden, the refined scrollwork of the parterres, shown in all its intricate detail in the Milheusser print *(see fig. 48)*, is of particular interest. Especially noteworthy is the design of the first parterre compartment, displaying griffins in its outer corners and, once again, the monogram of Frederik Hendrik and Amalia of Orange in its middle section.[112] While the parterre designs of Honselaarsdijk have been analysed by a few scholars,[113] those of Ter Nieuburch remain largely unstudied. Interestingly, one can see direct connections between Ter Nieuburch's parterre layouts, other parterre layouts in Holland, and French parterre designs. Indeed, as mentioned above, there are striking resemblances between the Ter Nieuburch and the French parterre designs from the school of the Mollets, which points to André Mollet as their most likely designer.[114] The account books do not specifically mention Mollet in the context of parterres at Rijswijk, but his employment at Honselaarsdijk and his frequent travels to Rijswijk as general overseer of the Stadholder's gardens seem to confirm this assumption. Besides, Mollet's recently found original payment account refers to the 'Rijswijk parterres' in the margin. Though this notation is a mistake and should read 'Honselaarsdijk parterres', the fact that the contemporary treasurer found it logical to associate Mollet with Rijswijk makes Mollet's involvement in the new parterre designs there in the early 1630s even more likely.

For our purposes it is important to note that several designs in André Mollet's garden treatise *Le Jardin de plaisir*,[115] though less intricate and stylistically somewhat bolder, are similar to the Ter Nieuburch parterres, showing the same floral ornamentation and features such as the cornucopia and the griffin. In particular the first parterre layout behind the Ter Nieuburch palace is articulated in a manner typical of André Mollet, dividing the parterre by means of one or more concentric circles.[116] This parterre must have been specially admired within the Dutch court circle, for its design was used in at least two other gardens, at the court of Groningen and at Vianen, owned by Frederik Hendrik's relatives.

Ter Nieuburch's garden was obviously an important showcase for the latest fashion in garden ornamentation, since apart from Groningen and Vianen many of its decorative features were found in various other Dutch gardens at the time. Until recently it was not known who designed the garden ornaments of Ter Nieuburch, or those of Honselaarsdijk and the other stadholderly gardens. The recent discovery of a rare printbook published by a certain Isaac Leschevin *(fig. 70)*[117] clarifies many aspects of the decorative features in Frederik Hendrik's garden. This printbook, which carries no title but is listed as *Portals and Palisades*, was published in Utrecht in 1635; it contains a series of twelve prints showing designs for architectural trellis-work structures and *berceaux* in a classicizing style *(figs. 71 and 72)*, which were to become an important source for the future court gardeners, including, most remarkably, Jan van der Groen.[118] The book is dedicated to the 'Tres haut & magnanime Prince' *(see fig. 70)*, which can only refer to the Prince of Orange, Frederik Hendrik. In his dedicatory foreword Leschevin explains that he wrote this booklet in order to be of use to the interested reader and to serve society as a whole. He adds that it describes agricultural matters, about which, as about all other sciences, 'His Excellency is very knowledgeable'. In the hope that it may please the Prince, Leschevin asks forgiveness for the simple style of his designs and ends his foreword signing 'De Viane ce 6. de Ianvier 1635. Vostre humble Serviteur Isaac Leschevin Iardinier'.

From this text it can be concluded that Leschevin was gardener of the Stadholder's close friend and relative Johan Wolfert van Brederode and responsible for laying out the gardens around the Batestein castle at Vianen. Furthermore, whether or not as a consequence of his printbook, Leschevin was invited to come to The Hague to assist in decorating the gardens of Ter Nieuburch. Though Leschevin's name does not appear in any of the records of payments, his involvement at Ter Nieuburch is borne out by the text on the cartouche in the top right-hand corner of the Milheusser print, dedicated by Leschevin and Borchgaert Frederic to the Stadholder. Indicated as 'son petit labeur Isaac Leschevin, jardinier du Son Exelence mon Seignieur de Brederode', Leschevin used the same words he used in his book to dedicate this print to the 'tres haut et magnanime Prince Frederic Henri' *(see fig. 47)*. In doing so, he was assisted by Ter Nieuburch's gardener-in-chief, as the text shows: 'accompagné de maistre Borchgaert Frederic: jardinier de son Altesse a la maison dudict Nieubourg proche de Risvic'. Borchgaert Frederic is also mentioned several times in the account books of 1643-44 as having completed and supervised work in the Ter Nieuburch garden (993 fols. 190, 244vo, 245).

The text on the cartouche and in the printbook indicates that Leschevin, assisted by Borchgaert Frederic, must have designed at least part of the ornament of the garden at Ter Nieuburch, including the semicircular *berceaux*, the decorative gateways, the palisades and porticoes encompassing the various garden plots. Very similar designs for palisades, cut hedges, porticoes, topiary in architectural forms (obelisks, columns, vases and balls) were shown in Leschevin's printbook. A comparison of the printbook designs with the

70. Title-page of Isaac Leschevin, *Portals and Palisades*, 1635, dedicated to Frederik Hendrik, showing structures in the Stadholder's gardens. The Metropolitan Museum of Art, New York

TRESHAVT & magnanime Prince:

CONSIDERANT QVE LES HOMMES AV-QVELS Dieu a donné ceste exelence de prevaloir a tous autres Creatures, en fin tomberoient en la condition des Ignorans, s'ils passoient ceste vie en innutilite, & sans l'estude qu'ils ont suivy, & du travail qu'ils ont pris pour servir a la societé des hommes. Ie me suis advisé que pour eviter ce silence parresseuse, & pour ne tomber au sepulchre d'inutilité, je me suis resolu de faire vn livret, quy appartient a lagriculture, a laquelle jay pris hardiesse de la dedier a vostre Excelence, comme estant d'hovez des graces & cognoissance de toute sience, esperant que vostre Excelence, la recevera pour agreable : suppliant & priant vostre Excelence, d'excuser la simplicite du stile, en attendant que Dieu me donnera la grace, de faire chose que j'espere qu'il vous soit plus agreable. Auquel je prie le Seignieur Dieu maintenir vostre Excelence, en prosperite, & conduire vos desirs a heureuse fin. De Viane ce 6. de Ianuier 1635.

Vostre humble Serviteur
Isaac Leschevin Iardinier.

D'AVTANT.

Qve les particles ou plustot portalles & palissades & belles hayes sont les enrichissement des Iardins. I'ay trouve que tous ces ouvrages faits en bois, sont propres, beaux & proufitables, faictes de petites lattes de sapin & cercle de tonneau avec leurs mesures clouez avec petits cloux ; Durent trois fois autant que les autres ouvrages en bois quy sont faictes de bois simples & liez avec des oysiers lesquels se pourissent plustot, sans ce que quand en Hiver que toutes les foeuiles des arbres sont tombes, demeurent beaucoups plus beaux a veoir que les autres.

Ce qui m'a incité, a mettre ce petit livre en lumiere, estant proufitable pour tous Iardiniers, & delectable pour tous Amateurs de Iardins esperant de bref l'augmenter.

DEWYLE,

Dat die Portallen ende Pallisaden, ende schoone Haghen zijn die cieraet vande Hoven. Soo heb ick gevonden, dat alle die vvercken in hout ghemaeckt zijn, proper, schoon ende profytelijcker ghemaeckt (met kleyne latten van vuerne hout, ende houpen met hare maten) ghespijckert met kleyne spijckers, dueren drymael soo langh als die andere wercken, dat met slechte hout ende teene ghebonden is : d'welcke eerder verrotten, sonder dan als in de Winter, die bladers van de Boomen ghevallen zijn, blijven veel schoonder aen te sien dan die andere.

Het welcke my beweegt heeft te laten in't licht comen, ofte te laten drucken dit kleyn boeck, profijtelijck zijnde voor alle Hovenieren, ende aengenaem van alle liefhebbers van hoven, hopende in corte tijt het selve te vermeerderen.

t'VTRECHT,
By Salomon de Roy, ordinaris Drucker der Heeren Staten s'Landts
van Vtrecht, Anno M. DC. XXXV.

71. Print from Isaac Leschevin's *Portals and Palisades*, 1635, with models for trellis-work used in the Stadholder's gardens.
The Metropolitan Museum of Art, New York

72. Print from Isaac Leschevin's *Portals and Palisades*, 1635, design for a semicircular palisade with five *berceaux* and central fountain.
The Metropolitan Museum of Art, New York

ornaments of the Ter Nieuburch and Vianen gardens, where Leschevin was active, indicates that the prints showed the garden ornament actually executed at Batestein. Apparently some of these designs were also used, in a slightly different form, for the garden at Ter Nieuburch.

One of Leschevin's designs for a trellis-work portico entitled 'Pallissade en forme de Portail' *(see fig. 71)* was the model for the two trellis-work hedges or porticoes set up at the edge of the Ter Nieuburch garden on either side of the main transverse axis behind the palace, offering a framed view of the surrounding fields and canals. The source for this design was not difficult to find; it provides further insight into the contemporary dissemination of artistic style in garden design throughout Northern European courts: the idea for the design

73. Print from Salomon de Caus's *Hortus Palatinus*, 1620, showing trellis-work in the garden of Heidelberg, copied by Isaac Leschevin.

Photo courtesy Kurpfälzisches Museum, Heidelberg

came from a well-known contemporary garden printbook, also kept in the stadholderly library, namely Salomon de Caus's *Hortus Palatinus (fig. 73)*.[119] Comparison of the two engravings shows that Leschevin copied de Caus's print of a palisade in the gardens of Heidelberg. The only difference between the two designs was that Ter Nieuburch's palisade consisted of wood only, while Heidelberg's one was partly constructed of stone. Both designs show a palisade with several portals, each having three openings in the form of a Serlian window. These portals in turn were separated by twisted columns holding a voluted gable with three *oculi*. The wall between the portals had two semicircular openings and carried vases with dwarf trees. More connections can be found between Ter Nieuburch's garden ornamentation and the *Hortus Palatinus*. Not only the palisades but also the garden sculptures of Ter Nieuburch reveal direct inspiration from the Heidelberg gardens.

SCULPTURE IN THE TER NIEUBURCH GARDEN

The sculptural decoration of the Ter Nieuburch garden occupies a special place in the history of Dutch garden sculpture. Here, the international artistic connections, aesthetic taste and political aspirations of the House of Orange found their reflection in an impressive array of antique and modern statues, vases and fountain-works. The most prominent statues in the garden of Ter Nieuburch were two reclining figures, or river gods, on a rock in the centre of the two ponds at the rear of the building. In addition to these figures, a monumental fountain and two large statues stood as decorative focal points on the central axis. Until recently, little was known about the sculptural decoration of Ter Nieuburch or, for that matter, about any of the statues decorating Frederik Hendrik's gardens. The garden sculpture of Ter Nieuburch was believed lost or ruined after the demolition of the palace and the garden in the late eighteenth century. However, in the course of this study it was discovered that, in addition to the statue busts presumably originating from Ter Nieuburch's grotto, the two reclining river gods are still in existence. They can be recognized in the reclining figures lining the entrance staircase of the Royal Beach Pavilion, the so-called Paviljoen von Wied or 'De Witte' at Scheveningen *(figs. 74, 75 and 76)*.[120] How these river gods escaped the ruin of the garden of Ter Nieuburch is still unknown, and when and how they came to The Hague or Scheveningen also needs further research. But the consequences

74. Statue of the River God, once decorating the pond in the garden of Ter Nieuburch, now flanking the Paviljoen von Wied at Scheveningen, looking northward. Photo courtesy Rijksdienst voor de Monumentenzorg, Zeist, 1982

75. Statue of the River God, once decorating the pond in the garden of Ter Nieuburch, now flanking the Paviljoen von Wied at Scheveningen, looking southward.

76. Detail of the face of one of Ter Nieuburch's River Gods, showing the robust lines of its features, accentuated by the influence of the elements and time. Photo courtesy Rijksdienst voor de Monumentenzorg, Zeist, 1982

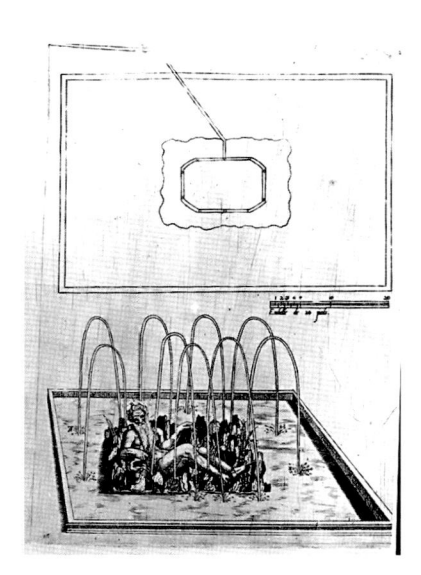

77. The River God decorating the Heidelberg garden, published in Salomon de Caus's *Hortus Palatinus* and taken as example for Ter Nieuburch.
Photo courtesy Kurpfälzisches Museum, Heidelberg

of this recent discovery of what is believed to be the only remaining monumental group of garden statues in The Netherlands dating from the first half of the seventeenth century are considerable.

Of special interest is the connection between Ter Nieuburch's river gods and those in the contemporary garden of Heidelberg, shown in Salomon de Caus's *Hortus Palatinus (fig. 77)*.[121] Like the Heidelberg statue, which still stands in the Hortus Palatinus today,[122] those of Ter Nieuburch are executed in a slightly robust style *(see fig. 76)* and encompassed by a network of water-spouts. Remarkably, a third river god – a colossal reclining Neptune decorating the Berlin gardens of the Stadholder's daughter Louise Henriette, who in 1646 married the Elector of Brandenburg[123] – can now be added to this group, which confirms a continued interest in certain sculptural topoi within the House of Orange. Though the close stylistic comparisons suppose direct links between the Dutch and German sculpture groups, their mutual prototype may have been Fontainebleau, where Henri IV had his gardens decorated with reclining river gods constructed by the Italian engineers Tommaso and Alessandro Francini.[124] Naturally, as a type, such reclining river gods have a long history, going back to antiquity and epitomized by the famous *Nile* and *Tiber* decorating the Belvedere statue court.[125] As personifications of water, river gods traditionally were part of other 'images of territory' in gardens, several examples of which survive in original sixteenth-century Italian Renaissance gardens.[126] It should be noted, finally, that in all the later prints of Ter Nieuburch, as well as in Jan de Bisschop's drawing of circa 1660, the two statues of the river gods featuring so prominently in the Milheusser print of 1644 *(see fig. 48)* are missing. It is possible that the statues were simply not represented, or, more likely, that they were taken away from Ter Nieuburch after Frederik Hendrik's death and brought somewhere else, though any documentary reference to such an undertaking is lacking.

Be that as it may, a direct link between the Heidelberg and Ter Nieuburch garden layouts, shown by the above examples, is particularly intriguing in the light of the 'chronicle of the Palatinate'. In 1620, even before the completion of the gardens, Friedrich V, Elector Palatine, and his wife Elizabeth of Bohemia fled to Holland to set up court at The Hague and Rhenen under the protection of their uncle Frederik Hendrik. Whether their gardener Salomon de Caus was invited to come with them and thus could have had a hand in the layout of the Stadholder's gardens, including the decoration of the gardens of Ter Nieuburch, is an interesting question which cannot be answered without further documentary evidence. That de Caus's work was well known and appreciated in Holland, however, can be gathered from the enthusiastic description of the Heidelberg gardens and waterworks in Huygens's 1620 travel journal mentioned above. De Caus's popularity is also obvious from the presence of his complete works in Frederik Hendrik's library[127] and the use of his prints from the *Hortus Palatinus* for the decoration of the Ter Nieuburch garden. The involvement of Friedrich V and Elizabeth of Bohemia in the Stadholder's estates is also relevant. Though they had a palace at Rhenen especially rebuilt for them, they often spent time at The Hague and on those occasions would frequently stay at Rijswijk. Here again, a letter by Huygens to Amalia written in September 1645 points the way:

> La Reine de Boheme a eu subject de m'escrire une lettre de Riswijck, ou elle dit qu'il faict fort beau et propre.[128]

From this letter, and several other letters from Elizabeth to her scholarly friend René Descartes, it can be concluded that 'la Reine de Boheme' was regularly invited to stay at Ter Nieuburch and greatly enjoyed the beauty of the palace and its gardens: at the time of her visit in the autumn of 1645 the garden must have reached its full-grown glory, as shown in the then just published Milheusser print.

In addition to the two river gods, the Milheusser print depicts various other monumental sculptures decorating the main parterre garden behind the house. Three large statues can be distinguished, forming appropriate accents on the main axis running from the palace southward through the whole parterre garden *(see fig. 48)*. On the face of it, these sculptures constitute a fountain structure topped by a statue at the centre of the parterre directly behind the house; it is followed by an imposing, classically-clad helmeted figure holding a spear in the middle of the garden, and concluded by a statue of a male figure with one uplifted hand standing in the last parterre section. Careful observation and comparison show that these three sculptures represented, respectively, a fountain of Ceres or Venus Lactans, a statue of Minerva, and an unidentifiable figure, possibly Apollo or Hercules.[129] As will be seen in chapter VI, Ter Nieuburch's statues were pivotal 'bearers of meaning' in the Stadholder's garden iconology.

In their attempt to emulate the Roman gardens of antiquity, as it were, Frederik Hendrik and Amalia stimulated the taste for classical statuary. In this context, Sandrart's remark about rare, modern or antique pieces of sculpture in the gardens 'zu Reswick [Rijswijk] und Hontslardick'[130] should be remembered. It is particularly interesting to observe the impact which Frederik Hendrik's and Amalia's fascination with antique sculpture had on garden ornamentation, especially at Ter Nieuburch. The mention of an antique marble figure of a reclining Cleopatra[131] at Ter Nieuburch is a case in point. Amalia, being 'exceedingly jealous' of this Cleopatra statue, had it brought over to Rijswijk just days before Maria de' Medici's arrival at the palace. According to a contemporary commentary,[132] Amalia thus hoped to impress the French royal visitor during her trip to Holland in 1638.

The statue of Minerva, situated at the epicentre of the Ter Nieuburch garden, is of special importance because of its central meaning within the iconology of the Stadholder's gardens and those of his courtiers. In fact, Frederik Hendrik's relative and military adviser Prince Johan Maurits van Nassau-Siegen would decorate his gardens at Cleves with a similar statue of Minerva, a copy of which still stands in the gardens today.[133] The immediate forerunner of this *Minerva* at Ter Nieuburch has disappeared, together with the entire seventeenth-century palace and garden complex of Ter Nieuburch. Sadly enough, though the Rijswijk palace was much admired and imitated for its architectural and ornamental innovations at the time of Frederik Hendrik's death, the estate would fall into complete neglect and eventual ruin soon after Amalia's own death in 1675.

TER NIEUBURCH AFTER FREDERIK HENDRIK
UP TO THE PRESENT

The last great role the palace and gardens of Ter Nieuburch played was as the setting of the Treaty of Rijswijk of 1697. In commemoration of this conference leading to the Peace of Rijswijk, the old Milheusser print of 1644 was reissued. Entirely new prints, showing the late-seventeenth-century layout of the garden, were published, including the engraving by I. van Vianen and A. Beek, and the print by J.A. Rietkessler *(see figs. 63 and 65)*. Though the form and inner division of the garden and its compartments remained the same, as can be seen in Beek's print *(see fig. 63)*, some changes were made in the planting and the garden's decoration. Most conspicuous was the replacement of decorative parterres with easier-to-keep dwarf-tree plantations, referred to in contemporary records of payments as *arbres nains*. These dwarf-tree compartments are also clearly visible in the other late-

Drawing by Jan de Bisschop, c. 1660, of the statue of Hercules and Cacus at Honselaarsdijk. RPK (see fig. 28)

COURTLY GARDENS IN HOLLAND 1600-1650

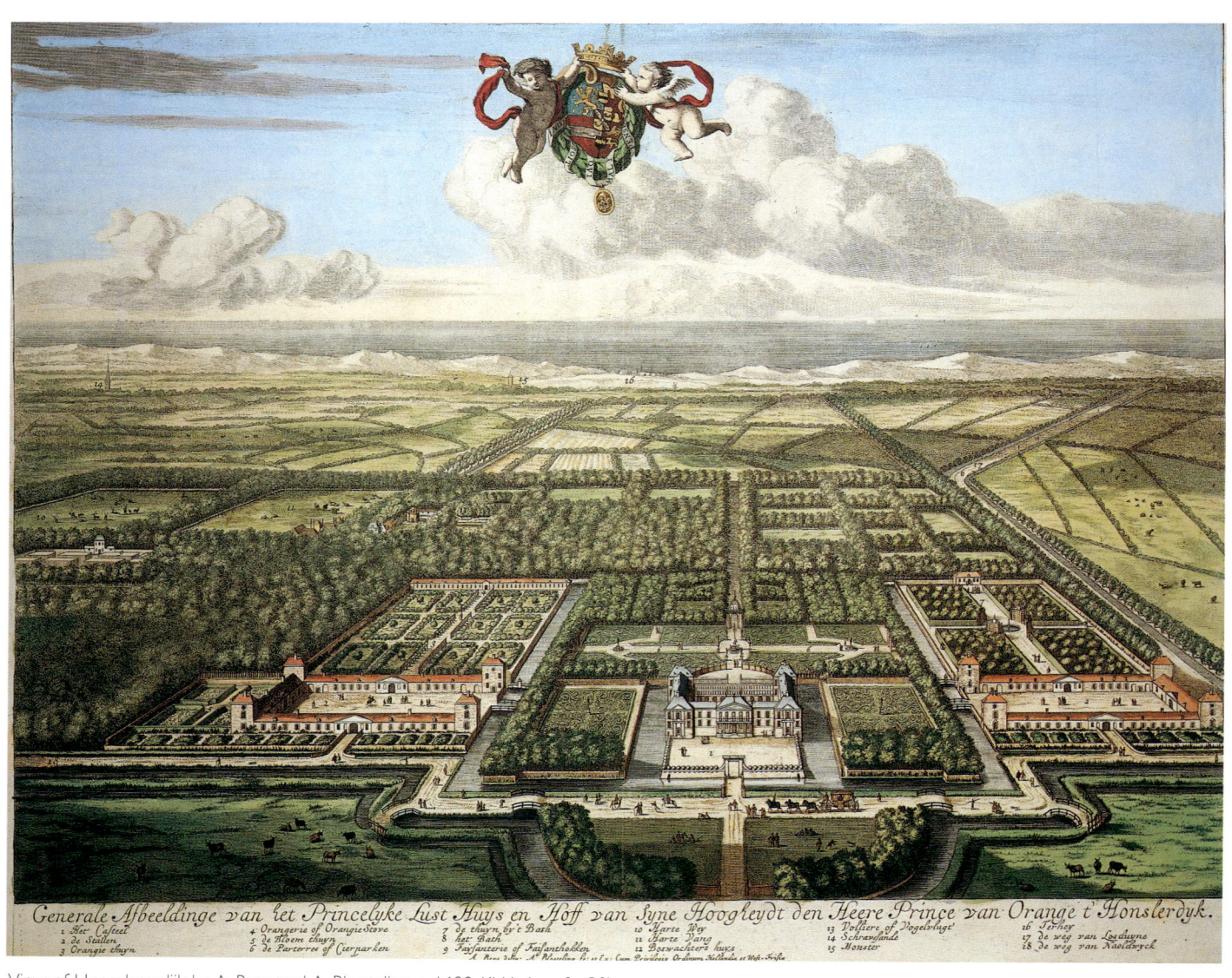

View of Honselaarsdijk by A. Bega and A. Blooteling, c. 1680. KHA (see fig. 30)

COURTLY GARDENS IN HOLLAND 1600-1650

78. Detail of Nicolaas Cruquius's map of Delfland, 1712, showing the lime plantation of Ter Nieuburch with its circular ponds and diagonal avenues.
Collectie Bodel Nijenhuis, Universiteitsbibliotheek, Leiden

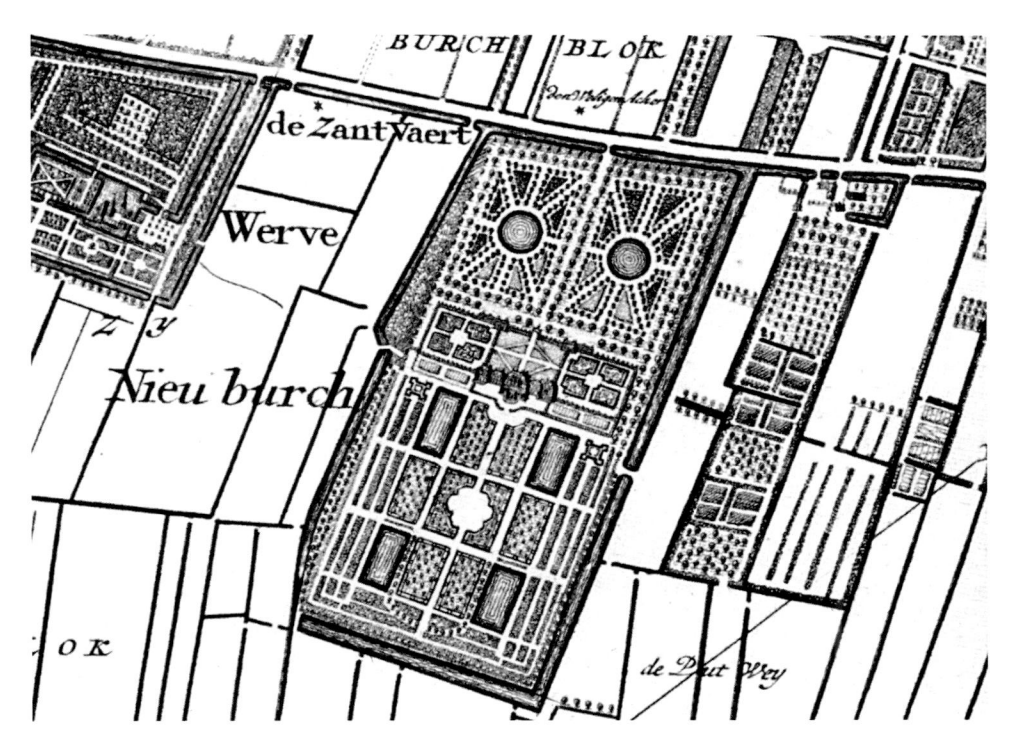

seventeenth- and early-eighteenth-century prints of Ter Nieuburch.

Whereas Honselaarsdijk was still mentioned frequently in the account books describing new projects in the palace and garden after 1660, Ter Nieuburch is but mentioned rarely and only in connection with the most necessary repairs to the palace and gardens. The last major improvements to the house and garden were undertaken in the 1690s under William III's architect Jacob Roman (999 fols. 194vo, 226, 247) and the earlier-mentioned gardener-in-chief Willem Brederoo [Brederode] (999 fols. 251, 273). After this short revival, palace and gardens were neglected and soon after William III's death in 1702 fell into disrepair, brought on by complications concerning his inheritance.

In 1711 Gysbert de Cretser commented in his *Beschrijvinge van 's Gravenhage* that 'the magnificent Palace ter Nieuburch, built by Frederik Hendrik in 1634 and chosen as glorious centre for the Peace negotiations of 1697' showed the first signs of decay. De Cretser expressed the hope that the King of Prussia would prevent further dilapidation of house and garden, at least to avoid total ruin of the Rijswijk court.[134] Improvements and changes were indeed undertaken by the King of Prussia in the early eighteenth century, as the map of Delfland by Cruquius shows, a detail of which is reproduced here *(fig. 78)*. The main innovations in the gardens visible on this map must have occurred between 1697 and 1712, when it was published; they included the addition of two round ponds in the centre of the lime-tree plantation. This plantation was now cut through by a system of straight and diagonal paths, creating a radial pattern in typical early-eighteenth-century mode. However, in spite of the King of Prussia's efforts, Ter Nieuburch would not survive the onslaught of time.

Even after the reinstatement of the House of Orange-Nassau in 1732[135] and the return of part of the Nassau Domains in the hands of William IV of Orange (1711-1751), lack of sufficient funds prevented the proper and continued upkeep of the Ter Nieuburch estate. Three Englishmen travelling through The Netherlands in 1743 commented on the neglect of the estate at the time:

We went also to Ryswyck a small village remarkable only for the peace made hear [*sic*] & call'd by the name of the place & for a large old stone house now much out of repair where

79. Poster announcing the public auction on 26 July 1786 of the remaining materials of the palace and garden of Ter Nieuburch. Algemeen Rijksarchief

80. The column in the Rijswijk public park, erected in 1793 in memory of Ter Nieuburch's palace and garden, where the Rijswijk Peace Treaty was signed. Gemeentearchief, The Hague

the plenipotentiaries met.[136]

In 1785, under William V (1751-1806), a last serious attempt was made to save Ter Nieuburch. First, both wings were demolished and the grounds prepared for lease as farmland, vegetable gardens and timber production, thus repeating the history of Honselaarsdijk. As this was not sufficient, the royal architect P.W. Schonk was soon ordered to demolish the remaining sections of the building. The building material – valuable Bentheimer stone, bricks and wooden beams – was subsequently sold by public auction. The poster announcing this auction, held on 26 July 1786 *(fig. 79)*, survives today as a sad reminder of the final ruin of this once glorious estate.[137] To commemorate Ter Nieuburch as the setting of the Peace of Rijswijk, the architect P.W. Schonk designed a memorial column ('De Naald'), which was erected at the site in 1793 *(fig. 80)*.[138] Small saplings are seen, planted in a semicircle surrounding the memorial, and a stone obelisk set on the main axis, in the centre of the then newly-opened public park.

Ter Nieuburch met with the same fate that befell Honselaarsdijk: the grounds were altered over the centuries to fit the changing tastes of garden design. With the layout, the function of Ter Nieuburch changed as the Rijswijk park was increasingly used for horticultural instead of representative and recreational purposes. By the end of the nineteenth century more than one third of the southern part of the park was cut off to be used for fruit and vegetable cultivation. But in spite of these changes, seventeenth-century features such as the central axis and the remaining ponds were still part of the network of undulating paths of Ter Nieuburch's nineteenth-century landscape park visible on an early-twentieth-century map *(fig. 81)*. It is interesting to see that on this map the central axis which once directed the orientation of Frederik Hendrik's garden layout again was taken as a guideline, this time to hold together the radiating street pattern of modern urban Rijswijk.

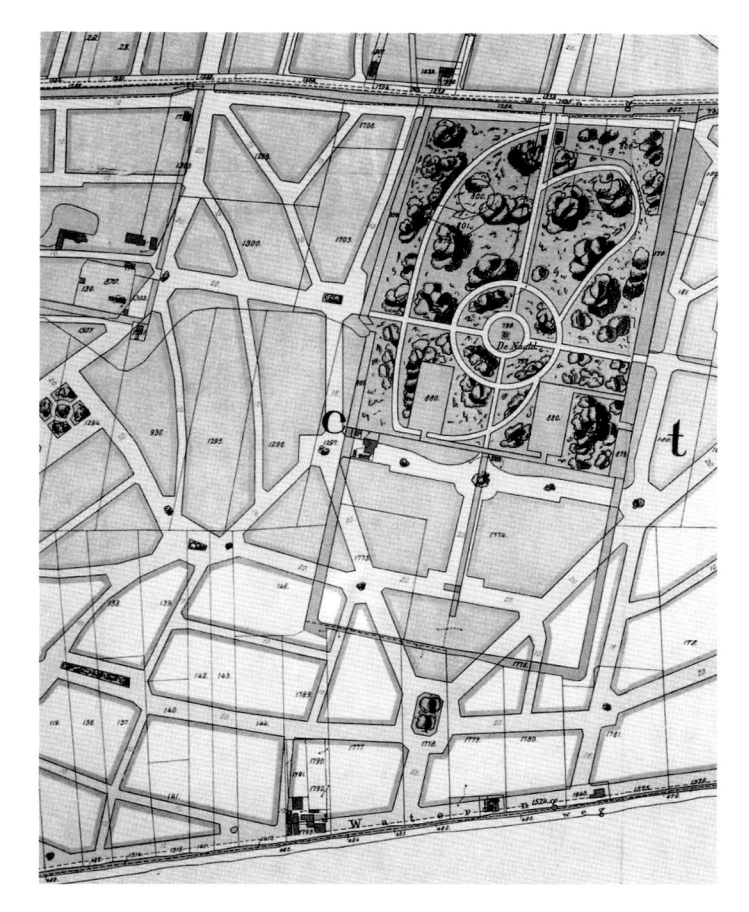

81. Plan by Johannes Mutters of 1906 of the extension of Rijswijk, showing the persistent influence of Ter Nieuburch's original layout on the twentieth-century design of street patterns.
Photo courtesy Gemeentearchief Rijswijk

82. Map of the Rijswijk public park in its present situation (1987), showing how the southern part of the garden has been cut off and built over (centre).
Photo courtesy Gemeentearchief Rijswijk

Even today, some details of the original seventeenth-century contour and inner divison of Ter Nieuburch can be found in the Rijswijk park known as the Rijswijkse Bos *(fig. 82)*. In the first place, the outline of the grounds, defined by the framework of canals, can still be recognized. Also, the main cross axes of the seventeenth-century layout, which determine the location of the obelisk, still define the system of paths in the present park. The park's northern edge, where the main entrance still is, as well as the western and eastern borders of the estate have basically remained intact. The urbanization of the region has encroached upon the southern border, where a complex of municipal buildings was constructed over two of the four rectangular ponds which once enclosed the ornamental parterres of Frederik Hendrik's garden.

HAGA·COMITIS·IN·HOLLANDIA

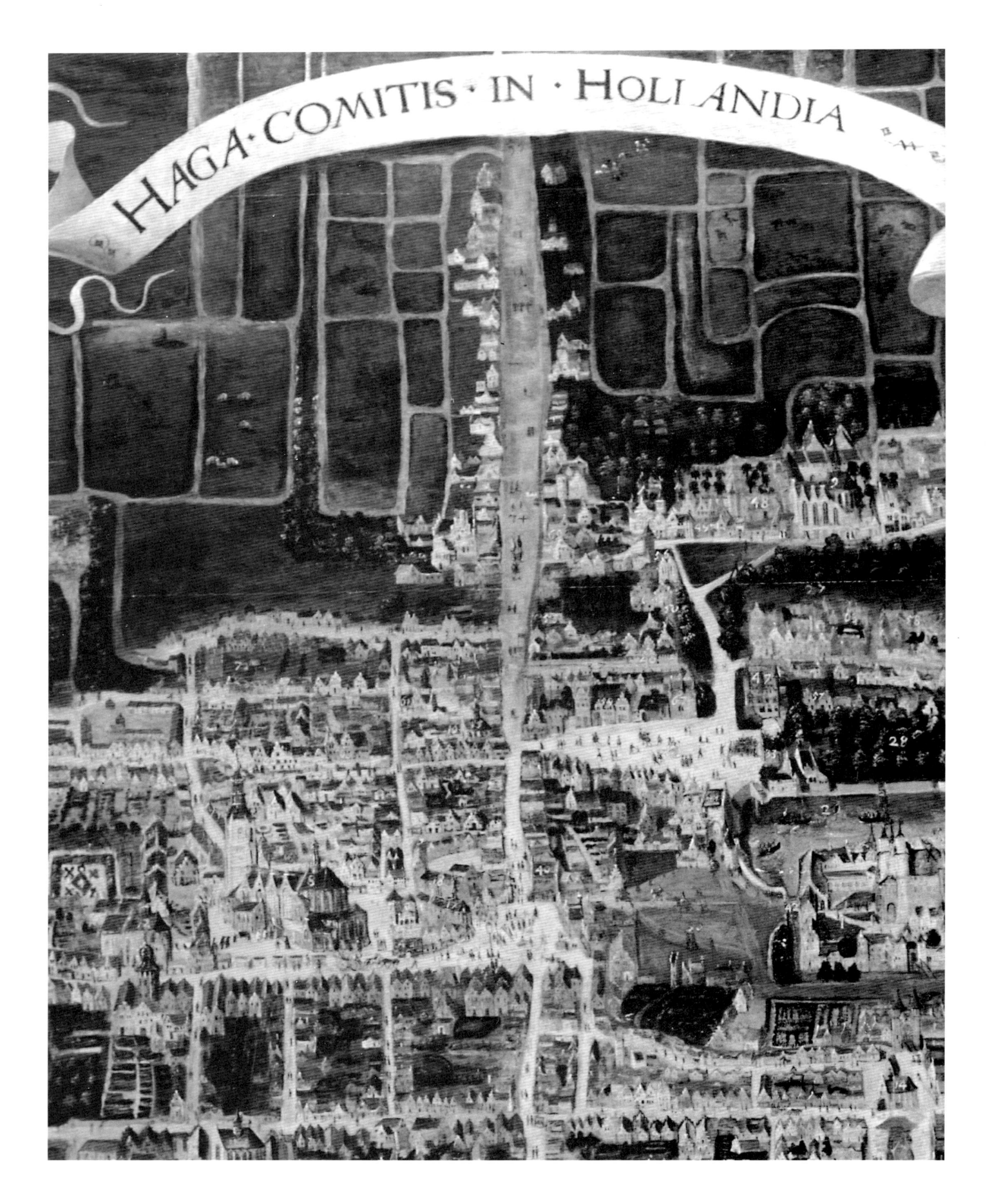

CHAPTER III

THE OTHER GARDENS OF FREDERIK HENDRIK AND AMALIA

83. Plan of The Hague in 1570 by Cornelis Elandts, showing (centre) the elongated area divided by canals of the later Noordeinde gardens.
Haags Historisch Museum, The Hague

The palace and garden of the Oude Hof (Old Court), today known as the Paleis Noordeinde, and the Huis ten Bosch (House in the Wood) hold important positions in the history of the properties of Frederik Hendrik and Amalia. Whereas Honselaarsdijk and Ter Nieuburch have almost completely disappeared, the Paleis Noordeinde and the Huis ten Bosch and their gardens survive and have even kept their original function as the residence of the Orange family. Though neither of these buildings was created by Frederik Hendrik, the way Honselaarsdijk and Ter Nieuburch were, they fall within the category of buildings under discussion. In fact, the Paleis Noordeinde may be considered the point of departure of Frederik Hendrik's lifelong involvement with building projects and garden layouts, for it was here that he spent his childhood years. The Huis ten Bosch, on the other hand, may be seen as the end-point of this creative process: completed after his death by his wife Amalia, it stands as a memorial to Frederik Hendrik's accomplishments as a statesman, warrior and Maecenas.

The other gardens to be reviewed here are gardens which Frederik Hendrik inherited from his brother Prince Maurits, such as those of the Prinsenhuis at Vlissingen (Flushing) and the Buitenhof at The Hague, which were completed under Frederik Hendrik. Furthermore, the gardens around the old castles of Breda, Buren, Zuylesteyn and Ysselsteyn will be discussed, which, though dating back to earlier times, are examples of gardens which Frederik Hendrik improved to such an extent that one can truly speak of new garden layouts.

PALEIS NOORDEINDE

The Old Court, developed from earlier structures on the site built by Willem Goudt in 1533, was extended by the Brandtwyck family in 1566.[1] In 1591 the States of Holland placed the house at the disposal of Louise de Coligny, Frederik Hendrik's mother, widow of William I of Orange. In 1609 it was granted to her and her son, then just twenty-five years old, in recognition of William the Silent's diplomatic accomplishments.[2] While the major rebuilding and extension of the old house would not be undertaken until more than twenty years later, already at that time Frederik Hendrik started to enlarge the grounds by acquiring the surrounding tracts of undeveloped grassland (1043 fol. 169vo). Under Frederik Hendrik certain existing orchards and garden sections[3] were incorporated into a newly-designed, monumental garden complex, as can be concluded from the account books and by comparing late-sixteenth- and early-seventeenth-century maps of the area.

A plan of The Hague by Cornelis Elandts *(fig. 83)*,[4] showing the layout of the city in 1570, provides one of the earliest views of the cluster of buildings and polderland which later would grow out to become the 'Court at the North End', or Noordeinde.[5] In this area

III. OTHER GARDENS

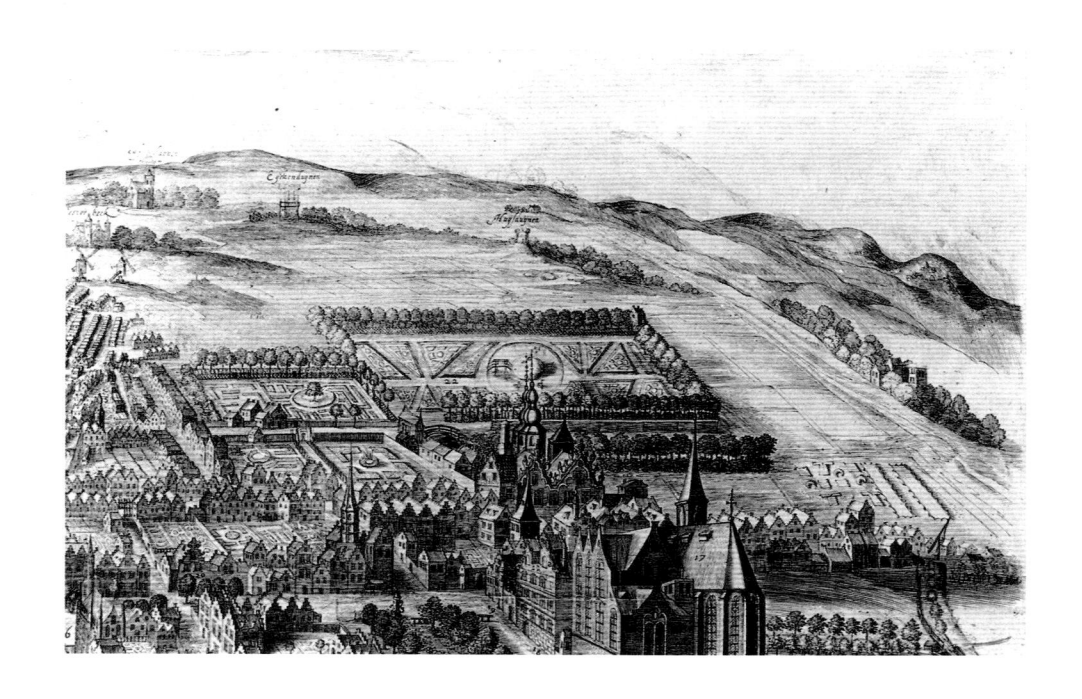

84. Bird's-eye view of The Hague by Nicolaas de Clerck and Johannes van Londerseel (detail), 1615, showing the rectangular Noordeinde garden with central pond.
Gemeentearchief, The Hague

lay the main thoroughfare of the outer north-western edge of town, along which the Paleis Noordeinde was built and from which it took its name. On this map the building complex is shown to be surrounded by a wooded tract of land, consisting mainly of orchards. North of the property, parallel to the street, a large, rectangular meadow, enclosed within a system of canals, stretched out. This tract, ending right under the banner inscribed 'Haga Comitis in Hollandia', defines the exact area which would later become the famous garden of the Paleis Noordeinde. Thus, as was the case at Honselaarsdijk and Ter Nieuburch, at Noordeinde the existing form and division of the surrounding meadow and polderland dictated the shape and boundary of the later garden. Unlike the Honselaarsdijk and Ter Nieuburch gardens, however, the Noordeinde garden was not laid out in direct relation to the palace, as we shall see.

The first improvements to the grounds were undertaken when Louise de Coligny set up her residence there in 1592.[6] As early as 1603 new stables were built, and Louise also commissioned the construction of 'a dwelling for the gardener'.[7] In 1609 a large tract of land, measuring four morgens and thirteen Rijnlandse roeden, or circa nine acres, was bought by Frederik Hendrik from the neighbouring St. Nicolaas Hospice for 4,800 pounds artois (1043 fol. 169[vo]).[8] This elongated, rectangular terrain, visible on all consecutive seventeenth-century plans of The Hague, would constitute the main garden area of the Noordeinde palace.

In 1614 Frederik Hendrik extended the Noordeinde property even further by purchasing a section of land for 1,400 pounds artois (1043 fol. 170[vo]). This yard, or *erff*, was situated immediately behind the palace proper, adjoining the living quarters of his mother; according to the description in the records of payments, it was acquired 'in order to make a small garden with a grotto'.[9] It is difficult to ascertain who was responsible for designing this grotto. However, one may suppose that Jacques de Gheyn, who about the same time was commissioned to design the gardens and grotto of Frederik Hendrik's brother Maurits at the Buitenhof, was also involved in the Noordeinde gardens and grotto.[10]

In the middle of the improvement of palace and garden, Friedrich V, Elector Palatine, and Elizabeth Stuart, just having been married in England, visited the Noordeinde in 1613

85. Map of The Hague (detail) by Cornelis Bos and Jacob van Harn, 1616, with the new Noordeinde gardens to the west and north-west of the palace complex. Gemeentearchief, The Hague

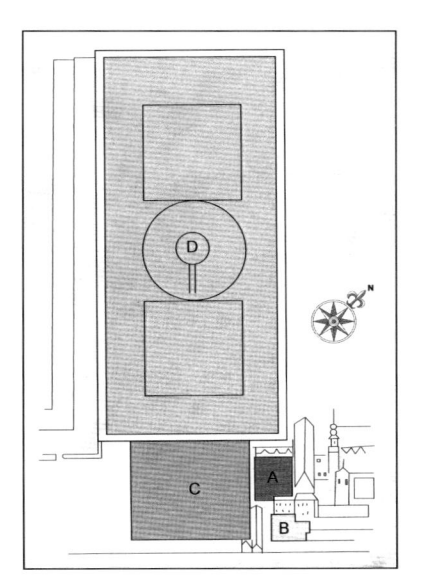

86. Reconstruction drawing of the Noordeinde gardens: (A) courtyard garden, (B) Amalia's Flower Garden, (C) *berceaux* garden, (D) Princesse Thuyn.

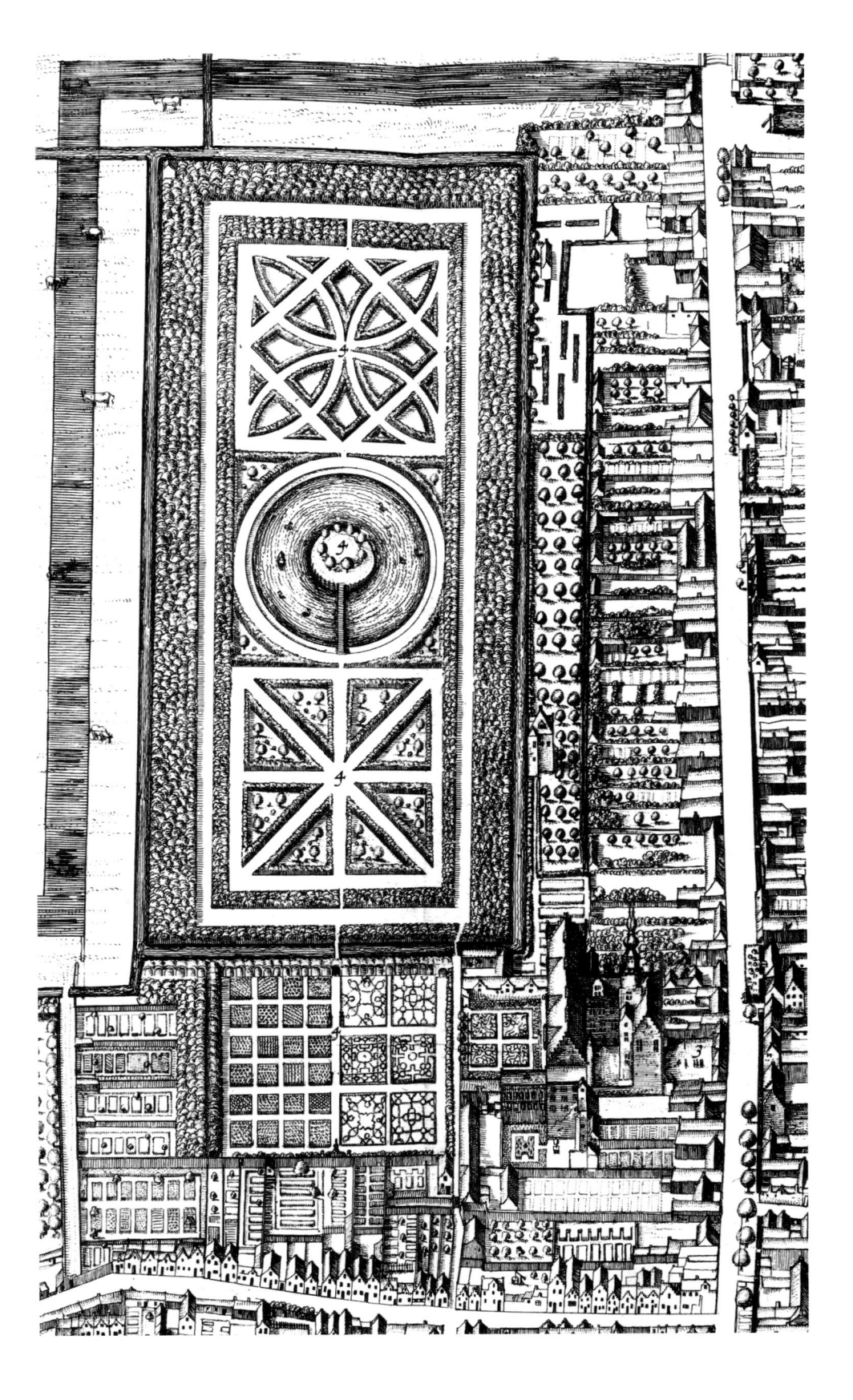

III. OTHER GARDENS

on their way to Heidelberg. The necessary embellishments for this high visit were undertaken in a great hurry, as is shown by a letter which Louise wrote to her friend, the Duchesse de Touars:

> Je suis si empêchée à préparer mon logis pour recevoir cette grande compagnie, que voilà tout ce que je vous puis dire.[11]

What the Noordeinde palace and grounds looked like at that time can be seen in a bird's-eye view of The Hague by Nicolaas de Clerck and Johannes van Londerseel dated 1615 *(fig. 84)*.[12] In the upper right-hand corner of the map one may distinguish the rough outline of two garden sections behind the palace, enclosed by rows of trees. The old courtyard garden to the left of the palace gave access to the large rectangular garden area with central pond and island running perpendicularly to the palace and extending to the Noordwal, or northern boundary, of The Hague. This large elongated terrain constituted the most important part of the Noordeinde garden known as the 'Groote Thuyn' (1043 fol. 170) or 'Princesse Thuyn' (Large or Princess's Garden),[13] which was developed by the Stadholder on the newly-acquired grassland.

A more detailed overview of the new inner arrangement of the whole garden complex under Frederik Hendrik and his mother is offered by the 1616 map of Cornelis Bos and Jacob van Harn *(fig. 85)*,[14] where the Noordeinde premises are designated as 'The Court of the Princess of Orange or the Residency of France'. Added to this map is a second picture *(fig. 86)*, indicating more clearly the various garden sections, numbered A to D. The old inner courtyard (A) shows a strict geometrical division in various garden plots consisting of flower and vegetable beds, separated by a central path and surrounded by hedges. Another courtyard garden (B) is situated south of this enclosed garden and would later be known as 'Amalia's flower garden'. West of these small courtyard gardens, a larger garden enclosed by *berceaux* and divided into two sections, a kitchen and a parterre garden, opened out (C). The Princesse Thuyn (D) lay to the north of this '*berceaux* garden' and was accessible via a bridge over the Middenvaert part of the canal which surrounded the entire terrain. This garden was divided into three square sections, the central one of which held the round pond with circular island accessible only by a small bridge. The two square garden plots on either side of the central pond were outlined by hedges, *berceaux* and shrubbery, planted in decorative shapes. The garden can again be defined by its enclosed character, surrounded as it was by canals, hedges and double rows of trees. It is not known who designed this new garden area, but, as mentioned earlier in the context of the grotto, Jacques de Gheyn may also have worked here for Frederik Hendrik.[15] Indeed, the decorative, trapezoid roof construction of this grotto, built against the southern wall of the small *berceaux* garden, is visible on the Bos and Van Harn map. How the garden looked in the first decades of the seventeenth century can also be gauged from Brereton's travel account, which describes the garden and its ornamentation and plantation in some detail:

> ...the Prince of Orange his garden, the fairest and most spacious platt that ever I saw in my life, and the vastest covered walks: the plot seems to be four square; walks covered round about it, and in middle of the plot here is a fair round moat, about sixteen or twenty yards wide, and in the middle thereof a little island round, wherein is a round covered walk and a kitchen-garden within the walk. In the middle of the garden are poor young cyprus trees.[16]

Details admired by Brereton, such as the covered walks or *berceaux* enclosing the garden,

87. Map of 1649 by Joan Blaeu (detail), The Hague, with the Buitenhof garden in the centre and the Noordeinde gardens at the upper left.
Collectie Bodel Nijenhuis, Universiteitsbibliotheek, Leiden

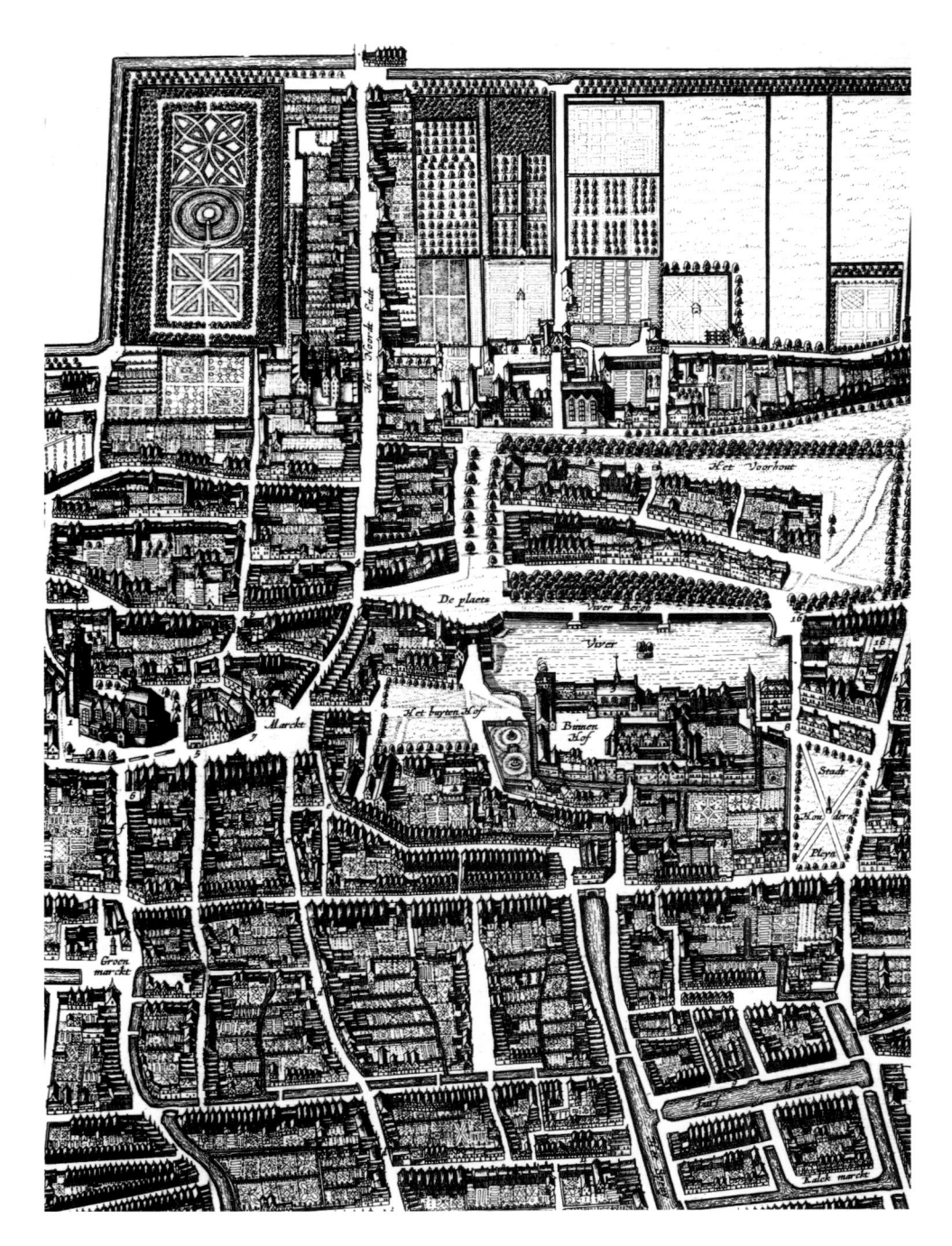

the round island with its circular walk planted with trees – apparently cypresses (unlikely survivors of the Dutch climate!) – are all clearly depicted on the contemporary maps.

In Joan Blaeu's 1649 plan of The Hague *(fig. 87)*[17] the old *berceaux* garden has changed and instead of taking on the function of a kitchen garden is now entirely laid out as a pleasure garden. Its many herb and vegetable beds have given way to flowers and boxwood, as the garden is divided into four square plots decorated with *parterres de broderie*. Overall, the layout of these small, walled-in garden sections shows continued preoccupation with the principle of the more intimate, enclosed garden spaces of the Renaissance. Throughout the century this basic form and outline of the various garden sections of the Paleis Noordeinde would be retained, though their inner planting and decoration would change with the taste of the time. Blaeu's map is also useful for showing the situation of the

III. OTHER GARDENS

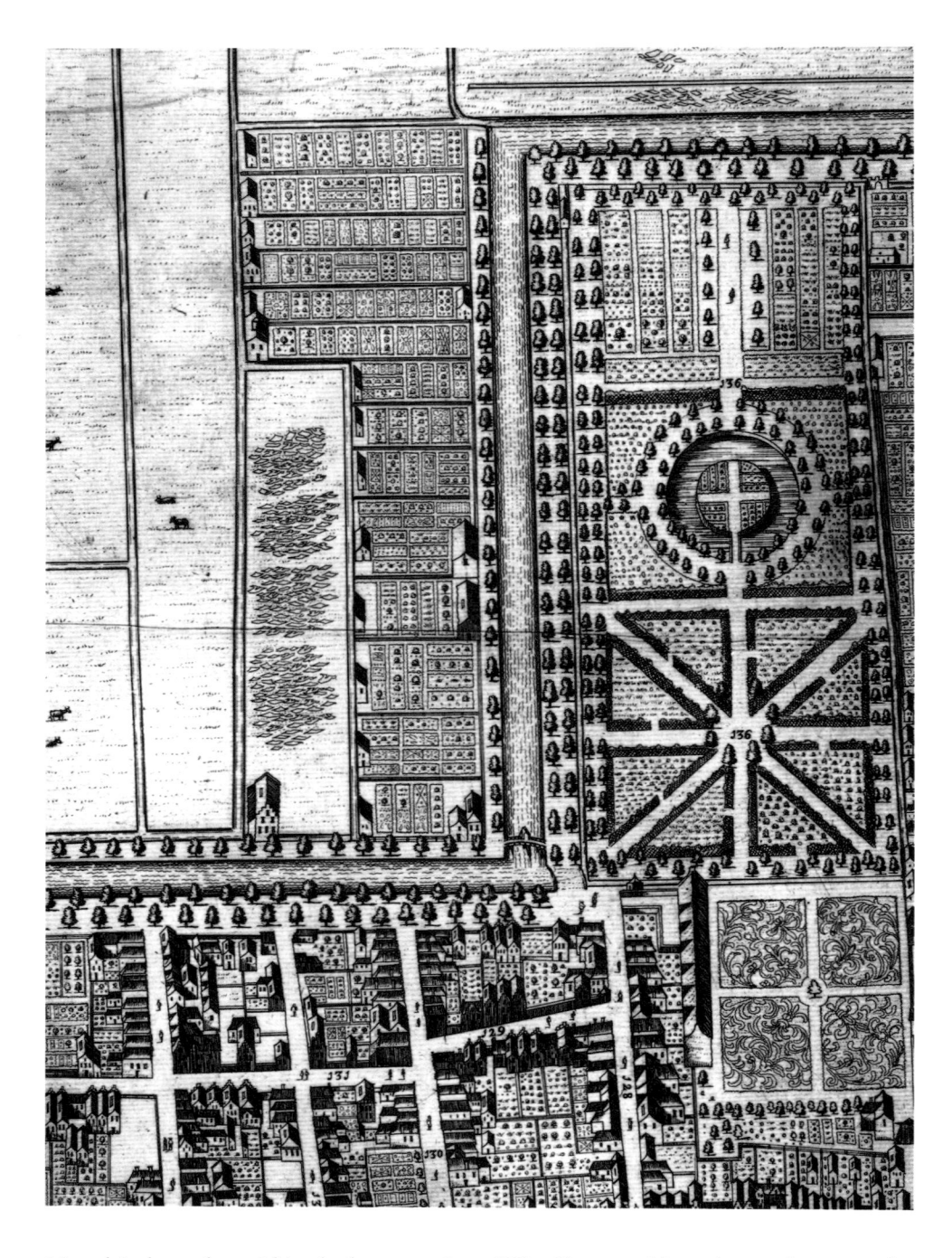

88. Detail of a map by Cornelis Elandts showing the mid-seventeenth-century situation of the Noordeinde, with arabesque parterres in the old garden and vegetable beds in the Princesse Thuyn (on top).
Collectie Bodel Nijenhuis, Universiteitsbibliotheek, Leiden

Noordeinde garden within the larger setting of The Hague, with to the south-east, at the centre of the town, the Old Ducal Court, or Binnenhof, surrounded by a pond, or *viver*.

A mid-seventeenth-century map of The Hague by Cornelis Elandts *(fig. 88)*[18] for the first time gives a detailed view of the decorative *parterres de broderie* in the old *berceaux* garden of the Noordeinde. The decoration of this garden, aligned with the rear façade of the palace, also features in a drawing by Constantijn Huygens Junior dated 1665.[19] In contemporary accounts, this garden section is called the Oude Thuyn and Kleine Thuyn; behind it lay the Princesse or Groote Thuyn. While the old *berceaux* garden, or Small Garden, was a pure pleasure garden, the layout of the Princesse Thuyn changed, taking on utilitarian purposes. On the Elandts map the third compartment of the Princesse Thuyn is seen to be laid out as a kitchen garden with vegetable beds. Interestingly, the visual evidence provided by this map can be corroborated by a contemporary description of the garden in a document which until now has received little attention. It concerns a contract between a certain Cornelis Dijck, 'Gardener of His Highness', and the Council of the Domains, dated 1667 and entitled [Notulen van de Raad] *Onderhout van de Hoven ende Thuynen in 't Noordeynde* (Instructions for the Upkeep of the Gardens in the Noordeynde; *see Appendix, Document VI)*.[20] The gardener's yearly income was set at 400 Carolus guilders, for which sum he was expected to do the following work:

> The gardener has to shave, bind, clean, repair and maintain the arbours, hedges, parterres, paths and galleries of the old garden [court] laying south of the Middenvaert [central canal] or the large garden, which is situated between the Middenvaert and the properties of the houses in the Molenstraet; he is not allowed to sow or plant anything but what will lead to the further embellishment and pleasure of the old garden, and can only do so with specific knowledge and by order of Her Highness [Amalia]. With regard to the two new gardens and orchards situated north of the Middenvaert and to the north and south of the round pond, the gardener should sow and plant a variety of vegetables (*Aertvruchten*) useful for the table and kitchen of Her Highness. And especially in the part north of the Round pond, since this part has not any hedges any more and has been prepared as a kitchen garden. He also has to cut back, bind up, repair and maintain the shrubbery and trees of the paths, avenues and arbours in this area according to the requirements of the work. Furthermore, the gardener overall has to keep clean the paths and covered walks of all the gardens and orchards mentioned above, including the avenues, so that one can always and at any time go and walk in them without being hindered by weeds, waste or dirt. The gardener also has to clean at least twice a year the canals running through and around the aforesaid orchards and Round pond, including the Middenvaert. If any of the fruit-trees or other trees or shrubberies should die or wither or, if Her Highness desires to have changes made, the gardener has to improve and change the garden accordingly, provided that the trees and plants necessary to do so will be delivered to him. Also, if Her Highness would like to have some more arbours in addition to those which have been constructed before, the gardener has to make them, provided that the shrubs, wood and twigs, wicker and materials necessary for that purpose will be supplied. He will also receive all the twigs, wicker, firs, trellis and other materials necessary to repair and maintain the covered walks, hedges, columns, arbours, pyramids, palisades and other works referred to above. If the gardener does not keep the garden according to the above conditions, and has been warned once or twice, yet still remains negligent in following or completing his instructions, one is allowed to prosecute him and have him complete matters at his own expense; any extra costs will be subtracted from his income without opposition. The gardener shall also take care that sections pointed out to him in the gardens will be sowed and planted with all kinds of vegetables and *Aertvruchten* in such a way that, depending on the season and time [of year], they will daily provide the kitchen [with fresh produce]. The gardener is allowed to take his own share of all the *Aertvruchten* which the gardens and orchards will yield above the quantity necessary for the Table and Kitchen of Her Highness. But when it comes to the Artichokes, Melons, Strawberries and Asparagus, these will entirely be to the disposal of Her Highness and the gardener will not be able to enjoy them, except for what is allowed by Her Highness. The gardener will receive the sum of four hundred guilders yearly for all the above, and will be paid two hundred guilders twice yearly. The first [payment] has been accounted for this last December 1660 and is to be paid out by the Treasurer and

Steward General of His Highness, Mr. Pieter Ardes. Furthermore, the gardener will enjoy free living quarters, provided and maintained by His Highness. Excluded are any provisions of food, drink, beer or light from Her Highness's kitchen or cellar, either directly or indirectly, in spite of previous different arrangements. The above contract took effect on the first of January 1660 and will expire on the last of December 1672. When Her Highness is not completely satisfied with the gardener, Her Highness is allowed to let him go after the first year or any time afterwards. Made up and agreed upon in the Chamber of aforesaid Council and Treasury of His Highness at The Hague this 17 February 1667.

From this contract one gets a good impression of the inner division, planting and decoration of the Noordeinde garden. It becomes clear that its upkeep was divided according to its sections. The elongated garden with its central pond, the Princesse Thuyn, laid out by Frederik Hendrik, was now known as the 'new garden', while the existing courtyard garden filled with parterres and surrounded by *berceaux* was known as the 'old garden'. Both sections were decorated with arbours, covered walks or trellis-work galleries and parterres, in accordance with the contract cited above. The large new garden was planted with dense rows of primarily lime-trees and shrubs. The contract states that the large Princesse Thuyn, partly laid out as a pleasure garden, also functioned as an orchard and kitchen garden, providing food for Her Highness the Dowager Princess Amalia's table. The aesthetic and the useful compartments of the Princesse garden were separated by the central pond, the area north of it comprising the orchard and kitchen gardens.

The description in the gardener's contract of the new inner division of this third garden section as an orchard-kitchen garden fits the plan of The Hague by Elandts *(see fig. 88)*, where, apart from the land north of the pond, even the central island is seen to be laid out as a vegetable garden. These orchard and kitchen gardens needed continuous care, and new fruit-trees were planted there under the supervision of the Stadholder's gardener-in-chief Jan van der Groen (996 fols. 220, 232), whom we have encountered before as the author of the well-known treatise on gardening *Den Nederlandtsen Hovenier*.

Apart from the planting, the garden was filled with various waterworks, among them the old grotto. New works which commenced under the supervision of Pieter Post in the small *berceaux* garden included the layout of a new grotto by the French *grottier-fontainier* Joseph Dinant (995 fol. 90vo),[21] who also designed the grottoes in the gardens of Honselaarsdijk and Ter Nieuburch. The grotto was situated against the southern wall surrounding the *berceaux* garden and was partly covered by a roof structure. This roof needed repair by 1664, when the mason Reyer Pieterssen was paid for demolishing the old roof and replacing it with a new one, as well as completing masonry work in the grotto (996 fols. 187 and 216vo).

Under Frederik Hendrik extensive alterations were made not only to the gardens but, from 1639 on, also to the palace. The new building activities comprised major extensions on all sides and the construction of a completely new *corps de logis* with a classical façade. The transformation of the Paleis Noordeinde into a truly regal residence was undertaken in connection with the pending marriage of William II and Mary Stuart, who were to take up residence here. Due to the delay of the construction of the new royal apartments and façade of the building, William II and Mary moved into the stadholderly quarters in the Binnenhof instead and remained there. After Frederik Hendrik's death in 1647 no other major changes were undertaken at the Noordeinde, apart from the completion of the original renovation plans under Amalia, who, as a widow, was given the use of the palaces of Ter Nieuburch and Noordeinde. Amalia herself moved into the quarters at the rear which had direct access to the small, walled-in garden, later referred to as 'Amalia's Blomhof' *(see*

89. View of the recently restored Paleis Noordeinde, with white stuccoed, classical façade designed by Jacob van Campen and the later Prussian gates.
Photo archive of the author

fig. 86, B).[22]

The rebuilding of the Paleis Noordeinde according to Jacob van Campen's designs resulted in the creation of a more unified and symmetrical layout, aligning better with the surrounding garden. Van Campen's design was based on the proportional principles of classical architecture and comprised the construction of a central *corps de logis* and two wings with open arcades surrounding a central *cour d'honneur*, which have recently been restored *(fig. 89)*. For the decoration of the new façade, Van Campen closely followed classical vocabulary, directly adapting examples from Scamozzi's *L'Idea dell'architettura universale*.[23] From several entries in the accounts we can conclude that Pieter Post, who functioned as general overseer and was charged with the execution of the works in collaboration with Van Campen, was also responsible for the interior renovations of the Noordeinde.[24] As at Honselaarsdijk and Ter Nieuburch, the interior was decorated with great splendour, as can be seen from an inventory of 1632[25] and from contemporary travel accounts. In addition to the description of the palace by de la Serre recounting Maria de' Medici's stay here in 1638[26] there exists a later description of the palace and grounds by a certain Jacob de Hennin. Whereas de la Serre tells us about the richness of the interior decoration, its precious tapestries and magnificent furniture – calling it, in short, a 'truly Royal abode'[27] – de Hennin concentrates on the layout and decoration of the garden.

In a curious booklet by Jacob de Hennin, entitled *De Zinrijke Gedachten toegepast op de Vijf Zinnen van 's Menschen Verstand* (Meaningful Thoughts Applied to the Five Senses of Man's Reason),[28] a detailed description is given of the gardens of the Paleis Noordeinde and their sculptural decoration. Even though this booklet was not published until 1681, its description fits the gardens' layout and decoration as they were at the end of Frederik Hendrik's reign, and at the very time when Amalia took up residence at the Noordeinde. De Hennin describes the old Voortuin, or *berceaux* garden *(see fig. 86, C)*, and, to its north, the large rectangular garden with central pond, which he calls the Oude Prinsentuin. He mentions Amalia's flower garden and the Pauwentuin, or Peacock Garden, clearly referring to the garden courtyards at the rear of the building *(see fig. 86, A and B)*.

Studying de Hennin's passages on the layout of the garden in greater detail, we can make some remarkable discoveries concerning the decorative aspects of the mid-

III. OTHER GARDENS

seventeenth-century courtly gardens. One aspect is the use of mirrors as an important *trompe-l'oeil* feature in contemporary garden architecture. According to de Hennin's description,[29] Amalia's flower garden contained mirrors which were set against the wall of a colonnaded garden pavilion (*kabinet*).[30] These mirrors served to enlarge the boundary of the enclosed garden, as they reflected its sculptural ornaments and plantation. Here in Amalia's flower garden, the mirrors reflected the central marble fountain, statues of putti, known as *kinderkens* (small children), as well as classical statues, identified by de Hennin as Diana, Neptune and Aquarius. They were placed among a large collection of exotic flowers, plants and trees for which Amalia's flower garden was famous. Many of the pots in which the exotic plants were set were delivered in 1647 by the sculptor Otto Reyerssen (994 fol. 204[vo]), who was also responsible for bronzing the stone statues in the garden of The Hague (1043 fol. 225). As at Honselaarsdijk, at the Noordeinde Reyerssen delivered and painted various 'heads' or busts (994 fol. 205: 'eenige hoofden in de Thuyn op de Cingel'), among them probably statues in Amalia's flower garden. To this archival documentation and de Hennin's description, information can be added from another source – a contemporary inventory of Amalia's possessions describing objects in the Noordeinde garden.

This list, made up in 1667, of Amalia's art treasures kept at Ter Nieuburch, the Huis ten Bosch and the Paleis Noordeinde[31] mentions two lead figures of women standing 'on the staircase in the small garden of the Noordeinde',[32] a lead figure representing Fame standing in the centre of a small fountain[33] and eight different kinds of lead animals.[34] Other objects enumerated in the inventory, presumably also present in the Noordeinde garden, included two large mirrors,[35] several little and larger putti or Cupids[36] and four life-size statues in full armour, cut of white marble and representing the illustrious princes of Orange, William I and II, Maurits and Frederik Hendrik.[37]

It is quite interesting that the statues mentioned by de Hennin as standing in Amalia's flower garden can be related to the objects listed in this inventory. Presumably the 'two mirrors' recorded in the list are identical with those described by de Hennin as 'these beautiful large Mirrors'. Likewise there may be a connection between de Hennin's 'statues after the best antique', one of which was identified as Diana, and the 'two women' mentioned in the list. One may also assume a correlation between the marble 'sleeping child' and 'little Cupids with bows' referred to in Amalia's inventory and the 'marble children' in de Hennin's description. Most important, the similarity of the description of the statues representing the Princes of Orange in the inventory and de Hennin's account of statues of 'the entire house of Orange cut and cast after life'[38] seems to confirm that they related to the very same set of statues; it corroborates their presence in Amalia's Noordeinde flower garden. To this information we can further add Sandrart's account of Amalia's tour in 1637 of the most famous Amsterdam 'curiosity cabinets' of well-known collectors-virtuosi. When she expressed her special admiration for a life-size marble Cupid sharpening a bow, made by François Du Quesnoy for Lucas van Uffelen's collection, the Magistrates of Amsterdam felt obliged to offer the statue to Amalia, after which she happily returned to The Hague to place it in her *Zier- und Lustgärtlein* at the Noordeinde.[39]

The flower garden filled with so many art objects, exotic plants and reflecting wall surfaces appears to have been treated as a kind of open-air *Wunderkammer* or 'curiosity cabinet' in itself.[40] Thus the garden extended, as it were, the spatial function of the pavilion and adjoining rooms in the palace building which contained Amalia's gallery and porcelain cabinet.[41] An iconological connection between interior and exterior decoration of the Noordeinde palace can be seen in the presence of tapestries and paintings with dynastic themes[42] and the actual set-up of life-size statues of the Princes of Orange in the adjacent

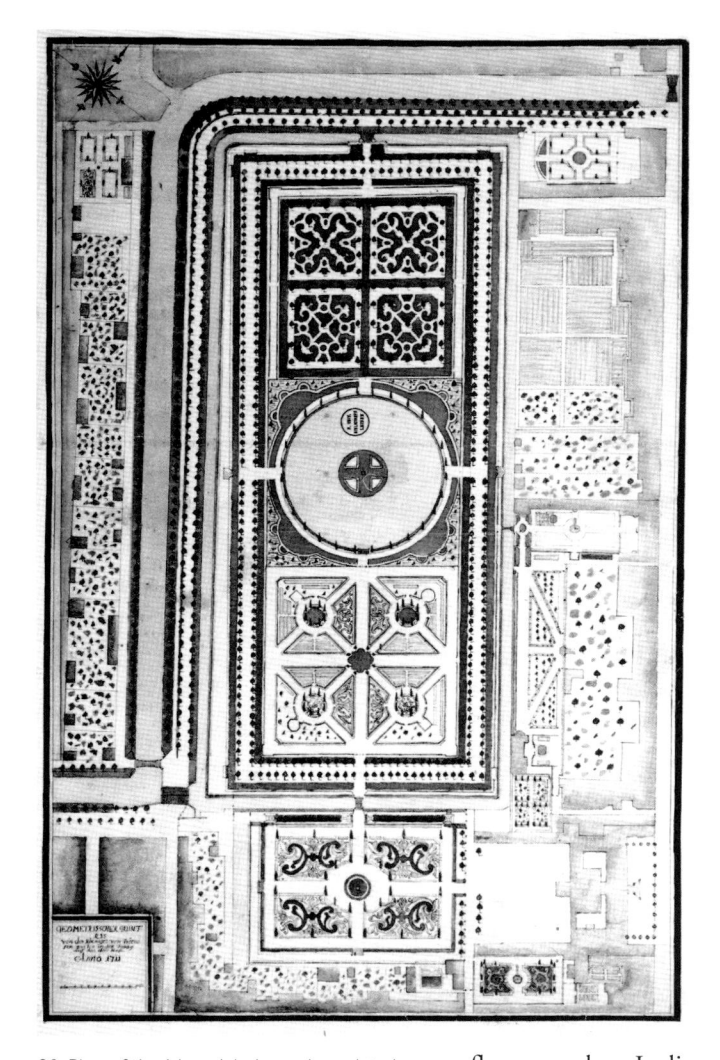

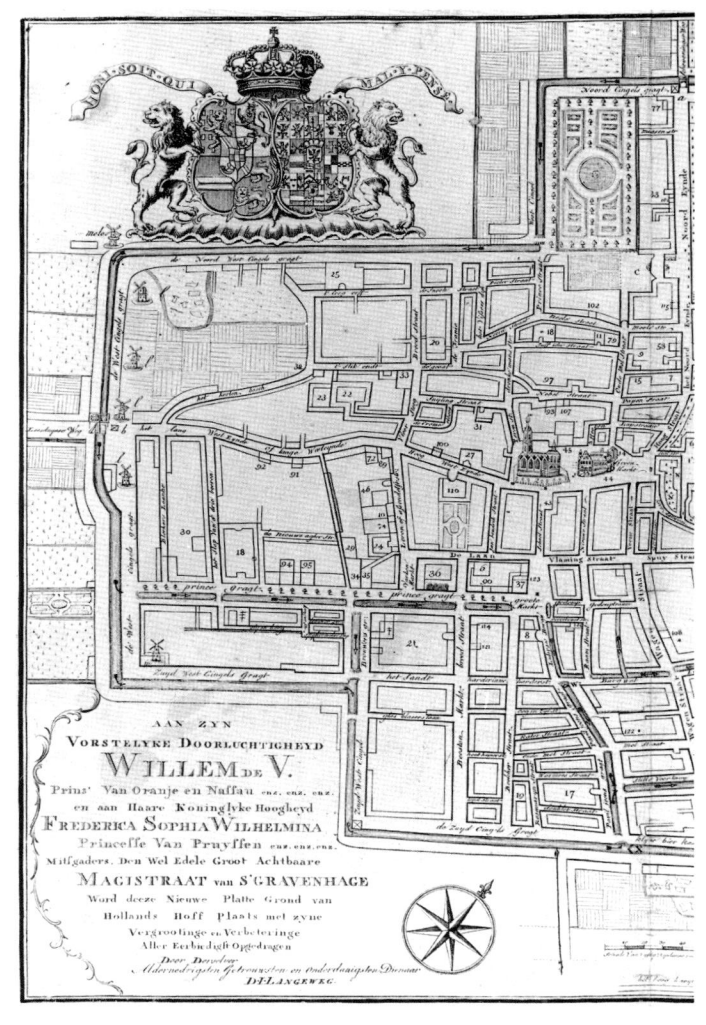

90. Plan of the Noordeinde gardens, dated 1711, by an unknown artist, in the style of Daniel Marot, showing newly-laid-out French parterre designs.
Collectie Bodel Nijenhuis, Universiteitsbibliotheek, Leiden
see colour plate 13

91. Map by D.I. Langeweg, 1767, showing the situation of the Noordeinde gardens under William V (upper right), consisting primarily of utilitarian areas.
Gemeentearchief, The Hague

flower garden. In line with an old tradition developed in Renaissance Italy,[43] the inner decoration of the Noordeinde palace comprised two large painted perspectives of the Stadholder's own estates, Honselaarsdijk and Ter Nieuburch. These perspectives were painted by Reijnier Claessen, who was paid 160 pounds artois each in November 1647 (994 fol. 92). Unfortunately the paintings have not come down to us; they would have constituted the most important single visual testimony of the splendour of the Stadholder's gardens. A last reference to the perspectives is found in 1689, when they were admired by the Swedish architect Nicodemus Tessin during his visit to the Paleis Noordeinde.[44] Tessin also walked through the gardens, which, like those in the beginning of the century, were found to be spacious and densely grown.[45]

After William III's death in 1702, Friedrich of Prussia, claiming to be the sole legal heir, sent ambassadors to take up residence in the Paleis Noordeinde and began making improvements to both palace and garden. In maintaining and embellishing the Noordeinde palace as well as Honselaarsdijk and Ter Nieuburch, Friedrich of Prussia was assisted by the States of Holland, who granted him an annual sum of 10,976 guilders.[46] From 1711 date two plans of the Noordeinde grounds, one of which is shown here *(fig. 90)*.[47] This plan shows that the basic form of the garden was retained and only the parterres were modernized according to the latest French fashion, then dictated by André Le Nôtre's style principles.[48] Providing a good view of early-eighteenth-century practices of garden ornamentation, this plan clearly shows the familiar outline of the three garden sections.

III. OTHER GARDENS

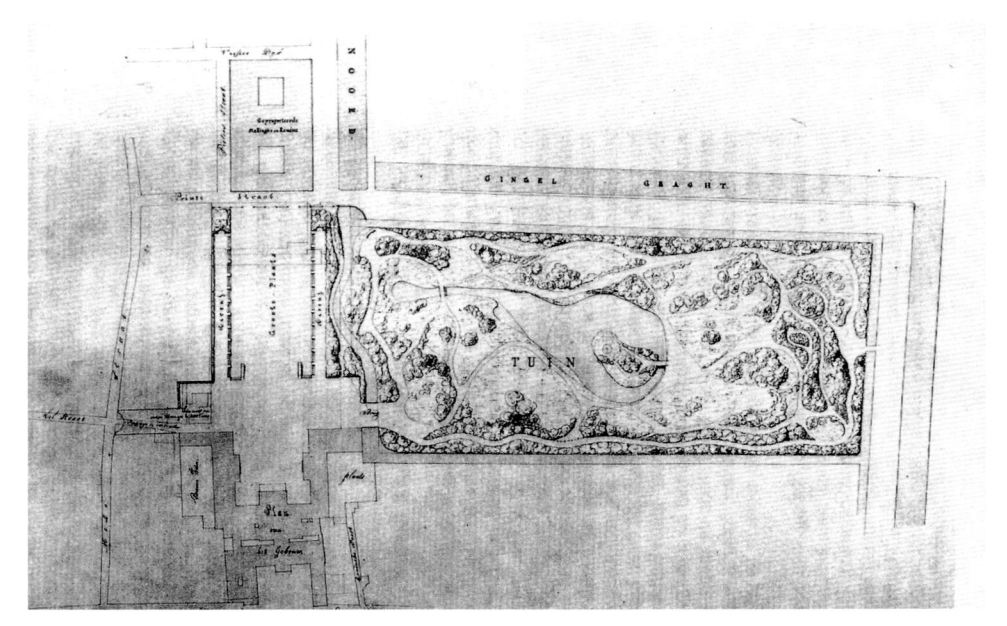

92. Unexecuted plan of the Noordeinde gardens by Jan de Greef, 1819, showing undulating forms of the wooded area and pond in landscape style. Algemeen Rijksarchief

Amalia's flower garden can be recognized at the lower right, now comprising a rectangular instead of a square area, decorated by two ornamental parterres surrounding a central fountain. It is this garden section which throughout the following centuries would remain basically intact. In fact, today it comprises the private, enclosed garden of the Orange family.

From the late seventeenth century onward, and all through the eighteenth century, the garden underwent several metamorphoses. In 1754, after the Noordeinde palace had returned into the hands of the Orange family,[49] the gardens were totally restored and replanted, and many of the ornamental parterres, especially those in the old *berceaux* garden, were again laid out as kitchen-garden plots *(fig. 91)*.[50] The most drastic change occurred in 1778,[51] when the geometrical layout of the garden was replaced with a landscape garden which, like Honselaarsdijk, was decorated in the then fashionable Chinese style with 'English shrubberies' (1135 fols. 198-198vo) and a Chinese pavilion on the island in the pond.[52] At this time the Noordeinde garden was referred to in the archival documents as the 'Nationale tuin'.[53] By the late eighteenth, early nineteenth centuries the garden was described as follows: 'The innermost garden is in a good condition, the large garden in excellent condition, filled with many rare indigenous and foreign plants and shrubs, being daily opened to the public.'[54] Consecutive changes in the Noordeinde garden included a new landscape design under the garden architect Johan David Zocher and the architect Jan de Greef *(fig. 92)*. This particular design was not executed, but a similar landscape layout was, the basic form of which still constitutes the layout of the Noordeinde garden park today, which is open to the public.[55]

HUIS TEN BOSCH

The Huis ten Bosch, originally called Sael van Oranje (Hall of Orange), occupies a special place in the range of residences laid out for the Orange family. Built according to the wishes of Frederik Hendrik's wife Amalia by Pieter Post,[56] with the assistance of Jacob van Campen and under supervision of the Prince and Huygens, the Huis ten Bosch stands out amidst the other country residences for its monumental central composition, to which the garden was carefully fitted.

COURTLY GARDENS IN HOLLAND 1600-1650

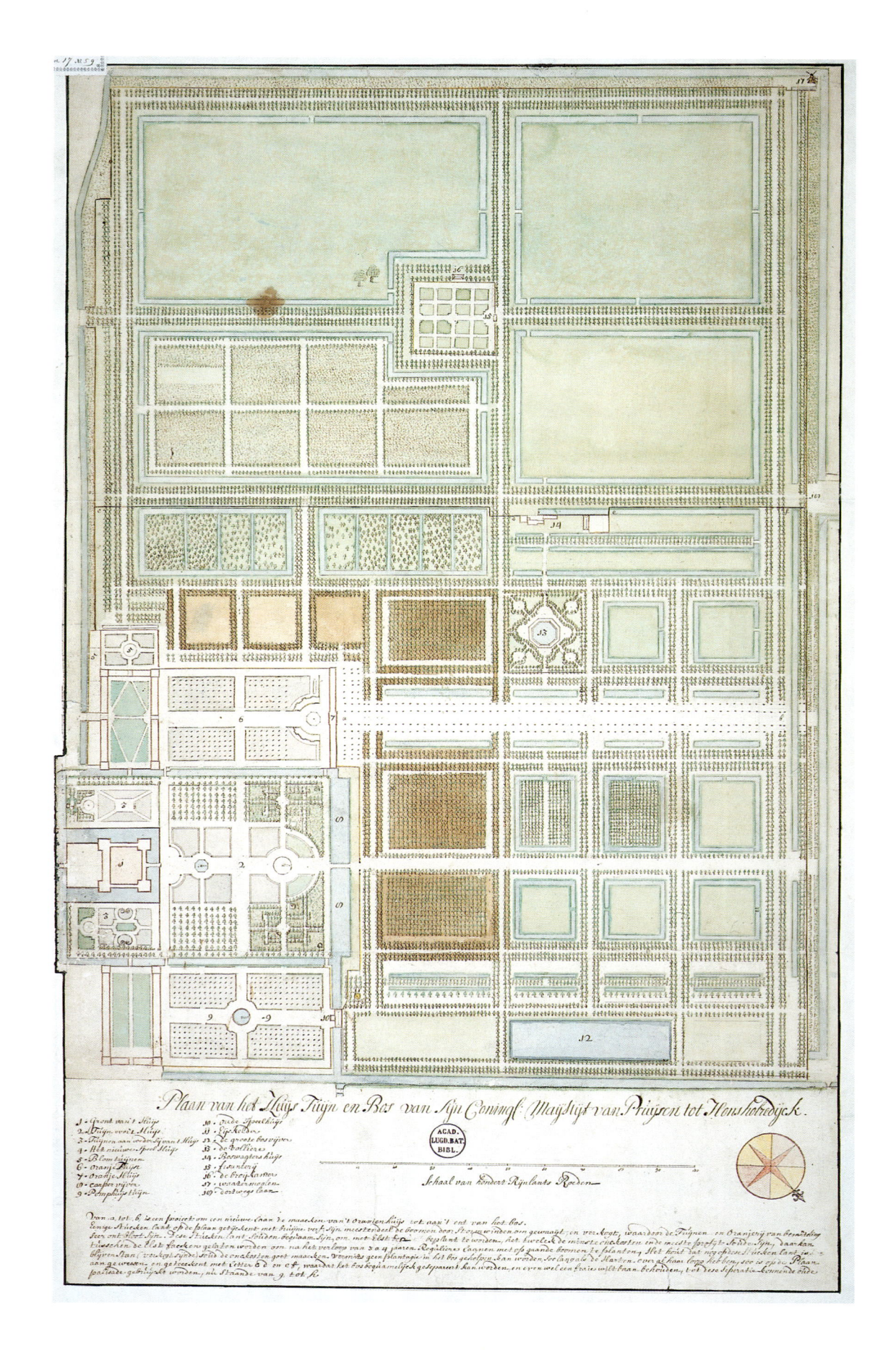

Map of Ter Nieuburch by Floris Jacobsz van der Sallem, c. 1630. ARA (see fig. 42)

Plan attributed to B. de Baes of Honselaarsdijk in the early eighteenth-century. CBN (see fig. 38) *(previous page)*

93. Plan by Pieter Florisz van der Sallem, 1645, of the Huis ten Bosch palace and garden complex, drawn after designs by Pieter Post.
Algemeen Rijksarchief

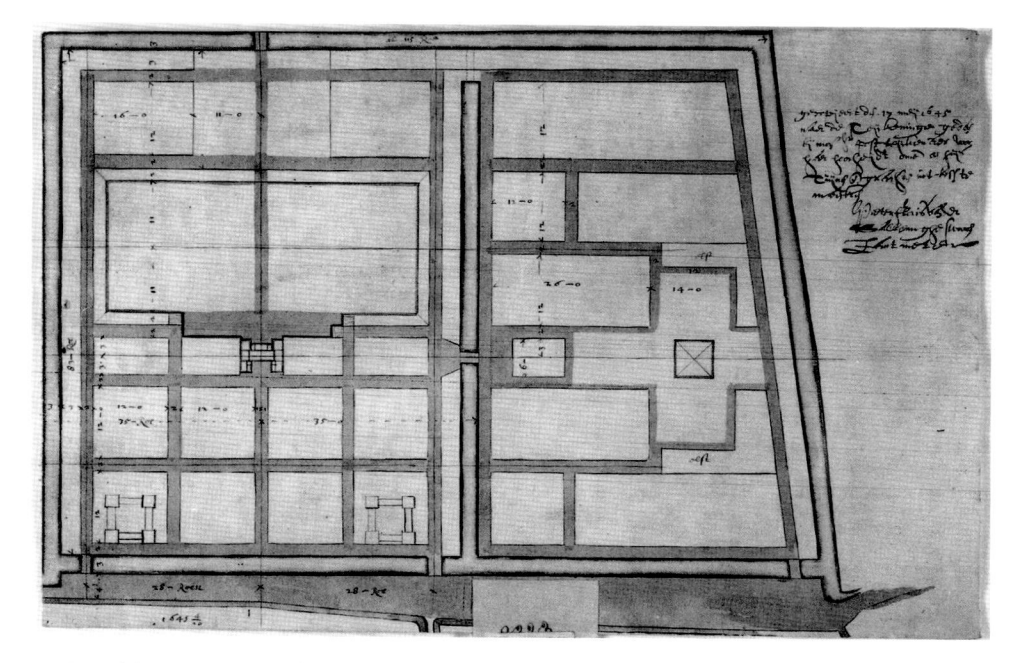

In addition to Honselaarsdijk and Ter Nieuburch, Amalia desired a summer retreat in the immediate vicinity of The Hague, and in 1645 the Chamber of Accounts granted her an uncultivated piece of meadow and duneland to the east of the Hague Woods, described as 'a tract of certain Alderwoods, meadow, lowlands, hollows and wilds, lying at the eastern end of the Haagsche Bosch on the north-west side of the Bezuidenhoutscheweg'.[57]

Thus situated behind the dunes on humid holm grounds, the terrain first had to be properly drained to provide for the layout of a garden. A map of 1645 by the land-surveyor Pieter Florisz van der Sallem after a design by the architect Pieter Post *(fig. 93)*[58] shows the early layout of the palace and grounds. The grounds follow a simple grid plan of squares and rectangles intersected by canals and paths. The whole area was divided into two large rectangular sections, separated by a canal. The first rectangular area comprised the palace proper and the main pleasure garden, the other, situated to the east, more orchards, meadows and woods. A letter to Amalia confirms that when Van der Sallem drew his plan the necessary works for the preparation of the garden had already begun:

> As soon as I arrived here I sent for Mr. Post, who arrived last Monday. Meanwhile I went to inspect the earth works on which the foremen are working hard at present and found everything in good order and well begun; also the surveyor Pieter Florissen [van der Sallem] is going to inspect the plot of the Elstslote [Alder stream] and will measure it as soon as the peat slush has been thrown out.[59]

The final layout of the gardens closely followed the original plan of Post and Van der Sallem, but the form of the palace itself was changed. Instead of a rectangular building with two projecting wings, a more centralized design with a cross-shaped hall was finally chosen by Amalia, as is shown by Post's later prints of the Huis ten Bosch *(figs. 94 and 95)*.[60] As can be gathered from a letter by Huygens, Frederik Hendrik also had strong opinions about the building design, and only after some initial doubt would agree to his wife's ideas, provided that the building remained simple.[61] Apparently these wishes were granted, for the palace, defined by its well-proportioned, unostentatious flat red brick façades, is relatively modest.

The complex seen as a whole, including the gardens, demonstrates the same sober character of a simple, well-balanced series of symmetrically arranged geometric blocks or

III. OTHER GARDENS

94. Pieter Post's bird's-eye view of the Huis ten Bosch, showing forecourt, lateral houses and main pleasure garden with octagonal pavilions behind the palace. Gemeentearchief, The Hague

'garden islands'. As such, the palace and garden reveal mathematical principles also employed by Post elsewhere, for example in the layout of the Vredenburg estate, consisting of a similar division in square plots divided again into smaller compartments. Like the building's façades, the garden of the Huis ten Bosch was decorated sparsely, mainly with *parterres de broderie* and some sculptures along the main axes. A good impression of the finished project is provided by Jan van der Heyden's paintings in the Metropolitan Museum of Art in New York and the National Gallery in London, showing the French-inspired arabesque parterre

95. Ground-plan of the Huis ten Bosch by Pieter Post, showing the division of house and garden in geometrically arranged blocks, held together by a system of axes.
Koninklijke Bibliotheek

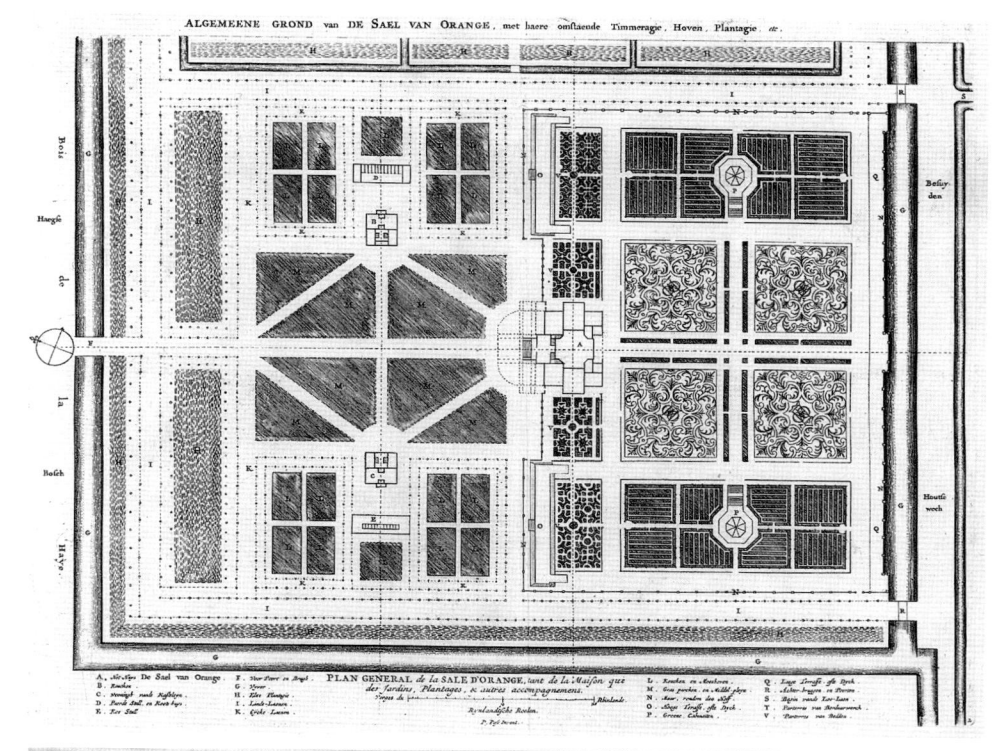

96. Garden of the Huis ten Bosch with *parterres de broderie* and classical statues lining the central axis, in a painting by Jan van der Heyden, c. 1668.
The Metropolitan Museum of Art, New York
see colour plate 14

designs adorned with classical sculpture and trellis-work obelisks *(fig. 96)*.[62]

There are closer similarities between house and garden, both in form and in content. The form of the centrally domed hall is reflected in the shape of the two pavilions flanking the main parterre garden behind the palace (P on Post's engraving). The decoration of this central hall, painted by the well-known artists of the day under the orchestration of Van Campen, extols the virtues of the Stadholder. This element of dynastic pride is continued in the decoration of the parterres centring on the monogram of Frederik Hendrik and Amalia, as in the garden of Ter Nieuburch. Standing in the central hall, looking through

III. OTHER GARDENS

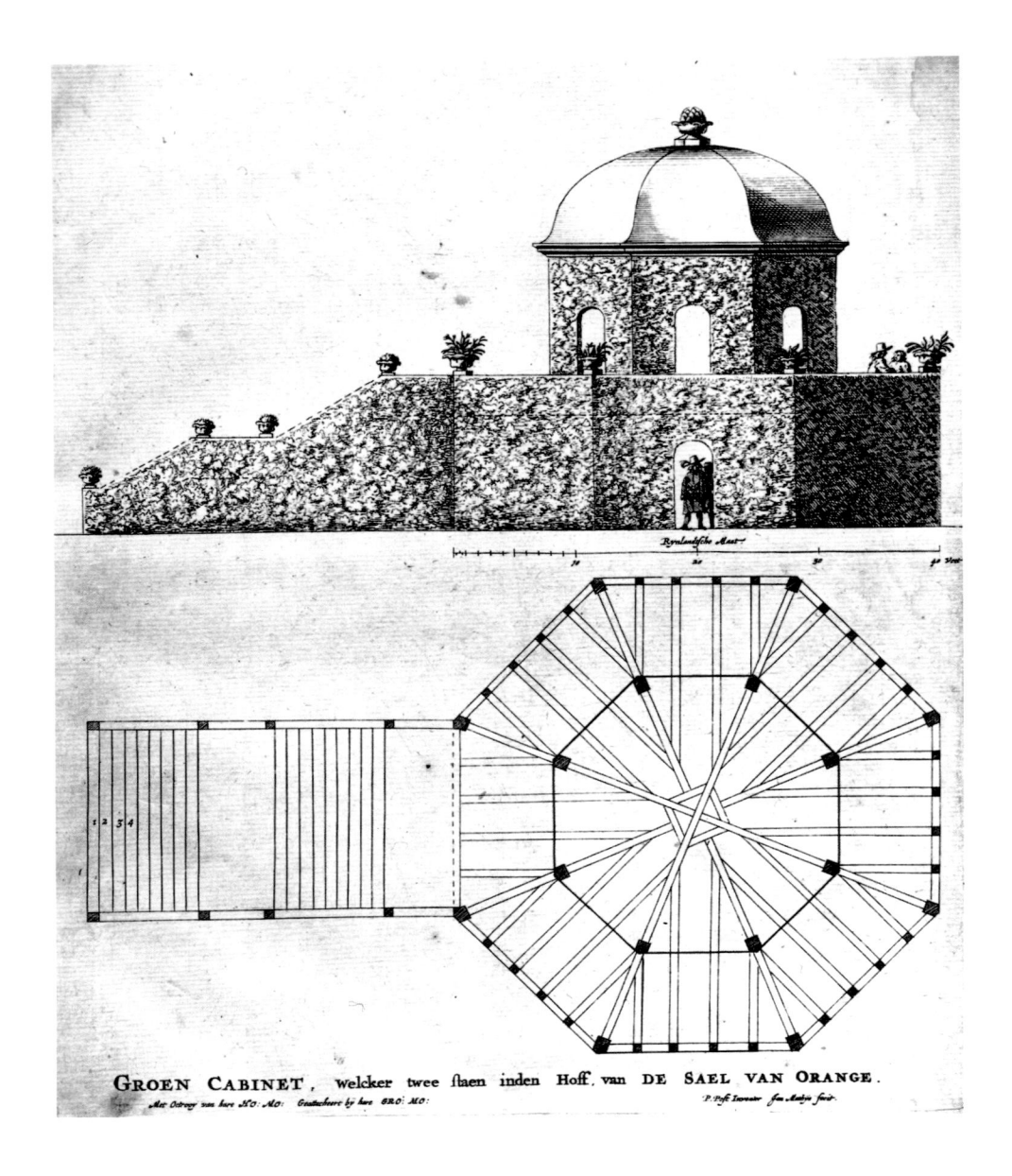

97. Print by Pieter Post showing the design for the ivy-overgrown, round pavilions in the Huis ten Bosch garden, reflecting the shape of its centralized dome.
Photo courtesy Utrecht University

the three large glassed terrace doors shaped like a triumphal arch, one could thus overlook the symbolic landscape of the garden ruled by the Orange family.

That such visual and iconological connections between palace and garden were clearly intended is further demonstrated by the dotted lines in Post's print, indicating the main transverse axes which connect house and garden. These dotted axes emphasize three main intersections in the total layout of the palace and garden complex, while the middle of the centrally-domed hall has been taken as the main vantage point. The house stands exactly in the middle of the open terrain so that the point where the terrace extends into the canal at the end of the rear parterre garden to the south and the point where the diagonally-cut lawn of the forecourt opens up to the north are equidistant from the centre of the hall. The same distance from the centre of this forecourt northward brings one to the main entrance gate of the property; thus, using the same module, one can dissect the whole layout of the garden.

The detailed arrangement and plantation of the garden are clearly indicated in the text on Post's print *(see fig. 95)*. After entering the grounds over a central bridge and passing

COURTLY GARDENS IN HOLLAND 1600-1650

through avenues of lime-trees and a plantation of alder-trees, one stood on the forecourt flanked by the kitchen building and stables. Behind these lay the kitchen gardens, encompassed by rows of oak-trees. From there diagonal paths led directly to the front entrance of the palace with its monumental staircase. The garden sections on either side of the palace contained flower- and herb-beds. The garden compartments nearest to the building were carefully enclosed within walls and conceived as *giardini segreti*. The outer compartments lay behind a high terrace or dike, from where the whole garden area could be overlooked. A similar high terrace or dike was thrown up at the rear of the main garden, which was surrounded by walls and rows of trees. The architecture of the garden as a whole, like that of Honselaarsdijk and Ter Nieuburch, can be defined by its enclosed character reminiscent of late-sixteenth-century garden-architectural principles, according to which each garden section is an important part of the whole, yet conceived as a separate entity.

Details of the parterre decoration can be compared with the parterres at Ter Nieuburch and Honselaarsdijk. Indeed, the style and decoration of the main parterre of the Huis ten Bosch, in simplified form, seem to be derived from those of the first parterre compartment in the garden of Ter Nieuburch, which, as mentioned above, also centred on the combined monogram of Frederik Hendrik (Henry) and Amalia (H.A.V.O.). It was painted no fewer than eight times in the cupola of the Huis ten Bosch and could also be found on the pulpit of the Honselaarsdijk chapel, thus constituting a powerful image expressed in various artistic media in the court residences.[63]

Since the parterres of Honselaarsdijk and Ter Nieuburch were designed by André Mollet, and given the fact that the parterres of the Huis ten Bosch were characterized by the same French arabesque motifs, it would seem possible that these parterres also were based on designs by Mollet. Whether Mollet made the designs while in Holland or whether the parterres were based on designs by Post inspired by Mollet is difficult to determine. Not without meaning is the fact that the same gardener – the Stadholder's gardener-in-chief Borchgaert Frederic, who worked at Ter Nieuburch during the 1640s – was responsible for the layout of the parterres at the Huis ten Bosch, as can be inferred from an entry in the records of payments stating that Borchgaert Frederic, gardener of Ter Nieuburch, was paid for the expenses of the parterres and borders in the 'hoff int haechse bosch', or Huis ten Bosch (993 fol. 428[vo]).[64] The gardener Isaac Leschevin, who worked together with Borchgaert Frederic and with him published the bird's-eye view of the Huis ter Nieuburch, may very well have been responsible for the trellis-work decoration, such as the obelisks, shown in Post's prints and Van der Heyden's paintings of the Huis ten Bosch.

The design of the Huis ten Bosch garden is also important for the way it was created, because it tells us something about the process and practice of garden design at the time. The plan by Pieter Florisz van der Sallem is proof of the important role of the land-surveyor in the process of laying out gardens. The involvement of a land-surveyor is not surprising in itself, given his special skills in measuring and mapping the grounds and his knowledge of drainage systems, which was the basis of every garden laid out in the Dutch lowlands. However, the garden layout of the Huis ten Bosch was the result of a direct collaboration between land-surveyor and architect, as can be deduced from the text on Van der Sallem's plan which states that it is a copy after a drawing by Pieter Post. The later print of the Huis ten Bosch shows that Van der Sallem's measurements and division of the plots intersected by the necessary drainage canals were closely followed. The architect Post was responsible for the further, mathematical and aesthetic layout of the compartments and their ornamentation, including hedges, arbours and pavilions. A detailed engraving showing the plan and elevation of the octagonally-shaped pavilions overgrown by ivy on either side of the main parterre garden was included in Post's print series of the Huis ten Bosch *(fig. 97)*.[65]

98. Plan of the gardens of the Huis ten Bosch by Daniel Marot, c. 1734, showing his partly executed design for the gardens in rococo style.
Gemeentearchief, The Hague

In the travel journal of the brothers Guido and Giulio De Bovio, written two years after Amalia's death in 1677, the palace and gardens of the Huis ten Bosch are described as follows:

> Il palazzo riguarda in un gran giardino per la parte di dietro, che è distinto in più compartimenti quadrati di fiori; nel mezzo vi sono 4 statue di pietra, e dalle bande per due scale si va ad altretanti padiglioni di verdura. Nel resto non visono nè acque, nè statue; ci mostrarono alcuni agrumi, che benchè piccioli, sono di molto pregio in queste parti. Il giardino è cinto di mura, et all'intorno ha un largo fosso d'acqua. L'ingresso della villa è delizioso per gli alberi ben disposti; e di qua e di là del detto palazzo vi sono due case uniformi, che servono per la commodità dei giardinieri e per li custodi di questo luogo delizioso.[66]

This description fits in all respects the depiction of the estate in the print series of Pieter Post, showing its unchanged form at the end of Frederik Hendrik's life and its lasting general appearance under Amalia. De Bovio mentions four stone statues in the middle of the garden – the sculptures standing on the central axis – but does not identify them. A closer look at Van der Heyden's paintings shows four tall figures clad in long tunics *à l'antique* which, though apparently stone statues, probably were of painted lead.[67] From the written and visual evidence at hand, it is difficult to identify the statues, even though two of the figures carry as attributes an urn and a cornucopia respectively, symbolizing Winter and Summer of the Four Seasons. Four other statues, which seem to compete with the classical ones in the garden, are life-size representations of the Princes of Orange,[68] described by De Bovio as '4 statue di marmo bianco alte al naturale, rappresentano altrettanti principi della Casa d'Oranges',[69] which lined the entrance staircase at the front of the building.

The palace and garden of the Huis ten Bosch survive today, albeit in altered form, as the residence of the Dutch royal family. The building's centralized form was changed by the early-eighteenth-century extension of the palace with lateral wings. The geometrical

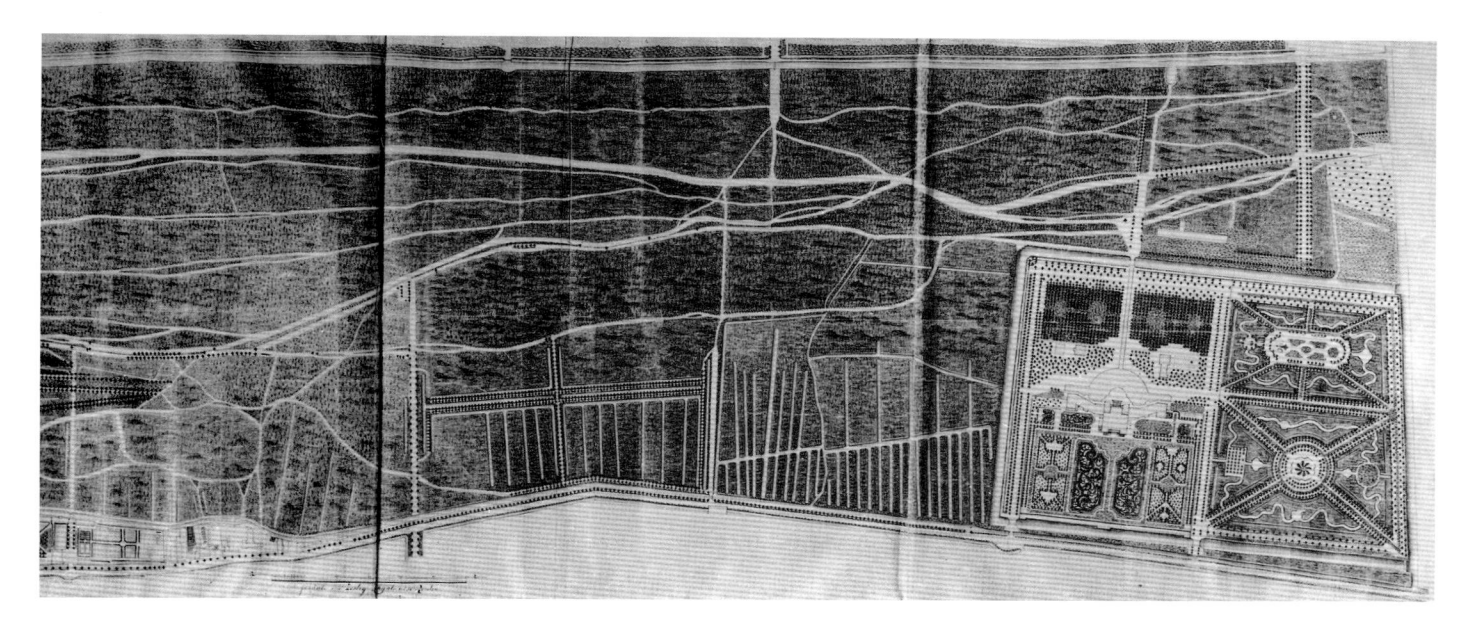

99. Plan of the Huis ten Bosch by Huybert van Straalen, 1778 (detail), showing gardens in the late picturesque style combining geometric and undulating landscape features.
Algemeen Rijksarchief

100. Plan of the Haagsche Bosch by Ary van der Spuij, showing the mid-nineteenth-century situation of the gardens of the Huis ten Bosch in landscape style.
Gemeentearchief, The Hague

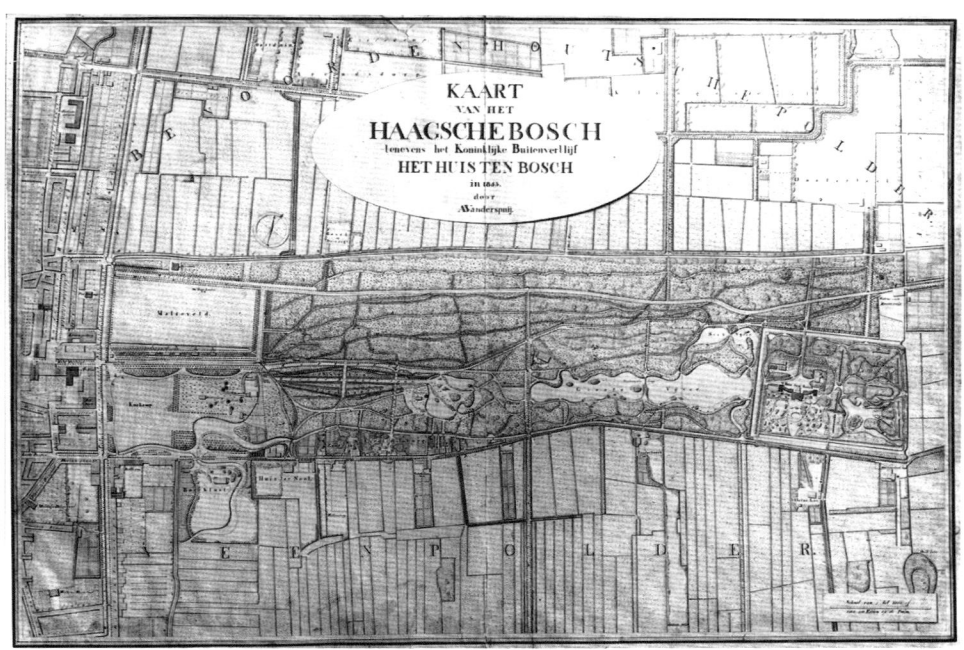

garden has disappeared, as the garden was modernized in the course of the centuries to fit the changing tastes. The earliest changes already occurred under Frederik Hendrik's grandson, Stadholder William III, from 1686 onward. He commissioned his friend, the well-known dilettante garden architect Philips Doublet, husband of Huygens's daughter Susanna and owner of the neighbouring estate Clingendael, to redesign part of the garden in the latest French style. Using André Le Nôtre's design for the parterre in front of the Orangerie at Chantilly as a model, Doublet redecorated the main parterre area behind the palace.[70]

In the first half of the eighteenth century no major alterations were undertaken, until the dispute with the King of Prussia concerning the inheritance of William III's properties was settled. After the Huis ten Bosch had been returned into the hands of the Orange family, and on the occasion of the marriage of William IV to Anna of Hanover in 1734, palace and garden underwent a complete renovation. Daniel Marot's monumental designs

III. OTHER GARDENS

for the garden date from this time *(fig. 98)*.[71] Marot's plan, characterized by the soft lines of the rococo style in garden architecture, for the first time shows an attempt to unify the two large, separated rectangular parts of the grounds. The main pleasure garden and the orchard garden to its east were to be connected by means of a huge, elongated basin. However, only part of Marot's design was executed – primarily the layout of the main garden and the addition of two wings to the palace.

A map of the area of 1778 by Huybert van Straalen shows the late-eighteenth-century layout of the garden and its situation at the eastern end of the Hague Woods *(fig. 99)*.[72] The main pleasure garden still echoes Marot's design for this garden section, while the other part to its east is conceived as a 'forest garden'. This section is laid out in what may be defined as a late example of the picturesque style, in that irregular landscape features are combined with traditional, formal shapes.[73] At the Huis ten Bosch the wooded area consisted of carefully arranged tree groups and shrubbery, cut through by diagonal avenues and undulating paths surrounding open areas with parterres.

In the early nineteenth century these last vestiges of the geometric garden design gave way to a new layout in the landscape style. The contemporaneous design by the landscape architect J.D. Zocher, recognizable in all its detail in a later map by A. van der Spuij *(fig. 100)*, shows the extension and modernization of the garden and the addition of a parade ground in front of the building.[74] The formal garden behind the palace and its larger eastern section were now joined to create a vast park with undulating paths and lakes, the layout of which still is the basis of the present-day garden park.[75]

THE BUITENHOF GARDEN

At the time Frederik Hendrik was laying out the garden at the Paleis Noordeinde, his brother Prince Maurits was working on the layout of a garden adjacent to the stadholderly quarters in the centre of The Hague. This was the garden called the Buitenhof (Outer Court), named after its situation adjoining the outside walls of the old court of the Counts of Holland, known as the Binnenhof *(see fig. 87)*. A closer look at this garden, which after Maurits's death in 1625 was finished by Frederik Hendrik, can contribute to a better understanding of the layout and decoration of Frederik Hendrik's other gardens at the Noordeinde, Honselaarsdijk and Ter Nieuburch.

Prince Maurits's building project, consisting of a 'Lusthuys met Gallerije' (pleasure house with gallery and garden), is clearly visible in a print by Hendrick Hondius published in his *Institutio artis perspectivae (figs. 101 and 102)*.[76] The new arcaded gallery, containing a grotto with waterworks and an aviary, opened on a walled-in, rectangular garden remarkable for its design with two large, circular *berceaux*. Hondius added a detailed description of the garden which, fifteen roeden and four voeten long by eight roeden and four voeten wide (circa 55 x 30 metres), contained four square arbours in the corners and four round ones in the middle, surrounding a central pavilion. This pavilion was decorated on the inside with *trompe-l'oeil* architecture and nature in the form of columns and foliage painted against a blue sky.[77] All the *berceaux* or leaf-covered walkways (*galderyen*) were made of green painted oak pillars, along which the foliage of beech-trees (*buken-boomen*) could grow. The opening within the two circular *berceaux* was decorated with *parterres de broderie*[78] encompassing a central, sculpturally decorated stone fountain. Eight large bronze urns made after the antique manner ('naer de maniere van de Anticquen') surrounded these fountains. Rare flowers, herbs and fruit-trees, including orange-trees, apples, figs, olives and laurel, were planted in rows of pots lining the circular *berceaux* and

101. Print by Hendrick Hondius, 1620, with orthographical overview of the Buitenhof garden, begun by Maurits and completed by Frederik Hendrik c. 1625, based on the perfect mathematical figures of circle and square.
Koninklijke Bibliotheek

102. Print by Hendrick Hondius, 1620, scenographic overview of the Buitenhof garden, showing the inner layout and decoration with two circular *berceaux* with central fountains and classical urns, designed in part by Jacques de Gheyn.
Photo Rijksprentenkabinet, Rijksmuseum, Amsterdam

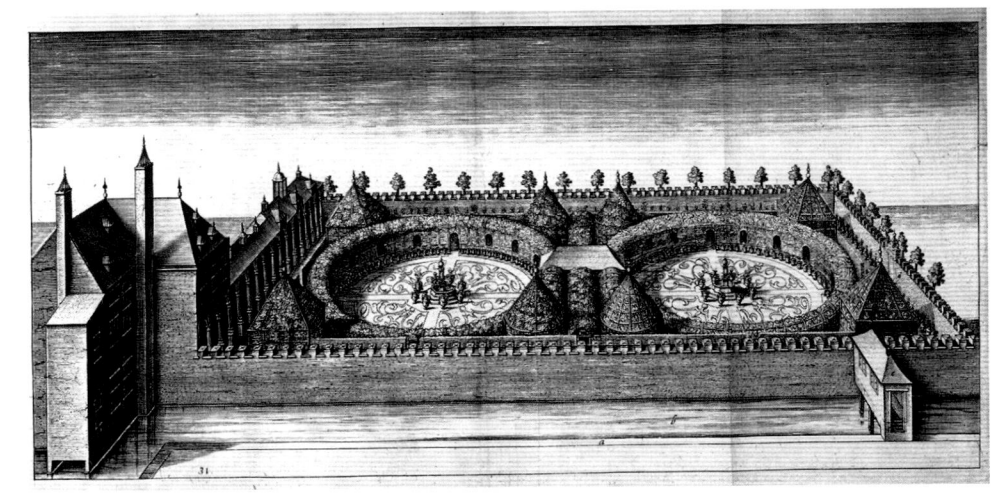

III. OTHER GARDENS

the garden wall. Finally, lime-trees were planted outside the crenellated garden wall to form a green screen hiding the lead roof and protecting the garden from cold winds. A later description of the garden in the verses of Jacob van der Does in *'s Graven-Hage, met de voornaemste plaetsen en vermaecklijkheden*[79] adds further information: apart from its many curiosities such as the costly decorated grotto and the exotic flowers, there was a tilt-yard inside the garden by the mid-century. While the characteristic outline of the two circular *berceaux* can be distinguished on most late-seventeenth-century maps, by the early eighteenth century the geometrical garden had been changed into a *palmasie of kaatsbaan*, an area for the game of pall-mall, according to the description of The Hague by Gysbert de Cretser.[80]

The form and decoration of the Buitenhof garden were considered important works of art at the time of Frederik Hendrik, and the garden was admired by Dutch as well as foreign visitors, among them John Evelyn, whom we encountered already in the previous chapter as the admirer of Ter Nieuburch's lime-tree plantation. Evelyn described the Buitenhof garden as 'full of ornament, close walks, statues, marbles, grots, fountains, and artificial music',[81] a description reminiscent of the *Wunderkammer*-like aspects of Amalia's garden at the Noordeinde. It is interesting that a dichotomy existed between the architectural form and the decoration of the garden and its grotto, defined as 'the final great illusionistic firework display of Dutch mannerism'.[82] The ornamentation of the garden was 'mannerist' – to use a rather flexible term in garden art, referring generally to a certain element of eccentric, refined artifice[83] – but when it comes to the structure of the garden, direct connections can be drawn between its design concept and classical architectural theory.[84] These connections with the classical past were already recognized at that time. For example, in his autobiography written between 1629 and 1631, Constantijn Huygens refers to the Buitenhof pleasure house and garden complex as 'a small villa in the city'.[85] Huygens's autobiography also provides further clues with respect to the designer of this garden:

> The proof [of such monumental building] one can find in the pleasure house, which he [Prince Maurits] had set within the garden [of the Buitenhof], and which also was designed by Ghein. Thereby [in designing this garden] he primarily relied on support from Ghein, who was not unwilling to refresh his own mind, tired out by more vigorous endeavours undertaken until then, by agreeing to do more enjoyable work in making decorations such as galleries, flower-beds, fountains and other fine things. He exerted himself for his master, who was not unthankful and knew how to reward him. And indeed, Ghein worked for a very high sum first for Maurits and afterwards for Prince Frederik Hendrik.[86]

From this passage one can conclude that 'Ghein', referring to Jacques de Gheyn II, was the designer of the Buitenhof's garden ornamentation, including the gallery holding the grotto and aviary, as well as its parterres and fountains.[87] A close friend of the Huygens family, de Gheyn, who came from a well-known Antwerp family and, like Hendrick Hondius, belonged to the cultural-artistic milieu of late-sixteenth-century Flanders, was a most versatile artist.[88] Famous for his miniature paintings and botanical drawings, at the end of his life de Gheyn apparently also took to architectural designs, of which the Buitenhof garden is proof.

Another remark in Huygens's autobiography should be mentioned here, since it provides a first clear insight into the relationship between Prince Maurits's gardens and those laid out by Frederik Hendrik. Huygens writes that before the work at the Buitenhof was finished, de Gheyn had died (1629) and his son Jacob, or Jacques de Gheyn III, completed his father's job which, according to Huygens, consisted in the very clever imitation of steep rocks standing in water 'after the example of the Italians'.[89] Huygens refers to the completion of the grotto work in the gallery of the Buitenhof garden where, supposedly, a semi-flat wall was covered with rockwork, fossils, coral and shells and set in a shallow water basin to make it look like a real grotto. The same impression of a grotto constructed as a wall-grotto made of rocks and shells fitted together is given by the description of the Buitenhof garden by the brothers De Bovio:

> Vedessimo però il giardino, ch'è molto galante. In esso vi è una grotta, fatta di rottami di pietre, che ben connessi assieme fanno una bella vista; più indentro vi sono due uccelliere grandi, in mezzo di ciascheduna delle quali vi è una fontana fatta a grottesco, che serve di ricovero agli uccelli, che bevono l'acque che cascano fra quei fossi. Nel mezzo vi è una gran pergola, dalla quale si va in certi ben aggiustati gabinetti, l'uno dei quali ha le pareti tutte ricoperte di conchiglie e di specchie.[90]

Further evidence concerning the design of the Buitenhof grotto is provided by two drawings by Jacques de Gheyn II, already discussed in chapter II *(see fig. 67)*, which show a wall with a mannerist rock landscape set in deep relief, including monsters, shells, coral and pumice-stone. Though the drawings relate to designs for a wall of decisively three-dimensional character with lively monsters, omitted in Huygens's and De Bovio's descriptions of the Buitenhof grotto, they generally have been identified as designs for the grotto of the Buitenhof garden.[91] Recently two other designs executed by de Gheyn and his son have been connected with the waterworks of the Buitenhof.[92] One drawing shows Neptune blowing on a conch, the other a fountain, the form of which seems directly relates to the forms of the fountains visible in Hondius's print, which were set in the parterres at the centre of the two circular *berceaux*. In view of de Gheyn's subsequent work for Maurits's successor Frederik Hendrik, similar designs may have been planned originally for the grottoes in Frederik Hendrik's gardens at the Noordeinde, Honselaarsdijk and Ter Nieuburch; they will be further discussed in chapter VI. If the Buitenhof grotto was executed exactly according to de Gheyn's design, it certainly constituted the most extensive, fantastic and stylistically most 'manneristic' of the series of grottoes the Oranges had built in their residences.[93]

Details of the gardens' decoration, including illusionistic paintings, waterworks and grottoes with artificial music, to all intents and purposes reflected the mannerist world of gardens in the late-sixteenth-century Flemish era, best represented by David Vinckboons's fanciful 'gardenscapes'[94] and, in some respects, Vredeman de Vries's garden designs. More specifically, connections can be made with contemporary grottoes and automata described by Salomon de Caus in his *Hortus Palatinus*, showing constructions in the gardens laid out at Heidelberg around 1620.[95] While its framework is highly classical, the decoration of the Buitenhof garden can be linked with the phantasmal, mannerist world of late-sixteenth- and early-seventeenth-century garden art, with strange ornamental grottoes and waterworks, where architecture touches upon alchemy, magic and science.

Another garden of the Stadholder, that of the Paleis Noordeinde, decorated with grottoes, sculpture and devices such as mirrors with optical effects, also reflected the idea of an enchanted, mysterious space first shown in the Buitenhof garden. In many respects, the Noordeinde and Buitenhof gardens, with their *giochi d'acqua*, grotesque figures and exotic vegetation, carried on the tradition of the great 'gardens of marvels',[96] where the garden and its galleries offered a means to display natural wonders, exotic rarities and precious antiquities in a carefully arranged 'natural' setting. To the most famous examples of such gardens at that time belonged, besides Pratolino's and Rudolf II's gardens at Prague, the gardens of Henry Prince of Wales at Richmond and Henry IV at Saint-Germain-en-Laye; the last one Frederik Hendrik knew well, both through his travels and from prints.[97]

From the description by De Bovio it can be inferred that at least until 1677 the *berceaux*, or *gran pergola*, as well as the connecting pavilion still existed in the Buitenhof garden. The pavilion was described earlier by Hondius as representing 'a starry northern sky', and De Bovio mentioned that it was decorated by shells and mirrors. According to de Cretser, the two *berceaux* and the central pavilion were demolished sometime in the early eighteenth century.[98] During the following centuries the Buitenhof garden and its surrounding area were gradually absorbed by the city. Until recently a parking lot, the space has now been taken up by government buildings in the centre of The Hague.

THE GARDEN OF THE PRINSENHUIS AT FLUSHING

The garden surrounding the Prinsenhuis at Flushing, or Vlissingen, should be reviewed briefly as the other important garden Frederik Hendrik inherited from his brother Prince Maurits in 1625. Like the Buitenhof garden in The Hague, the Flushing garden was characterized by a layout featuring the double circle of two large *berceaux*. Unfortunately, this important building and garden complex also no longer exists. A proper reconstruction is made difficult for lack of sufficient archival documentation, which was destroyed by fire in 1809.[99]

Originally built by Frederik Hendrik's father William I from 1580 onward, the Flushing house and garden were further enlarged and embellished by Prince Maurits about 1620. This date can be derived from the sparse archival sources in the Nassau Domains, including plans and records of payments. Of nine surviving drawings or plans for rebuilding the court or Prinsenhuis at Flushing one is dated 1617 and, significantly, according to the text on the map is made by Prince Maurits's architect-engineer Simon Stevin.[100]

As Hopper has shown,[101] Simon Stevin is of special importance for the development of garden architecture at the Dutch court.[102] In his publications on the ideal city, Stevin for the first time explained classical Italian principles advanced by Vitruvius and Alberti and adapted them to Flemish-Dutch circumstances.[103] Through his work, and that of Dutch engineers working abroad, the art of Dutch fortifications and architecture spread outside Holland, particularly to Northern Germany, Denmark and Scandinavia.[104] At the Dutch court, Stevin was tutor in mathematics to both Prince Maurits and Frederik Hendrik, instructing them, among other topics, on building according to classical rule.[105] He first worked for Prince Maurits and later for Frederik Hendrik, serving as an accountant and army engineer.[106] In fact, Stevin was still listed in Frederik Hendrik's records of payments during the early 1620s (1030 fol. XXXX^{vo}) and was later remembered by Huygens as 'unequalled in mathematics'.[107] He was regularly asked by the Stadholder to verify new inventions of measuring instruments, as well as to proofread various mathematical, mechanical and naval studies sent to the court to be granted publishing rights.[108] Even though no specific information as to his direct involvement with garden architecture at court has come down to us, his innovative ideas provided a direct impetus to the further development of geometric garden design. Actually, geometrical garden layouts such as those of Flushing and the Buitenhof at The Hague seem to carry his mathematical stamp.[109]

103. Plan, attributed to Simon Stevin, of the Prinsenhuis and garden at Flushing, with triangular labyrinth and rectangular section of eight compartments.
Algemeen Rijksarchief

III. OTHER GARDENS

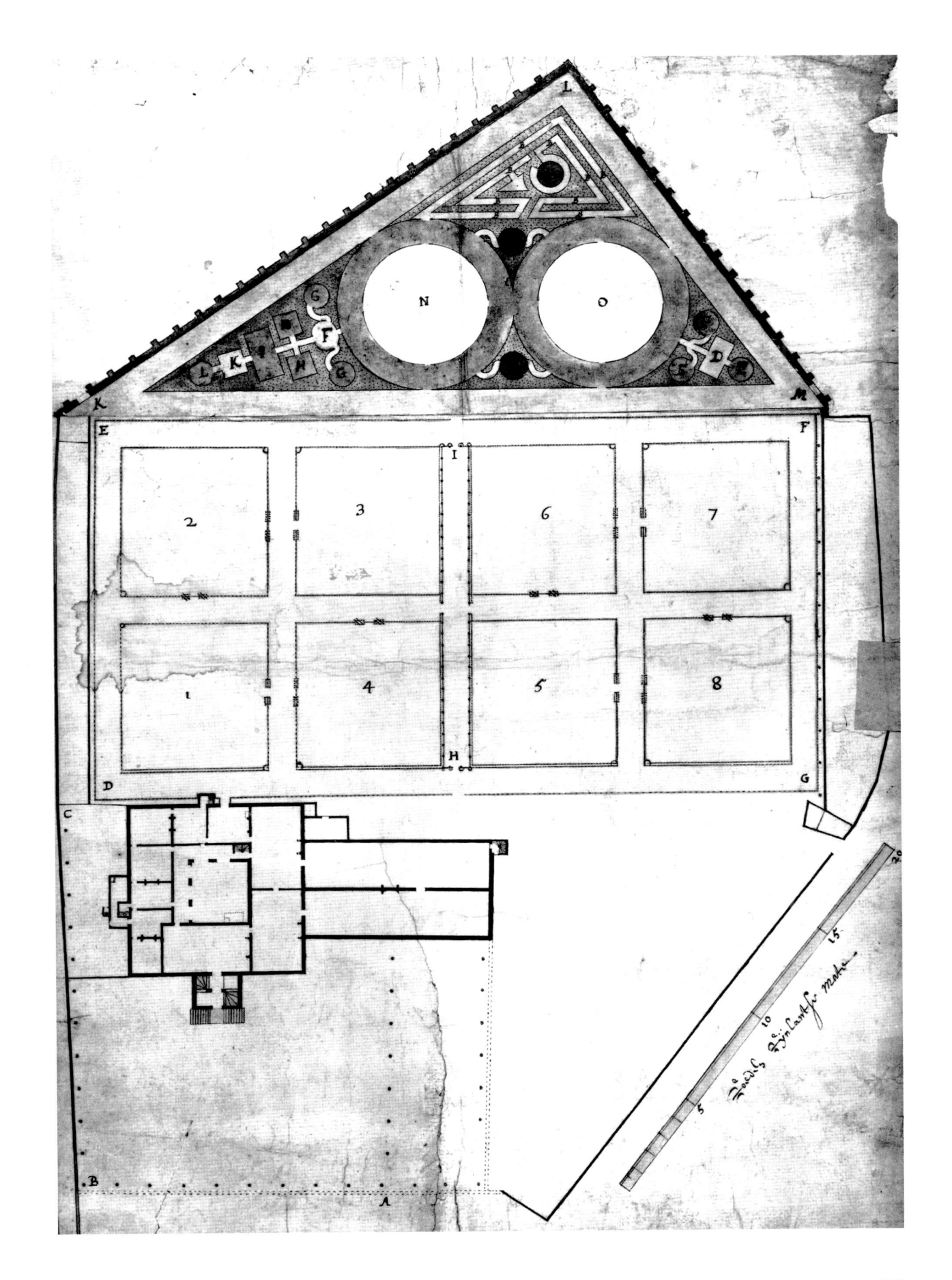

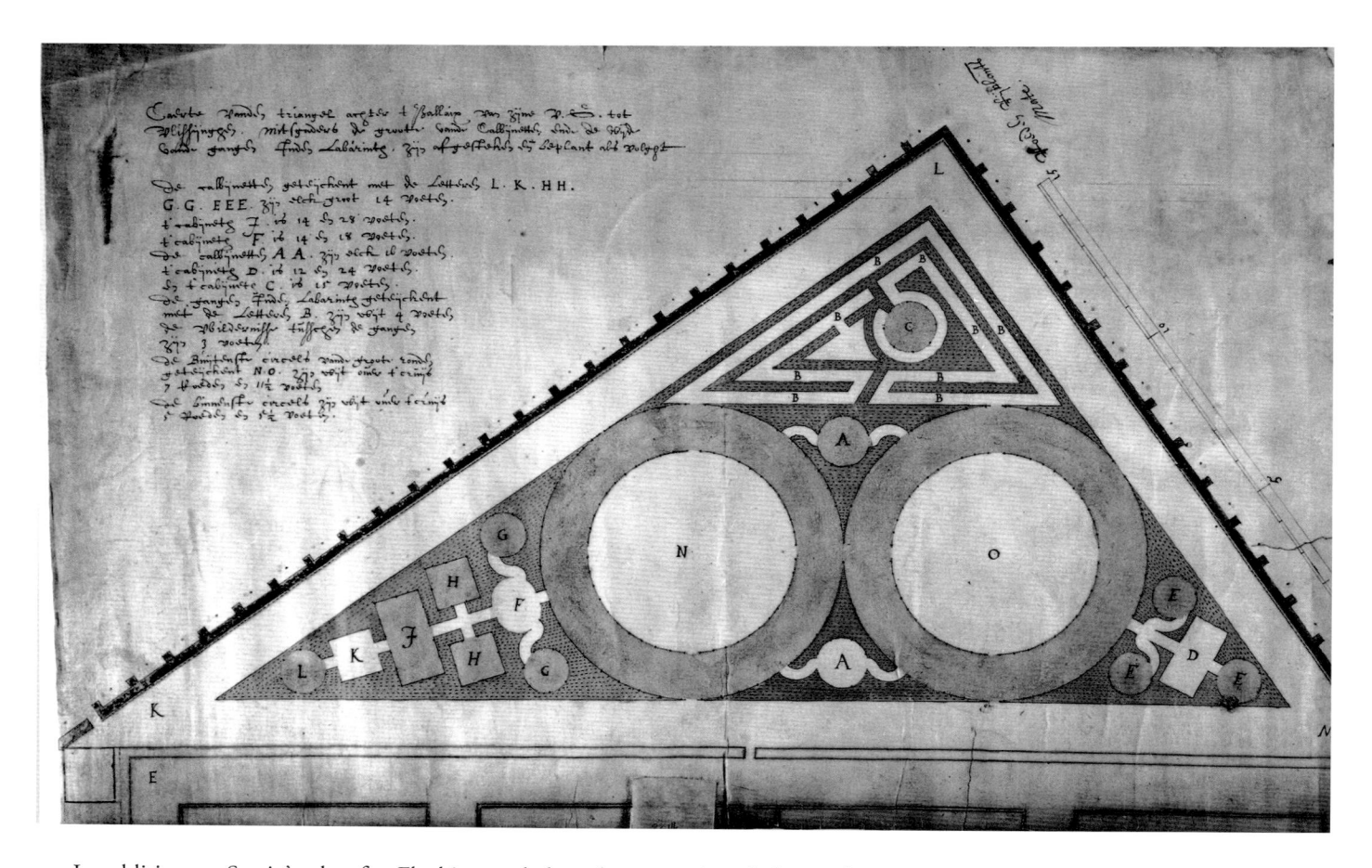

104. Detail of the triangular garden at Flushing, containing a labyrinth and two circular *berceaux* enclosed with crenellated walls.

Algemeen Rijksarchief

In addition to Stevin's plan for Flushing and the others mentioned above, there are accounts describing the purchase of fruit-trees and payments for further planting of the grounds which indicate that the garden of the Prinsenhuis was laid out between 1620 and 1626.[110] The other plans of the Prinsenhuis grounds, generally believed to be further elaborations of Stevin's original building project,[111] show that design ideas for the garden developed slowly during these years. Whether Stevin, who died in 1620, was originally involved in the design of the garden and therefore the author of its double-circle motif remains unclear. The garden's more exact layout, including the two joined circles, is found for the first time several years after Stevin's death, on two plans dating from 1623 and 1624 *(fig. 103)*,[112] one of which is attributed to the engineer Jacob Schoutens.[113] On the plan shown here a rectangular main parterre area can be seen, with behind it a triangular garden section, enclosed with a crenellated wall. This parterre area is divided into eight equally large square beds; the triangular garden section holds the two joined circles surrounded by small cabinets and a triangular labyrinth in the outer corners. A detailed overview of this rear garden section, appropriately called and indicated as the 'Triangel' on the seventeenth-century plan, is included among the series of plans of the Prinsenhuis *(fig. 104)*.[114]

While the general design of the garden had to be adjusted to fit Flushing's bulwarks (designed earlier by Stevin), the choice of this peculiar, triangular garden may also have been dictated by Prince Maurits's personal predilection for mathematics, particularly his fascination for the art of triangulation.[115] Maurits's interest in this branch of mathematics was shared by Simon Stevin, who describes trigonometry very thoroughly in 'Driehouckhandel', part of his mathematical work *Wisconstighe Ghedachtnissen* dedicated to Prince Maurits.

Though the square and later the rectangle were more suitable and generally preferred for garden designing,[116] the geometry of the triangle had a special fascination for several Dutch garden architects. Throughout the seventeenth century Dutch garden architects seem to have delighted in experimenting with various geometrical forms, following the contemporary credo advanced by the English gardener-botanist John Parkinson that 'every man will please his own fancie'.[117] Since many of the Stadholder's gardens and those of his courtiers, as we shall see, were based on some kind of geometrical form, it is of interest to note what the general opinion was about the ideal geometrical garden form at the beginning of the century. Parkinson, to take his remarks as an example, wrote:

> To prescribe one forme for every man to follow, were to great presumption and folly: for every man will please his owne fancie, according to the extent he designeth out for that purpose, be it orbicular or round, triangular or three square, quadrangular or foure square, or more long than brought. I will onely shew you here the severall formes that many men have taken and delighted in, let every man chuse which him liketh best, or may most fitly agree to that proportion of ground he hath set out for the purpose. The orbicular or round forme is held in its owne proper existence to be the most absolute forme, containing within it all other formes whatsoever; but few I thinke will chuse such a proportion to be joyned to their habitation, being not accepted anywhere I thinke, but for the generall Garden to the University at Padoa. The triangular or three square is such a forme also, as is seldome chosen by any that may make another choise, and as I thinke is onely had where another forme cannot be had, necessity constraining them to be therewith content. The four square forme is the most usually accepted with all, and doth best agree to any mans dwelling ...[118]

Ironically, it appears that the very geometrical forms which are described here as most unpractical for garden designing, the circle and the triangle, were chosen most frequently in the Dutch court environment. The role of the circle is discussed in chapter VI; here it should be noted that the triangle was the recurrent form for gardens at The Hague: Pieter Post's design for the Mauritshuis garden and the outline of Huygens's adjacent property were dictated by the triangle. Even later in the century the triangle was a popular feature of Dutch gardens; the most famous examples were the gardens of Gunterstein and the Hortus Medicus of Amsterdam.[119] Moreover, in the late seventeenth and early eighteenth centuries the triangle was recommended as the ideal shape for a garden in Pieter de la Court's treatise *Byzondere aenmerkingen*, which confirms the hold this geometrical form had on Dutch garden architecture.[120]

THE GARDENS OF BUREN

In 1629 Frederik Hendrik began work at Buren in order to restore and improve the old castle, as can be gathered from the accounts and ordinances of the Nassau Domains.[121] In addition to the restoration of the ancestral castle, the gardens also were enlarged and embellished, as can be inferred from payments to various gardeners for the delivery of trees in the years 1632 and 1633 (1042 fols. 253, 254, 254vo and 992 fol. 145). Most important for the aesthetic component of the gardens' decoration were payments to the French garden architect André Mollet in 1632 (2586 fols. 157-160) and 1633 (1042 fol. 232vo) for the layout of his highly intricate parterres made of boxwood, shells and little colored stones, like those at Honselaarsdijk.

Before the layout of parterres and the planting of trees at Buren could begin, part of the grounds was dug out to create new *dreven*, or drives (1039 fol. 273vo); the earliest references to them can be found in the accounts of 1629.[122] As these avenues were to run between the city of Buren and the castle, work on them was combined with the laying out of new pastures and orchards. The grounds were extended by the acquisition of an old orchard which was used in part for the construction of a large square in front of the castle (1039 fol. 272vo). This orchard was owned by the widow of the former steward of the Buren estate, Jacques van der Steene, who from 1627 onward had already received more than 50,000 pounds artois for expenses in connection with the work on the castle and grounds (1039 fols. 216, 216vo, 217, and 1040 fol. 211vo). In 1635 the deputy steward of Buren, Julius Sagemans, and the mason Jacob Outhamer received large payments for 'the improvements and repairs to His Highness's Castle and gardens at Buren', including improvements to the building at the entrance of the large pleasure garden, or 'grooten Thuin', as well as the house of the gardener above the castle's gate (1043 fols. 240-241).

More detailed information on the garden's inner appearance can be found from 1630 onward; it describes the clipping and binding of the beechwood *berceaux* in the large and small pleasure gardens ('grooten als cleynen lusthoff', in 2584 fols. 111-113vo). Important for the 'sylvan' appearance the Buren gardens must have had was the acquisition by the gardener Andries Hoorendonck of large amounts of laurel or bay-trees, beech, elm and lime-trees from 1630 onward. Supplemented on a regular basis until 1650 with new deliveries under the gardeners Willem Cornelisz van der Stoop (2590 fols. 130-131vo) and Reyer Langelaar (2594 fols. 121vo-123), these trees were planted on the ramparts and along the monumental entry avenues, which needed constant care. In 1633 no fewer than one thousand young shoots of alder-trees were paid for to replace the woods cut down in the previous year (2587 fols. 153-155). To these common trees, special fruit-trees, including apricots and peaches, as well as dwarf trees (*arbres nains*), were added in later years, as is shown by the accounts of 1638 (2591 fol. 148) and 1640 (2593, fols. 147-148vo) under gardener Simon Langelaer and in 1641 under Reyer Langelaer (2594 fol. 121vo-123).

Important information on the artistic rather than vegetational component of the Buren garden can be found in the entry of 1632, which describes the completion of a new gallery in the small pleasure garden ('nieuwe galerie inden cleynen Lusthoff'), for the decoration of which the painter Andries Andriesz Boscoop recieved 290 Carolus guilders (2586 fol. 159vo). A description like that is especially noteworthy because it shows the use and display of other media in the garden. The presence of such a painted gallery is reminiscent of the gallery of the Noordeinde, as well as that of the Buitenhof, at The Hague, which provide a place for exhibiting sculpture and rarities while at the same time forming a convenient spatial transition between building and garden.

A second building activity, with further improvements to the castle and grounds, took place about ten years later. Most of the records of payments for these improvements date from this time, including the further inner decoration of house and garden.[123] Both projects involved the Stadholder's architects at The Hague: Jacob van Campen for the early building activities and Pieter Post for the later ones.[124] As usual, all building activities were closely examined by the Prince himself, who in the summer of 1636, accompanied by Constantijn Huygens and Jacob van Campen, visited the castle to inspect the work on buildings and grounds and to discuss further improvements.[125] By 1642, when the gardens were completed and must have reached their full-grown appearance, Frederik Hendrik proudly showed his Buren property to Henrietta Maria, Queen of England, who, after having admired the gardens of Johan Wolfert van Brederode at Vianen, now had an opportunity to see the 'grand Jardin de Buren' as well, as Huygens wrote.[126]

The general appearance of the Buren gardens by the mid-1630s can be seen on a little-

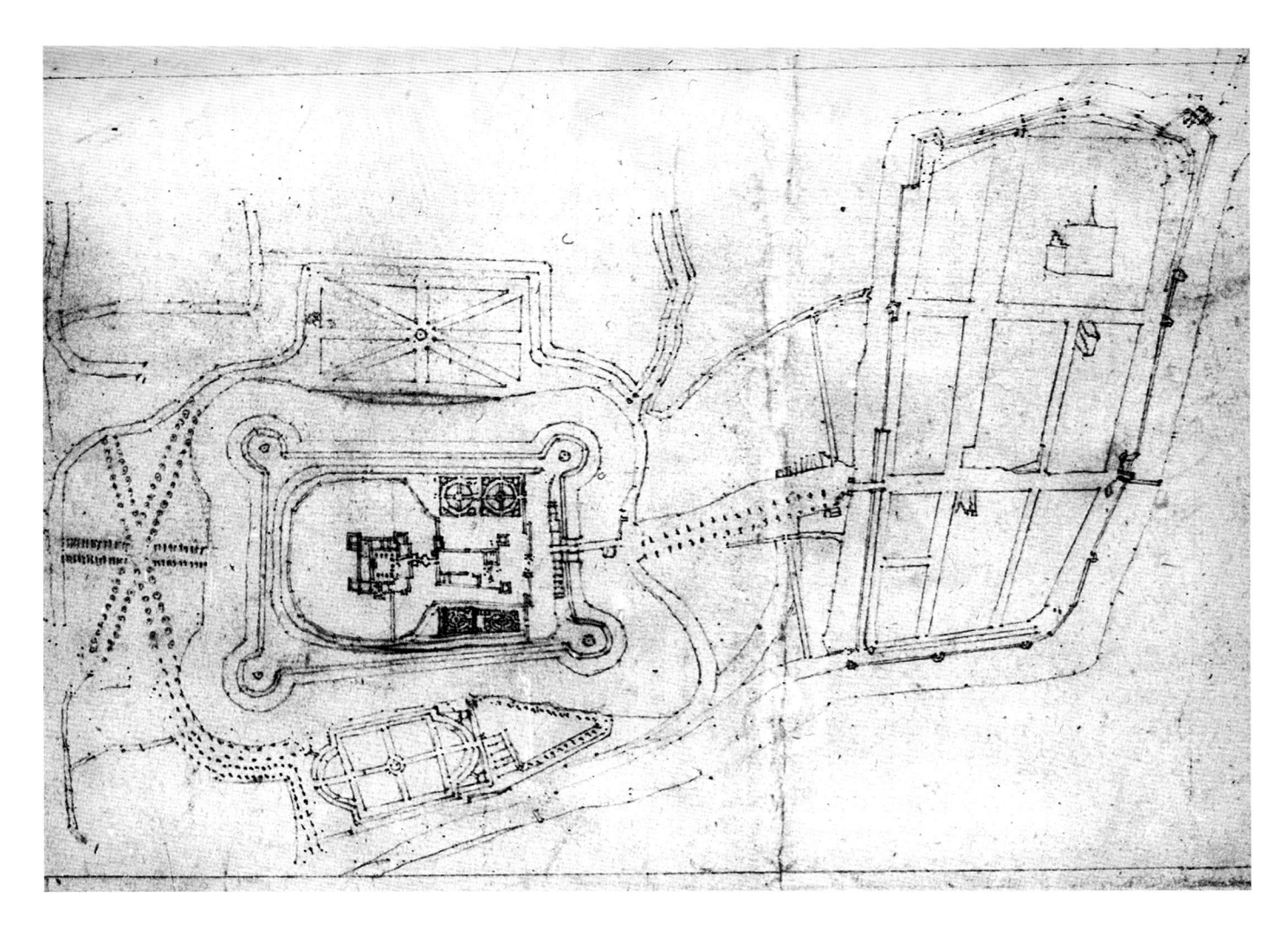

105. Plan of the castle of Buren in the map book of Johan Maurits van Nassau-Siegen, c. 1635, with layout of gardens on and off the island and repeated use of circle motifs.
Koninklijk Huisarchief

known map kept in the Koninklijk Huisarchief. The map book in the archival records of Johan Maurits van Nassau-Siegen entitled *Niederländische Fortificatien, Holländische Militaria* contains a hand-drawn plan of the castle of Buren *(fig. 105)*.[127] While the maps in this book were made for military purposes – to show the layout of the castle and the fortifications of the city in order to study their strategic defence[128] – the map depicted is of special art-historical value because it is a precise rendering of Buren's garden layout. It is not dated, but some of the other maps are – in verso, between 1630 and 1633, when the map of Buren, stylistically similar, must also have been drawn. Comparisons between the visual evidence on the map and archival information corroborate this dating.[129]

On the map one can recognize the city of Buren, with its simple grid plan and the church to the right, while the rectangular area of the fortified castle with its four round ramparts is situated to the left or west of the city. The castle is built in the water and the ramparts themselves are also surrounded by a moat or ring of water, called *ringgracht*. The gardens were laid out on the castle island as well as on the grounds of the mainland or outer banks flanking it. Avenues of trees planted radially stretch behind the castle complex and continue the axis formed by the approach avenue which leads from the city to the castle's ramparts. On either side of the castle island, on the mainland, there is a large, rectangular garden section. The one to the north looks like an area planted with hedges or possibly parterres, divided by diagonal paths. The garden area south of the castle complex has the form of a hippodrome, or a square with apsidal ends, and is divided into four sections

III. OTHER GARDENS

centring on what seems to be a fountain. Considering the layout of this hippodrome-shaped area, traditionally planted with low vegetation, this garden space may very well have been decorated with parterres. However, part of the function of this garden section may also have been that of a racetrack (*renbaen*), as can be inferred from descriptions of the Buren garden in the accounts.[130] Be that as it may, these two garden areas on either side of the castle must be the ones laid out by Mollet, given the fact that Mollet was paid for laying out two parterres on both sides of the Buren castle ('pour les parterres du Chasteau de Buere qui sont aux deux costez') in 1633.[131]

For the planting of these gardens on the *wallen*, or banks, of the Buren castle the gardeners Anthony Jansz Backer and Andries Hoorendonck, as well as Johan ter Borch, secretary of Buren, were reimbursed in the spring of 1640 (992 fol. 378). Concurrently, the city's master carpenter was paid for building a wooden fence or balustrade at the foot of the west bank (992 fols. 370, 443), and the gardener Willem Cornelisz van der Stoop was paid more than 100 guilders for the delivery of beech-trees, rose-bushes, peach-trees and strawberries to be planted in the *renbaen* as well as in the 'Great Garden' and the garden 'on the embankments' of the castle (992 fol. 417).[132] Several other entries, dated 1640 and 1647, discuss the planting of flowers in this *renbaen* (992 fol. 417) and the building of a new bridge behind the castle of Buren (993 fol. 462[vo]).

Interestingly, much of the plant material in the gardens of Buren was shipped from Honselaarsdijk. Besides the local gardener Abraham Blerisse (1042 fol. 253), Gijsbrecht Thonissen, gardener-in-chief at Honselaarsdijk, was involved in handling part of the new plantations at Buren (1042 fol. 254[vo]). First a large quantity of fruit-trees, such as cherry, pear, peach and apricot, was brought from Honselaarsdijk to Buren (1042 fols. 253, 253[vo], 254[vo]), together with several wagonloads of trees and shells (1042 fol. 253[vo] and 1041 fol. 251[vo]). In addition to these fruit-trees, the rarer fig-tree (1042 fol. 254) was planted in the gardens of Buren.

When it comes to the design of the garden, the most interesting sections at Buren were those laid out on the castle island itself. On either side of the forecourt one can recognize a rectangular garden divided into two squares with inscribed circles. Though the southern garden area appears to be somewhat squeezed due to the lack of space in this corner, the circles are still clearly visible on the map. In both gardens the circles, most likely again circular *berceaux*, have round pavilions in the four outer corners, but apparently lack a pavilion in the centre. Though it is difficult to distinguish all the details on this very finely-drawn map, the two squares containing the circles seem to be divided by a path, or maybe a transversely placed, tunnel-shaped *berceau*. Whatever the exact appearance may have been, it is significant that the twin-circle motif again features in the Buren garden and that this now familiar motif was used not once but twice.

By 1640 the cabinets and *berceaux* must have been old enough to need major repair. The master carpenter Cornelis Vermeulen was paid the sum of 378 guilders 11 stuyvers for 'the welding of the decayed arches and poles of the *berceaux* in the gardens around the house of Buren' (992 fol. 447). Repair was needed again seven years later, when Vermeulen received 725 guilders for 'all the repairs in the gardens of Buren, including the Galleries and Cabinets of His Highness's Pleasure grounds' (993 fol. 461).

The gardens with their circles have long since disappeared. The Buren castle and its gardens were demolished in 1804, leaving only meagre fragments including a few columns and parts of the old fortified walls. The original location of the castle and its grounds can be recognized in the rectangular open space used for recreation today, while parts of the ramparts serve as a cemetery.[133] Significantly, comparison of their names reveals that many of the architects, gardeners and workmen responsible for the layout and upkeep of Buren's

106. Map of the Breda castle and garden complex called the Valkenberg, from Joan Blaeu's *Toonneel der Steden*, 1649. Photo courtesy Gemeentearchief Breda

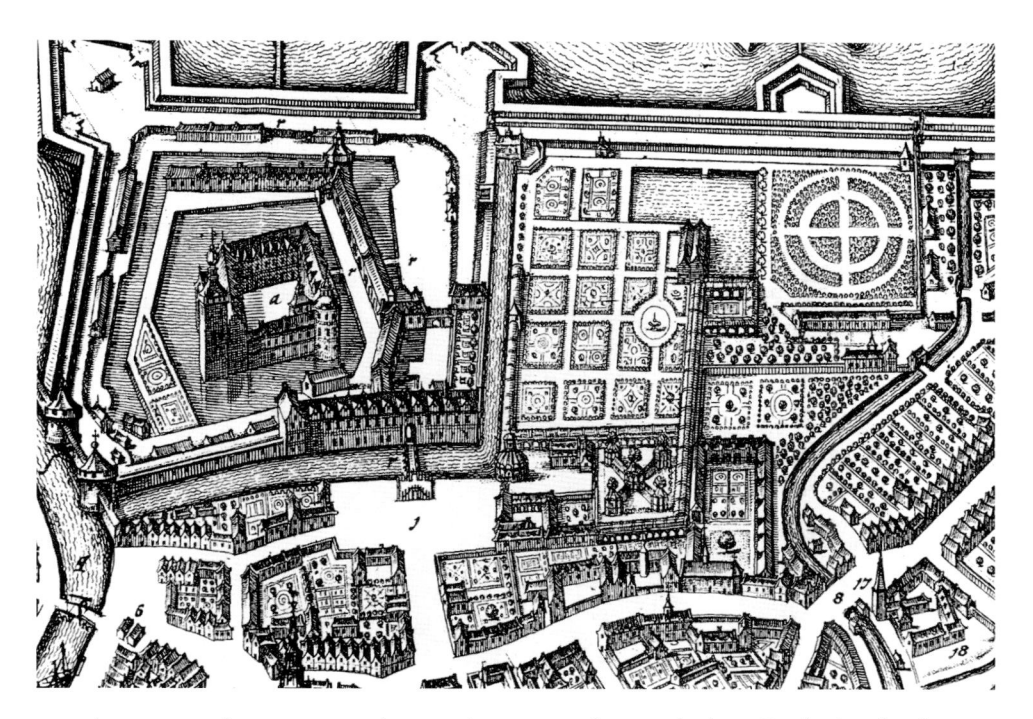

grand seventeenth-century gardens and avenues also worked at Breda in the famous Valkenberg park, part of which still survives today.

THE GARDENS OF BREDA

The castle and garden of Breda, in the south-east of Holland in the province of Brabant, hold a central position in the history of the Republic as the southernmost estate owned by the Orange-Nassau family. From this most strategically placed 'Orange stronghold' the Stadholder started his military campaigns, and here, in the gardens of the Valkenberg, he used to take a rest from the battlefield. On various occasions the Valkenberg garden became a battlefield itself, as attacks were launched from its entrenchments. Later, the Valkenberg would regain its traditional place as a realm of peace, when political agreements were settled at Breda in the garden's green pastures. Easily the most 'historic' of all the stadholderly gardens, it was here that Charles II, King of England, took up residence in 1660, and here, a mere seven years later, the peace treaties following the Second Anglo-Dutch War were negotiated.[134] What is more, it was presumably in the Valkenberg garden that Frederik Hendrik and Amalia first met during one of the outdoor parties held in honour of Friedrich V, Elector Palatine, and Elizabeth of Bohemia.[135] Situated to the east of the Breda castle and surrounded by the city's bulwarks, which were only dismantled in 1870, the garden with its originally fourteenth-century layout, its outline, form and function underwent many changes. Until 1882 the official property of the House of Orange, the Valkenberg is now a public park based on the form of a late-nineteenth-century landscape park measuring circa seven hectares, or about twenty acres.[136]

Only scarce information is provided by the archival records of the Nassau Domains on the history of the Breda gardens. However, a reconstruction is possible by linking this information to source material gathered in other archives. Thus, important documentation in the Municipal Archives of Breda, newly-recovered visual evidence in the Koninklijk Huisarchief and the Bodel Nijenhuis Collection combined with

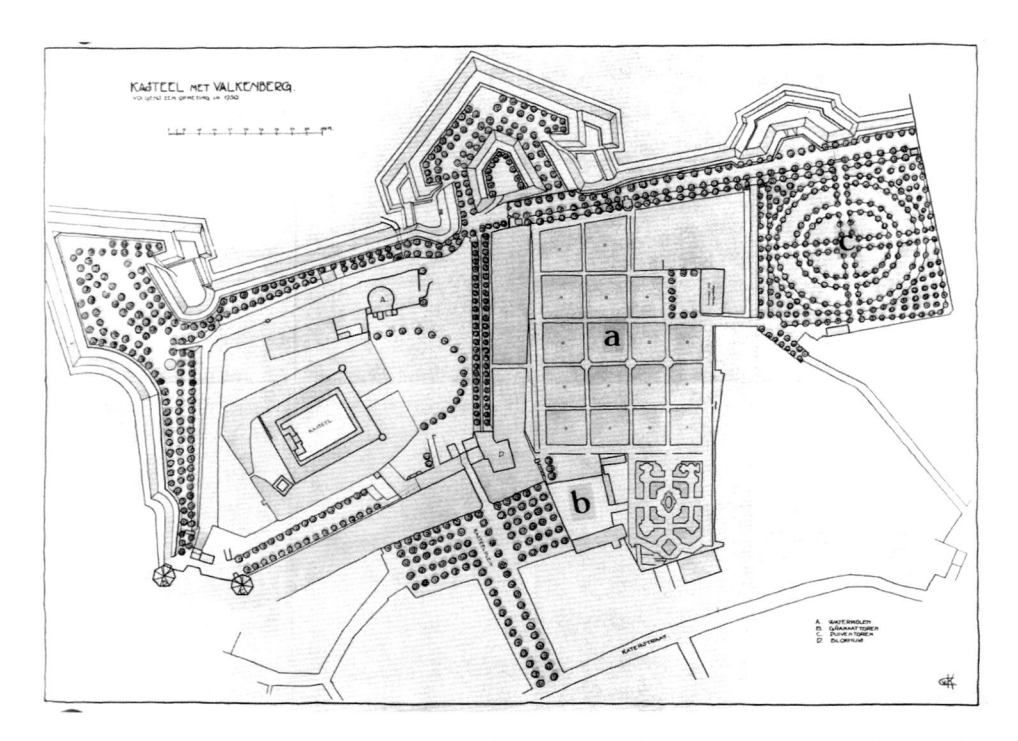

107. Detail of the Valkenberg gardens (right) at Breda, containing (a) the main parterre garden, (b) the courtyard garden, (c) circular wooded area.
Bibliotheek Landbouwuniversiteit, Wageningen

descriptions in seventeenth-century travel journals and current literature,[137] provide a clear picture of the seventeenth-century history of the Valkenberg garden.

To begin with, the visual evidence offered by a few contemporary maps of the province of Brabant makes it possible to obtain a general impression of the situation of the house and garden under Frederik Hendrik. A map published by Joan Blaeu in 1649 in *Toonneel der Steden (fig. 106)* showing the earlier situation of palace and garden of about 1625 provides an overview of the layout of the area shortly before the Stadholder's improvement of the grounds. Unlike the gardens of Honselaarsdijk and Ter Nieuburch, those of Breda had no direct relationship with the castle. As is most often the case with old fortified castles, its gardens were situated on the mainland to the east, separated from the castle proper by an agglomeration of buildings and several *fosses* and canals. The garden is still known as the Valkenberg, a name borrowed from an adjoining parcel of land with a falcon-house dating from the early sixteenth century.[138]

Already described in the sixteenth-century travel journal of the Bishop of Acqui as 'eminently graceful gardens',[139] in the beginning of the seventeenth century the Valkenberg garden consisted of three main parts *(fig. 107)* – a large parterre area (a), south of it a section containing the stables, several small courtyards and the lime-tree garden (b), and to the north-east a square wooded area (c), separated from the parterre garden by a large L-shaped fish-pond. The gardens were surrounded by other planted areas, incorporating gardens of the neighbouring residences the Begijnhof and the Capucijnenhof, which were acquired in the late seventeenth and the late nineteenth century, respectively, and still are part of the Park Valkenberg as it survives today.[140]

A detailed study of Blaeu's map *(see fig. 106)* shows that the parterre garden consisted of a checkerboard arrangement typical of sixteenth-century garden layouts. It was divided into seventeen square plots, each of which contained, possibly already at the time of Frederik Hendrik, a centrally-placed statue clearly visible in later representations of the garden.[141] The earliest mention of flower and grass parterres decorated with sculpture date back to the sixteenth-century journal of the Bishop of Acqui. The separate square wooded area to the north-east was characterized by two concentric circular paths cut through by

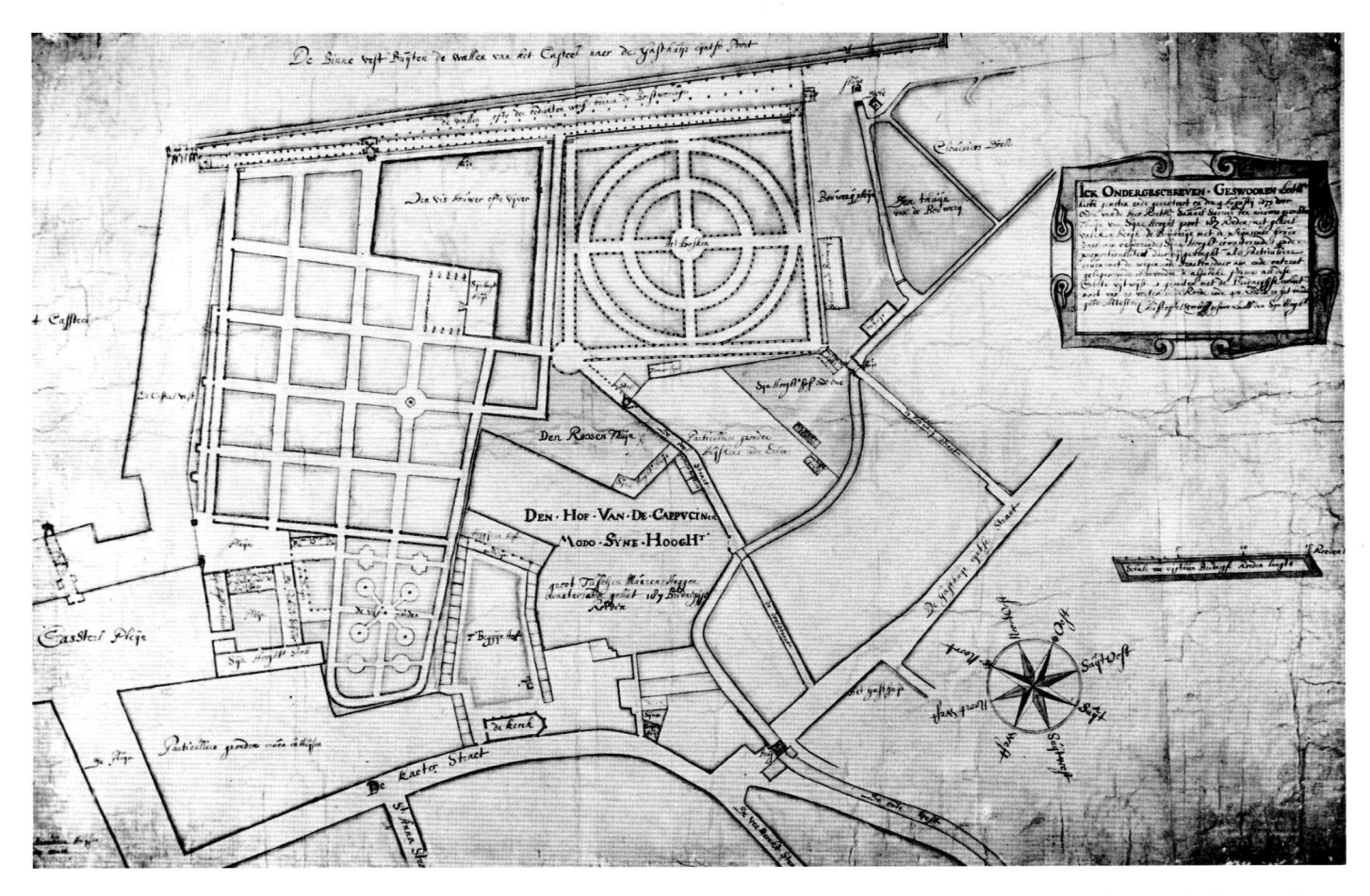

108. Plan of the Valkenberg gardens at Breda by Christoffel Verhoff, 1679, showing parterre garden, fish-pond and wooded 'Bosken' with circular paths.
Photo courtesy Gemeentearchief Breda

crossroads and known as the little wood, or 'Bosken', also referred to as the 'Warande' or 'Labyrinth'. The large fish-pond dates from the sixteenth century, for it was cleaned and restored in 1610.[142]

For a proper survey of the Valkenberg's seventeenth-century layout it is useful to compare Blaeu's plan from the first quarter of the century with a detailed plan from the last quarter. This plan by the land-surveyor Christoffel Verhoff, signed and dated 1679 *(fig. 108)*,[143] clearly shows the situation and layout of the Valkenberg grounds during Frederik Hendrik's reign and shortly before further improvements were undertaken by his grandson William III, who extended the gardens by incorporating the adjoining parcel of the Capucijnenhof in the south-east corner of the property. Though Verhoff was commissioned to draw his plan in order to show the newly-proposed extension of the surface area with the Capucijnenhof parcel (indicated on the plan as measuring 187 Bredase roeden), he added several other details, most remarkably 'den Roosen Thuijn', or rose garden, at the centre of the plan below the circular 'Bosken'. To the east of this little wood and bordering the Cloverniers Doelen, the Valkenberg's agricultural section with orchard and kitchen gardens is indicated on the plan as 'Den Thuijn van de Bouwerij', or garden of the farm. The buildings in the garden still include the house near the fish-pond, indicated on Verhoff's plan as 'Sijn Hooghts Huys', or His Highness's House, also known as the House of Pergamont after the chamberlain of Hendrik III of Nassau (1483-1538).

For the upkeep and good repair of such an extensive area, containing pleasure gardens with *berceaux* and parterres as well as orchard and kitchen gardens to provide fruit and vegetables, several gardeners were required. A rare survey of all the head-gardeners who were hired for the Valkenberg gardens from 1560 to 1770 and their respective instructions

III. OTHER GARDENS

is provided by a Registry kept among the collection of documents of the Nassau Domains in the ARA.[144] Among the items in this Registry, the *Letter of Instruction for the gardener Andries Hoorendonck at Breda (see Appendix, Document VII)*,[145] dated 16 April 1621, should be singled out as the oldest surviving document detailing the rights and responsibilities of the gardeners at the Dutch court. As can be determined from this letter, the gardeners received their instructions from the estate steward, a certain Balthasar Baldi called 'Directeur van den Hof van Valkenberch', and a Mr. Willeboorts, the general *controlleur*, or technical supervisor, of the buildings, woods and plantations of the Breda domains.[146] Given the importance of this document, a few remarks are in order, as they pertain to the early history of the Valkenberg.

Firstly, in Hoorendonck's Letter of Instruction the gardener was urged to put his greatest effort to perfecting the 'sieragien, plantagien ende culturen' (ornaments, plantations and cultures) in the garden, referring respectively to the ornamental flower-beds, the avenues and *berceaux*, and the orchard and kitchen garden in the adjacent farmland or *bouwerije* outside the garden proper, or 'buyten het parck gelegen'. The gardener was not permitted to sell the fruit of the orchard for his own profit but had to reserve it for use by His Sovereign Grace (Prince Maurits and, from 1622 onward, Frederik Hendrik). However, some exceptions to the rule were granted in case of the absence of His Grace and after the Governor of Breda, Justinus van Nassau, and the concierge had received their due portions of the best fruits and herbs. Then, depending on the surplus of fruit and its susceptibility to rotting in the summer heat, the gardener could sell the remainder, provided he kept an exact account of the sale to the best profit of His Sovereign Grace.

Hoorendonck – who also took care of the gardens at Buren, according to the account books of the Nassau Domains over the years 1638-40 (992 fols. 187, 313b, 378b, 386, 388) – received a yearly income of 300 Carolus guilders. The salary having been raised from 150 guilders in the beginning of the century, the amount of 300 guilders would remain the standard yearly income for the head-gardener until the mid-century. By 1653 the gardener Pieter van Bruheze would receive on top of the standard 300 Carolus guilders wages a bonus of 150 guilders, provided that he had done his work well. Such a bonus system is also described in a 1623 *Letter of Instruction for Michiel van Bruheze*,[147] who collaborated with and succeeded Hoorendonck as gardener of the Valkenberg. Michiel van Bruheze would not only enjoy the free use of a house but also, 'if he acquits himself [of his work] with dedication and diligence, he will receive yearly by special decree the amount of 100 or 150 Carolus guilders'.[148] Michiel van Bruheze apparently did acquit himself well of his duties, since every year from 1638 to 1648 a special stipulation in the account books reads: 'Michiel van Bruheze hovenier van den hoff van de Valckenbergh tot Breda de extraordinaris gagie van honderd vijfftig guldens nevens sijne ordinaris gagie van drie hondert guldens' (to Michiel van Bruheze, gardener ... the extra bonus of one hundred and fifty guilders in addition to his normal salary of three hundred guilders) (992 fol. 327 and 993 fols. 170, 216, 317).

Though it is difficult to ascertain the real value of such wages at the time, an idea of the modest sum of money such an income represented can be had by comparing Hoorendonck's 300 guilders with the French gardener André Mollet's *tractement* of 800 guilders yearly at Honselaarsdijk in 1633-34 (1042 fol 232vo), and a similar amount of 750 guilders for the Dutch gardener Jan van Dijck, who was responsible for planting the seventeen parterres of the Valckenberg garden in 1639 (992 fol. 274).

In every respect, the gardeners of the Valkenberg had to work hard for their wages, not only in tending the trees and plants but also in carefully supervising the flow of visitors in

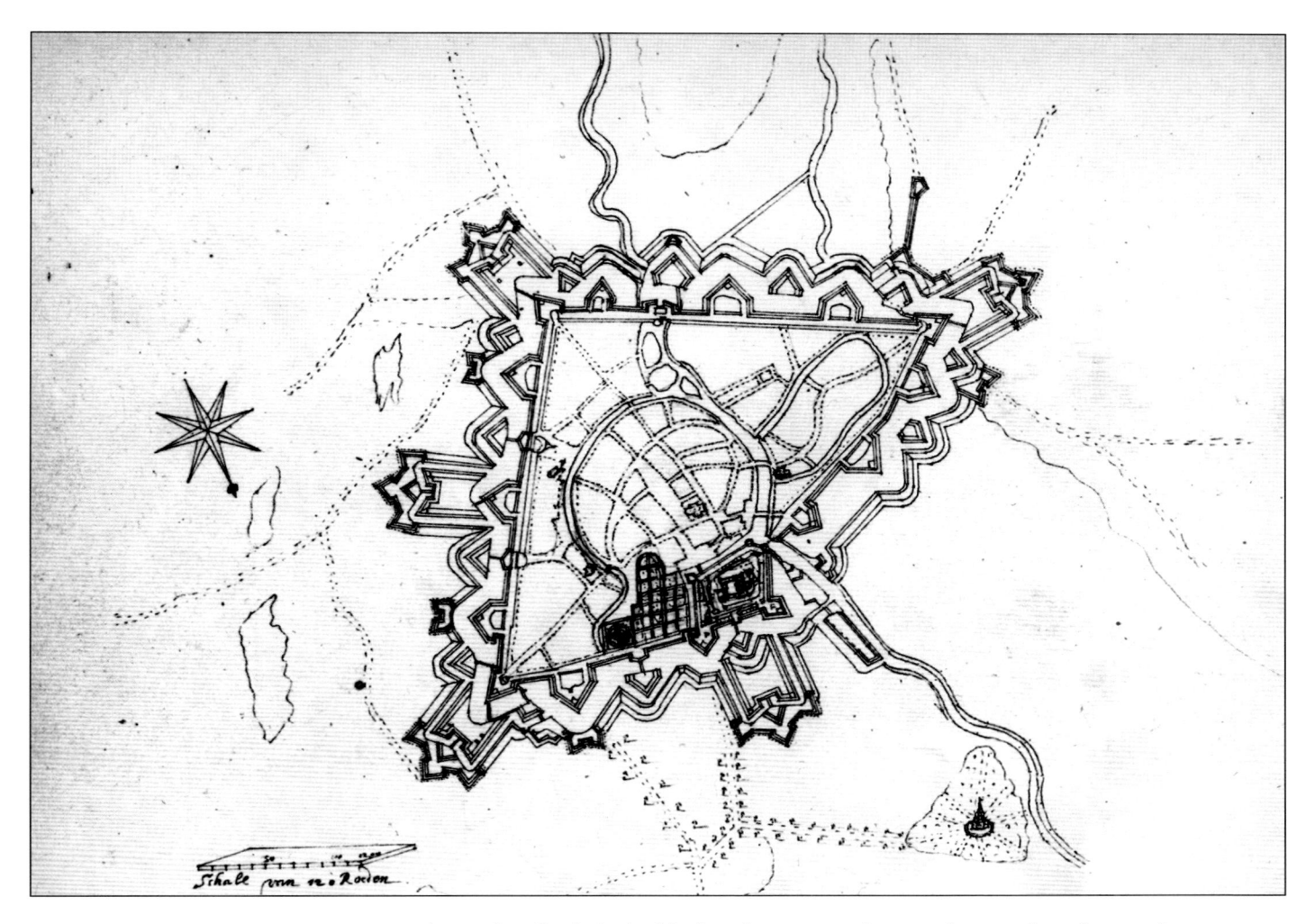

109. Fortifications of the city of Breda as drawn in Johan Maurits's map book, c. 1635. Castle and Belcromsche Bosch with pavilion to the north-west.
Koninklijk Huisarchief

the garden. In their double function as a gardener and a guard, under no circumstances were they to permit soldiers, young men or children into the garden, who could ruin the plantations and the *blomme parcken*, or flower-beds. The head-gardener was only allowed to show the garden to officers, foreign visitors and 'people of stature'. In spite of the gardener's attempts to guard the gardens, certain 'ruffians' did manage to ruin statues and plants over the years. It is nevertheless fortunate that the Valkenberg garden did ultimately receive enough 'people of stature' to provide us with a description of it.

Among the many foreign dignitaries who visited the garden were the English author and war correspondent William Lithgow and the brothers Moretus with their father, heirs of the well-known Antwerp printing house Plantijn-Moretus. Both visited Breda during a peaceful interval following many periods of war, in 1637 and 1668, respectively. Each came away with a different impression after their visits. If Lithgow was enthusiastic about the Valkenberg garden, calling it 'a pleasant, spacious and conspicuous garden, full of sweet, savoury and fructiferous trees, where on some are summerhouses and banquetting roomes erected',[149] Father Moretus and his sons were somewhat disappointed. Whether as a result of war, public vandalism or neglected care, the Moretus family found the garden to be in worse condition than in the days of Prince Maurits and Frederik Hendrik. Nevertheless they admired the many fine walking places, the arbours, woods and also the *caetsbaen*, for the game of fives and the *maillebaen* for pall-mall. They were most impressed, however, by the layout and decoration of the central parterre, which contained a sundial made of boxwood and also included the Prince of Orange's coat of arms:

III. OTHER GARDENS

> Om the gaen in de hovinge, staende nevens het kaetspel in welcke dat te noteren syn vele wandelingen van hagen, perielen [sic, priëelen] ende lommeringen; oock een warande ende in het middelste parck [parterre section] is notabel eenen wyser [zonnewijzer] met palm uytgebeelt, waer nevens de wapens van de Prins van Oranien winens [sic, wiens] rendtmeester syne wooninge alhier heeft.[150]

The reference to the boxwood parterre cut partly in the shape of the Prince of Orange's coat of arms is of special importance, as it coincides with the parterre decorations containing heraldic imagery and monograms in the gardens of Honselaarsdijk, Ter Nieuburch and the Huis ten Bosch. As such, these parterre layouts are typical of the general tendency to portray heraldic imagery in contemporary courtly gardens throughout Europe. The presence of a sundial, in Dutch *zonnewijzer* but in Breda described as a *wyser*, made of boxwood or 'met palm uytgebeelt', reflects the popularity of this object of ornamentation.[151] Moreover, as an image of the passing of time, central also in contemporary emblematic literature, the sundial was seen as symbolizing the brevity of life, adding to the sense of ephemerality in the garden.[152]

As the Valkenberg garden was situated within the fortification system of Breda, its changing appearance can be studied on some of the maps of that time. One of the most interesting representations is from a plan which, like the map of Buren, belonged to the hand-drawn maps bundled in Johan Maurits van Nassau-Siegen's *Niederländische Fortificatien, Holländische Militaria*. This finely-drawn plan of Breda *(fig. 109)*[153] shows how the gardens were incorporated with the extensive bulwarks of the city. Furthermore, north of the city, beyond the fortifications proper and accessible by means of bridges, lay what may be considered another part of the Breda gardens: a large wooded area known as the Belcromsche Bosch.[154] In the middle of this stretch of land lay a wooded area transected by avenues centring on an octagonal pleasure house or hunting pavilion. The architecture of this pavilion, known as the Speelhuys, was quite remarkable.[155] Several grand drives are seen to lead up to this house which, originally built by Prince Maurits in 1620, stood on a hill called the Konijnenberg, or Rabbit Hill; it was the centre of the Belcromsche Bosch until its demolition in 1834.[156] Part of this wood was fenced in as a zoological garden, part again as a tract for the play of pall-mall.[157]

In these maps of the Valkenberg and Breda gardens *(see figs. 106-109)* the contrast and yet remarkable interplay between fortified city and open garden space are clearly portrayed. The close and enduring connection between fortifications or military architecture and garden architecture, which has been considered briefly in the context of Stevin, ultimately would result in the design of bastion-shaped garden sections during the reign of William III and after.[158] Already in the mid-seventeenth century, however, several Englishmen travelling through Holland were struck by the layout of small parks on the ramparts of Dutch fortified towns. Actually Edward Southwell recorded that the fortifications of Breda were made into gardens: 'the Ramparts serve as a Tarrass walk'.[159] The tree-lined ramparts of Breda and many other seventeenth-century Dutch towns would function as public walking spaces and thus exemplify, as it were, an early, simplified version of this garden-architectural phenomenon relating fortress to garden.[160]

The close link between the layout of fortifications and that of gardens, which diametrically reflects the elements of 'architecture of war' and 'architecture of peace', would result in the ruin of garden layouts during military campaigns. At Breda, during the two sieges of the city in 1625 and 1637, the Belcromsche Bosch was destroyed and its trees cut down. Not only the wood but also the gardens within the bulwarks proper were ravaged by the digging of entrenchments in order to defend or attack the castle, as Huygens explained in a letter to Amalia:

...le gouverneur auroit faict certain retranchement au jardin de Valckenbergh, pour y disputer, ce semble, le chasteau.[161]

During the years following the second siege of Breda Frederik Hendrik began to renovate, improve and transform Breda's castle and gardens. Especially important for the history of these gardens are the entries in the Nassau records of payments between 1637 and 1640 to the various gardeners. In the spring of 1638 Michiel van Bruheze, referred to in the records as the 'gardener of the two courts' at Breda, improved the smaller courtyard gardens, one of which contained aviaries (992 fol. 378) and was situated in the area below the large parterre garden. At the same time the payment account for the gardener Jan van Dijck – who, as we have seen, received no less than 750 guilders for his work in this main parterre garden – read as follows:

>...for the planting of the parterres in the garden of the Valckenberg at Breda, namely the planting of the 17 compartments and their decoration with colours, such as palm, camomile as well as other herbs and crushed stone after the requirements of the work at 44 guilders 2 stuivers each compartment, making altogether 750 Carolus guilders ... March-April 1639 [992 fol. 274].

This account corroborates the accuracy of the maps which depict the seventeen compartments of the main garden filled with flowers, herbs and *parterres de broderie*, exactly according to the description. These parterres were particularly admired by a later visitor, the Polish clergyman Adam Samuel Hartmann, who wrote that the 'Prince's garden' was especially nice because of its artful *quartieren*, or compartments.[162]

While Hartmann also liked the beautiful green arbours, he particularly enjoyed the *Irrgarten*, or labyrinth, referring to the dense wooded area planted with fir-trees and *Ruspen beumen*. Contrary to other visitors at the time, Hartmann found but few flowers and fruits in the Valkenberg garden, but he may not have seen the orchard or kitchen-garden areas.

In addition to the new planting of the garden, Frederik Hendrik also had several buildings repaired and erected round and in the Valkenberg garden complex in 1638. These include the house of the gardener between the courtyard gardens and the main parterre garden (992 fol. 179) and the house in the centre of the parterre garden adjacent to the fish-pond, described as 'the house standing on the Valckenberg at the pond' (992 fols. 179, 181, 378) and known in older documents as the House of Pergamont.[163] Both buildings, including a gallery and aviary connected to the gardener's house, were repaired by the master bricklayer Jan Woutersz van Rijckevorsel, who was also paid for reconstructing the wall between the Valkenberg garden and the Capucijnenhof (992 fol. 230).

The supervisor of all the works at Breda in the late 1630s and early 1640s was the stonemason Laurens Drijffhout, brother of the Stadholder's master mason at The Hague, Bartholomeus Drijffhout. Over the years Laurens Drijffhout regularly received payments for 'stone works' in the Valkenberg, including the repair of a water-mill (992 fols. 348, 349, 350 and 993 fols. 140-141)[164] and the restoration of the above-mentioned octagonal Speelhuys outside the fortification of Breda in the Belcromsche Bosch (993 fols. 140). Laurens Drijffhout's work, generically indicated as 'stonework' but amounting to more than 2,000 guilders, may also have included the further decoration of the garden, for example with sculpture. In point of fact, his brother Bartholomeus Drijffhout, who worked at Honselaarsdijk and The Hague,[165] is mentioned in various entries in the records of payments of 1639 concerning the transportation and setting-up of statues in the gardens of Honselaarsdijk (992 fols. 277, 278, 333). Besides, like his brother's work at Honselaarsdijk and the Paleis Noordeinde, Laurens Drijffhout's work exceeded that of a mere stonemason. He also served as an architect, since he was paid for making several drawings of elevations and ground-plans for the buildings at Breda (992 fol. 139). It was probably to discuss these drawings in greater detail with the Prince that Drijffhout was summoned to stay at The Hague for a few months in the spring of 1642 (993 fol. 141).

Further entries, specifying general labour expenditures, describe works at the pavilion in the Valkenberg, referring to the house next to the fish-pond, and various smaller pavilions visible on the Blaeu map as standing on the heightened terrace which enclosed the garden to the north. Major work on this terrace took place in 1644 when Dirck van der Mijlen was paid the large sum of 5,738 guilders for the construction of a wall to be set against it (993 fol. 317). The terrace, which was covered by a roof and was more like an open gallery, afforded a far vista over the whole garden and the surrounding plantations, including the town and steeples of Breda.[166] From this position Constantijn Huygens Junior enjoyed overlooking the whole Valkenberg layout, as his drawing depicting this very view shows.[167]

In the accounts of the late 1630s and early 1640s, the *caetsbaen* and the *maillebaen* are singled out in addition to the gardener's house, the *escurie* and the *volière* (992 fol. 377 and 993 fol. 139). Obviously the game of pall-mall was very much in fashion at court, since similar tracks or alleys, as we know, were laid out at Buren and Honselaarsdijk at the time (992 fol. 142a). Indeed, grassy tracts for pall-mall graced most of the contemporary and later stadholderly gardens, which reminds us of the French gardener Boyceau's advice to include such expanses for exercise and all kinds of ball games. Boyceau's remark must have been taken to heart in France, too, since no less person than the King himself greatly favoured the game and actually had his gardens redesigned to fit alleys of appropriate length. Thus the gardens of the Tuileries were fitted out with an extra long alley for playing pall-mall, as two Dutch gentlemen observed on visiting Paris during their 'Grand Tour' in 1656-58: 'Il y a [at the Tuileries] un fort beau jeu de mail, et qu'on a mesme agrandi depuis le Roy se plaist à cet exercise.'[168]

Frederik Hendrik enjoyed the Valkenberg not only for the game of pall-mall but particularly for walking and discussing new construction plans for this palace complex and his other estates. True to Castiglione's well-known characterization of a veritable sovereign, the Stadholder persisted in fulfilling his dual princely obligation as strategic military commander and inspiring Maecenas. Even during the siege of Breda in the summer of 1637, Frederik Hendrik continued to occupy himself with architecture and gardening, and apparently had a house built surrounded by meadows in the outskirts of Breda, which he used for his headquarters. Constantijn Huygens, in a letter to Amalia, described how delighted the Stadholder was with this new building in the midst of nature, 'threatening to like it even more than Honselaarsdijk'. Moreover, Huygens continued, the structure was indeed worth to be contemplated by the great architects:

> ...le nouveau bastiment que S. Alt.e y a faict adjouster d'une belle chambre de bois, aveq un joli cabinet, le tout gazonné au dehors, ou il se plaist à merveilles, et proteste de l'admirer plus que Honselerdijck. Aussi est-ce une superbe structure et digne que les grands architectes la viennent contempler.[169]

A year later, after Frederik Hendrik had won back the city of Breda, Huygens again described the Prince's activities to Amalia, reporting on his jubilant entry into Breda and his careful inspection of all the new work on the castle.[170] In the summer of 1639 Frederik

110. Plan of the Valkenberg garden by an unknown artist, possibly Daniel Marot or Jacob Roman; layout and decoration from the late seventeenth, early eighteenth centuries.
Collectie Bodel Nijenhuis, Universiteitsbibliotheek, Leiden
see colour plate 15

111. Alternative plan from the late seventeenth, early eighteenth centuries of the Valkenberg gardens, showing the grand parterre gardens near the L-shaped fish-pond.
Collectie Bodel Nijenhuis, Universiteitsbibliotheek, Leiden

III. OTHER GARDENS

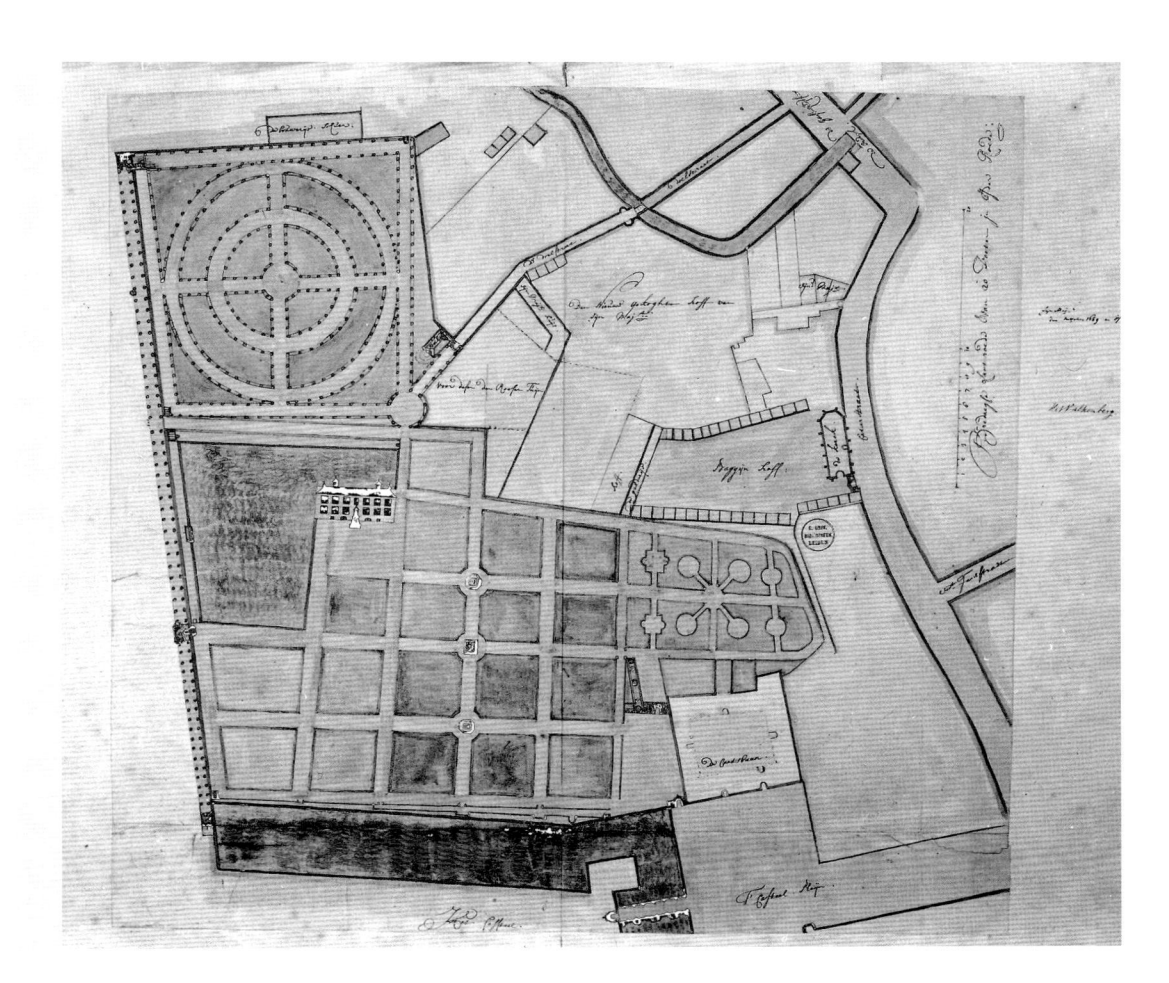

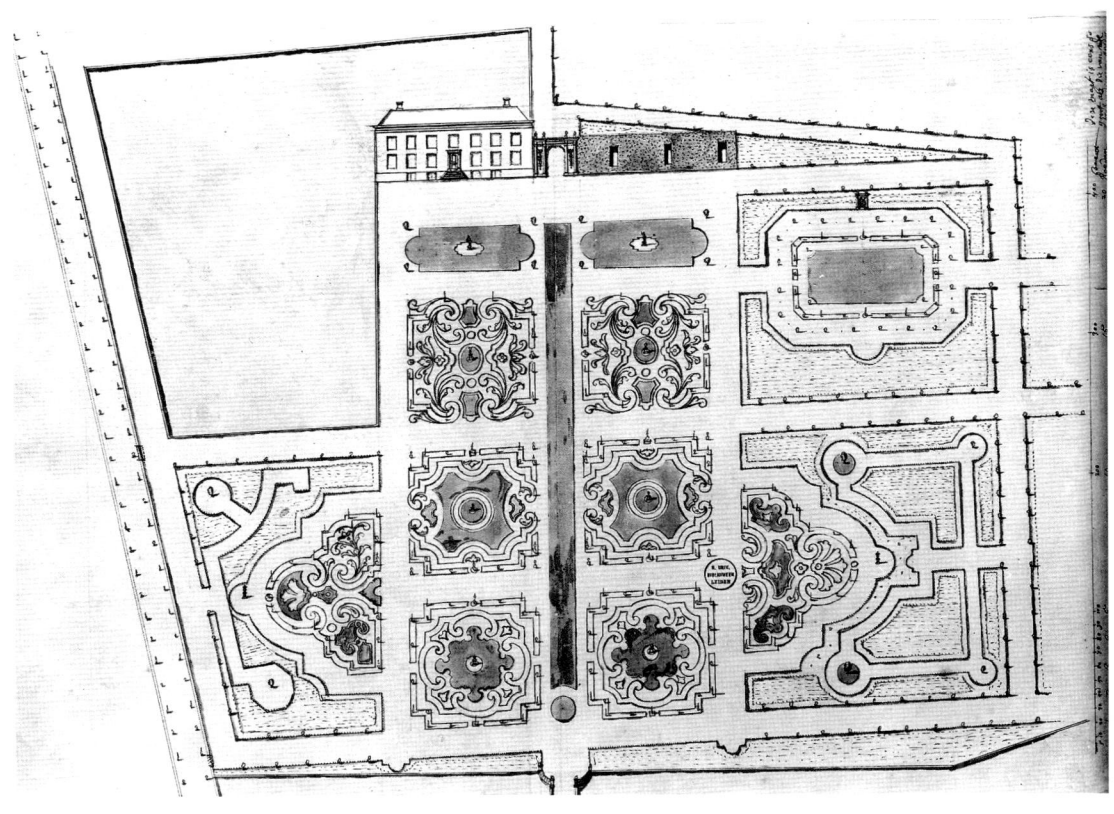

112. Drawing by Pieter de Swart of the Valkenberg's main parterre garden with statues, including *Hercules* in the first parterre lower left.
Breda Museum. Photo courtesy Gemeentearchief, Breda

Hendrik enjoyed a long walk in the newly-planted Valkenberg gardens and also travelled through the Liesbosch, a wooded area near Breda, to look at the various new plantations.[171] In this context it is important to remember that many of the plants decorating the Stadholder's gardens in The Hague came from this south-eastern area in The Netherlands. In fact, the centre of the tree-plantation region was the city of Meurs, often referred to in Huygens's letters and in the records of payments involving new supplies of fruit-trees. It was at Meurs that the Stadholder wished to spend the whole summer, Huygens declared, so much did he enjoy the surrounding landscape and the pure air.[172]

Like his grandfather, William III also enjoyed Breda and its surroundings, and during his reign the castle and garden underwent major changes. Under this Stadholder-King two new wings were added to the old castle by the architect Jacob Roman, which were begun in 1688 and completed in 1696.[173] Not only the building but also the garden was completely renovated and extended, as the plan by Christoffel Verhoff shows *(see fig. 108)*. Two recently discovered colour drawings *(figs. 110 and 111)*,[174] which geographically and stylistically belong to the same period as does the Verhoff plan, give a clear picture of the Valkenberg garden's late-seventeenth-century layout and ornamentation.

These drawings are not signed or dated. However, because of their close similarity to the Verhoff plan of 1679 they must date from between 1689 and 1702 when William III was King of England, as is further corroborated by the reference to William III as 'His

140   COURTLY GARDENS IN HOLLAND 1600-1650

Majesty'. Since Jacob Roman designed the architectural works for William III at Breda, and, from a stylistic point of view, these drawings may be compared with designs made in William III's court surroundings, it is possible to attribute the two drawings to Roman and his circle, including the architect-decorator Daniel Marot.[175]

Though the ornamentation of the Breda garden differed, its form and inner arrangement remained basically the same since Frederik Hendrik. In the first place, one can recognize exactly the same garden outline that is shown in Blaeu's map and Johan Maurits's military plan of the early 1630s *(compare figs. 106 and 109)*. The main parterre garden, its fish-pond and the square area with its two concentric circles, enclosed with the long heightened terrace to the north, a broad canal to the west and an agglomerate of buildings on the south and east, are still immediately recognizable in this late-seventeenth-century drawing. Also clearly visible *(see fig. 110, lower right)* is the indirect access from the palace to the garden, which could only be reached via the bridge over the moat and after crossing the 'Casteel Pleijn', or piazza, in front of the castle. From this piazza, to the east, three gates led via the *caetsbaen* to the old *berceaux* garden, which still retained its quality as an enclosed *giardino segreto*. Unchanged, though apparently heightened,[176] is the large parterre garden proper, divided into seventeen square plots as in the time of Frederik Hendrik.

The second drawing *(see fig. 111)* provides an alternative, modernized version of the layout of the parterre garden. Following the latest French style forms developed at the court of Louis XIV, the parterre area is now to end in two stepped exedrae, forming, as at Honselaarsdijk, Ter Nieuburch and Buren, a huge oval or hippodrome-shaped garden area. The exedrae and other compartments in the garden are filled with parterres of ornamental scrollwork, which replaced and stylistically updated the form of Frederik Hendrik's boxwood and flower compartments. Apart from the flowers, boxwood and herbs grown in the parterres under Frederik Hendrik, there was, according to the text in this drawing, a rose garden in the Valkenberg, between the fish-pond and the garden with the circular paths, undoubtedly the same 'Roosen Thuijn' as indicated on Verhoff's plan of 1679. The pleasure house, already renovated under Frederik Hendrik, had been rebuilt, showing a typical late-seventeenth-century, sober classical façade. Other garden structures visible in this drawing, which already existed under Frederik Hendrik, include a small pavilion, possibly containing a grotto, on the heightened terrace enclosing the Valkenberg garden to the north.

When it comes to the garden ornamentation and detailed plantation, information is scarce and hard to find. However, a comparison between early-seventeenth-century maps and the late-seventeenth-century drawings shows that the three fountains (only one in Blaeu's map) decorating the central crossroads in the parterre garden at the time of Frederik Hendrik *(see fig. 106)* were replaced with a group of statues and vases set up throughout the parterre garden by William III *(see fig. 111)*.[177] A view of the parterre garden and its sculptural decoration is offered by a rare drawing by Pieter de Swart *(fig. 112)*,[178] after which Immink fashioned a print. This drawing and print, dating from 1743, show that the basic arrangement of the seventeenth-century garden layout was retained into the eighteenth century. Of the seventeen statues originally set up in the parterres only one survives, most significantly (once again) a figure of Hercules, visible in the first parterre in the lower left corner. A reproduction of this *Hercules*, standing in a newly-reconstructed formal parterre, still decorates the Valkenberg park today.[179]

As in the case of most of the other gardens under review, only fragmentary information has come down to us about the history of the Breda gardens in the interval between the reigns of Frederik Hendrik and William III. However, Huygens's correspondence shows that in 1656, in order to pay the high cost of the upkeep of the Valkenberg property, plans were made to lease the gardens. It remains unclear whether these plans were ever put into effect, for serious disagreements arose between Huygens and David de Wilhem as protectors of the Nassau Domains on the one hand, and the governor of Breda on the other, who refused to lease the Valkenberg gardens.[180] Whether the governor succeeded in holding off the lease is doubtful, but in any case the gardens evidently continued to flourish and were kept in good condition. This can be concluded from a letter written in 1682 by Huygens's daughter Susanna, who expressed her admiration for the layout by stating that on walking through the Valkenberg gardens, then fully grown and flourishing, she fancied herself in paradise:

> Nous partimes de Haenwyck pour Breda la ou nous arivasmes vers le soir, d' assé bonne heure pour nous promener encore au Valkenberg la ou il fait beau à merveille et le Receveur ij est logé comme dans un Paradis.[181]

If Susannna Huygens-Doublet believed herself to be in paradise, this idyllic state would soon be disturbed by the great number of uninvited 'commoners' who stole their way into the park and threatened its pristine condition. Indeed, one of the most remarkable aspects of the Breda garden, which can be inferred from various documents, is the increasingly public role which the Valkenberg seems to have played. Its double function as a private and a public space can be first gleaned from the early-seventeenth-century *Instructions for the Gardener Hoorendonck*, describing the damage to the statues and the trampling of plants by careless 'soldiers and children'.[182] The references to vandalism were picked up again a century later, to become a familiar theme in letters written by the eighteenth-century stewards of the Valkenberg estate.[183] Ironically, of all the gardens under review the Valkenberg garden, which had suffered most from the public, would survive to the present. Expanded and modernized throughout the next centuries,[184] the Valkenberg garden, to quote Susanna Huygens-Doublet, still is a small paradise in the centre of the city of Breda. Recently restored and reorganized to function properly both as a city park and as a main thoroughfare from the town centre to the station,[185] the Valkenberg, in its metamorphoses from wooded area to courtly garden and public park, is an excellent example of the continuous adaptation of the garden to different requirements in an ever-changing environment.

THE GARDENS OF ZUYLESTEYN

As soon as Frederik Hendrik had become the owner of the old manorial estate of Zuylesteyn (also spelled Zuylestein or Zuilenstein) at Leersum,[186] plans were made for the extension and improvement of the old castle and its plantations. One of the oldest *ridderhofsteden* (knightly manors) in the province of Utrecht, the fourteenth-century castle of Zuylesteyn was destroyed by bombs in the Second World War. Fortunately, enough documents and visual material exist to make a reconstruction of its mid-seventeenth-century situation possible. This is all the more interesting because castle and garden remained virtually unchanged since the time of Frederik Hendrik. Though robbed of its building, even the castle's environment is of great historical value, as it constitutes one of the only surviving examples of an area originally holding a geometrical garden layout.[187]

Zuylesteyn is not only of interest for its geography but also for its architectural history, demonstrating as it does the great variety of building at the time.[188] It is a good example

113. Plan of the Zuylesteyn castle and garden complex c. 1630, shortly before Frederik Hendrik's improvements to the castle and grounds.
Algemeen Rijksarchief

114. Plan of the first extensions of the gardens and plantations of Zuylesteyn and the changes into regular garden plots and orchard areas.
Algemeen Rijksarchief

III. OTHER GARDENS

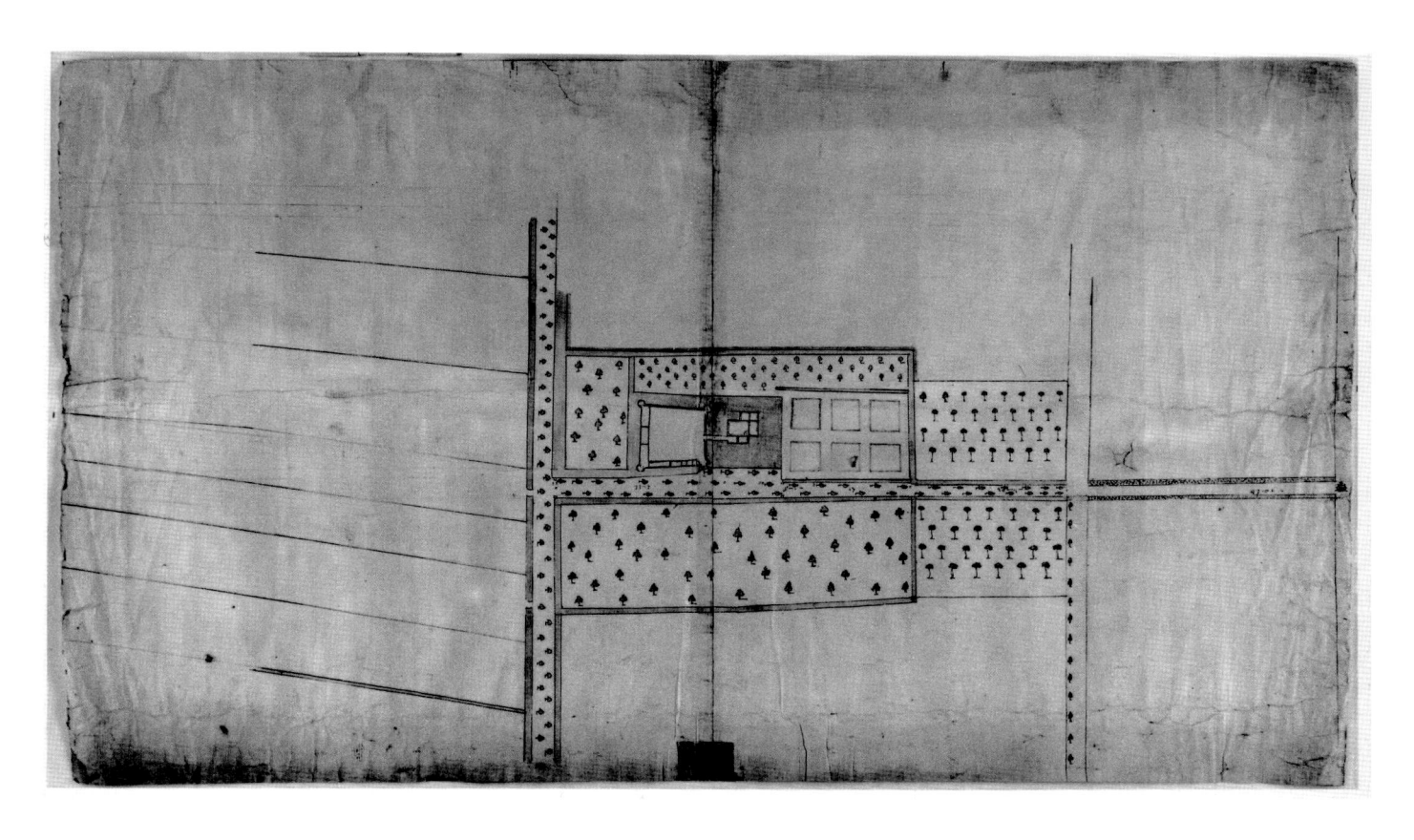

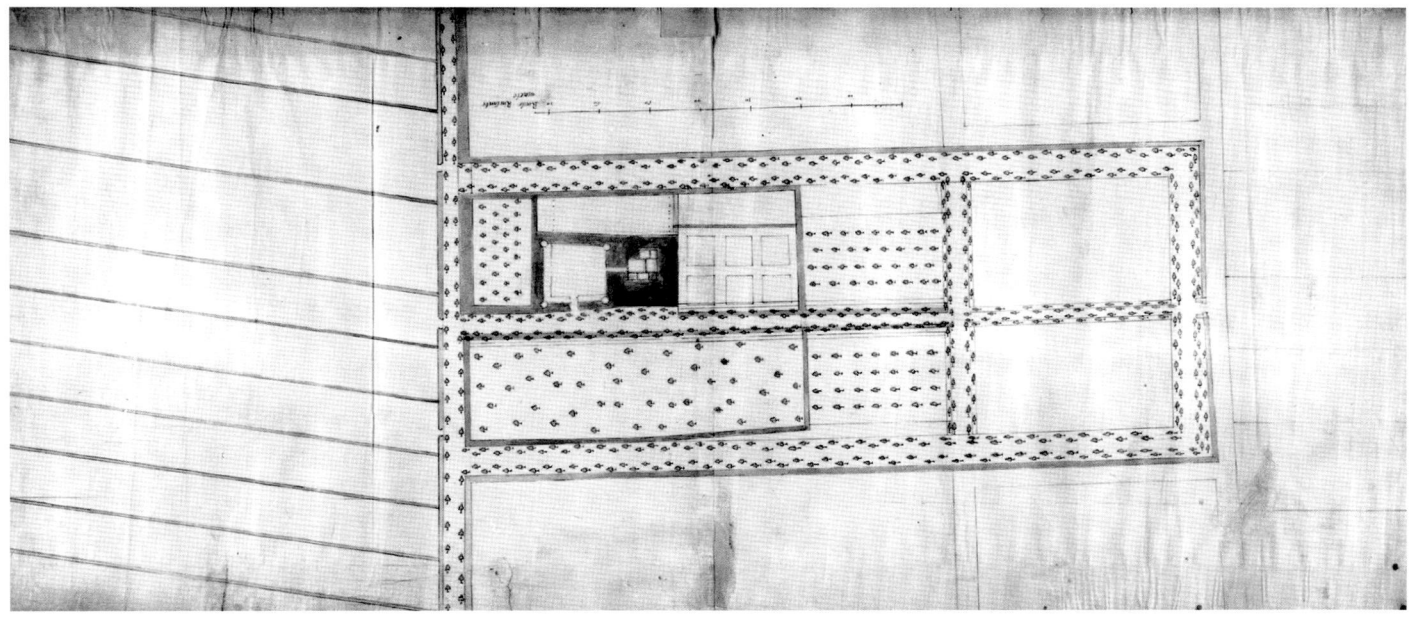

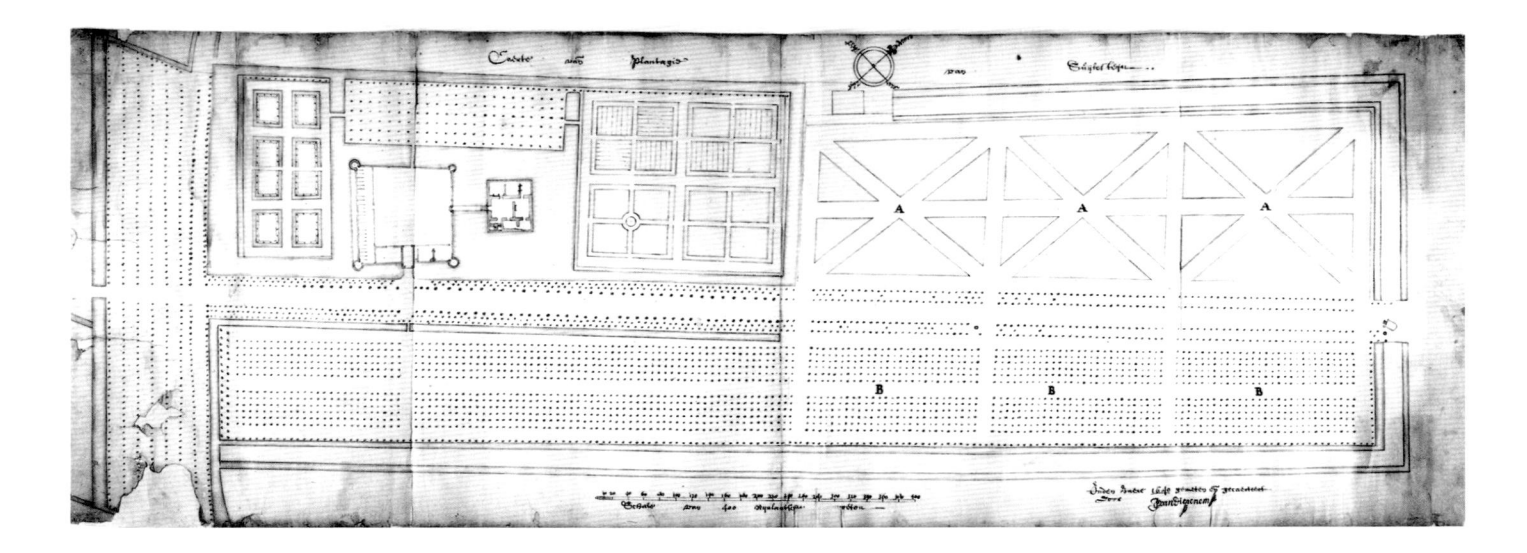

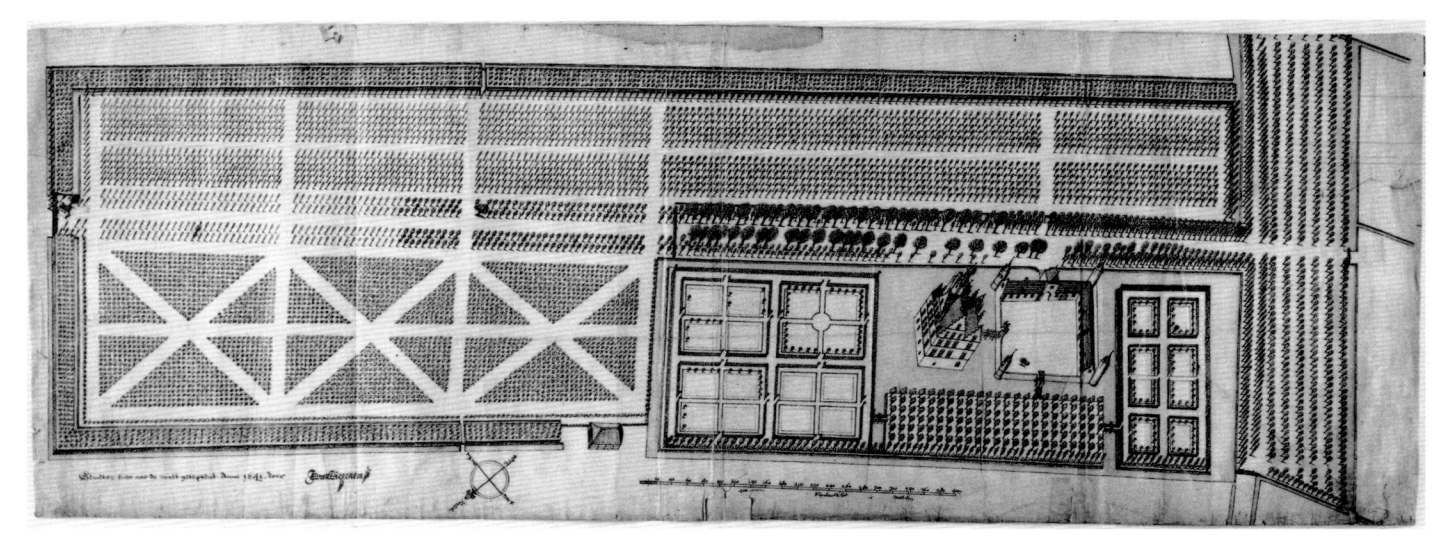

of the Stadholder's principles of building and restoration. The existing structure and character of the medieval castle were taken as the main point of departure for the renovation of the building, rather than the latest notions of 'good architecture', that is, the classical style. This historical approach resulted in the creation of a castle which looked more 'castle-like' than ever before.[189] The gardens fit this principle of conservatism and were laid out as separate, enclosed garden plots or islands, surrounded by water and primarily planted as orchards. The method of holding on to medieval forms and adjusting new structures to the medieval style of the existing building has important art-historical implications, particularly since there is a tendency to appreciate mostly the new and to neglect the older style traditions.

A series of ten maps, four of which will be shown here, is of central importance for the history of Frederik Hendrik's gardens at Zuylesteyn *(figs. 113-116)*.[190] These maps make it possible to reconstruct the gardens of shortly before, during and after Frederik Hendrik's ownership. Furthermore, a unique document concerning rules set up by the Stadholder for the upkeep of the gardens helps to complete their history, providing details about their layout and plantation.

From the evidence at hand it becomes clear that what we saw at Honselaarsdijk, Ter Nieuburch and the Huis ten Bosch applies again to Zuylesteyn, namely that the first step

115. Plan by Jan van Diepenen, 1640, showing the clear division of the Zuylesteyn gardens on geometric islands and the arrangement of the plantations. Algemeen Rijksarchief

116. Bird's-eye view of Zuylesteyn in the winter by Jan van Diepenen, 1641, showing the detailed arrangement of trees and garden compartments. Algemeen Rijksarchief

COURTLY GARDENS IN HOLLAND 1600-1650

undertaken by the Stadholder was the acquisition of surrounding lands and farms to expand the property (1043 fol. 304vo). It was followed by the levelling and reorganization of the grounds into orderly, linearly arranged plots of land, and the procedure was concluded by the careful plantation and decoration of the grounds in order to create a veritable pleasure garden. Concurrently, proper drainage systems were developed, and the new mathematically arranged plots of land were enclosed within a tight framework of canals and moats. The arrangement of trees in long rows and radial patterns was to accentuate the linearity and orderliness of the terrain.

At Zuylesteyn, as at most of Frederik Hendrik's other gardens, much attention was given to orchards and tree plantations, and relatively little to pure ornamental sections. Interestingly, the planting of the Zuylesteyn gardens was done in conjunction with the planting of the gardens at the Huis ter Nieuburch, as can be inferred from an entry in the accounts of 1631, mentioning the payment of more than 457 pounds artois for the transportation of 100,000 *plansoenen* or compartments of hornbeam and beech-trees from Meurs to be planted at Zuylesteyn and Ter Nieuburch (1040 fol. 221).

The first map of Zuylesteyn *(see fig. 113)*, drawn circa 1630, shows the old situation of the garden at the time when Frederik Hendrik dispatched his *fabryck meester*, the architect Willem van Salen, to inspect and make a report on the newly-acquired property (1039 fol. 273). The forecourt is still in its irregular form; it contains the stables and the castle built on separate islands which are encircled by a moat and connected by a bridge. This castle complex is surrounded by the larger plantation area; it is divided into several not clearly defined sections cut through by canals and tree plantations in random arrangement. Immediately east of the castle lies a garden section which is divided into six smaller compartments. A comparison with a later map *(see fig. 114)* shows the first improvements to the grounds. The plantation was extended eastward, and the new section of land was divided into two large, rectangular plots held within a framework of canals which were bordered by avenues planted with double rows of trees. The canal system surrounding the property was regulated and equally extended to create the typical elongated outline of the whole estate.

A third map *(see fig. 115)*, which consists of a planting plan indicated by the letters A and B and is signed and dated 1640 by the main land-surveyor of the province of Utrecht, Jan van Diepenen, clearly shows the improvements to the building complex and its gardens. The garden area surrounding the castle, itself a completely square unified building complex now, is divided into three clearly defined garden sections connected by bridges. The island situated to the west of the forecourt-island holds the vegetable garden enclosed with hedges; the island north of the castle complex, directly accessible from the forecourt-island, is planted as an orchard. The garden island to its east holds the garden proper, now divided into four instead of the former six compartments.

The main garden, visible from the principal rooms in the castle, contained compartments for vegetables and herbs as well as ornamental parterres, all enclosed once again with hedges and trees. While these ornamental parterres are not represented in detail on Van Diepenen's maps, we know of their existence from the gardener's contract. The type of parterres laid out at Zuylesteyn can be deduced from the fact that André Mollet was involved in the layout of the gardens. It is likely that Mollet, as the supervisor of His Highness's gardens, was sent to Zuylesteyn in 1634 in order to plan the parterres and to inspect the general progress of the work (1043 fol. 243).

Behind this main garden section, separated from the rest of the property by the moat, lay three tree compartments pierced by a central axis and diagonal walks. The rest of the terrain was given to further tree plantations. The situation of house and garden in their more or less completed form in 1640-41, at the time Frederik Hendrik presented Zuylesteyn to his son Frederik van Nassau,[191] is beautifully rendered in two bird's-eye views by Jan van Diepenen; they provide a most unusual 'seasonal' impression of the layout, showing a summer and a winter panorama of the whole property. The winter view is shown here *(see fig. 116)*. It is signed and dated 1641, and offers an impressively detailed picture of each tree's exact position and silhouette. Clearly visible is the newly-laid-out grand entrance avenue leading up to the moated castle complex and cutting the property in two. A heightened terrace or dike can be seen to enclose the plantation on all sides. The castle and gardens of Zuylesteyn have many of the general characteristics found in the other gardens laid out under Frederik Hendrik. As a 'donjon type' the Zuylesteyn castle may be compared with the castles of Buren and Breda. Furthermore, the gardens are characterized by the same 'piecemeal' tendencies typical of the Stadholder's and other seventeenth-century Dutch gardens, in that the various sections are laid out on separate islands with little integration among them, all tightly enclosed in a larger framework of moats and canals.

There are relatively few references in the archives detailing the building activities at Zuylesteyn. However, one document provides information on the dike surrounding the property: in 1634 the concierge of Zuylesteyn was commissioned to organize the construction of an embankment measuring twelve feet, or circa four metres, in width.[192] A year later Gijsbrecht Thonissen, gardener-in-chief at Honselaarsdijk, was paid 334 pounds 12 schillings for the delivery of fruit-trees (1041 fol. 251vo). Apparently Thonissen was commissioned to provide the Stadholder's estates with fruit-trees, since a year later he delivered twenty peach- and nine apricot-trees at Buren, for which he received 59 pounds artois (1042 fol. 254vo). Willem Dimmer, estate steward of Ysselsteyn, was paid more than 24,000 pounds in October 1632 for works executed at Zuylesteyn, including the arrangement of the new plantations (1041 fol. 252). His colleague, Julius Sagemans, under-steward of the county of Buren, received no less than 2,048 pounds for his work concerning the Zuylesteyn plantations in 1634 and 1635 (992 fol. 144). In 1639 a certain Willem Cornelisz van der Stoop, also responsible for many of the trees planted in the Stadholder's garden at Buren (992 fol. 313/2), was paid 97 pounds artois for elm- and pear-trees delivered at Zuylesteyn (992 fol. 313), and two years later for the delivery of 1,300 elm-trees (992 fol. 313 and 993 fol. 38). During these years Van der Stoop collaborated with Hendrick van Hattem, the Stadholder's *plantageur*.

From 1640 on, when the basic layout of the gardens had reached its completion, until about 1647, Hendrick van Hattem was frequently mentioned, indeed more than twenty times, for 'expenditures at the gardens and plantations of Zuylesteyn' and for 'expenditures at and planting of the gardens and plantations at Zuylesteyn, Buren, Honselaarsdijk and Ter Nieuburch' (992 fols. 361, 440 and 993 fols. 24, 131, 154, 188, 208, 220, 414vo, 415vo, 419). As far as can be gathered from the records of payments, Van Hattem was not only responsible for acquiring and transporting trees but also for supervising their correct planting in the plantations, where he was assisted, curiously enough, by the land-surveyor Jan van Diepenen. Van Hattem also acquired rare plants and flowers for the Stadholder's gardens, and for all his work at the various estates over a period of about ten years he received more than 150,000 Carolus guilders!

From the accounts it can be inferred that the improvement and planting of the garden at Zuylesteyn was part of a larger project involving, in the first place, the garden of the neighbouring estate of Buren, but also gardens in the Westland area, namely Honselaarsdijk and Ter Nieuburch. The new planting project also extended to Ysselsteyn, another house owned by Frederik Hendrik in this central region of Holland (1042 fol.

117. Bird's-eye view of Zuylesteyn by Daniel Stoopendael, c. 1690, showing the fully-grown gardens and plantations. (detail) Bibliotheek Landbouwuniversiteit, Wageningen

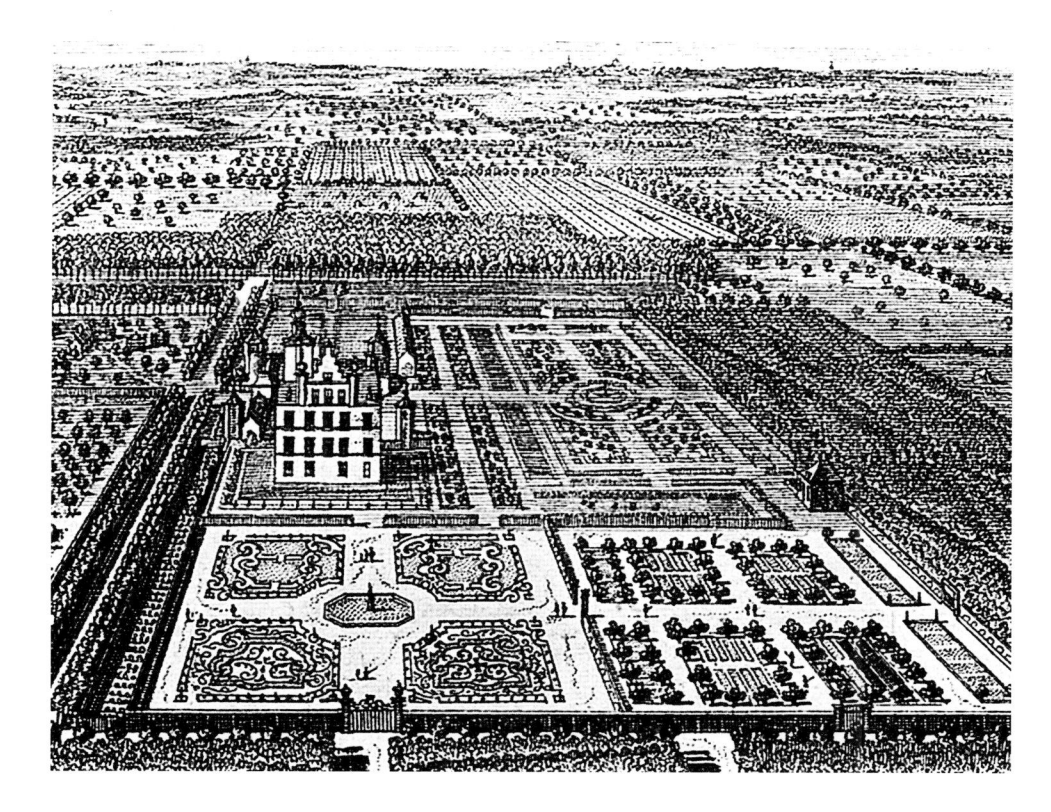

255vo), to be discussed below; it shows the extent of Frederik Hendrik's combined enterprises. The relationship between the building projects can also be seen from the yearly entries in the records of payments stating that 'no further acquisitions have been made at present apart from the advancement of the notable new buildings and considerable amelioration of the houses at Honselaarsdijk, Buren, Ysselsteyn and Nieuburch'.

Connections between the various building activities are shown as well by the fact that the Stadholder commissioned the same group of individuals to work in the The Hague and Utrecht areas. Not only did a specific group of architects and stonemasons, such as Post and the brothers Drijffhout (992 fol. 370), travel throughout Holland to work on many of the Stadholder's projects, but also was the same group of gardeners and plantation masters used at his various estates. Mollet and Van Hattem, as well as lesser-known figures such as Gijsbrecht Thonissen (1042 fol. 254vo) and Arent Pietersz Blom, both gardeners at Honselaarsdijk (992 fol. 386), are mentioned in the account books concerning the garden projects of The Hague and Utrecht. Moreover, the gardener Willem Cornelisz van der Stoop, purveyor of trees at Buren and Zuylesteyn (992 fol. 417 and 993 fols. 38, 181), and the gardener Simon Langelaer of Buren (993 fol. 404 and 994 fols. 39, 41vo, 93vo, 197)[193] are mentioned as working or delivering plants at several of the Stadholder's estates both in the neighbourhood of The Hague and in the centre and east of Holland.

The Stadholder's land-surveyors, too, travelled extensively throughout Holland. For example, Jan van Diepenen, apart from working at Zuylesteyn, was paid for travels to Buren and for maps made of that city (993 fols. 202 and 257vo). Another important piece of information from archival records, in particular from a document found in the Koninklijk Huisarchief, is the dual role of the land-surveyor as cartographer and 'garden architect', which we met earlier at Ter Nieuburch in the person of the land-surveyor Floris Jacobsz van der Sallem (1040 fol. 214) and at Honselaarsdijk and the Huis ten Bosch in that of his son Pieter Florisz van der Sallem, whose work involved drawing maps, laying out the grounds and arranging the plantations. Likewise, Jan van Diepenen is frequently mentioned in the records of payments for maps and measurements, and for making ground-plans and elevations (992 fols. 276, 277, 442 and 7993 fols. 54, 62, 184vo). Van Diepenen's detailed plans of the Zuylesteyn garden, precisely delineating its division in blocks, the drainage canals and the position of trees, also indicate deeper involvement than what we associate today with 'mere' land-surveying; it included the work of a 'plantation master'. Van Diepenen's extensive responsibilities are recorded in an unusual document dating from 1640, entitled *Memorie voor Hendrick van Hattem ende Johan van Diepenen … tot Suylesteyn (see Appendix, Document VIII)*[194] and describing in detail the steps undertaken in improving and replanting the gardens of Zuylesteyn. Curiously enough, the text of this document refers to the very map reproduced above *(see fig. 116)*, showing the planting material used.

The document also has a bearing on another important archival find, a gardener's contract dated 1635, entitled *Conditien ende voorwaerden … Jacob van Alenburch, Thuijnman (see Appendix, Document IX).*[195] It exactly describes the responsibilities of the gardener and the rules and regulations set up by the Stadholder: the gardener must take care of the trees, specified as oak-, elm- and lime-trees, and is responsible for the more detailed work of planting and keeping flowers and fruits and for the more 'artistic' work of creating parterres and *berceaux*. Fruits from the ground, such as melons, and fruits from the trees and the trellis-work walls are to be nurtured for a regular provision of His Highness's table. The gardener is held responsible for keeping clean all the paths, constantly clearing them from debris, so that they would at all times be ready for the Stadholder and his visitors to walk on. The gardener's work further entails the cutting and binding of low boxwood and high beech hedges, restoring old and setting up new *berceaux*, 'prielen ende wercken van plaisantie' (arbours and works of pleasure), shaping the portals, pyramids and other *ars topiaria*. In addition to pleasure gardens, part of the Zuylesteyn estate contained farms, as can be seen from a letter signed by 'Henry de Nassau' in the autumn of 1640, urging a certain Peter van Salsveld to restrain henceforth all the animals, be it horses, cows, sheep, pigs or others, so that they could not do further damage to the young trees planted at Zuylesteyn.[196]

The gardens of Zuylesteyn in their full-grown glory can be studied in detail in a late-seventeenth-century bird's-eye view by Daniel Stoopendael *(fig. 117)*[197] which helps to complete our survey of Frederik Hendrik's gardens. The only apparent differences between the late-seventeenth-century layout and the early-seventeenth-century Zuylesteyn under Frederik Hendrik are the moats and canals surrounding the castle and gardens, which in accordance with late-seventeenth-century fashion now consist of dry ditches. When we look westward over the main road to Utrecht towards the rear of the house, the various garden sections, already visible on Van Diepenen's earlier maps, are distinguishable on Stoopendael's print, with the advantage that this map is accompanied by a legend. Surrounding the castle lay the three main garden sections, enclosed within a stone wall: first the ornamental parterre garden, to its north the vegetable garden and behind it, encompassed by fish-ponds, the 'grand rear garden' containing a round grass parterre. Between the vegetable and the grass parterre gardens lay a small building indicated as the pleasure house, which was already depicted on Van Diepenen's mid-seventeenth-century maps.

Outside the main garden, surrounded by a high hedge, were the larger plantation areas, including the wooded areas transected by radial walks, described in the legend as *bois étoilez*. Southward, on the other side of the grand entrance avenue leading to the house, lay the main orchard garden which, like all other garden blocks, was neatly enclosed within a wall of high hedges. Though the castle no longer exists, the layout and main axes of its avenues and surrounding woodlands have survived and can be recognized in the present landscape.[198] Even the contour and the pattern of the seventeenth-century garden are for a large part still distinguishable in the remaining embankments and the block-like form of the ground surrounding the still existent outbuildings at Zuylesteyn.

THE GARDENS OF YSSELSTEYN

The last garden to be studied as part of the properties restored and improved by Frederik Hendrik is the garden of the nearby estate of Ysselsteyn (also spelled IJsselstein, Iselstein or Eijselsteijn). The upkeep of the Ysselsteyn garden was already discussed in the above-mentioned gardener's contract of 1635.[199] From this document it can be inferred that the Ysselsteyn and Zuylesteyn gardens were kept by the same gardener, Jacob van Allenburgh (or Alenburch). In addition to him, a certain Gijsbrecht van Alphen also worked as a gardener at Ysselsteyn; he is mentioned in the accounts from 1646 onward, receiving a salary of 129 guilders yearly.[200] As at Zuylesteyn, it was silviculture and orchards supplying fruit for the court table at The Hague for which the Ysselsteyn garden was most praised. Relatively few references in the records of payments provide further detailed insight into the projects undertaken at Ysselsteyn. However, the scarce accounts do reveal that the improvement of the building and grounds was started before 1627, thus preceding those at Zuylesteyn. Furthermore, in 1630 the steward of Ysselsteyn, Willem Dimmer, who also worked at Zuylesteyn, received more than 10,000 pounds artois for the improvement of the building (1040 fol. 212[vo]), and additional payments, each of them defined as 'for further improvements and repairs to His Highness's House at Ysselsteyn', were made in the following years (1043 fol. 242[vo]). In 1632 the architect Adriaen Willeboordsen Spierinxhouten was reimbursed for the amount of 55 pounds artois for expenditures and various trips undertaken for the Stadholder in 1627 and 1631 to inspect Ysselsteyn (1041 fol. 333[vo]). First mention of improvements to the gardens occurs in the accounts of 1633, when Willem Dimmer received more than 500 pounds artois for expenditures in the Ysselsteyn *lusthof*, or pleasure grounds (1042 fol. 255[vo]). During the 1630s references to the Ysselsteyn estate do not point to important changes to building and garden but confirm the estate's steady upkeep,[201] for which the same foremen and gardeners working at Zuylesteyn – among them Jacob van Allenburgh, Hendrick van Hattem and Jan van Diepenen as surveyor – were again responsible *(see Appendix, Document IX)*. Changes would occur, however, in the early 1640s, together with further improvement of the nearby estate of Buren.

By 1644 work was in progress to modernize the Ysselsteyn palace and garden, as can be seen from a letter by Pieter Post to the registrar Buysero, which includes information for Huygens about the work at Buren and Ysselsteyn. In this letter, Post states that Her Highness (Amalia) liked the plans and estimates of the building and garden well enough, but that she would prefer the newly-begun construction work to be done 'in the antique or Roman manner'.[202] The content of Post's letter is conducive to a better understanding of the current stadholderly work proceedings, particularly of Post's use of the term 'constructing in the antique or Roman manner' – a rare example of a direct reference to the application of classical style in architectural design. Another important conclusion to be drawn from Post's letter is Amalia's involvement with the building activities at Ysselsteyn. Indeed, since Amalia judged the designs and supervised the work at Ysselsteyn, Huygens was kept abreast not only of her opinions but of the latest developments in general.

The lack of sufficient further archival information and visual evidence makes it difficult to reconstruct the history of the Ysselsteyn castle and its gardens in greater detail. This is the more unfortunate since the building projects undertaken here, though perhaps of secondary importance compared with the large-scale undertakings at The Hague, could complete our vision of Frederik Hendrik's overall building enterprises in the area, executed by the same group of architects, masons, gardeners and land-surveyors that assisted in the other stadholderly gardens. Additional information about the activities at Ysselsteyn could reveal the possible application of specific restoration and replanting methods. Especially tantalizing is the mention of plans of the Ysselsteyn castle and gardens by Pieter Post,[203] whose involvement with Ysselsteyn has not been recorded before and could be of special interest with respect to his work at other estates in the 1640s. Be that as it may, examples of the Stadholder's building activities presented in this chapter provide a first insight into building methods and architectural thought at the Dutch court of the time, which would have important repercussions for the overall development of architecture in Holland.

CHAPTER IV

ARCHITECTURE, THEORY AND PRACTICE AT THE STADHOLDER'S COURT

> There is a middle line dividing Hofwijck into parts
> Of which the left and right sides do not differ;
> An East, a Western gate, an East, a Western path,
> An island East, one West, together form a pair;
> An orchard in the midst, a courtyard, house and pond,
> South on the river Vliet to while the time away.
> This put together on the Golden Balance to weight
> The needle would stand in the house, both scales straight.
> Who censures this distribution shows contempt for himself
> And the fairest which God created. Before I began to dig,
> I took this wise rule as guideline for my actions;
> I looked at myself; more no one needs to do.
> Two windows for Sight, two for Smell, two Ears,
> Two shoulders at right angles, two hips where they belong.
> On either side a thigh, a knee, a leg, a foot;
> It is, I said, God's work and therefore perfectly good.[1]

In the Introduction I briefly discussed the new, unifying architectural style, defined as Dutch classicism, which developed in Holland during the first three decades of the seventeenth century. The evolution of a new building and garden style took place after a long period of gestation which had its roots in late-sixteenth-century developments in science, mathematics and technology. During the early seventeenth century the knowledge of mathematics and geometry, stimulated by recent developments in the science of fortification and land-surveying, came to have a renewed and vital influence on the discipline of architecture and garden architecture.[2] Early references to the importance of mathematics, then seen as a common basis for the art of perspective in painting and the art of proportion in architecture, are found in two important Dutch theoretical works – Carel van Mander's *Schilder-Boeck* (1604)[3] and Salomon de Bray's *Architectura moderna* (1631).[4] Art and architecture, both urban and landscape architecture, thus became closely linked through their mutual mathematical foundations. The interest in the exact sciences and their relationship with art and architecture is also reflected in a series of publications on the subjects of fortification, mathematics, architecture and perspective. Particularly relevant are the standard works by Hendrick Hondius and Simon Stevin,[5] both of whom were involved in garden layouts, respectively at the stadholderly court at The Hague and at Flushing.

From the early seventeenth century onward, garden architecture became as much an object of serious artistic and theoretical consideration as was architecture itself. The engravings published in 1583 in Antwerp by the native Dutch architect-theoretician[6]

Johan Vredeman de Vries in *Hortorum viridariorumque formae (fig. 118)*[7] are good examples of the new relationship between architecture and garden art. Even the classical architectural terminology was used to characterize the different gardens. They were arranged according to the three architectural orders – Doric, Ionic and Corinthian – and embodied abstract, academic design, based on an intricate geometrical arrangement of architectural elements and plant material.[8] With his garden designs Vredeman de Vries demonstrated for the first time that gardens were more than a mere 'ornament to the building', as Serlio still defined them.[9] Novel, too, was the technically advanced manner in which Vredeman de Vries presented his gardens in large perspective views, which, also exhibited in Du Cerceau's French architectural representations, were soon to be copied in Dutch garden prints.[10]

By translating the erudite classical grammar into the modern Netherlandish idiom, de Vries's designs, and the art and architecture they showed, became available to a larger public. Conversely, the idea of publishing works for the common people can be seen as another attempt in that period to have the vernacular accepted as a scientific language. This was supported not only by de Vries's fellow-countryman Simon Stevin but also by René Descartes, who published his scientific findings in French instead of in Latin.[11] The

118. Print from Johan Vredeman de Vries's *Hortorum viridariorumque formae*, 1583, showing the geometrical design in classical, so-called Corinthian style.
The Metropolitan Museum of Art, New York

advancement of the vernacular paralleled the search for a new architectural vocabulary and found a common ground in the growing sense of national identity. The way burgeoning nationalism was mirrored in architecture is perhaps best shown by Philibert Delorme's efforts to add a sixth 'French Order' to the classical canon of the Orders, to the consternation of Italian architectural purists like Scamozzi.[12]

With this search for a new architectural and stylistic language, another Flemish publication would influence early-seventeenth-century architectural thought in The Netherlands, namely Peter Paul Rubens's *Palazzi Moderni di Genova*. As one of the foremost proponents of the classical formal language in the Southern Netherlands,[13] Rubens belonged to a larger, international circle of learned professionals and dilettantes[14] which included not only the Flemish-born architects Wenzel Cobergher and Jacob Francart[15] but also personalities such as Huygens and Van Campen at the Dutch court. In fact, Rubens and Huygens's exchange of ideas on classical architecture, written down in a series of important letters,[16] shed light on various questions regarding contemporary design and building methods in both the Southern and the Northern Netherlands. Thus, the letters of these erudite men are a pre-eminent example of the persistent cultural ties between the two countries (Holland and Belgium), despite religious-political differences and territorial boundaries.[17] Not only were direct contacts between the two countries upheld, but Flemish art was especially appreciated in Holland and at the Dutch court: the account books of the Nassau Domains confirm that a large part of the sculptures and paintings as well as the exotic plants which decorated the Stadholder's palaces and gardens came directly from the Southern Netherlands.

Through these contacts and the exchange of Flemish printbooks by de Vries and Rubens and other Flemish as well as French, Italian and German architects-theoreticians, the knowledge of garden art and architecture was stimulated at the Dutch court.[18] A large body of architectural works of the day was collected by the Stadholder and the elite circles of humanists round him, and, not surprisingly, much of the debate on new style developments in Holland centred round the internationally-oriented court at The Hague. In order to grasp fully the unique position of the court amidst the artistic transformations taking place at the time, and to analyse Frederik Hendrik's gardens properly, it is therefore necessary to consider the kind and degree of architectural knowledge available in the Dutch Republic during this period.

As to the development and diffusion of architectural knowledge at the Dutch court, two points should be made. Firstly, as we have observed, the resurgence of classical theory and design at the Dutch court was not an isolated occurrence but reflected similar architectural interests in European aristocratic circles, from the Southern Netherlands to Sweden. Secondly, none of the classical treatises which have come down to us actually describe gardens or provide a model for an 'ideal classical garden'. As a consequence, seventeenth-century garden layouts designed according to classical principles were largely dependent on the architect's own interpretation and his opinion on the most important aspects of the new classical idiom.[19]

NEW ARCHITECTURE AT COURT: CONSTANTIJN HUYGENS'S TRAVELS AND CORRESPONDENCE

At the Dutch court the most eminent advocates of a 'modern' architectural style centred round the Stadholder. Frederik Hendrik, as patron of the arts and through his close personal involvement in contemporary building projects, stimulated the development of a new architectural vocabulary, once even defined as the 'Frederik Hendrik style'.[20] This new vocabulary, characterized by mathematical measure and fixed rules ('maat en vaste regelen'),[21] evolved round new notions of strict symmetry, rectilinearity and impeccable proportion derived from classical treatises. At first tentatively expressed in the palaces and gardens of the Stadholder, the classical style then spread in a wider circle of artistically-inclined humanists, of which Constantijn Huygens, Jacob van Campen and Johan Maurits van Nassau-Siegen were the core.

In 1625, soon after Frederik Hendrik began his building projects, Huygens became closely associated with the Dutch court, officially as secretary to the Stadholder, as we have seen, but actually also as the Stadholder's artistic adviser. The connection of the Huygens family with the House of Orange, which would have so many important consequences in the sciences, the arts and literature, would span the entire century and would not end until Huygens's death in 1687, at the age of ninety-one. Even then, Huygens's sons Christiaan, renowned scientist at the Académie française, and Constantijn, who would become secretary to William III, in many ways would continue their father's legacy as artistic advisers, as they in turn were involved in the new building activities under William III.

Frederik Hendrik's passion for building and the construction of Honselaarsdijk and Ter Nieuburch have been called the most important element in a final break with the earlier Flemish-Dutch building tradition[22] – rightfully so, since Honselaarsdijk and Ter Nieuburch clearly express a new 'classical approach' to building. As mentioned before, this did not simply mean the superficial addition of classical ornament, as may be seen in Hendrick de Keyser's works, but the thorough application of classical mathematical ideals

119. Bird's-eye view by Matthaeus Merian of Heidelberg, depicting Salomon de Caus's richly decorated terraced garden layout along the Rhine valley.
Photo courtesy Kurpfälzisches Museum, Heidelberg

of form and space to the entire plan and arrangement of the building and gardens. Completed, both palace and garden ensembles anticipated the further unfolding of the new classical style in Holland, first fully expressed in two town houses built at The Hague in the 1630s, the Mauritshuis and the Huygens House, and a little later in several country houses, including Huygens's *villa suburbana* named Hofwijck (1640) and one of the palaces of Frederik Hendrik and Amalia themselves, the Huis ten Bosch at The Hague (1645).

Particularly indicative of this unfolding of a new artistic sense in Holland, and a precious source of information on the degree of contemporary architectural knowledge, are the catalogue of books kept in the library of the Orange family[23] and a catalogue of the library of the Huygens family.[24] Both libraries attest to the current interest in classical and contemporary arts and architecture, for they held an extensive collection of works on architectural theory, including various editions of Vitruvius, Alberti, Vignola, Scamozzi, Serlio, Palladio, Cattaneo, Colonna, Du Cerceau, de L'Orme, Böckler, Furttenbach and Vredeman de Vries, as well as Rubens's work on the palaces of Genoa. In addition to these publications, a long list of works on the related fields of military architecture or fortification, mechanics, mathematics and perspective, among them works by Marolois, de Caus, Hondius and Stevin, were kept in these libraries. It is significant to note the presence of a number of treatises on garden architecture which, in addition to de Vries's *Hortorum viridariorumque formae*, included Jacques Boyceau's *Traité du jardinage*, Salomon de Caus's *Hortus Palatinus* and *Les Raisons des Forces mouvantes*, and Joseph Furttenbach's *Architectura recreationis* and *Architectura privata*. The availability of these works indicates familiarity with the whole body of classical and contemporary architectural theory and garden architecture. Moreover, many of these treatises directly inspired the form and layout of the Stadholder's gardens.

Through the study of these books, and thanks to visits to the palaces of his godfather Henri IV in France as well as to several other European courts, Frederik Hendrik first developed his interest in a new architectural style at court.[25] His military and political duties often forced him to delegate work on his buildings and gardens to his close advisers, among them the much-respected dilettante architect Constantijn Huygens. By following Huygens's career as 'building consultant' at court and studying his role as the actual architect of some buildings and gardens designed after his own interpretation of classical treatises, much can be learned about the artistic reasoning behind, and actual construction of, Frederik Hendrik's palaces and gardens. As a result of Huygens's search for scientific-artistic principles and his objective, scholarly study of classical architectural treatises and Renaissance structures, new directions could be taken in the art of building in the Dutch court environment. Huygens's own comments in his early travel journals[26] and his extensive correspondence provide a good picture of this new aesthetic process.

More so than Frederik Hendrik himself, Huygens had the opportunity to study buildings and gardens outside Holland. At the centre of Huygens's interest in architecture was the first-hand knowledge of contemporary building practices he had obtained during his travels abroad, and which he had augmented by the study of all major architectural treatises, from Vitruvius to contemporary French and Italian authors.[27] Indeed, during his first trip to England in 1618 at the age of twenty-two, Huygens visited the various palaces at and round the English court. On that occasion he may have met the English royal architect Inigo Jones,[28] who was among the first to apply classical principles to architectural designs. Huygens admired some of his works[29] and, in playful defiance, tried to exceed Jones's new architectural style when constructing his own house at The Hague:

I have built a house, had prints made of it and will send them to you; Inigo Johns [*sic*] will see that his manner does not differ much from this one ...³⁰

The 'manner' Huygens refers to in his letter is the new classical style of building, based on Vitruvius, Alberti and Palladio, among others. He not only knew these classical works but also studied the original classical monuments when travelling through Central and Southern Europe.

As early as 1620, during his trip to Northern Italy in the retinue of the Dutch embassy to Venice, Huygens admired at first hand surviving buildings of the classical past and the Renaissance, studying amphitheatres and palazzi in Venice (Palazzo Ducale, the Libreria by Sansovino and Scamozzi), Verona (Palazzo Bevilacqua by Sanmicheli) and Vicenza (Teatro Olimpico by Palladio).³¹ Evidently much impressed by these classical buildings, Huygens was most fascinated by Palladio's Teatro Olimpico, which he called a 'bastiment moderne, mais à la verité tel qu'en Europe ne se peut veoir chose plus belle'.³² When looking back on his trip to Italy many years later, he speaks of 'veteris praecepta Vitruuj / Exemplis firmata novis et marmere vivo' (the old precepts of Vitruvius confirmed by new examples and living marble).³³

120. Mid-seventeenth-century German grotto garden filled with beds of rare flowers and sculptural ornament, from Joseph Furttenbach's *Architectura privata*. The Metropolitan Museum of Art, New York

121. The Cleves garden by Jan van Call, c. 1680, with Minerva statue and view from the Springenberg terraces and garden islands to the Rhine valley. Rijksprentenkabinet, Rijksmuseum, Amsterdam

During this same trip Huygens also visited the palace of Friedrich V, Elector Palatine at Heidelberg, laid out by Salomon de Caus shortly before its destruction during the siege of the city in 1620 *(fig. 119)*.[34] Here he must have admired the garden terraces filled with intricate parterres and classical sculptures, such as the *River Gods*, and the remarkable sound-filled grottoes with *automata*.[35] In his writings Huygens expressed the opinion that the fountain and grotto in this garden compared favourably with, indeed even excelled, those of France. Moreover, Huygens's description, and admiration, of de Caus's waterworks at Heidelberg subsequently had implications for the type of fountains and grottoes decorating the gardens of Frederik Hendrik, which in many respects echo de Caus's style.

Comparable to the form and decoration of the Heidelberg garden were the designs shown in the contemporary German architectural treatises of Joseph Furttenbach. Both Huygens and the Stadholder must have been familiar with these works, for copies were to be found in their libraries. Furttenbach's designs constituted a mixture between his observations on modern villa gardens studied during his sojourn in Italy and his personal interpretation of Italian classical style principles, adapted to a Nordic climate and to local socio-geographical circumstances. The title of one of his treatises, *Architectura recreationis*, which described architecture both on a practical and on a metaphysical level, is particularly meaningful in the context of Holland's growing nationalism and garden art: *recreationis* not only meant exercise or 're-creation', but was used here in a political-nationalistic sense, denoting the architecture of 'resurgence', or the rebuilding of the country after many years of war.[36]

Furttenbach's garden designs in this treatise, his *Architectura privata (fig. 120)*,[37] and Dutch courtly gardens have many points in common. Especially noteworthy are his designs of fortressed palace and garden ensembles, which not only can be compared with the early donjon-form of Honselaarsdijk but also with the bastioned outlines of the Valkenberg gardens at Breda and other medieval stronghold components in Dutch seventeenth-century gardens. Furttenbach's intimate garden courtyards decorated with rare flowers and intricate grottoes seem to depict the very gardens laid out at The Hague at that time, from the courtly gardens at the Noordeinde to those in the central square of the city, the Stadhoudersplein. Furttenbach's description of grottoes filled with artifice and *exotica*, including shell-encrusted waterworks, painted cosmological imagery and remarkable

IV. ARCHITECTURE, THEORY AND PRACTICE

mirrors,[38] seems to portray the very garden laid out by Johan Maurits across from the Mauritshuis, containing parterres with exotic plants and a large circular grotto with shells and no fewer than thirty-nine mirrors.[39]

Huygens particularly admired Johan Maurits's garden at Cleves *(fig. 121)*,[40] situated on the border with Germany and begun in 1647 on the latter's appointment as Stadholder of the Elector of Brandenburg. The garden of Cleves contained the impressive terraced Springenberg park and the intimate pleasure garden of the Prinzenhof, laid out in collaboration with Jacob van Campen.[41] When in 1652 Huygens, accompanied by his son, the young scientist Christiaan Huygens, walked through the garden, they both found it to be 'très plaisante'.[42] They were not the only ones to comment on the beauty of the Cleves garden. If we may believe Johan Maurits's own claims, thousands of people came to admire the garden and gave excited reports, going so far as to say that it was 'better than anything to be found in Rome or France'.[43]

Some of the most important aspects of the Cleves garden, with its landscape-architectural features and sculptural monuments, warrant a brief review, as they pertain to developments in garden art at the Dutch court. Firstly, Cleves's unique natural situation was fully exploited, resulting in an Italianate terraced garden with a Palladian amphitheatre on the steep hillside of the Springenberg, as well as the characteristically Dutch block-like islands or *insulae* in the boggy planes of the Rhine valley. A network of radiating avenues, similar to the perspectival alleys in the Honselaarsdijk and Ter Nieuburch prints, connected the various monuments and trophies, from the Column of Mars to the statue of Minerva, carrying familiar allusions to the art of War and Peace and the virtue of the Van Nassau ancestral line.[44] Interestingly, a copy of the statue of Minerva, conspicuously placed at the centre of the gardens of Ter Nieuburch, also was the central monument of the Cleves garden, holding similar iconographical allusions.[45]

Secondly, the hedged orchard-roundel of the Prinzenhof, divided into eight sections reminiscent of a compass card,[46] showed the continuing fascination with the circular motif in the seventeenth-century garden, from Heidelberg to Honselaarsdijk. In its large-scale form of a *rond-point*,[47] it was later epitomized by the circular orchard in the garden of Enghien,[48] from which William III was to draw inspiration.[49] It was the aspect of the *insulae* at the foot of the Springenberg which made the Cleves garden resemble the Stadholder's layouts and Huygens's own gardens most closely.

In addition to outlining his architectural impressions in his travel journals, Huygens liked to exchange thoughts on the new mode of building in letters to his friends and relatives. This is especially fortunate since Huygens's correspondence is an important source for our understanding of the development of architectural thought at court and in Holland in general. The extent to which the ancient writers were esteemed and studied by contemporary scholars can be inferred from the correspondence with humanists and dilettante gentlemen-architects moving in Dutch court circles. The most important correspondents included Jacob van Campen, Johan Albert Bannius,[50] Johan Brosterhuisen,[51] Joachim Wicquefort,[52] Daniel Heinsius[53] and, outside Holland, Peter Paul Rubens. The letters of Brosterhuisen and Wicquefort, in particular, should be mentioned here as they provide in condensed form an excellent example of the current understanding of classical architectural theory.

The first sentence of a letter written in the spring of 1635 to Wicquefort immediately confirms Huygens's all-consuming preoccupation with classical studies, 'whenever he could steal some time away from his public duties'. Referring to the construction of his house at The Hague, which was designed according to classical precepts, Huygens quotes the most important classical building treatises, the translation of which he strives to undertake for the sake of posterity. He asks Wicquefort to assist him in the endeavour of comparing carefully the various editions of classical texts in order to come forth with an exact, correct transcription:

> Tout ce que je puis derobber au publicq s'employe à l'architecture antique. C'est l'humeur ou m'a porté ce petit bastiment, que j'iray entamer, s'il plaisoit à ce troisiesme hiver de la saison. J'en suis desjà si avant, que je furette soigneusement les choses plus obscures, et prens plaisir à sçavoir en theorie, ce que la prattique ne me demandera jamais. Cela me faict rechercher tous les bons textes de Vitruve et tous les commentateurs ch'egli s'è terato adosso, par un stile dur, scabreux, fantasque et si esloigné de la grace du siecle qu'on luy attribue, que dernierement j'ay osé doubter aveq M. Heinsius, si Auguste l'a jamais ouy parler. Par tant de preface je pretends de vous induire à m'assister de vostre entremise en la recherche de ces livres. Les Italiens m'alleguent un Giovanno Jucundo, Cesare Cesariano, G. Baptista Caporali, Daniele Barbaro, patriarcha d'Aquileia, et Bernardino Baldi, abbate di Ganstalla, et en parlent aveq bien du faste. De tout cela rien ne se recouvre pardeça les monts. Non pas Leon Baptista Alberti, seulement en son Latin original, que je desire tant conferer aux versions. Prestez moy, Monsieur, de grace la faveur de vos habitudes vers ces beaux climats du midy. Je couve quelque dessein, qui aveq le temps se pourroit esclorre au bien de la posterité, et elle vous en aura ce qu'il faudra d'obligation. Je prevoy bien les peines où je vous engage, mais c'est pour le passé, sur les asseurances de la bonne volonté que vous m'avez tesmoignée, et pour l'advenir, à dessein de me tenir tousjours prest de pardeçà à vous faire ressentir mes ressentimens ...[54]

In numerous other letters written during the 1630s to his scholarly friends, Huygens urgently requested Alberti's original Latin commentary and other Italian commentaries on Vitruvius to enable him to grasp and calculate precisely the new harmonic rules. As Johan Brosterhuisen writes in 1642 regarding his own as well as Huygens's and Van Campen's combined efforts to publish books on classical architecture:

> With my translation of Vitruvius I have advanced halfway through the last book. Mr. Van Campen advises me to translate thereafter Palladio's last book, on the temples of the ancients, and next the last chapters of the second last book on the public buildings; this, then, could be printed following the translation of Vitruvius, unless you would not agree. 'My Wotton' [Henry Wotton], who is said to be Vitruvius's precursor, is ready to be printed but has only been waiting for a story of the origin of architecture that Mr. Van Campen has planned.[55]

Thus, about 1630, for the first time in Dutch architectural history, the classical style began to be approached not merely as a decorative adjunct but as a fundamental rule: expressed not only in the use of the classical orders and ornamental motifs on building façades but also in the whole form and composition of house and garden.

Central to the issue of the contemporary evolution in architectural style in Holland is the terminology which frequently appears in Huygens's letters and other commentaries on architecture. The words 'proportion', 'symmetry' and 'regularity' belong to the most frequently used and soon-to-be-standard vocabulary of the new building style. Of special interest in this context is the correspondence between Huygens and Rubens, which has yet to receive detailed scholarly attention,[56] particularly considering the above-mentioned observations on the enduring cultural-artistic links between the Southern and Northern

Netherlands in the first half of the century.[57] For example, in one of his letters to Rubens, Huygens uses the words 'égalité reguliere' and 'architecture ancienne et moderne',[58] which appear again and again, not only in his letters but also in his poetry, exemplified by the quotation with which this chapter opens. With Rubens, Huygens shared both admiration for classical architecture and a negative opinion on Gothic architecture. In 1622, in his foreword to *Palazzi di Genova*, Rubens hailed the slow disappearance of Gothic style in architecture in favour of 'true symmetry', as he called it, in accordance with 'the rules of the ancients'.[59] Similarly, in 1653 Huygens used the word 'Gothic' depreciatingly in a poem of praise for Jacob van Campen, who had struck 'the foul Gothic scales from the eyes of the blind, badly building Dutch'.[60] As early as 1635, Huygens had asked Rubens's advice for the design of the house at The Hague. Rubens would be glad to hear, Huygens wrote, that with this house 'l'architecture ancienne', which they both cherished so passionately, would be revived:

> Vous ne serez pas marry d'apprendre, que je pretens faire revivre là dessus un peu de l'architecture anciene, que je cheris de passion, mais ce n'est qu'au petit pied, et jusqu' à ou le souffrent le climat et mes coffres.[61]

Of course, Huygens added, 'It [the revival of classical architecture] cannot be done but on a small scale [petit pied], and only as far as the climate and my finances will allow.' Huygens's last words are significant, for they are a reminder of the climatological and financial limitations imposed by the Dutch situation on the practical application of any classical architectural theory. Remarkably enough, Huygens's words echo almost literally the apologies given by the architect Salomon de Bray in his *Architectura moderna*. Urging his reader to compare the greatness of modern Dutch buildings with the buildings of the ancients, de Bray at the same time begs them to be lenient, explaining that any derivation from the classical ideals is due to the softness of Holland's marshy grounds and the lack of natural stone, as well as possible (financial) limits imposed by the owner.[62]

THE URBAN DEVELOPMENT OF THE HAGUE AND THE STADHOLDER'S 'NATURAL INCLINATION TOWARDS ARCHITECTURE'

One of the earliest examples in Holland of the application of this new, classical vocabulary in architecture is found in the urban development of The Hague, namely the construction of the central piazza, or *plein*, and the houses surrounding it. While garden and urban design clearly have dissimilar approaches, a comparison between the stadholderly gardens and the design of the Plein at The Hague is justified, for urban and landscape architecture were imagined as being closely linked and having the same mathematical foundation. This well-documented building project demonstrates the Stadholder's expert knowledge of classical architecture, as well as his close personal commitment to the successful completion of the new layout of The Hague which, be it on a more modest scale, in many ways reflected the efforts undertaken earlier by his godfather Henri IV of France.[63] Moreover, and not surprisingly in view of the Stadholder's involvement, direct links exist between the construction of the Plein and its town houses and that of the Stadholder's country houses, particularly Ter Nieuburch, which was completed during the same period.

The urban building project included the Mauritshuis (begun in 1633) and Huygens's own house, the so-called House on the Plein (1634), across from the Mauritshuis. The buildings

Painting by A.J. van der Croos of Ter Nieuburch in c. 1634 Rijswijk Museum (see fig. 46)

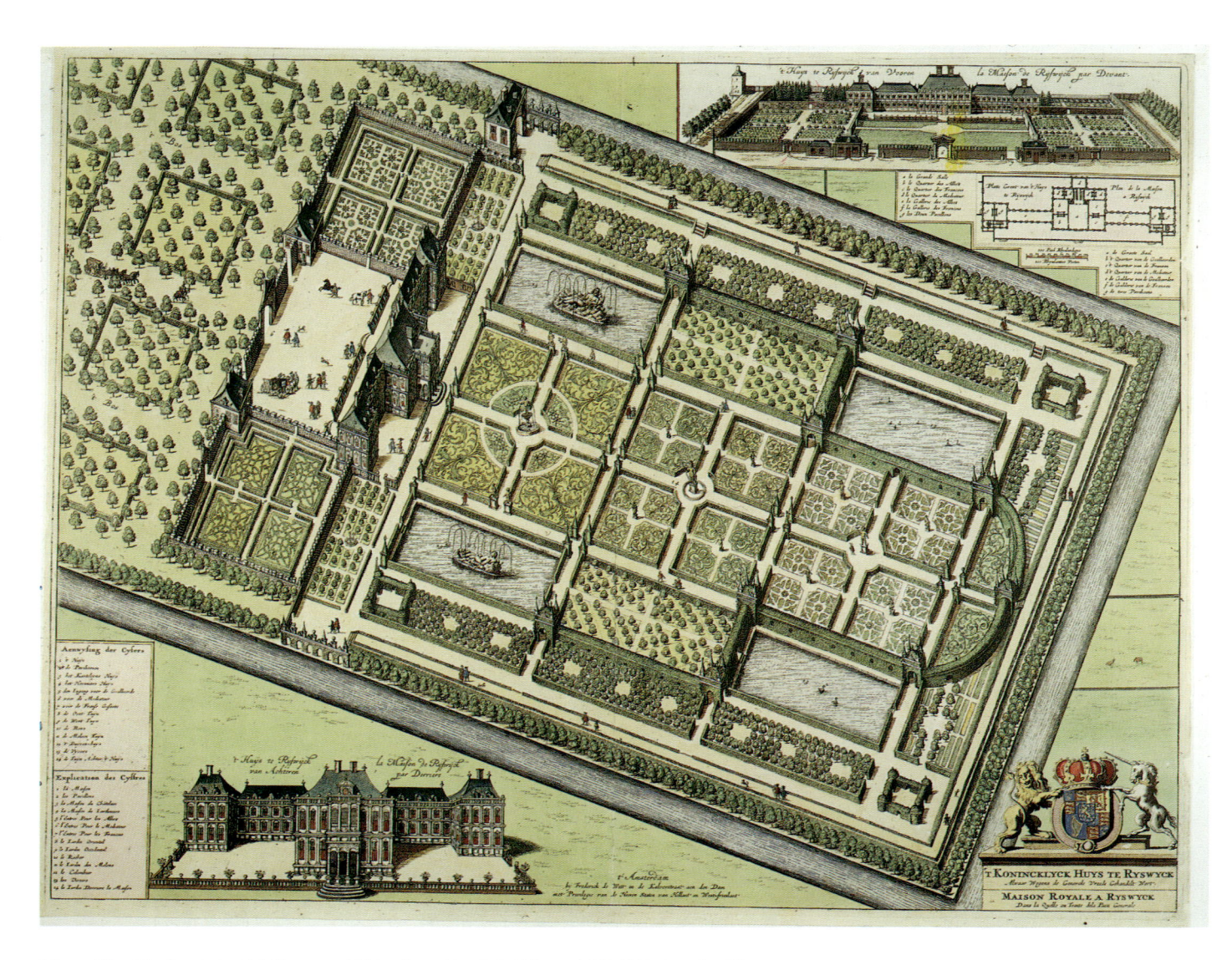

View of Ter Nieuburch by J.J. Milheusser, 1644, reissued by F. de Witt, c. 1697. KHA (see fig. 47)

COURTLY GARDENS IN HOLLAND 1600-1650

122. Plan for the new layout of the Plein (a) at The Hague's centre, adjoining the Ducal Court (b), Mauritshuis (c) and Huygens's house (d).
Algemeen Rijksarchief

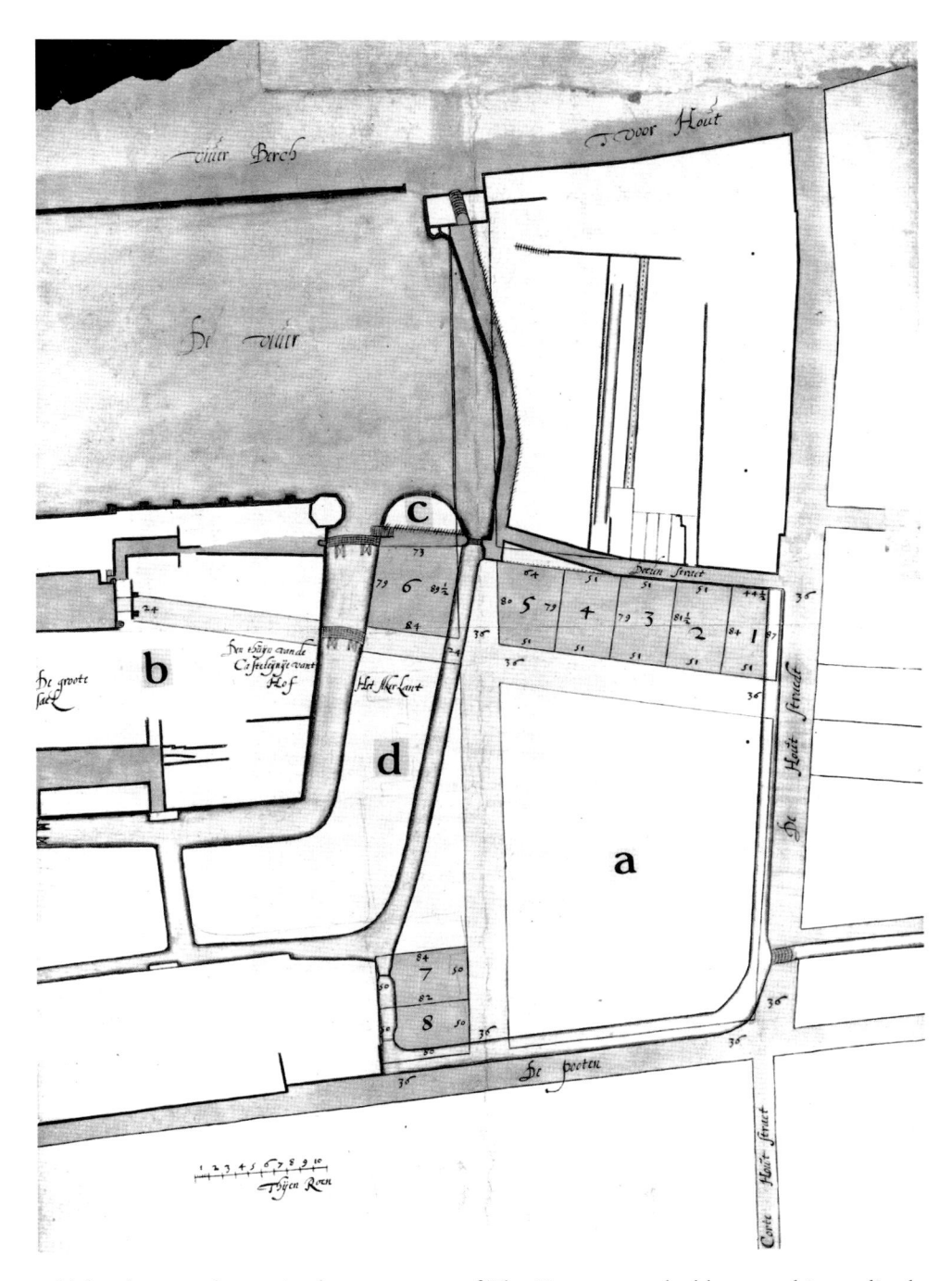

which subsequently rose in the new centre of The Hague, on valuable ground immediately east of the Binnenhof, or Ducal Court *(see fig. 87)*, for the first time manifest a full grasp of the essential nature of classical architecture: a design of solid forms and well-proportioned space instead of merely an aggregate of decorative motifs or accumulative blocks.[64]

As can be concluded from contemporary correspondence, it was largely due to the Stadholder's personal insight and efforts that the urban improvement of The Hague took place. The Plein and Huygens's house were laid out according to Frederik Hendrik and Huygens's personal ideas and directions, closely following classical architectural rules. In their endeavours Huygens and the Stadholder were assisted by Jacob van Campen and the well-known dilettante architect Prince Johan Maurits van Nassau-Siegen, owner and co-designer of the Mauritshuis.

IV. ARCHITECTURE, THEORY AND PRACTICE

Describing his house to his neighbour Johan Maurits, Huygens relates with mounting enthusiasm how both houses embellish the newly-laid-out area of the Plein *(fig. 122)*.[65] He boasts how spacious the new piazza is from which broad streets diverge and how all 'disorder' is admirably 'regulated' ('touts desordres reglez'), thus alluding once more to the classical dictum of regularity and symmetry. Huygens closes his letter with an apology for the tediousness of his long discourses on architecture, explaining that to bother only 'one master' about architecture is not quite enough, and, referring to Frederik Hendrik as his other 'victim', he admits to architectural discussions with the Stadholder in spite of his many duties:

> J'ay accoustumé de desennuyer mon maistre (comme il vous en souvient) par des discours d'Architecture au fort de ses grandes affaires.[66]

Numerous other letters in Huygens's correspondence again and again attest to the fact that Frederik Hendrik never wearied of discussing architectural matters. Even during military campaigns the Stadholder spent hours studying and ordering his architectural operations at Honselaarsdijk, Ter Nieuburch and his other palaces. To be entertained by such matters during his many occupations was of great importance and certainly the most agreeable of his diversions, the Stadholder himself and Huygens stated several times.[67] Further correspondence and documents show that architecture and gardening were not just seen as an 'agreeable diversion' or *divertissement*[68] by the Stadholder but approached as a serious study, involving close personal scrutiny of works in progress and even the development of his own alternative designs. Indeed, when it comes to the urban development of the open area adjacent to the Binnenhof in the early 1630s *(see figs. 87 and 122)*, it was thanks to Frederik Hendrik's foresight that a spatial, geometrically arranged square was created, approachable by broad avenues.

Both the piazza and the avenues leading to it, which still embellish The Hague's city centre today, greatly improved the area around the Old Ducal Court. However, the project only narrowly escaped plans for an agglomerate of small parcels with houses, crossed by narrow streets. When Frederik Hendrik saw the initial, mediocre plans submitted by a Treasury Advice Committee, which had subdivided the area in as many plots as possible in order to profit from their sales, he immediately brought the project to an end.[69] On suspending the original project, Frederik Hendrik commented dryly that he would rather be remembered as being a squanderer than be accused of the terrible crime of having ruined The Hague.[70] According to a letter by Huygens, it was due to Frederik Hendrik's 'natural inclination towards architecture' that the embellishment of The Hague was undertaken:

> …le tout à l'instance de S Ex.ᵉ qui, par affection naturelle qu'il porte à l'architecture, ne cesse d'animer un chascun à l'embellisement de la Haye, et à mesme intention m'a honoré de ce beau present.[71]

Apparently Frederik Hendrik regularly visited the new building site to 'warmly encourage' Huygens, and insisted on coming on foot to judge personally the progress of the houses on the Plein, as can be seen from a letter written to the German general Milander:

> Outre que Monseigneur mon maistre m'aiguillone chaudement, desirant veoir ma maison sur pied: pour y avoir contribué beaucoup de son ordonnance et pour estre – vous le savez mieux que moi – assez nouvellier en bastimens.[72]

123. Huygens's house on the Plein, designed by Huygens with the cooperation of Van Campen and others and built in classical style on precepts of the ancients. Gemeentearchief, The Hague

These telling comments, referring to the Stadholder as being 'quite novel' in architecture – a fact apparently even known abroad ('vous le savez mieux que moi') – clearly show Frederik Hendrik's interest in and practical understanding of building and designing in the classical mode.[73] The results of the Stadholder's and Huygens's knowledge of classical architectural principles would be evident in the design of Huygens's house in a very special way, as we shall see.

HUYGENS'S HOUSE AT THE HAGUE AND HIS COUNTRY HOUSE HOFWIJCK AT VOORBURG

The application of classical principles to architecture and garden architecture is best exemplified by Huygens's town house on the Plein at The Hague and his country house Hofwijck at Voorburg, just outside the city. The design history of Huygens's town house warrants a closer look, particularly since Frederik Hendrik, as appears from the correspondence, gave direct advice on its construction.

Though Huygens's house was demolished in 1876, a record of how it was remains in the form of prints and drawings *(fig. 123)*[74] as well as several letters and notes by Huygens describing its design. An unfinished treatise entitled *Domus*[75] includes a rough draft which discusses Huygens's plans and motives for building this house, created, as he writes, to demonstrate the revival of Dutch architecture. As was the case with the layout of the Plein itself, the principles followed in designing and erecting the house were based on the strict

IV. ARCHITECTURE, THEORY AND PRACTICE

mathematical system of the ancients, in that the Vitruvian human body was taken as a main point of departure. Yet, contemporary architecture, too, observed by Huygens during his various travels, influenced the design. Thus, while in detail classically Italian, the overall layout of Huygens's house was French: it had a U-shaped ground-plan consisting of a main *corps-de-logis* with two perpendicular wings surrounding a *basse-cour*. This basic idea of the form would soon find its expression in other Dutch buildings, such as Arent van 's Gravesande's Lakenhal at Leiden. The innovative design of the ground-plan, strictly based on the classical Italian mode with its symmetrical arrangement and unusual double staircase (*keizerstrap*, or imperial staircase), strongly resembled the layout of the Mauritshuis and, what is more, the layout of the vestibule and staircase at the Ter Nieuburch palace. Indeed, Ter Nieuburch's central pavilion with double staircase, built in 1630-33 and first shown clearly in the series of preliminary designs, must have been the 'master model' for Huygens's town house.[76] In point of fact, Huygens himself mentions that his house was built in consultation with the Stadholder, who advised on the correct orientation of the building according to Vitruvius's theories on the four winds.[77] And none other than the Stadholder's architect, Simon de la Vallée, who was involved in Ter Nieuburch's design, made suggestions about the ground-plan.[78] Van Campen, too, assisted by advising on the proper foundations and the general scheme of the house, while neighbour Johan Maurits van Nassau-Siegen was consulted about its general layout.[79] Finally, Huygens also recorded the involvement of his wife, Susanna Hoefnagel, whose practical suggestions resulted in the final rectangular shape of the house.[80]

The results of Huygens's classical studies, especially of Vitruvius, were apparent in the division of the house, as its main rooms were planned exactly according to the principles of symmetry and harmonic proportion propagated by Vitruvius and his commentators. As appears from Post and Van Campen's designs for the Mauritshuis, the Huis ten Bosch and the Paleis Noordeinde, one of the most favoured commentators among the Dutch court architects was Scamozzi.[81] A learned architect writing and designing for cultured men,[82] Scamozzi particularly appealed to Huygens. Consequently it may have been one of Scamozzi's diagrams of the 'Vitruvian man' published in 1615 in *L'Idea dell'architettura universale*, showing 'the extent to which Geometry embraces the human body',[83] which Huygens used when designing his houses and gardens, as we shall see presently. In any case, the Vitruvian analogy between the human figure and the ideal architectural form which Scamozzi depicted was clearly expounded in Huygens's written work, as is shown by this chapter's opening verses and Van Pelt's publication.[84]

Huygens not only followed Vitruvius's precepts in building his house according to the ideal proportions of the human body,[85] he also crowned the pediment with three female figures. They symbolized Vitruvius's three basic principles of good architecture, *Firmitas*, *Utilitas* and *Venustas*, emphasized again in Alberti's later commentary.[86] (Three similarly sculpted female figures decorated the pediment of the palace of Honselaarsdijk and may have expressed the same virtues, though it was believed that they personified Hope, Faith and Love.[87]) In the case of Huygens's house, the chimneys also were topped by the terrestrial and celestial spheres.[88] Subtle as their presence may be, these spheres and their meaning are of central importance for an understanding of Huygens's house as a *domus cosmographica*. Moreover, the spheres will turn out to have major ramifications for an iconological interpretation of Frederik Hendrik's gardens, where two circles or spheres reappear mysteriously as the central component of the whole design.[89]

In Holland as well as abroad the building projects undertaken at court were seen as a revival of the classical, Graeco-Roman past following the 'dark age' of architectural illiteracy under the Goths and the Vandals, as is shown by contemporary comments by

124. Bird's-eye view of Huygens's country estate Hofwijck at Voorburg, showing an elongated orchard garden in geometrically arranged blocks.
Gemeentearchief, The Hague

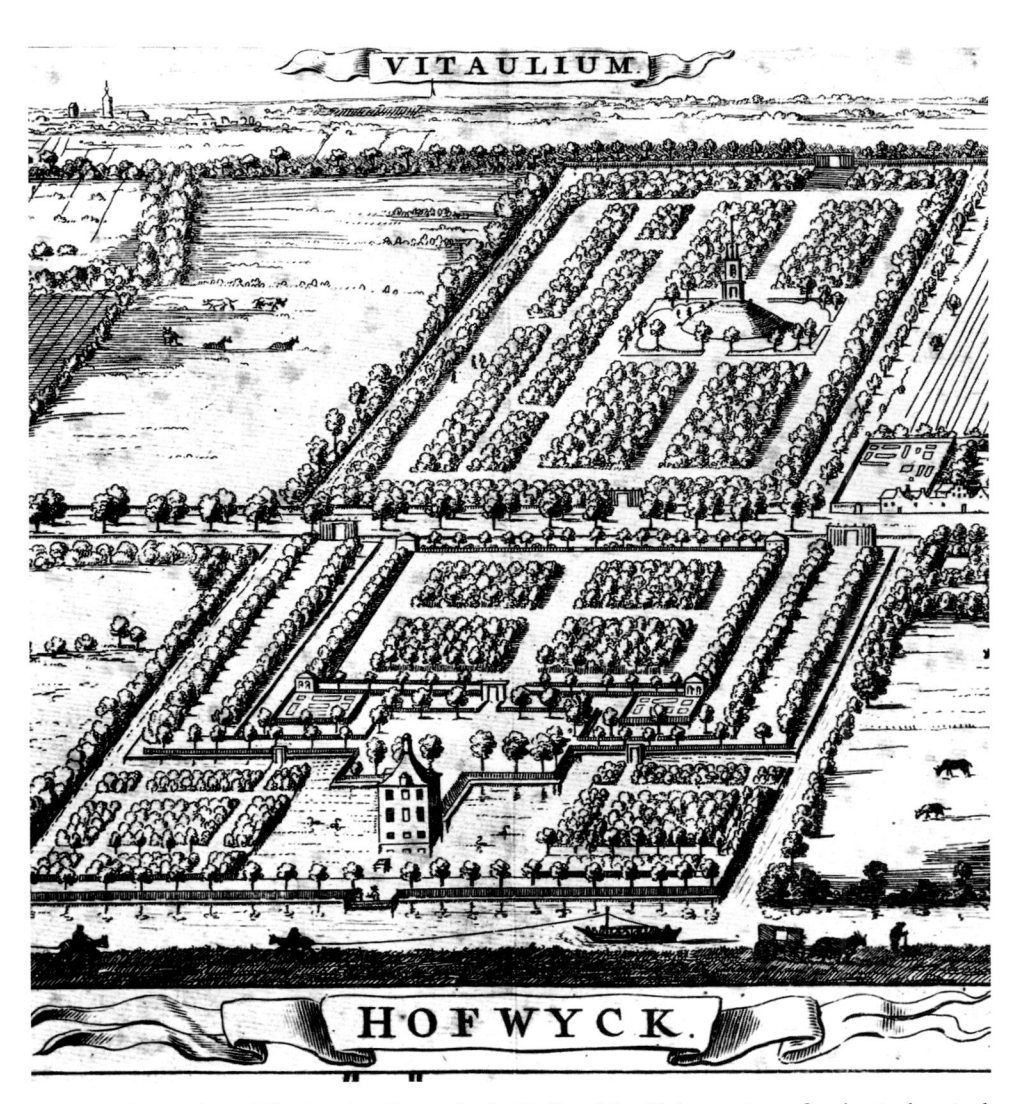

interested Dutch and foreign intellectuals. In Holland itself the notion of a classical revival found its expression in elaborate allusions to a 'New Rome' and to the mythical Batavia of ancient times; it was illustrated by the dedicatory poem on the Van Berckerode print. Huygens's epitaph for the architect Jacob van Campen developed the same historical and architectural theme, in that former Gothic Heresy is said to have been driven away by older Roman Truth.[90]

The way foreign intellectuals responded to the stylistic developments at court, associating its architecture with particular structures from classical antiquity, deserves special attention.[91] For example, an international group of literati commented on the design of Huygens's town house on the Plein by comparing it with buildings from the classical past. Referring to Pliny's *Letters*,[92] the well-known French man of letters J.-L. Guez de Balzac went so far as to say that the prints of Huygens's house at The Hague gave him no less pleasure than the two descriptions Pliny gave of his villas.[93] Louis XIII's secretary-adviser Valentin Conrart, a pivotal figure in French literary circles, later secretary of the Académie française, also admired the design.[94] One Dutch friend and scholar even wrote that the prints depicting the house were to him a commentary on Vitruvius, ending his letter by wishing that the house would remain standing for centuries as a memorial to Huygens's genius.[95] Similar complimentary remarks were extended in contemporary travel journals regarding the construction of the Stadholder's palaces, particularly Ter Nieuburch;

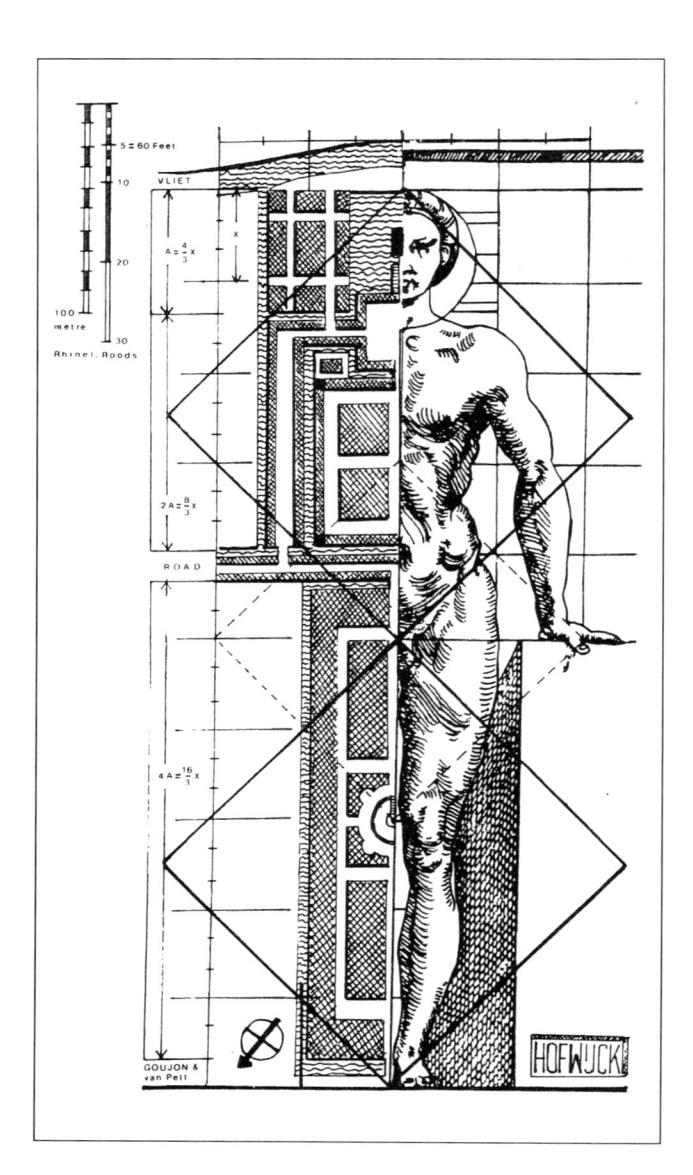

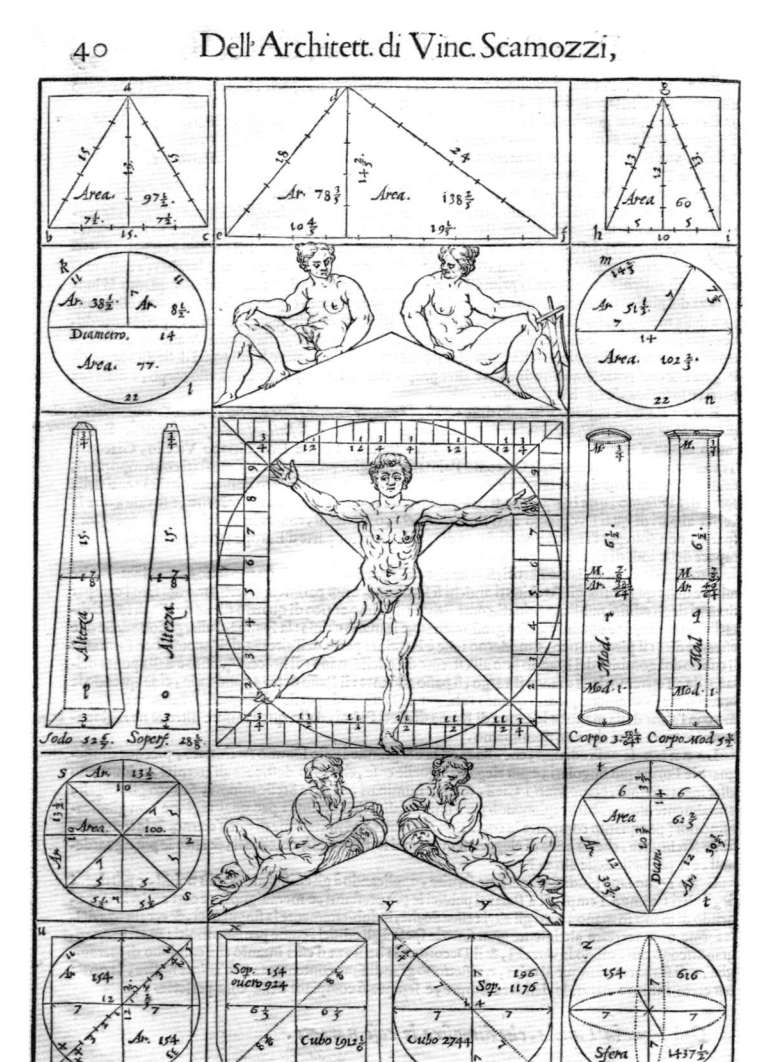

the 'regularity' of the whole building, its symmetry and the use of the classical orders in the palace's façade were hailed as particularly impressive and 'correct'.[96]

Classical principles can also be recognized in the layout of the garden behind Huygens's house on the Plein, the triangular form of which may have been derived from architectural treatises but at the same time must have been dictated by the shape of the remaining plot of land, called the Aeckerlandt.[97] Triangular in shape, this garden, like Prince Maurits's older garden at Flushing, seemed to follow classical geometrical ideals. While the various geometrical shapes of the triangle are clearly described and depicted in Serlio's *Tutte l'Opere d'architettura et prospettiva* and Scamozzi's *L'Idea dell'architettura universale*, they also were known in Holland through the mathematical publications of Prince Maurits's own engineer Simon Stevin, which contained a special section on Trigonometry.[98] Apart from its form, the garden was of special interest because of its decoration, enclosed as it was by a wall painted with scenes from Holbein's *Dance of Death*.[99] Though little is known about these ephemeral objects today, murals and painted perspectives apparently were a common feature of garden ornamentation, as garden architects were advised in contemporary treatises, such as André Mollet's, to place painted perspectives at the end of alleys to create the illusion of far views.[100]

125. Plan of Hofwijck as reconstructed with the ideal Vitruvian figure superimposed on the layout, the house corresponding to the head, etc.
Photo after reconstruction drawing by R.J. van Pelt

126. Vincenzo Scamozzi's diagram of the 'Vitruvian Man' from his *L'Idea della architettura universale*, 1615, which may have inspired garden design at the Dutch Court. The Metropolitan Museum of Art, New York

166   COURTLY GARDENS IN HOLLAND 1600-1650

Classical principles also were the foundation of Huygens's country estate, which was laid out in three carefully proportioned plots surrounding a small square, moated house designed as a centralized, classical pavilion *(fig. 124)*.[101] The garden layout of Hofwijck is of particular consequence, for it is here that the connection with the Stadholder's gardens, laid out along similar lines according to principles advocated in classical treatises, first appears. Moreover, the same architects involved in the design of Hofwijck, Jacob van Campen and Pieter Post, were working for the Stadholder. In both the Hofwijck garden and the Stadholder's gardens – especially Honselaarsdijk and Ter Nieuburch, but also the Huis ten Bosch and the Noordeinde – a new sense of the unity of form and space, rhythmically composed and divided, is evident in the design. How these classical principles were translated into garden architecture, and how they were consequently perceived, can be studied in the layout of Hofwijck, the history of which is well documented.

The layout of the Hofwijck garden and its metaphysical meaning are described by Huygens in his country-house poem *Vitaulium. Hofwijck*. A precise analysis of the text of this poem suggests that the plan of Hofwijck was designed according to strict mathematical principles following Vitruvian and Albertian precepts, and that its design forms a microcosm, reflecting the harmonious relations of the larger universe.[102] The verses with which this chapter opens, quoted from Huygens's *Hofwijck*, are the crux of the anthropomorphic vocabulary of the poem and indicate direct links between the form of the garden, its division in two equal halves and three main sections, and the shape of the human body. This verse and the accompanying illustrations taken from *Hofwijck* must suffice here to explain the connection Huygens drew between word and image, as he wrote how the ideal human body and its cosmological imagery are the basis of his garden design.

As to the plan of the garden, its very shape (circa 120 x 400 metres) seems to express what Huygens wrote in his verses on the ideal of the human body. The garden's structure and severe symmetrical arrangement can be related to Renaissance theory on absolute symmetry and the universal outstretched human figure as it was formulated by Alberti, the left corresponding exactly to the right.[103] The study by Van Pelt, which gives a cosmological interpretation of the whole layout along Neoplatonic and Pythagorean lines, suggests that in the layout of Hofwijck, which consists of three plots intersected and divided by canals, one can recognize the basic outline of the 'Vitruvian man': the moated house is supposed to represent the head, the middle section the chest, and the orchard with central mound the knees and legs of the outstretched human body *(fig. 125)*.[104] A comparison with the illustration of Scamozzi's 'Vitruvian man' *(fig. 126)*,[105] together with what we know about the predilection for his designs at court, seems to corroborate such an analysis.

This 'physical' analysis is then taken a step further and extended into the spiritual realm: according to Van Pelt's study, using Post's print and Huygens's own poem, this anthropomorphic plan is believed to symbolize not only the macro- and microcosms but also, in philosophical terms, the path of redemption.[106] A walk through the garden, described by Huygens as a walk towards God, according to this study, was perceived as symbolizing the three components not only of man's physical but also of his metaphysical nature – body, soul and mind, as one moves through the three parts which constitute the garden, beginning at its end in the orchard and ending in the moated house.

In spite of the subtlety of such an analysis which combines word and image, the question remains whether the conclusions presented in Van Pelt's study are altogether correct. One of the obstacles encountered in Van Pelt's work is the gap between the written text and the actual execution of the garden layout. While a sincere effort is made to bridge this divide between the theoretical and the practical or 'actual' design, the geographical realities may not have been taken sufficiently into consideration. In fact, one of the topographical elements left out is the public road which split the Huygens estate in two, and the irregularities in the boundary of the estate, which make it necessary to adjust the figure of the 'Vitruvian man' to fit the grid plan of the garden. Besides, Huygens's poem was written ten years after the creation of the estate, when the garden had matured, thus possibly influencing its original interpretation. All told, however, we should not entirely discard the hypothesis that the garden layout and its parts, if not in actual sense then certainly abstractly, were thought of in such classically inspired, Platonic and Pythagorean terms, by which certain proportions had a particular meaning, as Wittkower, and more recently Naredi-Rainer, have pointed out for the realm of architecture.[107] Huygens himself, foreseeing difficulties due to a literal interpretation of his text, admitted that art had to be stretched somewhat to allow for the discrepancies between the dimensions of the plots and the ideal human proportion: 'Art did not suffer violence, but let itself be slightly stretched …'[108] In other words, if the real garden of Hofwijck did not conform in all its details to absolute classical rule, the fictitious garden in Huygens's mind did. Thus, in spite of our hesitations about the actual superimposition of the 'Vitruvian man' at Hofwijck, the cosmological imagery connected with this ideal figure is the basic background against which the creation of Huygens's garden should be seen, as will be discussed in further detail in chapter VI.

After the limitations of a literal interpretation and the difference between abstract design ideas and their materialization have been established, the cosmological imagery of the ideal man appears more credible in the light of studies of the Huygens house and the Mauritshuis as *domus cosmographica*.[109] In these studies a close analogy between the basic form and layout of the Mauritshuis and the form of the Roman theatre given by Vitruvius in *De Architectura*[110] is demonstrated and presented as proof of the adaptation of classical form and related metaphysical thought at the Dutch court. The plan of the Roman theatre consisted of a circle with four inscribed equilateral triangles which, according to Vitruvius, could be compared with the astrological figure used to measure the musical harmony of the stars.[111] Because of Vitruvius's 'cosmological' analogy, in the sixteenth and seventeenth centuries this geometrical shape was regarded as an image of the cosmos.[112]

While discrepancies between the actual dimensions of the Mauritshuis and its purported architectural prototype also make its interpretation as a cosmological image uncertain, in this particular case the remarkable decoration of the interior appears to substantiate a cosmological analogy. Decorated with allegories of the four corners of the world and portraits of rulers from the ancient and the recent past, including, among the Roman Emperors, the Princes of Orange and rulers of the House of Nassau,[113] the interior appears to follow contemporary cosmography to the letter.[114] More important, as will be shown in the following chapters, to these examples one can add the classical-inspired layout of the Buitenhof garden with its two circles. Indeed, the Buitenhof design, like the Hofwijck garden, may be interpreted as an architectural example of the general re-emergence of cosmological thinking expressed in contemporary Dutch humanist literature.[115]

In Frederik Hendrik's garden layouts we can recognize an equal fascination for the axiom of all classical architecture, that is, the principles of symmetry and proportion, which were partly derived from Vitruvian, Pythagorean and Albertian theory.[116] At the same time, similar differences or 'gaps' to those encountered at Hofwijck can be seen to crop up between theory and practice in the Stadholder's garden designs. For our inquiry it is important to realize that, ever since Wittkower's well-known book was published,[117] there has been a tendency in modern literature to overemphasize an analysis along Platonic, symbolic lines.[118] In fact, it is important to realize that principles other than spatial geometry and harmonic proportion play an essential part in the creation of buildings and, as will be shown here, in garden architecture as well.

Paradoxically, the key to an alternative approach to the interpretation of classical architecture was offered by Renaissance commentators themselves, in particular Alberti. As recent studies have pointed out, Alberti did not necessarily mean his architectural values to be fixed rules, as Wittkower has interpreted them.[119] Alberti even allowed for modifications and measures of freedom in the creative process of building, much in the way flexibility was allowed in the closely related art of classical *rhetorica*.[120] Alberti emphasized the problems which the architect would encounter during the creative process of design and construction; following Vitruvius's remarks,[121] he allowed for the modification of ideal form and proportion to accommodate the nature of the site as well as the function and purpose of the building. These qualitative principles of usefulness and convenience, summarized in the already familiar Vitruvian triad *Firmitas*, *Utilitas* and *Venustas*,[122] in addition to quantitative criteria such as spatial mathematics and harmonic proportion, were an integral part of the art of building and garden designing.

FREDERIK HENDRIK AS PATRON AND DESIGNER OF GARDENS

An overview of the urban development of The Hague and the layout of a *villa suburbana*, both following classical rules, serves as an introduction to the unfolding of Dutch classicism and the part Frederik Hendrik played in it. Frederik Hendrik's role in other architectural undertakings and his passion for and personal involvement in the construction of his own palaces and gardens are further expressed in numerous letters of Huygens to Amalia. A selection of the most important ones is added here.

In 1638 the citizens of Breda eagerly awaited the arrival of Frederik Hendrik, who came to inspect the new bulwarks and the architectural changes to the castle of Breda,[123] including the renovated gardens of the Valkenberg.[124] Another letter describes the long days spent by Frederik Hendrik discussing the restoration projects at the castle of Buren with Jacob van Campen:

> …Tout ce que nous avons de nouvelles pardeça, c'est que demain S. Ex^e va faire une promenade jusqu'à Buren, en intention de n'y coucher qu'une nuit. J'aij eu ordre d'ij appointer aussi le S^r van Campen, qui veut dire, qu'on n'ij passera le temps à des choses de fascheuse importance…[125]

and we can add to this:

> …La plus part des heures s'emploije à considerer le Bastiment aveq le S^r van Campen et ce qu'il ij aurait moijen de faire; qui sont toutes choses plus tot de speculation, que d'aucun dessin effectif, hormis le changement du degré qui est bien necessaire, et la reparation du toict et quelques croisées au haut de la maison [de Buren].[126]

It can be concluded from these letters, and several others written in the same vein, that Frederik Hendrik personally supervised and even directed details of roof repair and window construction. He was equally involved in aspects concerning the interior decoration of his palaces, as is shown by a letter of Huygens to Amalia about the wall decoration of the gallery at Ter Nieuburch in 1636, which shows that Frederik Hendrik preferred flower designs to grotesque motives and planned to prepare an essay discussing his ideas:

> Monsieur le Comte Maurice, parti d'icy ... a eu ordre de representer à V.Ex.e ce que Monseigneur le Prince trouve à redire au patron de fueillage, desseigné à la galerie de Rijswijck. En general S.Ex.e voudroit que tout ressemblast à des fleurs et fueilles plustost qu'à de la grottesque; que le fonds fust d'une couleur gaye et vive et que surtout les armes fussent attachées à l'ouvrage par l'un ou l'autre rapport ou lien de bonne grace. Je croy qu'il sera à propos que S.Ex.e en voye encor un essay, si V.Ex.e n'en rencontre quelqu'un qu'elle juge luy debvoir satisfaire asseurement.[127]

If Frederik Hendrik was so committed to the structural problems of his architectural enterprises and their inner decoration as appears from these letters, one may expect an equally close involvement in the garden layout and ornamentation of his estates. And, indeed, the correspondence frequently refers to his control of matters concerning the improvement of the gardens:

> Avant hier au soir ... [S.A.] demeura bien deux heures à ordonner les jardins et Bastiments de Honselardick...[128]

In 1632 Frederik Hendrik also sent direct orders to André Mollet to change certain aspects of the parterres then being laid out at Honselaarsdijk:

> I received your letter with the orders of His Excellency concerning the parterres; the manager [*intendant*] And. [André] Mollet will put things right. But one must also take care of the water drainage. Catshuysen [estate steward] promises to do his best at Honselaersdijk.[129]

In reply to Frederik Hendrik's detailed inquiries Mollet sent a letter describing his works on the parterres.[130] Apart from the layout of the gardens and its parterres, Frederik Hendrik also personally oversaw the planting with trees and flowers. In answer to a request from the Stadholder, the court counsellor David de Wilhem wrote to Huygens that he would do his best as regards the planting of the trees in the gardens, though he rather wished the Prince would commission him to fulfil other projects.[131]

Most fascinating of all is a remark in the correspondence between Huygens and Amalia about Frederik Hendrik's personal abilities as a designing garden architect:

> Son Altesse vient de recevoir une lettre de V.A. par un messager de Buren hier, et me commande d'en envoyer un expres pour porter ceste boitte, et deux plans du jardin à Rijswijck, pour lequel M. van Campen avoit encore formé un autre dessein, qui me plaisoit assez, mais S.A. a preferé ceux-ci, qui sont de sa propre ordonnance ...[132]

From this letter it may be concluded that Frederik Hendrik prepared his own designs for the new garden layout of the Huis ter Nieuburch at Rijswijk, and that he preferred his own plans to Van Campen's. Fortunately, some of the preliminary drawings survive, though we cannot be sure whether any of these recently discovered plans actually relate to the one designed by the Stadholder himself. Nevertheless it is significant that Ter Nieuburch's final garden plan was for a large part dictated by the Stadholder's own architectural insights, and certainly by his and Amalia's personal taste. Frederik Hendrik and Amalia also collaborated in setting up the iconographical programme of the interior of the Paleis ter Nieuburch. A contemporary manuscript, written in the Stadholder's hand, gives a detailed description of the members of the European royalty who were to be portrayed in the galleries.[133]

Throughout his lifetime Frederik Hendrik drew pleasure from personally showing his gardens to royalty, ministers and other distinguished visitors at court. When Queen Henrietta Maria of England, on the occasion of the forthcoming marriage of William II and Mary Stuart, visited Frederik Hendrik at Buren, she met the Stadholder on her return from a walk through the gardens, whereupon he invited her to see the gardens of Buren in all their detail:

> La Reine … partiroit sur les trois heures vers Buren, s'y achemina aussi promptement, et y trouve S.M.[té] arriveé une demie heure auparavant, qui desjà avoit faict le tour des jardins, avant qu'entrer en sa chambre, comme elle dit estre sa coustume partout. … S.A. s'en retournant au logis du drossart, et ayant mené la Reine apres disner au grand jardin, qu'elle n'avoit encor vue.[134]

In addition to giving tours through his own gardens, Frederik Hendrik seized every opportunity to see the gardens of other prominent garden owners and botanical virtuosi. He frequently visited the gardens of his relatives, courtiers and friends, among them those of the Count of Solms, near Utrecht,[135] and Count Johan Wolfert van Brederode at Vianen.[136] It was on such occasions, we can imagine, that these gentlemen-soldiers would retire to their libraries after a walk through their gardens and discuss matters of architecture, art and horticulture.

BUILDING PRACTICE AND GARDENING AT COURT

Earlier publications have generally neglected to research in depth the artistic leadership behind Frederik Hendrik's architectural enterprises and garden designs. While this literature singles out various individuals as possible designing architects, it still remains unclear who was responsible for the total design concept of the Stadholder's palaces and gardens. Though opinions on the attribution of the works at Honselaarsdijk and Ter Nieuburch differ, most authors assume that the building projects were primarily in the hands of Jacob van Campen and Simon de la Vallée, and at a later stage in those of Pieter Post.[137] For the Ter Nieuburch palace, the perspective painter Bartholomeus van Bassen is added to the list of possible designers-architects.[138] For the gardens André Mollet is usually mentioned as the sole architect.[139] More recent literature emphasizes the role of the patron; it is suggested that the plan for the gardens of Honselaarsdijk was developed by Frederik Hendrik himself, assisted by his elder brother Maurits and with the collaboration of Jacques de Gheyn.[140]

Though a number of theories have been put forward about the person(s) responsible for the design of the Honselaarsdijk and Ter Nieuburch houses and garden complexes, none of these theories can be verified with certainty, since the documents available to us simply do not provide conclusive evidence. However, whereas a closer study of archival documentation of the Nassau Domain may not produce such evidence as to *the individual* responsible for designing Frederik Hendrik's palaces and gardens, these documents yield important information. Looking into the question of *how* the palaces and gardens were constructed instead of *by whom* leads to a better understanding of the development of

Frederik Hendrik's gardens. Through this approach of concentrating on the method of design rather than the possible designer a proper assessment can be made of Frederik Hendrik's palaces and gardens. Moreover, by studying more closely the creative process, larger questions about formal and stylistic origins, especially seen in the light of the contemporary influx of architectural theories from abroad, can be answered.

IDENTITY AND RESPONSIBILITY OF ARCHITECTS IN THE BUILDING PROGRAMME

In order to answer the question of the identity of the designer, we must first have a general impression of the way archival documents describe, or fail to describe, the involvement of certain individuals in the building enterprises at court. One problem immediately becomes apparent when reviewing the records of payments. These records only mention who was involved, without describing his exact function or position within the larger building programme. Careful study of the records shows that, even though a person's name is followed by a formal title in the accounts, such as 'architect', 'garden architect', 'draughtsman' or 'supervisor', these titles do not necessarily explain their actual role in the building projects. Thus, despite the fact that Bartholomeus van Bassen carried the important title of 'perspective painter and architect' and was credited for making designs of the whole building complex with gardens and surrounding lands of Ter Nieuburch[141] and certain sections of Honselaarsdijk,[142] this should not be interpreted as implying that he was the actual 'designing genius' behind the project, as some authors believe.[143] Instead, Van Bassen's drawings should be seen as an integral part of the work performed by a painter-draughtsman, providing Frederik Hendrik with a clear overview of the current state of the building, as Slothouwer points out.[144] Van Bassen's involvement as draughtsman rather than designer is confirmed by the fact that he is mentioned only once in the records of payments of Ter Nieuburch and Honselaarsdijk. Furthermore, though Van Bassen was well paid for his involvement at Honselaarsdijk,[145] he only received a modest sum for his work at Ter Nieuburch (80 pounds), which once again casts doubt on his role as the actual designing architect of the palace and grounds.

A similar case is that of Arent van 's Gravesande, later a famous architect in Leiden,[146] involved in the works at Ter Nieuburch and Honselaarsdijk. In the accounts he is referred to as 'architect', but actually he had a more subordinate position comparable to today's supervisor-in-chief.[147] At the same time, Gerrit Druivestein and Pieter van Bilderbeeck were named as 'architects', though they functioned as inspectors, checking and surveying the old and new works at Ter Nieuburch.[148] In the records of payments Arent van 's Gravesande is also referred to as 'draughtsman' (*teijckenaer*)[149]; he did indeed provide drawings for certain details of the buildings, such as the entrance gate and staircase at Honselaarsdijk[150] and the terrace with balustrade at Ter Nieuburch.[151] At Honselaarsdijk, Arent van 's Gravesande closely collaborated with other artists, designers and craftsmen. In this context his collaboration with Simon de la Vallée, referred to in the account books as 'the French architect', should be noted (1042 fol. 244).

Simon or Jacques de la Vallée, as he is called in the accounts, was the first person to be hired by Frederik Hendrik as official architect and can be considered as the 'architect-in-chief' during his years at the Dutch court from 1633 to 1637, though the extent of his activities remains vague. We do know that he completed the improvement of the whole *corps de logis* and front courtyard at Honselaarsdijk, which, originally rounded in shape, was extended into a monumental square area.[152] De la Vallée and Van 's Gravesande are mentioned as working together, with a host of other craftsmen including a painter and a blacksmith or ironworker, as 'building managers' or 'directors of the works' at Honselaarsdijk.[153] In this capacity de la Vallée also seems to have worked at Ter Nieuburch (1042 fol. 298). In addition to supervising the newly-begun works there, he may also have been responsible for certain designs, one of which could have been an ideal plan of Ter Nieuburch, namely the 'French plan' copied after the Luxembourg palace and gardens described above *(see fig. 51)*. Further investigation of Simon de la Vallée and his work may be fruitful, especially in view of Huygens's remark that he made suggestions for the design of his house on the Plein. Such an investigation could refute some of the opinions expressed by the la Vallée specialist Nordberg, who, reacting against earlier beliefs that the development of Dutch classicism depended on de la Vallée,[154] believed that his influence in Holland was slight and found that his later designs have little in common with Dutch classicism.[155] It should be mentioned that Nordberg was not familiar with the strongly French-inspired, classical preliminary designs for Ter Nieuburch. Be it as it may, de la Vallée was much respected at court, receiving an extra bonus upon his departure, while his son Jean in later years was reimbursed for his stay in Holland when travelling from Paris back to Sweden (997 fol. 306vo).

The stonemason Bartholomeus Drijffhout is frequently mentioned in the account books and seems to have had a function similar to that of Arent van 's Gravesande, combining his craft as a stonemason with that of executing drawings of plans and elevations. Though Drijffhout was paid for several drawings of elevations for Ter Nieuburch and Honselaarsdijk,[156] without further detailed information it is difficult to conclude that he was the designer of the Ter Nieuburch façade. Rather, it would seem that he provided a detailed drawing of how the brick and natural stone should be used. Like Van 's Gravesande, who would make a name for himself as city architect of Leiden, Drijffhout would later enjoy fame as a designing stonemason-architect at the Paleis Noordeinde, working under Pieter Post.[157] In both cases, the construction of Frederik Hendrik's palaces was the crucial stepping-stone for these men's careers as craftsmen-artisans-architects, as well as for many others. During the construction of Ter Nieuburch, Drijffhout and Van 's Gravesande were joined by a group of workmen – stonemasons, bricklayers, plumbers, woodworkers and other specialized craftsmen from the region of The Hague and Leiden – to complete the building tasks. This is shown in the recently recovered *bestecken* for Ter Nieuburch dating from 1633.[158]

For the later building activities in the 1640s Jacob van Campen and Post seem to be the leading personalities; both are frequently mentioned in the accounts from 1637 onward as 'painters-architects'. It is difficult here to give Van Campen and Post their proper places in the complicated network of Frederik Hendrik's building programme. Pieter Post, though involved since the late 1630s, was officially appointed court architect in 1645, a position he held until his death in 1669.[159] As the Stadholder's architect, Post succeeded Simon de la Vallée, who tendered his resignation in 1637 and left for Sweden with his son Jean.[160]

Jacob van Campen never had an official appointment as court architect, but was introduced to the Prince by his secretary Constantijn Huygens and became involved in the Stadholder's building activities in 1635.[161] In Van Campen we may recognize for the first time the genius of the architect-designer responsible for the design of the Mauritshuis and the Town Hall of Amsterdam. Van Campen also assisted Huygens in designing his house on the Plein at The Hague, and he was admired as the architect who had rescued Vitruvius from oblivion and thus brought back 'the light to the Earth'.[162] As he did in his above-quoted epitaph, in his poem *Hofwijck*, too, Huygens hailed Jacob van Campen as the genius who with his architectural *ratio* was able to lift off the foul Gothic shell from the faces of the blindly building Dutch.[163]

In 1636 Van Campen began his career at court. In addition to some architectural designing, it comprised the total interior decoration of the Stadholder's palaces. Starting with Buren[164] and followed by Honselaarsdijk (1636), Ter Nieuburch (1638)[165] and the Paleis Noordeinde (1640), his work would culminate after Frederik Hendrik's death in the completion of the famous 'mausoleum' Huis ten Bosch (1647-50).[166] At Honselaarsdijk and Ter Nieuburch, in constant consultation with the Stadholder, Van Campen would function as a designing co-ordinator, leaving the realization of his design ideas to others, such as Pieter Post, the stonemason Bartholomeus Drijffhout and several well-known Dutch and Flemish painters including Paulus Bor, Pieter de Grebber, Gerard van Honthorst, Moyses van Uyttenbrouck and Jacob Jordaens.[167]

Of particular interest, both from a stylistic and from an iconographical point of view, was Van Campen's ability to combine architecture, wall decoration and painting to create a unified whole.[168] At Honselaarsdijk the decoration of the large entrance hall, the staircase and the great reception hall on the first floor (or *piano nobile*), which provided a panoramic view over the whole garden, bears witness to this unifying principle. The total effect was complemented by the painted vaults of the reception hall, which show people from all over the world peering over a balustrade at Frederik Hendrik's painted triumphs while welcoming visitors.[169]

At first working as a painter-designer, Van Campen also came to supervise the sculptural decoration of the Stadhouder's palaces, the ornamentation of the outer pediment of Honselaarsdijk[170] and the sculptural programme of part of the gardens of Honselaarsdijk and Ter Nieuburch.[171] From 1637 onward, after de la Vallée's departure, Van Campen was engaged as architect proper and, as we have seen, was active as garden architect assisting Huygens and Johan Maurits in their garden endeavours. Most important, Van Campen not only advised Frederik Hendrik on gardens but made actual garden designs, notably for the grounds of Ter Nieuburch, some of which may be recognized among the surviving preliminary designs for the palace *(see figs. 53-56)*.[172]

With the reconstruction of the Paleis Noordeinde in 1640, however, Van Campen's role as leading architect at the Dutch court may be said to have reached its climax. On the other hand, Post's role should not be underestimated, as Slothouwer tends to do in referring to his 'simplicity' as opposed to Van Campen's 'monumentality'.[173] The records clearly show that Post collaborated with Van Campen at the Paleis Noordeinde, where he was *opsichter op de Timmeragie*, or supervisor of construction and carpentry.[174] Furthermore, Post and Van Campen could have collaborated not only in constructing the Noordeinde palace but also in improving the gardens, where Post is mentioned in connection with a new grotto (995 fol. 90vo). Whereas Van Campen was responsible for designing the Noordeinde façade inspired by a design of Scamozzi,[175] and may be considered the 'man of ideas', Post's strength was the honest, diligent approach of the architect-technician.[176] While admiration for Van Campen waned in court circles owing to his difficult, unpredictable character and his inability to complete his commissions in time,[177] Post became more appreciated for his dependability to finish the work. Not surprisingly, it was Post who was appointed stadholderly architect, not Van Campen.

If Post during the early stages of his career can be considered an architect-technician rather than a designer-architect, over the years he developed strong designing skills, as demonstrated by his extension plans for Honselaarsdijk which include a monumental design for the garden and grounds *(see fig. 17)*.[178] Several letters quoted in previous chapters referred not only to these plans[179] but also to other designs and estimates (*bestecken*) made by Post for the Stadholder's buildings and gardens, among them Buren and Ysselsteyn.[180]

Post's *chef-d'oeuvre*, however, was the Huis ten Bosch, designed after Scamozzi's Villa Badoer, as noted in chapter III.[181] In the gardens of the Huis ten Bosch several aspects of the Honselaarsdijk and Ter Nieuburch gardens were to be found again, for instance the importance of a carefully conceived mathematical ground division, the unity of palace and garden and the relation of the whole complex to its surroundings by means of a system of axes. Some features characteristic of the Honselaarsdijk and Ter Nieuburch layouts are seen again at the Huis ten Bosch, though in an almost exaggerated form – the strict symmetry of the layout and the severe 'regimentation' of the grounds in carefully proportioned blocks. The adherence to classical ideals of absolute symmetry and exact proportion, resulting in a certain stiffness of the layout, is also typical of Post's designs for other Dutch country houses, such as Rijxdorp and Vredenburg.[182]

The frequent mention of Post's name in Huygens's correspondence with his family and friends, particularly where the layout of new country houses is concerned from the early 1640s onward, is further evidence of Post's ability as an architect. In fact, Post's country estates retain a special place in the history of Dutch country-house architecture, as their form and layout betray the clear influence of the elements of palace architecture, skilfully combined with classical design features. Post's monumental designs for Vredenburg, the Huis Het Zant (not executed), Rijxdorp and Heeze, carried out between 1639 and 1665 in a style emulating that of the Stadholder's palaces, were meant for high-ranking court officials in need of a representative abode.[183] By having Post design not only their homes but the interiors and surrounding grounds as well, these courtiers could boast of owning a veritable unified work of art.[184]

When it comes to the more modest country-house projects, Post's involvement in the garden of Huygens's country house Hofwijck[185] was an important stepping-stone leading to many new commissions for the layout of estates belonging to Huygens's relatives and friends. Thus, at the time Post was assisting in designing the grounds and country house of Hofwijck, he was also working for Huygens's brother-in-law Philips Doublet at Clingendael, an estate situated on the border of The Hague,[186] and for Arent van Dorp at the neighbouring country seat of Arentsdorp.[187] All three building structures are characterized by the same classical form and style, being centralized pavilions standing in water. Not surprisingly, when a new city architect was sought in Leiden, Huygens recommended Post, calling him the best architect in the country and the most suitable man for this function.[188]

It would appear that Post was already committed to making architectural designs at an early stage of his career. While he first collaborated with Van Campen in executing important architectural commissions, during the 1640s Post gradually developed his own circle of patrons. It is also known that early on Post translated Van Campen's notoriously unclear first sketches into clear working drawings for workmen to follow at the various projects at court, as well as later at the Town Hall of Amsterdam.[189] Hence, considering the many times his name occurs in the records of payments during the 1650s and 1660s (Nassause Domeinraad 995-996), it is not surprising that it finally was Post who as leading architect and designer supervised and directed the work in progress at Honselaarsdijk and Ter Nieuburch.[190]

At Ter Nieuburch, Post was assisted by the *concierge-fontainier* Joseph Dinant, with whom he would also collaborate in the layout of new grottoes in the gardens of the Paleis Noordeinde (995 fol. 90vo). The frequency with which, besides Post, Dinant is mentioned as supervisor of the works at Ter Nieuburch, as well as at Honselaarsdijk, suggests a high degree of responsibility.[191] Originally invited from France to arrange the waterworks and grottoes in Frederik Hendrik's gardens in the early 1630s, Dinant had made a career that was distinguished by a quarter century of trustworthy service, during which he had progressed from a *fontainier-grottier* to an indispensable 'general foreman'. At court he was highly favoured by the Stadholder and continued his employ even after Frederik Hendrik's death. Actually, after the death of his son Otto George he was granted the privilege of having his grandson Frederic Dinant inherit the title. Later, Frederic Dinant is mentioned as the new *fontainier-grottier* of 'the fonteinen en grotten tot Honsholredijck, Rijswijck en in Den Haag'.[192] The grottoes 'at The Hague' referred to the grotto in the garden of the Paleis Noordeinde which, as new documentary evidence shows, was made by Dinant about 1653 (995 fol. 90vo). During his lifetime Joseph Dinant received a generous salary, including a bonus in 1653 for his 'extraordinary services' in completing new grottoes at 'Rijswijk, Honselaarsdijk and elsewhere', totalling more than 3,000 guilders (995 fol. 114vo).

Whereas much attention has been lavished on André Mollet's role in Frederik Hendrik's gardens and the consequent French-inspired style of their design, ironically enough Joseph Dinant's role has been overlooked. This is unfortunate since his influence seems to have been considerable, as shown by the wealth of new archival evidence available to us now. Obviously, in view of larger questions concerning the designer(s) of the courtly gardens and their stylistic origin, more attention should be paid to Dinant. For example, in the layout of the waterworks and grottoes at court we can find direct stylistic connections with France. By further developing the art of the grotto in the courtly gardens, Dinant followed in the footsteps of Jacques de Gheyn, who until his death in 1629 had advised Maurits and Frederik Hendrik in laying out their gardens and grottoes. Furthermore, Dinant may also have influenced the actual design of the courtly gardens, especially those of Ter Nieuburch, where as 'supervisor' – and in association with the architects Van Campen and Post – he may have been involved in the layout as a whole.[193]

Thus far, we can conclude from archival documentation that Frederik Hendrik's palaces were not designed by one 'genius', nor completed under one architect-designer or supervisor. The work was undertaken with the collaboration of a large group of 'architects-designers', craftsmen and artists, often exchanging their more or less specific trade and craftsmanship for other activities. The 'hierarchy' among these workmen-architects also fluctuated, depending on who was available at a particular place and at a particular time. The artists, architects, artisans, craftsmen and gardeners came from a large variety of educational backgrounds and places, both in and outside Holland, such as Belgium and France, or were hired either from the immediate surroundings of The Hague or from around the country, including the cities of Breda, Delft, Haarlem and Meurs. The aspect of 'teamwork' did not only apply to building constructions but, as a closer analysis of the account books shows, the layout of the Stadholder's gardens as well.

THE STADHOLDER'S GARDENS: THEIR DESIGNERS AND THEIR SOURCES

Though Morren, Slothouwer and other scholars offer a very precise survey and analysis of the architecture of the Stadholder's palaces, they are not much interested in garden architecture. Even Slothouwer's exhaustive study of Frederik Hendrik's palaces fails to give a complete list of documents specifically dealing with these gardens. In the case of Honselaarsdijk and Ter Nieuburch, André Mollet is frequently and rather easily referred to

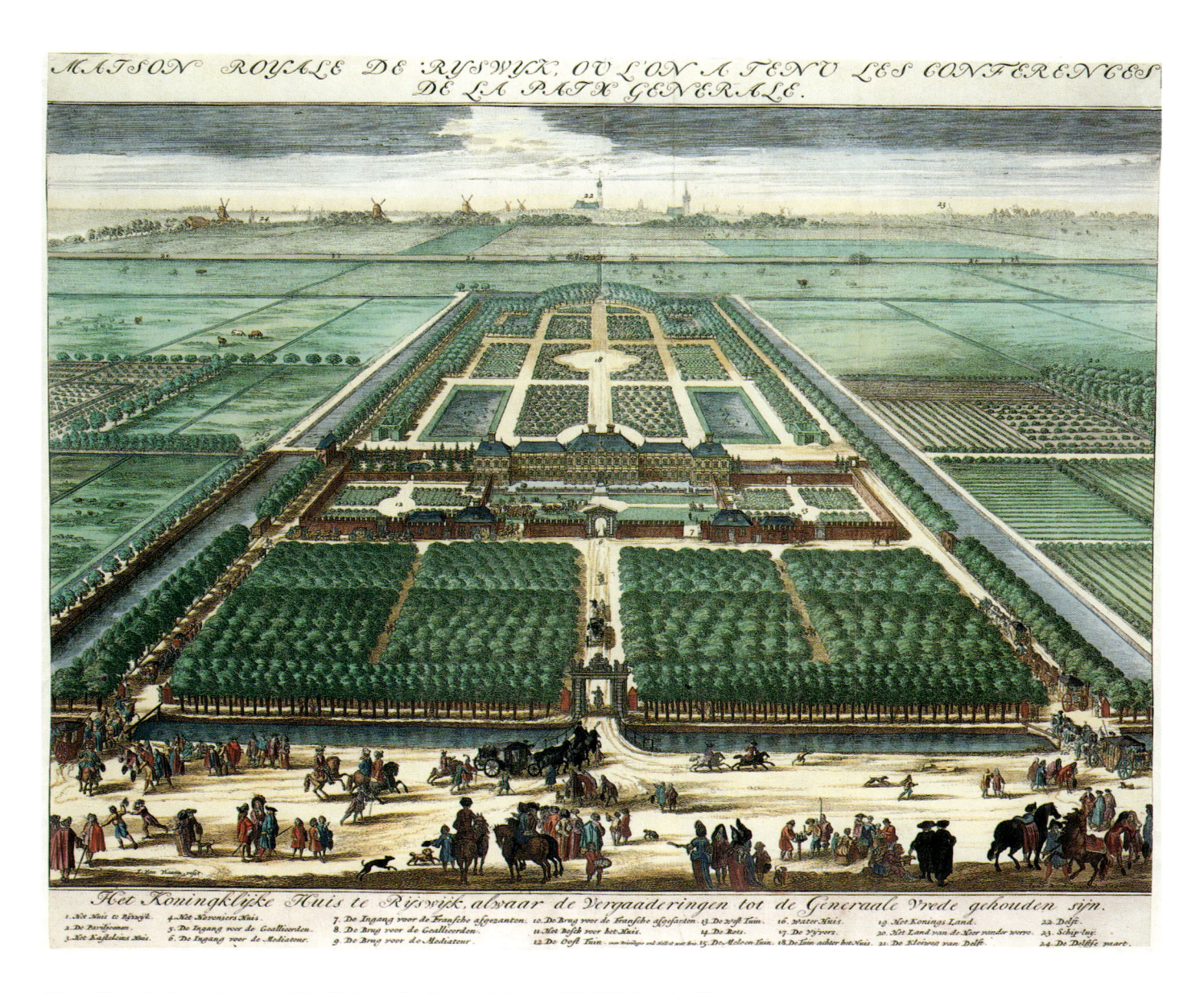

View of Ter Nieuburch during the Rijswijk Peace Conference, A. Beek, 1697. KHA (see fig. 63)

COURTLY GARDENS IN HOLLAND 1600-1650

Design for a grotto in one of the Stadholder's gardens. RPK (see fig. 68)

as the leading architect-designer.[194] The history of the Honselaarsdijk garden as represented in a series of maps *(see figs. 8, 9 and 13)* has shown that its form and basic layout as well as the division of its inner compartments had already been established before Mollet's arrival at the Dutch court.[195] Based on the evidence provided by the records of payments, and as previously mentioned, Mollet was not responsible for designing the total complex of Frederik Hendrik's garden layouts, but primarily for the very intricate *parterres de broderie*.

In spite of the fact that Mollet was not the actual designer of the Honselaarsdijk garden as a whole,[196] his responsibilities as parterre designer, supervisor and a kind of plantation master were comprehensive: he designed not only the parterres at Honselaarsdijk (1042 fol. 232[vo]) but also those of many other gardens owned by the Stadholder, and probably even those of his relatives and friends. Closer reading of the records of payments shows that Mollet designed parterres at Buren (1042 fol. 232[vo]), Zuylesteyn (1043 fol. 243) and most likely also at Ter Nieuburch.[197] Close similarities between Ter Nieuburch's parterre layouts and those at Vianen and Groningen suggest Mollet's direct involvement, and at least proves inspiration by his style of parterre designing, which would later inspire the parterres of the gardens owned by the Stadholder's daughters in Germany, as we shall see. The architect Pieter Post and the gardener Borchgaert Frederic were also inspired by Mollet's typically intricate, embroidered parterre designs when laying out the parterres of the Huis ten Bosch (993 fol. 428[vo]), which resemble the parterre ornamentation of Frederik Hendrik's other gardens.

In addition to being the designer of parterres, Mollet also supervised the actual layout and planting of the parterre compartments in the various gardens. Given the swirling forms of the designs, the layout of *parterres de broderie* was precision work and needed constant instruction by an expert. Mollet's function as a supervising professional is indicated by several entries in the account books, which mention him as *opsichter*, or 'superintendent'.[198] This function, as the descriptions in the records of payments show, implies that Mollet supervised the working process of the new parterre layouts, including their plantation and decoration with boxwood, gravel and stone.[199] Entries in the records of payments describe payments to labourers, gardeners and carpenters working together with Mollet; they show the degree of teamwork necessary to complete such complicated parterre layouts.[200] Besides for overseeing and directing the work in progress, Mollet is paid for acquiring and transporting the necessary material for the parterres. The extent of Mollet's involvement with Frederik Hendrik's garden layouts can be inferred from the records of payments: apparently Mollet had to travel regularly from one side of the country to the other to oversee the parterre layouts at the various estates, since numerous entries concern travelling expenses and expenditures for provisions during his inspection of the new parterres in Frederik Hendrik's gardens.[201]

One other aspect of Mollet's work should be mentioned here: his role as a draughtsman, which further widens our understanding of his place at court. One archival document specifically mentions that Mollet provided Frederik Hendrik with 'various drawings' (1042 fol. 232[vo]).[202] Though the subject and nature of these designs can only be guessed, it seems most likely that they were models for further parterre layouts and their decoration, not for entire garden layouts.[203] At first it seems that if these drawings involve designs for gardens at all, they must relate solely to details of certain garden parts, since the form and structure of the Stadholder's gardens, certainly of Honselaarsdijk, had already been determined. However, it is not impossible, indeed quite logical, that Mollet made suggestions regarding the layout of Ter Nieuburch, since the cultivation and decoration of its freshly-laid-out grounds occurred at the time of his arrival at court (1633), for which purpose he may have made some drawings. There might even be a connection between the 'various drawings' referred to in Mollet's payment account and the '21 designs' originally made for Ter Nieuburch's layout *(see figs. 51-59)*.

In this context we should remember one of the preliminary designs for Ter Nieuburch, the so-called 'French drawing' *(see fig. 51)*, which, though dated 1636 – after Mollet had left the court – stylistically stems from the Mollet environment. It is most remarkable that the close resemblance between certain elements in Ter Nieuburch's 'French drawing', the Milheusser print and Mollet's second ideal plan in his *Jardin de plaisir*, which will be discussed in the next chapter, seems to point once again to Mollet as the possible designer of part of the Stadholder's gardens. If so, this would confirm the belief that his role exceeded that of mere parterre-designer, which was already substantiated by references to Mollet's responsibilities as *desseigneur* (designer), *intendant* (manager) and *opsichter* (supervisor) in the Huygens correspondence.[204]

THE QUESTION OF 'AUTHORSHIP' AND SEVERAL IMPORTANT GARDENERS AT COURT

We have seen that there remain a few important questions about the style and form of the Stadholder's gardens which hinge on the presence of Mollet and his function as garden architect in Holland. These questions will be discussed in the next chapter, but one point should be mentioned here about the question of 'authorship'. When analysing the Honselaarsdijk and Ter Nieuburch gardens, historians all too readily look for one genius, preferably a foreign designer, concluding that it must have been Mollet or another person of French origin who was responsible for the layout. Thus Slothouwer simply stated that the Honselaarsdijk garden was designed by François [*sic*] Mollet, meaning André Mollet, without further details.

In the same vein, the role of another gardener, Louis D'Anthoni – whom we already encountered as gardener-in-chief at Ter Nieuburch – has been analysed. Slothouwer presumed that the entire Ter Nieuburch garden was laid out by this Louis D'Anthoni, whose name occurs in the records of payments concerning the gardens of Ter Nieuburch over the years 1631-38.[205] Erroneously, Slothouwer changed Louis D'Anthoni's name to François D'Anthoin.[206] Several other authors concluded from the name Louis D'Anthoni that he must have been French, even though he may have been a native of Holland and his name is spelled differently in the various account books and gardener's contracts as D'Anthoni, D'Anthonie or D'Anthoin.[207] The attribution of the Ter Nieuburch garden to Louis D'Anthoni or D'Antoin, whether a Frenchman or not, cannot be ascertained by studying the documents in detail. True, Louis D'Anthoni is regularly mentioned in the records of payments and referred to as 'His Highness's gardener' or *hovenier*, receiving a yearly salary of 600 pounds artois (1040 fol. 222 and 1042 fol. 302vo). However, his involvement with the layout of the gardens should not automatically lead to the conclusion that D'Anthoni also designed the garden of Ter Nieuburch. As a matter of fact, in most entries D'Anthoni received payments for the planting of trees (1041 fol. 253vo and 992 fol. 132) or sowing of new seed (1043 fol. 258vo), never for drawings or designs.[208] In one entry (1043 fol. 278) he is described as 'the gardener of the garden plots on either side of the House ter Nieuburch', referring to the Orangerie, herbal and vegetable gardens flanking the courtyard; in another he is mentioned for the 'yearly upkeep of the garden' (1041 fol. 278vo: 'jaer onderhouts'). Louis D'Anthoni's recently found gardener's instructions *Conditions and Stipulations of the Gardener Louis D'Anthoin (see Appendix,*

Document III),[209] now show conclusively that he was a gardener responsible for the general upkeep of the grounds, rather than a garden architect providing designs.

Obviously, some gardeners did work both as planters and as designers. For example, the gardener-in-chief Anthony van Thooren, who is mentioned in the records of payments for Honselaarsdijk from 1645 to 1658,[210] was paid in 1652 the sum of 138 guilders for work completed in 1646, 'designing and planting' the parterres on the west side of the house Honselaarsdijk (995 fol. 46a^{vo}), and 86.5 guilders (995 fol. 46b^{vo}) for 'drawing and making' the parterres in the 'old garden' at Honselaarsdijk.[211] Unfortunately the exact nature of these designs is unknown; they may have been decorative designs or practical working drawings for other gardeners to follow in laying out the parterres. Apart from making these designs, Van Thooren also acquired rare plants (995 fol. 46f^{vo}), fruit-trees (995 fol. 21) and vegetables (995 fol. 85) for the gardens; he was responsible for planting the new parterres (995 fol. 46e^{vo}) and was the general overseer of the labourers in the garden of Honselaarsdijk (995 fols. 47, 68vo, 110, 111, 111vo, 163, and 996 fols. 10vo, 13). At the same time, throughout the 1650s, the gardener Blaserus Jacobsz[212] collaborated with Van Thooren and shared the same responsibilities according to the records (995 fols. 47a, 69, 85vo, 154vo, and 996 fols. 11vo, 12, 12vo, 13), but he is not mentioned as having provided any designs for the gardens. Other gardeners mentioned regularly in the records of payments are Gijsbrecht Thonissen, as 'head-gardener', and Arent Pietersz Blom as the 'flower-man', or plant purveyor. They were both active at Honselaarsdijk in the 1630s and part of the 1640s and were involved in the maintenance and planting of the garden rather than in its actual design.

Another person who should be mentioned here is Dirk de Milde, key figure of the whole silviculture of Honselaarsdijk, but apparently also involved in the completion of the palace, that is, the construction of the annexes. The records of payments show that he received monthly payments for the 'oncosten gevallen in de Bosschen ende warande van Honsholredijck' (upkeep of the woods and pleasure grounds of Honselaarsdijk) – such payments being reported in the accounts from 1637 to 1647 (inv. nos. 993 and 994). Since de Milde is referred to in the accounts as *opsichter* (surveyor), *warantmeester* (park or pleasure-ground master) in addition to *boschbewaerder* (forester), his role obviously was much vaster than that of mere forester. His work ranged from the yearly upkeep of the pall-mall in front of Honselaarsdijk, for which he received 100 guilders (992 fol. 412 and 993 fol. 145ff), the delivery and planting of trees (992 fol. 331), the digging of ponds and canals (993, fol. 49) to the raising of palisades (993 fol. 203) and fences in and round the garden (993 fols. 46, 71, 149). He also built dovecotes (992 fol. 149b) and cages for the pheasants and other birds in the menagerie (992 fol. 272), as well as houses for the deer in the deer-park (993 fol. 148vo). He was reimbursed for work on the sewer system and bridges (993 fol. 142), and for laying an 'Italian floor' on the terrace or open gallery of the estate (993 fol. 423vo).

The high point and end of Dirk de Milde's career was marked by the construction of the galleries and pavilions on the west side of Honselaarsdijk (993 fols. 220vo, 291). This last building project cost more than 60,000 guilders (993 fol. 291), for which de Milde (993 fols. 220vo, 291), collaborating with Arent van 's Gravesande and stonemason Bartholomeus Drijffhout (993 fol. 436), received his share. Upon his death in 1647, de Milde was succeeded by Jan Herison as *boschbewaerder* (994 fol. 18).

Other gardeners mentioned during the 1640s and 1650s include Gijsbrecht's son Anthony Gijsbrechtsz as new 'head-gardener' at Honselaarsdijk, Balthasar van Engelen, *hovenier* at Antwerp, Hendrick van Hattem, the *plantagieur* [*sic*], and, lastly, Borchgaert Frederic, chief gardener at Ter Nieuburch. While these men may be considered as traditional gardeners, functioning as botanists and plant purveyors rather than garden architects, Borchgaert Frederic's role should be highlighted because it involved larger questions of garden design.[213]

Milheusser's print *(see fig. 47)* specifically mentions Borchgaert Frederic as 'His Highness's gardener at Rijswijk' ('maistre Borchgaert Frederic, jardinier de son Altesse a la maison dudict Nieuburg proche de Risvic'). As the text on this cartouche indicates, Borchgaert Frederic was assisted by Isaac Leschevin, gardener of 'Seigneur de Brederode' at Vianen. Frederic's name on the cartouche, and the fact that he dedicated this print to the Stadholder, prove that his activities exceeded those of a mere gardener. Indeed, Isaac Leschevin's printbook *Portals and Palisades* in the Metropolitan Museum (described in chapter II) reconfirms the notion of an artistic involvement by both Frederic and Leschevin in the Stadholder's gardens. Both gardeners must have been responsible for designing and setting up the trellis-work decoration and other ornamentation in the garden of Ter Nieuburch, and possibly also in some of the other stadholderly gardens. As the records of payments indicate, in the spring of 1646 Frederic also worked at the Huis ten Bosch, laying out the parterres of the main garden shown in Post's print (993 fol. 428vo).

Another gardener who combined the abilities of a plantation master with those of a designer – or rather, a historian – and who is remembered in the annals of the history of garden art for writing an important garden treatise, is Jan van der Groen. His father-in-law was the gardener and plant purveyor at Honselaarsdijk, Arent Pietersz Blom, whom he officially succeeded by 1659 as 'Hovenier van Sijn Doorluchtige Hoogheydt, den Heere Prince van Orangien', or gardener of the Prince of Orange.[214] As early as 1652, however, Van der Groen was paid for providing flowers for the 'new and old gardens' at Honselaarsdijk (995 fols. 83, 83vo); he was still mentioned as working there as 'gardener of the Prince of Orange' in 1670. From 1660 on Van der Groen also worked in this capacity in the gardens of the Paleis Noordeinde at The Hague, where he received payment for the planting of new shrubs and fruit-trees in 1665 (996 fols. 220vo, 232).

In short, the archival records indicate that Van der Groen worked at the Paleis Noordeinde from 1659 to 1665, at Honselaarsdijk from 1665 to 1670,[215] and from 1670 until his death in 1672 at the Huis ter Nieuburch as well.[216] It is possible that, since he was often in The Hague at the Paleis Noordeinde, he has also worked at the nearby Huis ten Bosch, but there is no documentary evidence to confirm this. Though Van der Groen, like his father-in-law, was a 'flower-man', or *bloemist*, in the first place, and in the records of payments is reimbursed primarily for acquiring and planting flowers and trees in the stadholderly gardens, his real and long-term contribution to Dutch garden art consists in his publication of the only original Dutch treatise written in the seventeenth century, entitled *Den Nederlandtsen Hovenier* (1669). This treatise is most unusual in that it combines practical horticultural advice with theoretical information, from the 'blessedness of country life' to traditions of garden designing.[217] It is especially relevant here because it was written by one of the Stadholder's own chief gardeners, and because it shows the direct influence from designs made by a previous gardener, namely Isaac Leschevin. Though Van der Groen was hired shortly after Frederik Hendrik's death, his work belongs to the early-seventeenth-century tradition of garden art. Actually the first three engravings in his treatise depict Frederik Hendrik's gardens at Rijswijk, Honselaarsdijk and the Huis ten Bosch, respectively. Van der Groen is chiefly concerned with horticulture. He gives an overview of the trees, plants, flowers and vegetables grown in The Netherlands during the second half of the seventeenth century, many of which presumably also grew in the Stadholder's gardens. A detailed comparison of the plants mentioned in his book with those named in the lists arranged by month in the gardener's contracts of Honselaarsdijk and Ter Nieuburch – as well as in the album with watercolours

Hortus Regius Honselaerdicensis in the Biblioteca Nazionale in Florence *(see fig. 29)* – yields important new horticultural information on the rare plants grown in Holland at that time.[218]

More important, in the context of contemporary garden art, is that Van der Groen's treatise supplies the interested reader and garden dilettante with two hundred models of flower-beds (*bloem-perken*), parterres, labyrinths (*dool-hoven*), arbours (*priëelen*), lattice-work (*lat-werken*) and sundials (*zonnewijzers*), as well as engravings of princely palaces and gardens (*lusthoven*) marked as 'after the Dutch and French fashion'.[219] As can be deduced from a careful comparative study of his book and contemporary garden-architectural works, in collecting his material Van der Groen drew from earlier French, Flemish and German sources, such as Böckler's *Nova Architectura Curiosa* (1664), D. Loris's *Le Thrésor des Parterres de l'Univers* (1579), J. Vredeman de Vries's *Hortorum viridariorumque formae* (1583), D. Rabel's *Livre de différents desseigns de parterres* (1630) and P. Lauremberg's *Horticultura Libris II* (1632), as well as Isaac Leschevin's work *Portals and Palisades*.[220] Consequently some of the designs were rather outdated by the 1670s, after Van der Groen's treatise had been published. However, many of his designs must have been considered fashionable during the reign of Frederik Hendrik.

Particularly significant from a stylistic point of view is Van der Groen's short historical survey of garden architecture with special attention to France. According to Van der Groen, the first to bring order in pleasure houses and gardens were the Romans, followed – and later surpassed – by the Italians. The art of gardening thus spread throughout Europe, where, Van der Groen continues, France is the example *par excellence* of garden architecture and ornamentation:

> At present it is especially France which excels all other countries in these delights [gardening], where one sees not only the Royal Houses and Courts as Fontaine-Bleau, St. Germain, &c. but also almost uncountable Princes, Counts and Noblemen flaunt and display their Palaces and Gardens like earthly Paradises.[221]

Those who are familiar with Holland, Van der Groen adds, know that there is no lack of such delights there either. Indeed, relative to the country's size, one can count here as many manors, country estates and homesteads as there are in France, although generally speaking they are not as splendid and magnificent. Yet, Van der Groen remarks, the palaces of Honselaarsdijk, Ter Nieuburch and the Huis ten Bosch rank with the most distinguished in France.[222] Van der Groen's further observations in his introduction are well suited to the situation of the Stadholder's gardens, or, for that matter, to gardening in the flat, low, humid and windswept Dutch countryside in general. He particularly discusses land reclamation and stresses the necessity of proper earthworks and drainage systems, as well as tree plantations as a shield against cold winds.[223] From an aesthetic point of view, Van der Groen's remarks on the 'regularity' of the garden, described as 'bilateral symmetry' ('beyde zijden gelijkformigh'),[224] can be related to the strict symmetrical layout of the Stadholder's gardens of Honselaarsdijk, Ter Nieuburch and the Huis ten Bosch. Van der Groen's treatise was written for the interested, well-informed individual who, with his text in hand, would be able to design, lay out and plant his own garden. Thus, the dilettante owner was approached as if he were an expert, at a time when the notion of garden architecture as a separate specialism had just begun to take root in Holland, stimulated by the developments at Frederik Hendrik's court.

ASPECTS OF BUILDING PRACTICES AND GARDEN LAYOUT AT COURT

In earlier literature describing the Stadholder's architectural projects, two important aspects of building practices in Holland have generally been neglected. The first concerns the position of the seventeenth-century architect and garden architect in Holland, the second the role of local artisans, artists and craftsmen. In early-seventeenth-century Holland the function of the architect, let alone the garden architect, had not yet developed into a specialized occupation.[225] In France, on the other hand, the social position of the architect was much more established and, thanks to the many monumental commissions of the court, much more independent: the architect was seen as a superior designing genius, responsible not only for the execution of the project but also for its actual design.[226] In Holland the architect was still seen as a craftsman executing the ideas of his patron, without having much influence on the final result of the design.[227] Only with the influx of Franco-Italian architectural thought, and the large-scale building commissions of the Stadholder's court, would the notion about the architect and his social position begin to change in Holland. The emergence of the type of gentleman-designer-architect of which Van Campen and Huygens were such outstanding examples has to do with precisely this initial lack of 'specialists' combined with a great surge of building and garden-design projects. Throughout the century, the dilettante garden architect, generally the well-educated owner of an estate who practised architectural designing, would remain important for the development of Dutch seventeenth-century garden architecture.[228]

The second aspect concerns the role of local artists and the way Frederik Hendrik's projects were undertaken, as we look more closely into the *process* and *practice* of designing palaces and gardens. Archival documents show that the building project was divided into sections and each section was commissioned to a different contractor.[229] This procedure, and the large range of persons involved, leads to a different perspective of Frederik Hendrik's architectural enterprises. The construction of Honselaarsdijk and Ter Nieuburch should perhaps not be seen as one great, total project, but essentially as a piecemeal affair.

Likewise we should reconsider the tendency to concentrate on a top layer of artists, preferably attributing a work of art to one particular 'genius'. Some architects who are considered to be of secondary importance and are not counted among the artists of this top layer may still have had considerable influence. Dirk de Milde, whose work is described above, must certainly have had an effect on the plantation and building activities at Honselaarsdijk during his decade of service there. This limited recognition of 'second-rate' architects can lead to serious flaws in historical surveys of the development of architecture in a particular period. In the case of Frederik Hendrik's palaces and gardens, it has led to fallacies about the stadholderly garden layouts, in that the role of foreign architects and gardeners is exaggerated at the cost of less famous, regional architects, gardeners and workmen.

As the account books show, these local artists and architects often worked together, yet the interesting aspect of 'teamwork' has largely remained unnoticed. This disregard of regional architects has immediate consequences for the stylistic analysis of the courtly gardens. Past analysis of Frederik Hendrik's and other Dutch gardens, as we have seen already, focused in the first place on foreign influences: the gardens were compared with French or Italian designs, in spite of discrepancies in time and place and notwithstanding the obvious influence and involvement of a large group of Dutch regional architects and gardeners, who worked according to specific Dutch traditions in gardening.[230] Executed by Dutch workmen, certain apparent, even unique Dutch form features, such as the

127. The strict, mathematically exact arrangement of trees and fruit-trees in the utilitarian and plantation areas of Honselaarsdijk, c. 1640.
Algemeen Rijksarchief

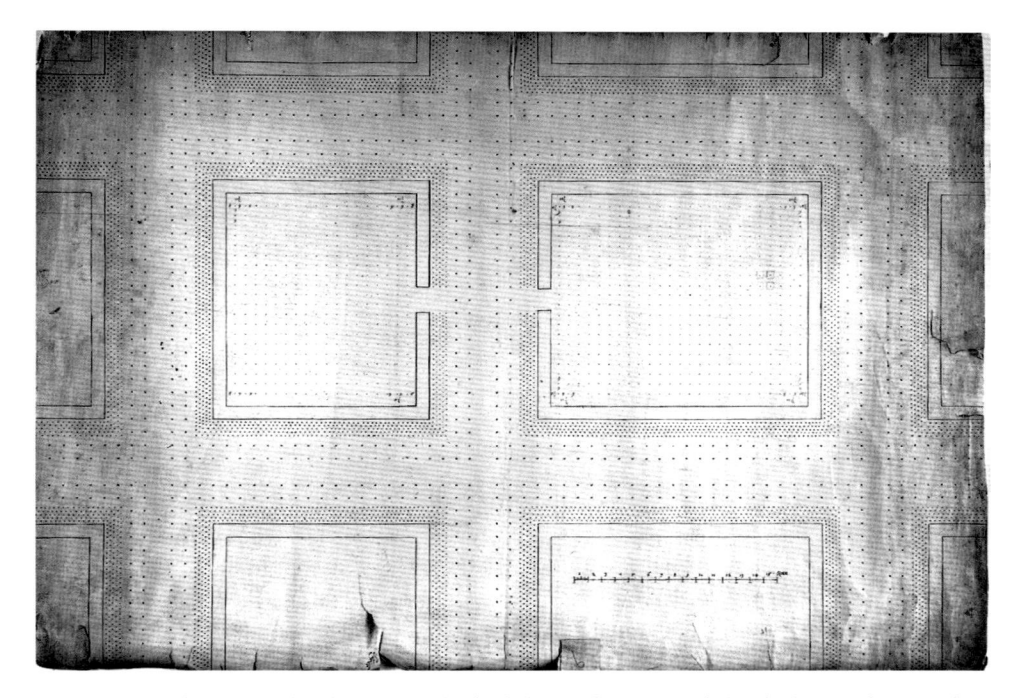

avenues, canals and embankments, which did not fit, or outdid, ideal French or Italian models, would be brushed aside as 'flaws' in the design, or simply ignored.

A review of the account books brings to light another surprising element – the system of *work division* round Frederik Hendrik's palaces. The accounts frequently mention map-makers and land-surveyors when the Stadholder was in the process of acquiring and developing a new piece of land. Unfortunately the crucial part played by these map-makers and land-surveyors in the actual design of the garden has remained unstudied.[231] Land-surveyors were not only active measuring and mapping, but their responsibilities extended to the actual layout of the grounds, as shown by a plan of the Huis ten Bosch *(see fig. 93)* which was made by the land-surveyor and map-maker Pieter Florisz van der Sallem in 1645.[232] The text in the upper right-hand corner of the map states that this plan was drawn by Van der Sallem after a design by Post.[233] Remarkably, the garden plan was completed by a land-surveyor, in collaboration with an architect. Post's engraving of the Huis ten Bosch *(see fig. 95)* shows close collaboration with Van der Sallem when it came to the general disposition of the ground masses and system of water drainage of the garden compartments. After approving the basic disposition of the various plots, the architect Post was then responsible for the aesthetic aspects of the layout and its architectural features, such as the parterres and garden pavilions.

At Honselaarsdijk and Ter Nieuburch Van der Sallem was similarly involved in the initial disposition of the garden plots. This is confirmed by frequent references to his work in the accounts of 1632 to 1663.[234] In these accounts Van der Sallem is mentioned as sharing responsibilities with an architect for the first development and basic layout of newly-acquired land into fertile garden grounds.[235] Several maps in the Nassau Domain, which on stylistic grounds can be attributed to Pieter Florisz van der Sallem, show the layout and planting of new garden plots as orchards and vegetable gardens, consisting of a mathematically precise, rigid arrangement of rows of trees and vegetable beds *(fig. 127, compare with figs. 22 and 23)*.[236] A similar role, involving measuring, levelling of canals and drawing of a proper ground division, can be attributed to the land-surveyor of Utrecht, Johan van Diepenen, who worked for Frederik Hendrik at Zuylesteyn (992 fol. 442) *(see figs. 115 and 116)*. Such a 'dual' role is not surprising given the fact that land-surveyors and engineers, unlike late-sixteenth- and early-seventeenth-century architects, received a formal education based on geometrical and mathematical principles. For example, when the engineer Simon Stevin was sent by Prince Maurits to inspect and suggest improvements to fortifications, he was accompanied by a land-surveyor responsible for preparing a detailed concept of the proposed extension plans.[237] Thus, the contribution of engineers and land-surveyors to the theory and practice of building and laying-out gardens also should be seen against the wider background of seventeenth-century science and technology, the evolution of which had such important ramifications for the development of garden architecture under Frederik Hendrik.

Combining the main issues reviewed here – that is, the abstract design idea (*lineamenta*), the design process and the final material reality of the executed plan (*materia*)[238] – we may again paraphrase Huygens's remark that art needed to be stretched somewhat to fit his artistic wishes. Huygens's comment can be compared not only with Alberti's allowances for modifications in design but also with Vitruvius's own remark that, after all calculations have been made, 'it is the part of wisdom to consider the nature of the site, or questions of use or beauty, and modify the plan. …'[239] These recommendations may be taken as a key to understanding Dutch courtly garden layouts and their design process; they link, on the one hand, the wish for perfect architectural design based on *ratio* and developed in the intellectual world of the Dutch humanists at court, with, on the other hand, the necessity to modify the ideal design in order to fit particular Dutch topographical conditions involving the engineer, the land-surveyor and the architect-gardener.

Finally, it is here that we touch upon the essential difference between architecture and gardens, namely that, in Alberti's words, the *materia* does not consist of stone but of living plant material. The nature of the garden's beauty (*pulchritudo, concinnitas*)[240] does not lay in the measured outline and proportion of the parts, but in nature itself – the trees, plants and flowers which constitute the garden, as they are influenced by the elements (wind, weather). Being of organic quality, the *materia* of garden architecture is much more transient and in a constant flux compared with static, stone buildings. However, by their exact arrangement in rows and grids, the trees in the garden do acquire architectural quality and function as 'living columns' which enhance the rhythm of the layout. The rare, colourful and fragrant plants and flowers in decorative parterres, punctuated with water surfaces and sculptural highlights (*ornamentum*),[241] lend a sense of movement and variety (*varietas*)[242] to the garden layout, delighting the mind, the senses and the soul. The careful balance between (classical) theoretical knowledge and practical application, with the final effect and enjoyment of the garden in mind, provides us with the clearest answers to questions about the style and form of the Stadholder's gardens.

CHAPTER V

STYLE AND FORM OF THE STADHOLDER'S GARDENS

The description of the Stadholder's gardens in the preceding chapters has shown that their style and form differ. Classical Italian as well as contemporary French influences, to a varying degree mixed with Dutch traditions, can be recognized at the basis of Frederik Hendrik's building projects. Furthermore, in the decorative details of the gardens' ornamentation a great variety of features can be distinguished, ranging from regional Dutch to Flemish and German, which stylistically belong to the late Renaissance and early baroque periods, showing a mix of continuing 'mannerist' and new classical style tendencies. The differences in style of the Stadholder's garden layouts and ornamentation, brought about by various causes – which will be discussed in this chapter – indicate that it is difficult to find one architectural style definition to fit all gardens. It may be questioned, in fact, whether looking for one definition is at all desirable, given the apparent confusion and the limits imposed by a purely stylistic approach to Dutch garden architecture. Indeed, study of the courtly gardens of this period will make clear that it is essential to weigh carefully all the sources of inspiration and the degree in which they influenced one another within the total design. Before analysing the style and form of the Stadholder's gardens and their ornamentation, it may be useful to look more closely at some of the obstacles to be faced, which depend largely on the adopted system of analysis.

It should be realized from the outset that a serious stylistic analysis of Dutch gardens – and, for that matter, of garden architecture in general – is hampered by the lack of a satisfactory method to describe them. This is of course in part due to the fact that gardens by their very nature are largely organic and ephemeral in character and therefore do not entirely fit in the categories of art and architecture through the ages.[1] However, other problems arise which have not been tackled sufficiently to make objective stylistic analyses easier. Since the vocabulary used to analyse gardens is derived from the art-historical discipline and its terminology to denote style and form in painting and architecture, words are often lacking to describe all the aspects of garden art. This lack of a precise vocabulary is immediately related to the traditional method, also borrowed from art history, to divide artistic style developments into blocks or periods of time, and, what is more, according to national origin.

On top of that, artistic development or stylistic progress is by tradition believed to move exclusively from the south northward, as the art of Italy still remains the source and absolute artistic standard in art history. For garden-historical research these art-historical traditions have had some serious consequences. A fair analysis of Dutch courtly gardens, for instance, was thwarted by the tendency to measure their development against garden art in Italy and France. The same system of formal and stylistic analysis used to explain the layout and decoration of Italian and French gardens was applied to Dutch gardens, regardless of the huge discrepancies in time, place, climate and function. Instead of concentrating on one particular stylistic analysis one should embrace different analytical approaches which can give new insights and perspectives. At the same time it is essential to recognize the danger of focusing solely on what is innovative in garden architecture. There

COURTLY GARDENS IN HOLLAND 1600-1650

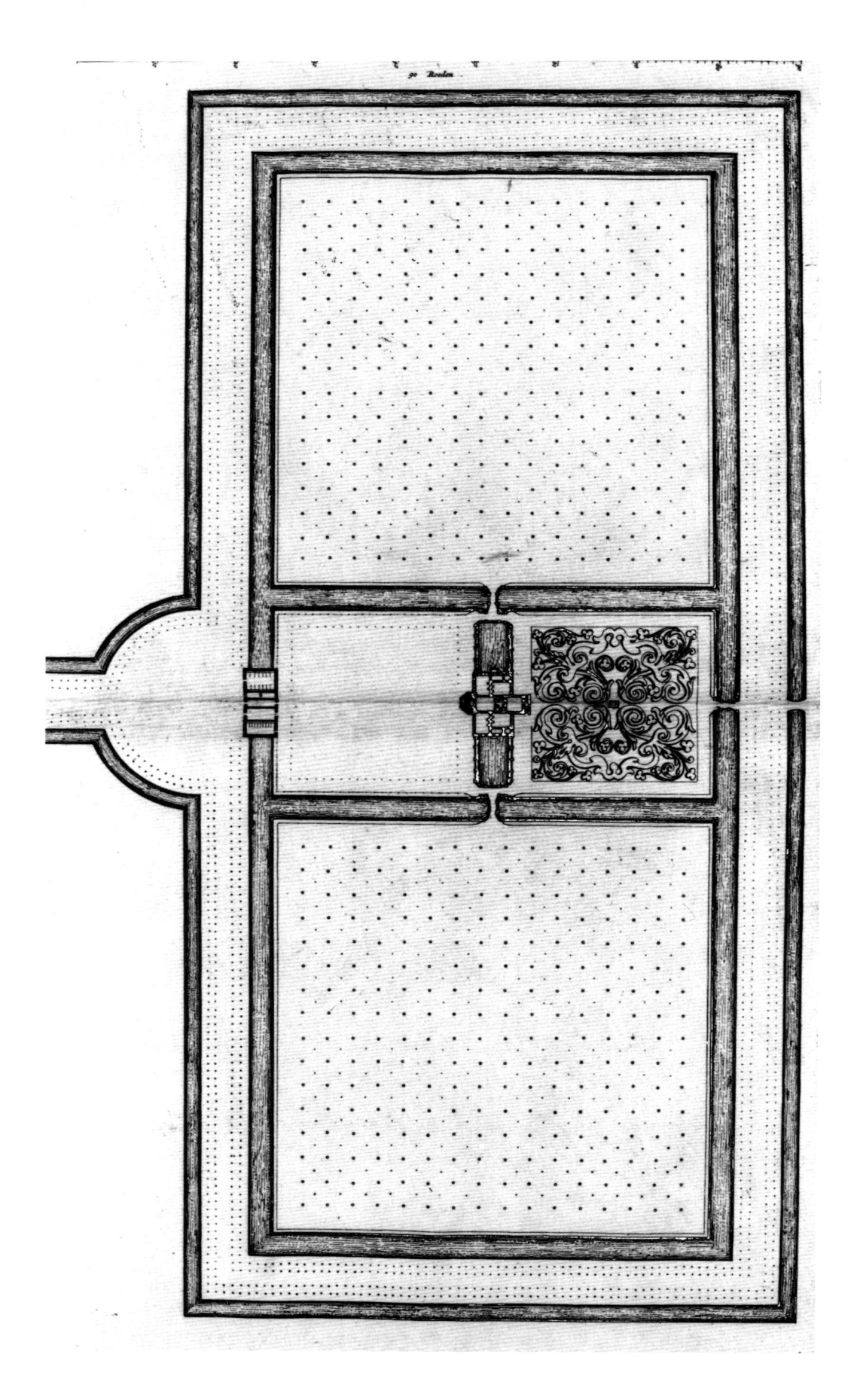

128. Design by Philips Vingboons for an ideal country estate in strict geometrical style, enclosed by canals and with a semicircular-ending avenue. Koninklijke Bibliotheek. Photo courtesy Utrecht University

is a tendency to prefer 'the new' and neglect 'the old' in garden history by only paying attention to the latest stylistic innovations and ignoring existing traditions. Disregard of the preservation of important traditions in garden architecture means repeating the same mistake which has constantly impaired the proper characterization of the Dutch garden. It is all the more regrettable because indigenous traditions and specific regional architectural preferences, including the artistic ideas of Frederik Hendrik and Amalia, carried much weight with the final design, form and style of Dutch gardens.

As we have seen, in most earlier literature (Bienfait, Morren, Slothouwer and Vermeulen) the Dutch courtly gardens have simply been called 'French', a term which was generically applied without specifying what exactly is meant by 'French influence', and without distinguishing between early- and late-seventeenth-century French inspiration – a crucial distinction which we will now be able to make. The undefined and exaggerated emphasis on the French contribution highlighted by earlier publications has obscured other, concurrent seventeenth-century artistic influences, especially the impact of classical architectural theory at the Dutch court. Paradoxically, now that the traditional Dutch suspicion of 'the classical' as inherently 'élitist' and therefore 'un-Dutch' has been overcome, care should be taken not to call everything 'classical' all of a sudden. Overemphasis on the impact of classical theory in turn hinders an understanding of more varied and subtle international artistic exchanges, especially the remarkable French and Dutch stylistic exchanges which, surprisingly, already occurred before the mid-seventeenth century. However, neither the impact of French garden-artistic know-how nor that of classical Italian theory should blind us to the infiltration of stylistic influences from other sources, which, apart from regional origins, came from Flemish and German cultural backgrounds. Hence, only by combining the diverse stylistic influences and by remaining open to different analytical approaches can one attempt to understand more fully the complex elements and aspects of the Stadholder's gardens.

Thus far, the analysis of the Stadholder's gardens has shown that there was a considerable difference between building in theory and building in practice. Discussing the study of 'l'architecture antique' in a letter to Wicquefort, Huygens expressed this difference well when he stated that he enjoyed researching more 'obscure' things and took pleasure in knowing in theory that which (building) practice never demanded.[2] This discrepancy between theory and practice meant that even if harmonic proportional models, as discussed by Wittkower, were available, they were not necessarily used or belonged to 'the norm' when it came to actual designing and building.[3] Often the architects, as they did at the Dutch court, continued to follow local traditions and measuring systems, such as that of quadrature, as we shall see. Moreover, when classical form principles were applied, they were and are not necessarily easily recognized in the final garden design, depending on the degree in which the ideal form was adapted to fit the natural circumstances of the site. Conversely, it has sometimes been difficult to assess to what degree classical proportions were applied deliberately during the actual design process, or recognized in the garden layout after its completion.

Fundamentally, the design of a garden is in the first place dictated by the topographical circumstances, as is shown by the differences in appearance of two 'Dutch' gardens designed within the same humanist circle of the Dutch court but laid out in different landscapes: the Stadholder's flat, horizontal gardens in the Westland's level polders, and Johan Maurits's Italianate garden terraces at Cleves, on the hilly German border. We have seen that within their various layouts the gardens of Frederik Hendrik combine certain 'conservative' and 'innovative' features. Instead of interpreting older style forms in a negative way, as is done in most literature, we should reconsider them as expressing the continuity of specific regional traditions in Dutch garden art and the patron's personal taste and financial resources. Once again, it is necessary to determine how the notion of 'conservatism' versus that of 'innovation' is defined in Holland at the time, and which elements of the layout and ornamentation of the Stadholder's gardens are identified by these notions.

A critical analysis of Frederik Hendrik's buildings and gardens and their description in seventeenth-century literature will result in new thoughts on the Stadholder's artistic accomplishments. Linked to this analysis is a close examination of the most striking formal components and decorative features of his gardens, with special emphasis on Honselaarsdijk and Ter Nieuburch.

HONSELAARSDIJK AND THE APPROACH AVENUE

An analysis of the most striking aspects of Frederik Hendrik's estates should appropriately start with the grand entrance avenue of Honselaarsdijk.[4] This imposing access way, ending in a semicircular piazza or amphitheatre, was the dominant feature of the layout of Honselaarsdijk, as it provided a dramatic, focal introduction to the building complex and its gardens. The avenue was the central axis of the total layout, carrying one's vista into the seemingly infinite space continuum of the flat polderland.

The map by the land-surveyor and cartographer Floris Jacobsz van der Sallem, dated circa 1615 *(see fig. 10)*, shows that Frederik Hendrik started his building enterprises by planning the monumental access way to Honselaarsdijk. By so doing, the Stadholder established a trend, as it were, which can also be recognized in the improvements undertaken at Breda and Buren, and much later in his grandson's palaces at Soestdijk and Het Loo. In fact, impressive entry avenues were to be a common feature of the Dutch seventeenth-century estate, as many topographical maps and bird's-eye views of the period show.[5] A detailed picture of the completed avenue at Honselaarsdijk can be studied on the map finished by Floris Jacobsz in 1625 *(see fig. 13)*.[6] The effect of this long, straight road on its surroundings and the implications of its dominant axis for the whole garden layout can be seen on maps of the larger Westland area *(see figs. 3 and 4)* and the Van Berckerode map *(see fig. 12)*. As these maps show, the centre of the avenue aligned with the central axis dividing the main pleasure garden into two strictly arranged, symmetrical halves. It was, as it were, the pivot on which hinged not only the garden layout but the whole surrounding landscape, as can be seen in a reconstruction drawing combining the front and the never executed rear avenue, with their total length of more than three kilometres *(see figs. 14 and 15)*.

The termination of the front and rear avenues was marked by a spacious semicircular piazza. In chapter I we have seen how the rear avenue also could have functioned as an alternative frontal approach, taking into account that the back of the palace, according to French conceptions, was to have been the front. In that case, the plan of the 'rear' avenue *(see fig. 14)* seems to reflect the initial struggle of Frederik Hendrik and his advisers with the unorthodox orientation of the Honselaarsdijk palace. Apparently, in their attempt to build according to contemporary French architectural principles and models, they experimented with alternative approaches and entrances to the palace before deciding on the final version.

In these maps we recognize the striking new form of the semicircular piazza, a kind of amphitheatre with trees, originally planned at either end of the long avenues, one in front, one at the rear of the palace. This semicircular piazza became a major issue in the larger question of foreign, particularly French, influences at Honselaarsdijk. It gave rise to some serious misconceptions about the origin of the palace's design – misconceptions which have their roots in the belief that the Dutch garden is a mere extension of French or Italian garden art. Moreover, the existence of this monumental avenue ending in a semicircle or amphitheatre, and the fact that the French garden architect André Mollet worked at Honselaarsdijk between 1633 and 1635, led to the assumption that Mollet designed this avenue. Thus, following Sten Karling's conclusion that the general design of the Honselaarsdijk garden was developed by Mollet,[7] Roy Strong assumed that the avenue and the amphitheatre were modelled after the amphitheatre of the Wilton gardens, where Mollet may have worked before he entered into the service of Frederik Hendrik.[8] Mollet's outline of the classic French garden in his treatise *Le Jardin de plaisir*, which in many respects fits the layout of Honselaarsdijk, supported the conclusion that Mollet was the designer of the Honselaarsdijk garden. Indeed, according to Mollet,[9] the first and foremost embellishment of a grand estate is a large avenue, which, planted with a double row of trees, is to run perpendicularly to the castle, ending in a semicircle:

> Premièrement, nous dirons que la maison Royale doit être située en un lieu avantageux pour la pouvoir orner de toutes choses requises à son embellissement, dont la première est d'y pouvoir planter une grande avenue à double ou triple rang, soit d'ormes femelles, soit de tilleuls (qui sont les deux espèces d'arbres que nous estimons les plus propres à cet effet), laquelle doit être tirée en alignement perpendiculaire à la façade devant la maison, au commencement de laquelle sera fait un grand demi-cercle ou un carré.[10]

In spite of the points in common between Mollet's text and Honselaarsdijk's situation, the account books and the maps by Floris Jacobsz of 1615 and 1625 prove decisively that the layout of Honselaarsdijk and its avenue predate Mollet's arrival in Holland.[11] Therefore, the question of the 'authorship' of the avenues must be reconsidered. What, then, were the earliest sources for the idea of such an access way with semicircular concourse, and where can we find similar prototypes?

The principle of a monumental entrance way with a large open area to ensure visitors and their entourage a smooth arrival in coaches or on horseback without getting in each other's way had already been extolled by Alberti in his *De re aedificatoria*, substantially completed by 1452.[12] Alberti's treatise was certainly known at court, as a copy was kept in Frederik Hendrik's library.[13] Undoubtedly, Frederik Hendrik was as familiar with Alberti's writings as he was with the works of the other major ancient authors describing the layout of their suburban villas, such as Pliny. Another, contemporary source for the design of the avenue at Honselaarsdijk may have been Scamozzi's *L'Idea dell'architettura universale*.[14] Scamozzi not only recommended that the line of the approach avenue should terminate at the main façade of a palace in order to emphasize its grandeur, but also mentioned the necessity of having a large, crescent-shaped concourse just in front of a building to provide more space for the incoming and outgoing guests. Scamozzi also described the importance of the width of this avenue and suggested the planting of trees for beauty and shade.[15] In many respects, Scamozzi's detailed description coincides with the actual form and layout of the Honselaarsdijk avenue which is bordered by eight rows of trees (four on either side with three tracks), terminating in a semicircle. Despite the obvious correlations between Scamozzi's text and Honselaarsdijk's avenue, and his influence on Huygens, Post and Van Campen, it is unlikely that his treatise directly inspired this particular form feature.[16] As the maps show *(see fig. 13)*, the avenue was in fact planned as early as 1615, at the very

Hic ubi tota stupens de se Natura triumphum
    Ducier audaci victa labore videt,
Hic ubi se Batavis tumidus submittere Collis
    Cogitur, & Laterem subter Arena latet,
Hic ubi de sterili sabulo frondescere jussa
    Populus umbrosam spondet adulta viam,

Judice me, vili suspensis cardine clathris
    Lignea magnificum Janua fœdat opus.
Eia, Viri proceres, solido de Marmore Portam
    Addite; pro modulo nostra papyrus erit:
Ecce, Patres, opera tantum pars altera restat,
    Dimidium facti fecit Episcopius.

                    CONSTANTER.

129. Print by Romeyn de Hooghe of Huygens's design for the entrance gate shaped like a triumphal arch to the Scheveningse Weg, connecting The Hague with the North Sea.
Gemeentearchief, The Hague

time Scamozzi's book was published in Venice and before it could have arrived in Holland and inspired architectural design.

Whether or not the designer of the monumental axial avenue of Honselaarsdijk was inspired by classical architectural treatises, there is no doubt that he was aware of classical theories. However, it is difficult to say where at this early date one must look for a possible direct visual link. In England there were some avenues dating from the Tudor period, but axial avenues terminating in semicircles are believed to have been unknown until later in the century.[17] In France the long approach way with apsidal ending is not known until the middle of the century, when it is found in the earliest layout of Versailles.[18] Later examples can be found at Richelieu, though there the shape of the semicircle is used in reverse.[19] It is important to note that in France the avenue, with or without apsidal termination, was considered essential to garden designing, and that not only Mollet but also his 'forerunner' in garden architecture, Jacques Boyceau, devoted a whole section to this element in his *Traité du jardinage* of 1638.[20] In Sweden, avenues with apsidal termination do not become a regular feature until the 1640s. They are seen to develop, not surprisingly yet significantly, after the arrival of Frederik Hendrik's own architect Simon de la Vallée and can be recognized in the layouts of the palace of Ekolsund about 1640.[21] In the latter part of the century imposing avenues ending in amphitheatres occur as a standard motif in the works of Simon de la Vallée's son Jean, for example at Östermalma and Eskilstuna, laid out in the 1650s and 1660s.[22] Though a rectilinear structure terminating in a semicircle can be found in plans of Palladio's villas – for instance, the Villa Maser and the Villa Sarego[23] – as well as in palace and garden plans designed by Jacques Androuet Du Cerceau,[24] no immediate model showing an avenue ending in a semicircle laid out before, and in the style of, Honselaarsdijk can be identified.

When searching for the origin, particularly a foreign prototype of the striking new feature of Honselaarsdijk's monumental avenue-cum-amphitheatre, one should first ask oneself if such a search for an 'origin' or 'foreign model' is justified. Couldn't this feature have been developed locally, out of sheer necessity to accommodate peculiarities of the Honselaarsdijk grounds? In a broader sense, could this layout have other than aesthetic purposes? Since the situation of the palace on an island surrounded by a moat did not leave much room for major changes in the area immediately in front of the main entrance to the palace, as we have seen, another area had to be constructed to solve this space problem and provide room for the carriages to unload and turn. The semicircular opening at the end of the avenue, just in front of the moat surrounding the rectangle of the palace and garden, must then have been deliberately planned for this purpose.

A possible regional source for this avenue and amphitheatre can be tested against the evidence found in the archives. Close examination of the maps and new documentary data once and for all refute the notion of a French architect (Mollet) and possibly even a foreign source. In fact, until further evidence concerning the precise origin or direct model of this avenue-cum-amphitheatre can be found, one may presume this design to be a regional invention.

A regional source rather than foreign origins of the formal concept of the Honselaarsdijk avenue is all the more logical if we remember the late-sixteenth-, early-seventeenth-century Dutch expertise in the field of military architecture, involving the science of fortification and perspective as well as land-surveying and engineering.[25] Indeed, in view of the precise maps and measurements made by Floris Jacobsz van der Sallem for this avenue and the whole system of avenues *(shown in figs. 13 and 14)*, and given the fact that cartographers-surveyors were directly involved in larger questions of design and drainage, a Dutch source seems evident.

V. STYLE AND FORM

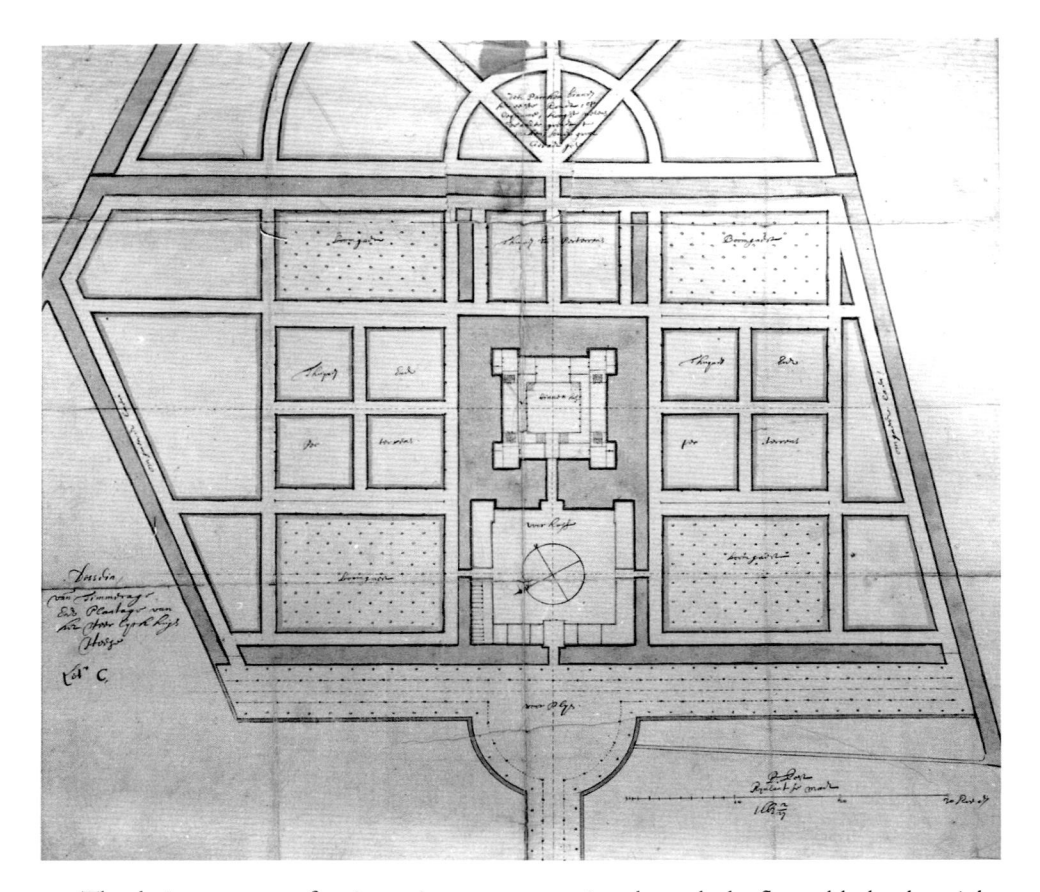

130. Plan by Pieter Post for the castle and garden of Heeze, 1663, of strict geometrical design, with semicircular-shaped avenues and parterre areas. Photo courtesy Rijksdienst voor de Monumentenzorg, Zeist

The design concept of an imposing avenue, cutting through the flat polderland straight as an arrow and connecting a building structure with its physical surroundings by way of a semicircle, had a lasting effect on Dutch landscape architecture. William III and his architect Maurits Post (1645-1677), son of Pieter Post, must have had Honselaarsdijk's impressive access way in mind when designing the *grande allée* of Soestdijk later in the century.[26] Earlier, in 1645, an avenue similar to the one at Honselaarsdijk was planned by a dilettante garden architect, Joan Huydecoper, possibly in collaboration with the Amsterdam city architect Philips Vingboons, in a design for a country house along the river Vecht.[27] Vingboons himself published engravings of his ideal plans for country residences in his *Afbeelsels* of 1648. One of these designs shows a house set in a totally geometrical garden landscape, very similar to the Honselaarsdijk layout, and approachable over a similar avenue terminating in a semicircular piazza *(fig. 128)*.[28]

Later in the century, in 1653, the basic idea of such a monumental avenue, now penetrating the dune landscape, was picked up and further developed by Huygens in his famous design for the Scheveningse Weg *(fig. 129)*, the monumental stone road connecting The Hague with the North Sea.[29] This extended road was regarded as the Dutch Via Appia, glorified in Huygens's long and famous poem *De Zee-straet*.[30] In his explanation of the plan, Huygens borrowed from ancient writers, extolling the importance of broad, cleanly paved avenues leading to, and lending grandeur to, the city.[31] The Scheveningse Weg, completed in 1663 and still in existence today, not only was of general commercial and aesthetic interest but also provided better access to Frederik Hendrik's palaces in and outside The Hague, as it ran from the sea to the Paleis Noordeinde and from there would join the road leading directly to the Huis ter Nieuburch at Rijswijk.

Another architect from the court who was influenced by Honselaarsdijk's monumental access way and amphitheatre, and its effect within a strict geometrical landscape, was Pieter

131. Design by Pieter Post, 1646, for a large semicircular, open gallery at Honselaarsdijk with a wide view over the gardens and connecting side buildings.
Algemeen Rijksarchief

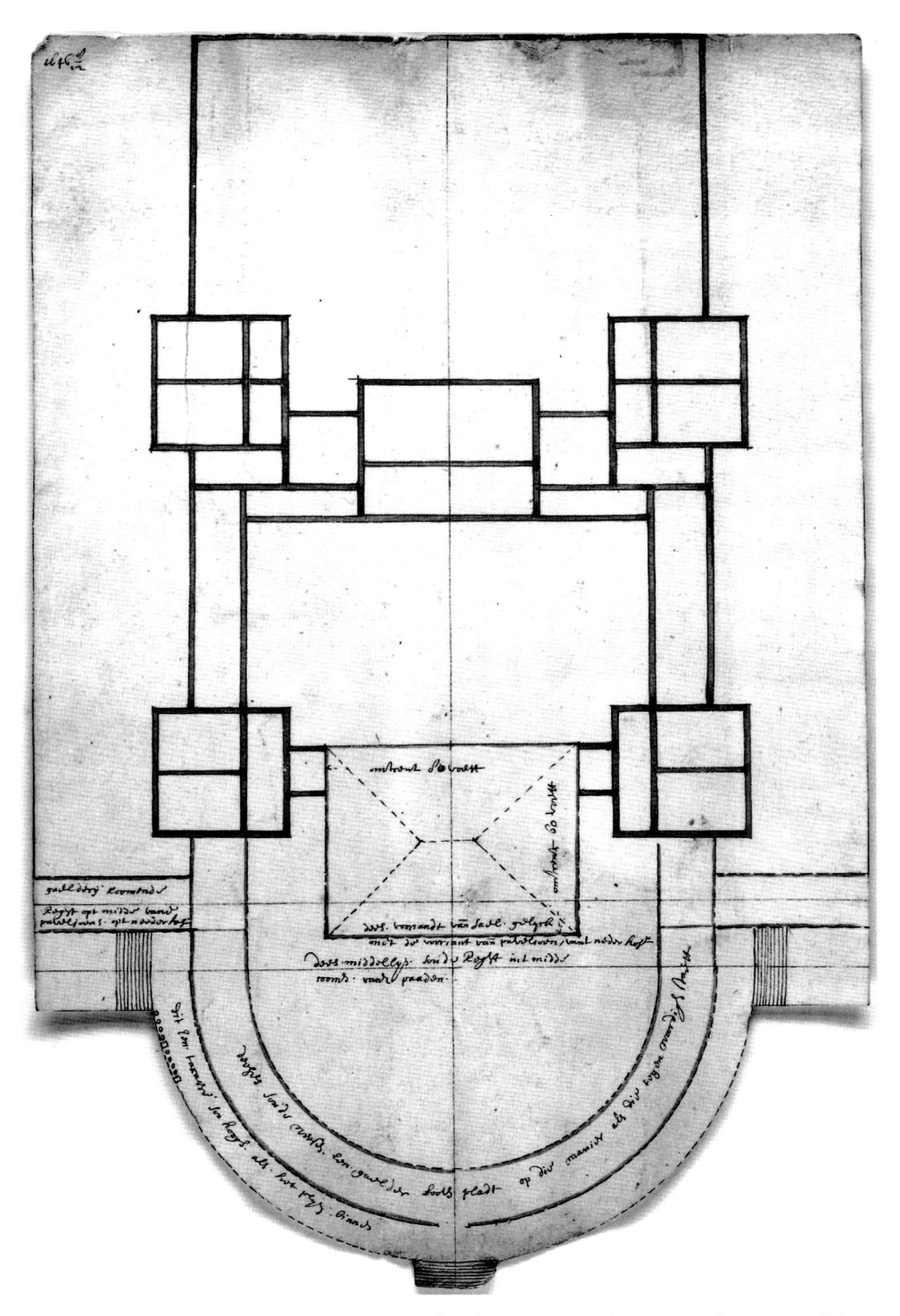

Post. In the early 1660s he made designs for the Heeze castle in Noord-Brabant. These designs, though only partly executed, are significant because they can be shown to relate to Honselaarsdijk's palace and avenue complex with the typical amphitheatrical openings at the front and rear of the castle island *(fig. 130)*.[32] At Heeze the idea of the apsidal or semicircular form is taken a step further by Post: it does not only involve the approach road but the larger design of the entire garden, where this all-embracing, semicircular form is repeated twice at a growing scale within the garden proper. Post used the semicircle in combination with three diagonally radiating axes, thus creating a strikingly new, dynamic

V. STYLE AND FORM

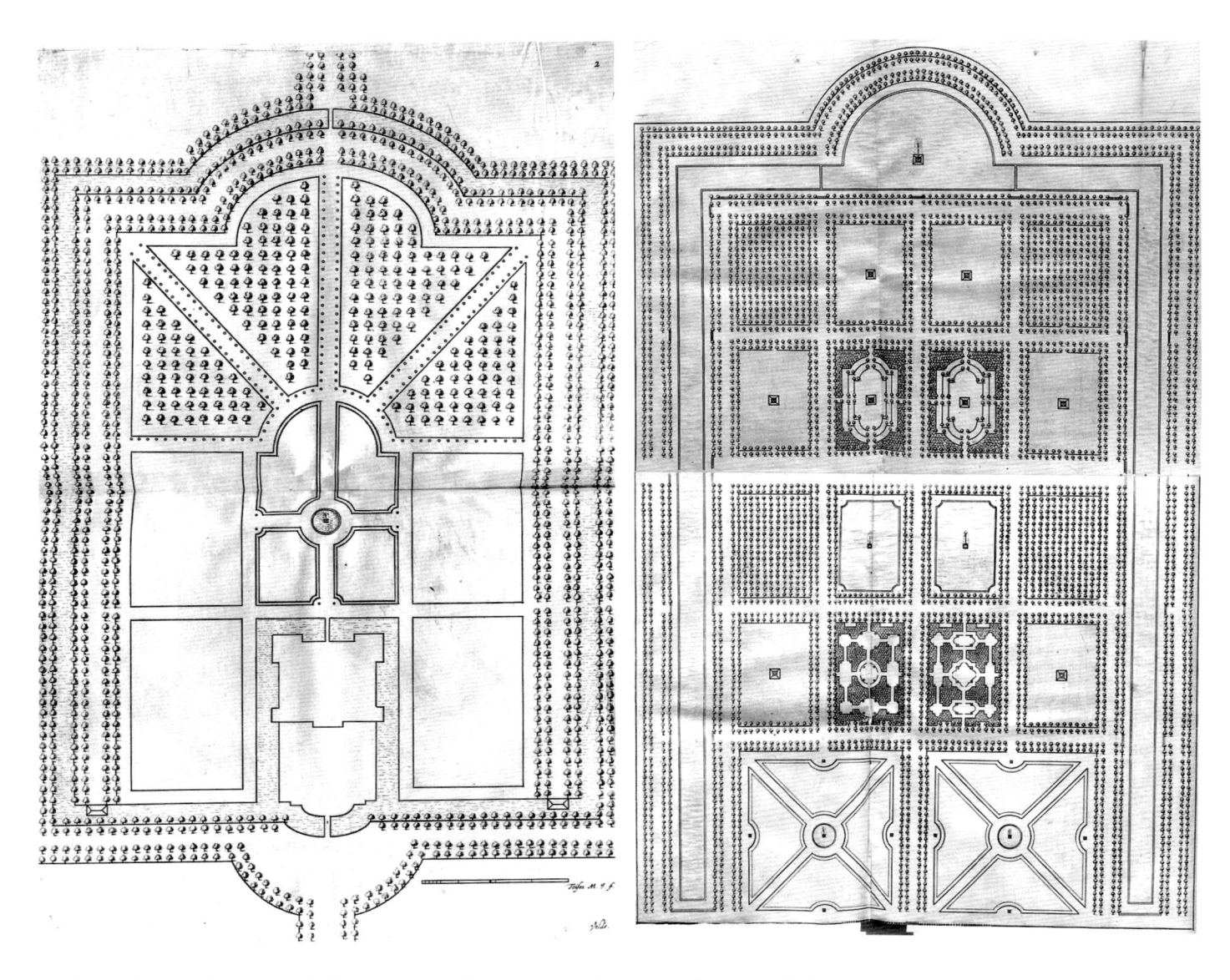

garden-architectural unity which anticipates late-seventeenth-century baroque design principles. Here we can definitely repudiate the notion that Post, unlike Van Campen, was only a practical technician rather than a daring designer-architect in his own right.[33]

Not only at the Heeze castle but also at Honselaarsdijk Post offered original and progressive design solutions. A little-noticed drawing by Post, signed and dated 1646 and showing solutions for the connection of the Honselaarsdijk palace with the annexes *(see fig. 17)*, expresses a similar boldness of design. Here the strict rectilinearity of the moat surrounding the castle on the island would be altered to a semicircle, from which similarly-shaped, increasingly larger strips of land, decorated with *parterres de broderie*, would radiate. The semicircular shape of the garden section would also penetrate the architecture of the palace itself, where Post planned to build a huge half-round gallery with glazed loggia in the centre, commanding a wide view of the whole garden layout *(fig. 131)*.[34] Only in the later part of the century, under William III, would the dynamic form of the semicircular exedra be fully exploited in the Honselaarsdijk garden, where we see the layout of a large open concourse immediately behind the castle island, just as Post had originally envisaged it *(compare figs. 31 and 33)*. Again, as in the case of the avenue, no immediate prototype of such a bold architectural solution can be found, considering that the

132. André Mollet's ideal plan no. 2 for a palace and garden complex, showing a layout comparable to that of the Honselaarsdijk gardens.
The Metropolitan Museum of Art, New York

133. André Mollet's ideal plan no. 1 for a palace and garden complex, showing a layout comparable to that of the Ter Nieuburch gardens.
The Metropolitan Museum of Art, New York

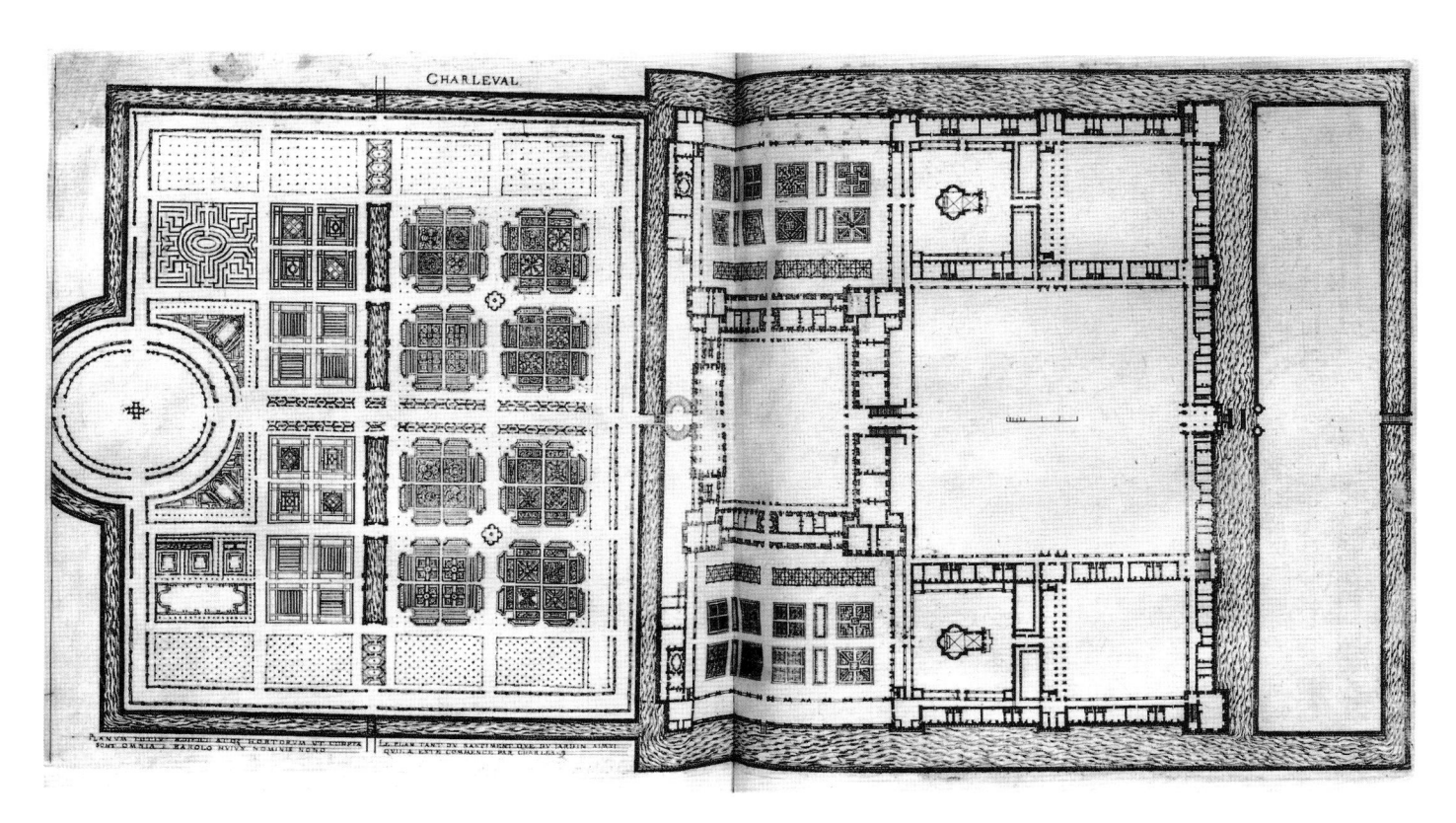

134. Plan of Charleval by Jacques Androuet Du Cerceau from his *Les Plus Excellents Bastiments de France*, 1576-79, showing geometrical gardens with rectilinear outlines bordered by canals.
The Metropolitan Museum of Art, New York

combined length of the building and its annexes would exceed 400 metres, which would express a grandeur unusual even by French and Italian standards.

The above examples illustrate that contemporary Dutch artists and architects were perfectly capable of putting forward their own innovative design ideas, including the use of dynamic shapes such as the diagonal and the semicircle. Moreover, instead of being influenced necessarily by foreign stylistic developments, at Honselaarsdijk the opposite is the case: Dutch design ideas inspired foreign architects. The recurrence of the avenue-cum-piazza, and the division of the grounds and setting of the garden within the familiar framework of canals as exemplified by the designs of Mollet and de la Vallée, confirm this process of mutual rather than one-sided inspiration. The recognition of Dutch influence on French garden architecture has quite revolutionary consequences for our traditional view on European garden art, that artistic inspiration generally moves from the south to the north.[35] In what manner foreign architects were influenced by Dutch garden architecture, and by which aspects exactly, is best explained by studying André Mollet's treatise and his two ideal garden plans.

HONSELAARSDIJK'S GARDEN DESIGN AND ANDRÉ MOLLET

Florence Hopper was the first to draw attention to the remarkable resemblance between one of the ideal garden plans in André Mollet's *Le Jardin de plaisir (fig. 132)*[36] and the general layout of Honselaarsdijk.[37] She noted the inaccuracy of statements made by former scholars who described the Honselaarsdijk layout, with its canals and ornamental garden axially aligned with the palace, as a 'French type'.[38] According to Hopper, the significance of Honselaarsdijk for the development of the Dutch garden had been obscured by the erroneous opinion that its layout was French-inspired and designed by André Mollet. Not

V. STYLE AND FORM

only did Mollet arrive after the basic layout had been established, he was even indebted to gardens he saw in Holland during his two-year stay at the Dutch court. In point of fact, Mollet acknowledged that his ideas were based on what he learned and practised in France, England and Holland,[39] witness his preface to the reader in *Le Jardin de plaisir*, which was written for gardeners in 'les lieux du Midi' as well as 'les climats froids et les pays du Nord':[40]

> … ce qui dépend du jardin de plaisir, suivant ce que j'en ai appris et practiqué en travaillant tant en France et en Angleterre qu'en Hollande, où j'ai eu l'honneur de servir les Rois et Princes, et étant maintenant au service d'une si auguste Princesse que Sa Majesté de Suède, je me suis efforcé à faire de mon mieux pour donner quelque intelligence aux jardiniers et curieux.[41]

Studying Mollet's ideal garden plans, including the first one *(fig. 133)*,[42] one is indeed tempted to conclude that his concept of the classic French garden was influenced by that of the Dutch garden, characterized as it is by a very flat, rectilinear layout within a strict rectangular framework, accentuated by trees and canals.[43]

While some clear general comparisons can be drawn between Mollet's two ideal garden designs and a few of the mid-sixteenth-century layouts in Du Cerceau's *Les Plus Excellents Bastiments de France* – especially Charleval *(fig. 134)*,[44] the Tuileries[45] and Anet[46] – such connections are largely due to their layouts on equally level terrain outlined by canals; on the other hand, there remain serious discrepancies in the inner compartmental arrangement of these gardens and the relationship between garden and building.[47] Indeed, there is less affinity between Mollet's plans and Du Cerceau's than between Mollet's concept and early-seventeenth-century Dutch designs, which not only are characterized by a similar layout on level terrain intersected by water, but seem to be arranged according to the same principles of form and inner disposition.

Within the scope of this comparison, the general design of the Honselaarsdijk garden under Frederik Hendrik *(see fig. 12)* appears to have been the direct model for Mollet's second ideal plan in his treatise *(see fig. 132)*, as Hopper has pointed out.[48] A comparison of Mollet's second ideal plan with the rediscovered original plan of the Honselaarsdijk garden *(see fig. 11)*[49] makes the similarities between the two gardens perfectly clear when it comes to their general outline, severe inner order and characteristic framework of canals and rows of trees. If one superimposes Mollet's design on the original garden plan of Honselaarsdijk, many lines actually are seen to converge *(compare figs. 11 and 132)*. Obviously, the prominent feature unifying both designs is the monumental access way, terminating in the familiar semicircle or *demi-lune*, clearly visible in later prints of the estate *(see fig. 30)*. Also directly comparable are the moated building and its forecourt (in Mollet's plan elegantly curved) and the way in which building and garden are balanced within the whole plan. Moreover, the size of the palace in Mollet's design more or less fits that of Honselaarsdijk,[50] and its form, with the square rear pavilions and the small lateral towers in front (rectangularly instead of octagonally drawn by Mollet), reflects the early building phase of the Honselaarsdijk palace structure, as depicted in this original plan *(see fig. 11)*, which was the form familiar to Mollet before Post's improvements in the early 1640s. Even such details as the two garden pavilions built over the canal at the southern outer corners of the garden are found in Mollet's plan.[51] In addition to the enclosing framework and inner arrangement of the garden, the proportional relationship of the total garden form, width to length 3:4, is directly comparable.[52] Following classical precepts, Mollet stressed the importance of correct proportions, the ideal garden being one third longer than wide:

> la proportion requise ordinairement à tous les jardins, à savoir un tiers plus long que large, ou plus, afin que toutes les séparations qui se pourraient y faire puissent avoir la forme de parallélogramme.[53]

Furthermore, the way Mollet describes his ideal plan no. 2 in detail could also be roughly used to explain the layout of Honselaarsdijk:

> Le dessin 2 est un autre plan général, mais moindre que le précédent, et d'environ 200 toises de long sur 150 de large, le château étant environné d'eau, comme aussi l'aire, ou superficie, de notredit lieu, si faire se peut, avec la demi-lune et la grande avenue au devant de celui-ci. A l'arrière, on peut faire le parterre en broderie folio 5, et sur les côtés on peut ajuster les bosquets décrits sur notre premier dessin. De plus, sur les côtés du château, on peut faire le parterre en broderie et les compartiments de gazon folios 16 et 24, ou bien, au lieu desdits parterres, on pourra mettre sur l'un des côtés les orangers, myrtes, jasmins d'Espagne et autres arbres rares, et à l'autre, les fleurs rares et quelques autres petits arbrisseaux toujours verts et mis par ordre en compartiments, qui correspondent au dessin des bosquets pour observer la symétrie requise à la construction de toute oeuvre, en y ajoutant les fontaines et statues en lieux propres. Puis, au bout dudit parterre, sont trois allées tendant au même centre, lesquelles doivent être plantées de charmes pour faire de hautes palissades; à six pieds de celles-ci sont marqués les lieux pour planter les cyprès d'espace, ou quelques autres beaux arbres bien faits et biens choisis comme des sapins, car quoiqu'ils soient communs en ces pays, néanmoins, s'ils sont plantés dans les jardins en lieux convenables et entretenus comme il appartient, il est évident qu'ils feront un très bel effet. Et dans les séparations que font lesdites allées, on peut planter des arbres fruitiers, ou bien en faire potager dont lesdites palissades hautes pourront empêcher la difformité, car autrement nous n'approuvons pas que ledit jardin de plaisir soit interrompu d'herbages ni d'arbres fruitiers, à moins qu'ils ne soient plantés en espalier et d'en faire un jardin bien à part. Reste à dire que la ceinture de notre plan postérieur est une grande allée double avec sa demi-lune ou ovale, du milieu de laquelle sort encore une grande allée en forme d'avenue pour correspondre à celle du devant du château, le tout entouré d'eau qui se communique l'une à l'autre, ainsi qu'il se peut voir sur notredit plan, car l'eau nous semble être un des principaux ornements du jardin de plaisir.[54]

Many of the aspects described by Mollet are close to the actual layout (proportion and inner division), decoration (parterres, fountains, statues) and plantation (palisades, fruit- and orange-trees, rare flowers) of the Honselaarsdijk garden. There are two exceptions, however: Honselaarsdijk's pleasure garden is somewhat smaller than Mollet advises,[55] and the Honselaarsdijk layout lacks diagonal alleys, which in Mollet's plan are seen to radiate from the exedra of the inner parterre towards the stepped *demi-lune* of the rear garden enclosure. In comparison with Mollet's plan – which with its elongated rather than square garden sections and its curvilinear parterre with *patte d'oie* (goose-foot) introduces a more dramatic organization of the garden's inner arrangement – the inner spatial organization of the Honselaarsdijk layout under Frederik Hendrik is much more 'static'.[56] In emphasizing transverse and parallel axes instead of diagonals, and in its solid checkerboard image, it seems to adhere to more traditional garden features and the typical 'mathematics' of the Dutch polderland. Dictated to a large extent by the exigencies of the natural landscape, now recognized for its aesthetic possibilities and exploited to fit classical rule, the mathematical pattern and cadence of these Dutch gardens would thus have an enduring imprint on Mollet's mind as reflected in his treatise.[57]

It should be remembered, however, that by the time Mollet's treatise was published in 1651 bold diagonal and curvilinear form features were already introduced in Holland, as is shown by Post's design for the extension of the Honselaarsdijk gardens and his designs for Heeze, and by several other mid-seventeenth-century gardens laid out by Post and Vingboons. At the end of Frederik Hendrik's reign, one could already witness the increased use of the *anse de pannier* and *patte d'oie* which provided more movement and perspectival effect in Dutch gardens, anticipating artistic developments in the latter part of the century. Moreover, by 1650 the Honselaarsdijk garden itself had undergone a metamorphosis, in that its closed, block-like appearance had diminished through the adaptation of a monumental, French-inspired parterre layout over the whole width of the garden. Visible only in later prints *(see figs. 30, 31 and 33)*, this remarkably modern parterre garden is generally attributed to William III's undertakings in garden architecture, but was actually laid out at the end of Frederik Hendrik's life.

The adornment of the garden with such large-scale *parterres de broderie* was the core of the total visual effect of the garden layout. The delicate form, colour and fragrance of the plants and flowers of these parterres were carefully chosen to enhance the visitors' pleasure and to bring *variété* to the whole design. In addition to their decorative purpose, plants and trees clearly have a formal purpose as well, which can be explained by using classical architectural terms. Trees can be seen to ensure *ratio* and *varietas* by defining the garden's contour and spatial layout. Trees also intensify the sense of order and regularity through their arrangement in neat rows and compartments, and they bring the necessary vertical contrast to the horizontal parterre sections. Mollet arranged the various trees, or *arbres sauvages*, according to their function and appearance, using terminology borrowed from architecture to describe their purpose.[58] Besides the more common fir-tree with its admirable pyramidal shape, Mollet specifically suggested the use of the cypress-tree, which, even though unsuitable for cold climates, was to be preferred for its beautiful effect:

> pour planter les cyprès d'espace, ou quelques autres beaux arbres bien faits et biens choisis comme des sapins, car quoiqu'ils soient communs en ces pays, néanmoins, s'ils sont plantés dans les jardins en lieux convenables et entretenus comme il appartient, il est évident qu'ils feront un très bel effet.[59]

In addition to the cypress-tree, Mollet mentioned the tall, fast-growing and easily replaceable Dutch elm-tree as ideal for the pleasure garden and most suitable for *allées*.[60] Among the flowers described by Mollet, the tulip is particularly admired for the great variety of its colours and its curious shape:

> Mais les tulipes surpassent de beaucoup en beauté et rareté ... par leur admirable panache et bigarrures en une infinité de couleurs ... jusqu'à cinq ou six sur une même fleur, ce qui les fait estimer des curieux parmi toutes les autres fleurs.[61]

This survey of Mollet's suggestions regarding plant material must suffice here to demonstrate that much of the design and total (spatial) effect of gardens depended on the choice and arrangement of plant material. This tends to be overlooked by architectural historians. During his years at the Stadholder's court, Mollet became influenced not only by the design but also by the plants of the courtly gardens, and was thus able to bring back to France new ideas on Dutch garden art and nature.

Important documentary evidence concerning the general esteem in which French architects, and the French style, were held at the Dutch court is found in the above-cited letter written in 1643 by Huygens to the Stadholder's agent in France, Mr. Tassin.[62] As we have seen, in this letter Huygens discussed the last modernization of Honselaarsdijk at the end of Frederik Hendrik's reign, and specified the new extension and renovation plans for certain sections of the palace and garden, including the improvement of the area immediately behind the palace, which contained the circular *berceaux*. This garden needed to be modernized according to the latest fashion or, as Huygens wrote, 'maintenant se pourra tailler à la mode'.[63] Whether or not directly in response to this letter, a new, French-inspired plan for the garden was made up and total reorganization of style, form and decoration of the main pleasure garden took place. As the late-seventeenth-century engravings show *(see figs. 30 and 31)*, this new garden consisted of one single expansive parterre area, interrupted only by three fountains set on the transverse axis, for the construction of which Joseph Dinant received payments in the beginning of 1647 (993 fols. 452, 465).

Two major conclusions can be drawn from this new garden appearance. Firstly, Frederik Hendrik's garden layouts, like all gardens, were by their very nature partly organic, and therefore subjected to constant change and frequent modifications. Secondly, the Stadholder insisted on having French architects and French garden architects contribute their ideas to the renovation plans for Honselaarsdijk.[64] The Stadholder's wish to have French garden architects give their design ideas is especially significant, for it demonstrates the position France and the French garden architect had already obtained as *arbiter elegantiae* before the middle of the century. This predilection for French examples can also be gleaned from the Stadholder's gardener-in-chief Jan van der Groen's treatise *Den Nederlandtsen Hovenier*, which stated, as we have seen in the preceding chapter, that at that time France excelled in the art of the garden.[65]

Van der Groen's remark, Mollet's parterre designs and the modernization of the Honselaarsdijk garden in the mid-1640s are indicative of the increasing artistic exchanges between the two countries. The growing cultural predominance of France at the end of Frederik Hendrik's life foretold the 'internationalism' of the arts within the Northern European court environment in the latter half of the century. A springboard for the later development of a particular Franco-Dutch style at William III's court, perhaps the earliest example of this phenomenon of 'artistic internationalism', can be found in the design of the Ter Nieuburch garden.

TER NIEUBURCH: FRENCH-DUTCH STYLISTIC EXCHANGE AND THE BOYCEAU-MOLLET CIRCLE

Significant similarities as well as discrepancies can be pointed out when comparing Honselaarsdijk and Ter Nieuburch. First of all, Ter Nieuburch was built as a summer residence and modelled accordingly as a long, horizontal palace, which did not have to fit any important existing structures on the spot. Honselaarsdijk originally served as a hunting palace and its form was dictated by its building history and original function as a stronghold, surrounded by a moat. This aspect of the moat, absent in the layout of Ter Nieuburch, resulted in a closer visual and actual relationship between house and garden, the unity of which was enhanced by the elongated, embracing form of the one-storey elevation of the palace. Furthermore, Ter Nieuburch's pleasure garden was twice the size of Honselaarsdijk's (within a rectangular framework); it measured circa 300 x 600 metres, against Honselaarsdijk circa 180 x 250 metres (excluding a semicircular piazza). Of a similar oblong form, Ter Nieuburch's garden was surrounded by a raised terrace within the familiar rectilinear canal system, and extended south-eastward towards Delft rather than following Honselaarsdijk's north-west orientation. Also, Ter Nieuburch's original garden design was directly modelled after a French example, the Palais du Luxembourg, although this source is not immediately in evidence in the final layout as depicted by Milheusser.

One of the recently discovered preliminary drawings of Ter Nieuburch *(see fig. 58)* provides us with an excellent geometrical overview of the whole garden, comparable to the geometrical sketch-plan of Honselaarsdijk *(see fig. 11)*. In this drawing Ter Nieuburch's geometrical scheme is again distinguished by a well-proportioned arrangement of square and rectangular compartments, echoing those of the palace structure – the square form of the pavilions and loggia and the rectangular form of the connecting galleries. The carefully thought-out relationship between size and proportion of the garden compartments and those of the building structures was already visible in the other preliminary drawings. One of them, the 'great fountain design' *(see fig. 56)*, clearly showed how the rear garden was to mirror the exact size, form and decoration of the courtyard with central fountain in front of the palace. The geometrical layout of the Ter Nieuburch garden expressed the same concern for symmetry and proportion as did Honselaarsdijk. The disposition of the parts, divided length- and breadthwise into three and multiples of three sections, reflected the tripartite division of the Honselaarsdijk garden. Such a tripartite arrangement was considered as possibly having a classical harmonic meaning,[66] but it is more likely that the use of the number three and its multiples was related to standard building practice, where this number was applied frequently, as Post's and Vingboons's rectangular ground-plans demonstrate.[67] The use of the number three and its proportional derivatives was also advised as most suitable for ground-plans by Renaissance architects like Palladio, without, however, implying any specific symbolic associations.[68]

Although the contour and main division of the terrain may not follow classical proportional rule *per se*, direct classical inspiration can be recognized in certain aspects of Ter Nieuburch's inner structure. The semicircular ending of the main parterre shows the reintroduction of an age-old Italianate architectural form – or, to be precise, a derivative of it – namely that of the hippodrome, which already had become a popular feature in contemporary French gardens. The hippodrome, originally derived from the ancient horse track and slowly adapted as a characteristic of garden architecture in Roman times, described by Pliny,[69] had developed into an important garden feature of Italian Renaissance villas, including the layouts of the Belvedere,[70] the Villa Madama[71] and the Villa Giulia,[72] among others. Introduced for the first time at Ter Nieuburch, this feature would inspire many subsequent Dutch gardens and can be recognized as a central attribute of many late-seventeenth-century garden layouts, the most famous examples of which are Heemstede and Zeist.[73] The 'hippodrome form' of Ter Nieuburch was not directly inspired by an Italian example; it was designed after a contemporary French model, that of the Luxembourg garden, which in turn was copied from the hippodrome-shaped theatre area in the Boboli gardens.[74]

In spite of the various classicizing compositional features of the Ter Nieuburch garden, only certain aspects of its layout are inspired by classical theory. Instead of being Italian or French, the general appearance of the garden is undeniably Dutch, that is, its overall spatial effect and contoured layout are largely dictated by the idiosyncrasies of the Dutch landscape. Other details can be ascribed to the Stadholder's personal views, as we shall see. Moreover, Ter Nieuburch already expressed at least one of the late-seventeenth-century French-inspired elements: a monumental parterre area with curvilinear termination consisting of intricately embroidered arabesque patterns after the latest French fashion. The manner in which the parterre was conceived, however – an agglomerate of several small beds filled with intricate boxwood decoration, rare flowers and statues enclosed by arbours – seems to adhere still to sixteenth-century principles of garden designing. In this respect, at the instigation of the Stadholder, Ter Nieuburch followed existing garden traditions which concentrated on separate ornamental nuances, evidenced also by such famous layouts as Heidelberg with which the Stadholder was familiar. Vestiges of earlier, indigenous traditions which also may have been preferred by the Stadholder[75] can be recognized in the lateral *giardini segreti* flanking the forecourt and holding rare plants and herbal plots, as well as an Orangerie and grotto with refined shell-work, all encompassed by 'medieval' crenellated walls.

Even if Ter Nieuburch harks back to older traditions, these rich ornamental elements are not necessarily 'traditional', for they are an inherent part of any garden style: contemporary architects relied as much on ornamentation as a means to enhance the garden's total appearance. Boyceau and Mollet devoted much space in their treatises to describing the detailed ornamentation of the garden. They recommended its decoration not only with parterres, grottoes and fountains but also, as we have seen, with paintings to provide perspectival views at the end of avenues.[76] They also advised the display of sculpture in surrounding galleries, thus adhering in all respects to the theme of the garden as 'open-air museum'.[77]

Though less monumental or dramatic in orchestration and ornamentation than the French garden, in general set-up Dutch gardens largely follow the compositional layout and plantation schemes of the French pleasure garden, characterized by the succession of a terrace, parterres, orchards and a wooded area. Among the Stadholder's gardens, Ter Nieuburch is unusual in its layout, in that the large wooded or orchard area lay in front of the palace instead of behind the house and garden where it was commonly situated, forming a natural backdrop for the rest of the garden and a protection against the winds. The effect of having to go through a shaded wood before entering the bright, open courtyard must have been impressive. The choice of situating this lime-tree wood was probably due to original plantations in the immediate vicinity, as seen in early maps of Ter Nieuburch.

How the form and layout of garden sections could give meaning to the whole palace complex can be seen by looking at the plantation's function in later years. The layout of Ter Nieuburch's lime-tree plantation, divided into three entrance avenues, would become the central feature of the protocol during the peace negotiations of 1697: the two adversaries would enter the property over the bridges and along the avenues at opposite ends, while the mediator approached it from the centre. The tripartite division of the wooded area mirrored that of the rear pleasure garden, which itself reflected the interior division of the palace. In 1697 this division was accentuated once again, as each party was restricted to opposite rooms in the west and east pavilions, while the mediator occupied the rooms in the central pavilion.

The style and form of this central pavilion constituted an appropriate link between the architectural and the sculptural decoration of Ter Nieuburch. From its centre protruded an unusual, rusticated two-storey loggia, from the balustraded rooftop of which one could overlook the whole garden and surrounding landscape, as far as the towers of Delft. Its shape, sharply projecting from the central pavilion in the middle of a raised terrace, to our knowledge was the first structure of its kind in Holland.[78] Quite unsuitable for the cold Dutch climate, the style and form of this loggia were indeed inspired by classical Italian designs. Actually the gable above the loggia[79] appears to be derived from designs in Serlio's fourth book on architecture, *Regole generali di architettura*,[80] and his *Extraordinario Libro*.

Serlio's gable design inspired not only one of the gables at Fontainebleau[81] but also Du Cerceau's roof and gable designs in his *Les Trois Livres d'Architecture*.[82] Both examples may have been another source for the Ter Nieuburch loggia, though this cannot be ascertained. It is of special interest that similar monumental Italianate loggia's, unpractical for the northern climate, became a recurrent feature of mid-seventeenth-century English palace architecture.[83] The loggia may thus be considered a popular element used to 'classicize' palace and garden.

Because of its explicit three-dimensional character, the loggia of Ter Nieuburch is a separate entity, as it were, functioning as a garden loggia in its own right. As such, it can be related to similar Italianate structures, epitomized by the classical garden loggia in

135. One of André Mollet's parterre or labyrinth designs from his *Le Jardin de plaisir*, comparable to parterres in Ter Nieuburch's preliminary designs.
The Metropolitan Museum of Art, New York

136. One of Jacques Boyceau's parterre designs from his *Traité du Jardinage*, with the motif of the inner circle for decorational monograms, as at Ter Nieuburch.
The Metropolitan Museum of Art, New York

Rubens's Antwerp residence, which also was based on Serlian designs.[84] Not only the style and form of Ter Nieuburch's garden loggia but also those of the garden's sculptural decoration can be related to classical models. At the same time, several details of the garden's ornamentation show links with the Southern Netherlands and Germany, specifically with statues in the gardens at Heidelberg and Cleves; they will be discussed in the next chapter.

Now that the complexities associated with a stylistic analysis of Ter Nieuburch's garden have been demonstrated, it is essential to isolate the French elements of its layout. Of primary relevance is Ter Nieuburch's initial 'French plan' *(see fig. 51)*, modelled on the Palais du Luxembourg. This French conceptional design demands detailed examination

V. STYLE AND FORM

especially in the light of André Mollet's presence at court, and the unfolding of French taste here and in Dutch cultural circles in general. Nowhere else is the influence of France on contemporary Dutch taste and mores more succinctly expressed than in the travel journal of the Englishman William Brereton, who, visiting the court at The Hague in 1634, remarked: 'The ladies and gentlemen here are all Frenchified in French fashion.'[85] The 'Frenchness' of Ter Nieuburch's preliminary design was confirmed by the use of the French toise as a unit of measure indicated in the drawing. Interestingly, the use of the toise was defined in detail by Mollet, who explained that artists generally prefer this measure, as distinct from the aune used by merchants.[86] Though the name of the person who made this 'French plan' for Ter Nieuburch still remains unknown, his identity is clear after careful weighing of all the facts and visual data: if not Mollet himself or possibly Simon de la Vallée, both present at the Dutch court, it must have been a French architect working within the Boyceau-Mollet circle in Paris. A brief survey of Boyceau and Mollet's views on garden architecture as set down in their treatises, and a comparison with Ter Nieburch's design history, will bear this out.[87]

Whereas Ter Nieuburch's so-called 'French plan', or French design concept, was not executed in the end, several of its most important features were, as is clearly shown by the Milheusser print *(see fig. 47)*. In the first place, Ter Nieuburch's total composition, unifying building and garden, its rectilinear canal-enclosed form, strong axial alignment and inner arrangements in strict mathematical units are directly comparable. Secondly, the tripartite division of the layout and the placement of the building halfway between a wooded section and a parterre area are the same in the conceptional and the final design *(compare figs. 47, 51 and 58)*. While these aspects partly depended on natural circumstances of the site with which the designer must have been familiar, more decorative architectural details, such as the raised terrace with oval stairs surrounding the pleasure garden, as well as its monumental parterre, were not. Indeed, these were exact copies of the heightened terraces and the unusual form of the oval stairs at the Luxembourg, itself an adaptation of features in the Florentine Boboli garden.[88] The stylistic boldness of the parterre in Ter Nieuburch's original concept and the radiating avenues through the wooded entrance area can thus be directly related to its French antecedent.[89]

In Ter Nieuburch's 'French plan' the whole pleasure garden behind the house is conceived as one single, vast parterre, divided into two square sections, each of a concentric octagonal shape punctuated by roundels. Ter Nieuburch's original parterre design, planned as a grand decorative eye-catcher visible from the main representative rooms in the palace, can be stylistically compared with Boyceau's parterre at the Luxembourg. At the same time this grand parterre can be seen as a variant of one of Mollet's ideal parterre designs *(fig. 135)*.[90] Ter Nieuburch's other parterres depicted in the Milheusser print, particularly the first main parterre with an inscribed inner circle containing the monogram of Frederik Hendrik and Amalia, must also have been designed by Mollet, who in turn may have been inspired by one of Boyceau's parterre designs, which are very similar *(fig. 136)*.[91] However, the motif of the concentric inner circle containing crowned monograms was already used in Salomon de Caus's famous parterres for the Heidelberg garden; this shows the difficulty of attributing certain ornamental patterns to one individual designer.[92]

More important, Mollet's first ideal plan in his treatise *(see fig. 133)* appears to be based in its entirety on Ter Nieuburch's layout, in much the same way as his second ideal plan was inspired by Honselaarsdijk. In fact, detailed examination of Mollet's first ideal plan shows that he must have combined features visible in Ter Nieuburch's conceptional 'French design', the Milheusser print and Boyceau's Luxembourg plan *(compare figs. 47, 51 and 60)*. At this point one may wish to ask in what way these three sources were welded together and how Mollet depicted and described his Ter Nieuburch-inspired first ideal plan.

Mollet's first ideal plan in schematic form roughly reflects the layout of Ter Nieuburch's chief parterre garden situated behind the palace structure. The main points in common between Mollet's ideal garden and Ter Nieuburch's layout are immediately apparent, such as the situation of the garden on level terrain and its strict rectilinear enclosure. Instead of using an entirely straight layout, Mollet had his garden terminate in a *demi-cercle*, just as he did in his subsequent ideal garden design based on Honselaarsdijk. Such an apsidal termination was characteristic for Boyceau's Luxembourg garden design, but it can also be found in other well-known French garden layouts, including Charleval and the Tuileries mentioned earlier.

The dimensions chosen by Mollet for his ideal garden design were circa 310 x 220 toises, or about 600 x 400 metres. Advertised as an ideal size for all truly stately gardens,[93] it would have come close to the dimensions of Ter Nieuburch's layout, were it not that the surface area had been shortened unexpectedly due to the impossibility to acquire the last parcels of land leading to the Rijswijkse Vliet canal, as maps of the region show *(compare figs. 134 and 44-47)*. Mollet's pleasure garden, being about one third longer than wide, reflected his as well as Boyceau's earlier contention that an oblong shape or parallelogram should be chosen for a garden, so that long alleys could be created to provide opportunities for perspectival effects. Following classical precepts, Mollet stressed the proper proportion of the surrounding canals, which should be measured precisely in relation to the dimensions of the paths and parterres. Devoting much space to a description of the exact appearance of the consecutive compartments as *parterres de broderie* and *compartiments de gazon*, or grass parterres, Mollet expressed the absolute necessity of variety in the garden. Its importance was also stressed by Boyceau; ultimately it was derived from the classical principle of *varietas*, described by Alberti as 'a most pleasing spice' and the visual highlight of a whole design.[94] Finally Mollet, pointing to the planting of trees in long double *ceintures* and heeding Boyceau's strict warnings, touched upon the essential aspect of gardening according to classical rule – that of symmetry, which referred here to Alberti's principle of bilateral correspondence in size and shape of all parts. According to the French garden architect, symmetry, both of the total design and of its diminutive parts, should be observed at all cost. Only within a strict symmetrical layout can the second prerequisite be obtained: the compositional unity of building and garden. Symmetry and compositional unity between palace and garden are indeed strictly applied, as both Mollet's design and Ter Nieuburch's plan show.

It is remarkable that the form of the central parterre section in Mollet's ideal plan, if reduced by one row of compartments to make up for Ter Nieuburch's diminished surface area, exactly reflects the central parterre depicted in the Milheusser print *(see figs. 47 and 133)*. In point of fact, Mollet's design copied Ter Nieuburch's rhythmical arrangement of parterres neatly paired along the central axis and framed by four ponds in the outer corners; in Mollet's plan they are indicated as undecorated rectangular compartments. The two large parterres immediately behind the building in Mollet's ideal plan are stylistically similar to the massive parterres visible in Ter Nieuburch's 'French design' *(see fig. 51)*. In turn, these parterres can be related to parterre layouts in two of the best-known gardens at the time, the Tuileries and Saint-Germain-en-Laye.[95]

An analysis of Mollet's ideal designs and his experience as garden architect in Holland shows the direct influence these Dutch courtly gardens had on his work.[96] While the Stadholder's gardens benefited from Mollet's expertise in creating innovative decorative parterres, Mollet benefited from the compositional features of the Stadholder's garden, modelling his two ideal pleasure gardens after them. In so doing, he took the main landscape-architectural characteristics of the Dutch garden – its flat, strictly enclosed geometrical terrain filled with, and surrounded by, water – and carried them over into a new aesthetic framework.

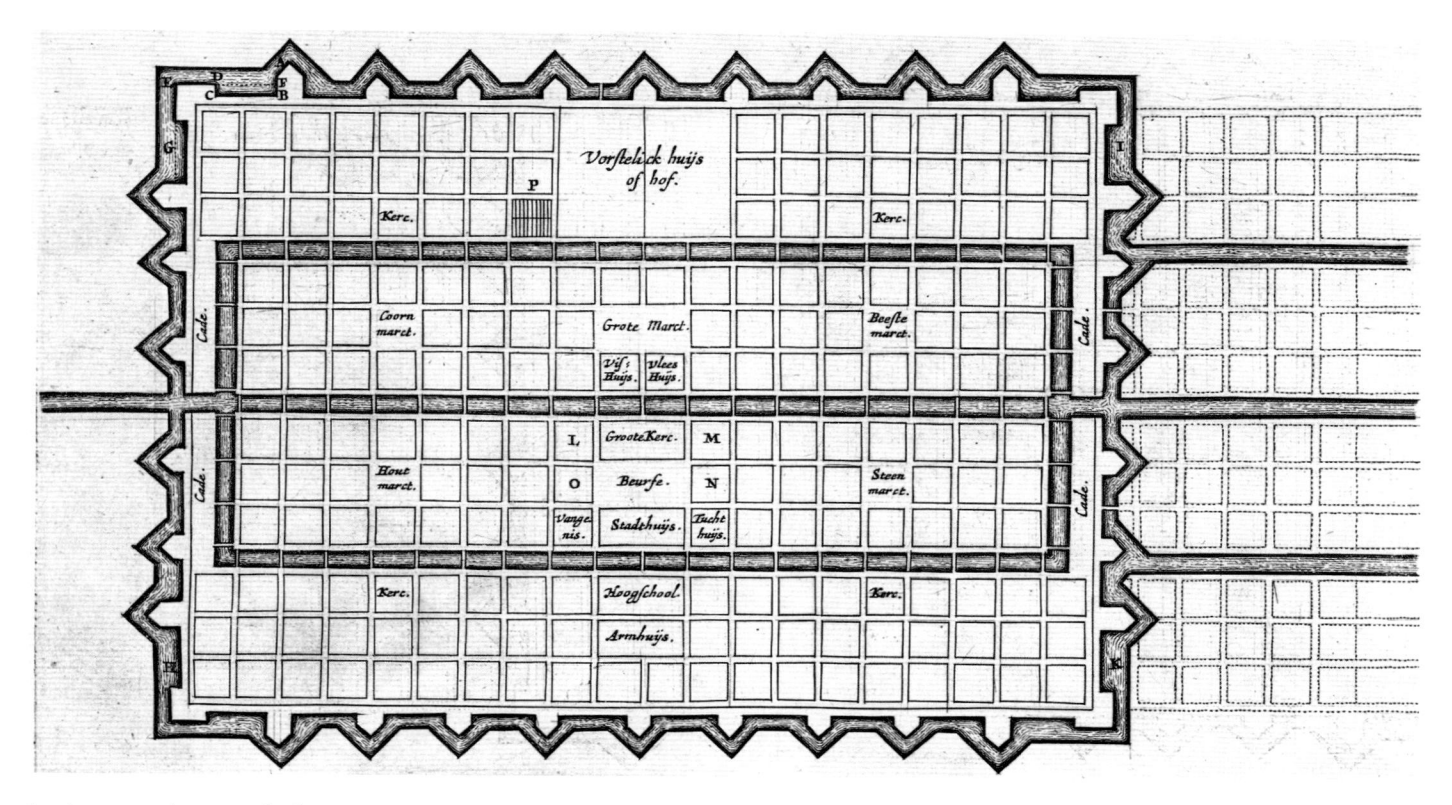

137. Simon Stevin's plan of an ideal city, based on a strict geometrical 'checkerboard pattern', also typical of contemporary garden designs. Photo courtesy Utrecht University

HONSELAARSDIJK AND TER NIEUBURCH: THE STADHOLDER AND DUTCH CLASSICISM

Thorough examination of Mollet's designs and his function at court makes it clear that the overall composition of the Honselaarsdijk and Ter Nieuburch layouts as depicted in the Van Berckerode and Milheusser prints *(see figs. 12 and 47)*, which used to be defined as 'French', predates contemporary French designs and the arrival of French architects at the Dutch court. What is more, both Honselaarsdijk and Ter Nieuburch, when it comes to their rectilinear framework and mathematical projection, inspired French garden design,[97] reversing the traditional art-historical belief that artistic influence moves northward. In the past, the historical development of the Dutch garden was often randomly compared with French garden history.[98] Fortunately, in more recent years the influence of classical Italian theory on Dutch garden design has received wider attention.[99] However, the specific Dutch and/or Flemish traits, as well as the personal taste of the patron, have not been studied sufficiently, and it is in this respect that one ultimately may expect to find answers to specific queries regarding the Dutch courtly gardens.

What were the personal thoughts and tastes of the Stadholder in the field of garden architecture, and how where they expressed at Honselaarsdijk and Ter Nieuburch? The picture which emerges from studying Frederik Hendrik's intellectual pursuits and artistic endeavours is that of a man who perceived his gardens not only as an aesthetic but also as an iconographical challenge. To the Stadholder the garden was an emblem of 'setting up court', at all its various levels of meaning, from the mastery of land reclamation to creating,

138. Simon Stevin's plan of an army camp, corresponding in form and layout to contemporary city planning and related to garden architecture.
Photo courtesy Utrecht University

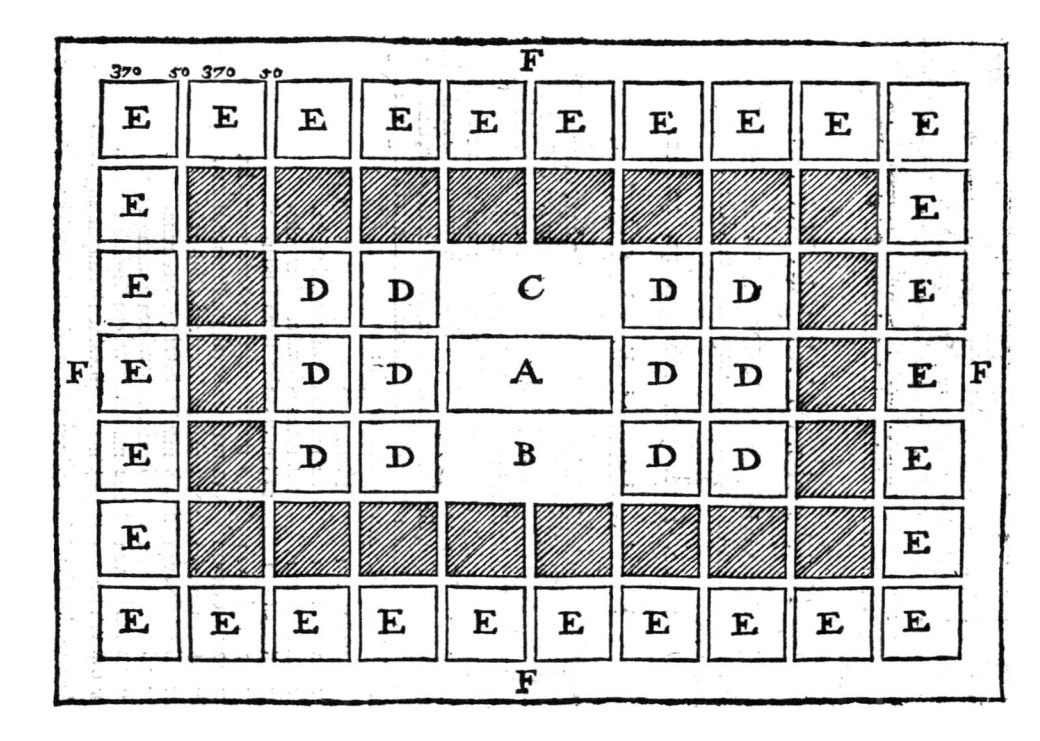

against all odds, a nation in which the arts and sciences could flourish. Naturally, the Stadholder knew how to benefit from the garden-architectural knowledge and experience developed elsewhere, particularly in Italy and France. Indeed, Frederik Hendrik and his architectural advisers applied the refined ancient mathematical laws of *ratio* as they had evolved from the Graeco-Roman past to be newly-adapted and interpreted by the architectural theorists of the Renaissance.[100] Similarly the Stadholder used the great skill which the French had developed in decorating gardens with embroidered tapestries of plant material and coloured stones, adding grace and *variété* to the garden.[101]

Honselaarsdijk and Ter Nieuburch were true *ensembles*, revealing the Stadholder's wish to make structure and garden appear as one single unit, laid out according to strict geometrical and arithmetical rules. Also noteworthy, yet often overlooked, are the aspects and features which the Stadholder chose not to apply to his gardens, even though the body of information was available to him. Instead of subscribing to all the aspects of contemporary garden design, such as more dynamic elongated compartments forwarded by Boyceau and Mollet, the Stadholder preferred the equilibrium of static square blocks, as the series of conceptual drawings of Ter Nieuburch show. The somewhat static arrangement of space which keeps the eye focused within the garden rooms instead of leading it outward into the surrounding countryside may be related to the patron's interest in exhibiting works of art for aesthetic as well as allegorical purposes.

In conclusion it remains to be seen how exactly Frederik Hendrik applied certain geometrical-mathematical predilections to the layout of his gardens, and how they were adapted to fit the Dutch landscape. In the preceding chapter it was explained that the Stadholder started to improve Honselaarsdijk and Ter Nieuburch at the very time when science and technology were developing dramatically, especially in the field of (military) architecture.[102] While Vredeman de Vries initially had been a motivating force in setting up garden architecture as a scientific discipline, from the late sixteenth century onward the resulting mathematical-architectural developments were stimulated by the Princes of Orange themselves and the learned men around them. To this circle belonged the engineer Simon Stevin, referred to by Huygens as a 'mathematical genius',[103] and encountered in

V. STYLE AND FORM

the previous chapters as the probable 'instigator' of various geometrical garden designs at court.[104] Stevin's connection with the court was in any case a lasting one, since even during Frederik Hendrik's reign he was regularly asked to review new inventions of measuring instruments, and to proofread various mathematical, mechanical and naval studies sent to the court for publishing rights.[105]

Concurrent with these developments, the knowledge of classical architectural theory was expanding rapidly at the Dutch court, fuelled by erudite men such as Huygens and Van Campen. As his advisers were well aware of the latest influx of Italian and French treatises on the topic, Frederik Hendrik himself proved to be particularly significant for the evolution of architectural style in Holland. As much at home on the battlefield as in the garden,[106] the Stadholder manifested an interest in and expert knowledge of the 'new' mathematical and engineering sciences as well as the classical building principles, soon to be expressed by his personal involvement in city planning, architecture and garden designing.[107]

THE STADHOLDER'S VISION OF SYMMETRY IN *CITTÀ, CASTRA* AND *GIARDINO*

Frederik Hendrik's knowledge of classical theory and his particular concern for symmetry and correct proportion are clearly reflected in the garden layouts of Honselaarsdijk and Ter Nieuburch, both as regards the total composition and elongated shape of the gardens and as to the disposition of the parts.[108] At Honselaarsdijk the rectangular form of the pleasure garden with its bastioned corners and the distribution of the larger plantation area in blocks or *carrés*,[109] all according to the traditional 'checkerboard pattern', can be related to the grid plan of the new city layouts of the time. The wooded area planted in front of Ter Nieuburch and the tree plantations at Zuylesteyn fit the same rules of regimented order, actually referred to as *ordre* in the garderner's contract *(Appendix, Document IX)*.[110] As Hopper and Taverne have pointed out,[111] such symmetrical organization and strict regimentation can be compared with designs from the realms of military architecture and city planning. Good examples are Stevin's design for an ideal city *(fig. 137)*[112] and contemporary designs by other Dutch engineers commissioned in and outside Holland for town planning or military fortifications. Particularly extensive, in this context, were the works undertaken by Dutch engineers in Denmark and Northern Germany (Schleswig-Holstein), sent there by Frederik Hendrik to assist his godfather, Christian IV of Denmark, in building fortified cities.[113] That the comparison between town and garden planning is justified is evidenced by Stevin's own remark on the ideal city, the form and distribution of which is comparable to the actual layout of Honselaarsdijk. Stevin writes that a city should follow the shape of a four-sided rectangle laid out on level terrain, so that it can be suitably divided into smaller rectangular blocks (read: compartments) of courtyards, houses, market-places and other places which cannot conform well to other shapes.[114]

When comparing city and garden architecture with city planning and military architecture, one is struck by the systematic arrangement of compartments at Honselaarsdijk and Ter Nieuburch, planted as they are with neat rows of trees reminiscent of military cordons of soldiers standing in perfect symmetrical order. This same tendency towards 'regimentation' would be displayed in the layouts of Buren and the Huis ten Bosch, and in numerous other Dutch gardens, such as Pieter Post's Vredenburg and Philips Vingboons's ideal plans for country houses. A direct relationship between the ideal form of the city – or, in this case, the garden – and Dutch military architecture is also shown by the

COURTLY GARDENS IN HOLLAND 1600-1650

Painting of Huis ten Bosch by Jan van der Heyden, c. 1668. Metropolitan Museum, New York (see fig. 96)

Plan of the Noordeinde gardens in 1711, by unknown artist. CBN (see fig. 90) *(previous page)*

similarity between Stevin's ideal city plan and his scheme for an army camp *(fig. 138)*.[115] Moreover, commenting on the Renaissance definition of *symmetria*, Stevin used anthropomorphic terms, in the very same way Huygens would, to stress 'likesidedness'. Stevin stated: 'lijksijdigheydt is der rechter en slijnckerdeelen eens lichaems overeencommingh in form grootheydt ende gestalt' (likesidedness means that the right and the left part of a body are the same in form, size and shape).[116] And besides, Stevin added, if one does not have any feeling for symmetry one may as well give up becoming an architect (*bouwmeester*) altogether.[117]

As can be seen from Huygens's poetic writings on Hofwijck (see the preceding chapter), the preference for absolute symmetry was derived from Alberti's harmony of nature, in which, like the members of an animal or human body, the parts on the right side correspond to those on the left in shape, number and size.[118] Absorbed by similar *problemata*, Frans van Schooten, professor in mathematics at Leiden University and Stevin's School for Engineers, who was responsible for training most of the outstanding building engineers of the day, in a long letter to the Stadholder and Huygens defended the utmost importance of mathematics. He stated that mathematically-educated craftsmen, landsurveyors/cartographers and engineers, 'not only greatly served this country, but also [that of] His Majesty of Sweden …'[119] The draughtsman responsible for the mathematical illustrations in Descartes's *Dioptrique*, Van Schooten also was the 'young man' referred to in Descartes's letter to Mersenne regarding the need for precise drawings of the Luxembourg garden layout to design a garden in Holland.[120] The importance of a sound mathematical education is also expressed in a letter by Huygens's friend, the mathematics teacher D. de Morlot, who, remarking on the education of Frederik Hendrik's son William II, wrote: 'la géometrie estoit une des principales sciences que devoit bien savoir Monsieur le Prince Guillaume …'[121] In this respect a series of contemporary mathematical studies by Johan Maurits van Nassau-Siegen, kept in the Koninklijk Huis Archief,[122] should also be taken into account, since they demonstrate geometrical exercises with triangles and circles which were the basis of his as well as Prince Maurits's and Frederik Hendrik's thoughts on garden architecture.

The transparency of the boundaries of architectural design – or, in other words, the connections between *città ideale*, *castra* and *giardino* – can be recognized in early-seventeenth-century Dutch garden architecture. The relationship between the different fields of architecture and their mutual classical, mathematical foundation was certainly not lost on architects in Dutch court circles.[123] It must have been on Frederik Hendrik's mind when he laid out his gardens, where mathematical proportions and the geometry of space seem to be applied in accordance with classical rules.

Turning our attention for a moment from issues of design to the decorative aspects of the Stadholder's gardens, we can draw direct lines not only between the structural form of his gardens and classical principles but also between their ornamentation and classical symbolism. The decorative programme of Frederik Hendrik's gardens, centring on classical sculpture and statues of Roman warriors, indicates overall associations with a heroic past, in particular the age of the Batavians during the Roman Empire.[124] Thus, the Stadholder's palaces and gardens can be seen as representative monuments expressing the power and prestige of the House of Orange, in which Rome and the classical past prevail as the exemplary archetype. In this respect we have already pointed out Nootman's dedicatory poem in the Van Berckerode print *(see fig. 12)*, in which the then popular typological simile comparing Batavians with Romans is reflected and Honselaarsdijk, as 'Batavian stronghold', is hailed as a new Rome.[125] To Nootman's text we could add Huygens's verses on the rebirth of Roman Truth in architecture[126] which echo exactly Vondel's poetic expression, referring to Van Campen and the Town Hall of Amsterdam as 'copying Rome on a small scale'.[127]

In spite of this Roman 'rhetoric', one wonders how the classical principles of symmetry and proportion were actually embodied in the plans of the Stadholder's gardens. The symmetry of the main garden plans of Honselaarsdijk and Ter Nieuburch shown by Van Berckerode and Milheusser *(see figs. 12 and 47)*, where parterre corresponds to parterre, *berceau* to *berceau* and orchard to orchard, certainly recalls Frederik Hendrik's and Huygens's obsession with absolute symmetry, witness remarks in contemporary letters. Apparently Huygens's emphasis on absolute symmetry and pure proportion was well known; he himself wrote that swirling lines made him 'dizzy and feverish'.[128] Huygens's friend Balzac hesitated to send him a plan of his garden in France, afraid as he was to present irregular objects to someone with such a 'perfect eye ... trained to look at architecture in a scientific manner'.[129] Likewise, Frederik Hendrik's brother Prince Maurits felt uncomfortable if the walls of his fortifications on both sides did not exactly correspond, according to Stevin.[130] Prince Maurits and Huygens applied the same concepts of symmetry and proportion derived from classical theory to their garden layouts. Prince Maurits did so in his princely gardens at Flushing and in the Buitenhof at The Hague in the early 1620s, and Huygens in the garden of Hofwijck at Voorburg about 1640.[131] Frederik Hendrik himself showed a similar concern for strict symmetry when vetoing the Commissioner's plan for the Plein at The Hague, proposing the layout of a spacious piazza encompassed by a network of straight, broad avenues instead of narrow, undulating streets. At the same time, he employed classical rules of symmetry and proportion for the design of his gardens, as shown by their particular shape and form.

In certain details of the layout of the Honselaarsdijk and Ter Nieuburch gardens, particularly the inner arrangement of smaller compartments, one can also recognize concern for classical symmetry and proportion. First of all, as we have seen, Honselaarsdijk's rectangular form with its bastioned corners and Ter Nieuburch's rectangular outline, while also generally applied by Post and Vingboons, can be associated in principle with Stevin's preference for a rectangle and are reminiscent of his design for an ideal city.[132] Furthermore, in the balanced division of the garden, centred round an axis, one can witness a literal application of Stevin's 'Albertian' definition of symmetry.[133] Though it is questionable whether, just as at Hofwijck, the application of absolute symmetry went too far, in that the palace represented the head and the garden's axis the spine, the principle of absolute symmetry undoubtedly underlay the designs of the Stadholder's gardens.

HONSELAARSDIJK AND TER NIEUBURCH: THE STADHOLDER AND HARMONIC PROPORTION

The total plans of the Honselaarsdijk and Ter Nieuburch gardens *(see figs. 11, 12 and 47, 58, respectively)* clearly echoed Frederik Hendrik and his advisers' concern with principles of symmetry. Moreover, the whole form and inner disposition of these gardens may possibly be regarded as Dutch interpretations of classical harmonic proportion. In fact Hopper, basing her research in part on Wittkower's pioneering work in the field of harmonic proportion in architecture and the problem of musical consonances,[134] went so far as to say that the Honselaarsdijk garden may have been one of the first examples in Northern Europe of a total plan based on one of the Pythagorean harmonic ratios.[135]

Hopper coupled her strictly classical interpretation of the Honselaarsdijk layout with a new definition of such a garden, labelling it 'the prototype of the Dutch Classical Canal

Garden'.[136] A classical interpretation like that was long overdue and opened up entirely new research areas for the history of Dutch garden architecture. However, as mentioned before, it is not always easy to determine to what extent classical theories were precisely and deliberately applied. It was often impossible to put pure theory into practice, because one was dealing with nature and organic material rather than stone. Steeped in classical literature as they were, the Stadholder and his advisers must have been aware of the significance of certain numbers and ratios within the Pythagorean theory and their deeper religious-philosophical meaning as interpreted by Renaissance theorists like Alberti. Nevertheless, the question remains whether they applied them deliberately when designing their gardens, and if so, how exactly.

While a clear answer will probably never be found, the publications by Hopper, Taverne and Van Pelt, based in part on Wittkower, show that harmonic ratios were indeed applied to Dutch gardens. It was found that Huygens's garden was undoubtedly based on harmonic (musical) ratios. Given the friendship between the two men and their common interests, the Stadholder's gardens may also have been inspired by harmonic ratios.[137] Two examples must suffice here to show how proportional relationship found in one of the Stadholder's gardens, Honselaarsdijk, can indeed be analysed in terms of classical ideals of musical harmony.[138] Honselaarsdijk's rectangular pleasure garden was laid out to the ratio of 4 to 3, or, in classical geometrical terms, a square and one third. This proportion can be compared to Pythagorean musical harmony and related to the simple consonant ratio, called 'concord' or *sesquitertia*, recommended by Alberti for modestly-sized layouts.[139] This same proportional relationship was illustrated by Serlio[140] and picked up by Stevin.[141] It developed into a popular standard size for smaller garden plans and was first described by Olivier de Serres,[142] then by André Mollet[143] and later by Dézallier d'Argenville in his early-eighteenth-century garden treatise.[144] Frederik Hendrik, who knew Henri IV's gardens at Fontainebleau and Saint-Germain-en-Laye and was much impressed by their layouts and decorations, may also have been inspired by the ratio of 4 to 3 employed for sections in these famous pleasure gardens.[145]

Likewise, not only the general form of the Honselaarsdijk garden but also its inner layout may have been based on ancient mathematical precepts. In this light, Honselaarsdijk's inner division into three compartments on either side of a central axis cannot have been accidental, according to Hopper, and may be seen as expressing contemporary interest in Neoplatonic philosophy.[146] In a Christian-Humanist context the number three was indeed 'Il numero primo e divino', as Wittkower has pointed out,[147] and it was at the centre of the Pythagorean-Platonic philosophy expressing cosmic order and harmony. Yet it is important to remember once again that Frederik Hendrik's design ideals had to be adjusted to fit the specific traditions of parcel division of the Dutch polderland. Moreover, the number three and its proportional derivatives, as we have seen, belonged to a standard size in building practice, quite separate from the classical tradition and its symbolic numerology. Besides, the actual size and form of the garden, too, were conditioned by the natural geography of the terrain. The development of Honselaarsdijk showed that its final form was conditioned in part by existing structures, moats and dike systems. As the history of the series of ground acquisitions for Ter Nieuburch shows, the surface area was considerably smaller than originally foreseen, and the final design and its proportions had to be modified *(compare figs. 44, 47 and 51)*. The same goes for the three-partite structure of the Noordeinde garden, which, even though it could be associated with classical harmonic proportional systems and their symbolic significance, actually was divided into three parcels long before Frederik Hendrik acquired the land *(see figs. 83 and 85)*, and certainly before anyone in Holland could have become familiar with classical architectural theory. In short, it seems that the form and layout of the Honselaarsdijk, Ter Nieuburch and other stadholderly gardens depended mostly on the natural situation and the historical development of the estates, and only in part on classical precepts.

In spite of reservations about the impact of classical theory on the form and layout of the Stadholder's gardens, it is plausible that classical thoughts permeated the inner division of these gardens. Particularly intriguing within this framework of ideas at court and the interpretation of classical principles of harmonic proportion is the curiously laid-out second garden compartment of Honselaarsdijk.[148] This compartment, situated directly behind the palace, consisted of a rectangle or double square with inscribed circles, also defined as bi-cycles or di-cycles,[149] formed by hedges. The predominance of the two perfect geometrical figures, the circle and the square, according to Hopper,[150] cannot be coincidental: it must be related to classical symbolic ratios and, more specifically, to the outstretched Vitruvian human figure with its cosmological significance. Considering that Prince Maurits's garden at the Buitenhof had the same form of a double square with two circular *berceaux*, and that Huygens's garden at Hofwijck, although different in shape, was perceived as reflecting the form of the Vitruvian human figure, such analogies with the layout of Honselaarsdijk seem justified.

In the next chapter detailed attention will be given to this unusual form motif of the twin circles within a square and its meaning in the Stadholder's gardens. Here, however, it is important to note that preference for this motif was more widely spread than the two examples discussed by scholars thus far. The identical form motif can be recognized in at least five other courtly gardens at the time. Of immediate consequence for our understanding of the dissemination of classical form in gardens is the fact that there was a direct source for this geometrical layout, and that it can be found in classical treatises which, significantly, were kept in the library of the Orange family, such as Scamozzi's *L'Idea dell'architettura universale* and Serlio's *Architettura in sei Libri*. What is more, the specific geometrical form of the circle in the square and its variations is shown by Serlio in his First Book on Geometry, describing in detail the making of a 'Circle in a foure square'.[151] It is this very treatise, translated in Antwerp in 1585 and republished in Dutch in Amsterdam in 1606, which may have inspired Prince Maurits, whose gardens at Flushing and somewhat later at The Hague (Buitenhof) were the first to be laid out according to the geometrical principles of the perfect circle and square. Furthermore, two of Serlio's perspective and cubic drawings[152] can be compared with Hendrick Hondius's perspective drawing of the Buitenhof garden, the layout of which is immediately related to the design of the garden behind the palace of Honselaarsdijk, confirming the classical Italian origin of this particular garden layout.

REGIONAL INFLUENCES AND FLEMISH-DUTCH TRADITIONS: QUADRATURE

The library of the Orange family was filled with classical, Italian and French treatises. However, an approach which overemphasizes any one of these sources without reckoning with the influence of local geographical peculiarities, earlier regional traditions of gardening and land division, and the patron's artistic taste, has to be regarded as incomplete. Indeed, environmental and topographical conditions as well as vestiges of regional traditions played an important role in the final conformation of the Honselaarsdijk garden. First of all, the form of the moated castle and garden, expressing the peculiar character of a medieval stronghold, was carefully retained by Frederik Hendrik,

139. Reconstruction drawing of the Honselaarsdijk garden, showing the strict geometrical construction and proportions based on quadrature.

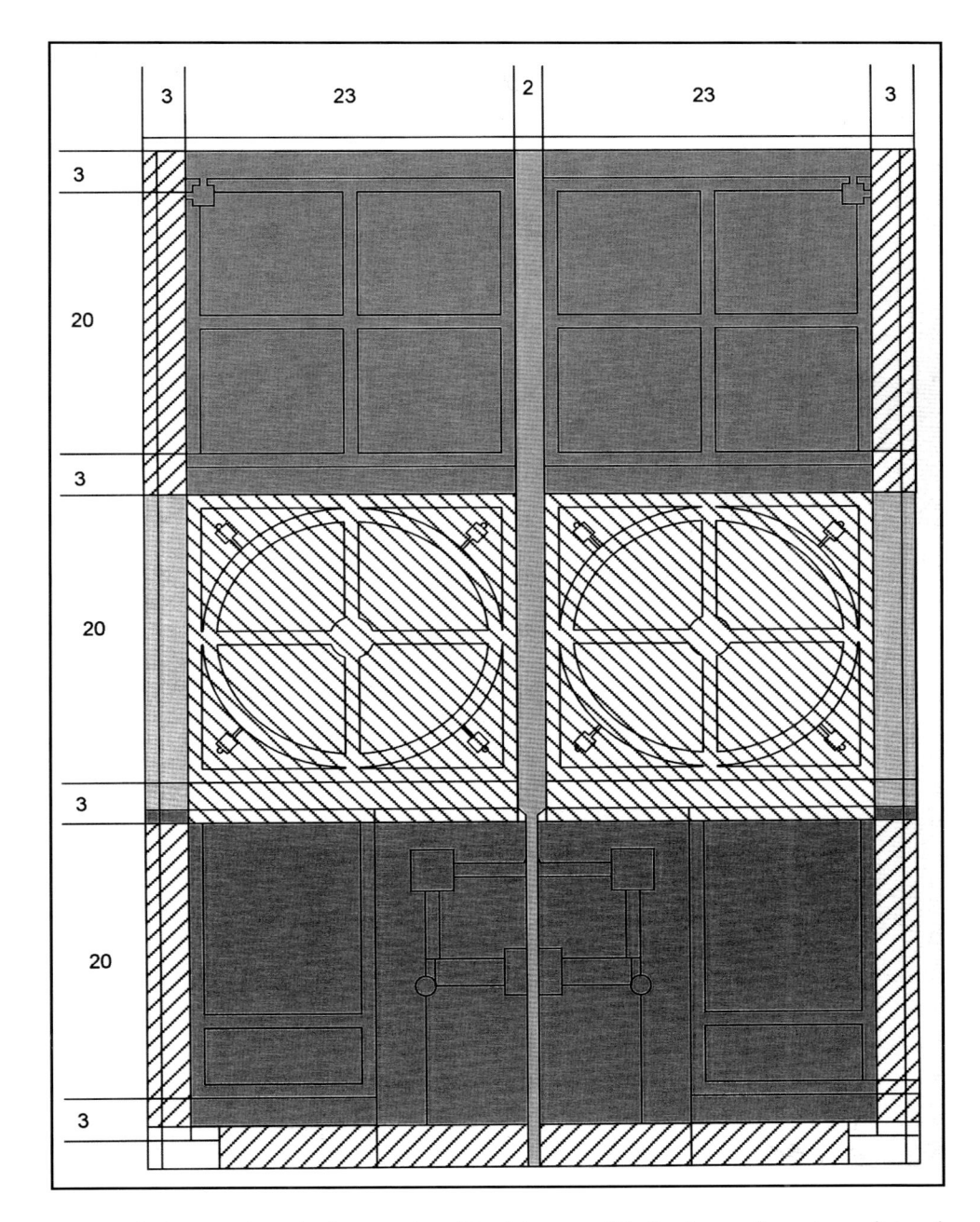

apparently because it evoked memories of feudal power. His fondness of certain traditional features with an 'image' of, or association with, the heroic Batavian past can also be recognized in the crenellated walls surrounding sections of his gardens at Ter Nieuburch and those of the Buitenhof. It is in the detail of the crenellated wall, lending a fortress-like appearance to the layout, that connections can be drawn between contemporary gardens and military architecture. The fortress-like form and image of the garden were also reflected in the protruding corners of the two lateral garden sections in front of the building. The idea of the garden as a paradise protected in a bastioned straightjacket, as it were, was also prominently extolled at the time by the German architect Joseph Furttenbach, whose books,[153] containing ideal garden designs, were undoubtedly known to Frederik Hendrik, because some of them were kept in his library.

Throughout the century the form idea of the fortress-like estate or *donjon*, which originally had a strategic function, can be seen to re-emerge in Dutch gardens, where it

V. STYLE AND FORM

gradually became appreciated for purely aesthetic reasons. We can notice the dissemination of this basic form of the moated house and garden, from Honselaarsdijk and Hofwijck to the famous late-seventeenth-century layouts of Clingendael, Heemstede and Zeist. Given the need to defend oneself and the omnipresence of water in the Low Countries, it is unlikely, however, that Honselaarsdijk constituted the absolute genesis of this type of layout.[154] Other predetermined factors and topographical conditions, such as the natural flatness of the terrain, influenced both the early- and the late-seventeenth-century garden designs reflecting this *donjon* principle. In this context we should also call to mind the method applied by the Stadholder when restoring an old, originally medieval estate such as Zuylesteyn. Frederik Hendrik's predilection for the past could be recognized in the careful way certain features were retained, including the moat and garden islands, while the total restoration of the castle was in close sympathy with its medieval origins.[155]

Evidence furnished by the series of maps surviving from the early building history of the Honselaarsdijk palace shows that the architect must have taken into account the Dutch topographical and certain other predetermined factors when designing the gardens. Factors which he had to consider, apart from the presence of the old medieval moat and castle island, included the partly existing canal system and dikes, particularly the old dike west of the estate *(see figs. 8, 9 and 10)*. Since the land division and part of the surrounding dike system existed already before the Stadholder's acquisition of the castle and its terrain, one may again question the reliability of an analysis of its final rectangular shape as being inspired by classical principles of proportion. In planning the gardens it was, in the first place, necessary to adjust the design to the peculiarities of the countryside, the flatness of which provided a natural wide perspective but precluded the layout of monumental cascades, while its humidity made a network of drainage canals unavoidable. As a protection against the strong north-western winds from the sea, rows of trees were planted to surround the garden, enhancing the closed character of the whole layout. As we have seen, certain aspects of the garden's shape and inner conformation, such as the rectangular form and 'checkerboard' division, resulted not only from contemporary regional mathematical advances but also from existing local traditions, involving methods of dividing grounds into elongated strips of land and the system of medieval quadrature.

Quadrature is one of the oldest mathematical systems. Already applied by the ancients, it was practised throughout the ages in the field of arts and crafts and survived in Frederik Hendrik's time.[156] Related to the system of quadrature in Holland were the traditional ideal of 'good craftsmanship' and the application of 'proper measurements'. These beliefs excluded any specific philosophical connotations when applying certain measurements, and they were still essential to the architectural trade, in spite of the influx of classical theory.[157] It is important to note that most early-seventeenth-century Dutch craftsmen-architects regarded geometric schemes or systems of measurement in the first place as a helpful framework for designing a new plan, and generally were unaware of, or ignored, their classical-symbolic implications. One medieval geometric rule of thumb, which continued to be used as a standard proportional scheme, even in the erudite court circles, was that of medieval quadrature.[158] It was here, however, that its application became again connected with Pythagorean numerological meaning and related to the ancient principles of measurement adapted by Renaissance theorists. Indeed, the system of quadrature is a geometrical progression based on the ratio between one of the sides of a square and its diagonal – a system already applied in classical antiquity and specifically mentioned by Vitruvius,[159] as well as by Palladio in the Renaissance.[160]

The layout of Honselaarsdijk as drawn in the original plan and depicted in the Van Berckerode print *(see figs. 11 and 12)* seems to be based on this very rule of thumb.[161] A

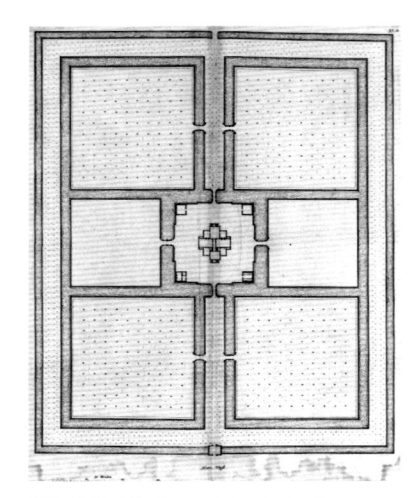

140. Philips Vingboons's ideal plan for a country house and garden, divided into mathematically arranged plots within a larger grid plan of canals.
Koninklijke Bibliotheek. Photo courtesy Utrecht University

141. Pieter Post's bird's-eye view of the Vredenburg gardens, showing their geometrical division in island blocks, with strict arrangement of trees.
Koninklijke Bibliotheek

PERSPECTIVE UYTBEELDINGE van VREDEN-BURGH, met hare omstaande Timmeragie, Hoven, Plantagie, etc. Gebouwt door den Hr. FREDERICK ALEWYN, aen de Noord-zyde van de Zuyder-wech, inde BEEMSTER.

P. Post Inventor

REPRESENTATION en PERSPECTIVE de VREDEN-BURG, tant de la Maison que des Jardins, Plantages, etc. Bâti par le Sr. FREDERIC ALEWYN, au côté du Nord du Zuyder-weg, dans le BEEMSTER.

reconstruction drawing of the Honselaarsdijk garden following this plan shows that the total plan can be neatly divided into squares and rectangular compartments according to this geometrical system of quadrature. The total plan of the Honselaarsdijk garden can be divided into two rows of three perfect squares measuring 23 x 23 Rijnlandse roeden (1 Rijnlandse roede = 3.76 metres), held within the framework of the outer canal *(fig. 139)*. The size of the three squares on either side of the central axis, including the strip of land formed by the surrounding walkway and canal, measured 23 x 26 roeden. The width of this added strip of land is obtained by transferring the measurement of half the squares' diagonal by means of compasses and drawing part of a circumference. Thus, at Honselaarsdijk we can recognize, apart from classical principles of proportion, the application of an old medieval tradition and system of architectural measurement originating from ancient writers.

The detailed inner structure of the garden, too, can be read from this reconstruction drawing. Taking the width of the frontal façade of the building as point of departure, the architect drew a simple scheme of squares and rectangles. The whole area of the main pleasure garden measured 73 x 54 Rijnlandse roeden and was divided into seven 'isles' or parts, whereas the palace island (including the bridge) and its two lateral plots each measured 13 x 24 roeden width to length[162] and the four compartments behind the palace 23 x 20 roeden. All the garden plots were surrounded by a path measuring two roeden, while the whole garden was encompassed by a canal of one and a half roeden. Similar mathematical schemes for arranging the various parts within a garden plan can be recognized in designs by Post, such as his plan for the Huis Vredenburg *(fig. 140)*,[163] and in plans by Vingboons, such as his ideal plan of a country estate *(fig. 141)*.[164] In these examples the gardens are seen to be composed of clear-cut square or rectangular sections which echo the shape of the stone building itself, held within a larger grid plan of canals. Such layouts are of special interest for demonstrating the new classical-baroque idea of incorporating house and garden within one and the same, carefully designed geometrical-proportional framework.

Particularly expressive of these new objectives of unifying building structure and garden is the mathematical method applied in seventeenth-century Holland, by which the proportional division of the elevation of the building often was taken as the standard measurement for its whole plan, and even for the surrounding terrain. Only scant material is left of authentic seventeenth-century architectural drawings with clear indications of the proportional set-up of the elevation and subsequent total design of the surrounding grounds. At Honselaarsdijk such methods are vaguely recognizable but remain hypothetical: the width of the front façade of the Honselaarsdijk palace, including the two lateral octagonal towers, measured 14 roeden, a scale also taken as point of departure for the surrounding grounds, as shown in the geometrical sketch-plan of the Honselaarsdijk garden *(see fig. 11)*. Since no other contemporary drawing with the exact proportion of the Honselaarsdijk elevation survives, it is difficult to use it to determine further detailed proportional relationships between façade and garden. A more likely 'candidate' for such geometrical and proportional analyses would be the Huis ten Bosch, the stone floor pattern of which, shown in detail in Post's prints, recalls the form of the garden's compartments and parterres.

The only project of this kind whose original proportional scheme survives is the plan of the elevation of the Schielandhuis in Rotterdam, designed by Jacob Lois in 1662 with the collaboration of Pieter Post.[165] The schematic principle used to divide the façade of the Schielandhuis is particularly important for our analysis of the proportional system of Honselaarsdijk's inner garden structure. The façade of the Schielandhuis, consisting of a

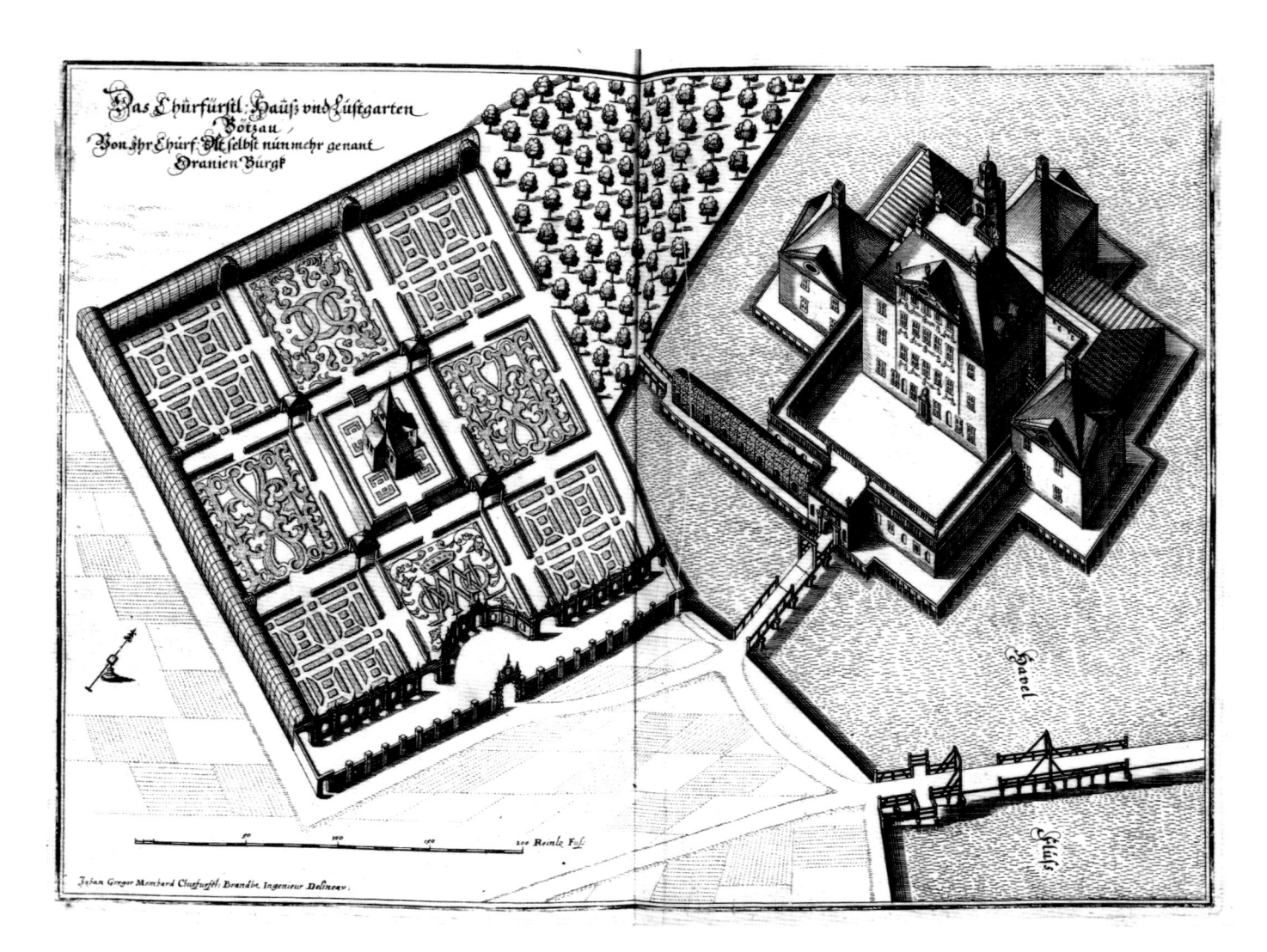

142. Bird's-eye view of Oranienburg by Matthaeus Merian, *Topographia Electoratus Brandenburgici*, showing Dutch-inspired gardens c. 1650, with parterres designed by André Mollet.
Collectie Bodel Nijenhuis, Universiteitsbibliotheek, Leiden

rectangle with a proportion of 1 to 2, is built up of two perfect squares with inscribed circles. The same mathematical scheme can be recognized in the Honselaarsdijk garden, where the compartment behind the palace proper consisted of two squares with inscribed circles *(see figs. 11 and 12)* – a scheme which will be analysed in greater detail in the next chapter. It is no coincidence, however, that the plan of the entire pleasure garden of Honselaarsdijk, including the space of the semicircular piazza in front of the palace, can also be interpreted as being composed of two blocks, with the proportion of 1 to 2. The first block would comprise the length of the semicircular piazza, palace island and moat; the second, equally large block, the rest of the main pleasure garden. Seen in this way, the outline or silhouette of Honselaarsdijk, consisting of a rectangle with a semicircular ending, can be connected to the form of Ter Nieuburch's main parterre garden *(compare figs. 12 and 47)*, which also consists of a rectangular area ending in a semicircle, there formed by monumental *berceaux*.

V. STYLE AND FORM

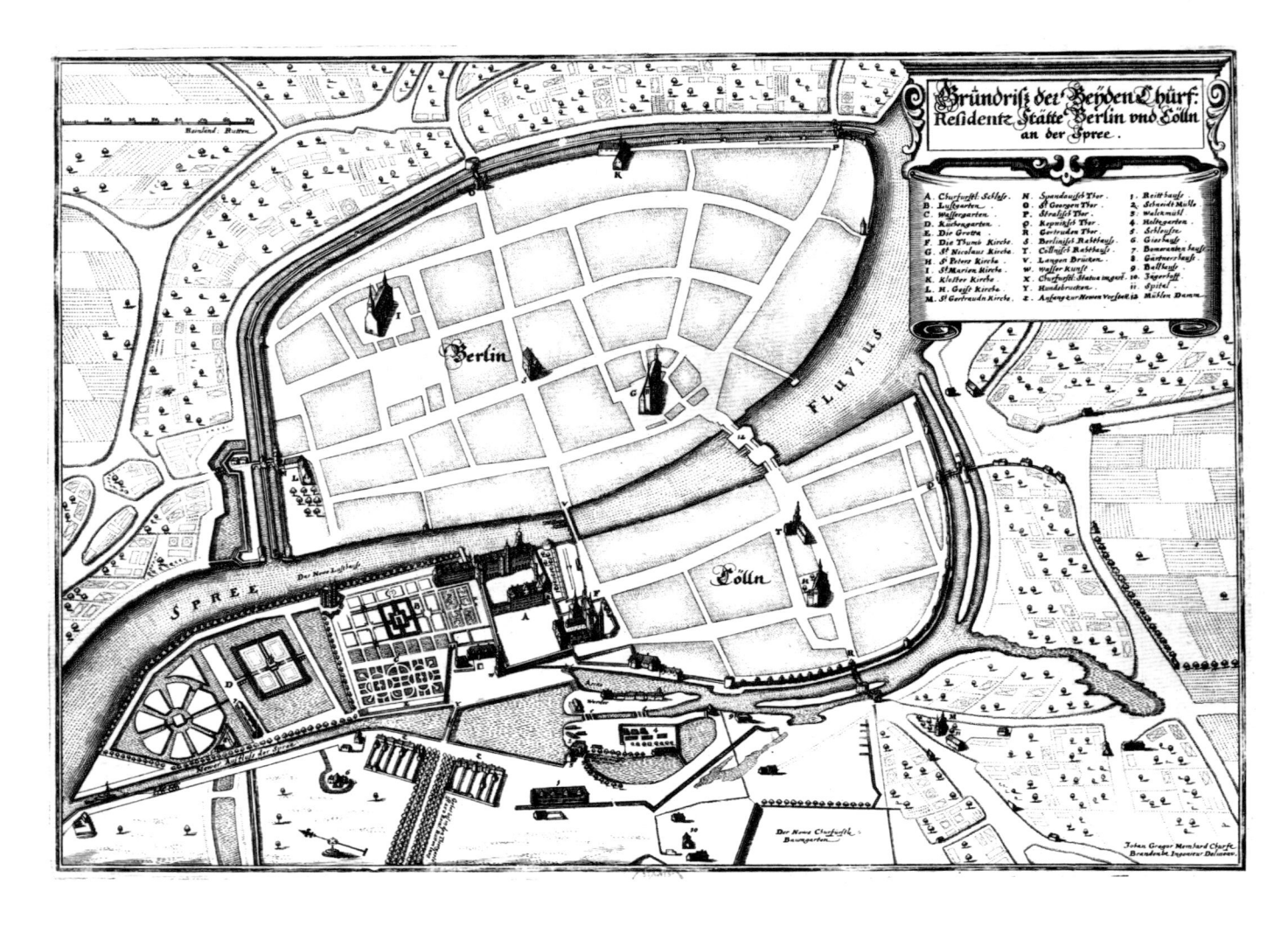

THE INFLUENCE OF FREDERIK HENDRIK'S GARDENS ABROAD

The style and form of the gardens of Honselaarsdijk and Ter Nieuburch would inspire garden architecture not only in Holland but also abroad. In addition to Denmark and Sweden, it was especially Germany where the art of gardening would be influenced, and from there further eastward. Through the efforts of the daughters of Frederik Hendrik and Amalia the style, form and decoration of Dutch gardens became known in Germany. Each of the Orange daughters had a palace built in their various principalities, which amusingly they named in unison Oranienbaum, Oranienburg, Oranienhof and Oraniensteyn.[166] Thanks to the building activities of Louise Henriette, Electress of Brandenburg (1627-1667),[167] and Henriette Catharina, Princess of Anhalt-Dessau (1637-1708),[168] the Orange family's artistic endeavours were continued after the Stadholder's death. Round the palaces of Oranienburg at Bötzow and Oranienbaum at Wörlitz, the Princesses of Orange laid out monumental gardens and, bringing Dutch gardeners and sculptors from Holland, set the tone for the influx of Dutch court culture. They also imported trees and plants from Holland and introduced exotic botanical species, as well as the more mundane Dutch potato.[169] All of this is a topic for further research; here, only the gardens laid out by Louise Henriette will be briefly reviewed to demonstrate the close stylistic connections between these German layouts and Frederik Hendrik's gardens.

143. Detail of Johann Gregor Memhardt's plan of Berlin in a print by C. Merian, showing the Brandenburg Dutch-style gardens along the river Spree under the Elector Friedrich Wilhelm of Brandenburg and Louise Henriette of Orange. Staatsbibliothek, Preussischer Kulturbesitz, Berlin

144. Classical Dutch sculptures in the Brandenburg garden, Berlin, under Louise Henriette showing putti and Roman Emperors drawn by J.S. Elssholtz in *Hortus Berolinensis*, 1657.
Staatsbibliothek, Preussischer Kulturbesitz, Berlin

145. Classical Dutch sculptures in the Brandenburg garden, Berlin, showing Flora, Ceres and sundials with putti drawn by J.S. Elssholtz in *Hortus Berolinensis*, 1657.
Staatsbibliothek, Preussischer Kulturbesitz, Berlin

The palace and garden of Oranienburg *(fig. 142)*, depicted in Matthaeus Merian's *Topographia Electoratus Brandenburgici*, are described as a most beautiful site in Bötzow near Berlin, named Oranienburg because of the Electress's extraordinary fondness of this place and the efforts she made to build palace and garden.[170] The print by Merian, after a drawing of circa 1649 by the architect-engineer Johann Gregor Memhardt, shows a garden which formally adheres to older architectural traditions, forced in part by the existing medieval moated castle complex with a separated and unaligned garden area. Perhaps best described as a mixture between Furttenbach and mid-seventeenth-century Dutch garden tradition, this rectangular 'garden island', all enclosed by *berceaux*, contained geometrical parterres centred on a heightened pavilion with a grotto. Ornamental aspects such as the decorative palisades and monogrammed parterres can be compared with those in the gardens of the Stadholder. Especially noteworthy is the return of André Mollet's famous design of the western parterre at Honselaarsdijk, which, with the omission of the Dutch lion, is copied twice on either side of Oranienburg's central garden pavilion *(see figs. 25, 26 and 142)*. Louise Henriette must have delighted in this enclosed garden with central grotto pavilion, since its exact form and layout can be recognized in the garden island which is only accessible by a bridge, at the centre of the Brandenburger palace complex at Berlin.

The Berlin garden of Friedrich Wilhelm and Louise Henriette, again designed by Memhardt and shown in Merian's Berlin city plan of 1652 *(fig. 143)*,[171] combined many of the features of Honselaarsdijk and Ter Nieuburch, or what we have come to associate with typical Dutch qualities: large horizontal expanses of parterres and water areas, alternated by *berceaux* and tree-lined avenues, and a large circular kitchen-garden area. The similarities between this layout and contemporary Dutch gardens are not only due to Louise Henriette's aesthetic sense and wish to emulate her father's gardens but also to the Berlin garden's situation on the low, humid banks of the river Spree. The geographical limitations also accounted for the lack of absolute symmetry and the irregular outline of the layout. However, it is especially in the remarkable decorational programme that one can witness the influence of the Stadholder's gardens, their layout and classicizing style language which, by means of an impressive array of garden sculptures, were meant to recreate the gardens of the House of Orange.[172]

While the Brandenburg palace garden and its ornamentation merits a detailed study, a few aspects of the garden's sculptural decoration should be discussed here to emphasize the unfolding of Dutch garden-artistic inspiration in Germany. Displayed as vertical highlights in the immense horizontal expanse of the latest French *parterres de broderie*, the numerous statues in the garden lent an air of classical elegance to this river-garden landscape along the Spree. Remarkably enough, a record exists of the garden sculptures, which were described by the Brandenburger court physician and botanist Johann Sigismund Elssholtz in his *Hortus Berolinensis* of circa 1657.[173] Among the statues depicted, several can be recognized as having come straight from Frederik Hendrik's gardens, while others are copies of the Stadholder's Dutch classical garden sculptures *(figs. 144 and 145)*.[174]

One of the most striking statues in the Berlin garden, set on the central axis in the first parterre garden right behind the palace,[175] was a life-size harnessed figure of Friedrich Wilhelm of Brandenburg himself,[176] copying François Dieussart's famous series of statues of the Princes of Orange then standing at the Huis ten Bosch (see 993 fol. 428vo and 995

146. Neptune Fountain in Louise Henriette of Orange's Brandenburg garden, Berlin, drawn by J.S. Elssholtz in *Hortus Berolinensis*, 1657, and inspired by Ter Nieuburch's *River Gods*.
Staatsbibliothek, Preussischer Kulturbesitz, Berlin

fol. 31).[177] Other statues adorning the garden included a colossal fountain figure of Neptune *(fig. 146)*,[178] in imitation of the river gods at Ter Nieuburch which in turn had been inspired by the Heidelberg statue of the Rhine,[179] and a series of busts of Roman emperors, alternating with small marble putti,[180] all of which reproduced the particular style, form and meaning of the Stadholder's garden sculpture.[181]

Several of the statues mentioned here are still in the German estates of the Princesses of Orange today, where they are rare examples of surviving seventeenth-century Dutch garden sculpture. They not only let us have a closer look at the stylistic details of contemporary garden sculptures influenced by Dutch court art, but also give an idea of the iconological content developed in the Stadholder's gardens. If we see them in a larger perspective, we can conclude that at both the Dutch and the German court reviewed here the placing of statues in gardens was not accidental or a mere matter of decorum. Rather, positioned in such a way that they balanced the whole composition, they helped to focus the eye and sharpen the mind by adding meaning to the garden space.[182] Conversely, the garden space enhanced the symbolism of the sculptures by linking them to the eternal cycles of nature and time.[183] It is of special interest, therefore, to consider the way in which the sculptural ornamentation of the Dutch courtly gardens was combined with the recurrent feature of the double circle – a formal feature which offers the clue both to the gardens' design principles and to their symbolic meaning.

COURTLY GARDENS IN HOLLAND 1600-1650

CHAPTER VI

AN ICONOLOGICAL INTERPRETATION OF THE DUTCH COURTLY GARDEN: SCULPTURAL ORNAMENTATION AND THE MOTIF OF THE TWIN CIRCLES

147. *Cupid Cutting a Bow* by François Du Quesnoy, originally decorating the Stadholder's Dutch gardens and later the Brandenburg garden in Berlin. Staatliche Museen, Preussischer Kulturbesitz Berlin

The most remarkable aspect of the Dutch courtly gardens discussed in the previous chapters was their rich sculptural ornamentation and the recurrence of one central motif – that of two connected circles. The statues and the circular motif not only had an aesthetic purpose but also served as central carriers of meaning. The Stadholder's elaborate iconological garden programme, centred as it was on the glorification of the patron, adhered to age-old traditions, yet was distinctive in the way it expressed allegory within a particular Dutch context. Therefore an analysis of Frederik Hendrik's gardens is not complete without reviewing his sculptural programmes and the double circle as a central garden motif. Set against the broader history of garden design and symbolism, such an analysis deepens our understanding of contemporary philosophical thought about garden design in Holland and in Northern Europe in general.

Until recently little was known about the ornamentation of the Stadholder's gardens, apart from some fragmentary details. With the help of Drossaers and Lunsingh Scheurleer's publication of the Orange family inventories, combined with new archival information, its history can now be reconstructed. It shows a startling departure from earlier impressions that the court, or even Holland at large, had no place on the stage of European sculptural developments.[1] In fact, the evidence from prints, inventories and records of payments, together with information from recent literature, affords new insights in the important aesthetic and iconographic function of sculpture at the Dutch court. The resulting reconstruction of at least part of the garden ornamentation shows that it was, in both style and theme, classically inspired.[2] This is not to say that this sculpture was of Italian provenance. Actually most statues came from France and Flanders or were executed in Holland itself, as the account books indicate. Visiting the garden after Frederik Hendrik's death, Jacob de Hennin commented on the sculpture of Honselaarsdijk as representing 'all the Beauties of Antiquity'[3] and, despite their obvious pagan subject matter, called them 'a truly great blessing from God':

> behold how this stately garden is adorned and decorated with so many antique, modern and various memorable and fair statues and figures made of marble or lead, gilded or bronzed, cut, hewn or cast, that not only the eye is supremely satisfied but one's whole soul and heart are lifted up to God, to thank and praise Him eternally for all His great mercies towards us.[4]

Whether of classical origin or after the classical mode, the stadholderly garden ornamentation testifies to Frederik Hendrik's taste for classical statues, a passion already noticed by the contemporary art critic Sandrart, who judged the Stadholder's collection among the most outstanding in Europe.[5] Seen in a larger context, the classical decoration of the Stadholder's gardens is indicative of the contemporary 'taste for the antique' at the Northern European courts, where some originals but mostly casts and copies after classical statues were imported from Italy or France and, as the account books testify, from the Southern Netherlands.[6]

In addition to this 'classicizing' element, some other aspects of the art of garden ornamentation need to be discussed briefly. To the Dutch court the then current fashion of creating 'encyclopedic collections', in combination with Holland's unique position as a seafaring empire and centre of exotic wares, was of the utmost importance. The wish to exhibit marvellous objects from around the world, and the tendency to admire the 'mysterious and wondrous', were part of the background of the early-seventeenth-century sculpture collection under discussion. All categories of collectible items, such as *Scientifica*, *Artificia* and *Naturalia*,[7] were not only to be found inside the collector's cabinet but could also be recognized in the artificial and natural objects present in a garden. An example of the remarkable interaction between *Ars* and *Natura* is the way statues of stone and of organic material were exhibited in the Stadholder's gardens. Species of rare plants imported from overseas would take on the role of monuments in their own right, and de Hennin indeed referred to them as such when describing flowers and antique statues in the Honselaarsdijk garden in one and the same sentence.[8] The plant as monument continued playing this role even in the later layout of Honselaarsdijk under William III, whose famous collection of rare plants was celebrated in an impressive series of coloured illustrations in the *Hortus Regius Honselaerdicensis*.[9] Each exotic plant is singled out and depicted as a separate artistic entity standing in a vase or on a pedestal.[10]

The role and appreciation of garden sculpture in Holland are of particular interest if we consider that natural stone is not quarried in this country and needed to be imported from abroad at high cost and effort. Whether due to these circumstances or, as contemporary art critics maintain, to the different 'mentality' of the Dutch, the art of sculpting was perhaps not held in the same esteem, or developed to the same degree, as were other artistic media in Holland.[11] Be this as it may, at court the art of sculpture certainly was developed and held in high esteem. Here, thanks to the efforts of the Stadholder and his advisers Jacob van Campen and Constantijn Huygens, sculpture had a central position in the decoration of the palaces and gardens, perpetuating the classical notion of the crucial relationship between the arts of building and sculpting.[12] An overview of the history of the most important garden statues, a few of which have recently been rediscovered, will demonstrate this point. Three statues or groups of statues, the *Hercules and Cacus* at Honselaarsdijk, the *River Gods* and the *Pallas Athena* or *Minerva* at Ter Nieuburch, will receive special attention, as they are particularly significant for the history of Frederik Hendrik's garden ornamentation and its iconology.

A HISTORY OF THE STADHOLDER'S MAIN GARDEN STATUES

The earliest reference to sculpture in the account books occurs in 1634, describing the acquisition of two stone statues, a *Mars* and a *Venus*, made by the famous Southern Netherlandish sculptor Artus Quellinus (1609-1668) (1043 fol. 223[vo]), who in all respects

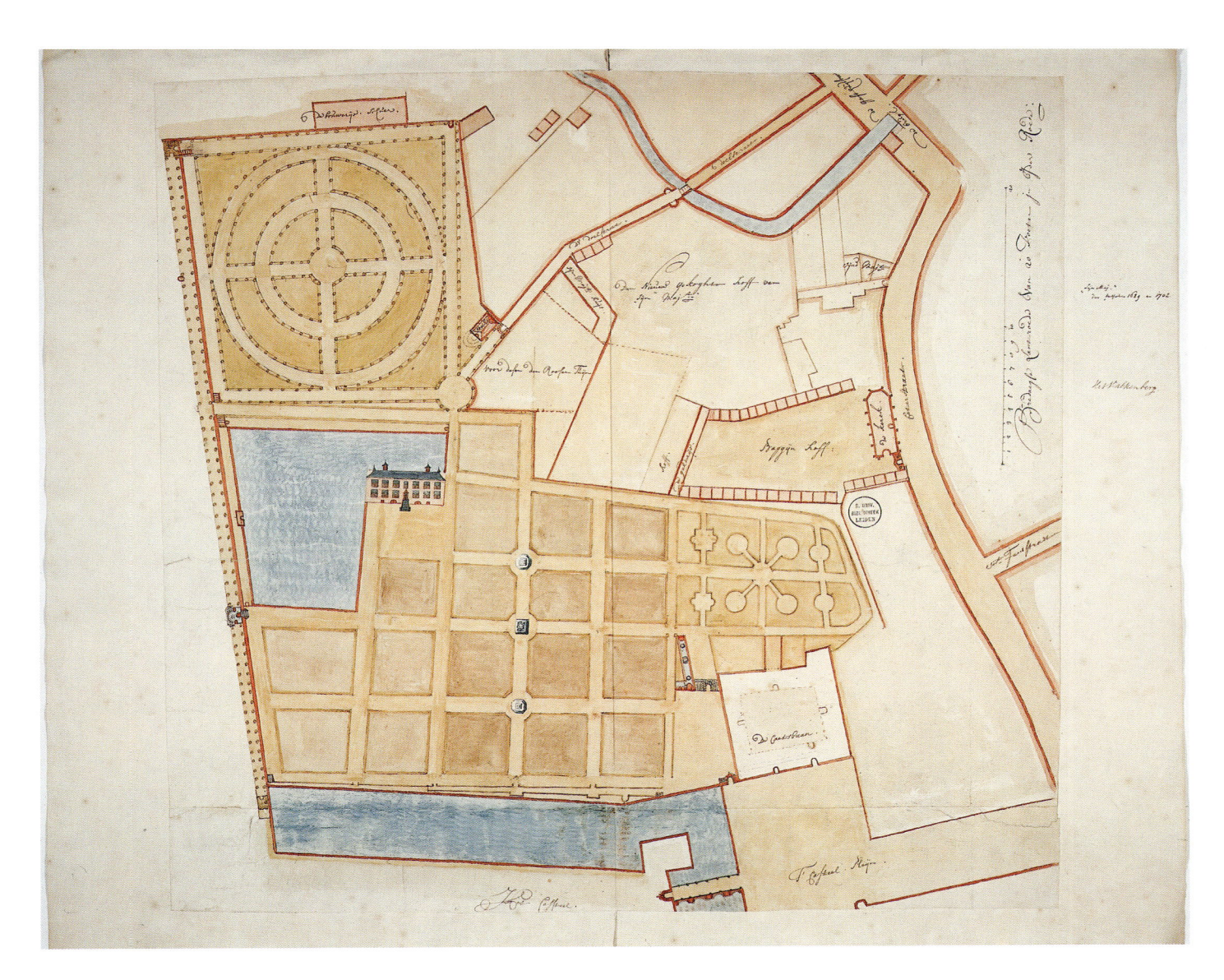

Plan of the Valkenberg garden by unknown artist, showing layout in c. 1700. CBN (see figure 110)

COURTLY GARDENS IN HOLLAND 1600-1650

Statue of Minerva Tritonia by Quellinus (replica) in the Springenberg garden, Kleve. Photo: Annegret Gossens, Museum Kurhaus Kleve (see fig. 149)

may be said to have set the tone for the influx of sculptors and sculpture from the Southern Netherlands to the Dutch court. Constantijn Huygens himself would be reimbursed in the summer of 1640 for paying more than 550 Carolus guilders (992 fol. 400) to commission no fewer than five stone statues by an unknown artist in Antwerp to decorate the Dutch palace gardens.[13]

As the account books of the Nassau Domains indicate, Quellinus's *Mars* and *Venus* were acquired for the Stadholder in Antwerp by the Amsterdam merchant Joachim de Wickevoort for 300 pounds artois, and transported by the shipper Cornelis Beron (1043 fol. 224[vo]) via the port of Lillo to Naaldwijk, where they were set in the gallery or in front of the Honselaarsdijk palace.[14] At the same time, the sculptor (*beeltsnijder*) Otto Reijersen, responsible for the placing, painting or 'bronzing' and upkeep of the statues in most of the Stadholder's gardens at The Hague and surroundings, received 52 pounds artois for bronzing three tall stone statues, two of which stood in the open gallery giving access to the garden, the third in the western parterre at Honselaarsdijk (1043 fol. 225). Of one of these three statues – the one standing in the western parterre garden – Jan de Bisschop made a drawing which not only shows this statue of Hercules and Cacus in its original setting but also clearly demonstrates the classical origins of its style *(see fig. 28)*.[15] A decade later Quellinus would make several other statues for the Stadholder, including a larger-than-life statue of a 'Palas'.[16] Interestingly, it may be this very *Pallas Athena* or *Minerva* which is depicted in the Milheusser print at the centre of the grand parterre garden of Ter Nieuburch *(see fig. 48)*,[17] a copy of which would also grace the gardens of Johan Maurits van Nassau-Siegen at Cleves some years later.[18]

In addition to Artus Quellinus, several other well-known Flemish-born sculptors received important commissions from the Stadholder's court, among them François Dieussart[19] and François Du Quesnoy.[20] Du Quesnoy's *Cupid Cutting a Bow (fig. 147)*, today in the Bode Museum (Staatliche Museen) in Berlin, is indeed one of the 'small children' or 'Cupidoken' described in the Orange family inventories.[21] It is this statue, presented to Amalia by the city of Amsterdam in 1637, which later passed into the hands of the Brandenburg family.[22] Copied in its own day to stand out of doors in the Brandenburg garden in Berlin,[23] Du Quesnoy's charming putto is an excellent example of the then very popular form of a Cupid, or *kinderken* (*kindje*, small child), to be seen in many Dutch seventeenth-century gardens. As allegorical representations of the Four Seasons, the Four Elements or certain virtues and activities,[24] these putti are the appropriate 'backdrop' against which the larger statues, such as Honselaarsdijk's *Hercules and Cacus*, should be seen.

THE STATUE OF HERCULES AND CACUS AT HONSELAARSDIJK

Among the groups of statues lining the Stadholder's parterre gardens, the statue identified as *Hercules and Cacus*[25] was by far the most impressive. It was round this statue, set up in Honselaarsdijk's west parterre garden visible from the Stadholder's own quarters, that the whole allegorical theme of the garden evolved. Standing as a symbol of the great Herculean labours, it can be interpreted as symbolizing the person and reign of the Stadholder himself, as well as the Dutch struggle for freedom against Spanish oppression. Of classical origin, the theme, composition and pose of this statue group were apparently much *en vogue* at the time. Already a popular sculptural figure-type in the Renaissance,[26] Hercules was especially appropriate for gardens because of his connection with the Garden of the Hesperides.

Hercules and Herculean themes were at the centre of the garden symbolism from the Medicis to the d'Estes, the Villa d'Este being the example *par excellence*.[27] As such the Herculean theme was also chosen by the House of Orange, where William I was the first to make use of this allegorical image, as would all his descendants, from Prince Maurits to William III. Following in the footsteps of his grandfather Frederik Hendrik, William III would carry the theme to new heights, using it in sophisticated decorational programmes of his palace and garden ensembles.[28] Significantly, in the inventory of Amalia's possessions at Ter Nieuburch a *Hercules Defeating Someone Else* made of alabaster is mentioned as part of the Stadholder's sculptural collection, representing another example of the same topos, if not the very statue originally standing at Honselaarsdijk.[29] Equally tantalizing is the listing under garden statuary of a marble *Cain and Abel* – probably referring to a *Hercules and Cacus* with which it was often confused – in the mid-eighteenth-century inventory of Honselaarsdijk.[30] Furthermore, in the days of Frederik Hendrik a Hercules figure may also have adorned the last parterre in the garden of Ter Nieuburch,[31] though the depiction of this statue in the Milheusser print is too vague to lead to a definite conclusion. However, the existence of a Hercules figure in Frederik Hendrik's garden of the Valkenberg at Breda is certain. A copy of this originally seventeenth-century statue representing Hercules leaning on his club, reminiscent of the well-known *Hercules Farnese*, still decorates the Valkenberg park today.[32]

148. Drawing by Cornelis Pronk, c. 1740, showing a statue of Hercules and Cacus (left borderline) in the Bentinck garden at Sorgvliet, comparable to the one at Honselaarsdijk.
Gemeentearchief, The Hague

The origin of the particular form and pose of the Honselaarsdijk *Hercules and Cacus* is difficult to determine. Many different versions of Hercules and Cacus statues were known at the time, the most famous being those by Michelangelo and Baccio Bandinelli of the early sixteenth century,[33] followed by Giovanni Bologna's thematically and compositionally related *Samson and the Philistine* of 1565 and Adriaan de Vries's small bronze of 1612. Nevertheless, the Honselaarsdijk statue does not seem to relate to any of these versions. Most curious is the presence of a statue of Hercules and Cacus in another Dutch garden, in what looks like the same pose as that of the Honselaarsdijk version. Depicted in a recently recovered early-eighteenth-century drawing by Cornelis Pronk of the garden of Sorgvliet, laid out by William III's adviser Hans Willem Bentinck, the statue stood on the heightened terrace walk surrounding the garden *(fig. 148).*[34] While the provenance of the Sorgvliet *Hercules and Cacus* cannot be ascertained, from an iconographical point of view this statue fits in with the rest of the Sorgvliet garden programme, which is interpreted as an apotheosis of the House of Orange.[35]

The theme and form of the Honselaarsdijk *Hercules and Cacus* must have held special fascination not only for collectors but also for contemporary artists. Besides Jan de Bisschop, the painter Jan Weenix (1642-1719) depicted this statue in one of his seaport scenes,[36] while the portrait painter Caspar Netscher (c. 1635-1684) most appropriately chose this statue as the central background feature of his portrait of William III's spouse, Queen Mary Stuart II.[37] Moreover, the Hercules-and-Cacus theme was also used in the decorative arts: two statuettes of Hercules and Cacus, copied after the particular pose of Honselaarsdijk's statue and described as 'Hercule qui représente le Roi Guillaume vainquant le Giant Cacus',[38] crowned William III's Coin Cabinet, completing the heroic-patriotic images of the historic medals kept there. Significantly, the Hercules-and-Cacus topos remained a popular feature for sculpture in Dutch gardens right into the next century. A good example is the early-eighteenth-century statue of Hercules and Cacus made by Jan van Baurscheit the Elder (1669-1728) for a Haarlem country estate, which today adorns the gardens of the Rijksmuseum in Amsterdam.[39] The symbolic theme represented by the Honselaarsdijk Hercules statue was further enhanced by its position at the centre, indeed under the very foot of the boxwood-embroidered Dutch Lion in the west parterre, directly under the Stadholder's apartments. In a sense, this bellicose 'theme' can be seen to comprise part of the whole structural and decorative composition of the Honselaarsdijk garden. It extended from the circular *berceaux* as symbols of two hemispheres under the Stadholder's rule, to Artus Quellinus's statues of Mars and Venus symbolizing War and Peace, set on either side of the entrance staircase in front of the palace. A similar theme, balancing the alternating intervals of war and peace, could be found at Ter Nieuburch, where Minerva, protectress of the Militia as well as of Wisdom, Peace and the Arts, with the obvious reference to the virtuous and intelligent deeds of the peace-loving warrior-patron Frederik Hendrik, stood at the centre of the garden.

THE STADHOLDER'S GARDEN STATUES AND THE ROLE OF HUYGENS AND VAN CAMPEN

In addition to these statues, a few others decorated the Honselaarsdijk and Ter Nieuburch gardens, courtyards and façades; they are of interest as examples of sculpture made by local artists, and because of the apparent involvement of Huygens and Van Campen. The pediment of Honselaarsdijk's entrance façade, comparable to those of the Noordeinde and the Mauritshuis,[40] held twelve children in relief carved by the Haarlem sculptor Jan Jansz

149. The statue of Minerva Tritonia by Artus Quellinus for Johan Maurits van Nassau-Siegen's garden at Cleves, copied after Ter Nieuburch's Minerva statue. Städtisches Museum Haus Koekkoek (photo shown), now in Museum Kurhaus, Kleve
see colour plate 16

de Vos.[41] Similar stone figures of little children and two dogs, executed by the Hague sculptor Pieter Adriaensz 't Hooft (992 fol. 185),[42] adorned the entrance gate and bridge leading to Honselaarsdijk.[43] Watchfully standing at the entrance, the two figures of dogs can be associated with the original function of Honselaarsdijk as a hunting palace – a function which is further borne out by the inner decoration of the palace with many hunting scenes.

About the same time, Pieter Adriaensz 't Hooft, a sculptor of some note and well known in The Hague, was also commissioned by Constantijn Huygens to make statues for his house on the Plein at The Hague. Apparently the two female figures, both personifying Good Fortune and decorating the main entrance hall as a welcome to visitors, were meant as a special tribute to Huygens's master Frederik Hendrik, symbolizing his good reign.[44] It is important to note that the source of Huygens's statues, possibly designed by Jacob van Campen,[45] was both classically Italian and Netherlandish, in that Italian emblem books and designs by Rubens for the Arcus Ferdinandus were used as prototypes for, respectively, the form and meaning of the figures.[46] In spite of these prototypes, the style of the statues is best defined as sturdy Dutch classicism. Characterized by a slight awkwardness in detail, their style and form seem to come close to the style and form of some of the statues in the Stadholder's palaces and gardens, notably the two *River Gods* of Ter Nieuburch.

In 1639 the largest group of sculptures for the decoration of the stadholderly gardens arrived from France (992 fol. 277). This shipment comprised numerous cast statues and effigies ('gegoten beelden en tronijen'), nine of which were sent to Honselaarsdijk, the others elsewhere, presumably to Ter Nieuburch, the Huis ten Bosch and the Noordeinde. Some of the effigies may have been related to the busts and heads described in Amalia's inventory of 1667, which lists sculpture decorating these palaces and gardens.[47] This listed sculpture may also refer to another set of statues acquired by Frederik Hendrik, including three children of Italian marble and six 'antique heads' or busts, for which a certain Nicolaes van Beyeren received 370 guilders in 1638 (992 fol. 133).

A rare, surviving painted view of one of the Stadholder's gardens, *Huis ten Bosch* by Jan van der Heyden (1637-1712),[48] clearly depicts four monumental classical statues facing each other on either side of the central axis. It must have been these statues which are mentioned in the inventory as 'four lead statues in the garden of the Oranjezael'.[49] The prominence of the statues, carefully copied after classical prototypes, is convincing proof of Frederik Hendrik's and Amalia's passion for statues *à l'antique* and the contemporary practice of casting and collecting classical statues.

It would seem logical that the Stadholder, though himself versed in matters of classical art, should turn again to knowledgeable advisers when collecting classical statues. It is not surprising that, as notes in the Stadholder's order book indicate, Jacob van Campen, designer and painter of many works of art in the classical style – notably the inner decoration of the Huis ten Bosch – played a leading role in the decoration of the gardens.[50] As documentary evidence shows, it was Van Campen, assisted by Huygens, who orchestrated and supervised the acquisition and installation of the statues for the Stadholder. Huygens was also instrumental in choosing artists to execute sculptural works, which is illustrated by the use of the same sculptor, Pieter 't Hooft, at Honselaarsdijk and in Huygens's house. Thus we may conclude that Van Campen and Huygens were once again responsible for advising the Stadholder on the sculptural decoration of his gardens, just as they had been for the general layout.[51]

Further evidence from the account books shows that the master stonemason Bartholomeus Drijffhout, active in the architectural construction of the Stadholder's palaces, was also responsible for the transportation, unpacking, hoisting and careful positioning of the statues and vases in the gardens of Honselaarsdijk and Ter Nieuburch (992 fols. 277, 278, 333), often under the supervision of Van Campen (992 fol. 333).[52] Some of the vases, or 'pots', placed by Drijffhout, most likely of painted lead, can be seen to decorate the balustrades of the terraces surrounding the Honselaarsdijk and Ter Nieuburch palaces in the various prints. In 1638 Drijffhout brought not only several 'stone children' to Honselaarsdijk but also 'some marble figures' to Ter Nieuburch (992 fol. 178). The remarks about the placement of sculptures, especially the rare and extremely costly marble statues, warrant a closer look, especially since they involve Amalia as patron of the arts.

The statues brought to Ter Nieuburch and here referred to as coming from Amsterdam may have included the well-known marble statue of a reclining Cleopatra, once in the collection of the Amsterdam merchant family Van Reynst.[53] As we have seen in chapter II, on visiting the Van Reynst Collection in Amsterdam in 1638 Amalia was so struck by the beauty of this classical figure that the city of Amsterdam persuaded Van Reynst to part with

150. Busts of Frederik Hendrik (left), Anhalt-Dessau and William II, in the Gothic House, Wörlitz, brought from Holland to the Oranienbaum grotto.
Staatliche Schlösser und Gärten, Oranienbaum, Wörlitz. Photo H.-D. Kluge

it.[54] Amalia had the sculpture brought to Ter Nieuburch and placed it in the garden or gallery there, just in time to be admired by Maria de' Medici.[55] This marble *Cleopatra* may have been a copy after the famous *Sleeping Ariadne* in the Vatican, which had become a very popular classical garden topos also in The Netherlands.[56] As such, the *Cleopatra* soon after was admirably depicted in Jan de Bisschop's famous Dutch compilation of antique sculpture, the *Icones & Paradigmata*, dedicated to Huygens's eldest son Constantijn and containing etchings drawn in part after statues in Dutch collections, including those of the Stadholder.[57] The inventories of Princess Amalia's possessions in the Huis ter Nieuburch list two sculptures representing Cleopatra, one seated, one reclining;[58] neither of them is preserved in The Netherlands today, making it difficult to assess their style and form. The trend set by Amalia and Frederik Hendrik resulted in a long tradition of collecting and exhibiting classical sculpture in the garden, which paralleled, as we have seen, the re-creation of a classical *museion*, or 'museum out of doors', along the lines of the famous collection of the Belvedere Court in Rome.[59]

THE RIVER GODS IN THE GARDEN OF TER NIEUBURCH

A good and, we may add, rare surviving example of the specific style and form of the Stadholder's garden sculpture is offered by the recently discovered statues of the two river gods, once decorating the two rectangular ponds of Ter Nieuburch *(see fig. 48)*. Like the statues in the entrance hall of the Huygens house, these statues are defined by a lack of refined detail. However, the roughness of their carving is accentuated by the worn-out condition of these statues, which stood in the open air flanking the staircase of the Pavilion von Wied at Scheveningen *(see figs. 74-76)*.[60] The reclining stone figures, originally placed conspicuously on rockwork in the two lateral ponds, constitute the most important classically-inspired sculptural decoration of the Ter Nieuburch garden. Enveloped by a shower of spouts, they embellished it with a pleasing, vertical play of water. Though these river gods can be connected to Henri IV's river gods at Fontainebleau and Friedrich V's examples at Heidelberg, the more immediate source of Frederik Hendrik's statues seems to have been Salomon de Caus's *River Gods*, representing the rivers Rhine, Neckar and Main. This German link is all the more important because the owners of the Heidelberg garden were the Stadholder's relatives who had been granted refuge in The Hague. Not only did their presence stimulate cultural life there, it also inspired undertakings in garden architecture, as shown by a letter describing Elizabeth of Bohemia's admiration for the garden of Ter Nieuburch.[61] Similarly, as we have seen, another connection with Germany could be made, for Ter Nieuburch's river gods inspired the Neptune fountain in the Brandenburg garden laid out by the Stadholder's daughter Louise Henriette *(see fig. 146)*.[62] Symbolizing the lands under the rule of Friedrich Wilhelm, the Great Elector, this statue followed an age-old theme in garden iconology, popular in contemporary European gardens.

At Rijswijk, the Ter Nieuburch river gods personified Holland's two largest rivers, the Rhine and the Maas, defining the territory dominated by the Prince of Orange. They thus create an appropriate framework for the rest of the garden's iconology, which centred on topoi of good government and the cycles of nature. In fact, a series of statues set at the centre and on pillars at the entrance of the various parterre compartments, though not all clearly identifiable, seem to follow long-standing traditions in garden ornamentation and represent the conventional symbolism of the Four Seasons and the Four Elements, thus completing the topographical iconography of the river gods.

The first compartment behind the palace with the familiar combined monogram of Frederik Hendrik and Amalia, which centres on a fountain with water-spouts topped by the figure of a Venus Lactans or Ceres,[63] was the point of departure for the whole allegorical programme. Following contemporary tradition, this programme concentrated on the glorification of the Stadholder: his peaceful reign is symbolized by the monogrammed parterre, while its fountain spouts forth the water of the 'Dutch Spring', the regenerative powers of nature, the return of the Muses and the flowering of the arts and sciences.[64] Such allegorical allusions to the garden as a place of peace, fertility and love, or *locus amoenus*, belonged already to an established tradition in sixteenth-century garden layouts. For our purposes it is noteworthy that during the period of the Eighty Years' War, the garden as *locus amoenus* was again a most popular theme in Dutch literature, as is also shown by Huygens's writings.[65]

The triumphant centre-piece of Ter Nieuburch's main parterre garden was a statue of Minerva, goddess of peaceful arts and sciences and protectress of Rome, *casu quo* of Holland as a 'new Rome'. Recognizable in the Milheusser print by her helmet, tunic and long spear, this statue can be seen to complete the allusion to the garden as a peaceful place and the person of the Stadholder as a great Maecenas. It was this monumental statue which was made by the Flemish sculptor Artus Quellinus not long before he started his distinguished career in Amsterdam in 1648, working under Van Campen at the Town Hall.[66] Because it was much admired for its classical elegance, Quellinus was commissioned to fashion another Minerva about two decades later. Resembling the Stadholder's statue in style, form and meaning,[67] this impressive marble *Minerva Tritonia*

151. Sleeping Cupid Resting on a Shield by François Dieussart, brought over by Henriette Catharina to Oranienbaum from the Noordeinde or Ter Nieuburch. Staatliche Schlösser und Gärten, Oranienbaum, Wörlitz. Photo H.-D. Kluge

in turn would form the decorative and symbolic centre-piece of Johan Maurits van Nassau-Siegen's Springenberg garden at Cleves *(fig. 149)*.[68]

There are more comparisons to be made between the gardens laid out by Johan Maurits and those of the Stadholder. In itself this is not surprising, since they were created in the same humanist court circles involving Huygens, Van Campen and Post.[69] One aspect of the Cleves garden decoration is worth pointing out because we see a similar arrangement in the Stadholder's gardens, namely the twelve busts of Roman Emperors decorating the Cleves Orangerie garden.[70] Another twelve busts of Roman Emperors were reported at Honselaarsdijk,[71] though it is not known where they were placed. At Ter Nieuburch, where similar busts existed, they actually may have decorated the lateral *giardini segreti*, one of which contained the Orangerie garden and grotto. However, such an analysis depends to some extent on the interpretation of Amalia's inventory, which does not distinguish clearly between statues placed inside the palace and those standing outside in the garden.

Particularly interesting is the mention of antique busts in the Ter Nieuburch *grootte*, probably a misspelling of the Dutch word *grotte*, meaning grotto: 'Three heads of marble on the architrave of the first bench of the north-west of the grotto of the Huis ter Nieuburch.'[72]

Allusions to the garden as a place celebrating the Stadholder and the Orange dynasty, in the wake of the Great Roman Emperors, may have led to the decoration of the Orangerie-cum-grotto at Ter Nieuburch. Roman busts would have been an appropriate antique counterpart of the rest of the garden decoration, and of busts of the Princes of Orange which also must have decorated the grotto. In this respect we should remember the contemporary designs for grottoes *(see figs. 67 and 68)* containing busts and reliefs of the Princes of Orange's effigies, which could be related to the Ter Nieuburch grotto.[73] Most remarkably, two of the busts of the Princes of Orange survive today at Wörlitz near Oranienbaum, the estate of Henriette Catharina von Anhalt-Dessau.[74] Originally placed in the grotto in the garden of Oranienbaum, the busts' present setting in three wall niches inside the Gothic House at Wörlitz *(fig. 150)*[75] closely resembles the wall decoration shown in one of the original seventeenth-century designs *(compare fig. 68)*, except that the bust of the Stadholder's son-in-law Johann Georg II von Anhalt-Dessau is now placed at the centre and flanked by Frederik Hendrik and William II.[76] This arrangement matches not only the listing in the Orange inventories[77] but also that in an eighteenth-century description of the Oranienbaum grotto itself[78] and may in fact illustrate the very layout and decoration of the Stadholder's original grotto at Ter Nieuburch. It is worth noting the bust of the Stadholder himself, which can be attributed to François Dieussart on the basis of a letter from the painter Gerard van Honthorst to Constantijn Huygens referring to Dieussart's commissions for the Dutch court.[79]

The sculptural commissions mentioned in this letter included a small statue of a 'Sleeping Cupid resting on a shield', which is described in the Orange family inventories among Amalia's garden sculpture at the Paleis Noordeinde and Ter Nieuburch *(fig. 151)*.[80] Remarkably, this very statue, and its probable counterpart *Cupid Bending a Bow*,[81] also survive today at Oranienbaum. These statues of small putti are excellent examples of the charming, at times somewhat standardized classicizing style of the Stadholder's garden statues, typical of the formal language of sculpture developed during the 1630s in Northern European court circles.[82]

Stylistically, in Ter Nieuburch's grotto design *(see figs. 66 and 68)* with its impressive classical architectural wall decoration, the development of the ornamental features of the Stadholder's garden comes to a close. We recognize a stylistic development from the mannerist wonderland of the late-sixteenth-century grotto filled with mysticism and music, exemplified by de Gheyn's grotto of the Buitenhof, to Joseph Dinant's shell-incrusted Ter Nieuburch grotto, which, by way of large screened windows, opened up the rest of the garden and heralded the less fantastic but spatially and decoratively innovative grotto designs of the French baroque.

THE STADHOLDER'S GARDEN ICONOLOGY AND THE MOTIF OF THE TWIN CIRCLES

An iconological analysis of the Stadholder's gardens is not complete without a discussion of one important structural feature, the twin circles or double circle. In point of fact, this feature of the double circle within a rectangle – or, if you will, a double square with inscribed circles – is so dominant and returns so frequently in Frederik Hendrik's gardens that one supposes to find here the clue to their geometrical design principle and deeper meaning.

One of the most remarkable aspects of Frederik Hendrik's gardens is indeed the recurrence of this motif, be it in the shape of two circular *berceaux* or, as at Honselaarsdijk, uncovered circular hedges.[83] Among the various Dutch gardens of that time it occurred as many as six times in the garden layouts of the 1620s and early 1630s. It is also significant that this form-motif does not seem to have any immediate precedents in Northern Europe and only occurs in the direct environment of the Dutch court. In Frederik Hendrik's gardens the twin-circle motif was found not only at Honselaarsdijk but also at The Hague (Buitenhof), Flushing (Prinsenhuis) and Buren. It was also adopted by Ernst Casimir, Count of Nassau-Dietz, in his gardens at Groningen and by Johan Wolfert van Brederode at Vianen, both relatives of Frederik Hendrik.[84] Of these six gardens, the layout of the Flushing one, in the province of Zeeland, is probably the oldest, followed by that of the Buitenhof garden at The Hague. Both these gardens were owned by Frederik Hendrik but had originally been laid out under his brother Prince Maurits in the early 1620s, thus preceding the layout of the Honselaarsdijk garden.[85] A short historical and chronological survey of the gardens with the double circle is needed in order to uncover the motif's source and its specific meaning for the Stadholder.

The double circle first appeared in the garden at Flushing, the layout of which was begun circa 1620 and completed about 1626.[86] The original plan for the Prinsenhuis was made by Prince Maurits's architect-engineer Simon Stevin,[87] who may have been the designer of the garden, though more precise plans of its layout, including the two joined circles, were dated after his death *(see fig. 103)*.[88] A detailed overview of the rear section of the garden shows a triangular area enclosed by a crenellated wall. This section, appropriately called and indicated as the 'Triangel' on the seventeenth-century plan, is included among the series of plans of the Prinsenhuis *(see fig. 104)*,[89] showing a layout consisting of two joined circles with cabinets and a labyrinth in the outer spandrels.

The Flushing garden is distinctive in that the motif of the joined circles is set within the geometrical framework of a triangle, while in all other instances, as we shall see, they were held within a rectangular enclosure. This combination of two basic geometrical forms in one garden design shows the preoccupation of the Dutch Stadholders with geometry and in particular with the form of the circle and the art of triangulation. Interestingly, when it comes to the execution of these geometrical shapes in the Flushing garden, only here do the two circles actually touch each other, without any division by means of a path or hedge. Furthermore, the size of the circles and cabinets and the width of the paths, or 'hallways' in the 'wildernesses', are all planned with great precision, as seen on the plan *(see fig. 104)*. Here the size of the circles, at their widest point, measured seven Rijnlandse roeden and 11.5 voeten, or about 28 metres, while in comparison those in the Honselaarsdijk garden were three times as large (circa 21 Rijnlandse roeden). However, the circular walks in the Flushing garden were exactly the same size as those laid out by Prince Maurits in his garden of the Buitenhof at The Hague.

The Buitenhof garden became more widely known than the Flushing garden, chiefly thanks to the engravings published by Hendrick Hondius in his *Institutio artis perspectivae*.[90] Hondius's bird's-eye view of the Buitenhof gives a good impression of the total layout of this city garden, while his plan and perspective demonstrate the geometric structure of the whole design concept, consisting of two squares with inscribed circles *(see figs. 89 and 90)*. It should be noted that the general design concept, or 'idea', of the garden layout engraved by Hondius shows a garden which ideally should be twice as large as the actual size of the Buitenhof garden, which measured circa 56 by 29 metres.[91] This also explains in part Hondius's remark that the Buitenhof garden was as beautiful and well ordered a garden as one could find, 'naer sijne grootte' (considering its size), which refers to its relative smallness.[92]

Much larger in size and of somewhat different shape were the twin circles in the Honselaarsdijk garden. Here they were formed by uncovered hedges instead of closed *berceaux*. Moreover, the circles were not perfectly round but appeared somewhat stretched, resulting in ovals rather than circles. The oval shape of the roundels is already noticeable on the old plan of the garden *(see fig. 11)* and was later repeated in the small total plan of the Honselaarsdijk area, shown in the upper right-hand corner of Van Berckerode's print *(see fig. 12)*. More important is that at Honselaarsdijk a tree-lined path divided the two ovals, which are not joined by a connecting structure, as in the garden of the Buitenhof. The prominent position of the two ovals in the Honselaarsdijk garden, and the fact that Van Berckerode adjusted these ovals and depicted the hedges as being more or less circular in his bird's-eye view, make it clear that the Honselaarsdijk garden definitely belongs to the larger group of courtly gardens using the joined-circle motif in their layouts.

A closer study of the other garden plans with the joined-circle motif shows that minor discrepancies in details of the layout also occurred in other gardens. While a tunnel-like *berceau* divided the two circles at the Buitenhof, as well as those in gardens of Buren, Groningen and Vianen, at Flushing the central *berceau* and pavilion were omitted altogether and the two circles touched directly.

In the case of the Buren garden one can recognize the device of the two circles not once but twice *(see fig. 105)*. The circles can be distinguished in the two rectangular garden compartments flanking the forecourt. Due to the lack of space on the castle island, the circles in the southern garden appear somewhat compressed. In both gardens the circles, most likely again circular *berceaux*, have round pavilions in the outer four corners but, as far as we can tell from this map, no pavilion in the centre. Though it is difficult to distinguish all details on this very finely-drawn map, the two squares containing the circles seem to be divided by a path, or perhaps a transversely placed, tunnel-shaped *berceau*. The exact details of the garden layout being as they may, it is significant that the joined- or twin-circle motif is again seen here, and is even repeated. Whether the circles were the result of Frederik Hendrik's improvements to the grounds in the early 1630s or whether they dated from earlier times, their continued existence and preservation indicate the Stadholder's special regard for this motif.

The garden behind the Prinsenhof, or Princely Court, in the centre of the city of Groningen has been reconstructed and is the only place where the double-circle motif still survives.[93] The garden with its circular *berceaux* is shown in a bird's-eye view of Groningen by Egbert Haubois, presenting the situation of the layout as it must have been about 1634 *(fig. 152)*.[94] In many respects the map by Haubois and a contemporary description of the Groningen garden[95] echo Hondius's description of the Buitenhof garden at The Hague, not only in the garden's structure but also in its inner decoration, which contains the coat of arms of Ernst Casimir and his spouse.[96] Again, the designer of the Groningen garden is not known. The layout coincided with the extension of the city in the mid-1620s,[97] according to a plan by the city's architect (*stadsbouwmeester*) Gerwert Peters. Though Peters is mentioned as having provided the plan (*proiect*) for the reorganization of the vacant grounds into a garden,[98] it is unlikely that he designed the inner division of the garden. He certainly did not develop the idea of the circles, since the motif had already been used in the Stadholder's gardens at Flushing and The Hague.

In 1632 an engraving was published of the garden at Vianen, owned by one of Ernst Casimir's close friends and brothers-in-arms Johan Wolfert van Brederode, who again used the motif of the twin circles as the focal point of his garden. The engraving by Hugo

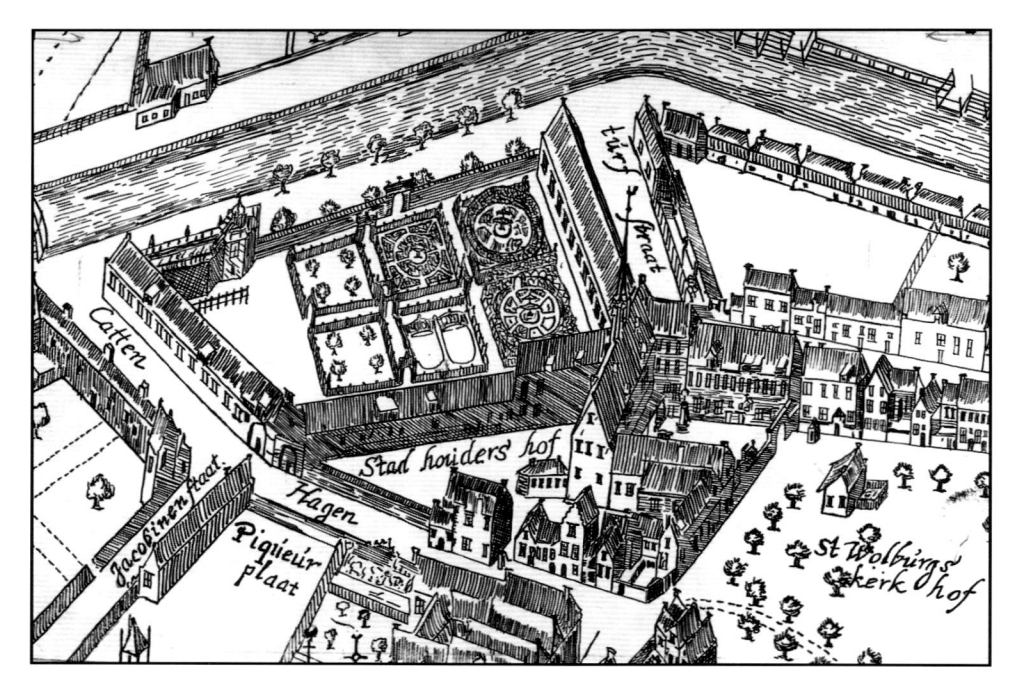

152. Map of Groningen (detail) by Haubois, c. 1660, showing the layout of the Prinsenhof gardens with the twin-circle motif.
Gemeentearchief, Groningen

Allaerdt entitled *Den Hoff van de Heer van Breederode tot Vianen* gives a good overview of Van Brederode's garden of the Batestein castle at Vianen, near Utrecht *(fig. 153)*.[99] According to the inscription in the cartouche on the lower right, the print is dedicated to Van Brederode by his gardener Isaac Leschevin ('Dedie son petit labeur Isaac Leschevin'), who also worked for the Stadholder at Ter Nieuburch. The garden was L-shaped and laid out below the ramparts overlooking the canal (*stadsgracht*) on one side of the castle of Vianen. The development of the garden can be followed by comparing a mid-seventeenth-century map by Jacob van Deventer[100] and two later maps of the area, one published by Johannes Blaeu[101] in 1649 and an anonymous hand-drawn map from the early eighteenth century.[102] The map of 1632 gives a detailed overview of the inner division and ornamentation of the garden, showing four walled-in square garden plots filled with parterres and a rectangular area with the familiar twin-circle motif. The layout and decoration of this garden section exactly follow the layout of Prince Maurits's Buitenhof garden again, copying its octagonal fountains and the parterres decorated with similar kinds of arabesque patterns and heraldic devices. Furthermore, just as at the Buitenhof and Flushing, the garden of Batestein is surrounded by a crenellated wall which, with its connotations of warfare and a traditional medieval stronghold, was particularly appropiate for gardens owned by warriors such as Prince Maurits, Frederik Hendrik and Johan Wolfert van Brederode. The close relationship between the Stadholder and Van Brederode is indicated not only by the execution of exactly the same garden design but also by the employment of the same gardener, Isaac Leschevin, whose printbook was dedicated to the Stadholder and showed designs for palisades and portals used in the gardens of Vianen and Ter Nieuburch.[103] Moreover, we know that throughout his lifetime, whenever his military campaigns brought him to this region in the centre of Holland, Frederik Hendrik visited Vianen and, accompanied by the proud owner, enjoyed a walk through the Batestein gardens, hailed by Huygens as 'the ultimate exertion of man and nature'.[104]

COURTLY GARDENS IN HOLLAND 1600-1650

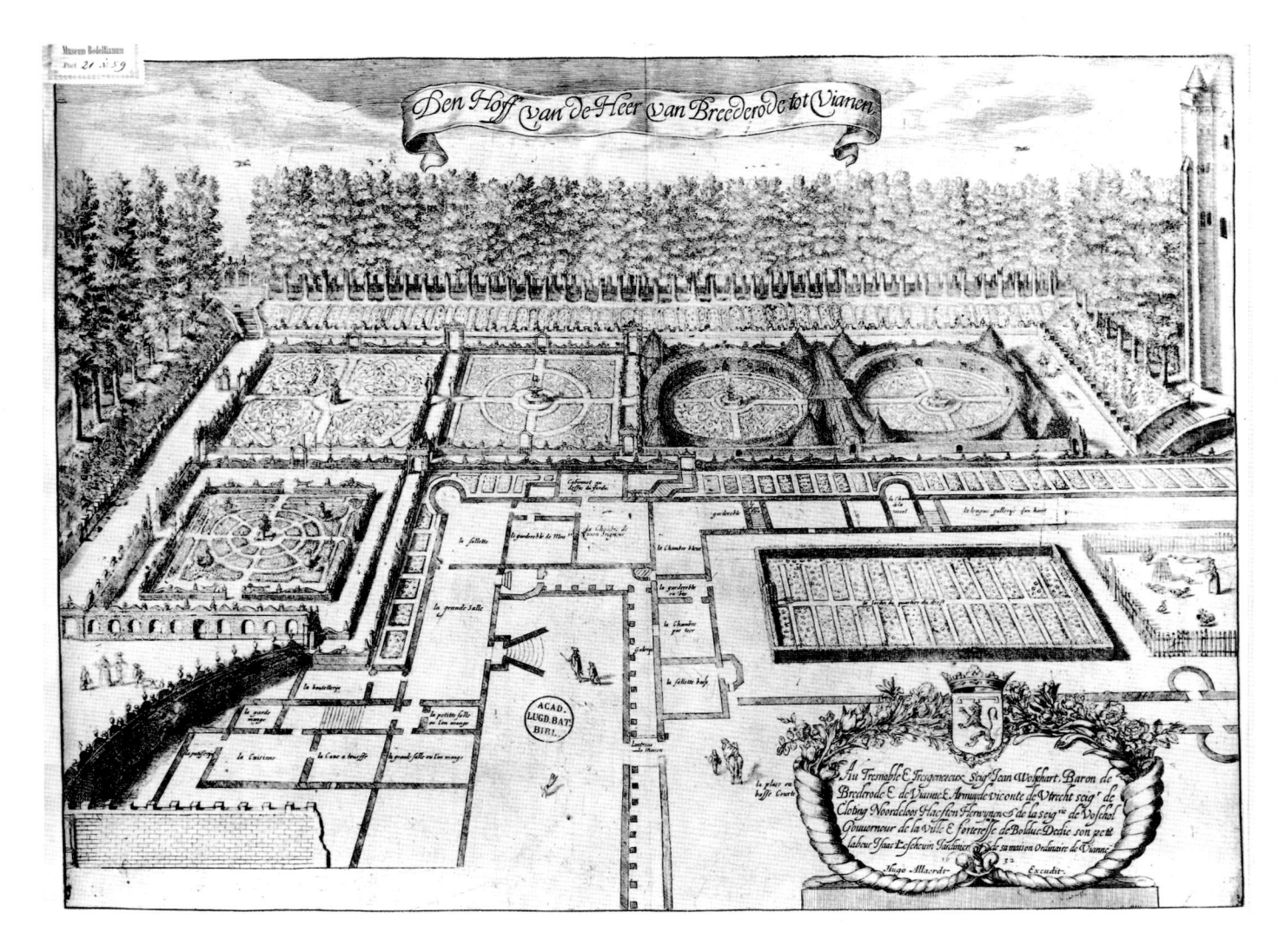

153. Print by Hugo Allaerdt, 1632, of the gardens of Vianen, showing the influence of the Stadholder's gardens in their decoration and the twin-circle motif. Collectie Bodel Nijenhuis, Universiteitsbibliotheek, Leiden

THE DESIGNER(S) OF THE DOUBLE-CIRCLE MOTIF

In spite of the resemblance between the courtly garden layouts described here, it is not known who was ultimately responsible for designing the joined-circle motif. However, certain suggestions can be made as to the possible designing genius behind the circular form in these six gardens. The stadholderly architect-mathematician Simon Stevin, as the designer of the Princely house at Flushing where the motif was first used, would seem a likely candidate. As described in the preceding chapters, Stevin was a man of an astonishing range of virtuosity, writing works on mechanical and military engineering, mathematics, accounting, perspective and architecture.[105] Connections between Stevin's work and the principle of the twin-circle motif are found in his book *Wisconstighe Ghedachtnissen: vande Deursichtighe*. As he writes in his preface, the book was the result of his discussions with Prince Maurits, who had expressed the wish to know the mathematical theory behind perspective drawing.[106] In the book, knowledge of classical architectural theory centres on concepts of absolute symmetry developed by Alberti, and closely followed in Prince Maurits's fortifications.[107] Related to it are Stevin's theories on the ideal city and army camps, which should have a rectangular shape, like the framework of the gardens under review.[108]

In addition to Stevin, one could also point to Hendrick Hondius as the possible master

VI. AN ICONOLOGICAL INTERPRETATION

designer of the twin-circle motif, by virtue of his book on perspective containing a description, bird's-eye view and detailed perspective plan of one of the circular garden layouts, the Buitenhof garden. Indeed, Huygens attested to Hondius's knowledge of the art of perspective, extolling his scientific exactitude in studying anatomy, particularly the human figure, to which the design of the twin-circle motif can be related if examined in a classical, Vitruvian context.[109]

The design of this motif could also be traced to Jacques de Gheyn II, who is mentioned specifically by Huygens as the designer of the Buitenhof garden and as working both for Maurits and for Frederik Hendrik.[110] Even if Huygens's remarks about de Gheyn's authorship are to be interpreted as referring to the ornamentation of the Buitenhof's garden rather than its total structural design,[111] de Gheyn's knowledge of classical architecture and the art of perspective is well documented and makes his involvement with the basic design of the garden likely.[112] De Gheyn was a gentleman-virtuoso who was known not only for his architectural knowledge but also for his miniature paintings and studies of plants and animals. He designed grottoes and waterworks and also had a general knowledge of alchemy, mechanical science and engineering, involving magical moving monsters and other *automata*.[113] Huygens himself describes how knowledgeable de Gheyn was about *gezichtkunde* (optics) and the rules of *doorzichtkunde* (perspective), these disciplines being the key to understanding the design principles of the twin-circle motif.

Thus it would appear that Stevin, Hondius and de Gheyn, each for their own particular backgrounds, are the three most likely candidates for designer of the twin-circle motif. Having narrowed our focus to these three, we should not forget how closely involved the individual garden owners were, certainly in choosing, but even in personally inventing, the design for their gardens. Prince Maurits in particular should be singled out as a knowledgeable dilettante architect. In the introduction to the reader in his *Wisconstighe Ghedachtnissen*, Stevin remarks how Prince Maurits frequently practised drawing groundplans and elevations for fortifications.[114] Maurits's fascination with trigonometry, documented by Stevin, and the occurrence of the triangle as basic form in the Flushing garden containing the two circles, cannot be mere coincidence and is further evidence of the owner's practical involvement. It seems likely that in designing the Flushing garden there existed a collaboration between Prince Maurits, who provided the mathematical concept, and Stevin, who translated its abstract geometrical form into architectural reality.[115] Similarly, at The Hague Prince Maurits's original idea may have been materialized by de Gheyn, who was responsible for the ornamentation of the Buitenhof garden.[116] Following Maurits, his brother Frederik Hendrik and Johan Wolfert van Brederode who were known for their erudition in the mathematical arts and sciences were able to invent their own garden designs at Honselaarsdijk and Vianen.

Whoever the designer may have been – and a collaboration between one of the above-mentioned owners and their garden advisers is likely – he clearly demonstrated architectural virtuosity and awareness of the classical ideal of perspective and proportion in garden architecture. Indeed, the nature of the design, as we shall come to analyse it, shows that the personality of the designer conforms to the 'true architect' expounded by Vitruvius, having an all-round education and being acquainted with every branch of the whole encyclopedia of knowledge,[117] be it skill in painting, geometry, knowledge of the art of perspective, arithmetic, philosophy, music or knowledge of astronomy.[118]

ORIGIN AND DEEPER MEANING OF THE CIRCLE AND TWIN-CIRCLE MOTIF

A more precise understanding of the circle and twin-circle motif in Dutch seventeenth-century garden architecture requires closer study both of the origin of its mathematical form and of its iconological history. In the first place the gardens discussed here were the result of a dialogue between architectural theory and practice.[119] Their design was based on the abstract conception of mathematics and proportion, its *lineamenta* (design idea), to quote Alberti, being superior to its practical realization, or execution in material form (*materia*).[120] In accordance with this classical approach to the supremacy of the 'design idea' over execution are Hondius's prints of the Buitenhof garden, which show, first, the fundamental geometrical skeleton of the garden, or orthographical depiction, followed by a real view from above, or scenographical illustration. The first engraving depicts the general design concept and its three-dimensional volume, thus expressing the connection between garden architecture, perspective and cubic theory, while the second engraving visualizes the garden's material reality.[121]

From a mathematical point of view, the layout of the gardens with the twin circles demonstrates the predominance of two perfect geometrical figures, the circle and the square.[122] In mathematical terms the circle was considered the most perfect of the two, having no beginning or end, running eternally and comprising the largest possible area in a given circumference. From an aesthetic point of view, the circle was appreciated for its intrinsic beauty. Indeed, within the context of garden art, the circle is commended by the English botanist John Parkinson for its 'most absolute forme', though for practical reasons it is not very suitable to add to one's mansion.[123] Fascination with the circle is also reflected in studies entirely devoted to it and the problem of measuring its diameter and circumference.

An example of the passion for the art of the circle in the Dutch court environment, soon to be expressed in the design of the stadholderly gardens, is Ludolf van Collen's (or Van Keulen's) standard work on the circle, entitled *Van den Circkel*, published in Delft in 1596. Van Collen was professor in Leiden at the engineering school founded by Prince Maurits to teach mathematics, geometry and the art of fortification. Surrounded by the symbols of his profession, Van Collen is represented by Jacques de Gheyn in his series of portraits of illustrious men *(fig. 154)*.[124] Van Collen's passion for mathematics, particularly the circle, is shown by his book, in which he managed to calculate pi to 35 decimal places, since then called 'Ludolf's number'.

However, another contemporary publication, blending mathematics and martial arts, provides an even closer explanation of the circle's meaning, namely Girard Thibault's *Académie de l'Espée ... par Reigles Mathématiques sur le fondement d'un Cercle Mystérieux*. One of the engravings in this work depicts the ideal positions which two swordsmen could take within the mathematical confines of the circle and the square situated in a garden *(fig. 155)*.[125] Thibault explains that his successful fighting method, learned in Spain, was based on the 'mystical circle', here shown below each swordsman, while the circle's proportions are given with recourse to Vitruvius and Albrecht Dürer.[126] Moreover, another closely related print in this book *(fig. 155a)* was dedicated specifically to Prince Maurits. Maurits's heraldic shield, military paraphernalia and device 'Je Maintiendrai' are depicted above the statue of Hercules, which corresponds to statues in the side niches representing Hercules slaying the Hydra and Hercules and Antaeus. Referring to Prince Maurits's mathematical and to his military expertise, the form of the 'mystical circle' can be seen here as combining architectural form and Herculean iconology, at the basis of both the Buitenhof and other stadholderly gardens.

154. Drawing by Jacques de Gheyn showing the portrait of Ludolf van Collen, a famous mathematician who wrote an influential work on the Art of the Circle. Fondation Custodia, Institut Néerlandais, Paris

155. Four pairs of swordsmen round a 'mystical circle' within a square, as depicted in Thibault, *Académie de l'Espée*, 1628, and expressing the relation between martial arts and mathematics, the basis of current garden design and symbolism. Rare Book and Manuscript Library, Columbia University, New York

155a. A print in Thibault, *Académie de l'Espée*, 1628, dedicated to Prince Maurits, showing swordsmen within the 'mystical circle', set against a palatial background decorated with statues of Hercules. Rare Book and Manuscript Library, Columbia University, New York

Apart from being the focus of such theoretical works, the circle came to be an important geometrical form in Dutch architecture and garden architecture, thus continuing a long-standing tradition in the history of architectural design which harks back to the classical past and the Italian Renaissance. Indeed, during the Renaissance the circle and the square and their derivatives (polygonals) were the basis of designs for centralized buildings, ideal city plans[127] and also gardens, expressing, as Wittkower put it, the almost magical power the circle had over the Renaissance architect.[128] In The Netherlands this interest in the circle was expressed in the building designs of the Stadholder's own architects, such as Arent van 's Gravesande's design of a round church for the Marekerk at Leiden (1640)[129] and Pieter Post's design for the Huis ten Bosch.

In using the circle also in his gardens, the Stadholder relied on a number of earlier garden designs, one of which was the famous Hortus Sphaericus of the Botanical Garden at Padua *(fig. 156),*[130] which represented an important model in the history of garden architecture. At the time, the design of the Paduan Botanical Gardens was well known in Holland, where it was suggested for the Leiden Hortus Botanicus during the planning of its layout in the late

VI. AN ICONOLOGICAL INTERPRETATION

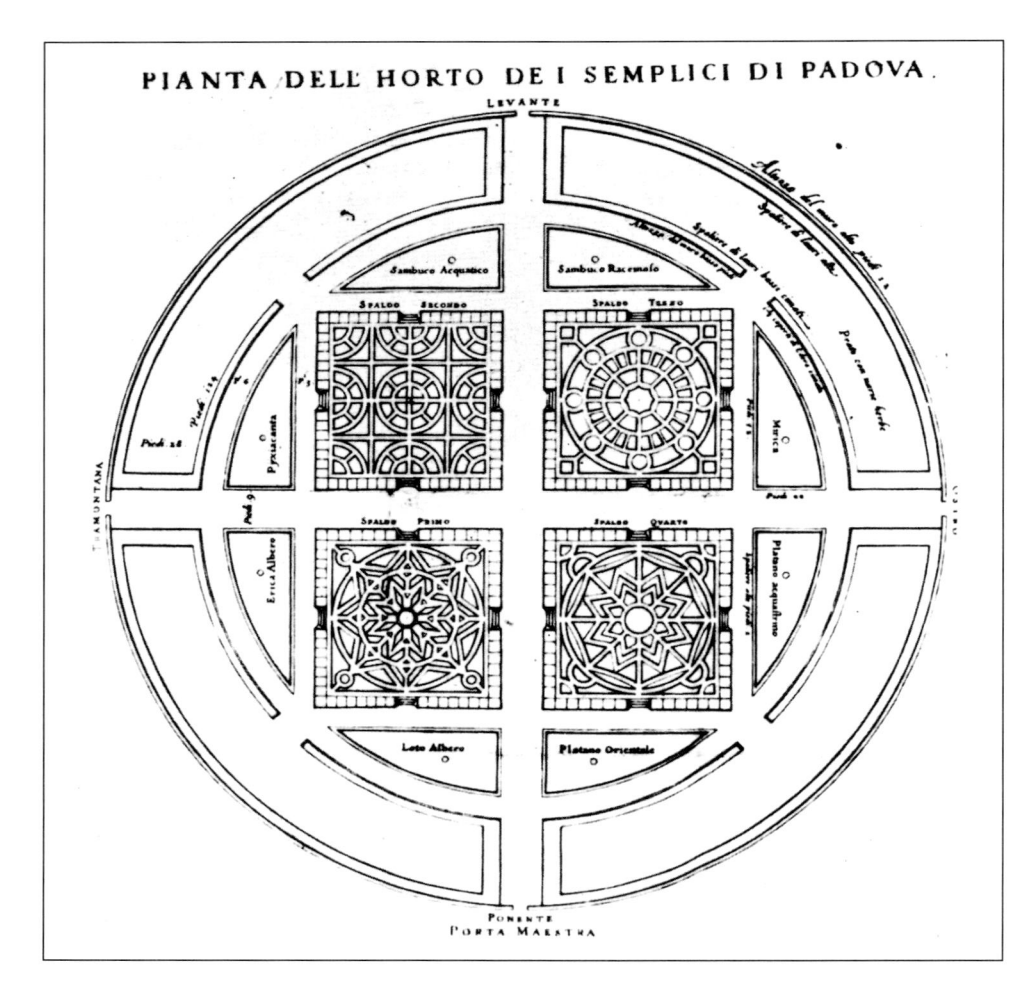

156. Plan of the Botanical Garden of Padua, based on the circle and reflecting cosmological thought and imagery in its form and inner layout.
Biblioteca dell'Orto Botanico, Padua

sixteenth century.[131] The Stadholder must also have been familiar with two other famous Italian Renaissance circular gardens, Francesco Colonna's fictional circular garden of Venus on the island of Cithera *(fig. 157)*[132] and Francesco Soderini's mid-sixteenth-century garden set within the remains of Augustus's round Mausoleum.[133] Another example may be the sixteenth-century layout of the garden at Petraia *(fig. 158)*, which depicts the only double-circle motif in garden art prior to the Stadholder's own layouts.[134]

In Northern Europe, too, the circle occurred frequently in sixteenth- and early-seventeenth-century garden designs.[135] Versions of the twin-circle motif were employed by Johan Vredeman de Vries in his late-sixteenth-century Flemish garden designs *(fig. 159)*.[136] Similarly, Johan Maurits van Nassau-Siegen employed a large circular structure in the garden of the Mauritshuis at The Hague. Furthermore a monumental circular orchard garden, divided into eight radiating compartments accessible through eight gates, was the centre of Johan Maurits's garden laid out about 1640 on the terrain surrounding the Prinsenhof at Cleves *(fig. 160)*.[137] At about the same time a very similar, huge circular orchard, planted with seven different kinds of trees, was created for the Duke de Aremberg, at the centre of his monumental gardens at Anguien [Enghien], just south of Brussels in the Southern Netherlands *(fig. 161)*.[138] Later that century, a circle inscribed in a triangle and divided into eight sections, possibly conceived as a compass rose, graced the famous Hortus Botanicus of Amsterdam,[139] substantiating the conclusion that in seventeenth-century Holland the geometry of the circle, with or without symbolic connotations, had become a guiding principle in the construction of gardens.

157. Print of Colonna's imaginary round garden on the island of Cithera, divided into concertric circles and influenced by cosmological imagery.
The Metropolitan Museum of Art, New York

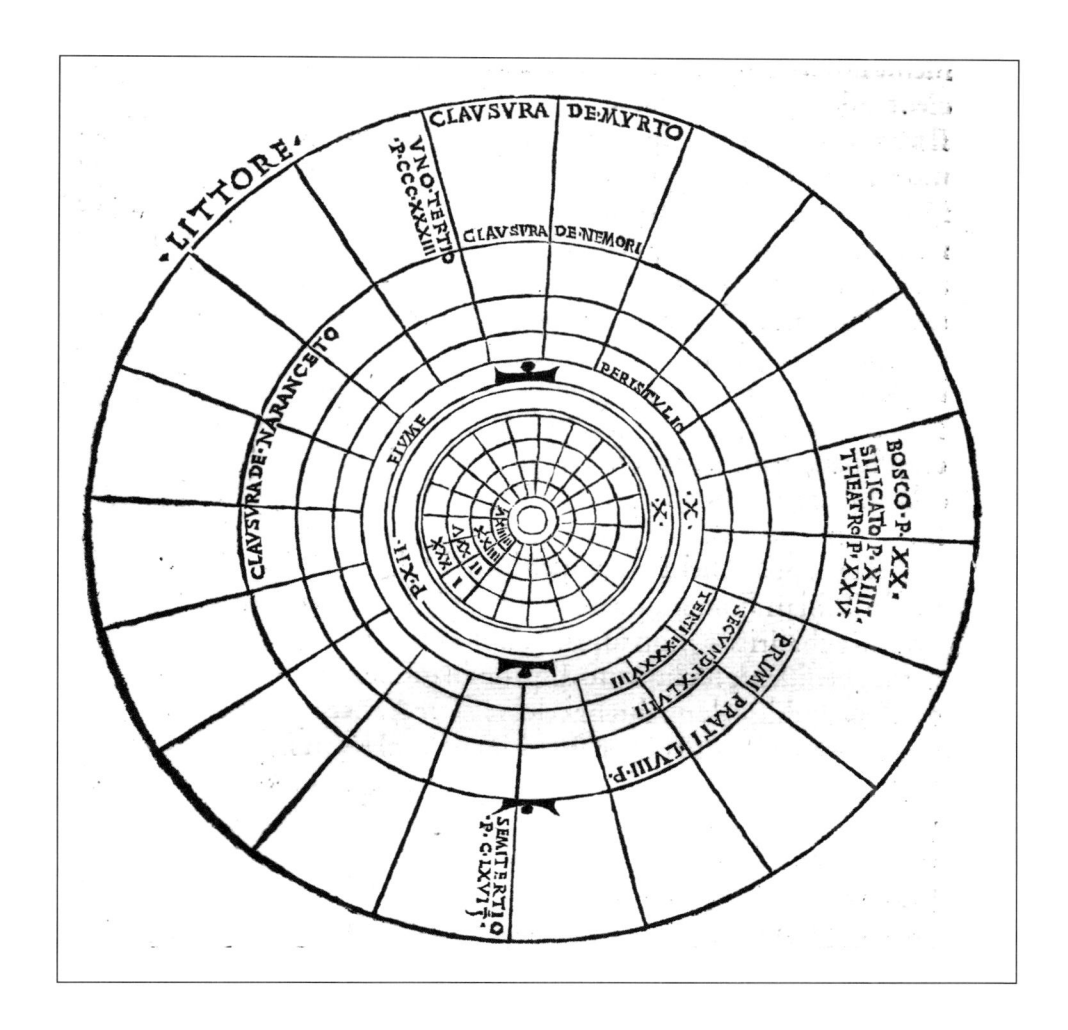

158. Painting by Utens, 1599, of the Villa Petraia, Florence, the only example of the use of the twin-circle motif prior to the Stadholder's gardens.
Galleria Palatina, Palazzo Pitti, Florence

VI. AN ICONOLOGICAL INTERPRETATION

159. Print by Johan Vredeman de Vries, showing the ideal garden design based on the circle and the square, with circular *berceaux*, laid out as a labyrinth.
The Metropolitan Museum of Art, New York

160. Print by Romeyn de Hooghe, depicting Johan Maurits's circular orchard garden at Cleves with eight entrances, influenced by cosmological imagery.
Bibliotheek Landbouwuniversiteit, Wageningen

161. Print by Romeyn de Hooghe, depicting the great circular wood cut through by alleys in the gardens of the Duke of Aremberg at Enghien, near Brussels, c. 1540.
Bibliotheek Landbouwuniversiteit, Wageningen

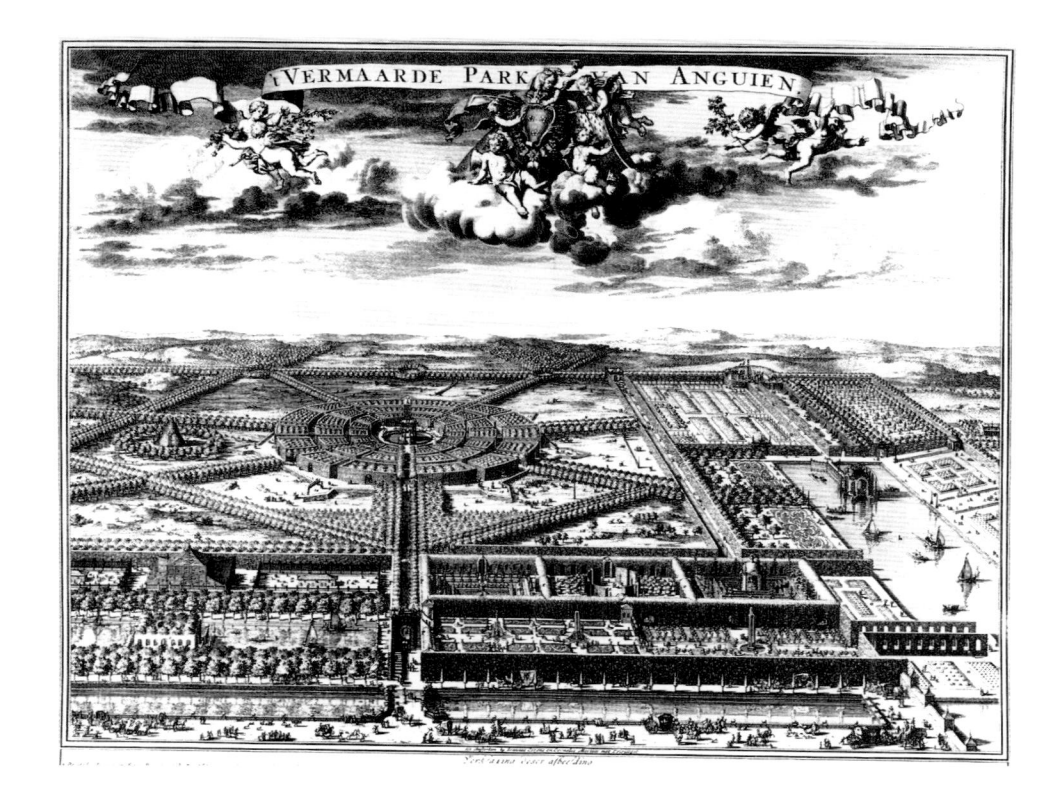

THE CIRCLE IN GARDEN ARCHITECTURE AND THE SCIENCE OF COSMOLOGY

In many if not all of the cases in which the circle or circular form is found in garden architecture, its layout evidently had cosmological overtones. This is proved by a number of surviving documents describing the iconological programme of a particular garden, and by the general plan or inner layout of gardens which are so clearly comparable to traditional cosmological diagrams that one cannot doubt their origin. Moreover, the great interest in the garden and cosmological imagery during Frederik Hendrik's lifetime is reflected in the explicit references to astrological works in the garden treatises of Claude Mollet and Jacques Boyceau. One contemporary treatise was even entirely dedicated to the subject: D. Loris's *Le Thrésor des Parterres de l'Univers*, which contains an illustration of a garden plan based on an astrological design symbolizing the sun and the zodiac in its circular centre.[140]

A short survey of a few cosmological diagrams is needed to show how their models influenced not only art and architecture but also sixteenth- and seventeenth-century garden design. Besides, these cosmological diagrams are particularly useful, for they reflect in very compact, geometrical schemata the whole gamut of current knowledge and concepts of the universe and its manifestations, involving astrology and astronomy (the planets, the zodiac), alchemy (the metals), Nature (the elements and the seasons) and Time (Hours, Days, Years and the Age of Man) – manifestations which we find in every garden layout and which occupied every gardener.

The design of the Paduan Botanical Garden can again be taken as the main point of departure, as its form and layout were the embodiment of classical and Renaissance cosmological thought. Because of the proportional relationship of its perfect circular form and geometrical inner layout, consisting of four parterre compartments based again on the circle and the square, the Paduan garden represented the well-known micro-macrocosm analogy, symbolizing the harmony between the world and the universe.[141] How the form and meaning of the Padua garden relate to cosmology, to man's image of the world, nature and the larger universe is best explained by comparing it with the three perhaps most widely-known sixteenth-century cosmological diagrams (figs. 162, 163 and 164). The first diagram (fig. 162) relates to the general vision of the universe in the Renaissance as derived from the Aristotelian and Ptolemaic traditions, in which the universe is seen as a complex of concentric spheres surrounding a stationary Earth.[142] At the centre is the Earth, encompassed by four concentric spheres, one for each of the Four Elements. Surrounding the spheres of the Four Elements are the seven planetary spheres, one for each of the Seven Planets,[143] as each sphere is labelled, holding the appropriate astronomical symbol.[144]

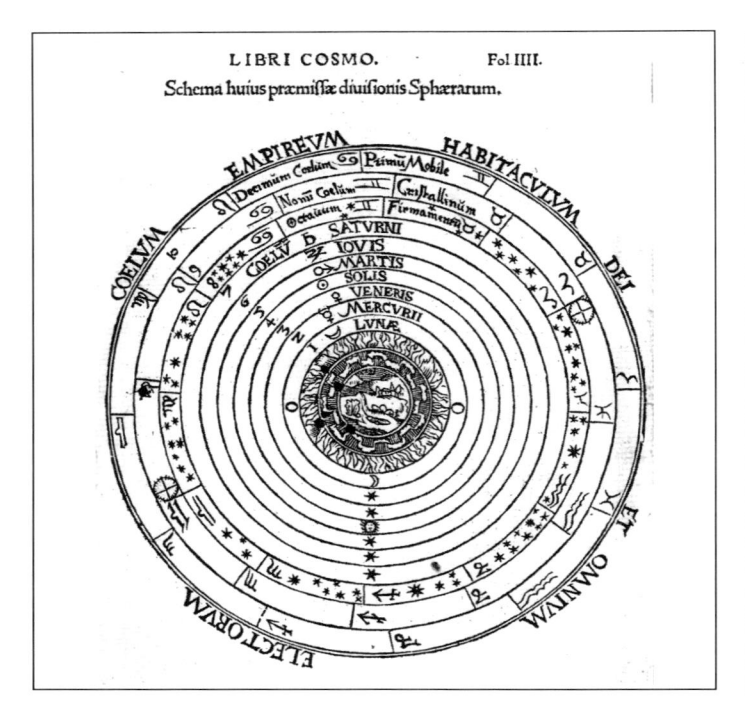

The second important diagram is that of the Pythagorean Tetrad (fig. 163), illustrating the doctrine of the *tetraktys* based on the premiss that there are four fundamental qualities, and that these qualities define the Four Elements.[145] The original, simplest statement of the tetrad appears in the figure shown here, based on the motif of the squared circle and showing the Four Elements and the Four Qualities set within the eight small circles surrounding the brim of the larger circle, with the sign of Christ (IHS) in the centre.[146] Throughout the ages and into the seventeenth century, the tetrad was seen as the abstract schema *par excellence* for the macro- and microcosmoi, reproducing in miniature their exhaustive fullness.[147] In later years this cosmological diagram became increasingly complex; for example, set within the Platonic context of contemporary science and philosophy, a *scala intellectualis* or *spiritualis* would be added to the cosmic scheme of the tetrad.[148]

The last important diagram relates to the human microcosm, expressed in the famous *homo ad circulum* and *homo ad quadratum*. In many ways, this diagram can be connected with the other examples of man in relation to his universe, yet it concentrates solely on the form of the human figure, the parts of the body and their proportions. Several versions are represented here (fig. 164).[149] In the upper left-hand corner, Leonardo's well-known example of the human figure standing both in the square and in the circle is shown. To the right of this diagram is Robert Fludd's expanded version, depicting the microcosm of man in the context of the macrocosm, in which the members of the body correspond to the signs

162. Cosmological diagram showing the pre-Copernican geocentric universe with static earth at the centre, surrounded by the spheres of the planets.
The Henry E. Huntington Library, San Marino, California

163. Theological version of the Pythagorean Tetrad with Christ at the centre, depicting the universe and the relationship between the Four Qualities and the Four Elements.
British Library, London

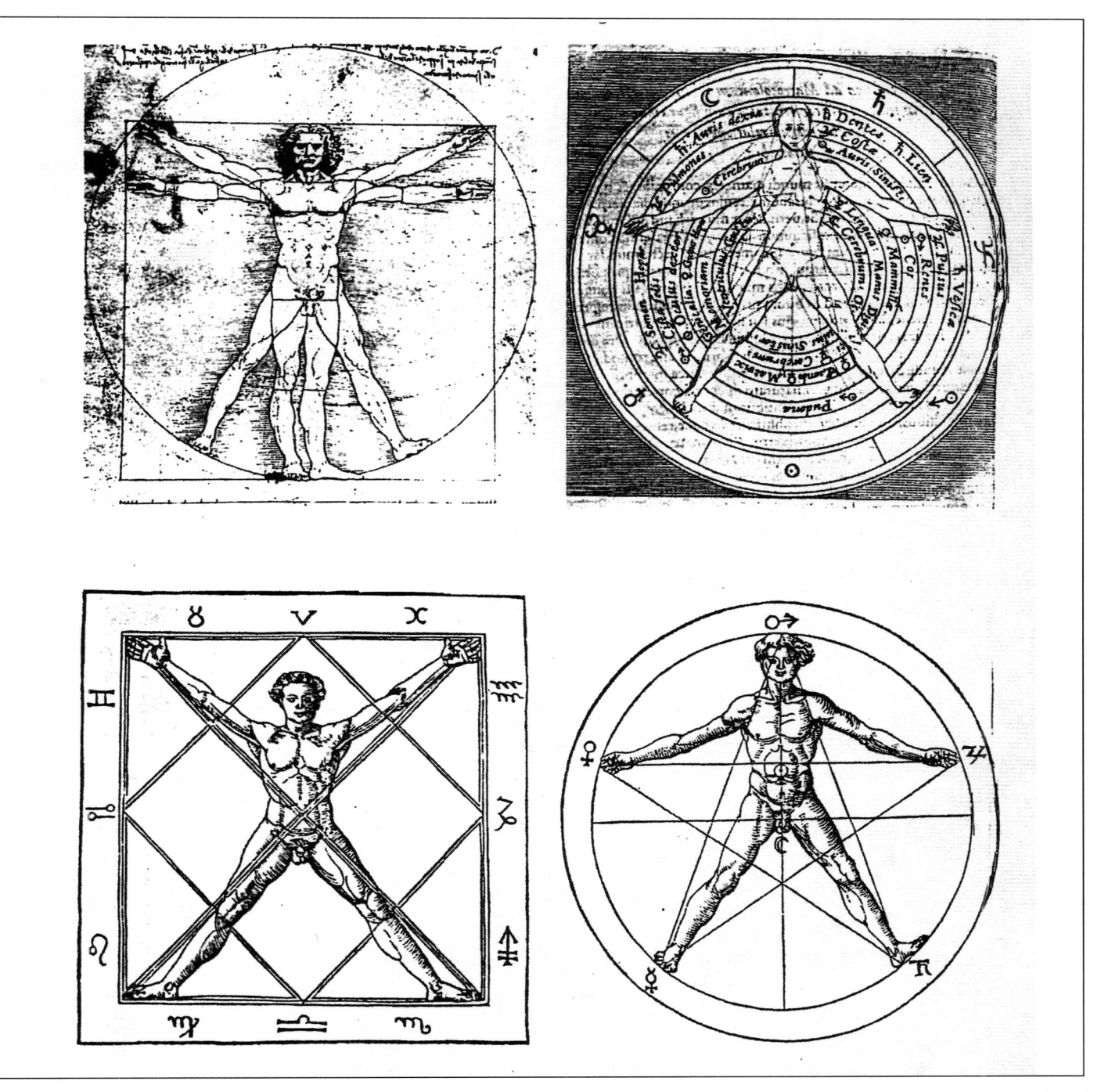

164. The human microcosm as visualized by Leonardo, Fludd and von Nettesheim, depicting the relationship between man and the universe.
Photo courtesy F.A. Yates

of the zodiac and the planets. The two other examples show Agrippa von Nettesheim's representations of the human figure in a square and a circle, again symbolizing the cosmos.[150]

Content and representation of these diagrams point to older traditions and ultimately have their sources in classical antiquity. In point of fact, all of these diagrams were based on the 'Vitruvian man', developed in Vitruvius's *The Ten Books on Architecture*. The third book on Temples contains the famous passage about the proportions of the human figure. As proof of the harmony and perfection of the human body, Vitruvius describes how a well-built man, with extended arms and legs, fits exactly into the most perfect geometrical figures, the circle and the square, a description which is well portrayed in Leonardo's

VI. AN ICONOLOGICAL INTERPRETATION

165. Tycho Brahe's observatory and garden complex Uraniborg on the island of Hveen, Copenhagen, 1591, based on the cosmological diagram of the tetrad. Woodcut from Brahe, *Astronomiae*, 1598. Bodleian Library, University of Oxford

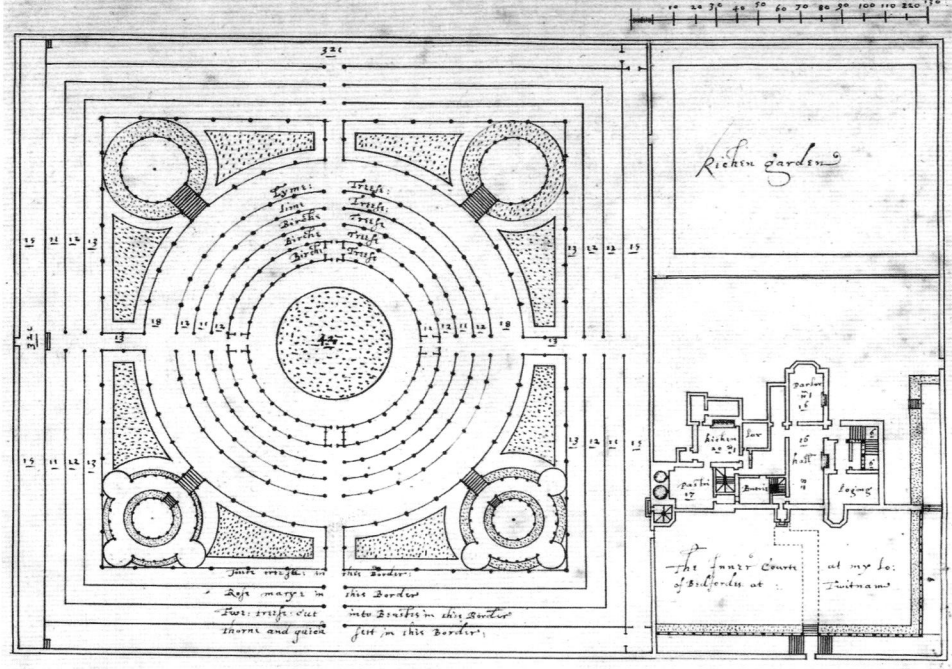

166. The Countess of Bedford's garden at Twickenham Park, based on the diagram of the pre-Copernican universe. Drawing by R. Smythson, ca. 1609.
British Architectural Library, RIBA, London

COURTLY GARDENS IN HOLLAND 1600-1650

167. Plan of Salomon de Caus's gardens of Heidelberg reflecting in its inner form and layout several 'microcosmoi', based on cosmological diagrams.
Photo courtesy Kurpfälzisches Museum, Heidelberg

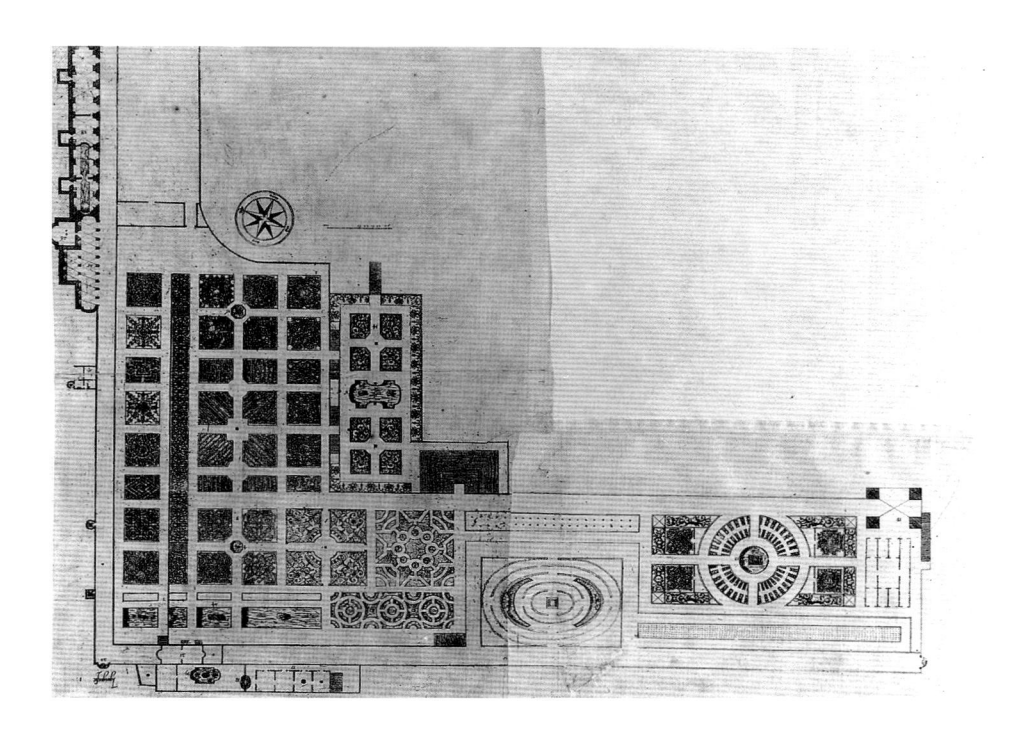

drawing of the 'Vitruvian man' *(see fig. 164)*.[151] Again, in compact form, these four schemata illustrate Renaissance commentaries on harmony and proportion, the human figure being of central importance and holding *Divina proportio*: from its body all measures and their denominations are derived and in it are to be found all and every ratio and proportion by which God revealed the innermost secrets of nature.[152]

In Northern Europe, immediately preceding the layout of the Stadholder's gardens, these diagrams directly influenced the structure and/or constituent parts of three gardens, two of which originated from the same scientific-philosophical milieu as did the garden of the Dutch court. The first layout, designed about 1591, was that of the garden of the world-renowned Danish astronomer Tycho Brahe on the island of Hveen, near Copenhagen *(fig. 165)*.[153] The total scheme of Tycho Brahe's palace-observatory, appropriately called Uraniborg after the Muse of Astronomy, was based on the circle and the square, reflecting the cosmic diagram of the tetrad *(see fig. 163)*,[154] in which the exedrae in the enclosing wall corresponded to the circles containing the Four Seasons in the tetrad model.[155] At the centre of the plan stood Tycho Brahe's famed observatory, which, decorated with a Pegasus on the rooftop,[156] symbolized at the same time the centre of the universe and the centre of scientific pursuit. An early-seventeenth-century example of a circular garden based on the first of the cosmological diagrams shown above – that of the Ptolemaic or pre-Copernican, geocentric universe – can be recognized in the garden of Lady Harington, Countess of Bedford at Twickenham Park *(fig. 166)*,[157] the layout of which consisted of hedges planted in concentric circles and mounds in the four outer spandrels, reflecting the Earth in the centre encompassed by the spheres of the planets *(see fig. 162)*.[158]

The last important garden whose inner division and decoration were clearly based on cosmological diagrams was Salomon de Caus's garden at Heidelberg *(fig. 167)*. This garden, designed for Friedrich V and his wife Elizabeth, was based on a complex iconological scheme involving several macro- and microcosmoi which visualized various great cosmological cycles, such as the Cycles of the Planets, the Years, the Seasons, Days, Hours, as well as the Cycle of Life.[159] Other parterres were laid out according to specific schemata which copy traditional cosmic diagrams reflecting the spheres of heaven and earth in all

VI. AN ICONOLOGICAL INTERPRETATION

their fullness. How these cosmic-harmonic diagrams were translated into an actual garden design at Heidelberg can best be observed in the large circular parterre called the Orange parterre. This parterre compartment was laid out as a complex diagram of eight equal sections, among them the eight roundels each holding an orange tree. The form of this parterre resembled musical diagrams published by de Caus in his *Institution Harmonique* and *Horologue Solaire*, which in themselves were derived from sixteenth-century Italian cosmic-harmonic diagrams, including complex versions of the tetrad model.[160]

In The Netherlands men of letters were undoubtedly familiar with these comprehensive, cosmological images and their metaphysical meanings. Besides, they had the opportunity to study actual garden designs, such as those at Padua, Denmark and Heidelberg which reflected these cosmological thoughts. And moreover the intellectual milieu of the Dutch Calvinist court, as described in chapter IV, showed a profound interest in classical and Renaissance literature and philosophy, including cosmological works and thoughts. It was with such cosmological diagrams in mind, ultimately based on Vitruvian and Pythagorean harmonic theories, that the Stadholder's garden and the gardens of his courtiers were designed, and it was from them that they derived their deeper meaning.

THE STADHOLDER'S GARDENS AND THE TWIN-CIRCLE MOTIF

The cosmological meaning of the Stadholder's gardens and those in his environment is best rendered by Everhart Meyster's country-house poem *Des weerelds Dool-om-berg ontdoold op Dool-in-bergh*, detailing the iconographical programme of the garden of Doolomberg ('Wander about the Mountain') near Amersfoort in the centre of Holland.[161] Laid out about 1655, shortly after Frederik Hendrik's death, this garden belongs to the artistic and ideological milieu of the first part of the century. In the middle of the larger garden complex of Doolomberg there was a circular labyrinth with a central mound *(fig. 168)*.[162] As can be deduced from Meyster's poem, in which the garden is literally called a microcosm, the geometrical labyrinth with central mound stands for the wandering Christian soul lost in the labyrinth of a sinful world from which only God can save him.[163] In Meyster's garden there is a fusion between classical, cosmological and religious sources,[164] in which the two sections of the garden complex, Doolomberg and Doolinberg, are referred to as 'earthly' and 'heavenly realms', respectively ('naar het Hemelsche … naar 't aardsch gedoopt').[165] This remark is of special relevance to our search for the links between garden design and cosmological thought, demonstrating a correlation between this garden with central mound and cosmological diagrams. Indeed, the position of the four smaller mounds surrounding the circular labyrinth in Doolomberg is related to the form of the Theological Tetrad *(see fig. 163)*, containing the Four Elements in the four smaller circles with God at the centre.[166] Thus there is a direct relationship between the Doolomberg labyrinth and its three-terraced mound, symbolizing the Road to God, and the diagram of the Theological Tetrad representing a *scala spiritualis*, or pilgrimage of the soul, towards the central figure of the Creator or God.[167]

Arousing much curiosity at the time, the Doolomberg garden complex was particularly admired by Constantijn Huygens, who spent whole days wandering through the gardens while talking with its ingenious owner.[168] In Meyster, Huygens found his equal, for not only was Meyster also a poet and dilettante architect, his gardens reflected cosmological and esoteric truths similar to those which have been recognized in the Hofwijck garden. As described above, Huygens and Van Campen and their patrons were aware of classical

168. View of Doolomberg, Amersfoort, c. 1660, showing the influence of cosmological thought and imagery on the shape of the garden with central mound. Bibliotheek Landbouwuniversiteit, Wageningen

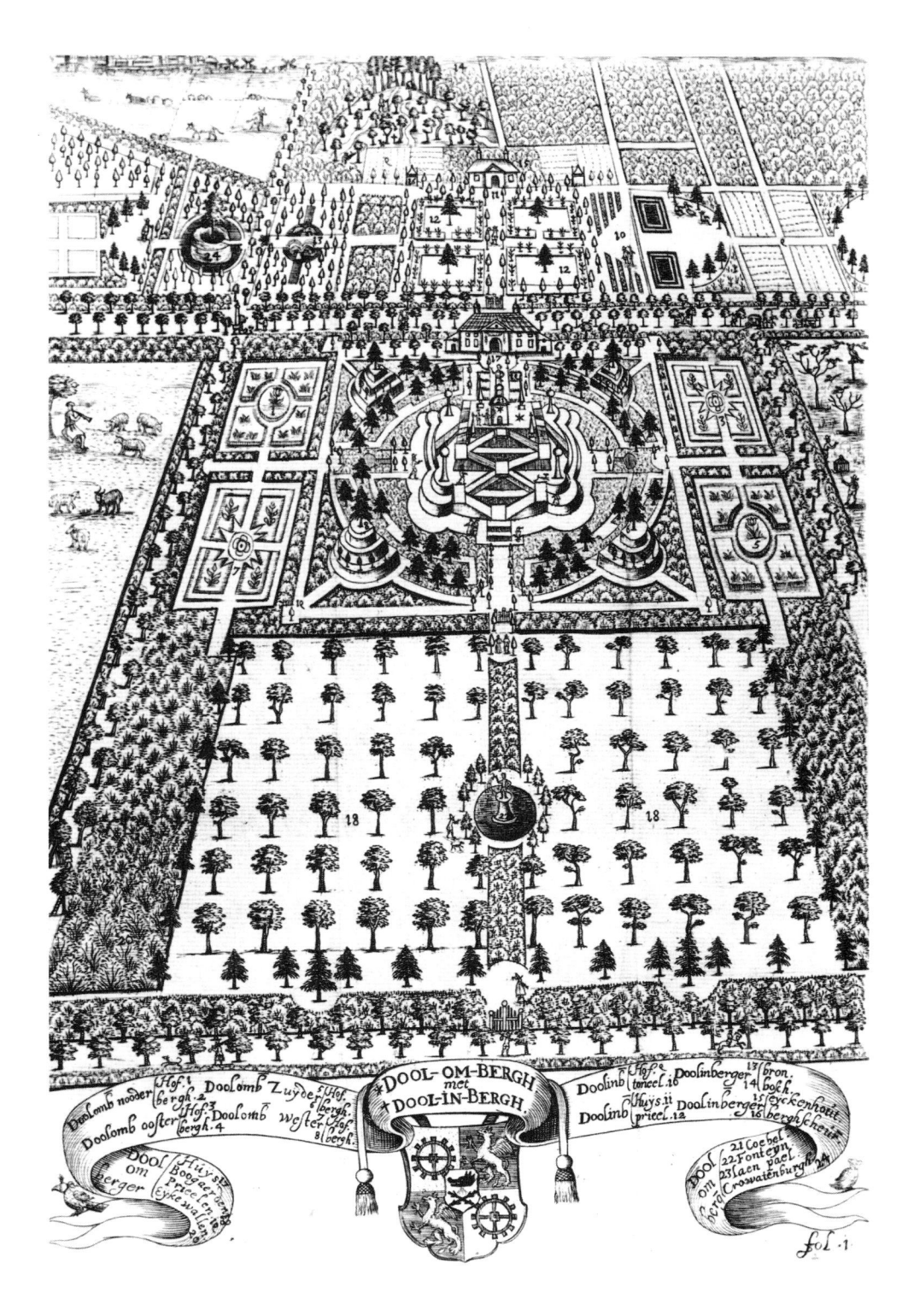

theories by Vitruvius, Plato and Pythagoras, and of Renaissance theorists such as Alberti and Palladio. Proof of their familiarity with the classical past and methods of thinking were Huygens's translation of Vitruvius and his study of many other classical and Renaissance authors, especially Alberti, all of which is evident in the design of his house at The Hague and his *villa suburbana* at Voorburg. Like the house of his neighbour Johan Maurits, which was recognized above as having been inspired by Vitruvius's circular diagram of the Roman theatre,[169] Huygens's house may be interpreted as a *domus cosmographica*, especially since comments by contemporary architects clearly point in that direction.[170] Indeed, the use of harmonic proportions in Huygens's house was commented on by Henry Wotton, who described the house as 'a sound piece of good Art ..., ravish the beholder by a secret Harmony in the Proportions'.[171]

The same harmonic proportions hidden in the ideal Vitruvian figure as interpreted by Renaissance architects are believed to underlie the Hofwijck garden, as we have seen in the preceding chapter *(see fig. 125)*. This notion was founded on a comparison of the text of Huygens's poem *Hofwijck* with the actual structure of the Hofwijck garden, undertaken in a study by Van Pelt. In spite of certain reservations regarding this study – in which Huygens's text appears to have been used too much *ad verbum*[172] and the discrepancies in the proportions of the estate and those of the ideal human body have not sufficiently been taken into consideration – we can arrive at some important conclusions. Whereas theories on the anthropomorphic form of the garden, supposedly recognizable in the tripartite layout of the terrain and its proportions (in which the villa was believed to represent the head, the central orchard the chest and arms, and the elongated wooded area the legs and knees[173]), may not be accurate in actual fact, they are true in an abstract sense, as suggested above. We have already seen that Huygens himself expressed the necessity to look at his poem and garden plan in this abstract way, allowing for a discrepancy between the ideal and the actual layout. Huygens's platonic-cosmological thoughts, expressed in the superimposition of the 'Vitruvian man' on his garden at Hofwijck, are worth considering as the general 'idea' behind garden designing in the environment of the Stadholder's court.

The Hofwijck garden was divided into three sections which, apart from corresponding to three parts of the human body, have been analysed as reflecting the human mind, or the three levels of contemplation, set forth in Huygens's poem. Similar religious-cosmological mysticism was the core of the Doolomberg poem and the actual layout of the garden. This proves that it is not unreasonable to analyse contemporary garden architecture along such cosmological lines and according to Platonic-philosophical thought, in that the garden reflects as it were the model of the tetrad with an added *scala spiritualis*. Indeed, hidden in the anthropomorphic form of the Hofwijck garden, a progressive direction can be seen, or a pilgrimage towards God, in which the soul, wandering through the various spheres, moves from the earthly (orchard) to the heavenly realm represented by the house. Interestingly, this same iconography, centring upon a linear progression of the soul and coupled to the corresponding levels of the heavenly spheres and harmonic proportions, can also be recognized in the layout of other contemporary gardens, notably the Heidelberg one,[174] albeit not in the actual but in the abstract sense again.[175] Whether directly expressed in garden architecture or indirectly as the thought behind its form, the concept of Vitruvian symmetry, the Platonic idea of the reascension of the soul and theories on musical harmony, so well expressed in Huygens's poetic and architectural thoughts, still were at the forefront of seventeenth-century cosmological thinking, as new, increasingly complex cosmological diagrams were developed visualizing modern cosmological thought.[176]

The gardens of the Stadholder and his courtiers containing the circular *berceaux* set within a square can be compared to the same cosmological thoughts and imagery present in the Dutch gardens shown above. Here, in contrast with what we see at Hofwijck, the actual form and proportions of the gardens mirror cosmological imagery, based on the Vitruvian *homo ad circulum* and *homo ad quadratum*. In line with the harmonic principles found in earlier Italian and Northern European layouts, including the above-mentioned Dutch gardens, the structures of the Stadholder's garden containing two squares with inscribed circles can be related to Pythagorean and later to Albertian theories on musical harmony, in which space is translated into musical ratios.[177] Expressed in these musical-harmonic terms, the garden compartments at Flushing, The Hague, Buren, Vianen and Groningen, containing the double-circle motif, had a proportion of length to width of 2 : 1, which relates to the double tone, or diapason – a harmonic ratio advised by Alberti for medium-sized plans.[178]

Now that we have examined the complex iconology of contemporary garden architecture, situating the Stadholder's gardens within the realm of ancient and Renaissance harmonic-cosmological thinking, we may wonder whether the double-circle motif had a special reference to the Princes of Orange and their retinue. Perhaps a remark by Huygens about the Buitenhof garden *(see figs. 101 and 102)* is a clue to how the Stadholder's symbolic gardens containing two circles within squares were viewed in Holland at the time. In one of his epigrams, entitled 'Hortus principis Mauritii dikuklos, 's Princen Huys-thuyn', part of *Haga Vocalis*, a seventh book of epigrams published in the collection *Momenta desultoria* (1644), which also includes playful references to several other places in The Hague, Huygens describes Maurits's garden at the Buitenhof as follows:

In Hortulum Principis Mauritii *dikuklon*
Quidni Mauritius geminos calcauerit orbes?
Orbis Alexandro non satis unus erat.[179]

This sentence can be interpreted in different ways, but the *dikuklon* undoubtedly refers to the structure of the two joined circular *berceaux*. Huygens here plays on the two meanings of the word *orbis*, which can be read as 'circle' or as 'world', cleverly referring to the circular *berceaux* in the garden. He paraphrases Juvenalis, who in his *Satirae* wrote: 'Unus Pellae iuveni non sufficit erat' (one world was not enough for the young man), in clear reference to Alexander the Great and his unbridled urge for conquest.[180] From this verse we may conclude that the two spherical *berceaux* symbolized the two halves of the world. Besides, if we carry Juvenalis's verses about Alexander's campaigns over to seventeenth-century Holland and to Frederik Hendrik as commander-in-chief of the Dutch army, the two circular *berceaux* would allude to the Stadholder's military accomplishments. Thibault's print showing the ideal positions of two fighting soldiers within a 'mystical circle' *(see fig. 155)* can be related to these verses; at the same time, the circles also symbolize the two earthly spheres.

Another interpretation of the two circular *berceaux* may be offered. Because of the strong cosmological tradition at the Dutch court, the two circular *berceaux*, or the twin-circle motif, could also symbolize the earthly and heavenly spheres. In contemporary emblem books two paired globes are represented as such *(fig. 169)*, symbolizing both the macrocosm and man's inner spiritual strife.[181] The very large number of emblem books published in The Netherlands from the sixteenth century onward, especially in Holland during the reign of Frederik Hendrik, indicates the widespread preoccupation with symbolism of this kind and the strong tendency to think in emblematic terms in general.[182]

Other examples of the two globes carrying this symbolism are those in the late-seventeenth-century garden of Het Loo, laid out by Frederik Hendrik's grandson William III.[183] Two globes representing, respectively, Heaven and Earth belonged to the most prominent decorative and symbolic features of the garden and, set opposite each other on either side of the central axis, held together the whole layout of the Loo garden and its iconography, surrounded as they were by allegorical statues representing the Four Parts of the World, and the Four Seasons *(fig. 170)*.[184] Walter Harris, William III's physician, gave the following detailed description of these globes:

169. Late-sixteenth-century emblem with two paired globes symbolizing the earthly and heavenly spheres and expressing man's inner spiritual strife.
Photo courtesy A. Henkel and A. Schöne

170. Print by Romeyn de Hooghe, c. 1690, showing the Earth globe fountain in the gardens of Het Loo, Apeldoorn, having cosmological symbolic meaning. Bibliotheek Landbouwuniversiteit, Wageningen

Turning out of the aforesaid Walk, from the Fountain of Venus, into a Cross-Walk on the right, we meet with a Fountain in the middle, wherein is erected a Celestial Globe, placed on a Marble Pedestal, between which Pedestal and the Globe there are four naked Boys in Marble, incircling one another in their Arms. About the Globe the twelve signs of the Zodiack are curiously painted, the Stars Gilded, and out of abundance of the Stars there do spout out Jettes on all sides of the Globe. Again, turning from the Fountain of Venus on the left hand the same distance in this Cross-walk, as we did before from thence on the right to the Celestial Globe, there is, I say, on the left such another Noble Fountain, in the middle of which is erected as a Terrestrial Globe. On this Globe, Europe, Asia, Africa and America, the four parts of the World, are exactly painted, and out of the several parts of it there do spring a great number of Spouts, which throw up water from all parts round it, as in the former Globe. This is likewise placed on the high Pedestal, round which there are four naked Boys in Marble, the first with a crown on his head, the second with a Turbant, the third a Negro in his short frizled hair, and the fourth with long hair hanging down his back: The four Boys representing the Inhabitants of the four parts of the Earth.[185]

In an earlier description of the Loo gardens, the English traveller Southwell had remarked that there were two large globes and that they spouted water, 'the Terrestrial Globe from

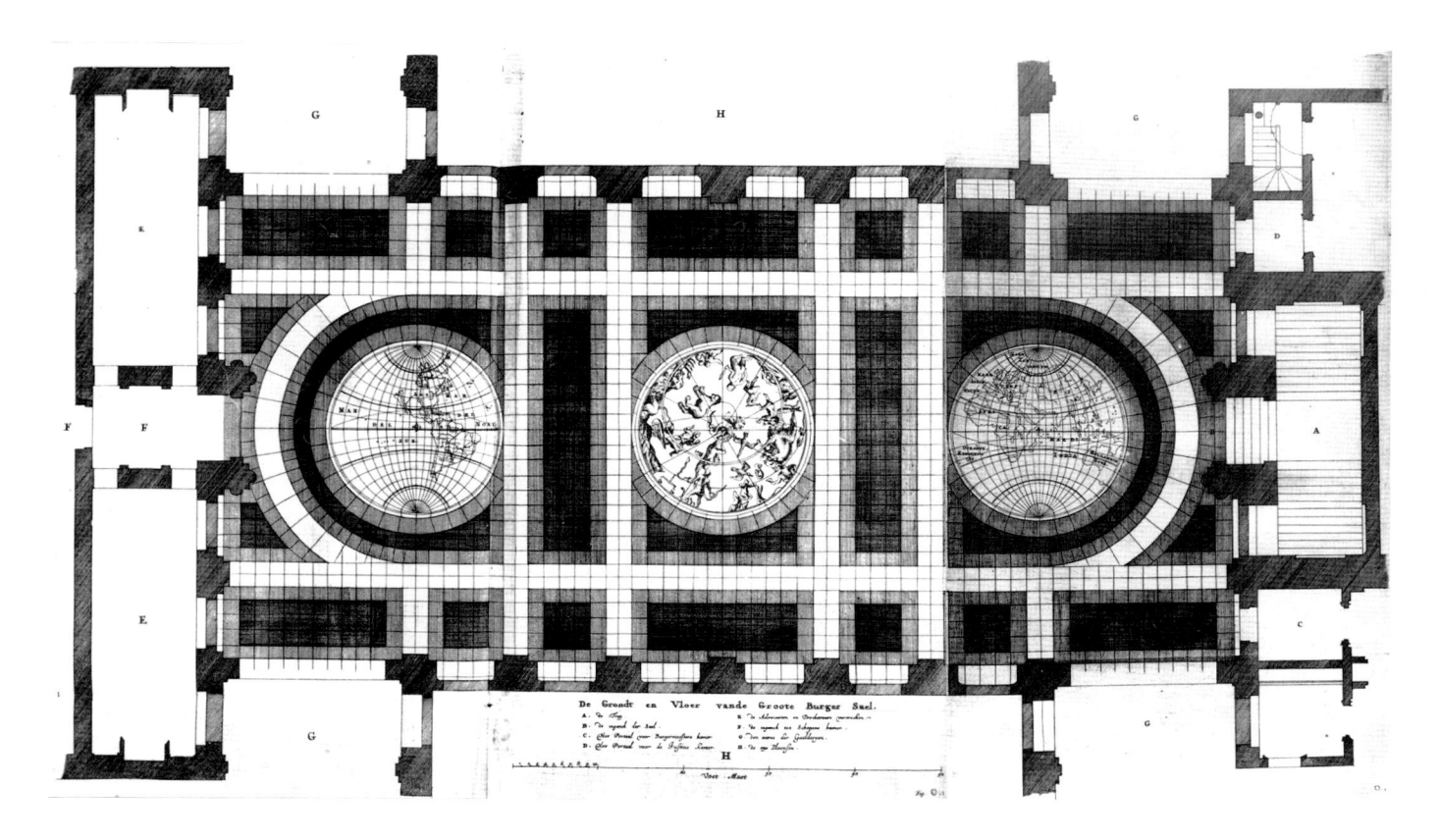

171. Floor plan of the Burgerzaal in the Amsterdam Town Hall, representing the two halves of the world and the heavens. Print by Jacob Vennecool.
Photo courtesy Utrecht University

the Chief Ports [cities], the Celestial from the noted Stars'.[186]

From these descriptions it is clear that a traditional cosmological programme was represented in the Loo gardens. Recently restored, it is not impossible that already in the seventeenth century the globes were turned in order to have Holland and Het Loo as central point of orientation, symbolizing at the same time Dutch hegemony over the seas and William III's reigning power. Similarly, the celestial globe may originally have been turned and oriented to render the position of the starry sky as it was at the time of Mary II Stuart's birth on Wednesday 30 April 1662, at one o'clock in the morning.[187] The cosmological symbolism of the gardens of Het Loo, glorifying the Stadholder-King (with a personal reference to his function and character) as the 'earthly' ruler and the Queen as his 'heavenly' or spiritual counterpart, would thus be complete.

It is also important to note that two globes or spheres decorated the roof of Huygens's newly-built house at The Hague.[188] The earthly and the heavenly sphere not only added to the building's symbolism as a *domus cosmographica* but also capped the chimneys of the apartments of Huygens and his wife *(see fig. 123)*.[189] The depiction of the terrestrial and celestial globes as focal point in Thomas de Keyser's famous portrait of Huygens is no coincidence either and refers to Huygens as a *homo universalis*.

More important is the occurrence of the twin-circle motif with cosmographical undertones in contemporary architecture and cartography. In developing the iconographical programme of the Amsterdam Town Hall, the stadholderly architect Jacob van Campen created his own true *domus cosmographica*. In the centre of the town hall was the Great Hall for the citizens, the Burgerzaal, the pavement of which was decorated with large spheres representing the maps of the terrestrial hemispheres and the northern hemisphere of the sky *(fig. 171)*. Painted above it in the central compartment of the ceiling, whose divisions mirrored those of the floor below, the southern celestial hemisphere was to have been represented.[190] Surrounding the southern hemisphere, the Fall of Phaeton to the

VI. AN ICONOLOGICAL INTERPRETATION

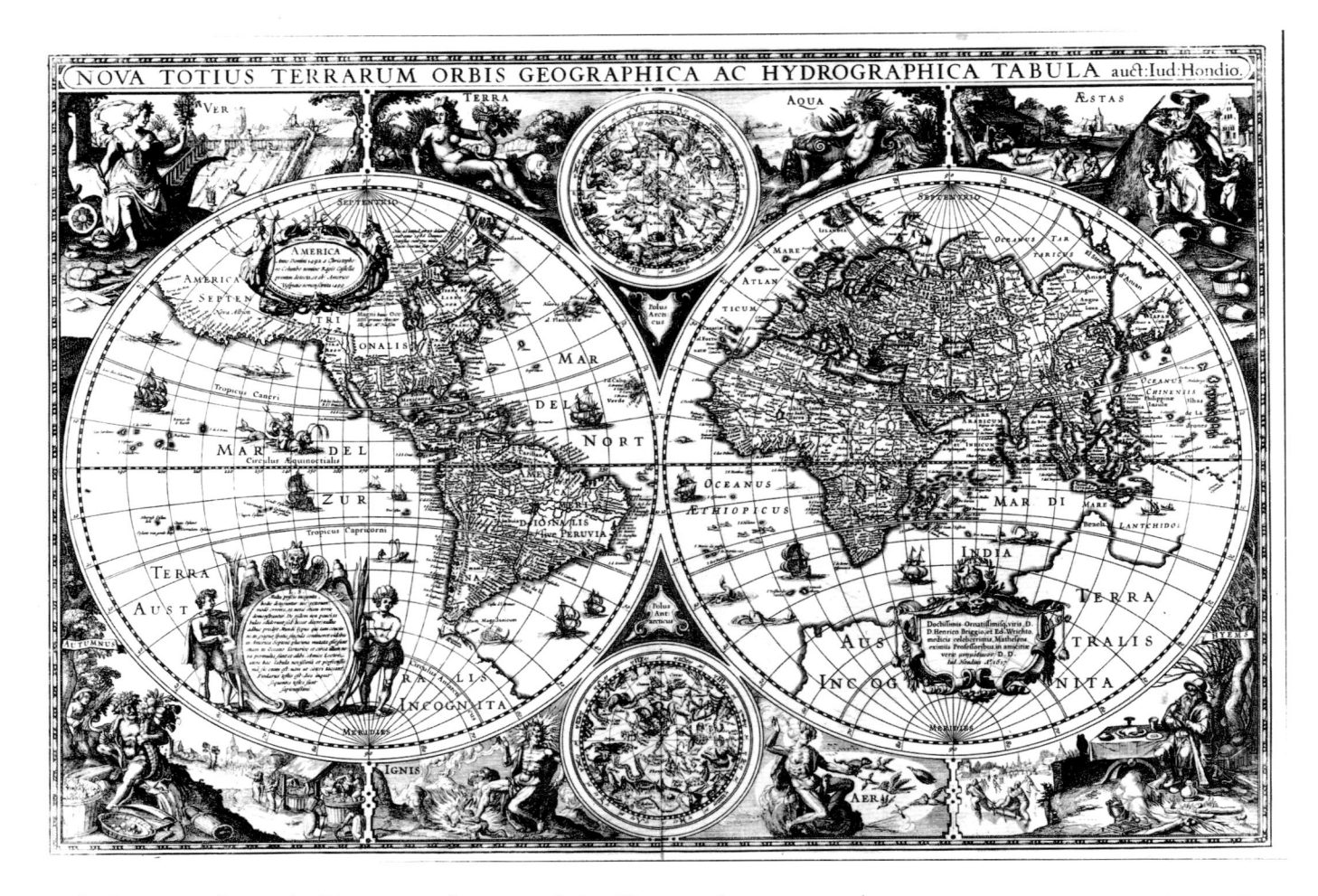

south, Boreas to the north, Neptune to the east and the Giants to the west must have represented the Four Elements, Fire, Air, Water and Earth. The Four Elements are again represented by sculptural figures set on the spandrels of the large arches which lead from the Burgerzaal to the surrounding galleries.

Symbols of the seasons and of the times of day, as well as further signs of the zodiac, also appear in the Burgerzaal, completing its cosmological iconography as a universe of space and time to surround the onlooker. In the words of a contemporary writer describing the Burgerzaal's decoration: 'You can ... make your way across the whole world in a moment.'[191] From his place in the universe the spectator would take part in Holland's hegemony over the seas: depicted in the map on the floor were Albert Tasman's discoveries of the coasts of Australia, proudly marked as 'New Holland'. The symbolic programme of the Burgerzaal is extended into the galleries flanking the hall, where the seven planets are depicted as standing figures on the end walls.[192] In all respects, the iconographical scheme of the Burgerzaal and its surrounding galleries suggests a direct link with the iconography of the diagrams above. Even more remarkable is that the programme as it was executed with the motif of the double circle or twin hemispheres at its centre can be compared with the motif of the double circle in the Stadholder's gardens. Indeed, the sentence quoted above would very well fit the effect of standing in the centre of the circular *berceaux* in the Stadholder's gardens, revelling in a living universe of sounds and scents. At the same time, the form of the twin circles can be associated with the usual way the world is represented in contemporary cartography. Good examples are the *mappae mundi* made by the famous cartographers and publishers Jodocus Hondius and Johannes and Willem Jansz Blaeu, and

172. Jodocus Hondius's Mappa Mundi, 1617, of the two halves of the world, the sky and emblematic representations of the Four Seasons and the Four Elements. Maritiem Museum Prins Hendrik, Rotterdam

173. Print by Romeyn de Hooghe of the Orangerie garden at Cleves, decorated with the twelve Roman Emperors, classic urns, rare plants and instruments. Bibliotheek Landbouwuniversiteit, Wageningen

the Antwerp cartographer Abraham Ortelius. These maps are in themselves an amalgam of contemporary cosmology, borrowing motifs from print series and emblems of famous artists for a lavish decoration of the cartouches in the borders.[193]

In 1617 Jodocus Hondius II published a world map entitled *Nova Totius Terrarum Orbis Geographica Ac Hydrographica Tabula*, in which not only an accurate view of the world is given as it was known in the early seventeenth century but also a complete overview of contemporary cosmology *(fig. 172)*.[194] The eastern and western hemispheres are surrounded by emblematic representations of the Four Seasons and the Four Elements.[195] Flanking the two smaller maps of the northern and southern skies, shown complete with the zodiac and signs of the planets, four classical deities are seated, traditionally identified with the Four Elements.[196] The Four Seasons, also represented by classical allegorical figures, are seated in the outer spandrels surrounding the large circular hemispheres.[197]

A comparison of this map by Jodocus Hondius with the plan of the Buitenhof garden by Hendrick Hondius (Jodocus's brother) *(see fig. 101)* shows remarkable analogies between the two geometrical layouts. The familiar twin-circle motif, represented by two hemispheres in the map, corresponds to the *berceaux* in the garden, though in this particular case the two halves are not connected. As we have seen, in the Buitenhof garden the two hemispheres were divided by a central pavilion, but at Flushing the two circles were

VI. AN ICONOLOGICAL INTERPRETATION

174. Title-page of Salomon de Caus's *Hortus Palatinus*, with allegorical figures representing all the disciplines of the Arts and Sciences based on number. Photo courtesy Kurpfälzisches Museum, Heidelberg

indeed connected. Hondius's remark that the Buitenhof pavilion was decorated as a dome of heaven with a *trompe-l'oeil* sky may not be without meaning. We can only speculate whether the round and square pavilions in the spandrels surrounding the circular *berceaux*, by means of painted or sculptural decoration, also represented the Four Elements and the Four Seasons as they do in the maps.

Lack of further documentation on the decoration of these pavilions, and on other parts of the courtly gardens with the twin-circle motif, does not obscure the fact that, overall, those gardens attempted to convey a cosmological message. This deliberate cosmological meaning was expressed, if not in the design of the garden as a whole, in those particular garden sections which, containing twice a circle in a square, were based on classical harmonic number systems, in which the dimensions of all the details follow one and the same predetermined numerical module.[198]

For our inquiry it is of interest to note that the cosmological significance of the architectural design was carried over to the ornamentation of the garden. The extension of harmonic theory to mechanical and technical matters found expression in the grottoes laid out by Jacques de Gheyn, such as those at the Buitenhof, and in several other courtly gardens *(see fig. 67)*.[199] Indicative of the wider court contacts and a mutual interest in larger philosophical questions relating to *Ars* and *Natura*, de Gheyn's grotto designs, a mixture of the scientific and the weird, resemble those at Heidelberg. Admired by Huygens for their ingenious waterworks and bizarre decoration,[200] these grottoes were published in Salomon de Caus's *Hortus Palatinus* and *Les Raisons des Forces mouvantes*, which were among the books in the Stadholder's library.

The grottoes or adjacent spaces often functioned as an open-air museum, or *rariteiten kabinet*, exhibiting curious objects, stones, shells, exotic flora and fauna.[201] A good example is offered by Johan Maurits's gardens of the Prinsenhof at Cleves, where niches in the garden wall alternately exhibited classical sculpture (busts of the Roman Emperors and philosophers), statues of the Four Seasons, rare plants and orange-trees set among peculiar objects and scientific instruments, mirrors and telescopes *(fig. 173)*.[202]

The same blend of science, nature and cosmology is expressed in contemporary garden treatises, the title-pages of which echo cosmographical imagery. Good examples are Parkinson's *Theatrum Botanicum*, Carolus Clusius's *Rariorum plantarum historia* and especially Salomon de Caus's *Hortus Palatinus*, which on its title-page has allegorical figures representing all the arts and sciences based on number, including alchemy *(fig. 174)*.[203] This kind of symbolism is also expressed by the album mentioned above, entitled *Hortus Regius Honselaerdicensis*, which contains water-colour drawings of the rare plants in the Honselaarsdijk garden *(see fig. 29)*.[204] On the title-page the four parts of the earth are prominently represented by four allegorical figures, showing that the Honselaarsdijk garden realm is a true *theatrum botanicum* and *theatrum mundum*, centring on the magnanimous personality of the Prince of Orange.

References to the garden as a theatre of the world with at its centre the glorification of the patron are not a new element in garden art. While the iconographical programme of the Amsterdam Town Hall set within the cosmological framework of the double hemispheres proudly extolled the virtues of the Dutch burgher and his Batavian ancestors,[205] the Stadholder's gardens laid out with the twin-circle motif glorified the House of Orange. Thus, in the courtly gardens, at the centre of their 'cosmic' double circles, there were decorative parterres containing the Stadholder's coat of arms. Part of the sculptural decoration of the gardens appeared to fit the glorification of the patron within a general cosmographical framework.[206]

Such heraldic imagery could be found at the Buitenhof, at Groningen and in Van Brederode's garden at Vianen. The Dutch Lion decorated the Honselaarsdijk garden, but it was laid out in the parterre flanking the castle, not in the double circle, as a pendant of the parterre with the statue of Hercules slaying Cacus. At Ter Nieuburch the monogram of Frederik Hendrik and Amalia surrounded the fountain in the middle of the first parterre compartment.[207] This monogram flanked the two reclining allegorical figures of the Rhine and the Maas, symbolizing Dutch territory.[208]

It is interesting that contemporary works on cosmography, particularly André Thevet's *La Cosmographie universelle*,[209] maintained that geography, topography as well as ethnography were an essential part of any proper cosmography. Thevet added that especially 'prosopography', or the history of illustrious persons, should be included, as it aimed 'to bring to life from the sombre and forgotten tombs of antiquity the actions, bearing and fame of illustrious persons', and to extoll their virtues, magnanimity and erudition.[210]

Frederik Hendrik's palaces, like his gardens, were decorated with images praising the virtues of the Orange family set within a larger framework of cosmological symbolism. The galleries at Honselaarsdijk and Ter Nieuburch were decorated with portraits of members of the European ruling houses and with topographical scenes illustrating the palaces of the Orange family and other European rulers, set among and compared with illustrious men from the present and the Graeco-Roman past.[211] The same themes were part of the decorative programme of the Stadholder's gardens, notably Ter Nieuburch and Honselaarsdijk,[212] but also the Noordeinde and Huis ten Bosch gardens. Another good example was Johan Maurits's garden at Cleves; in its Orangerie the busts of twelve Roman Emperors were exhibited. In all these cases, particularly at Honselaarsdijk and Ter Nieuburch, cosmological symbolism, expressed in the mathematical form and ornamentation of the garden, served to unify palace and garden.

All things considered, the motif of the double circle in the gardens of the Stadholder and his courtiers is best explained along political-dynastic lines, the circles standing for the

175. Willem Buytewech's allegorical representation of Holland personified by a woman seated in an enclosed garden with orange-tree, guarded by the lion. Historisch Museum, Stichting Atlas van Stolk, Rotterdam

micro- and macrocosmoi, not only in a worldly but also in a universal setting. Huygens's pun comparing the circular *berceaux* of the Buitenhof garden with the 'two worlds', and its owner with Alexander the Great, corroborates such a political-dynastic analysis. Seen in a political-historical context, the form of the garden takes on a new meaning, as it can be compared with the then popular image used in medals,[213] seals and political prints alike *(see fig. 1)*[214] of the young Dutch Republic as an enclosed, circular garden guarded by a rampant lion holding a sword and defending its territory against enemy forces *(fig. 175)*.[215] Indeed, nothing but the symbol of the circular garden protected by the Dutch Lion, both central decorative motifs in the Honselaarsdijk garden, would fit so well the image of Frederik Hendrik as statesman, warrior and gardener. This symbol expresses the Stadholder's ability to defend the Dutch territory, to stimulate its mercantile and agricultural growth and increase its wealth, and, above all, to secure the Hortus Batavus.

CONCLUSION

The reconstruction of the palaces and gardens of Stadholder Frederik Hendrik and Amalia of Orange-Nassau by means of visual and documentary evidence has shown that the Dutch courtly garden set a new standard for garden architecture and iconology in the seventeenth-century Netherlands. The Stadholder's gardens belonged to the most important architectural accomplishments of the day and inspired the art of garden design and garden sculpture at home and abroad. A model for Holland's cultural-artistic resurgence and a vehicle for Dutch political and philosophical thought, the Stadholder's garden may be seen as an emblem of the Dutch Golden Age. Reintroduced as an important art form at court and stimulated by Frederik Hendrik and Amalia themselves, garden architecture increasingly became the focus of attention in literary and artistic circles, celebrated by philosophers, poets and painters. Gardens became the stage for a variety of daily activities and entertainment, from banquets to the game of pall-mall.

Gardens by tradition were an ideal setting for various artistic media, and the Stadholder's gardens were no exception, decorated as they were with sculpture, painted perspectives, optical illusions such as mirrors, and automata or mechanical devices. Planted with exotic flowers and containing rarities like shells and corals in addition to animals from all four continents, the gardens were a veritable 'theatre of the world'. Today only a few of the Stadholder's gardens have survived, albeit in a much altered form based on nineteenth-century landscape designs (Huis ten Bosch) and with a new function as public parks (Ter Nieuburch and the Noordeinde).

Study of the history of Stadholder Frederik Hendrik's gardens, gathered from seventeenth-century archival documents, architectural theory and practice, as well as contemporary literature and personal correspondence, resulted in some important new observations concerning stylistic development, function and meaning of early-seventeenth-century Dutch gardens. Careful analysis of the existing documents and correspondence lead to the conclusion that the Stadholder's palaces and gardens did not depend on the ideas of one principal architect but were the result of teamwork, with Frederik Hendrik and Amalia at the centre and Constantijn Huygens, Jacob van Campen and Pieter Post, among others, as their collaborators. French architects and *fontainiers*, such as André Mollet, Joseph Dinant and Simon de la Vallée, also played an important part. For certain other specific features, particularly the remarkable motif of the double circle, the engineer Simon Stevin, assisted by such erudite men as Jacques de Gheyn and Hendrick Hondius, must have been responsible. Of special interest was the role of land-surveyors and map-makers, including Floris Jacobsz, Pieter Florisz van der Sallem and Jan van Diepenen, who not only drew maps of the Stadholder's gardens but were also actively involved in their basic layout. Most significant was the role of the Stadholder himself, who, as the archival documents and the Huygens correspondence demonstrate, functioned both as an inspiring patron and as a designing architect in his own right. Indeed, Frederik Hendrik not only offered specific proposals for the urban development of The Hague but also provided actual drawings for the layout of the gardens at Ter Nieuburch. Princess Amalia joined him in the designing process of the various palaces and gardens, including the composition of the Huis ten Bosch and the decoration of Ter Nieuburch. The Stadholder's secretary Constantijn Huygens, one of the famous *uomini universali* of the century, was the faithful and knowledgeable adviser and supervisor of all building activities undertaken at court.

In addition to the experience gained by the Stadholder during his travels in England, France and Germany (notably during his stay at the French court of his Godfather Henri IV), the main sources of the new architectural ideas and styles expressed in his palaces and gardens came from contemporary print books and theoretical works imported from France, Italy, the Southern Netherlands and Germany. Vitruvian theories expounded in classical treatises, architectural designs by Palladio, Serlio and Du Cerceau, as well as garden designs described and illustrated by Vredeman de Vries, de Serres, Boyceau, the Mollets, de Caus and Furttenbach inspired, and in some cases directly influenced, the design of the Stadholder's gardens and their decoration. In this context, the print book by Isaac Leschevin proves to be especially valuable, since his models for portals and palisades – originally designed for Frederik Hendrik's relative Johan Wolfert van Brederode at Vianen – also appeared to form the core of the trellis-work decoration in the gardens of Honselaarsdijk and Ter Nieuburch. Leschevin's designs, which later influenced Jan van der Groen and were based in part on the prints by the German garden architect Salomon de Caus, are of further interest because they show the dissemination of garden form and ornamentation throughout Northern Europe.

Two major stylistic influences can be discerned in the Dutch seventeenth-century garden, namely Italian and French form principles, which, adapted to the peculiarities of the Dutch countryside, were mixed to a greater or lesser degree with Dutch features and artistic traditions. Generally it can be said that in the first half of the century the Stadholder's gardens and Dutch garden architecture at large derived their compositions from two main sources: on the one hand, Dutch traditions, involving land division and land reclamation, and the art of quadrature; on the other hand, classical ideals of form and harmonic proportion, originally put forth by architectural theorists such as Vitruvius and Pythagoras and Italian Renaissance architects, from Alberti to Palladio. Actual contemporary French architecture and garden architecture also directly inspired Dutch garden art, as was explicitly shown in the designs made for Ter Nieuburch By the mid-century the prevalent tendencies in garden art were increasingly reshaped by design principles developed at the French court.

An effort was made here to examine more closely the stylistic origins of Honselaarsdijk and Ter Nieuburch, their traditional denotation as 'baroque' or 'classical' and 'Italian' or 'French' being too rudimentary and restrictive. In older literature simply referred to as 'French baroque layouts', and today, more accurately, defined as 'prototypes of the classical Dutch Canal Garden', the sources of the Stadholder's gardens actually were more varied and complex. Any particular definition should be used with care, as Dutch gardens do not seem to fit in specific style categories, and in a way every garden is unique in its own right. Apart from the landscape, Dutch social-political circumstances influenced the Stadholder's gardens, which clearly differed from French and Italian garden layouts, even though, for want of better terms, the same vocabulary to describe their diverse components and style elements is used. Overall, the vocabulary to denote style and form in garden art, borrowed from art history, is relatively limited and does not entirely fit the ephemeral nature of the ever-changing garden. The problem of too limited a vocabulary and too rigid style definitions in part results from the mistake of focusing on the garden as a finished product and neglecting its ongoing creative process. Thus, Honselaarsdijk's clearly distinguishable stylistic development expressed by two different layouts under Frederik Hendrik was generally overlooked: the first garden design may be described as the 'Italian classical' layout depicted on Van Berckerode's print, which by 1645 had developed into the 'French baroque' design dominated by the open expanse of a hippodrome-shaped parterre layout, shown in later seventeenth-century prints by Bega and Blooteling.

CONCLUSION

The tendency to focus on one genius designer-architect leads to various misconceptions regarding the layout of Dutch gardens in general and those of Honselaarsdijk and Ter Nieuburch in particular. One always assumed that André Mollet designed the Stadholder's gardens, because of his presence at the Dutch court and his design of the parterres of Honselaarsdijk. Close similarities between the Honselaarsdijk layout and Mollet's ideal plan in *Le Jardin de plaisir* (1652) would seem to confirm this assumption, yet Honselaarsdijk's basic layout, already completed at the time of Mollet's arrival in Holland (with the exception of the parterres), proved to have served as a model for Mollet's ideal garden plan – a fact acknowledged as much by Mollet himself in the introduction to his treatise. First discussed by Hopper, it shows that Dutch gardens contributed to French garden art. Besides, as more detailed investigation revealed, the first ideal plan printed in Mollet's book may also be directly related to one of the Stadholder's gardens, that of Ter Nieuburch, which further establishes important French-Dutch artistic relations at the time.

The design process of the Stadholder's architectural undertakings is very important, particularly in the building history of Ter Nieuburch, which can be followed by aligning a series of surviving drawings. One of these, here referred to as the 'French plan', is especially noteworthy, as it copied the Luxembourg palace and garden complex and superimposed its layout on the Dutch polderland. Documentary evidence shows that several other, toned-down versions were made for Ter Nieuburch, among them designs drawn by Jacob van Campen and one by the Stadholder himself. Given Mollet's presence at The Hague, as well as that of the French architect Simon de la Vallée, in the early 1630s, their involvement with the original design process of Ter Nieuburch seems likely. Be this as it may, the concurrent use of the Luxembourg garden plan as a model for another Dutch garden, near Bergen, is significant. Suggestions for the design of this garden were made by the renowned French scientist René Descartes, who, as one of Huygens's close friends and a member of the court's international learned élite, was personally responsible for ordering the necessary prints and drawings in Paris.

In spite of such international artistic exchanges, the accommodation of local features (flat, humid holmgrounds) and practical considerations (water drainage into canals), as well as existing traditions of land reclamation and subdivision (elongated strips of land and quadrature), remained at the centre of the design and layout of the Stadholder's gardens, to which 'classical Italian' ideals of proportion and dynamic early 'French baroque' solutions were carefully fitted. While the exact degree of the mutual influence of nature and art is difficult to ascertain, it can be confirmed here that the form and layout of the stadholderly gardens were dictated by the natural condition of Holland's delta land, rather than being solely the result of aesthetic considerations or architectural theory. The inclusion of this finding in a study can lead to different results. For example, the tripartite composition of the Honselaarsdijk and Noordeinde gardens, which were analysed in terms of classical thought on proportional harmony, in fact simply resulted from the natural conformation of the terrain. The need to weigh carefully artistic thought against topographical circumstances is also borne out by the differences between the 'plane geometry' of the Stadholder's gardens at The Hague and the 'verticality' of Prince Johan Maurits van Nassau-Siegen's Italianate terraced garden on the Springenberg at Cleves, both of which, despite stylistic discrepancies, were developed within the same artistic-humanist milieu.

Several of the Stadholder's gardens show a tendency towards a certain rigidity in their subdivision and enclosure and a lack of integration of the various parts laid out on separate 'islands' girded by canals. Again, such a strict layout reflects the mathematics of the Dutch landscape itself, presented in contemporary bird's-eye views as neatly patterned strips of grassland interspersed with villages, farms and estates and cut through by a network of waterways. Only at Ter Nieuburch and the Huis ten Bosch the buildings and gardens were fully integrated within a more unified design. Here, palace and garden were not separated by means of ditches and moats, as was the case in most of the older castle complexes (Honselaarsdijk, Buren, Zuylesteyn), where the integration with existing structures resulted in the division of building and garden.

Contrary to most of the actual garden layouts, contemporary prints and drawings by Pieter Post and Philips Vingboons show experimentation with diagonal lines and semicircular forms in garden design. This proves that the tendency towards rectilinearity typical of the Dutch garden was intentional, and that it was not the result of unfamiliarity with new, dynamic 'baroque' style principles, as alleged in the literature. Aspects such as the strict framework of canals and moats, the extensive tree-lined avenues and wide, natural views over the flat countryside are not only characteristic of Frederik Hendrik's garden layouts; they are part of the idiosyncrasies with which the 'Dutch garden' generally became associated. These very aspects were to influence garden layouts abroad, as exemplified by the courtly gardens in Sweden and the famous later seventeenth-century gardens of Herrenhausen at Hanover. More importantly, these layouts were preceded by the gardens of Oranienburg (near Berlin) and Oranienbaum (Wörlitz) laid out, respectively, by Frederik Hendrik's daughters Louise Henriette, Electress of Brandenburg, and Henriette Catharina, Princess of Anhalt-Dessau, who inherited their father's passion for garden architecture and sculpture. By attracting Dutch architects, gardeners and sculptors to their German courts, they not only carried Dutch garden architecture and ornamentation abroad but also assured the continuation of the Orange family's cultural-dynastic aspirations as expressed in the gardens' iconology.

The study of contemporary travel journals shows that, if the Stadholder's gardens were admired for their wide views, orderly plantations and collections of rare flowers, the actual palace structures and decorations were sometimes found to be relatively modest. Indeed, all things considered, the gardens laid out by the Stadholder, and Dutch gardens in general, express on a smaller scale and in more modest form the architectural and decorative features of contemporary Italian and French palace complexes. In this respect they fit well the Dutch poet Joost van den Vondel's dictum 'We're copying Rome in the small'. Most enlightening are Salomon de Bray's remarks in the introduction to his *Architectura moderna*. He points to Holland's swampy grounds, devoid of stone, and limited financial means to justify any want of grandeur or deviation from classical standards in its architecture.

Certain deviations from classical standards can indeed be recognized in the Stadholder's buildings and gardens. While particular 'conservative' architectural features are retained both in the palaces and in the gardens (fortress-like towers, bastion or donjon principles, separate garden rooms or islands, crenellated garden walls, knot-design parterres), these traits should not necessarily be criticized as being 'regressive', as the literature would have it; they should be studied from the viewpoint of current architectural notions and contemporary methods of restoration, of which Zuylesteyn is a good example. Remarkably, similar 'medieval' features are typical of Vredeman de Vries's and Furttenbach's garden-architectural designs, confirming the continued popularity of traditional fortress architecture. Some of these traditional features in the Stadholder's palaces and gardens are also due to the patron's own predilection for a specific architectural style and form (castle island, moats), in which castle and garden in their form of the medieval 'keep' were seen as a 'Batavian stronghold', involving associations with a heroic, feudal past. Moreover, as de

Bray had mentioned, financial considerations had to be kept in mind when examining the final design of palace and garden; Huygens admitted as much in his letter to Rubens describing the house at The Hague. Ter Nieuburch's monumental first design proposal, based on the Luxembourg palace and garden, was decidedly toned down in order to fit the topographical situation, but probably also because of the high cost of laying out such a garden. In fact, a surge for building and planting often occurred after new funds were available out of the treasures of the *zeeprijzen*, or sea prizes, obtained through piracy.

Visual evidence and the records of payment clearly show that tree and plant cultivation took up a large part of the gardens' layout, expressing the general aspect of *utile dulci*, the useful combined with the pleasurable. Throughout the centuries the Stadholder's garden supplied vegetables and fruit for the kitchen, as well as flowers for decorative purposes which were valued for their rarity. All plants are clearly marked in the account books, printed in the Appendix. The importance of silviculture, related to Calvinist religious-philosophical thought, appears from the poetry of Jacob Cats and Constantijn Huygens, which describes land reclamation in biblical terms as the re-creation of Paradise. Concurrent with this religious undertone, reclaiming the land and tending the orchard on Dutch territory also took on a political meaning. In this light, Cats's remarks admonishing the Stadholder to take his responsibilities as 'Praeceptor Hollandiae' by becoming at once gardener and statesman acquire their full meaning.

In addition to general design issues, the ornamentation of the Stadholder's gardens, which was not merely incidental to the layout but constituted an essential part of its overall visual effect, function and meaning, deserves detailed attention. The gardens' ornamentation was instrumental in unifying building and garden and to a large extent could be analysed in the light of the interior decoration of the palace, which it enhanced. Significantly, the well-known Southern Netherlandish sculptors Artus Quellinus, François Du Quesnoy and François Dieussart were directly involved in sculptural works for the Stadholder's gardens, while other statues were shipped from the Southern Netherlands or France. The presence of monumental statues was the more remarkable because stone and marble had to be shipped from abroad at great cost and effort. From a stylistic point of view, the ornamentation of the Stadholder's gardens varied: the grottoes decorated with pumice-stone, coral and mechanical devices to create a mysterious bizarreness belonged to the world of late-sixteenth-century Netherlandish art, while the large-scale *parterres de broderie* derived from current French decorative practice. The sculptural decoration, finally, was classical, in some cases actually stemming from Roman antiquity. The particular classicizing style of the Stadholder's statues, later expressed by the German garden sculpture of the Princesses of Orange, defies exact categorization. Until more detailed research of Dutch court sculpture produces a more appropriate terminology, the Stadholder's garden statues, from the larger gods and goddesses to the smaller *kinderkens*, are perhaps best described as being of a charming, somewhat robust classicism, typical in general of stylistic trends in sculpting at mid-seventeenth-century Northern European courts.

The celebration of the patron, his virtues and those of his family and his reign is the theme which permeates the decorative programme of these gardens. As such, the garden iconography adheres to age-old traditions in garden art and ornamentation glorifying the patron. The symbolism of the Stadholder's reign finds its expression above all in the recurring combined monogram HAVO of (Frederik) Henry and Amalia of Orange. The figures of the struggling Hercules and the Dutch Lion in the parterres of Honselaarsdijk, the river gods representing the Rhine and Maas, and the Minerva statue at Ter Nieuburch also symbolize the Stadholder's role as warrior and Maecenas, as they were set within the great universal cycles of nature and time.

The impact of the Stadholder's garden design and ornamentation on contemporary and later garden architecture was considerable. All in all it may be said that the garden-artistic activities under Frederik Hendrik and Amalia prepared the way for garden design during the reign of their grandson William III. Increased inspiration by French garden architecture would be the core from which Dutch garden architecture developed during Frederik Hendrik's later building activities from the third decade of the century onward. Certain features, such as that of the medieval 'donjon', the rectilinear framework of canals and the semicircular shape of the 'hippodrome' – first introduced in Frederik Hendrik's gardens – would dictate the basic outline and arrangement of Dutch gardens throughout the seventeenth and early eighteenth centuries (Clingendael, Heemstede, Sion, Zeist). The iconology of the Stadholder's garden also influenced later garden ornamentation. Thus the ornamentation of the gardens of Frederik Hendrik's grandson William III at Het Loo would again evolve round the symbolism of Hercules set within the universal cycles of nature and time, held together by the two great fountains carrying the earthly and heavenly spheres. Moreover, at Het Loo, the river gods were present once again, with their specific reference to the territory ruled over and defended by the Prince of Orange. References to the House of Orange and its virtues can also be found in other gardens during the reign of William III, including those of Sorgvliet, laid out by his adviser Hans Willem Bentinck. At Sorgvliet the well-known simile of Holland as a garden defended by the Princes of Orange was expressed not only in stone monuments glorifying the Princes' bravery but also in the very presence of a statue of Hercules and Cacus, featured so prominently in the Honselaarsdijk garden.

The revival of Roman antiquity in the Stadholder's gardens and the wish to evoke a heroic past are apparent in the placing of busts of the twelve Roman Emperors (Honselaarsdijk, Ter Nieuburch) and of classical vases (the urns in the Buitenhof garden) and antique statues or copies of them (represented in Jan van der Heyden's paintings of the Huis ten Bosch, for example) in most of the Stadholder's gardens. Even though clear references to these statues and vases are made in contemporary accounts, in later descriptions (Jacob de Hennin) and in the inventories of the Stadholder's palaces and gardens, further investigation is necessary to complete the research in this area. Future studies should also concentrate on painted objects and perspectives in gardens, a topic which has received little attention, yet has important implications for the role of the garden as a setting for other artistic media. In this context it should be mentioned that in Frederik Hendrik's time even Rubens was involved in the decoration of a garden, having painted the walls of a gallery surrounding the Habsburg garden in Brussels with Belgium-Dutch battle scenes. Of particular interest is Rubens's depiction of Mars being expelled by the Archduchess Isabella, personifying Peace, which was very much in the spirit of a central scene soon to be painted in the great hall of the Huis ten Bosch.[1] It was the exchange between Rubens and Huygens, both foremost proponents of the new, classically-inspired architecture at the courts of the Spanish Habsburgs and the Prince of Orange, respectively, which demonstrated continued cultural ties between the Southern and Northern Netherlands, despite religious-political differences and territorial borderlines.

The iconography of War and Peace expressed in the Stadholder's gardens and heralded by the statues of Mars and Venus flanking the entrance of Honselaarsdijk has a long history in gardens and their ornamentation, be it in sculpted or painted form. In its celebration of the Stadholder, his victories and good government, and the grandeur of the Orange family, the great hall of the Huis ten Bosch continued the decoration of the galleries at Honselaarsdijk, Ter Nieuburch and Buren, where depictions of the European reigning houses, their palaces and most important victories were hung on the walls. Thus direct lines can be drawn between the interior and exterior decoration of the Stadholder's palace complexes, both in form and content, the garden decoration being an appropriate extension of the palace's inner decorative programme, which centres on the good reign of the Stadholder.

The image of the garden as the realm of Peace finds its expression in the double circle, which, representing the Earthly and Heavenly spheres and/or the two Halves of the World, symbolized at the same time the macro- and microcosmoi and the two continents. A key to the deeper meaning of these circles in the Stadholder's gardens with reference to the owner is offered by relating this cosmological imagery to a print in Thibault's treatise on the martial arts dedicated to Prince Maurits, in which the soldier's perfect stance within the confines of a mystical circle is explained.

It is at this point, when considering the double circle with its deeper cosmological and metaphysical meaning, that connections can be drawn between the Stadholder's and other European gardens. In Denmark, notably in the gardens laid out by Tycho Brahe on the island of Hveen (c. 1590), in England in the gardens of Twickenham park (c. 1610) and in Germany in Salomon de Caus's garden at Heidelberg (1615-20), the geometrical form of the circle with cosmological overtones can be recognized. Furthermore, these gardens, like those of the Stadholder, continued the sixteenth-century tradition of the garden as a *rariteitenkabinet*, or collection of curiosities, full of exotic objects and strange mechanical devices, best exemplified by Rudolf II's gardens at Prague and Henri IV's at Saint-Germain-en-Laye. It can thus be said that Frederik Hendrik shared the desire, at the same time expressed at other Northern European courts – such as those of James I and Charles I of England, Friedrich V Elector Palatine and Christian IV of Denmark – to make their palaces and gardens into real 'microcosmoi', by combining Nature, the Arts and Science.

NOTES

INTRODUCTION

1 Jacob Cats's verse, quoted in Van der Groen, *Nederlandtsen Hovenier*. Translated from the Dutch by the author. The original Dutch text is as follows:
> Al wat men Holland noemt en zijn maar weynigh steden
> En Hollants vrienden selfs en zijn maer weynigh Leden
> En al van kleyn begrijp, maer des al niet te min,
> Daer schuylen over al verscheyde wonders in
> Soo wie maer eens betreet den ringh van Hollants kusten;
> Die vint een schoon Priëel van alderhande lusten:
> Al wat den hemel send, of uyt der aerden groeyt,
> Dat komt hier met de zee ter haven ingevloeyt.
> Godt is gelijk een son, die duysent gulde stralen,
> Laet op dees kleynen Thuyn geduerigh nederdalen!
> Wat oyt aen boomen hingh, of op de velde stont,
> Dat komt hier aen het volk gevallen in den mont.

2 A good example of such symbolic, visual imagery is provided by the title-page of *Respublica Hollandiae et Urbes* by Hugo de Groot (Hugo Grotius), showing a rampant lion protecting an enclosed garden which symbolizes Holland itself, appropriately surmounted by Stadholder Frederik Hendrik's coat of arms and framed by garlands with oranges. See also Hunt in Maccubbin and Hamilton-Phillips, *Age of William and Mary*, pp. 234-243. Compare Schama, *Embarrassment of Riches*, pp. 69-70, on patriotic images.

3 For further reading see Schama, *Embarrassment of Riches*, pp. 24-27, on moral geography and the primal Dutch experience of the struggle to survive rising waters.

4 Mountague, *Delights of Holland*, p. 70. See also de Jong, *Natuur en kunst*, p. 35.

5 Compare Fremantle, *Baroque Town Hall*, p. 5, describing Holland as a delta country won by its inhabitants fencing sea and inland waterways.

6 Moneys received from piracy are referred to in the account books of the Nassau Domains as 'Zeeprinsen' or 'Zeeprijsen'. See Slothouwer, *Paleizen*, p. 6.

7 For further reading see de Jong, *Natuur en kunst*, pp. 17-18.

8 Pieter Post in a letter to L. Buysero, dated 12 July 1644: 'De Timmeringh was naer de antijckse of Romeijnse manier.' Letter published by Lunsingh Scheurleer in Van Deursen et al., *Veelzijdigheid als levensvorm*, p. 48. Compare Terwen and Ottenheym, *Pieter Post*, p. 35.

9 Clear examples of the role of the garden as an open-air museum have recently been given by de Jong, *Natuur en kunst*, pp. 204-211, independently of my own studies in this area. For further reading see also Bergvelt and Kistemaker, *Wereld binnen handbereik*. Page 120 refers to the Stadholder's collection of paintings, pp. 34 and 269 describe his interest in antiquities, mentioning how Frederik Hendrik and his entourage, including Huygens, were the first visitors to Johannes Smetius's collection of antiquities in 1633. These antique objects were uncovered in Nijmegen, which was considered the capital of the Batavians, according to Tacitus. The Stadholder also visited the world-famous gardens and collection of *naturalia* and *artificia* in Bernardus Paludanus's estate at Enkhuizen; see ibid., p. 265.

10 Compare Luijten et al., *Dawn of the Golden Age*, pp. 112-113.

11 This terminology was used to describe the garden of Sorgvliet laid out by Hans Willem Bentinck, the decoration of which glorified the House of Orange, in particular William III's military and artistic deeds. See Sellers in Hunt, *Dutch Garden*, here especially p. 129. For further reading on the garden as a Landscape of War and Peace see Warnke, *Political Landscape*.

12 *Tuinkunst. Nederlands jaarboek voor de geschiedenis van tuin- en landschapsarchitectuur.*

13 Hopper's 'André Mollet' and Van Pelt's 'Man and Cosmos', which for the first time shed light on the application of classical theory in Dutch gardens. Another important stimulus to rethinking Dutch gardens and architecture is the recent publication of two monographs on Dutch seventeenth-century architects – Terwen and Ottenheym, *Pieter Post*, and Huisken et al., *Jacob van Campen*, which show the development of seventeenth-century architecture and the classical ideal at the Stadholder's court.

14 The articles published in Hunt, *Dutch Garden*, have made a significant contribution to furthering our knowledge of the Dutch garden. While these articles concentrate principally on the period of William and Mary, especially Hunt's ' "But who does not know what a Dutch Garden is", The Dutch Garden in the English Imagination', pp. 175-206, must be mentioned, as it touches on general problems of how to analyse and define gardens. Furthermore, various sections in de Jong's book *Natuur en kunst*, while concentrating primarily on gardens in the latter part of the century, also provide a most valuable perspective of seventeenth-century garden styles and iconography in general, demonstrating the continuation of certain practices and traditions originating from the court of Frederik Hendrik. Important aspects of Dutch seventeenth-century gardens and garden culture are also discussed in de Jong and Dominicus-van Soest, *Aardse paradijzen*, published in connection with an exhibition on Dutch gardens in the Noordbrabants Museum, 's-Hertogenbosch, and the Frans Halsmuseum, Haarlem.

15 Compare the remarks in Huisken et al., *Jacob van Campen*, p. 7.

16 Compare also Hopper in Jellicoe et al., *Oxford Companion to Gardens*, p. 392. For new publications on the topic of western-style influence on Eastern and Central European architecture, see for

instance Bracker, *Bauen nach der Natur*. In this book the influence of Dutch classicist architecture on the art and architecture of Germany and Poland is discussed. Important remarks can also be found in Kaufmann, *Court, Cloister and City*, pp. 248-249, describing the influence of Dutch, French and Italian classical architecture in Poland and, on pp. 280-281, general Flemish-Dutch artistic leadership in seventeenth-century Central European architecture and sculpture.

17 For a clear overview of the main archival sources consulted in the Algemeen Rijksarchief during this research see Van Hoof et al., *Archieven van de Nassause Domeinraad*, especially pp. 74-75, Register van Ordonnanties, and Rekeningen van de Thesaurier en Rentmeester-Generaal (List of Commissions, and Accounts of the Comptroller and Estate Steward), 1620-65. Consult also the pages with entries for each estate, arranged by region.

18 A portrait of Frederik Hendrik surrounded by a garland of blossoming orange branches, held together by his heraldic device and the emblem bestowed on him by the Knights of the Order of the Garter, a ribbon with the epigram 'Honi soit qvi mal y pense'. In the top corners the Stadholder's personal motto 'Patriaeque Patrique' can be found. This print, combined with a poem describing Frederik Hendrik's virtues and military victories, is published in Scriverius, *Beschrijvinge van Holland, Zeeland & Vriesland*, p. 585.

19 See Hopper, *Journal of Garden History*, II, 1 (1982), p. 33.

20 For collecting and the ideal of the complete gentleman as described by Francis Bacon in his *Gesta Grayorum*, see Kenseth, *Age of the Marvelous*, p. 9. Compare also Filipczak, *Picturing Art*, p. 93.

21 Cats, *Hof-gedachten*, pp. 14-15:
Prince Hendrick, zynd een vorst tot planten seer genegen
Quam dickmael hier besien des Heeren goede segen
Sijn Hoogheyt was verstelt, als hy by wylen vont,
Dat gul en weligh hout hier op gewassen stont.
Ick seyd' hem, machtig Vorst, ghy koopt verscheyde landen,
En dat tot hoogen prijs, en krijgt maer dorre zanden.
En maeckt'se tot een bosch, en uyt verachte stof
Verheft een schoon prieel, of wel een lustigh hof.
Dit is recht Princen werck, en 'tsal oock Hollandt baten
En ghy staet hoogen lof hierover na te laten. ...
Het sou niet dienstigh syn slechts voor n mensch alleen,
Maer 't sou aen 't Vaderlandt oock baten in 't gemeen.

22 See for a good example of the change of desolate wilderness into real paradise Johan Maurits van Nassau-Siegen's efforts in Brazil in 1639, as described by Diedenhofen in Van den Boogaart, *Johan Maurits van Nassau-Siegen*, pp. 197-236, especially p. 197.

23 The expression *Architectura Recreationis*, or Architecture of Resurgence, derives from the title of one of Furttenbach's works on garden architecture described in Dietzel, *Furttenbachs Gartenentwürfe*, p. 16, and will be further explained in chapter IV.

24 Huygens's house on the Plein, or central plaza, in The Hague, situated across from the Mauritshuis. The house was designed by Huygens himself, assisted by Jacob van Campen. See also Van der Haagen, *Jaarboek Die Haghe* (1928-29), pp. 6-39. See also Kamphuis, *Oud Holland*, 77 (1962), pp. 151-180.

25 Worp, *Briefwisseling*, II, RGP 19, letter 2109, Constantijn Huygens to Amalia of Orange, dated 4 June 1639. The text quoted here is only partly copied by Worp; for a complete quotation see Slothouwer, *Paleizen*, p. 348.

26 Defined in Rosenberg et al., *Dutch Art and Architecture*, p. 393, as a 'momentous style transitional to classicism'. In Slothouwer, *Paleizen*, pp. 2, 3 and 365, as 'Classic Baroque' or even 'Frederik Hendrik style'. The development of architecture in Holland at the time and the problem of style definitions will be discussed in detail later in the book.

27 Rosenberg et al., *Dutch Art and Architecture*, pp. 390-395. See also Slothouwer, *Paleizen*, introduction, pp. 1-6.

28 Slothouwer, *Paleizen*, preface, p. V.

29 Rosenberg et al., *Dutch Art and Architecture*, pp. 383-390.

30 Slothouwer, *Paleizen*, pp. 3-4.

31 Friedrich V's mother was Louise Juliana of Nassau, the daughter of William the Silent. Thus, Frederik Hendrik was Friedrich V's uncle.

32 Slothouwer, *Paleizen*, p. 6. See also Blok, *Frederik Hendrik*, pp. 62, 181-183 and 189-191, concerning life at the court of The Hague with the Palatine family. Also Van Sypestein, *Hof van Bohemen*. See especially the exhibition catalogues celebrating court life and patronage during the reign of Frederik Hendrik and Amalia (Keblusek and Zijlmans, *Vorstelijk vertoon*, and Van der Ploeg et al., *Vorstelijk verzameld*).

33 See Hopper in Jellicoe et al., *Oxford Companion to Gardens*, p. 391. For further reading on the development of country-house poetry and culture in general within the environment of the Dutch court see de Vries in Hunt, *Dutch Garden*, p. 81 and notes.

34 The Stadholder's own zoological collection and menagerie with exotic animals at Honselaarsdijk were well known; they were mentioned in Tulp, *Drie Boecken*. The Stadholder's shells, stones and corals, exhibited in his garden grottoes, also belong to the realm of collecting exotic rarities. See Bergvelt and Kistemaker, *Wereld binnen handbereik*, pp. 9 and 44. Furthermore, Holland's premier botanical and medical gardens were those laid out under the auspices of the Stadholder at Breda. The inaugural speech at the opening of the gardens in 1647 refers to the Stadholder as a plant collector and exponent of a long tradition of 'Great Men' with botanical interests. The speech was given by the supervisor of the Medical Gardens, Johan Brosterhuizen, one of Europe's foremost botanical cognoscenti. He was also a close friend of Huygens and the Stadholder, as the Huygens correspondence indicates; see chapter IV. See also de Jong, *Natuur en kunst*, pp. 47-48.

35 See cat. no. 139, in Hunt and de Jong, *Anglo-Dutch Garden*, pp. 288-289. Attributed to Stephanus Cousyns (?-1709), the album depicts a plant collection as we could expect it to have grown at Honselaarsdijk by the mid-century (with the exception of a few species introduced later). However, the rare plants shown here came from the Leeuwenhorst estate at Noordwijkerhout, acquired by the Stadholder's grandson William III in 1692. The album is kept in the Biblioteca Nazionale, Florence.

CHAPTER I

1 Also spelled Hontsholredijk, Honselerdijk, Honselerdijk or Honsholredyck. The spelling varies over the centuries and per individual. In this text I have followed the modern, general spelling of Honselaarsdijk, also used by Morren, *Honselaarsdijk*, pp. 1-5, for the history of the name and its early medieval origin. Slothouwer writes 'Honselaarsdyk'; Bienfait, *Oude Hollandsche tuinen*, 'Honselaersdijk'. Other variations also occur today, however. The name is derived from 'Hundeshel', 'Huntsel' or 'Hontsolerdike', a small hamlet on the spot, after which the estate was first called 'Hontsele' and the castle 'Hontshol'.

2 Floris Jacobsz van der Sallem, after 1586, and his son Pieter Florisz, after 1635, were the official 'land-measurers' (*landmeters*), in modern terms cartographers, of the Dike Reeves and Polder Office (Hoogheemraadschap) of Delfland, the polder area in which Honselaarsdijk is situated. Their name is also spelled 'van der Salm'. The map is kept in the Archives of the Hoogheemraadschap Delfland at Delft, inv. no. OAD 704.

3 The map by Cruquius (also spelled Kruikius) is part of a series of printed plans originally published in 1712 and recently republished in facsimile, entitled *Kaartboek van het Hoogheemraadschap van Delfland* (Alphen aan den Rijn: Canaletto, 1981). The originals are kept in the Collectie Bodel Nijenhuis (CBN), the Leiden University Library and the Municipal Archives of The Hague (GAH), topographical department. The coloured version of this map was made by Cornelis Koster after Cruquius's 1712 series and published in 1750 by Isaac Tirion; it is kept in the Rijksprentenkabinet, Rijksmuseum, Amsterdam (RPK).

4 According to the Stadholder's gardener-in-chief, Jan van der Groen, it took two hours to travel from The Hague to Honselaarsdijk. See Van der Groen, *Nederlandtsen Hovenier*. This book was republished under the same title in facsimile, augmented with a commentary and list of plants, by C.S. Oldenburger-Ebbers and D.O. Wijnands, respectively. See p. 22.

5 The deed was signed 16 April 1612 and is printed in a postscriptum by Frederiks in Fruin, 'Het Ambacht van Naaldwijk', *Bijdragen voor Vaderlandsche Geschiedenis*. See also Morren, *Honselaarsdijk*, pp. 9-11. The buyer would pay a sum of 360,000 guilders for the Seigniories of Naaldwijk, Honsholredijk, Wateringen and the Honderland with all *appendentien ende dependentien* (appendants and dependencies).

6 'Het heerlyck huys off sloth van Honsholredijck met sijn grachten, cingelen, plantagen, neerhoff, boomgaerden, bloemen, cruythoff, duyfhuijs ende visscherije … jaarlijks 500 ar. opbrengende.' The document is kept in the KHA; it is entitled 'Staet in 't corte van 'tgeene volgen soude de heerycheijt van Honsholredyck ende Wateringen'. See also Morren, *Honselaarsdijk*, p. 10, note 1.

7 For the early medieval history of this area and the castle see

Morren, *Honselaarsdijk*, p. 1. Since the thirteenth century the old castle was one of the homes of the Lords of Naaldwijk.

8   Morren, *Honselaarsdijk*, p. 5.

9   The estate was confiscated because of Aremberg's siding with the Spanish. See Morren, *Honselaarsdijk*, p. 7.

10 In 1609, as a consequence of the Twelve Years' Truce, Honselaarsdijk was restored to the Aremberg family, who sold the property to Frederik Hendrik in 1612.

11 Morren, *Honselaarsdijk*, pp. 8-9.

12 GAL, inv. no. 460, fol. 97. See also Morren, *Honselaarsdijk*, p. 4, with a detail of this map.

13 Morren, *Honselaarsdijk*, p. 4. Slothouwer, *Paleizen*, p. 41, calls the flanking towers octagonal, even though it is difficult to recognize this shape in the vague depiction of the map.

14 Balthasars, *Kaarten*.

15 Compare also Meischke and Ottenheym, *Jaarboek Monumentenzorg 1992*, pp. 118-119.

16 GAN, *Kaartboek van Naaldwijk* details, fols. 1 and 34. Using clear arguments, the editors dated this work about 1620; see Kok, *Kaartboek*, pp. 3ff.).

17 Written notes belonging to these series of maps indicate that already in 1618 the house and orchard of Honselaarsdijk were enlarged: '… Het huijs ende Boomgaert van Honsholredijk is inden Jare sestienhondert achtien de plantinge vergroot …' See Kok, *Kaartboek*, fol. 25. Compare also Meischke and Ottenheym, *Jaarboek Monumentenzorg 1992*, pp. 118-119.

18 ARA, NDR, inv. no. 6691 [old no. NDR, Eerste Afdeling, Vervolg, no 1475], map fol. xiiii [14], detail of upper half of folio. Though this particular sheet of paper with the map of Honselaarsdijk is not signed or dated, a similar plan, also bound in this map book, showing the same situation and in all aspects related to this plan, is signed Floris Jacobsz and dated 1615. See also Hopper, *Bulletin KNOB*, 3-4 (1983), p. 108, who first discovered the early date of this and several other maps in the ARA. Compare also Hopper, *Journal of Garden History*, II, 1 (1982), pp. 31 and 33.

19 For further information about the various building campaigns see Terwen and Ottenheym, *Pieter Post*, pp. 46-56.

20 ARA, map department, VTH 3344 C. Scale on drawing indicated as 14 Rijnlandse roeden. The style of this drawing and comparisons with documentary evidence indicate a date of circa 1630-35.

21 GAH, topographical department, Honselaarsrdijk, groot 1. The exact date of Van Berckerode's print remains a point of conjecture, but I believe it was 1639. In any case, a *terminus post quem* of 1638 seems to be applicable, the year in which the *maillebaan* was completed, here visible along the main entrance avenue. A *terminus ante quem* of 1639-40 can be put forward, the year in which large statues were set in the garden to complete its decoration, which cannot be found in the print yet.

22 Pieter Nootman wrote many pieces for the Amsterdam and The Hague Chambers of Rhetoric, several of which were performed by the theatre group Young Batavians. Most of his dramas and polemic poetry centred on the heroic deeds of the House of Orange, of which he was a strong supporter. His works are part of a long line of political writings on the early history of Holland or 'Batavia', which was a popular genre from the late sixteenth century onward and included well-known works such as Scriverius's *Beschrijvinghe van out Batavien*.

23 De Jong and Dominicus-van Soest, *Aardse paradijzen*, pp. 27 and 55. For further reading on cartography and perspective views see pp. 30-31 and 42-58. Compare also Alpers in Woodward, *Art and Cartography*, pp. 51-97.

24 De la Serre, *Histoire de l'Entrée*, pages not numbered.

25 Ibid.: 'Durant le temps que la Reyne y sejourna, Elle le passa doucement, soit en l'entretien ordinaire de son Altesse, dont l'esprit et l'humeur sont également admirables, soit dans le nouveau divertissement des promenades que sa Majesté faisoit souvent en particullier, suivie seullement de ses Dames et Filles d'honneur, dans les beaux Jardins et le grand Parc de cette superbe Maison; et comme tous les objects champestres qui pouvoient contenter l'esprit par les yeux, s'y trouvoient en abondance; la Reyne ne s'y ennuyoit jamais.'

26 The measure used in this polder area of Holland was the Rijnlandse roede, equalling 3.7674, or 3.77, metres. The scale visible in Van Berckerode's print is in Rijnlandse roeden.

27 Mentioned by de la Serre in his description of Honselaarsdijk, quoted above.

28 The completion of this avenue can be confirmed by the accounts at the time: ARA, NDR, inv. no. 1036 [old no. 775], fol. 155vo (*not* mentioned in Slothouwer): '… met den voorn. Catshuijsen gedaen aenden selven vergoet de somme van tien duijsent drie hondert vijff ende vijfftich ponden acht schellingen artois die d'selve bij sloote van reeckeninge vande nieuwe laen bij Sijnne Vorst. Gen. in de jaeren 1625 & 1626 voor den huijse van Honsholredijck doen maecken te boven gecomen is, als meer uijtgegeven dan ontfangen hebbende …' The essence of this entry translated into English reads: '… closing of the account of the new avenue commissioned by His Highness in the years 1625 & 1626 to be made in front of the house of Honsholredijck [sic] … 10.355:8:0.' It should be noted that the currency used in Holland at the time is the *pond artois*, the Flemish pound, which equalled about six Dutch florins or Carolus guldens. See Lessing, *Woordenboek*, vol. 12, s.v. Pond Artoys.

29 ARA, NDR, inv. no. 6691 [old no. NDR, Eerste Afdeling, Vervolg no. 1475], map fol. xxii [22], detail. See Hopper, *Bulletin KNOB*, 3-4 (1983), pp. 107-108.

30 Ibid., p. 109.

31 ARA, map department, VTH 2360. On the strength of stylistic

32 Reconstruction drawing by the author.
33 The book has recently been republished with a commentary by D. Thomson.
34 The accessibility of the old stronghold by means of a bridge on the rear or garden side towards the north is visible on Floris Balthasars's map of Delfland of 1611 and on several other maps in the *Kaartboek van Naaldwijk*.
35 Slothouwer, *Paleizen*, p. 367.
36 See remarks made about these towers in Morren, *Honselaarsdijk*, p. 11, and Slothouwer, *Paleizen*, p. 41.
37 See ARA, NDR, inv. no. 1039 [old no. 778], fol. 213vo, and inv. no. 1040 [old no. 779], fol. 211. See also Slothouwer, *Paleizen*, pp. 261-262.
38 ARA, NDR, inv. no. 6691 [old no. NDR, Eerste Afdeling, Vervolg no. 1475], map fol. lxiiii [64].
39 Worp, *Briefwisseling*, II, RGP 19, letter 1264, Constantijn Huygens to David de Wilhem, dated 23 October 1635. See Slothouwer, *Paleizen*, p. 342: '… De Prins is er ontevreden over, dat Honselaersdijk van 't jaar nog niet gereed komt.'
40 Worp, *Briefwisseling*, II, RGP 19, letter 1485, Constantijn Huygens to David de Wilhem, dated 17 October 1636: 'Zorg goed voor het bebouwen van den grond te Honselaersdijk; de Prins vindt het erg, dat er vorig jaar geen zorg voor is gedragen.'
41 Leiden University Library, Department of Western Manuscripts, Hug. 37. Letter written by David de Wilhem to Constantijn Huygens, dated 23 November 1636. Only in part in Worp, *Briefwisseling*, II, RGP 19, letter 1493.
42 For Post's designs to connect the annexe buildings with the main palace by means of long hallways see Slothouwer, *Paleizen*, pp. 61-64.
43 For the history of Pieter Post's 1646 building plans see Terwen in Van den Berg et al., *De stenen droom*, pp. 298-306.
44 ARA, map department, NADO 4 sheet 1, Plan by Pieter Post (not signed or dated), showing the old situation to the right and the new one to the left. Also published by Slothouwer, *Paleizen*, p. 65 and, with a reconstruction drawing (in which the front galleries with octagonal towers are rendered too short), p. 69, fig. 22.
45 For excellent reconstruction drawings of the built and unbuilt Honselaarsdijk palace see Meischke's text and illustrations in Morren, *Honselaarsdijk*, pp. 148-185.
46 The description of similar bath apartments is given by the Swedish architect Nicodemus Tessin in Siren, *Nicodemus Tessin Studieresor*, p. 76. Tessin mentioned in his travel journal that Honselaarsdijk's bath apartments could be compared with those built by Hans Willem Bentinck at Sorgvliet, containing marble seats in the corners of the lowered bathing pool. At Sorgvliet two side-pools provided hot and cold water, following classical Roman prototypes (*caldarium* and *tepidarium*). A clear description of the Roman-style baths at Sorgvliet, comprising the bath and two adjacent cabinets or *guarderobes*, is offered by the *Bentinck Inventory*, dated 1710, in the GAH, Notarieel Protocol no. 687, fols. 503-527, which will be published in a separate study. The inventory of the Sorgvliet estate (which follows that of the House on the Voorhout at The Hague), especially fol. 520 'in de Badkamer', describes the rich interior decoration of the bath apartments, with paintings, mirrors, chandeliers, couches and lacquered cabinets. Unfortunately no detailed description of the further interior decoration of the baths in the annexe buildings at Honselaarsdijk is given.
47 ARA, map department, NADO 4 sheet 2, GF 87336, attributed to Pieter Post. Dated in the upper left-hand corner 12 August 1646. For the other related design see chapter V, fig. 131. Compare also Terwen and Ottenheym, *Pieter Post*, p. 53.
48 Terwen in Van den Berg et al., *De stenen droom*, p. 301.
49 The capture of this Portuguese ship's silver treasure by the Dutch captain Piet Hein occurred in 1628, shortly before major land acquisitions and further garden extensions and adornments would be undertaken. From that date onward, regular mention is made of payments to be covered by funds from the 'sea prices' ('te betaelen uijt de penningen vande Zeeprijsen').
50 Worp, *Briefwisseling*, II, RGP 19, letter 1254, David de Wilhem to Constantijn Huygens, dated 6 October 1635. Only partly published by Worp.
51 Siren, *Nicodemus Tessin Studieresor*, p. 74.
52 Page 7. See for further consideration of de Bray's remarks chapter IV.
53 Of special interest in this context is the remark by the English traveller Sir William Brereton about the diminished height of one of the Stadholder's palaces, Ter Nieuburch: '… this house was intended a story higher, but that the foundation would not admit it. It is most proportioned in length.' See Brereton, *Travels in Holland*, p. 32. For a further discussion of Brereton's travel journal see the next chapter.
54 ARA, map department, VTH 2363/1 and 2363/14 (detail left).
55 See also Slothouwer, *Paleizen*, p. 268.
56 ARA, NDR, inv. nos. 6595, 6596, 6597 and 6602-6605ff. [old nos. NDR FOLIO, 1213, 1225, 1246-1256 and 1266-1272ff.].
57 ARA, NDR, inv. no. 992 [old no. 735], fols. 51, 52 and 59, all contain references to Pieter Florisz van der Sallem's survey work and maps.
58 Worp, *Briefwisseling*, II, RGP 19, p. 114, note 7. Simon van Catshuysen is mentioned as *kastelein*, or castellan, and *rentmeester*, meaning steward or estate manager.
59 Ibid., II, RGP 19, p. 252, note 6. Johan 'sHerwouters was comptroller of the 'Kamer van onzen Rade ende Rekeninge' (Chamber of our Council and Treasury) and in 1648 became

Amalia of Orange's Treasurer General.

60 Ibid., III, RGP 21, letter 2491, Constantijn Huygens to Amalia of Orange, dated 19 August 1640 (incomplete). A complete version is published in Slothouwer, *Paleizen*, pp. 348-349.

61 ARA, NDR, inv. no. 8118 [old no. 1190], no. V, dated 20 June 1646.

62 ARA, map department, VTH 2362. Probably drawn by Pieter Florisz van der Sallem.

63 ARA, map department, VTH 2363/9

64 The drawings for these extensions of the lower court area are mentioned in the accounts as being made in 1639-40. See ARA, NDR, inv. no. 992 [old no. 735], fol. 376, dated 21 March 1640. See also Slothouwer, *Paleizen*, p. 60.

65 ARA, NDR, inv. no. 992 [old no. 735], fols. 317, 337 and 368. Compare the entries in the accounts describing payments to respectively Floris Jacobsz and his son Pieter Florisz van der Sallem, who assisted his father in later years and officially took over his job as a land-surveyor and map-maker in 1635. See also *Kaartboek van Naaldwijk*, p. 6.

66 Worp, *Briefwisseling*, III, RGP 21, letter 3021, Constantijn Huygens to Amalia of Orange, dated 12 June 1642.

67 Ibid., II, RGP 19, letter 1260, David de Wilhem to Constantijn Huygens, dated 16 October 1635: '… par ordre de Madame la Princesse, Pierre d'Espaigns qui sera le congierge a Ryswyck …'

68 Drossaers and Lunsingh Scheurleer, *Inventarissen*, I, RGP 147, p. 239.

69 Hopper, *Journal of Garden History*, II, 1 (1982), p. 33.

70 Simon de la Vallée is also called Jacques de la Vallée. See Slothouwer, *Paleizen*, p. 367, and compare the account in the ARA, NDR, inv. no. 1042 [old no. 781], fol. 244vo: '… Jaques [sic] de la Vallée architect'. For further literature see also Nordberg, *De La Vallée*, pp. 67ff.

71 Simon de la Vallée may also have been responsible for important changes involving the exterior of Honselaarsdijk, namely the form and terracing of the open arcade on the garden façade as well as the changing of the semicircular forecourt into a more monumental square court. For de la Vallée's work in the interior, particularly the staircase, see Slothouwer, *Paleizen*, pp. 54-55. Compare also Meischke, *Nederlands Kunsthistorisch Jaarboek*, 31 (1980), pp. 86-103.

72 Hopper, *Journal of Garden History*, II, 1 (1982), p. 32, and *Bulletin KNOB*, 3-4 (1983), p. 105.

73 In recent literature the old mistake is continued and Honselaarsdijk and Ter Nieuburch are attributed to Mollet; see Goossens in Huisken et al., *Jacob van Campen*, p. 225.

74 Slothouwer, *Paleizen*, p. 367. Slothouwer is not referring to François but to André, son of Claude. Why Slothouwer used the name François is not clear, for none of André's brothers carried that name.

75 Karling in MacDougall and Hamilton Hazlehurst, *French Formal Garden*, pp. 12ff. and 19-21 for Mollet's work at the Dutch court.

76 Hopper, *Journal of Garden History*, II, 1 (1982), p. 34, and *Bulletin KNOB*, 3-4 (1983), p. 112.

77 Worp, *Briefwisseling*, II, RGP 19, letter 1254, David de Wilhem to Constantijn Huygens, dated 6 October 1635. Worp did not publish the complete text and paraphrased whole sections. This description of Mollet is only found in the original letter, kept at the Leiden University Library, Department of Western Manuscripts, Hug. 37.

78 ARA, NDR, inv. no. 1043 [old no. 782], fol. 243: 'Betaelt aen André Mollet opsichter van Sijne Hoocheits Thuynen de somme van sesentwintich ponden veertien schellingen voor reys ende teercosten by hem verleit, gaende door last van Sijne Hoocheit naer *Suylesteijn* om de Thuynen aldaer te besichtigen…. Marty XVIC vier en dertich.' We can thus conclude that as *opsichter* Mollet supervised the layout of the new parterres at Zuylesteyn, just as he did at Honselaarsdijk at that time. For the history of Zuylesteyn see Meischke in Hoekstra et al., *Liber Castellorum*, pp. 270-278, in particular p. 276 and note 5.

79 ARA, NDR, inv. no. 1041 [old no. 780], fol. 252: 'nieuwe wercken, als plantagien.'

80 ARA, NDR, inv. no. 1042 [old no. 781], fol. 232vo: '… terwijlen hij verscheiden teickeningen voor Sijnne Hoocheit heeft gemaeckt' (while he has made several drawings for His Highness). See also Slothouwer, *Paleizen*, p. 264.

81 ARA, NDR, inv. no. 1042 [old no. 781], fol. 232vo: '… sijn tractement van VIIIC pond artois jaerlicx.'

82 At Breda the gardener Michiel Bruheze received 300 pounds artois yearly; see ARA, NDR, inv. no. 992 [old no. 735], fol. 181. The gardener at Zuylesteyn made 300; Gijsbrecht Theunissen at Honselaarsdijk made 200 pounds a year for the upkeep of the parterres; see NDR, inv. no. 1042 [old no. 781], fol. 247vo, and inv. no. 1043 [old no. 782], fol. 232/3. At the Paleis Noordeinde, Joost Jansz van Hoorenbeeck received an income of 150 pounds artois for the yearly upkeep of the aviaries in the garden.

83 ARA, NDR, inv. no. 1042 [old no. 781] fol. 344vo: 'Betaelt aen Jacquis [sic] de la Vallee frans architect d'somme van vier hondert ponden hem bij Monsr de Vaulsin [?] door last van S.H. belooft tot reisgelt ende vacatien om sich alhier te coomen vertoonen volgens 't accoort met hem dienaengaande aengegaen … Juny 1633.'

84 ARA, NDR, inv. no. 564 [old no. 601], fol. 194vo: '… Joseph Dinant als fontainier ende Grottier geniet voor gagie jaerlijcx 500:0:0 ende voor costgelt tot eene gul. daechs 365:9:9.' See Slothouwer, *Paleizen*, p. 329.

85 ARA, NDR, inv. no. 1041 [old no. 780], fol. 250, and no. 1042 [old. no. 782], fols. 218, 225vo and 243: '… André Mollet opsichter van Sijne Hoocheits Thuynen …'

86 ARA, NDR, inv. no. 1043 [old no. 782], fols. 232-33: '... door de directie van ...'
87 Worp, *Briefwisseling*, II, RGP 19, letter 1254, David de Wilhem to Constantijn Huygens, dated 6 October 1635. See also Slothouwer, *Paleizen*, p. 342. Original text in Dutch: 'Uw brief met de bevelen van Z.E. aangaande de parterres heb ik ontvangen; de intendant And. Mollet zal het in orde maken. Maar er moet ook voor waterafvoer worden gezorgd. Catshusen [*sic*] belooft zijn best te zullen doen op Honselaersdijk.'
88 Leiden University Library, Department of Western Manuscripts, Hug. 37, dated 6 October 1635, David de Wilhem to Constantijn Huygens.
89 Hopper, *Bulletin KNOB*, 3-4 (1983), p. 114.
90 Further remarks about Mollet's parterres can be found in later letters by David de Wilhem to Huygens, referring to answers given by Mollet about the parterres. See Worp, *Briefwisseling*, II, RGP 19, letter 1260, dated 16 October 1635. This letter is only partly published and paraphrased by Worp. The original version in the Leiden University Library, Department of Western Manuscripts, Hug. 37, reads: '... Pour le parterre vous voire ici joincts la response de Monsieur Mollet a la quelle je me rapports.'
91 ARA, NDR, inv. no. I, Journalen, 2 January 1632 to 29 December 1635. Minutes, dated 9 June 1633 (pages in document are not numbered).
92 Contrary to what Morren states in *Honselaarsdijk*, p. 17, that Mollet 'liet zich voor zijn arbeid vorstelijk betalen' (let himself be paid royally), Frederik Hendrik and Amalia found his request quite reasonable, as the quoted text from Mollet's account shows.
93 ARA, NDR, inv. no. I, Journalen, 2 January 1632 to 29 December 1635. Minutes, dated 9 June 1633. This section of the text is in Dutch: 'De voorn heer Brouaert Raedt en Tresorier Gnael verhoort hebbende dat Mevrouwe de Princesse hem last hadde gegeven, dat soo wanneer Andre Mollez [*sic*], zoone van de hovenier van de Coninck van Frankrijk gedaen soude hebben mettet ordonneren ende doen opmaecken der parterres van Buren ende Honsholredijck, dat men hem soude afrekenen voldaen van sijne reyscosten, moeijten, ende andere oncosten bij hem gedaen. Daaronder met begrepen de hantwerckers oft arbeijders die daeraan gevrocht hebben. Ende gesien de declaratie daervan bij voorsz. Andre Mollez overgegeven, hierna volgende.'
94 ARA, NDR, inv. no. I [old no. I]. Journalen van de Raad, 2 January 1632 to 29 December 1635. Minutes of the Council, dated 9 June 1633. This section of the original text is in French and contains many spelling errors. See the last entry in the Appendix for the original French text.
95 ARA, NDR, inv. no. I, Journalen, 2 January 1632 to 29 December 1635. Minutes, dated 9 June 1633. The original text of this document ends again in Dutch. See the last entry in the Appendix for the original Dutch text.

96 Not Frederik Hendrik's own coat of arms, as is erroneously believed by Karling in *French Formal Garden*, p. 19. A depiction of Frederik Hendrik's coat of arms and personal motto 'Patriaeque Patrique' can be found in Scriverius, *Beschrijvinge van Holland*, p. 585, reproduced in the introduction (see fig. 2). See also Blok, *Frederik Hendrik*, p. 249. It should be mentioned, however, that a lion also is part of Frederik Hendrik's own coat of arms.
97 Described in ARA, NDR, inv. no. 1042, fol. 232vo: '... twee parterren te Honselerdijck, een van sooden ende palm met wit, root ende swarten ende het ander geheel van palm seer aerdigh gemaeckt.'
98 Pointed out by Hopper, *Journal of Garden History*, II, 1 (1982), pp. 34-35.
99 The Metropolitan Museum of Art, New York, Harris Brisbane Dick Fund, 1926 (26.104.5).
100 Karling in MacDougall and Hamilton Hazlehurst, *French Formal Garden*, p. 19 and plates IX and X. Karling mistakenly writes that folio 29 in Mollet's treatise illustrates the Honselaarsdijk turf parterre. It should be folio 23.
101 Mollet's design folio 14 measured circa 47 x 34 toises, equalling 94 x 68 metres, while the area on the side of the Honselaarsdijk palace left room for a parterre of circa 28 x 23 toises, or 56 x 46 metres (cf. the actual size for the parterre on the opposite side of the palace).
102 Hopper, *Journal of Garden History*, II, 1 (1982), p. 34, and *Bulletin KNOB*, 3-4 (1983), p. 112.
103 It is not completely clear whether the eight arbours (*cabinetten*) mentioned here actually refer to the eight arbours in the corners of the central garden plot with the two circles, or whether they refer to the arbours (each consisting of three small structures) in the parterre gardens, including the two arbours which extend into the enclosing moat.
104 First the design, then the construction and lastly the painting of the wooden arcades for the *berceaux* on either side of the parterre garden are described in great detail in the following accounts: ARA, NDR, inv. no. 1043 [old no. 782], fol. 219vo and 229vo; for the actual construction of the arches, inv. no. 1043 [old no. 782], fol. 232, concerning *patronen* (designs) made for the arches; and finally inv. no. 1043 [old no. 782], fol. 228vo, concerning the painting of the wooden trellis-work arches.
105 Slothouwer, *Paleizen*, p. 52. Slothouwer's analysis of the Honselaarsdijk grotto and Orangerie is vague, as he frequently confuses information about Rijswijk's grotto and Orangerie with that about Honselaarsdijk's. It is not clear where Frederik Hendrik's Orangerie, apparently containing a grotto, was exactly situated, but probably it was part of the annexe buildings situated west of the palace. We only have a representation of the late-seventeenth-century Orangerie built by Van Swieten and Roman under William III.
106 The *fonteijnsteen* referred to in the account probably was the special

kind of pumice or limestone quarried near Tivoli.

107 Probably he worked for the court after this date, though no specific mention is made in the records of payments. However, in later entries, dated June 1680, Dinant's heirs, probably his children and/or grandchildren — Maria, Daniel and (then deceased) Paulus Dinant — receive a last payment from the Treasurer General. See ARA, NDR, inv. no. 997 [old no. 740], fols. 249vo and 250.

108 Morren in *Honselaarsdijk*, p. 19, mentions the setting of statues in the Honselaarsdijk garden but omits the important fact that these statues came from France. Slothouwer in *Paleizen*, p. 271, does not include the archival sources with more detailed descriptions on the placement of 'nine statues sent from France' in the Honselaarsdijk garden. He only mentions documents with brief remarks about the transportation of statues from Rotterdam to Honselaarsdijk. See ARA, NDR, inv. no. 992 [old no. 735], fol. 333; the 'placing of statues', mentioned in the account book, NDR, inv. no. 992 [old no. 735], fol. 389, and 'ironwork delivered to the stone statues' in the Honselaarsdijk garden, mentioned in inv. no. 992 [old no. 735], fol. 391.

109 Drossaers and Lunsingh Scheurleer, *Inventarissen*.

110 Sandrart, *Accademia Todesca*, I, book II, p. 41.

111 RPK, inv. no. A 1587. Another version of this drawing is in the GAH, topographical department, Honselaarsdijk, klein 37.

112 Neurdenburg, *Beeldhouwkunst*, p. 19. Neurdenburg prefers the interpretation of the statue as 'Hercules and Cacus' to its identification as 'Cain and Abel'. Even in the seventeenth century there was much confusion about their representation, as evidenced by a reference to them as 'Hercules and Daphne'. See Morren, *Honselaarsdijk*, p. 56. Furthermore, a similar sculpture in a painting by Jan Weenix also has been identified as 'Cain and Abel' or 'Samson Killing a Philistine'. See Schloss, *Oud Holland*, 97 (1983), p. 76.

113 The statues represented William I, Maurits, Frederik Hendrik and William II. They are mentioned in the inventories of Amalia's sculpture at Ter Nieuburch and Noordeinde; see Drossaers and Lunsingh Scheurleer, *Inventarissen*, I, RGP 147, p. 259, no. 617 and the note, referring to their probable original placement at the Huis ten Bosch. See Lunsingh Scheurleer, *Oud Holland*, 84 (1969), pp. 29-66. Compare also Neurdenburg, *Beeldhouwkunst*, p. 122.

114 Their possible function as garden statues can be derived from another statue which was copied after these Dutch examples, namely that of Friedrich Wilhelm, Elector of Brandenburg. After his marriage to Louise Henriette of Orange in 1646, the Elector had his own life-size figure modelled on those of the Princes of Orange by Dieussart and set it up in the gardens of Berlin, as will be further discussed in chapter VI.

115 Drossaers and Lunsingh Scheurleer, *Inventarissen*, II, RGP 148, p. 501, no. 500; see also nos. 501-503 for other iron pots inside the garden.

116 See for further references to the acquisition of plants and flowers in the Honselaarsdijk garden, ARA, NDR, inv. no. 992 [old no. 736], fols. 238, 252, 285 and 469.

117 ARA, NDR, inv. no. 566 [old no. 603], fols. 24-26: *Reglement waer naer Meester Hendrick Quellenburch in het onderhouden van alle de Thuynen van het huys tot Honsholredyck sigh sal hebben te gedragen ... Actum 's-Gravenhage*, 13 February 1686.

118 Biblioteca Nazionale, Florence, Ms. Pal. 6BB85. The *Hortus Regius Honselaerdicensis* is attributed to Stephanus Cousyns. See Hunt and de Jong, *Anglo-Dutch Garden*, pp. 288-289, plate IV. For further reading on the collections of rare plants in Holland throughout the seventeenth century, see J. Kuijlen et al., *Paradisus Batavus*.

119 London, Museum of Natural History, Sloane Herbarium, MSS. George London, folio H.S. 91.

120 These special hotbeds, hothouses and glass cases were developed mostly under William III and probably did not yet exist at the Frederik Hendrik's time. See on this subject Jacques and Van der Horst, *Gardens of William and Mary*, pp. 177-180, and especially Geytenbeek, *Oranjerieën*, pp. 9-44.

121 'Her Highness' must refer to William III's wife Mary II Stuart.

122 Timber production and deer parks were essential features of many estates at the time. See for other examples Taigel and Williamson, *Journal of Garden History*, 1-2 (1991), pp. 9-10.

123 Leiden University Library, Department of Western Manuscripts, Hug. 37, David de Wilhem to Constantijn Huygens, dated 6 October 1635.

124 ARA, NDR, inv. no. 992 [old no. 735], fol. 267: delivery of trees in 1639, and inv. no. 993 [old no. 736], fol. 71, again refer to delivery of trees to 'the old garden of Honsholredijck' in August 1641. Inv. no. 993 [old no. 736], fol. 238, describes water ditches made by him in the new plantation. Gijsbrecht Theunissen's, or Thonisz's, place as a gardener was taken over by his son Anthonis Gijsberts in 1643. Compare Morren, *Honselaarsdijk*, p. 17.

125 The date of their presence at Honselaarsdijk is 1640-41, not 1642-43, as Morren states in *Honselaarsdijk*, p. 19.

126 ARA, NDR, inv. no. 1043 [old no. 782], fols. 21 and 215vo, describe trees arriving from Koevoort (Coevorden), Meurs and Diest. See NDR, inv. no. 994 [old no. 737], fols. 38vo and 41a, describing various other trees brought over from Meurs. See NDR, inv. no. 993 [old no. 736], fol. 84, referring to trees coming from Antwerp. NDR, inv. no. 992 [old. no. 735], fol. 255, describes trees imported all the way from France.

127 ARA, NDR, inv. no. 992 [old no. 735], fol. 332, inv. no. 993 [old no. 736], fol. 84, and inv. no. 994 [old no. 737], fol. 29, for example.

128 Compare entries in the accounts of the ARA, NDR, inv. no. 993 [old no. 736], fols. 193vo, 238, 252 and 285. The crash of the tulip market occurred in 1637. See Blok, *Frederik Hendrik*, p. 188. See also Jacques and Van der Horst, *Gardens of William and Mary*, pp. 182-184.

129 ARA, NDR, inv. no. 993 [old no. 736], fol. 84, and many following entries in the account books over the years 1641-47. For his appointment as *plantagueur* see also NDR, inv. no. 562 [old no. 599], fol. 71, and compare Morren, *Honselaarsdijk*, p. 21, note 1.

130 Chaps. XIV and XV, pp. 82-83.

131 Ibid., p. 82.

132 Ibid., p. 83.

133 See for the history of the Dutch *Hofdicht*, or country-house poem, Van Veen, *Soeticheydt*, pp. 9 and 28-34.

134 Van der Groen, *Nederlandtsen Hovenier*, facs. ed., p. 26: 'Den Hofbouw, en 't buyten-leven, is, naer 't seggen van veel Geleerden, het vermakelijkste, voordeelighste, gesontste, ja menighmael ook wel het salighste leven, dat men sou kunnen wenschen, voor die gene, die aen geen beroep, in de Steden vast gebonden is.' See also Hunt and de Jong, *Anglo-Dutch Garden*, p. 16.

135 Worp, *Briefwisseling*, II, RGP 19, letter 1646, Constantijn Huygens to Amalia of Orange, dated 18 August 1637. Partly printed in Slothouwer, *Paleizen*, p. 343.

136 Worp, *Briefwisseling* III, RGP 21, p. 222, note 2: Charles de Lannoy is mentioned in 1633 and 1641 as Frederik Hendrik's Groom of the Chamber; he later held an important position in the army.

137 Ibid., letter 2838, Constantijn Huygens to Amalia of Orange, dated 29 August 1641.

138 Ibid., letter 2426, Constantijn Huygens to Amalia of Orange, dated *dernier* June 1640. Worp published the letter partly translated into Dutch. Slothouwer in *Paleizen*, p. 348, quotes from the original French text.

139 Dodt van Flensburg, *Archief voor kerk en wereldlijke geschiedenis*, vol. V, p. 348, referred to in Morren, *Honselaarsdijk*, p. 33, note 1.

140 Examples of such increasingly open garden spaces with intricate parterres can be found at the Château Neuf at Saint-Germain-en-Laye, featuring the terrace with the well-known hippodrome-shaped parterre garden, the gardens of the Château du Luxembourg in Paris, to be discussed later, and the gardens of the Château de Richelieu. For further reading see Woodbridge, *Princely Gardens*, pp. 129-147.

141 KHA, K XX 156.

142 In the end the chapel was not built in this rather awkward position above the bridge leading from the palace to the garden, but placed in the annexe buildings.

143 Worp, *Briefwisseling*, III, RGP 21, letter 3220, Constantijn Huygens to Tassin, dated 16 February 1643. See Slothouwer, *Paleizen*, pp. 62 and 350-351.

144 Worp, *Briefwisseling*, IV, RGP 24, letters 3601 and 3614, L. Buysero (registrar) to Constantijn Huygens, dated 13 and 14 July 1644.

145 CBN, inv. no. P17 N62, shows a unique colour-printed version of this print in the so-called Teyler procédé. Our illustration comes from Bienfait, *Oude Hollandsche tuinen*, plate 74.

146 ARA, NDR, inv. no. 994 [old no. 737], fol. 18, and also 993 [old no. 736], fol. 469: new bulbs in new west garden, and 994 [old no. 737], fol. 72vo: flowers in the new garden. See also inv. no. 994 [old no. 737], fol. 80, describing the delivery of fruit- and other trees in the new west garden. Dirck de Milde made a fence round the new garden on the west side of the palace; see inv. no. 993 [old no. 736], fol. 431vo and fol. 466vo. References to the new garden, situated east of the new gallery, are also found in inv. no. 993 [old no. 736], fol. 457.

147 ARA, NDR, inv. no. 993 [old no. 736], fol. 465, discusses the costs for material needed to construct the fountains; inv. no. 994 [old no. 737], fol. 36vo, the payments for the workmen, and fol. 85vo describes the costs for the stone imported from Tivoli.

148 Sellers in Hunt and de Jong, *Anglo-Dutch Garden*, p. 137.

149 The gardeners mentioned in the accounts as *hoveniers* at Honselaarsdijk in the 1650s and 1660s are Blaes Jacobsz, Jacob Verbruggen and Anthonie van Tooren.

150 Hoogewerff, *Twee reizen*, p. 242. English translation: 'Six miles away you can see a villa of the Prince of Orange called Onselerdic [*sic*] which is very elegant because of the multiplicity of bosquets, statues and delicious fountains, adjoining to a park which is not big but very interesting, they are putting everything into a better state.' See also Jacques and Van der Horst, *Gardens of William and Mary*, p. 37.

151 GAH, topographical department, Honselaarsdijk, groot 4.

152 RKD, topographical department, The Hague. Drawing in brown ink. Unknown author; on stylistic grounds to be attributed to Cornelis Pronk and dated about 1730.

153 LUW, department of special collections, inv. no. 01.1048.02

154 GAH, topographical department, Honselaarsdijk, klein 10.

155 See for Roman also Bienfait, *Oude Hollandsche tuinen*, pp. 92-93.

156 LUW, Springer Collectie, no. 01.1049.10.

157 Japikse, *Correspondentie*, I, RGP 23, letter 206, Bentinck to Willem III, dated 1 March 1698: '… les orangers a Versailles sont extremement beaux et gros et grand en nombre, les teges [sic, tiges] belles et hauttes, mais les testes ne sont pas comme celles de Honslaerdick.'

158 Ibid., letter 200, William III to Bentinck, dated 23 February 1698: 'Je croi aussi que vous poures bientost chasse et voir des jardinages que vous saves estre deus de mes passions.'

159 Sellers, *Journal of Garden History*, VII, 1 (1987), pp. 1-43.

160 Since I completed my research, which involved the discovery of numerous maps and prints, some of these have been published in a new, augmented edition of Morren's *Honselaarsdijk*, figs. 226-228.

161 Ibid., pp. 67-70, and Slothouwer, *Paleizen*, pp. 84 and 370.

162 The print is kept in the RPK, inv. no. 1936:434. It is made by Pierre Loofs and probably dated c. 1715. See Thieme and Becker,

Künstlerlexicon, s.v. Pieter Loofs.
163 ARA, map department, VTH 2363/18. A similar map, of the same area of Honselaarsdijk's garden, signed and dated by de Baes in 1735, is also kept in this map department, under no. OSK H 72.
164 CBN, inv. no. P17 N59. Anonymous. Made during Prussian ownership, the plan is entitled 'Plaan van het Huijs Tuijn en Bos van Sijn Coning Maijstijt van Pruijsen tot Honsholredijck'. Compare de Vries, *Kaarten met geschiedenis*, p. 111.
165 Hirzel, *Albrecht Hallers Tagebücher*, p. 114. See also Morren, *Honselaarsdijk*, p. 75.
166 Morren, *Honselaarsdijk*, pp. 73-74, and Slothouwer, *Paleizen*, pp. 86 and 370.
167 Morren, *Honselaarsdijk*, pp. 75ff., and Slothouwer, *Paleizen*, p. 86. The architect David van Stolk was asked to draw up an estimate of the possible restoration of the castle and annexe buildings. After much deliberation whether to demolish the old castle or to restore it, the Princess of Orange decided on a compromise, and in 1758 the most-needed repairs were finally undertaken.
168 ARA, map department, VTH 2363/15. The date of the map (1762) can be derived from the text on it, which is dated eight years after William IV's reign began in 1754: 'Anno Octavo Gubernationis Eminentia Regiae Principis Arausicanae et Nassoviae …'
169 ARA, Resolutien NDR, 9 October 1778: '… soogenoemde Engelse bloem- en heester tuinen'. See also Morren, *Honselaarsdijk*, p. 82, and Slothouwer, *Paleizen*, p. 87. The changes in the garden were undertaken at the suggestion of the architect Philip Willem Schonck.
170 Photograph taken March 1978, after the restoration of the building.
171 Hopper, *Bulletin KNOB*, 3-4 (1983), p. 114.
172 Map entitled 'Kaart voor vakantie en vrije tijd, Zuid-Holland Noord'. Published by Provinciale VVV Zuid-Holland, 1989. Scale 1 : 50,000.

CHAPTER II

1 The close links between the two buildings are borne out by the original *bestecken* in the ARA, NDR, inv. no. 4694 [old no. NDR FOLIO, 1413], in which both buildings are frequently compared. More specifically, one entry describes the dismantling of the stone balustrade surrounding the forecourt of Honselaarsdijk and its reconstruction on the new garden terrace behind the building of Ter Nieuburch, while another entry urges woodcutters to copy wooden roses in the ceiling 'as seen at Honselaarsdijk'. See the 'Besteck waer nae Sijn Excie Prince van Orangien wil besteden het timmer ende ijserwerck tot twee Gallerijen ende twee Pavillioenen volgens parfijl [profiel], gront ende stant teijckeninge daervan zijnde: …' 'gewulfte … met zijn Rosen als te zien is op hontsholredijck.' See also the 'Besteck waerna van wegen Sijn Excie mijn heere den Prince van Orangie etc. wil besteden het maecken van een Balustrade die gestelt sal worden aen de Suytsijde voor hoochgemelte Sijn Excies gebouw tot Rijswijck in maniere als volgt: …' 'Den aennemer sal alle de Balusters tot honsholredijck staende aff breecken, tot Rijswijck voeren, ende daer wederstellen.'
2 As mentioned in chapter I, Brereton's remark on the diminished height of Ter Nieuburch seems to confirm de Bray's comments on the limitations of Dutch architecture due to the softness of the ground. Even though Brereton makes the interesting remark that Ter Nieuburch's building would have been higher had the foundations been less weak, no further references as to a major change of building plans have been found.
3 Brereton, *Travels in Holland*, p. 32.
4 De Parival, *Délices*, second edition, 1669, p. 115. This text is slightly different in the first edition of 1651, p. 141. Compare Vermeulen, *Nederlandsche Historiebladen*, I (1938), p. 115 and note 4.
5 For further reading on the early history and previous owners of the old estate or *hofstede* 'genaempt Ter Nyeuburch' see Chandali and Huitsing, *Ter Nieuwburg*, pp. 6-7.
6 Vernatti lived at Rijswijk from 1620 to 1628. See Vermeulen, *Nederlandsche Historiebladen*, 1 (1938), p. 129 and note 6.
7 'In Julio XVIc dertich tijde deser heeft Sijnne Furstelicke Doorluchticheit van Filibert Vernatti gecocht eene wooninge genaemt Ter Nieuburch bij Rijswijck gelegen met hare boomgaerden, cingelen, waranden ende veertien margen [sic] een hond ses ende tnegentich roeden landts daeraen gehoorende, ende dat voorde somme van dertich duisent ponden artois, welkce [sic] wooninge Sijnne Hoochgemelte Furstelicke Doorluchticheit teenemael geraseert ende inde plaetse vandien een seer treffelick gebouw gestichtet heeft …' ARA, NDR, inv. no. 1039 [old no. 778], fol. 218. Compare Slothouwer, *Paleizen*, p. 289. The original deed of purchase, dated 18 July 1630, is kept in the ARA, NDR, inv. no. 4667 [old no. NDR FOLIO, 1405].
8 ARA, map department, VTH 2399 A and B.

9   On the first map, map A, a note by Floris Jacobsz written at the top of the map indicates that it is now outdated and that a new one has been made, referred to as map B: 'Dese caerte en dient niet meer alsoo eene andere daer naer is gemaeck' (This map is no longer of use since another one has been made). The second, improved map must be the one referred to in a deed of purchase of Lambert van der Horst's grounds (indicated on the map), dated 13 March 1631.

10 One Rijnlandse morgen = 0.85 ha, thus 38 x 0.85 = 32.30 or 33 ha. 1 hectare = 2.47 acres, thus 33 x 2.47 = 81.51 or 80 acres. The actual pleasure garden measured c. 620 x 310 metres, or 192,200 square metres. 1 hectare = 10,000 sq. metres, thus 19.2 or 20 ha, equalling 49 or 50 acres.

11 On Floris Jacobsz' second, more refined map the parcels of land are numbered A to G.

12 A.J. van der Croos made as many as thirteen paintings of the same topic. This version depicts the palace and grounds as seen from the south-west. For further reading and other illustrations see Dumas, *Haagse stadsgezichten*, pp. 345-349 and 520-527.

13 GAH, topographical department, Rijswijk–Van Vredenburchweg, groot 1. The Milheusser and Van Berckerode prints are remarkable for belonging to the earliest panoramic views of specific Dutch castles and country estates with gardens.

14 CBN, inv. no. P16 N51.

15 The names of specific garden plots are indicated in a later publication of the print by Frederik de Wit, issued on the occasion of the Peace of Rijswijk in 1697; the old copperplates featuring Frederik Hendrik's earlier layout were simply reprinted, with an added frontal view, ground-plan and rear elevation of the palace.

16 In Bienfait, *Oude Hollandsche tuinen*, plate 50, the drawing is mentioned as being in the collection of Mr. I.Q. van Regteren Altena in Amsterdam. The present whereabouts are unknown.

17 This idea of a correlation between the axis and the tower of the church at Delft was first suggested by Slothouwer, *Paleizen*, p. 91.

18 KHA, K XX 181.

19 The plans were discovered during the study of copies of old maps in the GAH, topographical department, Rijswijk–Van Vredenburchweg, Huis ter Nieuburg, zeer groot 2, 3, 4, 5 and 6 (original missing in ARA), groot 7 and klein 59. With the assistance of J.J. Terwen, emeritus professor Leiden University, I then checked the remaining originals in the ARA, map department, VTHR 392 (fig. 59), 393 (fig. 58), 394 A, B, C, D and E (figs. 51, 55, 53, 57 and 56, respectively).

20 Drawing VTHR 394 A (I) (fig. 51), which has been published by Van der Haer, *Jaarboek Die Haghe* (1955), pp. 50-53.

21 That originally there were twenty-one designs can be concluded from the fact that these were mentioned in an inventory of maps of the Nassau Domains of 1729, entitled *Inventaris van de Caerten gehorende tot de Domeynen en Goederen nagelaten bij Sijne Con[e] Maj[t] van Groot Britten* (ARA, map department). It is also noted on the back of one of the maps; see Van der Haer, *Jaarboek Die Haghe* (1955), p. 53.

22 ARA, map department, VTHR 393 (fig. 57), is inscribed *in dorso*: 'Nieuwe Grotte te Rijswyc geconstrueert [? ... 15] 1643 30 April.' The date appears to have been written by a seventeenth-century hand. The other map, VTHR 394 A (I) (fig. 51), is dated *in dorso* '1636', also in original seventeenth-century handwriting. The rest of the text *in dorso* reads: 'Rijswijk no. 1 & a', in what appears to be nineteenth-century handwriting.

23 ARA, map department, VTHR 394 A (I) (fig. 51). A copy (fig. 52) is kept in the GAH, topographical department, Rijswijk–Van Vredenburchweg, zeer groot 3, which shows the lines of the design more clearly.

24 Worp, *Briefwisseling*, II, RGP 19, letter 1909, Constantijn Huygens to Amalia of Orange, dated 2 August 1638. See for the complete text Slothouwer, *Paleizen*, p. 344.

25 Coope, *De Brosse*, pp. 110-134 and figs. 135-136.

26 Slothouwer, *Paleizen*, p. 101.

27 Vermeulen, *Handboek*, III, p. 55, first mentions Simon de la Vallée, but on p. 109 quotes Bartholomeus van Bassen as designer of Ter Nieuburch. Slothouwer in *Paleizen*, p. 100, points at this inconsistency, yet on pp. 52 and 54 seems to make the same mistake when he, too, refers to de la Vallée as having been involved in the design of Ter Nieuburch, based on 'examples by Jacques Androuet Du Cerceau'.

28 Karling in MacDougall and Hamilton Hazlehurst, *French Formal Garden*, pp. 3-25, especially pp. 20-21, believes that Simon de la Vallée in laying out Fiholm, for example, was influenced by Mollet, who already worked in Sweden since 1635. But, as Karling himself admits, one should not overstress Mollet's influence on de la Vallée since, as is shown above, the latter knew modern French examples. Moreover, working at the Dutch court, both Simon de la Vallée and André Mollet obviously were acquainted with contemporary Dutch garden architecture, which expressed the same rectilinearity and composition in square plots planted with orderly rows of trees.

29 Nordberg, *De La Vallée*, pp. 128-131 and 135-141.

30 Dinant is still mentioned in 1657 as *concierge* at Ter Nieuburch, involved in supervising or 'attesting to' the works ('geattesteert by Dinant'); see ARA, NDR, inv. no. 995 [old no. 738], fol. 221.

31 Worp, *Briefwisseling*, III, RGP 21, letter 3220, Constantijn Huygens to Tassin, dated 16 February 1643. See Slothouwer, *Paleizen*, pp. 62 and 350-351. The rest of the letter from which this important excerpt is taken has been quoted in chapter I.

32 Adam and Milhaud, *Descartes Correspondance*, V, p. 147, letter 330, R. Descartes to C. Huygens, dated 31 January 1642.

33 Adam and Tannery, *Oeuvres de Descartes, Correspondance*, IV, p. 99, letter of L. Buysero to R. Descartes, dated 8 March 1644.

34 Schaper, *Tuinkunst*, I (1995), pp. 23-45, especially pp. 25-28.

35 Adam and Milhaud, *Descartes Correspondance*, V, p. 73, letter 315, R. Descartes to M. Mersenne, dated 17 November 1641.
36 Ibid., p. 143, letter 329, C. Huygens to R. Descartes, dated 25 January 1642.
37 Ibid., p. 213, letter 351, C. Huygens to R. Descartes, dated 6 September 1642, and a note of gratitude on receiving the book by R. Descartes to C. Huygens, dated 6 October 1642.
38 Compare Schaper, *Tuinkunst*, I, p. 27. Further research in the rare book and print departments (including the Metropolitan Museum of Art, New York, where I was kindly assisted by Mrs. Elisabeth Eustis) has not uncovered any other large-scale garden treatises in those years, except for the book by Boyceau. The fact that Huygens refers to it as 'the book of parterres' confirms that the work in question must have been Boyceau's book, which is full of parterre designs.
39 Text in Faugère, *Journal de voyage*, p. 86. The remainder of the text describes the Tuileries and reads: 'La grande allée est merveilleuse pour la hauteur des arbres qui la forment et la grande ombre qu'ils causent. Aux costés on trouve des cabinets de charpenterie, couverts de quelques verdures. Il y a un fort beau jeu de mail, et qu'on a mesme agrandi depuis que le Roy se plaist à cet exercice; car outre la longueur du jardin qu'il avoit, on luy a donné un repli, qui le fait venir jusques à la grande allée. On voit tout auprès un fort beau ject d'eau, proche duquel est un labyrinthe planté de cyprès. Il y a d'ordinaire bon nombre de bourgeois et de bourgeoises sur le bord de ce bassin, qui y prennent le frais et s'y reposent apres s'est pourmenés, en voyant pourmener les autres. Le grande monde n'y aborde que sur le soir, quand on va au Cours et quand on en revient. On y est quelquefois jusques bien avant dans la nuict, et alors il y a souvent assemblée et bal, qui est d'autant plus agréable qu'on y est avec toute sorte de liberté.'
40 Slothouwer, *Paleizen*, p. 101, already mentioned the relationship with the school of Salomon de Brosse but, ironically, came to this conclusion without knowing about the 'French plan', copied after the Luxembourg and direct proof of such stylistic connections.
41 Karling in MacDougall and Hamilton Hazlehurst, *French Formal Garden*, p. 5.
42 Woodbridge, *Princely Gardens*, p. 134. See also Nordberg, *De La Vallée*, pp. 35-38. In Coope, *De Brosse*, de la Vallée's involvement in the Luxembourg palace is not mentioned at all.
43 For important similarities between the Stadholder's gardens and Jean de la Vallée's designs in Sweden see Karling, *Trädgardskonstens*, pp. 388ff., especially the illustrations on p. 421 for Vänngarn, p. 435 for Ekolsund, p. 461 for Stermalma, based on Philips Vingboons's ideal garden design. See for further reading on Philips and Justus Vingboons and Simon and Jean de la Vallée's architectural designs in Sweden, Ottenheym, *Philips Vingboons*, pp. 132-134. See also Hopper's remarks in Jellicoe et al., *Oxford Companion to Gardens*, p. 391. For Mollet's work in Sweden compare his design for Jacobsdahl with wide, open parterres, shown in André Mollet, *Jardin de plaisir*, facs. ed., p. 114, fig. 16.
44 Bibliothèque Nationale, Paris, inv. no. C 87659.
45 Woodbridge, *Princely Gardens*, p. 137.
46 Bibliothèque Nationale, Paris, inv. no. C 87659.
47 The Metropolitan Museum of Art, Harris Brisbane Dick Fund, 1926 (26.104.2). For other illustrations of the central parterre in the Luxembourg garden see Hamilton Hazlehurst, *Boyceau*, figs. 24-25.
48 Coope, *De Brosse*, p. 131, note 61. See also Hamilton Hazlehurst, *Boyceau*, pp. 48-49.
49 Professor Hamilton Hazlehurst made this remark in a letter to the author, in which Ter Nieuburch's designs and their resemblance to the Luxembourg layout were discussed.
50 Compare also the last parterre model entitled 'Moitie d'un Parterre Quarre de mesme Ordonnance que le grand de Luxembourg'. See also Hamilton Hazlehurst, *Boyceau*, figs. 24-25.
51 Ibid., p. 57.
52 One drawing in the ARA, map department, VTHR 393, has a scale saying '20', which refers to 20 Rijnlandse roeden, indicating a local measuring system. The others have no scale but can be related stylistically to this Dutch drawing.
53 Brereton, *Travels in Holland*, p. 32.
54 For further reading on Van Campen's role as 'interior decorator' see Buvelot in Huisken et al., *Jacob van Campen*, pp. 129-132.
55 See Bok in Huisken et al., *Jacob van Campen*, p. 52 and notes 335-336, concerning a book with drawings made by Van Campen. See also Buvelot, ibid., pp. 129-132, and Ottenheym, ibid., p. 174, about Van Campen's involvement in the interior decoration and the layout of the garden of Ter Nieuburch.
56 GAH, topographical department, Rijswijk–Van Vredenburchweg, zeer groot 7. Compare for the original the ARA, map department, VTHR 394 C.
57 GAH, topographical department, Rijswijk–Van Vredenburchweg, Huis ter Nieuburch, zeer groot 6. The original in the ARA is missing, only this copy survives.
58 GAH, topographical department, Rijswijk–Van Vredenburchweg, zeer groot 5, corresponding to ARA, map department, VTHR 394 B.
59 GAH, topographical department, Rijswijk–Van Vredenburchweg, Huis ter Nieuburch, zeer groot 4, corresponding to ARA, map department, VTHR 394 E.
60 ARA, map department, VTHR 392. Text *in dorso*: 'Verclaringe vant gebou, perck ende stallinge tot Rijswyck …' Various details, numbered 1-37, are described at the left on the map. A separate document, VTHR 394 F, contains a legend for a stable complex entitled 'Desclaration des batimens des écuries de Rhijswick', which, on closer reading, does not pertain to VTHR 392.
61 GAH, topographical department, Rijswijk–Van Vredenburchweg,

klein 59. Compare this drawing with the original in the ARA, map department, VTHR 394 D.

62 ARA, NDR, inv. no. 4694 [old no. NDR FOLIO, 1413]: 'Besteck waer nae van wegen Sijn Excie mijn heere Den Prince van Orangie etc. besteet sal werden het maecken leveren ende stellen van een greijne houte plating rontom beyde de vijvers die jegenwoordich gemaeckt werden aende Zuytsijde vant Gebouw van Hoochgemelte Sijn Excie te Rijswijck ter hoogte van drie of vier duijm beneden het Somer water.' Dated September and December 1636.

63 GAH, topographical department, Rijswijk–Van Vredenburchweg, zeer groot 2. Compare the original in the ARA, map department, VTHR 393.

64 The scale of twenty Rijnlandse roeden, equalling seventy-five metres, which would make the total length of the palace's façade about one hundred metres, corresponds to the final size of the building in later engravings of the Huis ter Nieuburch. The length of the garden façade engraved by J.A. Rietkessler (published in Slothouwer, *Paleizen*, p. 117, fig. 37), indicated in 'pieds Rhinlandiques' or Rijnlandse voeten (0.313 metres), totalled about 330 Rijnlandse voeten or circa 102 metres.

65 ARA, map department, VTHR 393. Text *in dorso*: 'Nieuwen Grotte te Rijswyc, geconstruert [? … 15] 1643 30 April.'

66 ARA, NDR, inv. no. 4694 [old no. NDR FOLIO, 1413]. These gardener's regulations are among the bundle of *bestecken*.

67 ARA, NDR, inv. no. 4669 [old no. NDR FOLIO, 1407].

68 ARA, NDR, inv. nos. 4668 and 4670, 4671, 4672 and 4673 [old nos. NDR FOLIO, 1412 and 1408, 1409, 1410 and 1406].

69 De Beer, *Diary John Evelyn*, II, pp. 41-42.

70 Brereton admired these fig- or sycamore-trees in the forecourt of Ter Nieuburch in 1634; see Brereton, *Travels in Holland*, pp. 32-34. In Jacques and Van der Horst, *Gardens of William and Mary*, pp. 116-117, the wrong conclusion is drawn from this travel account, namely that Brereton referred to the lime-tree grove in front of the palace, which was clearly not the case.

71 ARA, NDR, inv. no. 566 [old no. 603], fols. 20vo-23.

72 ARA, NDR, inv. no. 566 [old no. 603], fol. 22: '… en blom en alderhande groene blaen om de schotelen mede te verciemen.' Compare also the description of flower decorations at Ter Nieuburch by the Sieur de la Serre, later in this chapter.

73 What is meant by 30 'roeden voeten' is not exactly clear, but thirty voeten, or Rijnlandse voeten, would be thirty times 0.314 metres, equalling circa nine and a half metres.

74 The exact measurements are again unclear, but if three Rijnlandse voeten are meant, the embankment would be circa one metre high and four metres wide.

75 The *pleijn*, or terrace, with its balustrade behind the house needed to be heightened, levelled and partly reconstructed after the completion of the whole building complex in 1636, as is shown by the two builder's estimates, ARA, NDR, inv. no. 4694 [old no. NDR FOLIO, 1413], the *Conditie ende Voorwaerden .. van het aenhogen ende effenen van seecker stuck lant off pleijn gelegen achter of aende Suijtsijde vant gebouw .. te Rijswijk* and the *Besteck .. van een Balustrade .. aende Suijtsijde .. tot Rijswijk*, both signed and dated by 'sHerwouters, 1636.

76 Important sentence from this entry: '… ende noch in proiect staat gemaeckt te worden, welck Sijne Hoocheit gelast heeft in allerijl te doen maecken ende int leger toesonden te worden … Jan. 1633.'

77 ARA, NDR, inv. no. 4694 [old no. NDR FOLIO, 1413]. These builder's estimates will receive separate attention in a forthcoming publication in the *Bulletin KNOB*.

78 Dubuisson-Aubenay, *Ex Itinerario Batavico*, 1638, Bibliothèque Mazarine, Paris, MS 4407. See Slothouwer, *Paleizen*, p. 303.

79 Slothouwer, *Paleizen*, p. 303.

80 ARA, NDR, inv.no. 4694 [old no. NDR FOLIO 1413]. The *Besteck van het Schrijnwerck alsmede Anticq Snijderije opt' huys des heeren Prince van Orange tot Rijswijck* (Builder's Specifications of the Joiner's Work and Antique Carving) relates in particular to the interior and 'antique' wood panelling. The document is signed by Constantijn Huygens and Alewijn Claessen van Assendelft and dated 15 March 1636. Van Assendelft also worked at Honselaarsdijk during that period, as can be found in the Honselaarsdijk records of payments; see NDR, inv. no. 992 [old no. 735], fols. 15 and 188.

81 ARA, NDR, inv. no. 992 [old no. 735], fol. 129, shows that Van Campen received the sum of 3,175 guilders to pay several painters for their work in the gallery of Ter Nieuburch. See also Buvelot in Huisken et al., *Jacob van Campen*, pp. 129-132.

82 Sr. de la Serre, *Histoire de l'Entrée*, pages not numbered; see s.v. Ryswick for a description of Ter Nieuburch.

83 For further reading and illustrations of the original designs for these lost paintings by Honthorst see Chandali and Huitsing, *Ter Nieuwburg en de Vrede van Rijswijk*, pp. 14-15, and Haak, *Golden Age*, pp. 42-43.

84 Heldring, *Jaarboek Die Haghe* (1967), pp. 66-71. On p. 69 Heldring expresses the belief that the manuscript containing a list of names of the persons to be depicted was written by Frederik Hendrik himself.

85 Worp, *Briefwisseling*, II, RGP 19, letter 1309, David de Wilhem to Constantijn Huygens, dated 24 November 1635. The original text is in Latin and states that the French sculptor, most likely Jacques Martin, has returned to his country and that the architect Simon de la Vallée knows someone else, who is much better.

86 KHA, K XXV and XX 182a.

87 KHA, K XX 169.

88 KHA, K XX 169 (detail).

89 That this building must have been the pump house is supported by a later print by I. van Vianen and A. Beek (see fig. 63), where, though in slightly different form, it is indicated as the *Waterhuis*.

90 It is very likely that the grotto remained unchanged at the same location after its completion in the mid-1640s until the restoration of house and garden for the Peace Conference in 1697. That its layout remained the same is also probable, if we consider the exceptional expensiveness of designing such a grotto with fountain works, and the lack of any mention of major changes at Ter Nieuburch in the archival records. After 1660 no major improvements seem to have been undertaken in the palace and gardens, except necessary repairs.

91 For further reading on the Idstein garden and the magnificent coloured design drawings for its grotto see Lentz and Nath-Esser, *Die Gartenkunst*, II, 2 (1990), pp. 165-216.

92 Worp, *Oud Holland*, 9 (1891), p. 106. See also Bienfait, *Oude Hollandsche tuinen*, p. 42.

93 De Beer, *Diary John Evelyn*, II, p. 41. See also Sieveking, *Temple*, pp. 200-201, dated 19 August 1641.

94 Brom, *Bijdragen en Mededeelingen van het Historisch Genootschap*, XXXVI (1915), p. 126: '… In esso vi è una grotta, fatta di rottami di pietre, che ben connessi assieme fanno una bella vista.'

95 See for further reading two recent publications on the topic of collecting 'marvels' and the world of the garden: Bergvelt and Kistemaker, *Wereld binnen handbereik*, p. 21, for a reproduction of Jan Weenix's portrait of Agneta Block and Sybrand de Flines with their art and *naturalia* collection in the garden of Vijverhof, and Kenseth, *Age of the Marvelous*, pp. 85ff., on 'a World of Wonders in One Closet Shut', as well as pp. 159ff. on the marvellous in theatres, festivals and gardens.

96 Boyceau, *Traité du jardinage*, chap. XI, 'Des Grotes', p. 80.

97 The Pierpont Morgan Library, New York, no. 1954.3. The drawing was first published in Stample, *Master Drawings*, 3 (1965), pp. 381-384, plate 27.

98 RPK, inv. nos. 1950:82 and 220:337 / 1956:125. Published in I.Q. van Regteren Altena, *Oud Holland*, 85 (1970), pp. 33-44, figs. 6 and 9.

99 Stample, *Master Drawings*, 3 (1965), p. 381.

100 Designs for grotesque double images are published in Floris, *Veelderleij niewe inventien*. See Stample, *Master Drawings*, 3 (1965), p. 382, fig. 1.

101 De Caus, *Forces mouvantes*. See also Strong, *Renaissance Garden*, p. 101, fig. 57.

102 The most famous example of such a grotesque head, shaped like a gigantic open mouth, is the *Mouth of Hades* of the Sacred Grove in the gardens of Bomarzo. See for further reading Darnall and Weil, *Journal of Garden History*, 1 (1984); title-page for an illustration.

103 Worp, *Bijdragen en Mededeelingen van het Historisch Genootschap*, XV (1894), pp. 78-79.

104 I.Q. van Regteren Altena uses the word *schelpenpaviljoen* (shell-pavilion) in *Oud Holland*, 85 (1970), pp. 33-44.

105 In ibid., p. 41, Van Regteren Altena already pointed out the possible connection between these designs and the work undertaken at the Stadholder's palaces. His ideas are now corroborated by findings in this study.

106 Slothouwer, *Paleizen*, pp. 81-83. See also Van Regteren Altena, *Oud Holland*, 85 (1970), pp. 41-43, fig. 10. Instead of Dirck de Wilde, the name was spelled de Milde; as mentioned in the accounts of the Nassau Domains, he was responsible for the works in the chapel.

107 Clearly recognizable are the letters H, A, V and two O's, referring to *H*enry (Frederik Hendrik used to sign documents with this name), *A*malia, *V*an (of) and *O*ranje. This same monogram was used on the pulpit of the Honselaarsdijk chapel, now at Wateringen; see Slothouwer, *Paleizen*, fig. 27, pp. 83 and 110, and Morren *Honselaarsdijk*, p. 33. Both Slothouwer and Van Regteren Altena missed the important fact that the monogram was a central feature of the Stadholder's garden decoration as well. It can also be found on various art objects, for example a gold case with enamelled portrait of Frederik Hendrik by Henri Toutin, in the Rijksmuseum, Amsterdam. See Fock, *Apollo*, CX, no. 214 (December 1979), p. 473, fig. 19.

108 Van Regteren Altena, *Oud Holland*, 85 (1970), p. 43.

109 ARA, NDR, inv. no. 4697 [old no. NDR FOLIO, 1417].

110 A description of the grotto in the gardens of Oranienbaum referring to these busts, which today are in the Gothisches Haus at Wörlitz, is given by Beckmann, *Fürstenthum Anhalt*, III, p. 393, cited in W. Boeck, *Zeitschrift des deutschen Vereins für Kunstwissenschaft*, 4 (1937), p. 39. Compare Van Regteren Altena, *Oud Holland*, 85 (1970), pp. 39-42 and fig. 8. See chapters V and VI for further consideration of the Stadholder's garden sculpture in Germany.

111 Van Regteren Altena, *Oud Holland*, 85 (1970), p. 42, refers to the two busts as 'nearly identical', except that the head of the actual statue leans somewhat more to the left than it does in the drawing.

112 The letters H, A, V and O, topped by a crown, are clearly recognizable within the central roundel of the main parterre.

113 See in particular Karling in MacDougall and Hamilton Hazlehurst, *French Formal Garden*, pp. 19-21.

114 Bienfait, Slothouwer and Karling all mention the likelihood of this relationship, but do not go into the question in further detail.

115 Plates 6 and 13.

116 Compare the designs by André, Jacques and Noël Mollet for their father Claude Mollet's *Théâtre des plans et jardinages*, reproduced by Karling in MacDougall and Hamilton Hazlehurst, *French Formal Garden*, figs. 10-12.

117 The Metropolitan Museum of Art, New York, Harris Brisbane Dick Fund, 1942 (42.141).

118 Ibid.

119 De Caus, *Hortus Palatinus*, plate 17.

120 The rediscovery of these two river gods from Frederik Hendrik's

gardens, first noticed and identified by L.J. van der Klooster, director of the RKD topographical department, and Th.H. Lunsingh Scheurleer, emeritus professor of Leiden University, was aided by further research on the Paviljoen von Wied by Caroline Sillem. Her findings were published as 'Beschrijving van het Paviljoen', in Rosenberg, *Koninklijk paviljoen*, pp. 22-23. See also de Jong and Schellekens, *Het beeld buiten*, p. 51.

121 Plate 24. Compare this statue of the Rhine with the figure of a reclining river god in de Caus's print from the same period, entitled *Les Raisons des forces mouvantes* and shown by Zangheri in Mosser and Teyssot, *Western Gardens*, p. 68.

122 For further reading on the Heidelberg garden see Zimmerman in Mosser and Teyssot), *Western Gardens*, pp. 157-159. See also Patterson, *Journal of Garden History*, 1 and 2 (1981), pp. 67-105 and 179-203.

123 See for a more detailed analysis chapter V. For further reading see Wendland, *Berlins Gärten und Parke*, pp. 20ff. and the reproduction of the Neptune fountain on p. 32.

124 Woodbridge, *Princely Gardens*, pp. 124-127.

125 Haskell and Penny, *Taste and the Antique*, pp. 272-273.

126 Good examples are the river gods of the Villa Lante at Bagnaia and the Villa Farnese, Caprarola. For images of territory and geography, the Medici garden at Castello near Florence is a good example. See for further reading Lazzaro, *Italian Renaissance Garden*, pp. 146-148 and 167-189. For the iconographical programme of the Castello garden see Wright, *Medici Villa*.

127 KB, Department of Old Prints and Manuscripts, MS 78 D 14. De Caus's books are listed under nos. 277-279.

128 Worp, *Briefwisseling*, IV, RGP 24, letter 4125, Constantijn Huygens to Amalia of Orange, dated 23 September 1645.

129 Compare de Jong, *Natuur en kunst*, p. 77, who identifies the three sculptures as a Venus fountain, a Minerva and a Hercules. While Minerva is clearly distinguishable because of her familiar pose and attributes of helmet and spear, the others cannot be identified with certainty. The female figure topping the fountain, represented in the Milheusser print as a figure upholding her breast from which water is flowing, seems to be a Ceres because of this gesture, unless she represents a so-called Venus Lactans type. A conflation of the two types is not impossible, given their mutual aquatic setting and closely related symbolic meaning. See for further discussion chapter VI. For further reading see Lazzaro, *Italian Renaissance Garden*, pp. 151-153 and 174-176.

130 Sandrart, *Accademia Todesca*, I, book II, p. 41.

131 Logan, *Verhandelingen van de Koninklijke Nederlandse Akademie van Wetenschappen*, 99 (1979), p. 55.

132 Ibid., pp. 11-59, especially p. 55, note 45. See chapter VI for further consideration of garden sculpture.

133 For further reading and illustrations see Diedenhofen et al., *Fonteijn van Pallas*, pp. 8ff. See also de Jong and Schellekens, *Het beeld buiten*, p. 53. For Johan Maurits and his gardens and the art of his age see the catalogue published in conjunction with the 300th anniversary of his death, Van den Boogaart, *Johan Maurits van Nassau-Siegen*. See also Diedenhofen in *Soweit der Erdkreis reicht*, pp. 165-188, and Hilger, ibid., pp. 189-194.

134 De Cretser, *Berschrijvinge van 's Gravenhage*, pp. 121-122: 'Maar het is te beklagen, dat het zelve Hof ... weder tot zyn ruine zal geraken, waar van men reeds de beginselen al begint te zien, ten ware dat zyne Koninklyke Majesteit van Pruyssen, die daar van tegenwoordig Possesseur is, daaraan ernstig de hand geliefde te houden.'

135 Both Ter Nieuburch and the Huis ten Bosch were returned by Prussia to the Orange family on that occasion. Slothouwer, *Paleizen*, p. 130, states that Ter Nieuburch was given back to the Orange family in 1754, not 1732. Compare Loonstra, *Het Huys int Bosch*, pp. 65-66, describing the agreement between the House of Nassau and the Prussian line in 1732.

136 KB, Department of Old Prints and Manuscripts, MS 133 L 32, p. 3. Travel Journal of John Mucklow, John Eliot and Samuel Wilson, 12 June-30 July 1743.

137 ARA, NDAH, copy of this poster in the GAR, s.v. Rijswijk, Huis ter Nieuwburg.

138 GAH, topographical department, Rijswijk–Van Vredenburchweg, klein 54.

CHAPTER III

1. For the early history of the Paleis Noordeinde see Den Boer, *Noorteynde*, pp. 8-19, and Slothouwer, *Paleizen*, pp. 134-136 and 375-376. See also Morren, *Jaarboek Die Haghe* (1899), pp. 371ff., and Van Pelt, *Jaarboek Vereniging Oranje-Nassau Museum* (1979), pp. 11-19.

2. Slothouwer, *Paleizen*, pp. 138-139. Den Boer, *Noorteynde*, p. 22.

3. Under Willem Goudt orchards and plain gardens were situated behind the house. In 1582 the heirs of Adriana van Persijn, widow of Van Brandtwyck, already bought a piece of land from the St. Nicolaas Hospice to enlarge the property. See Den Boer, *Noorteynde*, pp. 14-15.

4. Haags Historisch Museum, The Hague, panel inscribed 'Haga Comitis in Hollandia', inv. no. HH 51-ZJ. The plan was made in 1663. For further reading see Dumas, *Haagse stadsgezichten*, pp. 66 and 380-381.

5. Frederik Hendrik called it 'Onsen Huijse int Noorteijnde' (Our House at the North End); see Den Boer, *Noorteynde*, pp. 8-9. Though the palace was situated at the western edge of town, it is called North End because of the way Holland is traditionally depicted on maps: turned sideways, the western shoreline on top.

6. A map of The Hague by Jacques de Gheyn dated 1597 shows the old palace complex. Behind a cluster of buildings lays a simple garden, consisting of two rectangular beds enclosed by walls. See Den Boer, *Noorteynde*, p. 9.

7. Ibid., pp. 18-20.

8. Compare ibid., pp. 15-23, and Van Pelt, *Jaarboek Vereniging Oranje-Nassau Museum* (1979), p. 16. Already in 1582, and again in 1609 and 1614, mention is made of enlarging the property through the acquisition of 'large meadows' from the St. Nicolaas Hospice. Later entries in the archival records of the early 1630s refer to payments for new tracts of land as well as continued instalments paid for these earlier acquisitions; compare ARA, NDR, inv. no. 1040 [old no. 779], fol. 179, and NDR, inv. no. 1043 [old no. 782], fol. 170vo, with ARA, NDR, inv. no. 1043 [old no. 782], fols. 169vo and 180vo.

9. Extract from ARA, NDR, inv. no. 1043 [old no. 782], fol. 170: '… Ende is van dit stuckgen erff gemaeckt een Tuyntgen ende Grotto gevoecht aent quartier vant huijs daer haere fürstel. Gen. Hoochlofl. mem. Sijne Hoocheits Vrouw Moeder in logerende was …' (And of this piece of land are made a small garden and grotto, added to the quarter of the house where her Highness's right honourable memory, His Highness's Mother was living …)

10. Worp, *Oud Holland*, 9 (1891), p. 114. See also Den Boer, *Noorteynde*, p. 23.

11. Marchegay, *Correspondance de Louise de Coligny*, p. 277, Louise de Coligny to Madame de La Trémoille, duchesse de Touars, dated May 1613.

12. GAH, topographical department, Den Haag, and Haags Historisch Museum, The Hague, inv. no. HH 89-ZJ. For further reading see Dumas, *Haagse stadsgezichten*, pp. 16-17.

13. Bienfait, *Oude Hollandsche tuinen*, p. 45, and Peters, *Landsgebouwen*, p. 175.

14. CBN, inv. no. P16 N51, detail of middle upper section of this map.

15. Den Boer, *Noorteynde*, p. 23.

16. Brereton, *Travels in Holland*, p. 28.

17. Detail of Joan Blaeu's plan of The Hague from his *Toonneel der Steden*, published in 1649. CBN, inv. no. P16 N56.

18. Detail of the map of The Hague after the Blaeu map executed by C. Elandts, here shown in a later edition dating from 1681. CBN, inv. no. P 16 N 62.

19. The layout of the parterres in the old *berceaux* garden behind the palace's rear or garden façade can be recognized in a drawing in the Collectie de Grez, Koninklijke Musea voor Schone Kunsten, Brussels, inv. no. 1753. The drawing is made by Constantijn Huygens, inscribed and dated recto 'Vande Haegschen Toren: 4 Jun. 1665'; it shows a panorama of The Hague taken from the Grote Kerk or Sint-Jacobskerk over the Noordeinde palace towards the sea. A copy, attributed to A. Rademaker, in the GAH is reproduced on the cover and on p. 62 of Den Boer, *Noorteynde*, as well as in Slothouwer, *Paleizen*, p. 145, fig. 49, where an attribution to J. de Bisschop instead of Rademaker is proposed. See for commentary on the original version by Constantijn Huygens Junior, Heijbroek, *Met Huygens op reis*, pp. 53-54. See also Van Lakerveld, *Opkomst en bloei*, p. 160, cat. no. 68. In addition see Duparc, *Landscape in Perspective*, pp. 130-131, cat. no. 43.

20. ARA, NDR, inv. no. 566 [old no. 603, Notulen van de Raad, vol. 26, dated 17 February 1667], pages not numbered, separate sheets arranged according to date and following fol. 20.

21. The description in the record of payments mentions reimbursement to Dinant for 'the new grotto in the garden at the Cingel of the Court' (Noordeinde), which seems to indicate that there already existed a grotto in the garden.

22. See for a clear overview of the palace's interior division and access to outside garden areas Den Boer, *Noorteynde*, p. 40.

23. Van Pelt, *Jaarboek Vereniging Oranje-Nassau Museum* (1979), pp. 26-29. For the influence of Scamozzi in Holland see Terwen, *Bulletin KNOB*, 65 (1966), pp. 129-130.

24. ARA, NDR, inv. no. 562 [old no. NDR (Gemengde Domestiquen), no. 599], fol. 51vo. See Slothouwer, *Paleizen*, pp. 31 and 325: 'Acte voor Pieter Post, architect tot Haarlem omme opsicht te hebben op de timmeragie alhier int Noordtejjnde … 30 April 1640.' Or: 'Pieter Post … to have supervision over the carpentry here in the Noordeinde.'

25. Drossaers and Lunsingh Scheurleer, *Inventarissen*, I, RGP 147, pp. 179-292.

26. De la Serre, *Histoire de l'Entrée*, pages not numbered. See also

27 De la Serre, *Histoire de l'Entrée*: '… ce Palais paressoit une maison vrayment Royalle.' See also Den Boer, *Noorteynde*, p. 82.
28 Concerning the garden of the Paleis Noordeinde, pp. 106-111.
29 De Hennin, *Zinrijke Gedachten*, p. 110: '… let toch hoe al deze schoone groote Spiegels respondeere op den gantschen Hof en Fontein …' (… see how all these beautiful large Mirrors reflect the whole Court and Fountain …)
30 The open, arcaded, mirrored pavilion later contained Amalia's porcelain cabinet. ARA, NDR, inv. no. 993 [old no. 736], fol. 293, and NDR inv. no. 994 [old no. 737], fols. 121-122. See also Den Boer, *Noorteynde*, p. 47, notes 57-58.
31 Drossaers and Lunsingh Scheurleer, *Inventarissen*, I, RGP 147, pp. 258-259.
32 Ibid., p. 259, no. 613: 'Twee figuren van vrouwen van loot gemaeckt op de trap in 't cleyne tuyntje in 't Noordeynde staende.'
33 Ibid., p. 259, no. 614: 'Een figure van een faem in 't midden van een fonteyntje staende, van loot.'
34 Ibid., p. 259, no. 615: 'Acht loode dieren van verscheyde soorten.'
35 Ibid., p. 259, no. 616: 'Twee groote spiegels.'
36 Ibid., p. 258, nos. 606 and 610-12: 'Een marmer Cupidoken die een boochjen schaeft; Een kindeken slaepende van marber, rustende op een schildeken; Een Cupidoken van marber dat een booghjen schaefft; Een Cupidoken van marber dat een boochjen buygt.' See chapter VI for further information.
37 Ibid., p. 259, no. 617: 'Vier statuen in vollen harnas, alle gehouwen in witten marber soo groot als 't leven, denoterende de doorlugtige princen van Orangen, Willem, Maurits, Frederick Hendrick ende Willem de laeste, alle onsterffelijcker memorie.' For an illustration see Neurdenburg, *Beeldhouwkunst*, p. 122, figs. 91-92. Compare chapter VI for further information, including on the Elector of Brandenburg's copy after these life-size statues.
38 De Hennin, *Zinrijke Gedachten*, p. 110: 'Daar ziet gij nu het geheele Huis van Nassau en Orangie, alle na 't leven afgegoten en gesneeden / het schijnt zy alle levendigh daar staan.' (There you see the whole family of Nassau and Orange, all cast and cut 'after life'/ it is as if they stand there alive.) For a more detailed discussion of these statues see chapters V and VI.
39 Sandrart, *Accademia Todesca*, II, book III, p. 348. Compare again the Cupids referred to in Amalia's inventory. See Drossaers and Lunsingh Scheurleer, *Inventarissen*, I, RGP 147, pp. 258-259, nos. 606, 611-12 and 629. The Cupid is described by Sandrart, *Accademia Todesca*, I, book II, p. 41, as 'ein in Lebens-Grösse nackend stehender Cupido, der ihm einen Bogen schneidet'. Thus no. 611, called in the inventory 'Een Cupidoken van marmer dat een booghje schaefft', exactly fits Sandrart's description of the statue. For further consideration of these putti see chapter VI.
40 Earlier examples of the garden gallery-cum-grotto functioning as an open-air *Wunderkammer* were Isabella d'Este's garden rooms known as the *grotto* and *studiolo* at Mantua; see Brown, *Gazette des Beaux-Arts*, 89 (1977), pp. 155-171. Another sixteenth-century Italian example was Francesco I's hanging garden in the Loggia dei Lanzi in Florence; see Kreutner, *Kunstgeschichtliche Studien für H. Kauffmann*, pp. 240-251. It is of interest to note that garden and grotto elements became an intrinsic element of the whole *Wunderkammer* concept, in which interior spaces took on rustic decorations, such as the Tribuna in the Uffizi, with its encrusted dome crowned by a weather vane. In this context we are reminded of the Mauritshuis with its vast collection of 'marvels' from all over the world and the galleries inside the Ter Nieuburch palace, painted according to Frederik Hendrik's own distinct wishes – not with grotesque decoration, but with floral elements. For the idea of the *Wunderkammer* and examples in Italy see the good recent survey by Zangheri in Mosser and Teyssot, *Western Gardens*, pp. 59-68. See for further reading also Hunt, *Garden and Grove*, chap. 6: 'Cabinets of curiosity', pp. 73-83. See also Impey and MacGregor, *Origins of Museums*.
41 For a reconstruction of the interior function of the rooms in the Paleis Noordeinde see the plan in Van Pelt, *Jaarboek Vereniging Oranje-Nassau Museum* (1979), pp. 54-55, nos. 23, 25 and 26. See for a bird's-eye view Den Boer, *Noorteynde*, pp. 40-41, nos. 12, 13 and 19.
42 The iconography of the great hall, representing the story of Dido and Aeneas – portrayed as founders of Troy – referred to Amalia and Frederik Hendrik as historic founders of the Orange dynasty. See Drossaers and Lunsingh Scheurleer, *Inventarissen*, I, RGP 147, inventory of 1702, pp. 483-503, no. 110.
43 Perspective paintings of the owner's properties and gardens decorated the walls of rooms in many Italian Renaissance villas, including the Villa d'Este at Tivoli, the Villa Lante at Bagnaia, the Belvedere and the Villas Giulia and Medici in Rome. See for reproductions of the last three examples Coffin, *Villa in Renaissance Rome*, pp. 77, 87, 162, 218 and 221.
44 Siren, *Studieresor*, p. 77: 'Im alten Printzen Hoff … undt in einer Cammer zweij zimlich grosse gemahlte perspectiven von Hundzlardick undt Rosswick.'
45 Ibid., p. 77: 'Der garten hieran ist ziemlich gross, wie meine plante von Haag ausweist, die plantage war sehr hoch gewachsen.'
46 ARA, NDR, inv. no. 1002 [old no. 745], fol. 159. See also Den Boer, *Noorteynde*, p. 72, note 46.
47 CBN, inv. nos. IX-10-56 (shown here) and IX-10-66. Made during Prussian ownership, the plan is entitled 'Geometrisscher Gruntris von des Koeniges von Pröeussen garten in den Haag auff das alte Hoff'. Compare de Vries, *Kaarten met geschiedenis*, p. 110.
48 Similar parterre designs and ornamentation can be found in the treatise by Le Nôtre's follower: Dézallier d'Argenville, *La Théorie et la Practique du Jardinage*.

49 In 1754 Honselaarsdijk and the Noordeinde were bought back by Anna of Hanover, William IV's widow, for 70,000 pounds, with an additional 5,000 pounds for the furnishings in both palaces. See ARA, NDR, inv. no. 994 [old no. 737], fols. 121-122. See also Den Boer, *Noorteynde*, p. 76.

50 The restoration of house and garden was undertaken by the stadholderly architect David Stolk; see Den Boer, *Noorteynde*, pp. 76-77. Under Prussian rule, the Noordeinde garden was opened to the public and the neighbouring houses received permission to join their gardens with that of Noordeinde. The restoration of the gardens included new earth, new embankments, retaining walls and large-scale planting of trees and shrubs. The island, decorated with a late-seventeenth-century statue by Xaveri, was made accessible by way of a little cable ferry boat. By 1757 the restoration of the garden was advanced far enough that miniature naval manoeuvres could be held in the large pond. See Den Boer, *Noorteynde*, p. 77.

51 The remodelling of palace and garden was undertaken under the direction of the architect Philip Willem Schonck from 1778 onward. See ARA, Resolutiën Nassausche Domeinraad, dated 9 October 1778. See ARA, NDR, inv. nos. 4688 and 4692. At the same time the ceilings of the then demolished Huis ter Nieuburch were brought over to the Paleis Noordeinde to decorate its main stairwell; see Slothouwer, *Paleizen*. pp. 153 and 310, in a letter written by Princess Wilhelmina to her daughter, dated May 1791: 'Le plafond de l'escalier est orné des peintures de celui de Ryswyk.' We may wonder whether at that occasion also certain statues, such as the *River Gods*, were moved from Ter Nieuburch's gardens to the Noordeinde or elsewhere in The Hague, before being brought to the Paviljoen von Wied at Scheveningen.

52 ARA, NDR, inv. no. 4692 [old no. 9194.1], fol. 81vo. An early-nineteenth-century inventory of the house and garden refers to the Chinese pavilion on the island in the pond: 'Chineesche Salon op het Eylandje in den vijver.' In ARA, NDR, inv. no. 6750 [old no. 7146.1], concerning the 'Westland bestecken en conditien' dated 9 June 1811, this pavilion is mentioned as having undergone repairs and standing in the 'National Garden', the new name of the Noordeinde garden: 'eenige reparatien aan de koepel op het Eilandje in de warande in de *Nationale Tuin* in Den Haag'. An old picture of the Chinese pavilion in 1890 is included in Den Boer, *Noorteynde*, p. 89. See also pp. 82 and 87 for the landscaping in 'Chinese style' of the Noordeinde garden in the late eighteenth century.

53 ARA, NDR, inv. no. 4692 [old no. 9194.1], fol. 81vo. Compare the previous note.

54 ARA, NDR, inv. no. 4688 [old no. 9193.1]. The document is entitled *Rapporten wegens de Gebouwen en Tuinen rondom Den Haag* and states: '... De binnentuyn is in een goede staat ... de groote tuyn in een zeer goede staat en voorsien van veele curieuse uyt- en inheemsche planten en gewassen, sijnde dagelijks voor het publicq open.'

55 De Greef's design is kept in the ARA, topographical department, inv. no. WCAP 1515-1517. Compare Den Boer, *Noorteynde*, pp. 102-103. See also Slothouwer, *Paleizen*, pp. 165 and 313-314, and Oldenburger-Ebbers, *Tuinengids*, p. 220.

56 In his *De Sael van Orange ghebout bij haere Hooch[t] Princesse Douariere van Orange*, Pieter Post states specifically that the palace was the 'brain child' of the Dowager Princess Amalia. Van Campen was involved in its design and construction; see Huisken et al., *Jacob van Campen*, pp. 22 and 77-81.

57 ARA, NDR, inv. no. 4675 [old no. NDR, Oude Inventarissen, fol. 1263, no. 2]. Compare also ARA, map department, inv. no. VTH 4698. See Slothouwer, *Paleizen*, p. 183, and Loonstra, *Huijs int Bosch*, p. 15: 'Een partije van seeckere elst-ackers, weye, valleye en wildernisse, gelegen op 't Oosteijnde van 't Haegsche Bosch, aan de noordwestzijde van de besuijdenhoutschen wech.'

58 ARA, map department, VTH 3323. Signed and dated in the upper right-hand corner 'Pieter Florisz van der Sallem, 17 May 1645' and accompanied by the following text: 'gecopyeert den 17 Meij 1645 naer de teijckeninge gedaen bij Monsr Post teyckenaer voor haer hoocheydt omme een huijs, tuijnen ende grachten int bosch te maecken' (copied on 17 May 1645 after the drawing done by Mr. Post, draughtsman of Het Highness, to build a house, gardens and canals in the wood).

59 KHA, archief Frederik Hendrik, no. A 14-VII-13. Unknown writer, but possibly David de Wilhem as member of the Council Chamber of the Domain and supervisor of the works, to Amalia van Solms, dated 7 July 1645: 'Op mijn aencompst alhier inden Hage hebbe terstont Mons.[r] Post ontboden die op Maendach lestelijk tegen den avont hier is aengecomen; ondertusschen hebbe het Aerdewerck waerin de Aennemers sterck doende sijn wesen besichtigen, en bevonden dat alles bij haer wel is met goeder orde werde aengevangen, gelijck oock den landtmeter Pieter Florissen t' stuck de Elstslote gaet besichtigen en opmeten soo rasch de Baggert daer uijt geworpen is.' (Upon my arrival here in The Hague I immediately sent for Mr. Post, who arrived here last Monday in the evening; meanwhile I went to see the earthwork where the contractors are working hard, and found all to be in good order and well begun, just as the surveyor Pieter Florissen will inspect and measure the piece of land of the Elstslote as soon as the mud has been thrown out.)

60 GAH, topographical department, Huis ten Bosch, and KB, Department of Rare Books and Manuscripts, no. 1292 C 33, Pieter Post, *De Sael van Orange*. The engravings of the Huis ten Bosch were published again in *Les Ouvrages d'architecture de Pierre Post*.

61 Worp, *Briefwisseling*, IV, RGP 24, letter 4034, Constantijn Huygens to Amalia of Orange, dated 20 July 1645. See also

Slothouwer, *Paleizen*, p. 351. 'En me hastant d'obeïr aux commandemens de V.A. par la prompte depesche de ce messager porteur des desseins de son Bastiment ... S.A. a recognu aveq patience les changemens du dessein de V.A. au Bois, et ne les a pas tant voulu gouster d'abord, comme apres quelque information qu'elle a souffert qu'on luij en fist, projectant mesme de restreindre le Bastiment, de sorte que la salle eust esté salle, et entrée et toutes choses, retraicte des lacquais et des honestes gens. Mais enfin la justice s'est trouvée du costé de V.A. qui, je m'asseure, trouvera tout contentement dans la joincte.'

62 The Metropolitan Museum of Art, New York, Anonymous Gift, 1964 (64.65.2). The version in the National Gallery, London (which shows the statues most clearly), is reproduced in de Jong and Dominicus-Van Soest, *Aardse paradijzen*, p. 92. Another version, in the Hamburger Kunsthalle, Hamburg, also by Jan van der Heyden, is reproduced in Keblusek and Zijlmans, *Vorstelijk vertoon*.

63 Slothouwer *Paleizen*, p. 207, believed that Constantijn Huygens designed the combined monogram, but there is no direct evidence for such an assumption.

64 ARA, NDR, inv. no. 993 [old no. 736], fol. 428vo: 'To Borchgaert Frederick gardener, for the expenses concerning the parterres and flower borders in the garden of the Court in the Hague Wood.'

65 Post, *Sael van Orange*. Van der Heyden made a painting using Post's garden pavilion as central architectural feature; see de Jong and Dominicus-Van Soest, *Aardse paradijzen*, p. 93.

66 Brom, *Bijdragen en Mededeelingen van het Historisch Genootschap*, XXXVI (1915), p. 119.

67 KHA, archief Frederik Hendrik, no. A 14-XIII-16, 618. See Drossaers and Lunsingh Scheurleer, *Inventarissen*, I, RGP 147, p. 259, no. 618. Compare also Loonstra, *Huijs int Bosch*, p. 46: 'Vier loode beelden in de thuyn aen de Orangezael, gemaeckt bij ... [no name added].'

68 The description of these four marble statues corresponds with the four life-size statues of the Princes of Orange described in Amalia's 1667 inventory, no. 617. According to de Hennin, *Zinrijke Gedachten*, p. 110, similar statues stood in Amalia's flower garden at the Paleis Noordeinde in the late 1670s. It is not clear whether de Hennin refers to a different or to the same group of statues; in the latter case they must have been transported to the Noordeinde garden from the Huis ten Bosch sometime between 1677 and 1681. The statues of the four Princes of Orange were commissioned by Amalia from François Dieussart in 1646; see ARA, NDR, 993 [old no. 736], fol. 428vo. See also Slothouwer, *Paleizen*, p. 335. They were brought to Berlin by the King of Prussia and, until their destruction in the Second World War, were kept at Potsdam. See Drossaers and Lunsingh Scheurleer, *Inventarissen*, I, RGP 147, p. 259, no. 617 and accompanying note. For an illustration see Neurdenburg, *Beeldhouwkunst*, p. 122, figs. 91-92. Compare also the copy made after these statues of the Princes of Orange by the Elector of Brandenburg, further considered in chapters V and VI.

69 Brom, *Bijdragen en Mededeelingen van het Historisch Genootschap*, XXXVI (1915), p. 118.

70 See Sellers, *Journal of Garden History*, VII, 1 (1987), pp. 31-32.

71 GAH, topographical department, Haagsche Bosch, zeer groot 1.

72 ARA, map department, VTH 3328 B. Map of the Haagsche Bosch, signed and dated Huybert van Straalen, 4 Maart 1778.

73 Wiebenson, *Picturesque Garden in France*, and Hunt and Willis, *Genius of the Place*. Compare also Pevsner, *Picturesque Garden*.

74 GAH, topographical department, Haagsche Bos, zeer groot 11. The early-nineteenth-century plan by Jan David Zocher is kept in the LUW; it is reproduced in Loonstra, *Huijs int Bosch*, p. 111. Van der Spuij, whose plan dates from 1853, shows the garden almost half a century later, in its mature form. Other nineteenth-century ideas and plans for changes in the Huis ten Bosch garden are kept in the ARA, Archief Kroondomeinen, no. 54. See Loonstra, *Huijs int Bosch*, pp. 108-111, notes 24 and 25.

75 During the remodelling of the garden about 1948, Zocher's early-nineteenth-century layout remained largely untouched, except for the sections in front of the building which, interestingly, hark back to Daniel Marot's eighteenth-century plan. See for illustrations Loonstra, *Huijs int Bosch*, p. 121.

76 KB, Department of Rare Books and Manuscripts, no. 1292 C 33 [old no. 1376 B 73], Hendrick Hondius, *Institutio artis perspectivae*, plates 30 and 31, with accompanying description. The Buitenhhof garden and these prints have been analysed in depth by Hopper, *Journal of Garden History*, II, 1 (1982), pp. 26-29.

77 Hondius, *Institutio*, Beschrijvinge van de dertichste Figure: 'pavillioen ... het welcke van binnen is geschildert met loofwerck ende pylasters, als oft men daer door sage tegen een blaeuwe locht ...'

78 Hopper, *Journal of Garden History*, II, 1 (1982), p. 28, believes that the parterres bore the pattern of the Prince's coat of arms, but it is difficult to distinguish its decoration clearly, which resembles a generic flower motive.

79 Pages 124-125.

80 De Cretser, *Beschrijvinge van 's Gravenhage*, p. 18.

81 De Beer, *Diary John Evelyn*, II, p. 41. See also Hopper, *Journal of Garden History*, II, 1 (1982), p. 27.

82 Van Regteren Altena, *Jacques de Gheyn*, I, p. 141.

83 What is defined as 'mannerism' in sixteenth- and early-seventeenth-century painting and sculpture does not necessarily apply to garden art; artifice, intricacy and eccentric curiosities to some extent form a natural part of gardens, and certainly of grottoes. Seen chronologically, the term far extends the usual boundaries in garden art, where the fascination for artifice and 'the monstrous' continued into the eighteenth century. For further

84 Hopper, *Journal of Garden History*, II, 1 (1982), pp. 26-29.
85 A.H. Kan (ed.), *De jeugd van Constantijn Huygens door hemzelf beschreven* (Rotterdam, 1971), p. 70. See also Hopper, *Journal of Garden History*, II, 1 (1982), p. 27.
86 Worp, *Oud Holland*, 9 (1891), pp. 106-136, here especially p. 114. See also Bienfait, *Oude Hollandsche tuinen*, p. 42, and Hopper, *Journal of Garden History*, II, 1 (1982), p. 27.
87 Hopper, *Journal of Garden History*, II, 1 (1982), p. 27, on de Gheyn. Huygens's *galerijen*, translated here as *berceaux*, may refer to the circular *berceaux* or just to arbours in general.
88 For further reading on de Gheyn and his cultural-artistic milieu see Van Regteren Altena, *Jacques de Gheyn*, and Meij, *De Gheyn Drawings*.
89 Worp, *Oud Holland*, 9 (1891), p. 114. See also Bienfait, *Oude Hollandsche tuinen*, p. 42, and Meij, *De Gheyn Drawings*, p. 91.
90 Brom, *Bijdragen en Mededeelingen van het Historisch Genootschap*, XXXVI (1915), p. 126.
91 See Meij, *De Gheyn Drawings*, pp. 90-91. See also Van Regteren Altena, *Oud Holland*, 85 (1970), pp. 33-44, and Stample, *Master Drawings*, 3 (1965), pp. 381-383.
92 Van Regteren Altena, *Jacques de Gheyn*. For the fountain design see ibid., vol. II, no. 161, p. 213, fig. 438. For the Triton drawn by de Gheyn III see ibid., vol. I, p. 140, fig. 107, and vol. III, no. 12.
93 Meij, *De Gheyn Drawings*, p. 91.
94 A good example is his *Bathers* in the Princeton University Art Museum, where a shady grotto area is represented, including a fountain crowned by statues of Hercules and Antaeus and surrounded by rustic walls filled with shells, pumice-stones and coral.
95 De Caus, *Hortus Palatinus*, I, pp. 26-31, and II (facsimile edition of the 1620 edition), figs. 21-23 and 25-26.
96 For a recent publication on the subject with good background information, see Zangheri in Mosser and Teyssot, *Western Gardens*, pp. 59-68.
97 Abraham Bosse published prints by Alessandro Francini of the waterworks and grottoes at Saint-Germain-en-Laye and Fontainebleau in 1624. See Woodbridge, *Princely Gardens*, pp. 120-121, 125 and 129.
98 De Cretser, *Beschrijvinge van 's Gravenhage*, p. 18.
99 FLUSHING: Den Hoed, *Bulletin KNOB*, 15 (1962), pp. 337-347, here especially p. 337. For further research consult Van Hoof et al., *Archieven van de Nassause Domeinraad*, pp. 527-533, and especially the accounts of the stewards, ARA, NDR, inv. nos. 14975-14996.
100 This and other plans concerning the rebuilding of the Prinsenhuis are kept in the ARA, map department, inv. nos. VTH 3509-3514. Plan no. 3509 has a text on the back attesting to Stevin's authorship: 'Plante van Syns Exties huys tot Vlissingen, overgelevert by Simon Stevin op den XIen Martij 1617.' See for further reading Vermeulen, *Oudheidkundig Jaarboek*, 5 (1936), pp. 43-47, especially pp. 45-46 and fig. 3. See also Bienfait, *Oude Hollandsche tuinen*, p. 60; Den Hoed, *Bulletin KNOB*, 15 (1962), p. 338, fig. 4; and Schmidt in *Opstellen voor Hans Lochner*, pp. 79-88, especially p. 85.
101 Hopper first pointed to the important connections between Stevin and the art of garden designing in *Journal of Garden History*, II, 1 (1982), pp. 25-27, and *Bulletin KNOB*, 3-4 (1983), p. 99.
102 For further reading see Crone and Struik, *Simon Stevin*. See also Dijksterhuis, *Simon Stevin*. Compare Hopper, *Journal of Garden History*, II, 1 (1982), pp. 37-38, notes 1 and 2.
103 Stevin in *Materiae politicae*. Compare Hopper, *Journal of Garden History*, II, 1 (1982), p. 25 and note 3.
104 See Taverne, *In 't land van belofte*, pp. 81-90 about Christian IV in Denmark, pp. 94-102 about cities and fortifications in Sweden under Gustaf Adolf II and later Queen Christina. Compare also Hopper, *Bulletin KNOB*, 3-4 (1983), p. 99 and note 2.
105 Stevin, *Wisconstighe Ghedachtnissen*. For the effect of his work on Frederik Hendrik's architectural activities see Taverne, *In 't land van belofte*, pp. 49 and 82, describing how the Stadholder helped assembling Dutch engineers to be sent to Denmark to work for Gustav IV in 1626.
106 Stevin, native of Bruges, came to Holland and settled in Leiden in 1581. Already known as a pioneer in mathematical research, engineering and political theory, he later would be acclaimed as the founder of modern hydrostatics and as a proponent of the use of Dutch as a scientific language. See also Vermeersch, *Bruges and Europe*, p. 83.
107 Worp, *Briefwisseling*, III, RGP 21, letter 3044, Constantijn Huygens to J.A. Bannius, dated July 2, 1642: '… Stevinius Belgicos in mathematica non semel praemisere.' As can be concluded from the correspondence, Huygens knew Stevin's scientific works intimately. Compare, for example, his discussion of Stevin's theory on the weight of water published as *De Beghinselen des Waterwichts* (1584), with his French friend the scientist-philosopher Mersenne, in Worp, *Briefwisseling*, III, RGP 21, letter 2386, Huygens to M. Mersenne, dated 3 June 1640.
108 See, for example, Van Deursen, *Resolutiën*, p. 460, no. 502, dated 18 June 1615: Jan Hendricxsz, collector general of the Admiralty at Dokkum, requests the right to publish 'Gulden Zegel des Zeevaerts'. It is decided to have the book first researched by Stevin and Marollois [Samuel Marolois, the French fortress engineer]. Ibid., p. 582, no. 139: Stevin is sent to attend a demonstration of the instruments of Abraham de Huysse for longitudinal measurements at sea.
109 Compare also Hopper, *Journal of Garden History*, II, 1 (1982), pp. 25-27.
110 Den Hoed, *Bulletin KNOB*, 15 (1962), p. 343. See also Schmidt in *Opstellen voor Hans Lochner*, p. 84.

111 ARA, map department, VTH 3510 and 3511, respectively dated 1623 and 1624 on the back of the sheet. See Vermeulen, *Oudheidkundig Jaarboek*, 5 (1936), pp. 45-46. For a description of the texts on the back of the maps, see also Schmidt in *Opstellen voor Hans Lochner*, pp. 84-85, fig. 3.

112 ARA, map department, VTH 3510. See also Den Hoed, *Bulletin KNOB*, 15 (1962), fig. 7, and Schmidt in *Opstellen voor Hans Lochner*, p. 85, fig. 3.

113 ARA, map department. 'Inventaris van de Caerten gehorende tot de Domeijnen en goederen nagelaten bij Sijne Con^e Maj^t van Groot Britten Willem de derde glor: mem: soo als die naer resumtie en Inventarisatie gedaen in de maend van Decemb: 1729 ter Griffie van opgem^e Sijne Maj^t zijn bevonden en berusten.' See for Flushing pp. 42-44. According to notes in pencil in the margin, nos. 3509 and 3511a are made or 'copied' by Jacob Schoutens, and the stylistically similar drawing no. 3510 (reproduced in this book) probably was also made by him.

114 ARA, map department, VTH 3514.

115 Dijksterhuis, *Simon Stevin*, p. 42.

116 Parkinson, *Garden of Pleasant Flowers*, facs. ed., chap. III, p. 3. Parkinson ultimately prefers the square form, the triangle being too unpractical and seldom chosen if another can be had. Jacques Boyceau and André Mollet in their later treatises forward the rectangle or parallelogram as the ideal garden form because of its optical effect, which was to be a main concern for later seventeenth-century garden architects.

117 Ibid.

118 Ibid.

119 For an illustration of Gunterstein see Bienfait, *Oude Hollandsche tuinen*, pp. 178-179, plate 226. For an illustration of the Hortus Medicus of Amsterdam see *Journal of Garden History*, 2-3 (1988), p. 275, fig. 121, and Wijnands et al., *Een sieraad voor de stad*, p. 69.

120 See also Bienfait, *Oude Hollandsche tuinen*, pp. 254-255, for a description and illustration of de la Court's triangular ideal garden plan.

121 BUREN: ARA, NDR, inv. no. 1039 [old no. 778], fols. 216, 216vo, 217, 234, 272vo and 273; NDR, inv. no. 1040 [old no. 779], fols. 211vo, 227vo; and NDR, inv. no. 1042 [old no. 781], fol. 253, and inv. no. 1043 [old no. 782], fols. 240-244 and 349. Important for many references to the layout, plantation and decoration of the gardens at Buren are the records of payments during the Stadholder's reign in the ARA, NDR, inv. nos. 2584-2603ff. [old nos. 5642-5661ff.]. These accounts of the various stewards state expenditures on a monthly basis. The most important activities and expenditures from 1630 to 1650 are referred to here and copied below in the appendix. For further information on the garden and new avenues at Buren see also ARA, NDR, inv. nos. 2509 and 2510 [old. nos. NDR FOLIO, 1788-1791 and 1793]. For further research consult Van Hoof et al., *Archieven van de Nassause Domeinraad*, pp. 128-151, and especially the accounts of the stewards, ARA, NDR, inv. nos. 8415-8435.

122 ARA, NDR, inv. no. 2509 [old no. NDR FOLIO, 1790].

123 A detailed history of the building activities at Buren undertaken by Frederik Hendrik remains to be written. A short survey is given in de Beaufort and Van den Berg, *Nederlandse monumenten*, p. 95. References to these building activities, including a new entrance stairway to the castle, addition of a kitchen, restoration of the great Knight's Hall and west tower, construction of a gallery and a watermill, reconstruction of the ramparts, repairs to the bridges, stables etc. in ARA, NDR, inv. no. 992 [old no. 735], fol. 370, and NDR, inv. no. 993 [old no. 736], fols. 162, 189, 201-202, 210, 248, 249, 257vo, 267, 404, 412, 413, 458, 461, 461vo, 462, 462vo, 463 and 463vo. Important for the history of the gardens, apart from those discussed in my text, are references to maps made by Jan van Diepenen in 1644 of the Buren castle and gardens in fols. 202 and 257vo, which can be related to some of the descriptions in an early-eighteenth-century inventory of maps of the Nassau Domains, mentioned above and kept in the ARA, map department, entitled 'Inventaris van de Caerten behorende tot de Domeijnen'. A plan which would have been of special interest for our purposes but is now missing is described in this map inventory as 'grondteekening van 't Casteel te Bueren met syn gragten, wal, hoven ende Plantagien gelyk het ao 1644 was leggende gemeeten en gecarteerd door J.C. van Diepenen' (ground-plan of the Castle of Bueren with its moats, bank, gardens and plantations as it was situated and measured anno 1644 by J.C. van Diepenen).

124 Worp, *Briefwisseling*, IV, RGP 24, letter 3614, L. Buysero to Constantijn Huygens, dated 14 July 1644: 'Ick hebbe aen Monsieur Post d'intentie ende begeerte van S.H.^{t} geschreven aengaende het gereet maken der bestecken voor den grooten ende cleynen thuyn, alsmede aengaende de estimatie van 't gebouw; hiernevens gaet het rapport van syne Buerensche reyse, daertoe my referere, ende sullen wegens de stellinge der wapenen in 't wulffsel van de gallery d'intentie van S.H.^{t} verwachten.' (I have written to Mr. Post about the intentions and wishes of His Higness regarding the completion of the estimates for the great and the small garden, including the estimate of the building; enclosed is the report of his travel to Bueren, to which I refer, and we shall expect His Higness's intentions as to the placement of the coat of arms in the ceiling of the gallery [new gallery at Buren].) Where Buysero writes about 'the great and the small garden' it is not clear from the text whether he refers to the gardens at Honselaarsdijk or to those at Buren. Though from the wording of the letter he seems to refer to the Honselaarsdijk gardens, these were ususally called 'the old and the new garden', while part of the gardens at Buren were indeed referred to as 'the great garden'; see ARA, NDR, inv. no. 992 [old no. 735], fol. 417, and NDR, inv. no. 993 [old no. 736], fol. 463.

125 Worp, *Briefwisseling*, II, RGP 19, letters 1424 and 1427, Constantijn Huygens to Amalia of Orange, dated 25 and 28 August 1636.

126 Ibid., III, RGP 21, letter 3007, Constantijn Huygens to Orange, dated 3 June 1642: 'Son Altesse … ayant mené la Reine apres diner au grand jardin, qu'elle n'avoit encor veu.'

127 KHA, archief Johan Maurits van Nassau-Siegen, inv. A 4-1476, fol. 56. The map has been published in de Beaufort and Van den Berg, *Nederlandse monumenten*, pp. 90-100, especially p. 92, fig. 66.

128 The map of Buren is folded in the middle, has punch marks for copy purposes and, like many other maps showing traces of red seals as they were sent as letters, points to the habit of taking such maps along on military expeditions.

129 In de Beaufort and Van den Berg, *Nederlandse monumenten*, p. 92, the map is also dated circa 1630.

130 Closer study of this section reveals that its function as a place to run horses is probable, because next to it a building is depicted which, divided into compartments, looks like a stable.

131 ARA, NDR, inv. no. 1 [old no. 1, Journalen van de Raad], dated 9 Juni 1633.

132 It is not entirely clear which garden section is referred to by the 'Great Garden', but one may assume that it is the large garden section within the ramparts, or the so-called *berceaux* garden with the double circles.

133 De Beaufort and Van den Berg, *Nederlandse monumenten*, pp. 92, 94 and 96.

134 See Hallema, *Jaarboek 'De Oranjeboom'*, XVIII (1965), pp. 130-154, and XIX (1966), pp. 1-31; especially XVIII, p. 149. The negotiations were actually held in the shady arbours of the Valkenberg garden.

135 Ibid., XVIII (1965), p. 142.

136 For a short and general survey of the history of the Valkenberg park see Dragt, *Groen*, 1 (1996), pp. 9-12, and Kerkhoven, ibid., pp. 13-17. For a more detailed study see Dragt's report 'Park Valkenberg te Breda'. This report was written in conjunction with the restoration of the park in 1993-94 and is kept in the GAB. For further information on the Valkenberg see also Oldenburger-Ebbers, *Tuinengids*, p. 252.

137 BREDA: For the seventeenth- and early-eighteenth-century history of the Valkenberg gardens see especially Hallema's two articles in *Jaarboek 'De Oranjeboom'*, XVIII (1965) and XIX (1966). For a general survey see Dragt and Kerkhoven in *Groen*, 1 (1996), pp. 9-17. For further research consult Van Hoof et al., *Archieven van de Nassause Domeinraad*, pp. 318-354, and especially the accounts of the stewards, ARA, NDR, inv. nos. 8415-8435.

138 For the history of the name and a description of the Valkenberg in the early eighteenth century see Van Goor, *Stadt en Lande van Breda*, p. 63.

139 The travel journal of Petrus Vorstius, Bishop of Acqui, written by his secretary Cornelis Ettius and published as *Nouveaux Mémoires de l'Académie Royale*, 1537. See Hallema, *Jaarboek 'De Oranjeboom'*, XVIII (1965), p. 135.

140 LUW, Department of Special Collections, inv. no. 01.2089.02. On the later changes of the Valkenberg gardens as a result of the opening of a railroad in 1858, the late-nineteenth-century dismantling of the Breda fortifications and the northward expansion of the city, see F.A. Brekelmans, *Bulletin KNOB*, 68 (1969), and G. Otten, *Jaarboek van de Geschied- en Oudheidkundige Kring van Stad en Land van Breda 'De Oranjeboom'*, XXXXIV (1991), mentioned by Dragt, *Groen*, 1 (1996), p. 12, note 7. Compare also Oldenburger-Ebbers, *Tuinengids*, p. 252.

141 The sculptures shown in later prints at the centre of each parterre date from the reign of William III, who may have replaced earlier statues. No detailed information exists about their provenance or further history. Compare Hallema, *Jaarboek 'De Oranjeboom'*, XIX (1966), pp. 24-25, who only briefly refers to the white-painted statues while discussing late-seventeenth-century alterations to the Valkenberg gardens.

142 Melchior Maes de Loeckere received the large sum of 1107 Rijnse guilders for cleaning out the fish-pond. See ibid., XVIII (1965), p. 140.

143 GAB, no. 1966-36. Verhoff's plan was first published in ibid., XVIII (1965), fig. 17, between pp. 46 and 47. At that time the plan was kept in the Koninklijke Militaire Academie, or Royal Military Academy, at Breda; it is now in the GAB, inv. no. 1966-36.

144 ARA, inv. no. 7951 [old no. NDR, Register 1023-XIII], fols. 289-325. See also Hallema, *Jaarboek 'De Oranjeboom'*, XVIII (1965), pp. 138 and 153, note 12. Eight gardeners are mentioned specifically from 1600 till 1770 in this Registry, which also includes their Letters of Instruction. The head-gardeners of the Valkenberg garden were: Mattheus van den Houte (1560-1600), his son Govert Mattheusz van den Houte (1600-1621), succeeded by Andries van Hoorendonck (1621-1623), Michiel van Bruheze (also Bruhese, 1623-1647), succeeded by his son Pieter van Bruheze (1647-after 1661, when his contract was renewed). There is a hiatus during the Stadholderless Period of 1650-1672. The first gardener mentioned again in the eighteenth century is Willem van Loo, in 1733.

145 ARA, NDR, inv. no. 7951 [old no. NDR, Register 1023-XIII], fols. 296-297. See Hallema, *Jaarboek 'De Oranjeboom'*, XVIII (1965), p. 140, and for a copy of the text of this document *Jaarboek 'De Oranjeboom'*, XIX (1966), pp. 26-27.

146 For the names and responsibilities of the stewards, comptroller and supervisors see ibid., XVIII (1965), p. 141.

147 Document dated 23 November 1623. See Hallema, *Jaarboek 'De Oranjeboom'*, XVIII (1965), p. 144, who does not specify the folio

number. However, Michiel van Bruheze's Letter of Instruction must be among the archival records describing the responsibilities of all other gardeners at the Valkenberg, and it must precede those of his successor, Pieter van Bruheze; see ARA, NDR, inv. no. 7951, fols. 300-301 [old no. NDR, 1023, quoted by Hallema: NDR, Register 1023-XIII, fols. 300-301].

148 ARA, NDR inv. no. 7951 [old no. NDR, 1023], fols. 300-301 (see remarks in the previous note). Document dated 23 November 1623: '… Indien hij hem neerstelycken en vlijtelycken draecht ende quijt, op onse speciale ordonnantie hij jaerlicx sal genieten hondert gulden off hondert ende vijftich carolus gulden…' Compare Hallema, *Jaarboek 'De Oranjeboom'*, XVIII (1965), p. 143.

149 Lithgow, *True and experimentall discourse*. Compare Hallema, *Jaarboek 'De Oranjeboom'*, XVIII (1965), p. 144.

150 On the description by the Moretus family see Hallema, *Jaarboek 'De Oranjeboom'*, XVIII (1965), p. 151. The text is only partly published by Hallema, who refers for the rest to an article by M. Stabbe in *Taxandria*, 31 (1924), p. 82.

151 See for further reading on sundials in the garden and their meaning, Coffin, *English Garden*, pp. 8-26; here especially p. 15, describing the decoration of sundials with heraldic imagery combined with portraits of the princely owner.

152 Ibid., pp. 8-10.

153 KHA, archief Johan Maurits van Nassau-Siegen, inv. A 4-1476, fol. 59.

154 Kalf, *Nederlandsche monumenten*, I, pp. 52-53.

155 Roest van Limburg, *Kasteel van Breda*, p. 139, shows this unusual octagonal pleasure house which was demolished in 1824. It had three floors, each with a gallery commanding a magnificent view over the countryside.

156 Ibid., p. 139, showing the Speelhuys in the 1743 print by Immink after P. de Swart.

157 Kalf, *Nederlandsche monumenten*, I, p. 52.

158 Intrigued by the possibilities of form and meaning, architects would design actual fortification-shaped sections within the gardens proper, which sometimes were used for the re-enactment of historical battle scenes. Famous examples of such 'fortification gardens' are those designed by Charles Bridgeman at Blenheim; see Willis, *Charles Bridgeman*, figs. 24-25. See also J.D. Hunt's remarks on 'ramparts as Tarrass walks' in Dutch and Flemish cities, in *Dutch Garden*, p. 186, showing Stephen Switzer's 'fortification garden'.

159 Fremantle, *Nederlands Kunsthistorisch Jaarboek*, 21 (1970), pp. 39-69, here p. 67. See also Hunt, *Dutch Garden*, p. 186.

160 Willis, *Charles Bridgeman*, figs. 24-25. Compare also Hunt, *Dutch Garden*, pp. 185-186.

161 Worp, *Briefwisseling*, II, RGP 19, letter 1725, Constantijn Huygens to Amalia of Orange, dated 30 September 1637.

162 Prümers, *Zeitschrift der historischen Gesellschaft für die Provinz Posen*, XV (1900), p. 108. See Hallema, *Jaarboek 'De Oranjeboom'*, XVIII (1965), p. 149.

163 It is not clear what is meant exactly by 'op de vijver' and whether this relates to a pavilion in the pond – one adjacent to, or overhanging, the water, as was a popular practice at the time in Holland. Compare Cats's platform overhanging the fish-pond at Sorgvliet; see Hunt, *Dutch Garden*, p. 179.

164 The tower with the water-mill was demolished in 1826; see Kalf, *Nederlandse monumenten*, I, p. 33.

165 Slothouwer, *Paleizen*, p. 29. During the building activities at the Paleis Noordeinde, Bartholomeus Drijffhout was promoted to *controlleur*.

166 A later version of this terrace can still be seen in an eighteenth-century print by B.F. Immink reproduced in Roest van Limburg, *Kasteel van Breda*, p. 179.

167 Reproduced in Heijbroek, *Met Huygens op reis*, pp. 41 and 64, the drawing is dated 15 July 1665 and today is in the Gronings Museum, Groningen.

168 Faugère, *Journal de voyage*, p. 86.

169 Worp, *Briefwisseling*, II, RGP 19, letter 1646, Constantijn Huygens to Amalia of Orange, dated 18 August 1637.

170 Ibid., II, RGP 19, letter 1918, Constantijn Huygens to Amalia of Orange, dated 12 August 1638: 'Van morgen, voor zonsopgang, trokken wij naar Breda, waar de burgerij zich verheugde over de komst van Z.H., die de nieuwe werken bezichtigde, op het kasteel middagmaalde met de gedeputeerden der Staten en daarna het heele gebouw nauwkeurig bezichtigde.' (This morning, before sunrise, we left for Breda, where the citizens rejoiced about the arrival of His Highness, who looked at the new works, shared his afternoon meal with the State Deputies and afterwards closely inspected the whole building.)

171 Ibid., II, RGP 19, letter 2195, Constantijn Huygens to Amalia of Orange, dated 5 August 1639.

172 Ibid., II, RGP 19, letter 2206, Constantijn Huygens to Amalia of Orange, dated 18 August 1639.

173 Van Goor, *Stadt en Lande van Breda*, p. 61. See also Roest van Limburg, *Kasteel van Breda*, pp. 176-177, and compare Springer, *Oude Nederlandsche tuinen*, p.15. See also Kalf, *Nederlandsche monumenten*, I, pp. 38-39.

174 CBN, inv. nos. XI-8-69 and XI-8-68.

175 The text in the two drawings is in Dutch, which would point to the hand of Roman rather than Marot, who wrote in French. However, the drawings could have been made by a third person after designs by Roman and/or Marot. Important is that details of the parterre ornamentation, particularly the harp motif in the scrollwork, are closely related to designs for the parterres by Daniel Marot made for the gardens of Het Loo and shown in his *Oeuvres*, most completely published by Jessen, *Ornamentwerk*, and more recently

176 See Kalf, *Nederlandsche monumenten*, I, p. 52.
177 See GAB, Stamboeknummer 4021, for more information on the original seventeen statues in the Breda garden. See also Hallema, *Jaarboek 'De Oranjeboom'*, XVIII (1965), p. 136.
178 GAB, no. 1989-2258.
179 See Hallema, *Jaarboek 'De Oranjeboom'*, XVIII (1965), p. 147, and Kerkhoven, *Groen*, 1 (1996), p. 17, for an illustration of the original seventeenth-century statue and its modern replica.
180 Worp, *Briefwisseling*, V, RGP 28, letter 5479, David de Wilhem to Constantijn Huygens, dated 23 May 1656, and letter 5483, dated 30 May 1656, same to the same.
181 Christiaan Huygens, *Oeuvres complètes*, VIII, letter 2179, Susanna Huygens-Doublet to her brother Christiaan Huygens, dated 27 June, 1682.
182 ARA, inv. no. 7951 [old no. NDR, Register 1023-XIII], fols. 296-297. See also Hallema, *Jaarboek 'De Oranjeboom'*, XIX (1966), pp. 26-27. For a good impression of the problem of vandalism see the letter written circa 1710 by the estate steward Josias Eckhart to the Council of the Domains, in the NDR, inv. no. 7951 [old no. NDR, Register 1023-XIII], fols. 363-364, copied by Hallema, ibid., pp. 27-28. Eckhart insisted on hiring guards to resolve this problem. See also remarks concerning vandalism in the later *Instructions for the Gardener Willem van Loo*, dated 25 September 1733, in the NDR, inv. no. 7951 [old no. NDR, Register 1023-XIII], fols. 379-380, and published in Hallema, ibid., pp. 29-30.
183 Two further letters, dated 29 June 1705 and 28 October 1717, respectively, also discuss vandalism in the Valkenberg gardens. See ARA, NDR, inv. no. 7951 [old no. NDR, Register 1023-XIII], fol. 337: 'Op de remonstrantie van de rentmeester van de Domeynen tot Breda, Mr. Josias Eckhart remonstrerende dat de Thuijnman van het Valkenbergh aldaar hem heeft geklaagt over de moetwilligheden die door eenig slegt en moetwillig volk die haer loopplaets aldaar bij dage en nagte komen te nemen werde gepleegt, versoeckende dat den raad tot voorkominge van verdere disorders sodanige placcaeten gelieve te emaneren waerbij aen een yder wie het oock soude mogen wesen, niet alleen verboden werde na de klokke van negen uren des avonds in het Valkenburg te mogen wandelen ofte van te vooren daerinne zijnde te mogen blijven, maer ook geen boomen, heggen, parken bloemen, banken, thuijnhuijsen, ofte wat des meer is, te mogen scheuren, breeken &ca of eenige moetwilligheden te plegen, of seeckere swaere poene daerteegen te statueeren. Sij dese remonstrantie gestelt in handen vande heere Commissaris eerstdaegs gaende op de verpagtinge der Thienden tot Breda, omesigh opde klagten hierneven gemelt nader t'informeren, en van sijne bevindinge aen desen rade rapport te doen. Actum inden rade van bij Sijne Kon. Maj.^{t} van Groot Brittagne glor. Mem. aengestelt geweest, en bij resol. van haar Ho. Mo. in qualiteijt als Executeurs vande Testamenten van Prins Fredr. Hendr. mede glor. Mem. en van hoogstged. Sijne Maj.^{t} geauthoriseert in 's Gravenhage den 29 Junij 1705.' For similar complaints in a later document, describing the apparent duplication of the key which let everyone through the garden gate, despite the frequent changes of the locks, see ARA, NDR, inv. no. 7951 [old no. NDR, Register 1023-XIII], fol. 369ff.: 'Nietegestaende alle onse aengewende devoiren en veranderinge vande sloote vande Valkenberg ... hebben wij niet kunnen beletten dat de sleutels wederom oneijndig vermengvuldig sijnde ... portier dient te worden aengesteld.' Breda, dated 10 October, 's-Gravenhage, 28 October, 1717.
184 The layout of the Valkenberg landscape park is based on the design by the Belgium landscape architect Pierre Lieven Rosseels (1843-1921), whose *Plan voor het Valkenberg Breda*, dated 1885-86, is kept in the GAB. For an illustration and further reading see Dragt, *Groen*, 1 (1996), p. 12, and Oldenburger-Ebbers, *Tuinengids*, p. 252.
185 For the recent restoration and restructuring of this inner city park see Dragt and Kerkhoven, *Groen*, 1 (1996), pp. 11-12 and 13-17.
186 ZUYLESTEYN: By buying the rights of the property from both Johan van Renesse and Godard van Reede for the total sum of 35,000 pounds artois (see ARA, NDR, inv. no. 1039 [old no. 778], fols. 229vo, 230 and 234vo), Frederik Hendrik ended the year-long dispute about the ownership of Zuylesteyn. See Van der Wijck and Enklaar-Lagendijk, *Zuylesteyn*, p. 6. Compare also Van Hoof et al., *Archieven van de Nassause Domeinraad*, p. 188, and especially ARA, NDR, inv. nos. 3949-3951.
187 Ibid., p. 5.
188 Meischke in Hoekstra et al., *Liber Castellorum*, pp. 270-278, especially p. 270.
189 Ibid., p. 270.
190 ARA, map department, VTH 3039-10, 3039-5, 3039-9 and 3039-6, respectively.
191 KHA, archief Frederik Hendrik, no. A 14-VII-9, contains the original deed of gift.
192 ARA, NDR, inv. no. 1 [old no. NDR 1], Journaal van de Raad, or Journal of the Stadholder's Council, 2 January 1632 until 29 December 1635. Compare Meischke in Hoekstra et al., *Liber Castellorum*, p. 276.
193 Simon Langelaer was mentioned primarily for bringing rose-water and fruits from Buren to The Hague for Amalia of Orange.
194 KHA, archief Frederik Hendrik, no. A 14-VII-9.
195 Ibid.
196 Ibid. This document is held among the gardener's contracts and regulations for Zuylesteyn's upkeep.
197 LUW, Department of Special Collections, inv. no. 01.1005.01/01.1054.01.
198 Tromp and Henry-Buitenhuis, *Historische buitenplaatsen*, p. 139.

199 KHA, archief Frederik Hendrik, no. A 14-VII-9: *Conditien ende voorwaerden ... Jacob van Alenburch, Thuijnman ... als hovenier in Sijne hoven, Boomgaerden ende Plantagien tot Zuylesteyn ende Ysselsteyn*, dated 31 August 1635. This gardener signed his name Jacob van Allenburgh.

200 ARA, NDR, inv. no. 686 [old no. NDR, 577, 'Amptboek'], fol. 444.

201 YSSELSTEYN: ARA, NDR, inv. nos. 4826-5156 [old nos. 8415-8528], showing the accounts of the estate steward Willem Dimmer of 1633-36. For further research consult Van Hoof et al., *Archieven van de Nassause Domeinraad*, pp. 222-235. See especially ARA, NDR, inv. nos. 4827-4856, including the accounts of the stewards Willem and Jan Dimmer of 1621-50, which could yield further information about the building and upkeep of the Ysselsteyn estate under Frederik Hendrik.

202 Pieter Post in a letter to the registrar L. Buysero, dated 12 July 1644: 'Tot Bueren sijnde hebbe haar hooght. laaten sien de teijckeninghe of menuijten, tot den bouw als hooven van Eijselstijn, de ordonnantie geviel haer hooght. wel, dan soude beeter gevallen daer in hebben, dat het nieuwe werck dat men daer aen maaken soude te weeten de timmeringh was naer de antijckse of Romijnse manier. Hebbe van dit goet vinden van haer hooght. aen den heer van Zuijlichem geschreeven, uijt Bueren.' (At Buren I showed Her Highness the drawing or minutes for the building and gardens of Ysselsteyn, the ordinance pleased Her Highness, but she would like it even better if the new work, namely the woodwork, would be after the antique or Roman manner. Having obtained Her Highness's permission, I wrote to the Lord of Zuylichem from Buren.) Part of a letter published by Lunsingh Scheurleer in Van Deursen et al., *Veelzijdigheid als levensvorm*, p. 48. Compare also Terwen and Ottenheym, *Pieter Post*, p. 35.

203 A search for these and other maps described in the above-mentioned inventory of all the maps of the Nassau Domains, dated 1729 and entitled *Inventaris van de Caerten gehorende tot de Domeynen en Goederen nagelaten bij Sijne Con^e Maj^t van Groot Britten*, would be helpful. Important are nos. 3 and 6, described as plans by Pieter Post and dated 1640, for the restoration of the Ysselsteyn castle and gardens.

CHAPTER IV

1 Huygens, *Vitaulium*, p. 39. My translation; for other English translations see Hopper, *Journal of Garden History*, II, 1 (1982), p. 40, note 43, and Van Pelt, *Art History*, IV, 2 (1981), pp. 152 and 156. For the publication of the whole poem *Hofwijck* see Worp, *Gedichten*, IV, pp. 266-338.

2 Marolois, *Opera Mathematica*, has a title-page showing architecture among the sciences, in which Vitruvius has taken his proper place in the company of Euclid (mathematics), Archimedes (fortifications) and Vitellius (geodesy). See Ottenheym, *Philips Vingboons*, p. 158, fig. 215.

3 Van Mander, *Schilder-Boeck*, p. 299. Van Mander refers to the use of proper proportion, taking that of the human body as an example, which is derived from Vitruvius's architectural work: 'Dees proporty in ghebouw oft figuere noemt Vitruvius ...' Vitruvius, *Libri decem*, Liber III, chap. 1.

4 De Bray, *Architectura moderna*. In his foreword to the reader, de Bray explains that the engravings in the book provide the opportunity to compare contemporary architecture in Holland with the architecture of the ancients and to judge and measure the buildings according to the true reason of Mathematical Building ('... ende de selve met de ware redenen der Wiskonstighe Bouwinge proeven ende naer meten'). Compare also Ottenheym, *Philips Vingboons*, p. 162.

5 Important Dutch books published at the time, demonstrating the relationship between these disciplines and mathematical science, are Hendrick Hondius, *Fortificatie* and *Architectuur*. Of the utmost importance for the art of fortification and city planning is Stevin's 'Van de oirdeningh der steden', in *Materiae politicae*. See also Ottenheym, *Philips Vingboons*, pp. 158-159. For further reading see Hopper, *Journal of Garden History*, II, 1 (1982), pp. 25-29, and Taverne, *In 't land van belofte*, pp. 49-81 and 545.

6 Term used in Vercelloni, *European Gardens*, p. 47.

7 The Metropolitan Museum of Art, New York, The Elisha Whittelsey Collection, The Elisha Whittelsey Fund, 1949 (49.95.2629[1]). Compare also the facsimile edition of this book, published after Theodoor de Bray's edition of 1587.

8 See Mehrtens in Mosser and Teyssot, *Western Gardens*, p. 104.

9 Serlio, *Five Books on Architecture*. Unabridged reprint of the English edition of 1611, translated from the Dutch edition of 1606. For the remark on gardens as ornaments see the heading of the print depicting mazes and knots in his book IV, chap. 12, fol. 69vo.

10 On the use of perspective in Vredeman de Vries's work see Mehrtens in Mosser and Teyssot, *Western Gardens*, pp. 103 and 105, notes 13-15. See also de Jong and Dominicus-Van Soest, *Aardse paradijzen*, p. 57. Compare Hopper, *Journal of Garden History*, II, 1 (1982), p. 28.

11 A good example are Stevin's mathematical exercises for Prince Maurits published in Dutch, *Wisconstighe Ghedachtnissen*. Descartes published his historic work *Discours de la Méthode* (Paris, 1636) in French. See also Vermeersch's comment in *Bruges and Europe*, p. 83, and Geyl, *Netherlands*, p. 217, about Descartes's linguistic efforts.

12 Delorme tried to do this in his *Premier Tome de l'Architecture*; see Kruft, *History of Architectural Theory*, p. 100.

13 Rubens's importance in relation to Dutch architectural development is discussed in Fremantle, *Baroque Town Hall*, p. 98.

14 One of Frederik Hendrik's own relatives, Count Jan III of Nassau-Siegen (1583-1638), may have belonged to this group. Half-brother of the 'Dutch' Johan Maurits, Count Jan had become a Catholic and fought for the Spanish against his own relatives. He and his wife Ernestine de Ligne owned a grand palace at Renaix (Ronse), south-east of Antwerp, surrounded by monumental, geometrically aligned gardens; it is shown in Goetghebuer, *Choix des monumens*, plates XXXIII-XXXV. Comparable to the architecture at the Dutch court, the Ronse palace design and decoration followed classical building principles expounded by Serlio and Scamozzi. Comparisons can be made between elements in this design and Italian architecture, for example Poggio Reale in Serlio's *Five Books on Architecture*, book III, chap. 4, fol. 72. For further reading on Count Jan see Worp, *Briefwisseling*, II and III, RGP 19 and 21, s.v. Nassau-Siegen and de Ligne. Compare also Mout in Van den Boogaart, *Johan Maurits van Nassau-Siegen*, pp. 13-38, especially p. 36.

15 For further reading on these architects-painters see Plantenga, *Architecture religieuse*, pp. 32-49, demonstrating, for example, the influence of Serlio in Cobergher's centralized churches.

16 The letters are kept in the Koninklijke Academie voor Wetenschappen (Library of the Royal Academy of Sciences) in Amsterdam.

17 The continuing contacts between the two countries, even after the Twelve Years' Truce of 1609-21, have been pointed out by Albert Blankert in *The Art Bulletin*, LXXVII (March 1995), pp. 145-148, in his critique of the recent exhibition of early-seventeenth-century art at the Rijksmuseum, Amsterdam, entitled *Dawn of the Golden Age*. According to Blankert, the authors overstressed the artistic dividing lines between the Northern and Southern Netherlands, to the detriment of our cultural understanding of that period. Though Blankert writes at length about the art of painting, the same criteria apply to the analysis of architecture. Also, architectural historians can be 'mesmerized by accidental borders' (p. 148). For further reading on the separation of the Southern and Northern Netherlands see Geyl, *Netherlands*, pp. 14-17.

18 For further reading on de Vries's gardens and classical architecture see Mehrtens in Mosser and Teyssot, *Western Gardens*, pp. 103-105.

19 This was discussed by Dietzel, *Furttenbachs Gartenentwürfe*, p. 12.

20 This definition was used by Vermeulen, *Handboek*, pp. 206-212. For other important literature on this topic see Fremantle, *Baroque Town Hall*, chap. IV. See also Slothouwer, *Paleizen*, introduction pp. 1-12; Kamphuis, *Oud Holland*, 77 (1962), pp. 151-180; and Ottenheym, *Philips Vingboons*, pp. 153-160.

21 Defined as such by the mid-seventeenth-century architect Philips Vingboons; see Ottenheym, *Philips Vingboons*, p. 156.

22 Rosenberg, Slive and Ter Kuile, *Dutch Art and Architecture*, p. 393. No further detailed explanations are given in their text.

23 KB, unpublished manuscript, Hs. no. 78 D 14, dated 1686. A first general survey of this catalogue was given by Byvanck, *Oranje-Nassau Boekerij*. See for a further survey Kuijpers and Renting, *Boeken van Oranje*. For a detailed survey and analysis see especially Renting and Renting-Kuijpers, *Seventeenth-Century Orange-Nassau Library*. See also Chroust, *Oud Holland*, 15 (1897), pp. 11-23, for a survey of the library of Frederik Hendrik's older brother Prince Maurits of Orange, which Frederik Hendrik inherited in 1625.

24 Auction catalogue 1688, kept in the Museum Meermanno Westreenianum, The Hague, and published in *Catalogus van de bibliotheek van Constantijn Huygens*. His library held more than 2,850 works. See also Bots in Van Deursen et al., *Veelzijdigheid als levensvorm*, p. 15, note 30; Kamphuis, *Oud Holland*, 77 (1962), p. 153; and Plantenga in *Verzamelde opstellen*, p. 31.

25 In 1610, at the age of fourteen, Frederik Hendrik spent a year at the French court as page of Henri IV. In 1619 he again travelled to France and on his way stopped briefly at Heidelberg. In 1612-13 the Stadholder sailed to England to witness the wedding of Frederik V of the Palatine and Elizabeth Stuart. For a survey of Frederik Hendrik's trips abroad see Poelhekke, *Frederik Hendrik*, pp. 39-41.

26 Huygens's early travel journals are published by Worp in *Bijdragen en Mededeelingen van het Historisch Genootschap*, XV (1894), pp. 62-152.

27 Compare also Fremantle, *Baroque Town Hall*, pp. 100-102.

28 Kamphuis, *Oud Holland*, 77 (1962), pp. 151-52. Compare also Fremantle, *Baroque Town Hall*, p. 101.

29 Constantijn Huygens was present at the opening of the Banqueting House in 1622. See Worp, *Briefwisseling*, I, RGP 15, letter 122, Huygens to his parents in 1621. Also via Nicolas Stone, son-in-law of Hendrick de Keyser, knowledge of contemporary architecture in England may already have come to Holland.

30 Worp, *Briefwisseling*, II, RGP 19, letter 1765, Constantijn Huygens to N.N., dated 11/21 November 1637. See also Slothouwer, *Paleizen*, pp. 344.

31 Worp, *Bijdragen en Mededeelingen van het Historisch Genootschap*, XV (1894), pp. 62-152.

32 Huygens made this remark in his French travel journal, published by Worp, ibid. See also Kamphuis, *Oud Holland*, 77 (1962), p. 152.

33 Worp, *Gedichten*, VIII, 'De Vita Propria', p. 200, Liber 1, verse 744-745. See also Kamphuis, *Oud Holland*, 77 (1962), p. 152, note 6.

34 Worp, *Bijdragen en Mededeelingen van het Historisch Genootschap*, XV (1894), pp. 77-79.

35 For further reading see Patterson, *Journal of Garden History*, 1 and 2 (1981), pp. 67-105 and 179-203.

36 Compare also Hennebo, *Gartenkunst*, III, p. 103, who refers to garden architecture after Germany's Thirty Years' War as 'Gärten in der Zeit des Wiederaufbaues'.

37 The Metropolitan Museum of Art, New York, The Elisha Whittelsey Collection, The Elisha Whittelsey Fund, 1954 (54.512.2). Furttenbach's own enclosed courtyard garden at Ulm shown in his *Architectura privata*, 1641. See Gollwitzer, *Gartenlust*, coloured engraving opposite p. 24.

38 In his *Neues Itinerarium Italiae* Furttenbach describes a single large mirror reflecting whole gardens which he had seen in Italy. Compare Diedenhofen in Van den Boogaart, *Johan Maurits van Nassau-Siegen*, p. 220.

39 For the further history of these mirrors and shells of the so-called 'hoorensaal' (*horens*, or conches), which later were brought over to the Bentinck garden at Sorgvliet, see Diedenhofen in Van den Boogaart, *Johan Maurits van Nassau-Siegen*, p. 220, note 116. Compare Sellers in Hunt, *Dutch Garden*, pp. 112-114. See also J.J. Terwen, *Nederlands Kunsthistorisch Jaarboek*, 31 (1980), pp. 104-121. For a comparable circular grotto with cosmological decoration see also Lentz and Nath-Esser, *Die Gartenkunst*, II, 2 (1990), pp. 165-209 and figs. 6-8.

40 RPK, inv. no. RP-T-A-1918. The gouache by Jan van Call of c. 1680 in the RPK gives a clear overview of the whole layout: from the amphitheatre on the Springenberg, over the three ponds and the statue of Minerva, we can see the garden islands below in the Rhine valley and the town of Hochtelen in the distance. Compare de Jong and Dominicus-van Soest, *Aardse paradijzen*, p. 94.

41 See Diedenhofen's various detailed publications: in Van den Boogaart, *Johan Maurits van Nassau-Siegen*, pp. 197-236; in Hunt, *Dutch Garden*, pp. 49-80. For his most recent publication see *Klevische Gartenlust* and *Fonteijn van Pallas*, pp. 41-56.

42 Christiaan Huygens, *Oeuvres complètes*, I, letter to Lodewijk Huygens, dated 24 May 1652. See Bienfait, *Oude Hollandsche tuinen*, p. 62.

43 'Many people say that neither Rome nor France can boast anything like it.' See the letter of Johan Maurits to the Elector of Brandenburg dated December 1678, in the German Central Archives at Merseburg, Rep. 34, no. 39.3g, fol. IV, quoted by Diedenhofen in Hunt, *Dutch Garden*, p. 75.

44 Diedenhofen in Hunt, *Dutch Garden*, pp. 56-61, 74 and 217. For further iconographical explanations compare chapter VI.

45 De Jong in Diedenhofen et al., *Fonteijn van Pallas*, p. 39.

46 A compass card or roundel showing the direction of the winds is illustrated in Boyceau's contemporary *Traité du jardinage*, book I, chap. VII, p. 14, 'De l'Air & des Vents', as essential information for the proper planting of gardens. The presence of large roundels in gardens may be related to this kind of figures.

47 See Jellicoe et al., *Oxford Companion to Gardens*, pp. 121 and 478.

48 See Delannoy, *Le Parc d'Enghien*, 2 vols. (Enghien: Delwarde, 1979).

49 De Jong, *Natuur en kunst*, pp. 30 and 33, note 75 with further references.

50 Worp, *Briefwisseling*, II, RGP 19, letter 1417, C. Huygens to J.A. Bannius, dated 11 August 1636. Johan Albert Bannius was a scholar and Roman Catholic clergyman. The letter's content is as follows (translated from the Dutch in Slothouwer, *Paleizen*, pp. 342-343, the original being in Latin): 'To complete my work I need the Latin commentary by Daniel Barbarus on Vitruvius, in order to calculate justly and precisely the new kind of harmony. The Italian translation I borrowed from my inseparable friend Van Campen, but now I should like to look into a Latin copy, which I am longing to receive from you, and then I shall submit my work to Your Honour and to your judgement, if you permit.'

51 The learned botanist and supervisor of the Medical Gardens at Breda.

52 Worp, *Briefwisseling*, II, RGP 19, letter 1046, Constantijn Huygens to J. Wicquefort, dated 5 December 1634, and p. 54, letter 1088, same to the same, dated 8 March 1635. See also Slothouwer, *Paleizen*, p. 341. Joachim Wicquefort was a scholar and agent of Saxony, Weimar and Hessen-Cassel.

53 Worp, *Briefwisseling*, II, RGP 19, letter 1087, Constantijn Huygens to D. Heinsius, dated 7 March 1635. The commentaries he desires to have, which he specifically mentions in his letter, are those by Daniele Barbaro, Johannes Jucundus (or Giovanni Giocondo), Cesare Cesariano, Giovanni Battista Caporali and Bernardinus Baldus. See for the titles of their works Worp, *Briefwisseling*, II, RGP 19, p. 53, notes 3-7. See also Slothouwer, *Paleizen*, p. 341. Daniel Heinsius was a well-known scholar and author.

54 Worp, *Briefwisseling*, II, RGP 19, letter 1088, Constantijn Huygens to J. Wicquefort, dated 8 March 1635.

55 Worp, *Briefwisseling*, IV, RGP 21, letter 2942, Brosterhuisen to Constantijn Huygens, dated 6 February 1642: 'De heer van Campen raadt mij aan, daarna het laatste boek van Palladio, over de tempels der ouden, te vertalen en dan de laatste hoofdstukken van het voorlaatste boek over de publieke gebouwen; dat zou dan achter de vertaling van Vitruvius gedrukt kunnen worden, tenzij gij dat niet goed vindt. "Mijn Wotton", die de voorloper van Vitruvius moet weesen, is ghereedt om gedruct te werden, maer hij heeft alleen ghewacht nae een verhael van den oorsprongh der bouwcunst, dat de heer van Campen ontworpen heeft ...' See also

Slothouwer, *Paleizen*, p. 350. The book referred to by Brosterhuisen, created in collaboration with Huygens and Van Campen, was never published. Henry Wotton (1568-1624), whom Huygens mentions in this letter, wrote *The Elements of Architecture collected by Henry Wotton, Knight, from the best Authors and Exemples*. Wotton was the English envoy extraordinary at The Hague and a personal friend of Huygens's father.

56 A mutual research programme of the Catholic University of Leuven, Belgium, and the University of Utrecht in Holland has been set up to study the continuing architectural relations after the division of the two countries. The project includes a closer study of the correspondence between Rubens and Huygens, recently published by Ottenheym in *Bulletin KNOB*, 1 (1997), pp. 1-11; compare p. 10, note 1.

57 A good introduction to the issues brought up in their correspondence is Fremantle, *Baroque Town Hall*, pp. 98-100.

58 Worp, *Briefwisseling*, II, RGP 19, letter 2149, Constantijn Huygens to Peter Paul Rubens, dated 2 July 1639: 'Je pense m'acquitter d'une vielle debte, en vous offrant ces tailles douces. Au moins ma maison me semond d'un peu de mention que je vous ay faict autrefois de ce bastiment. Soit obligation anciene ou nouvelle importunité, voyci le morceau de brique que j'ay eslevé à la Haye, en un lieu, que j'ose bien nommer des plus illustres du village. ... C'est ce qui me porta à ceste égalité reguliere de part et d'autre, que vous trouverez en ces departemens, que vous sçavez avoir tant pleu aux anciens, et que les bons Italiens d'aujourd'huy recherchent encor aveq tant de soin. ... Je vous prie de jetter l'oeil sur le reste, et de m'en dire franchement vostre advis. Si vous ne me donnez que l'approbation que, possible, j'auray meritée en quelqu'endroict, j'estimeray que vous me cachez la censure qui me pourroit servir d'instruction et à d'autres d'advertissement. Mon dessein estoit d'adjouster à ces imprimez – dont je garden les planches à moi seul – une sorte du dissertation latine à mes enfants, par où, apres moy, ils demeurassent informez des raisons et justifications de mon faict, et me fusse-je laissé entrainer, à ceste occasion, en des considerations non inutiles sur le subject de l'architecture anciene et moderne .. [Je] retourneray à vous faire part de mes resversies, sachant combien vous avez deferé à ceste estude par le passé et aveq combien d'applaudissement.' Compare also ibid, letter 2272. With the exception of Ottenheym's article in *Bulletin KNOB*, 1 (1997), pp. 1-11, Huygens's letters to Rubens have not been studied sufficiently by scholars, even though they make an interesting connection between Rubens and the study of classical architecture. When mentioning Rubens's knowledge in these matters, Huygens no doubt not only refers to the *Palazzi di Genova* but also to the design of Rubens's own house at Antwerp. For a short, general survey of Rubens and architecture see A. Blunt, *The Burlington Magazine*, CXIX (September 1977), pp. 609-621.

59 'Vediamo que in queste parti, si và poco à poco invecchiando & abolendo la maniera d'Architettura, che si chiama Barbaro, ò Gothica; & che alcuni bellisimi ingegni introducono la vera simmetria di quella, conforme le regole de gli antichi, Graeci e Romani, con grandissimi splendore & ornamento della Patria ...'

60 De Jongh, *Nederlands Kunsthistorisch Jaarboek*, 24 (1973), pp. 85, 94 and 130. Huygens used the term 'Gotsche schell' in his poem *Hofwijck*, published in 1653; he used a similar terminology in his epitaph for Van Campen in 1658, quoted above. For further reading see also Spies in Huisken et al., *Jacob van Campen*, pp. 229-232.

61 Worp, *Briefwisseling*, II, RGP 19, letter 1301, Constantijn Huygens to Peter Paul Rubens, dated November 1635. The letter continues as follows: 'Tant y a, au chaud de ces contemplations, je ne doibs guere prendre de peine à vous faire croire le desir que j'auroy de vous gouverner chez moy, qui excellez en la cognoissance de ceste illustre estude, comme en toute autre chose, et m'en pourriez faire des leçons, sed fata obstant.'

62 De Bray, *Architectura moderna*, introduction, p. 7: '... mogende naer zijn welgevallen en eygen selfs oordeel, dese onse tydtsche Gebouwen, by die van de oude vergelijcken, ende deselve met de ware redenen der Wis-konstighe Bouwinge proeven, ende naer meten. Biddende alleenigh dese onse Bouwe eenige nootsaeckelijke gebreeckinge te verontschuldigen, soo vermits onse weecke en moerachtige grounden (al-hoe-wel geheydt) niet alle toe en late datmen geerne soude willen, als oock vermits in dese landen alle steen van so juysten en begeerden grootte, als wel by den ouden is geweest, niet en zijn te bekomen, bovendien heeft onsen Bouwmeester, staende onder de Bouw-heere, en sijne Meesters, oock dikwils benepen en gedrongen geweest; meer haer believen, als zijn selfs geweten te volgen. So vele heeft ons goed geacht die te verontschuldigen; maer om weder ter ander syde deselve te loven, en met prijsinghe hooghe te verheffen, dat en sullen wy niet doen, dewyle goede saecken sich selven prijsen ...' (... may he, after his own pleasure and opinion, compare our current buildings with those of the ancients, and judge and measure them according to true reason of Mathematical Building. I only pray that the reader will forgive us the necessary deficiencies due to our soft, swampy grounds which (although provided with piles) do not allow all one wishes for; furthermore, in this country one is not able to obtain the right pieces and appropriate sizes of stone like the ancients had; moreover, our architect, dependent on the patron and his advisers, is often limited and confined to follow his masters' wishes rather than his own principles. If it seemed right to excuse our own architecture, at the same time we refrain from praising and lifting it up too highly, since good work praises itself ...)

63 For further reading see Ballon, *The Paris of Henri IV*.

64 Terminology taken from Fremantle, *Baroque Town Hall*, p. 91.

65 ARA, map department, VTH 3308a. See also Kamphuis, *Oud Holland*, 77 (1962), p. 160, fig. 4.

66　Worp, *Briefwisseling*, II, RGP 19, letter 1763, Constantijn Huygens to Count Johan Maurits van Nassau, dated 17 November 1637. For the complete text see Slothouwer, *Paleizen*, pp. 343-344.

67　Worp, *Briefwisseling*, III, RGP 21, letter 2838, Constantijn Huygens to Amalia of Orange, dated 29 August 1641: 'Charles Lanoy [de Lannoy] revient hier et donna contentement à S.A. de beaucoup des choses, concernant les ouvrages à la Haye et Honselardijck, hormis la garderobbe de S.A. et la maisonnette de bois au jardin … Parmi les occupations de S.A. c'est le premier et plus aggreable de ses divertissements, que d'estre entretenue de ces matieres.'

68　For the use of the word *divertissement* in Huygens's correspondence see ibid., II, RGP 19, letter 2109, Constantijn Huygens to Amalia of Orange, dated 4 June 1639, quoted above in the Introduction. See also ibid., II, RGP 21, letter 2838, quoted in the previous note.

69　The plan submitted by the Committee was described by Huygens as a series of small lots and a design prompted by 'greed' rather than grandeur and aesthetics; see Huygens's manuscript *Domus*, KB, inv. no. XLVIII, fol. 738vo, and its recent publication by Blom et al., and Kamphuis, *Oud Holland*, 77 (1962), p. 157. A series of maps showing the initial plans for the development of the piazza is kept in the ARA, map department, VTH 3305-3309 (12 maps). No. 3308a is the plan which was executed. Map 3308c shows thin pencil lines indicating the places of Huygens's and Johan Maurits's houses. See also Kamphuis, *Oud Holland*, 77 (1962), p. 157, notes 25-28.

70　KB, remark from Huygens's manuscript *Domus*, inv. no. XLVIII, 738vol, and its recent publication by Blom et al. See Kamphuis, *Oud Holland*, 77 (1962), pp. 156-157, notes 25-27. For the history of Frederik Hendrik, Huygens and the Plein at The Hague see also Van der Haagen, *Jaarboek Die Haghe* (1928-29), pp. 6-39.

71　Worp, *Briefwisseling*, I, RGP 15, letter 897, Constantijn Huygens to J. Wicquefort, dated April 1634.

72　Ibid., II, RGP 19, letter 1025, Constantijn Huygens to General Milander, dated 17 October 1634. Milander was a colonel, later a general, in the Hessian army and a close friend of the Huygens family. He supplied part of the building material for Huygens's house and the Mauritshuis; see letters RGP 19, nos. 983 and 989.

73　Compare also Fremantle's commentary in *Baroque Town Hall*, pp. 104-106, concerning these letters and the Stadholder's 'affection naturelle', and the changes at The Hague.

74　GAH, topographical department, Het Plein. Photo Kamphuis, *Oud Holland*, 77 (1962), p. 162, fig. 6, of P. Post's engraving.

75　Huygens himself writes that his Latin treatise has 'remained in the pen', in other words, has not been written; see Worp, *Briefwisseling*, II, RGP 19, letter 2151, Constantijn Huygens to V. Conrart, dated 2 July [1639]. However, a number of abstracts of his first ideas concerning such an architectural treatise survive in his manuscript *Domus* (published by Blom et al.), and in miscellaneous notes in the KB; see Kamphuis, *Oud Holland*, 77 (1962), p. 153, note 9, and p. 154, note 12.

76　This connection is already discussed in older literature; it is now confirmed by new evidence brought on by the preliminary designs of Ter Nieuburch. See Lunsingh Scheurleer, *Oud Holland*, 77 (1962), pp. 181-205. See also Kuyper, *Dutch Classicist Architecture*, pp. 62 and 252, note 6, and Terwen, *Nederlands Kunsthistorisch Jaarboek*, 33 (1982), p. 176.

77　Kamphuis, *Oud Holland*, 77 (1962), p. 179: 'Uit Vitruvius over de windstreken. Dat op gezag van de Prins en volgens ons oordeel het oosten het beste beviel.' (From Vitruvius concerning the four winds. That on the Prince's authority and in our opinion the east pleased best.) For Vitruvius's theories on the winds see Vitruvius, *Ten Books on Architecture*, book I, chap. 6, pp. 24-31.

78　Kamphuis, *Oud Holland*, 77 (1962), p. 180: 'De plattegrond. Dikwijls aangegeven. Ook La Vallée.' (The plan. Often referred to. Also La Vallée.)

79　Ibid., p. 154, note 13, and p. 180: 'Lof voor Van Campen. Graaf Maurits en ik waren het met elkaar eens.' (Praise to Van Campen. Count Maurits and I agreed.) See also Kuyper, *Dutch Classicist Architecture*, pp. 61-62.

80　Kamphuis, *Oud Holland*, 77 (1962), p. 180: 'het vernuft van mijn vrouw.'

81　See Terwen, *Nederlands Kunsthistorisch Jaarboek*, 33 (1982), pp. 169-189, especially p. 170, on the great popularity of Scamozzi's book, considering the total number of editions published at the time. Compare also Ottenheym in Huisken et al., *Jacob van Campen*, p. 156: Van Campen preferred two contemporary Italian books, Palladio's of 1570 and Scamozzi's of 1615.

82　Terminology and interpretation by Kruft, *Architectural Theory*, p. 99.

83　Book I, part I, p. 38 and plate 40. Compare Kruft, *Architectural Theory*, p. 99 and fig. 55.

84　Van Pelt, *Art History*, IV, 2 (1981), pp. 154-156.

85　Vitruvius, *Ten Books on Architecture*, book III, chap. 1, pp. 72-73. Cf. also Vitruvius's remarks on symmetry, book I, chap. 2, p. 14.

86　Ibid., book I, chap. 3, p. 17. For further reading on Huygens and the sculpture in his house at The Hague see Lunsingh Scheurleer, *Oud Holland*, 77 (1962), pp. 181-205 and for the sculptures on the pediment pp. 198 and 201. For Vitruvius's influence in Holland in the world of literati see Bodar, *Bouwen in Nederland*, pp. 55-105 and for the pediment of Huygens's house pp. 66-67. For its relation with figures crowning the pediment of the Amsterdam Town Hall see Goossens in Huisken et al., *Jacob van Campen*, p. 208. On Alberti's thoughts on Vitruvius's principles of architecture see his *Art of Building*, book I, chap. 9, p. 23, and book VI, chap. 1, p. 426.

87　Neurdenburg, *Beeldhouwkunst*, p. 19. See also Goossens in Huisken et al., *Jacob van Campen*, pp. 204-205, who relates the statues on the Huygens House to Honselaarsdijk and the Amsterdam Town Hall, comparing them with façades in classical treatises, such as Palladio's Temple of Castor and Pollux.

88 This decorative feature of Huygens's house was particularly admired, as can be concluded from a letter written to Huygens and including an epigram on these spheres; see Worp, *Briefwisseling*, II, RGP 19, letter 2105, G. Wendelius to Constantijn Huygens, dated 1 June, 1639: 'Een vriend van mij, die in Den Haag geweest is, vertelde mij, dat gij daar zulk een prachtig huis gebouwd hebt met een aardbol en hemelbol boven de schoorsteenen, en verzocht mij daarop een paar puntdichten te maken, die hierbij gaan.' (A friend of mine told me that you built such a beautiful house at The Hague, with an earthly and a celestial sphere on top of the chimneys, and asked me to write some eprigrams on them, which are enclosed herewith.)

89 This will be discussed in further detail in chapter VI.

90 Huygens's verse is paraphrased here, the original reading as follows: 'Die 't Gotsche krulligh mall met staetigh Roomsch vermanden, En dreef ouw' Ketterij voor ouder Waerheit heen.' (Who bound Gothic's mad twirl with stately Roman, and dislodged old Heresy for older Truth.) Compare de Jongh, *Nederlands Kunsthistorisch Jaarboek*, 24 (1973), p. 85; also Spies in Huisken et al., *Jacob van Campen*, p. 230. See the use of the term Gothic in Huygens's and Rubens's correspondence mentioned above.

91 For interesting comparisons between the assimilation of the classical idiom and ideas on classicism in Northern Europe, especially in England in circles of the learned elite, see Gent, *Albion's Classicism*, pp. 29-78.

92 Plinius Secundus, *Epistulae*, book II, chap. 17, and book V, chap. 6; see Pliny the Younger, *Letters*, chap. VI, pp. 376-393.

93 Worp, *Briefwisseling*, III, RGP 21, letter 2297, J.-L. Guez de Balzac to Constantijn Huygens, dated 25 January and 1 February 1640: 'La figure [print] de la vostre [maison] ne me plaist pas moins que les deux descriptions que Pline nous a laissés des deux siennes.' Interestingly, in the circles of literati in Scotland at the time, similar associations with contemporary architecture and Pliny's villas were made; see Gent, *Albion's Classicism*, p. 57.

94 Worp, *Briefwisseling*, II, RGP 19, letter 2151, Valentin Conrart to Constantijn Huygens, dated 2 July 1639.

95 Ibid., II, RGP 19, letter 2267, G. Wendelius to Constantijn Huygens, dated 25 October 1639: 'Die prenten zijn voor mij een commentaar op Vitruvius. Moge het huis eewenlang bestaan als eene herinnering aan U.' The text is in Latin and this section was translated by Worp from the original kept in the library of Leiden University.

96 See for Dubuisson-Aubenay's remarks Slothouwer, *Paleizen*, p. 303.

97 For the history of the area of the Aeckerlandt see Van der Haagen, *Jaarboek Die Haghe* (1928-29), pp. 6-39, and more specifically Kamphuis, *Oud Holland*, 77 (1962), p. 160, fig. 4.

98 Stevin, *Wisconstighe Ghedachtnissen*, 'Driehouckhandel', XI, i, 1. See also Dijksterhuis, *Stevin*, p. 104 on 'Gonio- en Trigonometri', and *Science in the Netherlands*, p. 42. For further reading see also Crone and Struik et al., *Principal Works of Simon Stevin*, and Kemp, *Art Bulletin*, 68, 2 (1986), pp. 237-252, especially pp. 240-241.

99 *Oeuvres complètes de Christiaan Huygens*, I, letter 10, Christiaan Huygens to his brother Constantijn, dated 14 August 1646: 'J'aij peint en nostre jardin des grandes figures comme le vif, avecq du charbon mis dans l'huijle et du craijon blancq, contre les aijs qui separent nostre jardin d'avecq celuij du comte Maurice [Mauritshuis garden], ce sont des figures d'Holbeins Dodendans, que, de petites comme le petit doict qu'elles sont, j'ay aggrandies à la hauteur susdite.'

100 Mollet, *Jardin de plaisir*, facs. ed., p. 31: 'Aux extrémités de ces allées, on posera de belles perspectives peintes sur toile …'

101 GAH, topographical department, Voorburg. The engraving is from Huygens's country-house poem *Hofwijck*.

102 See Van Pelt, *Art History*, IV, 2 (1981), pp. 150-174, and Bodar, *Bouwen in Nederland*, p. 67. For a literary analysis see de Vries in Hunt, *Dutch Garden*, pp. 81-97.

103 See Alberti, *Art of Building*, p. 310, and below for the further discussion of related classical terminology.

104 In his *Domus mea*, published in Worp, *Gedichten*, III, p. 31, Huygens calls his town-house a human being with mouth, ears, nose and eyes, and further, shoulders, breasts, arms, ribs, stomach as well as intestines; it smiles at the passers-by and invites the tired traveller to enter, offering 'humanitas' to every stranger: '… Adi libenter hanc domum: Iam nunc Homo, Humanitatem pollicetur aduenis.' See Bodar, *Bouwen in Nederland*, p. 99. The Hofwijck garden is also described in Huygens's poem *Hofwijck* as having a corporeal form and its various sections representing parts of the human body. For further reading see Worp, *Gedichten*, IV, pp. 266-338, and especially Van Pelt, *Art History*, IV, 2 (1981), pp. 150-174. See also Hopper, *Journal of Garden History*, II, 1 (1982), p. 33 and note 43. Compare also de Vries in Hunt, *Dutch Garden*, p. 83. De Vries's critical analysis of the text confirms that Huygens used the 'Vitruvian man' as the ideal model for Hofwijck. However, instead of Van Pelt's three-part division, de Vries distinguishes a fourth section in the layout, namely the road cutting through the estate, referred to in the text as representing the human waist.

105 The Metropolitan Museum of Art, New York, Harris Brisbane Dick Fund, 1942 (42.60.2).

106 Van Pelt, *Art History*, IV, 2 (1981), pp. 150-174.

107 Wittkower, *Architectural Principles*, pp. 4-126, on the problem of harmonic proportion in architecture and musical consonances and the visual arts, also discussed by Naredi-Rainer, *Architektur und Harmonie*, pp. 11-25.

108 Huygens, *Hofwijck*, p. 5: 'De konst leed geen geweld, maer liet sich wel wat recken, Ter liefde van mijn lust, En soo van dusend

trecken, Bleef d'een en ander vast.' (Art did not suffer violence, but let itself be slightly stretched, to answer my desire. And so after many plans were sketched, one and the other were fixed.) See Van Pelt, *Art History*, IV, 2 (1981), pp. 152-153.

109 Lunsingh Scheurleer and Van Pelt in Van den Boogaart, *Johan Maurits van Nassau-Siegen*, pp. 143-196.

110 For a current translation and illustration see Vitruvius, *Ten Books on Architecture*, book V, chap. 6, pp. 146-150.

111 Ibid., p. 146.

112 Yates, *Theatre of the World*, pp. 112-116, has pointed at the metaphysical importance of Vitruvius's design and the contemporary notion that if buildings incorporated this design, they became an allusion to the cosmos or the *Fabrica Mundi*. Compare Van Pelt in Van den Boogaert, *Johan Maurits van Nassau-Siegen*, pp. 194-196.

113 Among the portraits of the rulers of the House of Orange and Nassau, all of whom had fought for the Dutch Republic, was one of Adolf of Nassau as King of the Romans. See Lunsingh Scheurleer in Van den Boogaart, *Johan Maurits van Nassau-Siegen*, p. 146. For further remarks on the simile between 'Roman' and 'Batavian' see chapter VI.

114 See ibid., pp. 188-189, and chapter VI.

115 For an excellent commentary on Huygens's *Hofwijck* and the world of humanist thinking in which it was created, see de Vries in Hunt, *Dutch Garden*, pp. 81-97.

116 Symmetry is defined differently depending on what classical text or Renaissance commentary is used. Alberti speaks of the necessity to have every element arranged in its level, alignment, number, shape and appearance; that right matches left, top matches bottom, adjacent matches adjacent, and equal matches equal. See Alberti, *Art of Building*, p. 310. Vitruvius's *symmetria* is translated as 'commensurability' and refers to symmetry as the result of proportional relationship. Proportion, in turn, is defined as a correspondence among the measures of the members of an entire work, and of the whole to a certain part selected as standard; on it depends the beauty of the entire design. See Vitruvius, *Ten Books on Architecture*, book I, preface, p. 3. Vitruvius uses the word *eurhythmia* to refer to perfect beauty; see Onians, *Bearers of Meaning*, p. 37. This definition and the related idea of a uniform system of proportion throughout the design also cover in part Alberti's central concept of beauty, or *concinnitas*, defined as the harmony and concord of all the parts achieved in such a manner that nothing can be taken away or altered except for the worse. The key to beauty or correct proportion in Alberti is harmonic ratio, and, according to Wittkower, *Architectural Principles*, p. 33, more specifically Pythagoras's system of musical harmony. For a concise survey of Alberti's terminology and its meaning see his *Art of Building*, pp. 420-428. For new thoughts on Alberti's text, which move away from the Platonic interpretation to discuss his remarks on aesthetic experience, see Smith, *Architecture in Early Humanism*, p. 92, and pp. 89-97 for the term *concinnitas* referring to the principle of 'antithesis' or harmony of contrasting qualities in the context of classical architecture and rhetoric practice. Compare also Van Eck, *Organicism*, pp. 40-62.

117 Wittkower, *Architectural Principles*, pp. 101ff.

118 Ottenheym, *Philips Vingboons*, p. 160. Research in this area has lead to empty arithmetics, connected in part to too strong a supposition that the use of proportional measurements and geometry always needs to be filled with symbolism and deeper meaning. Compare also the publications by Smith, *Architecture in Early Humanism*, p. XVIII, and Van Eck, *Organicism*, p. 40.

119 Wittkower, *Architectural Principles*, p. 7, interprets the definition of beauty as a fixed law, which seems to contradict Alberti's own allowances for freedom in design (discussed by Wittkower himself on pp. 55-56) and the general ability to make all necessary changes for the appropriate use and convenience, or *utilitas*, of a building. See Alberti's use of the Vitruvian triad in Alberti, *Ten Books on Architecture*, p. 426. Compare for further commentary on this issue E.R. de Zurko, 'Alberti's Theory of Form and Function', *The Art Bulletin*, 39 (1957), pp. 142-145.

120 For recent new interpretations of classical thought and Renaissance commentaries see Smith, *Architecture in Early Humanism*, pp. xviii and 80-120. For the important relation between architecture, aesthetics and eloquence see ibid., pp. 133ff. Compare also Van Eck, *Organicism*, pp. 45-47 with a critical analysis of Wittkower's interpretation, and p. 40 for the relation between architecture and rhetorical concepts, and the issue of flexible formulations versus a fixed body of principles.

121 Compare Vitruvius, *Ten Books on Architecture*, book VI, chap. 2, pp. 174-175: 'After the standard of symmetry has been determined, and the proportionate dimensions adjusted by calculations, it is the part of wisdom to consider the nature of the site, or questions of use or beauty, and modify the plan by diminutions or additions in such a manner that these diminutions or additions in the symmetrical relations may be seen to have been made on correct principles, and without detracting at all from the effect.'

122 See Alberti, *De re aedificatoria*, pp. 426-427.

123 Worp, *Briefwisseling*, II, RGP 19, letter 1918, Constantijn Huygens to Amalia of Orange, dated 12 August 1638. See chapter III, note 170.

124 Ibid., II, RGP 19, letter 1725, Constantijn Huygens to Amalia of Orange, dated 30 September 1637: '... le gouvernuer auroit faict certain retrenchement au jardin de Valckenbergh, pour y disputer, ce semble, le chasteau ...' A later visit by the Stadholder to his Breda castle and the gardens of the Valkenberg took place two years later; see ibid., II, RGP 19, p. 481, letter 2195, Constantijn Huygens to Amalia of Orange, dated 5 August 1639.

125 Ibid., II, RGP 19, letter 1424, Constantijn Huygens to Amalia of

Orange, dated 25 August 1636. For the complete text see Slothouwer, *Paleizen*, p, 343.

126 Worp, *Briefwisseling*, II, RGP 19, letter 1427, Constantijn Huygens to Amalia of Orange, dated 27 August 1636. For the original French text see Slothouwer, *Paleizen*, p. 343.

127 Worp, *Briefwisseling*, II, RGP 19, letter 1449, Constantijn Huygens to Amalia of Orange, dated 20 September 1636. See Slothouwer, *Paleizen*, p. 343.

128 Worp, *Briefwisseling*, III, RGP 21, letter 2426, Constantijn Huygens to Amalia of Orange, dated 30 June 1640. For the original French text see Slothouwer, *Paleizen*, p. 348 .

129 'Uw brief met de bevelen van Z.E. aangaande de parterres heb ik ontvangen; de intendant And. Mollet zal het in orde maken. Maar er moet ook voor waterafvoer worden gezorgd. Catshuysen belooft zijn best te zullen doen op Honselaersdijk. 6 8bris. 1635. Raptim Hagae.' Worp, *Briefwisseling*, II, RGP 19, letter 1254, Constantijn Huygens to David de Wilhem, dated 6 October 1635. See Slothouwer, *Paleizen*, p. 342.

130 Worp, *Briefwisseling*, II, RGP 19, letter 1260, David de Wilhem to Constantijn Huygens, dated 16 October 1635: 'Hierbij gaat een brief van den Heer Mollet over het perk.' (Enclosed is a letter by Mr. Mollet regarding the parterre.) Unfortunately this letter is lost.

131 Ibid., II, RGP 19, letter 1466, David de Wilhem to Constantijn Huygens, dated 9 October 1636: 'Ik zal mijn best doen ten opzichte van het planten der boomen. Maar ik zou liever willen, dat de Prins mij andere dingen opdroeg, b.v. eene regeling van zaken met de Oost- en West-Indische Compagnie.' (I shall do my best as regards the planting of the trees. But I'd rather the Prince gave me other things to do, such as settling business with the East or West India Company.) The trees referred to are those planted at Honselaersdijk, as is clarified by a later letter describing the work at Honselaersdijk and questioning the planting of these trees: see ibid., letter 1493, David de Wilhem to Constantijn Huygens, dated 23 8b (October) 1636: 'Catshuijsen verzekert mij dat er hard gewerkt wordt op Honselaersdijk, maar ik zal er ook op toezien. Hoe moeten de boomen geplant worden?' (Catshuijsen assures me that one is working hard at Honselaersdijk, but I shall attend to it myself. How should the trees be planted?)

132 Ibid., II, RGP 19, letter 1909, Constantijn Huygens to Amalia of Orange, dated 2 August 1638. See Slothouwer, *Paleizen*, p. 344.

133 Heldring, *Jaarboek Die Haghe* (1967), pp. 66-71.

134 Worp, *Briefwisseling*, III, RGP 21, letter 3007, Constantijn Huygens to Amalia of Orange, dated 3 June, 1642.

135 Johan Albrecht II, Count of Solms, colonel in the Dutch army. See Worp, *Briefwisseling*, III, RGP 21, letter 2578, Constantijn Huygens to Amalia of Orange, dated 17 November 1640: 'A midi Messieurs les Estats d'Utrecht l'ont traicté en un beau et grand festin, apres que S.A. eust employé la matineé à veoir le jardin de M. le comte de Solms.'

136 Ibid., III, RGP 21, letter 3004, Constantijn Huygens to Amalia of Orange, dated 30 May 1642: 'Z.H. is gisteren te Vianen aangekomen, heeft gewandeld … Van morgen heeft Z.H. het bosch van den heer van Brederode bekeken …' (His Highness arrived yesterday at Vianen, took a walk … This morning His Higness looked round the woods of the lord of Brederode …) Count Johan Wolfert van Brederode was related to Frederik Hendrik by his previous marriage to Anna of Nassau and in 1638 remarried Amalia's sister, Louise van Solms.

137 Bienfait, *Oude Hollandsche Tuinen*, pp. 48-51, believes that Honselaarsdijk was constructed under three guiding architects, Jacob van Campen, Simon de la Vallée and Pieter Post, with Constantijn Huygens as adviser, without mentioning the actual designer of the building. Concerning Ter Nieuburch, pp. 51-53, Bienfait quotes Bartholomeus van Bassen as the architect-designer. Slothouwer, *Paleizen*, pp. 19-20, 27-31, 100 and 366-367, is more specific, distinguishing between the roles of various individuals indicated as 'architects' in the records of payments, including Arent Arentsz van 's Gravesande and Bartholomeus van Bassen. Of central importance were, according to Slothouwer, Simon de la Vallée (official architect 1634-37), Jacob van Campen (never officially hired but involved since 1632) and Pieter Post (involved from the late 1630s onward and since 1645 the Stadholder's official court architect). For Ter Nieuburch see ibid., pp. 27-31 and 371-373, where Slothouwer again quotes Simon de la Vallée as possible designer. Plantenga in *Verzamelde opstellen*, p. 28, believes that Jacob van Campen was the designer of both Honselaarsdijk and Ter Nieuburch. Before Plantenga, Hudig, *Frederik Hendrik*, p. 23, named Van Campen as the designing architect. Vermeulen, *Nederlandsche Historiebladen*, I (1938), p. 117, wrote that Bartholomeus van Bassen designed Ter Nieuburch, not Jacob van Campen, as these earlier authors believed. Van Bassen was also the central figure in Vermeulen's *Handboek*, III, p. 109. However, in the same book, p. 55, he attributed Ter Nieuburch to Simon de la Vallée, as he did in his article in *Nedelandsche Historiebladen*, I (1938), p. 122. In his *Bouwmeesters*, pp. 54-55, too, Vermeulen attributed the architectural designs of both Honselaarsdijk and Ter Nieuburch to Simon de la Vallée. Recently Den Boer, *Noorteynde*, p. 33, did the same. For further comment see the text below.

138 See also the preceding note. Bienfait, *Oude Hollandsche tuinen*, pp. 51-52: '… new house reconstructed according to plans by the painter-architect Bartholomeus van Bassen'. Here Bienfait must have followed the ideas put forward by Vermeulen in *Nederlandsche Historiebladen*, I (1938), p. 117, and also in his *Handboek*, III, p. 109. Vermeulen drew this hasty conclusion from an entry in the Ter Nieuburch records of payments, ARA, NDR, inv. no. 1042 [old no. 781], fol. 258vo, where one can read that Van Bassen provided plans for the house and grounds of Ter Nieuburch. As mentioned above, later Van Bassen would indeed work as a

designing architect, namely for the Koningshuis at Rhenen; see Terwen, *Nederlands Kunsthistorisch Jaarboek*, 33 (1982), p. 173, fig. 3.

139 This mistake has again been made in the recent publication on Van Campen; see Goossens in Huisken et al., *Jacob van Campen*, p. 225.

140 Hopper, *Journal of Garden History*, II, 1 (1982), p. 33.

141 ARA, NDR, inv. no. 1042 [old no. 781], fol. 258vo, where Barthout van Bassen, 'perspectijffschilder ende architect', was paid for making two perfect plans ('grontteijckeningen') of all the grounds belonging to the Huis ter Nieuburch, including plans of the house, gardens and plantations, and also 'two large drawings ("standteijckeningen") of the elevation of the afore-said building in the state in which it is now and is still projected to be completed ("in proiect staet"), which His Highness ordered to be made in all haste and to be sent to him in the army … January 1633'.

142 ARA, NDR, inv. no. 1039 [old no. 778], fol. 213vo. See Slothouwer, *Paleizen*, pp. 27 and 48.

143 Bienfait, *Oude Hollandsche tuinen*, pp. 51-52, and Vermeulen, *Nederlandsche Historiebladen*, I (1938), p. 117, and *Handboek*, III, p. 109.

144 Slothouwer, *Paleizen*, pp. 27-28.

145 ARA, NDR, inv. no. 1039 [old no. 778], fol. 213vo. Van Bassen received 373 pounds, which is a large sum for only providing models and drawings, according to Slothouwer, *Paleizen*, p. 27; yet he is only mentioned once and specifically referred to as *schilder* (painter). However, if the word *modellen* refers to very complex and detailed wooden models of the whole edifice, this could very well justify the high price paid for Van Bassen's work. Compare also the remarks on Van Bassen in notes 138 and 141.

146 Kuyper, *Dutch Classicist Architecture*, pp. 89-97. 's Gravesande's most important buildings at Leiden are the Lakenhal and the Marekerk, both initiated in 1639.

147 See for example ARA, NDR, inv. no. 1041 [old no. 780], fol. 273, describing Arent van 's Gravesande's role 'to direct and advance the building at Rijswijk', and 1042 [old no. 781] fol. 279, 'for the making of the necessary drawings … as well as having supervision over the workmen and their progress'. See also Slothouwer, *Paleizen*, p. 26.

148 ARA, NDR, inv. no. 1042 [old no. 781], fols. 260vo, 264vo and 268vo, where Pieter van Bilderbeeck is called 'architect from Leijden' and Gerrit van Druijvestein (*sic*) *fabrijck*, or builder-architect, of The Hague.

149 ARA, NDR, inv. no. 1042 [old no. 781], fols. 234 and 236, and inv. no. 1043 [old no. 782], fol. 227.

150 For drawings in general see ARA, NDR, inv. no. 1040 [old no. 779], fol. 5.211: '… over eenige teeckeninge bij hem ten dienste vant voorscreve gebouw gemaeckt.' For drawings and a model for the staircase see inv. no. 1042 [old no. 781], fol. 244. See also Slothouwer, *Paleizen*, pp. 263-264.

151 ARA, NDR inv. no. 1041 [old no. 780], fol. 255: '… eenige teickenin. van poorten, balusters etc.', and fol. 260vo: 'verscheijden teijckeningen bij den selven vande voorschreve poorte ende balustrade gemaeckt.' See Slothouwer *Paleizen*, pp. 289-290.

152 Slothouwer, *Paleizen*, p. 52. See also Meischke, *Nederlands Kunsthistorisch Jaarboek*, 33 (1982), p. 191.

153 ARA, NDR, inv. no. 1043 [old no. 782], fol. 266vo: 'Mr. Evert, schilder, Gerrit Druivestein architect, Allert Claessen smith, la Vallee architect ende Arent Arentsen teijckenaer gesamentlick te Honselerdijck tot directie vande wercken aldaer …' See Slothouwer, *Paleizen*, p. 265. De la Vallée and Van 's Gravesande also collaborated in the completion of the grand central staircase at Honselaarsdijk, designed by de la Vallée as part of his modernization plan for the whole central pavilion; see ARA, NDR, inv. no. 1042 [old no. 781], fol. 244. For this staircase Van 's Gravesande also provided a wooden model; he is specifically referred to in the accounts as architect and *schrijnwercker*, or joiner; compare ARA, NDR, inv. no. 1041 [old no. 780], fol. 261vo. Van 's Gravesande also made models for specific building units at Ter Nieuburch, such as that for the central entrance porch and balustrade which he sent to Amsterdam to be used by stonemasons working for the court there; see ARA, NDR, inv. no. 1042 [old no. 781], fol. 229vo. He shared his position as joiner with other persons, such as Alewijn Claesz van Assendelft, who himself was responsible for making a model of the entire edifice of Honselaarsdijk, referred to in ARA, NDR, inv. no. 992 [old no. 735], fol. 188.

154 Vermeulen believed that de la Vallée's role was all-important for the development of the new Dutch classical style, see *Handboek*, III, pp. 115-120. Slothouwer and Nordberg's publications, as well as the more recent studies by Meischke and Ottenheym, do not refer to de la Vallée as an architect who played a key role in the development of architecture in Holland.

155 Nordberg, *De La Valleé*, pp. 84-85.

156 ARA, NDR, inv. no. 992 [old no. 735], fol. 188.

157 Slothouwer, *Paleizen*, pp. 29-30.

158 See the entries in the Appendix under ARA, NDR, inv. no. 4694 [old no. NDR FOLIO, 1413].

159 Slothouwer, *Paleizen*, pp. 31 and 325-326, quotes from the account books, ARA, NDR, inv. no. 562 [old no. 599], fol. 152: 'Acte voor Pieter Post, schilder and architect, omme Sijnne Hooch[t] te dienen als schilder ende architect in desselfs gebouwen, … 14 Febr. 1645 … dat midts de goede experientie ende ervarenheijt die wij bevonden hebben inden persoon van Pieter Post, schilder ende architect tot Haerlem wij den selven aengenomen hebben … omme hem als schilder ende architect te gebruijcken in onse gebouwen waer vooren wij hem over zijne vacatien soo wanneer hij in onsen dienst buijten de stadt sal reijsen toegevoucht hebben ses

guldens s'daechs ende vier gulden over montcosten, behalven de wagenvrachten ende teeckeningen bij hem te maecken ...' (Deed for Pieter Post, painter and architect, to serve His Highness, as painter and architect, in his buildings, ... 14 Feb. 1645 ... that, due to the great experience and skill we found in the person of Pieter Post, painter and architect at Haarlem, we have appointed the same ... to be our painter and architect in our buildings, and for his travels in our service outside the city he will receive a daily fee of six guilders, as well as four guilders food allowance, excluding [reimbursements] for the cart-loads and the drawings to be made by him ...) ARA, NDR, inv. no. 562 [old no. 599], fol. 208vo describes a later, augmented Deed of Appointment for Pieter Post, which shows how pleased Frederik Hendrik was with his work. Post is called a fine, capable man with whom everyone has an excellent working experience: 'Acte voor Pieter Post, als schilder ende Architect van Sijne Hoocheijt ... 9 Febr. 1646 ... in het gebruijcken van zijnen dienst in onse gebouwen nu eenige jaren herwaerts, Ende ons daeromme volcomentlijck vertrouwende tzijner cloeckheijt experientie en bequaemheijt, Wij den selven hebben aengenomen ... tot onsen Schilder ende Architect ordinaris van onse gebouwen, met laste ende bevel omme daerinne alles wel ende getrouwelijck te verrichten ende uijt te voeren tgene wij hem van tijt tot tijt sullen goetvinden hem te ordonneren ende te bevelen, waer voren wij hem tot Gagie ende huijshuijre toevougen de somme van duijsent car. gulden jaerlijx, behalven de teeckeningen ende concepten bij hem te maecken ... midts dat hij Post gehouden sal sijn op Maij toecomende sijne residentie te comen nemen alhier inden Hage ...' (Deed for Pieter Post, His Highness's painter and architect ... 9 Feb. 1646 ... having made use of his services in our buildings during several years, and having relied completely on his vigorousness, experience and competence, we have appointed the same ... as our ordinary painter and architect of our buildings, with the order to carry out and execute therein well and with precision everything which from time to time we shall see fit to request from him, for which work and for house rental he will receive the sum of one thousand carolus guilders yearly, excluding the drawings and first drafts to be made by him ... provided that he, Post, in the coming month of May will take up his residency here in The Hague ...)

160 Slothouwer, *Paleizen*, pp. 31 and 325-327. Detailed information from the account books, ARA, NDR, inv. no. 562 [old no. 599], fol. 4, shows Simon de la Vallée's 'Letter of Resignation', describing his position as architect at the Dutch court with an income of 800 pounds artois yearly and permission to leave for Sweden: 'Acte van ontslaginge van Jacques de la Vallée uijt sijnen dienst als architect van Sijne Hooch[ts] gebouwen ... May 1637.'

161 The contract for the decoration of the pediment of Honselaarsdijk is dated 10 January 1636. See Meischke, *Nederlands Kunsthistorisch Jaarboek*, 33 (1982), p. 198.

162 Worp, *Briefwisseling*, III, RGP 21, letter 3462, Constantijn Huygens to J. Bannius, dated 10 February 1644. For the text of Huygens's poem see Slothouwer, *Paleizen*, p. 351: '... Campius oppressi vindex sub nube Vitruvj ... Qui lucem terris redderet ...'

163 Worp, *Gedichten*, IV, p. 282, vss. 617-620. Compare also Spies in Huisken et al., *Jacob van Campen*, p. 229.

164 In 1636 Van Campen designed the decoration of the gallery at the castle of Buren and rebuilt staircases and windows, as shown by letters in the Huygens correspondence. See Worp, *Briefwisseling*, II, RGP 19, letters 1424 and 1427, Constantijn Huygens to Amalia of Orange, dated 25 and 27 August 1636, respectively, describing Van Campen's discussions with the Stadholder about improvements at Buren. See for the complete text in its French original Slothouwer, *Paleizen*, p. 342. Compare Buvelot in Huisken et al., *Jacob van Campen*, p. 128.

165 An entry in the account books (see ARA, NDR, inv. no. 992 [old no. 735], fol. 129, dated April 3, 1638) mentions that Van Campen received 3175 Carolus guilders to pay the respective painters in the gallery of Ter Nieuburch. See Slothouwer, *Paleizen*, p. 300. Compare also Buvelot in Huisken et al., *Jacob van Campen*, p. 129.

166 See Brenninkmeyer-De Rooij, *Oud Holland*, 96 (1982), pp. 133-185, and Buvelot in Huisken et al., *Jacob van Campen*, pp. 121-141. For the Huis ten Bosch compare also Terwen and Ottenheym, *Pieter Post*, pp. 63-70. For Honselaarsdijk see Meischke, *Nederlands Kunsthistorisch Jaarboek*, 31 (1980), pp. 86-103, and ibid., 33 (1982), pp. 191-205.

167 Slothouwer, *Paleizen*, pp. 34-36, 55-56 and 202.

168 Compare Fremantle, *Baroque Town Hall*, p. 187, describing Van Campen's designs for the Amsterdam Town Hall, which result in the welding of all the arts into a unifying scheme. See also the remarks by Buvelot in Huisken et al., *Jacob van Campen*, p. 127.

169 Slothouwer, *Paleizen*, pp. 55-56. See also Buvelot in Huisken et al., *Jacob van Campen*, pp. 122-127, and p. 124 with illustrations of the *omgaende gallerije*, or balustrade, with figures painted in the great reception hall at Honselaarsdijk.

170 Fremantle, *Oud Holland*, 80 (1965), pp. 65-108. See also Goossens in Huisken et al., *Jacob van Campen*, pp. 203-205.

171 Van Campen's involvement with garden statues at Honselaarsdijk can be inferred from two entries in the accounts, dated 16 December 1639, showing that Bartolomeus Drijffhout received payment for his work involving the placement of statues in the gardens, all according to Van Campen's declaration. Compare the entry in the ARA, NDR, inv. no. 992 [old no. 735], fol. 333, about statues coming from Rotterdam to Honselaarsdijk. According to Worp, *Briefwisseling*, II, RGP 19, letter 1909, Huygens to Amalia of Orange, dated 2 August 1638, Van Campen may also have assisted in the sculpture programme for Ter Nieuburch's garden. Compare Goossens in Huisken et al., *Jacob van Campen*, pp. 223-224.

172 Worp, *Briefwisseling*, II, RGP 19, letter 1909, Constantijn Huygens to Amalia of Orange, dated 2 August 1638.

173 Slothouwer, *Paleizen*, p. 34. See also Weissmann, *Oud Holland*, 20 (1902), pp. 166 and 169.

174 ARA, NDR, inv. no. 562 [old no. 599], fol. 51vo, and compare Slothouwer, *Paleizen*, pp. 31 and 325: 'Acte voor Pieter Post, architect tot Haerlem, omme opsicht te hebben op de timmeragie alhier int Noordteijnde … 30 April 1640.' For Post's collaboration with Van Campen see also his letter to Huygens of 23 October 1640, describing his decision to meet Van Campen in The Hague to discuss matters concerning the Noordeinde palace. See Worp, *Briefwisseling*, III, RGP 21, letter 2558. For further reading see Terwen and Ottenheym, *Pieter Post*, pp. 38-43, particularly p. 39: while Van Campen was the designer, the actual execution of the work, including the reconstruction and decoration of the great hall and the new apartments, was in Post's hands.

175 Slothouwer, *Paleizen*, p. 144. According to Van Pelt, *Jaarboek Vereniging Oranje-Nassau Museum* (1979), pp. 26ff., the façade was based on a design from Scamozzi's *L'Idea dell'architettura universale*. Compare also Den Boer, *Noorteynde*, pp. 37-40.

176 The pleasure of working with Post is clearly expressed in the contract of stadholderly architect quoted above. See ARA, NDR, inv. no. 562 [old no. 599], fol. 208vo.

177 The displeasure with Van Campen is shown in a letter by Huygens to Amalia of Orange, dated 3 September 1649; see Worp, *Briefwisseling*, V, RGP 28, letter 4975. See also Slothouwer, *Paleizen*, pp. 354-355.

178 For further reading see Terwen and Ottenheym, *Pieter Post*, pp. 47-49.

179 Worp, *Briefwisseling*, IV, RGP 24, letter 3601, L. Buysero to Constantijn Huygens, dated 13 July 1644.

180 Ibid., IV, RGP 24, letter 3614, L. Buysero to Constantijn Huygens, dated 14 July 1644. Compare also Post's letter to Buysero, dated 12 July 1644, in the Fondation Custodia, Paris; see Lunsingh Scheurleer in Van Deursen et al., *Veelzijdigheid als levensvorm*, pp. 48-50. For a short description of these letters see also Blok, *Pieter Post*, pp. 13-14.

181 For a detailed description of the building history see Terwen and Ottenheym, *Pieter Post*, pp. 56-72; also Loonstra, *Huijs int Bosch*, pp. 14-27.

182 For further reading on Rijxdorp and Vredenburg see Terwen and Ottenheym, *Pieter Post*, pp. 88-99 and 103-107, especially p. 97, showing an early garden plan for Vredenburg by Post dated 7 September 1641 (kept in the RMZ). This drawing clearly shows the strict regimentation. The geometrical forms of the triangle and semicircle are developed in the garden at Rijxdorp; see ibid., p. 106. Post also experimented with semicircular forms at the Huis Het Zant (ibid., p. 102) and at Heeze (p. 116), both comparable with the 1646 design for Honselaarsdijk.

183 See Terwen and Ottenheym, *Pieter Post*, chap. IV, pp. 88ff.

184 The term used today to denote such a unified whole is *Gesamtkunstwerk*.

185 Worp, *Briefwisseling*, III, RGP 21, letter 2558, P. Post to Constantijn Huygens, dated 23 October 1640: 'Neevens deesen wert gesonden een teijckeningh tot de plantagie.' (In addition, a drawing for the plantation has been sent.) Compare also the following letter by Post to Huygens, in which Post remarks about having sent a note to Van Campen about the trees for the garden and the iron for the chimney (Worp, *Briefwisseling*, III, RGP 21, letter 2655, dated 24 February 1641): 'Ick hebbe aen Monsr. van Campen geschreeven, soo van de boomen als van het eijser op de schoorsteen.' (I have written to Mr. Van Campen about the trees and the iron on the chimney.) The plantation referred to in the first letter and the trees in the second are believed to belong to the estate Hofwijck, mentioned in several other letters sent by Huygens to Post, vice versa, at the time.

186 Ibid., III, RGP 21, letter 2654, P. Post to Constantijn Huygens, dated 24 February 1641: 'Soo t Mijnheer gelieft, gelieft aen den heer van 'sAnnelandt te laaten weeten van mijn comst in den Haagh.' (If you do not mind, would you please let the lord of St. Annelandt [Philips Doublet's official title] know of my arrival at The Hague.) For the further history of Clingendael see Sellers, *Journal of Garden History*, VII, 1 (1987), pp. 8-9.

187 It would be of great interest to uncover to what extent Post was involved in designing and building Hofwijck, Clingendael and Arentsdorp, given the important typological (pavilion-type structure), chronological (1640s) and conceptual (architectural theory within family circle) links between the country houses and their owners. The similarity of the houses mentioned here was first noted by Van der Wijck, *Nederlandse buitenplaats*, pp. 21 and 61-63, and further developed in Sellers, *Journal of Garden History*, VII, 1 (1987), p. 9 and note 14. A reference to Post's involvement with 'a plantation', probably referring to the plantation of the Hofwijck garden, is given in Worp, *Briefwisseling*, III, RGP 21, letter 2558, P. Post to Constantijn Huygens, dated 23 October 1640, quoted above.

188 Ibid., V, RGP 28, letter 5389, Constantijn Huygens to J. Golius, dated 29 January 1655. See also Blok, *Pieter Post*, p. 40.

189 Blok, *Pieter Post*, p. 18. Post may also have provided drawings for the Amsterdam Town Hall after Van Campen's ideas. His brother Anthonie Post was paid 312 guilders 7 stuivers for drawings and models made by Pieter Post for the newly-built Town Hall, as mentioned in the accounts *extra ordinaris* of the City of Amsterdam, dated 5 April 1647.

190 See Terwen and Ottenheym, *Pieter Post*, chap. III.

191 For Dinant's important role as supervisor, apart from his function as *concierge-fontainier*, see the many entries in the records of payments, particularly ARA, NDR, inv. no. 994 [old no. 737],

fol. 112, and inv. no. 995 [old no. 738], fols. 65, 90vo, 114vo and 221.

192 Morren, *Honselaarsdijk* pp. 59-60.

193 Dinant is mentioned as supervising the work together with the comptroller 'sHerwouters: 'geattesteert bij den Controlleur 'sHerwouters ende den Grottier Joseph Dinant'; see ARA, NDR, inv. no. 993 [old no. 736], fols. 12a, 12b, 47b, and inv. no. 994 [old no. 737], fol. 85vo. Many other entries are described as having been 'declared by Joseph Dinant', or 'op declaratie van Joseph Dinant concierge van de huijse to Rijswijck'; see ARA, NDR, inv. no. 994 [old no. 737], fol. 112. For his work on the grottoes at Ter Nieuburch see ARA, NDR, inv. no. 992 [old no. 735], fol. 409, and inv. no. 993 [old no. 736], fol. 442vo. For the grottoes and fountains at Honselaarsdijk see ARA, NDR, inv. no. 993 [old no. 736], fols. 452vo, 465; inv. no. 994 [old no. 737], fol. 36vo; and inv. no. 995 [old no. 738], fol. 114vo. One of the reasons why I believe that Dinant may have been involved in details of the garden layout is the versatility of his craftsmanship. In 1634 he was paid for making a special sort of paper stucco for the interior decoration of Her Highness's chamber cabinet at Honselaarsdijk, as indicated in ARA, NDR, inv. no. 1043 [old no. 782], fol. 2322vo. Besides, the existence of a plan of the Ter Nieuburch garden drawn up in the French toise instead of the local Dutch Rijnlandse roede, and thus to be attributed to a Frenchman, could point to Dinant as draughtsman. However, he was not the only Frenchman at court at the time, as mentioned in chapter II, and in spite of his capabilities it remains unlikely that Dinant's activities extended to that of designing architect.

194 Morren, *Honselaarsdijk*, p. 17, and Bienfait, *Oude Hollandsche tuinen*, p. 49, stated that Mollet was invited to lay out the parterres at Honselaarsdijk, without being specific as to the possible designer of the garden as a whole. Bienfait's description on pp. 49 and 52 is more carefully balanced, differentiating between parterre layout and total design of the gardens. While referring briefly to other gardeners (Jan Versyll and Louis D'Anthoni), Bienfait also concentrated on Mollet as the principal, guiding garden architect. Compare Springer, *Oude Nederlandsche tuinen*, pp. 5-7, who attributed Honselaarsdijk's and Ter Nieuburch's garden layouts to Claude and André Mollet. Vermeulen, *Nederlandsche Historiebladen*, 1 (1938), p. 119, mentioned Louis D'Anthoni as gardener, without further commentary. Kuyper, *Dutch Classicist Architecture*, pp. 140-141, stated: 'One Louis D'Anthonio (or d'Antoni) served as a gardener, but there are some indications that André Mollet, who made the broderies at Honselaarsdijk, was also the overseer of the Prince's other gardens.'

195 Hopper, *Journal of Garden History*, II, 1 (1982), p. 33, and *Bulletin KNOB*, 3-4 (1983), p. 109.

196 Ibid., p. 34, and ibid, p. 112.

197 ARA, NDR, inv. no. 1 [old no. NDR 1], Journal of the Stadholder's Council, dated 9 June 1633, where 'Rijswijk parterres' is written in the margin, instead of 'Honselaarsdijk parterres'.

198 André Mollet is mentioned as 'Opsichter van Sijne Hooch[ts] Tuijnen' (superintendent of His Highness's gardens) in ARA, NDR, inv. no. 1042 [old no. 781], fols. 236 and 250, and inv. no. 1043 [old no. 782], fols. 218, 225vo and 243. He is also called 'Franschen architect hovenier' (French architect-gardener) in ARA, NDR, inv. no. 1042 [old no. 781], fol. 231vo, and 'Fransch hovenier' (French gardener) in ARA, NDR, inv. no. 1042 [old no. 781], fols. 232vo, 244vo.

199 Mollet's responsibility is described in ARA, NDR, inv. no. 1043 [old no. 782], fol. 232d, according to which Gijsbrecht Tonissen, gardener at Honselaarsdijk, is paid 200 pounds for the yearly upkeep of 'two new parterres in the garden belonging to the House at Honselaarsdijk, made under the direction of André Mollet …'

200 ARA, NDR, inv. no. 1043 [old no. 782], fols. 218vo, 219, 219vo and 221vo. Compare ARA, NDR, inv. no. 1043 [old no. 782], fol. 218: 'André Mollet supervisor … for costs made during five days at Honselaarsdijk to complete the new *perck* …' In the subsequent records of payments the various gardeners are paid for the planting of the new *perck*, which can mean compartment or flowerbed and may refer to the construction of parterres at Honselaarsdijk. For the planting of the garden see ARA, NDR, no. 1043 [old no. 782], fol. 218vo: 'Arent Pietersz Blom … 820 pounds 11 schillings for putting white poplar shrubs and elm shrubs at Honselaarsdijk in the new *perck* …' See also ARA, NDR, no. 1043 [old no. 782], fols. 220 and 221vo, for planting willow and fruit trees and shrubs. For the upkeep of the new parterres made by Mollet see ARA, NDR, inv. no. 1042 [old no. 781], fol. 233vo: 'Paid to the steward Catshuysen … 1,220 pounds 7 schillings 2 dernier for dayly wages, freights, consumptions and other costs to plant the two parterres at Honselaarsdijk … June 1633.' See also ARA, NDR, no. 1042 [old no. 781], fol. 247: 'Gijsbrecht Thonissen gardener … 250 pounds … for the upkeep of the two new parterres … Dec. 1633', and no. 1043 [old no. 782], fol. 232d: 'Gijsbrecht Thonissen … an addition of 200 pounds for the yearly upkeep of the two new parterres in the garden of the house at Honselaarsdijk, made under the direction of Andre Mollet …' Furthermore, regarding payments for the making of wooden structures such as fences or *plancken heijninge* and arches or arcades in the newly-begun *perck*, and the 'two gardens of House Honselaarsdijk', see ARA, NDR, inv. no. 1043 [old no. 782], fol. 219, and no. 1043 [old no. 782], fol. 219vo: '300 pounds for the construction of 34 pine-wooden arches or arcades in the two gardens of the house Honselaarsdijk.' These arches or arcades must be those surrounding Mollet's two parterre compartments on either side of the palace, visible in Van Berckerode's print, as is substantiated by the following description in inv. no. 1043 [old no. 782], fol. 229vo: 'Paid to Wouter Hendricsz and Willem Heijningen, carpenters, the sum of 505

pounds ... for the completion of 35 pine-wooden arches or arcades made and constructed in the two new gardens of the parterres on either side of the house Honselaarsdijk ... Dec. 1633.' For the original Dutch texts see the Appendix.

201 The most important entry is the account for all the work executed for the Stadholder, ARA, NDR, inv. no. 1042 [old no. 781], fol. 232vo: 'Paid to André Mollet, French gardener, the sum of 1,050 pounds for reimbursements and for directing the making of the parterres commissioned by His Highness at Honselaarsdijk and Buren, that is, 400 for the two parterres at Honselaarsdijk, one of turf and boxwood [palm] with white, red and black [stones or gravel] and the other entirely of boxwood, and 300 for two boxwood parterres at Buren, 300 for his travel money to come from and return to France, and 50 pounds for costs incurred at The Hague while making several drawings for His Highness ... and his yearly salary of 800 pounds and including a daelder [2.5 pounds] for daily wages ... June 1633.' One entry, concerning Honselaarsdijk (ARA, NDR, inv. no. 1043 [old no. 782], fol. 225vo), seems to imply that Mollet was responsible for more than the layout of parterres alone, namely for overseeing the plantation of other compartments in the gardens. In this entry Mollet is paid 11 pounds, 10 schillings for travelling expenses for his work in the summer of 1634 at Honselaarsdijk in order to 'direct the gardens and plantation there'. In other entries Mollet is paid for the transportation of several wagonloads of building and planting materials, or 'freights', as well as travelling expenses and provisions during his journeys to the various gardens ('wagenvracht en teercosten', 'verteerde costen', 'reiscosten'). In ARA, NDR, inv. no. 1043 [old no. 782] fol. 225vo, Mollet receives 11 pounds artois, 10 schillings for his journey to Honselaarsdijk 'om de thuijnen ende plantage aldaer te beleijden' (to direct [the work in] the gardens and the plantation there). Similarly, in ARA, NDR, inv. no. 1043 [old no. 782], fol. 243, Mollet is paid 26 pounds 14 schillings for his 'reijs ende teercosten ... naer Suilesteijn om de thuijnen te besichtigen' (journey to Zuylesteyn to inspect the gardens). ARA, NDR, inv. no. 1042 [old no. 781], fol. 231vo, describes the reimbursement of 9 pounds for the landlord of the local inn at Honselaarsdijk for 'consumptions by the French architect-gardener and other workmasters [employees]' in May 1633. Compare ARA, NDR, inv. no. 1042 [old no. 781], fol. 244vo, for references to subsequent costs incurred at the inn by Mollet, the steward Catshuijsen and the architect Jacques [sic] de la Vallée. Compare also the Appendix.

202 ARA, NDR, inv. no. 1042 [old no. 781], fol. 232vo. The sentence reads: '... costs incurred at The Hague while he has made various drawings for His Highness'. Compare ARA, NDR, inv. no. I [old no. I], Journal of the Stadholder's Council, dated 9 June 1633: 'Et pour la despense qu'il a faicte a la haye en faisant les susdits dessins cinquante livre.'

203 Since Mollet, according to the record of payments, stayed at The Hague while making these drawings, his work may have involved designs for parterres in Frederik Hendrik's gardens, such as those later used at the Huis ten Bosch, or possibly designs for the parterres at Ter Nieuburch or the Paleis Noordeinde.

204 See the discussion of Mollet's role in chapter I. For his responsibilities as *intendant*, *desseigneur*, architect, etc. in the Huygens correspondence, compare Worp, *Briefwisseling*, II, RGP 19, letter 1260, D. de Wilhem to Constantijn Huygens, dated 6 October 1635. See the text in its original version in the Leiden University Library, Dept. of Western Manuscripts, Hug. 37.

205 As we have seen in chapter II, Louis D'Anthoni (or D'Antoin) started working at Ter Nieuburch at the end of 1631 or the beginning of 1632, according to the *Conditions and Stipulations* (see Appendix, Document III). He is first mentioned in the records of payments of January 1633 (see ARA, NDR, inv. no. 1040 [old no. 779], fol. 22) as having worked at Ter Nieuburch during the past year and a half, that is, since the middle of 1631. He is last mentioned in the accounts of March 1638 (see ARA, NDR, inv. no. 992 [old no. 735], fol. 132).

206 Slothouwer, *Paleizen*, p. 373: 'François D'Antoine was responsible for the layout of the gardens.' Compare also p. 296: 'Louis D'Anthoni ... who must have been a Frenchman and was therefore probably called Antoine.'

207 See Bienfait, *Oude Hollandsche tuinen*, p. 52, and Vermeulen, *Nederlandsche Historiebladen*, I (1938), p. 119.

208 In his function as gardener-in-chief, Louis D'Anthoni was preceded by the *thuynman*, or gardener, Levert Janssen Versyll, described in ARA, NDR, inv. no. 1040 [old no. 779], fol. 214, and succeeded by Borchgaert Frederic (spelled 'Borchert Frederick' in the accounts) in the early 1640s. Compare ARA, NDR, inv. no. 993 [old no. 736], fols. 190, 244vo and 245. From 1651 onward this position was taken over by Cornelis Joosten; see ARA, NDR, inv. no. 995 [old no. 738], fol. 5vo. Borchgaert Frederic was not just a gardener; he was presumably also involved in larger artistic questions of garden design, for it was he who, together with the gardener Isaac Leschevin, dedicated the impressive print of Ter Nieuburch by Milheusser to Frederik Hendrik, as we have seen in chapter II. However, Borchgaert Frederic is also paid for delivering earth and manure (ARA, NDR, inv. no. 993 [old no. 736], fols. 190, 244vo and 245) and for bringing new orange-trees to the Ter Nieuburch garden, without there being any reference to payments for drawings or designs.

209 ARA, NDR, inv. no. 4694 [old no. NDR FOLIO, 1413]. See also chapter II and the Appendix.

210 The first payment to Van Thooren occurred in September 1645, see ARA, NDR, inv. no. 993 [old no. 736], fol. 313vo, the last payments date from the spring of 1658, for work completed in 1654; see ARA, NDR, inv. no. 996 [old no. 739], fols. 10vo and 13.

Anthony van Thooren was gardener of 'His Highness's old and second new gardens', while Blaes Jacobsz is usually indicated as gardener of the 'old and first new gardens' of Honselaarsdijk.

211 If the garden 'on the west side of the house' was the garden section holding the *parterres de broderie* laid out by Mollet on either side of the palace, it would mean that the parterres only survived for a period of ten to twelve years, since Van Thooren had already provided the drawings in 1646, according to the accounts. Another possibility is that the garden on the west side of the house actually refers to the *newly*-laid-out garden situated in the larger plantation area of Honselaarsdijk, outside the original pleasure garden here referred to as the 'old garden'. It is likely that other parterres were laid out in addition to those shown in the Van Berckerode print, or that the parterres referred to are not decorative parterres but kitchen-garden beds. In the account books ARA, NDR, inv. nos. 995 [old no. 738] and 996 [old no. 739], a distinction is made not only between the 'old garden' (the old main garden on the island proper) and the 'new garden', but also between the 'first new garden' (most likely the larger plantation area to the west of the main island) and the 'second new garden' (probably the larger garden section to the east of the main garden).

212 Also spelled 'Blaes Jacobsz' and, in ARA, NDR, inv. no. 996 [old no. 739], fol. 12, 'Blaes Jacobsz Verbruggen'.

213 For the other gardeners working at Breda, Buren, Zuylesteyn and Ysselsteyn see chapter III and the Appendix.

214 Compare also Van der Groen, *Nederlandtsen Hovenier*, facs. ed., p. 11.

215 In a document in the GAH, Notarieel Archief, 341, fols. 157 and 161-162, dated 18 October 1670, Van der Groen is still described as 'hovenier van Zijne Hoogheid op Honsholredijk'. See also Van der Groen, *Nederlandtsen Hovenier*, facs. ed., p. 11.

216 GAH, Notarieel Archief, 228, fols. 399-399vo, dated 21 October 1671. Inventory of his property was made up, Notariële Archieven, 640, fols. 206-208vo, dated 5 January 1672. See also Van der Groen, *Nederlandtsen Hovenier*, facs. ed., p. 12.

217 Compare also the commentary by de Jong in Hunt, *Dutch Garden*, pp. 13-48, especially pp. 13-23.

218 See also Van der Groen, *Nederlandtsen Hovenier*, facs. ed., pp. 17-18. For a list of later-seventeenth-century plants in the princely gardens see pp. 161-177.

219 Ibid., p. 19, showing the original title-page describing the decoration with engravings: '… Verrijkt met verscheyde Kopere Figueren, uytbeeldende Prinçelijke Lust-hoven en Hof-steden, na de Nederlandse en Françe ordre …'

220 See for this overview of Van der Groen's sources *Nederlandtsen Hovenier*, facs. ed., p. 10, and Jellicoe et al., *Oxford Companion to Gardens*, p. 579. For the influence of Leschevin's work on Van der Groen, see Sellers, 'De tuin van een krijgsman' in Koenhein et al., *Johan Wolfert van Brederode*, pp. 99-114.

221 Van der Groen, *Nederlandtsen Hovenier*, facs. ed., p. 31: '… doch voornamelijk steekt Vrankrijk tegenwoordigh boven alle andere Landen in desen heerlijkheyt uyt, alwaer men niet alleen de Koninklijke Huysen en Hoven Fontaine-Bleau, St. Germain, &c. maer ook byna ontallijcke Princen, Graven, en Edellieden haer Palleysen en Lust-hoven als aerdsche Paradijsen, siet pronken en pralen.

222 Ibid., pp. 33-34.

223 Ibid., p. 30.

224 Ibid.

225 Slothouwer, *Paleizen*, p. 25, remarks upon the fact that at court no leading architect seems to have existed and no specialized education for architects had as yet been developed.

226 Mollet, *Jardin de plaisir*, facs. ed., pp. 99 and 115.

227 See Slothouwer, *Paleizen*, pp. 24-25.

228 For the Doublet family and Huygens as dilettante garden architects and their role in the development of garden art during the last quarter of the seventeenth century see Sellers, *Journal of Garden History*, VII, 1 (1987), pp. 1-42.

229 Different contractors meant different working teams. Compare Slothouwer, *Paleizen*, p. 25.

230 See for an overview of this art-historical method used to analyse French and Italian gardens Sellers, *Rutgers Art Review*, IX-X (1988-89), pp. 137-139, notes 5, 6 and 7. For the idea of the 'Dutch Garden' in history see Hunt in Maccubbin and Hamilton-Phillips, *Age of William and Mary*, pp. 234-243.

231 For information on *landmeters kunst*, or the art of land-surveying, see Taverne, *In 't land van belofte*, and Muller and Zandvliet, *Admissies als lantmeter*.

232 ARA, map department, VTH 3323. The land-surveyor and map-maker was also responsible for levelling the ditches or canals, as can be concluded from an entry in the records of payments, ARA, NDR, inv. no. 994 [old no. 737], fol. 140, where Pieter Florisz is paid for maps as well as *waterpassen van slooten*, or levelling of ditches/canals, at Honselaarsdijk in 1648.

233 The text reads: 'Gecopieert den 17 Mey 1645 naer de teyckeninge gedaen by Mr. Post, teyckenaer voor haer hoocheydt omme een huys tuynen en grachten int bosch te maecken. Pieter Floris van der Sallem gesworen Lantmeter.'

234 When land was acquired from Nicolaas van Wouw for the extension of the grounds of Honselaarsdijk in 1638, measurements and maps were completed by Pieter Florisz van der Sallem; see ARA, NDR, inv. no. 992 [old no. 735], fol. 337. Two years later he recieved payment for the precise measurement of grounds and gardens at Honselaarsdijk, and for providing several maps (*caerten*); see ARA, NDR, inv. no. 992 [old no. 735], fol. 368. Payments for his work at Honselaarsdijk began in 1632 and continued till 1663, after which Johan van Swieten is mentioned as *landmeter*, or surveyor. References to Pieter Florisz occur in the following entries

in the account books: ARA, NDR, inv. no. 993 [old no. 736], fols. 249, 253 a-b, 423, 445 a-b and 445vo a-b. In inv. no. 994 [old no. 737], fols. 77vo and 140 a-b, he is reimbursed for the 'waterpassen van de slooten' (levelling of the small water canals); compare also inv. no. 995 [old no. 738], fols. 12vo and 226, and inv. no. 996 [old no. 739], fols. 8vo, 28 and 164vo. His father Floris Jacobsz is mentioned in the account books concerning Ter Nieuburch; see ARA, NDR, inv. no. 1041 [old no. 780], fol. 255vo, dated February 1632.

235 The following document clearly describes what was expected of the land-surveyor, including precise measurements and exact mapping. The document is kept in the KHA, archief Frederik Hendrik, inv. no. A 14-VII-8: 'Sijne Hooch[t] authoriseert hier mede Sijmon van Catshuijsen sijnen Rentmr. van Naeltwijck omme door eenen geswooren lantmeter te doen behoorlijcke grondt Caertinghe vande thien morgen lants gecocht vande Erffgen. van Jo.[r] Jan de Hutter gemeen leggende in een Camp van 20 morgen ende eenige roeden aencomende voor de hoeff Pieter Philipssen Heemskerck, mits dat het gedeelte van Sijne Hoocht sal genomen werden aende westzijde, ende Pieter Philipsz Heemskerck aende oostzijde, ende daervan te doen maken eene pertinente Caerte. Actum opden huijse tot Honsholredijck desen IIIe July XVIC sevenendertich.' (His Highness commands Sijmon van Catshuijsen his Steward at Naeltwijck to have a good map made by an official land-surveyor of the ten morgen [8 Rijnlandse acres] piece of land acquired from the heirs of Squire Jan de Hutter situated in a general area of 20 morgens [16 Rijnlandse acres] and a few roeden [a few square metres] land, touching upon the farmstead of Pieter Philipssen Heemskerck, on the understanding that His Highness's piece will be taken on the west side and Pieter Philipsz Heemskerck's on the east side, and to make a good plan of these grounds. Done in the House at Honsholredijck on this third of July 1637. [Signed Pieter Florisz van der Salm and Buysero, the treasurer].) Further descriptions of the surveyor's job, measuring the lands and waterways and providing detailed maps (in this case of the Orangepolder area, bordering the Honderlandt), are given in a document dated September 1644, also kept in the KHA, inv. no. A 14-VII-14.

236 ARA, map department, VTH 2363-6 and 2363-16, showing details of the new east garden c. 1640.

237 This was the case in 1598, when Stevin was accompanied by the land-surveyor David van Orliens to inspect the fortifications at Harderwijk. Van Orliens's report and his detailed drawings for the layout of new fortifications survive. See Taverne, *In 't land van belofte*, p. 57, note 20.

238 For Alberti's definition and its interpretation in modern literature see his *Art of Building*, pp. 422-423.

239 Vitruvius, *Ten Books on Architecture*, book VI, chap. 2, pp. 174-175. See also note 121.

240 For beauty, or *pulchritudo*, as described by Alberti, see his *Art of Building*, p. 420, and for beauty in relation to *concinnitas*, p. 422.

241 For comments on Alberti's definition of beauty and ornament (*pulchritudo et ornamentum*) see ibid., p. 420.

242 See ibid., pp. 24 and 426. For a further discussion on the crucial element of *variety* in the garden, and Mollet's architectural ideas, see chapter V.

CHAPTER V

1. Some of the ideas put forward here have been discussed in an earlier publication in the *Rutgers Art Review*, IX-X (1988-89), pp. 137-139.
2. Worp, *Briefwisseling*, II, RGP 19, letter 1088, Constantijn Huygens to J. Wicquefort, dated 8 March 1635: '… que je furette soigneusement les choses plus obscures, et prens plaisir à savoir en theorie ce que la practique ne me demandera jamais.'
3. See Van den Heuvel's review of Huisken et al., *Jacob van Campen*, in *Bulletin KNOB*, 4 (1996), p. 140, describing the need to refine the analyses of (the use of) ideal harmonic models in architecture, as done by Smith in *Architecture in Early Humanism*.
4. See Hopper in Jellicoe et al., *Oxford Companion to Gardens*, p. 260.
5. Another example is the avenue of the Clingendael estate; see Sellers, *Journal of Garden History*, VII, 1 (1987), p. 4, fig. 4, shown on the map of Delfland. Compare the avenue of the Hof at Bergen, visible on the provincial map of Noord-Holland; see Schaper, *Tuinkunst*, 1 (1995), pp. 25-27.
6. Hopper, *Bulletin KNOB*, 3-4 (1983), p. 107.
7. Karling in MacDougall and Hamilton Hazlehurst, *French Formal Garden*, pp. 18-21.
8. Strong, *Renaissance Garden in England*, p. 161. See also Hopper, *Bulletin KNOB*, 3-4 (1983), p. 109.
9. Hopper, *Bulletin KNOB*, 3-4 (1983), pp. 112-113, note 67.
10. Mollet, *Jardin de plaisir*, facs. ed., p. 31. 'First we should say that the Royal house must be sited to its best advantage so that it can be adorned with all things necessary to its embellishment, the first of which is to be able to plant a large avenue with a double or triple row of female elms or lime-trees (the species of trees we esteem most suited to this effect) which must be planted at right angle to the front of the château, at the beginning of which there should be a large semicircle or square …'
11. Hopper, *Bulletin KNOB*, 3-4 (1983), p. 109.
12. Alberti, *Art of Building*, book V, chap. 2, p. 121: '… the Houses of Princes … should have an Entrance from the Master Way and especially from the Sea or River; and … they should have a large open Area, big enough to receive the Train of an Ambassador, or any other Great Man, whether they come in Coaches, in Barks or on Horseback.' Compare Hopper, *Bulletin KNOB*, 3-4 (1983), p. 108, and later comments in Jacques and Van der Horst, *Garden of William and Mary*, p. 106.
13. Alberti's *De re aedificatoria* is included in the list of books of the stadholderly library kept in the KB, Department of Rare Books and Manuscripts, inv. no. 78 D 14.
14. See also Hopper, *Bulletin KNOB*, 3-4 (1983), p. 108.
15. Vol. II, pp. 356-360: Libro Ottavo, 'Delle strade fatte dagli antichi', and pp. 360-362: Libro Ottavo, chap. XXVII, 'Delle strade antichi in piano'.
16. Hopper, *Bulletin KNOB*, 3-4 (1983), p. 108, and Jacques and Van der Horst, *Gardens of William and Mary*, pp. 106-107.
17. Two exceptions may be the avenues at Twickenham Park and New Hall, Essex, which were designed between 1609 and 1618 and in 1623, respectively. See Jacques and Van der Horst, *Gardens of William and Mary*, p. 106.
18. Ibid., p. 106. See also Woodbridge, *Princely Gardens*, pp. 197-199, fig. 207.
19. Pérouse de Montclos, *Histoire de l'Architecture française*, p. 225, fig. 257.
20. Book III, chap. IV, p. 72: 'Des allees & long promenoirs.' Boyceau's advice on p. 71 is also important: to make an oblong rather than a square garden, which results in long avenues with pleasant perspectives. See also Hamilton Hazlehurst, *Boyceau*, p. 60.
21. Nordberg, *De La Vallée*, fig. 28.
22. Karling, *Trädgardskonsten*, p. 399, fig. 166, showing the palace and city plan of Eskilstuna. For the palace of Östermalma see p. 463, fig. 194. For the plan of Hässelby see p. 483, fig. 210. Note that Karling attributed the general plan of Ekolsund, which Nordberg attributed to Simon, to Simon's son Jean de la Vallée, p. 435, fig. 179.
23. Wittkower, *Architectural Principles*, fig. 47a, Villa Sarego from Palladio's *Quattro Libri*, Liber II, plate 49. See Chastel in *Vierhundert Jahre Palladio*, p. 54, fig. 4.
24. Thomson, *Du Cerceau*, facs. ed., pp. 164-165 and 210-211.
25. Hopper, *Bulletin KNOB*, 3-4 (1983), pp. 105-109.
26. See the plan of Soestdijk's grand entrance avenue with semicircular termination dated 1674 and kept in the CBN. The plan is shown in Tromp, *Huijs te Soestdijck*, pp. 26-27.
27. Ottenheym, *Philips Vingboons*, p. 43, figs. 40a and 40b.
28. Ibid., pp. 66, 191 and 224, ideal plan I 56. KB, Department of Rare Books and Manuscripts, inv. no. KW 1298 C 5, uit Vingboons, *Afbeelsels*, plate 56.
29. GAH, topographical department, Scheveningse Weg. See also Blok, *Pieter Post*, p. 76. Considering the friendship between Post and Huygens, Blok wonders if Post could have assisted Huygens with the planning of the Scheveningse Weg, or have been involved in designing the monumental entrance gate shaped like a triumphal arch.
30. Constantijn Huygens, *De Zee-straet* (1653), in Worp, *Gedichten*, VII, pp. 327-334. See also Strengholt, *Constanter*, p. 109, engraving by Romeyn de Hooghe after a drawing by Jan de Bisschop. The road was laid out according to Huygens's own drawings and plans and was completed in 1665; see Worp, *Briefwisseling*, V, RGP 28, pp. XVII-XVIII, and VI, RGP 32, p. X, notes 7-8.
31. Constantijn Huygens, in his 'Ontwerp by den Heere van Zuylichem aangaande eenen Steenwegh op Schevening', printed

31 following his poem *De Zee-straet*, reprinted in de Cretser, *Beschrijvinge van 's Gravenhage*, pp. 45-46.
32 Collection Kasteel Heeze. The design is signed and dated by Pieter Post, 27 February 1663. See for further reading Van Oirschot, *Bulletin KNOB*, 16 (1963), pp. 94-96.
33 Slothouwer, *Paleizen*, p. 34, and Weissmannn, *Oud Holland*, 20 (1902), pp. 166 and 169.
34 ARA, map department, VTH 3344 B, dated 8 August 1646. For further reading see Terwen in *De stenen droom*, pp. 268-306, especially p. 301, fig. 5.
35 Another example of art-historical research neglecting northern influence on southern art – in this case the English and Dutch influence on details of the French châteaux – is given by Rosenfeld, *Journal of the Society of Architectural Historians*, L, 3 (1991), pp. 317-321.
36 The Metropolitan Museum of Art, New York, Harris Brisbane Dick Fund, 1926 (26,104.5). Mollet, *Jardin de plaisir*, facs. ed., plate 2, described in the text on p. 32.
37 Hopper, *Journal of Garden History*, II, 1 (1982), pp. 40.
38 Karling in MacDougall and Hamilton Hazlehurst, *French Formal Garden*, p. 19.
39 Hopper, *Journal of Garden History*, II, 1 (1982), p. 34.
40 Mollet, *Jardin de plaisir*, facs. ed., p. 10.
41 Ibid., p. 10: 'Au Lecteur'.
42 The Metropolitan Museum of Art, New York, Harris Brisbane Dick Fund, 1926 (26.104.5).
43 Hopper, *Journal of Garden History*, II, 1 (1982), p. 34.
44 The Metropolitan Museum of Art, New York, Harris Brisbane Dick Fund, 1930 (30.32).
45 See on the Tuileries and their influence on Mollet the postscript by M. Conan in Mollet's *Jardin de plaisir*, p. 112.
46 Thomson, *Du Cerceau*, facs. ed., pp. 210-211.
47 For the terminology compare Hopper, *Journal of Garden History*, II, 1 (1982), pp. 33-37, and *Bulletin KNOB*, 3-4 (1983), pp. 112-115.
48 Mollet, *Jardin de plaisir*, facs. ed., p. 38, no. 2. See also Hopper, *Journal of Garden History*, II, 1 (1982), p. 34.
49 ARA, map department, VTH 3344 C. The maker and date of this rather roughly drawn plan are unknown, but a comparison between the information provided by the records of payments, describing the construction of fences, arches, arcades and the planting of trees, and the actual depiction of the terrain, indicating the placing of trees and arbours by means of points, suggests a date about 1633. See the account books in the ARA, NDR, inv. no. 1043 [old no. 782], fols. 219, 219vo, 229vo and 232a.
50 The palace in Mollet's plan is 29 toises wide by 21 long, or (1 toise being circa 2 metres) 58 x 42 metres, while Honselaarsdijk's palace structure measured 55 x 41.5 metres.
51 Hopper, *Journal of Garden History*, II, 1 (1982), p.34.
52 Mollet, *Jardin de plaisir*, facs. ed., p. 32. The size of the second ideal garden design was 200 x 150 toises. See also Hopper, *Journal of Garden History*, II, 1 (1982), p. 34, note 55.
53 Mollet, *Jardin de plaisir*, facs. ed., p. 32. Quoted in part by Hopper, *Journal of Garden History*, II, 1 (1982), p. 34.
54 Mollet, *Jardin de plaisir*, facs. ed., p. 32.
55 Mollet advises a garden of circa 200 x 150 toises, or 400 x 300 metres, compared with Honselaarsdijk's main garden of circa 320 x 240 metres.
56 Compare Hopper, *Journal of Garden History*, II, 1 (1982), pp. 34 and 37.
57 See for the terminology Hamilton Hazlehurst, *Boyceau*, p. 57.
58 Mollet, *Jardin de plaisir*, facs. ed., pp. 27-29. Mollet's terminology used to describe the function of the trees is similar to that used for architectural elements in building: '[arbre] beau et utile; il croit également en pyramide; propres et utiles à la décoration du jardin de plaisir; arbre toujours vert et propre.'
59 Ibid., p. 32. Quoted above in the description of ideal design no. 2.
60 Ibid., pp. 28-29: 'L'orme, ou ormeau ... La meilleure espèce pour les allées du jardin de plaisir ... Il se nomme ipre, ou ipreau, mot qui est dérivé d'une place dans les Flandres où on en élève en grande quantité.'
61 Ibid., p. 26.
62 Tassin was the agent, or *intendant*, of the Duc d'Orléans and also looked after the interests of the Orange family in France. For more information on Tassin see Worp, *Briefwisseling*, II, RGP 19, p. 444, and Slothouwer, *Paleizen*, p. 62.
63 Worp, *Briefwisseling*, III, RGP 21, letter 3220, Constantijn Huygens to Tassin, dated 16 February 1643. See Slothouwer, *Paleizen*, pp. 62 and 350-351.
64 Certain designs signed and dated by Post in 1646 can be linked to the building projects mentioned by Huygens in this letter. Post made designs for wings connecting the stables and the main building and for the proposed construction of a chapel over the bridge leading from the palace to the garden, as well as for a new layout of the main garden behind the palace. See also Slothouwer, *Paleizen*, pp. 60-63, figs. 16-18. The designs are kept in the ARA, map department, NADO.
65 Van der Groen, *Nederlandtsen Hovenier*, facs. ed., p. 31.
66 The number three was seen as the 'numero uno et divino', see Wittkower, *Architectural Principles*, pp. 27 and 102-105. Compare Hopper, *Journal of Garden History*, II, 1 (1982), p. 34.
67 See Terwen and Ottenheym, *Pieter Post*, pp. 222-223, and Ottenheym, *Philips Vingboons*, pp. 160-164.
68 See Ottenheym, *Philips Vingboons*, pp. 160-161, and Ottenheym in Huisken et al., *Jacob van Campen*, p. 157.
69 Pliny's description of the 'hippodrome' in his gardens strongly influenced the development of this form as an important garden feature. See Pliny the Younger, *Letters*, I, book V, chap. VI,

pp. 389-393. The best factual Roman example is the famous 'hippodrome' or 'stadion' of the Villa Adriana; for further reading and illustrations see R. Vighi, *Villa*.

70 For further reading see Ackerman, *Journal of the Warburg and Courtauld Institutes*, 14 (1951), pp. 70-91 and for an illustration p. 74. See also Coffin, *Villa in Renaissance Rome*, p. 82, fig. 49.

71 For the Villa Madama and its hippodrome-shaped garden see Coffin, *Villa in Renaissance Rome*, p. 247, fig. 150.

72 See ibid., p. 152, fig. 98.

73 See Bienfait, *Oude Hollandsche tuinen*, figs. 298 (Heemstede) and 109 (Zeist).

74 See Gurrieri and Chatfield, *Boboli Gardens*, plate 7.

75 Compare Kuyper, *Dutch Classicist Architecture*, p. 141. For further reading on the clinging to traditions and disregarding classical influence see Gent, *Albion's Classicism*, pp. 224-227.

76 Mollet, *Jardin de plaisir*, facs. ed., p. 31.

77 Boyceau, *Traité du jardinage*, p. 82.

78 Fremantle, *Oud Holland*, 80 (1965), p. 80.

79 Ottenheym, *Philips Vingboons*, pp. 32-33.

80 Serlio's architectural treatise, which first appeared book by book from 1537 onward, was later compiled and published in several editions. These included *Five Books of Architecture* (London, 1611) and *Tutte l'opere d'architettura et prospettiva ... diviso in sette libri* (Venice, 1619), both accessible in recent facsimile editions. For the gable designs which influenced Ter Nieuburch compare *Five Books of Architecture*, Dover reprint, book IV, chap. 6, fols. 30-32.

81 The Aile de la Belle Cheminée; see Ottenheym, *Philips Vingboons*, p. 32.

82 Plate 14.

83 See Gent, *Albion's Classicism*, pp. 109-147, on the loggia in Tudor and Early Stuart England.

84 Blunt, *The Burlington Magazine*, CXIX (September 1977), p. 613.

85 Brereton, *Travels in Holland*, p. 33. Compare Fremantle, *Baroque Town Hall*, p. 103, notes 2 and 3. See also Brenninkmeyer-De Rooij in *De Rembrandt à Vermeer*, pp. 47-86, especially p. 49.

86 Mollet, *Jardin de plaisir*, facs. ed., p. 31.

87 For detailed information on Boyceau's contribution to French garden design and the Luxembourg see Hamilton Hazlehurst, *Boyceau*, pp. 26 and 56ff.

88 Ibid., p. 56.

89 Ibid., pp. 55 and 60, on the importance of radiating alleys.

90 The Metropolitan Museum of Art, New York, Harris Brisbane Dick Fund, 1926 (26.104.5). Mollet, *Jardin de plaisir*, plate 29, depicting an octagonal labyrinth planted with palisades in double rows.

91 The Metropolitan Museum of Art, New York, Harris Brisbane Dick Fund, 1926 (26.104.2).

92 Compare de Caus, *Jardin Palatin*, facs. ed., plate 5, with fig. 48 above, showing details of Ter Nieuburch's monogrammed parterre.

93 Mollet, *Jardin de plaisir*, facs. ed., p. 32: 'Premièrement, le dessin I est un plan général à construire à l'arrière de quelque grand palais ou maison de plaisance, lequel est d'environ 310 toises de long sur 220 de large, ce qui est la proportion requise ordinairement à tous les jardins, à savoir un tiers plus long que large ...' Compare Hopper, *Journal of Garden History*, II, 1 (1982), p. 34.

94 Alberti, *Art of Building*, book I, chap. 9, pp. 24 and 426.

95 Indeed, the pattern used by Mollet – a square with central fountain cut diagonally into four sections – created a separate entity, yet was part of a bigger unit of four parterres, together repeating the same motif on a larger scale. A most popular motif at the end of the seventeenth century, such a parterre pattern can also be found in Holland in the garden of the Paleis Noordeinde.

96 Hopper, *Journal of Garden History*, II, 1 (1982), p. 34, discusses connections between Honselaarsdijk's layout and Mollet's ideal design no. 2. To this can now be added the comparison between Ter Nieuburch's layout and Mollet's first ideal plan.

97 Hopper, ibid., first mentioned Mollet's indebtedness to Holland and his dependence on, rather than his contribution to, the Dutch canal garden.

98 Hopper, ibid., writes: 'In Holland itself the historical development of the Dutch garden is often equated, in simplistic terms, with France and England, while Italy, a major source of inspiration, ... is rarely mentioned.' The mention of England here must refer to the late-seventeenth-century Dutch garden, defined as the 'Anglo-Dutch garden', and to the subsequent 'Dutch taste' in gardening, used as a synonym of 'regressive' garden design in eighteenth-century England. Compare also the analysis of the Honselaarsdijk layout by Strong in *Renaissance Garden in England*, p. 161, and by Karling in *French Formal Garden*, pp. 19ff., where the Honselaarsdijk garden is still attributed to Mollet and inaccurately compared with the layout of the Wilton garden in England.

99 Hopper, *Journal of Garden History*, II, 1 (1982), p. 32.

100 For the chief principles in classical architecture and the changing meaning of architectural terminology, such as *symmetry* and *concinnitas*, see Vitruvius, *Ten Books on Architecture*, book III, chap.1, p. 72, and Alberti, *Art of Building*, book IX, chap. 5, pp. 302-303 and 421. Compare also Wittkower, *Architectural Principles*, p. 33. His opinions have been criticized in recent publications on classical architectural thought and terminology, for instance by Van Eck, *Organicism*, pp. 45-56 and p. 48 on *concinnitas*. Compare also notes 116 and 119 in chapter IV.

101 The two basic principles are the aspects of elegance or grace and variety, to which Mollet refers in his *Jardin de plaisir*, p. 32, using *diversifier* several times, while Boyceau warns against monotony and stresses variety in laying out and decorating the gardens in his *Traité du jardinage*, book III, chap. 1, p. 69. Compare also Hamilton-Hazlehurst, *Boyceau*, pp. 29 and 32.

102 Hopper, *Journal of Garden History*, II, 1 (1982), p. 25.

103 Worp, *Briefwisseling*, III, RGP 21, letter 3044, Constantijn Huygens to J.A. Bannius, dated 2 July 1642: '… Stevinius Belgicos in mathematica non semel praemisere.' Compare also chapter III.

104 Compare Hopper, *Journal of Garden History*, II, 1 (1982), pp. 25-27.

105 See Van Deursen, *Resolutiën*, RGP 151, p. 460, no. 502, dated 18 June 1615: a book on navigation is checked by Stevin and Marolois before publication; and, p. 582, no. 139: Stevin inspects navigational measuring instruments. Compare also chapter III.

106 Term borrowed from Hamilton Hazlehurst, *Boyceau*, p. xii.

107 Fremantle, *Baroque Town Hall*, pp. 104-106, and Hopper, *Journal of Garden History*, II, 1 (1982), p. 33.

108 See Hopper, *Journal of Garden History*, II, 1 (1982), p. 33, referring to the proportional layout and, on p. 25, to the elongated shape of the gardens, and Prince Maurits's predilection for the rectangle as the most suitable form for the Dutch flat landscape.

109 Term used by Mollet in his *Jardin de plaisir*, facs. ed., p. 32, describing the garden compartments in his first ideal garden plan.

110 Zuylesteyn, 21 October 1640, Instructions for the gardener Hendrick van Hattem. KHA, archief Frederik Hendrik, no. A14-VII-9: 'Memorie voor Hendrick van Hattem ende Johan van Diepenen … tot Suylesteyn. Eerstelyck, de Eycken heesters sullen geplant werden opde *ordre* als de Ypen die Suytwaerts op staen, … oock de Ypen, die voor op de middeldreve ontrent de Cappelle staen sullen werden uijtgenoomen, ende eycke heesters inde plaets geset op de selve *ordre* als de Suytwaerts op staen.' (Instructions for Hendrick van Hattem and Johan van Diepenen … at Suylesteyn. First, the oak shrubbery will be planted in the same manner as the elm-trees standing southward, … also the elm-trees which are standing along the central alley near the chapel shall be taken out, and oak shrubs planted instead in the same manner as those standing southward.)

111 Hopper, *Journal of Garden History*, II, 1 (1982), p. 25, and Taverne, *In 't land van belofte*, pp. 99 and 102.

112 From Stevin's 'Van de oirdeningh der steden'. See also Taverne, *In 't land van belofte*, pp. 35-37, fig. 1.

113 Ibid., p. 83, on Christian IV's activities as city builder attracting Dutch engineers with the help of Count Ernst Casimir van Nassau and Frederik Hendrik (1626). The royal Danish engineer Axel Arup studied with Frans van Schooten at Leiden. See for the activities of Gustaf Adolf II of Sweden pp. 95-97, figs. 23 and 24, designs for the city extension of Gotenburg (1624) and Jönköping (1619) by Dutch engineers and an example of Dutch town planning abroad. For further reading see also Roding, *Christiaan IV*, pp. 37-140, and Römelingh et al., *Art in Denmark*, pp. 1-68ff.

114 Ibid., p. 39: 'De viersydige rechthouck op een plat even landt is myn bedunken der Steden bequaemste Form, om daer in te crijgen geschickte rechthoekige blocken, erven, huysen, hooven, marcten en plaetsen, welcke in andere formen soo niet vallen en connen.' (The four-sided rectangle on a flat even terrain is in my opinion the most suitable form for a city, to be divided in appropriate rectangular blocks, courts, houses, yards, markets and places which do not fit rightly in other shapes.) Stevin's outspoken preference for the rectangle is unusual and is not found in the rest of the contemporary literature; compare Taverne, ibid., p. 415, note 34. See also Hopper, *Journal of Garden History*, II, 1 (1982), pp. 25-26.

115 'Teyckening eens leghers, diens form langduerlic de zelve mocht blijven', from Stevin's *Castrametatio*, p. 45. See also Taverne, *In 't land van belofte*, pp. 38-39, fig. 2.

116 Ibid., p. 415, note 33.

117 Stevin, *Materiae politicae*, p. 16. See Taverne, *In 't land van belofte*, p. 415, note 33.

118 Alberti, *Art of Building*, book VII, chap. 5, p. 199, describing his morphological analogy: 'What is more, just as the head, foot, and indeed any member must correspond to each other and to all the rest of the body in an animal, so in a building, and especially a temple, the parts of the whole body must be so composed that they all correspond to one another, and any one, taken individually, may provide the dimensions of all the rest.' And p. 303: 'This they evidently learned from Nature: to animals she has given ears, eyes, and nostrils matching on either side, but in the center, single and obvious, she has set the mouth.'

119 Worp, *Briefwisseling*, IV, RGP 24, letter 4320, F. van Schooten, Jr. (1615-1661) to Constantijn Huygens, dated 4 February 1646. Van Schooten mentions Paen, Van Belcum and Gilot as important engineers, and 'no lesser land-surveyors [*landtmeeters*], accounting-masters [*reeckenmeesters*] and other experienced artists, who from no other instruction but this [mathematical school at Leiden] daily practise their skills.'

120 See Adam and Milhaud, *Descartes Correspondance*, V, p. 73, letter 315, R. Descartes to M. Mersenne, dated 17 November 1641. This letter is discussed and in part quoted in chapter II. For the Dutch garden which Descartes planned to design using the layout of the Luxembourg, see Schaper, *Tuinkunst*, 1 (1995), pp. 25-28.

121 Worp, *Briefwisseling*, II, RGP 19, letter 2229, D. de Morlot to Constantijn Huygens, dated 13 September 1639.

122 Johan Maurits's exercises, which he entitled 'Geometrische Problemata', in the KHA, archief Johan Maurits van Nassau-Siegen, inv. no. A 4-1476, are bundled with drawings of fortress-cities.

123 See Mout in Van den Boogaart, *Johan Maurits van Nassau-Siegen*, pp. 13-38, especially on the *schola militaris* and his career at court, pp. 33-38. See also Hopper, *Journal of Garden History*, II, 1 (1982), pp. 25 ff.

124 Most significantly, the Amsterdam Town Hall was decorated with scenes celebrating the Batavians as the heroic Dutch ancestors who fought the Romans before becoming their allies. See Fremantle,

Baroque Town Hall, pp. 48-49. See also Scriverius, *Beschrijvinghe van out Batavien* and *Beschrijvinge van Holland*, and various other histories of the Batavian past, and the heroic deeds of the Stadholder. Compare also the remarks in the Introduction regarding Huygens's visit to Johannes Smetius's collection of antiquities in Nijmegen, which is considered the capital of the Batavians, and further notes in chapter VI.

125 This comparison of Batavians with Romans (symbolizing Holland versus Spain) became very popular at the time; it found expression in the poetry of Huygens and Joost van den Vondel (*Inwijdinghe van het Stadthuys t'Amsterdam*), as well as in paintings by Rembrandt (for example the heroic revolt of the Batavians against the Romans in *The Conspiracy of the Batavians*, described by Tacitus in his *Germania* and executed for the Amsterdam Town Hall). For the further use of this literary-artistic typological simile comparing Batavian with Roman, the city of Amsterdam with Rome and the Dutch Republic with the Roman Republic, see Blankert, *Kunst als regeringszaak*. Compare de Jongh, *Nederlands Kunsthistorisch Jaarboek*, 24 (1973), p. 89, note 26, and Ottenheym, *Philips Vingboons*, p. 118 and note 256. See Fremantle, *Baroque Town Hall*, p. 49.

126 See de Jongh, *Nederlands Kunsthistorisch Jaarboek*, 24 (1973), p. 85, and also Spies in Huisken et al., *Jacob van Campen*, p. 230. Compare the description of Huygens's verses in chapter IV.

127 Vondel, *Werken*, III, p. 526: 'Wy bootzen 't groote Rome na in 't kleen, Nu Kampen bezigh is met bouwen ...' See also Spies in Huisken et al., *Jacob van Campen*, p. 228.

128 See Bienfait, *Oude Hollandsche tuinen*, p. 65.

129 Worp, *Briefwisseling*, III, RGP 21, letter 2297, J.L. Guez de Balzac to Constantijn Huygens, dated 25 January–1 February 1640: 'Il n'y a pas une pierre, où il n'y ayt une incongruité en architecture, et qui ne blesse la veue de ceux qui voyent avecque science. Tellement que si vous me faisiés jamais l'honneur que vous voulés que je recoive chez vous, je serois contraint, de peur de vous presenter des objects irreguliers, de vous faire dresser des tentes sur le bord de ma riviere, apres avoir cherché quelque charme pour vous rendre invisible ma maison.'

130 Stevin, *Materiae politicae*, p. 16. See Taverne, *In 't land van belofte*, p. 415, note 33: Prince Maurits would feel uncomfortable if symmetry was failing: 'dat gaet mij tegen 't hart'. Compare Hopper, *Journal of Garden History*, II, 1 (1982), p. 26.

131 Hopper, *Journal of Garden History*, II, 1 (1982), p. 33. See also Van Pelt, *Art History*, IV, 2 (1981), pp. 150-174.

132 Taverne, *In 't land van belofte*, pp. 35-37, fig. 1.

133 Stevin, *Materiae politicae*, pp. 11-16. Stevin's definition was derived from Alberti, *De re aedificatoria*, book VII, chap. 5, p. 199, and book IX, chap. 5, p. 301. Compare also Taverne, *In 't land van belofte*, p. 415, note 33, and Hopper, *Journal of Garden History*, II, 1 (1982), p. 33.

134 Wittkower, *Architectural Principles*, pp. 107-142.

135 See Jellicoe et al., *Oxford Companion to Gardens*, pp. 80 and 260.

136 See ibid., pp. 391-392.

137 Term borrowed from Wittkower, *Architectural Principles*, p. 140.

138 Hopper's articles in *Journal of Garden History*, II, 1 (1982), pp. 33-37, and *Bulletin KNOB*, 3-4 (1983), pp. 109-112, have been taken as point of departure.

139 Alberti, *Art of Building*, book IX, chaps. 5 and 6, pp. 305-306. On harmony and the ratio of 1 to 2 see also Wittkower, *Architectural Principles*, pp. 45-46 and 101ff. on the problem of harmonic proportions in architecture. Compare Hopper, *Journal of Garden History*, II, 1 (1982), p. 29.

140 Serlio, *Architettura*, Libro Primo, p. 27. See Serlio, *Five Books of Architecture*, Dover reprint, book I 'of geometrie', chap. 1, fol. 11vo. Compare Hopper, *Journal of Garden History*, II, 1 (1982), p. 33.

141 Stevin, *Materiae politicae*, chap. 4, 'Van de Form der Steden'. See Taverne, *In 't land van belofte*, pp. 37-39. Stevin borrowed from Vitruvius, Alberti and Pietro Cattaneo.

142 De Serres, *Théâtre*, p. 457. Speaking of the *jardin de potager*: 'le meilleur sera tenir le Iardin un peu plus long que large, non en quarré parfait ...' See Hopper, *Journal of Garden History*, II, 1 (1982), p. 40, note 49.

143 Mollet, *Jardin de plaisir*, facs. ed., p. 32 (referring to his ideal plan no. 1): '... un plan général ... lequel est d'environ 310 toises de long sur 220 de large, ce qui est la proportion requise ordinairement à tous les jardins, à savoir un tiers plus long que large, ou plus ...' Compare this with Mollet's thoughts on proportion cited earlier in this chapter.

144 Dézallier d'Argenville, *Théorie et Practique*, facs. ed., chap. III, p. 20: 'La proportion generale des Jardins est, d'être un tiers plus longs que larges ...'

145 Karling in MacDougall and Hamilton Hazlehurst, *French Formal Garden*, p. 7 and figs. 7 and 8. Compare Hopper, *Journal of Garden History*, II, 1 (1982), p. 33 and note 49

146 Hopper, *Journal of Garden History*, II, 1 (1982), pp. 33-34.

147 Wittkower, *Architectural Principles*, p. 103 and note 2.

148 Compare Hopper, *Journal of Garden History*, II, 1 (1982), p. 29.

149 Terminology used by Kuyper, *Dutch Classicist Architecture*, p. 140.

150 Hopper, *Journal of Garden History*, II, 1 (1982), p. 29. See also Wittkower, *Architectural Principles*, pp. 14-16 and figs. 2a-c, 3 and 4.

151 Serlio, *Five Books of Architecture*, Dover reprint, book I, chap. 1, fol. 2vo.

152 Serlio, *Architettura*, Libro Secundo, fig. 39, and *Five Books of Architecture*, Dover reprint, book II, 'of perspective', chap. 2, fols. 4 and 5 and also fols. 6vo and 7vo. Compare Hopper, *Journal of Garden History*, II, 1 (1982), p. 28.

153 *Architectura civilis*, *Architectura universalis* and *Architectura*

154 Hopper, *Journal of Garden History*, II, 1 (1982), p. 32.

155 Meischke in Hoekstra et al., *Liber Castellorum*, p. 270.

156 See an excellent overview in Ottenheym, *Philips Vingboons*, pp. 160-172, on measuring systems and proportions for the ideal villa in seventeenth-century Holland.

157 Ottenheym, *Philips Vingboons*, p. 161.

158 This geometrical rule was also still popular in Italy, where it had already been integrated into the classical systems of measurements. See for further reading von Naredi-Rainer, *Architektur und Harmonie*, pp. 11-25. See also Scholfield, *Proportion in Architecture*. About medieval quadrature see Shelby, *Gothic Design Techniques*. Compare Ottenheym, *Philips Vingboons*, p. 161 and note 392.

159 Vitruvius, *Ten Books on Architecture*, book VI, chap. 3, pp. 176-180.

160 Palladio, *Quattro Libri*, Liber 1, chap. 2, where he includes the root of 2 in his series of harmonic ratios: 3 to 4, 2 to 3, 3 to 5, 1 to 2, and 1 to the square root of 2.

161 It is difficult to ascertain which depiction of the Honselaarsdijk layout is the most accurate. For example, the architectural sketch-plan of the garden differs from Van Berckerode's version in that the garden compartments are not rendered as perfect squares and the circles in the first garden plot are not perfectly round but rather oval.

162 The inner size and the actual island (excluding the bridge) measure 13 x 20 instead of 13 x 24 Rijnlandse roeden. Other relative measurements and proportional relationships between the various garden parts are indicated on the drawing.

163 KB, Department of Rare Books and Manuscripts, inv. no. 1292 C 33, Post, *Ouvrages d'architecture*, p. 6.

164 KB, Department of Rare Books and Manuscripts, inv. no. KW 1298 C 5, Vingboons, *Afbeelsels*, plate 53a. The mathematical scheme for Vingboons's design of an ideal country estate is taken from Ottenheym, *Philips Vingboons*, p. 162, fig. 218.

165 The proportional scheme of the elevation was drawn by Jacob Lois in 1662; it is discussed by Terwen in Meischke and Terwen, *Trippenhuis*, pp. 172-173. Pieter Post was also involved in the design and construction of the building, as contemporary accounts indicate; see Blok, *Pieter Post*, pp. 50-51. A clear analysis of the mathematical scheme of the Schielandhuis with sketches explaining the step-by-step process is given by Ottenheym, *Philips Vingboons*, pp. 161-162.

166 For general reading see Alex et al., *Anhaltische Schlösser*, pp. 34-35 and 60-61. For Oraniensteyn (Oranienstein) see Heck, *Oranienstein*. For the artistic influence of the Orange family in Germany in gerneral, see also the exhibition catalogue *Onder den Oranjeboom*, Oranienburg, August-November 1999 and Apeldoorn, Paleis Het Loo, December 1999-March 2000.

167 See Wendland, *Berlins Gärten und Parke*. See also Boeck, *Oranienburg*, pp. 14-18 and 26-34. Compare Hennebo and Hoffmann, *Deutsche Gartenkunst*, II, pp. 104-105 and 114-117.

168 See Alex et al., *Anhaltische Schlösser*, pp. 35ff.

169 Boeck, *Oranienburg*, p. 15.

170 Merian, *Topographia Brandenburgici*, pp. 76-77: 'Dieses ist ein schöner lustiger Orth 4 Stunden von Berlin und drei Stunden von Spandau an dem Fluss der Havel gelegen ... So haben höchstgedachte G. Churfürstliche Durchl. dero Frau Gemahlin diesen Orth mit allen darzu gehörigen ... und den Dienst des Churfürstlichen Ingenieurs Johan Gregorii Memhards nicht allein das Schloss in solche artige Form wie hie zu sehen ausgeführt, sondern auch dabey dieser schöne Garten angeleget ... Und weil höchstgedachte Churfürstin ein solch sonderbares Belieben und Vergnügen an diesem Orthe haben, und an dessen Erbauung so viel wenden, so hat der Churfürst demselben den Nahmen Oranienburg gegeben.' Compare also Hennebo and Hoffmann, *Deutsche Gartenkunst*, II, pp. 104-105 and 114-116.

171 Staatsbibliothek zu Berlin, Preussischer Kulturbesitz, Kartenabteilung, Kart. 11 294 R. See Wendland, *Berlins Gärten und Parke*, p. 19.

172 Ibid., pp. 39-40.

173 Ibid., p. 20, and for illustrations of these statues pp. 32 and 39.

174 Handschriftenabteilung, Ms. boruss. quart. 12, S. 51, 67 and 81. Several Dutch sculptors were involved in the Berlin gardens, among them Otto Mangiot from Brabant, who fashioned a copy of François Du Quesnoy's *Cupid Cutting a Bow*, while the sculptor Georg Larson made no fewer than twelve statues of small children, or putti, for the Berlin gardens in 1654. Compare also Wendland, *Berlins Gärten und Parke*, p. 20, and for illustrations of these statues pp. 32 and 39.

175 Ibid., p. 32.

176 The statue is by the Flemish sculptor François Dieussart, who made several statues for the Orange and Brandenburg families. See Wendland, *Berlins Gärten und Parke*, pp. 15-44, especially p. 32 showing the statue, and p. 39 showing Dieussart's statue of the Elector as a putto holding a crown. For Dieussart's other work see chapter VI.

177 The stylistic resemblance between these statues is clearly shown by comparing the illustration in Wendland, *Berlins Gärten und Parke*, p. 32, fig. 32, of a page from the *Hortus Berolinensis*, with those in Neurdenburg, *Beeldhouwkunst*, p. 122, figs. 91 and 92. For further reading on these life-size, white-marble statues by Dieussart, for which he was paid 940 Carolus guilders in 1646, see the accounts in ARA, NDR, inv. no. 993 [old no. 736], fol. 428vo [b] (Honselaarsdijk). Compare Neurdenburg, *Beeldhouwkunst*, p. 21. See also Drossaers and Lunsingh Scheurleer, *Inventarissen*, I, RGP 147, p. 259, no. 617, referring to the figures of the Princes of

Orange by Dieussart, which were brought over to Berlin in the eighteenth century and were kept in Potsdam until their destruction in the Second World War.

178 Handschriftenabteilung, Ms. boruss. quart. 12 S 51.

179 For an illustration see Wendland, *Berlins Gärten und Parke*, p. 32, fig. 31, and compare Salomon de Caus's design of a colossal figure in his *Raisons des Forces mouvantes*, and Heidelberg's statue of the Rhine, both depicted by Zangheri in Mosser and Teyssot, *Western Gardens*, p. 68.

180 Compare Wendland, *Berlins Gärten und Parke*, p. 32, figs. 30-31, showing the fountain (p. 39, fig. 38), figures of Venus and Ceres, and also the putti as sundials made by the Dutch sculptor Peter Streng. The drawings of these sculptures in the *Hortus Berolinensis* of 1657 were made by Elssholtz.

181 Many of the statues in Louise Henriette's Berlin palace were dispersed in the early eighteenth century, in part to the palace of Charlottenburg in Berlin and the garden at Potsdam, today a section of the Dahlem Botanical Gardens. Compare Wendland, *Berlins Gärten und Parke*, pp. 43-44. For sculpture in Oraniensteyn, home of the Stadholder's daughter Albertina Agnes, compare Drossaers and Lunsingh Scheurleer, *Inventarissen*, II, RGP 148, pp. 121ff. and 159ff.

182 Placement of sculptures in groups of two, four or twelve reflects the careful (symmetrical) arrangement of the garden parts themselves. Following classical theory, Vredeman de Vries already remarked on the crucial connection between sculpture and architectural design. See de Jong and Schellekens, *Het beeld buiten*, p. 15. Compare also Goossens in Huisken et al., *Jacob van Campen*, pp. 201-203.

183 Compare the remarks by Gerard de Lairesse in his *Groot Schilderboek* on the mutual influence of sculpture and its surroundings. His remarks are useful, even though they refer to the interior of the Amsterdam Town Hall, not to an outdoor garden space. See Goossens in Huisken et al., *Jacob van Campen*, p. 212.

NOTES CHAPTER VI

1 Neurdenberg, *Beeldhouwkunst*, p. 7, already stated: 'Is our country [Holland] in the seventeenth century the land of painters and not of sculptors? ... That the art of sculpting would mean but little to our country is a pronouncement that is for a large part based on a lack of knowledge instead of a thorough study.' Owing to the scope of her work, Neurdenberg could not concentrate on the important role of the court in the development and dissemination of the art of sculpting in The Netherlands. In Rosenberg, Slive and Ter Kuile, *Dutch Art and Architecture*, pp. 419-422, only four pages are reserved for the art of sculpture in Holland. On page 422 Ter Kuile states: 'The fact that foreigners such as Quellin and Dieussart found employment at the court of Prince Frederick Henry shows that it was not easy to find good sculptors in the country itself.' Here the traditional view that Dutch sculptors are rare and their works poorly executed is perpetuated without further explanation.

2 The classical theme and subject matter of the gardens' sculptural decoration can be inferred from various sources. Most important are the statues listed in the inventories of Ter Nieuburch and Honselaarsdijk, dated 1667 and 1755 respectively, and published by Drossaers and Lunsingh Scheurleer in *Inventarissen*, I, RGP 147, pp. 258-260, and II, RGP 148, pp. 500-501, of which a short analysis concerning references to garden statues follows here. These inventories include part of the sculpture originally acquired by Frederik Hendrik; they describe classical gods and goddesses. Not all statues mentioned in these lists date from the time of Frederik Hendrik; some date from the time of William III and later, when major changes took place after the estates had come into the hands of the Prussian rulers. It is certain that the statues specified below were still standing in the main garden in the 1680s under William III, when several detailed series of prints were made showing statues mentioned in the inventories and contemporary travel journals. The decoration of Honselaarsdijk's main garden included no. 497, 'four intertwined dolphins holding a child', which must be the Hercules fountain represented in late-seventeenth-century prints by C. Allard, A. Bega and A. Blooteling, and C. Danckerts. See Slothouwer, *Paleizen*, p. 53. This, or another version of the Hercules-dolphin fountain, later decorated the gardens of Het Loo, where the Hercules theme was continued. Another statue representing the Hercules theme is possibly mentioned in the 1755 inventory, where 'A marble statue of Cain and Abel' may be Honselaarsdijk's famous statue of Hercules and Cacus, though the later history and whereabouts of this statue are unknown. Surrounding Honselaarsdijk's central fountain were eight gilded lead statues which may have represented 'Pretense', Andromeda, Apollo, Lucretia, a 'Greek Venus' (Aphrodite?), Diana and Ceres – all listed in the 1755 inventory. See Drossaers and Lunsingh Scheurleer, *Inventarissen*, II, RGP 148, pp. 500-501, nos. 490-496.

These lead statues were admired by Nicodemus Tessin; see Siren, *Studieresor*, p. 74: '.. einen 8eckigen bassin, mit 8 bleijern Statuen herumb, so sämptlich vergult wahren und einen guten effect im Auge thaten.' Whether the Stadholder or William III acquired the statues mentioned in this inventory is not clear. De Hennin, too, refers to them as decorating and surrounding the three fountains at Honselaarsdijk; these fountains were constructed circa 1647 as part of the garden improvements undertaken at the end of Frederik Hendrik's life. The second, westernmost fountain was topped by a gladiator, possibly the one listed in the 1755 inventory under no. 498 as 'een Gladiator'. Its counterpart, set above the fountain at the eastern end of the garden and representing a female figure with child, may have been the stone statue of 'Venus met Cupido' listed under no. 489 in the 1755 inventory. These last two statues are reproduced in the augmented republication of Morren, *Honselaarsdijk*, pp. 55, 211 and 221 (see the prints in the centre, showing different gladiators) and 214, drawn by I. de Moucheron. Many other classical statues were mentioned by de Hennin in *Zinrijke Gedachten*, pp. 8-10, as standing in the Honselaarsdijk garden, including a Venus, Cleopatra, Flora, Helena, Paris, Narcissus, Orpheus and Mercury.

3   De Hennin, *Zinrijke Gedachten*, p. 9: 'Let toch eens op de representatie dezer statuen en beelden naa't leeven gemaeckt, daar in dat men ziet al de Schoonheden des Antijks.' And compare p. 109, in translation: 'What wonderful figure of Diane that is, standing on it [the fountain] next to Neptune and Aquarius, ... all of the best antique.'

4   Ibid., p. 8.

5   Sandrart, *Accademia Todesca*, I, chap. 2, p. 41.

6   Haskell and Penny, *Taste and the Antique*, chap. V, p. 35.

7   See for these divisions and their terminology Kenseth, *Age of the Marvelous*, pp. 88ff.

8   De Hennin, *Zinrijke Gedachten*, p. 8: '... deftige vruchten en fruiten ende alderhande uytheemsche gewassen ... Aanschouwt verders hoe dien deftigen hof is verciert en opgepronkt met soo veele antique ...'

9   See cat. no. 139 in Hunt and de Jong, *Anglo-Dutch Garden*, pp. 288-289. Attributed to Stephanus Cousyns (?-1709), the album depicts the later-seventeenth-century plant collection of the Leeuwenhorst estate at Noordwijkerhout, acquired by the Stadholder's grandson William III in 1692. With a few exceptions, most rare plants were known in Holland by the mid-century.

10 I owe this observation to Guus Kemme.

11 Gerard de Lairesse, *Groot Schilderboek*, vol. II, book 9 on sculpture ('Verhandelinge van de Beeldhouwerije'). Lairesse wrote: 'In deze landen word de Beeldhouwerij niet veel geacht. Hier is geen of weinig voordeel te maaken met marmer, noch andere steen; en schoon hier of daar een tuin, of zo iets is, daar men nu en dan een beeld of kindtje van hartsteen te maaken vind, dat is te gering voor een braaf meester. Het is zoo niet als in Italien.' (In these countries, sculpture is held in low esteem. Little or no profit is to be made with marble or another stone; and even though there may be a garden here or there where one finds to make a statue or a small child of stone, it is not sufficient for a good master. It is not like in Italy.) See Neurdenburg, *Beeldhouwkunst*, p. 15. Compare also the painted statues in the outer niches of the façades of Huygens's Hofwijck and his son-in-law Philips Doublet's Clingendael, as well as 'painted trophies' or monuments with painted representations in the later-seventeenth-century garden of Hans Willem Bentinck at Sorgvliet. For Clingendael see Sellers, *Journal of Garden History*, VII, 1 (1987), pp. 33-35, and for Sorgvliet see Sellers in Hunt, *Dutch Garden*, pp. 121-122.

12 On Van Campen, the Dutch court and the art of sculpture compare also Goossens in Huisken et al., *Jacob van Campen*, pp. 201-226, especially pp. 201-202.

13 See also Neurdenburg, *Beeldhouwkunst*, p. 20, and *De Nederlandsche Spectator* (1875), p. 110.

14 Compare also Slothouwer, *Paleizen*, p. 58, doubtless the two statues on either side of the staircase in front of the building.

15 Van Gelder, *Latin-American Art*, p. 51.

16 Neurdenburg, *Beeldhouwkunst*, pp. 20 and 174. Compare Worp, *Briefwisseling*, IV, RGP 24, letter 4259, Michiel Le Blon to Constantijn Huygens, dated 27 January 1646. In this letter we read that Quellinus 'de Palas, levensgroot, met verscheyde andere beelden voor zijn Hoocht heeft gemaect, eer hy naer Italien ginck' (made the Palas [Pallas Athena, or Minerva], life-size, with several other statues for His Highness before he left for Italy). See Goossens in Huisken et al., *Jacob van Campen*, p. 224.

17 While it is certain that the Ter Nieuburch *Minerva* is the one made by Quellinus, as a comparison with his later Minerva version shows, there is a time difference of a whole year between the statue's depiction in the Milheusser print (end of 1644) and its mention in Le Blon's letter (beginning of 1646).

18 See Diedenhofen et al., *Fonteijn van Pallas*, and cover picture.

19 See Thieme and Becker, *Künstlerlexicon*, Band X, p. 225, s.v. Dusart (c. 1600-c. 1661). Compare also Avery, *François Dieussart*, pp. 205-235.

20 François Du Quesnoy (1597-1643), also referred to as Duquesnoy or, in Rome, 'Il Fiammingo'.

21 Skulpturen-Sammlung, inv. no. 540. Drossaers and Lunsingh Scheurleer, *Inventarissen*, I, RGP 147, p. 258, no. 606: 'Een marmer Cupidoken die een boochje schaeft', or the statue of no. 611: 'Een Cupidoken van marmer dat een booghjen schaefft.' Compare Lunsingh Scheurleer's notes on p. 258. Today the Bode Museum is part of the Staatliche Museen in Berlin.

22 Fransolet, *François Du Quesnoy*, pp. 80-81, note 1; according to Sandrart's description, the statue came into the possession of the Brandenburgs after the death of Amalia in 1675. According to a

German commentator (Galland), the statue was given to the Elector by the Stadholder; compare Wendland, *Berlins Gärten und Parke*, p. 40. The statue's presence in the Bode Museum was confirmed by the director of the sculpture collection. The members of the staff at Oranienbaum in Wörlitz were also helpful in locating the Orange family's stone putti, some of which are part of their own collection. I am grateful to Th.H. Lunsingh Scheurleer, emeritus professor of Leiden University, and Betsy Rosasco of the Princeton Art Museum for their helpful suggestions regarding these and other 'lost' garden sculptures.

23 Wendland, *Berlins Gärten und Parke*, p. 39, fig. 39, depicting a copy by the Flemish-Dutch sculptor Otto Mangiot after Du Quesnoy's *Cupid Cutting a Bow*. Another sculptor from Holland, Georg Larson, also copied Dutch sculpture, including twelve putti displayed in Louise Henriette's Berlin gardens, as mentioned in chapter V.

24 De Lairesse specifically refers to these stone children as the only regular commissions the Dutch sculptor could always count on; see *Groot Schilderboek*, book 9: 'In deze landen word de Beeldhouwerij niet veel geacht. Hier is geen of weinig voordeel te maaken met marmer, noch andere steenen, schoon hier en daar een tuin, of zo iets is, daar men nu en dan een beeld van kindtje van hartsteen te maaken vind, dat is te gering voor een braaf Meester. Het is zoo niet als in Italien.' (In these lands the art of sculpture is not much esteemed. There is no or hardly any profit to be made of marble, or other stone, though there may be a garden, or something like it, for which one can make a statue or a small stone child, that is not sufficient for a good artist. It is not like in Italy.) For later versions of such statues see Artus Quellinus the Younger's remaining series of three children representing the Four Seasons in de Jong and Schellekens, *Beeld buiten*, p. 57.

25 This is the interpretation given by Neurdenburg, *Beeldhouwkunst*, p. 19.

26 See Lazzaro, *Italian Renaissance Garden*, p. 131.

27 For a detailed example of the Hercules iconography in the garden, influencing the choice of directions and vistas, see Coffin, *Villa d'Este*, and Lazzaro, *Italian Renaissance Garden*, pp. 95-99.

28 A very detailed survey of the iconography of Hercules in the building and garden of William III's Paleis Het Loo, as well as of the heroic imagery centring on the figure of Hercules in contemporary art at the Dutch court, is given by de Jong in *Natuur en kunst*, pp. 91-97. See also pp. 81-83, showing Chevalier's Penningen Cabinet (Cabinet for Coins and Medallions), etched by R. De Hooghe, and illustrating the use of Herculean symbolism in furniture. See also p. 86, depicting the Hercules fountain at Het Loo and the thematically related fountain of Honselaarsdijk shown in Valck, *Veues et Perspectives*. See for an illustration Morren, *Honselaarsdijk*, pp. 210-211, and for similar illustrations of the fountain in prints published by C. Allard and C. Danckerts, ibid., pp. 218-221. The motif of Hercules squeezing water from the snakes in his hand may be compared with Hercules constraining snakes in his crib, depicted in Zincgreffius, *Emblemata*.

29 The statue is not directly mentioned or identified in contemporary documents. Amalia's 1667 inventory of Ter Nieuburch lists a *Hercules Defeating Someone Else*, made of 'albaster'. See Drossaers and Lunsingh Scheurleer, *Inventarissen*, I, RGP 147, p. 260, no. 646.

30 In the Honselaarsdijk inventory of 1755 a *Cain en Abel* or *Hercules en Dafné* of marble is listed. In 1757 this statue was brought to the gardens of the Huis ten Bosch, but was replaced by statues of Jupiter and Mercury from the castle of Breda. See Drossaers and Lunsingh Scheurleer, *Inventarissen*, II, RGP 148, p. 500, no. 487.

31 De Jong in *Natuur en kunst*, p. 77, identifies this statue as such.

32 See Hallema, *Jaarboek 'De Oranjeboom'*, XIX (1966), p. 147, and for the modern replica Kerkhoven, *Groen*, 1 (1996), p. 17. See also de Jong and Schellekens, *Beeld buiten*, p. 63. In the Rijksmuseum van Oudheden at Leiden a reduced version of the *Hercules Farnese* is kept, which once stood in the Leiden Hortus Botanicus and originally came from the famous collection of Van Reynst in Amsterdam, who had acquired it from the Vendramin Collection in Venice.

33 See Weinberger, *Michelangelo*, vol. II, plates 70-75.

34 GAH, topographical department, Sorgvliet. Drawing by Cornelis Pronk, circa 1740, recently acquired by the GAH (topographical departmemt, Kl. A 3441). The statue must have been placed in the Sorgvliet gardens sometime in the early eighteenth century, for it is not yet shown in Jan van de Aveelen's prints of circa 1690. Given the close resemblance between the Sorgvliet and Honselaarsdijk versions of *Hercules Slaying Cacus*, we may speculate if this statue came from Honselaarsdijk and was given by William III to Bentinck as a keepsake for his lifelong friendship and trusted service.

35 See Sellers in Hunt, *Dutch Garden*, pp. 121-122 and 129.

36 An example is his *The Pleasaure Party*, depicted in Schloss, *Oud Holland*, 97 (1983), p. 76, fig. 8.

37 See also Van Raay and Spies, *Willem en Mary*, p. 14. Compare de Jong and Schellekens, *Beeld buiten*, p. 79, and de Jong, *Natuur en kunst*, p. 79.

38 Chevalier, *Histoire de Guillaume*. See also de Jong, *Natuur en kunst*, p. 79, note 109, and p. 83, for an illustration of this Cabinet in an etching by R. De Hooghe.

39 De Jong and Schellekens, *Beeld buiten*, pp. 78-79.

40 The pediments of these buildings have all been attributed to Van Campen as designer and Huygens as adviser.

41 Fremantle, *Oud Holland*, 80 (1965), p. 66.

42 These statues of children and dogs were made and delivered in 1638 by Pieter 't Hooft, who received 152 guilders for his work,

43 They are visible in a drawing by Abraham Beerstraten of circa 1660, kept in the RPK and depicted in Lunsingh Scheurleer, *Oud Holland*, 77 (1962), p. 192, fig. 13.
44 Ibid., p. 194.
45 Ibid., p. 196.
46 Ibid., pp. 188-194.
47 Drossaers and Lunsingh Scheurleer, *Inventarissen*, I, RGP 147, pp. 258-260.
48 Several versions of this view, dated 1660-70, exist, one in the Metropolitan Museum of Art in New York, another in the National Gallery in London, reproduced in Hunt and de Jong, *Anglo-Dutch Garden*, p. 133.
49 Drossaers and Lunsingh Scheurleer, *Inventarissen*, I, RGP 147, p. 260, no. 618
50 Compare also Goossens in Huisken et al., *Jacob van Campen*, p. 223.
51 For Van Campen and the role of sculpture compare ibid., p. 211, mentioning Van Campen's collaboration with Drijffhout and 't Hooft and, pp. 224-226, Van Campen's possible involvement in the sculptural programmes of the Stadholder's gardens.
52 ARA, NDR, inv. no. 992 [old no. 735], fol. 333. On 14 December 1639 Drijffhout was paid 96,12 Carolus guilders for 'providing models and drawings, the writing down and gathering of estimates, as well as the delivery of plaster, among other things, needed to put up the statues in the gardens at Honselaarsdijk, as declared and certified on the reverse by Mr. Van Campen.'
53 Logan, *Verhandelingen*, 99, pp. 11-59.
54 Ibid., p. 55, note 45: '… veele antique statuen van Venetien aen sijn broeder heeft gesonden, waervan een raer van Cleopatra in marble, het niet willende vercopen, door begeerte van de stadt Amsterdam tselve de princesse heeft vereert met goede recompenses, daervan de selve princesse seer amoureuse sijnde ende ialours, sorgende dat de coniginne van Vranckryck daer sinne toe mochte crijgen, het daechs voor haer aencomste hadde laten verbrengen in haer lust pallais tot Rijswijck, dat den prince met grote costen daer heeft doen bouwen.' (… many antique statues from Venice sent to his brother, among them a rare Cleopatra of marble; not wanting to sell it, after good recompenes [he did], because the city of Amsterdam wished to present it to the princess; the same, being very enamoured and jealous of the statue, making sure that the Queen of France would be impressed by it, only days before her arrival had it brought over to her pleasure palace at Rijswijk, which the Prince had built there at great costs.)
55 Drossaers and Lunsingh Scheurleer, *Inventarissen*, I, RGP 147, p. 260, and notes for nos. 637 and 641. William II also mentioned a statue of Cleopatra in a letter to his father Frederik Hendrik in August 1639.
56 Later a similar *Sleeping Ariadne* or *Cleopatra* can be found as one of the central decorative features of the Bentinck garden at Sorgvliet, which was laid out as a tribute to Frederik Hendrik's grandson William III's reign and virtues. See Sellers in Hunt, *Dutch Garden*, pp. 118-119. The theme itself was inspired by the Fountain of Cleopatra in Francesco Colonna, *Hypnerotomachia*. Compare MacDougall, *Art Bulletin*, 57 (1975), pp. 357-365.
57 Van Gelder and Jost, *Jan de Bisschop*, II, pp. 116-117, no. 35.
58 Drossaers and Lunsingh Scheurleer, *Inventarissen*, I, RGP 147, p. 260, nos. 637 and 641, respectively.
59 This idea of the garden as a museum is mentioned in an early-eighteenth-century description of the Papendrecht estate, north of Amsterdam, by Van Hoogstraten and Schuers in *Groot algemeen woordenboek*. They wrote that many pieces of antique marble could be found in the gallery of the house and were placed in the gardens the same way they were kept in and round Rome in the buildings and gardens of the cardinals. In Dutch: '… zeer vele stukken van antyk marmer … in de galerije, het huis en de tuinen geplaatst …, op gelycke wijze als de zelve binnen en buiten Rome in de gebouwen en tuinen der kardinalen bewaart worden.' See also de Jong and Schellekens, *Beeld buiten*, p. 63.
60 See Sillem in Rosenberg, *Koninklijk paviljoen*, pp. 22-23.
61 Worp, *Briefwisseling*, IV, RGP 24, letter 4125, Constantijn Huygens to Amalia of Orange, dated 23 September 1645. See the quotation from this letter in chapter II, p. 29.
62 The statue, stylistically close to the other river-god versions at Heidelberg and Ter Nieuburch, also was encircled by a shower of water-spouts, as depicted by Elssholtz in *Hortus Berolinensis*. See Wendland, *Berlins Gärten und Parke*, p. 32, fig. 31.
63 See also de Jong, *Natuur en kunst*, p. 77, who identifies the fountain as a Venus fountain. Yet the female figure topping the fountain, represented in the Milheusser print as a figure upholding her breasts from which water flows, because of this gesture is more likely to be a Ceres, or possibly a Venus Lactans. A conflation of the two types is not impossible either, given their mutual aquatic setting and closely related symbolic meaning, which centres on love and fertility. However, at Ter Nieuburch the four smaller statues at the entrance of the fountain parterre seem to represent the Four Seasons, traditionally linked to Ceres. Furthermore, Venus was usually either accompanied by Cupid (as later at Het Loo) or recognizable by her famous spiral pose (*Venus de' Medici*). As part of a fountain, Venus was often wringing her hair in imitation of Giambologna's famous *Florence Venus* at Castello. Ter Nieuburch's fountain figure with its peculiar pose and gesture of overflowing breasts is vaguely reminiscent of the Ceres which was part of Ammannati's Juno fountain. For further reading see also Lazzaro, *Italian Renaissance Garden*, pp. 151-153 and 174-176.
64 For the continuation and further explanation of these iconological themes during the time of William III see de Jong, *Natuur en kunst*, pp. 76-79.

65 See ibid., p. 77, note 98.
66 On Van Campen and Quellinus see Goossens in Huisken et al., *Jacob van Campen*, pp. 212-221.
67 The statue was praised by the famous Dutch poet Joost van den Vondel in *Poëzij*, I, 410, explaining its complex symbolism. See also Hilger in *Soweit der Erdkreis reicht*, pp. 189-194.
68 Statue in Museum Kurhaus Kleve. Diedenhofen in Van den Boogaart, *Johan Maurits van Nassau-Siegen*, pp. 211-212.
69 For example, the layout of the Sonnenberg castle and gardens in many ways can be compared with the gardens of Honselaarsdijk and Ter Nieuburch. For further reading see Terwen in Van den Boogaart, *Johan Maurits van Nassau-Siegen*, pp. 54-141, here pp. 112-113, figs. 52-53.
70 Diedenhofen in ibid., pp. 217 and 222, fig. 123.
71 Neurdenburg, *Beeldhouwkunst*, p. 19.
72 Drossaers and Lunsingh Scheurleer, *Inventarissen*, I, RGP 147, p. 259, no. 624; compare also nos. 621 described as a Cajus Martius Coriolanus, and the following nos. 625-636, referring, among others, to statues of Marcus Antonius, Julius Caesar, Octavianus and Claudius.
73 Also relating to the decoration of this grotto is information from Amalia's inventory, describing busts of the Princes of Orange as well as of Roman Emperors and philosophers on the various *rustbanken*, benches or couches, which were set either in the garden or in the palace. See Drossaers and Lunsingh Scheurleer, *Inventarissen*, I, RGP 147, pp. 258-260. nos. 624, 633, 634, 640 and 642. One of them, no. 624, is described as follows: 'drij hooffden van marber op de architrave van de eerste sitbanck van 't noortwesten van de grootte [grotte?] van 't Huys Ter Nieuburch', probably referring to the grotto of Ter Nieuburch.
74 See for further reading Alex et al., *Anhaltische Schlösser*, pp. 58-61. Another series of busts of the Stadholder and his relatives was made by François Dieussart for Johan Maurits van Nassau-Siegen, and presented to the Elector of Brandenburg in 1652. See Avery, *Bulletin van het Rijksmuseum*, 19 (1971), pp. 150ff., and *François Dieussart*, pp 205-235. See also Lunsingh Scheurleer in Van den Boogaart, *Johan Maurits van Nassau-Siegen*, p. 162, note 22, and Van der Ploeg and Vermeeren, *Princely Patrons*, pp. 232-235.
75 After the demolition of the Oranienbaum garden grotto in 1794 due to the redesigning of the garden in Anglo-Chinese style, the busts were put inside the Gothic House at Wörlitz. Here, in the Summer Dining-Room, they admirably fit the iconography of the space, which is decorated with a ceiling showing the apotheosis of the House of Orange. This ceiling originally came from the Dessau Castle. (Information kindly provided by the staff of Oranienbaum.)
76 The bust of Friedrich Wilhelm of Brandenburg is mentioned in the Orange family inventory as grouped with the busts of the Princes of Orange. At Oranienbaum the Elector of Brandenburg's effigy was replaced with that of Prince Johann Georg II von Anhalt-Dessau, which today is at the centre, flanked by Frederik Hendrik and William II in the arrangement of the Gothic House at Wörlitz. The bust of Johann Georg was made by Johann Michael Döbel in 1700.
77 Drossaers and Lunsingh Scheurleer, *Inventarissen*, I, 147, p. 258, no. 607: 'Drij figuren van marber, halflijvig, van de doorluchtige princen Frederick Willem, cheurvorst van Brandenburg, Frederick Hendrick ende Willem de laetste, de twee leste onsterffelijker memorie.' (Three figures out of marble, half-body, of the illustrious princes Frederick Willem, elector of Brandenburg, Frederick Hendrick and Willem the Last [Willem II], the last two of immortal memory.) Compare also Lunsingh Scheurleer's notes on p. 258, regarding no. 607. As mentioned in the preceding note, the Elector of Brandenburg was replaced with Johann Georg II von Anhalt-Dessau at Oranienbaum.
78 Beckmann, *Historie des Fürstenthums Anhalt*, III, p. 393: 'Eine kostbare Grotte, mit schwartz und weissen Marmel, auch Seulen und andern Stücken ausgezieret, worunter auch kostbare Brustbilder, das eine von Dero Herrn Vater Printz Friedrich Henrichen, das andere von Dero Herrn Gemahl, das dritte von Dero Herrn Bruder Printz Wilhelmen zu sehen.' Beckmann's text is also cited in Boeck, *Zeitschrift des deutschen Vereins für Kunstwissenschaft*, 4 (1937), p. 39. Compare also Van Regteren Altena, *Oud Holland*, 85 (1970), p. 42 and note 17.
79 Worp, *Briefwisseling*, III, RGP 21, letter 2802, Gerard Honthorst to Constantijn Huygens, dated 28 July 1641. Honthorst asks Huygens to persuade the Stadholder to sit for half an hour for a quick clay model, so that Dieussart can complete his bust in a more lifelike manner. In this letter Honthorst, 'knowing how great a lover of the arts (*liefhebber*) he [Frederik Hendrik] is', also recommends Dieussart's artistic expertise to the Stadholder. This would result in some important acquisitions and commissions; see ARA, NDR, inv. no. 993 [old no. 736], fol. 90, and inv. no. 995 [old no. 738], fol. 31. Compare also Neurdenburg, *Beeldhouwkunst*, p. 21.
80 Drossaers and Lunsingh Scheurleer, *Inventarissen*, I, RGP 147, p. 258, no. 610: 'Een kindeken slaepende van marber, rustende op een schildeken.' See Worp, *Briefwisseling*, III, RGP 21, letter 2802, Gerard Honthorst to Constantijn Huygens, dated 28 July 1641, in which Honthorst reminds Huygens of the fact that Dieussart already made a statue for the court, namely the 'Sleeping Cupid which her Highness has of marble'.
81 Drossaers and Lunsingh Scheurleer, *Inventarissen*, I, RGP 147, p. 258, no. 612: 'Een Cupidoken van marber dat een boochjen buygt.' This statue may indeed correspond to a similar statue of 'a child bending a bow' kept, together with Dieussart's *Sleeping Cupid*, in the Oranienbaum collection at Wörlitz. (Information kindly provided by the staff of Oranienbaum.) The *Cupid Bending a Bow* may also have been made by Dieussart or by Du Quesnoy,

82 Neurdenburg, *Beeldhouwkunst*, mentioned this topic of an international court style only in passing, and further research as well as more refined terminology are needed to define the Dutch contribution to this Northern European classicizing style development in sculpture.

83 Hopper in *Journal of Garden History*, II, 1 (1982), p. 29: '… the prominence given to the twin circles, appearing as celestial spheres in the guise of *berceaux*, must have contained a specific reference to the Prince of Orange and Stadholder of the United Provinces, since a similar motif was later employed by Frederick Hendrick in the gardens of Honselaarsdijk after he succeeded Maurice.'

84 Ernst Casimir was Frederik Hendrik's cousin. Johan Wolfert van Brederode was first married to Anna van Nassau (who died in 1636) and in 1638 remarried Louise Christina, Countess of Solms, Amalia's sister.

85 The actual pleasure garden, situated immediately behind the castle and containing the two circles, is depicted for the first time in the Van Berckerode print of circa 1638-39, and also in the older sketch-plan of Honselaarsdijk's main pleasure garden, dating from the early to mid-1630s.

86 Den Hoed, *Bulletin KNOB*, 15 (1962), p. 343. See also Schmidt, *Opstellen voor Hans Lochner*, p. 84.

87 ARA, map department, VTH 3509-3514. Plan no. 3509 has a text on the back proving Stevin's authorship: 'Plante van Syns Ex^ties huys tot Vlissingen, overgelevert by Simon Stevin op den XIen Martij 1617.' See Vermeulen, *Oudheidkundig Jaarboek*, 5 (1936), pp. 45-46 and fig. 3. See also Bienfait, *Oude Hollandsche tuinen*, p. 60, and Den Hoed, *Bulletin KNOB*, 15 (1962), p. 338, fig. 4. Compare Schmidt, *Opstellen voor Hans Lochner*, p. 85.

88 ARA, map department, VTH 3510 and 3511, respectively dated 1623 and 1624 on verso. See Vermeulen, *Oudheidkundig Jaarboek*, 5 (1936), pp. 45-46, for a description of the texts on the back of the maps. See also Schmidt, *Opstellen voor Hans Lochner*, pp. 84-85, fig. 3.

89 ARA, map department, VTH 3514.

90 Plates 30 and 31.

91 According to the size indicated by Hondius on his plan and perspective, the ideal garden plan would measure more than 31 x 16 Rijnlandse roeden (circa 115 x 58 metres), instead of the 15 x 8 roeden (56 x 29 metres) mentioned as the size of the Buitenhof garden in the accompanying text. The ideal plan is thus twice as large as the actual Buitenhof garden.

92 Hendrick Hondius, *Institutio artis perspectivae*: 'Beschrijvinghe van de dertichste Figure: … welcken Hoff (naer sijne grootte) soo schoon is, ende soo wel geordoneert, als ick meene, dat men eenen konnen sien.'

93 Schmidt, *Opstellen voor Hans Lochner*, p. 79.

94 GAG, topographical department, map by E. Haubois. Schmidt, ibid., p. 81, cautiously states that it must be the situation between 1634 and 1637, that is, between the time when the map was first engraved and its publication in 1637. Only the second edition of this map, dating from 1643, is known today, in a copy by Johannes Blaeu, *Toonneel der Steden van de Vereenighde Nederlanden* (Amsterdam, 1649).

95 There exists a detailed description of the garden, written by Charles Ogier, a French envoy who visited it in 1636, and published in Ogier, *Dziennik podrózy*, p. 280. It is quoted in Schmidt, *Opstellen voor Hans Lochner*, p. 88, note 13: 'Near and behind the church is the Stadholder's house, which is called "curia". It is a fairly large and comfortable house with a lovely and well-kept garden; in particular two round *berceaux* of bent trees, which are so impenetrable and densely grown that in the afternoon they not only keep out the rays of the sun but hardly admit any daylight. They surround plots with all kinds of flowers. There are flowers and plants from far-off regions, which are carefully kept by the able gardener. There are also all kinds of fruit-trees. Moreover, there is a beautiful view on the fields. The houses and gardens of our sovereigns usually are not so well kept, as a result of the laziness and impertinence of the personnel.'

96 The coat of arms is not mentioned by Ogier in his description of the garden, but there is no reason to believe that it was not there from the outset, since such heraldic elements in gardens were quite common at the time.

97 The Groningen garden was probably completed by 1632, when Ernst Casimir was killed in battle. Thereafter only maintenance expenses were noted in the account entries; see Rijksarchief te Groningen, Staten archief, inv. no. 6, fols. 3109, 3112, 3122vo and 3127vo. See also Schmidt, *Opstellen voor Hans Lochner*, p. 80, note 8.

98 The extension of the grounds and the layout of a garden according to a plan by Peters were described as 'extensie ofte ampliatie vant 'tselve met de ledige plaetse daerachter tot een gaerde, volgens seker proiect bij den bouwmr. Gerwert Peters daervan gemaect' (the extension or amplification of the same [court] with the vacant ground behind it into a garden, according to a plan made by the architect Gerwert Peters). See Schmidt, *Opstellen voor Hans Lochner*, p. 80, note 8.

99 CBN, Port. 21, no. 59.

100 Van Deventer, *Nederlandsche steden*, fig. 98.

101 *Toonneel der Steden*. See also Renaud, *Bulletin KNOB*, 11 (1958), p. 118, fig. 1.

102 Peter van Meurs, *Oud Holland*, 32 (1914), fig. opposite p. 206, showing the situation of the garden (indicated as 'Bloem Park')

within the L-shaped fortification system surrounding the Batestein castle.
103 This largely unknown printbook in the Metropolitan Museum, New York, is further examined by Sellers in Koenhein et al., *Johan Wolfert van Brederode*, pp. 99-114.
104 See de Meyere and Ruijter, *Kasteel Batestein*, p. 37.
105 For a survey see Crone and Struik et al., *Principal Works of Simon Stevin*.
106 Ibid., vol. 5, p. 785.
107 Dijksterhuis, *Science in the Netherlands*, p. 116. It concerns anthropomorphic and zoomorphic symmetry. Compare Alberti, *Art of Building*, book VII, chap. 5, p. 199, describing his morphological analogy.
108 Hopper, *Journal of Garden History*, II, 1 (1982), pp. 25-26.
109 Worp, *Oud Holland*, 9 (1891), p. 109: 'Corporis humani membra, non contemnenda methodo, suis dimensionibus singula et majusculo volumine efformanda dabat ... hac anatome praeuia singulorum artuum exactam notitiam adeptus non fuisset.'
110 Ibid., p. 114.
111 Hopper, *Journal of Garden History*, II, 1 (1982), p. 27 translates Huygens's *galerijen* as *berceaux*; however, it is not clear whether Huygens is referring to the circular *berceaux* or just to arbours in general.
112 Compare ibid., pp. 27-28.
113 For further reading see Van Regteren Altena, *Jacques de Gheyn. Three Generations*, and Meij and Poot, *Jacques de Gheyn, Drawings*.
114 Stevin, *Wisconstighe Ghedachtnissen*, p. 4. See also Crone and Struik et al., *Principal Works of Simon Stevin*, vol. 2 B, pp. 800-801.
115 This is also suggested by Hopper, *Journal of Garden History*, II, 1 (1982), p. 28, who assumes that Prince Maurits made the design.
116 Ibid., p. 28.
117 Yates, *Theatre of the World*, p. 25.
118 Vitruvius, *Ten Books on Architecture*, book I, chap. 1, pp. 5-13. See also Yates, *Theatre of the World*, p. 25.
119 This expression is used in a slightly different context by Kemp in *Art Bulletin*, 68, 2 (1986), p. 242.
120 See Alberti, *Ten Books on Architecture*, prologue, p. 5, and book I, chap. 1, pp. 7-8 and 422-423. In his prologue Alberti argues that architecture consists of two parts, the *lineamenta*, deriving form the mind, and the *materia*, deriving from nature. Compare Yates, *Theatre of the World*, pp. 27-28, and Hopper, *Journal of Garden History*, II, 1 (1982), p. 29.
121 Hopper, *Journal of Garden History*, II, 1 (1982), p. 28.
122 Terminology taken from ibid., p. 29.
123 Parkinson, *Garden of Pleasant Flowers*, facs. ed., p. 3: '... the orbicular or round forme is held in its owne proper existence to be the most absolute forme, containing within it all other formes whatsoever, but few I thinke will chose such a proportion to be joined to their habitation, being not accepted any where I think, but for the generall Garden to the University at Padoa.' See for Parkinson also chapter III.
124 Collection Frits Lugt, inv. no. 3428. Meij, *Jacques de Gheyn Drawings*, p. 50, cat. no. 30, shows Van Collen's portrait, including military and fencing attributes as well as the circle and its diameter. Van Collen's portrait was made by Jacques de Gheyn, who, also employed by Prince Maurits, must have known him personally.
125 The two engravings from Thibault's *Académie de l'Espée* reproduced here are plates IIII [*sic*, IV] and XXVI, made by Crisp. de Pas [Crispijn van der Passe] and Schelte à Bolswert, respectively.
126 This explanation is derived in part from the texts added to the exhibition of seventeenth-century Dutch books, curators E. Wyckhoff et al., entitled 'The Books & the Arts in Seventeenth-Century Holland', Columbia University, Butler Library, Rare Book and Manuscript Library, New York., April-July 1996.
127 For the use of the circle and centralized buildings see Wittkower, *Architectural Principles*, figs. 5 and 6. For ideal city plans see Filarete's Sforzinda shown in Visentini, *L'Orto Botanico*, p. 99. In Holland the cities of Coevorden and Naarden are good examples of centralized, polygonal city designs. See Taverne, *Land van belofte*, pp. 58 and 60; for ideal fortified cities designed by Simon Stevin and Frans van Schooten, pp. 54 and 65.
128 Wittkower, *Architectural Principles*, p. 19.
129 Kuyper, *Dutch Classicist Architecture*, pp. 19-21 and 357.
130 Porro, *L'horto de i semplici di Padova*. Visentini, *L'Orto Botanico*, p. 116.
131 One of two recently discovered garden designs in the Leiden Gemeentearchief – previously described as 'ceiling designs', though they actually were parterre designs, one of them an early copy of the Padua Botanical garden – substantiates this. The Leiden drawing is probably a copy of the design brought to Holland by a certain Bernardus Paludanus, physician at Enkhuizen, who had completed his medical studies in Padua (1578-80) and was asked to become the first *prefectus horti*. See Terwen-Dionisius, *Uit Leidse bron geleverd*, pp. 392-401. For further reading see also the extended article by the same author in *Journal of Garden History*, 4 (1990), pp. 213-235.
132 The Metropolitan Museum of Art, New York, Gift of J. Pierpont Morgan, 1923 (23.73.1). Colonna, *Hypnerotomachia*, plate preceding p. 'u'.
133 An engraving of this garden was published in Sadeler, *Vestigi delle antichità*. See also Lazzaro, *Italian Renaissance Garden*, p. 76, fig. 67.
134 Mignani, *Le Ville Medicee*, pp. 30 and 67-70. The lunettes were painted at the end of the seventeenth century. Unfortunately, no further documentation as to the possible meaning of these circles and their direct source seems to exist.
135 Rudolph II's gardens at Prague were laid out according to the

derivatives of the circle and the square; see Evans, *Rudolf II and His World*, p. 121. See also Strong, *Renaissance Garden in England*, p. 122. Other interesting circular gardens or parts of gardens can be recognized in Furttenbach's early-seventeenth-century ideal garden plans for palaces in Germany; see, for example, Dietzel, *Furttenbachs Gartenentwürfe*, plate 24.

136 The Metropolitan Museum of Art, New York, The Elisha Whittelsey Collection, The Elisha Whittelsey Fund, 1949 (49.95.2629[4]}. Vredeman de Vries, *Hortorum viridariorumque formae*, facs. ed., plates 15, 24 and 25.

137 LUW, Department of Special Collections, inv. no. R381 D08 (1986). Diedenhofen in Hunt, *Dutch Garden*, pp. 71-72, fig. 23.

138 Published by J. Covens and C. Mortier, c. 1690. LUW, Department of Special Collections, inv. no. 01.1101.01. Delannoy, *Le Parc d'Enghien*.

139 See Hunt and de Jong, *Anglo-Dutch Garden*, p. 275, fig. 121. The Hortus Botanicus of Amsterdam was designed in 1683 by Bastiaan Stoopendael. See also Wijnands et al., *Een sieraad voor de stad*, p. 69.

140 See A. Lecoq in Mosser and Teyssot, *Western Gardens*, pp. 69-80. For further reading on circular and other geometrically-shaped gardens as representations of the universe, or the garden as a *pentacolo*, see also Tongiorgi Tomasi and Carpeggiani in ibid., pp. 81-83 and 84-87, respectively.

141 At the same time this garden, like other circular gardens, was interpreted not only as an image of the world or the macrocosm but as Paradise itself, including the well-known topos of the sacred garden or *hortus conclusus*. The topos of this enclosed garden is of central importance to the development of the circle, and it is immediately connected with the form of the Padua garden. It is a fusion of classical-cosmological and medieval-religious sources: imagery is taken from Pythagorean theory and combined with biblical descriptions of the enclosed or sacred garden of the Song of Salomon. The typical embodiment of a *hortus conclusus* comes from Henry Hawkins's book in which the garden is envisaged as having a circular form, contained within a fortress-like enclosure which is surrounded by a high, crenellated wall with a single gate. The garden is laid out geometrically, with flower-beds arranged along two roads with a fountain in the middle. For other examples of the imagery of Paradise and the *hortus conclusus* see Visentini, *L'Orto Botanico*, p. 73, which shows an example drawn by the Limbourg brothers of the Earthly Paradise from the *Très Riches Heures du Duc de Berry*. Other representations include Prest, *Garden of Eden*, pp. 6-10, showing the 'Little Paradise Garden' of the Oberrheinischer Meister (c. 1410), and a woodcut by Ludolphus of Saxonia, *Leven Jhesu Christi*, 1503. For further reading see Lucia Tongiorgi Tomasi, *Journal of Garden History*, 1 (1983), pp. 1-34. See also Visentini, *Comunità*, 182 (1980), pp. 259-338, and his *L'Orto Botanico*.

142 British Library, Department of Printed Books. Heninger, *Cosmographical Glass*, pp. 36-39. This diagram shows the pre-Copernican, geocentric universe according to Peter Apian's often reprinted early-sixteenth-century *Cosmographicus liber*, fol. 4. It is of interest to note that similar geometrical diagrams of the universe are legion in the Renaissance, testifying to a widely accepted convention which, in spite of new scientific-astronomical evidence refuting the traditional vision of a geocentric and finite universe, was dominant far into the seventeenth century.

143 These seven planets are the Moon, Mercury, Venus, the Sun, Mars, Jupiter and Saturn.

144 The eighth sphere or heaven is labelled 'the firmament' and holds the signs of the zodiac and numerous stars. The ninth heaven is the 'crystalline sphere', while the tenth heaven, or *primum mobile*, forms the boundary between our finite universe and the 'empyreal heavens', the habitation of God and the Saints. Two special markers indicate the vernal and autumnal equinox, at the beginning of Aries and at the beginning of Libra, respectively.

145 Heninger, *Cosmographical Glass*, p. 102.

146 The illustration is taken from Clavius, *In sphaeram Joannis*, which is based on Finé's *Protomathesis*. See Heninger, *Cosmographical Glass*, p. 106. The Four Elements and Four Qualities are placed diagonally across from their opposites, indicating at the same time the various transmutations and compatibilities among the elements and qualities, thus interrelating the 'cosmoi' of the physical world, the year, and man. The original, Pythagorean Tetrad has a dragon in the centre, whereas this later Christian derivative, or Theological Tetrad, has the letters IHS in the central medallion, thus making Christ the centre of the universe with its intricate systems of forces and counterforces.

147 Heninger, *Cosmographical Glass*, p. 107.

148 In this case, the cabbala, Christianity and cosmology were included in the model of the tetrad; see ibid., pp. 190-191, figs. 115-116.

149 Versions are taken from Yates, *Theatre of the World*, p. 18, plate 2.

150 Mössel, *Urform des Seins*, p. 373, plate 280.

151 Vitruvius, *Ten Books on Architecture*, book III, chap. 1, pp. 72-75. See also Wittkower, *Architectural Principles*, p. 14.

152 Pacioli, *Divina Proportione*, p. 129. See also Wittkower, *Architectural Principles*, p. 15.

153 Shelfmark Arch. Bc.3, signature H2verso. See for further reading Orum-Larsen, *Journal of Garden History*, 2 (1990), pp. 97-106; here p. 101, fig. 5. The strict geometrical layout consisted of an enclosed square area divided into four sections according to the points of the compass, centring on a circular piazza. Each section contained an orchard and parterres with a pavilion set in each of the four exedrae of the enclosing wall. For further reading on garden architecture and science in the late sixteenth century see Dreyer, *Tycho Brahe*.

154 In this case the Pythagorean version, though only the theological

version is depicted in this book. As already mentioned, the Pythagorean Tetrad has a dragon, the Theological Tetrad the letters IHS in the central medallion. Heninger in *Cosmographical Glass*, pp. 166-168, believes that Brahe had the Theological Tetrad in mind, focusing on Christ. Given the name Uraniborg for his observatory – which, topped by Pegasus, represented Mount Parnassus itself – I believe that Brahe was inspired not so much by the Christian as by the classical model, or the Pythagorean Tetrad.

155 Heninger, *Cosmographical Glass*, pp. 106-107 and 166-167, figs. 97 and 98. Unfortunately, Orum-Larsen did not recognize this important connection with the form of the tetrad, though he remarks that the master designer probably had a symbolic 'esoteric' motivation when creating Uraniborg. Indeed, Orum-Larsen suggests that the four parts of the garden may symbolize Aristotle's Four Elements and the central building the centre of man's vision of the earth, while the five rows of trees visible in the original design of Uraniborg may symbolize the five planets. See Orum-Larson, *Journal of Garden History*, 2 (1990), p. 100.

156 Ibid., pp. 99 and 103.

157 Strong, *Renaissance Garden in England*, pp. 120-121, fig. 72. The garden was laid out about 1609.

158 The same geometry of the circle and the square, and the same cosmological symbolism, dictated Walter Jones's garden at Chastleton House in Oxfordshire, as well as the early garden at Wilton, near Salisbury in Wiltshire, laid out sometime before 1623 by William Herbert, 3rd Earl of Pembroke. See Strong, *Renaissance Garden in England*, pp. 121-123.

159 For our purpose, it is interesting to note that the garden as a whole manifests an attempt at universal numerical reconciliation, in that some parterre layouts can be directly related to harmonic musical diagrams, borrowed from Pythagorean-Platonic musical harmony. For further reading see Patterson, *Journal of Garden History*, 1 and 2 (1981), pp. 67-105 and 179-203, respectively.

160 According to Patterson, *Journal of Garden History*, 1 (1981), pp. 84-85, this diagram is derived from Gioseffo Zarlino's harmonic diagram. The relationship between garden-architectural space and music is further developed in the grottoes filled with moving-water mechanisms and musical instruments, for which de Caus even composed music. Musical harmonic diagrams ultimately originate from cosmic schemes such as the tetrad, to which the Orange parterre can be related. This larger cosmic connection is borne out by the direction of the star form within the parterre, which exactly corresponds to the points of the compass in the orientation of the garden, thus reflecting, as it were, the heavens in horticulture. Furthermore, the huge circular parterre laid out at the end of the Heidelberg garden and conceived as a 'botanical clock' also resembled the basic diagram of the tetrad, this time in its expanded form as a compass rose, with the world at its centre, surrounded by spheres of the planets.

161 Bienfait, *Oude Hollandsche tuinen*, pp. 208-210. See also Hamer and Meulenkamp, *Bulletin KNOB*, 86 (1987), pp. 3-14. Compare Huisken et al., *Jacob van Campen*, pp. 47-48.

162 LUW, Department of Special Collections, inv. no. 01.2012.02 (R352 G04). Meyster, *Des weerelds Dool-om-berg*, p. 49: 'Dit Dool-om-bergsche Oog-in-al vertoont een pleyn, Daar men 't heel al beoogt van s'werelds kloot in 't kleyn, een Mycrocosmon zelfs, na 't leven veel gelijcker, Alst kleyn na 't groot eens om gekeerde verrekijker …' (This Dool-om-berg Oog-in-al presents an area where one beholds the universe of the globe in the small, a microcosm in itself, much closer to life than the small into the large through an inverted telescope.' See also Hamer and Meulenkamp, *Bulletin KNOB*, 86 (1987), p. 12.

163 Ibid., p. 14.

164 Thus the mound symbolizes not only the centre of the universe but also the mountain from where Satan showed all the kingdoms of the world to Christ (Matthew 4:8-9).

165 Hamer and Meulenkamp, *Bulletin KNOB*, 86 (1987), p. 9.

166 Heninger, *Cosmographical Glass*, p. 165, fig. 96, showing God enthroned in a tetrad of Evangelists (in other cases the Four Elements instead of the Evangelists), can also be connected to the design of Dool-om-berg. The later seventeenth-century garden layout of Sorgvliet, owned by Hans Willem Bentinck, also had two mounds which can be analysed along cosmological lines.

167 The meaning of the three terraces constituting the central mound in the Doolomberg garden has been described as representing the Trinity; see Hamer and Meulenkamp, *Bulletin KNOB*, 86 (1987), p. 9. See also Heninger, *Cosmographical Glass*, p. 183, fig. 109: the mound representing the ascent in an alchemical context is visually comparable to representations of Mount Parnassus. Keeping in mind the contemporary urge to syncretize, we may ultimately relate the three terraces also to contingent systems of cosmology, such as the symbolism of the 'three worlds' of the cabbala (the empyreal, the ethereal and the elementary) and the three levels of creation, as represented in Renaissance diagrams; see Heninger, *Cosmographical Glass*, pp. 87-98. Furthermore, a late-sixteenth-century emblem, itself based on the original tetrad model and showing a labyrinth surrounded by four small semicircles containing the Four Elements, is also directly comparable to the design of the Dool-om-berg garden. See de la Perrière, *Théâtre des Bons Engins*, and Hamer and Meulenkamp, *Bulletin KNOB*, 86 (1987), p. 9, fig. 6.

168 Huygens visited Meyster's estate in 1669 and described his trip in 'Uijtwandeling vanden … augusti tot … septemb. 1669'; see Worp, *Gedichten*, VII, p. 289. See also Van Veen, *De soeticheydt des buyten-levens*, p. 41.

169 Lunsingh Scheurleer and Van Pelt in Van den Boogaart, *Johan Maurits van Nassau-Siegen*, pp. 142-197, here especially pp. 190-194, figs. 107-109. The ground-plan consisted of a circle within

which four equilateral triangles are placed in such a way that their corners divide the circumference into twelve equal parts, as has been pointed out in chapter IV.

170 Moreover, given Huygens's accomplishments as a musician, it is not surprising to find that in his buildings, and also in his gardens, he used Vitruvian and Pythagorean musical harmonic proportions, in which the distance of the tones on a musical scale were translated into actual measurable space. Thus the external and internal measurements of the spaces in huygens's house copied classical proportion: the two main halls were cubic in form, defined in musical terms as a 'monochord', while the width of the principal rooms was half their length, representing a 'diapason'. See Alberti, *Art of Building*, book IX, chaps. 5 and 6, pp. 305-308. Compare also Van Pelt, *Art History*, IV, 2 (1981), p. 170, fig. 3. See Fremantle, *Baroque Town Hall*, p. 99, and Wittkower, *Architectural Principles*, pp. 117-126, for the terminology of musical proportions.

171 Wotton, *Elements of Architecture*, p. 9. See also Fremantle, *Baroque Town Hall*, p. 99.

172 Van Pelt did not take fully into account either rhetorical tradition or poetic freedom, or Huygens's florid style typical of contemporary country-house literature. For style, poetic freedom and the degree of imagination in Huygens's poem see de Vries in Hunt, *Dutch Garden*, pp. 85-86, where Huygens offers an idealized version of reality when talking about Hofwijck, asking us to imagine Hofwijck's layout in its fully-grown state of a century later.

173 Van Pelt, *Art History*, IV, 2 (1981), p. 154, fig. 2.

174 Patterson, *Journal of Garden History*, 2 (1981), p. 190, fig. 2, a reconstruction of the supposed structural model of the Hortus Palatinus, demonstrating a progression from the Mundane through the Celestial to the Super Celestial world.

175 Again, as at Hofwijck, one has to be careful and see how literal, and to what extent, abstract philosophical thought actually could have been translated into the architectural reality of the garden. In fact, the recent analysis by Patterson, like that by Van Pelt on Hofwijck, neglects to mention how strongly the form of the garden depended on the topographical site. The resulting discrepancies between the abstract thought and its architectural expression in the Heidelberg garden render such direct comparisons again unlikely, and only useful in theory.

176 Good examples of new cosmological diagrams are those designed by Robert Fludd in his influential cosmological work *Utriusque cosmi historia*. Following Huygens's thinking, Fludd depicts a diagram showing the ideal Vitruvian man within his microcosm, in which the earthly and heavenly spheres correspond to man's bodily and intellectual components, comparable to the ascent of the soul, or *scala spiritualis*. Man is divided into three regions, the intellectual or angelic region in the macrocosm, the middle region, comparable to the celestial world, and the elementary region, comparable to the material, sublunary world of the Four Elements. The cycle of day and night is reflected in the bipartite image of diurnal man, and lastly man's proportion is represented in relation to musical harmony, illustrated by the double circle which is indicated as a 'diapason'. See also Heninger, *Cosmographical Glass*, pp. 27-28, fig. 18; pp. 144-145, fig. 84; and p. 152, fig. 90.

177 Compare Hopper, *Journal of Garden History*, II, 1 (1982), pp. 33-34.

178 Wittkower, *Architectural Principles*, p. 115. Compare Hendrick Hondius, *Institutio artis perspectivae* and the remark about the garden's relative smallness. Compare also Hopper, *Journal of Garden History*, II, 1 (1982), p. 29 and note 29.

179 Worp, *Gedichten*, II, p. 229. The poem was written on 20 April 1631. Compare also Kuyper, *Dutch Classicist Architecture*, p. 131.

180 Schmidt, *Opstellen voor Hans Lochner*, pp. 167-168, gives a good explanation of this text and corrects Kuyper's translation and interpretation in *Dutch Classicist Architecture*, pp. 131 and 280, note 1.

181 Henkel and Schöne, *Handbuch*, p. 42. The image has the inscription 'Ad eser uno de dos', which can be interpreted as follows: Earthly life is as far removed from eternal life as the earth is removed from the sky. Man can but follow one of the two, and only he who attempts to improve himself will be happy.

182 Fremantle, *Baroque Town Hall*, pp. 61-62.

183 That the set-up of globes or the heavenly and earthly spheres in gardens was a widespread tradition at the time can be confirmed by their representation in an embroidered garden, namely in the first wall-hanging of Stoke Edith, reproduced on the cover of Hunt and de Jong, *Anglo-Dutch Garden*. Compare also the description of spheres in the garden of Het Loo: 'hemelcloten van coper staende op witte, kleyne, marbre statuen' (heavenly [and earthly] spheres of brass, standing on white, small, marble statues), mentioned in the inventory of 1713 published in Drossaers and Lunsingh Scheurleer, *Inventarissen*, I, RGP 147, p. 683, no. 975.

184 LUW, Department of Special Collections, inv. no. R350 E22 (1786).

185 Harris, *Description of the King's Royal Palace*, pp. 16-18. See also the Dutch translation with commentary and reproduction of prints of the gardens in Van Everdingen-Meyer, *Beschrijving van 's konings paleis*, pp. 35 and 39-40.

186 Van Asbeck and Aardoom, *Groen*, 6 (1984), pp. 278-282.

187 This date and hour were taken as a point of departure for the orientation of the celestial globe during its recent restoration, although there is no direct proof of this being the original, seventeenth-century orientation. See Van Asbeck and Aardoom, *Groen*, 6 (1984), p. 280.

188 Two spheres also decorated, and still do, the roof of the Bibliotheca Thysiana at the Rapenburg in Leiden, built in 1635, at the same time Huygens's house was built. They were designed by Arent van

189 The terminology used here is borrowed from Lunsingh Scheurleer in Van den Boogaart, *Johan Maurits van Nassau-Siegen*, pp. 142-190.
190 Fremantle, *Baroque Town Hall*, pp. 42-43 and fig. 26, the plan of the Burgerzaal, from Vennecool, *Afbeelding van 't Stadt Huys*.
191 Zoet, *Werken*, p. 183. See Fremantle, *Baroque Town Hall*, p. 42.
192 Fremantle, *Baroque Town Hall*, p. 45.
193 Heijbroek and Schapelhouman, *Kunst in kaart*, p. 19.
194 For further reading see ibid., p. 37.
195 In a map by Petrus Plancius, which shows the double hemisphere for the first time in such an elaborate border of decoration, the four parts of the world instead of the four seasons are represented in the outer spandrels. Plancius's map also includes a compass and an armillary sphere, set between the two large hemispheres. See for a colour representation the advertisement of John Potter Ltd. in *Antiques* of June 1989 (pages not numbered).
196 Ceres for the Earth, Neptune representing Water, Jupiter (here Apollo) for Fire and Juno (here a male figure, possibly Ganimede) for Air. The allegorical figures on this map were taken from famous late-sixteenth-century Flemish print series, such as those by Nicolaes de Bruyn and Johannes Sadeler after drawings by Maerten de Vos and Hans Bol. See Heijbroek and Schapelhouman, *Kunst in kaart*, p. 38.
197 Another famous map, made by Willem Jansz Blaeu, adds the Labours of Man to the iconography found in Hondius's map. See ibid., p. 71.
198 In this context, the eight roundels for the placement of bronze urns around the octagonal fountains, as shown in Hondius's print, must be part of a larger numerical system. These roundels, comparable to those in the orange-tree parterre at Heidelberg, may have been intended to denote the cycle of an octave which holds all musical consonants together.
199 Van Regteren Altena, *Oud Holland*, 85 (1970), pp. 33-44.
200 Huygens greatly admired these grottoes during his visit to Heidelberg in 1620. See the description in chapter IV. See also Worp, *Bijdragen en Mededeelingen van het Historisch Genootschap*, XV (1894), p. 79.
201 Archival documentation demonstrates Frederik Hendrik's interest in shells, stones, coral and pumice, imported from overseas to decorate the grottoes at Honselaarsdijk, Ter Nieuburch and the Paleis Noordeinde. See the records of payments ARA, NDR, inv. no. 992 [old no. 735], fols. 335, 409 and 439. A famous late-seventeenth-century collection was the grotto and porcelain cabinet of William III and Mary at Het Loo, recently restored. William III's close friend and adviser, Hans Willem Bentinck, mentioned before, had a well-known collection of rarities exhibited in his Orangerie at Sorgvliet, near The Hague.
202 LUW, Department of Special Collections. Diedenhofen in Hunt, *Dutch Garden*, pp. 72-74, fig. 25.
203 The discipline of alchemy is represented by the five most perfect polyhedra, symbolizing five regular solids. Throughout the ages these regular solids, imbued with unique qualities, held a special fascination for mathematicians, scientists and architects, who saw these forms as elementary models in the fabrication of our universe and came to associate the shape of each regular solid with one of the Four Elements and Ether. In this theory, the familiar form of the cube, centre of Hondius's engraving showing the bare three-dimensional cubic skeleton of the Buitenhof, was identified with the element Earth – an appropriate element for a garden.
204 See Hunt and de Jong, *Anglo-Dutch Garden*, colour-plate 4, cat. no. 139, pp. 288-289.
205 Fremantle, *Baroque Town Hall*, pp. 48-49. The symbolic programme included the deeds of the Dutch ancestors, the ancient Batavians, who rebelled against the powerful Romans, who later became their allies. From this story developed the well-known Batavians-Romans analogy, referred to in the Introduction and chapters IV and V. Compare especially the interior decoration of the Mauritshuis with its depiction of the rulers of the House of Orange and Nassau, including a portrait of Adolf of Nassau, King of the Romans, and the Princes of Orange, who fought for the Dutch Republic to establish a 'New Batavia'. Compare also Lunsingh Scheurleer in Van den Boogaart, *Johan Maurits van Nassau-Siegen*, p. 146.
206 As was mentioned earlier in this chapter, Sorgvliet belonged to a well-known late-seventeenth-century garden which glorified the House of Orange, both for its military-political accomplishments and for its artistic patronage. Here monumental trophies showing the deeds of the House of Orange were set up round Mount Parnassus and the Labyrinth. The Sorgvliet mound and labyrinth are also important examples of the influence of cosmographical diagrams in garden architecture; they are comparable to the mound of the Doolomberg garden. For further reading see Sellers in Hunt, *Dutch Garden*, pp. 121-122.
207 Significantly, this monogram is in itself a double circle formed by the connected O's of Orange, holding the letters H and A for Henry, as Frederik Hendrik signed his name, and Amalia.
208 The parterre with the coat of arms of the Stadholder and his wife was part of the larger sculptural programme, which may very well have included the Four Seasons and the Four Elements or Four Parts of the World. Even though they are difficult to distinguish in detail in the Milheusser print, the posture of the statues, their attributes and positions in the garden seem to indicate such an iconographical content, as was mentioned earlier in this chapter.
209 See also Lunsingh Scheurleer in Van den Boogaart, *Johan Maurits van Nassau-Siegen*, p. 189.
210 Thevet, *Les vrais pourtraits*. See Lunsingh Scheurleer in Van den

Boogaart, *Johan Maurits van Nassau-Siegen*, p. 189.

211 Drossaers and Lunsingh Scheurleer, *Inventarissen*, I, RGP 147, pp. XXII-XXIII. For sculpture in the gardens of Ter Nieuburch and the Paleis Noordeinde see pp. 258-259, nos. 617 and 624-636, including busts of Marcus Aurelius, Seneca, Julius Caesar, Octavianus and Claudius. Compare an entry in the account books, ARA, NDR, inv. no. 992 [old no. 735], fol. 418, mentioning payment to the painter Soutmans for a print series offered to the Stadholder, containing ten portraits of the Counts of Nassau and the Princes of Orange. For the decoration of the Mauritshuis compare also chapter IV.

212 See for the sculptural 'programme' of Frederik Hendrik's gardens the description of de Hennin, *Zinrijke Gedachten*, for example p. 10, mentioning the 'twelve Roman Emperors' among a series of other Graeco-Roman figures apparently decorating the garden of Honselaarsdijk. Compare also Neurdenburg, *Beeldhouwkunst*, p. 19.

213 The symbolic representation of Holland as a Lion, the so-called Leone Belgico, set within a circular enclosed garden, is often found in contemporary seals and medals. For an illustration of a late-sixteenth-century medal with this representation see Hunt and de Jong, *Anglo-Dutch Garden*, p. 58, fig. 31. Compare also for further literature and commentary the Introduction.

214 This image of the rampant lion crowned with Frederik Hendrik's coat of arms and standing in a garden was used on the title-page of Hugo de Groot's *Respublica Hollandiae et Urbes* (see fig. 1). Compare also Hunt in Maccubbin and Hamilton-Phillips, *Age of William and Mary*, p. 234, fig. 270. For other illustrations of the political struggle between the Dutch and the Spanish, represented in various late-sixteenth- and early-seventeenth-century emblems using the image of the lion set in two circular enclosures, see Van Gelder and Wittemans et al., *Marnix van St. Aldegonde*, fig. 60. See also the notes in the Introduction.

215 The political print shown here is an *Allegory of the Twelve Years' Truce* by Willem Buytewech, representing 'Hollandiae', personified by a woman seated within a kind of grotto structure which is crowned by Frederik Hendrik's coat of arms and those of the Seven Provinces. 'Hollandiae' is surrounded by petitioners representative of all the social classes, a citizen, a merchant, a farmer and a soldier. In the centre of the garden is the orange-tree, withered but standing, symbolizing the Orange dynasty. The entrance to the garden is protected by the Dutch Lion. See Haverkamp-Begemann, *Willem Buytewech*, p. 14 and cat. no. vG17. See also de Jong in Hunt, *Dutch Garden*, p. 15, fig. 2. For further reading on the history of depicting Holland as a garden see Van Winter, *Nederlands Kunsthistorisch Jaarboek*, 8 (1957), pp. 29-121.

CONCLUSION

1 See for this description of John Evelyn visiting the gardens in 1644 Sieveking, *Sir William Temple*, p. 201: 'There is a faire terrace which looks to the Vine-yard, in which, on pedestalls, are fix'd the statues of all the Spanish Kings of the House of Austria. The opposite walls are paynted by Rubens, being a history of the late tumults in Belgia; in the last piece the Arch Duchesse shutts a greate payre of gates upon Mars, who is coming out of hell, arm'd, and in a menacing posture. On another, the Infanta is seen taking leave of Don Philip.' This description fits the theme depicted in the great hall of the Huis Ten Bosch, depicting Victory entering through doors opened by Hercules and Minerva; see Loonstra, *Huijs int Bosch*, p. 129. Compare also Brenninkmeyer-De Rooij, 'Notities', *Oud Holland*, 96 (1982), pp. 133-185, especially pp. 165-170 and fig. 43 illustrating a print from Gevartius's *Pompa Introitus Ferdinandi*, after Rubens's design for the Temple of Janus.

APPENDIX

Archives: Algemeen Rijksarchief, The Hague. Koninklijk Huisarchief (if indicated as such).
Documents: De Archieven van de Nassause Domeinraad 1581-1811, abbreviated to :
ARA, NDR, inv. no. ... call number 1.08.11, inv. no. ...

Content: Accounts & Decrees of the Gardens of Honselaarsdijk, Ter Nieuburch, Paleis Noordeinde and Huis ten Bosch, the gardens of Breda, Buren, Zuylesteyn and Ysselsteyn. Gardener's Contracts and Instructions, years 1620-1690.
Note: The numbers at the end of each entry constitute the total cost in pounds artois (£), subdivided in schellingen (sch), stuivers (sts) and dernier (dr).
Note: In 1997 all documents in the Archives of the Nassau Domains were assembled in one inventory system and renumbered accordingly. The old number system, which distinguished various separate archival collections – Nassau Domeinraad Hingman (Main Archive, Hingman's Inventory) and Nassause Domeinraad Folio (Hulshof's Inventory), among others – are now unified. For the sake of clarity, and to keep important standard literature on the topic current, the old numbers have been added in brackets to the new inventory numbers. For a comprehensive survey and further details on the Nassau Domains Archives see M.C.J.C. van Hoof, E.A.T.M. Schreuder and B.J. Slot (eds.), *De Archieven van de Nassause Domeinraad 1581-1811*. The Hague: Algemeen Rijksarchief, 1997. See pp. 694-742. for concordance of the old and new inventory numbers.

REKENINGEN VAN DE THESAURIER EN RENTMEESTER-GENERAAL EN REGISTER VAN ORDONNANTIES VOOR DE THESAURIER EN RENTMEESTER-GENERAAL EN RENTMEESTERS VAN DE PRINSEN VAN ORANJE EN DE DOMEINRAAD, OVER DE JAREN 1620-1665.

ACCOUNTS AND DECREES OF THE COMPTROLLER AND CHIEF ESTATE STEWARD AND STEWARDS OF THE PRINCES OF ORANGE AND THE COUNCIL OF THE DOMAINS, 1620-1665

HONSELAARSDIJK

NDR, inv. no. 1027 [768] (year 1620)

1027 fol. 41
Betaelt aen Adriaen Dircksz. Mr Timmerman ... twee en dertich ponden negen schellingen artois ter saecke van reyscosten en vacatien ... XXII £ IX sts

Betaelt aen den selven ... de somme van negen en t' sestich ponden vijff schellingen artois, voor reyscosten en vacatien ... LXIX £ V sts

NDR, inv. no. 1028 [769] (year 1621): lacks further information

NDR, inv. no. 1029 [770] (year 1622): lacks further information

NDR, inv. no. 1030 [771] (year 1623)

1030 fol. 40 verso
Betaelt aen Catarina Cray als moeder van de vier naegelaeten kinderen van wijlen Mr Simon Stevin in sijn leven Superintendant van Sijne Vorstelijke Gen. Comtoiren van de finantie, met naemen Frederick, Hendrick, Susanna en Levina, de somme van vierhondert ponden artois voor een Jaer lijffpensie, de voorsz. vier kinderen elck van hondert ponden artois toegevoecht ... den lesten december XIV^C drie en twintich ...

NDR, inv. no. 1031 [772] (year 1624): lacks further information

NDR, inv. no. 1034 [773] (year 1625)

1034 fol. 168
...betaelings ten behoeve vant gebouw te Honselerdijck gedaen, beloopende de somme van III^M VI^C XL £ sulcx dat de heerlickheijt van Naeldwijck met de selve somme alsin verbetert is ...

NDR, inv. no. 1035 [774] (year 1626): lacks further information

NDR, inv. no. 1036 [775] (year 1627)

1036 fol. 155 (Slothouwer, p. 261)
... vergoet de somme van acht en twintich duijsent acht hondert vijff ende veertich ponden negentien schell. twee dernier artois die hij, bij slote van reeckeninge vande drie pavillioenen bij Sijne Vorst. Gen. inde jaren 1621, 1622, 1623 ende 1624 aenden huijse Honsholredijck doen maecken te boven gekomen is, als meer uitgegeven dan ontfangen hebbende ...
[total in pounds artois] ... 28845:19:2

1036 fol. 155 verso
… met den voorn. Catshuijsen gedaen aenden selven vergoet de somme van tien duijsent drie hondert vijff ende vijfftich ponden acht schellingen artois die d'selve bij slote van reeckeninge vande nieuwe laen bij Sijnne Vorstl. Gen. in de jaeren 1625 & 1626 voor den huise van Honsholredijck doen maecken te boven gecomen is, als meer uijtgegeven dan ontfangen hebbende …
[total in pounds artois] … 10355:8:0

NDR, inv. no. 1037 [776] (year 1628): lacks further information

NDR, inv. no. 1038 [777] (year 1629)

1038 fol. 202 (Slothouwer, p. 261)
Sijnne furstelijcke Doorluchticheit heeft doen besteden het quartier vant huis te Honsholredijck achter naer den tuijn aende Naeldwijcse sijde leggende, 't selve te maecken ende vollueren, te weten een pavillioen op den hoff westelick vant pavillioen twelck lest gemaeckt is, ende een galerie vant selve pavillioen aff tot aent leste gemaeckt werck welck suijdelijck vant selve gebou gelegen is een opene gallerie op pilasters noordelick vant gebou welck van dit voorscreve nieuw aengenomen pavillioen langs den thuin naert leste gemaeckte pavillioen gaen sal. Te betalen in drie paijen waer van de helft vant eerste verschijnen soude als 't heijwerck voor goet opgenomen soude sijn, ende de wederhelft als de eerste cruiscosijnen vant selve aengenomen gebouw staen sullen, het tweede termin als 't voorsz. werck ondert dack ende de affhangende goten gehangen sullen sijn, ende het derde ende leste termin als alle t'geheele werck volgens d'aengenomen conditie sal sijn volpresen ende opgenomen, ende sijn aennemers vant selve werck gebleven Fop Oenissen ende Jan Ariensen Bijl beijde van Haerlem voorde somme van LV M ponden artois, maeckende XVIII^M III^C XXXIII £ VII sts VIII dr artois voor elcken termin … als blijckende is bij de maentreeckeninge vande domeijnen van Martio XVIC negenentwintich

NDR, inv. no. 1039 [778] (year 1630)

1039 fol. 213 verso (Slothouwer, p. 262)
… betaelt de somme van seven ende twintich duijsent acht hondert drie ende t'seventich ponden tien schellingen artois … over de wederhelft van den eersten termin vant westelick pavillioen van den huise te Honsholredijc ende de gallerie die aldaer op den thuin respondeert ende streckende is tottet groote middelpavillioen aengenomen bij Fop Oenissen ende Jan Ariensen Bijl beide van Haerlem int geheel voorde somme van LV^M £ … mitsgaders III^C LXXIII £ X sts betaelt aen Barthout van Bassen schilder ter saecke van verscheijden teijckening ende modellen ten behouve van gebouw van Honsholredijck gemaeckt als anders, uijtwijsens de maentreeckeninge vande domeinen Julij …

1039 fol. 214 verso (Slothouwer, p. 262)
… betaelt aan Adriaen Willeboortsen Spierencxhoeck de somme van sestien duijsent seven hondert negen ende tsestich ponden vier schellingen artois … voor de welcke hem inde jaren XVI^C XXV ende XVI^C ses ende twintich aenbesteet was, t'noordtoostelicke groote pavillioen met de gallerien ende camers die vant selve nieuwe pavillioen naet huis te Honsholredijck strecken. Item noch VIIIC £ overt heijen vant selve werck buiten den bestelden was IIII^C LXXXV £ op reeckeninge van de muijr die vande helft vande gracht vant huijs loopt …

1039 fol. 234
… In den jaere XVI^C dertich tijde deser en sijn geen meerdere acquisiten der domeynen gedaen dan de verbeteringen vande notabele nieuwe Gebouwen ende reparatien soo aenden Casteele ende Thuynen te Buren, ende aende huyse te Honsholredijck ende Nieuburch gemaeckt ende gedaen …
X^N Somma: M^C LXX^M IX^C LXXXV £ XIII sts XV dr

NDR, inv. no. 1040 [779] (year 1631)

1040 fol. 119
… Sijne furstelicke doorluchticheit heeft van Sijne Genaede den Grave van Arenberge gecost ende vercregen de heerlickheit van Naeltwijc, Honsholredijck, Wateringe, den Opstal, 't Honderlandt &. Ende het erftmaerschalckschap van Hollandt aende selve heerlickheit gehorich Rentm^r daervan is Symon Hendricsz. Catshuijsen derwelcke bijt Sloten Sijnner verreckeninge van de domeinen der voorschrevene heerlick^t onder den Jaere XVIC eenendertich tijde deser schuldich gebleken is de somme van sestien duijsent vijfhondert vier en vijftich ponden ses dernier artois die den rendant aan de selve Catshuijsen bij liquidatie ontfangen ende profiteren sal wegens verscheijden notabele porterende … die hij nopende de gebouwen ende plantagien van Honsholredijck betaelt hadde … 16554:0:6

1040 fol. 208
Uijtgave gedaen ter saecke van Sijne furstelicke doorluchtich^{ts} huis te Honsholredijck onder Naeltwijck gelegen.
Den Rendant heeft betaelt de somme van twaelfhondert vijf en vijftich ponden tien schellingen artois te weten XII^C VI £ X sts overt maecken ende vollueren van een houten heijnninge in de Tuin te Honsholredijck om de abricosen, persicken ende kerssen tegens te setten lanch CXIVI roeden een voet ses duijm tot VIII £ V sts de roede bij Jacob Janssen Timmerman aengenomen ende de verdere L £ VII sts Sijne furstelicke doorluch^{ts} commissarissen int opnemen vant voorsz. werck geoordeelt den voornoemde Timmerman noch te competeren … mey tijde deser [1631] … 1255:10:0

1040 fol. 209

… betaelt d'somme van sevenenveertich ponden vijff schellingen artois over de verteeringen ende wagenvrachten bij Sijnne Furstelicke doorluchticheits commissarissen gadaen ende verteert soo int besichtigen ende daerna int besteden vande groote riolen in de Tuin te Honselerdijck dienende omt overvloedich water welck de boomen aldaer verderven af te leijden … Augusti [1631] … 47:5:0

1040 fol. 209 verso

… betaelt twee en twintich ponden tien schellingen artois over vijff wagenvrachten van den rendant inde maent September Jaers deser tweten te Honsholredijck te voeren om de wercken aldaer te doen vorderen …

1040 fol. 209 verso

betaelt de somme van achtien hondert elf ponden sestien schellingen te weeten XIIII^C XXXI £ X sts. over tmaecken ende volueren vande groote ende cleine riolen in den Thuijn te Honselerdijck bij Jan Gijbersch, Laurens Arentsz. ende Cornelis Jansz metselaers de groote riolen a VIII £ X sts de roede, ende cleine à XXX £ den hoop sonder maet opgenomen, Item II^C £ aende voornoemde metselaers bij besteck belooft bij den hoop sonder maet voort maken ende volueren van de riolen in de twee palm tuijnen neffens thuijs te Honselerdijck leggen, XXX £ voor verscheijden gegoten blauwe tegels om te leggen op de monde van de beckens daer de voorsz riolen beginnen ende vergaderen, om deselve desnootsijnde te openen ende te connen reinigen, XIIII £ XIX sts … over arbeitsloon vande aerde te verspreiden die door het graven vande voorschreve riolen overgeschoten was, ende de resterende hondert en ses ponden sestien schellingen over verscheijden cleine wercken ten dienste vant huijs ende thuijnen te Honsholredijck gedaen … October [1631] … 1811:16:0

1040 fol. 223 verso

aende Erfgenaemen van wijlen Mr Leonard de Voogt in sijn leven Raetsheer in den hooge Rade in Hollandt de somme van vijfduijsentachtentachtich ponden dertich schellingen acht dernier artois over den lesten termin van drie van XV^M VI^C LXVI £ VIII sts V dr bij henluijden bedongen voor seckere wooninge int westlant gelegen die Sijne Furst. doorl in Mey XVI^C negenentwintich gecost heeft …

1040 fol. 227 verso

In den Jaere XVI^C eenendertich tijde deser en sijn geen meerdere acquisiten der domeinen gedaen, dan de voorsz. verbeteringe vande notable nieuwe gebouwen ende merckelijcke verbeteringen soo aende huijsen te Honsholredijck, Buren, Iselstein ende Nieuburch gemaeckt ende gedaan, waarvan hier voorn aparte capittelen tonen, welck hier durende is voor
X^n Somma XCL^M CI £ XVI dr

1040 fol. 5.211 (Slothouwer, p. 263)

… betaelt aen Arent Arentsz architect de somme van tien ponden over eenige teeckeninge bij hem ten dienste vant voorscreve gebouw gemaeckt blijckende bij de maentreeckeninge van Decemb. XVI^C eenendertich …

NDR, inv. no. 1041 [780] (year 1632)

1041 fol. 238 verso
… ten dienste van den huijse van Honsholredijck in den jaere XVI^C sesen twintich …

bier voor de arbeijders	CXII £ II sts
ter saecke vanden hoff	VI^C VIII £ XIX sts
onderhouden vande carpers	XII £
dispensie van stal aldaer	XXXII £ XIX sts
expenditures buildings & gardens 1626	III^M XLVII £ III sts IIII dr

1041 fol. 240
ter saecke vanden hoff	V^C VIII £ XIX sts VI dr
expenditures buildings & gardens 1627	IIII^M V^C LXVIII £ XI sts VIII dr

1041 fol. 241
ter saecke vanden hoff	XVI^C XXXI £ II sts VII dr
expenditures buildings & gardens 1628	V^M IIII^C XVIII £ XV sts VII dr

1041 fol. 242 verso
ter saecke vanden hoff	X^C LXXXIIII £ XIIII sts IX dr
expenditures buildings & gardens 1629	VI^M V^C XVII £ VIII sts VII dr

1041 fol. 243
oncosten vanden hoff	VII^C XL £ XVI sts
expenditures buildings & gardens 1630	III^M VI^C XVI £ XII sts

1041 fol. 244
aen oncosten van hoff	VIII^C LIIII £ VIII sts IX dr
expenditures buildings & gardens 1631	III^M III^C XXXVI £ V sts VI dr

1041 fol. 247
aen oncosten vanden hoff	VI^C XLVIII £ X sts VII dr
expenditures buildings & gardens 1632	IIII^M VI^C XXII £ XVII sts V dr

APPENDIX HONSELAARSDIJK

1041 fol. 251 verso
Aen Gijsbrecht Tonissen hovenier van Sijnne hooch^t te Honsholredijck d'somme van drie hondert vier ende dertich ponden twaelff schellingen over leveringen van eenige fruitboomen als andere dachgelden ende reijscosten bij hem verleidt ende verdient om d'selve te Suijlestein te gaen planten
Julij 1632 … III^C XXIIII £ XII sts

1041 fol. 333 verso
… Adriaen Willeboortsen Spierinxhouten [houck?] architect … over verscheyden vacatien ende costen bij hem selve gedaen ende besteet in diverse reysen die hij ten dienste van S.H. te Yselstein nopende 't gebou aldaer in den Jaere 1627 ende voorts in den jaere 1631 te Honsholredijck gedaen heeft …
… 76:5:0

NDR, inv. no. 1042 [781] (year 1633)

1042 fol. 229 verso (Slothouwer, p. 263)
Betaelt aen Alewijn Claesz van Assendelft, schrijnwercker tot Delft d'somme van vijffhondert acht ende vijfftich ponden acht schell. over seecker model vant huis te Honsholredijck bij denselven door last vanden rentm^r Symon Hendricsz Catshuijsen gemaeckt ende gelevert …

1042 fol. 231 verso (Slothouwer, p. 263)
Betaelt aen Huijch Jansz, weerdt te Honsholredijck de somme van negen ponden voor teercosten bijden Franschen architect hovenier ende andere werckmrs inde maendt Meij XVI^C drie endertich tsijnen huijse gedaen …

1042 fol. 232 verso (Slothouwer, p. 263)
Betaelt aen Andre Mollet, Frans hovenier, de somme van tien hondert vijfftich ponden over sijn vacatien ende beleit vant maecken vande parterren die Sijne Hoocheit door den selven te Honsholredijck ende te Buuren heeft doen maecken te weten IIII^C £ voor twee parterren te Honselerdijck een van sooden ende palm met wit, root ende swarten ende het ander geheel van palm seer aardich gemaeckt III^C £ voor twee parterren van palm te Buren, III^C voor sijn reisgelt ende weder van ende naer Vranckrijck als L £ voor teercosten bijden selven inden Hage gedaen, terwijlen hij verscheiden teickeningen voor Sijne Hoocheit heeft gemaeckt ende dit alvooren hem sijn tractement van VIII^C £ jaerlicx beneffens een daelder daechs aen costgelt was geordonneert. Bij specificatie ende quitantie overgenomen op de maendtreeckeninge van Junij XVI^C drie en dertich …

1042 fol. 233 verso
Betaelt aen Symon Hendricsz. Catshuijsen Rentmeester van Naeldwijck de somme van twaelff hondert twintich ponden seven schellingen twee dernier, voor soo bij hem betaelt ende verschooten is aen dachgelden, vrachten, verteeringe ende andere oncosten omme het planten vande twee parterren te Honsholredijck hierboven vermelt …
op de maendtreckeninge van Junij [1633] … XII^C XX £ VII sts II dr

1042 fol. 234 (Slothouwer, p. 264)
Betaelt aen Arent Arentsz. 's Gravesandt, architect ende teickenaer de somme van tien ponden seventien schellingen over verscheiden vrachten ende anders bij den selven inde maendt Julio XVI^C drie endertich ten dienste vant voorscreve gebouw verschooten …

1042 fol. 236 (Slothouwer, p. 264)
Vergoet aen Andre Mollet, opsichter van Sijnne Hooch^{ts} Tuijnen de somme van dertich ponden over verscheiden vrachten ende andere oncosten bij den selven ten dienste van Sijnne Hoocheit verschoten …

1042 fol. 239 (Slothouwer, p. 264)
Vergoet aenden architect La Vallee de somme van negen ponden voor wagenvrachten bij hem betaelt om ten dienst vant gebouw na Honselerdijck te gaen …

1042 fol. 240
Betaelt aen Dirck Jansz. metselaer, opsichter vant gebouw te Honsholredijck ende Rijswijck de somme van achtien ponden voor soo verre bij hem gegeven is aen de metselaers, steenhouwers, timmermr ende dergelijck aent gebouw te Honsholredijck wercken welck Haere Hoocheit inde Maendt September tijde deser daer sijnde …

1042 fol. 242
Betaelt aen Jan van Dalen Mr steenhouwer tot Amsterdam de somme van twaelff hondert twee en twintich ponden achtien schellingen voor leverantie van XIXXXIX groote roode ende graue tegelen omme te Honsholredijck op de binnenplaets en de buyten comende vant huijs inde Thuijn te beleggen … XII^C XXII £ XVIII sts

1042 fol. 242 verso (Slothouwer, p. 264)
Betaelt aen Dirck Jansz. metseler van Naeldwijck de somme van vierhondert vier en dertich ponden thien schellingen voor soo veel bij hem uitgekeert is aen dachgelden vande metselaers die gevrocht hebben aen t'overtrecken met tras ende clinckert de galerij kelders op de binnenplaets vant huijs te Honselerdijck, welcke met het sacken vant gebouw geborsten ende ondicht waren geworden de nichen, cornissen, pilasters, poortkens, borstweringen, festons op de beijde einden vande gallerie die op den tuin siet, te stellen aende brugge, die naer den hoff streckt eenen nieuwen boge te metselen, de balusters daer op te stellen ende deselve te plaveijen, den trap vande selve brugge te leggen, als om vast te stellen alle de bollen die op de pedestallen vande ballustrade boven opde gallerie comen …

1042 fol. 244 (Slothouwer, p. 264)
Betaelt aen Arent Arensz. sGravesandt, architect ende schrijnwercker de somme van vierende twintich ponden overt maecken ende hermaken van een houten model ter ordonnantie vanden architect la Vallee, diennende tot den grooten trap te Honselerdijck …

1042 fol. 244 verso (Slothouwer, p. 264)
Betaelt aen Huijch Jansz, weerdt te Honselerdijck de somme van drie endertich ponden twaelff schellingen artois, over de verteringe tot sijnent gedaen bijden rendant, neffens den rentm^r Catshuisen, Jacques de la Valle architect, den Fransen hovenier ende eenige werkmrs, tot diverse reisen inde maenden Julij, Augusti, September ende October XVI^C drie en dertich, daerinne mede begrepen sijnde het staen van des rendants peert

1042 fol. 246
Betaelt aen Maertijn Leenderts Vischcoopster de somme van hondert drie en sestich ponden artois voor leverantie van een quantiteit van Snoecken, Carpers ende andere rivieren visch bij Sijne Controlleur Montaigne door last van Hare Hoocheit gecocht ende inde grachten vant huijs te Honsholredijck doen setten … CLXIII £

1042 fol. 247 verso
Betaelt aen Gijsbrecht Thonissen hovenier van Sijnne hoocheit te Honsholredijck de somme van twee hondert vijfftich ponden artois te weeten II^C £ denselven bij die van Sijne hoocheits Raeden toegevoecht tot onderhout vande twee nieuwe parterren d'eene van zoden, schelpen, rooden gestampten steen ende palm, ende d'ander van palm alleen, die aldaer in den voorsomer van 't Jaer tijde deser ende hier voorsz. vereeckent sijn ende dat vanden eersten aff dat deselve sijn gemaeckt tot op lesten december XVI^C drie en dertich, ende de verdere L £ voor dachgelden van denselven Gijsbrecht Tonissen ende andere bij hem geemployt tot het planten van de voorsz parterres …
Decembris [1633] … II^C L £

1042 fol. 248
Betaelt aen Arien Philipsz. metselaer de somme van twee ende twintich ponden omme het plaveijen van een gedeelte vant padt inden tuijn voor de trap van de brugge als men vant huijs in den hoff comt, als voor eenig ander buijtenwercken … XXII £

1042 fol. 250
Vergoet aen Andre Mollet opsichter van Sijne hoocheits Tuijnen, de somme van ses ponden tien schellingen voor wagenvracht ende teercosten gaende in December XVI^C drie en dertich ten dienste van voorscreve gebouw naer honsholredijck … VI £ X sts

Expenditures buildings & gardens 1633   XIX^M IX^C LXXXVII £ XIIII sts III dr

1042 fol. 253 verso
Betaelt de somme van drie en sestich ponden soo voor leverantie van twaelff wagens [?] soo schelpen, als voor vracht vande selve ende eenige fruitboomen van hier [Den Haag/Honselaarsdijk] naer Bueren te voeren … Martio 1633 … LXIII £

1042 fol. 254
Betaelt de somme van seven en seventich ponden soo over leverantie van twaelff vijgeboomen a vijf ponden tien schellingen tstuck en verder in den thuijn van Bueren gestelt sijn, als oock eenig andere werck … [?] ten dienste van t' huijs aldaer gedaen … May XVI^C drie en dertich LXXVII £

1042 fol. 254 verso
Betaelt aen Gijsbrecht Thonissen hovenier de somme van negen ende vijfftich ponden artois voor twintich persick ende negen abricoos boomen bij hem in de Thuijn tot Bueren gelevert … September sestien hondert drie en dertich tijde deser … LIX £

1042 fol. 343
Betaelt aen Catarina Cray weduwe van wijlen Mr Simon Stevin de somme van vier hondert ponden artois omme een jaer lijfpensie bij Sijnne furstel Gen. Prince Maurits H. L. M. ten lijve van Frederick, Hendrick, Susanna ende Levina haere kinderen toegevoecht … lesten December XVI drie en dertich … IIII^C £

1042 fol. 344 verso
Betaelt aen Jacquis de la Vallee frans architect d'somme van vier hondert ponden hem bij Monsr de Vaulfin [?] door last van S. hooch^t belooft tot reisgelt ende vacatien om sich alhier te comen vertoonen volgens 't accoort met hem dienaengaende aengegaen … Juny [1633] … IIII^C £

NDR, inv. no. 1043 [782] (year 1634)

1043 fol. 21
Betaelt aen Hendrick Kermir schipper van Koevoort d'somme van twee hondert vijfftich ponden voor vracht van 4000 beuckenboomen, 2000 jonge heesters, ende eenige jonge plantsoenen bij hem uijt de Graefschap Meurs tot Delft toe gebracht om te Honselerdijck geplant te worden [Febr. 1634].. II^C L £

1043 fol. 215 verso
… verscheiden schuijtvoerders van Diest d'somme van eenenvijfftich ponden tien schellingen voor schuitvracht vande voorscreve boomen van Diest tot honselerdijck te brengen … [Febr. 1634] … LI £ x sts

APPENDIX HONSELAARSDIJK

1043 fol. 218 (only partly in Slothouwer, p. 265)
Betaelt aen Andre Mollet opsichter van Sijnne Hoocheits thuijnen de somme van sessendertich ponden, over verteerde costen bij hem in vijff dagen te Honselerdijck gedaen, om het nieu perck aldaer te doen als voor verscheijden wagenvrachten bij den selven verstreckt …
April 1634 … XXXVI £

1043 fol. 218 verso
Betaelt aen Arent Pietersz. Blom de somme van acht hondert twintich ponden elf schellingen voor XIX^C XXIIII abeel heesters ende III^C LIIII Ypen heijsters om te Honselerdijck int nieuwe perck te stellen, bij den selven Blom op diverse plaetsen gecost als voor eenige reiscosten ende vrachten bij hem verleit … VIII^C LXX £ XI sts

1043 fol. 219
Betaelt aen Cornelis van der Veen timmerman de somme van achthondert voor de gerede penningen hem belooft over het maecken van een plancken heijninge rontsomme het nieuwe aengevangen parck te Honselerdijck … Aprillis [1634] … VIII^C £

1043 fol. 219 verso
Betaelt aen Willem Jacobssen, Wouter Heijndricz ende Jan Jacobssen de somme van drie hondert ponden ter saecke sijluiden in de twee Thuinen van huis Honselerdijck aengenomen hebben te maecken leveren ende stellen vier en dertich greinnen houte bogen oft arcaden henluiden bij den Controlleur 'sHerwouters aenbesteet … III^C £

1043 fol. 220
Betaelt aen Arien Nijben, Jan Cornelissen ende Tonis Jasparsz. t'samen de somme van vierhondert veertich ponden veertien schillingen over elsen ende willigen boomen die sijluiden to het nieuwe perck van Sijnne hoocheit te Honselerdijck gelevert hebben … Aprillis [1634] …
IIII^C XL £ XIIII sts

1043 fol. 221 verso
Betaelt aen Gijsbrecht Tonissen ende Jan Harmisz. tsamen de somme van drie hondert seven ende tseventich ponden vier schillingen over leverantie van aelbessen, flamboisen, ijpen, roosch haselaer ende andere boomen omme int nieuwe parck te Honselerdijck te planten … Junij XVI^C vierendertich … III^C LXX VII £ IIII sts

1043 fol. 223 verso (Slothouwer, p. 265)
Vergoet aen Joachim de Wickevoort coopman tot Amsterdam de somme van drie hondert ses en twintich ponden tien schellingen bij hem betaelt aen Artus Quellinus beelthouwer tot Antwerpen over twee hartstene beelden eenen Mars ende eenen Venus beijde grooter als t leven …

1043 fol. 224 verso
Betaelt aen Cornelis Beron schipper van Lillo de somme van twintich ponden voor schipvracht van de selve beelden van Lillo in den hage te brengen … XX £

1043 fol. 225 (Slothouwer, p. 265)
Betaelt aen Otto Reijerssen beeltsnijder de somme van twee en vijfftigh ponden tien schellingen ter saecke hij te Honselerdijck gebronseert heeft drie groote hardtsteene beelden, waervan opde open gallerie naer den Thuin ende tderde int Westel parterre staen …

1043 fol. 225 verso
Betaelt aen André Mollet opsichter van Sijne hoocheits Thuijnen de somme van elff ponden tien schellingen over reiscosten bij hem verleijt in de maenden Meij, Junij ende Julij XVI^C vierendertich naer Honselerdijck om de thuijnen ende plantage aldaer te beleijden …
Augusto 1634 … XI £ X sts.

1043 fol. 226 verso (Slothouwer, p. 265)
Betaelt de somme van vijftien ponden twaelff schellingen voor verteeringen gedaen bij wijlen den Raedt ende Tresorier Brouart beneffens mr. Evert [E. van der Maes] schilder, Gerrit Druivestein architect, Allert Claessen smith, la Vallee architect ende Arent Arentsen teijckenaer gesamentlick te Honselerdijck tot directie vande wercken aldaer geweest sijnde …

1043 fol. 227 (Slothouwer, p. 265)
Vergoet aen Arent Arentssen s Gravesant teijckenaer de somme van ses en twintich ponden negentien schellingen voor reis ende teercosten bij hem verleit, gaende in Julio ende Augusto jaers deser reeckeninge ten dienste ende vorderinge vande gebouwen te Honselerdijck ende Rijswijck verscheijden reisen naer Amsterdam, Leijden, Delft …

1043 fol. 228 verso (Slothouwer, p. 266)
Betaelt aen Hans Bogaert schilder de somme van hondert dertich ponden, ter saecke hij met olijverwe geschildert heeft de nieu houte boogen die Sijnne Hoocheit te Honsholredijck inden thuin geordonneert heeft te doen maken als mede dat hij gerootverft heeft de balustrade op de brugge aende sijde vanden hoff, item de ciersels op de tirasse vant huis siende opden hoff waer inne twee steene gebronseerde figuren gestelt sijn …

1043 fol. 229 verso
Betaelt aen Wouter Hendricsz. ende Willem Heijningen timmerlieden de somme van vijff hondert vijff ponden in voldoeninge van VIII^C V £ die sijluiden bij besteck bedongen hadden voor vijffendertich greinen houte boogen off arcaden bij haer gemaeckt ende gestelt in de twee thuijnen van de parterres aan wedersijden van het huis te Honselerdijck … December 1634 … V^C V £

1043 fol. 232
Betaelt aen Arent Laurenssen Timmerman d'somme van CVIII £ voor vier houte Bogen bij hem tot patroonen gemaeckt ende gelevert om inden Tuijn van huis te Honselerdijck te stellen …
Meert 1634 … CVIII £

1043 fol. 232 verso (Slothouwer, p. 266)
Betaelt aen Joseph Dinant fontenier d'somme van CL £ over het pampier werck bij hem gemaeckt ende gelevert welck bij Sijn Hooch^t geordonneert was totde camer ende cabinet van Hare Hooch^t opt huijs te Honselerdijck ende naermaels niet en gedient heeft …

1043 fol. 232 (Slothouwer, p. 267)
Betaelt aen Evert vande Maes schilder alhier inden Hage d'somme van XX £ over verscheide teickeningen bij hem gemaeckt tot de ciersels vant gebouw te Honselerdijck als andersints …

1043 fol. 232
Betaelt aen Gijsbrecht Tonissen hovenier tot Honselerdijck de somme van twee hondert ponden voor soo verre hem bij die van Sijne hoocheits Raden Jaerlicx toegevoucht is voor het onderhouden van twee nieuwe parterres in den Tuijn aenden huijse te Honsholredijck door de directie van André Mollet gemaeckt …

1043 fol. 233 verso
Aen Symon Catshuijsen wegens de slooten sijner reeckeninge is noch vergoet de somme van drie duijsent hondert ses en veertich ponden seven schellingen twee dernier over de wercken, reparatien ende onderhoudingen aen ende ten dienste van Honselerdijck in den Jare XVI^C vierendertich gemaeckt ende gedaen als namentlijck aen Timmer ende Schrijnwerck …

… aen de ijser ende cooper werck	CXVIIII £ III sts X dr.
… aen steen ende metselwerck	LXXVIII £ XVIII sts VI dr.
… aen schilderwerck ende vergultwerck	LXXII £ I sts
… aen meubeleren van huise	XXII £ XII sts
… aen bier voor de arbeiders	CXXIX £
… aen reparatien aende glasen	CXIIII £ VI sts VIII dr.
… aen reparatien vande daecken	LXVIII £ XIX sts
… aen d'onderhoudinge van de hoff	IIII^C XXXIII £ IX sts VIII dr.
… voort schoonmaecken vande huise	IX^C XL £ V sts IIII dr.
… voort onderhout van de Carpers	XII £
… aen extraordinaris partijen	IIII^C LXXVIII £ VII sts VIII dr.

Bedragende de bovenstaende partien tsamen ter voorsz. somme van drie duijsent hondert ses en veertich ponden seven schellingen ende twee dernier … III^M CXLVI £ VII sts II dr.

1043 fol. 235
Aen voornoemde Catshuijsen noch vergoet de somme van dertien hondert een ponden vier schellingen acht dernier voor … tot onderhoudinge ende verbeteringe vande warande aende huise te Honselerdijck …

1043 fol. 236 verso (Slothouwer, p. 267)
Betaelt aen Hendrick Cornelisz. Bilderbeeck ende Pieter Pietersz. Deneijn aennemers vande hardtsteene balustrade inden thuin tot Honselerdijck volgens den bestecke in date den IXe Octob. XVI^C vierendertich de somme van drie duisent vier hondert ponden …

1043 fol. 239 verso
Betaelt aende weduwe van wijlen Cornelis Matternissen Timmerman de somme van elffhondert vijffenveertich ponden veertien schellingen negen dernier per restende in voldoeninge van II^C IXI roeden vijff voeten houten heijninge als van pecken ende branden vande palen totte selve heijninge bij hem om 't parck te Honselerdijck gemaeckt volgens 't besteck … Augusto 1636 … XI^C XLV £ XIII sts IX dr.

1043 fol. 243
Betaelt aen André Mollet opsichter van Sijne Hoocheits Thuijnen de somme van sesentwintich ponden veertien schellingen voor reijs ende teercosten bij hem verleit, gaende door last van S.H. naer Suilesteijn om de Thuijnen aldaer te besichtigen … Martij XVI^C vierendertich … XXVI £ XIIII sts

BOUW, ONDERHOUD EN BESTEKKEN. BUILDING, UPKEEP AND ESTIMATES

NDR, inv. no. 6743 [7146] (year 1636) (Slothouwer, p. 267)

Op huijden den 11e Januarij 1636 heeft mr Jan Vos woonachtich tot Haerlem aengenomen ter bestedinge van de H^{re} van Zuijlichem ende J. van Campen uijt den name van S. Exc^{ie} binnen de maendt Aprillis naestcommende tot Honsholredijck te leveren ende in de groote frontispice aldaer te voegen twaelff kindertjens halff rond gehouwen in bequamen Bentemer steen volgens de teeckeninge hem daer van te leveren, bij den voorn. H^r van Campen tot genoegen van den welcken hij aenemer yder van derselver kindertjens alvoorens van eerde sal hebben te boetseren ende vorders ter approbatie vanden selve op te maecken, welverstaende dat yder kind binnen den muur gestelt sal wesen ter diepte van thien rijnlandtsche duijmen. Ende sal hem aennemer voor yder der voorn. kinderen betaelt worden de somme van ses ende dertich Carls guld^s te voldoen, de eene helft wanneer hij bewijsen sal de helft van sijn werck volhouwen te hebben ende de resterende helft wanneer hij het ganttsche werck vollvoert ende als vooren inden muijr sal hebben gevoecht. Waertoe hem buijten sijnen laste de steijgeringe sal werden gestelt, alsmede een oftemeer metselaers toegevoecht naer hij van noode sal hebben. Endtelijck sal hij noch in consideratie vande vragt van Haerlem op Honsholredijck genieten een vereeringe van thien Guldens sonder yetwes meer, hoedanich het soude mogen wesen van hoochgemelte Sijne Ex^{cie} desen aengaende te pretenderen. Aldus gedaen ter goeder trouwen bij de voorz. Besteders ende aennemer geteeckent in 's-Gravenhage ter dage ende jaere alsboven. Ende was onde^t C. Huygens J. van Campen Czn. ... Jan Janszoon de Vos den aennemer is ordonnantie verleent in voldoeninge van dit Bestek den 6 Augusti 1636 gedepecheert bij S. Raedt Huygens.

ACCOUNTS OF THE COMPTROLLER, DECREES OF THE COUNCIL, continued

NDR, inv. no. 992 [735] (years 1635-1640):

992 fol. 14
Otto Reijersz. Schaijck, potbacker, over geleverde blompotten ende commen bij hem inden Thuijn van Honsholredijck gelevert ... April 1637 ... 365:10:0

992 fol. 15
... te betaelen uijt de penningen vande zeeprinsen aen Alewijn Claessen van Assendelft, de somme van seven hondert drijendertich guldens ses stuijvers, zes deniers, over de eersten termijn van drijen vande somme van 2200 gul. ... voor het beschieten met wage schot vande gewulffde sael tot Honsholredijck met sijn pijlasters, lijsten ende anders ... 17 April 1637

992 fol. 19
... Bartholomeus en Laurens Drijffhout over het cieren van de bordestrap op Honsholredijck, soo in hartsteen, hout als metselwerck ordonneert ...
Maert en April 1637 ... 520:10:0

992 fol. 36 (Slothouwer, p. 268)
... te betaelen uijt de penningen procederende vande zeeprinsen aen Pieter Cornelissen van Kouwenhoven, timmerman ende Claes Dirckxsen Dorthoven, metselaer, de somme van twee duijsent twee hondert guldens, in voldoeninge vanden tweeden ende derden lesten termijn haer competerende over het opmaecken ende voltrecken vant speelhuijs inden Noordwesthouck vant bosch tot Honsholredijck ...
15 Junij 1637

992 fol. 36
... te betaelen aen Nicolaes Smijter een duysent acht hondert vijffentwintich guls. over het maken van seker aerdewerck van slooten en wallen om de warande aent huijs te Honsholredijck, bestaende in drijhondert vijffentsestich roeden tot thien guls de roede volgens de besteck daervan sijnde in dato April 1637

992 fol. 53
... Aen Hilario Oliva de somme van seshondert vierentsestich guls. over ses en dertich Orange ende Citroenboomen, midtsgaeders twee Chineesche boomkens bij hem ten dienste van Sijne Hooch^t gelevert, de Orange ende Citroen boomen tot achtien guldens t stuck, ende de twee Chineesche ter acht guls. t stuck, beloopende tsamen de voorn. somme van 664:0:0

992 fol. 58
... Jacob Mesen Holsteijn Pr Jansz. en Willem Michilsz. alle aerdewerckers de somme van achthondert vijffenvijfftich guls. dat sijluyden hebben gemaeckt ende voltrocken tot Honsholredijck 't verwijden vande binnengracht op de oostzijde langs de nieuwe wal vande warande van acht op twintich voeten volgens 't bovenstaende Besteck in dato ...
13 Julij 1637 ... 855:0:0

992 fols. 51 and 52
... aankoop van d'Erfgenamen van 'tWeeskindt van Boon Dircxz Bosch ende Geertchen Claesz. over Coop van Wooninge met aller der landen daeronder gehoorende aller gelegen inden ambachte van Naeltwijck ... Sept. 1637 ... 10705:0:0

992 fol. 59
... Betaelinge aen Pieter Philipsz. Heemskerck de somme van sestien hondert guls. van acht hondt Landts leggende tot Honsholredijck binnen de vacken en zayingen daervan gemaeckt ende bij den landtmeter op de caerte gefigureert, bij Sijne Hooch^t van voorn. Pieter Philipsz. van Heemskerck gecocht tot twaelff hondert gul. den morgen, omme geappliceert te werden tot vegrootinge vande warande aende voorsz. huijse van Honsholredijck, volgens den bovenstaende contracte ...

Alsoo bij Acte van metinge gedaen bij geswooren landtmeter Pieter Florisz. van der Salm op den 7 Maert 1637 dese partije landts groot is bevonden acht hondt een en veertich roeden, soo moet desen ordonn. verhoocht worden volgens de conditien met LXXXII guls, en dien volg. ende tsamen aende vercooper betaelt werden sestienhondert twee ende tachtich carolus guldens ... 1682:0:0

992 fol. 60
... Conditien vant op 8 hont ende 141 roeden lants gelegen onder Honsholredijck bij Sijne Hooch^t gecocht van Pieter Pietersz. 't Hart Junij 1637 ... 1357:12:10

992 fol. 61
… Pieter Adriaensz. Coningh, over coop van sijne hoffstede met ses hondt landts gelegen op Honsholredijck … 2115:0:0

992 fol. 67
… Nicolaes de Smijter vant voltrecken ende opleveren vande wal ende slooten om de warande tot Honsholredijck lesten 4e termijn, met een vereeckeninge van 100 gul. … 1032:1:8

992 fol. 71
… Dirck de Milde Boschbewaerder tot Honsholredijck op sijne declaratie van oncosten gevallen inde maendt Nov. 1637 … 124:10:0

992 fol. 100
… Dirck de Milde Boschbewaerder tot Honsholredijck over de oncosten gevallen in de boschen gedurende de maend Dec. 1637 … 48:15:0

992 fol. 105
… Dirck de Milde Boschbewaerder tot Honsholredijck over de oncosten gevallen in de boschen gedurende de maend Jan. 1638 … 49:18:0

992 fol. 113
… Dirck de Milde Boschbewaerder tot Honsholredijck over de oncosten gevallen in de boschen gedurende de maend Febr. 1638 … 55:10:0

992 fol. 133 (Slothouwer, p. 269)
… omme te betaelen uijt de penningen vande zeeprinsen, aenden selven Nicolaes van Beijeren de somme van drije hondert tseventich Car. guldens, soo ter saecke van drije steene kinderkens, te weten twee van Italiaensche marber ende een van pleijster, bij hem vercocht voorde somme van twee hondert twintich guldens alsmede over ses antijcke hooffden met corpusden van pleijster bij hem vercocht voorde somme van hondert vijftich guldens, maeckende tsamen de voorn. somme van drij hondert ende tseventich guldens, dewelcke bij de voorn. van Beijeren ten dienste van Sijne Hooch[t] sijn gelevert opden huijse van Honsholredijck … 23 April 1638

992 fol. 141
… Pieter Philipsz. Heemskerck over coop van vier morgen een hondt Teelandts gelegen tussen Honsholredijck en Naeltwijck … 4733:6:8

992 fol. 141 [a]
Oncosten …aen rentm[r] Catshuijsen gevallen inde Bosschen ende Warande van Sijne Hooch[t] tot Honsholredijck … 102:16:0

992 fol. 142
Contract van coop van drie morgen 3 hont vrij patrimoniael lant, gelegen tussen Naeltwijck ende Honsholredijck.
Den XXI May 1638 … aen Juff[r] Angenieta van Cockelbergch weduw wijlen secretaris van Wijll … eerst de somme van dry duysent drie hondert vijffentwintich guls. … 3361:0:0

992 fol. 142 [a] (Slothouwer, p. 269)
… Alsoo Pieter Cornelissen van Couwenhoven, timmerman aengenomen heeft … te maecken ende leveren alle het houtwerck tot de maliebaan voor onsen huijse van Honsholredijck, lanck omtent 200 twintich roeden met het ijserwerck daertoe dienende, item een greene brugge over de vaert, die de maliebaan traverseert, den hoop voor de somme van seventhien hondert vijffentwintich Car. guldens … Maer alsoo de voorn. maliebaen bij meetinge is bevonden 15 roeden corter te wesen als twee hondert twintich roeden, waervoor den aennemer volgens de conditien moet gecort werden van yeder roede vijff gul. acht stuijvers … 30 Julij 1638 … 1725:0:0

992 fol. 143
… Dirck de Milde Boschbewaerder tot Honsholredijck van de oncosten gevallen in de Boschen aldaer [Honsholredijck] gedurende de maend April 1638 ter somme van een hondert en twintich gulden drie stuyvers … 120:3:0

992 fol. 144
… te betaelen uijtte penningen procederende vande zeeprinsen aen Bruijn Arentsz., Ary Jacobsz., Franck Janssen ende Jaspar Janssen, aerdewerckers, de somme van acht hondert guldens, over den eersten en derden termijn hen competerende volgens de bovenstaende attestatie als aengenomen hebbende het maken van een maliebaan inde laen off dreve gelegen aende Zuijdtzijde vant huijs Honsholredijck …
XXII May 1638

992 fol. 145
… Gijsbrecht Teunissen hovenier … omme uyt de penningen vande zeeprinsen te betaelen aende selve Gijsbrecht Teunissen de somme van elff hondert negenentzeventich Carolus guldens negentien sts 6 dr. Ter sake van 2969 ypeboomen à 6 sts 't stuck bij hem ten dienste van Sijne Hooch[t] in den Jare 1637 gelevert tot de plantagie vande nieuwe warande tot Honsholredijck …
[May 1638] … 1179:19:6

992 fol. 146 [a]
… Anthonis Dircksen Clock woonende tot Leyden … omme uyt de penningen vande zeeprinsen te betalen aen selven Anthonis Dircksen Clock de somme van seven hondert seventien Carolus guldens seventien stuyvers, ter sake van 100 abele boomen à 10 sts 't stuck, 30 ypeboomen à 9 sts tstuck, met 55000 else boomkens het duysent tot 9 gulds 10 sts, bij hem in dienst van Sijne Hooch[t] in den Jare 1638 gelevert tot de plantagie vande warande tot Honsholredijck
[May 1638] … 717:17:0

992 fol. 146 [b]
… Gijsbrecht Thonisz. de somme van hondert vier en dertich gulden negen stuyvers ter sake van verscheyde perzick, abricosen als kerse boomen bij den selve ten dienste van Sijne Hooch^t in de nieuwe Thuijn tot Honsholredijck soo in den voorleden Jare 1637 als in den Jare 1638 gelevert … 134:9:0

992 fol. 146 [c]
… Symon Jansz. Patijn …aengenomen heeft het vollen van sekere sloot lanch ontrent vijfftich roeden, gelegen aende westzijde vande Laen voor de huijse van Honsholredijck, voor de somme van twee hondert car. guldens.

992 fol. 147
… Dirck Janssen Metselaer volgens bovenstaend besteck in dato October 1637 aengenomen heeft het straetwerck op de Nederhoff vande huijse van Honsholredijck te verleggen daert gesackt was, voor de somme van sesentachtich guls twaelff stuyvers … 86:12:0

992 fol. 148 [a] (Slothouwer, p. 269)
Alsoo Anthonis Gerritsz. timmerman … aengenomen heeft het maecken van twee houte balustraden voor de parterre Thuijnen tot Honsholredijck ter lenghte van 26 roeden, item acht cabinetten met palen ende latten te besetten, alles voor de somme van hondert vierentwintich Carolus guldens
23 Mei 1638 … 124:0:0

992 fol. 148 [b]
… Jaspar Jansz, Jacob Meesen Holsteyn, Pieter Jansz. ende Willem Michielsz. aerdewerckers … eenige aerdewercken inde nieuwe warande aende huijse tot Honsholredijck als namentlijck tmacken van Grippen, hoogen ende effenen vande paden, ende het toehalen ofte vullen vande onder slooten, te samen voor de somme van twee duysent vier hondert Carolus gulds. … 2400:0:0

992 fol. 148 [c]
… omme te tellen aen Hilario Olive [cf 992 fol. 53] de somme van vijfftich car. guls. die Sijne Hooch^t den selven is schenckende … 50:0:0

992 fol. 149 [a]
Alsoo Bastiaen Jansz. ende Hendrick Claessen van Rijn volgens de bovenstaende conditie in dato 1 Aprilis 1638 aengenomen heeft het uytlagen van twee Elstackers gelegen aen de oostzijde vande oude warande van Honsholredijck en met deselve aerde de paden aldaer op te hoogen voor de somme van … 225:10:0

992 fol. 149 [b]
… Dirck de Milde opsichter vande warande te Honsholredijck … oncosten
Julij 1638 …152:14

992 fol. 149 [c]
… Dirck de Milde opsichter vande warande te Honsholredijck sal doen maken een Tortelduyvenhock midtgaders vijff houten roosters in de gracht vande warande om visch daerin te houden … bedragende Timmerwerck de somme van 162 guls 11 sts en anders vant IJserwerck 47 guls 13 sts, makende tsamen tweehondert tien guls. vier sts.
Julij/Augusto 1638 …210:4:0

992 fol. 155
… Dirck de Milde Boschbewaerder tot Honsholredijck van de oncosten gevallen in de Boschen ende warande van Honsholredijck in de maend May 1638

992 fol. 177
… Dirck de Milde opsichter vande waranden te Honsholredijck … oncosten
October 1638

992 fol. 178
Betaelt aen Bartholomeus Drijffhout Steenhr. over de arbeijdt, reys en teercosten bij hem gedaen ende verschooten ten dienste van Sijne Hoocheit int halen tot diverse reysen van Amsterdam eerst eenige steene kinderkens, dewelcke heeft gebracht ende gevoert op den huijse van Honsholredijck ende andersinds alsmede noch eenige marmere figuren mede bij hem gevoert op den huijse Ter Nieuburch in den Jaere 1638 … 89:0:0

992 fol. 185 [a] (Slothouwer, p. 270)
… te betalen uijt de penningen vande zeeprinsen aen Pieter 't Hooft, de somme van een hondert twee ende vijfftich guldens, over leverantie van twee hertsteen honden met drije kinderkens bij hem gelevert ende gestelt op pilasters opde brugge ende bovende poort voor de huijse van Sijne Hooch^t tot Honsholredijck, uytwijsende de bovenstaende cedulle ende attestatie van Van Campen
3 December 1638 … 152:0:0

992 fol. 185 [b]
… Dirck de Milde opsichter vande bosschen ende warande van Honsholredijck oncosten in de maendt November 1638 … 45:1:0

992 fol. 188
… aen Bartholomeus Drijffhout steenhouwer de somme van vier en dertich guldens, ter sake van eenige reparatien aende Huijse van Honsholredijck, 't maecken van een standt teekening van 't voorste vanden selve Huijse …
Dec 1638 … 34:0:0

992 fol. 192
… silverwerck t'welck Monsr de Lopez tot Parijs ten dienste van Sijne

Hooch^t heeft doen maecken ende alhier overgesonden ende ontfangen is …
Dec. 1638 … 18341 gul 13 sts

992 fol. 228
… Dirck de Milde opsichter vande bosschen ende warande van Honsholredijck …

992 fol. 233
… aen Pieter Florisz. vander Salm Landtmeter de somme van 66 gulds, over de caert bij hem gemaeckt ende gecopieert ten dienste van Sijne Hooch^t … 66:0:0

992 fol. 241
… Dirck Pietersz. Vischcooper de somme van hondert drij en veertich car. gul. over leverantie van vande snoucken, carpers en andere riviervisch dewelck op XIIII en XXV Nov. 1638 bij Dirck Pietersz. sijn gelevert inde wateringe achter de warande van Sijne Hooch^t tot Honsholredijck … 143:0:0

992 fol. 242 (Slothouwer, p. 333)
Den XVII februarij 1639 is gedeponeert ordonnan op d'attestatie van d'heer van Zuylichem ten behoeve van de schilder Rembrandt als volgt. Sijne Hooch^t ordonneert aen Thijman van Volbergen sijn Tresorier ende Rentm^r Gnael. te betaelen aenden schilder Rembrandt, de somme van twaelff hondert vier en dertich Carolus guldens, over twee stucken schilderij wesende t'eene de begraeffenisse ende het ander de Verrijsenisse van onse Heer Christus, bij hem gemaeckt ende gelevert aen Sijne Hooch^t … 1234:0:0

992 fol. 247
… Dirck de Milde opsichter vande bosschen ende warande van Honsholredijck oncosten in de maendt Februarij 1639 … 35:16:0

992 fol. 255
Den IXde Maert 1639 … te betaelen aen Daniel Jacob de somme van vierhondert sesentachtich guls. thien stuyvers over de fruijtboomen bij hem gebracht uijt Vranckrijck ende gelevert ten dienste van Sijne Hooch^t … Tyman van Volbergen ende Controll. s'Herwouters … 486:10:0

992 fol. 259
… Dirck de Milde opsichter vande bosschen ende warande van Honsholredijck oncosten in de maendt Febr. 1638 … 80:16:0

992 fol. 260
Theunis Gerritsz. Timmerman aengenomen heeft … het maecken van beyde de hecken aen het Bosch ofte Warande van Honsholredijck voor de somme van 100 car. gul.

992 fol. 261 (Slothouwer, p. 271)
… Alsoo Anthonis Gerritsz. timmerman, aengenomen heeft … het maken vande bancken in acht cabinetten opde huijse tot Honsholredijck voor de somme van acht hondert Carolus guldens … 21 Mrt. 1638 … 800:0:0

992 fol. 263
… Catshuijsen 1639 te Honsholredijck wesende … 123:6:0

992 fol. 267
… Gijbrecht Theunissen, hovenier tot Honsholredijck de somme van drij en vijfftich guls. sesthien stuyvers ter sake van roseboomen, bremboisen ende planten van camperfoelje bij hem gelevert ten dienste van Sijne Hooch^t in den Jaere 1639 tot Honsholredijck … 53:16:0

992 fol. 268
… Dirck de Milde opsichter vande bosschen ende warande van Honsholredijck oncosten in de maendt Februarij 1639 … 72:2:8

992 fol. 269
… Dirck Pietersz. Viscooper de somme van sevenenvijfftich guls. over leverantie van snoecken ende andere cleynvisch gelevert tot Honsholredijck [febr. 1639] … 72:2:8

992 fol. 271
… Theunis Dirckz Clock de somme van negen hondert vijffendertich guls. elff stuyvers over de Ypen ende Abeele midtsgaders fruijtboomen bij hem gelevert ten dienste van Sijne Hooch^t tot Honsholredijck in den Jaeren 1638 ende 1639 … 935:11:0

992 fol. 272
… Dirck de Milde … in dato XXI feb. 1639, het maecken van een houte koye om fesanten, patrijzen, quartels ende tortelduyven in te houden in de warande tot Honsholredijck … 468:0:0

992 fol. 277
Den 13. May 1639 Is gedeponeert opt Billet van Bartholomeus Drijffhout geattesteert bij Sr. van Campen, ordonnans als volcht, Sijne Hooch^t ordonneert hiermede sijne Tres^r ende Rentm^r Gnael. Thijman van Volbergen te betaelen uyt de Zeeprinsen, aen Bartholomeus Drijffhout mr. steenhouwer … de somme van twee ende vijfftich guls. sesthien stuyvers over den arbeij bij hem ende sijn knechts gedaen int ontpacken ende opt landt in een Thuijn dragen van alle de gegoten beelden ende tronijen, dewelcke uyt Vranckrijck aen Sijne Hooch^t gecoomen sijn, daer van hij negen beelden tot Honsholredijck gebracht ende gecost heeft als anders, beiden blijkende bij 't billet aen d'andere sijde vermelt 3 May 1639 … 52:16:0

992 fol. 278
Den XIII May 1639 Is gedeponeert opt Billet van Bartholomeus Drijffhout geattesteert bij Sr. van Campen, ordonnans als volcht, Sijne Hooch[t] ordonneert hiermede sijne Tres[r] ende Rentm[r] Gnael. Thijman van Volbergen te betalen uyt de penningen van de Zeeprinsen aen Bartholomeus Drijffhout de somme van sestich guls. een sts. vier dr. over 't geene hij heeft gedaen ende verschoten int vervoeren naer Honsholredijck ende aldaer met sijn knechts op petestalen vast te setten eenige potten en beelden etc. ende 't maecken van een Besteck vande stallingen, Gallerije ende Coetshuijsen dienend op Capel werff zullende te maecken, als over 't maecken vande Caerte van 't binnen ende buytenhoff mitsgaders de Vijverbergh ende andersints breedt blijckende bij bovenstaande declaratie ende attestatie van Sr van Campen
… 60:1:4

992 fol. 278
… te betalen uyt de penningen vande Zeeprinsen aen Bartholomeus Drijffhout de somme van vierendertich guls. over t maecken ende overslaen van eenige Bestecken ende Teeckeningen soo van Stallinge, aen de Zuydzijde vant huys tot Honsholredijck als van de heynwerck om de Thuijn ende Cappelle werff aldaer … 34:0:0

992 fol. 282
… uyt de penningen van de Zeeprinsen te betalen aen Anthonis Gerritsz. Timmerman de somme van seventhien guls. sesthien stuyvers achtien p. over arbeyt ende gelevert hout bij hem gedaen in het afschulten van een wijnkelder op onse huyse van Honsholredijck
… 17:16:18

992 fol. 282
… uyt de penningen van de Zeeprinsen te betalen aen Anthonis Gerritsz. Timmerman de somme van twintich gul. drij stuyvers over arbeijt ende gelevert hout bij hem gedaen in het afschulten vande nieuwe plantagie bij het Bosch aen onse huyse tot Honsholredijck
… 20:3:0

992 fol. 285
… Dirck de Milde opsichter vande bosschen ende warande van Honsholredijck oncosten in de maendt April 1639

992 fol. 285
… Arent Pietersz. Blom, de somme van drijentseventich guls. twee stuyvers over verscheyde planten, bloemen ende saet bij hem gelevert ten dienste van Sijne Hooch[t] ende geplant inde Thuijn tot Honsholredijck
[April 1639] … 73:2:0

992 fol. 287
… aen Juffrouwe Johanna van Schreve [Sneeck?] weduwe van wijlen Jacob vander Burch van Oudaen … eerste de somme van tweeduysent achtenegentich guls. waer op dat beloopen de cooppenning van twee margen vijff hondt eenentwintich roeden vrij patrimoniaal landt gelegen int ambacht van Naeltwijck, bij Sijne Hooch[t] van haer luyden in qualiteit voorsz. gecocht tot 700 Car. gul. den mergen volgens den bovenstaende contracte in dato XVIII Aprilis 1639

992 fol. 290
… Dirck de Milde opsichter vande bosschen ende warande van Honsholredijck oncosten in de maendt May 1639 … 148:1:8

992 fol. 297
… Dirck de Milde opsichter vande bosschen ende warande van Honsholredijck oncosten in de maendt Junij 1639 … 165:10:0

992 fol. 301
… Dirck de Milde opsichter vande bosschen ende warande van Honsholredijck oncosten in de maendt Julius 1639 … 190:9:0

992 fol. 307
… Dirck de Milde opsichter vande bosschen ende warande van Honsholredijck oncosten in de maendt Augusto 1639 … 171:12:0

992 fol. 313
… Dirck de Milde opsichter vande bosschen ende warande van Honsholredijck oncosten in de maendt September 1639 … 116:3:0

992 fol. 316
… Gerrit Jans van Lier Steenhouwer de somme van een hondert dertich guls. vier sts. over Teyckeninge, besteck ende anders bij hem gedaen van eenige wercken ten dienste van Sijne Hooch[t] gemaeckt soude worden tot Honsholredijck in de Jaren 1638-1639 … 130:4:0

992 fol. 317
Floris Jacobsz. Landtmeter, de somme van vier hondert vijfentachtich guls. vier sts. over verscheyde metingen van Landen, maecken van Caerten, en reyscosten bij hem door Ordre en ten dienste van Sijne Hooch[t] gedaen tot Honsholredijck in de jaren 1636, 37 ende 1638
… 485:4:0

992 fol. 318
… te betaelen aen Dirck Fransz. metselaer, de somme van twee hondert drijenveertich guls seventien stuyvers acht p. over verdiende dachgelden ende verscheyden materialen bij hem door ordre ende ten dienste van Sijne Hooch[t] in Jaere 1639 gelevert tot het maecken ende stellen van achtien pedestallen in desselfs Thuijnen tot Honsholredijck, volgens d'attestatie van Mons[r] van Campen
XVIII Oct. 1639 … 243:17:8

992 fol. 318

… aen Jasper Jansz. woonende tot Rijswijck de somme van sesendertich car. guls. over sekere quantiteyt schelpen bij hem ten dienste van Sijne Hooch^t in den jaere 1639 gelevert ende bij Boschwachter de Milde inde Maliebaan achter den huyse van Honsholredijck verstroijt … 36:0:0

992 fol. 319 (Slothouwer, p. 271)

Alsoo Dirck de Milde aengenoomen heeft … het maecken van een houte duijfhuis inde warande tot Honsholredijck voor de somme van drij hondert en vijftich Car. Gul …
20 Oct. 1639 … 350:0:0

992 fol. 319

… Abraham de Verwer schilder tot Amsterdam de somme van vier hondert car. guls. waermede Sijne Hooch^t de schilder is vereerende, ter sake van twee stucken schilderijs zijnde de Louvre van Parijs in twee verscheijden gesichten bij hem aen Sijne Hooch^t gelevert
XXI Oct. 1639 … 400:0:0

992 fol. 325

… Dirck de Milde opsichter vande bosschen ende warande van Honsholredijck oncosten in de maendt October 1639 … 128:10:0

992 fol. 331

… Dirck de Milde de somme van vijff hondert twee guldern sesthien sts. over 1676 Ypeboomen bij hem gelevert tot ses sts. het stuck ten dienste van Sijne Hooch^t totte plantagie vande oude ende nieuwe warande tot Honsholredijck in desen Jaere 1639
VIII Dec. 1639 … 502:16:0

992 fol. 331

… Dirck de Milde opsichter vande bosschen ende warande van Honsholredijck oncosten in de maendt Novembris 1639
9 Dec. 1639 … 308:3:8

992 fol. 332

… aen Wiquefort, de somme van drij hondert gulden voor een Cristallen commeken met een decksel, drij hondert gul. voor een schelpe van agathe, twee hondert vijftich guld. voor een blompotjen met een deckstel van Cristal, ende vijff hondert gul. voor een ovalen copken met een deckstel van crystall vanden sleven Wiquefort gecocht, monterende tsamen …
XIII Dec. 1639 … 1350:0:0

992 fol. 332

… Balthasar van Engelen de somme van twee hondert tachtich guls. ter sake van een granaat ende vijff orangie boomen bij hem ten dienste van Sijne Hooch^t gelevert in desen Jaere 1639 volgens bovenstaend billet en attestatie vande Controlleur 's Herwouters, 's Gravenhage
XIII Dec. 1639 … 280:0:0

992 fol. 333 (Slothouwer, p. 271)

… te betalen aen Bartholomeus Drijffhout mr. steenhouwer en Pieter Cornelisz. hofftimmerman, de somme van eenentnegentich gul. achtien st. soo over eenige schuijt, wagenvrachten, dachgelden als anders bij haer verschoten ende betaelt int overbrengen van diversche beelden van Rotterdam opden Huijse van Honsholredijck …
6 Dec. 1639 … 91:18:0

992 fol. 333

… Bartholomeus Drijffhout de somme van sesenegentich guls. twaelff sts. over het maecken van modellen ende teeckeningen, 't schrijven ende collationeren van bestecken, mitsgaders leveringe van plaester als anders noodich tot het stellen vande Beelden in desselfs Thuijnen tot Honsholredijck, volgens de declaratie ende attestatie van Sr van Campen aen d'ander sijde deser …
XVI Dec. 1639 … 96:12:0

992 fol. 334

[Contract ende Betaelinge voor aankoop nieuw land bij Naeltwijck] … te betaelen aen Nicolaus van Wouw de somme van ses duysent ses hondert thien car. guldens III sts. IIII dr. metten interest van dien jegens … waerop dat beloopen de cooppenningen van zeven mergen vierhondert seventsestich roeden landt gelegen tusschen Naeltwijck ende Honsholredijck bij Sijne Hooch^t vanden voorsz. van Wouw gecocht tot acht hondert ende vijfftich Car. gul. den margen, volgens den bovenstaende contracte in dato 1 Januarij 1638 .. maeckende tsamen sesduysent sevenhondert vijfftich gulds. III sts. IIII dr.
15 Dec. 1639 … 6760:3:4

992 fol. 335 (Slothouwer, p. 271)

… te betaelen aen Pieter Cornelisz. timmerman en Claes Dircksz. metselaer, de somme van drij hondert tzeventich guldens 15 sts 9 p. over gedaenen arbeijt ende diversche materialen bij haer ten dienste van Sijne Hooch^t … gelevert aent speelhuijs in desselfs warande tot Honsholredijck
22 Dec. 1639 … 377:15:9

992 fol. 336

… te betaelen aen Nicolaes Frederick Mulder, casteleijn vant huijs van Sijn Gen. Graeff Mauritz, de somme van vijff hondert drijenvijfftich car. gul. ter sake van een model vanden huijse van Honsholredijck bij hem gemaeckt ende gelevert ten dienste van Sijne Hooch^t inden jaere 1639 …
27 Dec. 1639 … 553:0:0

992 fol. 337

Alsoo bijde metinge dese Landen gedaen bij geswooren Landtmeter Pieter Florisz. vander Salm volgens d'acto daervan sijnde in dato 14 Jan. 1638 deselve groot sijn bevonden seven mergen en vijffhondert ende

APPENDIX HONSELAARSDIJK

vijff roeden, ende die volgens negenendertich roeden meer als in contracte … maecken in geldt vijffenvijfftich gulden vijff stuyvs.
XV Maert 1639 … 55:5:0
… aen Nicolaus van Wouw mogen betaelen … 6760:3:4
[total] … 6815:8:4

992 fol. 343
… Dirck de Milde opsichter vande bosschen ende warande van Honsholredijck oncosten in de maendt December 1639
3 Jan. 1640 … 81:9:8

992 fol. 347
… Arien Leendert Timmerman aengenomen heeft volgens den Besteck daervan sijnde in dato IX Januarij 1640, het maken ende stellen van een hout palissade inde warande van Sijne Hooch^t tot Honsholredijck, ter lengte van ontrent ses hondert roeden tegens vijff car. guls. de roede, te betalen in drij termijnen, te weten een derde part gelevert op den handt, tweede derde part als het hout ter plaetse gebracht ende gelevert sal sijn, ende het leste derde part als het werck opgenomen ende gepresen zal sijn
XI Jan. 1640 … 1000:0:0

992 fol. 352
… Anthonis Dircksz. Clock de somme van seshondert eenenveertich car. guls. ter sake van boomen bij hem ten dienste van Sijne Hooch^t gelevert inde nieuwe thuijn tot Honsholredijck inde Jaere 1639 …
28 Jan. 1640 … 641:0:0

992 fol. 360
… Samuel van Damme Smit tot Leyden de somme van 400:0:0 die Sijne Hooch^t hem is avancerende op de ijsere baille bij hem aengenomen te maecken op de logie tot Honsholredijck
10 Febr. 1640 … 400:0:0

992 fol. 361
… Dirck de Milde opsichter vande bosschen ende warande van Honsholredijck oncosten in de maendt Jan. 1640
VI Febr. 1640 … 57.10.0

992 fol. 367
Op de reeckeninge van Jacob van Campen vande betalingen bij hem ten dienste van Sijne Hooch^t gedaen, geleverde schilderijen, gesneden steen ende houtwerck, verschooten reijscosten, wagenvrachten als anders … vierduysent negentich gul. tien schellingen … volgens den schriftelijcke last ende ordre van Sijne Hooch^t in dato 5 Julij 1637 …
Febr. 1640 … 4090:10:0

992 fol. 368
… Pieter Floris vander Sallem Lantmeter woonende alhier in den hage, de somme van drij hondert achtenveertich car. guls. hem competerende voor verscheyde Caerten, metingen van Landen, Thuijnen als anders bij hem ten dienste van Sijne Hooch^t tot Honsholredijck ende elders in den voorleden Jare 1639 gedaen ende gemaeckt
XIII Febr. 1640 … 348:0:0

992 fol. 376 (Slothouwer, pp. 271-272)
… te betalen uyt de penningen vande zeeprinsen aen Jan Gerritsen van Lier, steenhouwer de somme van negenentnegentich gulden drij sts. over de teijckeningen bestecken ende anders bij hem ten dienste van Sijne Hooch^t in de jaren 1639 ende 1640 vande stallingen ende coetshuijsen te maecken tot Honsholredijck …
21 Maert 1640 … 99:3:0

992 fol. 379
… Dirck de Milde opsichter vande bosschen ende warande van Honsholredijck oncosten in de maendt Maert 1640
VI Maert 1640 … 52:15:0

992 fol. 384
… Anthonis Gerritsz. Timmerman tot Honsholredijck … het maecken ende stellen van een nieuwe brugge van goet greijnen hout over de nieuwe Vaert naede Gantel inde Dortwecht … 100:0:0

992 fol. 385
… Dirck de Milde opsichter vande bosschen ende warande van Honsholredijck oncosten in de maendt Maert 1640
VI April … LXXXIX XVIII st

992 fol. 385
… te betalen uyt de penn. vande zeeprinsen aen Symon van Catshuysen aennemer de somme van thien duysent car. gul.
XVII April 1640 … 10000:0:0

992 fol. 386
… aen Arent Pietersz. Blom de somme van ses ende tachtich gulden thien stuyvers over verscheyde plantsoenen van bloemen bij hem ten dienste van Sijne Hooch^t aen Andries Hoorendonck gewesen hovenier tot Bueren inden Jare 1639 gelevert om bij denselve aen de wallen ende inde percken aldaer gepoot te werden
[April 1640] … 86:10:0

992 fol. 388
… aen Arent Pietersz. Blom de somme van hondert vier gulden twaelff stuyvers over verscheyde plantsoenen van bloemen bij hem ten dienste van Sijne Hooch^t aen Andries Hoorendonck, gewesen hovenier tot Bueren inden Jare 1639 gelevert om bij denselve aen de wallen ende inde percken aldaer gepoot te werden
[April 1640] … 104 XII sts.

992 fol. 389 (Slothouwer, p. 272)
… te betalen uyt de pen. vande zeeprinsen aen Matthieu de Bus, schilder, de somme van twee duysent vijff hondert vijff en tachtich gul. over verscheijden vergult ende schilderwercken bij hem ten dienste van Sijne Hooch[t] gedaen ende gemaeckt in verscheijden quartieren ende camers op den huijse van Honsholredijck …
28 April 1640 … 2585:0:0

992 fol. 389 (Slothouwer, p. 272)
… te betalen aen Pr Cornelissen van Couwenhoven, hofftimmerman, de somme van twee hondert ses ende tachtich Car. gul. voor soo veel als bij hem is verdient ende aen andere mrs. ende luijden verschooten, aen oncosten gevallen int brengen, voeren, opwinnen ende stellen van verscheijden beelden mitsgaders het inlaten en stellen van een ijsere baille voor onsen huijse tot Honsholredijck, in den jare 1640 …
30 April 1640 … 286:0:0

992 fol. 390 (Slothouwer, p. 272)
… te tellen aen Jacob van Campen de somme van twee duysent vijff [hondert] Car. gul. die S.Ht hem is toevougende ende vereerende over sijne gedane diensten ende schilderijen bij hem opden huijse Honsholredijck gelevert
30 April 1640 … 2500:0:0

992 fol. 391 (Slothouwer, p. 272)
… te betalen uijt de pen. vande zeeprinsen aen Jan Jansz. de Vos de somme van hondert drij ende tnegentich gul. vier stuijvers hem per reste noch competerende over ses steene kinderkens bij hem ten dienste van Sijne Hooch[t] gelevert ende leggende over de ijsere baille op den huijse van Honsholredijck
27 April 1640 … 193:4:0

992 fol. 391 (Slothouwer, p. 272)
… te betalen uijt de penningen vande zeeprinsen aen Cornelis Gerritsz. Smit de somme van veertich gul. sesthien stuijvers over ijserwerck bij hem gelevert aende steene beelden staende inde thuijnen van Sijne Hooch[t] tot Honsholredijck … ende attestatie van Sr. van Campen …
24 April 1640 … 40:16:0

992 fol. 391
Op declaratie van Pr Post is ordonn. gedeponeert … aen Pr Post, architect de somme van twee hondert dertien gul. thien sts. over verscheyden teeckeningen vacatien, reijs ende teercosten bij hem gedaen ten dienste van S.H. inde jaren 1637, 1639 ende 1640 …
XXX April … 213:10:0

992 fol. 392
… te tellen aen Jacob van Campen de somme van IIIMVC Car. gul. die S.H. hem is toevougende tot vervullinge van sijne gedaene oncosten soo van huijshuere als onderhout van sijn Persoon, terwijl hij sich in den hage ten dienste van S.H. heeft opgehouden …
VI May 1640 … 3500:0:0

992 fol. 393
… Wooning en 52 morgen, 1 hondt 75 roeden landts Ond[r] Ambacht in Naeltwijck bij S.H. gecocht van Leendert Quirijnsz. vanden Burch voor 900 gul. den mergen
XX April 1640 … 47612:10:0

992 fol. 400
… Dirck de Milde Boschbewaerder tot Honsholredijck op sijne declaratie van oncosten gevallen inde maendt April 1640 … 90:4:0

992 fol. 400 (Slothouwer, p. 333)
… te rembouseren aen Sijne Raedt ende Secretaris Huygens, de somme van vijffhondert negenentsestich car. gul. XVIII sts. II dr. over gelt somme bij hem verschoten aen vijff steene beelden tot Antwerpen doen maecken ten dienste van Sijne Hooch[t] ende twee flessen Orangewater vandaer ontboden
IX May 1640 … 569:18:2

992 fol. 409
… Dirck de Milde Boschbewaerder tot Honsholredijck op sijne declaratie van oncosten gevallen inde maendt May 1640 …
V Junij 1640 … 125:19:0

992 fol. 410
Alsoo Anthonis Gerritsz, Timmerman aengenomen heeft … het maken ende stellen van twee nieuwe hecken, het versetten van een oudt heck inde warande van Sijne Hooch[t] tot Honsholredijck, voor de somme van 410 Car. guls. In het leger tot Walcheren …
XXIII Junij 1640 … 410:0:0

992 fol. 412
… Dirck de Milde aengenomen heeft volgens de conditien in dato den 17 May 1639 daervan gemaeckt, het schoon onder houden vande maliebaan te Honsholredijck voor den tijd van dry eerst comende Jaeren, jaers voor de somme van hondert car. gul. … te betaelen ende dat in voldoeninge vant eerste jaer
XXVIII Junij 1640 … 100:0:0

992 fol. 417
… Dirck de Milde Boschbewaerder tot Honsholredijck op sijne declaratie van oncosten gevallen inde maendt Junij 1640 …
IX Julij 1640 … 209:15:2

992 fol. 419
… Dirck de Milde Boschbewaerder tot Honsholredijck op sijne

declaratie van oncosten gevallen inde maendt Julio 1640 …
X Aug. 1640 … 147:14:0

992 fol. 429
… Dirck de Milde Boschbewaerder tot Honsholredijck op sijne declaratie van oncosten gevallen inde maendt Sept. …
III Sept. 1640 … 163:6:8

992 fol. 439
Alsoo Cornelis Cornelisz. aengenomen heeft volgens een besteck daarvan in dato IX Jan. 1640 het maken ende stellen van een houte palisade rondtom de groote dreve recht voor het huys te Honsholredijck ter lengte van ontrent vijff hondert roeden, t eynde mate teynde gelde, tegens seven guls. vijff stuyv. de roede, te betaelen in dry Termijnen …
XXIII Oct. 1640 … 1000:0:0

992 fol. 442
… aen Arent Pietersz. Blom hovenier, de somme van 108 guls. achthien stuiv. over diverse soorten van bloemen bij hem inde potten ende op rabatten inde Thuijnen tot Honsholredijck inden Jare 1639 geplant ende gelevert
1 Oct. 1640 … 108:18:0

992 fol. 447
… Dirck de Milde Boschbewaerder tot Honsholredijck op sijne declaratie van oncosten gevallen inde maendt Oct. 1640 …
V Nov. 1640 … 192:5:8

992 fol. 449
… Pieter Florisz, Landtmeter … over de vacatien bij hem ten dienste van S.H. inden Jare 1639 int meten ende carteren van sekere wegen gelegen in Naeltwijck, Monster, 's Gravesande, Honsholredijck ende Poeldijck
XII Nov. 1640 … 20:0:0

992 fol. 457
… Dirck de Milde Boschbewaerder tot Honsholredijck op sijne declaratie van oncosten gevallen inde maendt Nov. 1640 …
6 Dec. 1640 … 163:8:0

NDR, inv. no. 993 [736] (years 1641-1647)

993 fol. 5
… Dirck de Milde Boschbewaerder tot Honsholredijck van de oncosten gevallen in de Bosschen ende warande van Honsholredijck in de maendt Dec. 1640
5 Jan. 1641 … 259:4:8

993 fol. 6
… Bartholomeus Dircksz van Klinckenberch, m^r Timmerman tot Warmont … het maecken van een Wip-Watermolentje inde warande van Sijne Hooch^t tot Honsholredijck, voor de somme van vijffhondert ende vijfftich car. guls. te betaelen als het voorn. molentjen gangbaer ende voorgoet opgenomen, ende geprezen soude sijn …
11 Jan. 1641 … 550:0:0

993 fol. 11
… Dirck de Milde Boschbewaerder tot Honsholredijck van de oncosten gevallen in de Bosschen ende warande van Honsholredijck in de maendt Jan.
IIII Febr. 1641 … 158:8:0

993 fol. 11 (Slothouwer, p. 272)
… te betalen uijtte penningen vande zeeprinsen aen Moyses Uyttenbroeck schilder, de somme van negen hondert vijftich Car. guldens, over twee stucken schilderijen bij hem gemaeckt ende gelevert ten dienste van Sijne Hooch^t op den huijse van Honsholredijck …
26 Febr. 1641 … 950:0:0

993 fol. 13
… Cornelis Gerritsz Smyt, de somme van negenentseventich ponden seventhien schellingen acht dernier over ijserwerck door hem ten dienste van Sijne Hooch^t in de Jaere 1640 gelevert tot den nieuwe heckens inde warande van Honsholredijck ende aende nieuwe brugge in den Dortwech bij den Gantel …
XIII Febr. 1641 … 79:17:8

993 fol. 14
… Theunis Dircksz Clock … de somme van sevenhondert ponden vier schellingen over Elst, asperge-planten midtsgaders kers, persicke ende abricose boomen bij hem inde Jaere 1640 ten dienste van Sijne Hooch^t in desselffs Thuijnen tot Honsholredijck gelevert …
XXVI Febr. 1641 … 708:4:0

993 fol. 15 (Slothouwer, p. 272)
… te betalen aen Pieter Jansz de Hout, leijdecker ende pompemaker de somme van een hondert Carolus guldens, over het onderhouden van 't schalie [leien] ende pannendack, mitsgaders de loode gooten aende huyse van Honsholredijck voor den jare 1640 …
26 Febr. 1641 … 100:0:0

993 fol. 21
… Goris Claessen aengenomen heeft … het omspitten van eenig landt in Sijne Hooch^{ts} warande tot Honsholredijck tot ses guls. en vijff stuyvers ijder hondt …
XI Maert 1641 … 32:16:4

993 fol. 25 [a]
… Huych Jansz de somme van vierentsestich guldens over verteerde costen bij twee Engelse 'tsijner huyse gedaen die besich sijn geweest beid't planten van eenige boomen in Sijne Hooch[ts] warande tot Honsholredijck van Dec. 1640 tot Maert 1641 …
XVIII Maert 1641 … 64:0:0

993 fol. 25 [b]
… Huych Jansz Schipper tot Honsholredijck, de somme van tachtich Car. guldens over eenige vrachten met boomen bij hem ten dienste van Sijne Hooch[t] gehaelt tot Delft, tsedert de maendt November 1640 totten 11 Maert deser Jaers 1641 …
XVIII Maert 1641 … 80:0:0

993 fol. 26
… Rosier Hirver ende Jan Aderen de somme van hondert drieendertich guldens twee stuyvers over den arbeydt bij hem gedaen in Sijne Hooch[ts] warande tot Honsholredijck inde maenden van Dec. 1640 ende Jan. 1641
18 Maert 1641 … 133:2:0

993 fol. 25
… Huijch Jansz, Schipper tot Honsholredijck, de somme van tachtich Car. guls. over eenige vrachten met boomen bij hem ten dienste van Sijne Hooch[t] gehaelt tot Delft, tsedert de maendt Nov. 1646 totten VI Maert deser Jaers 1641 ….
XVIII Maert 1641 … 80:0:0

993 fol. 26
Alsoo Dirck de Milde aengenomen heeft het maecken van drije verwulfde riolen tegens achthien guldens de roede ende vier ongewulfde toegedeckte riolen tegen twaelff gulds. thien stuyvers de roede …
18 Maert 1641 … 602:2:8

993 fol. 34
… Dirck de Milde Boschbewaerder tot Honsholredijck van de oncosten gevallen in de Bosschen ende warande van Honsholredijck in de maendt Maert 1641
11 April 1641 … 150:0:0

993 fol. 36
… te rembouseren aen Dirck de Milde sijne warantm[r] tot Honsholredijck, de somme van seshondert vier ende vijfftich gulds. acht stuyvers over gelijcke somme bij hem betaelt ende verschoten aende coop van boomen, stellen van een pomp ende andersints gespecificeert … in dato 26 Oct. 1640
28 April 1641 … 641:8:0

993 fol. 46
… Dirck de Milde aengenomen heeft het maecken ende stellen van een houte palissade rondtom de groote dreve recht voor het huys te Honsholredijck voor seven gul. ende thien stuyvers de roede …
April 1641 … 3391:17:6

993 fol. 49
… Dirck de Milde aengenomen heeft het maecken van een vijver, grachten, slooten ende greppels aen onse huyse tot Honsholredijck voor de somme van acht duysent guls. …
V May 1641 … 1200:0:0

993 fol. 51
Contract voor landt gecocht [1 mergen 64 roeden] onder Honsholredijck bij Sijne Hooch[t] van Arent Philipsz Backer …
XVIII May 1641 … 1671:0:0

993 fol. 71
… Gijsbrecht Thonissen, hovenier tot Honsholredijck, over geleverde boomen inden ouden Thuijn op Honsholredijck …
V Aug. 1641 … 78:11:0

993 fol. 71
… Dirck de Milde … het maecken van verscheyde steene hecken inde warande tot Honsholredijck … te betaelen in drij termijnen …
Aug. 1641 … 600:0:0

993 fol. 75
te vergoeden en rembouseren aen sijnen rentm[r] tot Steenbergen Daniel Noirot de somme van hondert negenentseventich guls. vijfthien stuyvers over gelijcke somme bij hem verstreckt ende betaelt aen incoop ende andere oncosten van 340 eyckeheesters, bij hem ten dienste van Sijne Hooch[t] gecocht ende gesonden op Honsholredijck … Schepen van Bergen op Zoom, den …
30 Sept. 1641 … 179:15:0

993 fol. 79
… Dirck de Milde Boschbewaerder tot Honsholredijck van de oncosten gevallen in de Bosschen ende warande van Honsholredijck in de maendt Sept. 1641 … 165:8:0

993 fol. 83
… Dirck de Milde Boschbewaerder tot Honsholredijck van de oncosten gevallen in de Bosschen ende warande van Honsholredijck in de maendt Oct. 1641 … 155:3:0

993 fol. 84
… Balthasar van Engelen, hovenier van Antwerpen, de somme van twee hondert vierendesestich guls. over acht orange boomen bij den selven van

Engelen in desen Jaere 1641 ten dienste van Sijne Hooch[t] gelevert ...
XXVI Nov. 1641 ... 264:0:0

993 fol. 84
... te tellen aen Hendrick van Hattem, sijnen plantagueur de somme van seshondert guldens, omme geemployeert te worden tot betalinge van incoop van boomen en andere te doene oncosten totte plantagies van Honsholredijck, Bueren ende Zuylesteijn, volgens den laste van Sijne Hooch[t] aen hem gegeven ...
XXVII Nov. 1641 ... 600:0:0

993 fol. 89
... aen Joseph Dinant, sijne fonteynier de somme van drij hondert negenenegentich guls. vier stuyvers bij hem gedebouseert ende betaelt spp aen materialen als arbeydtsloon van Timmerluyden ende metselaers die gerepareert hebben het huys, waerinne de voorsz. Dinant alhier is woonende
5 Dec. 1641 ... 399:4:0

993 fol. 90 (Slothouwer, p. 333)
... te tellen aen Francesco Dieussart beelthouder vande coninck van Engelandt de somme van vijfthien hondert Carolus guldens, ter sake van twee albaste beelden van Sijne Hooch[t] ende Princesse van Engelandt, bij hem aen Sijnne Hooch[t] gepresenteert.
21 Dec. 1641 ... 1500:0:0

993 fol. 90 [b]
... Dirck de Milde Boschbewaerder tot Honsholredijck van de oncosten gevallen in de Bosschen ende warande van Honsholredijck in de maendt Nov. 1641 ...
23 Dec. 1641 ... 137:3:8

993 fol. 131
... te tellen aen Hendrick van Hattem, sijnen plantagueur de somme van seshondert guldens, omme geemployeert te worden tot betalinge van incoop van boomen en andere te doene oncosten totte plantagies van Honsholredijck, Bueren ende Zuylesteijn ...
III Febr. 1642 ... 600:0:0

993 fol. 131
... Arent Pietersz Blom, de somme van twee hondert drijentwintich guls. eene stuyver, ter sake van verscheyde soorten van bloemen, bollen ende saet van bloemen bij hem inde Jaren 1640 ende 1641 gelevert ten dienste van Sijne Hooch[t] ende geplant inden nieuwe Thuijn bij huyse tot Honsholredijck ...
4 Febr. 1642 ... 223:1:0

993 fol. 133
... Jan ende Andries de Walsche, de somme van drij hondert tweeendertich guls. ses stuyvers ter sake vande nombre van 1100 populierboomen bij haer gecocht ten dienste van Sijne Hooch[t] tot vijffthien guls. het hondert, mitsgaders over vrachten ende vacatien ende andere oncosten bij haer gedaen ende verschoten int overbrengen vande selve boomen van het dorp Sleijde [?] uyt Vlaenderen tot binnen de stadt Delft ...
XVII Febr. 1642 ... 332:6:0

993 fol. 142 [a]
... Dirck de Milde Boschbewaerder tot Honsholredijck van de oncosten gevallen in de Bosschen ende warande van Honsholredijck in de maendt Februari 1642 ...
IX Maert 1642 ... 234:13:0

993 fol. 142 [b]
... Dirck de Milde aengenomen heeft het maecken ende leveren van twee sluysdeuren voor een brugge, ende noch een deurcken voor een riool inde warande tot Honsholredijck ...
8 Maert 1642 ... 200:0:0

993 fol. 143
... Dirck de Milde ... het maecken van een vijver, grachten, slooten ende greppels aen onse huyse tot Honsholredijck ... tweede termijn
8 Maert 1642 ... 8000:0:0

993 fol. 145
... te betaelen aen Balthasar van Engelen de somme van negen hondert vierentwintich Car. guls. over een stuck schilderij, sijnde een herder ende herderinne, bij hem ten dienste en op ordre van Sijne Hooch[t] gecocht vande Erfgenamen van Petrus Pauwelus Rubens tot Antwerpen, met eenige andere oncosten daaronder gevallen ...
X April 1642 ... 924:0:0

993 fol. 145
... Dirck de Milde ... schoon onder houden vande maliebaan te Honsholredijck ...
10 April 1642 ... 100:0:0

993 fol. 145 verso (Slothouwer, p. 334)
... Thomas Willeboorts schilder tot Antwerpen de somme van een duysent Carolus guldens, over twee schilderije d'eene van Dido ende haere suster, ende d'ander van Venus ende Adonis bij hem gemaeckt ende gelevert ten dienste van Sijne Hooch[t] in desen Jaere 1642 ...
13 April 1642 ... 1000:0:0

993 fol. 148
... Dirck de Milde Boschbewaerder tot Honsholredijck van de oncosten gevallen in de Bosschen ende warande van Honsholredijck in de maendt April 1642 ...
XII May 1642 ... 172:3:8

993 fol. 148 verso (Slothouwer, p. 272)
Alsoo Dirck de Milde … heeft gemaeckt ende gelevert, een hoijberch met drij hartenhuijsen in de warande tot Honsholredijck, de somme van seven hondert guldens …
16 May 1642 … 700:0:0

993 fol. 149 (Slothouwer, p. 272)
Alsoo Dirck de Milde aengenomen heeft … het maecken van een afheijninge inde warande tot Honsholredijck ter lengte van ontrent 200 roeden, tot preservatie van schaerhout tegen de harten, voor de somme van vijff hondert ende twintich Carolus guldens …
16 Mei 1642 … 520:0:0

993 fol. 150
… Dirck de Milde … schoon onder houden vande maliebaan te Honsholredijck jaarlijcx …
Mei 1642 … 100:0:0

993 fol. 151 verso (Slothouwer, p. 273)
… te betalen aen Pieter Monicx, schilder alhier in den Hage, de somme van twee duijsent acht hondert guldens, over dat hij ten dienste van Sijne Hooch[t] heeft geschildert het speelhuijs in den nieuwen thuijn aen de Huijse van Sijne Hooch[t] tot Honsholredijck, bestaende in verscheijden lantschappen, fruijten, blommen ende vogeltjens …
27 Mei 1642 … 2800:0:0

993 fol. 151 verso
… te betalen aen Thonis Dircxz. Clock de somme van hondert acht ende twintich Car. guls. twaelff stuyvers voor eenige fruytboomen, Asperge planten ende anders bij hem ten dienste van Sijne Hooch[t] gelevert in den nieuwe thuijn tot Honsholredijck …
27 May 1642 … 128:12:0

993 fol. 154
… te tellen aen Hendrick van Hattem sijnen plantagueur de somme van een duysent twee hondert Car. guldens omme bij hem geemployeert te werden soo int coopen van boomen, als andere oncosten aende plantagies van Sijne Hooch[t] aengedaen …
1 Junij 1642 … 1200:0:0

993 fol. 158 verso
… te tellen aen Hendrick van Hattem sijnen plantagueur de somme van een duysent twee hondert Car. guldens omme bij hem geemployeert te werden soo int coopen van boomen, als andere oncosten aende plantagies van Sijne Hooch[t] aengedaen …
Junij 1642 … 300:0:0

993 fol. 158 verso
… Dirck de Milde Boschbewaerder tot Honsholredijck van de oncosten gevallen in de Bosschen ende warande van Honsholredijck in de maendt Junij 1642 … 122:13:0

993 fol. 159 (Slothouwer, p. 334)
… te betalen aen Thomas Willeboorts schilder woonende tot Antwerpen, de somme van een duysent drij hondert een ende tachtich guldens voor ses stucken schilderije bij hem tot last van S.Hooch[t] tot Antwerpen gecocht
9 Junij 1642 … 1381:0:0

993 fol. 161
… Dirck de Milde Boschbewaerder tot Honsholredijck van de oncosten gevallen in de Bosschen ende warande van Honsholredijck in de maendt Julio 1642 … 204:13:8

993 fol. 161 verso
Op de reckeninge van Dirck Pietersz. van geleverde visch in de Vijver tot Honsholredijck …
25 Aug. 1642 … 252:18:0

993 fol. 167
… Hendrick van Hattem sijne plantagueur, de somme van acht hondert Car. guldens omme geemployeert te werden tot betaelinge van de incoop van boomen en andere te doene oncosten totte plantagien van Sijne Hooch[t] tot Honsholredijck, Rijswijck, Bueren ende Zuylesteijn
XX Oct. 1642 … 800:0:0

993 fol. 169
… Dirck de Milde Boschbewaerder tot Honsholredijck van de oncosten gevallen in de Bosschen ende warande van Honsholredijck in de maendt Sept. 1642 …
4 Nov. 1642 … 122:4:0

993 fol. 169
Op de quitantie vande huijshuere betaelt bij den hovenier tot Honsholredijck aen Gerrit Jansz. Lindebleude … het contract metten hovenier gemaeckt in dato 30 Oct. 1632, waer bij hem een vrije wooninge werdt belooft. Dese huere van veertich guld. over het jaer verscheen 1 Nov. 1636 aenden hovenier sal mogen remboueren de somme van veertich car. gul. …
Nov. 1642 … 40:0:0

993 fol. 169
… noch gelijcke ordonnans over twee en een half jaeren huyshuere bij voorsz. hovenier betaelt aen Cornelis Gerritsz. van Egmont van 1 Nov. 1636 tot 1 May 1639, etc.
Nov. 1642 … 282:0:0

993 fol. 170
… Dirck de Milde Boschbewaerder tot Honsholredijck van de oncosten gevallen in de Bosschen ende warande van Honsholredijck in de maendt October 1642
XI Nov. 1642 … 129:19:0

993 fol. 179 verso
… Dirck de Milde Boschbewaerder tot Honsholredijck van de oncosten gevallen in de Bosschen ende warande van Honsholredijck in de maendt Dec. 1642 …
14 Jan. 1643 … 347:17:0

993 fol. 188
… te tellen aen Hendrick van Hattem, sijnen plantagueur de somme van negen hondert Car. guldens, omme geemployeert te worden tot betalinge van incoop van boomen en andere te doene oncosten totte plantagies van Honsholredijck, Rijswijck, Bueren ende Zuylesteijn …
VI Maert 1643 … 900:0:0

993 fol. 188
… aen Cornelis Jacobsz. … de somme van negen en negentich gulden thien stuyvers over verscheyden roose, negelantier, elst ende Lindeboomen, bij hem ten dienste van Sijne Hooch^t gelevert inde warande ende ontrent de vijver tot Honsholredijck …
VI Maert 1643 … 99:10:0

993 fol. 188 verso
… Dirck de Milde Boschbewaerder tot Honsholredijck van de oncosten gevallen in de Bosschen ende warande van Honsholredijck in de maendt Febr. 1643 …
IX Maert 1643 … 105:0:0

993 fol. 189
… aen Dirck Pietersz. vischvercooper, over riviervisch bij hem gelevert inde vijver tot Honsholredijck …
31 Maert 1643 … 153:0:0

993 fol. 193 verso
… aen Arent Pietersz. Blom, de somme van hondert en twaelff Car. guls. vijfftien sts. over verscheijdene plantsoenen van bloemen mitsgaders kersen ende persicke boomen bij hem ten dienste van Sijne Hooch^t gelevert in den nieuwen thuijn tot Honsholredijck …
XI April 1643 … 112:15:0

993 fol. 194
… Dirck de Milde Boschbewaerder tot Honsholredijck van de oncosten gevallen in de Bosschen ende warande van Honsholredijck in de maendt Maert 1643 …
XVIII April 1643 … 215:18:0

993 fol. 197
… Dirck de Milde Boschbewaerder tot Honsholredijck van de oncosten gevallen in de Bosschen ende warande van Honsholredijck in de maendt Febr. 1643 …
18 May 1643 … 127:17:8

993 fol. 198
… salaris verdient bij Pieter Florisz. vander Salm, Landtmeter over verscheydene Caerte ende grondt teckeningen bij hem gemaeckt ende gecopieert tsedert Febr. 1642 tot Febr. 1643 … sal mogen betalen de somme van ses ende sestich Car. guls.
XII May 1643 … 66:0:0

993 fol. 203
… te betalen aen Dirck de Milde de somme van vier hondert seven ende negentich guldens drij stuyvers over 't versetten vande pallisade heyninge bij de dreve voor 't huys van Sijne Hooch^t tot Honsholredijck, met het maecken van vijffentwintich roeden ende twee voet nieuwe palissade ende geleverde nagels, bedragende tsamen de voorn. somme van …
18 Junij 1643 … 497:3:0

993 fol. 205 verso
… Pieter Cornelisz. van Kouwenhoven ende Arent Lourisz. Noom m^r Timmerluyden … besteck in dato XXIIII April 1641 … lesten termijn betalinge van pavillioen ende borstweringe van een muyr tot Honsholredijck …
Junij 1643 … 4322:14:8

993 fol. 206
… Dirck de Milde Boschbewaerder tot Honsholredijck van de oncosten gevallen in de Bosschen ende warande van Honsholredijck in de maendt Junio 1643 …
XXVII Julij 1643 … 122:8:0

993 fol. 208
… Dirck de Milde Boschbewaerder tot Honsholredijck van de oncosten gevallen in de Bosschen ende warande van Honsholredijck in de maendt Julio 1643 …
XXIIII Aug. 1643 … 160:13:0

993 fol. 208
… te tellen aen Hendrick van Hattem, sijnen plantagueur … oncosten van plantagien monterende alles te samen de somme van drij duysent vier hondert seven ende tsestich car. guls. seventien sts. acht dr. mogen betaelen …
XVI Aug. 1643 … 3467:17:8

993 fol. 208 verso
… te tellen aen Hendrick van Hattem, sijnen plantagueur … oncosten van plantagien monterende alles te samen de somme van ses hondert car. guls.
22 Aug. 1643 … 600:0:0

993 fol. 210
… Dirck de Milde Boschbewaerder tot Honsholredijck van de oncosten gevallen in de Bosschen ende warande van Honsholredijck in de maendt Aug. 1643 …
28 Sept. 1643 … 198:13:6

993 fol. 213 verso
… Dirck de Milde Boschbewaerder tot Honsholredijck van de oncosten gevallen in de Bosschen ende warande van Honsholredijck in de maendt Sept. 1643 …
28 Oct. 1643 … 159:10:0

993 fol. 217
… Dirck de Milde Boschbewaerder tot Honsholredijck van de oncosten gevallen in de Bosschen ende warande van Honsholredijck in de maendt Oct. 1643
XXI Nov. 1643 … 147:19:8

993 fol. 220
… te tellen aen Hendrick van Hattem, sijnen plantagueur … oncosten van incoop van boomen voor plantagien monterende de somme van hondert car. guls.
7 Dec. 1643 … 100:0:0

993 fol. 220
… te tellen aen Dirck de Milde aennemer vande stallinge ende vier pavilloenen te maecken aende Westsijde van Sijne Hooch^{ts} Huyse van Honsholredijck, de somme van vijff duysent Carolus guldens …
7 Dec. 1643 … 5000:0:0

993 fol. 220
… Dirck de Milde Boschbewaerder tot Honsholredijck van de oncosten gevallen in de Bosschen ende warande van Honsholredijck in de maendt Nov. 1643 …
IX Dec. 1643 … 114:3:0

993 fol. 234
… Dirck de Milde Boschbewaerder tot Honsholredijck van de oncosten gevallen in de Bosschen ende warande van Honsholredijck in de maendt Dec. 1643 …
13 Jan. 1643 … 193:19:0

993 fol. 238
… te betalen aen Arent Pietersz Blom hovenier, de somme van hondert en dertich car. guls. vier sts. ter sake van verscheyde soorten van Bollen ende planten van bloemen, bij hem inde nieuwe Thuijn van Sijne Hooch^t tot Honsholredijck in de maendt Septemb. 1643 gelevert … geattesteert bij Jacob Cornelisz. Bode [hovenier]…
VI Febr. 1643 … 113:4:0

993 fol. 238
… te betalen aen Thonis Dircxz Clock, de somme van hondert en dertich car. guls. over de nombre van duysent bollen van tulpen tot achtentsestich gul. ende hondert ende twintich kerseboomen voor twaelff stuyvers 't stuck tot twee en zeventich guldens beloopende tsamen de voorn. somme van 130:0:0 bij hem in Sijne Hooch^{ts} nieuwe thuijn tot Honsholredijck in Augusto ende Novemb. 1642 gelevert … geattesteert bij Jacob Cornelisz. Bode [hovenier] …
11 Febr. 1644 … 130:0:0

993 fol. 238
… aen Gijsbrecht Thonisz. hovenier vande ouden thuijn tot Honsholredijck, over waterlossingen ende greppelen bij hem gemaeckt inde nieuwe plantagie aent mastbosch annex 't landt bij de wooninge bij Sijne Hooch^t gecocht van Leendert Quirijnz. vander Burch anno 1643 … ter somme van veertich car. guls. sesthien sts. …
V Febr. 1644 … 40:16:0

993 fol. 239 verso
… aen Salomon Pietrsz. Seijs de somme van drij hondert acht ende seventich car. guls. ter sake van duysent abeele boomen tot XXV guls. het hondert, met eenige plantsoenen van bloemen ten dienste van Sijne Hooch^t gelevert inde warande tot Honsholredijck geattesteert bij den boschwachter Dirck de Milde …
XIX Febr. 1644 … 370:0:0

993 fol. 240 verso
… aen Philips Pauwelsz. Vos, Inwoonder van Naeltwijck … sal mogen betaelen de somme van een hondert ende negentich Car. Guls. over schade ende pretenties van affgravinge ende ongebruyck van landt geemployeert totte warande ende 't pleyn van Sijne Hooch^t tot Honsholredijck …
XXII Febr. 1644 … 190:0:0

993 fol. 241
… aen Maerten Maertensz. pachter vande wooninge ende landen bij Sijne Hooch^t gecocht van Heyster Ariaens vande Made, gelegen onder Naeltwijck sal mogen betaelen de somme van een hondert ende dertich Car. Guls. over schade ende pretenties van affgravinge ende ongebruyck van landt geemployeert totte warande ende 't pleyn van Sijne Hooch^t tot Honsholredijck …
XXII Febr. 1644 … 130:0:0

993 fol. 241
… aen Jan Jansz. van Foreest ende Vranck Oliviersz. sal mogen betaelen de somme van een hondert ende dertich Car. Guls. over schade ende pretenties van affgravinge ende ongebruyck van landt geemployeert totte warande ende 't pleyn van Sijne Hooch^t tot Honsholredijck ..
XXII Febr. 1644 … 180:0:0

993 fol. 241
… Gelijcke ordonnantie op de requeste van Willemtjen Pieters ende verder inwoondersse van Naeltwijck …
XXII Febr. 1644 … 300:0:0

993 fol. 241
… Gelijcke ordonnantie op de requeste van Pieter Davidsz. …
XXII Febr. 1644 … 100:0:0

993 fol. 241
… Gelijcke ordonnantie op de requeste van Pieter Pietersz. 't Ert … affgraevinge ende ongebruyck van landt geemployeert totte warande ende vijver van Sijne Hooch^t tot Honsholredijck …
XXII Febr. 1644 … 400:0:0

993 fol. 242
… Alsoo Adriaen Leendertsz. Timmerman alhier in den hage … het maecken ende stellen van een houte pallissade inde warande tot Honsholredijck, ter lengte van ontrent ses hondert roeden, tegens vijff Car. guls. de roede, te betaelen in drij termijnen …
XXII Febr. 1644 … 570:8:0

993 fol. 245 verso
… Dirck de Milde Boschbewaerder tot Honsholredijck van de oncosten gevallen in de Bosschen ende warande van Honsholredijck in de maendt Febr. 1644 …
16 Maert 1644 … 159:19:0

993 fol. 249
… Dirck de Milde Boschbewaerder tot Honsholredijck van de oncosten gevallen in de Bosschen ende warande van Honsholredijck in de maendt Maert 1644 …
XI April 1644 … 142:9:0

993 fol. 249
… te betalen aen Pieter Florisz. vander Salm over verscheyde copijen van Caerten in 1641 ende 1642 gemaeckt …
April 1644 … 81:0:0

993 fol. 252
… te betalen aen Arent Pietersz. Blom hovenier de somme van een hondert ses ende vijfftich Car. guls. ses sts. over verscheijden soorten van bollen ende planten van bloemen bij hem in de ouden thuijn van Sijne Hooch^t tot Honsholredijck, in desen Jare 1644 gelevert … geatteteert bij hovenier Anthonij van Thooren …
12 May 1644 … 156:6:0

993 fol. 253 [a]
… aen Pieter Florisz. vander Salm Landtmeter, over metingen ende caerten bij hem gedaen ende gemaeckt aengaende Naeltwijck, Honsholredijck sedert 29 Augustij 1642 totten eersten Julij 1643 …
XVI May 1644 … 197:0:0

993 fol. 253 [b]
… aen Pieter Florisz. vander Salm Landtmeter, over metingen ende caerten bij hem gedaen ende gemaeckt aengaende Naeltwijck, Honsholredijck sedert April 1643 totten 24 Maert 1644 …
May 1644 … 125:12:0
[Total] … 322:12:0

993 fol. 254
… te betalen aen [Frans?] Post schilder bij den heere Grave Mauritz Generael vande West Indien de somme van acht hondert Car. guls. van een groot stuck schilderij vande gelegenheyt over Landschappen in Westindien bij hem gemaeckt …
29 May 1644 … 800:0:0

993 fol. 254 verso
… Dirck de Milde aengenomen heeft het maecken ende stellen van een heijning off staketsel ter hoogte van vijff voeten, ende lengte van ontrent hondert roeden om een stuck landts gelegen ten noorden van het speelhuys tot Honsholredijck, sijnde tusschen de vijver ende 't selve speelhuys, ijder roede voor 24 stuyvers …
13 May 1644 … 112:3:0

993 fol. 257
… Dirck de Milde Boschbewaerder tot Honsholredijck van de oncosten gevallen in de Bosschen ende warande van Honsholredijck in de maendt April 1644 …
XVI Junij 1644 … 185:9:0

993 fol. 257
… Dirck de Milde Boschbewaerder tot Honsholredijck van de oncosten gevallen in de Bosschen ende warande van Honsholredijck in de maendt May 1644 …
16 Junij 1644 … 158:10:0

993 fol. 257
… te betalen aen Guillaume Blom salaris van visitatie vande wercken tot Honsholredijck …
14 Junij 1644 … 127:0:0

993 fol. 262
… Dirck de Milde Boschbewaerder tot Honsholredijck van de oncosten gevallen in de Bosschen ende warande van Honsholredijck in de maendt Junio 1644 …
4 Aug. 1644 … 145:2:8

993 fol. 262
… te tellen aen Hendrick van Hattem, sijnen plantagueur de somme van seshondert guldens, omme geemployeert te worden tot betalinge van incoop van boomen en andere te doene oncosten totte plantagies van Honsholredijck, Rijswijck, Bueren ende Zuylesteijn, volgens den laste van Sijne Hooch^t aen hem gegeven …
Aug. 1644 … 600:0:0

993 fol. 264 verso
… Dirck de Milde Boschbewaerder tot Honsholredijck van de oncosten gevallen in de Bosschen ende warande van Honsholredijck in de maendt Augusto 1644 …
17 Sept. 1644 … 229:16:0

993 fol. 267
… Dirck de Milde Boschbewaerder tot Honsholredijck van de oncosten gevallen in de Bosschen ende warande van Honsholredijck in de maendt September 1644 …
XVII Oct. 1644 … 160:16:8

993 fol. 270
… te tellen aen Hendrick van Hattem, sijnen plantagueur de somme van vijffhondert guldens, omme geemployeert te worden tot betalinge van incoop van boomen en andere te doene oncosten totte plantagies van Honsholredijck, Bueren ende Zuylesteijn, volgens den laste van Sijne Hooch^t aen hem gegeven …
XIII Nov. 1644 … 500:0:0

993 fol. 270 verso
… Dirck de Milde Boschbewaerder tot Honsholredijck van de oncosten gevallen in de Bosschen ende warande van Honsholredijck in de maendt October 1644 …
21 Nov. 1644 … 458:1:0

993 fol. 274 verso
… te betaelen aen Dirck de Milde, extraordinaris wercken ende reparatien inde warande gedaen inde Jare 1641 …
31 Dec. 1644 … 1227:6:12

993 fol. 284 verso
… Dirck de Milde Boschbewaerder tot Honsholredijck van de oncosten gevallen in de Bosschen ende warande van Honsholredijck in de maendt Nov. 1644 …
11 Jan. 1645 … 160:4:0

993 fol. 285
… aen Arent Pietersz. Blom over Tulpa bollen etc. bij hem gelevert inde nieuwe thuijn tot Honsholredijck anno 1643 ende 1644 … ter somme van een hondert vier ende sestich car. guls. twaelff sts. …
18 Jan. 1645 … 164:12:0

993 fol. 287
… Dirck de Milde Boschbewaerder tot Honsholredijck van de oncosten gevallen in de Bosschen ende warande van Honsholredijck in de maendt Dec. 1644 …
28 Jan. 1645 … 208:5:0

993 fol. 289 verso
… te tellen aen Pieter Post schilder ende architect van sijne gebouwen de somme van duysent carolus guldens die Sijne Hooch^t hem voor een extraordinaris is vereerende ende schenckende over de goede diensten ende debuoiren bij hem nu eenige Jaren herwaerts aen Sijne Hooch^t gedaen …
13 Febr. 1644 … 1000:0:0

993 fol. 291 (Slothouwer, p. 273)
… Alsoo Dirck de Milde aengenomen heeft … het maecken ende opbouwen van sekere stallingen ende vier pavilloenen aende Westzijde van onsen Huijse tot Honsholredijck, voor de somme van drijentsestich duijsent vijff hondert guldens, te betalen in drij termijnen.
24 Febr. 1645 … 63500:0:0

993 fol. 291 verso
… Dirck de Milde Boschbewaerder tot Honsholredijck van de oncosten gevallen in de Bosschen ende warande van Honsholredijck in de maendt Jan. 1645 …
22 Febr. 1645 … 180:8:0

993 fol. 295
… aen Francisco Veghens schilder tot Antwerpen de somme van twee hondert ende vijfftich car. guls. over een stuck schilderije sijnde blommen ende fruytagies bij hem gemaeckt ende aen Sijne Hooch^t gelevert …
29 Maert 1645 … 250:0:0

993 fol. 295 verso
… Dirck de Milde Boschbewaerder tot Honsholredijck van de oncosten gevallen in de Bosschen ende warande van Honsholredijck in de maendt Februari 1645 …
10 Maert 1645 … 178:18:0

993 fol. 295 verso
… Dirck de Milde Boschbewaerder tot Honsholredijck van de oncosten gevallen in de Bosschen ende warande van Honsholredijck in de maendt Maert 1645 …
12 April 1645 … 302:0:8

993 fol. 301
… Dirck de Milde Boschbewaerder tot Honsholredijck van de oncosten gevallen in de Bosschen ende warande van Honsholredijck in de maendt April 1645 …
23 May 1645 … 173:6:0

993 fol. 313 verso
… aen Anthonij van Thoren hovenier vande ouden Thuijn tot Honsholredijck, over geleverde mis, sant, bloemen roseboompjes etc. inde voorsz. thuijn, beloopende in alles ter somme van drijhondert tweeentwintich guls. 16 sts.
15 sept. 1645 … 322:16:0

993 fol. 403
… aen Dirck de Milde … schoon onder houden vande maliebaan te Honsholredijck, jaren 1642 …   IIII Jan. 1646 … 100:0:0
ende jaren 1643, 1644 … 200:0:0

993 fol. 403
… Dirck de Milde Boschbewaerder tot Honsholredijck van de oncosten gevallen in de Bosschen ende warande van Honsholredijck in de maendt December 1645 …
XVI Jan. 1646 … 174:11:0

993 fol. 409 verso
… Dirck de Milde Boschbewaerder tot Honsholredijck van de oncosten gevallen in de Bosschen ende warande van Honsholredijck in de maendt Januarij 1646 …
XVI Febr. 1646 … 229:6:0

993 fol. 410
… aen [Pieter de] Grebber schilder tot Haerlem de somme van drie hondert car. guls. over de ronde schilderije van Ganimedes bij hem voor Sijne Hooch^t geschildert ende gelevert tot de Eedtsael in 't quartier vande Coniginne in 't hoff van Sijne Hooch^t in 't Noorteynde alwaer de selve boven inde solder is gestelt …
23 Febr. 1646 … 300:0:0

993 fol. 410 verso [b] (Slothouwer, p. 335)
… aen Gonsalo Coquis [Conques] schilder van Antwerpen … ter sake van een schilderije van dansende herders ende herderinnen bij hem aen S.H. gelevert lesten Febr. 1646 …
Febr. 1646 … 250:0:0

993 fol. 413
… Dirck de Milde Boschbewaerder tot Honsholredijck van de oncosten gevallen in de Bosschen ende warande van Honsholredijck in de maendt Febr. 1646 …
XIX Maert 1646 … 234:18:0

993 fol. 414 verso
… aen Hendrick van Hattem plantaguem^r van Sijne Hooch^t dezelfde despence ende uytgevels tot van de bepootinge vande plantagien tot Bueren, Honsholredijck, Rijswijck ende Suylesteijn van April 1642 tot April 1643 … ter somme van twee duysent vier hondert ses ende dertich Car. guls. eene sts. …
28 Maert 1646 … 2436:1:0

… Gelijcke ordonnantie ter sake als voorsz. van 28 Julij 1643 tot in Mayo 1644 ter somme van …
Maert 1646 … 1758:15:3

… Gelijcke ordonnantie ter sake als voorsz. van Augusto 1644 tot Februarij 1645 ter somme van …
Maert 1646 … 1247:0:8

993 fol. 414 verso
… aen Adriaen Steenbergen over 't opsicht bij hem gedaen int opdoen van 't hoy …
28 April 1646 … 108:0:0

993 fol. 416 verso
… aen Cornelis Cornelisz. over arbeytsloon van 't schoon onderhouden van 't ackerlandt bij Naeltwijck int jaer 1645 …
18 Maert 1646 … 43:0:0

993 fol. 419 verso
… Dirck de Milde Boschbewaerder tot Honsholredijck van de oncosten gevallen in de Bosschen ende warande van Honsholredijck in de maendt Maerto 1646 …
27 April 1646 … 239:14:0

993 fol. 423
… aen Pieter Florisz vander Salm … maecken van caerten t sedert 14 Julij 1644 …
18 May 1646 … 324:10:0

993 fol. 423 verso (Slothouwer, p. 273)
Op de rekeninge van Dirck de Milde over 't leggen van een Italiaensche vloer inde open galderij bij 't huijs te Honsholredijck in Martio 1646
18 May 1645 … 2363:3:0

993 fol. 424 verso
… aen Dirck de Milde over extraordinaris oncosten gedaen aen 't stuck landts achter 't speelhuys bij de vijver aen 't huys tot Honsholredijck in April 1646 … de somme van vijf hondert en 't seventich gul. eene sts acht dr. … over het beleggen met sooden ende andere oncosten gedaen aen 't stuck landts hierboven vermelt …
28 May 1646 … 579:1:8

993 fol. 426
… aen Dirck de Milde … oncosten maliebaan …
XXVIII May 1646 … 100:0:0

993 fol. 428 verso [a]
… aen Mr Borchaert Fredrick hovenier … over oncosten aende parterres ende rabatten inden Hoff in't Haechsche Bosch …
[Juni 1646] [no amount]

993 fol. 428 verso [b] (Slothouwer, p. 335)
… aen Mr Francisco Dieussart Beelthouwer de somme van negen hondert veertich gul. ses sts. over vier blocken witte marmor steen ende andere oncosten daar op gevallen bij hem Mr Francisco ten dienste van Sijne Hooch{t} gecocht om daer van te maecken eenige beelden in de bovenstaende reckeninge …
2 Junij 1646 … 940:6:0

993 fol. 431
… Dirck de Milde Boschbewaerder tot Honsholredijck van de oncosten gevallen in de Bosschen ende warande van Honsholredijck in de maendt May 1646 …
20 Junij 1646 … 201:6:0

993 fol. 431 verso
… Dirck de Milde heeft aengenomen te maken een nieuwen Thuijn ende heyninge daerom aende westzijde van 't huys tot Honsholredijck te samen voor veerthien duysent drij hondert ponden … sal mogen betalen de somme van vier duysent seven hondert sesentsestich gul. derthien sts. vier dr. ende dat over den 1e termijn van drijen …
Junij 1646 … 4766:13:4

993 fol. 431 verso
… aen Dirck de Milde Boschbewaerder tot Honsholredijck van de oncosten gevallen in de Bosschen ende warande van Honsholredijck in de maendt Junij 1646 …
28 Julij 1646 … 160:11:0

993 fol. 434
… aen Dirck de Milde Boschbewaerder tot Honsholredijck van de oncosten gevallen in de Bosschen ende warande van Honsholredijck in de maendt Julio 1646 …
Augusto 1646 … 226:9:8

993 fol. 436 (Slothouwer, p. 273)
… Op de declaratie vande dachgelden ende andere oncosten gevallen int opnemen vande wercken te Honsholredijck gemaeckt bij Dirck de Milde … ten behoeve van Adriaen van 's Gravesande ende Barth. Drijffhout … elck haer contingent, sal mogen betalen de somme van ses en tnegentich gul. elf stuijvers …
8 Sept. 1646 … 96:11:0

993 fol. 439 (Slothouwer, p. 273)
… Alsoo mr Arien Leendertsz. Cleij mr. metselaer, ende Mr Cornelis Leendertsz. mr. timmerman, aengenoomen heeft … het maecken van twee pavillioenen met twee galderijen ende twee agtkantige torens aen onsen Huijse tot Honsholredijck, ende dat voor een somme van een hondert ende twaelf duijsent gul. te betalen in vier termijnen …
4 Oct. 1646 … 112000:0:0

993 fol. 439
… aen Dirck de Milde Boschbewaerder tot Honsholredijck van de oncosten gevallen in de Bosschen ende warande van Honsholredijck in de maendt Augusto 1646 …
24 Oct. 1646 … 215:4:8

993 fol. 439
… aen Dirck de Milde Boschbewaerder tot Honsholredijck van de oncosten gevallen in de Bosschen ende warande van Honsholredijck in de maendt Sept. 1646 …
25 Oct. 1646 … 153:8:0

993 fol. 441
… aen Henry de la Valle de somme van hondert gul. die Sijne Hooch{t} hem tot eene gratuiteyt is schenckende …
18 Nov. 1646 … 100:0:0

993 fol. 441 verso
… aen Daniel de Bruyn coopman tot Antwerpen de somme van drijduysent gul. ter somme van een camer tapijten sijnde landtschappen
27 Nov. 1646 … 3000:0:0

993 fol. 442
… Rembrant schilder tot Amsterdam de somme van twee duysent vier hondert car. gul. ter sake dat hij ten dienste van Sijne Hooch{t} heeft gemaeckt ende gelevert twee schilderijen, d'eene vande Geboorte Christi ende d'andere vande besnijdinge Christi …
XXIX Nov. 1646 … 2400:0:0

993 fol. 444
… Berckenrode [Balthazar Florisz van Berckerode ?] over Caertjes anno 1641 …
IIII Dec. 1646 … 15:0:0

993 fol. 445 [a]
… aen Pieter Florisz vander Salm … over 't meten ende Caerten vande Loosduynse Vaert bij hem gedaen 'tsedert augustus 1643 tot Junij 1645 …
21 Dec. 1646 … 104:10:0

993 fol. 445 [b]
… aen Pieter Florisz vander Salm … over verscheyde metinge ende carteringe vande Buytengorssinge vant Honderlandt, alsmede van eenige binnenlanden … sedert Aug. 1643 tot den lesten Oct. 1645 …
21 Dec. 1646 … 268:18:0

993 fol. 445 verso [a]
… aen Pieter Florisz vander Salm … over 't meten van den nieuwen ende oude Thuijn [Honselaarsdijk?], 't maecken van Caerten als andersints bij hem gedaen op 't huys ter Nieuburch bij Rijswijck in den Jare 1645 …
21 Dec. 1646 … 23:0:0

993 fol. 445 verso [b]
… aen Pieter Florisz vander Salm … over gedaene metinge …
21 Dec. 1646 … 14:0:0

993 fol. 445 [a]
… aen Dirck de Milde Boschbewaerder tot Honsholredijck van de oncosten gevallen in de Bosschen ende warande van Honsholredijck in de maendt Oct. 1646 …
24 Dec. 1646 … 191:17:8

993 fol. 445 [b]
… aen Dirck de Milde Boschbewaerder tot Honsholredijck van de oncosten gevallen in de Bosschen ende warande van Honsholredijck in de maendt Nov. 1646 …
24 Dec. 1646 … 192:19:0

993 fol. 451 verso
… Hans Golsus heeft aengenomen 't maecken van een orgel inde preek sael tot Honsholredijck den 22 Dec. 1646 …
III Jan. 1647 … 600:0:0

993 fol. 452 verso
… Op de declaratie van J. Dinant over eenige behoeften totte aengenoomene fonteijnen ende grotte tot Honsholredijck … ter somme van negen en tsestich gulden …
8 Jan. 1647 … 69:0:0

993 fol. 455
… Op 't besteck van een deel hartehocken, 3 hoybergen een nootstal, heyning van ontrent 36 roeden lengte een wedde om paerden te wassen & ten behoeve van Sijne Hooch[ts] huys & stallinge tot Honsholredijck aengenomen bij Dirck de Milde …
22 Jan. 1647 … 5971:15:0

993 fol. 455 verso (Slothouwer p. 273)
… het maecken van 't schrijnwerck ofte belegsels inde sael vande ZuijdtOost gallerije van 't Nederhoff van Sijne Hooch[t] tot Honsholredijck aengenoomen bij Dirck de Milde volgens de bestecke in dato 1e Julij 1646 … de somme van ses hondert Car. gul. …
22 Jan. 1647 … 600:0:0

993 fol. 456
… Alsoo Dirck de Milde aengenoomen heeft volgens den voorstaende bestecke in dato 19e May 1644, het maken van twee distincte huijsingen, te weten d'deene tusschen de twee Noort-West ende tusschen de twee Noord-Oost pavilioenen van Sijne Hooch[ts] Huijs tot Honsholredijck, yder voor de somme van negenthien duijsent vijff hondert gul., maeckende over de twee te samen de somme van negen en dertich duijsent Car. gul. …
22 Jan. 1647 … 39000:0:0

993 fol. 457
… aen Dirck de Milde over 't vloeren van 2 Camers aen 't Oosteynde van de open Gallerije tegens den nieuwen Thuijn tot Honsholredijck …
22 Jan. 1647 … 1330:0:0

993 fol. 464 verso
… aen Theunis ende Arie Willemsz. … koemis à ses gulden thien stuyvers 't schip gevaert ende gelevert bij Theunis ende Arie Willemsz. inde nieuwen West Thuijn van Sijne Hooch[ts] Huys tot Honsholredijck …
VII Febr. 1647 … 650:0:0

993 fol. 465 [a] (Slothouwer, p. 273)
… te tellen aen Joseph Dinant sijnen grottier de somme van twee duijsent Car. gul. omme daer uijt te vervallen ende betalen de loode pijpen ende ander gereetschap, die bij hem Dinant sijn doen maecken tot Amsterdam voor de drie fontijnen die gemaeckt sullen worden tot Honsholredijck …
11 Febr. 1647 … 2000:0:0

993 fol. 465 [b]
… aen Dirck de Milde Boschbewaerder tot Honsholredijck van de oncosten gevallen in de Bosschen ende warande van Honsholredijck in de maendt Dec. 1646 …
18 Febr. 1647 … 213:11:0

993 fol. 466 verso [a]
… Dirck de Milde heeft aengenomen volgens den bovenstaande bestecke het ophogen ende maecken van een nieuwen Thuijn ende heyninge daerom aende Westzijde van 't huys tot Honsholredijck te

samen voor de somme van veerthien duysent drie hondert Car. guldens ... sal mogen betaelen de somme van vier duysent seven hondert sesentsestich gul. deerthien sts. vier dr. ende dat over den IIe en III termijn ...
23 Febr. 1647 ... 4766:13:4

993 fol. 466 verso [b]
... Dirck de Milde ... schoon onder houden vande maliebaan te Honsholredijck ...
23 Febr. 1647 ... 100:0:0

993 fol. 469
... aen Arent Pietersz. Blom hovenier van Sijne Hooch[t] over geleverde bollen ende Blommen inde West Thuijn tot Honsholredijck inden Jaere 1646 ...
XXV Febr. 1647 ... 84:1:0

993 fol. 475
... aen Dirck de Milde Boschbewaerder tot Honsholredijck van de oncosten gevallen in de Bosschen ende warande van Honsholredijck in de maendt Jan. 1647 ...
4 Maert 1647 ... 184:1:0

NDR, inv. no. 994 [737] (years 1647-1650)

994 fol. 13 (Slothouwer, p. 274)
Alsoo mr. Arien Leendertsz. Cleij, metselaer, ende mr. Cornelis Leendertsz, timmerman, aengenoomen hebben ... het maecken van 2 pavillioenen met twee galerijen ende twee achtcantige toorens aen onsen huijse tot Honsholredijck, ende dat voor een somme van een hondert ende twaelff duijsent gul. te betaelen in vier termijnen ...
22 May 1647 ... 11200:0:0

994 fol. 14 verso
... aen Simon van Catshuijsen Rentm[r] vande Domeijnen van Naeltwijck te betalen aen voorn. aenenemer de voors. duysent carolus gul. over het maecken van een sloot aende westzijde vande warande tot Honsholredijck ...
May 1647 ... 1000:0:0

994 fol. 18
... als Jan Herison bij Sijne Hooch[t] gestelt tot sijnen Boschbewaerder tot Honsholredijck de somme van ses hondert Car. gul.
11 Junij 1647 ... 600:0:0

994 fol. 18
... aen Theunis en Arij Willemsz over acht ende vijfftich schepen koemis à ses gulden thien 't schip gevoert ende gelevert by Theunis en Arij Willemsz inden nieuwen westhuijn van Sijne Hooch[ts] huijs tot Honselaersdijck ...
12 Junij 1647 ... 377:0:0

... aen Theunis en Arij Willemsz over twee ende negentich schepen koemis inde voorsz thuijn ...
12 Junij 1647 ... 598:0:0

994 fol. 18 verso
... aen Theunis ende Arie Willemsz ... acht ende vijfftich schepen koemis à ses gulds. thien sts 't schip ... in den nieuwen westhuijn van Sijne Hooch[ts] huijse Honsholredijck ...
12 Junij 1647 ... 377:0:0

... aen Theunis ende Arie Willemsz ... twee en negentich schepen koemis inde voorsz thuijn ...
12 Junij 1647 ... 598:0:0

994 fol. 18 verso
... Bastiaen ende Symon Jansz Patijnen inwoonders van Naeltwijck ... soo vaert wech als sloot aende westzijde vande warande noch competerende ...
Junij 1647 ... 1000:0:0

994 fol. 21
... Antoine Deschamps sijnen stalmeester de somme van een duijsent ses hondert negen ende tachtich guls. negentien sts over reys ende teercosten ... reyse naer Parijs ...
1 Julij 1647 ... 1689:19:0

994 fol. 22 (Slothouwer, p. 274)
Alsoo Arent Laurensz. Oom mr. timmerman tot Rijswijck ... aengenoomen heeft het maecken van drie achtkante fonteijn putten in den thuijn achter onsen huijse tot Honsholredijck met een waterback op een van de pavillioenen aldaer voor de somme van vijff duijsent Car. gul. te betaelen in drie termijnen ...
11 Julij 1647 ... 5000:0:0

994 fol. 26 verso
... Pieter Florisz van der Salm ... seven ende veertich Car. gul. over verscheyde metingen ende caerteringen van Sijne Hooch[ts] landen in 't Westland in 1646 ...
5 Aug. 1647 ... 47:0:0

994 fol. 27
... Op andere declaratie van den voorsz Pieter Florisz vander Salm Landtmeter de somme van twee hondert acht ende dertich gul. over 't maecken ende copieren van enige caerten als anders bij hem gemaeckt in den jaere 1646 ...
5 Aug. 1647 ... 238:0:0

994 fol. 27
… Pieter 't Hooft steenhouwer over gelevert marmersteen ende arbeijtsloon tot Honsholredijck …
12 Aug. 1647 … 71:16:0

994 fol. 28 verso and 29
… Bartholomeus Drijfhout veertich gul. ende Beaumont ende Pauw veertich gul. over 't opnemen van het werck van Dirck de Milde te Honsholredijck …
Aug. 1647 … 40:0:0

994 fol. 29
… Balthasar van Engelen hovenier tot Antwerpen de somme van ses hondert car. gul. over twaelff Orange boomen bij hem ten dienste van Sijne Hooch^t geleverd …
8 Aug. 1647 … 600:0:0

994 fol. 36 (Slothouwer)
Alsoo Ary Leendertsz. Cleij en Cornelis Leendertsz Roels … het maecken van twee pavillioenen annex aen onsen huijse tot Honsholredijck …
XX Oct. 1647 … 18000:0:0

994 fol. 36 verso
… te tellen aen Joseph Dinant sijnen Grottier de somme van duijsent car. gul. omme daer uijt te vervallen ende te betalen de werckluijden die bij hem werden geemployeert tot het maecken van drie fonteinen tot Honsholredijck …
25 Oct. 1647 … 1000:0:0

994 fol. 38
… Alsoo Bastiaen en Simon Jansz Patijnen inwooners tot Naeltwijck aengenomen hebben volgens den besteck daervan sijnde in dato 4 May 1647 het maken van eenige vaarten, slooten ende dreven tot vergrootinge vande warande achter de huijse van Honsholredijck …
3 Nov. 1647 … 2000:0:0

994 fol. 38 verso
… als Mr Anthonie van Thoor hovenier van sijne Thuijnen tot Honsholredijck de somme van hondert car. gul. ter vervallinge van sijne oncosten te doen op sijne reijse naer Rijnberch, Meurs ende andere quartieren daer omtrent, omme vandaer te halen eenige beucken als andere boomen ten dienste van Sijne Hoocheit …
7 Nov. 1647 … 100:0:0

994 fol. 39 verso
… alsoo declaratie van Simon Langelaer hovenier tot Buren over reijscosten bij hem gedaen in Aug. 1647 over eenig fruijt van daer naer den Hage te brengen aen hare Con. Hooch^t is ordonnans …
27 Aug. 1647 … 8:0:0

994 fol. 41 [a]
… Anthony van Tooren hovenier tot Honsholredijck … van 36.000 haechen ende Mey buecken, 600 buecken Stalboomkens bij mr. Geurt Sainct Gardenier tot Meurs aen hem gelevert ten dienste van Sijne Hooch^t alsmede de quitantie vande voorn. Geurt Sainct van 501 gul. Meursgelt bij hem ontfangen in betalinge vande voorsz. boomkens …
VI Dec. 1647 … 426:9:0

994 fol. 41 [b]
… Anthony van Thooren hovenier op 't huijs tot Honsholredijck … schipper Jan Jacobsz van Duynen die als doen mede gem. boomen ter Plantsoenen hadde affgebracht, verstaen … als desen schipper Pieter Hendrix sal mogen betalen de somme van hondert vijff ende twintig Car. guldens over de vracht van bovenstaende …
VI Dec. 1647 … 125:0:0

994 fol. 41 verso
… Simon van Langelaer, hovenier te Bueren over reijscosten in Nov. 1647
IX Dec. 1647 … 31:4:0

994 fol. 72 verso
… Op den rekeninge van Arent Pieterz Blom over geleverde bloemen inden nieuwen thuijn tot Honsholredijck in den Jaere 1647 …
1 Julij 1648 .. 27:5:0

994 fol. 77 verso
… Pieter Florisz vander Salm over gemaeckte caerten vacatien ende verdient salaris int westlandt heden den 7 Febr. 1647 …
IX Julij 1648 … 109:10:0

994 fol. 77 verso
… Pieter Florisz vander Salm overt maecken ende copieren van Caerten, metingen …
sedert januaris 1647 tot december 1647 de somme van … 150:15:0

994 fol. 80
… Cornelis Jacobsz van Brederoode over verscheydene soo Fruijt als andere boomen bij hem ten dienste van Sijne Hooch^t inden nieuwen Westhuijn tot Honsholredijck gelevert anno 1647 …
30 Junij 1648 … 594:4:0

994 fol. 85 verso (Slothouwer, p. 274)
… te betalen asen Sr. Willem Mulman, coopman tot Amsterdam de somme van XI^C XLVIII £ ter seacke van fonteijnsteen bij hem voor des selfs broeder Henrico Mulman tot Tyvoli buiten Roma doen coopen ende alhier tot Honsholredijck ten dienste van S. Hooch^t gelevert …
30 Sept. 1648 … 1148:0:0

994 fol. 87
… Dirck de Milde voort het onderhouden van de Maliebaan tot Honsholredijck …
6 Oct. 1648 … 100:0:0

994 fol. 88 verso
… Alsoo Dirck de Milde aengenoomen heeft volgens de bestecken daervan sijne in dato 20 Julij 1646 het maken van een nieuwe thuijn ende houte heijning daeromme aende westzijde van S. Hooch[ts] huijs tot Honsholredijck te samen voor een somma van veertien duijsent drie hondert Car. gul. te weten den nieuwen thuijn voor elf duijsent car. gul. ende een houten heijninge voor drie duijsent drie hondert gulden te betalen in drie termijnen [derde en lesten termijn] …
XIX Oct. 1648 … 4541:13:4

994 fol. 90 (Slothouwer p. 274)
… Alsoo Arent Lourisz Noom, mr. timmerman tot Rijswijck … aengenoomen heeft het maken van drie achtkante fonteijnputten inde thuijn achter onsen huijse tot Honsholredijck met een waterback op een vande pavillioenen aldaer, voor de somme van vijff duijsent Car. gul. …
31 Oct. 1648 … 5000:0:0

994 fol. 93 verso
… Cornelis van Stoop over geleverde Ypen boomen inden jare 1647 … [rentm[r] van Bueren mag hem betaelen] …
2 Sept. 1648 … 27:10:0

994 fol. 140
… Pieter Florisz vander Salm over het maecken ende plaetsen van Caerten ende waterpassen van slooten als andersints bij hem gedaen ten dienste van Sijne Hooch[t] inden Jare 1648 …
X Aug. 1649 … 92:11:0
… ibid. metinge van landen gelegen in het Westlandt …

994 fol. 159
… Cornelis Jacobsz Steenhuijsen woonende tot Naeltwijck … attestatie vande warantm[r] tot Honsholredijck van verscheyde sacken granen ende andere eetwaren bij Cornelis Jacobsz Steenhuijsen gelevert ten behoeve van Sijne Hooch[ts] wilt ende gevogelte tot Honsholredijck inden Jaren 1647 ende 1648
4 Febr. 1649 … 688:2:0

… gelijcke ordonnans … Cornelis Jansz vander Eest … in de maenden Nov. ende Dec. 1648 en Jan. 1649 …   271:15:0

994 fol. 168 verso (only partly in Slothouwer, p. 275)
… staet van oncosten gedaen bij den grottier Joseph Dinant aende grotten ende fonteijnen tot Honsholredijck inden jare 1649 … geverifieert en getekend bij den Controlleur vande Camer van Sijne Hooch[t] Pierre du Nois …
22 Junij 1650 … 3277:13:0

NDR, inv. no. 995 [738] (years 1651-1657)

995 fol. 3 verso
… Cornelis Simonsz vander Meer ende Ary Claessen Duyffhuys … over 't leveren van 42 schepen sandt yeder schip tot 26 stuyvers huys van Sijne Hoocheit tot Honsholredijck in den ouden Thuyn … gelevert in de maenden van Nov. ende Dec. 1650 …
IX Jan. 1651 … 54:12:0

995 fol. 5 verso
… Cornelis Joosten hovenier tot Rijswijck … geattesteert bij den hovenier vanden Thuynen tot Honsholredijck …
14 Febr. 1651 … 69:0:0

995 fol. 10
… Michiel Jans van Sweth … over gelevert cooren voor de harten beesten ende vogels tot Honsholredijck in Nov. 1650 …
XI Mrt. 1651 … 148:0:0
Ibid.:   Dec. 1650   135:0:0
          Feb. 1651   136:4:0

995 fol. 12 verso
… Pieter Floris van der Salm over vacatien ende metingen in 't Westlandt tsedert 22 April 1649 tot 20 Dec. 1649 …
14 Maert 1651 28:0:0

Ibid.:   Jan. 1650 - Apr. 1651   5: 0:0
          Jan. 1649 - 5 Dec. 1649   28:17:0
          Feb. 1650 - 22 Sept. 1650 15: 0:0

995 fol. 21
… Anthony van Thooren hovenier tot Honsholredijck … over boomen tot Meurs gehaelt in 1647 …
3 May 1651 … 87:11:8

995 fol. 26 verso
… Junius Nollemans ende Jacob Albertsz van Spijck … geatt. by den Concierge Joseph Dinant … over het schilderen en verwen van verscheyden groot hecken ende stacketten tot Honsholredijck …
22 Aug. 1651 … 489:19:0

995 fol. 28
… Michiel Jansz van Sweth over geleverde Cooy als anders voor de herten beesten ende vogelen tot Honsholredijck …
Maert 1651 … 136:12:0

Ibid.:   Apr. 1651   138:2:0
           May   145:6:0
           Jun.   145:18:0
           Jul.   145:0:0
           Aug.   145:0:0

995 fol. 31 (Slothouwer, p. 337)
… Opt contract van vier statuen van marber vande Princen Willem, Maurits, Frederick Hendrick en Willem is ordonnantie gedepescheert als volgt. Alsoo Francisco Dieussart beelthouwer aengenomen heeft volgens den bovenstaende contracte in dato 19 April 1648 te maecken ende te leveren vier witte marbere beelden representerende na 't leven de vier Princen inden voorsz. contracte vermelt, voor de somme van 4000 Car. gul. …
8 Nov. 1651 … 4000:0:0

995 fol. 36
… Aen Jan Herison warantm^r tot Honsholredijck … tot vervallinge van de oncosten te doen int overbruggen naer Aurick vande dieren ende vogelen aende heer Grave van Oostvrieslandt …
16 Dec. 1651 300:0:0

995 fol. 45 verso
… Bastiaen Jansz en Simon Jansz Patijnen eenige dreven, slooten ende andere aerdewercken inde nieuwe warande tot Honsholredijck inde Jare 1648
5 Febr. 1652 … 625:0:0

995 fol. 45 verso
… hout en metselwerck van vijff Bruggens op de Nederhoven tot Honsholredijck den 8 May 1649 …
Febr. 1652 … 2096:1:4

995 fol. 46
… Claes Dircksz Balckeneynde ende Arent Laurensz Heemskerck vant gelevert houtwerck aende Bruggen bij wijlen Rentm^r Catshuysen gemaeckt over de Naeltwijckse Vaert tot Honsholredijck in den Jare 1649 ….
5 Febr. 1652 …. 226:3:0

995 fol. 46 verso
… Anthony van Thooren, over arbeytloonen over 't teeckenen en planten vande parterres aen de westzijde van 't huys tot Honsholredijck
10 Febr. 1652 …. 138:0:0

995 fol. 46 verso
… Voorn. Van Thooren, over arbeyten van teeckenen ende maecken vande nieuwe parterre in den ouden Thuyn tot Honsholredijck in den Jare 1646
… 86:5:0

995 fol. 46 verso
… Voorn. Van Thooren, over missie by verscheyden persoonen gelevert inden Jare 1647
… 74:10:0

995 fol. 46 verso
… voorn. hovenier, over geleverde missie, gaerden aerde en anders by verscheydene personen in den Jare 1647
… 148:18:0

995 fol. 46 verso
… vande selven hovenier over arbeytsloon verdient aende parterres inden Jare 1647
… 95:4:6

995 fol. 46 verso
… op andere staet ende specificatie … over gecochte Granaet ende Orangie boomen in Augusto 1650
… 100:0:0

995 fol. 47
… voor voorn. hovenier tot Honsholredijck Anthony van Thooren over arbeytsloonen verdient by verscheyden persoonen in Sept. 1651 …
186:7:6

Ibid.:   Oct. 1651   124:3:6
           Nov. 1651   96:11:0
           Dec. 1651   179:8:0

995 fol. 47
… Blaserus Jacobsz Hovenier tot Honsholredijck over arbeytsloon verdient by verscheydene persoonen inden nieuwe Thuyn tot Honsholredijck in Sept.
Sept. 1651 … 95:18:0

Ibid.:   Oct. 1651   73:10:8
           Nov. 1651   70:1:0
           Dec. 1651   58:5:0

995 fol. 47 verso
… arbeyders die gewrocht hebben inde warande tot Honsholredijck in Augusto 1651 …
10 Febr. 1652 … 114:6:9

Ibid.:   Sep. 1651   94:14:0
           Oct. 1651   115:15:0
           Nov. 1651   74:2:0

995 fol. 47 verso

... Anthony van Thooren ... tottet coopen vande behoeften ...
415:15:0

995 fol. 52

... Op de requeste van Pierre Colombier hovenier ... costgelt van eenen gul. daagen van 1 Jan. 1651 tot den 8 Maert daeraenvolgende,
23 Maert 1652

995 fol. 54 verso

... Pieter Floris vander Salm over gedaene metingen ...
16 April 1652 130:2:0

995 fol. 59

... Johan Herison warantm^r tot Honsholredijck ... reise naer Emden met de Bere ende honden die hare hoocheden aende Grave van Oostvrieslandt hebben vereert ... waer te neemen Sijne Hoocheits Bosch ende warande tot Honsholredijck ...
25 May 1652 ... 74:14:0

995 fol. 62 verso

... Jan Herison ... int overbrengen van 't wildt bij hare Hoocheit aende Grave van Oostvrieslandt vereert ...
21 Aug. 1652 ... 462:14:0

995 fol. 68

... persoonen die in de warande tot Honsholredijck hebben gewrocht in January 1652 ...
26 Aug. 1652 ... 72:6:6

Ibid.:	Feb. 1652	69:10:0
	Mrt.	86:9:9
	Apr.	82:16:0
	May	84:19:0

995 fol. 68 verso

... Anthony van Thooren ... over verdient arbeytsloon by de persoonen die gewrocht hebben in de oude ende lesten nieuwe Thuyn tot Honsholredijck ...
Jan. 1652 ... 26 Aug. 1652 ... 75:17:0

Ibid.:	Feb. 1652	75:17:0
	Mrt.	146 19:0
	Apr.	236:10:0
	May	221:9:8

995 fol. 69

... Blaserus Jacobsz ... in den eersten nieuwe thuyn tot Honsholredijck ... in Jan. 1652 ...
26 Aug. 1652 ... 52:10:0

Ibid:	Feb. 1652	48:12:0
	Mrt.	73:9:0
	Apr.	98:8:0
	May	94:5:0

995 fol. 81

... Op de memorie van Monsieur Pieter Post architect van Sijne Hoocheit ... over leverantie vande Caerte ende boecken der uytbeeldinge vande begraeffenisse van Sijne Hoocheit Prins Frederick Hendrick hooch lofflijcker memorie ...
25 Sept. 1652 ... 486:0:0

995 fol. 83

... Jansz Vander Groen, over leverantie van eenige blommen en andere gewassen inde oude ende tweeden nieuwen Thuyn tot Honsholredijck inden Jare 1652 ... van dato 7 Febr. lestleden tottet coopen vande Bloemen ende ander plantsoen ... geatt. by den hovenier Anthony van Thooren ...
21 Oct. 1652 ... 56:0:0

995 fol. 83

... persoonen die gewrocht hebben inde nieuwen Thuyn tot Honsholredijck versoeckende prompte betaeling van wat verdient is in de maent Juny 1652 inden eersten nieuwe Thuyn te Honsholredijck ...
30 Oct. 1652 ... 97:2:0

Ibid.: in den ouden ende tweede nieuwe thuyn

	Jul. 1652	222:4:0
	Aug.	198:11:0
	Sep.	184:18:0

995 fol. 83 verso

... Jansz vander Groen over leverantie van Bloemen inden eersten nieuwen Thuyn tot Honsholredijck desen Jare 1652 ...
21 Oct. 1652

995 fol. 85

... Anthony van Thooren hovenier tot Honsholredijck, tottet coopen van messie, asperges, sant, kerssen, pruymen, persicken ende anders ...
5 Nov. 1652 ... 576:8:0

995 fol. 85 verso

... Blaes Jacobsz hovenier van Sijne Hoocheits eersten nieuwe Thuyn tot Honsholredijck ... tottet coopen vande Messie, Boomen, Gaerden, Thienden, Spijckers, Sandt, Planten, Bloemen, Saet ende anders
5 Nov. 1652 ... 244:6:0

995 fol. 85 verso
… Martin Geoffroy Tapissier …. 465:15.0 … Over sijn Travaile extraord. moeyten, mitsgaders tot verval van de oncosten op sijn retour naer Parijs …
21 April 1651 … 465:15:0

995 fol. 95
… Cornelis Gerritsz Timmerman over verdient arbeytsloon aende Beerhocken, honde hocken, kotten ende hertehocken, ende anders in de maand aug. tot nov. 1650 … geattesteert by Joseph Herison …
20 Febr. 1653 … 188:0:0

995 fol. 99
… besteck van een nieuwe brugge aen de oostzijde van 't huys tot Honsholredijck voor de somme van 640 car. gul. … (Febr. 1653)

995 fol. 103
… Arent Laurensz van heemskerck Timmerman tot Rijswijck de somme van twee duysent seven hondert en thien car. gul. over verdient arbeytsloon ende geleverde materialen aen het hecke gestelt inde Jare 1650 inden Thuyn achter huyse Honsholredijck … geattesteert bij den concierge ende fontainier Joseph Dinant …
1 Febr. 1653 … 2710:0:0

995 fol. 102
… Arent Laurensz van Heemskerck … de somme van vijff hondert vier ende negentich gul. ses stuyvers over geleverde materialen ende arbeytsloonen by hem geleverd ende verdient aende fonteyn op sijn Hoocheits huys te Honsholredijck … geattesteert by den Concierge Joseph Dinant …
1 Febr. 1653 … 594:6:0

995 fol. 106 verso
… Opt rapport van Architect Pieter Post wordt den schilder M. de Bus noch ses duysent negen hondert ende veertich guls. betaald …
14 Maart 1652 … 6940:0:0

995 fol. 109
… Mr Jansz Brasser glasemaker tot Honsholredijck over vijfftich nieuwe spiegelglasen inde ramen vande nieuwe pavillioenen opden huyse van Honsholredijck … rentm^r domeynen ende architect Pieter Post …
23 April 1653 … 171:3:6

995 fol. 110 verso
… Specificatie vande arbeyders die gewrocht hebben inde warande tot Honsholredijck in Junio 1652 …
May 1653 … 82:0:0

Ibid.:	Julio 1652	67:4:0
	Aug. 1652	67:4:3
	Sept. 1652	60:18:6
	Oct. 1652	67:3:6

995 fol. 111
… Anthony van Tooren hovenier van Sijne Hoocheit inde oude ende nieuwe Thuyn te Honsholredijck, vande personen die daer in gewrocht hebben in October 1652 …
12 May 1652 … 168:10:0

Ibid.:	Nov. 1652	93:4:0
	Dec. 1652	112:16:8
	Jan. 1653	79:2:0
	Feb. 1653	78:8:0
	Mrt. 1653	122:8:0

995 fol. 111 verso
… Blaserus Jacobsz hovenier vande nieuwe Thuyn tot Honsholredijck, mitsgaders andere arbeyders die inde selve gewrocht hebben in Oct. 1652 …
12 May 1653 … 77:3:0

Ibid.:	Nov. 1652	74:0:0.
	Dec. 1652	51:3:0.
	Jan. 1653	45:14:0
	Feb. 1653	52:10:6

995 fol. 114 verso
… Joseph Dinant concierge op de huyse tot Rijswijck ende fontainier de somme van drie duysent car. gul. die hem werden toegevoegt over de extraordinair diensten ende Travail bij hem gedaen in't maken van de grotten tot Rijswijck, Honsholredijck ende elders …
7 Juni 1653 … 3000:0:0

995 fol. 115 verso
… L. Drijffhout … soo vacatien ende dachgelden mitgdrs. reyscosten overt opnemen van verscheydene wercken tot Honsholredijck beginnende 8 Augusti tot uytgaande Sept. 1649 … geverifieert bij de architect Pieter Post.

995 fol. 125 verso
… verscheyden personen die gewrocht hebben in Sijne Hooch^{ts} oude ende nieuwe Thuynen op Honsholredijck …
… 237:12:2

995 fol. 126
… verscheyden personen die gewrocht hebben in Sijne Hooch^{ts} oude ende nieuwe Thuynen op Honsholredijck …

Ibid.:   May 1652   214:12:0
         Juny   178:13:6
         July   190:11:3
         Aug.   172:1:0
         Sep.   172:1:0
         Oct.   143:7:9

995 fol. 141
… Abraham de Klerk over gelevert hennipsaet voor 't Gevogelte tot Honsholredijck …
XI Febr. 1654 … 70:0:0

995 fol. 154 verso
… arbeyders gewrocht hebben inde warande tot Honsholredijck in de maent November 1652 …
28 April 1654 … 55:18:0

Ibid.:   Dec. 1652   50:18:0
         Jan. 1653   54:16:6
         Feb. 1653   48:7:6
         Mrt.   64:12:3
         Apr.   63:5:0
         Mei   63:1:0
         Jun.   41:4:6
         Jul.   40:17:9
         Aug.   51:16:6
         Sep.   52:11:6
         Oct.   44:12:6
         Nov.   36:18:0
         Dec.   30:16:0
         Jan. 1654   36:15:0
         Feb. 1654   30:2:0
         Mrt.   51:13:6

995 fol. 154 verso
… Blaes Jacobsz hovenier van Sijne Hooch^{ts} eersten nieuwen Thuyn tot Honsholredijck …
28 April 1654 … 116:10:0

Ibid.:   May. 1653   104:96:0
         Jun. 1653   84:5:0
         Jul.   82:2:3
         Aug.   78:15:0
         Sep.   88:8:0
         Oct.   67:16:0
         Nov.   66:17:0
         Dec. 1653   61:16:0

995 fol. 146
… Blaes Jacobsz hovenier … over oncosten gevallen in't coopen van noodiche behoeften in den Jare 1653 …
28 April 1654 … 323:1:0

995 fol. 146
… Gelijcke ordonnantie op gelijcke specificatie van Anthony van Thooren hovenier van Sijne Hoocheits Thuynen op Honsholredijck vant Jaer 1653 …
28 April 1654 … 385:6:0

995 fol. 146
… Anthony van Thooren …
26 April 1654 … 201:9:8

Ibid.:   May 1653   155:19:0
         Jun.1653   125:19:0
         Jul.   121:18:6
         Aug.   112:19:6
         Sep.   107:8:0
         Oct.   106:2:3
         Nov.   101:15:0
         Dec. 1653   11:8:0

995 fol. 151
… Pieter Florisz van der Sallem over vacatien ende verdient salaris inden Jaren 1651, 1652 ende 1653 …
… 112:0:0

995 fol. 163
… Anthony van Thooren hovenier vande oude ende nieuwe Thuyn tot Honsholredijck over arbeytsloonen vande persoonen die inde voorn. Thuynen gewrocht hebben in January ende Febr. 1654 …
29 Oct. 1654 … 45:0:0

Ibid.:	Mrt. 1654	137:15:0
	Apr. 1654	187:10:6
	May	243:10:2
	Jun.	216:5:11
	Jul.	206:5:3
	Aug.	201:10:0
	Sep.	178:3:9
	Oct.	159:11:0

995 fol. 164
… Blasius Verbruggen hovenier … verscheydene arbeytsluyden gewrocht hebben in Sijne Hoocheits eersten nieuwen Thuyn tot Honsholredijck … vande maendt Jan. 1654, 12 Nov. 1654 …   33:8:0

Ibid.:	Mrt. 1654	56:19:0
	Apr. 1654	100:6:0
	May	98:8:0
	Jun.	93:12:0
	Jul.	89:19:4
	Aug.	87:7:0
	Sep.	88:14:0
	Oct. 1654	72:12:12

995 fol. 184 verso
… Dirch Craey schilder … becleden, repareeren, uythalen, werder overschilderen van eenige schilderijen op den huys tot Honsholredijck … in den Jare 1651 …
16 Sept 1655 … 236:0:0

995 fol. 186
… Arbeyders gewrocht hebbende inde warande op Honsholredijck inde maent April 1654 …
28 October 1655 … 41:0:0

Ibid.:	May 1654	40:16:0
	Jun.	39:2:0
	Jul.	46:14:0
	Aug.	40:16:0

995 fol. 186
… noch van verscheydene persoonen over leverantie van boomen … ende sandt
… 65:4:0

995 fol. 186
… Anthonis Gerrits Timmerman over verdient arbeytsloon inde warande tot Honsholredijck tsedert Jan. 1652 totten eersten dec. 1653
… 141:6:0

995 fol. 191
… Jan Herison warantm^r tot Honsholredijck … tractementen en costgelden aende wiltschutten van Sijne Hoocheits tot Honsholredijck inde Jaren 1648, 1649, 1650 ende 1651 …
XXX Nov. 1656 … 3327:0:0

995 fol. 223 verso
… arbeyders gewrocht hebbende inde warande op Honsholredijck in't snoeyen van vier viercante Ypenboomen aldaer in den Jaere 1657 … geattesteert by den warantm^r Paulus Stappaert … rentm^r vande domeynen van Naeltwijck Frederick Schoon …
28 May 1657 … 79:4:0

995 fol. 223 verso
… Anthonis Gerritsz timmerman … over nodige reparatien inde warande op Honsholredijck, 6 April 1656 …
28 May 1657 … 34:12:0

995 fol. 226
… Pieter Florissen vander Salm Landtmeter over vacatien ende verdient salaris inden Jaeren 1654, 1655, 1656 …
23 Juny 1657 … 134:6:0

NDR, inv. no. 996 [739] (years 1657-1665)

996 fol. 8 verso
… Landtmeter Pieter Florisz vander Salm over vacatien ende verdient salaris inden Jaere 1657 …
April 1658 …   157:0:0

996 fol. 10 verso
… Anthony van Thooren hovenier van Sijne Hoocheits oude ende tweeden nieuwen Thuyn tot Honsholredijck … over de maent November 1654 … ordre ende last van haere hoocheden de voogden van Sijne hoocheit in dato
Maert 1658 … 75:11:0

996 fol. 11 verso
… Blaes Jacobsz … Sijne Hoocheits ouden ende tweeden nieuwen Thuyn tot Honsholredijck van de maent December 1654 …   62:11:0

Ibid.:	Jan. 1655	77:9:8
	Feb.	76:12:0
	Mrt.	161:8:0
	Apr.	151:7:0
	May	213:8:0
	Jun.	220:8:0
	Jul.	216:4:0
	Aug.	174:17:0

Sep.	156:11:0
Oct.	142:12:0
Nov.	124:14:0
Dec.	112:16:8
Jan. 1656	59:7:8
Feb.	41:6:0
Mrt.	103:1:0
Apr.	90:7:0
May	183:10:0
Jun.	142:17:8

996 fol. 12
… Blaes Jacobsz Verbruggen hovenier van Sijne Hoocheits eersten nieuwen Thuyn op Honsholredijck …
Nov. 1654 … 90:0:0

Ibid.:	Dec. 1654	70:7:0
	Jan. 1655	44:2:0
	Feb.	42:0:0
	Mrt.	137:11:0
	Apr.	106:8:8
	May	110:7:8
	Jun.	91:4:0
	Jul.	83:12:4
	Aug.	86:3:0
	Sep.	89:3:0
	Oct.	69:4:0
	Nov.	61:6:0
	Dec.	83:18:4
	Jan. 1656	40:16:0
	Feb.	36:0:0
	Mrt.	105:17:4
	Apr.	110:8:4
	Jun.	93:10:0

996 fol. 12 verso
… Blaes Jacobsz hovenier van Sijne Hooch[ts] eersten nieuwe Thuyn tot Honsholredijck over oncosten van incoop van noodige behoeften inden Jare 1654 … tottet coopen van Messie, Boomen Gaerden, Thienden, Sandt, Bloemen, Planten, Saet ende anders …
19 April 1658 … 249:2:8

996 fol. 13
… Anthony van Thooren … oncosten gevallen in't coopen van eenige noodige behoeften in den Jare 1654
[April 1658] … 360:10:0

996 fol. 14 verso
… Paulus Stappaert warantm[r] tot Honsholredijck over het stooren van Exters ende Crayen op twee distincte Schouwdagen …
Juni 1658 … 19:0:0

996 fol. 19
… besteck van eenige reparatien aen't Pavillioen ende het logement van de warantm[r] tot Honsholredijck … 4 Oct. 1656 naer voorgaende visitatie ende overlech gedaen by den architect Post …
20 ende 25 Sept. 1658 … 530:0:0

996 fol. 22
… Maria Margareta van Ackerlaken, sekere Genealogie geintituleert de Fonteyn van Orange …
13 Nov. 1658 … 50:0:0

996 fol. 28
… Pieter Florissen van der Salm Landtmeter over vacatien ende verdient salaris in den Jaere 1658 …
7 Maert 1659 … 101:15:0

996 fol. 31 verso
… Leendert Gillis Duyfhuys ende Mers Gerritsz van der Meer over verdient arbeytsloon inde warande tot Honsholredijck in Julio 1658 … geatt. by warantm[r] Paulus Stappaert … rentm[r] van de Domeynen van Naaltwijck Frederick Schoon … 18:0:0

996 fol. 32 [a]
… Leendert Gillis Duyfhuys ende Mers Gerritsz van der Meer over verdient arbeytsloon van het snoeien vande Boomen in de warande tot Honsholredijck …
Dec. 1658 tot April 1659 … 82:16:0

996 fol. 32 [b]
… Thonis Gerritsz Timmerman op Honsholredijck over arbeytsloon ende geleverde materialen tot het repareren van de palissade heyninge aen't Bosch tot Honsholredijck …
1657 tot Mey 1658 … 27:4:0

996 fol. 32 [c]
… Jan Pietersz Smit op Honsholredijck, geleverde materialen en arbeytsloon inde warande tot Honsholredijck …
1657-'58 … 32:0:0

996 fol. 60
… Pieter Post architect van Sijne Hoocheit over vracht ende teercosten gevallen op de keer ende wedersreyse naer Dieren, op de vercopinge vande houten heyninge om 't Parck aldaer …
8 Juny 1660 … 45:11:0

996 fol. 128
… Johan van Swieten Lantmeter, watermolen tot Nieuvaert … 103:1:0

996 fol. 162
… Erffgenamen van Cornelis Gerritsen van Egmont in sijn leven Smit op Honsholredijck … Boschbewaerder Johan Herrison … over arbeytsloon ende gelevert yserwerck aen het huys ende pallesaten in Sijne Hoocheits warande tot Honsholredijck in de jaren 1651, 52, 53 en 1654 …
… 179:7:6

996 fol. 164 verso
… Pieter Florisz van der Salm … vacatien ende verdient salaris Feb. 1659 - Jan. 1663 …
… 229:3:0

996 fol. 194
… Johan van Swieten Lantmeter …
… 289:3:0

996 fol. 197 verso
… Fabryck mr. Johan van Swieten …
10 Dec. 1664 … 134:0:0

ARA, NDR, inv. nos. 6945-6967 [7146-7168], the accounts of the estate steward Simon Catshuijsen provide further detailed information regarding the upkeep of the Westland region, including Naaldwijk and Honselaarsdijk.

NOTULEN VAN DE RAAD. NOTES OF THE COUNCIL.
1 Januari 1667
NDR, inv. no. 26 [NDR 26, 603]

Maendagh 31 January 1667
Weduwe vanden Thuynman tot Honsholredyck
Is binnen gestaen de Weduwe van den Thuynman ende versoeckt dat doch eenmael order mach worden gestelt tot betaling van haer achterstie, dat sij het niet langer conde uytstaen ende haer goet tot groote schade soude vercocht werden. is haer gesegt dat de Raede ende Rentm^r Schoon soude spreken …

Dinsdagh 1 February 1667
Weduwe vanden Thuynman tot Honsholredyck. Is binnen gestaen de Rentmeester Schoon ende is hem aengesecht ende belast dat hij de Weduwe vande hovenier van Honsholredijck soude hebben contentement te doen, ende oock van Haere Hooch^t daertoe sijn gelast geweest.

Maendagh 7 February 1667
Is gedisponeert op de remonstrantie van Paulus Stappaerts, Warantmeester tot Honsholredyck, aengaende 't snoeyen vande Boomen inde warande, ende 't repareren vande palissades, omme soo veel doenen de schade die de harten doen inde caren, bergen ende inde Thuynen.

TER NIEUBURCH

ACCOUNTS OF THE COMPTROLLER, DECREES OF THE COUNCIL, continued

NDR, inv. nos. 1039-999 [778-742] (years 1630-1694)

1039 fol. 218 (Slothouwer p. 289)
In Julio XVI^C dertich tijde deser heeft Sijnne Furstelicke Doorluchticheit van Filibert Vernatti gecocht eene wooninge genaemt Ter Nieuburch bij Rijswijck gelegen met hare boomgaerden cingelen waranden ende veertien margen een hond ses ende tnegentich roeden landts daeraen gehoorende, ende dat voorde somme van dertich duisent ponden artois, … elcke wooninge Sijnne Hoochgemelte Furstelicke Doorluchticheit teenemael geraseert ende in de plaets vandien een seer treffelick gebouw gestichtet heeft …
Julio 1630 … 30000:0:0

1039 fol. 219
… Heeft noch betaelt de somme van vier hondert acht ponden negen schellingen artois, soo over het dempen van eenige slooten ende wederom schieten van andere, also over eenige vrachten, reijs ende teercosten als andersins bij den concierge Langenhoven ter saecke vant Gebouw vant voorscreve huijs gedaen ende verleit …
1630 … 408:9:0

1039 fol. 220
… drie hondert ponden seven sts. vier dernier soo per rest van het dempen van eene binnensloot als ander verschot bij den Concierge Langehoven verleit …
1630 … 388:7:4

1039 fol. 220 verso
… twee duijsent twee hondert ende seven ponden twaelff sts vier dernier over verscheijden partien ten behoeve vant voorscreve Gebouw gedaen, als Dempen ende 't schieten vande slooten 't leveren van VII^C XXVI Lindeboomen, mitgaders 't planten vant Lant voor den voorschrevene huijse naer de gemene wech leggende …
1630 … 2207:12:4

1039 fol. 234
… In den jaere XVI^C dertich tijde deser en sijn geen meerdere acquisiten der domeynen gedaen dan de verbeteringen vande notabele nieuwe Gebouwen ende reparatien soo aenden Casteele ende Thuynen te Buren, ende aende huyse te Honsholredijck ende Nieuburch gemaeckt ende gedaen …
[1630] … X^N Somma: M^C LXX^M IX^C LXXXV £ XIII sts XV dr

NDR, inv. no. 1040 [779] (year 1631)

1040 fol. 213 verso
… Uytgave wegens het Gebou twelcke Sijne Furst. doorl. heeft doen maecken aent huijs genaemt Ter Nieuburch bij Rijswijck gelegen. Den Rendant heeft betaelt de somme van dertienhondert achtensestich ponden artois soo over leverantie van CXLIX Lindeboomen als voor .. (?) over arbeitsloon vant planten ent hoogen vande thuijnen vant huijs Ter Nieuburch, mitsgaders 't planten vande boomen aldaar van november XVI^C en dertich tot ultimo January Jaers deser verreckening bij den Concierge Langenhoven betaelt …
… 1368:0:0

1040 fol. 214
… heeft noch betaelt d'somme van twee duijsent driehondert en veertich ponden vijf dernier artois, te weten XIIII^C £ XVI sts VIII dr. over de twee derde paijen van XXI^C L £ V sts bij Levert Janssen Versijll Thuijnman bedongen voor de leverantie van XVIII^C LVII Lindeboomen om bij 't huijs Ter Nieuburch te planten sullende tresterende derde part betaelt worden op t einde van de somme deser Jaers, als wanneer men sien sal dat deselve boomen van goeder aart sullen sijn, III^C £ voor het dempen ende vollen van den Suyt-achterlaen ende Noortwaerts van den uytgeroeyden boomgaert metten sloot tussen den wal Cingel int weylant aent huijs Ter Nieuburch, CLXIIII £ III sts IX dr. over arbeitsloon bij den concierge Langenhoven in de maend februari Jaers deser verreckening betaelt, aen Floris Jacobsz Lantmeter over verscheijden vacatien ten dienste van t voorschrevene gebou gedaen, LXXV £ over leverantie van verscheijden soorten van planten, om in de Thuijnen van Rijswijck te setten, ende noch CVIII £ over leverantie van CVIII Lindeboomen omme ontrent thuijs Ter Nieuburch te planten, alles naerder blijckende bijde maendtreckeninge van de domeinen van Februarij tijde deser …
Febr. 1631 … 2341:0:5

1040 fol. 215
… betaelt de somme van dertien hondert acht ponden ses schellingen als namentlijck CXLVII £ VIII sts overt schieten vanden Sloot die door de weyde achter het huijs Ter Nieuburch gemaeckt is, Item II^C LXXXIII £ VI sts VIII dr. over een derde part van VIII^C L £ bij eenige arbeijders bedongen voor het hoogen toemaecken ende verlaten vanden Oost thuijn, mitsg. III^C £ insgelijcx over een derde part van II^C L £ bij eenige arbeijders, voor het aenhoogen ende toemaecken vande West thuijn aent huijs Ter Nieuburch bedongen …
[Febr. 1631] … 1308:6:0

1040 fol. 215
… ende noch V^C XXVII £ XI sts III dr. door den Concierge Langenhoven aen verscheijden leveranties ende arbeijders die in de maent Maert Jaers deser reeckeninge buyten de voorsiene aengenoomen wercken getreden …
Febr. 1631 … 527:11:3

1040 fol. 216
… heeft noch betaelt de somme van negentienhondert ses en tachtich ponden vijf schellingen artois te weten CXLVIII £ over koemis inde Thuijnen aent huijs Ter Nieuburch gelevert, Item LXXVIII £ XIIII sts over leverantie van XXXIIII Vijgeboomen à V £ VII sts tstuck, ende noch acht mistus peereboomen à II £ II sts yder, mitsgaders XII^C LXVI £ XIII sts IIII dr. over de resterende twee derde parten vant ophoogen toemaecken ende verlaten vande oost ende west thuijn aent huijs Ter Nieuburch … ende noch III^C XXII £ XVII sts VIII dr bijden concierge Langenhoven aen verscheijden arbeijders ten dienste vant Gebouw ende Thuijnen in de Maent Aprilis tijde deser betaelt …
April 1631 … 1986:5:0

1040 fol. 216 verso (only partly in Slothouwer p. 289)
… betaelt de somme van twintich duisent vier hondert eenenveertich p[onden acht schellingen artois, namentlick XX^M £ aen Symon Catshuisen betaelt over de twee paije van vieren van LXXX^M £ bij hem voorde opbouwinge vant groote middelpavillioen vant huis Ter Nieuburch bedongen, welcke voorschrevene tweede part verschenen is als wanneer de dorpels vande cruiscosijnen ront sommeren of de muren gelect sijn geweest, ende de verdere IIII^C XLI £ VIII sts over leverantie van duisent voet groene palm à III sts de voet, Item XL persickeboomen à II £ XII sts elck, CLVIII lindeboomen à I £ yder ende CXX kersseboomen à I £ II sts 'tstuck alle om inde thuijnen aent huijs Ter Nieuburch geplant te worden …
May [1631] … 20441:8:0

1040 fol. 217 verso
… betaelt d'somme van elfhondert een en twintich ponden drie schillingen artois, te weten III^C XLVII £ V dr over leverantie van LXXIX schepen koemis welcke inde moesthuijnen aent huis Ter Nieuburch gelevert sijn, II^C LXXIII £ XVIII sts over leverantie van II^{C}XLIX lindeboomen à XXII £ tstuck, III^C voor het dempen ende effenen van seeckere twee zuydslooten aende oost ende west thuijnen leggende, ende de verdere L £ betaelt aen Frans Janssen dewelcke aen partie lants, het welcke Sijnne Furst. doorl. met Jonkh^r van der Horst gepermiteert heeft in pacht hadde, omme daermede van den selve pacht te desisteren blijckende bij de maendt reckeninge van de domeinen …
Junij [1631] … 1121:3:0

1040 fol. 218
… vier ponden tien schellingen artois over drie wagenvrachten vanden rendant inde maendt Augustus Jaers deser reckeninge aent huijs Ter Nieuburch te voeren om de wercken ald^r te bevorderen ende besichtigen …
Aug. 1631 … 4:10:0

1040 fol. 218 verso
… twee hondert acht ponden seventien schellingen ses dernier artois bijden Concierge Langenhoven betaelt aen verscheijden arbeitsloonen vande wercken inde maendt Mey Jaers deser reeckeninge aent Gebou ende Thuijnen Ter Nieuburch gemaeckt ende gedaen …
[Aug. 1631] … 208:17:6

1040 fol. 219
… de somme van twee duisent zevenhondert acht endertich ponden dertich schellingen vier dernier artois te weten VIII^C LXXVIII £ IX sts VIII dr. over soo voorden Concierge Langenhoven betaelt heeft aen verscheiden leveraars ende arbeitslieden in de maenden Juny, July Augusti September ende October alle Jaers deser reeckeninge ten behouve vant Gebouw ende Thuijnen Ter Nieuburch ijetwes gedaen ende gelevert hebben, Item VII^C VI £ voor den eersten termin van XIX^C LXXV £ bij Adriaen Groenevelt Timmerman bedongen voor het affbreecken vant bouwhuijs vant huis Ter Nieuburch, ende om t'selve wederom op een andere plaetse te stellen, Mitsgaders IIII^C XLVI £ V sts aen den Schout ende Secretaris van Rijswijck betaelt, over henluyden gerechticheden int coopen permiteren ende aenbesteeden van verscheyden partien lants die Sijnne furstelicke D^t inden Ambachte van Rijswijck gecost, vermangelt als wercken aen doen nemen heeft ende noch VII^C £ VIII sts VIII dr. over het resterende derde part van II^M CI £ VI sts twelck Leendert Franssen thuijnman over leverantie van XVIII^C LVII lindeboomen, … Item verdere VII £ X sts over wagenvrachten bijden Rendant inde maent Octobr. Jaers deser reeckeninge ten dienste van voorschreve Gebouw verleyt …
Oct. 1631 … 2738:13:4

1040 fol. 221
… betaelt de somme van vier hondert sevenendevijftich ponden dertich schellingen te weten II^C III £ X sts over de vracht van Meurs van hondert duisent plansoenen van haech ende Mey buecken, om te Suylestein ende aent huijs Ter Nieuburch geplant te worden, Item CXLI £ IX sts over arbeijtsloon bij den Concierge Langenhoven inde Maent December Jaers deser reeckeninge ten dienste vant voorschreve Gebouw verstreckt, mitsgr. de verdere CXII £ XIIII sts over leverantie van ongecoleurde blompotten, als eenige koemis …
Dec. 1631 … 457:13:0

1040 fol. 222 (Slothouwer, p. 289)
… betaelt aen Louis d'Antonio hovenier van S. Vorst. Doorluchts. thuinen aent huijs ter Nieuburch de somme van sevenhondert ponden tot extinctie van alle pretensien van tractem^t die hij jegens S. Furst. D^t soude mogen hebben over seventien maenden die hij segt te Nieuburch gedient te hebben aleer S. Hoochgemelte Furst. D^t hem sijn ords tractement van VI^C £ jaerlicx gelieft heeft te accorderen, uijtwijsens de maendtrereckeninge vande domeijnen
January 1632 …

1040 fol. 222 verso
… aflossinge vant capitael van eene rente van II^C £ jaerlicx die Mr Jacob van der Does op de heerlickheit Naeldwijck spreeckende hadde, Item II^M VIII^C XL £ XVII sts in betaling van twee morgen drie hont drie entnegentich roeden lants inden plaspolder onder Rijswijck gelegen aen Sijnne furst. doorluchticheit vande kerckmrs. van Rijswijck in february Jaers deser Reeckeninge gecost, mitsgaders III^M IX^C XXVI £ in voldoeninge van vier margen sestien roeden, mede inde voorscreve plaspolder gelegen, van Jo^r Jacob de Bye in februario voorscreve doen coopen, ende noch XV^C LXV £ over de coop van ontrent vijff hont lants met huis berch ende geboomte daerop staende, met het recht vande Santvaert, oock inde plaspolder onder Rijswijck gelegen van Martije Claeszn Tetingerbrouck becomen …
Febr. 1631 … 11531:17:0

1040 fol. 224 verso [cf. 1042 fol. 307 verso]
… aen de erffgenamen van wijlen Jo^r Jan Prince ende Joff^r Margarita Ratallier sijne gewesene huisvrouwe de somme van ses duisent hondert twee ende vijfftich ponden vijff schellingen seven dernier artois te weten … voor de wooninge groot achtien morgen drie hondert drie en dertich roeden lants vrij allodiaal goet in den ambachte van Rijswijck gelegen, welck S.F.D. vande voornoemde erfgen. doen coopen heeft …
6152:5:7

1040 fol. 227 verso
… In den Jaere XVI^C een ende dertich tijde deser en sijn geen meerdere acquisiten der domeinen gedaen, dan de voorsz. verbeteringe vande notable nieuwe gebouwen ende merckelycke verbeteringen soo aen de huijsen te Honsholredijck, Buren, Iselstein ende Nieuburch gemaeckt ende gedaen …
December 1631: X^n Somma: XCL^M CI £ XVI sts V dr.

NDR, inv. no. 1041 [780] (year 1632)

1041 fol. 253 verso
… aen Louis d'Anthoni hovenier vande thuijnen aent huijs Ter Nieuburch de somme van drie en vijfftich ponden twaelff schill. over leverantie van eenige Rooselaers aertbesien, om inde voorschreve Thuijnen te planten …
Febr. 1632 … LIII £ XII sts

1041 fol. 254 verso
… Willem Foppen wegens Jan Claesz van Woerden de somme van vier ende twintich ponden dertien schillingen in voldoeninge van eenige pannen tot het Thuijnhuischen aent huijs Ter Nieuburch gelevert …
Febr. 1632 … XXIIII £ XIII sts

1041 fol. 255 verso
… Floris Jacobsz lantmeter de somme van vijff ende tachtich ponden artois over sijne vacatien int meten vande partien die Sijne hoocht inden ambachte van Rijswijck gecost heeft, als voor eenige Caerten te maecken
Febr. 1632 … LXXXV £

1041 fol. 257 verso
… Cornelis Leenersz de somme van ses ende twintich ponden vijff schillingen bij hem besteck bedongen voor het toemaecken van acht ackers tottet planten vande heggen, blijckende …
April 1632 … XXVI £ V sts.

1041 fol. 258
… Balthasar van Engelen de somme van twee hondert vijffentwintich ponden tien schellingen voor eenenveertich rooden ende blauwe vygeboomkens bij hem gelevert …
Aprilis 1632 … 225:10:0

1041 fol. 258 verso
… Franck Dircsen ende Jaspar Janssen werckluyden de somme van twee duisent vijff hondert vijff ende twintich ponden artois, bij henlieden volgende de Conditien vant besteck bedongen voor het hoogen vande plantagien voor het huijs Ter Nieuburch …
Aprilis 1632 … II^M V^C IXXV £

1041 fol. 260 verso (Slothouwer, p. 290)
… betaelt aen Arent Arentsz, architect, de somme van acht en twintich ponden voor verscheijden teijckeningen bij den selven vande voorschreve poorte ende balustrade gemaeckt …

1041 fol. 261 (Slothouwer, p. 290)
Inde maent Junij XVI C twee endertich tijde deser heeft den rendant geassisteert met Gerrit van Druijvestein, fabryckmeester vanden hage Pieter Bilderbeeck, architect ende eenige mrs. metselaers bestelt het graven ende metselen van riolen tot de waterlosinge vande binnen ende voorplaats, als oock de fondamenten vande balustrade ende groote voorpoort aent huijs Ter Nieuburch, ende ter dier oorsaecke drie mael aldaer geweest, betaelt voor de wagenvrachten de somme van seven ponden tien schell …

1041 fol. 261 verso (Slothouwer, p. 290)
… betaelt aen Arent Arentsz, architect, d'somme van achtendertich ponden achtien schellingen soo over reiscosten ende vacatien gaende naer Amsterdam om de modellen vande poort ende ballusters aende steenhouwers aldaer te brengen, als overt vorderen ende waernemen vant metsel ende graeffwerck totde fondamenten van voorsz. balustrade ende poorte uijtwijsens de maentreeckeninge van Junio 1632 …

1041 fol. 263 (Slothouwer, p. 290)
… betaelt aen Arent Arentsz, architect, de somme van dertien ponden tien schellingen over salaris, vacatien ende verscheijden diensten bijden selven int teickenen ende anders tot het werck vant huijs Nieuburch …

1041 fol. 264 verso
… Arien Cornelissen Groenevelt Timmerman … versetten ende weder opbouwen van het bouhuis … ende alhier op een andere plaets met eenige verbeeteringen gestelt is …
Augustus 1632 … XIII^C XXIII £

1041 fol. 271 verso
… Hendrick Sebastiaensen, aennemer vant ophoogen vant plein off groote binnenplaets vant huijs ter Nieuburch … ende overt aenhoogen vande balustrade ende andere buytenwerck bij hem gedaen …
Nov. 1632 … VIII^C XVII £

1041 fol. 273 (Slothouwer, p. 291)
… vergoet aen Arent Arentsz 'sGravesandt, architect die den rendant gebruijckt tot directie ende vorderinge vant gebou tot Rijswijck …

1041 fol. 278 verso
… aen Louis d'Anthoni de somme van ses hondert ponden over een Jaer onderhouts vande Thuijn, ende van sijn Tractement als hovenier tot Nieuburch
Dec. 1632 … 600:0:0

1041 fol. 279 (Slothouwer p. 292)
… Arent Arentsz van 'sGravesant architect … voort maecken vande nodige teickeninge tot het gebouw Ter Nieuburch, als om d'opsicht te hebben …
Januario 1633 … III^C £

1041 fol. 284 verso (Slothouwer, p. 292)
… Catshuisen … over tleggen vande fondamenten vande twee gallerien ende pavillions aen Sijnne Hooch^{ts} huijse te Rijswijck … 8770:5:0

1041 fol. 313
… Mr Cornelis Helminhuis Schoolmeester tot Rijswijck … Jaer verloops van drie distincte rentgens gehypotiquieert opte huijsingen ende erven welck totte Stalling tot Rijswijck geappliceert sijn …
II £ XV sts.

NDR, inv. no. 1042 [781] (year 1633)

1042 fol. 258 verso (Slothouwer, p. 292)
… betaelt aen Barthout van Bassen, perspectijffschilder ende architect inden Hage d'somme van tachtich ponden over tmaken ende leveeren van twee perfecte grontteijkeningen vant geheele landt onder 't huis Nieuburch gehoorende, met de grontteijkeninge vant huijs, tuijnen ende plantagien vandien, item twee groote standtteijkeningen vant voorscreve gebouw inder vougen als het nu is, ende noch in proiect staet gemaeckt te worden, welck Sijnne Hoocheit gelast heeft in allerijl te doen maecken ende int leger toesonden te worden, als om andere vacatien bij den selven van Bassen ten dienste van Sijnne Hooch^t gedaen, volgen de specificatie ende quitantie overgenomen op de maendtreeckeninge van Januarij XVI^C drie en dertich …
Jan. 1633 … 80 :0:0

1042 fol. 260 (Slothouwer, p. 292)
… aen Jan Cornelisz. Bol. voerman, die Gerrit Druvestein ende Pieter van Bilderbeeck, architecten, vier reisen te Rijswijck gevoert heeft, om 't gebou bij Symon Catshuijsen aengenomen, te visiteren ende priseren, om int opnemen vant selve werck te connen dienen …
Jan. 1633

1042 fol. 264 verso (Slothouwer, p. 293)
… Vergoet aen Gerrit van Langenhoven concherge vant huijs Ter Nieuburch d'somme van vijffendertich ponden voor soo veel bij hem op IIen Februarij XVI^C drie en dertich verschooten is, om opt huis Ter Nieuburch een maeltijt etens te versorgen, als wanneer den rendant beneffens mr. David de Willem, oock raet van Sijn Hoocheit geassist^t met Gerrit Druivestein ende Pieter van Bilderbeeck om int bijwesen van Symon Hendricxen Catshuisen ende sijne adsistenten met commissie van Sijn Hooch^t begonden op te nemen het groot middelpavillioen ende loge vant huis Ter Nieuburch den muir die de plaets ende de thuijnen omcingelt mitsgaders de twee pavillions tot de officien aldaer …
2 Febr. 1633 … 35:0:0

1042 fol. 266
… aen Arent Pieters bogaertman d'somme van drie ende twintich ponden vier schellingen artois, omme leverantie van LXI lindeboomen, om bij Sijnne Hoocheits huijs te Rijswijck geplant te worden, volgens d' ordonnantie … maendreeckeninge van Maert 1633 …
Maert 1633 … LXXIII £ IIII sts

1042 fol. 266
… aen Job Smal de somme van vierenvijftich ponden vijfftien schellingen voor XLIII lindeboomen bij hem à XXV sts tstuck gelevert ende om te Rijswijck geplant te worden …
Maert 1633 … LIIII £ XV sts

1042 fol. 266 verso
… aen Cornelis Dircsz Hensbroeck de somme van hondert ponden voor coeymis bij hem in de twee Tuijnen van Sijnne hoocheit te Rijswijck gelevert
Maert 1633 … C £

1042 fol. 269 verso
… vergoet aen Cornelis Langenhoven concherge vant huijs Ter Nieuburch d'somme van vijffentwintich ponden artois voor soo verre bij hem op XXIII Februarij XVI^C XXXIII aen cost ende dranck verschooten is, als wanneer de heeren gedeputeerden van de heeren Staten van Ierlandt thuijs Ter Nieuburch waren besichtigen ende aldaer bij d'heer president ende Raedt Brouaert ende den Rendant van Weijck Sijnne hoocheit getracteert sijn geweest …
Martij 1633 … XXV £

1042 fol. 284
… Den rendant heeft door last van Sijnne Hoocheit in Junij XVI^C drie en dertich ten onderstaen van den gerichten aldaer openbaer Sitdach gehouden, om op Sijn hoocheits welbefangen te besteden het verhoogen ende verlaten van weyden die achter het huijs liggen, ende sich stecken tot aen den Vliet oever toe, soo breet als het huijs ende Tuijnen daernevens sich verstrecken ende dat doorgaens ter hoochte ende waterpas van den groote dreve die voore aen berijts rijsende plantage langs loopende is, neffens de breede sloot, soudende deselve verhoochde ende verlatene weyden hebben, en een breede Sloot rondomme van 30 roeden voeten breet ende diep naer advenant, ende binnen den sloot rontomme eenen dijck boven 't verlatene ende verhoochde landt drie voeten hooch ende boven op de cruin vandien vier en twintich voeten breet, al van vasten cleysoorten ende cleyaerde gemaeckt. Van welck werck de minsten aennemers gebleven sijn voor de oost sijde vant selve werck Thijs Pietersz tot VII £ X sts yder roede viercandt, ende voorde west sijde Bruyn Jansz à VI £ V sts de roede viercandt, welck tsamen onder de morgen tellen [?] van d'selve weyden belopen soude hebben … Gerrit de Bye secretaris van Rijswijck soo voor deselfs vacatie ende besoigne in deser bestedingen gedaen …
Junio 1633 … XXVII £ XVIII sts

1042 fol. 288
… aen Jan Pietersz ende Jaspar Jansz aerdewerckers de somme van acht ponden voor hun salaris ten saecke sijluyden een overslach gemaeckt hebben van eenen dijck ende gracht rontomme de weyden die achter het huis Ter Nieuburch liggen …
1633 … VIII £

1042 fol. 292
… aen Jan Michielsz Blau Steenhouwer de somme van hondert drie ponden acht sts voor dachgelden van sijn volck, die de tegelen waermee de balustrade ofte wandelplaets geplaveit is gecant ende gepast hebben …
CIII £ VIII sts

1042 fol. 291 (only partly in Slothouwer, p. 295)
… aen Dirck Jansz metselaer de somme van twee duijsent ponden bij hem bedongen voort metselwerck vant maecken ende stellen vande balustrade, off terrasse die langs het huis te Rijswijk op de binnenplaets comt, deselve te plaveijen, den muur van de fondamenten van het gebouw welck nu gemaeckt wort, in den toecommen somer voltooien sal worden te verhoochen, om aldaer te plavijen, de riolen onder de aerde te maecken, als oock de ontfanger van de selve onder de plaets, ende die riolen die voorts buiten thuijs onder de aerde langs 'tgebouw leggen tot in de Suyt wateringe toe, 'twater vant huijs ende pavillioens uijtlopen, het fonderen ende stellen vande groote voorpoorte waerdoor men opt huijs ende binnenplaets comt …
Oct. 1633 … II^M £

1042 fol. 298 (Slothouwer p. 295)
… Betaelt aen Joseph Dinant d'somme van hondert vijfftich ponden ter saecke hij gemaeckt ende gelevert heeft de cartouches off grotteske ciersels van gestampt ende gepapt pampier tot het cabinet van Hare Hoocheit opt huijs Ter Nieuburch door den architect La Vallée geordoneert
Oct 1633 … CL £

1042 fol. 302 verso (Slothouwer p. 296)
… Betaelt aen Louis d'Antoni de somme van ses hondert ponden voor een jaer gagie hem als hovenier van Sijnne Hoocheits thuijnen aent huijs Ter Nieuburch verschenen ultima December XVI drie en dertich … VI^C £

1042 fol. 307 verso
In den eerste betaelt aen Jacob Vennecool ende Jan Barthout van Loo beijde procuratie hebbende vande gemeene erfgenamen van wijlen Jonch^r Johan Prine ende Joffrouw Margarita Rataller sijne huijsvrouw de somme van vijff duijsent hondert twee ende vijftich ponden sestien sts een dernier omme den derden ende lesten termijn die Sijnne hooch^t aenden voorn erfgenamen schuldig was, omme de coop van seeckere wooninge ende Landen groot achtien mergen CXXXIII roeden lants vrij allodiale goet in den Ambachte van Rijswijck gelegen, tegens VIII^C L £ de morgen sulcks verschenen op XXII februarij volgens het transport … V^M CL XII £ XVI sts

NDR, inv. no. 1043 [782] (year 1634)

1043 fol. 118
Ontfanck vande domeinen gehoorende ondert huijs Ter Nieuburch bij Rijswijck gelegen: Sijne Hoocheit heeft in de maent van Junij XVI^C dertich van Philibert Vernatti gecocht seeckere wooninge genaemt Ter Nieuburch bij Rijswijck gelegen met hare boomgaerden cingelen waranden ende veertien margen een hond ses ende tnegentich roeden landts daeraen gehoorende, met alle lijdende ende domineerende servitueren soo vande voorschreve huijsinge, landen ende emolumenten vanden Santsloot als andersins dienvolgens inden Jaere XVI^C XXXVI ontfangen van Gerrit van Langenhoven als rentm^r vande goederen onder voorsz huijse gehoorende de somme van vijfhondert twee en veertich ponden ses schellingen vijf dernier …

1043 fol. 251 verso
… Pieter Bilderbeeck architect de somme van twaelff ponden artois voor sijne vacatien hebbende neffens andere wederom op het werck gevisiteert, gecalculeert, geestimeert het besteck ende buytenwerck vant gebouw aent huijs te Rijswijck …
[1634] … XII £

1043 fol. 254
… Betaelt aen Arent Lourissen Oom Timmerman te Rijswijck de somme van vijff ende negentich ponden artois over leverantie van latten, dewelcke in beide de Thuijnen ter sijden thuijs Ter Nieuburch nodich waren …
Mey 1634 … XCV £

1043 fol. 254 verso
… Arent Arentsz Teijckenaar de somme van sevenentwintich ponden een schelling over reys en teercosten bij hem tot vorderinge vande gebouwen tot Rijswijck ende Honsholredijck tot verscheijden reysen soo naer Amsterdam ende Haarlem van IX Maert tot II Mey gedaen …
XXVII £ I sch

1043 fol. 258 verso
… Betaelt aen Louis d'Anthonij hovenier op 't huijs Ter Nieuburch de somme van dertich ponden LX sch over verscheijden saet, welck hij inde Thuijnen aldaer gesaijt heeft …
Mey 1634 … XXX £ LX sch

1043 fol. 261 verso
… Betaelt aen Symon de Wilde pompmaecker ende lootgieter de somme van hondert vijffentwintich ponden seven sch over verscheijden loodepompen bij hem ten dienste van de Conchergerie vant Huijs te Rijswijck gelevert … CXXV £ VII sts.

1043 fol. 271 verso
… Betaelt aen Pieter Arienssen Mr. steenhouwer in den hage de somme van drie hondert ende veertich ponden artois te weten III^C £ voor eene balustrade bij hem gemaeckt ende gelevert opt buitenbordes vant West pavillioen te Rijswijck waerdoor men in den Westthuijn van het huijs gaet … III^C XL £

1043 fol. 278
… Louis d'Anthonij hovenier van Sijne Hoocheits Thuijnen aen beijde zijden vant huijs Ter Nieuburch de somme van ses hondert ponden,

voor een Jaer sijner gagie vervallen en lesten dec. XVI^C vier ende dertich volgens quitantien overgenomen op de respective maentreeckeninge van Maert, Oct ende Dec …
Dec. 1634 … VI^C £

1043 fol. 287
… Betaelt aen Jacques Martin de Franse beeltsnijder ciercels aen de schoorsteenmantel van de slaepcamer … Hare Hoocheits quartier … V^C X £

1043 fol. 292 verso
… Betaelt aen Leendert Mauritsz schipper de somme van vier ende vijfftich ponden over leverantie van twaelff schepen aerde yder schip tot IIII £ X sts bij hem ten dienste van Sijne Hooch^{ts} Thuijnen aent huijs Ter Nieuburch gelevert …
[1635] … LIIII £

NDR, inv. no. 992 [735] (years 1637-1640)

992 fol. 14
… Joost Jansz ende Jaspar Jans beijde aerdewerckers over gemaeckt aerdewerck aende huijse tot Rijswijck … den VIII April 1637 … hebben voltrocken ende gemaeckt het aerdewerck geroijt int spitten ende verlaten vant aengehoogde landt ende verbinden vandien bij ende ontrent de vijvers op den hoffstede tot Rijswijck …
VIII April 1637 … 386:0:0

992 fol. 24
… te betaelen uijt de penningen vande Zeeprinsen aen Joost Janszen vander Poel ende Jaspar Jansz beijde aerdewerckers de somme van drijhondert guldens, voor den eersten ende tweede termijn hen competeerende volgens den bovenstaende attestatie als aengenomen hebben 't leggen ende maecken van 40 off 50 roeden wals off dijckx, gelegen langs de oost ende westzijde vant aengecochte landt aende Zuijdtsijde vant huijs Ter Nieuburch volgens 't Besteck daervan sijnde,
31 Maert 1637 … 300:0:0

992 fol. 41
… Joost Jansz vander Poel ende Jaspar Jansz … overt voltrecken vande twee wallen ofte dijcken achter den huijse Nieuburch tot Rijswijck … tweede lesten termijn …
… 611:5:0

992 fol. 96
… Louis d'Anthoni hovenier van Sijne Hoocheit in sijne Thuijnen tot Rijswijck gesteld aldus over schenckagie …
… 100:0:0

992 fol. 108
… Pieter Cornelisz Timmerman ende Claes Dircxz overt maken van een riool inden Thuijn tot Rijswijck …
[Jan. 1638] … 441:3:6

992 fol. 115
… omme te betaelen uijt de penningen vande Zeeprinsen aenden selven Thonis Lievensz de somme van hondert vijffthien guldens over het spitten, wijen ende schoonmaecken soo vande paden als andersints inde nieuwe Thuijnen achter Sijne Hoocheits huijse tot Rijswijck mitsgaders over het tweede gemais vant gras onder de Lindeboomen van de plantagie aldaer bij hem aengenomen …
[Febr.] 1638 … 115:0:0

992 fol. 117 (Slothouwer, p. 300)
… Alsoo Matthieu de Bus schilder ende vergulder … vergulden vande vensters ofte ramen ende deuren inde voorsz gallerije … ende onder elck conterfeijtsel van coningen ende prinsen, die tusschen de vensters gestelt zullen worden te maken de wapenen vande selve coningen ende prinsen etc.
17 Maert 1638 … 3042:0:0

992 fol. 129 (Slothouwer, p. 300)
… te tellen aan Jacob van Campen de somma van drieduysent een hondert ende vijffentseventich car. gul. omme daer uijt bij hem te betaelen de respective schilders in de bovenstaende memorie vermelt over de conterfeijtsels ende andere schilderingen bij haer gemaeckt ende gelevert totte gallerije opden huijse van Nieuburch.
3 April 1638 … 3175:0:0

992 fol. 132
… Louis d'Anthoni hovenier van Sijne Hoocheits Thuijnen tot Rijswijck op den Tresorier Gnael. Volbergen omme te betaelen aenden selven Louis d'Anthoni de somme van twee hondert eenennegentich guldens seventhien stuijvers, ter saecke van verscheijde fruijtboomen bij hem ten dienste van Sijne Hooch^t gelevert ende geplant in sijne voorsz Thuijnen tot Rijswijck
[Maart] 1638 … 291:17:0

992 fol. 178
Betaelt aen Bartholomeus Drijffhout Steenh^r over de arbeijdt, reys en teercosten bij hem gedaen ende verschooten ten dienste van Sijne Hoocheit int halen tot diverse reysen van Amsterdam eerst eenige steene kinderkens, dewelcke heeft gebracht ende gevoert op den huijse van Honsholredijck ende andersints alsmede noch eenige marmere figuren mede bij hem gevoert op den huijse Ter Nieuburch in den Jaere 1638
… 89:0:0

992 fol. 227 (Slothouwer, p. 300)
… uijt de penn. vande Zeeprinsen aen Pieter Soutman de somme van drij hondert ende vijftich guldens, ter sake dat hij op den huijse van Sijne Hooch{t} bij Rijswijck heeft gemaeckt ende gelevert conterfeijtsels vande coninck ende coninginne van Spagnien …
10 Jan. 1639 … 350:0:0

992 fol. 256
… aen Maerten Blom ende Sijmon van Langelaer de somme van twee hondert vijftich guls. over het spitten, wijen ende schoonmaken soo vande paden als andersints inden nieuwen Thuijn gelegen aende Zuydtsijde van Sijne Hooch{ts} huyse tot Rijswijck gedaen in den Jaere 1638 … 250:0:0

992 fol. 314
… Alsoo Claes Claesz Smyter aengenoomen heeft volgens den Besteck daervan sijnde in dato laetsten february 1639 het aenhoogen ende effenen van het landt beslooten tusschen de dijcken ende de nieuwe Thuyn, gelegen aende Zuytsijde van onsen huyse tot Rijswijck voor de somme van negen duysent Car. guldens te betaelen in vier termijnen …
27 Oct. 1639 … 2250:0:0

992 fol. 335 (Slothouwer, p. 301)
… te betalen aen Barent Jansz de somme van drije hondert veertich guldens, over verscheijde Indiaensche hoornen ende schelpen bij hem door ordre ende ten dienste van Sijne Hooch{t} gecocht ende gelevert om inde orangerie bij 't huijs Ter Nieuburch gebruijckt te werden aen 't grotwerck aldaer …
16 Dec. 1639 … 340:0:0

992 fol. 376
… uyt de penningen vande Zeeprinsen aen Pieter Cornelisz van Couwenhoven mr. Timmerman, alhier in den hage, ende Arent Lourisz mr. Timmerman tot Rijswijck, de somme van ses duijsent vier hondert vier ende sestich ponden artois vier sts ter sake van een muer ende houten logie bij haer aengenomen ende gemaeckt ten dienste van Sijne Hooch{t} voor d'Orangerie bij den huijse Ter Nieuburch mitsgaders over eenige andere wercken ende reparaties bij haer gedaen, soo als de Zuijdmuer vande voorsz Orangerie als andersints … geattesteert bij Controlleur s'Herwouters …
VIII Maert 1640 … 6464:4:0

992 fol. 388
… Uyt de penningen vande Zeeprinsen aen Bartholomeus Bosch de somme van thien hondert tsestich Car. gul. negen stuyvers over geleverde spijkers, staelhamers als ander ijserwerck bij hem gelevert inden jaere 1639 om in de Orangerye bij thuijs Ter Nieuburch gebruijckt te worden … controlleur 'sHerwouters …
28 April 1639 … 1060:9:0

992 fol. 409 (Slothouwer, p. 301)
… te rembouseren ende betaelen aen Joseph Dinant, fonteijnier van Sijne Hooch{t} de somme van ses hondert gul. bij hem gedebouseert ende verstreckt aen Arnoult Fortane, coopman tot Diepen, over 14 barcken met schelpen, eenige tacken wit corael ende swerte keijen, bij hem gelevert ten dienste van Sijne Hooch{t} tottet maken vande grotte, ontrent den huijse ter Nieuburch bij Rijswijck …
6 Juni 1640 … 600:0:0

992 fol. 439 (Slothouwer, p. 301)
… te betalen aen Willem Mulman, coopman tot Amsterdam, de somme van twaelff hondert zeventhien Car. gulden thien stuyvers ter sake vanden fonteijnsteen bij hem doen coopen tot Tivoli buijten Roomen, ende alhier gelevert ten dienste van Sijne Hooch{t} tottet maecken vande grotte ontrent Sijne Hooch{ts} huijse Ter Nieuburch bij Rijswijck, bedraegende met de assurantie van maeckelaerdij vracht ende oncosten daer op gevallen ter voorsz. somme van twaelff hondert seventhien gul. thien stuyvers …
3 Oct. 1640 … 1217:10:0

992 fol. 400
… S.H. ordonneert hiermede Johan Dimmer rentm{r} sijner baronie Yselsteyn te betalen aen Willem Cornelisz vander Stoop de somme van vierhondert acht entsestich Car. gul. over 640 Ypen ende 4000 Haechbuycke boomen, bij hem ten dienste van S.H. gelevert ende geplant aende huijse Ter Nieuburch bij Rijswijck …
III Mey 1640 … 468:0:0

992 fol. 418 (Slothouwer, p. 333)
… aen den schilder Soutmans de somme van hondert vijfftich Car. gul. die Sijne Hooch{t} aenden selve is vereerende ter sake hij aen Sijne Hooch{t} heeft gededicceert een boeck van acht off thien conterfeijtsels in folio vande Graven van Nassau ende Princen van Orange …
25 Julij 1640 … 150:0:0

992 fol. 439
… op den reckeninge van Willem Jorisz geattesteert bij Concherge Langenhoven enden hovenier vande Orangerije Ter Nieuburch … te betalen aen Willem Jorisz de somme van acht ende dertich Car gul. acht stuyvers ter sake vande 48 wagens mis tot 16 stuyv. yder wagen mette vracht bij hem gelevert tot S. H. inde Orangerije ontrent den huijse Ter Nieuburch bij Rijswijck …
III Oct. 1640 … 38:8:0

992 fol. 448
… aen Balthasar van Engelen hovenier woonende tot Antwerpen, de somme van drij hondert en tsestich Car. guls. voor de nombre van twaelff orangie boomen bij den selven gelevert inde Orangerije aende huijse van S.H. Ter Nieuburch bij Rijswijck …
VI Nov. 1640 … 360:0:0

992 fol. 457
… aen Arent Lourisz geseyt Noom, mr. Timmerman tot Rijswijck de somme van seven hondert vijff en veertich guls. achthien sts negen der. ter sake van leverantie van hout ende andere materialen, wercken ende reparatien bij hem gedaen ende gemaeckt ten dienste van S.H. inden selven thuijnen ende huijse Ter Nieuburch van Maert 1638 tot Dec. 1639 …
Dec. 1640 … 745:18:9

NDR, inv. no. 993 [736] (years 1641-1647)

993 fol. 12 [a]
… aen Gillis de Hertoch de somme van vijff hondert acht en dertich guldens achthien sts over ijserwerck ende andere materialen bij hem aen het Grotwerck van S.H. Huijs bij Rijswijck gelevert in den Jaere 1640 … ende attestatie van Controlleur 'sHerwouters ende den Grottier Joseph Dinant
XII Febr. … 1641 … 538:18:0

993 fol. 12 [b]
… Simon de Wilde de somme van achtien hondert dertich Car. gul. negen sts over loot, pijp ende fonteijnwerck bij hem ten dienste van S.H. aende Grotte van desselfs huijs tot Rijswijck gelevert inde Jaren 1639 ende 1640 … declaratie ende attestatie Controlleur 'sHerwouters ende fonteijnier Joseph Dinant …
XII Febr. 1641 1830:9:0

993 fol. 21
… Cornelis vander Stoop de somme van ses hondert Car. gul. ter sake van 600 Ype boomen van breet bladt tot 45 gul., ende 1100 gelijcke boomen tot 30. gul. thondert bij hem gelevert ten dienste van S.H. ende geplant ontrent S.H. huijse Ter Nieuburch bij Rijswijck gelegen …
V Maert 1641 … 600:0:0

993 fol. 23
… aen Balthasar van Engelen hovenier te Antwerpen de somme van twee hondert en vijfftich guld. over seven schoone Orangien boomen bijde selve ten dienste van S.H. in februario lestleden gelevert …
XIIII Maert … 250:0:0

993 fol. 47 [a]
… aen Arent Lourisz Timmerman, de somme van ses hondert drie en veertich Car. gul. ter sake van verdient arbeijdersloon ende eenig houtwerck bij hem gemaeckt ende gelevert ten dienste van S.H. tot het afstutten ende wederstellen van de Looffs inde Orangerije bij S.H. huijse Ter Nieuburch van 1e Maert totten eersten Nov. 1640 … contr. 'sHerwouters …
4 Mey 1641 … 643:18:0

993 fol. 47 [b]
… aen Arent Lourisz Timmerman, de somme van twee hondert drie en tachtich Car. gul. ter sake van verdient arbeijdersloon ende eenig houtwerck bij hem gemaeckt ende gelevert ten dienste van S.H. … soo inde Loofs als tot behoeff van het werck inde Orangerije ontrent S.H. huijse Ter Nieuburch … contr. 'sHerwouters ende den Grottier Joseph Dinant …
4 Mey 1641 … 283:14:0

993 fol. 47 [c]
… Alsoo Pieter Pietersz Post mr. metselaer, aengenomen heeft volgens den bovenstaende Besteck … het metselen van seker muijrwerck met bastaert Trab ende plaveien om de bedden inde Orangerije bij onsen huijse Ter Nieuburch tot ses guls. vijffthien sts de roede inde lengte, te betalen…
4 Mey 1641 … 648:0:0

993 fol. 48 (Slothouwer, p. 302)
… Alsoo Pieter Cornelisz van Couwenhoven, hofftimmerman alhier inden Hage, ende Arent Lourisz mr. timmerman tot Rijswijck aengenomen hebben (volgens den bovenstaende bestecke in dato 17e Juni 1640) het maecken van een pomphuijs tot het fonteijnwerck bij onsen huijse Ter Nieuburch voor de somme van vier duijsent twee hondert Car. gul. …
4 Mey 1641 … 4200:0:0

993 fol. 89
… Joseph Dinant … over de reparatien van sijn huys …
Dec. 1641 … 399:4:0

993 fol. 126 (Slothouwer, p. 302)
… Alsoo Pieter Pietersz Post mr. metselaer alhier in den Hage aengenoomen heeft … het opbreecken ende verleggen vande wandelplaats aende Noortseyde van het huijs Ter Nieuburch voor de somme van drie hondert veerthien guls. alsmede de haerden met tegelen te beleggen voorde somme van 70 gul. maeckende tsamen de somme van 384 gul. …
14 Jan. 1642 … 384:0:0

993 fol. 145
… Simon de Wilde pompemaecker alhier inden Hage de somme van seshondert acht entachtich guls. vijfftien stuyvers drie dr. over verscheijde rollen loot, pomppijpen, ende lood fonteijnpijpen, bij hem gelevert aent fonteijnwerck op de huijse van S.H. bij Rijswijck, … geattesteert bij den Contr. 'sHerwouters ende Joseph Dinant Grottier …
X April 1642 … 688:15:3

993 fol. 188
… te tellen aen Hendrick van Hattem, sijnen plantagueur de somme

van negen hondert Car. guldens, omme geemployeert te worden tot betalinge van incoop van boomen en andere te doene oncosten totte plantagies van Honsholredijck, Rijswijck, Bueren ende Zuylesteijn …
VI Maert 1643 … 900:0:0

993 fol. 189
… Dirck Pietersz vischcooper over riviervisch bij hem gelevert inde vijver tot Rijswijck den 8sten Jan 1643 …
lesten Maert 1643 … 65:12:0

993 fol. 190
… Op de cedulle vande veenaerde gebracht voor op de Lindeplantagie vant huijs Ter Nieuburch geattesteert bij den hovenier Borchert Frederick …
V Maert 1643 … 443:17:0

993 fol. 213
… Balthasar van Engelen hovenier woonende tot Antwerpen, de somme van twee hondert tachtich Car. guldens over de nombre van seven Orange boomen bijden selven gelevert inde Orangerije aenden huijse van S.H. Ter Nieuburch bij Rijswijck …
17 Oct. 1643 … 280:0:0

993 fol. 244 verso
… Vranck Dircxsz over 88 kruywagens koemis tot 2 sts 12 penningen den wagen, midtsgaders 't verplanten van eenige Lindeboomen voor S.H. huijs Ter Nieuburch … geattesteert bij Mr. hovenier Borchert Frederick …
IX Maert 1644 … 29:7:0

993 fol. 245
… Cornelis Cornelisz ende Louwereijs Hendrick over 97 wagens paerdemis yder wagen bedogen voor 18 sts … geatt. bij Mr hovenier Borchaert Frederick …
IX Maert 1644 … 87:6:0

993 fol. 247
… oncosten gevallen op tmeten ende taxeren vande huijsinge ende Stall tot Rijswijck …
XI April 1644 … 73:14:0

993 fol. 262
… te tellen aen Hendrick van Hattem, sijnen plantagueur de somme van seshondert guldens, omme geemployeert te worden tot betalinge van incoop van boomen en andere te doene oncosten totte plantagies van Honsholredijck, Rijswijck, Bueren ende Zuylesteijn, volgens den laste van Sijne Hooch^t aen hem gegeven …
Aug. 1644 … 600:0:0

993 fol. 285
… Cornelis Jansz van Slingelandt met sijn helpers gewijt hebbende de bassecourt vant huijs Ter Nieuburch in Aug. 1644 …
18 Jan. 1645 … 16:1:0

993 fol. 301
… Arent Lourisz Noom aengenomen heeft … het maecken van een glinte heijninge ter lengte van 25 roeden aen onse huijse Ter Nieuburch yder roede voor 15 guls.
23 Mey 1645 … 375:0:0

993 fol. 414 verso
… aen Hendrick van Hattem plantaguem^r van Sijne Hooch^t dezelfde despence ende uytgevels tot van de bepootinge vande plantagien tot Bueren, Honsholredijck, Rijswijck ende Suylesteijn van April 1642 tot April 1643 … ter somme van twee duysent vier hondert ses ende dertich Car. guls. eene sts. …
28 Maert 1646 … 2436:1:0

… Gelijcke ordonnantie ter sake als voorsz. van 28 Julij 1643 tot in Mayo 1644 ter somme van …
Maert 1646 … 1758:15:3

… Gelijcke ordonnantie ter sake als voorsz. van Augusto 1644 tot Februarij 1645 ter somme van …
Maert 1646 … 1247:0:8

993 fol. 436
… Bartholomeus Drijffhout over arbeijtsloon ende geleverde materialen op thuijs Ter Nieuburch 1644 ende 1645 …
XI Sept. 1646 … 35:3:8

993 fol. 442 verso (only partly in Slothouwer, p. 302)
… ordonneert hiermede Symon van Catshuijsen rentm^r vande domeijnen van Naeltwijck, te rembouseren aen Joseph Dinant, de somme van vijffhondert veerthien Car. gul. bij hem ten dienste van S. Hooch^t gedebourseert over 't coopen van verscheyden liphoornen, belhoornen ende perlem^r hoornen etc. breeder blijckende bij de bovenstaende rekeninge ende quytancie van Gerard van Kippen Cooppman woonende tot Amsterdam …
19 Nov. 1646 … 1514:0:0

993 fol. 445 verso [a]
… aen Pieter Florisz vander Salm … over 't meten van den nieuwen ende oude Thuijn [Honselaarsdijk?], 't maecken van Caerten als andersints bij hem gedaen op 't huys ter Nieuburch bij Rijswijck in den Jare 1645 …
21 Dec. 1646 … 23:0:0

993 fol. 446 (Slothouwer, p. 302)
… Op 'tbesteck waer nae mr. Arent Laurensz voornt. heeft aengenoomen het maecken van twee deuren in het Oost Pavillioen, om uijt Sijne Hooch[ts] quartier te comen inde Orangerije aende Huijse van Sijne Hoocht tot Rijswijck de somme van hondert vijff en dertich Car. gul …
19 dec. 1646 … 135:0:0

NDR, inv. no. 994 [737] (years 1647-1650)

994 fol. 112
… Op declaratie van Joseph Dinant concierge vande huijse tot Rijswijck, van 'tgeene bij hem is gedebourseert ende betaelt ten behoeve vant voorsz. huijs 'tsedert Mey 1646 tot den lesten Dec. 1648 …
19 Jan. 1649 … 419:13:0

NDR, inv. no. 995 [738] (years 1651-1657)

995 fol. 5 verso
Cornelis Joosten hovenier tot Rijswijck … geattesteert bij den hovenier vanden Thuynen tot Honsholredijck …
14 Febr. 1651 … 69:0:0

995 fol. 65
Joseph Dinant Concierge van het Huys Ter Nieuwburch …

995 fol. 114 verso
Joseph Dinant concierge op de huyse tot Rijswijck ende fontainier de somme van drie duysent car. gul. die hem werden toegevoegt over de extraordinair diensten ende Travail bij hem gedaen in't maken van de grotten tot Rijswijck, Honsholredijck ende elders …
7 Juni 1653 … 3000:0:0

995 fol. 221
Joseph Dinant Concierge van het Huys Ter Nieuwburch …
14 May 1657.

995 fol. 222
Mr. Robert Padee hovenier van Sijne Hoocheits Thuynen tot Rijswijck is … te betalen aende suppliant de somme van vijffhondert drie ende dertich gul. die hem noch per reste souden competeren volgens het contract met hem voor desen gemaeckt in dato 1 September 1653 wegen 't onderhout vande Thuynen hierinne vermelt, van den 1 September 1656 totten eersten December daer aen volgende … midts dat het waerneemens vande Orangerie ende andere pretensien inden Jaere 1656 daer onder begrepen …

NDR, inv. no. 996 [739] (years 1658-1666): lacks further information

NDR, inv. no. 999 [742] (years 1692-1694)

999 fol. 194 verso
… Over verdiende arbeytsloonen ende geleverde materialen in den jare 1691, 92 en 1693 ten dienste van Sijne Maj[t] op deselfs huys tot Rijswijck gedaen, geverifieert bij den Architect Romans …
29 Jan. 1694 … 596:2:4

999 fol. 226
… over verdiende arbeytsloonen en geleverde materialen in de jaren 1692, 1693 ende 1694 ten dienste van Sijne Maj[t] aen deselfs huys tot Rijswijck gedaen, geverifieert door den Heere Directeur Des Marets, geattesteert ende gereguleert bij den architect Romans …
13 Mey 1694 … 189:2:0

999 fol. 247
… voor Jan de La over arbeytsloon opt Huys tot Rijswijck gedaen, in dato 18 Aug. 1694 … 30:12:0

999 fol. 251
… over arbeytsloon ende geleverde materialen bij haer in den jaren 1691, 92, 93 ende 1694 ten dienste van S. Maj[ts] huys ter Nieuburch gedaen, alle geverifieert door den Heere Directeur Des Marets, geattesteert ende gereguleert bij den architect Romans ende den hovenier Willem Brederode …
1 Sept. 1694 … 96:18:8

999 fol. 273
… Gerrit van der Plas ende Bartholomeus Speijck bij haer in den Jaere 1692 ende 1694 ten dienste van S. Maj.[ts] huys en Thuyn Ter Nieuburgh gedaen …
2 Dec. 1694 … 131:0:0

PALEIS NOORDEINDE / OUDE HOF

ACCOUNTS OF THE COMPTROLLER, DECREES OF THE COUNCIL, continued

NDR, inv. nos. 1040-996 [779-739] (years 1631-1666)

1040 fol. 179
… Den Rendant heeft voor eerst betaelt de somme van hondert vijfenzeventich ponden artois aen Mr Jacob Dedel rentm[r] van St Nicolaes Gasthuijs van 'sGravenhage onder een Jaers rente vant selve Gasthuijs van Sijnne furstel. D[t] competerende voor rest van coop vant landt daer den Thuijn int Noorteinde mede vergroot is verschijnt dit jaer in Octob. 1631
Oct. 1631 … 175:0:0

1043 fol. 169 verso
… Sijne Hoocheit heeft oock inden jaere XVI^C negen van die vant St. Nicolaes Gasthuys in den hage gecocht een partie weylandt groot vier morgen XIII roeden daerinne den eigendom vande Gasthuysland begrepen is die in de Molenstraet uyt compt, met soodanigh vryheit ende lasten als voorsz Gasthuys dat besittende was, sijnde ten deele dat daer niemant in vermach andere achter uytganck te hebben, dan soo ende gelycke de huijsen van den Ontfanger Nierop ende vanden heer Beverweert in 't Noordeynde ende vanden Advocaat Berendrecht inde Molenstraet gelegen, altans hebbende sijn, ende dat voor de somme van vierduysent acht hondert ponden artois Capitaels … noch op Schielandt gehypotequieert welck voorsz Landt geemployeert is aenden groote Tuijn van Sijnne Hoocheits huijsinge int Noordteinde voornoemt … desen coop in dato XVII Octobris XVI^C negen berustende ter Camere van S.H. Raede ende Reckeninge … 4800:0:0

1043 fol. 170 verso
… Sijne hoocheit heeft noch gecocht van Thomas Carsiopijn een partij erff achter denselve huis int Noorteynde gelegen ende dat voor de somme van achtien hondert ponden artois … als opdracht daervan sijnde dato den 18 Augusti 1614 … ende is van dit stuckgen erff gemaeckt een Tuyntgen ende Grotto gevoecht aent quartier vant huis daer haere fürstel. Gen. hoochlof. mem. Sijne hoocheits Vrouw moeder in logerende was … 1800:0:0

1043 fol. 180 verso
… Aen Mr Jacob Dedel als rentm^r van het St Nicolaes gasthuijs in den haage betaelt de somme van hondert vijfentwintich ponden artois … van S.H. competeerende ter reste van coop van wijden daer den Thuijn int Noordteijnde mede vergroot is …
IX Oct. 1634 … 125:0:0

992 fol. 14
… Joost Jansz van Hoorenbeeck … waergenoomen ende gevoeyert de vogelkens van S.H. vogelkens huijs inden Thuijn aende Hoff …
April 1637 … 150:0:0

992 fol. 130
… Joost Jansz van Hoorenbeeck … jaergagie over 1638 … 150:0:0

993 fol. 144
… Joost Jansz van Hoorenbeeck … vogelkens in 't Noorteynde …
April 1642 … 150:0:0

993 fol. 193
… Joost Jansz van Hoorenbeeck … vogels inde vogelkoye int hoff …
April 1643 … 150:0:0

993 fol. 247
… Joost Jansz van Hoorenbeeck … vogels inde vogelkoye int hoff …
April 1644 … 150:0:0

993 fol. 297
… Joost Jansz van Hoorenbeeck … vogels inde vogelkoye int hoff …
April 1645 … 150:0:0

993 fol. 314
… Ary Leendertsz vander Cley … logie met sijne Camer ende Cabinetten achter int Hoff in 't Noorteynde …
Octob. 1645 … 4500:0:0

994 fol. 59 verso
… aen Joost Fransgen van Hoornbeeck de somme van hondert vijfftich Car. gul. … hij het hele jaer heeft waergenoomen en gevoeyert de Vogelkens van S.H. Vogelhuijs in de Thuijn aent Hoff …
XX Maert 1648 … 150:0:0

994 fol. 66
… Cornelis Jansen Bol Mr Timmerman aengenoomen heeft wegens den bovenstaende bestecke in dato 14 Febr. 1648 het maecken van een heynickmuyr met den gevolge vandien, aen onsen huyse int Noorteynde …
May 1648 … 975:0:0

994 fol. 67 verso
… Adriaen Leendertsz Cley … voort maecken van een stal en coetshuys int Noorteynde …
May 1648 … 280:0:0

994 fol. 85
… Op de acte van Pieter Florissen vander Salm ende verclaringe van Bartholomeus Drijffhout van 't schoonmaecken vande sloot tusschen de oude ende nieuwen Thuijn van Sijne Hoocheit int Noorteynde …
1 Sept. 1648 … 70:14:0

994 fol. 149
… Pieter Cornellissen van Couwenhoven, hoff timmerman heeft volgens den bovenst. bestecke in dato 22 May 1648 het maecken van een glintinge ende Coetspoorte langs S.H^{ts} Thuyn in't hoff int Noorteynde …
21 Dec. 1649 … 1750:0:0

994 fol. 204 verso
… Otto Reyerssen voor leverantie van eenige potten ten dienste van haere Hooch^t in 't Noordeynde in 1649 …
7 Dec. 1649 … 10.4.0

APPENDIX NOORDEINDE

994 fol. 205

… voor den selven Reyerssen … over 't verschepen ende verwen van eenige hoofden inden Thuyn op de Cingel [1649] … 35.3.0

995 fol. 90 verso

Op de specificatie van Joseph Dienandt … te rembouseren aen Joseph Dinant concierge vande huyse ter Nieuburg de somme van negen hondert ses ende sestich gul. vier stuivers over gels somme bij hem verstrecken in de jaren 1650 ende 1651 aen verscheyden materialen aende nieuwe grotte inden Thuyn op de Cingel van't hoff … breeder uytwijsende de bovenstaande specificatie, gevisiteert ende geattesteert bij den architect van Sijne Hoocheit Mr Pieter Post ende … aende Grotte vande Thuyn op de Cingel van't hoff …'s Gravenhage …
7 January 1653 … 966:4:0

996 fol. 187

… Ordonnatie voor Reyer Pietersen als aennemer vande te maecken wercken op de Singel alhier in Den Hage boven de grotto. Alsoo Reyer Pieterssen Mr. Metselaer in 'sGravenhage heeft aengenoomen volgens den Besteck van dato 29 Mey 1664 het affbreecken vande kap ende Timmerwerck over de grotte bezuyden de Cleyne Thuijn ofte ten Noorden vande cingel in 's Gravenhage voor de somme van derthien hondert vijffendertich Car. guls.
Actum Honselerdijck 13 Junij 1664 … 600:0:0

996 fol. 216 verso

… Reyer Pieterssen Dronck Mr Metselaer … wegen het vermaken van de Grotte van Sijne Hooch[t] op de Cingel alhier in Den Hage … Timmerwerck over de grotte bezuyden de Cleyne Thuyn ofte ten Noorden van de Cingel … Ende het maken van een nieuwe kap met het metselwerck over en aende voorn. Grotte, voor de somme van dertien hondert vijffendertich Car. gul. … betaeling 2e termijn …
28 Febr. 1665 … 825:0:0

996 fol. 218

… Johannes Post over het schilderen ende vergrooten van het stuck van Rubbens gestelt inde Schoorsteen van Hare Hoocheits Bedcamer ende Alcove in Sijne Hooch[ts] Hoff in't Noordeinde …
28 Febr. 1665 … 50:0:0

996 fol. 220 verso

… Jan vander Groen Hovenier van Sijne Hooch[ts] Thuyn op de Cingel alhier … avanceren ende tellen eene somme van een hondert vier ende seventich guls omme bij hem daeruyt gecocht te werden de Fruytboomen ende verdere oncosten tot het opmaken ende beplanten van den Thuyn in desen vermelt …
24 Maert 1665 … 174:0:0

996 fol. 232

… Jan vander Groen Hovenier van Sijne Hoocheits Thuynen alhier in Den Hage op de Cingel … tot incopinge van noodige Fruytboomen en andere groenten …
3 July 1665 … 343:18:0

996 fol. 271 verso

Sijn gehoort eenige voorschlagen gedaen bij den hovenier van Sijne hooch[ts] Thuynen ende hoven int Noorteynde nopender het opruymen ende dempen vande Sloot aende Noortsyde vant voorsz hoff … [in het jaer] 1666.

BUREN

ACCOUNTS OF THE COMPTROLLER, DECREES OF THE COUNCIL, continued

NDR, inv. no. 1039-996 [778-739] (years 1630-1666)

1039 fol. 216

… Uytgave gedaen ter saecke vande Gebouwen aen Sijnne fürstelicke doorluchticheits Casteele ende Thuynen te Buren. Den Rendant heeft by liquidatie met Jaquis vander Steene Rentmeester van Buren gedaen, aenden selven vergoet de s.v. vier duysent vijffhondert vier en negentich ponden vijff schellingen vijff dernier artois, over soo veele den selven Rentmeester nopende de Gebouwen te Buren in den Jaere sestien hondert sevenentwintich gedaen betaelt heeft … [1630] … 4594:5:5

1039 fol. 216 verso

… Aen denselve Van der Steene noch vergoet de somme van twee en twintich duysent vier hondert vier en dertich ponden seventien schellingen tien dernier artois, over gelycke betalingen bij hem over de Gebouwen te Buren inden jaere XVI^C acht en twintich gedaen …
[1630] … 22.434:17:0

1039 fol. 217

… Aen deselve Van der Steene noch vergoet de somme van dertien duysent drie hondert drie en dertich ponden acht schellingen een dernier … over de Gebouwen te Buren inden Jaere XVI^C XXIX gedaen …
[1630] … 13.333:8:1

… Item de somme van vier hondert een en veertich ponden elf schellingen over gelycke betalingen die over de gebouwen inden Jaere XVI^C dertich gemaeckt, gedaen heeft …
… 441:11:0

1039 fol. 234

… In den jaere XVI^C dertich tijde deser en sijn geen meerdere acquisiten der domeynen gedaen dan de verbeteringen vande notabele

nieuwe Gebouwen ende reparatien soo aenden Casteele ende Thuynen te Buren, ende aende huyse te Honsholredijck ende Nieuburch gemaeckt ende gedaen ...
[1630] ... X^N Somma: M^C LXX^M IX^C LXXXV £ XIII sts XV dr

1039 fol. 272 verso
... Op den staet van Lucretia Crayvangers wed^e van wijlen Jacques vander Steene in sijn leven Rentmeester van Buyren ...
... Item VII^C XX ponden haer toe gevoecht voor LX roen lants die van haeren Boomgaert afgegraven ende geappliceert sijn aen tplein voorden Casteele te Bueren XII ponden de roede ...
Aen de weduwe Lucretia Crayvangers totaal ... 2159:3:11 ... 720:0:0

1039 fol. 273 verso
... Item noch CXX ponden bets. [betaeld] aende voochden vant werck van wijlen Dirc Goetcoop voort afgraven van 80 roeden lant die tot de nieuwe dreeff gebruickt sijn ...
... 120:0:

1040 fol. 211 verso
... Jacques vander Steen in sijn leeven Rentm^r tot Buyren vergoet ... bij haer betaelt over de wercken ende reparatien aent Gebou te Buren inden Jare 1630 tot in January 1631 ...
Juny 1631 ... 14080:5:9

1042 fol. 232 verso (Slothouwer, p. 263)
Betaelt aen Andre Mollet, Frans hovenier, de somme van tien hondert vijfftich ponden over sijn vacatien ende beleit vant maecken vande parterren die Sijne Hoocheit door den selven te Honsholredijck ende te Buuren heeft doen maecken te weten IIII^C £ voor twee parterren te Honselerdijck een van sooden ende palm met wit, root ende swarten ende het ander geheel van palm seer aardich gemaeckt IIIC £ voor twee parterren van palm te Buren, III^C voor sijn reisgelt ende weder van ende naer Vranckrijck als L £ voor teercosten bijden selven inden Hage gedaen, terwijlen hij verscheiden teickeningen voor Sijne Hoocheit heeft gemaeckt ende dit alvooren hem sijn tractement van VIII^C £ jaerlicx beneffens een daelder daechs aen costgelt was geordonneert. Bij specificatie ende quitantie overgenomen op de maentreeckeninge van Junij XVI^C drie en dertich ...

1042 fol. 253
Uytgave nopende de verbeteringen ende reparatien gedaen aen Sijne Hooch^{ts} Casteel tot Bueren
... In den eersten betaelt aen Abraham Blerisse hovenier, de somme van twee hondert sestich ponden achtien schillingen onder kwitantie van CXVIII kerseboomen à XXVI sts tstuck met XXV pereboomen à XX sts yder dewelcke in Sijnne hooch^{ts} thuijn te Bueren geplant sijn ...
Febr. 1633 ... II^C LX £ XVIII sts

1042 fol. 253 verso
... Betaelt de somme van drie entsestich ponden soo voor leverantie van twaelff wagens soo schelpen, als voor vracht vande selve ende eenige fruijtboomen van hier [Den Haag] naer Bueren te voeren ...
Martio 1633 ... LXIII £

1042 fol. 253 verso
... Betaelt de somme van twaelff ponden artois voor leverantie van acht vrachten See schelpen ten dienste van Sijnne Hoocheits thuijnen te Bueren
April 1633 ... XII £

1042 fol. 254
... Betaelt de somme van seven en seventich ponden Soo over leverantie van twaelff vijgeboomen à vijf ponden thien schillingen tstuck en verder in de thuijn te Bueren gestelt sijn, als oock eenige andere Wercken [?] ten dienste van 't huijs aldaer gedaen ...
May 1633 ... LXXVII £

1042 fol. 254 verso
... Betaelt aen Gysbrecht Thonissen hovenier de somme van negen ende vijftich ponden artois voor twintich persick ende negen apricoos boomen bij hem inde Thuijn tot Bueren gelevert ...
Sept. 1633 ... LIX £

1043 fol. 240
... Vergoet aen Julius Sagermans substituut rentm^r tot Buren ... voor soo veel bij den selven betaelt is aen verscheyden leverantie en arbeiders die ten dienste van S.Hooch^{ts} Casteele tot Buyren soo aen nieuwe wercken gemaeckt als aan reparatien aen t'selve gebou yets gedaen ende gelevert hebben ...
Febr. 1635 III^M VII^C V £ XV sch IIII dr

1043 fol. 241
... Aen Jacob Outhamer M^r metselaer tot Buyren, soo overt maecken ende vernieuwen vande murage in het blauhuis staende aenden inganck vanden grooten Thuin tot Buyren, als vanden reparatien in het logement vanden hovenier boven de poorte vanden Casteele mitsgaders voor leverantie van eenige hardtsteene lijsten aende schoorsteenmantels aldaer gemaeckt ende gedaen ...
[Febr. 1635] ... 564:7:0

1043 fol. 349
... de somme van seventien hondert ponden acht schellingen seventien dernier die gemeene erffgenamen van wijlen Jacquis vander Steen in sijn leven Rentmeester van Buren ... noch schuldig sijn ... 1700:8:17

992 fol. 145
... Willem Cornelisz vander Stoop te betaelen de somme van hondert

twee ende sestich Car. guls. thien pen. over coop van 325 Ypenboomen breet bladt tot vijfftich guls. het hondert bij hem ten dienste van S.H. gelevert inden Hoff vande huijse te Bueren in den Jare 1632 …
May 1638 … 162:10:0

992 fol. 187
… Andries Hoorendonck sijnen hovenier tot Buren … over sijne reys ende teercosten bij hem gedaen int herwaerts comen van Buren ende wederom reysen herwaerts …
Dec. 1638 … 35:0:0

992 fol. 313 [a]
… aen Willem Cornelisz vander Stoop … ter sake van ypen, peereboomen, muscadel wijngaerden, doornboomkens ende pruymestammekens bij hem gelevert ten dienste van Sijne Hoocheit in desen Jare 1639 ende geplant beneden aende wal om den Casteele tot Buren … XXI Octob. 1639 … 224:0:0

992 fol. 313 [b]
… Andries Hoorendonck hovenier van Sijne Hoocheit[s] hoven tot Buren … over de reys ende teercosten bij hem gedaen op dese sijne reyse gints ende weder na Buren …
XXV Oct. 1639 … 30:0:0

992 fol. 370 [a]
… Bartholomeus Drijffhout m[r] Steenhouwer … over de besteck soo van de Trap op den huyse van Buren als de noortgalderij van het hoff int Noorteinde … 1639 ende 1640 gemaeckt …
XXV Febr. 1640 … 105:18:0

992 fol. 370 [b]
… Wouter Hendricksz m[r] timmerman wonende alhier in den Hage … het maken ende stellen van een bordestrap op onse huijse ende Casteele tot Bueren voor de somme van twee duysent Car. guls. te betalen in twee termijnen …
XXV Febr. 1640 … 2000:0:0

992 fol. 378 [a]
… Anthony Jansz Backer … over diversche plantsoenen van bloemen bij hem ten dienste van Sijne Hoocheit aen Andries Hoorendonck gewesen hovenier tot Bueren in den Jare 1639 gelevert ende gepoot aende wallen vande Casteele tot Bueren …
XV April 1640 … 63:10:0

992 fol. 378 [b]
… Julius Sagemans sub[t] Rentm[r] van Bueren, te betaelen aen Johan Terborch Secretaris der voorsz Stede … over diversche plantsoenen van bloemen bij hem ten dienste van Sijne Hoocheit aen Andries Hoorendonck gewesen hovenier tot Bueren in den Jare 1639 gelevert om bij denselve aende wallen ende percken aldaer gepoot te werden …
XV April 1640 … 104:12:0

992 fol. 386
… Aen Arent Pietersz Blom de somme van ses ende tachtich gulden thien stuyvers over verscheyde plantsoenen van bloemen bij hem ten dienste van S.H. aen Andries Hoorendonck, gewesen hovenier tot Bueren in den Jaere 1639 gelevert om bij denselve aende wallen ende inde percken aldaer gepoot te werden …
April 1640 … 86:10:0

992 fol. 388
… Aen Arent Pietersz Blom … over verscheyde plantsoenen van bloemen bij hem ten dienste van S.H. aen Andries Hoorendonck, gewesen hovenier tot Bueren in den Jaere 1639 gelevert om bij denselve aende wallen ende inde percken aldaer gepoot te werden …
… 104:7:0

992 fol. 417
… Willem Cornelisz vander Stoop … ter sake van eenige buecken, roose ende persicke boomen, midtsgaders verscheydene planten van aertbesien, bij hem gelevert ten dienste van Sijne Hoocheit ende geplant soo in de renbaan als in de grooten Thuyn ende opde wallen vande Casteele van Bueren …
XXVI July 1640 … 102:0:0

992 fol. 443
… Cornelis Vermeulen M[r] Timmerman volgens den annexe besteck in dato 28 April 1640 het maecken van een Glintinck, op de voet ofte Berm vande wal aande Westzijde vande Casteele tot Buren …
24 Octob. 1640 … 260:0:0

992 fol. 447
… Cornelis Vermeulen … over arbeytsloon ende gelevert hout tot 't repareren vande heckens vande dreeff, 't lassen vande vergaene boogen ende paelen vande berceaux inde Thuynen om de Huyse van Buren …
1 Nov. 1640 … 378:11:0

992 fol. 447
… Cornelis Vermeulen, M[r] Timmerman repareren vande Hecken vande dreef, 't lassen vande vergaene boogen ende paelen vande berceaux inde thuijnen om den huijse van Buren …
1 Nov. 1640 … 378:11:0

993 fol. 55
… Hendrick van Hattem … tot incoop van boomen ende andere te doene oncosten totte plantagien van Bueren …
Junius 1641 … 1000:0:0

993 fol. 131
... Hendrick van Hattem sijne plantagueur de somme van acht hondert Car. guls. omme ... incoop van boomen totte plantagie van Honsholredijck, Buren, Zuylesteijn ...
III Febr. 1642 ... 800:0:0

993 fol. 181
... Willem Cornelisz vander Stoop ... voor ses hondert vande Ypenboomen, ende onderhoudt der voorn. boomen in behoorlijcke waerden ...
22 Jan 1643 ... 433:12:0

993 fol. 188
... te tellen aen Hendrick van Hattem, sijnen plantagueur de somme van negen hondert Car. guldens, omme geemployeert te worden tot betalinge van incoop van boomen en andere te doene oncosten totte plantagies van Honsholredijck, Rijswijck, Bueren ende Zuylesteijn ...
VI Maert 1643 ... 900:0:0

993 fol. 202
... Jan van Diepenen over vacatien ende reyscosten naer Bueren ende afftekeninge van eenig werck aldaer ...
May 1643 ... 60:0:0

993 fol. 257 verso
... Jan van Diepenen ... besoignes van metinge ende Caerten vande Casteele tot Buren ...
Junius 1644 ... 393:0:0

993 fol. 262
... te tellen aen Hendrick van Hattem, sijnen plantagueur de somme van seshondert guldens, omme geemployeert te worden tot betalinge van incoop van boomen en andere te doene oncosten totte plantagies van Honsholredijck, Rijswijck, Bueren ende Zuylesteijn, volgens den laste van Sijne Hooch^t aen hem gegeven ...
Aug. 1644 ... 600:0:0

993 fol. 403
... Reyer van Langelaer ... over geleverde fruytboomen in 1644 en 45 tot Bueren ...
Jan. 1644 ... 18:19:0

993 fol. 404
... Simon van Langelaer hovenier tot Bueren over reyscosten van Bueren naer Breda bij hem gedaen anno 1645 ...
Jan. 1645 ... 24:0:0

993 fol. 414 verso
... aen Hendrick van Hattem plantaguem^r van Sijne Hooch^t dezelfde despence ende uytgevels tot van de bepootinge vande plantagien tot Bueren, Honsholredijck, Rijswijck ende Suylesteijn van April 1642 tot April 1643 ... ter somme van twee duysent vier hondert ses ende dertich Car. guls. eene sts. ...
28 Maert 1646 ... 2436:1:0

... Gelijcke ordonnantie ter sake als voorsz. van 28 Julij 1643 tot in Mayo 1644 ter somme van ...
Maert 1646 ... 1758:15:3

... Gelijcke ordonnantie ter sake als voorsz. van Augusto 1644 tot Februarij 1645 ter somme van ...
Maert 1646 ... 1247:0:8

993 fol. 415 verso
... gelijcke ordonnans ter saecke als voorsz 28 Julij 1643 tot in Mayo 1644 ...
28 Maert 1646 ... 1758:15:3

993 fol. 419
... gelijcke ordonnans ter saecke als voorsz van augusto 1644 tot Febr. 1645 ...
28 Maert 1646 ... 1247:0:8

993 fol. 458
... Simon van Langelaer hovenier tot Bueren over reyscosten ...
Jan. 1647 ... 36:0:0

993 fol. 461
... Alsoo Cornelis Vermeulen aengenoomen heeft volgens de annexe bestecke in dato den XVII Marty 1646 het repareren vande Gallerijen ende Cabinetten van Sijne Hooch^{ts} Lusthoven aende Casteele van Bueren ...
8 Febr. 1647 ... 725:0:0

993 fol. 461 verso
... Alsoo Ryck Geversz aengenoomen heeft volgens de annexe bestecke in dato 1 April 1645 het maecken ende stellen van twee hecken ofte Glinten over de wallen vande Casteele tot Bueren ...
8 Febr. 1647 ... 471:0:0

993 fol. 462
... Alsoo Goosen Cornelisz Versteech aengenoomen heeft volgens de annexe bestecke in dato 1 April 1645 het maecken ende repareren vande Brugge van Sijne Hooch^{ts} Casteele tot Bueren ...
8 Febr. 1647 ... 343:0:0

993 fol. 462 verso
... Cornelis Vermeulen ... over reparaties aende Staltooren vande

Nederhoff tot Bueren …
Febr. 1647 … 759:0:0

993 fol. 462 verso
… Cornelis Vermeulen … over 't maecken van een nieuwe Brugge bijde renbaen tot Bueren …
Febr. 1647 … 234:0:0

993 fol. 463
… Cornelis Vermeulen … over 't maecken van een schuer boven de watermolen aende dyck achter 't Casteele tot Bueren … 700:0:0

993 fol. 463 verso
… Cornelis Vermeulen … over 't maecken van een nieuwe Brugge aende grooten hoff tot Bueren …
Febr. 1647 … 160:0:0

994 fol. 39
… Simon van Langelaer hovenier tot Bueren … fruit voor Hare Hooch[t] tot Hage …
… 8:0:0

994 fol. 41 verso
… Simon van Langelaer … roosewater inden Hage … 31:4:0

994 fol. 30 verso
… alsoo declaratie van Simon Langelaer hovenier tot Buren over de oncosten bij hem gedaen in aug. 1647 over het fruyt van daer naer den hage te brengen als hare Con. Hooch[t] is ordonnans …
27 Aug. 1647 … 8:0:0

994 fol. 41 verso
… Simon van Langelaer, hovenier te Bueren over reyscosten in nov. 1647
IX Dec. 1647 … 31:4:0

994 fol. 90 verso
… Willem Cornelisz vander Stoop … over ypenbomen …
[Oct.1648] … 27:10:0

996 fol. 201 verso
… Anthony van Langelaar hovenier te Buren … voor het branden van rosewater …
12 Dec. 1664 … 36:12:0

BUREN ACCOUNTS OF THE COMPTROLLER, DECREES OF THE COUNCIL, continued

NDR, inv. nos. 2584-2603 [5642-5661] (years 1630-1650)
[Information concerning the upkeep and acquisition of plant material for the Buren gardens, as detailed in the accounts of the various estate stewards (Rentmeesters) of Buren during the years 1630-1650. For the period 1642-1650, only the total yearly expenditures are copied here, without repeating details of the upkeep of the grounds, which closely follows that of the preceding years.]

NDR, inv. no. 2584 [5642] (year 1630)

2584 fols. 111-113 verso
Onderhout van den Thuijn: Item betaelt aen diverse arbeyders die int geheele jaer met spitten ende spaijen wyen ende ypeboomen onder de berseaux te bynden soo inde grooten als cleynen lusthoff verdient hebben vermogens haere specificaties, onder de maent van January LXXVII £ VI sts
Aen Horendonck hovenier ter sacke van verscheyde boomen by hem gecocht ende betaelt als laurierboomen, lynboomen als anders … XLV £
total sum 1630: XII^C V £ XVII sts V dr

NDR, inv. no. 2585 [5643] (year 1631)

2585 fol. 111
Aen Horendonck hovenier .. boomen te knooten ende Berseaux te binden ende te onderhouden … doender sijn geweest 1631 …
total sum 1631: XVI^C LVI £ VII sts VI dr

NDR, inv. no. 2586 [5644] (year 1632)

2586 fols. clvii-clx
Leverantie van beuken, ypen, Schulpen [schelpen]

2586 fol. clix verso:
Betaelt aen Arien Andriesz Boscoop Schilder de somme van twee hondert en 't negentich guldens ter sake dat hy volgende seker besteck inden Jaere 1632 geschildert heeft de nieuwe galerie inden cleynen Lusthoff … II^C XV £

2586 fol. clx:
Betaelt aen Joost van Nieuwenhuysn ende Johan Simmonsz de somme van seven ende twintich guldens elf stuyvers over t'geene Andre Mollet, hovenier, aldaer 'tharen huyse verteert heeft inden Jare 1632, gedurende den tyt dat hy de parterres inde Lusthoven heeft gemaeckt gehadt. Dus competerende by quitantie .. XXVII £ XI sts
total sum 1632: XVI^C LXXXVII £ XII sts X dr

NDR, inv. no. 2587 [5645] (year 1633)

2587 fols. 153-155
fol. 155: voor duysent else pooten … die geimployeert zijn int planten van het bosch dat in den jare 1633 affgehouwen wierdt.
total sum 1633: XII^C XXI £ VIII sts IIII dr

NDR, inv. no. 2588 [5646] (year 1634)

2588 fols. 137-138
Reparatien van eenige roeden slooten door mijnen order gerepareert vermidts sijnne hoocheijts tuijn … XV £ XVIII sts IX dr
Reparatien gedaen aenden Casteele van Bueren ende dependentien, als van houtwerck, metselwerck yserwerck gedurende de jaere tijder deser ….
Uytgave totte onderhoudinge vande Thuijn opden Casteele van Buren ende onderhoudinge vande wallen ende Grachten vande Casteele van Buren

2588 fol. cxxxviii verso
Den Rendant heeft betaelt aen verscheijden arbijders die geduerende desen Jare 1634 inden thuyn ende hoven mitsgaders opde dreven ende opde wallen vande Casteele van Buren hebben gearbeijt, soo int spitten, graven, wijen, bomen te planten, de bersiaux te binden ende t'onderhouden, de somme daer toe hier Maentlijcks specificaties sijn beloopende sulxs als hier naer volgt …
total sum 1634: XIII^C XXIII £ IX sts

NDR, inv. no. 2589 [5647] (year 1635)

2589 fols. 135-136.
fol. 136: betaelt aende handen van Willem Cornelisz vander Stoop de somme van seven hondert ponden ende dat ter saecke van coop van seeckere veertien hondert IJpersbomen door last van Sijne hoochijt gecost als mede te zien is inde bijgaende attestatie vande heer Drosstaert ende den hovenier Horendonck, ende sijn d'selve bomen geplant opde dreven ende wallen vande Casteele .. VII^C £
total sum 1635: XVI^C LXIIII £ XII sts

NDR, inv. no. 2590 [5648] (year 1637)

2590 fols. cxxx-cxxxi verso
fol. CXXX verso Uytgaven tot onderhouding vanden Thuijn opde Casteele tot Buren: Den Rendant heeft betaelt aen verscheijden arbijders d'welcke geduerende desen Jare 1637 inden Thuyn ende hoven mitsgaders opde dreven ende opde wallen vande Casteele van Buren hebben gearbeijt, soo int spitten, graven, wijen, planten van bomen … de somme …
[*and added under monthly accounts:*] Aen Willem Cornelisz vander Stoop de somme van een hondert twee en sestig ponden thien schellingen over gedaene leverantie van drie hondert vijff en twintich Yppersbomen breet bladt, ieder hondert tot vijftich gulden. en sijn d'selve boomen door order van Sijne Hoochijt omde dreven geplant als mede opde wal vanden Casteele …

NDR, inv. no. 2591 [5649] (year 1638)

2591 fols. cxxxv verso-cxxxviii
… mest van peerden voor nieuw geplantte bomen en Iepers en Linden bomen Ende leverantie van partij fruijtbomen.
total sum 1638: XV^C LXIX £ X sts

NDR, inv. no. 2592 [5650] (year 1639)

2592 fols. 154-156 verso
… mest van peerden voor nieuw geplantte bomen, als mede het maeijen vant geen rontsomme de dreef ende plantagie …
total sum 1639: XIII^C XCIIII £ XVII sts X dr

NDR, inv. no. 2593 [5651] (year 1640)

2593 fols. 147-148 verso
… mest van peerden voor nieuw geplantte bomen, als mede het maeijen vant geen rontsomme de dreef ende plantagie …

… Simon Langelaer hovenier … veertien ponden acht schellingen voor eenige arbrenijns bomen …
total sum 1640: X^C XIIII £ XIIII sts

NDR, inv. no. 2594 [5652] (year 1641)

2594 fols. cxxi verso-cxxiid
… Reyer Langelaer hovenier … diverse quantiteyt van fruytboomen ende witte hagedoorn d'welcke inde Runnebaen [renbaen ?] achter het Casteel sijn gepoot … XXV £ VIII sts
… Reyer van Langenhoven gelevert aende hovenier tot Bueren seckere quantiteijt Jonge fruytboomen soo abricoosen als persicken die aen de voet vande wall aende suytsijde aldaer tegens de nieuwe glintingen sijn geplant door Last van S.H., ende sijn d'selve alreedts wel geavanceert, twee en veertich ponden vijfthien schellingen … XLII £ XV sch
… Laurens Evertsz … van gedaene leverantie van haech ende teenen daer de bersiaux inde tuynen van Sijne Hoocheyt mede sijn gebonden ende gerepareert in den jare 1641.
total sum 1641: XI^C II £ XIX sts

NDR, inv. no. 2595 [5653] (year 1642)

2595 fols. 123-124
total sum 1642: X^C XXXII £ XI sts

NDR, inv. no. 2596 [5654] (year 1643)

2596 fols. 123-124
total sum 1643: IX^C XLV £ XVIII sts

NDR, inv. no. 2597 [5655] (year 1644)

2597 fols. 121-121 verso
total sum 1644: IX^C LVIII £ XIX sts

NDR, inv. no. 2598 [5656] (year 1645)

2598 fols. 123-124
total sum 1645: XI^C XIIII £ I sts VI dr

NDR, inv. no. 2599 [5657] (year 1646)

2599 fols. 122 verso-124
planten van Ypenboomen op de dreef
total sum 1646: XI^C XC £ XIX sts

NDR, inv. no. 2600 [5658] (year 1647)

2600 fols. 123 verso-125 (3 blz.)
Iepen breedt blad tot reparatie van boomen in S. Hooch^ts plantagie
total sum 1647: IX^C LXXXI £ XIII sts IIII dr

NDR, inv. no. 2601 [5659] (year 1648)

2601 fols. 124-125
leverantie van Ypen boomen door Willem van der Stoop
total sum 1648: IX^C LXXXV £ XVIII sts

NDR, inv. no. 2602 [5660] (year 1649)

2602 fols. 124 verso-125 verso
total sum 1649: IX^C £ VI sts

NDR, inv. no. 2603 [5661] (year 1650)

2603 fols. 121verso-122 verso
total sum 1650: VIII^C LXVI £ XIX sts

BUREN, ACQUISITIONS, continued

NDR, inv. no. 2509 [NDR FOLIO, nos. 1790-1791]

Lijste van namen der persoonen d'welcke graven comen ofte boomgaerden sullen gebragt worden … in de Nieuwe Dreeft leggende tusschen den Stadt ende Casteele van Buren… Bedragende 'tsamen de somme van twee duijsent acht hondert seven en veertich gul. thien stuyvers. J.W. Saige, 's Gravenhage, Jaer 1629.

NDR, inv. no. 2509 [NDR FOLIO, nos. 1790-1791]

… Zeeckere lijste van zeeckere veerthien partijkens affgegraven boomgaertgens off deel der selven casteele van Buuren ten behoeve vande nieuwe dreve van Sijne Excellentie …
… Opdrachte van 14 persoonen over de voorszeide 14 parceelen affgegraven boomgaerts ten behoeve van Sijne Excellentie gedaen voor schout ende schepenen van Buuren. 30 maart 1631.
… worden omtrent seven ofte acht roeden affgegraven vande thuijn oft boomgaert vanden oudt Burgemr. Rijck vander Lingen …
    's Gravenhage dd. 28 maert 1636, J.W. Saige.

BREDA

ACCOUNTS OF THE COMPTROLLER, DECREES OF THE COUNCIL, continued

NDR, inv. nos. 992-996 [735-739] (years 1637-1666)

992 fol. 179
… Jan Woutersz van Rijckevorsel … het repareren van het huijs staende inde Valckenberg op den Vijver …
May 1638 … 180:0:0

992 fol. 181
… aen Michiel van Bruheze hovenier vande twee hoven tot Breda de somme van hondert ende vijfftich Car. guls. over een Jaer extraordinaris tractement bij S.H. toegevoegt boven sijn ordinaris gagie van 300 …
May 1638 … 150:0:0

992 fol. 230
… aen Jan Woutersz Mr Metselaer tot Breda … over reparatien en metselwerck bij hem gedaen ten dienste van Sijne Hooch^t tot Breda aende muer tusschen de Capucijnen hoff ende hoff van Valckenberg, item aende muer comende tegens de bouwerije ende aende trappen comende achter de voorsz hoff van Valckenberg tegens de pavillioenen …
January 1639 … 40:3:12

992 fol. 274
… Jan van Dijck hovenier … planten vande parterres inden hoff vande Valckenberg te Breda, als namentlijck de 17. parcken te planten ende cieren met sijne couleuren, soo van palm, camille als andere cruyden ende gestampte steen naer den eysen vant werck tot 44. guls. 2 sts yder parck, mackende tsamen over de 17 parcken 750 Car. gul. … ende nadien bij bovenstaande attestatie blijckt, dat 't voorsz werck volcomen ende naer behooren volgens de voorsz contracte ende Teeckeninge daer van gemaeckt sijnde is voltrocken, opgenomen ende gepresen …
Maert/April 1639 … 750:0:0

992 fol. 280
… Laurens Drijffhout opsichter van S.H. wercken tot Breda de somme van 38:7:0 over hartsteenwerck bij hem ten dienste van S.H. inden Jaere 1638 gelevert tot het maken ende repareren vande watermolen staende op de kasteel tot Breda tot de poort vant binnenhoff aende lange Galderije inhet huijs ende staende aende voorn. Galderije …
May 1639 … 38:7:0

992 fol. 327
… Michiel van Bruheze hovenier vande hoff vande Valckenberg tot Breda de extraodinaris gagie van hondert vijfftich guldens nevens sijn ordinaris gagie van drie hondert guldens …
XXI Nov. 1639 … 150:0:0

992 fol. 348
… Laurens Drijffhout opsichter van Sijne Hoocheit[s] wercken ende steenhouwer tot Breda … over verdiende dachgelden ende hartsteenwerck bij hem ten dienste van Sijne Hoocheit in de Jaere 1638 gedaen ende gelevert inde Valckenberg …
XIII Jan. 1640 … 112:4:8

992 fol. 377
… Albrechtsz van Bingen gedaen ende gelevert ten dienste van S.H. aent huijse ende pavillioen vant hoff van Valckenburch, hoveniershuijs, voliere, Escurie, Bouwen vande Caetsbaen tot Breda inde Jare 1637 …
July 1637 … 161:19:0

992 fol. 378
… Aert Rietmakers lootgieter … over loot ende arbeydtsloon bij hem gedaen ende gelevert ten dienste van Sijne Hoocheit aent huys ende Pavillioen van 'thoff van Valckenburch, hoveniershuys, voliere, Escurie, Bouwerije ende Caetsbaen tot Breda inde Jare 1637 ende 1638 …
1 Maert 1640 … 161:19:0

992 fol. 459
… aende Concherge vande huyse van Valckenbergh Elisabeth van Buerstede … over het schoonmaecken ende reynigen vande voorsz huyse …
1 Decemb. 1640 … 84:19:3

993 fol. 140
… Laurens Drijffhout voor gelevert hartsteenwerck ende arbeydtsloon bij hem verdient aen het speelhuys buyten Breda in de Jaere 1640 …
12 Maert 1642 … 36:10:0

993 fol. 141
… Laurens Drijffhout voor 't repareren ende hartsteenwerck bij hem gelevert inden Jaere 1638 in Valckenberg tot Breda … 112:4:8

993 fol. 170
… Michiel van Bruheze over extraord[s] gagie als hovenier tot Breda …
Nov. 1642 … 150:0:0

993 fol. 216
… Michiel van Bruheze hovenier vande hoff van Valckenberg tot Breda tot sijn extraord[s] gagie …
Nov. 1643 … 150:0:0

993 fol. 317
… Dirck vander Mijlen over 't maken vaneen muyr inde Valckenbergh tegens de tirassen vande wal tot Breda met eenich buytenwerck …
Nov. 1645 … 5738:10:0

993 fol. 317 verso
… Michiel van Bruheze … jaer extra[or] gagie …
Nov. 1645 … 150:0:0

994 fol. 65
… Pieter Michielsz van Bruheze hovenier tot Breda … extra[or] gagie … aen supplement als hovenier vanden Hoff van Valckenberch …
12 May 1648 … 150:0:0

994 fol. 164 verso
… Pieter van Bruheeze hovenier tot Breda vant hoff van Valckenberg tot Breda sijn gage …
16 May 1650 … 150:0:0

995 fol. 26
… Michiel Coenlaer hovenier vande hortus botanicus vande Illustre schoole tot Breda, over arbeijt ende dachgelden …
17 Julij 1651 … 60:0:0

995 fol. 149
… Pieter van Bruheze hovenier tot Breda [1654] [no amount] …

ZUYLESTEYN

ACCOUNTS OF THE COMPTROLLER, DECREES OF THE COUNCIL, continued

NDR, inv. nos. 1039-993 [778-736] (years 1630-1647)

1039 fol. 229 verso [cf. ARA, NDR, inv. no. 3949, dated 6 August 1630]
Den Rendant heeft noch betaelt aen de volmachtichde van Jo^r Godert van Reede heere van Amerongen de somme van drie en twintich duysent ponden artois in voldoeninge vande portie ende aen pacht welck deselve heer van Amerongen inden huyse van Suylestein int Sticht van Utrecht gelegen ende aencleven vandien met ende beneffens den heere van Mijdrecht was competerende …
XXIII September … 23:000:0:0

1039 fol. 230
… heeft noch betaelt aen de volmachtigde van d'heer van Renesse van der Aa, heer van Mijdrecht de somme van twaelf duysent ponden artois, mede in voldoeninge van S.E^{cie} aen pacht welck denselven inden voornoemden huise van Suylestein ende aencleven vandien was hebbende sulex dat Synne furstelicke doorluchticheit nu daermede volcommen eygenaer ende possesseur is vanden voorscreve huise met alle de voordeelen daeraen gehoorende …
September 1630 … 12:000:0:0

1039 fol. 234 verso
… Sijne fürstelicke doorluchticheit heeft in den Jaere sestienhondert ende dertich van Jonck^{er} Godert van Reede heere van Amerongen ende van d'heer Renesse van der Aa heere van Mijdrecht gecocht het heerlijck huys van Suylestein mette aencleving vandien, int Sticht van Utrecht staende ende gelegen.

1039 fol. 273
… Den Rendant heeft noch betaelt aen Willem van Salen als fabryckmeester de somme van sevenentsestich ponden seventien schellingen artois over reys ende teercosten gaende door last van Sijne furstelicke d^r naer thuys te Suylestein om 'tselve te besichtichen ende daervan rapport te doen …
Augusti 1630 … 67:17:0

1040 fol. 221
… betaelt de somme van vier hondert sevenendevijftich ponden dertien schellingen te weten II^C III £ X sts over de vracht van Meurs van hondert duisent plansoenen van haech ende Mey buecken, om te Suylestein ende aent huijs Ter Nieuburch geplant te worden, Item CXLI £ IX sts over arbeijtsloon bij den Concierge Langenhoven inde Maent December Jaers deser reeckeninge ten dienste vant voorschreve Gebouw verstreckt, mitsgr. de verdere CXII £ XIIII sts over leverantie van ongecoleurde blompotten, als eenige koemis …
Dec. 1631 … 457:13:0

1041 fol. 251 verso
… aen Gijsbrecht Tonissen hovenier van Sijnne Hooch^t te Honsholredijck, d'somme van drie hondert vier ende dertich ponden twaelff schillingen over leveringen van eenige fruijtboomen als andere dachgelden ende reyscosten bij hem verleidt ende verdient om d'selve te Suylestein te gaen planten …
Julij 1632 … III^C XXIIII £ XII sts

1041 fol. 252
… aen Willem Dimmer Rentm^r van Iselsteijn de somme van vierentwintich duysent drie hondert drie en tachtich ponden elff schillingen vier dernier die bij hem betaelt sijn nopende de nieuwe wercken, als plantagien door last van S.H. van den XXVIII Sept. 1630 aff tot den XXI Junij 1632 toe te Suylestein gemaeckt en doen planten …
Oct. 1632 … 24.380:11:4

1042 fol. 256 verso
… Betaelt aen Willem Dimmer, Rentmeester van Iselstein, de somme van dertien hondert vijff ponden twaelff schellingen artois, over verscheyden partien van wercken bij den selven betaelt, die in den Jaere XVI^C drie en dertich tijde deser aent huis ende plantagie te Zuylestein gedaen ende gemaeckt sijn …
Junio 1633 … 1305:12:0

1042 fol. 257 verso
… Betaelt aen Willem Dimmer, Rentmeester van Iselstein, nopende reparatien aenden huise te Zuylestein ende dependentien vandien gedurende den Jaere 1633 gedaen …
Junio 1633 … 3200:49:11

1043 fol. 243
… Betaelt aen André Mollet opsichter van Sijne hoocheits Thuijnen de somme van ses en twintich ponden veertien schillingen voor reys ende teercosten bij hem verleit, gaende door last van S.H. naer Suilesteyn om de Thuijnen aldaer te besichtigen …
V Martij 1634 … 26:14:0

1043 fol. 304 verso
… aen de heer Johan de Wilde de somme van veertien hondert ponden in betalinge van seeckere seven roeden ende twee mergen bosch leggende voor den huise van Suylestein bij hem op XXX July 1634 aen Sijnne hoocheit vercost …
… 1400:0:0

992 fol. 144
… Julius Zegemans sub^t rentm^r vant Graeffschap Bueren, van verschooten penningen overt maken vande nieuwe plantagie op Zuylesteijn annos 1634 ende 1635 …
May 1638 … 2048:0:0

992 fol. 246
… Jan Dircksz Metselaer aengenoomen heeft volgens der annexe besteck in dato den XXIII July 1637 't maecken vande nieuwe keuckens, mitsgaders een nieuw Coetshuys en 't verlengen vande groote poort op onsen huyse tot Zuylesteyn …
Febr. 1639 … 1250:0:0

992 fol. 313
… Willem Cornelisz vander Stoop … ter sake van ypen ende peereboomen bij hem gelevert ten dienste van Sijne Hoocheit in desen Jare 1639 die geplant sijn tot Zuylestein …
XXI Oct. 1639 … 97:10:0

992 fol. 361
… Hendrick van Hattem de somme van ses hondert Car. guls. omme bij hem geemloyeert te worden tot betalinge van te doene oncosten der plantagie tot Zuylestein die S.H. hem heeft gelast aldaer te laten doen …
IIII Febr. 1640 … 600:0:0

992 fol. 440
… Hendrick van Hattem … oncosten plantagie te Zuylestein …
XXIII Octob. 1640 … 1000:0:0

992 fol. 442
… Jan van Diepenen Landtmeter tot Utrecht … over de reyscosten ende vacaties bij hem gedaen ten dienste van Sijne Hoocheit …
XXIII Octob. 1640 … 85:0:0

993 fol. 38
… Cornelis vander Stoop hovenier over lesten termijn van drie van 1300 Ypenboomen breedt bladt gelevert te Zuylestein …
XXIX April 1641 …

993 fol. 53
… Reynier Dircksz van Langelaer over 12 abricose ende 12 persicke boomen bij hem gelevert inde Thuyn te Zuylesteyn …
May 1640 … 24:0:0

993 fol. 54
… Jan van Diepenen lantm^r over vacatien int ondersoecken van sekere landen by Zuylesteyn …
May 1641 … 60:0:0

993 fol. 55
… Hendrick van Hattem over oncosten vande plantagien by Zuylesteyn …
May 1640 … 2704:6:8

993 fol. 62
… Jan van Diepenen lantm^r over een stantteeckeninge bij hem gemaeckt van Zuylesteyn …
Juni 1641 … 165:0:0

993 fol. 24
… Hendrick van Hattem over te doene oncosten aende plantagie tot Zuylestein …
… 400:0:0

993 fol. 24
… Jan van Diepenen lantmeter te Utrecht over gemaeckte Caerten, reyscosten etc. …
… 126:0:0

993 fol. 131
… Hendrick van Hattem sijne plantagueur de somme van acht hondert Car. guls. omme … incoop van boomen totte plantagie van Honsholredijck, Buren, Zuylestein …
III Febr. 1642 … 800:0:0

993 fol. 154
… te tellen aen Hendrick van Hattem sijnen plantagueur de somme van een duysent twee hondert Car. guldens omme bij hem geemployeert te werden soo int coopen van boomen, als andere oncosten aende plantagies van Sijne Hooch^t aengedaen …
1 Junij 1642 … 1200:0:0

993 fol. 184 verso
… Jan van Diepenen lantm^r over 't copieren van Caerten, 't maecken van Teeckeningen, vacatien, reyscosten etc. …
Febr. 1643 … 192:0:0

993 fol. 188
… te tellen aen Hendrick van Hattem, sijnen plantagueur de somme van negen hondert Car. guldens, omme geemployeert te worden tot betalinge van incoop van boomen en andere te doene oncosten totte plantagies van Honsholredijck, Rijswijck, Bueren ende Zuylesteijn …
VI Maert 1643 … 900:0:0

993 fol. 208
… te tellen aen Hendrick van Hattem, sijnen plantagueur … oncosten van plantagien monterende alles te samen de somme van drij duysent vier hondert seven ende tsestich car. guls. seventien sts. acht dr. mogen betalen …
XVI Aug. 1643 … 3467:17:8

APPENDIX ZUYLESTEYN

993 fol. 220

... te tellen aen Hendrick van Hattem, sijnen plantagueur ... oncosten van incoop van boomen voor plantagien monterende de somme van hondert car. guls.
7 Dec. 1643 ... 100:0:0

993 fol. 262

... te tellen aen Hendrick van Hattem, sijnen plantagueur de somme van seshondert guldens, omme geemployeert te worden tot betalinge van incoop van boomen en andere te doene oncosten totte plantagies van Honsholredijck, Rijswijck, Bueren ende Zuylesteijn, volgens den laste van Sijne Hooch^t aen hem gegeven ...
Aug. 1644 ... 600:0:0

993 fol. 414 verso

... aen Hendrick van Hattem plantaguem^r van Sijne Hooch^t dezelfde despence ende uytgevels tot van de bepootinge vande plantagien tot Bueren, Honsholredijck, Rijswijck ende Suylesteijn van April 1642 tot April 1643 ...
28 Maert 1646 ... 2436:1:0

... Gelijcke ordonnantie ter sake als voorsz. van 28 Julij 1643 tot in Mayo 1644 ter somme van ...
Maert 1646 ... 1758:15:3

... Gelijcke ordonnantie ter sake als voorsz. van Augusto 1644 tot Februarij 1645 ter somme van ...
Maert 1646 ... 1247:0:8

YSSELSTEYN

ACCOUNTS OF THE COMPTROLLER, DECREES OF THE COUNCIL, continued

NDR, inv. nos. 1040-1042 [779-781] (years 1631-1633)

1040 fol. 212 verso

... Aen Willem Dimmer Rentmeester van Iselstein de somme van tien duysent drie hondert seven ponden drie schellingen artois by hem betaelt over de wercken soo nieuw als oudt die Sijnne Furstelicke doorl^t in den Jaere XVI^C negenentwintich aent huys te Iselstein doen maecken heeft ...
... 10.307:3:0

1041 fol. 333 verso

... Adriaen Willeboortsen Spierinxhouten [houck?] architect ... over verscheyden vacatien ende costen bij hem selve gedaen ende besteet in diverse reysen die hij ten dienste van S.H. te Yselstein nopende 't gebou aldaer in den Jaere 1627 ende voorts in den jaere 1631 te Honsholredijck gedaen heeft ...
... 76:5:0

1042 fol. 255 verso

... Vergoet aen Willem Dimmer Rentmeester van Iselstein de somme van vijff hondert seventich ponden sestien schellingen artois, voor soo verre de selve betaelt heeft aen Claes Jansz metselaer, ter saecke vant over leggen vanden Lusthoff van Sijnne hoocheit tot Iselstein ...
Junij 1633 ... 570:16:0

1043 fol. 242 verso

... Uytgave nopende de verbeteringen ende reparatien gedaen aen Sijne Hooch^{ts} huyse te Iselstein ...
[1634]

ARA, NDR, inv. nos. 4827-4856 [8416-8445], accounts of the stewards Willem and Jan Dimmer, 1621-1650, provide further detailed information on the building and upkeep of the Ysselsteyn estate.

GENERAL INFORMATION CONCERNING VARIOUS ESTATES

ACCOUNTS OF THE COMPTROLLER, DECREES OF THE COUNCIL, continued

NDR, inv. nos. 1039-993 [778-736] (years 1630-1647)

1039 fol. 234

... In den jaere XVI^C dertich tijde deser en sijn geen meerdere acquisiten der domeynen gedaen dan de verbeteringen vande notabele nieuwe Gebouwen ende reparatien soo aenden Casteele ende Thuynen te Buren, ende aende huyse te Honsholredijck ende Nieuburch gemaeckt ende gedaen ...
X^N Somma: M^C LXX^M IX^C LXXXV £ XIII sts XV dr

1040 fol. 227 verso

... In den Jaere XVI^C een ende dertich tijde deser en sijn geen meerdere acquisiten der domeinen gedaen, dan de voorsz verbeteringe vande notable nieuwe gebouwen ende merckelijcke verbeteringen soo aende huijsen te Honsholredijck, Buren, Yselstein, Nieuburch gemaeckt ende gedaen ...

1040 fol. 257

... Catarina Cray weduwe van wijlen Mr Symon Stevyn de somme van vier hondert ponden artois over een jaerlijffpensie bij Sijnne Fürstelicke Genade Prince Maurits hoochlofflicker memorie ten lijve van Frederick, Hendrick, Susanna ende Livina haere kinderen toegevoecht ... 400:0:0
X^N Somma: XCL^M CI £ XVI sts ... dr

1042 fol. 205
Den Raedt ende Tresorier Brouart ... de somme van sevenentsestich ponden seven schellingen voor reijs en teercosten bij hem verleit sijnde by Sijne hoocheit uyt het leger te Boxtel ontbooden, ende gelast met sich te brengen de architecten van Sijnne hoocheits Gebouwen ende Thuynen ...
[1633] ...   67:7:0

993 fol. 154
... Hendrick van Hattem ... soo int coopen van boomen als andere oncosten des plantagies van S.H. aengedaen ...
1 Junij 1642   ... 1200:0:0

993 fol. 158 verso
... Ibid.:   ... 300:0:0

993 fol. 167
... Ibid.:   ... 800:0:0

993 fol. 208
... H. van Hattem plantageur van S.H. monterende in alles ter somme van drij duysent vier hondert ende tsestich car. guls. seventhien sts ...
XVI Aug. 1643 ... 3467:17:8

993 fol. 208 verso
... Ibid.:
22 Aug. 1643 ... 600:0:0

993 fol. 220
... Ibid.:
7 Dec. 1643 ... 100:0:0

HUIS TEN BOSCH

993 fol. 428 verso
... Aen Mr Borchaert Fredrick hovenier ... over oncosten aende parterre ende rabatten inden Hoff in't Haechse Bosch ...
[Juni 1640] [no amount]

GRONINGEN

993 fol. 249
... Aende hoven en gaerden tot Groningen noodich, van wegen Sijn Hooch^t sal werden becostigt ...
... Elias Jansz hovenier tot Groningen over hout ende timmerwerck inde hoven aldaer gelevert anno 1641, 42, 43 ...
April 1644 ... 239:8:14

JOURNAL OF THE COUNCIL (years 1632-1635)

NDR, inv. no. I [NDR, I] **Journaal van de Rade van Sijne Ex^{tie}** beginnende vrijdach den 2de Jan. 1632 en lopende tot 29 Dec. 1635.

Den IX Junij present d'heeren Brouaert ende Willem.
... De voorn. heer Brouaert Raedt ende Tresorier Gnael. verhoort hebbende dat Mevrouwe de Princesse hem last hadde gegeven, dat soo wanneer Andre Mollez, zoone van de hovenier vande Coninck van Franckrijck gedaan soude hebben mettet ordonneren ende doen opmaecken der parterres van Buren ende Honsholredijck, Dat men met hem soude afrekenen voldaen van seyne reyscosten, moeyten, ende andere oncosten bij hem gedaen, Daaronder niet begrepen de hantwerckers oft arbeijders die daeraen gevrocht hebben. ende gesien de declaratie daervan bij voorsz Andre Mollez overgegeven, hiernaer volgende:

Pour les parterres du Chasteau de Burre qui sont aux deux costez, d'iceluij trois cent Livres dont je fait conte et cinquante quil a receu de Genr Monsr Dinance   300 £

Plus pour le parterre en Broderie et le Compartmnt.
de gazon de honsholredick quatre cent livres   400 £
Et pour ses voyages trois cent livres   300 £

Et pour la despense qu'il a faicte a la haye en faisant
les susdits dessins cinquante livres   50 £
...   1050 £

Ende bevonden wesende de voorsz declaratie niet te wesen exorbitant bedragende thien hondert vijftich guldens, verstaen dat den voorsz Raedt ende Tresorier Gnael. den voorsz Mollez sal mogen contenteren, als aff streckende 't geene hij daerop soude mogen hebben ontfangen, en hier vooren eensdeels vermelt is.

DOCUMENTS

FREDERIK HENDRIK'S GARDENS

GARDENERS' CONTRACTS, INSTRUCTIONS AND OTHER PAPERS

DOCUMENT I

HONSELAARSDIJK, 20 June 1646, layout of the new West Gardens
ARA, NDR, inv. no. 6744 [NDR FOLIO, 1330]

ESTIMATE FOR MAKING AND DIGGING A NEW WEST GARDEN AT HONSELAARSDIJK

Besteck vant maken en graven van een nieuwe Thuijn, mitsgaders een houten heijninge, om deselven tot Honsholredijck, aengenomen bij Dirck de Wilde [Milde], een Thuijn voor 11.000 L, ende de heijninge voor 3.300 L, in date 20 Junij 1646.

    Conditien ende Voorwaarden waernaer Sijne hoogheijt den Prince van Orangien wil besteden het ophoogen met sant ende te maecken een nieuwen Thuijn aende Westzijde vant huijs te Honsholredijck met een nieuwen sloot, mitgaders het verdelven ende het uyt roeijen vande boomen inder manieren als volcht, welcke voorsz. nieuwen Thuijn men soo lange ende breet sal maken als de tegenwoordige nieuwen Thuijn is gelegen aende oostzijde tot honsholredijck mette bermen ende slooten soo men den Aennemers aenwijsen sal, ende affpassen als de Elssenboomen uijtgeroeijt zijn.

    De Aennemers sullen gehouden wesen alle de ijpen boucken ende Eijcken boomen comende in de voorsz. te maecken Thuijn te laeten staen totten herfst offe totten tijt dat Zijn hoocheijt het goet sal vinden ende sullen alsdan de selve boomen moeten bequaem mette wortelen uijtroeijen omme weder uijt te comen verplanten, ende alle de Elssen boomen van stonden aen uijt te roeijen mette wortelen, welcke Elssen boomen de Aennemers tot haeren voordeel sullen hebben, doch sullen de selve datelijcken uijt de plantagien moeten brengen opde verbeurte vande selve boomen.

    De Aennemers sullen gehouden wesen alle de bovenste zooden comende opt voorsz. Velt eerst bovenaff te slaen ter dijckte van ses duijmen, ende alsdan onder de voorsz. duijmen noch twee roeden voeten diep te verdelven soo wel inde laechte als inde hoochte, ende alle de zooden wel cleijntgens te breecken ende onder opden bodem op eenen egaelen dickte te verspreijden.

    De Aennemers sullen gehouden wesen de voorsz. te maecken Thuijn als die dus omgespit is op te hoogen met goet wit sandt ende eenhalve voet hooger te maecken aende oost ende westzijde, als den tegenwoordigen Thuijn nu is, die aende oostzijde van Honsholredijck leijt, ende inde midde wegen noch een voet hooger te maecken ende aen weerszijde oost en West ten ront neergaende ende zuijden ende Noorden int waterpas te maecken sulcx alsmen den Aennemers aenwijsen sal sonder eenige laechtens daerinne te laeten.

    De Aennemers sullen gehouden wesen alst voorsz. werck met sandt opgehoocht is op zijn peijl het voorsz. Velt wederomme te herdelven ende om te spitten ende mengen het bovenste sandt mette cleij diese alrede verdolven hebben met het sandt soo veel alst doendelijcken is door den anderen, ende dat ter diepte alst voorgaende omgespit is omme alsoo een bequamen Thuijn te maecken, ende daer de ijpen, boucken, ende Eijcken boomen zijn blijven staen ende niet verdolven is omme de wortelen niet te quetsen, sullen als zij dieselve boomen uijtroeijen moeten verdelven ter diepte vant verdolven werck daeromme gelegen ende breecken alle de cluijten aen cleijne stucken ende maecken dat het oost ende West een voet toe rondt neergaet ende zuijden ende Noorden int waterpas sonder eenige hoochtens ofte laechtens daerinne te laeten ende oock alle de wortelen mette steenen soo den rest verdolven is schoon uijt te lesen tot contentment van Sijn hoocheijt.

    Den Aennemer sal noch gehouden wesen te maken een berm aende Westzijde langs de tegenwoordige te maecken Thuijn, de welcke boven breet wesen sal ses voeten ende hooch gelijckx de nieuwe te maecken thuijn, ende op ijder voethoochte een voet west op te doceren ofte breder te maecken omme dat men de heijninch daer bequaem ende vast op mach stellen.

    De Aennemers sullen gehouden wesen te maecken een nieuwe sloot aende Noordzijde vande nieuwe te maecken thuijn, ende dat soo lang als den voorsz Thuijn int westen strecken sal ende int oosten tot inde oude Gracht te verheelen, welcke sloot boven wijdt gemaeckt sal werden vierentwintig roede voeten. Ende de canten aen wederzijde erst schoon te doceren naerden eijsch. Ende dat totter diepte van vier voeten ondert laechste soomerwater int waterpas te maecken sonder eenige hoochtens daerinne te laeten ende de canten linie recht te maecken, ende van onder tot boven recht onder te rij te maecken, sonder eenige bochten ofte busten daerinne te laeten, ende een berm van ses voeten breet te maecken tusschen den Thuijn ende sloot hooch naer den eijsch vant werck, ofte op alsulcks hoochte als den Thuijn moet wesen, ende de canten langs de sloot daer den berm te laech is met sooden op te setten naerden eijsch van het werck, de spijs comende uijt de voorsz sloot te brengen op de bermen ende nieuwe te maecken thuijn in de laechten doorgaende te verspreijden waterpas gewijs soo ver die strecken mach.

    Den Aennemers sullen gehouden wesen de oude oostsloot comende langs den nieuwen te maken thuijn te verwijden ende maecken op vierentwintich voeten, ende dat op sulcken diepte als van de voorsz nieuwe sloot geseijt is soot zijn hoocheijt belieff, ende de berm langs de cant van de oude sloot te maecken naerden eijsch van't werck soo men aanwijsen sal.

    Den Aennemers sullen gehouden wesen het oude heck dat langs de voorsz oostsloot staet noch te nemen tot haeren voordeel omme soo wel te beter ende bequamer de spijs opt voorsz werck te connen brengen.

    Item de Aennemers sullen met haer eerste verdelven moeten blijven drie voeten rontomme vande stammen vande ijpen, boucken ende Eijckenboomen omme de wortelen niet te quetsen maer als zij de selve sullen uijtgeroeijt hebben sullent als dan spitten ende effenen als vooraen verhaelt is.

    Ende soo men de oude oostsloot niet en verwijdt sullen de aennemers gehouden wesen daer een breeden berm te maecken, tusschen den Thuijn ende sloot ende op te hoogen tot gelijck den Thuijn ende soo de canten vanden berm langs de sloot vereijsche met sooden op geset te werden sullen de aennemers het selfde gehouden wesen te doen ende dit alles naerden eijsch vant werck.

    De Aennemers sullen gehouden wesen haer selven te versorgen ende onderhouden op haer eijgen coste van schoupen, spaden, cordewagens, deelen, plancken, paelen, spickers, masten, het maecken van dammen het opnemen vandien het uijthoosen ende droogh houden vant water van gelijcken haer selven te versorgen van scheepen, schuijten, pramen, wagens ende paerden omme mede te carren. Oock het sandt haer selven te versorgen niet uijtbesondert dat sij van doen souden mogen hebben tot ophoginge ende verdelven vant voorsz werck ende het maecken vande slooten alles uijtwijsende dese voorsz Conditien ende dit alles op haer eijgen cost ende bier.

Sijne hoocheijt sal totte opsicht vant voornoemde werck stellen soodanige persoonen als het hem gelieven sal.

Den Aennemer sal genieten vrijdom van alle impositien soo van materialen als drinckebieren gelijck Sijne hoocheit is competerende.

Alle 'tvoornoemde werck sal moeten gedaen sijn voor het aenstaende saijsoen van planten, alsoo Sijne hoocheijt den voornoemden thuijn begeert met den aenstaende herfst te beplanten.

De betalinge sal geschieden in drie gelijcke termijnen, te weten den eersten termijn gereet, den tweeden als den thuijn op zijn behoorlijcke hoochte sal sijn gebracht, ende den derden lesten termijn als alle 'tvoornoemde werck volcomen gedaen opgenomen en gepresen sal sijn. op alle welcke conditien aennemer vant voornoemde werck is gebleven Dirck de Milde, ende dat voor een somme van elf duijsent car. guldens.

Noch heeft de voornoemden de Milde aengenomen den voorsz. Thuijn met een houten heijning te maken tegen het Westen ende Noorden ende dat soodanich ende van sulcke planten als inden Thuijn int Oosten is gestelt, mits datse sal wesen drie voeten hooger, gelijck de andere heijninge tegenwoordich oock soo veel verhoocht wordt. Ende sullen de palen dienvolgende oock naer advenant haer swaerte moeten hebben, alsmede denselven thuijn te maecken met soodanich houtwerck, paelen, latten ende glintingen even gelijck inden anderen Thuijn int oosten te sien is, oock alle 'tselve te verwen naer behooren als inden voorsz Thuijn, den voornoemde de Milde sal daer toe alles moeten leveren niets uijtgesondert. Ende dat voor de somme van drie duijsent drie hondert car. guldens.

Tot voldoeninge vande voorschreve wercken sal den Aennemer stellen suffisante Cautie.

Aldus bestelt ende aengenomen op approbatie van van Sijne Hoocheijt desen 20 Junij sestien hondert ses ende veertich, was ondertekent D. de Milde.

Legerstont. Sijne hoocheijt, gesien hebbende het bovenstaende Contract, heeft deselve naer sijne forme ende inhouden geratificeert ende geapprobeert, ratificeert ende approbeert tselve bij desen, Actum Breda desen 26 Junij sestien hondert ses ende veertich, ende was ondertekent F. Henry de Nassau.

Noch Legerstont. Sijne hoocheijt, Committeert ende authoriseert hiermede Mr. Cornelis Pauw sijnen Raedt, omme metten Rentm^r van sijne Domeijnen van Naeltwijck ende den Lantmeter Pieter Florissen van der Salm, mitsgaders met Mrs., hen des verstaende te visiteren ende op te nemen alle de wercken inden bovenstaende Besteck vermelt, wel lettende dat deselve wel ende naer behooren conform de Conditien sijn gemaeckt ende voltrocken, Actum in 's Gravenhage desen seventhienden februarij sestien hondert acht en veertich, was ondertekent G.P. d'Orange, in margine stont gecacheteert t'Cachet van Sijne Hoocheijt in rooden wasse met papieren ruijte overdeckt, onder stont: Ter ordonnantie van Sijne hooch^t ende gecontrasigneert L. Buysero.

DOCUMENT II

HONSELAARSDIJK, 13 February 1686, instructions for Hendrick Quellenburch
ARA, NDR, inv. no. 566 [603], fols. 24-26

REGULATIONS FOR MR. HENDRICK QUELLENBURCH FOR THE UPKEEP OF THE GARDENS OF THE HOUSE HONSELAARSDIJK

Reglement waer naer Meester Hendrick Quellenburch in het onderhouden van alle de Thuijnen van het huys Honsholredijck sigh sal hebben te gedragen.

Sal hij alle parterres, bedden, Rabatten ende paden geene uytgesondert suyver ende schoon van alle onkruydt onderhouden.

De Vruchtboomen sal hy tydelyck snoeyen ende binden inden uytgegane plaetsen andere weder in planten.

Sal alle Vlyt aenwenden om vroegh ende laet groente, Aertvruchten, Druyven, Kerssen etc. voor te telen, daer toe hem de noodige kassen, glasen, Rietmatten, Broeymis sal worden gelevert.

Alle dese Vruchten sal hy opden gerequereerden tyt naer den Hage seynden aen die dewelcke hem sal worden genoemt.

Sal alle de Loofwercken van palm, de Gras parterres net ende suyver onderhouden met scheeren ende wieden, de plaetsen die uytgegaen syn met nieuwe plantsoen weder vollen, de Gras parterres dickwils mayen ende het Gras cort houden.

Sal alle heggens, Cabinetten scheeren ende onderhouden met binden, de gront van onkruyt suyveren, ende met schoffelen ende kleuseren net ende Rouw houden.

Alle de planten, bollen ende saden van bloemen die hem ter handt gestelt syn, ende noch sullen werden, sal hy wel in acht nemen deselve trachtement alleen wel ende trouwelyck te bewaren, maer oock te vermeerderen, ende soo mogelyck in alle saysoenen bloeyende te houden ende hebben, om vandeselve alle weecken twee drye bouquetten ten dienste van Hare hooch^t te maken.

Sal van gelycken, d'Orange, Citroen, grenaden, Myrtis ende Jassemyn boomen, nevens alle andere vreemde bygewassen soo die daer in syn, ende noch staen te comen, sorghvuldiglyck in acht te nemen met Gieten, verplanten, ververschen van Aerden, uyt ende insetten op den gerequereerden tyt, d'overvloedige Vruchten ende bloemen van deselve affplucken, ende wel besorght naer den Hage seynden. Geene van dese boomen off by gewassen sal hy mogen vervreemden, noch oock geene bloemen, boomvruchten off Aert vruchten vercoopen op wat pretent het oock soude mogen syn.

De backen, potten tot de Orange boomen ende bygewassen, de Turff om des winters de kachels te stoken, als oock alle mist ende sant, sullen door den genomineerden by Syne hooch^t werden versorght, mits dat in tyts van alle gerequereerde werden gewaerschout.

Sal met alderhande gereetschap noodich tot het werck inde voorsz Thuynen te doen, als oock het wijen der selve tot synen eygen costen moeten versorgen.

Sal om de Broeymis te brengen tot de Meloenen ende andere Aertvruchten noodich, als oock om die Rypgeworden naer den Hage te transporteren, een paart met een karre tot syne vrye dispositie hebben, welck paert hy oock sal gehouden syn te gebruycken om de fonteyn back vol te pompen.

Sal mede hebben eene vrye woonplaets ende genieten soodanigen vrydom van import als Syne hooch^ts huys op honsholredyck is hebbende.

Alle het bovengemelte werck in alle de voorsz Thuynen, nevens het geene hier niet uytgedruckt noodich is tot haer vereyschte onderhout, sal hy gehouden syn te doen, met de hulpe van negen knechts, hier voor genietende jaerlycks voor syn persoonlyck Tractement eene somme van 800 Car. Guldens, voor vyff knechts die het geheele jaer sullen dienen voor haere Cost tegens drye guldens ter weeck eene somme van 780 guldens. Ende voor de cost van vier andere knechts die maer negen maenden, te weten vande 1 Febr. tot den 1 Novemb. sullen dienen, mede tegens drye guldens ter weeck, eene somme van 468 Car. guldens, de meester knecht sal genieten een Tractement van tachtich Car. guldens ende andere acht knechts sullen yder ten hoochsten goedgedaen werden een Gagie van sestich Car. guldens int jaer, Mits dat alle het geene bovengen. knechts minder sullen trecken als de voorsz sestich gul. jaerlycks, selve door den Tresorier Generaal Verhagen tot proffyte van S. hooch^t sal worden ingehouden, ende geensints strecken tot voordeel van de voornoemde Tuynman.

Dit alles sal den voornoemde Hendrick Quellenburgh betaelt worden by den Tresories Generael van S. hoocheyt, Dirck Verhagen, en dat van vierendeel tot vierendeel jaers het gereckte vierendeel. Te weten alleen van de somme concernerende het Tractement hem jaerlycks toegevoecht ende het Costgelt van de vyff knechts die het geheele jaer in dienst sullen blyven, als oock het jaerlycks Tractement der vyff voornoemde knechts. Het Tractement ende Costgelt van de resterende vier knechts sullen alleen in het geheel den 1 Novemb. betaelt worden naer het expireren vande negen maenden. Welverstaende dat dese knechts haer gelt wegens haer Tractement ontfangende daervan behoorlyck quitantie sullen moeten geven exprimerende de somme die sy sullen hebben genoten. Ende alles onder behoorlycke quitantie vanden voornoemde Hendrick Quellenburgh. Dit voorsz. Reglement sal syn aanvanck nemen met den 1 Mey 1686.

Syne Hooch^t approbeert dese conditie ende ordonneert dienvolgende Synen Tresorier Generael Dirch Verhagen de betalinge volgens de voorsz. Conditien te doen, dewelcke hem in syne Rekeninge sal valideren.

Actum in 's Gravenhage den 13 Feb. 1686.

DOCUMENT III

TER NIEUBURCH, 1632, instructions for Louis D'Anthoni. ARA, NDR, inv. no. 4694 [NDR FOLIO, 1413], among Bestekken or Builder's Estimates for works at Ter Nieuburch, 1632-1636.

CONDITIONS AND STIPULATIONS FOR THE GARDENER LOUIS D'ANTHOIN [ANTHONIE]

Conditien ende Voorwaerden waerop die van Rade ende Rekeningen van Sijne Ex^cie mijn heere Prince van Orange op desselfs welbehagen en aggreatie aengenomen hebben Louis D'Anthoin Thuijnman. Om Sijne Ex^cie te dienen als hovenier in Sijne hoven, Boomgaerden ende Plantagien tot Rijswijck.

Den voorsz. hovenier sal gehouden wesen in voorsz. hoven ende Boomgaerden te saeijen en te planten, alle soorten van Aert ende Boomvruchten die dienstich sullen wesen tot de Tafel ende Keucken van Sijne Ex^cie, t'sij tot Rijswijck ofte in den hage sulcx ende soo gelijck Sijne Ex^cie hem sal gelieven te ordonneren ofte te doen ordonneren.

Hij sal oock gehouden wesen de paden ende gangen, soo door als rontomme de voorsz. hoven ende Boomgaerden, mitsgaders vande plantagien, t'sij met snoeijen, wijen, ofte anders soo't best wesen sal, altijt net ende schoon te houden.

Noch sal hij gehouden wesen alle de heijningen ende pallissaden, oock alle prieelen ende wercken van plaijsantie die Sijne Ex^cie aldaer soude mogen doen maken, van oncruijt te reijnigen, te binden ende te scheeren, ende voorts te onderhouden naden eijsch vande selve wercken.

Indien eenich gewas vande selve wercken soude mogen uijtgaen ende verdorren, ofte dat Sijne Ex^cie daerinne iet begeerde verandert te hebben, soo sal den voorsz. hovenier gehouden wesen t'selve te beteren ende te veranderen, mits dat hem gelevert sullen werden de planten ende voorder hout daer toe nodig sijnde.

Indien oock eenige fruijtboomen, ofte ijpen ende Linde boomen staende buijten ofte binnen de thuijnen mochten uijtgaen ende verdorren, ofte dat Sijne Ex^cie eenige andere boomen begeerden geplant te hebben, d'voorsz. hovenier sal gehouden wesen t'selve oock te beteren, ende andere boomen te beplanten, mits dat hem mede gelevert sullen werden d'selve boomen, sonder dat hij hovenier eenich wassende off opgaende hout sal hebben aff te hacken, ten sij met voorgaende expresse last van Sijne Ex^cie dewelcke verstaet dat denselven hovenier noch ijemandt anders dienaengaende geen emolumenten sal hebben te pretenderen.

Hij sal oock gehouden wesen twee mael tenminste des Jaers, de nieuwe Graften ende slooten rontomme d'voorsz. hoven, Boomgaerden ende plantagien van allerleij vuijlicheijt te baggeren ende reijnigen ende de canten van oncruijt te ontblooten.

Indien Sijne Ex^cie eenige nieuwe prieelen begeerde gemaeckt te hebben, den voorsz. hovenier sal gehouden wesen d'selve te helpen maecken, te binden ende te scheeren, oock met piramijden, portalen, ende andere fraijicheden te vercieren, naden Eijsch van t'werck, mits dat hem gelevert sullen werden de thienen, Rijsen ende andere materialen die daertoe noodich sullen wesen, sonder ijets voor sijn dachgoet te trecken. Ende deselve gemaeckt wesende voorders te onderhouden als voor.

Alle Aert ende Boomvruchten sullen commen tot prouffijte ende ter dispositie van Sijne Ex^cie dewelcke hij hovenier sal hebben te plucken reijnigen ende bergen twee mael ter weecke, t'sij inde keucken van Sijne Ex^cie tot Rijswijck, ofte inden hage daer het deselve gelieven sal, sonder dat hij totte voorsz. boom ende aertvruchten eenighe pretensie ofte prouffijt sal hebben.

Den voorsz. hovenier sal voor al t'gene voorsz. is ende tot voldoeninge vande gene die hij tot sijne hulpe sal gebruycken, Jaerlijcx ontfangen ende genieten de somme van ses hondert car. guldens innegaende metten eerstendach des Jaers XVI^C tweendertich, die hem alle drie maenden betaelt sullen werden met hondert vijftich guldens smaels bij Sijne Ex^cies Tresorier Generael tegenwoordich ende toecommende.

Bovendijen sal hij hebben een vrije wooninge die hem gelevert ende onderhouden sal werden tot costen van Sijne Ex^cie.

Ende opdat alle dagen de vruchten vande voorsz. hoven ende boomgaerden te meer sullen mogen wassen, Sal Sijne Ex^cie daerinne alle Jaer tot wederroepens, doen brengen vijftich voederen, soo koe als peerdemisse, omme geemploijeert te werden daert den voorsz. hovenier in voorsz. thuijnen oirbaerlicxt sal vinden.

Ende omme te weten off den voorn. hovenier dese Conditien ende Voorwaerden wel ende deuchdelijck gestadich heeft onderhouden sal hij lijden dat Sijne Ex^cie soodanigen persoon stelle, die dagelijcx sal mogen comen besichtigen naer t'volvoeren van desen Contracte, als deslve daertoe sal gelieven te emploieren.

Des soo is expresselijck geconditioneert Indien Sijne Ex^cie bevonden dat hij metten voorsz. hovenier niet wel tot sijn contentement gedient en ware, dat hij denselven sal mogen afdancken.

Ten laatsten is mede geconditioneert dat Sijne Ex^cie d'voorsz. thuijnen voor t'eerste Jaer sal doen approprieren in bedden ende percken, waerinne den voorsz. hovenier mede sal wercken sonder dachgoet. Ende sal den voorsz. hovenier metten Soomer vant Jaer 1632 ende navolgende Jaren moeten winnen soo veel saet dat hij voor de voorn. thuijnen sal connen besaeijen van alle t'geene van noode sal wesen, off anderssints tot sijnen coste moeten versorgen. Ende soo wanneer hij quame te scheijden vande voorn. sijnen Dienst, dat hij t'gewonnen saet, t'welck alsdan onder hem sal berusten overleveren sal, aenden toekomenden thuijnman, die in sijne plaetse comen sal om t'selve te oirbaren ten prouffijte van Sijne Ex^cie.

Gedaen In s'Gravenhage den XX Februarij XVI^C twee ende dertich. Ter Ordonnantie van die vande Rade ende Reeckeninge van Sijne Ex^cie. G.W. Saige. Louis D'Antoins.

Sijne Ex^cie gesien hebbende de bovengeschrevene Conditien ende Voorwaerden bij die van Zijnen Rade op des selve welbehagen aengegaen met Louis d'Anthoin over het hovenierschap van Zijnen huijse tot Rijswijck, heeft deselve tot zijnen wederroepen geaggreert ende aggreert mits desen.

Gedaen in s'Gravenhage den lesten februarij XVI^C twee ende dertich.

DOCUMENT IV

TER NIEUBURCH, 1686, instructions for Willem Brederoo
ARA, NDR, inv. no. 566 [603], fols. 20 verso-23.

REGULATIONS FOR THE GARDENER AND CASTELLAN WILLEM BREDEROO ... FOR THE UPKEEP OF THE GARDENS OF TER NIEUBURCH

`Reglement waernaer Mr Willem Brederoo als hovenier ende Casteleyn in het onderhouden van S. hooch^ts huys ende thuynen van het selve huys Ter Nieuburch gelegen by Ryswyck sich sal hebben te reguleren.

Eerstelyck sal hij gehouden sijn de twee thuijnen gelegen aen wederzyden van het huys schoon te houden van alle oncruyt ende daerinne het geheele jaer voort te teelen alder hande groente, tot dienst van S. hooch^ts keucken.

Sal mede op den behoevelycke tyt moeten snoeyen ende binden alle de Boomen die Rontom de muijr off doorde Thuynen alreede geplant syn ofte alsnoch geplant sullen worden volgens d'ordre vande geenen die Syne hooch^t daertoe gelieven te stellen.

Al de rabatten daer de Arbrenains sullen staen, eens jaers om te spitten, een spit diep sonder de wortelen te beschadigen, ofte eenige groove groente (als suyringh, pietersely, peen off diergelyck) daer op te mogen teelen.

Sal oock alle de paden schoon en net moeten houden van alle oncruyt sonder die boll off mul te maken, en alle de palm eens 's jaers te scheeren inden behoorlycke tyt.

Alle de vruchten als peeren, appelen, persicken, abricoosen, pruymen, kerssen, druyven, aelbesien, kruysbesien, aerbesien wel te bewaren ende te plucken inder bequamen tyt, desselve te seynden in den Hage ofte elders daer Syne hooch^t sulcx sal goetvinden te ordonneren sonder yetwes daer van te mogen vercoopen.

De twee kleyne Thuynen tusschen de groote ende twee voorsz. Thuynen gelegen, sal hy gehouden syn mede wel te suyveren van alle oncruyt, en alles in teelen tot dienste van S. hooch^ts keucken.

Gelyck mede sal mogen geschieden met den geheelen grooten Thuyn, voorts de terrassen ofte dycken rontom desen Thuyn leggende schoon te houden van alle oncruyt, ende alle de heggens, prieelen off kabinetten te scheeren, ende te binden soo als behoort.

Sal oock alle de parterres als blomstucken, loffwercken off gras stucken, schoonhouden ende suyveren van alle oncruyt, mede de gras stucken dickwils mayen ende de kanten affsteken ende inde behoorlycke tyt eens sjaers de palm te scheeren.

Aengaende het snoeyen ende binden vande boomen wert alhier gehouden voor geprepareert Artlo 2.

Sal gehouden syn de vier vyvers inden grooten thuyn schoon te houden van alle gras en slym dat daer in soude mogen aenwassen off aengroeyen.

Alle de missie, sant ende aerde mitsgaders de noodige gereetschappen van broeybacken, Glasen, Rietmatten en wat verders mochte werden gerequereert, als Syne hooch[t] versorgen, mits op behoorlycken tyt waerschouwende, gelyck Syne hooch[t] mede een wyester, item en kar met een paert off een schuytje sal doen besorgen, om de provisie aende keucken dagelycks te transporteren, ende dat op soodaningen uyre als de dispenciers sullen ordonneren sonder eenig manquement.

Sal (als Casteleyn) den geheelen hoff moeten onderhouden, ende voorts bewaren ende schoonhouden dat hem ter handt gestelt sal werden. Ende sal hebben vrye woonplaetse ende genieten soodaningen vrydom van impost als voorgaende Casteleyns op het voornoemde Syn hocch[ts] huys altyt genoten hebben.

Sal naerstelyck van alles hebben te teelen ende sorge dragen datter in Syne hooch[ts] keucken werde gefurneert alderhande soorte van groente ende wortelen vroegh ende laet, het geheele jaar door van vierendeel jaars tot vierendeel jaars, in voegen als breeder wert gespecificeert in het register hiernaer volgende.

January February Maert
Suyringh, peterseli, kervel, Cleyne Latouw, sterck kers, pimpernel, dragon, minte ende ander toekruyt die tot sala behoort. Asperges, Endivye, Sellery, Suyckerpeen met alle andere wortelen, koolen ende alle soorten van Groen, om de Schotelen te versieren, gelyck maegde- ende andere palm Laurierblaen van alderhande slagh, etc.

April May Juny
Kropsala, porceleyn, fijn sala, groensala met alderhande toekruyt, gelyck pimpernel, trip madam, raquette spruyten van roosen ende van alles. Venckel, Annys, jonge peen, peulen, roomse boomen soo vroegh en soo laet alst mogelyck, artisiock, met alle bloemen met groene bladen om de Schotelen te versieren, en ander gemeyn groen.

July Augustus September
Endivie kropsala porceleyn kleyn en groot voor pottagie en sala, groen sala voor het gemeyn, met alle toekruyt het geheele jaar door. Artisiocken, bloemkolen ende alle andere koolen, Turcksche boomen seer vroeg ende laet scharsouaria, salsifie, suycker peen, meloenen, Comcommers, Champignons (soot mogelyck is) het geheele jaar door, met veel sult Comcommertjes en blom en alderhande groene blaen om de schotelen mede te versieren.

October November December
Endivie, seleri, Kropsala, Artisiock vet sala, alderhande koolen en alle soorten van wortelen, Ajuijn, Chalottes, peperwortel, Lepelbladen, het geheele jaar door te besorgen met alderhande fyn kruydt groen en gedrooght gelyck, Thym, Rosmarijn, sala, Marioleyn, ysop, vergulde saly, fyne saly, betony met al het dagelycx kruyt als suyring, peterselie, kervel, biet prey, biesloock, suyckerey wortelen met alle de andere wortelen en toekruyt ende alle soorten van groen off bloemen tot het versieren van schotelen t'geheele jaar door.

Alle het bovengenoemde werck in alle de voornoemde Thuynen nevens het geene (hier niet uytgedruckt) verder noodich is tot haer vereyschte onderhout, sal hy gehouden syn te doen, met de hulpe van twee knechts soo lange Syne hooch[t] niet ander sal comen te ordonneren, hier voor gemetende jaerlycx voor syn personeel Tractement eene somme van 900 Car. gulden, voor de twee kechts die het geheele jaar sullen dienen voor haeren kost drye gulden ter weeck eene somme van 312 gulden ende voorjaer Tractement 60 gulden yder eene somme van 120 gulden, makende te samen de somme van 832 gulden. Dit alles sal den voornoemde Willem Brederoo betaelt werden by den Tresorier Generael van S. Hooch[t] Dirck Verhagen ende dat van vierendeel jaaers tot vierendeel jaers het gereckte vierde part van dien, sullende dit voorsz. Reglement syn aenvang nemen met den 1 November 1685.

Syne Hoocheyt approbeert de bovenstaande Conditien ende ordonneert dienvolgende synen Tresorier ende Rentmeester Generael Dirck Verhagen de betalinge volgens de voorsz. conditien te voldoen, de welcke hem in uytgave syner reckeninge sullen valideren. Mits overbrengende voor de eerste Reyse dese ofte Copye Authentycq van dien met quitantie ende daer naer alleen quitantie.

Actum in 's Gravenhage desen 4 Febr. 1686.

Acte tot een derde knecht inde Thuyn tot Ryswyck.

Syne Hoocheyt ordonneert hier mede synen Tresorier ende Rentmeester Generael Dirck Verhagen te betalen aen Syne hooch[ts] Thuynman op Ryswyck Willem Brederoo, de somme van twee hondert sesthien gulden jaerlicx ingegaen met den 1 November 1685 als namentlyck hondert ses en vyftich gulden over Costgelt van een derde knecht int jaer ende de verdere sestich gulden wegens het Tractement, gelyck Syne hooch[t] hem, Brederoo nopende de twee andere knechts by het Reglement ende Acte vanden 4 deser maent toegelegt heeft. Ende desen off wel Copye Authentycq van dien voor de eerste mael met quitantie overbrengende ende naderhandt alleen quitantie sal de voorsz. F 216.0 Syne hooch[ts] Tresorier voornoemt in uytgeeff syner Rekeninge geleden worden.

Actum in 's Gravenhage desen 22 Febr. 1686.

DOCUMENT V

TER NIEUBURCH, 15 November 1671, decree of lease and instruction of care.
ARA, NDR, inv. no. 4697 [NDR FOLIO, 1417]

DECREE FOR THE UTILIZATION OF TER NIEUBURCH BY WILLEM VAN ODIJK, DURING HER HIGHNESS' LIFE [AMALIA VAN SOLMS OF ORANGE]

Acte waarbij haere hooght. voor haer leven lang het Huys ende Landerijen van Ter Nieuburg om te gebruijcken vergunt aen den Heere van Odijck [Willem van Nassau, heere van Odijck]:

Amalie Princesse Douariere van Orange ... Doen te weeten dat wy omme redenen Ons daer toe moverende vergunt ende geaccordeert hebben als wy gunnen en accorderen midts desen aen Heer Willem van Nassau, Heere van Odyck ...

... Dat hy geduyrende Ons leven sal hebben de directie ende Opsicht van't Huys Ter Nieuburgh, met de Thuynen, Boomgaerden, Plantagien, ende alle de appendentien ende dependentien van dien, de selve te bepooten, beplanten, besaeyen, de vruchten daervan provenierende te genieten ende trecken, het onnoodich Hout op sijn tydt te laten kappen, de Boerewooninge met de Landeryen daertoe specterende met uytgesondert tot synen proffijte te verpachten, de Pacht penningen te ontfangen en te genieten, Ende voorts alles ter gebruycken met soodanigen Recht, als wy daertoe syn hebbende, Met dien verstande nochtans, dat Hy, Heere van Odyck, niets en sal vermogen te maken ofte te breecken aen ende in het Groot Huys 't gene eenichsints van consideratie soude mogen wesen, dan met Onse kennisse, Sullende oock gehouden syn het gantsche Huys te laten t'onsen dienste, Behalve het Pavillioen ende Gallerie aende Westzyde, welcke Hy Heere van Odyck voor syn particulier sal mogen gebruycken.

... Ende sullen aen hem Heere van Odyck oock by Inventaris worden ter handen gestelt alle de Meubelen tot het Huys gehoorende, die hy gehouden sal syn wel ter doen bewaeren, onderhouden, schoonmaken ende gouverneren naer behooren. Wyders sal ons vry staen de Beelden, Schelpen, ende andere varieteyten, die in de Grotte staen naer Ons te neemen. Ende dit alles tot wederoepens. Actum in 's Gravenhage desen 15. November 1671. Amelie D'Orange; ondertekent door de griffier L. Buysero.

DOCUMENT VI

NOORDEINDE

1 January 1667 - 31 January 1667 and 1672. Instructions for Cornelis Dijck in the Notes of the Council of the Nassau Domains.
ARA, NDR, inv. no. 26 [26, 603], fols. 20 verso-23 and 24 verso.

THE UPKEEP OF THE GARDENS AT THE NOORDEINDE BY THE GARDENER CORNELIS DIJCK

Notulen van de Raad, 1 January 1667 - 31 January 1667 and 1672.

Onderhout van de Hoven ende Thuynen in 't Noorteynde.

Conditien ende voorwaerden waerop die van de Rade ende Rekeninge van Syne Hooch^t door Expresse Last ende op Approbatie van haere Hooch^t syn veraccordeert, met Mr. Cornelis Dijck, hovenier van Sijne hooch^t wegen het onderhoudt vanden Hoven ende Boomgaerden achter het hoff van Syne Hooch^t int Noordtende, alhier inden Hage.

Den Hovenier sal gehouden wesen te scheren te binden te reynigen te repareren ende te onderhouden de pryeelen, heyningen, parterres, paden ende gangen van den ouden hoff, leggende ten suyden vande Middel vaert, ofte den grooten hoff synde desen ouden hoff gelegen tusschen de genoemde Middelvaert ende Erven vande huysen inde Molenstraet, sonder oock in den ouden hoff iet te mogen sayen off planten dan 'tgeene strecken sal tot chiraet ende plaisier ten waer met kennisse ende ordre van haere Hooch^t.

Maer wat belangt de twee nieuwe hoven ende Boomgaerden leggende ten Noorden vande voorsz. Middenvaert, ende soo ten Noorden als ten suyden van de ronde vijver, daerinne sal hy gehouden syn te sayen ende planten alle soorten van aertvruchten die duurstich sullen wesen tot de taefel ende de keucken van Haere Hooch^t.

Ende besonder het gedeelte benoorden de Ronde vijver, alsoo daer geen heggen meer in syn, ende deselve tot keucken thuyn is geprepareert.

Hy sal oock gehouden wesen t'gewas ende Boomen waermede de voorsz. soo wegen, Alleen, oock alle de prieelen daerby en ontrent gelegen, te snoeyen, te binden, te repareren, ende te onderhouden naer den eysch van het werck.

Noch sal hy gehouden wesen generalyck alle de paden ende gangen van alle de voorsz. hoven ende boomgaerden als oock van alle de voorsz. Alleen, altyt schoon ende net te houden, omme daerinne ende daerdoor altyt te mogen gaen, ende wandelen sonder beletsel van eenich oncruyt, ruychte ofte vuylichheyt.

Noch sal hy gehouden wesen ten minste twee mael des Jaers de Slooten door ende rontomme de voorsz. Boomgaerden als oock de voorsz. Ronde vijver mitsgaeders de middelvaert te reynichen van oncruyt ende andere ruychte.

Indien eenige Fruijtboomen, ofte andere boomen ofte gewasch soude mogen uytgaen ende verdorren, off dat het Haere Hooch^t begeerden daerinne iet verandert te hebben, de voorsz. hovenier sal gehouden wesen 't selve te beteren ende veranderen, mits dat hem gelevert sullen werden de Boomen ende planten daertoe noodich synde.

Indien oock Haere Hooch^t eenige prieelen booven de geene die al eerder gemaeckt syn begeerde gemaeckt te hebben, sal den voorsz. hovenier gehouden wesen deselve te maecken, mits dat hem gelevert sullen worden t'gewas, hout, rysen, theenen ende materialen die daertoe noodich sullen wesen.

APPENDIX DOCUMENTS

Gelyck hem gelevert sullen werden alle ryssen ende theenen sparre latten ende andere materialen die noodich sullen wesen tot reparatie ende onderhoudt van de Gallerijen, heyningen, columnen, prieelen, piramiden, pallisaden ende andere wercken hiervoren verhaelt.

Indien den voorsz. hovenier volgens den voor verhaelde Conditien den hoff niet wel onderhoudt ende een ofte twee mael vermaent synde, onachtsaem blijft omme te doen of te maecken t'geene men hem belast, soo sal men volgh in mogen setten ende 'tselve t'sijnen coste laeten doen, ende hetgeene men daervan sal betaelen sal hem sonder tegen wercken aen syne bedongen penningen worden gecort.

Sal oock sorge dragen dat de quartieren die men hem inden voorsz hoff sal aenwijsen, met allerley groente ende Aertvruchten worden besayt ende beplant, omme naert sayson ende gelegentheyt van den tyt de keucken dagelijcks daermede te voorsien.

Jegens alle t'gene voorsz. sal den voors. hovenier syn proffyt mogen doen met alle de voorsz. Aertvruchten die in de voorsz. hoven ende Boomgaerden sullen waschen boven de genoemde die noodich sullen wesen tot de tafel ende keucken van haere Hooch.[t]

Maer wat belangt de Artichocken, meloenen, Aertbesien, Asperges, derselven sullen int geheel staen ter dispositie van haere Hooch[t] sonder dat de voorsz. hovenier van iet anders sal profyteren dan t'geene hem bij haere Hooch[t] sal werden vergunt.

Den voorschreven hovenier sal voor alle t'geene voorsz. is, jaerlicx ontfangen ende genieten de somme van vierhondert guldens die hem alle halve jaren betaelt sullen worden met twee hondert Car. guldens, daervan het eerste Jaer, is verschenen den lesten December 1660, te betaelen by de tresorier ende Rentmeester Generael van Syne Hooch[t] Mr. Pieter Ardes.

Bovendien sal hy hebben eene vrye wooninge die hem gelevert ende onderhouden sal werden tot coste van Syne Hooch.[t]

Sonder dat de voorsz. Hovenier spijse, drancke, bier off licht sal mogen crychen oft genieten uyt de keucken ofte kelder van haere Hooch[t] directelyck off indirectelyck, niet tegenstaende voor desen uyt seeckere consideratien anders gebruyckt is geweest.

Ende is het tegenwoordich contract inne gegaen metten eersten January 1660 ende sal het selve uytgaen metten lesten December 1672.

Dan indien haere Hooch[t] haer met den voorsz. hovenier niet wel ende tot contentement gedient mochte vinden, sal haere Hooch[t] denselve hovenier 'tsy met 't eerste jaer off daernaer altoos mogen afdancken.

Alhier gedaen ende veraccordeert, ter Camere van die vande voorsz. Rade ende Reckeninge van Syne Hooch[t] in 's Gravenhage desen 17 February sestien hondert seven ende sestich.

DOCUMENT VII

BREDA, VALKENBERG GARDENS
16 APRIL 1621, instructions for Andries Hoorendonck.
ARA, NDR, inv. no. 7951 [1023], fols. 296-297.

LETTER OF INSTRUCTION FOR THE GARDENER ANDRIES HOORENDONCK AT BREDA

Sijne Vorst. Gen. den Prince van Orangien heeft Andries Hoorendonck aengenomen als hij hem aenneempt bij dese tot zijnen ordinaris Hovenier van zijne thuynen tot Breda. Ende dat op de conditien ende voorwaerden hier nae volgende.

Eerstelyck dat hij alle arbeyt ende vlijt sal aenwenden tot het volmaecken der sieragien, plantagien ende culturen van Sijne Vorstel. Gen. hoven, so wel inde hoff van Valckenburch als inden potagerije off keuckenhoff off buyten inde parcke gelegen als op de bouwerije ende dat op sulcke forme ende maniere, als hem bij Balthasar Baldi van wegen Syne V. Gen. sal aengewesen ende geordonneert worden. Ende voor soo veele het noodich is ende het werck vereyscht sal daer toe met voorweten ende consent vanden voors. Baldi ende Contrerolleur Willeboorts, arbeijders op dachuren ten meeste oorbaer ende prouffijt mogen gebruycken, houdende hij ende den voors. Contrerolleur pertinente notitie vande dachuijren ende dagen die zij arbeyders sullen gemployeert worden. Ende verstaet S.V. Genade dat voors. arbeyders bij zijnen Rentmeester der Domeijnen van Breda van maent tot maendt op behoorlycke attestatie vanden gemelden Baldi ende contrerolleur sullen betaelt worden.

Hij hovenier sal geene vruchten vande hoven mogen tot zynen prouffijte vercoopen, dan sal deselve reserveren ten behoeve van Sijne Vorstel. Genade. Doch gedurende de absentie van Sijner Vorstel. Genade hoffhoudinge tot Breda sal den hovenier aen d'Heer Justinus van Nassau, Gouverneur van Breda; Item aende Conchierge laten volgen hare behoefftige cruyden mitsgaders alle de goede fruijten inden somer hier schicken. Ende belangende het surplus, twelck verderven soude cunnen, sal hij ten meesten prouffijte van S.V. Genade mogen vercoopen ende daer aff behoorlijcke notitie houden ende Reeckeninge doen, gelijck voor date deser is geschiet. Voorts sal den hovenier gehouden wesen goede opsicht te nemen op het innegaen ende uijtgaen des volcks inden hoff ende niet toelaten dat daerinne comen soldaten, Jongers ofte kinderen, die de plantagie ende blomme parcken souden mogen verderven. Doch Officiers, vreemde passagiers ende luyden van qualiteit sal hy den hoff met discretie mogen laten besichtigen. Ende dit alles op den eedt van getrouwicheydt, die hij ter camere van onsen Rade sal doen. Voor alle twelcke Syne Vorstel. Genade den voorn. Andries Hoorendoncq voor eene jaerlijcxe gaige heeft toegevoecht als hij toevoecht bij dese de somme van drie hondert car. gulden, innegaende het eerste Jaer den eersten May deses Jaers XVI[C] XXI, ende expirerende den lesten Aprilis XVI[C] XXII. Ordonnerende zijnen Rentmeester vande Domeynen van Breda aen hem Andries dvoors. gaige van halven tot halven Jare op behoorlycke quitantie te betaelen. Ende sal hem Rentmeester de betaelinge uyt crachte deser gedaen, soo dickmaels des noot zij, in Reeckeninge geleden worden. Mits voor deerste reijse overbrengende dese met quitancie, ende daer nae Jaerlijcxe quitantie. Ende dit alles bij provisie ende tot onsen wederroepens. Gedaen in 's Gravenhage den XVIen Aprilis XVI^c een ende twintich.

DOCUMENT VIII

ZUYLESTEYN, 21 October 1640, instructions for the Gardener and Surveyor.
Koninklijk Huisarchief, inv. no. A14-VII-9.

INSTRUCTIONS FOR HENDRICK VAN HATTEM AND JOHAN VAN DIEPENEN AT ZUYLESTEYN

Memorie voor Hendrick van Hattem ende Johan van Diepenen, vant' gene Syne hooch^t heeft geresolveert ende gelast dat gedaen sal worden tot Suylesteyn

Eerstelyck, vindt Syne hooch^t goet dat de Eycken heesters ter plaatse geteeckent opde Caerte mette letter B. sullen geplant werden opde ordre als de Ypen die Suytwaerts op staen, ofte soo als naerder goet gevonden sal worden. Dat oock de Ypen, die voor op de middeldreve ontrent de Cappelle staen sullen werden uijtgenoomen, ende eycke heesters inde plaets geset op de selve ordre als die Suytwaerts op staen.

Tot welcke eynde by den Lantmeter Jan van Diepenen de roynge [rooien] ende afpalinge sal werden gedaen.

Gelyck oock denselven Lantmeter sal afpalen ende royen de wegen ende dreven Zuytwaerts uyt naerde Riviere, ende oock naer Leersum, soo als t' selve by Syne hooch^t hem aengewesen is, ende alle t'selve opde Caerte afteeckenen ende aenwysen. Ende dat soo als doenlyck, omme noch van dit Saysoen de selve te beplanten met Eycken heesters, als het doenlyck ware.

Den voorsz van Hattem sal de wederhelft van het Mastboschken beplanten, mette plantsoenen die inde wederhelft te veel staen ende uytgenoomen moeten worden, ende voorts besayen met het Mastsaet, 't welck hem toegesonden sal werden.

De Fruytboomen die mede inde wech staen, sal hy uytroyen, ende de boomen laten vercopen ter profyte van Syne hooch^t. [Signed:] Jan van Diepenen, L. Buysero. Gedaen in 's Gravenhage desen XXI October 1640.

DOCUMENT IX

ZUYLESTEYN and YSSELSTEYN, 31 August 1635, instructions for Jacob van Alenburch. Koninklijk Huisarchief, inv. no. A14-VII-9.

CONDITIONS AND STIPULATIONS FOR THE GARDENER JACOB ALENBURCH AT ZUYLESTEYN AND YSSELSTEYN

Conditien ende voorwaerden waerop die vande Rade ende Reeckeninge van Si$_j$ne Ex^{tie} mijn heere den Prince van Orange op desselfs welbehagen aengenomen hebben Jacob van Alenburch, Thuijnman, om Sijne Ex^{tie} te dienen als hovenier in Sijne hoven, Boomgaerden ende Plantagien tot Zuylesteyn ende Ysselsteyn.

Den voorsz. hovenier sal gehouden wesen, soo veele Aertvruchten te sayen, telen ende planten in Sijne Ex^{ties} Thuynen tot Zuylesteyn ende, als totte keucken van Sijne ende Haere Ex^{ties} aldaer wesende van noode zal sijn. Doch sal hij hovenier vande resterende aertvruchten tottet gene voorsz. niet noodich weesende, zijn proffijt daermede mogen doen, Midts hij na dispositie accomodere den Concierge Frenijn tgene zijne keucken van groente is vereijschende, vermidts hij geen hoff is hebbende.

Item sal den voorsz. hovenier de voorsz. thuynen moeten laten spitten, graven ende daer in leveren het saet ende 25 of 30 voederen missie met het geende daer toe behoort, midts dat hij attestatie jaarlijcx aen den Drossaert verthoont, sulcke Nombre van missie in de hoff gelevert te hebben.

Doch aengaende de boom vruchten, sullen desselve comen ter proffijte van Sijne Ex^{tie} maer sal den voorsz hovenier moeten onderhouden alle de voorsz boomen desselve rechten ende schoon houden.

Sal den voorsz hovenier mede op zijne coste moeten aenbinden alle Abricois ende persesboomen die geplant staen, ende noch geplant zouden mogen werden aende plancke heijninge, ende aende muijr van de Stallinge, ende daer toe leveren de teenen daertoe noodich. Edoch Sijne Ex^{ties} willigen, staende op de bouwinge niet te sullen tot deselve imploijeren.

Sal hij hovenier gehouden wesen alle de Paden ende Gangen, soo daer als rontomme de thuynen, Boomgaerden ende Plantagie 'tsij met wijen oft anders soo 't best wesen sal, altijdt temogen gaen ende wandelen, sonder belets van eenich oncruijt, ruijchte oft vuijlicheijt.

Noch sal hij hovenier alle de heyjninge ende Pallisaden oock alle prielen ende wercken van plaisantie alreede gemaeckt oft noch tot coste van Sijne Ex^{tie} te maecken, van oncruijt te reijnigen, ende te breijden ende te scheeren, alle de heggen ende palm vande voorsz hoven, naer den eijsch van t geheele werck ende de teenen te leveren.

Indien eenich gewasch vande selve thuijnen oft wercken zoude mogen uijtgaen ende verdorren, oft sal Sijne Ex^{tie} daerinne ijets begeerden verandert te hebben, soo sal den voorsz hovenier gehouden wesen 'tselve te beteren ende te veranderen midts dat hem gelevert zullen werden de planten ende houtwerck daertoe noodich zijnde.

Indien oock eenige Fruytboomen, Ypen, Eijcken oft Linde boomen mochten uijtgaen ende verdorren, oft dat Sijne Ex^{tie} eenige andere boomen begeerden geplant te hebben, sal den voorsz hovenier gehouden wesen 'tselve oock te beteren, ende andere boomen te planten, midts dat hem mede gelevert zullen werden deselve boomen.

Indien Sijne Ex^{tie} eenige Prieelen, die noch niet gemaeckt en zijn, begeerde gemaeckt te hebben, dan voorsz. hovenier sal gehouden wesen deselve te maecken, te binden ende te scheeren, oock met Piramiden, Portalen, ende andere fraijecheden te vercieren, na den eijsch van 't werck, midts dat hem gelevert zullen werden de theenen, Rijsch ende andere Materialen die daertoe noodich zullen wesen, tot opmaecken vande selve, maer het wijder onderhoudt tot laste vanden Aennemer.

Naer wat belangt de Meloenen, Deselve zullen alle staen ter dispositie van Sijne Ex^{tie} ten waere Sijne Ex^{tie} hem eenige der selver wilde toelaten.

Den voorsz. hovenier sal voor altgene voorschreven is ende tot belooninge van de gene die hij tot zijnen hulp zal gebruijcken, ontfangen ende genieten de somme van driehondert guldens jaarlijcx, te betalen door Sijne Ex^{ies} Rentm^r van Ysselsteyn in den tijdt wesende van vierendeel tot vierendeel Jaers, den welcken de voorsz. Jaerlijcxe betalinge zal valideren opt Slot zijnder Rekeninge tegens Sijne Ex^{ties} Tresorier-gnael, die dit Tractement zal hebben te brengen in Uijtgeeff opt Capittel vant onderhoudt vanden Huijse Zuylesteyn. …

Bovendien zal hij hebben eene cleyne vrije wooninge die hem gelevert ende onderhouden zal werden tot cost van Sijne Ex^{tie}.

Ingevalle soo bevonden worde dat den aennemer in eenige deser pointen nalatich werde, soo zal den Substituijt Drossaert van wegen Sijne Ex^{tie} de nalaticheijt doen repareren, en wat 't selve quam te costen, sal die gemelten aennemer aen sijne penningen gecort worden, sonder Contradictie. Ende sullen dese Conditien ingaen metten Jaere 1635, ende soo lange duijren als Sijne Ex^{tie} gelieven sal, ende anders niet. Gedaen in 's Gravenhage, den lesten Augustij XVI^c vijffendertich. G.W. Saige, Jacob van Allenburgh.

Rekeninge met Jacob van Alenburch hovenier van sijne Ex^{ties} thuijnen van Zuijlensteijn ende Ysselteijn. Heeft deselve Conditien ende Voorwaerden naer haere forme ende tendrz. geaggreert ende geapprobeert, gelijck deselve doet bij desen. Actum Arnhem den X November XVI^c XXXV.

Ter Ordonnans van Sijne Ex^{tie}: Jacob van Allenburgh, Jan van Diepenen, G.W. Saige.

BIBLIOGRAPHY

Ackerman, J.S. 'The Belvedere as a Classical Villa', *Journal of the Warburg and Courtauld Institutes*, 14 (1951), pp. 70-91.

— *Distance Points. Essays in Theory and Renaissance Art and Architecture.* Cambridge, Mass.: MIT Press, 1991.

Adam, Ch., and P. Tannery. *Oeuvres de Descartes. Correspondance.* 8 vols. Paris: Leopold Cerf, 1899.

Adam, Ch., and G. Milhaud. *Descartes Correspondance.* 8 vols. Paris: Librairie Félix Alcan and Presses Universitaires de France, 1936-63.

Alberti, L. B. *On the Art of Building in Ten Books.* J. Rykwert, N. Leach and R. Tavernor (transl.). Cambridge, Mass.: MIT Press, 1991.

— *De re aedificatoria. Ten Books on Architecture.* J. Rykwert (ed.). London, 1955.

Alex, E.; R. Engelhardt; D. Hempel; and M. and H. Ross. *Anhaltische Schlösser in Geschichte und Kunst.* Wörlitz: Landeshauptarchiv Sachsen-Anhalt, Staatliche Schlösser und Gärten Wörlitz, Oranienbaum, Luisium, 1991.

Alpers, S. *The Art of Describing. Dutch Art in the Seventeenth Century.* Chicago: University of Chicago Press, 1983.

— 'The Mapping Impulse in Dutch Art', in *Art and Cartography. Six Historical Essays*, by D. Woodward (ed.). Chicago and London: University of Chicago Press, 1987, pp. 51-97.

Apian, Peter. *Cosmographicus liber.* Antwerp: Gemma Frisius, 1533.

Asbeck, J.B. van, and L. Aardoom. 'De aardglobe- en hemelglobefonteinen', *Groen*, 6 (1984), pp. 278-284.

Avery, C. 'François Dieussart in the United Provinces and the Ambassador of Queen Christina', *Bulletin van het Rijksmuseum*, 19 (1971), pp. 143-164.

— 'François Dieussart (c. 1600-1661). Portrait Sculptor to the Courts of Northern Europe', in *Studies in European Sculpture.* London, 1981, pp. 205-235.

Ballon, H. *The Paris of Henri IV: Architecture and Urbanism.* Cambridge, Mass.: MIT Press, 1991.

Balthasars, Floris. *Kaarten van Rijnland, Delfland en Schieland uit 1611.* Facsimile edition, Alphen aan den Rijn: Canaletto, 1972.

Barbaro, D. *I dieci libri dell'architettura.* Venice, 1567.

Beaufort, R.F.P. de, and H.M. van den Berg. *De Nederlandse monumenten van geschiedenis en kunst. De Betuwe.* The Hague, 1968.

Beckmann, J.C. *Historie des Fürstenthums Anhalt.* Zerbst: Zimmermann, 1710-16.

Beer, E.S. de (ed.). *The Diary of John Evelyn.* 6 vols. Oxford: Clarendon Press, 1955.

Bergvelt, E., and R. Kistemaker (eds.). *De wereld binnen handbereik. Nederlandse kunst- en rariteitenverzamelingen, 1585-1735.* Zwolle: Waanders, 1992.

Bers, G., and C. Doose (eds.). *Der italienische Architekt Alessandro Pasqualini (1493-1559) und die Renaissance am Niederrhein.* Pasqualini Symposium. Julich: Fischer, 1994.

Bezemer Sellers, V. *See* Sellers, V. Bezemer.

Bienfait, A.G. *Oude Hollandsche tuinen.* The Hague: M. Nijhoff, 1943.

Bierens de Haan, J.C. *Rosendael, groen hemeltjen op aerd. Kasteel, tuinen en bewoners sedert 1579.* Zutphen: Walburg Pers and Stichting Vrienden der Geldersche Kasteelen, 1994.

Blaeu, J. *Toonneel der Steden van de Vereenighde Nederlanden.* Amsterdam: J. Blaeu, 1649.

Blankert, A. *Kunst als regeringszaak in Amsterdam in de zeventiende eeuw: rondom schilderijen van Ferdinand Bol.* Lochem: De Tijdstroom, 1975.

— Review of *Dawn of the Golden Age. Northern Netherlandish Art, 1580-1620*, by G. Luijten and A. van Suchtelen (eds.). *The Art Bulletin*, LXXVII (March 1995), pp. 145-148.

Blok, G.A.C. *Pieter Post (1608-1669). Der Baumeister der Prinzen von Oranien und des Fürsten Johann Moritz von Nassau-Siegen.* Dissertation. Aachen: Technische Hochschule, 1936. Siegen: Vorländer, 1937.

Blok, P.J. *Frederik Hendrik, Prins van Oranje.* Amsterdam: Meulenhoff, 1924.

Blom, F.R.E.; H.G. Bruin; and K.A. Ottenheym. *Domus. Het huis van Constantijn Huygens in Den Haag.* Zutphen: Walburg Pers, 1999.

Blom, A. van der. *Lieven de Key, Haarlems stadsbouwmeester: een Vlaamse emigrant en zijn rijke nalatenschap.* Haarlem: Schuyt & Co., 1995.

Blunt, A. 'Rubens and Architecture', *The Burlington Magazine*, CXIX (September 1977), pp. 609-621.

Böckler, G.A. *Nova Architectura Curiosa.* Nuremberg: R.J. Helmers, 1664.

Bodar, A. 'Vitruvius in de Nederlanden', *Bouwen in Nederland. Leids Kunsthistorisch Jaarboek*, 3 (1984). Delft: Delftsche Uitgevers Maatschappij, 1985, pp. 55-105.

Boeck, W. 'Die Fürstenbüsten im Gothischen Hause zu Wörlitz', *Zeitschrift des deutschen Vereins für Kunstwissenschaft*, 4 (1937), pp. 39ff.

— *Oranienburg. Geschichte eines preussischen Köningsschlosses.* Berlin: Poeschel & Trepte, 1938.

Boer, P. den. *'Het huijs int noorteynde'. Het Koninklijk Paleis Noordeinde historisch gezien. The Royal Palace Noordeinde in an Historical View.* Zutphen: Walburg Pers, 1986.

Bok, M.J. 'Familie, vrienden en opdrachtgevers', in *Jacob van Campen. Het klassieke ideaal in de Gouden Eeuw*, by J. Huisken et al. (eds.). Amsterdam: Architectura & Natura, 1995, pp. 27-52.

Boogaart, E. van den (ed.). *Johan Maurits van Nassau-Siegen (1604-1679). A Humanist Prince in Europe and Brazil.* The Hague: Johan Maurits van Nassau Stichting, 1979.

Bots, H. 'De kosmopoliet en virtuoos in geleerd Europa', in *Veelzijdigheid als levensvorm. Facetten van Constantijn Huygens' leven en werk*, by A.Th. van Deursen et al. Deventer: Uitgeverij Sub Rosa, 1987, pp. 9-19.

Boyceau de la Barauderie, Jacques. *Traité du jardinage selon les raisons de la Nature et de l'Art*. Paris: M. van Lochom, 1638.

Bracker, J. (ed.). *Bauen nach der Natur, Palladio: die Erben Palladios in Nordeuropa*. Ostfildern-Ruit: Verlag Hatje, 1997.

Brahe, Tycho. *Astronomiae instauratae mechanica*. Wandsbeck, 1598.

Bray, Salomon de. *Architectura moderna; ofte, Bouwinge van onsen tyt*. Amsterdam: C. Danckerts, 1631. Facsimile edition, Soest: Davaco, 1971.

Brekelmans, F.A. 'De stedelijke ontwikkeling van Breda', *KNOB Bulletin*, 68 (1969).

Brenninkmeyer-De Rooij, B. 'Notities betreffende de decoratie van de Oranjezaal in Huis ten Bosch', *Oud Holland*, 96 (1982), pp. 133-185.

— 'Correspondances et interactions entre peintres français et hollandais au XVIIe siècle', in *De Rembrandt à Vermeer. Les peintres hollandais au Mauritshuis de La Haye*. Exhibition catalogue. Paris: Galeries nationales du Grand Palais, 1986, pp. 47-86.

Brereton, William. *Travels in Holland, The United Provinces, England, Scotland and Ireland*, by E. Hawkins (ed.). London: The Chetam Society, 1844.

Bresc, G.; P. Rosenberg; and K. Tahara (photographs). *The Louvre. An Architectural History*. Paris: The Vendome Press, 1995.

Brom, G. 'Een Italiaanse reisbeschrijving der Nederlanden (1677-1679)', *Bijdragen en Mededeelingen van het Historisch Genootschap*, XXXVI (1915).

Brown, C.M. 'The Grotto of Isabella d'Este', *Gazette des Beaux-Arts*, 89 (1977), pp. 155-171.

Buitenhuis, T. (ed.). *Soeticheydt des Buyten-levens. Buitenplaatsen langs de Vliet en omgeving*. Delft: Delftse Universitaire Pers, 1988.

Buvelot, Q. 'Jacob van Campen als schilder en tekenaar' and 'Ontwerpen voor geschilderde decoratieprogramma's', in *Jacob van Campen. Het klassieke ideaal in de Gouden Eeuw*, by J. Huisken et al. (eds.). Amsterdam: Architectura & Natura, 1995, pp. 53-119 and 121-154.

Byvanck, W.G.C. *De Oranje-Nassau Boekerij en de Oranje-penningen in de Koninklijke Bibliotheek en in het Koninklijk Penning-kabinet te 's Gravenhage*. Haarlem: Bohn, 1898.

Carpeggiani, P. 'Labyrinths in the Gardens of the Renaissance', in *The Architecture of Western Gardens*, by M. Mosser and G. Teyssot (eds.). Cambridge, Mass.: MIT Press, 1991, pp. 84-87.

Cats, Jacob. *Ouderdom, buyten-leven en hof-gedachten, op Sorghvliet*. Amsterdam: J.J. Schipper, 1656.

Caus, Salomon de. *Les Raisons des Forces mouvantes*. Paris, 1624 (1st edition, Frankfurt and London: I. Norton, 1615).

— *Institution Harmonique*. Frankfurt: J. Norton, 1615.

— *Hortus Palatinus*. Frankfurt: De Bry, 1620.

— *Le Jardin Palatin*. Facsimile edition, Paris: Éditions du Moniteur, 1981.

— *Hortus Palatinus. Die Entwürfe zum Heidelberger Schlossgarten von Salomon de Caus, 1620*. With commentary by R. Zimmerman. 2 vols. Worms: Wernersche Verlagsgesellschaft, 1986.

— *Horologue Solaire*. Paris, 1624.

Chandali, D.R., and H.H. Huitsing. *Ter Nieuwburg en de Vrede van Rijswijk. Vorstelijk vertoon in een Hollands dorp*. Rijswijk: Gemeente Rijswijk, 1989.

Chastel, A. 'Le "Nu" de Palladio', in *Vierhundert Jahre Palladio*. Heidelberg: Carl Winter Universitätsverlag, 1982.

Chevalier, N. *Histoire de Guillaume III, Roy d'Angleterre, d'Écosse, de France et d'Irlande, Prince d'Orange &c. ... Par médailles, inscriptions, arcs de triomphe et autres monumens publics*. Amsterdam, 1692.

Chroust, A. 'Die Bibliothek des Prinzen Moritz von Oranien', *Oud Holland*, 15 (1897), pp. 11-23.

Clavius, Christopher. *In sphaeram Joannis de Sacro Bosco commentarius*. Rome, 1581.

Clusius, Carolus. *Rariorum plantarum historia*. Antwerp: Joan Moretus, 1601.

Coffin, D.R. *The Villa d'Este at Tivoli*. Princeton: Princeton University Press, 1960.

— *The Villa in the Life of Renaissance Rome*. Princeton: Princeton University Press, 1979.

— *The English Garden. Meditation and Memorial*. Princeton: Princeton University Press, 1994.

Collen, Ludolf van. *Van den Circkel*. Delft: Jan Andriesz., 1596.

Colonna, Francesco. *Hypnerotomachia Poliphili*. Venice, 1499.

Coope, Rosalys. *Salomon de Brosse*. London: A. Zwemmer, 1972.

Cosgrove, D. *The Palladian Landscape*. Philadelphia: Pennsylvania State Press, 1993.

Court van der Voort, Pieter de la. *Byzondere aenmerkingen over het aenleggen van pragtige en gemeene Landhuizen, Lusthoven, Plantagien en aenklevende cieraeden*. Leiden: A. Kallewier and J. Verbeek, 1737.

Cretser, G. de. *Beschrijvinge van 's Gravenhage*. Amsterdam: Jan ten Hoorn, 1711.

Crone, E., and D.J. Struik et al. *The Principal Works of Simon Stevin*. 5 vols. Amsterdam: C.V. Swets & Zeitlinger, 1955-66.

Dahlberg, Erik. *Suecia antiqua et hodierna*. Stockholm, 1661.

Dami, L. *Il Giardino Italiano*. Milan: Bestetti & Tumminelli, 1924.

Darnall, M.J., and M.S. Weil. 'Il Sacro Bosco di Bomarzo', *Journal of Garden History*, 1 (1984), pp. 1-94.

Delannoy, Y. *Le Parc d'Enghien*. 2 vols. Enghien: Delwarde, 1979.

Delorme, Philibert. *Le Premier Tome de l'Architecture*. Paris, 1567.

Dennis, M. *Court and Garden. From the French Hotel to the City of Modern Architecture*. Cambridge, Mass.: MIT Press, 1986.

Der Mensch, die Natur, die Baukunst. Baukunst nach der Natur. Die Erben Palladios in Nordeuropa. Exhibition catalogue. Hamburg: Museum für Hamburgische Geschichte, 1996.

Deursen, A. Th. van. *Resolutiën der Staten Generaal.* Rijks Geschiedkundige Publicatiën, 151. The Hague: M. Nijhoff, 1984.

Deursen, A. Th. van; E.K. Grootes; and P.E.L. Verkuyl (eds.). *Veelzijdigheid als levensvorm. Facetten van Constantijn Huygens' leven en werk.* Deventer: Uitgeverij Sub Rosa, 1987.

Deventer, Jacob van. *Nederlandsche steden in de 16de eeuw. Plattegronden.* Facsimile edition, with introduction by R. Fruin, The Hague: M. Nijhoff, 1916-23.

Dézallier d'Argenville, A.J. *La Théorie et la Practique du Jardinage.* Paris: J. Mariette, 1709. Facsimile edition, Milan: L.J. Toth, 1989. Reprint of the third, augmented edition, The Hague: Jean-Martin Husson, 1739.

Diedenhofen, W. 'Johan Maurits and His Gardens', in *Johan Maurits van Nassau-Siegen (1604-1679). A Humanist Prince in Europe and Brazil,* by E. van den Boogaart (ed.). The Hague: Johan Maurits van Nassau Stichting, 1979.

— 'Die Klever Gärten des Johann Moritz', in *Soweit der Erdkreis reicht. Johann Moritz von Nassau Siegen 1604-1679.* Exhibition catalogue. Cleves: Städtisches Museum Haus Koekkoek, 1979, pp. 165-188.

— ' "Belvedere", or the Principle of Seeing and Looking', in *The Dutch Garden in the Seventeenth Century,* by J.D. Hunt (ed.). Washington, D.C.: Dumbarton Oaks, 1990.

— *Klevische Gartenlust. Gartenkunst und Badebauten in Kleve.* Cleves: Freunde des Städtischen Museums Haus Koekkoek, 1994.

Diedenhofen, W.; E.J. Goossens; E. de Jong; and M.J.H. van Rooijen-Buchwaldt. *De Fonteijn van Pallas. Een geschenk van Amsterdam aan Johan Maurits.* Amsterdam: Stichting Koninklijk Paleis, and Cleves: Städtisches Museum Haus Koekkoek, 1994. Amsterdam: Architectura & Natura Pers, 1994.

Dietzel, Senta. *Furttenbachs Gartenentwürfe.* Nuremberg: Ernst Frommann & Sohn, 1928.

Dijksterhuis, E.J. *Simon Stevin.* The Hague: M. Nijhoff, 1943.

— *Simon Stevin. Science in the Netherlands around 1600.* The Hague: M. Nijhoff, 1970.

Does, Jacob van der. *'s Graven-Hage, met de voornaemste plaetsen en vermaecklijkheden. Op nieuws oversien.* The Hague: Hermannus Gael, 1668.

Dominicus-van Soest, M., and E. de Jong (eds.). *Aardse paradijzen. De tuin in de Nederlandse kunst 15de tot 18de eeuw.* Ghent: Snoeck-Ducaju & Zoon, 1996.

Donkersloot-de Vrij, Y.M. *Topografische kaarten van Nederland vóór 1750. Handgetekende en gedrukte kaarten, aanwezig in de Nederlandse rijksarchieven.* Groningen: Wolters Noordhoff, 1981

Dragt, G. 'Het Valkenberg te Breda: van bos en hoftuin tot stadspark', *Groen,* 1 (1996), pp. 9-12.

Dreyer, J.L.E. *Tycho Brahe. A Picture of Scientific Life and Work in the 16th Century.* New York: Dover Publications, 1936.

Drossaers, S.W.A., and Th. H. Lunsingh Scheurleer. *Inventarissen van de Inboedels in de verblijven van de Oranjes en daarmede gelijk te stellen stukken 1567-1795.* 3 vols. Rijks Geschiedkundige Publicatiën. Grote Serie, I-III, nos. 147-149. The Hague: M. Nijhoff, 1974-76.

Du Cerceau, Jacques Androuet. *Les Trois Livres d'Architecture.* Paris: Benoist Preuost, 1559.

— *Les Plus Excellents Bastiments de France.* Paris, 1576-79. Facsimile edition, with commentary by D. Thomson, Paris: Sand & Conti, 1988.

Dumas, Ch. *Haagse stadsgezichten 1550-1800. Topografische schilderijen van het Haags Historisch Museum.* Zwolle: Waanders, 1992.

Duparc, F.J. *Landscape in Perspective.* Exhibition catalogue. Cambridge, Mass.: Arthur Sackler Museum, Harvard University, and Montreal: Museum of Fine Arts, 1988.

Eck, C. van. *Organicism in Nineteenth-Century Architecture. An Inquiry into Its Theoretical and Philosophical Background.* Amsterdam: Architectura & Natura, 1994.

Elssholtz, Johann Sigismund. *Hortus Berolinensis.* Berlin, c. 1657

Evans, R.J.W. *Rudolf II and His World. A Study in Intellectual History, 1576-1612.* Oxford: Clarendon Press, 1973.

Everdingen-Meyer, L.R.M. van. *Een beschrijving van 's konings paleis en tuinen van Het Loo.* The Hague: Staatsuitgeverij, 1985.

Faugère, A.-P. (pub.). *Journal de voyage de deux jeunes Hollandais à Paris en 1656-1658.* Paris: H. Champion, 1899.

Filipczak, Z.Z. *Picturing Art in Antwerp, 1550-1700.* Princeton: Princeton University Press, 1987.

Finé, Oronce. *Protomathesis.* Paris: Gerardi Morrhij & Ioannis Petri, 1532.

Floris, Cornelis. *Veelderleij niewe inventien van antijksche sepultueren diemen nou zeere ghebruijkende is met noch zeer fraeije grotissen en compartimenten zeer beqwame voer beeltsniders antijcksniders schilders en alle constenaers.* Antwerp: Ieronijmus Cock, 1557.

Fludd, Robert. *Utriusque cosmi historia.* 4 vols. Oppenheim: Th. de Bry, 1617-19.

Fock, C.W. 'The Princes of Orange as Patrons of Art in the Seventeenth Century', *Apollo,* CX, no. 214 (December 1979), pp. 466-475.

Fockema Andreae, S.J., et al. *Kastelen, ridderhofsteden en buitenplaatsen in Rijnland.* Leiden: Gysbers & Van Loon, 1952.

Fransolet, M. *François Du Quesnoy. Sculpteur d'Urbain VIII 1597-1643.* Brussels: Palais des académies, 1942.

Frederiks, J.G., in 'Het Ambacht van Naaldwijk', by R. Fruin, *Bijdragen voor Vaderlandsche Geschiedenis,* series 3, vol. 3, p. 308.

Fremantle, K. *The Baroque Town Hall of Amsterdam.* Utrecht: Haentjes, Dekker & Gumbert, 1959.

— 'Jan Jansz. de Vos, Sculptor of Haarlem, the Author of Some

Notable Lost Works', *Oud Holland*, 80 (1965), pp. 65-111.

— 'A Visit to the United Provinces and Cleves in the Time of William and Mary. Described in Edward Southwell's Journal', *Nederlands Kunsthistorisch Jaarboek*, 21 (1970), pp. 39-69.

Furttenbach, Joseph. *Architectura civilis*. Ulm: Jonam Saurn, 1628.

— *Architectura universalis*. Ulm: Johan Sebastian Medern, 1635.

— *Architectura recreationis*. Augsburg: Johann Schultes, 1640.

— *Architectura privata*. Augsburg: Johann Schultes, 1641

— *Neues Itinerarium Italiae*. Ulm: Jonam Saurn, 1627. Facsimile edition, Hildesheim, 1971.

Galinsky, G.K. *The Herakles Theme. The Adaptions of the Hero in Literature from Homer to the Twentieth Century*. Oxford, 1972.

Geest, W. de. *Het Cabinet der Statuen*. Amsterdam, 1702.

Gelder, A. Enno van, and F. Wittemans et al. (eds.). *Marnix van St. Aldegonde*. Brussels and Amsterdam: Wereldbibliotheek, 1940.

Gelder, J.G. van. *Latin-American Art and the Baroque Period in Europe*. Acts of the 29th International Congress of the History of Art, III. Princeton: Princeton University Press, 1963.

Gelder, J.G. van, and I. Jost. *Jan de Bisschop and his Icones & Paradigmata. Classical Antiquities and Italian Drawings for Artistic Instruction in Seventeenth-Century Holland*. 2 vols. Doornspijk: Davaco, 1985.

Gent, L. (ed.). *Albion's Classicism. The Visual Arts in Britain, 1550-1660*. New Haven and London: Yale University Press, 1995.

Geyl, P. *The Netherlands in the Seventeenth Century, 1609-1648*. London: Cassell Publications, 1961.

Geytenbeek, E. *Oranjerieën in Nederland*. Alphen aan den Rijn: Canaletto, 1991.

Goetghebuer, P.J. *Choix des monumens, édifices et maisons les plus remarquables du Royaume des Pays-Bas*. Ghent: A.B. Stever, 1827.

Gollwitzer, G. *Gartenlust*. Munich: C. Wolf & Sohn, 1956.

Goor, Th. E. van. *Beschryving der Stadt en Lande van Breda*. The Hague: J. van den Kieboom, 1744.

Goossens, E.-J. 'De rol van de beeldhouwkunst', in *Jacob van Campen. Het klassieke ideaal in de Gouden Eeuw*, by J. Huisken et al. (eds.). Amsterdam, 1995, pp. 201-226.

— *Treasure Wrought by Chisel and Brush. The Town Hall of Amsterdam in the Golden Age*. Amsterdam: Royal Palace. Zwolle: Waanders, 1999.

Grisebach, A. *Der Garten. Eine Geschichte seiner künstlerischen Gestaltung*. Leipzig: O. Brandsterrer, 1910.

Groen, Jan van der. *Den Nederlandtsen Hovenier*. Amsterdam: Marcus Doornick, 1669. Facsimile edition, with preface by C.S. Oldenburger-Ebbers and D.O. Wijnands, Utrecht: Matrijs, 1988.

Groot, Hugo de. *Respublica Hollandiae et Urbes*. Leiden: Johannes Maire, 1630.

Gurrieri, F., and J. Chatfield. *Boboli Gardens*. Florence: Edam, 1972.

Haagen, J.K. van der. 'Het Plein, Huygens en Frederik Hendrik', *Jaarboek Die Haghe* (1928-29), pp. 6-39.

Haak, B. *The Golden Age. Dutch Painters of the Seventeenth Century*. New York: Harry N. Abrams, 1984.

Haer, L.J. van der. 'Een aanvulling op de bouwgeschiedenis van het Huis te Rijswijk', *Jaarboek Die Haghe* (1955), pp. 50-53.

Hallema, A. 'Historische gegevens betreffende het Bredase Stadspark. Bijdragen tot de geschiedenis van het Valkenberg inzonderheid in de 17de en 18de eeuw', *Jaarboek van de Geschied- en Oudheidkundige Kring van Stad en Land van Breda 'De Oranjeboom'*, XVIII (1965), pp. 130-154, and XIX (1966), pp. 1-31.

Hamer, D., and W. Meulenkamp. 'Nimmerdor en Doolomberg, twee 17e-eeuwse tuinen van Everhard Meyster', *Bulletin KNOB*, 86 (1987), pp. 3-14.

Hamilton Hazlehurst, F. *Jacques Boyceau and the French Formal Garden*. Athens, Ga.: University of Georgia Press, 1966.

Harris, Walter. *A Description of the King's Royal Palace and Gardens at Loo*. London: R. Roberts, 1699.

Haskell, F., and N. Penny. *Taste and the Antique. The Lure of Classical Sculpture 1500-1900*. New Haven and London: Yale University Press, 1981.

Haslinghuis, E.J., and H. Janse. *Bouwkundige termen. Verklarend woordenboek van de westerse architectuur- en bouwhistorie*. Leiden: Primavera Pers, 1997.

Haverkamp-Begemann, E. *Willem Buytewech*. Amsterdam: Menno Hertzberger, 1958.

Heck, H. *Oranienstein. Geschichte eines Barockschlosses*. Frankfurt: Ariel Verlag, 1967.

Heijbroek, J.F. (ed.). *Met Huygens op reis*. Exhibition catalogue. Amsterdam: Rijksprentenkabinet, and Zutphen: Terra, 1982.

Heijbroek, J.F., and M. Schapelhouman (eds.). *Kunst in Kaart: decoratieve aspecten van de cartografie*. Exhibition catalogue. Amsterdam: Rijksprentenkabinet, and Utrecht: Hes Uitgevers, 1989.

Heldring, H.H. 'De Portrettengalerij op het Huis Ter Nieuburch te Rijswijk', *Jaarboek Die Haghe* (1967), pp. 66-71.

Heninger, S.K. *The Cosmographical Glass. Renaissance Diagrams of the Universe*. San Marino, Calif.: The Huntington Library, 1977.

Henkel, A., and A. Schöne. *Handbuch zur Sinnbildkunst des XVI. und XVII. Jahrhunderts*. Stuttgart: J.B. Metzlersche Verlagsbuchhandlung, 1967.

Hennebo, D., and A. Hoffmann. *Der architektonische Garten: Renaissance und Barock*. Vol. 2 of *Geschichte der deutschen Gartenkunst*. 3 vols. Hamburg: Broschek, 1962-65.

Hennin, Jacob de. *De Zinrijke Gedachten toegepast op de Vijf Zinnen van 's Menschen Verstand*. Amsterdam: Jan Claasen ten Hoorn, 1681.

Heuvel, Ch. van den. Review of *Jacob van Campen. Het klassieke ideaal in de Gouden Eeuw*, by J. Huisken, K.A. Ottenheym and G. Schwartz (eds.). *Bulletin KNOB*, 4 (1996), pp. 138-140.

Hilger, H.P. 'Klevischer Helikon. Zur Interpretation der Statue der Minerva Tritonia im Amphitheater des Neuen Tiergartens zu Kleve', in *Soweit der Erdkreis reicht. Johann Moritz von Nassau Siegen 1604-1679*. Exhibition catalogue. Cleves: Städtisches Museum Haus Koekkoek, 1979, pp. 165-194.

Hirzel, Ludwig. *Albrecht Hallers Tagebücher seiner Reisen nach Deutschland, Holland und England 1723-1727*. Leipzig: Hirzel, 1883.

Hoed, J. den. 'Het Prinsenhuis te Vlissingen', *Bulletin KNOB*, 15 (1962), pp. 337-347.

Hoekstra, H.; H.J. Jansen; and I.W.L. Moerman (eds.). *Liber Castellorum, 40 variaties op het thema kasteel*. Zutphen: Walburg Pers, 1981.

Hondius, Hendrick. *Fortificatie, dat is stercke Bouwing*. Amsterdam: Jan Jansz., 1627

— *Architectuur, dat is Bouwkunde*. Amsterdam: Jan Jansz., 1628.

— *Institutio artis perspectivae*. The Hague, 1622.

Hondius, Petrus. *Dapes inemptae, of de Moufe-schans, dat is, de soeticheydt des buyten-levens vergheselschapt met de boucken*. Leiden: Jons Abrahamsz. van der Marsce, 1621.

Hoof, M.C.J.C. van; E.A.T.M. Schreuder; and B.J. Slot (eds.). *De archieven van de Nassause Domeinraad 1581-1811*. The Hague: Algemeen Rijksarchief, 1997.

Hoogewerff, G.J. (ed.). *De twee reizen van Cosimo de' Medici Prins van Toscane door de Nederlanden (1667-1669)*. Werken uitgegeven door het Historisch Genootschap, derde serie, no. 41. Amsterdam: Johannes Muller, 1919.

Hoogstraten, D. van, and J.-L. Schuer (eds.). *Groot algemeen historisch, geografisch, genealogisch, en oordeelkundig woordenboek*. 10 vols. Amsterdam: Brunel, Wetsteins, Waesberge, de Coup, Humbert, 1725-33.

Hooydonk, J. H. van. *Graaf Hendrik III van Nassau-Breda en zijn stad 1504-1538*. Publications of the Gemeentearchief Breda, Studies no. 10. Breda, 1995.

Hopper, F. 'André Mollet and the Dutch Classical Garden', *Journal of Garden History*, II, 1 (1982), pp. 25-40.

— 'De Nederlandse klassieke tuin en André Mollet', *Bulletin KNOB*, 3-4 (1983), pp. 98-115.

— 'Netherlands', in *The Oxford Companion to Gardens*, by G. and S. Jellicoe, P. Goode and M. Lancaster (eds.). Oxford: Oxford University Press, 1986.

— 'Daniel Marot, a French Garden Designer in Holland', in *The Dutch Garden in the Seventeenth Century*, by J.D. Hunt (ed.). Washington, D.C.: Dumbarton Oaks, 1990, pp. 131-158.

Hudig, F.W. *Frederik Hendrik en de kunst van zijn tijd*. Amsterdam: Menno Hertzberger, 1928.

Huisken, J. *'s Konings Paleis op den Dam. Het Koninklijk Paleis op de Dam historisch gezien. The Royal Palace on the Dam in a Historical View*. Zutphen: Walburg Pers, 1989.

Huisken, J.; K.A. Ottenheym; and G. Schwartz (eds.). *Jacob van Campen. Het klassieke ideaal in de Gouden Eeuw*. Amsterdam: Architectura & Natura, 1995.

Hunt, J.D. 'A Lion in the Garden. The Anglo-Dutch Garden', in *The Age of William III and Mary II. Power, Politics, and Patronage 1688-1702*, by R.P. Maccubbin and M. Hamilton-Phillips (eds.). A reference encyclopedia and exhibition catalogue. Williamsburg, Va., 1989, pp. 234-243.

— *Garden and Grove. The Italian Renaissance Garden in the English Imagination*. Princeton: Princeton University Press, 1986.

— (ed.). *The Dutch Garden in the Seventeenth Century*. Washington, D.C.: Dumbarton Oaks, 1990.

Hunt, J.D., and E. de Jong (eds.). *The Anglo-Dutch Garden in the Age of William and Mary. De Gouden Eeuw van de Hollandse Tuinkunst*. Exhibition catalogue and special double issue of *Journal of Garden History*, 2-3 (1988).

Hunt J.D., and P. Willis (eds.). *The Genius of the Place. The English Landscape Garden 1620-1820*. London: Paul Elek, 1975.

Huygens, Christiaan. *Oeuvres complètes de Christiaan Huygens, publiées par la Société Hollandaise des Sciences*, 22 vols. The Hague: M. Nijhoff, 1885-1950.

Huygens, Constantijn. 'Haga Vocalis', in *Momenta desultoria*. The Hague, 1644.

— *Vitaulium. Hofwijck. Hofstede vanden Heere van Zuylichem onder Voorburgh*. The Hague: A. Vlac, 1653.

— 'Ontwerp by den Heere van Zuylichem aangaande eenen Steenwegh op Schevening', in *De Zee-straet van 's Graven-hage op Schevening*. Reprinted in G. de Cretser, *Beschrijvinge van 's Gravenhage*. Amsterdam: Jan ten Hoorn, 1711, pp. 45-46.

— *Catalogus van de bibliotheek van Constantijn Huygens*. The Hague: W.P. van Stockum, 1903.

Impey, O.R., and A.G. MacGregor (eds.). *The Origins of Museums. The Cabinet of Curiosities in Sixteenth- and Seventeenth-Century Europe*. Oxford: Clarendon Press, 1985.

Israel, J. *The Dutch Republic. Its Rise, Greatness and Fall 1477-1806*. Oxford: Oxford University Press, 1995.

Jacques, D., and A.J. van der Horst. *The Gardens of William and Mary*. London: Christopher Helm, 1988.

Janson, E.M.Ch.M. *Kastelen in en om Den Haag*. The Hague: W. van Hoeve, 1971.

Japikse, N. (ed.). *Correspondentie van Willem III en van Hans Willem Bentinck, eersten Graaf van Portland*. 5 vols. Rijks Geschiedkundige Publicatiën. Kleine serie, nos. 23, 24, 26, 27 and 28. The Hague: M. Nijhoff, 1927-37.

Jehee, J.J. *Resultaten van het bouwkundig historisch onderzoek van het Paleis Noordeinde te Den Haag. Door de Rijksdienst voor de Monumentenzorg te Zeist, 1979-1983*. Zeist, 1985.

Jellicoe, G. and S.; P. Goode; and M. Lancaster (eds.). *The Oxford Companion to Gardens*. Oxford: Oxford University Press, 1986.

Jessen, P. *Das Ornamentwerk des Daniel Marot*. Berlin: Wasmuth, 1892.

Jong, E. de. '"Een Teycken van den soeten Vreed." Zur Interpretation des "Eiseren Mannes" am Springenberg', in *Soweit der Erdkreis reicht. Johann Moritz von Nassau Siegen 1604-1679*. Exhibition catalogue. Cleves: Städtisches Museum Haus Koekkoek, 1979, pp. 195-204.

— 'For Profit and Ornament. The Function and Meaning of Dutch Garden Art in the Period of William and Mary, 1650-1702', in *The Dutch Garden in the Seventeenth Century*, by J.D. Hunt (ed.). Washington, D.C.: Dumbarton Oaks, 1990, pp. 13-48.

— *Natuur en kunst. Nederlandse tuin- en landschapsarchitectuur 1650-1740*. Amsterdam: Thoth, 1993.

— 'Arte et marte. De Pallas Athene op de Kleefse Springenberg', in *De Fonteijn van Pallas. Een geschenk van Amsterdam aan Johan Maurits*, by W. Diedenhofen, E.J. Goossens, E. de Jong and M.J.H. van Rooijen-Buchwaldt. Stichting Koninklijk Paleis, Amsterdam, and Städtisches Museum Haus Koekkoek, Cleves. Amsterdam: Architectura & Natura Pers, 1994.

Jong, E. de, and M. Dominicus-van Soest. *Aardse paradijzen. De tuin in de Nederlandse kunst 15de tot 18de eeuw*. Ghent: Snoeck-Ducaju & Zoon, 1996.

Jong, E. de, and C. Schellekens. *Het beeld buiten. Vier eeuwen tuinsculptuur in Nederland*. Heino: Hannema-de Stuers Fundatie, 1994.

Jongh, E. de. '"'t Gotsche krulligh mall." De houding tegenover de gotiek in het zeventiende-eeuwse Holland', *Nederlands Kunsthistorisch Jaarboek*, 24 (1973), pp. 85-145.

Kalf, J. *Nederlandsche monumenten van geschiedenis en kunst*. Vol. I. *De monumenten in de voormalige Baronie van Breda*. Utrecht: Oosthoek, 1912.

Kamphuis, G. 'Constantijn Huygens, bouwheer of bouwmeester', *Oud Holland*, 77 (1962), pp. 151-180.

Kan, A.H. (ed.). *De jeugd van Constantijn Huygens door hemzelf beschreven*. Rotterdam: Donker, 1971.

Karling, S. *Trädgårdskonsten historia i Sverige*. Stockholm: Albert Bonniers Förlag, 1931.

— 'The Importance of André Mollet and His Family for the Development of the French Formal Garden', in *The French Formal Garden*, by E. MacDougall and F. Hamilton Hazlehurst (eds.). Washington, D.C.: Dumbarton Oaks, 1974, pp. 3-25.

Kaufmann, Th. DaCosta. *Court, Cloister and City. The Art and Culture of Central Europe 1450-1800*. Chicago: University of Chicago Press, 1995.

Keblusek, M., and J. Zijlmans (eds.). *Vorstelijk vertoon. Aan het hof van Frederik Hendrik en Amalia. Princely Display. The Court of Frederik Hendrik of Orange and Amalia van Solms in The Hague*. Exhibition catalogue. The Hague: Haags Historisch Museum, and Zwolle: Waanders, 1997.

Kemp, M. 'Simon Stevin and Pieter Saenredam. A Study of Mathematics and Vision in Dutch Science and Art', *Art Bulletin*, 68, 2 (1986), pp. 237-252.

— *The Science of Art. Optical Themes in Western Art from Brunelleschi to Seurat*. New Haven: Yale University Press, 1990.

Kenseth, J. (ed.). *The Age of the Marvelous*. Hanover, N.H.: Hood Museum of Art, Dartmouth College, 1991.

Kerkhoven, W. 'Het Valkenberg te Breda: vernieuwing van een binnenstadspark', *Groen*, 1 (1996), pp. 13-17.

Kleijn, K.; J. Smit; and C. Thunnissen. *Nederlandse bouwkunst. Een geschiedenis van tien eeuwen architectuur*. Alphen aan den Rijn: Atrium, 1995.

Koenhein, A.J.M., and P. Brederoo et al. (eds.) *Johan Wolfert van Brederode 1599-1655. Een Hollands edelman tussen Nassau en Oranje*. Zutphen: Walburg Pers, 1999.

Kok, M. (ed.) *Kaartboek van het Baljuwschap van Naaldwijk*. Facsimile edition published by the Genootschap Oud-Westland, Alphen aan den Rijn: Canaletto, 1985.

Kreutner, H. 'Der giardino pensile der Loggia dei Lanzi und seine Fontäne', *Kunstgeschichtliche Studien für H. Kauffmann*. Berlin: Wolfgang Braunfels, 1956, pp. 240-251.

Kruft, H.W. *A History of Architectural Theory. From Vitruvius to the Present*. London and New York: Zwemmer, and Princeton: Princeton Architectural Press, 1994.

Kruikius, N. *Kaartboek van het Hoogheemraadschap van Delfland*. Facsimile edition, Alphen aan den Rijn: Canaletto, 1981.

Kuijlen, J.; C.S. Oldenburger-Ebbers; and D.O. Wijnands. *Paradisus Batavus. Bibliografie van plantencatalogi van onderwijstuinen, particuliere tuinen en kwekerscollecties in de Noordelijke en Zuidelijke Nederlanden (1550-1839)*. Wageningen: Pudoc, 1983.

Kuijpers, J., and A.D. Renting. *Boeken van Oranje, De Oranje-Nassau Bibliotheek ten tijde van William III*. Exhibition catalogue. The Hague: Koninklijke Bibliotheek, 1988.

Kuyper, W. *Dutch Classicist Architecture*. Delft: Delft University Press, 1980.

— *The Triumphant Entry of Renaissance Architecture into the Netherlands. The Joyeuse Entrée of Philip of Spain into Antwerp in 1549. Renaissance and Mannerist Architecture in the Low Countries from 1530-1630*. 2 vols. Alphen aan den Rijn: Canaletto, 1995.

Lairesse, G. de. *Groot Schilderboek, waar in de schilderkonst in al haar deelen grondig werd onderweezen*. 1st edition, Amsterdam: Erfgenamen van W. de Coup, 1707. 2nd edition, Haarlem: Johannes Manhoorn, 1740.

Lakerveld, C. van (ed.). *Opkomst en bloei van het Noord Nederlandse stadsgezicht in de 17de eeuw. The Dutch Cityscape in the 17th Century and Its Sources*. Exhibition catalogue. Amsterdam:

Amsterdams Historisch Museum, and Toronto: Art Gallery of Ontario, 1977.

Lauremberg, P. *Horticultura Libris II*. Frankfurt am Main: Matth. Merian, 1632.

Lawrence, Cynthia. '"Worthy of Milord's House?" Rembrandt, Huygens and Dutch Classicism', *Kunsthistorisk Tidskrift*, LIV (1985), pp. 16-26.

Lazzaro, C. *The Italian Renaissance Garden*. New Haven and London: Yale University Press, 1990.

Lecoq, A.-M., 'The Garden of Wisdom and Bernard Palissy', in *The Architecture of Western Gardens*, by M. Mosser and G. Teyssot (eds.). Cambridge, Mass: MIT Press, 1991, pp. 69-80.

Lekkerkerk, P. *Paleis Noordeinde*. Zutphen: Walburg Pers, 1991.

Lentz, C., and M. Nath-Esser. 'Der Schlossgarten zu Idstein', *Die Gartenkunst*, II, 2 (1990), pp. 165-216.

Leschevin, Isaac. [Untitled, listed by the Metropolitan Museum, New York, as:] *Portals and Palisades*. Utrecht: Salomon de Roy, 1635.

Lessing, J.H. *Woordenboek der Nederlandse taal*. The Hague: M. Nijhoff, and Leiden: A.W. Sijthoff, 1949.

Lit, R. van, and M.C. van der Sman (eds.). *Buitenplaatsen in en om Den Haag*. Zwolle: Waanders, 1992.

Lithgow, William. *A true and experimentall discourse upon the beginning, proceeding and victorious event of this last siege of Breda*. London: printed by I. Okes for I. Rothwel, 1627. Published in *Taxandria*, XXIII (1916), pp. 225-229.

Logan, A.M.S. 'The "Cabinet" of the Brothers Gerard and Jan van Reynst', *Verhandelingen van de Koninklijke Nederlandse Akademie van Wetenschappen*, 99. Amsterdam, Oxford and New York: North Holland Publishing Company, 1979, pp. 11-59.

Loonstra, M. *'Het Huijs int Bosch'. Het Koninklijk Paleis Huis ten Bosch historisch gezien. The Royal Palace Huis ten Bosch in a Historical View*. Zutphen: Walburg Pers, 1985.

Loris, D. *Le Thrésor des Parterres de l'Univers*. Geneva, 1579.

Luijten, G.; A. van Suchtelen; R. Baarsen et al. (eds.). *Dawn of the Golden Age. Northern Netherlandish Art 1580-1620*. Exhibition catalogue. Amsterdam: Rijksmuseum, and Zwolle: Waanders, 1993.

Lunsingh Scheurleer, Th.H. 'Beeldhouwwerk in Huygens' Haagse huis', *Oud Holland*, 77 (1962), pp. 181-205.

— 'De woonvertrekken in Amalia's Huis in het Bosch', *Oud Holland*, 84 (1969), pp. 29-66.

— 'The Mauritshuis as "Domus Cosmographica"', in *Johan Maurits van Nassau-Siegen (1604-1679). A Humanist Prince in Europe and Brazil*, by E. van den Boogaart (ed.). The Hague: Johan Maurits van Nassau Stichting, 1979, pp. 142-190.

— 'Drie brieven van Pieter Post over zijn werk voor Constantijn Huygens en stadhouder Frederik Hendrik in de Fondation Custodia te Parijs', in *Veelzijdigheid als levensvorm. Facetten van Constantijn Huygens' leven en werk*, by A.Th. van Deursen, E.K. Grootes and P.E.L. Verkuyl (eds.). Deventer: Uitgeverij Sub Rosa, 1987, pp. 39-51.

Lunsingh Scheurleer, Th. H., and S.W.A. Drossaers. *Inventarissen van de Inboedels in de verblijven van de Oranjes en daarmede gelijk te stellen stukken 1567-1795*. 3 vols. Rijks Geschiedkundige Publicatiën. Grote Serie, I-III, nos. 147-149. The Hague: M. Nijhoff, 1974-76.

MacDougall, E. 'The Sleeping Nymph. Origins of a Humanist Fountain Type', *Art Bulletin*, 57 (1975), pp. 357-365.

Mander, Carel van. *Het Schilder-Boeck*. Haarlem: Paschier van Wesbusch, 1604. Facsimile edition, Utrecht, 1969.

Marchegay, P. *Correspondance de Louise de Coligny, Princesse d'Orange (1555-1620)*. Paris: A. Picard, 1887.

Marolois, Samuel. *Opera Mathematica ou Oeuvres Mathématiques, traictans de Géometrie, Perspective, Architecture et Fortification*. Amsterdam: Jan Jansz., 1617.

Mehrtens, U. 'Johan Vredeman de Vries and the Hortorum Formae', in *The Architecture of Western Gardens*, by M. Mosser and G. Teyssot (eds.). Cambridge, Mass: MIT Press, 1991, pp. 103-105.

Meij, A.W.F.M., and J.A. Poot (eds.). *Jacques de Gheyn als tekenaar 1565-1629* or: *Jacques de Gheyn II, Drawings*. Exhibition catalogue. Rotterdam: Museum Boymans-van Beuningen, and Washington, D.C.: National Gallery of Art, 1985-86.

Meischke, R. 'De grote trap van het huis Honselaarsdijk, 1633-1638', *Nederlands Kunsthistorisch Jaarboek*, 31 (1980), pp. 86-103.

— 'Het Kasteel Zuilenstein te Leersum', in *Liber Castellorum, 40 variaties op het thema kasteel*, by T.J. Hoekstra, H.J. Jansen and I.W.L. Moerman (eds.). Zutphen: Walburg Pers, 1981, pp. 270-278.

— 'De modernisering van de twee grote zalen van het Huis Honselaarsdijk in 1637 door Jacob van Campen', *Nederlands Kunsthistorisch Jaarboek*, 33 (1982), pp. 191-205.

Meischke, R., and K. Ottenheym. 'Honselaarsdijk. Tuin en park; speelhuis (1636) en Nederhof (1640-1644)', *Jaarboek Monumentenzorg 1992*. Zeist and Zwolle, 1993.

Meischke, R., and J.J. Terwen. *Het Trippenhuis in Amsterdam*. Amsterdam, 1983.

Merian, Matthaeus. *Topographia Electoratus Brandenburgici*. Frankfurt, 1652.

Meurs, P. van. 'De erfenis van de Brederodes', *Oud Holland*, 32 (1914), pp. 105-131, 190-215 and 233-259.

Meyere, J.A.L. de, and J.M.M. Ruijter. *Kasteel Batestein te Vianen. Aspecten uit de historie van het kasteel en zijn bewoners*. Alphen aan den Rijn: Stichting Stedelijk Museum Vianen, Repro Holland, 1981.

Meyster, E. *Des weerelds Dool-om-berg ontdoold op Dool-in-bergh*. Utrecht: Johannes Ribbius, 1669.

Mignani, D. *Le Ville Medicee di Giusto Utens*. Florence: Arnaud, 1980.

Miller, M. *The Garden as an Art*. Albany: State University of New York Press, 1993

Mirande, A.F., and G.S. Overdiep. *Het schilder-boek van Carel van Mander: het leven der doorluchtige nederlandsche en hoogduitsche schilders*. Amsterdam: Wereldbibliotheek, 1936.

Mollet, A. *Le Jardin de plaisir*. Stockholm: H. Kayser, 1651. Facsimile edition, with postface by M. Conan, Paris: Editions du Moniteur, 1981.

Mollet, Claude. *Théâtre des plans et jardinages*. Paris: C. de Sercy, 1652.

Morren, Th. 'Het tegenwoordige paleis in het Noordeinde en zijne eerste bewoners, 1533-1609', *Jaarboek Die Haghe* (1899), pp. 371-377.

— *Het Huis Honselaarsdijk*. Leiden: A.W. Sijthoff, 1908. Augmented facsimile edition, Alphen aan den Rijn: Canaletto, 1990.

Mössel, E. *Von Geheimnis der Urform des Seins*. Stuttgart: Deutsche Verlagsgesellschaft, 1938.

Mosser, M., and G. Teyssot (eds.). *The Architecture of Western Gardens*. Cambridge, Mass.: MIT Press, 1991.

Mountague, W. *The Delights of Holland: or a Three Months' Travel about that and the other Provinces*. London, 1696.

Mout, M.E.H.N. 'The Youth of Johan Maurits', in *Johan Maurits van Nassau-Siegen (1604-1679). A Humanist Prince in Europe and Brazil*, by E. van den Boogaart (ed.). The Hague: Johan Maurits van Nassau Stichting, 1979, pp. 13-38.

Muller, E., and K. Zandvliet (eds.). *Admissies als lantmeter in Nederland voor 1811*. Alphen aan den Rijn: Canaletto, 1987.

Muller, S. 'Het Koningshuis te Rhenen', *Bulletin KNOB*, 2 (1911), pp. 66-73.

Naredi-Rainer, P. von. *Architektur und Harmonie*. Cologne: Dumont, 1982.

Nehring, D. 'The Garden Designs of Joseph Furttenbach the Elder', in *The Architecture of Western Gardens*, by M. Mosser and G. Teyssot (eds.). Cambridge, Mass.: MIT Press, 1991, pp. 160-162.

Neurdenburg, E. *De zeventiende eeuwsche beeldhouwkunst in de Noordelijke Nederlanden*. Amsterdam: Meulenhoff, 1948.

Nieuwenhuis, H. *Stijltuinen: vijf eeuwen Nederlandse tuinkunst*. Zwolle: Waanders, 1981.

Nordberg, Av Tord O:son. *De La Vallée. En arkitektfamilj i Frankrike, Holland och Sverige*. Stockholm: Almqvist & Wiksell, 1970.

Ogier, Karol. In *Dziennik podrózy do Polski, 1635-1636*, by E. Jedrkiewicz (ed.). Vol. II. Gdansk: Biblioteka miejska i Towarzystwo przyjaciol nauki i sztuki, 1953.

Oirschot, A. van. 'Ontwerptekeningen van Pieter Post voor het Kasteel Heeze', *Bulletin KNOB*, 16 (1963), pp. 94-96.

Olde Meierink, B., et al. (eds.). *Kastelen en ridderhofsteden in Utrecht*. Utrecht: Matrijs, 1995.

Oldenburger-Ebbers, C.S. *De tuinengids van Nederland*. Rotterdam: De Hef, 1989.

— 'Garden Design in The Netherlands in the Seventeenth Century', in *The Architecture of Western Gardens*, by M. Mosser and G. Teyssot (eds.). Cambridge, Mass.: MIT Press, 1991, pp. 163-165.

Oldenburger-Ebbers, C.S.; D.O. Wijnands; and J. Kuijlen. *Paradisus Batavus. Bibliografie van plantencatalogi van onderwijstuinen, particuliere tuinen en kwekerscollecties in de Noordelijke en Zuidelijke Nederlanden (1550-1839)*. Wageningen: Pudoc, 1983.

Onians, J. *Bearers of Meaning. The Classical Orders in Antiquity, the Middle Ages, and the Renaissance*. Princeton: Princeton University Press, 1988.

Orum-Larsen, Asger. 'Uraniborg, the Most Extraordinary Castle and Garden Design in Scandinavia', *Journal of Garden History*, 2 (1990), pp. 97-106.

Otten, G. 'De ontmanteling van Breda en het Plan van Uitleg van Van Gendt 1869-1881', *Jaarboek van de Geschied- en Oudheidkundige Kring van Stad en Land van Breda 'De Oranjeboom'*, XXXXIV (1991)

Ottenheym, K.A. *Philips Vingboons (1607-1678) Architect*. Zutphen: Walburg Pers, 1989.

— *Timmermansoog en kennersblik*. Inaugural lecture. Rijksuniversiteit Utrecht. Utrecht: Faculteit der Letteren, 1995.

— 'De correspondentie tussen Rubens en Huygens over architectuur (1635-'40)', *Bulletin KNOB*, 1 (1997), pp. 1-11.

Ottenheym, K.A.; J. Huisken; and G. Schwartz (eds.). *Jacob van Campen. Het klassieke ideaal in de Gouden Eeuw*. Amsterdam: Architectura & Natura, 1995.

Ottenheym, K.A., and R. Meischke. 'Honselaarsdijk. Tuin en park; speelhuis (1636) en Nederhof (1640-1644)', *Jaarboek Monumentenzorg 1992*. Zeist and Zwolle, 1993, pp. 118-119.

Ottenheym, K.A.; W. Terlouw; and R. van Zoest (eds.). *Daniel Marot. Vormgever van een deftig bestaan*. Zutphen: Walburg Pers, 1988.

Ottenheym, K.A., and J.J. Terwen. *Pieter Post (1608-1669)*. Zutphen: Walburg Pers, 1993.

Pacioli, Luca. *Divina Proportione*. C. Winterberg (ed.), in *Quellenschriften*, by Eitelberger-Ilg. Vienna, 1889.

Palladio, Andrea. *I Quattro Libri dell'architettura*. Venice: Domenico de'Franceschi, 1570.

Parival, Jean de. *Les Délices de la Hollande*. Leiden: Pierre Leffen, 1651, and Amsterdam: Jan van Ravestein, 1669.

Park, K., and L.J. Daston. 'Unnatural Conceptions. The Study of Monsters in Sixteenth- and Seventeenth-Century France and England', *Past and Present. A Journal of Historical Studies*, 92 (August 1981), pp. 20-54.

Parkinson, John. *A Garden of Pleasant Flowers. Paradisi in Sole, Paradisus Terrestris*. London: Humphrey Lowes & Robert Young, 1629. Facsimile edition, New York: Dover Publications, 1976.

— *Theatrum Botanicum or An Universall and Complete Herball*. London: Tho. Cotes, 1640.

Patterson, R. 'The Hortus Palatinus at Heidelberg and the Reformation of the World'. Part I, 'The Iconography of the Garden', and Part II, 'Culture as Science', *Journal of Garden History*, 1 and 2 (1981), pp. 67-105 and 179-203.

Pelt, R.J. van. 'The Mauritshuis as Domus Cosmographica II', in *Johan Maurits van Nassau-Siegen (1604-1679). A Humanist Prince in Europe and Brazil*, by E. van den Boogaart (ed.). The Hague: Johan Maurits van Nassau Stichting, 1979, pp. 190-196.

— 'Aspecten van de bouwgeschiedenis van het Oude Hof', *Jaarboek Vereniging Oranje-Nassau Museum* (1979), pp. 11-68.

— 'Man and Cosmos in Huygens' Hofwijck', *Art History*, IV, 2 (1981), pp. 150-174.

— 'De wereld van Huygens' Hofwijck', *Bulletin KNOB*, 3-4 (1983), pp. 116-123.

Pérouse de Montclos, J.-M. *Histoire de l'Architecture française. De la Renaissance à la Révolution*. Paris: Editions Mengès, 1989.

Perrière, Guillaume de la. *Le Théâtre des Bons Engins*. Paris, 1539.

Peter-Raupp, H. *Die Ikonographie des Oranjezaal*. Hildesheim, and New York: Olms, 1980.

Peters, C.H. *De Landsgebouwen te 's-Gravenhage*. The Hague, 1891.

Pevsner, N. (ed.). *The Picturesque Garden and Its Influence outside the British Isles*. Washington, D.C.: Dumbarton Oaks, 1974.

Pfeiff, R. *Minerva in der Sphäre des Herrschersbildes. Von der Antike bis zur Französischen Revolution*. Münster and Hamburg, 1990.

Plantenga, J.H. 'Constantijn Huygens en de bouwkunst', in *Verzamelde opstellen*. Amsterdam: H.J. Paris, 1926.

— *L'Architecture religieuse dans l'ancien Duché de Brabant au XVIIe siècle*. The Hague: M. Nijhoff, 1926.

Pliny the Younger. *Letters*. With an English translation by W. Melmoth. The Loeb Classical Library. London: W. Heinemann, and New York: The Macmillan Co., 1915-24.

Ploeg, P. van der, and C. Vermeeren et al. *Vorstelijk verzameld. De kunstcollectie van Frederik Hendrik en Amalia. Princely Patrons. The Collection of Frederik Hendrik of Orange and Amalia van Solms in The Hague*. Exhibition catalogue. The Hague: Mauritshuis, and Zwolle: Waanders, 1997.

Poelhekke, J. *Frederik Hendrik, Prins van Oranje. Een biografisch drieluik*. Zutphen: Walburg Pers, 1978.

Pope-Hennessy, J. *Italian High Renaissance and Baroque Sculpture*. London: Phaidon Press, 1963.

Porro, G. *L'horto de i semplici di Padova*. Venice, 1591.

Post, Pieter. *Les Ouvrages d'architecture de Pierre Post, Architecte des leurs Altesses les Princes d'Orange*. Leiden, 1715.

— *De Sael van Orange ghebout bij haere Hooch[t] Amalie Princesse Douariere van Orange*. Amsterdam: F. de Witt, 1655.

Prest, J. *The Garden of Eden*. New Haven and London: Yale University Press, 1981.

Prümers, R. 'Tagebuch Adam Samuel Hartmanns über seine Kollektenreise im Jahre 1657-1659', *Zeitschrift der historischen Gesellschaft für die Provinz Posen*, XV (1900).

Raay, S. van, and P. Spies. *In het gevolg van Willem en Mary. Huizen en tuinen uit hun tijd*. Amsterdam: De Bataafse Leeuw, 1988.

Rabel, Daniel. *Livre de différents desseigns de parterres*. Paris, 1630.

Regteren Altena, I.Q. van. 'Grotten in de tuinen der Oranjes', *Oud Holland*, 85 (1970), pp. 33-44.

— *Jacques de Gheyn. Three Generations*. 3 vols. Boston, London and The Hague: M. Nijhoff, 1983.

Reid, J.D. *Classical Mythology in the Arts*. 2 vols. New York and Oxford: Oxford University Press, 1993.

Renaud, J.G.N. 'Kastelen in het riviergebied', *Bulletin KNOB*, 11 (1958).

Renting, A.D., and J.T.C. Renting-Kuijpers (eds.). *The Seventeenth-Century Orange-Nassau Library. The Catalogue Compiled by Anthonie Smets in 1686, the 1749 Auction Catalogue, and Other Contemporary Sources*. With notes by A.S. Korteweg. Utrecht: Hes Uitgevers, 1993.

Roding, J. *Christiaan IV van Denemarken (1588-1648). Architectuur en stedebouw van een Luthers vorst*. Dissertation. Alkmaar: Cantina Architectura, 1991.

Roest van Limburg, Th.M. *Het Kasteel van Breda*. Schiedam: Roelants, 1904.

Römelingh, J.; S. Heiberg; and L. Olof Larsson et al. 'Art in Denmark 1600-1650', *Leids Kunsthistorisch Jaarboek*, 2 (1983). Delft: Delftsche Uitgevers Maatschappij, 1984.

Rosenberg, H.P.R. (ed.). *Een koninklijk paviljoen en een museum aan zee. Het paviljoen 'De Witte' en het museum Beelden aan Zee in Scheveningen*. The Hague: Gemeente 's-Gravenhage, Dienst Ruimtelijke Ordening, 1994.

Rosenberg, J.; S. Slive; and E.H. ter Kuile. *Dutch Art and Architecture: 1600-1800*. Harmondsworth: Penguin Books, 1977.

Rosenfeld, M.N. Reviews of *Renaissance Paris. Architecture and Growth 1475-1600*, by D. Thomson, and *Das französische Schloss der Renaissance*, by W. Prinz and R. Kecks, in *Journal of the Society of Architectural Historians*, L, 3 (1991), pp. 317-321.

Rubens, P.P. *Palazzi Moderni di Genova. Raccolti e designati da P.P. Rubens*. Antwerp, 1622.

Rykwert, J.; N. Leach; and R. Tavernor. *Leon Battista Alberti. On the Art of Building in Ten Books*. Cambridge, Mass.: MIT Press, 1991.

Sadeler, A. *Vestigi delle antichità di Roma, Pozzuolo et altri luoghi*. Prague, 1606.

Sanderius, A. *Flandria illustrata*. Amsterdam: J. Blaeu, 1641.

Sandrart, J. von. *L'Accademia Todesca della Architectura, Scultura e Pittura. Oder Teutsche Academie der Edlen Bau, Bild und Mahlerey Künste*. 2 vols. Nuremberg: J.P. Miltenberger, 1675-79.

Scamozzi, Vincenzo. *L'Idea della architettura universale*. 2 vols. Venice, 1615. Facsimile edition, Ridgewood, N.J.: Gregg Press, 1964.

Schaap, E.B. *Bloemen op tegels in de Gouden Eeuw. Dutch Floral Tiles in the Golden Age*. Haarlem: Becht, 1994.

Schama, S. *The Embarrassment of Riches. An Interpretation of Dutch Culture in the Golden Age.* New York: Alfred A. Knopf, 1987.

Schaper, S.J. 'Het Hof in Bergen', *Tuinkunst*, 1 (1995), pp. 23-45.

Schloss, C. 'The Early Italianate Genre Paintings by Jan Weenix', *Oud Holland*, 97 (1983), pp. 69-97.

Schlosser, J. von. *Die Kunst- und Wunderkammer der Spätrenaissance.* Brunswick: Klinkhardt & Biermann, 1978.

Schmidt, V. 'De tuin van het Prinsenhof te Groningen', in *Werk. Opstellen voor Hans Lochner.* Groningen: Rijksuniversiteit Groningen, 1990, pp. 79-88.

Scholfield, P.H. *The Theory of Proportion in Architecture.* Cambridge: Cambridge University Press, 1958.

Schwartz, G.; J. Huisken; and K.A. Ottenheym (eds.). *Jacob van Campen. Het klassieke ideaal in de Gouden Eeuw.* Amsterdam: Architectura & Natura, 1995.

Scriverius, Petrus. *Beschrijvinghe van out Batavien.* Arnhem: Janszoon, 1612.

— *Beschrijvinge van Holland, Zeeland & Vriesland.* The Hague: Mr. Pieter Brugmans, 1667.

Segal, S., and M. Roding. *De tulp en de kunst*, Zwolle: Waanders, 1994.

Sellers, V. Bezemer. 'Clingendael. An Early Le Nôtre Style Garden in Holland', *Journal of Garden History*, VII, 1 (1987), pp. 1-48.

— 'Honselaarsdijk', in *The Anglo-Dutch Garden in the Age of William and Mary. De Gouden Eeuw van de Hollandse Tuinkunst*, by J.D. Hunt and E. de Jong (eds.). Exhibition catalogue and special double issue of *Journal of Garden History*, 2-3 (1988).

— 'Sources and Ideas for the Seventeenth-Century Dutch Garden', *Rutgers Art Review*, IX-X (1988-89), pp. 135-149.

— 'The Bentinck Garden at Sorgvliet', in *The Dutch Garden in the Seventeenth Century*, by J.D. Hunt (ed.). Washington, D.C.: Dumbarton Oaks, 1990, pp. 99-130.

— 'De tuin van een krijgsman: Batestein onder Johan Wolfert van Brederode en de hovenier Isaac Leschevin', in A.J.M. Koenhein (ed.), *De relaties tussen Brederode en Oranje-Nassau.* Zutphen: Walburg Pers, 1999.

Serlio, Sebastiano. *Regole generali di architettura sopra le cinque maniere degli edifici ... con gli essempi dell'antichità, che, per la magior parte concordano con la dottrina di Vitruvio.* Venice: Francesco Marcolini Da Forli, 1537.

— *Extraordinario Libro di Architettura de Sebastiano Serlio.* Venice: Giovambattista & Marchio Sessa fratelli, 1557.

— *Tutte l'opere d'architettura et prospettiva ... diviso in sette libri.* Venice, 1584 and 1619. Facsimile edition, Ridgewood, N.J.: Gregg Press, 1964.

— *The Five Books of Architecture.* Unabridged reprint of the English edition of 1611. New York: Dover Publications, 1982.

— *Architettura di Sebastiano Serlio, Bolognese, in sei Libri divisa.* Venice: Combi & La Nou, 1663.

Serre, S[r]. de la. *Histoire de l'Entrée de la Reine Mère du Roi Très-Chrétien dans les Villes des Pays-Bas et dans le Grand Bretagne.* Amsterdam: J.M.E. Meyer, 1848.

Serres, Olivier de. *Le Théâtre d'agriculture et mesnage des champs.* Paris: Abr. Savgrain, 1603.

Shearman, J. *Mannerism.* Harmondsworth: Penguin Books, 1984.

Shelby, L.R. (ed.). *Gothic Design Techniques.* Carbondale: Southern Illinois University Press, 1977.

Shumaker, W. *The Occult Sciences in the Renaissance: A Study in Intellectual Patterns.* Berkeley: University of California Press, 1972.

Sieveking, A.F. *Sir William Temple upon the Gardens of Epicurus, with Other XVIIth-Century Garden Essays.* London: Chatto and Windus, 1908.

Sillem, C. 'Beschrijving van het Paviljoen', in *Een koninklijk paviljoen en een museum aan zee. Het paviljoen 'De Witte' en het Museum Beelden aan Zee in Scheveningen*, by H.P.R. Rosenberg (ed.). The Hague: Gemeente 's-Gravenhage, Dienst Ruimtelijke Ordening, 1994, pp. 20-41.

Siren, Osvald. *Nicodemus Tessin D. Y:s Studieresor Danmark, Tyskland, Holland, Frankrike och Italien.* Stockholm: Norstedt, 1914.

Slothouwer, D.F. *De paleizen van Frederik Hendrik.* Leiden: A.W. Sijthoff, 1945.

Smith, C. *Architecture in the Culture of Early Humanism. Ethics, Aesthetics and Eloquence 1400-1470.* New York and Oxford: Oxford University Press, 1992.

Spies, M. 'De "Maetzang" van Van Campen: de stem van de literatuur', in *Jacob van Campen. Het klassieke ideaal in de Gouden Eeuw*, by J. Huisken, K.A. Ottenheym and G. Schwartz (eds.). Amsterdam, 1995, pp. 227-238.

Springer, L.A. *Oude Nederlandsche tuinen.* Haarlem: Joh. Enschedé en Zonen, 1936.

Stample, F. 'A Design for a Grotto by Jacques de Gheyn II', *Master Drawings*, 3 (1965), pp. 381-384.

Stevin, Simon. *Wisconstighe Ghedachtnissen vande Deursichtighe, Inhoudende 't ghene daer hem in ghenoeffent heeft den doorluchtichsten hoochghebooren Vorst ende Heere Maurits Prince van Oraengien.* Leiden: Ian Bouwensz., 1605.

— *Castrametatio, dat is legermeting.* Rotterdam, 1617.

— 'Van de oirdeningh der steden', in *Materiae politicae: burgerlijke stoffen.* Leiden: H. Stevin, 1649.

Stock, J. van der (ed.). *Antwerp. Story of a Metropolis, 16th-17th Century.* Exhibition catalogue. Antwerp: Hessenhuis, and Ghent: Snoeck-Ducaju & Zoon, 1993.

Stokstad, M., and J. Stannard et al. *Gardens of the Middle Ages.* Lawrence: University of Kansas, 1983.

Strengholt, L. *Constanter. Het leven van Constantijn Huygens.* Amsterdam: Querido, 1987.

Strong, R. *The Renaissance Garden in England.* London: Thames and Hudson, 1979.

Swillens, P.T.A. *Jacob van Campen. Schilder en bouwmeester*

(1595-1657). Assen: Van Gorcum, 1961.

Sypestein, C.A. van. *Het Hof van Bohemen in Den Haag in de XVII eeuw.* Amsterdam: J.C. Loman, 1886.

Taigel, A., and T. Williamson. 'Parks in the Seventeenth and Early Eighteenth Centuries', *Journal of Garden History*, 1-2 (1991), pp. 9-11.

Taverne, Ed. *In 't land van belofte: in de nieue stadt. Ideaal en werkelijkheid van de stadsuitleg in de Republiek 1580-1680.* Maarssen: G. Schwartz, 1978.

Terwen, J.J. 'Scamozzi's invloed op de Hollandse architectuur', *Bulletin KNOB*, 65 (1966), pp. 129-130.

— 'De herkomst van de Amsterdamse stadhuis-plattegronden', in *Miscellanea I.Q. van Regteren Altena.* Amsterdam: Scheltema & Holkema, 1969.

— 'Johann Moritz und die Architektur', in *Soweit der Erdkreis reicht. Johann Moritz von Nassau Siegen 1604-1679.* Exhibition catalogue. Cleves: Städtisches Museum Haus Koekkoek, 1979, pp. 127-142.

— 'The Buildings of Johan Maurits', in *Johan Maurits van Nassau-Siegen (1604-1679). A Humanist Prince in Europe and Brazil*, by E. van den Boogaart (ed.). The Hague: Johan Maurits van Nassau Stichting, 1979, pp. 54-141.

— 'De tuinen van het Mauritshuis', *Nederlands Kunsthistorisch Jaarboek*, 31 (1980), pp. 104-121.

— 'Mag de bouwkunst van het Hollands classicisme "Palladiaans" genoemd worden?', *Nederlands Kunsthistorisch Jaarboek*, 33 (1982), pp. 169-189.

— 'De uitbreidingsplannen van Pieter Post voor het Huis Honselaarsdijk', in *De stenen droom. Opstellen over bouwkunst en monumentenzorg*, by H.M. van den Berg et al. (eds.). Liber amicorum for C.L. Temminck Groll. Zutphen: Walburg Pers, 1988, pp. 298-306.

Terwen, J.J., and K.A. Ottenheym. *Pieter Post (1608-1669).* Zutphen: Walburg Pers, 1993.

Terwen-Dionisius, E.M. 'De eerste ontwerpen voor de Leidse Hortus', in *Uit Leidse bron geleverd.* Leiden: Gemeentearchief, 1989, pp. 392-401.

— 'Date and Design of the Botanical Garden in Padua', *Journal of Garden History*, 4 (1990), pp. 213-235.

Thevet, André. *La Cosmographie universelle.* 2 vols. Paris, 1575.

— *Les vrais pourtraits et vies des hommes illustres.* Paris, 1584.

Thibault, Girard. *Académie de l'Espée de Girard Thibault d'Anvers ou se demonstrent par Reigles Mathématiques sur le fondement d'un Cercle Mystérieux la Théorie et Pratique des vrais et iusqu'à présent incognus secrets du maniement des Armes à Pied et à Cheval.* Leiden: Bonaventura & Abraham Elzevier, 1628-30.

Thieme, F., and U. Becker. *Allgemeines Lexicon der bildenden Künstler von der Antike bis zur Gegenwart.* Leipzig: W. Engelmann, 1907-50.

Thomson, D. *Les Plus Excellents Bastiments de France par Jacques Androuet Du Cerceau.* Facsimile edition, Paris: Sand & Conti, 1988.

Thornhill, J. *Sir James Thornhill's Sketchbook Travel Journal of 1711. A Visit through the Low-Countries and East-Anglia*, by K. Fremantle (ed.). 2 vols. Utrecht: Haentjes, Dekker & Gumbert, 1975.

Tongiorgi Tomasi, L. 'Botanical Gardens of the Sixteenth and Seventeenth Centuries', in *The Architecture of Western Gardens*, by M. Mosser and G. Teyssot (eds.). Cambridge, Mass.: MIT Press, 1991, pp. 81-83.

— 'Projects for Botanical and Other Gardens: A 16th-Century Manual', *Journal of Garden History*, 1 (1983), pp. 1-34.

Tromp, H. *'Het Huijs te Soestdijck' Het Koninklijk Paleis Soestdijk historisch gezien. The Royal Palace Soestdijk in a Historical View.* Zutphen: Walburg Pers, 1987.

Tromp H., and T. Henry-Buitenhuis (eds.). *Historische buitenplaatsen in particulier bezit.* Utrecht: Het Spectrum, 1991.

Tulp, Nicolaas. *De drie Boecken der Medicijnsche Aenmerkingen.* 3 vols. Amsterdam, 1650.

Valck, G. *Veues et Perspectives de Honselardyck.* Amsterdam, 1695.

Veen, P.A.F. van. *De soeticheydt des buyten-levens, vergheselschapt met de boucken.* Utrecht: Hes Uitgevers, 1985.

Veenland-Heineman, K.M. (ed.). *Tuin & Park. Historische buitenplaatsen in de provincie Utrecht.* Utrecht: Uitgeverij Matrijs, 1992.

Vennecool, Jacob. *Afbeelding van 't Stadt Huys van Amsterdam.* Amsterdam: Dancker Danckerts, 1661.

Vercelloni, V. *European Gardens. A Historical Atlas.* Milan and New York: Rizzoli, 1990.

Verhoeff, J.M. *De oude Nederlandse maten en gewichten.* Amsterdam: P.J. Meertens Instituut, 1983.

Vermeersch, V. (ed.). *Bruges and Europe.* Antwerp: Fonds Mercator, 1992.

Vermeulen, F.A.J. 'Simon de la Vallée, architect van Frederik Hendrik 1633-1637', *Jaarboek Die Haghe* (1933), pp. 9-33.

— 'Simon Stevin bouwmeester van het Prinsenhuis te Vlissingen', *Oudheidkundig Jaarboek*, 5 (1936), pp. 43-47.

— *Bouwmeesters der klassicistische barok in Nederland.* The Hague: M. Nijhoff, 1938.

— 'Bouwgeschiedenis en beschrijving van het voormalig Huis Ter Nieuburch te Rijswijk', *Nederlandsche Historiebladen*, I (1938), Antwerp, pp. 115-133.

— *Handboek tot de geschiedenis der Nederlandsche bouwkunst.* 3 vols. The Hague: M. Nijhoff, 1923-41.

Vighi, R. *Villa Hadriana.* Rome: Tipografia Artistica, 1959.

Vingboons, Philips. *Afbeelsels der voornaemste Gebouwen uyt alle die Philips Vingboons geordineert heeft.* Amsterdam: Philips and Ioan Vingboons, 1648.

Visentini, M. Azzi. *L'Orto Botanico di Padova e il giardino del*

Rinascimento. Milan: Edizioni il Polifilo, 1984.

— 'Il giardino dei semplici di Padova: un prodotto della cultura del Rinascimento', *Comunità*, 182 (1980), pp. 259-338.

Vitruvius. *The Ten Books on Architecture*. Translated by M.H. Morgan. Cambridge, Mass.: Harvard University Press, 1914, and New York: Dover Publications, n.d.

Vondel, Joost van den. *Inwijdinghe van het Stadthuys t'Amsterdam*. Amsterdam, 1655.

— *De Werken van Vondel in verband gebracht met zijn leven, en voorzien van verklaring en aanteekeningen door Mr. J. van Lennep*. 12 vols. Amsterdam: M.H. Binger & zonen, 1855-69.

Vredeman de Vries, Johan. *Hortorum viridariorumque formae*. Antwerp: Joh. Galle, 1583, and Theodoor de Bray, 1587. Facsimile edition, Amsterdam: Van Hoeve, 1980.

— *Perspective*. New York: Dover Publications, 1968.

Vries, D. de (ed.). *Kaarten met geschiedenis 1550-1800. Een selectie van oude getekende kaarten van Nederland uit de Collectie Bodel Nijenhuis*. Utrecht: Hes Uitgevers, 1989.

Vries, W.B. de. 'The Country Estate Immortalized: Constantijn Huygens' Hofwijck', in *The Dutch Garden in the Seventeenth Century*, by J.D. Hunt (ed.). Washington, D.C.: Dumbarton Oaks, 1990, p. 81 and notes.

Waal, H. van de. *Drie eeuwen vaderlandsche geschied-uitbeelding, 1500-1800: een iconologische studie*. 2 vols. The Hague: M. Nijhoff, 1952.

Wander, P. *Haagse huizen van Oranje: vier eeuwen paleizen en huizen van de Oranjes in en om de residentie*. The Hague: Gemeentearchief 's-Gravenhage, 1982.

Warnke, M. *Political Landscape. The Art History of Nature*. London: Reaktion Books, 1994.

Weinberger, M. *Michelangelo. The Sculptor*. 2 vols. London and New York: Columbia University Press, 1967.

Weissmann, A.W. 'Jacob van Campen', *Oud Holland*, 20 (1902), pp. 165-170.

Wendland, F. *Berlins Gärten und Parke, von der Gründung der Stadt bis zum ausgehenden neunzehnten Jahrhundert*. Frankfurt, Berlin and Vienna: Propyläen Verlag, 1979.

Wiebenson, D. *The Picturesque Garden in France*. Princeton: Princeton University Press, 1978.

Wijck, H.W.M. van der. *De Nederlandse buitenplaats*. Alphen aan den Rijn: Canaletto, 1982.

Wijck, H.W.M. van der, and J. Enklaar-Lagendijk. *Zuylesteyn*. Alphen aan den Rijn: Canaletto, 1982.

Wijnands, D.O.; J. Kuijlen; and C.S. Oldenburger-Ebbers. *Paradisus Batavus. Bibliografie van plantencatalogi van onderwijstuinen, particuliere tuinen en kwekerscollecties in de Noordelijke en Zuidelijke Nederlanden (1550-1839)*. Wageningen: Pudoc, 1983.

Wijnands, D.O.; E.J.A. Zevenhuizen; and J. Heniger. *Een sieraad voor de stad. De Amsterdamse Hortus Botanicus (1638-1993)*. Amsterdam: Amsterdam University Press, 1994.

Willis, P. *Charles Bridgeman and the English Landscape Garden*. London: A. Zwemmer, 1977.

Winter, P.J. van. 'De Hollandse tuin', *Nederlands Kunsthistorisch Jaarboek*, 8 (1957), pp. 29-121.

Wittkower, R. *Architectural Principles in the Age of Humanism*. London and Worcester: Billing & Sons, 1973.

Woodbridge, K. *Princely Gardens. The Origins and Development of the French Formal Style*. London: Thames and Hudson, 1986.

Worp, J.A. 'Constantijn Huygens over de schilders van zijn tijd', *Oud Holland*, 9 (1891), pp. 106-136.

— 'Constantijn Huygens Journaal van zijne Reis naar Venetië in 1620', *Bijdragen en Mededeelingen van het Historisch Genootschap*, XV (1894), pp. 62-152.

Worp, J.A. (ed.). *De gedichten van Constantijn Huygens naar zijn handschrift uitgegeven*. 9 vols. Groningen: J.B. Wolters, 1892-99.

— *De briefwisseling van Constantijn Huygens*. 6 vols. Rijks Geschiedkundige Publicatiën, Grote Serie, I-VI, nos. 15, 19, 21, 24, 28 and 32. The Hague: M. Nijhoff, 1911-17.

Wotton, H. *The Elements of Architecture collected by Henry Wotton, Knight, from the best Authors and Examples*. London: John Brill, 1624.

Wright, D.R. *The Medici Villa at Olmo a Castello. Its History and Iconography*. Dissertation. Princeton: Princeton University Press, 1976.

Yates, F.A. *Theatre of the World*. Chicago: University of Chicago Press, 1969.

Zangheri, L. 'Curiosities and Marvels of the Sixteenth-Century Garden', in *The Architecture of Western Gardens*, by M. Mosser and G. Teyssot (eds.). Cambridge, Mass.: MIT Press, 1991, pp. 59-68.

Zimmerman, R. 'The Hortus Palatinus of Salomon de Caus', in *The Architecture of Western Gardens*, by M. Mosser and G. Teyssot (eds.). Cambridge, Mass.: MIT Press, 1991, pp. 157-159.

Zincgreffius, I.G. *Emblemata ethico politicorum*. Heidelberg, 1666.

Zoet, Jan. *Werken. De Zaale van Oranje, gebouwd by Haare Hoogheid Amelie van Solms*. Amsterdam, 1719.

Zurco, E.R. de. 'Alberti's Theory of Form and Function', *The Art Bulletin*, 39 (1957).

LIST OF ILLUSTRATIONS

1. Title-page of Hugo de Groot's *Respublica Hollandiae et Urbes*, 1630, depicting Holland as an enclosed garden guarded by the rampant Dutch Lion which represents the Stadholder. By permission of the Folger Shakespeare Library, Washington, D.C.
2. Frederik Hendrik portrayed in a garland of orange blossom, with verses glorifying his deeds and with his personal motto 'Patriaeque Patrique'. Scriverius, *Beschrijvinge van Holland, Zeeland en Vriesland*, 1667, p. 585. Courtesy Amsterdam University Library, Rare Books Department.
3. Map of the Westland by Floris Jacobsz or Pieter Florisz van der Sallem, c. 1638, with Honselaarsdijk in the centre, the North Sea on top. Archive Hoogheemraadschap Delfland, Delft, inv. no. OAD 704.
4. Map of the Hoogheemraadschap of Delfland by Nicolaas Cruquius, 1712, showing the situation and extended layout of Honselaarsdijk and its surroundings. GAH, topographical department.
4a. Detail of the map of the Hoogheemraadschap of Delfland by Nicolaas Cruquius, showing the early-eighteenth-century layout of the Honselaarsdijk garden. GAH, topographical department.
5. Map of the Hoogheemraadschap of Delfland, detail made by Cornelis Koster after Nicolaas Cruquius's map of 1712 and published by Isaac Tirion, c. 1750, showing Honselaarsdijk and Ter Nieuburch among rows of country estates in the polderlands surrounding Delft and The Hague. RPK, Atlas Ottens.
6. Earliest map of the Castle, or Slot, at Naaldwijk by Jan Pietersz Dou, 1609. Map book of the St. Catharijne Gasthuis. GAL, inv. no. 460, fol. 97.
7. Map of Delfland by Floris Balthasars, 1611, showing the old situation of Honselaarsdijk as a round 'donjon', with old dike system and avenues. GAH, topographical department.
8. Map from the map book of Naaldwijk, showing Honselaarsdijk c. 1620, with orchards and castle in round pond prior to the large-scale improvements. GAN, *Kaartboek van Naaldwijk*, detail fol. 1.
9. Map from the map book of Naaldwijk, showing Honselaarsdijk in 1620-25 with the first changes made to the garden layout and the approach avenue. GAN, *Kaartboek van Naaldwijk*, detail fol. 34.
10. Map by Floris Jacobsz van der Sallem, c. 1615, showing the situation of the castle on a round island and first indications of a grand avenue. ARA, NDR, inv. no. 6691, fol. 14.
11. Original plan of the new layout of Honselaarsdijk, c. 1633, showing the geometrical garden compartments and circular *berceaux*. ARA, VTH 3344ᶜ.
12. The gardens of Honselaarsdijk in Balthazar Florisz van Berckerode's bird's-eye view, c. 1638, showing the completion of the first geometrical garden layout under Frederik Hendrik. GAH, topographical department, Honselaarsdijk.
13. Map of the front approach avenue of Honselaarsdijk by Floris Jacobsz van der Sallem, signed and dated 1625. ARA, NDR, inv. no. 6691, fol. 22.
14. Unexecuted plan of the rear approach avenue of Honselaarsdijk, creating a monumental system of axes crossing the surrounding landscape. ARA, VTH 2360.
15. Reconstruction drawing of the combined front and rear avenues of Honselaarsdijk extending over several kilometres into the surrounding polder landscape.
16. Map by Floris Jacobsz van der Sallem, 1634, showing the finished building block of the castle and the further extension of the gardens. ARA, NDR, inv. no. 6691, fol. 64.
17. Plan by Pieter Post, 1646, for the connection of the Honselaarsdijk palace and annexes with extensive semicircular gardens. ARA, NADO 4, blad 2.
18. Reconstruction drawing showing the changes and further extension of the Honselaarsdijk garden between c. 1620 and 1638.
19. Reconstruction drawing showing the further extension of the Honselaarsdijk garden to the east and to the west, c. 1638-42.
20. Plan of the Honselaarsdijk garden by Pieter Florisz van der Sallem, 1639, showing the old and the new situation of the west gardens. ARA, VTH 2363-1.
21. Completed extension plans and exact regulation of compartments in straight blocks in a map by Pieter Florisz van der Sallem, 1640-42. ARA, VTH 2363-14 (detail left).
22. The pleasure house, or *speelhuys*, in the east garden of Honselaarsdijk, shown in a print published by J. Covens and C. Mortier, c. 1690. Historisch Museum, Stichting Atlas van Stolk, Rotterdam. Paleizen no. 8.
23. Extension plans of the new east garden and annexe buildings at Honselaarsdijk, replacing existing houses. ARA, VTH 2362.
24. Plan of the kitchen gardens, orchard and fish-pond in the new east garden of Honselaarsdijk, in accordance with strict geometrical arrangement. ARA, VTH 2363-9.
25. Detail of the Van Berckerode print, c. 1639, showing André Mollet's *parterres de broderie* at Honselaarsdijk, including the Rampant Lion made of boxwood, with the classical statue of Hercules and Cacus at the centre. Bienfait, *Oude Hollandsche Tuinen*, plates 45-46.
26. Design for a parterre from André Mollet, *Le Jardin de plaisir*, plate 23, used for the layout of the west parterre at Honselaarsdijk in 1632-33. The Metropolitan Museum of Art, New York, Department of Drawings and Prints.
27. Design for a parterre from André Mollet, *Le Jardin de plaisir*, plate 14, used for the layout of the east parterre at Honselaarsdijk in 1632-33. The Metropolitan Museum of Art, New York, Department of Drawings and Prints.
28. Drawing by Jan de Bisschop, c. 1660, showing the statue of Hercules and Cacus in the west parterre of Honselaarsdijk. RPK. inv. no. A 1587.

29. Exotic plants at Honselaarsdijk, in a water-colour album entitled *Hortus Regius Honselaerdicensis*, attributed to Stephanus Cousyns, c. 1685. Biblioteca Nazionale, Florence, Ms. Pal. 6BB85.
30. Bird's-eye view of Honselaarsdijk by A. Bega and A. Blooteling, c. 1680, showing the garden as originally planned by Frederik Hendrik. KHA, kast XX 156.
31. Bird's-eye view of Honselaarsdijk by Daniel Stoopendael, c. 1685-90, showing the situation of the garden and details of Honselaarsdijk's façade. GAH, topographical department, Honselaarsdijk.
32. Drawing attributed to Cornelis Pronk, c. 1730, of Honselaarsdijk's garden façade, with a view over the fountain with the eight gilded statues. Private collection.
33. Honselaarsdijk's parterre garden with central fountain as originally envisaged by Frederik Hendrik. Print by Petrus Schenck, c. 1690. LUW, Spr. 01104802.
34. Honselaarsdijk's grand parterre garden with mid-seventeenth-century fountain and statues as they were under William III, with Jacob Roman's triumphal arch. GAH, topographical department, Honselaarsdijk.
35. The Orangerie at Honselaarsdijk, built under William III by Johan van Swieten and Jacob Roman in sober brick style. Print by C. Danckerts. LUW, Spr. 01104910.
36. The new Orangerie at Honselaarsdijk as rebuilt under Prussian reign, in an engraving by Pierre Loofs, c. 1715. RPK, inv. no. 1936:434.
37. Plan of Honselaarsdijk by B. de Baes, 1746, showing the larger utilitarian garden sections with orchards, woods and fish-pond. ARA, VTH 2363-18.
38. Large plan of Honselaarsdijk attributed to B. de Baes, showing the new plantations and avenues in the garden during Prussian ownership. CBN, inv. no. P17N59.
39. Map of Honselaarsdijk by Johannes de Puyt, 1762, showing the 'picturesque' layout of the pleasure garden with sculpture in chinoiserie style. ARA, VTH 2363-15.
40. Eastern lower courts or stables at Honselaarsdijk, still known as 'Nederhof', the only remaining structure of the palace complex. Photo courtesy RMZ, 1978.
41. Map of the Honselaarsdijk area as it is today, intersected by a motorway and built over by greenhouses, its original framework of canals still visible. Map 'Voor vakantie en vrije tijd', Zuid-Holland-Noord, Provinciale VVV, 1989.
42. Map of Ter Nieuburch by Floris Jacobsz van der Sallem, c. 1630, with old orchards and farm shortly before the improvements by Frederik Hendrik. ARA, VTH 2399 A.
43. Map of Ter Nieuburch by Floris Jacobsz van der Sallem, c. 1630, showing the first improvement of grounds and newly-acquired parcels of land. ARA, VTH 2399 B.
44. Map of Delfland (detail) by Nicolaas Cruquius, 1712, showing the extension of Ter Nieuburch (left of centre) between Zandvaert and Rijswijkse Vaart. GAH, topographical department.
45. Reconstruction drawing of the extension of Ter Nieuburch by the acquisition of land parcels between Zandvaert and Vliet (orientation reversed).
46. Painting by Anthony Jansz van der Croos based on a sketch of c. 1634, depicting the recently completed Ter Nieuburch palace with still unfinished gardens, in a wooded holm-ground setting. Photo Collection Museum 'Het Tollenshuis', Rijswijk.
47. Bird's-eye view by J. Julius Milheusser, 1644, showing the palace and gardens of Ter Nieuburch as completed under Frederik Hendrik. GAH, topographical department, Rijswijk-Van Vredenburchweg.
48. Ter Nieuburch's *parterres de broderie* and sculpture, the River Gods, Venus-Ceres fountain and Minerva statue. Detail of Milheusser print, 1644. CBN, inv. no. P17N6.
49. Drawing by Jan de Bisschop, overlooking the ponds from the garden southward, to the garden façade of Ter Nieuburch's palace. Private collection.
50. Print by J. Gole showing the symbolic axis running from the garden of Ter Nieuburch to the Grote Kerk at Delft with monument of William I. KHA, kast XX 181.
51. Plan referred to as 'French plan' for the new layout of Ter Nieuburch based on the Palais and Jardin du Luxembourg in Paris. ARA, VTHR 394 A.
52. Copy of the 'French plan' for the layout of Ter Nieuburch, showing in stylized form the adaptation of the Palais and Jardin du Luxembourg in the Dutch polderland. Copy of ARA, VTHR 394 A in GAH, topographical department, Rijswijk-Van Vredenburchweg.
53. Plan of the new layout of Ter Nieuburch's palace. Rudimentary design, showing the concept of a central pavilion connected with side pavilions. ARA, VTHR 394 C.
54. Plan of Ter Nieuburch's palace structure with central loggia, front and lateral courts, and the layout of the orchard in strict compartments. Original missing in ARA, copy GAH, topographical department, Rijswijk-Van Vredenburchweg.
55. Alternative plan of Ter Nieuburch's palace, pavilions and lateral courts, including the stables in front of the courtyard. ARA, VTHR 394 B.
56. Plan or 'great fountain design' of Ter Nieuburch's palace and garden, including lateral courts, stables and two central fountains. ARA, VTHR 394 E.
57. Alternative design for the garden of Ter Nieuburch, showing its geometrical, square compartments, lateral ponds and enclosing canals. ARA, VTHR 394 D.
58. Final plan of the garden of Ter Nieuburch with central parterre area, four ponds, lateral arbours, surrounding terrace and canal system. ARA, VTHR 393.
59. Design for the stables at Ter Nieuburch, the precise location of which on the Ter Nieuburch estate is not clear. ARA, VTHR 392.

60. Plan of the Luxembourg palace and garden complex, shortly before 1627, showing the rudimentary design for gardens with surrounding terraces. Bibliothèque Nationale, Paris, inv. no. C87659.
61. Print of the Palais du Luxembourg, with semicircular enclosed gardens and parterres, used in Ter Nieuburch's original 'French design'. Bibliothèque Nationale, Paris, inv. no. C177.
62. The central parterre of the Jardin du Luxembourg, designed by Jacques Boyceau, as published in his *Traité du jardinage*, 1638. The Metropolitan Museum of Art, New York, Department of Drawings and Prints.
63. Print by I. van Vianen and A. Beek of Ter Nieuburch, showing the entry of the plenipotentiaries negotiating the Peace of Rijswijk in 1697. KHA, kast K, port. XXV.
64. Side view of Ter Nieuburch's rear elevation and garden, as designed under Frederik Hendrik and planted under William III, looking south-westward over the clipped *berceaux* and low shrubbery. KHA, kast XX 182 a.
65. Print by J.A. Rietkessler, 1697, of Ter Nieuburch, showing the plan and elevation of the palace and courtyard with lateral, enclosed gardens. KHA, kast XX 169.
66. Detail of J.A. Rietkessler's print of Ter Nieuburch, showing the grotto wall in the east or Orangerie garden beside the palace. KHA, kast XX 169 (detail).
67. Design by Jacques de Gheyn II for the grotto in the Buitenhof garden, c. 1620, showing a phantasmagoria of sea monsters, shells and organic shapes. The Pierpont Morgan Library, New York, inv. no. 1954.3.
68. Grotto design for one of the Stadholder's gardens. Classic architectural design, with bust of the Stadholder and famous monogram. RPK, inv. no. 1950:82.
69. Grotto design by G.H. van Scheyndel (attributed), with portraits of William I and Prince Maurits and details of coral and pumicestone. RPK, inv. nos. 220:337 and 1956:125.
70. Title-page of Isaac Leschevin, *Portals and Palisades*, 1635, dedicated to Frederik Hendrik, showing structures in the Stadholder's gardens. The Metropolitan Museum of Art, New York, Department of Drawings and Prints. The Harris Brisbane Dick Fund 1942, 42.141.
71. Print from Isaac Leschevin's *Portals and Palisades*, 1635, with models for trellis-work used in the Stadholder's gardens. The Metropolitan Museum of Art, New York, Department of Drawings and Prints. The Harris Brisbane Dick Fund 1942, 42.141.
72. Print from Isaac Leschevin's *Portals and Palisades*, 1635, design for a semicircular palisade with five *berceaux* and central fountain. The Metropolitan Museum of Art, New York, Department of Drawings and Prints. The Harris Brisbane Dick Fund 1942, 42.141.
73. Print from Salomon de Caus's *Hortus Palatinus*, 1620, showing trellis-work in the garden of Heidelberg, copied by Isaac Leschevin. Photo courtesy Kurpfälzisches Museum, Heidelberg.
74. Statue of the River God, once decorating the pond in the garden of Ter Nieuburch, now flanking the Paviljoen von Wied at Scheveningen, looking northward. Photo courtesy RMZ, 1982.
75. Statue of the River God, once decorating the pond in the garden of Ter Nieuburch, now flanking the Paviljoen von Wied at Scheveningen, looking southward. Photo courtesy RMZ, 1982.
76. Detail of the face of one of Ter Nieuburch's River Gods, showing the robust lines of its features, accentuated by the influence of the elements and time. Photo courtesy RMZ, 1982.
77. The River God decorating the Heidelberg garden, published in Salomon de Caus's *Hortus Palatinus* and taken as example for Ter Nieuburch. Photo courtesy Kurpfälzisches Museum, Heidelberg.
78. Detail of Nicolaas Cruquius's map of Delfland, 1712, showing the lime plantation of Ter Nieuburch with its circular ponds and diagonal avenues. CBN.
79. Poster announcing the public auction on 26 July 1786 of the remaining materials of the palace and garden of Ter Nieuburch. ARA, NDR, photo courtesy GAR.
80. The column in the Rijswijk public park, erected in 1793 in memory of Ter Nieuburch's palace and garden, where the Rijswijk Peace Treaty was signed. GAH, topographical department, Rijswijk-Van Vredenburchweg.
81. Plan by Johannes Mutters of 1906 of the extension of Rijswijk, showing the persistent influence of Ter Nieuburch's original layout on the twentieth-century design of street patterns. Photo courtesy GAR.
82. Map of the Rijswijk public park in its present situation (1987), showing how the southern part of the garden has been cut off and built over (centre). Photo courtesy GAR.
83. Plan of The Hague in 1570 by Cornelis Elandts, showing (centre) the elongated area divided by canals of the later Noordeinde gardens. Haags Historisch Museum, The Hague, panel inscribed 'Haga Comitis in Hollandia'.
84. Bird's-eye view of The Hague by Nicolaas de Clerck and Johannes van Londerseel (detail), 1615, showing the rectangular Noordeinde garden with central pond. GAH, topographical department.
85. Map of The Hague (detail) by Cornelis Bos and Jacob van Harn, 1616, with the new Noordeinde gardens to the west and north-west of the palace complex. GAH, topographical department.
86. Reconstruction drawing of the Noordeinde gardens: (A) courtyard garden, (B) Amalia's Flower Garden, (C) *berceaux* garden, (D) Princesse Thuyn.
87. Map of 1649 by Joan Blaeu (detail), The Hague, with the Buitenhof garden in the centre and the Noordeinde gardens at the upper left. CBN, inv. no. P16 N56.
88. Detail of a map by Cornelis Elandts showing the mid-seven-

teenth-century situation of the Noordeinde, with arabesque parterres in the old garden and vegetable beds in the Princesse Thuyn. CBN, inv. no. P16 N62.

89. View of the recently restored Paleis Noordeinde, with white stuccoed, classical façade designed by Jacob van Campen and the Prussian gates. Photo archive of the author.

90. Plan of the Noordeinde gardens, dated 1711, by an unknown artist, possibly Daniel Marot, showing newly-laid-out French parterre designs. CBN, inv. no. IX-10-56.

91. Map by D.I. Langeweg, 1767, showing the situation of the Noordeinde gardens under William V (upper right), consisting primarily of utilitarian areas. GAH, topographical department, The Hague.

92. Unexecuted plan of the Noordeinde gardens by Jan de Greef, 1819, showing undulating forms of the wooded area and pond in landscape style. ARA, WCAP 1515-1517.

93. Plan by Pieter Florisz van der Sallem, 1645, of the Huis ten Bosch palace and garden complex, drawn after designs by Pieter Post. ARA, VTH 3323.

94. Pieter Post's bird's-eye view of the Huis ten Bosch, showing forecourt, lateral houses and main pleasure garden with octagonal pavilions behind the palace. GAH, Huis ten Bosch, *Sael van Orange*, 1655.

95. Ground-plan of the Huis ten Bosch by Pieter Post, showing the division of house and garden in geometrically arranged blocks, held together by a system of axes. KB, Rare Books, 1292 C 33, Pieter Post, *Sael van Orange*, 1655.

96. Garden of the Huis ten Bosch with *parterres de broderie* and classical statues lining the central axis, in a painting by Jan van der Heyden, c. 1668. The Metropolitan Museum of Art, New York (64.65.2). Anonymous gift, 1964.

97. Print by Pieter Post showing the design for the ivy-overgrown, round pavilions in the Huis ten Bosch garden, reflecting the shape of its centralized dome. Photo courtesy Utrecht University.

98. Plan of the gardens of the Huis ten Bosch by Daniel Marot, c. 1734, showing his partly executed design for the gardens in rococo style. GAH, topographical department, Haagse Bos.

99. Plan of the Huis ten Bosch by Huybert van Straalen, 1778 (detail), showing gardens in the late picturesque style combining geometric and undulating landscape features. ARA, VTH 3328 B (detail).

100. Plan of the Haagsche Bosch by Ary van der Spuij, showing the mid-nineteenth-century situation of the gardens of the Huis ten Bosch in landscape style. GAH, topographical department, Haagse Bos.

101. Print by Hendrick Hondius, 1620, with orthographical overview of the Buitenhof garden, begun by Maurits and completed by Frederik Hendrik c. 1625, based on the perfect mathematical figures of circle and square. KB, Rare Books, 1292 C 33 (1376 B 73).

102. Print by Hendrick Hondius, 1620, scenographic overview of the Buitenhof garden, showing the inner layout and decoration with two circular *berceaux* with central fountains and classical urns, designed in part by Jacques de Gheyn. RPK.

103. Plan, attributed to Simon Stevin, of the Prinsenhuis and garden at Flushing, with triangular labyrinth and rectangular section of eight compartments. ARA, VTH 3510: '17 Mei 1623'.

104. Detail of the triangular garden at Flushing, containing a labyrinth and two circular *berceaux* enclosed with crenellated walls. ARA, VTH 3514: 'Caerte vanden triangel achter t palais ... Vlissingen'.

105. Plan of the castle of Buren in the map book of Johan Maurits van Nassau-Siegen, c. 1635, with layout of gardens on and off the island and repeated use of circle motifs.
KHA, *Niederländische Fortificatien*, A 4-1476, fol. 56.

106. Map of the Breda castle and garden complex called the Valkenberg, from Joan Blaeu's *Toonneel der Steden*, 1649. Photo courtesy GAB.

107. Detail of the Valkenberg gardens (right) at Breda, containing (a) the main parterre garden, (b) the courtyard garden, (c) circular wooded area. LUW.

108. Plan of the Valkenberg gardens at Breda by Christoffel Verhoff, 1679, showing parterre garden, fish-pond and wooded 'Bosken' with circular paths. Photo courtesy GAB, inv. no. 1966-36.

109. Fortifications of the city of Breda as drawn in Johan Maurits's map book, c. 1635. Castle and Belcromsche Bosch with pavilion to the north-west. KHA, *Niederländische Fortificatien*, A 4-1476, fol. 59.

110. Plan of the Valkenberg garden by an unknown artist, possibly Daniel Marot or Jacob Roman; layout and decoration from the late seventeenth, early eighteenth centuries.
CBN, inv. no. XI-8-69.

111. Alternative plan from the late seventeenth, early eighteenth centuries of the Valkenberg gardens, showing the grand parterre gardens near the L-shaped fish-pond. CBN, inv. no. XI-8-68.

112. Drawing by Pieter de Swart of the Valkenberg's main parterre garden with statues, including *Hercules* in the first parterre lower left. Breda Museum. Photo courtesy GAB, inv. no. 1989-2258.

113. Plan of the Zuylesteyn castle and garden complex c. 1630, shortly before Frederik Hendrik's improvements to the castle and grounds. ARA, VTH 3039-10.

114. Plan of the first extensions of the gardens and plantations of Zuylesteyn and the changes into regular garden plots and orchard areas. ARA, VTH 3039-5.

115. Plan by Jan van Diepenen, 1640, showing the clear division of the Zuylesteyn gardens on geometric islands and the arrangement of the plantations. ARA, VTH 3039-9.

116. Bird's-eye view of Zuylesteyn in the winter by Jan van Diepenen, 1641, showing the detailed arrangement of trees and garden compartments. ARA, VTH 3039-6.

117. Bird's-eye view of Zuylesteyn by Daniel Stoopendael, c. 1690,

showing the fully-grown gardens and plantations. LUW.

118. Print from Johan Vredeman de Vries's *Hortorum viridariorumque formae*, 1583, showing the geometrical design in classical, so-called Corinthian style. The Metropolitan Museum of Art, New York. Department of Drawings and Prints.

119. Bird's-eye view by Matthaeus Merian of Heidelberg, depicting Salomon de Caus's richly decorated terraced garden layout along the Rhine valley. Photo courtesy Kurpfälzisches Museum, Heidelberg.

120. Mid-seventeenth-century German grotto garden filled with beds of rare flowers and sculptural ornament, from Joseph Furttenbach's *Architectura privata*. The Metropolitan Museum of Art, New York. Department of Drawings and Prints.

121. The Cleves garden by Jan van Call, c. 1680, with Minerva statue and view from the Springenberg terraces and garden islands to the Rhine valley. RPK.

122. Plan for the new layout of the Plein (a) at The Hague's centre, adjoining the Ducal Court (b), Mauritshuis (c) and Huygens's house (d). ARA VTH, 3308 A.

123. Huygens's house on the Plein, designed by Huygens with the cooperation of Van Campen and others and built in classical style on precepts of the ancients. GAH, topographical department, Het Plein.

124. Bird's-eye view of Huygens's country estate Hofwijck at Voorburg, showing an elongated orchard garden in geometrically arranged blocks. GAH, topographical department, Voorburg.

125. Plan of Hofwijck as reconstructed with the ideal Vitruvian figure superimposed on the layout, the house corresponding to the head, etc. Photo after reconstruction drawing by R.J. van Pelt.

126. Vincenzo Scamozzi's diagram of the 'Vitruvian Man' from his *L'Idea della architettura universale*, 1615, which may have inspired garden design at the Dutch Court. The Metropolitan Museum of Art, New York. Department of Drawings and Prints.

127. The strict, mathematically exact arrangement of trees and fruit-trees in the utilitarian and plantation areas of Honselaarsdijk, c. 1640. ARA, VTH 2363-6.

128. Design by Philips Vingboons for an ideal country estate in strict geometrical style, enclosed by canals and with a semicircular-ending avenue. Vingboons, *Afbeelsels*, 1648, pl. 56. Photo courtesy Utrecht University.

129. Print by Romeyn de Hooghe of Huygens's design for the entrance gate shaped like a triumphal arch to the Scheveningsche Weg, connecting The Hague with the North Sea. GAH, topographical department, Scheveningse Weg.

130. Plan by Pieter Post for the castle and garden of Heeze, 1663, of strict geometrical design, with semicircular-shaped avenues and parterre areas. Photo courtesy RMZ.

131. Design by Pieter Post, 1646, for a large semicircular, open gallery at Honselaarsdijk with a wide view over the gardens and connecting side buildings. ARA, VTH 3344 B.

132. André Mollet's ideal plan no. 2 for a palace and garden complex, showing a layout comparable to that of the Honselaarsdijk gardens. The Metropolitan Museum of Art, New York. Department of Drawings and Prints.

133. André Mollet's ideal plan no. 1 for a palace and garden complex, showing a layout comparable to that of the Ter Nieuburch gardens. The Metropolitan Museum of Art, New York. Department of Drawings and Prints.

134. Plan of Charleval by Jacques Androuet Du Cerceau from his *Les Plus Excellents Bastiments de France*, 1576-79, showing geometrical gardens with rectilinear outlines bordered by canals. The Metropolitan Museum of Art, New York. Department of Drawings and Prints.

135. One of André Mollet's parterre or labyrinth designs from his *Le Jardin de plaisir*, comparable to parterres in Ter Nieuburch's preliminary designs. The Metropolitan Museum of Art, New York. Department of Drawings and Prints.

136. One of Jacques Boyceau's parterre designs from his *Traité du Jardinage*, with the motif of the inner circle for decorational monograms, as at Ter Nieuburch. The Metropolitan Museum of Art, New York. Department of Drawings and Prints.

137. Simon Stevin's plan of an ideal city, based on a strict geometrical 'checkerboard pattern', also typical of contemporary garden designs. Stevin, *Oirdeningh der Steden*, c. 1600. Photo courtesy Utrecht University.

138. Simon Stevin's plan of an army camp, corresponding in form and layout to contemporary city planning and related to garden architecture. Stevin, *Castrametatio*, c. 1617. Photo courtesy Utrecht University.

139. Reconstruction drawing of the Honselaarsdijk garden, showing the strict geometrical construction and proportions based on quadrature.

140. Philips Vingboons's ideal plan for a country house and garden, divided into mathematically arranged plots within a larger grid plan of canals. Vingboons, *Afbeelsels*, 1648, pl. 53a. Photo courtesy Utrecht University.

141. Pieter Post's bird's-eye view of the Vredenburg gardens, showing their geometrical division in island blocks, with strict arrangement of trees. KB, Rare Books, 1292 C 33, Post, *Les Ouvrages de Pierre Post*, 1715.

142. Bird's-eye view of Oranienburg by Matthaeus Merian, *Topographia Electoratus Brandenburgici*, showing Dutch-inspired gardens c. 1650, with parterres designed by André Mollet. CBN.

143. Detail of Johann Gregor Memhardt's plan of Berlin in a print by C. Merian, showing the Brandenburg Dutch-style gardens along the river Spree under the Elector Friedrich Wilhelm of Brandenburg and Louise Henriette of Orange. Staatsbibliothek, Berlin, Preussischer Kulturbesitz.

144. Classical Dutch sculptures in the Brandenburg garden, Berlin, under Louise Henriette, showing putti and Roman Emperors drawn by J.S. Elssholtz in *Hortus Berolinensis*, 1657. Staatsbibliothek Berlin, Preussischer Kulturbesitz.

145. Classical Dutch sculptures in the Brandenburg garden, Berlin, showing Flora, Ceres and sundials with putti drawn by J.S. Elssholtz in *Hortus Berolinensis*, 1657. Staatsbibliothek Berlin, Preussischer Kulturbesitz.

146. Neptune Fountain in Louise Henriette of Orange's Brandenburg garden, Berlin, drawn by J.S. Elssholtz in *Hortus Berolinensis*, 1657, and inspired by Ter Nieuburch's *River Gods*. Staatsbibliothek Berlin, Preussischer Kulturbesitz.

147. *Cupid Cutting a Bow* by François Du Quesnoy, originally decorating the Stadholder's Dutch gardens and later the Brandenburg garden in Berlin. Staatliche Museen zu Berlin, Preussischer Kulturbesitz, Sculpture Collection, inv. no. 540.

148. Drawing by Cornelis Pronk, c. 1740, showing a statue of Hercules and Cacus (left borderline) in the Bentinck garden at Sorgvliet, comparable to the one at Honselaarsdijk. GAH, topographical department, Sorgvliet.

149. The statue of Minerva Tritonia by Artus Quellinus for Johan Maurits van Nassau's garden at Cleves, copied after Ter Nieuburch's Minerva statue. Städtisches Museum Haus Koekkoek (photo shown) now in Museum Kurhaus, Kleve.

150. Busts of Frederik Hendrik (left), Anhalt-Dessau and William II, in the Gothic House, Wörlitz, brought from Holland to the Oranienbaum grotto. Staatliche Schlösser und Gärten, Oranienbaum, Wörlitz. Photo H.-D. Kluge.

151. *Sleeping Cupid Resting on a Shield* by François Dieussart, brought over by Henriette Catharina to Oranienbaum from the Noordeinde or Ter Nieuburch. Staatliche Schlösser und Gärten, Oranienbaum, Wörlitz. Photo H.-D. Kluge.

152. Map of Groningen (detail) by Haubois, c. 1660, showing the layout of the Prinsenhof gardens with the twin-circle motif. GAH, topographical department.

153. Print by Hugo Allaerdt, 1632, of the gardens of Vianen, showing the influence of the Stadholder's gardens in their decoration and the twin-circle motif. CBN, inv. no. P21 N59.

154. Drawing by Jacques de Gheyn showing the portrait of Ludolf van Collen, a famous mathematician who wrote an influential work on the Art of the Circle. Fondation Custodia, Institut Néerlandais, Paris, inv. no. 3428.

155. Four pairs of swordsmen round a 'mystical circle' within a square, as depicted in Thibault, *Académie de l'Espée*, 1628, and expressing the relation between martial arts and mathematics, the basis of current garden design and symbolism. Columbia University, Rare Book and Manuscript Library, Butler Library, New York.

155a. A print in Thibault, *Académie de l'Espée*, 1628, dedicated to Prince Maurits, showing swordsmen within the 'mystical circle', set against a palatial background decorated with statues of Hercules. Columbia University, Rare Book and Manuscript Library, Butler Library, New York.

156. Plan of the Botanical Garden of Padua, based on the circle and reflecting cosmological thought and imagery in its form and inner layout. Biblioteca dell'Orto Botanico, Padua.

157. Print of Colonna's imaginary round garden on the island of Cithera, divided into concentric circles and influenced by cosmological imagery. The Metropolitan Museum of Art, New York. Department of Drawings and Prints.

158. Painting by Utens, 1599, of the Villa Petraia, Florence, the only example of the use of the twin-circle motif prior to the Stadholder's gardens. Galleria Palatina, Palazzo Pitti, Florence.

159. Print by Johan Vredeman de Vries, showing the ideal garden design based on the circle and the square, with circular *berceaux*, laid out as a labyrinth. The Metropolitan Museum of Art, New York. Department of Drawings and Prints.

160. Print by Romeyn de Hooghe, depicting Johan Maurits's circular orchard garden at Cleves with eight entrances, influenced by cosmological imagery. LUW.

161. Print by Romeyn de Hooghe, depicting the great circular wood cut through by alleys in the gardens of the Duke of Aremberg at Enghien, near Brussels, c. 1640, published by J. Covens and C. Mortier, c. 1690. LUW.

162. Cosmological diagram showing the pre-Copernican geocentric universe with static earth at the centre, surrounded by the spheres of the planets. Apian, *Cosmographicus Liber*, 1533. The Henry E. Huntington Library, San Marino, California.

163. Theological version of the Pythagorean Tetrad with Christ at the centre, depicting the universe and the relationship between the Four Qualities and the Four Elements. British Library, London. Department of Printed Books.

164. The human microcosm as visualized by Leonardo, Fludd and von Nettesheim, depicting the relationship between man and the universe. Photo courtesy F.A. Yates from *Theatre of the World*, pl. 2.

165. Tycho Brahe's observatory and garden complex Uraniborg on the island of Hveen, Copenhagen, 1591, based on the cosmological diagram of the tetrad. Woodcut from Brahe, *Astronomiae*, 1598. Bodleian Library, University of Oxford, shelfmark Arch. Bc.3, signature H2verso.

166. The Countess of Bedford's garden at Twickenham Park, based on the diagram of the pre-Copernican universe. Drawing by R. Smythson, ca. 1609. The British Architectural Library, RIBA, London.

167. Plan of Salomon de Caus's gardens of Heidelberg reflecting in its inner form and layout several 'microcosmoi', based on cosmological diagrams. Photo courtesy Kurpfälzisches Museum, Heidelberg.

168. View of Doolomberg, Amersfoort, c. 1660, showing the influence of cosmological thought and imagery on the shape of the garden

with central mound. LUW.

169. Late-sixteenth-century emblem with two paired globes symbolizing the earthly and heavenly spheres and expressing man's inner spiritual strife. Photo from A. Henkel and A. Schöne, *Handbuch zur Sinnbildkunst*, p. 42.

170. Print by Romeyn de Hooghe, c. 1690, showing the Earth globe fountain in the gardens of Het Loo, Apeldoorn, having cosmological symbolic meaning. LUW.

171. Floor plan of the Burgerzaal in the Amsterdam Town Hall, representing the two halves of the world and the heavens. Print by Jacob Vennecool, *Stadthuys*, 1661. Photo courtesy Utrecht University.

172. Jodocus Hondius's Mappa Mundi, 1617, of the two halves of the world, the sky and emblematic representations of the Four Seasons and the Four Elements. Maritiem Museum Prins Hendrik, Rotterdam.

173. Print by Romeyn de Hooghe of the Orangerie garden at Cleves, decorated with the twelve Roman Emperors, classic urns, rare plants and instruments. LUW.

174. Title-page of Salomon de Caus's *Hortus Palatinus*, with allegorical figures representing all the disciplines of the Arts and Sciences based on number. Photo courtesy Kurpfälzisches Museum, Heidelberg.

175. Willem Buytewech's allegorical representation of Holland personified by a woman seated in an enclosed garden with orange-tree, guarded by the lion. Historisch Museum, Stichting Atlas van Stolk, Rotterdam.

ABBREVIATIONS

ARA	Algemeen Rijksarchief (National Archives)
CBN	Collectie Bodel Nijenhuis, Universiteitsbibliotheek, Leiden (Collection Bodel Nijenhuis, Leiden University Library)
GA	Gemeentearchief (Municipal Archives)
GAH	Gemeentearchief Den Haag (Municipal Archives, The Hague)
GAB	Gemeentearchief Breda (Municipal Archives, Breda)
GAG	Gemeentearchief Groningen (Municipal Archives, Groningen)
GAL	Gemeentearchief Leiden (Municipal Archives, Leiden)
GAN	Gemeentearchief Naaldwijk (Municipal Archives, Naaldwijk)
GAR	Gemeentearchief Rijswijk (Municipal Archives, Rijswijk)
KB	Koninklijke Bibliotheek (Royal Library)
KHA	Koninklijk Huisarchief (Royal House Archive)
LUW	Bibliotheek Landbouwuniversiteit Wageningen (Library Agricultural University, Wageningen)
NDAH	Nassaus Domeinarchief Hingman (Nassau Domain Archives in ARA)
NDR	Nassause Domeinraad (Nassau Domain Council)
RKD	Rijksbureau voor Kunsthistorische Documentatie (Netherlands Institute for Art History)
RMZ	Rijksdienst voor de Monumentenzorg (Netherlands Department for the Conservation of Monuments)
RPK	Rijksprentenkabinet, Rijksmuseum, Amsterdam (Print Room)

INDEX

A
Academie Française 154, 165
Acqui, Bishop of 132
Aderen, Jan 44
alchemy 123, 245, 259
Alberti, Leon Battista 124, 155, 156, 159, 167-169, 184, 189, 205, 209-211, 239, 251-253, 263
Alenburch (Allenburgh), Jacob van (see Appendix, Document IX, p. 393) 148, 149
Alexander the Great 253
Alkmaar (Noord-Holland) 72
Allaerdt, Hugo 236
Alphen, Gijsbrecht van 149
Amalia of Orange-Nassau, Countess van Solms-Braunfels (1602-1675) 11
 - and (antique) sculpture 96, 110, 118, 225, 226, 229-233, 266
 - builds Huis ten Bosch 101, 112, 113
 - designs interior decoration Ter Nieuburch 82, 169-171, 262
 - inventory list, sculpture 110, 232, 233
 - involvement as patron, surveyor 33, 35, 37, 51, 107, 108, 112, 113, 149, 169-171, 187, 262
 - mourning widow 89
Amersfoort 250
 - Doolinberg, Doolomberg 250
amphitheatre, semicircle 28, 50, 51, 188-196, 200, 204, 205, 217
Amsterdam 110, 191, 212, 225, 227, 229
 - Hortus Botanicus 242
 - Hortus Medicus 127
 - Town Hall (Paleis op de Dam) 173, 175, 209, 231, 255, 256, 259
Ancy-le-Franc 25
Androuet, see Du Cerceau
Anet 196
Anguien (Enghien) (Brussels) 242
Anna of Hanover 119
Anthoni, D'Anthoin, Louis (see Appendix, Document III, p. 388) 78-80, 178-179
Antwerp 42, 44, 84, 135, 151, 179, 203, 212, 225, 257
Apeldoorn
 - Loo, Het 188, 253-255, 267

Architecture, style and form
 - antique, Roman manner 9, 28, 38, 81, 120, 149, 160, 181, 267
 - Baroque 49, 61, 76, 194, 216, 233, 263, 264, 265
 - classical Italian influence 64, 66, 87, 95, 110, 123, 124, 155, 156, 164, 179, 181, 183, 185, 200, 201, 207, 208-212, 225, 228, 240, 263
 - Classical principles 12, 22, 76, 109, 122, 124, 151-163, 185, 216, 240, 263, 264
 - Classical theory studied at court 153, 159, 162, 187, 191, 206-212, 250-253, 263
 - dissemination artistic style 58, 72, 92, 153, 172, 181, 185, 199, 217- 221, 263, 267
 - Dutch Classicism, classical baroque 56, 76, 108, 109, 113, 151-153, 175, 195, 216, 229, 240
 - Flemish-Dutch artistic exchange 54, 87, 123, 151-153, 155, 159, 160, 181, 185, 203, 206, 212, 224, 225, 242, 266, 267
 - French-Dutch exchange 56, 155, 178, 187 189, 195-206, 263-65, 267
 - French influence 25, 28, 49, 58, 72, 111, 141, 164, 176, 178, 181-183, 185, 187-189, 191, 199, 200, 204, 207, 233, 263
 - German-Dutch artistic exchange 155, 157, 158, 185, 203, 217-221
 - Gothic 160, 174
 - harmonic proportion, musical harmony 168, 187, 200, 210-212, 252-253
 - Mannerism 87, 122, 123, 185, 233
 - medieval 144, 214, 216, 236
 - military features: bastion, bulwark, rampart 17, 18, 20, 21, 26, 54, 124, 126, 128, 129, 131, 136, 144, 155, 157, 184, 191, 199, 208-210, 212-214, 219, 236, 265
 - Rococo 59, 120
 - Renaissance 49, 105, 110, 112, 114, 185, 200, 201, 225, 233, 240, 246, 252, 266
 - ratio 198, 207
 - symmetry 159, 160, 167, 175, 181, 197, 200, 205, 208-210, 219, 237
 - variety (varietas) 198, 205, 207

Arcus Ferdinandus 228
Ardes, Mr. Pieter 107
Aremberg, Count of 17
Aremberg, Duke de 242
Arentsdorp, see Hague, The

Arentsz, Laurens 29
Aristoteles 246
Artemisia 89
Artificia 12, 224, 268
astrology 245
astronomy 238, 245, 246
Australia 256
avenues, grand approach, radiating 19, 20, 24, 25, 128, 129, 148, 158, 182-196, 204, 219
aviaries 12, 24, 45, 137,
axes, system of 23, 25, 50, 53, 67, 98, 99, 113, 114, 116, 129, 148, 149, 158, 188, 191, 220

B
Backer, Anthony Jansz 130
Bacon, Francis 12
Bad Kreuznach (Germany) 218
 - Oranienhof 218
Baes, B. de 58
Baldi, Balthasar, see Bernardino
Baldi, Bernardino 159
Balthasars, Floris 18
Balzac, J.-L. Guez de 165, 210
Bandinelli, Baccio 227
Bannius, Johan Albert 158
Barbaro, Daniele 159
Bassen, Bartholomeus van 171, 172
Bastion, see Architecture, military
Batavia, Batavians 12, 21, see Iconology
Batestein, see Vianen
Baurscheit The Elder, Jan van 227
Bedford, Lady Harington, Countess of 249
Beek, A. 96
Beemster (Noord-Holland) 113
 - Huis Vredenburg 113, 114, 208, 216
Bega, A. 49, 56, 263
Belgium 153, 176, 267
Belvedere (Rome) 95, 200
Bentheimer stone 80-81, 98
Bentinck, Hans Willem, Earl of Portland 58, 227, 267
Berckerode, Balthazar Florisz van 20-22, 25, 26, 31, 38, 39, 41, 46, 49, 165, 206, 209, 214, 235, 263
Bergen (Noord-Holland) 72, 264
Berlin 59, 95, 218-220, 225
 - Oranienburg (Bötzow) 85, 95, 218-221, 225, 265
 - Spree River 219, 220

Beron, Cornelis 225
Beyeren, Nicolaes van 229
Bienfait, A.G. 10, 187
Bilderbeek, Pieter van 172
Bisschop, Jan de 41, 66, 225, 227, 229
Blaeu, Johannes 104, 132, 138, 141, 236, 256
Blaeu, Willem Jansz 256
Blerisse, Abraham 130
Blom, Arent Pietersz 45, 147, 179, 180
Blooteling, A. 49, 263
Böckler, G.A. 155, 181
Bötzow, see Berlin
Bohemia 133
Bohemia, see Elizabeth Stuart, Queen of
Bologna, Giovanni 227
Bor, Paulus 174
Borch, Johan ter 130
Bos, Cornelis 104
Boscoop, Andries Andriesz 128
botany, botanical collections, illustrations 13, 122, 180, 181, 184, 218, 220, 238, 259
Bovio, Giulio and Guido, De 87, 118, 123, 124
Boyceau, Jacques de la Barauderie 45, 46, 72-74, 76, 155, 191, 199-206, 245, 263
Brahe, Tycho 249, 268
Brandtwyck, Family 101
Bray, Salomon de 31, 151, 160, 265
Breda 176
 - Breda, Castle, Valkenberg gardens 10, 46, 101, 131-142, 157, 169, 226
   - Begijnhof, Capucijnenhof, Cloveniers Doelen 132, 133, 137
   - Belcromsche Bosch 136, 137
   - Hercules statue 141, 226
   - parterre designs 138
   - Rose garden 133, 141
   - Stadholder's building in nature 138
   - surrounding wood, hunting pavilion 136
   - vandalism in garden 142

Breda, Siege of 136, 137, 138
Brederode, Johan Wolfert van 90, 128, 171, 234-236, 238, 259, 263
Brederoo (Brederode), Willem (see Appendix, Document IV, p. 389) 79, 80, 97
Brereton, Sir William 61, 62, 76, 104, 204
Breukelen (Utrecht) 127
 - Gunterstein 127
Brosse, Salomon de 69, 73, 74

Brosterhuisen, Johan 158, 159
Brouart, Th. 37, 47
Bruheze, Michiel van 134, 137
Bruheze, Pieter van 134
Brussels
 - Habsburg Court garden 267
Buitenhof, see Hague, The
bulwark, stronghold 17, 18, 20, 21, 26, 208-210, 236
Buren (Buren, Gelderland)
 - Castle and garden 10, 36, 37, 45, 69, 101, 127-131, 138, 146, 147, 169, 174, 177, 208, 234-236, 253, 265, 267
   - avenue, grand approach 128, 129, 188
   - castle island, military aspects 129, 265
   - circular berceaux 128, 130, 234-236, 253
   - hippodrome-shaped parterres 129, 130
   - sylvan character 45, 128
Buysero, L. 149
bulwarks, see Architecture, military
Bye, Jacob de 78

C
Calvinism 46, 266, 250, 266
Campen, Jacob van 158, 159, 165, 167, 189, 232, 250, 262
 - advisor sculptural decoration 224, 227-230
 - Amsterdam Town Hall 173, 175, 209, 231, 255, 256
 - Buren 128, 169, 174
 - Cleves gardens 158
 - Hofwijck 167, 173, 174
 - Honselaarsdijk 41, 167, 174
 - Huis ten Bosch 112, 115, 164, 167, 174
 - Mauritshuis 76, 164, 173
 - Nieuburch, Huis ter 68, 69, 81, 167, 170, 174
 - Noordeinde Palace 109, 164, 167, 174
 - responsibilities at court 171-176

Caporali, Giovan Battista 159
Castiglione, B. 138
Cats, Jacob 9, 12, 46, 266
Catshuysen, Symon van 27, 33, 35, 36, 170
Cattaneo, Pietro 155
Caus, Salomon de 87, 93, 123, 155, 204, 231, 249, 250, 259, 263, 268
Cesariano, Cesare 159
Chantilly 119

Charles I, King of England 41, 268
Charles II, King of England 131
Charleval 25, 196, 205
Christ 246, 250
Christian IV, King of Denmark 208, 268
Christina, Queen of Sweden 196
circle, see Architecture, see Garden
city, ideal 208-210, 237, 240
city planning 11, 160-163, 208-210, 262
classical baroque, see Architecture
Claessen, Reijnier 111
Clerck, Nicolaas de 104
Cleves 225, 264
 - Prinsenhof (Germany) 158, 203, 242, 259, 260
 - Springenberg park 158, 187, 203, 225, 232, 264
Clusius, Carolus 259
Cobergher, Wenzel 153
Collen (Keulen), Ludolf van 239
Colonna, Francesco 155, 242
Columella 46
Conrart, Valentin 165
Copenhagen (Denmark) 249
 - Uraniborg, Island of Hveen 249, 268
Copernicus 249
corps de logis 25, 108, 164
Cosimo III de'Medici 53
cosmology, theory of 164, 167, 168, 245-261, 268
country-house architecture 163, 175, 192, 208, 216
country-house poetry 10, 45, 46, 151, 167, 168, 173, 250
country life, ideal of 46, 180
Court, Pieter de la 127
Couwenhoven, Pieter Cornelisz van 85
Cretser, Gysbert de 97, 122
Croos, Anthony Jansz van der 63
Cruquius (Kruikius), Nicolaas 15, 63
curiosity cabinet, see also museion 87, 110, 122, 157, 201, 224, 230, 259-261, 268

D
D'Anthoni (D'Anthoin), see Anthoni
D'Este, Family 226
Danckerts, Cornelis 56
De Bovio, see Bovio
Delfland 15
Delft 15, 62, 176, 200, 201

- mausoleum William I 67, 89
- Nieuwe Kerk 67
- Sion 267

Delorme, see L'Orme, Philibert de
Denmark 10, 124, 208, 217, 250, 268
Descartes, René 72, 73, 95, 152, 264
Deventer, Jacob van 236
Dézallier d'Argenville, J.A. 211
Diepenen, Jan van (see Appendix, Document VIII, p. 393) 144-148, 183, 262
Dieren (Dieren, Gelderland) 32
Diest (Belgium) 44
Dietz (Germany) 218
- Oraniensteyn 218

Dieussart, François 41, 220, 225, 233, 266
Dijck, Cornelis (see Appendix, Document VI, p. 391) 107
Dijck, Jan van 134, 137
Dimmer, Willem 146, 149
Dinant, Frederic 176
Dinant, Joseph 35, 36, 39, 40, 50, 51, 70, 82-85, 88, 89, 108, 175, 176, 199, 233, 262
Dinant, Otto George 176
Dircksz, Boon (Boon Dircxz Bosch) 32, 33
Does, Jacob van der 122
Dohna, Frederik van 35
domus cosmographica, see Iconology
donjon, castle island 17, 18, 20, 26, 28, 129, 146, 157, 194, 196, 208-210, 212-214, 219, 236, 265, 267
Dorp, Arent van 175
Dou, Jan Pietersz 18
Doublet, Philips 119, 175
Dürer, Albrecht 239
Drijffhout, Laurens 137, 138
Drijffhout, Bartholomeus 41, 137, 173, 174, 179, 229
Drossaers, S.W.A. 223
Druivestein, Gerrit 172
Dubuisson-Aubenay, Mr. 81
Du Cerceau, Jacques Androuet 25, 152, 155, 191, 196, 202, 263
Du Quesnoy, François 110, 225, 266
Dutch burgher, Batavian ancestor 259
Dutch Classical Canal Garden, see Garden
Dutch Golden Age 10, 231, 262
Dutch Lion, see Iconology, lion
Dutch Republic 13, 21, 67, 261
Dutch territory, symbol of, see Iconology

Dutch tradition land-reclamation, cultivation, see Landscape

E
Earth 164, 168, 173, 181, 246, 247, 249, 253-258
Eighty Years' War 12, 231, 267
Ekolsund (Sweden) 70, 191
Elandts, Cornelis 101, 106, 108
Elizabeth Stuart, Queen of Bohemia 13, 95, 102, 131, 231
Elssholtz, Johann Sigismund 220
emblem books 253
Engelen, Balthasar van 44, 85, 179
Enghien (Belgium) 158
England 44, 45, 59, 61, 97, 102, 112, 155, 191, 196, 202
English flower-, shrubbery garden 112
Ernst Casimir, Count of Nassau-Dietz 234, 235
Eskilstuna (Sweden) 191
Evelyn, John 79, 87, 122

F
Flanders, Flemish art, science 44, 87, 123, 153, 181, 185, 203, 224, 225, 266, 267
Florence
- Boboli Gardens 181, 204
- Villa Petraia 242

Floris, Cornelis 87
Fludd, Robert 247
Flushing (Vlissingen, Zeeland)
- Prinsenhuis 101, 124-127, 151, 210, 212, 234-238, 253, 257-259
   - circular berceaux 125-127, 234-238, 257-259
   - triangular garden, labyrinth 125-127, 234

Fontainebleau 36, 95, 181, 202, 211, 231
fortifications 54, 124, 128, 129, 132, 136, 155, 157, 184, 208-210, 237
Francart, Jacob 153
France 61, 69, 72, 73, 87, 138, 155, 175, 181, 185, 191, 196
French architects at court 10, 35, 40, 49, 69-73, 175-178, 195-206
French style influence, see Architecture, see Garden
Francini, Alessandro and Tommaso 74, 95
Frederic, Borchgaert 80, 90, 117, 177, 179, 180

Frederik Hendrik, Prince of Orange-Nassau (1584-1647), Captain General of the United Provinces, Stadholder of Dutch Republic; signs his name as 'Henry de Nassau', referred to as Son Altesse, His Highness
- and double (twin-) circle motif 250-261
- and harmonic proportion 210-212
- architectural features, predilections for 153-160, 206-208, 212-214, 265
- bust of 88, 89, 233
- collector of sculpture 41, 223-233, 267
- commissions French architects 49, 50, 69, 199
- completes Buitenhof garden 86, 101
- designs gardens 67-69, 82, 169-171, 262, 267
- Hercules/Herculean labours, symbol of 225-227, 267
- historical restoration 142, 144, 150, 187, 212-214, 265
- inspects palaces and gardens 33, 35, 46-51, 112, 113, 128, 169-171
- library 155, 212, 263
- natural inclination towards architecture 160-163, 188
- Praeceptor Hollandiae 12, 261, 266
- prepares influx French style William III 50-56, 267
- symmetry, notions of 208-210, 252
- urban development The Hague 160-163, 262
- virtues as warrior-patron, ruler 101, 115, 168, 188, 225-227, 231, 261, 266-268

Frederik van Nassau-Zuylesteyn 146
Friedrich Wilhelm, Elector of Brandenburg 95, 158, 219, 231
Friedrich V, Elector Palatine, King of Bohemia 13, 95, 102, 131, 157, 231, 268
Friedrich I, King of Prussia 58, 97, 111, 119
Friedrich Wilhelm II, King of Prussia 58
Furttenbach, Joseph 155, 157, 219, 263, 265

G
game of fives (caetsbaan) 122, 128, 135
Garden Ornamentation
- automata 157, 238, 262
- berceaux, see also Iconology, circle, double 21, 22, 24, 49, 50, 66, 90, 104-106, 109, 120,

123-126, 128, 130, 141, 212, 217, 219, 227, 234, 235, 252, 253
- fountains 40, 43, 50, 51, 77, 110, 120, 123, 141, 220, 236, 259
- galleries 108, 128, 130
- grottoes 39, 40, 45, 82-89, 93, 108, 122, 123, 141, 157, 158, 174-176, 219, 232, 233, 238, 259, 266
- labyrinth 126, 134, 181, 250
- marvels, curiosities, exotica 87, 110, 122-124, 157, 158
- mirrors, optical effects 109, 110, 123, 158, 238, 262
- music, artificial 87, 123, 157, 233
- obelisks, pyramids 90, 98, 107, 114, 148
- pagoda, Chinese 59, 112
- paintings, illusionistic, perspective 109-111, 120, 123, 128, 166, 171, 174, 201, 238, 255-260, 262, 267
- palisades, portals 90-93, 148, 179, 197, 219, 263
- parterres 23, 37-39, 45, 73, 88-93, 105, 106, 108, 114, 120, 130, 132, 135, 137, 141, 145, 177, 179, 181, 194, 198, 204, 217-220, 236, 247
- pavilion, pleasure house, cabinet 31, 33, 39, 58, 110, 112, 115, 117, 120, 124, 128, 130, 133, 136, 138, 141, 219
- statues, vases, urns, see Sculpture
- sundial 135, 181
- topiary 90, 148
- trellis, lattice-work 39, 90-93, 108, 114, 117, 148, 180, 181, 197, 263

Garden, style and form
- and classical architectural orders 152
- anthropomorphic form 167, 252
- bastioned outline, see Architecture, military
- bizarreness in 87, 88, 259, 266
- chinoiserie 59, 112
- circle, circular garden 21, 50, 120, 123-127, 130, 141, 158, 212, 217, 220, 233-244, 250-261, 268
- circle, double (twin) circle motif 24, 120, 124, 158, 164, 212, 221, 227, 233-245, 250-261, 268
- Dutch Classical Canal Garden, character of 18, 19, 22, 23, 37, 64, 76, 102, 104, 117, 145, 158, 175, 181-184, 188, 195-210, 263-265

- Dutch Classical Canal Garden, definition 14, 76, 210, 263
- Dutch indigenous tradition 152, 182, 185, 187, 188, 191, 200, 201, 212-217, 263-265
- Dutch influence abroad 196, 199, 217-221, 266, 267
- French-Dutch artistic exchange, see Architecture
- French style examples 49, 50, 58, 68, 69, 181, 185, 199, 263, 264, 267
- grid system 61, 64, 264
- harmonic proportion, musical harmony 168, 187, 200, 210-212, 252-253, 263
- ideal geometric form 10, 126, 127, 197, 207, 212, 234, 239, 240, 242
- landscape garden, park 98, 112, 120, 131, 158, 262
- micro-macrocosm 167, 245, 246, 253
- mound, central 250
- museion, open-air museum 87, 110, 122, 123, 157, 158, 201, 224, 230, 268
- orientation layout, symbolic 67
- Paradise 142, 181
- picturesque style 120
- practice and process of designing 68, 117, 171-176, 182-184, 239, 262
- realm of peace (locus amoenus) 131, 231, 266-268
- rectilinear framework of canals 195, 196, 200, 205, 206, 216, 264, 267
- Renaissance gardens, Italian 95, 181, 183, 200, 240, 242, 263
- Rococo design 52, 120
- Roman gardens of antiquity 95-96, 181, 200
- style form, main principles 185-188, 263-265
- triangle, triangular garden 126, 127, 166

Gardener's contracts see Appendix, Documents
sGravesande, Arent van 164, 172, 173, 179, 240
Genoa 155
Germany 10, 124, 185, 187, 208, 217-221
Gheyn III, Jacob de 123
Gheyn II, Jacques de 87, 102, 104, 122, 123, 171, 176, 233, 238, 239, 259, 262
giardini segreti 64, 77, 117, 141, 201, 232
Gijbersch, Jan 29
Gijsbrechtsz, Anthony 179

Giocondo, Giovanni 159
globe, terrestrial, celestial 253-258
God 12, 46, 151, 167, 223, 249, 250
Gole, J. 67
Goudt, Willem 101
Graeco-Roman past 12, 207, 209, 260
Grand Tour 73, 138
Grebber, Pieter de 174
Greef, Jan de 112
Groen, Jan van der 43, 46, 51, 53, 89, 108, 180-181, 199, 263
Groningen 90
  - Prinsenhof 90, 177, 234, 235, 245, 253, 259
grotto, see Garden Ornamentation
Gunterstein, see Breukelen

H
Haarlem 176, 227
Habsburg Court, see Brussels
Haenwijck 142
Hague, The (Courtly Residence) 13, 62, 76, 147, 151, 173, 175, 192
- Aeckerlandt 166
- Arentsdorp 175
- Bezuidenhoutsche Weg 113
- Binnenhof (Old Ducal Court) 106, 108, 120, 161, 162
- Buitenhof garden 85, 87, 102, 120-124, 128, 168, 210, 233, 233-239, 253, 257-261
    - circular berceaux 120-124, 233-244, 253
    - grotto 122, 233, 258
- Clingendael 119, 175, 214, 267
- Hague Woods (Haagse Bos) 113, 120
- Huis ten Bosch 10, 88, 89, 101, 112-120, 155, 164, 174, 177, 180, 181, 183, 208, 216, 220, 229, 240, 260, 262
    - Amalia's summer retreat, designs for 111-113
    - as mausoleum 89, 101, 174, 267
    - centralized composition palace 112, 113
    - decoration central Hall 115, 267
    - mathematical division grounds, axes 115, 116
    - meadow and duneland, cultivation of 113
    - monogram Stadholderly pair 88, 89, 117
    - process, practice garden designing 117

- Huygens's House 161-169, 228, 251, 252, 255

- Mauritshuis 76, 85, 127, 155, 160-164, 168, 227, 242
- Molenstraat 107
- Noordeinde, Palace (Oude Hof, Old Court) 10, 104-120, 128, 157, 164, 173-176, 180, 211, 227, 229, 233, 260, 262
    - Amalia's flower garden 89, 104, 108-111, 122
    - meadowlands, orchards 102, 107, 108
    - grotto 89, 104, 108, 176
    - Princesse Thuyn with island 104, 106-108
    - sculpture 227-230, 233
- Plein, Het 160-163, 210, 228
- Scheveningse Weg 190, 192
- Sorgvliet 227
- St. Nicolaas Hospice 102
- urban development 160-163, 262

Haller, Albrecht 58
Hamilton Hazlehurst, F. 75
Hanover (Germany) 265
 - Herrenhausen 265
Harn, Jacob van 104
Harris, Walter 253
Hartmann, Adam Samuel 137
Hattem, Hendrick van (see Appendix, Document VIII) 45, 80, 146-149, 179
Haubois, Egbert 235
heaven 253-258, see Iconology, sphere
Heemskerck, Pieter Philipsz van 32
Heemstede (Utrecht) 200, 214, 267
Heeze (Noord-Brabant) 175, 193, 194
 - Heeze castle 175, 193, 194
Heidelberg (Germany) 157
 - Hortus Palatinus 88, 93, 95, 102, 123, 157, 158, 200, 204, 220, 231, 250, 259, 268
Heinsius, Daniel 158, 159
hemispheres, see Iconology
Hendrick III van Nassau 133
Hennin, Jacob de 109, 110, 223, 267
Henri IV, King of France 13, 73, 95, 155, 160, 211, 231
Henrietta Catharina, Princess of Orange-Nassau, Princess of Anhalt-Dessau 85, 89, 177, 218, 220-221, 233, 265
Henrietta Maria, Queen of England 41, 128
Henry, Prince of Wales 124
Hercules, see Sculpture, see Iconology

Herison, Jan 179
sHerwouters, J. 33
Heyden, Jan van der 114, 117, 118, 229, 267
hippodrome 35, 51, 58, 64, 129, 141, 200, 263, 267
Hirver, Rosier 44
Hoefnagel, Susanna 164
Hofwijck, see Voorburg
Holbein, Hans 166
Holland, garden of, see Iconology, Hortus Batavus
Holland, geography, topography, see Landscape
Holland, see Dutch Republic
Hondius, Hendrick 120-124, 151, 155, 234, 237, 239, 257, 258, 262
Hondius, Jodocus II 256-258
Hondius, Petrus 46
Honselaarsdijk, see Naaldwijk
Honselersdijk, village (Naaldwijk) 18, 33
Honthorst, Gerard van 82, 89, 174, 233
tHooft, Pieter Adriaensz 228, 229
Hoorendonck, Andries (see Appendix Document VII, p. 392) 128, 130, 134
Hopper, Florence 25, 195, 208, 210-212, 264
Horst, Jonkheer Lambert van der 78
horticulture 13, 43-46, 58, 79, 171, 179-181, 198, 218, 266
Hortus Botanicus, see Leiden
Hortus Palatinus, see Heidelberg
Hortus Medicus, see Amsterdam
Huis ten Bosch, see Hague, The
Huizinga, J. 10
humanism 11, 46, 158, 184, 187, 211, 266
Huydecoper, Johan 192
Huygens, Christiaan 51, 154
Huygens, Constantijn, Junior 106, 138, 154, 230
Huygens, Susanna Doublet 119, 142
Huygens, Constantijn (1596-1687) 26, 27, 81, 112, 128, 140, 155, 158, 184, 189, 192, 208, 209, 232, 233, 250-255, 262, 264
 - advisor sculptural decoration 41, 227-230, 233
 - and Jacob van Campen 159, 165, 173
 - and René Descartes 72, 73, 264
 - Buitenhof, description of 87, 122, 123, 253
 - classical architecture, notions of 76, 153-160
 - country-house poetry 45, 151, 167, 168, 173
 - cosmology, notions of 168, 251-253, 255

- harmonic proportion, notions of 210-212, 250-253
- Hofwijck, designer of 151, 163-169, 175, 209-212,
- Huygens's House on Plein, designer of 161-169, 228
- letters Amalia 33, 35, 46-48, 68-69, 76, 95, 136, 138, 169-171
- letters Rubens 153, 158, 159, 160, 266, 267
- letters Tassin 49, 50, 72, 199
- letters Wiquefort 158, 159, 187
- letters Wilhem, Le Leu de 27, 36, 142, 170
- portrait of 255
- symmetry, notions of 208-210
- travels 153-160
- urban development The Hague 160-163, 262

Hveen Island, see Copenhagen, Uraniborg

I
Iconology
- Batavia, mythical land, stronghold 165, 209, 212-214, 265
- Christian virtues (Hope, Faith, Love) 164
- circle and cosmology 211, 245-261, 268
- circle, double-circle motif, meaning of 120, 124, 223, 233-245, 250-261
- cosmic-harmonic diagrams 246-250, 268
- cultivation orchard, Calvinism 46, 266
- Cycles of Life, Nature, Time 82, 136, 221, 231, 245, 249, 253-258, 266
- Dance of Death 166
- domus cosmographica 164, 168, 251, 255
- European rulers, glorification of 82, 168, 260, 267, 268
- Four Parts of World 82, 168, 253-259
- Four Elements 225, 231, 246, 253-258
- Four Qualities 246
- Four Seasons 225, 82, 231, 249, 253-259
- Four Winds 164
- Garden of Hesperides 225
- Gothic Heresy-Roman Truth 165, 174, 209
- harmonic proportion and music 164-169, 210-212, 250-253, 263
- hemispheres, two halves world 227, 253-258, 268
- Herculean labours, themes 225, 226, 239, 267

- heroic past, feudal pretensions 21, 26, 208-210, 265, 267
- Homo ad circulum, quadratum, see Vitruvian man
- Hope, Faith, Love 164
- Hortus Batavus, Garden of Holland 9, 12, 21, 219, 261, 267
- House of Orange-Nassau, glorification of 82, 88, 174, 223, 225-227, 231, 233, 253, 255, 259-261, 266-268
- House of Orange-Nassau, dynastic aspirations, rule 21, 26, 82, 93, 110, 115, 116, 135, 136, 158, 168, 208-210, 225-228, 231, 259-261, 265, 268
- illustrious persons 168, 260, 267, 268
- Lion, Dutch, Rampant 9, 38, 39, 41, 219, 227, 259, 261, 266
- mappae mundi 256, 257
- Mars-Venus/Minerva, War-Peace 158, 227, 267
- micro-macrocosm 246, 253-261, 268
- Minerva, protectress Militia, Wisdom, Arts 96, 158, 227, 266
- monogram, heraldic imagery 88, 89, 115, 117, 136, 204, 219, 231, 236, 239, 259, 266
- mystical circle and martial arts 239, 268
- national identity 12, 153, 157, 206, 207, 261, 262
- path of redemption 167, 250
- realm of peace (locus amoenus) 131, 231, 266-268
- Rome, New 21, 164, 209, 231, 265
- scala intellectualis, spiritualis 167, 246, 250, 252, 253
- sphere/globe, terrestial/earthly, celestial/heavenly 164, 250, 253-258, 268
- territory, symbol of Dutch 95, 231, 259, 267
- tetrad: Pythagorean, theological 246, 249, 250
- theatrum mundum, botanicum 259-261, 262, 268
- utile dulci 45, 66, 79, 108, 262, 266
- Vitruvian Man, homo ad circulum/quadratum 147, 164, 167-169, 212, 238, 246-252
- Vitruvian virtues (Firmitas, Utilitas, Venustas) 164, 169
- war-peace, landscape of 12, 136, 158, 227, 231, 267
Idstein (Germany)

- Nassau Palace 85
IJsselstein see Ysselsteyn (Utrecht)
Ireland 82
Isabella of Habsburg, Archduchess 267
Italy 156, 157, 185

J
Jacobsz, Blaserus 179
James I, King of England 13, 268
Jansz, Cornelis 29
Johan Maurits van Nassau-Siegen 76, 96, 129, 136, 141, 158, 161, 162, 164, 174, 187, 209, 225, 232, 242, 259, 260
Johan Albrecht II, Count of Solms 171
Johan Georg II von Anhalt-Dessau 233
Jones, Inigo 155, 156
Jordaens, Jacob 174
Justinus van Nassau 134
Juvenalis 253

K
Karling, S. 189
Key, Lieven de 13
Keyser, Thomas de 255
Keyser, Hendrick de 13, 154
kitchen gardens 17, 79, 105, 107, 108, 133, 137, 219
Koster, Cornelis 15

L
labyrinth 126, 134
land-reclamation, -cultivation, see Landscape
Langelaer, Reyer and Simon 128
landscape gardens 98, 112, 120, 131, 158, 262
Landscape: geography, land-reclamation, cultivation
 - geography, topography, climate 14, 15, 25, 29, 31, 75, 102, 105, 142-144, 157, 160, 181, 184, 185, 187, 192, 196, 197, 200-202, 211, 212-217, 224, 263-265
 - land-reclamation, cultivation 9, 12, 22, 29, 31, 33, 46, 78, 80, 101, 102, 113, 144-146, 181, 183, 184, 206, 211, 263-265

Lannoy, Charles 47
Lauremberg, P. 181
Laurensz (Lourisz), Arent 85
Le Nôtre, André 111, 119
Leersum (Utrecht) 142

- Zuylesteyn 10, 36, 45, 79, 101, 142-149, 177, 183, 208, 265
  - cultivation orchard, silviculture 145-147
  - garden islands, separate 145, 265
  - historical restoration 142-144, 265
Leiden 11, 172, 173, 175, 209, 239
- Hortus Botanicus 240
- Lakenhal 164
- Marekerk 240
- St. Catharijne Gasthuis 18
Leonardo da Vinci 246-248
Leschevin, Isaac 89-92, 117, 180, 181, 236, 263
library House of Orange 155, 212, 263
Liesbosch (Breda) 140
Lillo (Antwerp, Belgium) 225
Lithgow, William 135
loggia, Italianate 64, 194, 201-203
Lois, Jacob 216
Londerseel, Johannes van 104
London, George 43
Loo, Het, see Apeldoorn
Loris, D. 181, 245
L'Orme, Philibert de 155
Louis XIII, King of France 165
Louis XIV, King of France 58, 138, 141
Louise de Coligny 13, 101, 102, 104
Louise Henriette, Princess of Orange-Nassau, Electress of Brandenburg 58, 85, 89, 95, 177, 218-221, 231, 265
Louvre, see Paris
Lunsingh Scheurleer, Th. H. 223
Luxembourg, Palais du, see Paris

M
Maas-river, see also Sculpture 17
macrocosm-microcosm, see Iconology
Mander, Carel van 151
mannerism, see Architecture
maps, mappae mundi 257
Marekerk, see Leiden
Maria de' Medici 22, 69, 81, 95, 109, 230
Marolois, Samuel 155
Marot, Daniel 119, 111, 120, 140, 141
Mars, see also Sculpture and Iconology 267
martial arts 239, 268
Martin, Jacques 82
Mary I Stuart, Princess of England 108
Mary II Stuart, Queen of England 227, 255

mathematics, science of 155, 184, 191, 197, 207-210, 214-217, 234, 237-240
Maurits, Prince of Orange-Nassau 17, 87, 88, 102, 110, 120, 122, 124, 134, 136, 171, 184, 209, 210, 212, 226, 236-239, 253, 268
mausoleum 67, 89, 101, 174, 242, 267
Medici, Family De 226
medieval, see Architecture
Memhardt, Johann Gregor 218, 219
menagerie 22, 24, 44, 45, 136
Merian, Mattheus 218
Mersenne, Martin 72, 209
Meurs (Mrs, Germany) 44, 79, 140, 145, 176
Meyster, Everhart 250
Michelangelo 227
Mijlen, Dirck van der 138
Milander, General 162
Milde, Dirck de (see Appendix, Document I) 32, 34, 44, 179, 182
Milheusser, J. Julius 63, 66, 69, 79, 80, 89, 90, 95, 96, 204, 206
military features, see Architecture, military
Mollet, Claude 36, 73, 245, 263
Mollet, André 25, 29, 69, 73, 134, 166, 170, 211, 262, 263
 - avenue, grand approach, Honselaarsdijk 25, 189, 191
 - ideal garden plan, Honselaarsdijk 38, 39, 90, 178, 195-206, 264
 - ideal garden plan, Ter Nieuburch 36, 199-206, 264
 - parterre Buren 37, 127, 130, 177
 - parterre Honselaarsdijk 37-39, 89, 117, 170, 177
 - parterre Ter Nieuburch 89, 90, 117, 177
 - role in courtly garden 35-40, 176-178, role in Zuylesteyn garden 145

monogram, Frederik Hendrik and Amalia, see Iconology
Monster (Zuid-Holland) 15
Moretus, Family 135
Morlot, D. de 209
Morren, Th. 10, 187
Mountague (Montague), William 9
museion, open-air museum, see Iconology
Muses 231
music 87, 123, 157, 233, 238
musical harmony, see Garden, see Iconology, harmonic
mystical circle 239, 268

N
Naaldwijk, Lords of 17
Naaldwijk (Westland, Zuid-Holland) 15, 225
 - Honselaarsdijk, palace and garden 15-60, 112, 136, 137, 138, 144-147, 158, 164, 182, 183, 214, 216, 219, 234-239, 259-261, 262-267
    - architects and gardeners 170-181, 194
    - as ideal garden plan 38, 39, 90, 178, 195-206
    - avenue, grand approach 19, 20, 24, 25, 188-195
    - axes, system of 22, 25, 50, 53, 188
    - berceaux, circular hedges 22, 39, 50, 199, 234
    - fountains 40, 43, 50, 51, 110, 157, 231
    - grottoes 39, 40, 88, 176
    - lower courts Domeinhof, Nederhof 28, 34, 59, 117
    - menagerie, faisanterie 22, 24, 33, 44, 51
    - modernization garden, c. 1645 48-51, 199, 263, 385-387 (Document I)
    - Orangerie 31, 51, 56-59
    - parterres 23, 37-39, 58, 117, 179
    - pleasure house (speelhuys) 33, 58

Naredi-Rainer, P. von 168
Naturalia 12, 224, 268
Neoplatonism, see Plato
Neptune 95, 123
Netscher, Caspar 227
Nettesheim, Agrippa von 247
Nile 95
Noordeinde Palace, see Hague, The
Nootman, Pieter 21, 209
Nordberg, Av Tord O:son 173

O
Östermalma (Sweden) 191
Oliva, Hilario 44
orangerie 31, 40, 51, 56-58, 82-89, 119, 178, 232, 260
Oranienbaum, see Wörlitz
Oranienburg, see Berlin (Bötzow)
Oranienhof, see Bad Kreuznach
Oraniensteyn, see Dietz

orchard 34, 43-46, 58, 102, 107, 108, 128, 133, 134, 137, 158, 179, 201, 242
Orléans, Duc de 72
Ortelius, Abraham 257
Outhamer, Jacob 128

P
Padua, Botanical Garden 127, 240, 245, 246, 250
pagoda, see Garden Ornamentation
painting, illusionistic 82, 115, 174
Palace Noordeinde, see Noordeinde (The Hague)
palisade, see Garden Ornamentation
Palladio, Andrea 155, 156, 159, 200, 214, 251, 263
pall mall (malie-, maillebaan) 32, 45, 122, 135, 136, 138, 179
Paradise, see Garden, see Iconology
Paris 138, 204
 - Louvre 72
 - Palais du Luxembourg 69, 72-75, 81, 173, 200, 203-205, 264, 266
 - Rue de Vaugirard 75
 - Tuileries 36, 72, 73, 138, 196, 205
Parival, Jean de 62
Parkinson, John 127, 239, 259
parterres, see also Mollet 23, 37-39, 45, 73, 88-93, 105, 106, 108, 114, 120, 117, 130, 132, 135, 137, 141, 145, 177, 179, 181, 200, 203, 210, 225, 266
Pauwelsen, Cornelis 78
pavilion, see Garden Ornamentation
Pavilion von Wied (Scheveningen) 93, 231
peace treaty 61, 78, 96-98, 131, 201
peace, realm of, see Garden, see Iconology
Pelt, R.J. van 164, 167, 211, 252
perspective, art and science of 110, 120, 121, 151, 152, 155, 158, 171, 184, 191, 201, 212, 237-239, 262, 267
Peters, Gerwert 235
Phaeton 256
Pieterssen, Reyer 108
Pietersz, Dirck 79
planets 245, 246, 253-257
Plantijn-Moretus, Family 135
Plants and trees in courtly gardens
 - aertvruchten (vegetables) 107
 - alder 113, 117, 128

- apples 120
- apricot 44, 128
- artichokes 107
- asparagus 107
- bay 128
- beech 44, 120, 128, 130, 145
- berries 45
- boxwood 29, 37, 79, 127, 137
- camomile 137
- cherry 43, 44, 79
- chinese trees 44
- cypress 104, 197, 198
- dwarf trees (arbres nains) 44, 79, 96, 128
- eglantine 45
- elm 44, 80, 128, 148, 198
- espalier 44
- fig 44, 79, 120
- fir tree 137, 197, 198
- hornbeam 79, 80, 145
- ivy 117
- jasmin 43, 197
- laurel 120
- lemon 43, 44
- lime 44, 59, 64, 78, 108, 117, 122, 128, 132, 148
- melon 43, 107, 148,
- muscadine grapevine
- myrtle 197
- oak 44, 63, 117, 148
- olives 120
- orange 43, 44, 197
- peach 44, 79, 128, 130
- pear 79
- pine 44
- pomegranate 43
- poplar 44
- potato 218
- rose 45, 130, 133, 141
- strawberries 107, 130
- tulip 198
- white poplar 44
- willow 44

Plato, Platonism 167, 168, 211, 246, 251, 252
Pliny the Younger 165, 189, 200
poetry, country-house 10, 45, 46, 151, 167, 168, 173, 250
polderland, see Landscape, topography
politics 11-13, 21, 201, 266

Portland, Earl of, see Bentinck
Post, Maurits 192
Post, Pieter 9, 27, 28, 50, 51, 127, 164, 167, 183, 189, 192-194, 196, 200, 208, 216, 232, 240, 262
 - Buren 128
 - Palace Noordeinde 108-110, 164, 173, 174
 - Heeze 193
 - Hofwijck 167, 175
 - Huis ten Bosch 112-118, 164
 - Zuylesteyn, Ysselsteyn 147-150
 - baroque designs, dynamic 28, 50, 51, 192-195, 198, 265
 - role at court 171-177

Prague 124, 268
Pratolino 124
Princeton (New Jersey) 89
Prinsenhof, see Cleves, see Groningen
Prinsenhuis, Flushing (Zeeland) 101, 124-127, 151
Pronk, Cornelis 56, 227
Prussia(n) 58, 59, 119
Ptolemeus 246
Puyt, Johannes de 59
Pythagoras, Pythagorean 167, 168, 210, 211, 214, 250-252, 263
 - harmonic proportion and musical harmony, see Garden, Iconology
 - Tetrad 246, 249, 250

Q

quadrature 29, 187, 212-217, 263
Quellenburch (Quellenburgh), Hendrick (see Appendix, Document II, p. 387) 43
Quellinus, Artus 54, 224, 225, 231, 266

R

Rabel, D. 181
ramparts, see Architecture, military
ratio, see Architecture, ratio
reclamation land, see Landscape
redemption, path of, see Iconology
Reijerssen (Reyerssen), Otto 41, 110, 225
Renaissance style, see Architecture
rethorica, classical 169, 210
Reynst, Family van 229
Rhenen (Gelderland) 95
Rhine river, valley 158

Richelieu (France) 191
Richmond (England) 124
Riddarhuspalatset (Sweden) 70
Rietkessler, J.A. 83, 85, 96
Rijckevorsel, Jan Woutersz van 137
Rijswijk (The Hague, Zuid-Holland)
 - Huis Ter Nieuburch (Nieuwburg, Huis te Rijswijk) 10, 28, 35, 36, 61-99, 136, 144-147, 158, 164, 182, 183, 211, 219, 220, 227-233, 236, 262-267
  - architects and gardeners 170-181
  - as ideal garden plan, Ter Nieuburch 36, 199-206
  - designs palace complex, preliminary 67-77, 80
  - French Plan and Luxembourg Palace 68-77, 173, 178, 200, 203-205, 264, 266
  - Grotto, shell-pavilion 82-89, 93, 176, 233
  - hippodrome-shape in garden 64, 217
  - lime-tree plantation 64, 78, 122
  - loggia, Italianate 64, 201-203
  - Orangerie 40, 82-89, 178
  - parterres 88-93, 117, 204-206
  - sculpture in garden 41, 93-99, 220, 224-231, 233
  - trelliswork structures 64, 89-93

Rijswijk (Zuid-Holland) 40, 45, 62, 63, 69, 98-99, 192
 - church 78
 - Heerewegh 63, 75
 - memorial column (De Naald) 98
 - Peace treaty (1697) 61, 96-98, 201
 - public park (Rijswijkse Bos) 61, 98, 99
 - Vliet River 63, 205
 - Vlietwegh, Kleiwegh 63
 - Vredenburchweg 63
 - Winston Churchill-laan 63
 - Zandvaert 63
 - Zandwegh, Heerewegh 63
Rijxdorp, see Wassenaar
River god, see Sculpture, see Iconology
Rococo, see Garden, style and form
Roman, Jacob 56, 97, 140, 141
Roman Emperors, see Sculpture
Roman gardens, emulation of 95, 220
Roman past 12, 207, 209
Roman style, see Architecture, see Garden
Roman theatre 251

Roman Truth, see Iconology
Roman warriors, see Sculpture
Rome 83, 231, 265
- Belvedere statue court 95, 230
- Mausoleum of Augustus 242
- New, a, see Iconology
- Via Appia 192
- Villa Giulia 200
- Villa Madama 200
Rotterdam (Zuid-Holland)
- Schielandhuis 216
Rubens, Peter Paul 153, 155-160, 203, 228, 267
Rudolf II, Holy Roman Emperor 124, 268

S
Sagemans, Julius 128, 146
Saint-Germain-en-Laye 36, 181, 211, 268
Salen, Willem van 145
Sallem (Salm), Floris Jacobsz van der 15, 19, 25, 26, 31, 34, 62, 63, 76, 78, 147, 188, 189, 191, 262
Sallem (Salm), Pieter Florisz van der 15, 31, 34, 51, 113, 117, 147, 183, 262
Salsveld, Peter van 148
Sandrart, J. von 41, 110, 224
Sanmicheli, Michele 156
Sansovino, Jacopo 156
scala intellectualis, spiritualis, see Iconology 247, 252
Scamozzi, Vincenzo 109, 153, 155, 156, 164, 167, 174, 175, 189, 212
Scandinavia 124
Schenck, Petrus 49, 56
Scheveningen (Zuid-Holland)
- Pavilioen von Wied (De Witte) 93, 231
- Scheveningse Weg 192
Schleswig-Holstein 208
Schonk, P.W. 98
Schooten, Frans van 72, 209
Schoutens, Jacob 126
science, see mathematics, see perspective 155
science and technology 11, 155, 184, 191, 207, 208, 237, 238, 259, 268
Scientifica 12, 224, 268
Sculpture
- and its role in courtly gardens 31, 40-43, 53, 54, 58, 88, 89, 93-96, 110, 118, 120-123, 137, 141, 157, 158, 164, 174, 201, 220, 221, 223-233, 266

- animal figures 110, 228
- antique statues, heads, busts 41, 93, 118, 223, 224, 229, 233, 266
- Apollo 96
- Aquarius 110
- Ariadne, Sleeping 230
- Cain and Abel 226
- Ceres 231
- Charles I, King of England, bust of 41
- children (kinderkens) 228, 229, 266
- children, twelve in relief 227
- Cleopatra 96, 229, 230
- collection Orange family 40, 41, 230,
- Cupid Bending a Bow 233
- Cupid Cutting a Bow 110, 225
- Cupid Sleeping, resting on shield 110, 233
- Cupid (putto, kinderken) 41, 110, 220, 225
- Diana 110
- Dogs, two 228
- Fame 110
- Firmitas, Utilitas, Venustas, female figures of 164
- Four boys 254, 255
- Four Elements 225
- Four Seasons 118, 225
- Frederik Hendrik, bust of 88, 89, 233
- Friedrich Wilhelm of Brandenburg, lifesize figure 220
- Globe 253-255
- Good Fortune, female figure of 228
- Henrietta Maria of England, bust of 41
- Hercules 96, 141, 225-227
- Hercules and Cacus 41, 53, 54, 224-227, 259, 266, 267
- Hercules Defeating Someone Else 226
- Hercules Farnese 226
- Hope, Faith, Love, female figures of 164
- Johann Georg II von Anhalt-Dessau, bust of 233
- Maas 231, 259, 266
- Main 231
- Mars 54, 158, 224, 227, 267
- Minerva (Pallas Athena) 96, 158, 225, 227, 231, 266
- Minerva Tritonia 96, 158, 231, 232
- Muses 231
- Neckar 231
- Neptune 95, 110, 220, 231
- Nile 95

- Pegasus 249
- plant as sculptural ornament 224, 266
- pots, urns, vases 23, 42, 43, 54, 110, 120, 223-230, 267
- Princes of Orange, life-size 41, 110, 118, 220
- Rhine 220, 231, 259, 266
- River gods 93-96, 157, 220, 224, 229-233
- Roman warriors 209
- Roman Emperors, busts of 168, 209, 220, 232, 233, 260, 267
- Roman theatre 168, 251
- Samson and the Philistine 227
- spheres, celestial, terrestial 164
- Tiber 95
- Venus, Venus Lactans 54, 96, 224, 227, 231, 242, 267
- Virtues 225
- William II, bust of 233

Serlio, Sebastiano 152, 155, 201-203, 211, 212, 263
Serre, Sieur de la 22, 81, 82, 109
Serres, Olivier de 211, 263
silviculture 43-46, 58, 128, 145, 149, 205, 266
Sion, see Delft
Slothouwer, D.F. 10, 36, 172, 174, 187
Soderini, Francesco 242
Soestdijk (Utrecht) 188, 192
Sorgvliet, see Hague, The
Southwell, Edward 136, 254
Spain 239, 267
spheres, hemispheres, see Iconology
Spierinxhouten, Adriaen Willeboordsen 149
Spuij, A. van der 120
Steene, Jacques van der 128
Stevin, Simon 124-126, 136, 151, 152, 155, 184, 207-211, 234, 237, 238
Stoop, Willem Cornelisz van der 128, 130, 146, 147
Stoopendael, Daniel 53, 147, 148
Straalen, Huybert van 120
Strong, R. 189
stronghold, see Architecture, military
style and form, see Architecture, see Garden
Swart, Pieter de 141
Sweden 10, 70, 173, 191, 209, 217, 265
- Eskilstuna 191
- Ekolsund 70, 191
- Östermalma 191

- Riddarhuspalatset 70
Swieten, Johan van 56
symmetry, absolute 159, 160, 167, 175, 181, 197, 200, 205, 208-210, 219

T
Tasman, Albert 256
Tassin, Mr. 72, 199
Taverne, Ed 208, 211
temple 247
Ter Nieuburch, see Rijswijk, Huis ter Nieuburch
Tessin, Nicodemus 31, 111
tetrad, see Iconology, see Pythagoras
The Hague, see Hague, The
Theunissen, Gijsbrecht 44
Thevet, Andr 259, 260
Thibault, Girard 239, 268
Thonissen, Gijsbrecht 130, 146, 147, 179
Thooren, Anthony van 34, 179
Tiber 95
Tivoli 40, 51, 83, 88
- Villa D'Este 226
topography, see Landscape
Touars, Douchesse de 104
tree cultivation 43-46, 58, 128, 145-149, 179, 205, 266
trees, see Plants
triangle, trigonometry 126, 127, 166, 234, 238
Tuileries, see Paris
Twickenham Park (England) 249, 268

U
Uffelen, Lucas van 110
universe 246, 249
Urania, Muse of Astronomy 249
Uraniborg, see Copenhagen
utile dulci 45, 66, 79
Utrecht 147, 171
Uyttenbrouck, Moyses van 174

V
Vallée, Simon de la 26, 35, 40, 69, 70, 73, 76, 164, 171-174, 191, 204, 262, 264
Vallée, Jean de la 173, 191
Vallée, Marin de la 73
Varro 46
Vecht River 192
Venice 156, 191
- Libreria 156

- Palazzo Ducale 156
Verhoff, Christoffel 133, 140, 141
Vermeulen, Cornelis 130
Vermeulen, F.A.J. 187
Vernatti, Filibert 62
Verona, Palazzo Bevilacqua 156
Versailles 191
Vianen 90, 128, 171, 177, 234-236, 253, 259, 263
- Batestein castle 90, 92, 128, 171, 177, 234-236, 253, 259, 263
Vianen, I. van 96
Vicenza
- Teatro Olimpico 156
Vignola, Jacopo Barozzi 155
Villa Badoer (Peraga) 175
Villa D'Este (Tivoli) 226
Villa Giulia (Rome) 200
Villa Madama (Rome) 200
Villa Maser (Veneto) 191
Villa Sarego (Veneto) 191
Villa Petraia (Florence) 242
villa suburbana 154, 169, 251
Vinckboons, David 123
Vingboons, Philips 192, 200, 208, 216, 265
Virgil 46
Visscher, Claes Jansz 21
Vitruvian Man 164, 167-169, 212, 238, 246-249, 250-252
Vitruvian triad 169
Vitruvian true architect 238
Vitruvius 124, 155, 156, 157, 159, 164, 165, 168, 173, 212, 214, 238, 239, 250, 263
Vlissingen, see Flushing
Vlooswijck, Barthout van 78
Vondel, Joost van den 209, 265
Voorburg (The Hague) 163
- Hofwijck 151, 163-169, 175, 209-212, 250-252
Vos, Jan Jansz de 227, 228
Vredeman de Vries, Johan 152, 153, 155, 181, 207, 242, 263, 265
Vredenburg, Huis, see Beemster
Vries, Adriaan de 227

W
war, see Landscape, see Iconology
warfare 12, 236
Wassenaar (Zuid-Holland) 175

- Rijxdorp (Rijksdorp) 175
- Zant, Huis Het 175
Weenix, Jan 227
Werven, Mr. van der 78
Westland 15, 146, 187, 188
Wickevoort, Joachim de 225
Wicquefort, Joachim 158, 187
Wilde, Simon de 85
wilderness 234
Wilhem, David Le Leu de 27, 36, 142, 170
Willeboorts, Mr. 134
Willem van Nassau-Odijk 89 (Document V, p. 391)
William I of Orange-Nassau (William the Silent) 12, 67, 88, 101, 110, 124, 226
William II, Prince of Orange-Nassau 32, 35, 51-56, 108, 110, 209, 233
William III of Orange-Nassau, King of England 32, 43, 45, 51-58, 97, 111, 119, 133, 140, 141, 158, 192, 194, 199, 226, 227, 253-255, 267
William IV of Orange-Nassau 97, 119
William V of Orange-Nassau 98
Wilton gardens (England) 189
Wittkower, R. 168, 169, 187, 210, 211, 240
world, two halves of, see Iconology
Worp, J.A. 36
Wotton, Henry 159, 252
Wou (Wouw), Nicolaus van 32
Wörlitz (Germany)
- Gothic House 89, 233
- Oranienbaum 85, 218, 233, 265

Y
Ysselsteyn (Utrecht)
- Ysselsteyn garden 10, 45, 101, 146, 147, 149-150
    - silviculture, fruit for court 45

Z
Zeist 200, 214, 267
Zilvervloot (Portuguese Silver Fleet) 9, 28, 266
Zocher, Johan David 112, 120
zodiac 245, 247, 254
zoo, see menagerie
zoological collections 13, 136, 224, 238
Zurck, Anthonis van 72
Zuylesteyn, see Leersum

This first edition was made possible in part by a grant from The Prince Bernhard Culture Foundation,
Dr. Hendrik Muller's Vaderlandsch Foundation and The M.A.O.C. Countess van Bylandt Foundation.

Design: Thijs van Delden †
Text editing: Henk Scheepmaker
Publisher: Guus Kemme †
Production: Slenderprint
Printed in the Czech Republic

Front cover painting: View of Honselaarsdijk by A. Bega and A. Blooteling c. 1680

Published by Architectura & Natura Press
Leliegracht 22
1015 DG Amsterdam
The Netherlands
ISBN 90 71570 78 9

© 2001 Vanessa Bezemer Sellers and Architectura & Natura Press, Amsterdam
in association with the August Kemme Foundation

Distributed outside the Netherlands by
Garden Art Press
5 Church Street
Woodbridge
Suffolk
IP12 1DS
U.K.

and in the U.S.A. by
Antique Collectors' Club
Market Street Industrial Park
Wappingers' Falls
NY 12590
U.S.A.